Main C
of Europe

2016

Contents

COUNTRIES

Dear Reader,

Welcome to the 35th edition of the 'Main Cities of Europe' guide.

This guide is aimed primarily at international business travellers who regularly journey throughout Europe but it is equally ideal for those wishing to discover the delights of some of Europe's most romantic and culturally stimulating cities for a short break or special occasion.

Entry into the MICHELIN guide is completely free of charge and it continues to be compiled by our professionally trained teams of full-time inspectors from across Europe, who make their assessments anonymously in order to ensure complete impartiality and independence. Their mission is to check the quality and consistency of the amenities and services provided by the hotels and restaurants throughout the year and our listings are updated annually in order to ensure the most up-to-date information.

Most of the establishments featured have been hand-picked from our other national guides and therefore our European selection is, effectively, a best-of-the-best listing.

In addition to its user-friendly layout, the guide contains practical and cultural information on each country and each city; suggestions on when to go, what to see and what to eat; and keywords which succinctly convey the style of each establishment.

Thank you for your support and please continue to send us your comments. We hope you will enjoy travelling with the 'Main Cities of Europe' guide 2016.

Consult the MICHELIN guide at:
www.ViaMichelin.com
and write to us at:
themichelinguide-europe@uk.michelin.com

Our Commitments:
Experienced in quality!

Whether they are in Japan, the USA, China or Europe, our inspectors use the same criteria to judge the quality of each and every hotel and restaurant that they visit. The MICHELIN guide commands a worldwide reputation thanks to the commitments we make to our readers - and we reiterate these below:

Anonymous inspections – Our inspectors make regular and anonymous visits to hotels and restaurants to gauge the quality of products and services offered to an ordinary customer. They settle their own bill and may then introduce themselves and ask for more information about the establishment. Our readers' comments are also a valuable source of information, which we can follow up with a visit of our own.

Independence – To remain totally objective for our readers, the selection is made with complete independence. Entry into the guide is free. All decisions are discussed with the Editor and our highest awards are considered at a European level.

Selection and choice – The guide offers a selection of the best hotels and restaurants in every category of comfort and price. This is only possible because all the inspectors rigorously apply the same methods.

Annual updates – All the practical information, classifications and awards are revised and updated every single year to give the most reliable information possible.

Consistency – The criteria for the classifications are the same in every country covered by the MICHELIN guide.

The sole intention of Michelin is to make your travels safe and enjoyable.

How to use this Guide

LOCATION

The country, the town, the district and the map.

RESTAURANTS

XxXxX to X
Red: Our most delightful places.

STARS

❀❀❀
Exceptional cuisine, worth a special journey!

❀❀
Excellent cooking, worth a detour!

❀
High quality cooking, worth a stop!

BIB GOURMAND

🅐
Good quality, good value cooking.

RESTAURANTS & HOTELS

The country is indicated by the coloured strip down the side of the page: light for restaurants, dark for hotels.

HOTELS

🏠🏠🏠 to 🏠
Red: Our most delightful places.

PARIS
PARIS
Population 2 243 833

CHAMPS-ÉLYSÉES, ÉTOILE, PAL

Le Petit Four (Martin)
2 rue François 1ᵉʳ (1st) Ⓜ Palais-Royal – ℘ 01 12
– www.petit.four.fr – Closed Sunday dinner
Menu 75 €, 185/215 € – Carte 112/170 € (boo
➜ Foie gras chaud au vinaigre de cidre. Saint
rôti au miel.
• Luxury • Inventive •
In the gardens of the Palais-Royal, sumptuo
rated with splendid "pictures under glass"
worthy of this historic monument.

Au Pied de Porc
15 bd Voltaire (11th) Ⓜ République – ℘ 01
– www.Pieddeporc.org – Closed in July an
Menu 9 €, 32/72 € – Carte 37/61 €
• Classic • Trendy •
Pigs trotters are the speciality of this re
late into the night since opened in 19
fruits designs.

ÉTOILE – CHAMPS-ÉLYSÉES
Rond-point des Champs-É

Palazzo Panthéon
2 rue Montaigne (8th) Ⓜ Franklin-R
– ℘ 01 45 12 24 24 – www.palazzo
145 rm �] – † 250/350 € †† 400/5
❀❀ *La Terrasse* – See restaura
• Palace • Stylish •
Classic style in the luxuriously red
gallery, stunning designer bar: th
ming, green-filled terrace, ensh
when the weather turns nice, is

Le Faubourg St-Thomas
15 r. des Ecuries (7th) Ⓜ St-Fran
– www.faubourgsainthomas.f
174 rm ⊜ 20 € – † 250 € †† 6
❀ *Café Honoré* – See rest
• Business • Modern
This "Faubourg" branch of S
tech rooms, 1930-style ba
decor, restful indoor garde

Élysée Hotel
112 rue Copernic (8th) Ⓜ (
– www.elyseehotel.fr – Clo
29 rm – † 90/120 € †† 15
• Family • Cosy •
Peninsula family hotel •
the sloping r

LOCATING THE ESTABLISHMENT

Use the coordinates to locate the establishment on the city plan.

PRACTICAL & TOURIST INFORMATION

Pages with practical information on every city: tourist sites, cultural attractions, annual events, public transport... and local cuisine!

FACILITIES & SERVICES

See also page 10.

ADDRESS & PRICES

All the information you need to make a reservation and find the establishment.
Prices : See also page 10.

DESCRIPTION OF THE ESTABLISHMENT

Atmosphere, style, character...

CLASSIFICATION BY DISTRICT

With the corresponding plan number.

KEY WORDS

If you are looking for a specific type of establishment, these key words will help you make your choice more quickly.
→ For hotels, the first word explains the **establishment type** (chain, business, luxury, etc); the second one describes the décor (modern, stylish, design, etc) and sometimes a third will be used to complete the picture.
→ For restaurants, the first word relates to the **type of cuisine** and the second to the **atmosphere**.

7

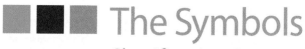

The Symbols
Classification & Awards

The MICHELIN Guide selection lists the best hotels and restaurants in each category of comfort and price. The establishments we choose are classified according to their levels of comfort and, within each category, are listed in order of preference.

Hotels and restaurants, classified by their comfort, from 5 to 1

Other recommended accommodation

Hotel with a restaurant

Restaurant with bedrooms

Pubs serving good food

Tapas bars

To help you make the best choice, some exceptional establishments have been given an award in this year's Guide. They are marked Stars ✿ (One, Two or Three) or Bib Gourmand ☺.

THE BEST CUISINE

Michelin stars are awarded to establishments serving cuisine, of whatever style, which is of the highest quality. The cuisine is judged on the quality of ingredients, the skill in their preparation, the combination of flavours, the levels of creativity, the value for money and the consistency of culinary standards.

For every restaurant awarded a star we include 3 specialities that are typical of their cooking style. These specific dishes may not always be available.

✿✿✿ **Three Stars: Exceptional cuisine, worth a special journey!**
Our highest award is given for the superlative cooking of chefs at the peak of their profession. The ingredients are exemplary, the cooking is elevated to an art form and their dishes are often destined to become classics.

✿✿ **Two Stars: Excellent cooking, worth a detour!**
The personality and talent of the chef and their team is evident in the expertly crafted dishes, which are refined, inspired and sometimes original.

✿ **One Star: High quality cooking, worth a stop!**
Using top quality ingredients, dishes with distinct flavours are carefully prepared to a consistently high standard.

GOOD FOOD AT MODERATE PRICES

🔴 **Bib Gourmand: Good quality, good value cooking**
'Bibs' are awarded for simple yet skilful cooking for under 37€.

PLEASANT HOTELS AND RESTAURANTS

Symbols shown in red indicate particularly pleasant or restful establishments: the character of the building, its décor, the setting, the welcome and services offered may all contribute to this special appeal.

🏠 to 🏠🏠🏠🏠🏠 **The most delightful hotels**
✗ to ✗✗✗✗✗ **The most delightful restaurants**

OTHER SPECIAL FEATURES

As well as the categories and awards given to the establishment, Michelin inspectors also make special note of other criteria which can be important when choosing an establishment.

LOCATION

If you are looking for a particularly restful establishment, or one with a special view, look out for the following symbols:

🕊 **Peaceful establishment**
≤ **Great view**

WINE LIST

If you are looking for an establishment with an excellent wine list, look out for the following symbol:

🍷 **Particularly interesting wine list**
This symbol might cover the list presented by a sommelier in a luxury restaurant or that of a simple restaurant where the owner has a passion for wine. The two lists will offer something exceptional but very different, so beware of comparing them by each other's standards.

The Symbols
Facilities & Services

March-April	Dates when closed, as indicated by the hotelier / restaurateur
Ⓜ ⊖	Nearest metro / underground station
🏡	Garden or park
🍴	Outside dining available
⤒ ⊠	Swimming pool: outdoor or indoor
⑱	Wellness centre: an extensive facility for relaxation and well-being
🜂 Ⅎ	Sauna – Exercise room
♿	Wheelchair access
🅰🅲	Air conditioning (in all or part of the establishment)
⫣	Establishment with areas reserved for non-smokers
✂	Tennis court
🎭	Restaurant offering lower priced pre and/or post theatre menus
🆅	Restaurant offering vegetarian menus (UK and Ireland)
♻	Private dining room
🛉	Equipped conference room
🅿	Car park
🚘 🚗	Valet parking – Garage
⊄	Credit cards not accepted

Prices

The prices are given in the currency of the country in question. Valid for 2016 the rates shown should only vary if the cost of living changes to any great extent.

MEALS

Menu 40/56	Fixed price menu - Lowest / highest price
Carte 65/78	À la carte menu - Lowest / highest price
♟	House wine included

HOTEL

30 rm	Number of rooms
86 rm - ♟ 650/750	Lowest and highest price for a single
♟♟ 750/890	and for a double room
28 rm ⌣ - ♟ 100 ♟♟ 180	Prices include breakfast
⌣ 20	Price of breakfast where not included in rate

City Plan Key

- Hotels
- Restaurants

SIGHTS

▬	Place of interest	🚪	Interesting place of worship

ROADS

▭▭▭	Motorway	❶	Junctions: complete
▭▭▭	Dual carriageway	❶	Junctions: limited
▭▭▭	Pedestrian street	🚆	Station and railway

VARIOUS SIGNS

🛈	Tourist Information Centre	✈	Airport
▣	Mosque	✚	Hospital
▣	Synagogue	▤	Covered market
♨	Ruins	▭	Public buildings:
▭	Garden, Park, Wood	H	Town Hall
		R	Town Hall (Germany)
🚌	Coach station	M	Museum
Ⓜ	Metro station	U	University
⊖	Underground station (UK)		

Michelin is committed to improving the mobility of travellers

ON EVERY ROAD AND BY EVERY MEANS

Since the company came into being – over a century ago – Michelin has had a single objective: to offer people a better way forward. A technological challenge first, to create increasingly efficient tyres, but also an ongoing commitment to travellers, to help them travel in the best way. This is why Michelin is developing a whole collection of products and services: from maps, atlases, travel guides and auto accessories, to mobile apps, route planners and online assistance, Michelin is doing everything it can to make travelling more pleasurable!

→ Michelin Apps

Because the notions of comfort and security are essential, both for you and for us, Michelin has created a package of six free mobile applications. A comprehensive collection to make driving a pleasure!

→ *Michelin MyCar* • *To get the best from your tyres; services and information for carefree travel preparation.*

→ *Michelin Navigation* • *A new approach to navigation: traffic in real time with a new connected guidance feature.*

→ *ViaMichelin* • *Calculates routes and map data: a must for travelling in the most efficient way.*

→ *Michelin Restaurants* • *Because driving should be enjoyable: find a wide choice of restaurants, in the UK, France and Germany, including the MICHELIN Guide's complete listings.*

→ *Michelin Hotels* • *To book hotel rooms at the best rates, all over the world!*

→ *Michelin Travel* • *85 countries and 30 000 tourist sites selected by the Michelin Green Guide. Plus a tool for creating your own travel book.*

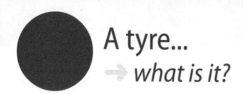

A tyre...
→ what is it?

Round, black, supple yet solid, the tyre is to the wheel what the shoe is to the foot. But what is it made of? First and foremost, rubber, but also various textile and/or metallic materials... and then it's filled with air! It is the skilful assembly of all these components that ensures tyres have the qualities they should: grip to the road, shock absorption, in two words: 'comfort' and 'safety'.

1 TREAD
The tread ensures the tyre performs correctly, by dispersing water, providing grip and increasing longevity.

2 CROWN PLIES
This reinforced double or triple belt combines vertical suppleness with transversal rigidity, enabling the tyre to remain flat to the road.

3 SIDEWALLS
These link all the component parts and provide symmetry. They enable the tyre to absorb shock, thus giving a smooth ride.

4 BEADS
The bead wires ensure that the tyre is fixed securely to the wheel to ensure safety.

5 INNER LINER
The inner liner creates an airtight seal between the wheel rim and the tyre.

Michelin
→ *innovation in movement*

Created and patented by Michelin in 1946, the belted radial-ply tyre revolutionised the world of tyres. But Michelin did not stop there: over the years other new and original solutions came out, confirming Michelin's position as a leader in research and innovation.

→ *the right pressure!*

One of Michelin's priorities is safer mobility. In short, innovating for a better way forward. This is the challenge for researchers, who are working to perfect tyres capable of shorter braking distances and offering the best possible traction to the road. And so, to support motorists, Michelin organises road safety awareness campaigns all over the world: «Fill up with air» initiatives remind everyone that the right tyre pressure is a crucial factor in safety and fuel economy.

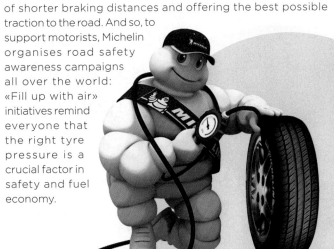

The Michelin strategy:
→ *multi-performance tyres*

Michelin is synonymous with safety, fuel saving and the capacity to cover thousands of miles. A MICHELIN tyre is the embodiment of all these things – thanks to our engineers, who work with the very latest technology.

Their challenge: to equip every tyre – whatever the vehicle (car, truck, tractor, bulldozer, plane, motorbike, bicycle or train!) – with the best possible combination of qualities, for optimal overall performance.

Slowing down wear, reducing energy expenditure (and therefore CO_2 emissions), improving safety through enhanced road handling and braking: there are so many qualities in just one tyre – that's Michelin Total Performance.

MICHELIN
Total Performance

Every day, **Michelin** is working towards sustainable mobility

OVER TIME, WHILE RESPECTING THE PLANET

Sustainable mobility
→ *is clean mobility... and mobility for everyone*

Sustainable mobility means enabling people to get around in a way that is cleaner, safer, more economical and more accessible to everyone, wherever they might live. Every day, Michelin's 113 000 employees worldwide are innovating:

- by creating tyres and services that meet society's new needs,
- by raising young people's awareness of road safety,
- by inventing new transport solutions that consume less energy and emit less CO_2.

→ *Michelin Challenge Bibendum*

Sustainable mobility means allowing the transport of goods and people to continue, while promoting responsible economic, social and societal development. Faced with the increasing scarcity of raw materials and global warming, Michelin is standing up for the environment and public health. Michelin regularly organises 'Michelin Challenge Bibendum', the only event in the world which focuses on sustainable road travel.

Selection by Country

AUSTRIA
ÖSTERREICH

VIENNA ●

● Salzburg

→ **AREA:**
83 878 km² (32 376 sq mi).

→ **POPULATION:**
8 507 786 inhabitants.
Density = 101 per km².

→ **CAPITAL:**
Vienna.

→ **CURRENCY:**
Euro (€).

→ **GOVERNMENT:**
Parliamentary republic and federal state (since 1955). Member of European Union since 1995.

→ **LANGUAGE:**
German.

→ **PUBLIC HOLIDAYS:**
New Years' Day (1 Jan); Epiphany (6 Jan); Easter Monday (late Mar/Apr); Labor Day (1 May); Ascension Day (May); Whit Monday (late May/June); Corpus Christi (late May/June); Assumption of the Virgin Mary (15 Aug); National Day (26 Oct); All Saints' Day (1 Nov); Immaculate Conception (8 Dec); Christmas Day (25 Dec); St Stephen's Day (26 Dec).

→ **LOCAL TIME:**
GMT+1 hour in winter and GMT+2 hours in summer.

→ **CLIMATE:**
Temperate continental with cold winters - high snow levels - and warm summers (Vienna: January 0°C; July 20°C).

→ **EMERGENCY:**
Police: ☏ **133**;
Medical Assistance: ☏ **144**;
Fire Brigade: ☏ **122.**
(Dialling **112** within any EU country will redirect your call and contact the emergency services.)

→ **ELECTRICITY:**
230 volts AC, 50Hz; 2 round pin sockets.

→ **FORMALITIES:**
Travellers from the European Union (EU), Switzerland, Iceland and the main countries of North and South America need a national identity card or passport (America: passport required) to visit Austria for less than three months (tourism or business purpose).
For visitors from other countries a visa may be required, in addition to a passport, especially for those wishing to stay for longer than three months. We advise you to check with your embassy before travelling.

VIENNA
WIEN

Population: 1 781 105

ReSeandra/Fotolia.com

Beethoven, Brahms, Mozart, Haydn, Strauss...not a bad list of former residents, by any stretch of the imagination. One and all, they succumbed to the opulent aura of Vienna, a city where an appreciation of the arts is as conspicuous as its famed cakes. Sumptuous architecture and a refined air reflect the city's historic position as the seat of the powerful Habsburg dynasty and former epicentre of the Austro-Hungarian Empire. Despite its grand image, Vienna has propelled itself into the 21C with a handful of innovative hotspots, most notably the MuseumsQuartier cultural complex, a stone's throw from the mighty Hofburg Imperial Palace. This is not a big city, although its vivid image gives that impression. The compact centre teems with elegant shops, fashionable coffee-houses and grand avenues, and the empire's awesome 19C remnants keep visitors' eyes fixed forever upwards. Many towns and cities are defined by their ring roads, but Vienna can boast a truly upmarket version: the Ringstrasse, a showpiece boulevard that cradles the inner city and the riches that lie therein. Just outside, to the southwest are the districts of Neubau and Spittelberg, both of which have taken on a quirky, modernistic feel. To the east lies Prater, the green lung of Vienna and further out lies the suburban area enhanced by the grandeur of the Schönbrunn palace.

VIENNA IN...

→ **ONE DAY**
A tram ride round the Ringstrasse, St Stephen's Cathedral, a section of the Hofburg Palace, cakes in a café.

→ **TWO DAYS**
MuseumsQuartier, Spittelberg, Hundert-wasserhaus, Prater.

→ **THREE DAYS**
A day at the Belvedere, a night at the opera.

PRACTICAL INFORMATION

ARRIVAL-DEPARTURE

✈ Wien-Schwechat Airport is 19km from the city centre.

The City Airport Express train to Wien Mitte takes 16min and leaves every 30min. A taxi will take around 30min.

GETTING AROUND

The city's buses, trams and metro are renowned for their impressive efficiency. You can purchase Rover tickets for 24hr or 72hr. There are around eighty bus routes in the city. Night buses run every half-hour; trams run every 5-10min and there are timetables at every stop. The Vienna Card, which allows unlimited travel on the whole of the city's public transport network for 48hr or 72hr and offers a discount to sights, cafes, restaurants and shops, can be bought from the Tourist Office, at your hotel or from ticket offices of the Vienna Transport Authority.

CALENDAR HIGHLIGHTS

January
New Year's Concert of the Vienna Philharmonic.

February
Opera Ball.

April
Vienna City Marathon.

May
Life Ball.

June
Donau Island Festival.

September
Literature Festival.

October
Viennale Film Festival, Long Night of the Museums.

November
Vienna Jazz Floor Festival.

EATING OUT

Vienna is the spiritual home of the café and Austrians drink nearly twice as much coffee as beer. It is also a city with a sweet tooth: cream cakes enhance the window displays of most eateries and is there a visitor to Vienna who hasn't succumbed to the sponge of the Sachertorte? Viennese food is essentially the food of Bohemia, which means that meat has a strong presence on the plate. Expect beef, veal and pork, alongside potatoes, dumplings or cabbage - be sure to try traditional boiled beef and the ubiquitous Wiener Schnitzel (deep-fried breaded veal). Also worth experiencing are the Heurigen, traditional Austrian wine taverns which are found in Grinzing, Heiligenstadt, Neustift and Nussdorf. You'll find plenty of snug cafés and bars too. If you want to snack, the place to go is Naschmarkt, Vienna's best market, where the stalls spill over into the vibrant little restaurants. When it comes to tipping, if you're in the more relaxed, local pubs and wine taverns, just round up the bill, otherwise add on ten per cent.

AUSTRIA - VIENNA

Palais Coburg Residenz

Coburgbastei 4 ✉ *1010* – Ⓜ *Stubentor* – ✆ *(01)*   Plan: **E2**
51 81 80 – *www.palais-coburg.com*
34 suites ⌸ – ♦695/2695 € ♦♦695/2695 €
• Grand Luxury • Historic • Modern •
This magnificent, classic building was built in 1840. It offers guests an imposing hotel setting that is more than matched by the luxurious, largely duplex suites and the excellent service. The Clementine restaurant serves international fare, has a winter garden feel and boasts an attractive terrace.
🌼🌼 **Silvio Nickol Gourmet Restaurant** – See restaurant listing

Sacher

Philharmonikerstr. 4 ✉ *1010* – Ⓜ *Karlsplatz* – ✆ *(01)*   Plan: **D3**
51 45 60 – *www.sacher.com*
133 rm – ♦530/915 € ♦♦530/915 € – ⌸ 38 € – 16 suites
• Grand Luxury • Classic • Personalised •
The rooms in this hotel that dates back to 1876 are elegant, modern and equipped with the latest technology. Traditional feel is still here, as is the attentive service. The suites and rooms on the top floor enjoy a wonderful roof terrace and an exclusive spa. Don't forget to visit the famous Café Sacher.
Anna Sacher • Rote Bar – See restaurant listing

Imperial

Kärntner Ring 16 ✉ *1015* – Ⓜ *Karlsplatz* – ✆ *(01)*   Plan: **E3**
50 11 00 – *www.imperialvienna.com*
138 rm – ♦379/819 € ♦♦379/819 € – ⌸ 41 € – 35 suites
• Palace • Grand Luxury • Historic •
This grand hotel was opened in 1873 to celebrate Vienna's World Expo, and still promises all the majesty of the Austrian Empire in its splendid interior. The lobby is stylish, the rooms and suites are lavish and elegant. Don't miss the fascinating 'Course of History'. The restaurant is decidedly upmarket and the Café Imperial is a classic Vienna coffee house.
🌼 **OPUS** – See restaurant listing

Park Hyatt

Am Hof 2 ✉ *1010* – Ⓜ *Herrengasse* – ✆ *(01)*   Plan: **D2**
2 27 40 12 34 – *vienna.park.hyatt.com*
143 rm – ♦425/520 € ♦♦425/520 € – ⌸ 35 € – 35 suites
• Historic • Luxury • Elegant •
This former bank building, constructed in 1915, combines historical style and modern design, including the latest technology. It is a genuinely luxury hotel complete with Arany Spa and a gold-plated pool in the former vaults. The aptly named The Bank restaurant serves international cuisine made using local produce.

The Ritz-Carlton

Schubertring 5 ✉ *1010* – Ⓜ *Karlsplatz* – ✆ *(01) 3 11 88*   Plan: **E3**
– *www.ritzcarlton.com/vienna*
202 rm – ♦345/550 € ♦♦345/550 € – ⌸ 34 € – 20 suites
• Business • Grand Luxury • Modern •
This luxury hotel is created from four individual buildings and set right on Vienna's Ringstraße. It offers a restrained and tasteful modern interior that is never ostentatious and has lots of period detail (the comfortable lobby was once a bank vault). There is an exclusive Guerlain Spa and impeccable service of the sort you would expect in a Ritz-Carlton. The Distrikt restaurant serves international cuisine and various cuts of steak.

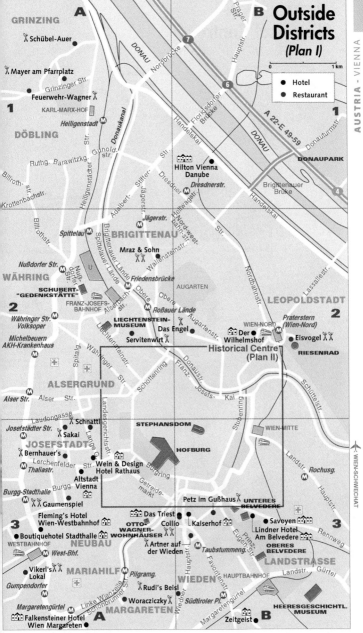

Outside Districts (Plan I)

AUSTRIA - VIENNA

0 _____ 1 km

● Hotel
● Restaurant

GRINZING

Schübel-Auer

Mayer am Pfarrplatz

Grinzinger Str.

Feuerwehr-Wagner

KARL-MARX-HOF

Heiligenstadt

DÖBLING

Ruthg. Barawitzkg.

Billroth-str.

Krottenbachstr.

Spittelau

Nußdorfer Str.

WÄHRING

SCHUBERT-
"GEDENKSTÄTTE"

FRANZ-JOSEFS-
BAHNHOF

Währinger Str.
Volksoper

Michelbeuern
AKH-Krankenhaus

ALSERGRUND

Alser Str.   Alser Str.

Laudongasse

Josefstädter Str.   Schnattl

Sakai

JOSEFSTADT

Bernhauer's

Lerchenfelder Str.
Thaliastr.

Burgg-Stadthalle

Gaumenspiel

Fleming's Hotel
Wien-Westbahnhof

Boutiquehotel Stadthalle

WESTBAHNHOF   West-Bhf.

NEUBAU

Vikerl's
Lokal

Gumpendorfer

Margaretengürtel

Falkensteiner Hotel
Wien Margareten

MARIAHILF

Pilgramg.

Linke Wienzeile

MARGARETEN

DONAU

Nordbrücke

DONAUKANAL

Prager Str.

Hauptstr.

Handelskai

Floridsdorfer
Brücke

DONAU

A 22-E 49-59

Donauturmstr.

DONAUPARK

Hilton Vienna
Danube

Dresdnerstr.

Nordwestbahnstr.

Brigittenauer
Brücke

Handelskai

Jägerstr.

Stifter
Str.

Dresdner
Str.

Adalbert

Jägerstr.

BRIGITTENAU

Mraz & Sohn

Brigittenauer Lände

Spittelauer Lände

Obere Donaustr.

Friedensbrücke

Wallensteinstr.

AUGARTEN

Obere Augartenstr.

Roßauer Lände

Nordbahnstr.

Lassallestr.

LEOPOLDSTADT

Praterstern
(Wien-Nord)

WIEN-NORD

RIESENRAD

Eisvogel

LIECHTENSTEIN-
MUSEUM

Das Engel

Servitenwirt

Der
Wilhelmshof

Historical Centre
(Plan II)

Liechtensteinstr.

Spitalg.

Währinger Str.

Landesgerichtsstr.

Schottenring

Donaust.
Franz-
Josefs-
Kai

Stubenring

WIEN-MITTE

Landstr. Rochusg.

STEPHANSDOM

HOFBURG

Burgring

Wein & Design
Hotel Rathaus

Altstadt
Vienna

Burgg.

Getreide-
markt

Das Triest

Collio

Kaiserhof

Petz im Gußhaus   UNTERES
BELVEDERE

Savoyen

Lindner Hotel
Am Belvedere

OTTO-
WAGNER-
WOHNHÄUSER

Artner auf
der Wieden

Taubstummeng.

Prinz-
Eugen-Str.

OBERES
BELVEDERE

LANDSTRASSE

Rennweg

Haupstr.

Rudi's Beisl

Woracziczky

WIEDEN

Südtiroler Pl.

Wieden

Favoritenstr.

HAUPTBAHNHOF

Landstr. Gürtel

Margaretengürtel

Schönbrunner

Zeitgeist

HEERESGESCHICHTL.
MUSEUM

WIEN-SCHWECHAT

25

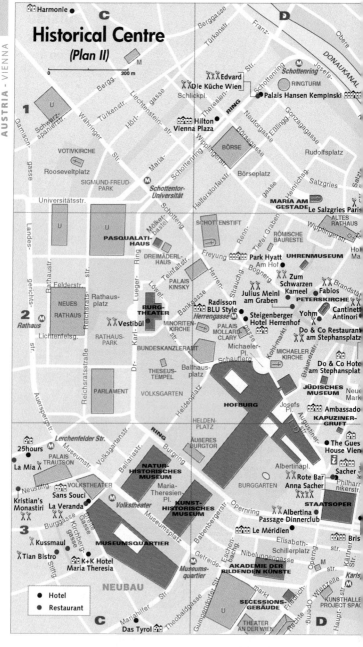

Historical Centre
(Plan II)

AUSTRIA - VIENNA

0   300 m

Harmonie

Edvard
Die Küche Wien
Palais Hansen Kempinski

Hilton
Vienna Plaza

BÖRSE

VOTIVKIRCHE

Rooseveltplatz

SIGMUND-FREUD-PARK

Schottentor-Universität

Rudolfsplatz

Börseplatz

MARIA AM GESTADE
Le Salzgries Paris

ALTES RATHAUS

Universitätsstr.

PASQUALATI-HAUS

SCHOTTENSTIFT

RÖMISCHE BAURESTE

UHRENMUSEUM

DREIMÄDERL-HAUS

Freyung   Park Hyatt
Am Hof

Zum Schwarzen
Kameel   Fabios

PALAIS KINSKY

Julius Meinl
am Graben   PETERSKIRCHE

NEUES RATHAUS

Rathaus-platz

BURG-THEATER

Radisson
BLU Style

Steigenberger
Hotel Herrenhof

Yohm   Cantinetta
Antinori

Vestibül

MINORITEN-KIRCHE

PALAIS MOLLARD-CLARY

Do & Co Restaurant
am Stephansplatz

RATHAUS-PARK

Lichtenfelsg.

BUNDESKANZLERAMT

Michaeler-Pl.
Schaufierg.

MICHAELER-KIRCHE

Do & Co Hotel
am Stephanspl.

THESEUS-TEMPEL

Ballhaus-platz

JÜDISCHES MUSEUM   Neue
Mark

PARLAMENT

VOLKSGARTEN

HOFBURG

Josefs-
Pl.

Ambassador

KAPUZINER-GRUFT

25hours

Lerchenfelder Str.

ÄUSSERES BURGTOR

HELDEN-PLATZ

The Guest
House Vien

PALAIS TRAUTSON

La Mia

VOLKSTHEATER

NATUR-HISTORISCHES MUSEUM

Maria-
Theresien-Pl.

Albertinapl.

BURGGARTEN

Sacher

Rote Bar
Anna Sacher

Kristian's
Monastiri

Sans Souci

La Veranda

Volkstheater

KUNST-HISTORISCHES MUSEUM

STAATSOPER

Kussmaul

Albertina
Passage Dinnerclub

Le Méridien

Bris

Tian Bistro

K+K Hotel
Maria Theresia

MUSEUMSQUARTIER

Museums-quartier

Elisabeth-
Schillerplatz

AKADEMIE DER
BILDENDEN KÜNSTE

NEUBAU

SECESSIONS-GEBÄUDE

KUNSTHALLE
PROJECT SPAC

● Hotel
● Restaurant

Das Tyrol

THEATER
AN DER WIEN

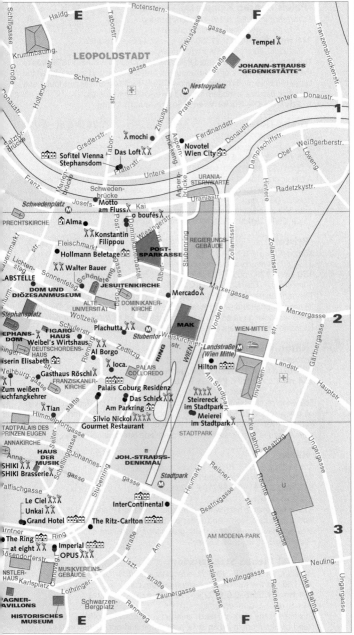

LEOPOLDSTADT

Tempel ✗

JOHANN-STRAUSS "GEDENKSTÄTTE"

Nestroyplatz

✗ mochi

Das Loft ✗✗

Novotel Wien City

Sofitel Vienna Stephansdom

URANIA-STERNWARTE

Schwedenplatz

Motto am Fluss ✗

o boufés ✗

PRECHTSKIRCHE

Alma ●

Konstantin Filippou ✗✗

Mercado ✗

REGIERUNGS-GEBÄUDE

Hollmann Beletage

POST-SPARKASSE

Walter Bauer ✗

ABSTELLE

DOM UND DIÖZESANMUSEUM

JESUITENKIRCHE

ALTE UNIVERSITÄT

DOMINIKANER-KIRCHE

Stephansplatz

FIGARO HAUS

Plachutta ✗✗

MAK

WIEN-MITTE

STEPHANS-DOM

Weibel's Wirtshaus ✗

DEUTSCHORDENS-HAUS

Al Borgo ✗

Ioca ●

Landstraße (Wien Mitte)

iserin Elisabeth

Gasthaus Röschl ✗

PALAIS COLLOREDO

Hilton

Veihburg-gasse

Zum weißen uchfangkehrer ✗

FRANZISKANER-KIRCHE

Palais Coburg Residenz

Tian ●

Das Schick ✗✗

Steirereck im Stadtpark ✗✗✗✗

Am Parkring

Silvio Nickol ✗✗✗✗

Meierei im Stadtpark ✗

Gourmet Restaurant

STADTPARK

STADTPALAIS DES PRINZEN EUGEN

ANNAKIRCHE

Anna-

HAUS DER MUSIK

JOH.-STRAUSS-DENKMAL

SHIKI ✗✗

SHIKI Brasserie ✗

Stadtpark

Valfischgasse

Le Ciel ✗✗✗

Unkai ✗✗

InterContinental ●

Grand Hotel

The Ritz-Carlton

arntner

The Ring

at eight ✗✗

Imperial

OPUS ✗✗✗

NSTLER-HAUS

Karlsplatz

MUSIKVEREINS-GEBÄUDE

AM MODENA PARK

AGNER-AVILLONS

HISTORISCHES MUSEUM

AUSTRIA - VIENNA

Palais Hansen Kempinski Vienna

Schottenring 24 ⊠ 1010 – Ⓜ Schottenring – 𝒞 (01)
2 36 10 00 – www.kempinski.com/wien Plan: **D1**
116 rm – ♦350/420 € ♦♦350/420 € – � 42 € – 36 suites
• Grand Luxury • Historic • Elegant •
This hotel is housed in the listed Palais Hansen, which was built in 1873 close to
the stock exchange. It offers luxurious yet tasteful rooms and suites with all the
latest technology (including your own iPad). Facilities: an elegant lobby and
attractive bar area, a modern spa and exclusive events rooms.
❀ **Edvard • Die Küche Wien** – See restaurant listing

Grand Hotel

Kärntner Ring 9 ⊠ 1010 – Ⓜ Karlsplatz – 𝒞 (01) Plan: **E3**
51 58 00 – www.grandhotelwien.com
205 rm – ♦458/558 € ♦♦458/558 € – � 34 € – 11 suites
• Grand Luxury • Classic •
A classic grand hotel with an imposing lobby and a sumptuous furnishing in a
period setting. The comfortable rooms exude real Viennese charm. "Grand Spa
No605". Don't miss the house speciality: `Guglhupf' – a delicious ring-shaped
cake. The Grand Café serves traditional cuisine. Nice pavement terrace.
❀ **Le Ciel • Unkai** – See restaurant listing

Bristol

Kärntner Ring 1 ⊠ 1010 – Ⓜ Karlsplatz – 𝒞 (01) Plan: **D3**
51 51 60 – www.bristolvienna.com
150 rm – ♦280/605 € ♦♦330/665 € – � 36 € – 15 suites
• Luxury • Traditional • Classic •
The traditional-style Bristol is run with great commitment and Viennese charm.
Its period lounge and saloon areas set the tone for the lovely interior. The Opera
suites are looking out on the Staatsoper, the Prince of Wales suite is genuinely
imposing. The restaurant serves both classic and regional cuisine.

Hilton Vienna Plaza

Schottenring 11 ⊠ 1010 – Ⓜ Schottentor-Universität Plan: **D1**
– 𝒞 (01) 31 39 00 – www.vienna-plaza.hilton.com
254 rm ⊠ – ♦229 € ♦♦249 € – 10 suites
• Business • Luxury • Design •
Following comprehensive renovation, this hotel on the Schottenring has taken
on a new splendour with its 20C-style lobby and timelessly comfortable rooms.
You can even treat yourself to a 10th floor suite complete with balcony and
view of Vienna. The Brasserie serves French and international cuisine.

Hilton

Am Stadtpark 1 ⊠ 1030 – Ⓜ Landstraße – 𝒞 (01) Plan: **F2**
71 70 00 – www.vienna.hilton.com
556 rm ⊠ – ♦199 € ♦♦219 € – 23 suites
• Chain hotel • Luxury • Contemporary •
A large conference hotel with a central location and a modern lobby full of artworks. Executive rooms and suites on the 10th to 15th floors with superior
accommodation, roof terrace with great views. Restaurant concept: "S'SPARKS
- Viennese. Simple. Good. Cuisine".

Sofitel Vienna Stephansdom

Praterstr. 1 ⊠ 1020 – Ⓜ Schwedenplatz – 𝒞 (01) Plan: **E1**
90 61 60 – www.sofitel-vienna-stephansdom.com
156 rm – ♦225/550 € ♦♦225/550 € – ⊠ 32 € – 26 suites
• Luxury • Business • Design •
This hotel is the work of French architect Jean Nouvel. It offers a harmonious
blend of ultramodern urban style both inside and out. Its minimalist design
has lots of glass, classic whites, greys and blacks. Unique view of Vienna.
Das Loft – See restaurant listing

AUSTRIA - VIENNA

 Le Méridien ⚲ ♨ 🏊 🖥 ♿ 🄰🄲 🛎

Opernring 13 ✉ 1010 – Ⓜ Karlsplatz – ☏ (01) 58 89 00
– www.lemeridienvienna.com
Plan: **D3**
294 rm – 🛏180/419 € 🛏🛏180/419 € – ⭸ 32 € – 17 suites
• Chain hotel • Design •

Behind its classic façade, this hotel features modern design, a host of art works and a special lighting concept. See and be seen in the Moët Champagne Bar, which serves choice snacks and, of course, champagne! The bar also boasts a DJ from breakfast to dinner.

 InterContinental ⚲ 🚣 🏊 ♨ ♿ 🄰🄲 🛎 🚗

Johannesgasse 28 ✉ 1030 – Ⓜ Stadtpark – ☏ (01)
71 12 20 – www.vienna.intercontinental.com
Plan: **E3**
444 rm – 🛏199/499 € 🛏🛏199/499 € – ⭸ 33 € – 15 suites
• Chain hotel • Business • Classic •

This business hotel close to the Stadtpark has a tasteful, elegant lobby and extensive conference facilities. If you are looking for that little something extra, try the 140 m² Presidential Suite on the 12th floor with its wonderful views over the city. Champagne lunch on Sundays (from September to May).

 Savoyen ⚲ ♨ ♿ 🄰🄲 🛎 🚗

Rennweg 16 ✉ 1030 – Ⓜ Karlsplatz – ☏ (01) 20 63 30
– www.austria-trend.at
Plan I: **B3**
309 rm – 🛏108/350 € 🛏🛏108/350 € – ⭸ 23 € – 43 suites
• Luxury • Contemporary •

The most imposing building of the former government printing works. Impressive atrium-style lobby and good conference facilities (including the largest venue in Vienna at 1 100 m²), providing modern-style in a historic setting. The rooms on the seventh and eighth floors have balconies. International cuisine.

 Ambassador ⚲ 🄰🄲 🛎

Kärntner Str. 22 ✉ 1010 – Ⓜ Stephansdom – ☏ (01)
96 16 10 – www.ambassador.at
Plan: **D2**
89 rm – 🛏272/500 € 🛏🛏346/626 € – ⭸ 25 € – 4 suites
• Townhouse • Classic •

The Ambassador is one of the city's most venerable institutions. The style is resolutely traditional, although never at the expense of modern comfort. It has marble columns in the atrium lobby and most of the rooms feature antique furniture. The themed rooms are dedicated to famous celebrities.

 Sans Souci ⚲ 🚣 🌐 ♨ 🖥 ♿ 🄰🄲 🛎

Burggasse 2 ✉ 1070 – Ⓜ Volkstheater – ☏ (01)
5 22 25 20 – www.sanssouci-wien.com
Plan: **C3**
60 rm ⭸ – 🛏224/359 € 🛏🛏254/404 € – 3 suites
• Townhouse • Traditional • Personalised •

High class boutique hotel in the Spittelberg artists' quarter. This epitome of urban lifestyle is located opposite the Volkstheater and nearby the major museums. Artworks including originals by Roy Lichtenstein, Allen Jones, Steve Kaufman.
La Veranda – See restaurant listing

 The Ring ⚲ 🚣 ♨ ♿ 🄰🄲 🚗

Kärntner Ring 8 ✉ 1010 – Ⓜ Karlsplatz – ☏ (01)
22 12 20 – www.theringhotel.com
Plan: **E3**
68 rm – 🛏219/518 € 🛏🛏259/518 € – ⭸ 32 € – 2 suites
• Townhouse • Modern • Contemporary •

This modern, well-run business hotel is housed in a historic townhouse. It has a luxurious touch and a pleasant, informal atmosphere. The heritage protected lift is not to be missed.
at eight – See restaurant listing

AUSTRIA - VIENNA

Steigenberger Hotel Herrenhof

Herrengasse 10 ⊠ 1010 – **Ⓜ** *Herrengasse – ℰ (01)* Plan: **D2**
53 40 40 – www.steigenberger.com/wien
196 rm – ♦169/430 € ♦♦169/430 € – ☐ 29 € – 10 suites
• Townhouse • Historic • Contemporary •
This lovely historic building is a comfortable hotel which caters for both business guests and tourists with a central location in the heart of the city and attractive rooms and suites in fresh, warm colours. The bar offers a lively venue.

Das Triest

Wiedner Hauptstr. 12 ⊠ 1040 – **Ⓜ** *Karlsplatz – ℰ (01)* Plan I: **B3**
58 91 80 – www.dastriest.at
72 rm ☐ – ♦279 € ♦♦299 € – 2 suites
• Business • Design •
The light, simple and elegant decor in this designer hotel is the work of Sir Terence Conran. Something of a home-from-home for its many regulars, it was once a posting house on the Vienna-Trieste route. It also has a smart bar.
Collio – See restaurant listing

Radisson BLU Style

Herrengasse 12 ⊠ 1010 – **Ⓜ** *Herrengasse – ℰ (01)* Plan: **D2**
22 78 00 – www.radissonblu.com/stylehotel-vienna
78 rm – ♦149/499 € ♦♦169/499 € – ☐ 24 €
• Townhouse • Historic • Design •
Cosmopolitan-style and high quality materials right up into the eaves characterise this former bank building. Even the old vault doors in the gym have been retained! If you like international cuisine, try the Sapori restaurant.

Lindner Hotel Am Belvedere

Rennweg 12 ⊠ 1030 – **Ⓜ** *Karlsplatz – ℰ (01) 79 47 70* Plan I: **B3**
– www.lindner.de
219 rm – ♦99/339 € ♦♦119/359 € – ☐ 22 € – 1 suite
• Business • Modern •
This hotel offers a perfect blend of contemporary style, quality and technology. If you like your privacy, try one of the individual saunas in the wellness suite. The leisure area on the seventh floor offers great views of the Belvedere Castle. The modern yet rustic Heuriger Am Belvedere serves regional food. Transport connections into the city are good.

Do & Co Hotel am Stephansplatz

Stephansplatz 12 ⊠ 1010 – **Ⓜ** *Stephansplatz – ℰ (01)* Plan: **D2**
2 41 88 – www.doco.com
45 rm – ♦249/395 € ♦♦249/399 € – ☐ 29 € – 2 suites
• Business • Design • Stylish •
The ultra-modern exterior of this hotel provides a real contrast to the other buildings around St Stephen's Cathedral. A very special designer hotel - fashionable and upmarket. The smokers' bar serves Euro-Asian fusion food from the show kitchen before transforming itself into a trendy club in the evening!
Do & Co Restaurant am Stephansplatz – See restaurant listing

The Guest House Vienna

Führichgasse 10 ⊠ 1010 – **Ⓜ** *Herrengasse – ℰ (01)* Plan: **D3**
5 12 13 20 – www.theguesthouse.at
36 rm – ♦247/307 € ♦♦247/307 € – ☐ 9 € – 3 suites
• Luxury • Townhouse • Modern •
Are you looking for understated, modern comfort and a discreet atmosphere? This boutique hotel behind the Albertina museum and the Opera offers high quality rooms in a Terence Conran interior. Excellent food from the great All Day Breakfast (bread and pastry baked on the premises) to dinner.

AUSTRIA - VIENNA

Kaiserhof

Frankenberggasse 10 ✉ *1040 –* Ⓜ *Karlsplatz – ℰ (01)*   Plan I: **B3**
5 05 17 01 – www.hotel-kaiserhof.at
70 rm ☷ – 🛏119/219 € 🛏🛏143/291 € – 4 suites
• Traditional • Art Deco • Modern •
Remarkable friendly service, Viennese charm, and a tasteful juxtaposition of modern and classic features characterise this beautiful 1896 hotel. There is a lovely breakfast room with a buffet service. Snack menu in the bar.

Hollmann Beletage

Köllnerhofgasse 6 (2nd floor) ✉ *1010*   Plan: **E2**
– Ⓜ *Stephansplatz – ℰ (01) 9 61 19 60 – www.hollmann-beletage.at*
25 rm ☷ – 🛏159/189 € 🛏🛏209/249 € – 1 suite
• Townhouse • Design • Modern •
The upmarket boutique hotel combines ornate mid-19C architecture and modern feel. Leafy terrace in the interior courtyard, small cinema (complete with popcorn machine), afternoon cakes and patisseries for residents... and an iPad for the length of your stay! Don't miss the 93m² Séparée Suite (own hammam).

Altstadt Vienna

Kirchengasse 41 ✉ *1070 –* Ⓜ *Volkstheater – ℰ (01)*   Plan I: **A3**
5 22 66 66 – www.altstadt.at
37 rm – 🛏109/260 € 🛏🛏149/280 € – 8 suites
• Historic • Design • Personalised •
From the outside you would never guess the tasteful and original combination of art, design and charm that awaits you behind the attractive old façade of this period hotel. The lovely high-ceilinged rooms are all different and genuinely individual. Central location close to all the major sights.

Hotel Rathaus - Wein & Design

Lange Gasse 13 ✉ *1080 –* Ⓜ *Rathaus*   Plan I: **A3**
– ℰ (01) 4 00 11 22 – www.hotel-rathaus-wien.at
– Closed 23-27 December
39 rm – 🛏130/160 € 🛏🛏170/210 € – ☷ 18 € – 1 suite
• Townhouse • Historic • Design •
The atmosphere is relaxing and homely thanks to the wonderful service and the charming building with its historical façade and modern interior. Breakfast is an impressively generous buffet, which can be enjoyed in the pretty interior courtyard. The wine bar offers a selection of some 450 Austrian wines.

Harmonie

Harmoniegasse 5 ✉ *1090 –* Ⓜ *Schottentor – ℰ (01)*   Plan: **C1**
3 17 66 04 – www.harmonie-vienna.at
63 rm ☷ – 🛏138/168 € 🛏🛏148/178 € – 3 suites
• Historic • Cosy • Contemporary •
This newly renovated 19C building is located close to the Palais Liechtenstein and easily accessible by tram (Line D). High quality, comfortable rooms in tasteful colours, charming service, a fresh breakfast and afternoon teas with delicious cakes. The Bistro serves a small selection of regional dishes.

K+K Hotel Maria Theresia

Kirchberggasse 6 ✉ *1070 –* Ⓜ *Volkstheater – ℰ (01)*   Plan: **C3**
5 21 23 – www.kkhotels.com
132 rm ☷ – 🛏125/250 € 🛏🛏125/290 €
• Business • Functional •
Located in arty Spittelberg, this hotel offers functional rooms. Ask for one with a view over the city. The spacious lobby has a bar that serves a small menu.

 25hours

Lerchenfelder Str. 1 ⊠ 1070 – **Ⓜ** *Lerchenfelder Str.*   Plan: **C3**
– 𝒞 (01) 52 15 10 – www.25hours-hotels.com
217 rm – †120/200 € ††120/200 € – ☑ 19 €
• Townhouse • Business • Personalised •
The message here is that "24 hours isn't enough". The interior mixes smart design and shabby chic, antique pieces and modern-style with imaginative allusions to the world of the fairground. For a note of originality, some of the rooms feature a bath on the balcony! The restaurant, '1500 foodmakers', serves pizzas and pasta dishes.

 Das Tyrol

Mariahilfer Str. 15 ⊠ 1060 – **Ⓜ** *Museumsquartier*   Plan: **C3**
– 𝒞 (01) 5 87 54 15 – www.das-tyrol.at
30 rm ☑ – †109/229 € ††149/299 €
• Townhouse • Personalised •
A beautifully restored corner building offering attractive, timelessly furnished rooms, an excellent breakfast and a small sauna decorated in gold tones. Contemporary art hangs on the walls throughout the hotel. Close to the museum quarter.

 Novotel Wien City

Aspernbrückengasse 1 ⊠ 1020 – **Ⓜ** *Nestroyplatz*   Plan: **F1**
– 𝒞 (01) 9 03 03 – www.novotel.com
123 rm – †99/199 € ††99/199 € – ☑ 18 € – 1 suite
• Chain hotel • Modern •
This modern business hotel is located right on the Aspern bridge. It offers seminar facilities and some executive rooms complete with French-style balcony terraces and great views from the top floor. It also makes a great base for tourists – children under 16 can sleep in their parents' room free of charge.

 Kaiserin Elisabeth

Weihburggasse 3 ⊠ 1010 – **Ⓜ** *Stephansplatz – 𝒞 (01)*   Plan: **E2**
5 15 26 – www.kaiserinelisabeth.at
63 rm ☑ – †130/145 € ††202/225 €
• Traditional • Classic •
The 400-year-old history of the hotel is reflected in the classic decor including paintings by Elisabeth and Kaiser Franz in the stylish lobby. Particularly comfortable superior rooms. Try some of the delicious Kaiserschmarrn for breakfast!

 Am Parkring

Parkring 12 ⊠ 1010 – **Ⓜ** *Stubentor – 𝒞 (01) 51 48 00*   Plan: **E2**
– www.schick-hotels.com
55 rm ☑ – †135/236 € ††175/347 € – 4 suites
• Business • Functional •
Am Parkring is located opposite the Stadtpark, on the upper floors of Vienna's high-rise Gartenbauhochhaus. It offers modern rooms with great views over Vienna, some with balconies. Be sure to ask for a room on the 13th floor.
Das Schick – See restaurant listing

 Der Wilhelmshof

Kleine Stadtgutgasse 4 ⊠ 1020 – **Ⓜ** *Praterstern*   Plan I: **B2**
– 𝒞 (01) 2 14 55 21 – www.derwilhelmshof.com
105 rm ☑ – †84/239 € ††94/259 €
• Townhouse • Personalised • Contemporary •
The Hotel is located close to the Prater, the exhibition centre and the city centre. It is a classic 19C townhouse, which has been transformed into an art hotel. The rooms offer an individual feel - the Atelier rooms and junior suites are particularly chic. Fresh buffet breakfast and unexpected garden.

Fleming's Hotel Wien-Westbahnhof

Neubaugürtel 26 ✉ *1070* – ⓜ *West-Bahnhof* – *ℰ (01)*   Plan I: **A3**
22 73 70 – *www.flemings-hotels.com*
173 rm ⌂ – ⓘ99/204 € ⓘⓘ115/204 € – 2 suites
• Business • Contemporary •
The business hotel close to the west railway station has been maintained in a thoroughly modern style. All the rooms possess glassed-in bathrooms. Restaurant with a brasserie-style atmosphere.

Alma

Hafnersteig 7 ✉ *1010* – ⓜ *Schwedenplatz* – *ℰ (01)*   Plan: **E2**
5 33 29 61 – *www.hotel-alma.com*
26 rm ⌂ – ⓘ111/181 € ⓘⓘ132/202 €
• Business • Townhouse • Modern •
A thoroughly modern hotel in a narrow side street, convenient parking just 3min away. Deluxe rooms with whirlpools, a small terrace with a Jacuzzi, and a wonderful view over Vienna from the roof. Water, tea and coffee are free all day.

Steirereck im Stadtpark (Heinz Reitbauer)

Am Heumarkt 2a ✉ *1030*   Plan: **F2**
– ⓜ *Stadtpark* – *ℰ (01) 7 13 31 68*
– *www.steirereck.at*
Menu 85 € (lunch)/142 € – Carte 94/113 € – *(booking essential)*
• Creative • Design • Formal •
Heinz Reitbauer has a style all of his own characterised not only by creativity but also by his regional references. In the tastefully elegant restaurant, the charming Birgit Reitbauer supervises an excellent service and lavishes every attention on her guests. Wonderful terrace with a view over the Stadtpark.
→ Karpfenmilch mit Fenchel, Mais und Stachelbeeren. Perlfisch mit Kürbis, Macadamianuss und Duftrosen. Pogusch Lamm mit Paradeiser, Topinambur und Monarde.
🅜 **Meierei im Stadtpark** – See restaurant listing

Anna Sacher – Hotel Sacher

Philharmonikerstr. 4 ✉ *1010* – ⓜ *Karlsplatz*   Plan: **D3**
– *ℰ (01) 51 45 68 40* – *www.sacher.com*
– *Closed July-August and Monday*
Menu 64/86 € – Carte 48/80 € – *(dinner only) (booking advisable)*
• Classic • Luxury •
Stylish green and fine wood interior adorned with original Anton Faistauer canvases radiates Viennese charm and elegance - a great place to enjoy international haute cuisine including Gut Dornau sheatfish with broccoli and garlic.

Silvio Nickol Gourmet Restaurant – Hotel Palais Coburg Residenz

Coburgbastei 4 ✉ *1010* – ⓜ *Stubentor*
– *ℰ (01) 51 81 81 30* – *www.palais-coburg.com*   Plan: **E2**
– *Closed 1-20 January, 7-31 August and Sunday-Monday*
Menu 148/188 € – Carte 108/147 € – *(dinner only)*
(booking advisable)
• Modern • Elegant • Luxury •
It is remarkable how much time and energy Silvio Nickol has invested here. He combines a wide range of ingredients (nothing but the best) and aromas with creative presentation skills to produce a cuisine that is innovative and full of contrast. The wine list is one of the best in Europe so keep your eyes open for the rarities!
→ Dorade, Tomate, Safran, Basilikum. Reh, Rüben, Eierschwammerl, Mais. Schokolade, Fragolino, Trauben, Hagebutte.

AUSTRIA - VIENNA

XXX ⊗ **Edvard** – Hotel Palais Hansen Kempinski Vienna 🏠 🅰🅺

Schottenring 24 ✉ *1010* – Ⓜ *Schottenring* – ℰ *(01)*   Plan: **D1**
2 36 10 00 80 82 – www.kempinski.com/wien – Closed 1-11 February,
August, Sunday-Monday and Bank Holidays
Menu 89/119 € – Carte 59/75 € – *(dinner only)*
• Modern • Elegant • Luxury •

One of the latest hotspots on the Viennese culinary scene. The chef and his team cook flavoursome, modern food with great finesse. It is served in an elegant setting in one of the quieter parts of the hotel accessible via a separate entrance. Accomplished front-of-house team.
➝ Schwein von Kopf bis Fuß. Pulpo, Paprika, Balsamico. Lamm, Polenta, Knoblauch, Gurke.

XXX ⊗ **Le Ciel** – Grand Hotel 🏠 ♿ 🅰🅺 ⇔ 🚗

Kärntner Ring 9 (7th floor) ✉ *1010* – Ⓜ *Karlsplatz*   Plan: **E3**
*– ℰ (01) 5 15 80 91 00 – www.leciel.at – Closed 12-15 February, 1-
29 August and Sunday-Monday*
Menu 58/98 € (dinner) – Carte 74/90 €
• Classic • Elegant •

Le Ciel is an upmarket seventh-floor restaurant with a lavish decor, elegantly set tables and a magnificent roof terrace. It serves ambitious cuisine based on the highest quality produce. Good value lunchtime menu.
➝ Kalbszunge mit Thunfisch, Champignons und Hagebutte. Taubenbrust mit Schwarzwurzel, Rotkrautessenz und Trüffel. Maroni mit Armagnac, Powidl und Limette.

XXX ⊗ **OPUS** – Hotel Imperial ♿ 🅰🅺

Kärntner Ring 16 ✉ *1015* – Ⓜ *Karlsplatz* – ℰ *(01)*   Plan: **E3**
50 11 03 89 – www.imperialvienna.com – Closed Monday
Menu 54/99 € – Carte 59/92 € – *(dinner only) (booking advisable)*
• Regional/country • Elegant • Luxury •

Located in an attractive, classical building, OPUS is decorated in the style of a 1930s Vienna workshop in elegant grey tones with chandeliers and art on the walls. The ambitious cuisine is creative and regionally inspired.
➝ Saibling und Flusskrebs, Kürbis, Salatherzen, Zitronengras. Heimischer Rehrücken, Quitte, Brokkoli, Mandelkrokant. Geeister Frischkäse, Vanille, Heidelbeere, Amaranth.

XX **Rote Bar** – Hotel Sacher ♿ 🅰🅺 🚗

Philharmonikerstr. 4 ✉ *1010* – Ⓜ *Karlsplatz* – ℰ *(01)*   Plan: **D3**
51 45 68 41 – www.sacher.com
Menu 60/67 € – Carte 39/78 €
• Austrian • Elegant • Traditional •

A mainstay of the Hotel Sacher, which epitomises the charm of this great Viennese establishment, Rote Bar is also a champion of Austrian cuisine. Treat yourself to a Wiener schnitzel or traditional rump of beef and soak up the atmosphere!

XX **Albertina Passage Dinnerclub** 🅰🅺

Opernring 4/1/12 (corner Operngasse) ✉ *1010*   Plan: **D3**
*– Ⓜ Karlsplatz – ℰ (01) 5 12 08 13 – www.albertinapassage.at – Closed
Sunday-Monday, 14 June-13 September: Sunday-Wednesday*
Menu 49/59 € – Carte 43/61 € – *(dinner only) (booking advisable)*
• Modern • Individual • Trendy •

A successful mix of music venue and upmarket restaurant. A lounge-like feel, a large bar area and live music along with excellent service and the modern international cuisine of Alexander Kumptner. Try the dishes from the charcoal grill.

AUSTRIA - VIENNA

XX **SHIKI**   ♿ 🅰🅲 ⟷

Krugerstr. 3 ✉ 1010 – Ⓜ Karlsplatz – ☏ (01) 5 12 73 97   Plan: **E3**
– www.shiki.at – Closed Sunday-Monday and Bank Holidays
Menu 65/85 € – *(booking advisable)*
• Japanese • Fashionable • Design •
SHIKI offers fine dining Japanese-style in the heart of Vienna, close to the Opera. The elegant restaurant decorated in dark tones offers a perfect marriage of tradition and modernity. It serves ambitious, seasonal cuisine ('Shiki' means the four seasons).
SHIKI Brasserie – See restaurant listing

XX
☺ **Vestibül**   🕮 🈂 ♿

Universitätsring 2 (at Burgtheater) ✉ 1010   Plan: **C2**
– Ⓜ Herrengasse – ☏ (01) 5 32 49 99 – www.vestibuel.at – Closed 23 July-15 August, Saturday lunch, Sunday and Bank Holidays
Menu 31 € (lunch)/69 € – Carte 36/79 € – *(booking advisable)*
• International • Classic • Brasserie •
Even though Christian Domschitz uses exclusively organic Austrian ingredients in his cuisine, there is no substituting the lobster in his Szegediner lobster with cabbage. The location in the charming historical setting of Vienna's celebrated Burgtheater is equally striking. Good wines served by the magnum.

XX **Das Loft** – Sofitel Vienna Stephansdom   ⇐ ♿ 🅰🅲 🈂

Praterstr. 1 ✉ 1020 – Ⓜ Schwedenplatz – ☏ (01)   Plan: **E1**
90 61 60 – www.sofitel-vienna-stephansdom.com
Menu 30 € (lunch)/78 € – Carte 58/88 € – *(bookings advisable at dinner)*
• International • Design • Fashionable •
This will take your breath away! An airy, high-ceilinged room on the 18th floor with glazed walls all around and an enormous view. There is nothing quite like it for an evening meal as the sun goes down over Vienna. Well chosen wine list.

XX
✿ **Walter Bauer**   🕮 🅰🅲

Sonnenfelsgasse 17 ✉ 1010 – Ⓜ Stubentor – ☏ (01)   Plan: **E2**
5 12 98 71 – Closed 25 July-19 August and Saturday-Monday lunch
Carte 53/74 € – *(booking advisable)*
• Classic • Cosy • Family •
Do you fancy some Viennese charm? Walter Bauer has been running this stylish, upmarket restaurant in the old town for 25 years. In the kitchen Mike Feierabend conjures up exquisite classic dishes characterised by great produce and fulsome flavour. The extensive wine list offers something for every budget.
→ Vitello Tonnato "warm". Lamm, Aubergine, Paprika. Topfenpalatschinken, Sabayon, Holunder.

XX **La Veranda** – Hotel Sans Souci   🈂 ♿ 🅰🅲 ⟷

Burggasse 2 ✉ 1070 – Ⓜ Volkstheater – ☏ (01)   Plan: **C3**
5 22 25 20 94 – www.laveranda-wien.com
Menu 55/65 € (dinner) – Carte 45/67 €
• International • Fashionable • Individual •
An extremely chic restaurant with a modern designer interior seemingly divided in two by the glazed corner façade. It serves seasonal food described as 'casual cuisine'. Good value set lunch menu on weekdays.

XX
☺ **Eisvogel**   🈂 ♿ 🅰🅲 ⟷ 🅿

Riesenradplatz 5 (Prater) ✉ 1020 – Ⓜ Praterstern   Plan I: **B2**
– ☏ (01) 9 08 11 87 – www.stadtgasthaus-eisvogel.at – Closed 1-10 January
Carte 23/51 € – *(bookings advisable at dinner)*
• Austrian • Elegant •
A restaurant full of life close to the Big Wheel at the Prater. You can sip an aperitif at the top (by reservation only) or savour the flavoursome Austrian food with a Mediterranean twist. The excellent goulash is one of the classics.

AUSTRIA - VIENNA

XX **Zum Schwarzen Kameel** 🏛 🍴 AC ⇄

Bognergasse 5 ✉ 1010 – ⓜ Herrengasse – ℰ (01) Plan: **D2**
5 33 81 25 – www.kameel.at
Menu 68/89 € (dinner) – Carte 36/75 € – *(booking essential)*
• Traditional • Friendly • Cosy •
One of Vienna's oldest restaurants (1618), fitted out in the much admired
Vienna Art Nouveau-style in 1901/02. Guests are offered international and
regional cuisine. The restaurant's own delicatessen and patisserie are great for
gifts.

XX **Fabios** 🍴 AC

Tuchlauben 6 ✉ 1010 – ⓜ Stephansplatz – ℰ (01) Plan: **D2**
5 32 22 22 – www.fabios.at – Closed Sunday
Carte 45/80 € – *(booking essential)*
• Italian • Trendy •
The Italian food served in this trendy restaurant is as modern and minimalist as
the interior design. Both the food and decor are well worth a visit. Chef Christoph Brunnhuber has already made his reputation in the kitchen – try his ravioli!

XX **Tian** 🏛 ⇄
🏵
Himmelpfortgasse 23 ✉ 1010 – ⓜ Stephansplatz Plan: **E2**
*– ℰ (01) 8 90 46 65 – www.tian-vienna.com – Closed 1-12 January,
18 July-10 August and Sunday-Monday, December: Sunday*
Menu 32 € (lunch)/127 € – Carte 42/75 €
• Vegetarian • Elegant • Fashionable •
Let Tirol-born Paul Ivic and his team introduce you to the gourmet world of
vegetables and cereals accompanied by a bottle of something from the extensive, handwritten wine list courtesy of sommelier Alexander Adlgasser. If you
fancy something a little more intimate, look at the wine bar in the basement.
→ Kokos-Curry, Crèmesuppe. Reduziert, Champignons, Kohlrabi. Sacher
entwurzelt, Nyangbo Schokolade, Marille, Karotte.

XX **Do & Co Restaurant am Stephansplatz** – Do & Co Hotel am Stephansplatz

Stephansplatz 12 (7th floor) ✉ 1010 ⇐ 🛏 🍴 �& AC ⇄ 🚗
– ⓜ Stephansplatz – ℰ (01) 5 35 39 69 Plan: **D2**
– www.doco.com
Carte 40/57 € – *(booking essential)*
• Euro-asiatic • Trendy •
An ultra-modern restaurant on the seventh floor with a great terrace and view
of St Stephen's Cathedral. Southeast Asian dishes including chicken kaow soy
and sushi alongside Austrian classics such as braised calves' cheeks and goose
liver.

XX **Collio** – Hotel Das Triest 🍴 �& AC

Wiedner Hauptstr. 12 ✉ 1040 – ⓜ Karlsplatz – ℰ (01) Plan: **B3**
*58 91 81 33 – www.dastriest.at – Closed Saturday lunch, Sunday and Bank
Holidays*
Carte 33/54 €
• Italian •
Collio offers a modern interior and a wonderful terrace in the gloriously green
inner courtyard outside. The food on offer is Italian, focusing especially on the
cuisine of northern Italy. Less expensive lunchtime menu.

XX **Die Küche Wien** – Hotel Palais Hansen Kempinski Vienna AC

Schottenring 24 ✉ 1010 – ⓜ Schottenring – ℰ (01) Plan: **D1**
2 36 10 00 80 80 – www.kempinski.com/wien
Carte 32/55 €
• Regional/country • Individual •
The second restaurant in the Palais Hansen focuses on new interpretations of
Viennese classics. Try the veal lights or sirloin of Wienerwald Weiderind beef in
the unique atmosphere of the 'living room', the winter garden or the kitchen.

AUSTRIA - VIENNA

XX   **Das Schick** – Hotel Am Parkring   AC ⌒
Parkring 12 ⊠ *1010 –* Ⓜ *Stubentor – ℰ (01)*   Plan: **E2**
*51 48 04 17 – www.schick-hotels.com – Closed Saturday lunch, Sunday
lunch and Bank Holidays lunch*
Carte 34/56 €
• Mediterranean • Fashionable • Elegant •
Das Schick offers a friendly atmosphere, seasonal cuisine with an upmarket
touch and a phenomenal view! That is the recipe that brings diners up here to
the 12th floor.

XX   **Unkai** – Grand Hotel   ⅋ AC ⌒
Kärntner Ring 9 (7th floor) ⊠ *1010 –* Ⓜ *Karlsplatz*   Plan: **E3**
*– ℰ (01) 5 15 80 91 10 – www.grandhotelwien.com – Closed Monday
lunch*
Menu 55/130 € – Carte 26/94 €
• Japanese • Minimalist •
A bright and modern restaurant offering authentic teppanyaki dishes served in
both low Japanese-style and more conventional European tables. Unkai Sushi
Bar in the basement serves sushi brunches on Saturdays, Sundays and public
holidays.

XX   **Cantinetta Antinori**   ⌂ AC ⇔
Jasomirgottstr. 3 ⊠ *1010 –* Ⓜ *Stephansplatz – ℰ (01)*   Plan: **D2**
5 33 77 22 – www.cantinetta-antinori.com
Carte 48/67 € – (booking advisable)
• Italian • Friendly • Cosy •
The Viennese offshoot of the original Florentine restaurant serves primarily
Tuscan cuisine, including succulent braised rabbit. It has a lively but stylish
atmosphere. Wide selection of high quality Antinori wines (available by the
glass).

XX   **at eight** – The Ring   ⌂ ⅋ AC ⌒
Kärntner Ring 8 ⊠ *1010 –* Ⓜ *Karlsplatz – ℰ (01)*   Plan: **E3**
2 21 22 39 30 – www.ateight-restaurant.com
Menu 45/62 € – Carte 47/59 €
• Traditional • Fashionable •
Simple, modern lines set the tone at this restaurant where the chairs are
dressed with covers and the tables with runners in the evenings. The seasonal,
classic but contemporary cuisine is accompanied by primarily Viennese wines.

XX   **Plachutta**   ⌂ AC
Wollzeile 38 ⊠ *1010 –* Ⓜ *Stubentor – ℰ (01) 5 12 15 77* Plan: **E2**
– www.plachutta.at
Carte 30/50 € – (booking advisable)
• Austrian • Traditional • Inn •
For years, the Plachutta family has been committed to Viennese tradition. They
serve beef in many forms in the green panelled dining room or on the large
terrace.

XX   **Kristian's Monastiri**   ⌂ ⇔
Neustiftgasse 16 ⊠ *1070 –* Ⓜ *Lerchenfelder Str.*   Plan: **C3**
– ℰ (01) 5 26 94 48 – www.kristians.monastiri.at
Carte 32/57 € – (dinner only)
• Regional/country • Cosy •
Not far from the Volkstheater you will find the outwardly somewhat unprepos-
sessing Monastiri. In both the slightly more casual smoking area and the more
elegant non-smoking area chef Jürgen Winter serves upmarket cuisine with a
strong regional slant. Try arctic char tartar with cucumber and hazelnuts.

AUSTRIA - VIENNA

XX **Gaumenspiel**

Zieglergasse 54 ⊠ *1070 –* ⑩ *Burgg-Stadthalle*   Plan I: **A3**
– ℰ (01) 5 26 11 08 – www.gaumenspiel.at
– Closed Sunday and Bank Holidays
Menu 40/49 € – Carte 39/56 € – *(dinner only)*
• International • Friendly •

A friendly restaurant in the 7th district that has made its mark as something of a culinary institution in Vienna. Choose from four menus in both the pleasant dining rooms and the pretty interior courtyard. Dishes include roasted pink wild duck breast and braised leg with shiitake mushrooms. Alternatively, you can eat in the lively bistro. Simple guestrooms.

XX **Al Borgo**

An der Hülben 1 ⊠ *1010 –* ⑩ *Stubentor – ℰ (01)*   Plan: **E2**
5 12 85 59 – www.alborgo.at – Closed Saturday lunch, Sunday and Bank Holidays
Carte 28/47 €
• Italian • Friendly •

Al Borgo enjoys a very central and yet secluded location in the heart of Vienna's 1st district. It serves classic Italian cuisine and a range of excellent seasonal dishes. Regular themed weeks.

XX **Konstantin Filippou**

Dominikanerbastei 17 ⊠ *1010 –* ⑩ *Stubentor – ℰ (01)*   Plan: **E2**
5 12 22 29 – www.konstantinfilippou.com – Closed 3 weeks August, Saturday-Sunday and Bank Holidays
Menu 39 € (lunch)/119 € – *(booking advisable)*
• Innovative • Minimalist • Fashionable •

In this minimalistic restaurant with its lovely wooden floors and shining ash wood tables Konstantin Filippou showcases his delicate, complex creations. In the main dining room you can even watch the chefs preparing the entrées. In summer the restaurant and its accomplished service move out into the garden.
→ Stockfischbrandade, Saiblingskaviar. Mieral Taube, Mandel, Kürbis, Johannisbeere. Passionsfrucht, Banane, Sherry, Kokos.
⊛ **o boufés** – See restaurant listing

XX **Julius Meinl am Graben**

Graben 19 (1st floor) ⊠ *1010 –* ⑩ *Stephansplatz*   Plan: **D2**
– ℰ (01) 5 32 33 34 60 00 – www.meinlamgraben.at
– Closed Sunday
Menu 39/85 € – Carte 47/79 € – *(booking essential)*
• Classic • Formal • Cosy •

This restaurant and its sister delicatessen (housed in the same building) come to life early in the morning. Ambitious food is served using the finest quality ingredients from breakfast through to dinner (make sure you try the stuffed quail with greengages) complete with a view over Vienna's pedestrian zone.

XX **Zum weissen Rauchfangkehrer**

Weihburggasse 4 ⊠ *1010 –* ⑩ *Stephansplatz – ℰ (01)*   Plan: **E2**
5 12 34 71 – www.weisser-rauchfangkehrer.at
Menu 34/50 € – Carte 27/59 € – *(booking advisable)*
• Austrian • Traditional • Formal •

Viennese cuisine including seasonal dishes, such as duo of Schneebergland duck and specials like calf's head brawn. These are served throughout the day in comfortable, traditional dining rooms. Wide range of wines and digestifs.

Kussmaul

Spittelberggasse 12 ⊠ 1070 – ⓜ Volkstheater   Plan II : **C3**
*– ℰ (01) 58 77 62 85 – www.kussmaul.at – Closed end July-mid August
and Saturday lunch, Sunday lunch*
Menu 58/100 € – Carte 50/71 € – *(booking advisable)*
• Creative • Fashionable • Design •
Mario Bernatovic and his team await you at Vienna's latest 'in' restaurant. Pleasantly uncomplicated with an open kitchen and modern design, it offers a taste
of urban flair and lifestyle. The food is creative, international and ambitious. Try
a seat at the chef's table. There is a shorter, simpler lunchtime menu and a café
serving light meals.

Meierei im Stadtpark – Restaurant Steirereck

Am Heumarkt 2a ⊠ 1030 – ⓜ Stadtpark – ℰ (01)   Plan: **F2**
7 13 31 68 – www.steirereck.at – Closed Saturday-Sunday
Carte 29/48 €
• Regional/country • Friendly •
The Steirereck's pleasantly light and airy milk and cheese bar is fitted out entirely in white with the occasional splash of fresh green. The food has a regional
slant so try the classics, which include Ritschert stew with wild duck and Steirereck goulash. Also taste one of the local pastries!

Schnattl

Lange Gasse 40 ⊠ 1080 – ⓜ Rathaus – ℰ (01)   Plan I: **A3**
*4 05 34 00 – www.schnattl.com – Closed 1 week Easter, 3 weeks August,
2 weeks Christmas, Saturday-Sunday and Bank Holidays*
Menu 17/32 € – Carte 34/46 € – *(lunch only)*
• Regional/country • Cosy •
This friendly, personally-run restaurant is set a little out of the way but remains
popular with regulars and theatregoers. They appreciate the classic cuisine and
warm, friendly atmosphere.

Le Salzgries Paris

Marc-Aurel-Str. 6 ⊠ 1010 – ⓜ Schwedenplatz – ℰ (01)   Plan: **D1**
*5 33 40 30 – www.le-salzgries.at – Closed Sunday and Bank Holidays,
January-November: Sunday-Monday*
Carte 39/67 €
• French classic • Brasserie • Fashionable •
This exuberant, lively bistro is decorated in warm colours and has a modern bar,
which is a real eye-catcher. The tried and tested French cuisine offers classic
dishes including entrecote.

SHIKI Brasserie – Restaurant SHIKI

Krugerstr. 3 ⊠ 1010 – ⓜ Karlsplatz – ℰ (01) 5 12 73 97   Plan: **E3**
– www.shiki.at – Closed Sunday-Monday and Bank Holidays
Carte 51/128 €
• Japanese • Brasserie • Design •
This minimalist-style brasserie with its large terrace is SHIKI's less formal eatery.
It offers a wider range of dishes from miso soup to tempura and sushi – the lat-
ter prepared before you as you sit at the sushi bar.

Sakai

Florianigasse 36 ⊠ 1080 – ⓜ Josefstädter Str. – ℰ (01)   Plan I: **A3**
7 29 65 41 – www.sakai.co.at – Closed Monday and Bank Holidays
Menu 25 € (lunch)/75 € – Carte 22/59 €
• Japanese • Minimalist •
Hiroshi Sakai, no stranger in Vienna, has now set up his own restaurant after 10
years at Unkai. He serves seasonally influenced, traditional Japanese cuisine.
Take a seat in the authentically simple surroundings and enjoy some sushi and
sashimi or better still, one of his sophisticated set Kaiseki menus.

AUSTRIA - VIENNA

X Petz im Gußhaus ✿

Gußhausstr. 23 ⊠ 1040 – Ⓜ Taubstummeng. – ☎ (01)   Plan I: **B3**
5 04 47 50 – www.gusshaus.at – Closed 1 week early February, 3 weeks
August and Sunday-Monday
Carte 32/55 € – *(booking advisable)*
• Austrian • Cosy •

Located not far from the Karlsplatz, this restaurant promises excellent, fully flavoured cuisine with international influences, as well as Austrian dishes. Try the
fried chicken with potato and cucumber salad, the lemon and veal ragout with
bone marrow dumplings, or the octopus in fennel and curry stock with risotto
balls. All served in a smart dining room.

X Motto am Fluss ✿

Franz Josef Kai 2 ⊠ 1010 – Ⓜ Schwedenplatz – ☎ (01)   Plan: **E1**
2 52 55 10 – www.mottoamfluss.at
Carte 35/58 €
• International • Fashionable • Friendly •

As befits its location on the banks of the Danube (by the jetty for the Twin City
Liner), this modern building with its glass façade is modelled on a boat. Smart
1950s interior style and international dishes. Less expensive at lunchtimes.

X Artner auf der Wieden 🛖

Floragasse 6 ⊠ 1040 – Ⓜ Taubstummengasse   Plan I: **B3**
– ☎ (01) 5 03 50 33 – www.artner.co.at – Closed Saturday lunch, Sunday
lunch and Bank Holidays lunch
Carte 27/53 €
• International • Fashionable • Design •

A great place for real Viennese cooking including Wiener Schnitzel and the delicious 'Kaiserschmarrn' dessert. Dishes from the the charcoal grill are also available. Join the busy business diners to sample the excellent value lunch menu.

X Tempel 🛖

Praterstr. 56 ⊠ 1020 – Ⓜ Nestroyplatz – ☎ (01)   Plan: **F1**
2 14 01 79 – www.restaurant-tempel.at – Closed 24 December-6 January
and Saturday lunch, Sunday-Monday
Menu 18 € (lunch)/55 € – Carte 28/48 €
• Regional/country • Bistro •

You may have to search for the slightly concealed entrance to the interior courtyard and lovely terrace that lead to this friendly restaurant. It serves flavoursome, contemporary Mediterranean cuisine and offers a good value lunchtime
menu.

X Bernhauer's 🛖

Pfeilgasse 2 ⊠ 1080 – Ⓜ Josefstädter Str. – ☎ (01)   Plan I: **A3**
9 57 59 83 – www.bernhauers.at – Closed August and Saturday-Monday
lunch
Menu 20 € (lunch)/60 € – Carte 34/67 €
• International • Fashionable •

The Bernhauer family's modern little restaurant is located in a plain corner
house in the heart of the Josefstadt quarter. The tasty international food specialises in dry aged beef steaks. In summer you can sit outside on the pavement.

X Das Engel 🛖🚭

Große Pfarrgasse 5 ⊠ 1020 – Ⓜ Schottenring – ☎ (01)   Plan I: **B2**
2 12 78 94 – www.dasengel.at – Closed 24 December-7 January, August
and Saturday-Sunday
Carte 28/46 € – *(dinner only)*
• International • Bistro •

Whether you think of it as an urban bar or a minimalist bistro, Das Engel is a
great place to enjoy some pleasantly pared down, tasty cuisine. Una Abraham
cooks both classic dishes such as boeuf bourguignon and Mediterranean fare.

AUSTRIA - VIENNA

✕ **Gasthaus Pöschl**

Weihburggasse 17 ✉ *1010 –* Ⓜ *Stephansplatz –* ✆ *(01)* Plan: **E2**
513 52 88 – www.gasthauspoeschl.com
Carte 30/43 € – *(booking advisable)*
• Traditional • Cosy • Family •

This long-established little restaurant is close to St Stephan's cathedral and the Franziskanerplatz. It serves traditional regional cuisine including Viennese-style fried chicken and plum doughnuts. It is best to book as the few tables under the lovely vaulted ceiling are in great demand.

✕ **Weibel's Wirtshaus**

Kumpfgasse 2 ✉ *1010 –* Ⓜ *Stubentor –* ✆ *(01)* Plan: **E2**
5 12 39 86 – www.weibel.at
Menu 30 € – Carte 26/47 € – *(booking advisable)*
• Austrian • Friendly •

Just a few minutes' walk from St Stephen's Cathedral, Weibel's Wirtshaus is the archetypal Viennese restaurant – warm and friendly, rustic and snug! It also has a charming garden in the small alleyway. The food is traditional and Viennese.

✕ **La Mia**

Lerchenfelder Str. 13 ✉ *1070 –* Ⓜ *Lerchenfelder Str.* Plan: **C3**
– ✆ *(01) 5 22 42 21 – www.lamia.at*
Carte 22/42 €
• Italian • Bistro • Rustic •

This informal bistro makes a lively alternative to Kristian's Monastiri next door (under the same management). The fresh Italian cuisine includes antipasti, pasta and grilled meats, such as fillet steak with rosemary potatoes, as well as pizzas baked in the wood-fired oven.

✕ **LABSTELLE**

Lugeck 6 ✉ *1010 –* Ⓜ *Stephansplatz –* ✆ *(01)* Plan: **E2**
2 36 21 22 – www.labstelle.at – Closed Sunday and Bank Holidays
Menu 16/56 € – Carte 35/52 € – *(booking advisable)*
• Regional/country • Design • Bistro •

Labstelle offers an attractive, upmarket bistro atmosphere with a relaxed bar area. It serves ambitious seasonal, regional fare including Arctic char, Marschfeld artichoke, parsnips and parsley. There is also a reduced lunchtime menu and a pretty interior courtyard.

✕ **loca.**

Stubenbastei 10 ✉ *1010 –* Ⓜ *Stubentor –* ✆ *(01)* Plan: **E2**
5 12 11 72 – www.bettereatbetter.com
Menu 44 € – Carte 38/49 € – *(dinner only) (booking advisable)*
• Regional/country • Cosy •

"Better eat better" is the slogan of this friendly little restaurant close to the Stadtpark. The menu includes dishes such as zander served with two sorts of pumpkin and *speck*. Don't be afraid to ask for the special theatre menus.

✕ **Servitenwirt**
☺

Servitengasse 7 ✉ *1010 –* Ⓜ *Roßauer Lände –* ✆ *(01)* Plan I: **A2**
3 15 23 87 – www.sevitenwirt.at
Menu 45/60 € – Carte 24/47 €
• Austrian • Friendly • Cosy •

If you are looking for flavoursome, authentic Viennese cuisine, that is exactly what you will find alongside the international fare at Servitenwirt. It is set in a quiet square close to the church. The clientele consists mainly of regulars and locals, with the addition of an occasional tourist or two.

X
🕾

mochi

Praterstr. 15 ⊠ 1020 – ⓜ Nestroyplatz – ℰ (01)   Plan: **E1**
9 25 13 80 – www.mochi.at – Closed 24 December-10 January and Sunday
Carte 17/46 € – *(booking essential at dinner)*
• Japanese • Trendy • Fashionable •

Take care not to overlook this small, outwardly unprepossessing restaurant.
Eduard Dimant offers authentic Japanese cuisine with the odd modern twist at
very reasonable prices - simple and delicious. Try the 'rolls', but also the gyoza
soup, sake teriyaki or tori karage. No reservations taken before 3pm.

X
🕾

o boufés

Dominikanerbastei 17 ⊠ 1010 – ⓜ Stubentor – ℰ (01)   Plan: **E2**
5 12 22 29 – www.konstantinfilippou.com – Closed Saturday-Sunday and
Bank Holidays
Carte 34/52 € – *(booking advisable)*
• Mediterranean • Bistro •

Located just next door to its gourmet counterpart, this relaxed restaurant with
its bare walls, high ceilings and minimalist decor, serves a varied menu. It ranges
from a charcuterie plate to keftedes (meatballs) with hilopites (small Green
pasta squares), as well as black pudding ravioli with cuttlefish, shellfish and
peas. The food is a accompanied by a choice of natural wines.

X
🕾

Tian Bistro

Schrankgasse 4 ⊠ 1070 – ⓜ Volkstheater – ℰ (01)   Plan: **C3**
5 26 94 91 – www.tian-bistro.com
Carte 18/26 €
• Vegetarian • Bistro • Friendly •

This is the more casual bistro-style alternative to the Michelin-starred vegetarian
restaurant of the same name. Here too, the simple, flavoursome food is vegetarian or vegan, ranging from cream of tomato soup to *flammekueche* and
crisp broccoli with creamed sweet corn. There is also an attractive, covered interior courtyard.

X

Mercado

Stubenring 18 ⊠ 1010 – ⓜ Stubentor – ℰ (01)   Plan: **E2**
5 12 25 05 – www.mercado.at – Closed Saturday lunch
Menu 69/89 € (dinner) – Carte 37/51 €
• Other world kitchens • Exotic • Cosy •

The ideal restaurant for those who like it hot! Mercado serves "Latin inspired
market cuisine" in a relaxed, Latin American atmosphere. Don't miss the pan-
fried octopus with potatoes and tamarind barbecue sauce – à la carte or served
"family-style".

X

Yohm

Petersplatz 3 ⊠ 1010 – ⓜ Stephansplatz – ℰ (01)   Plan: **D2**
5 33 29 00 – www.yohm.com
Menu 25 € (lunch) – Carte 32/64 €
• Asian • Fashionable •

A pleasant modern restaurant with a striking orange decor occupying two
floors. The open kitchen serves up contemporary twists on Southeast Asian cuisine that borrows liberally from around the globe. Good wine selection.

OUTER DISTRICTS   **PLAN I**

Hilton Vienna-Danube Waterfront

Handelskai 269 ⊠ 1020 – ⓜ Dresdnerstr. – ℰ (01) 7 27 77   **P**
– www.vienna-danube.hilton.com   Plan: **B1**
367 rm ⌧ – ♦169 € ♦♦189 €
• Chain hotel • Business • Contemporary •

The rooms in this former warehouse building are spacious, elegant and modern.
They offer views over the Danube or the city with executive rooms on the sixth
and seventh floors and the Executive Lounge on the eighth. The Waterfront restaurant and terrace also provide river views.

Park Royal Palace Vienna

Schlossallee 8 (by Mariahilfer Straße **C3**) ✉ 1140 – ✆ (01) 8 91 10 – www.austria-trend.at/prw

233 rm – 🚹87/280 € 🚹🚹87/280 € – ☕ 19 € – 21 suites

• Conference hotel • Functional •

The first thing to strike you on entering this conference hotel is the large atrium-style lobby with its modern straight lines and muted colours. The spacious suites offer the best views of Schöllbrunn Castle. Direct access to Vienna's Museum of Technology, which serves as an occasional venue for events.

Melia

Donau City Str. 7 (by A 22 B1) ✉ 1220 – Ⓜ Kaisermühlen – ✆ (01) 9 01 04 – www.melia.com

253 rm – 🚹165/390 € 🚹🚹165/390 € – ☕ 26 € – 5 suites

• Business • Chain hotel • Design •

Located in the modern DC Tower, this hotel is just a few underground stations from the city centre. The rooms are just as good as the location, they are all stylish, practical and offer the latest technology and floor-to-ceiling windows. The 57 restaurant (on the 57th floor) serves Mediterranean cuisine with an impressive view.

Kahlenberg Suite Hotel

Am Kahlenberg 2 (by Heiligenstädter Straße **A1**) ✉ 1190 – ✆ (01) 32 81 50 09 00 – www.kahlenberg.eu

20 rm ☕ – 🚹179/219 € 🚹🚹219/269 €

• Conference hotel • Modern •

Its location is on Vienna's local mountain. The amazing views, as well as the spacious, high quality, very modern rooms with panoramic windows, makes this a very unique hotel. This restaurant with a simple, elegant style has a wonderful terrace.

Falkensteiner Hotel Wien Margareten

Margaretengürtel 142 ✉ 1050 – Ⓜ Margaretengürtel – ✆ (01) 36 16 39 00 – www.falkensteiner.com

Plan: **A3**

195 rm – 🚹109/369 € 🚹🚹109/369 € – ☕ 20 € – 4 suites

• Business • Chain hotel • Modern •

This business hotel is set between Schönbrunn Castle and the city. It offers good conference facilities, easy connections into Vienna and an appealing mix of modern design and Biedermeier style. The seventh floor houses a leisure area complete with terrace for rest and relaxation.

Courtyard by Marriott Wien Messe

Trabrennstr. 4 (by Handelskai **B2**) ✉ 1020 – Ⓜ Praterstern – ✆ (01) 7 27 30 – www.courtyard-wien-messe.at

251 rm – 🚹99/260 € 🚹🚹149/360 € – ☕ 20 € – 7 suites

• Conference hotel • Contemporary • Modern •

Located in Exhibition Hall D, the hotel is ideal for business travellers but it is also close to the Prater, the race course and the stadium. The rooms are comfortable yet functional. Modern conference facilities and large fitness area. International classics and regional cuisine in a casual setting.

Zeitgeist

Sonnwendgasse 15 ✉ 1100 – Ⓜ Hauptbahnhof – ✆ (01) 90 26 50 – www.zeitgeist-vienna.com

Plan: **B3**

254 rm – 🚹78/128 € 🚹🚹93/286 € – ☕ 14 €

• Business • Functional • Design •

Located not far from the main railway station, Zeitgeist offers a variety of different room categories. These include Urban, Prestige (with view and terrace) and Zeitgeist Suite, which are all fashionable, minimalist in style and with the latest technology. The Pergola bistro serves international fare and there is also a good sauna and interior courtyard garden.

roomz Vienna

Paragonstr. 1 (by Landstr. Gürtel **B3***) ✉ 1110 – ✆ (01) 7 43 17 77 – www.roomz-vienna.com – Closed 19-26 December*
152 rm – †69/124 € ††79/134 € – ☕ 15 €
• Business • Design •

This well-run and practically equipped hotel has a young, colourful design. The underground station is a 10min journey from the Dom. Handy, nearby underground car park. The lobby with its open restaurant is also fashionable.

XX ✿✿

Mraz & Sohn

Wallensteinstr. 59 ✉ 1200 – Ⓜ Friedensbrücke – ✆ (01) 3 30 45 94 – www.mraz-sohn.at – Closed 1-6 January, 19-28 March, 13 August-4 September, Saturday-Sunday and Bank Holidays Plan: **A2**
Menu 65/112 € – *(dinner only) (booking advisable)*
• Creative • Individual • Fashionable •

When eating out at the Mraz family restaurant you can be sure of a creative cuisine: a beautifully presented menu offering up to nine courses. The interior (dark stone floor, grey tones, clean lines, art works) is as modern as the food.
➜ Kalbsbeuschel, Lauch, Carabineros. Wagyu Flanksteak, Steinpilze, Erdäpfel. Mais, Feige, Gries.

XX

Eckel

Sieveringer Str. 46 (by Billrothstraße **A1***) ✉ 1190 – ✆ (01) 3 20 32 18 – www.restauranteckel.at – Closed 8-22 August, 23 December-18 January and Sunday-Monday*
Carte 23/60 €
• Regional/country • Family • Traditional •

This family run business has a good number of regulars from the 19th district, one of the most attractive in Vienna. It offers comfortable dining rooms serving both classic regional fare and lobster specialities. Wonderful garden.

XX

dasTURM

Wienerbergstr. 7 (22 th floor, at Business Park Vienna, Turm D1) (by Wiedner Hauptstraße **B3***) ✉ 1100 – ✆ (01) 6 07 65 00 – www.dasturm.at – Closed 23 December-6 January, 1-7 February, 23 July-7 August, Saturday-Sunday and Bank Holidays*
Menu 30 € (lunch)/83 €
• Creative • Fashionable • Friendly •

The ascent in the all-glass external lift here is an experience in itself! On top the great view is accompanied by two ambitious and creative set menus: 'Kulinarische Ausblicke' and 'Kulinarische Einblicke'. Business lunch at midday. There is also a bar with a terrace just below on the 21st floor.

XX

Vikerl's Lokal

Würffelgasse 4 ✉ 1150 – Ⓜ Wien Westbahnhof – ✆ (01) 8 92 19 52 – www.vikerls-lokal.at – Closed 2 weeks end August and Saturday lunch, Sunday dinner-Monday Plan: **A3**
Menu 15 € (lunch)/58 € – Carte 32/51 €
• Traditional • Cosy • Friendly •

If you are looking for traditional Austrian cuisine served in friendly rustic surroundings, you will find them both at this long-established restaurant in the Vienna suburbs. The Trummer-Milkovits family serves such delights as braised oxtail in red wine sauce, as well as a popular, good value lunchtime menu.

X

Hill

Sieveringer Str. 137 (by Billrothstr. **A1***) ✉ 1190 – ✆ (01) 3 20 11 11 – www.hill-restaurant.at – Closed 1 week early January, 2 weeks August and Sunday-Monday*
Menu 45/85 € – Carte 51/66 € – *(dinner only)*
• International • Neighbourhood • Friendly •

A great restaurant located in the attractive 19th district and run with great commitment. The cuisine – a good mix of seasonal and regional dishes – is based on high quality produce and, above all, taste. Look out for the daily specials.

Freyenstein

Thimiggasse 11 (by Währinger Straße A2) ✉ 1180 – ℰ (0664) 4 39 08 37 – www.freyenstein.at – Closed 2-13 February, 10-14 May, 6-17 September and Sunday-Monday
Menu 34/48 € – *(dinner only) (booking advisable)*
• Traditional • Family • Individual •

Friendly, comfortable, casual and serving great food, this is just the type of restaurant you would love to find in your area! The menu changes regularly, offering 10 small dishes, two per course. Eating here is great fun!

Kutschker 44

Kutschergasse 44 (by Währinger Straße A2) ✉ 1180 – ℰ (01) 4 70 20 47 – www.kutschker44.at – Closed Sunday-Monday and Bank Holidays
Menu 38/43 € – Carte 32/60 € – *(dinner only)*
• Traditional • Fashionable •

The particularity of this informal, modern restaurant lies in the show kitchen situated in the bar. You can watch your choice from the contemporary, seasonal menu being prepared for you before you sit down to enjoy your meal.

Woracziczky

Spengergasse 52 ✉ 1050 – Ⓜ Pilgramgasse – ℰ (0699)   Plan: **A3**
11 22 95 30 – www.woracziczky.at – Closed 24 December-17 January, 8-28 August, Saturday-Sunday and Bank Holidays
Carte 22/44 €
• Austrian • Neighbourhood • Family •

The chef reserves a warm personal welcome for diners in this friendly, pleasantly informal inn (pronounced 'Vorashitkzy'). It is particularly popular for its casual atmosphere and local Viennese cuisine.

Rudi's Beisl

Wiedner Hauptstr. 88 ✉ 1050 – Ⓜ Taubstummengasse   Plan: **B3**
– ℰ (01) 5 44 51 02 – www.rudisbeisl.at – Closed Saturday-Sunday and Bank Holidays
Carte 16/46 € – *(booking advisable)*
• Regional/country • Simple • Neighbourhood •

Always busy and bustling, Rudi's Beisl is a down-to-earth eatery with lots of decoration on the walls – small, simple and snug! The friendly owner does the cooking himself: traditional fare such as schnitzel, boiled beef and pancakes.

Schübel-Auer

Kahlenberger Str. 22/Zahnradbahnstr. 17 (Döbling)   Plan: **A1**
✉ 1190 – ℰ (01) 3 70 22 22 – www.schuebel-auer.at
– Closed 23 December-February and Sunday-Monday, March-April and November-December: Sunday-Tuesday
Carte 15/28 € – *(open from 4pm)*
• Regional/country • Wine bar • Cosy •

Today the carefully refurbished former Auerhof (built in 1642 as a wine-grower's house) with its quiet interior courtyard makes a lovely restaurant. Located at the end of tramline D, it is easy to reach from the city centre.

Feuerwehr-Wagner

Grinzingerstr. 53 (Heiligenstadt) ✉ 1190 – ℰ (01)   Plan: **A1**
3 20 24 42 – www.feuerwehrwagner.at – Closed during Christmas
Carte 15/34 € – *(open from 4pm)*
• Regional/country • Wine bar • Rustic •

This typical, traditional Austrian wine tavern is greatly appreciated by regulars. Find a cosy, rustic decor with dark wood and simple tables. The terraced garden is particularly nice.

Mayer am Pfarrplatz

Pfarrplatz 2 (Heiligenstadt) ✉ 1190 – ✆ (01) 3 70 12 87 Plan: **A1**
– www.pfarrplatz.at
Menu 24/38 €
– Carte 20/35 € – *(Monday-Friday open from 4pm, Saturday-Sunday open from 12am)*
• Regional/country • Wine bar • Rustic •

A textbook traditional Austrian wine tavern: rustic furnishings, traditional Viennese folk music, and an attractive courtyard terrace. Of note: Beethoven lived here in 1817.

AT THE AIRPORT

NH Wien Airport

Einfahrtsstr. 1 ✉ 1300 – ✆ (01) 70 15 10 – www.nh-hotels.com
499 rm – †129/195 € ††129/195 € – ☕ 25 €
• Business • Modern • Classic •

The lobby, bar and restaurant area are spacious, the rooms well equipped and the hotel enjoys a convenient location close to the airport arrivals hall. All in all an ideal destination for the business traveller. The restaurant serves international cuisine alongside Austrian classics.

SALZBURG
SALZBURG

Population: 146 631

Gérald Schléwitz/Fotolia.com

Small but perfectly formed, Salzburg is a chocolate-box treasure, gift-wrapped in stunning Alpine surroundings. It's immortalised as the birthplace and inspiration of one of classical music's greatest stars, and shows itself off as northern Europe's grandest exhibitor of baroque style. Little wonder that in summer its population rockets, as the sound of music wafts from hotel rooms and festival hall windows during rehearsals for the Festspiele. In quieter times of the year, Salzburgers enjoy a leisurely and relaxed pace of life. Their love of music and the arts is renowned; and they enjoy the outdoors, too, making the most of the mountains and lakes, and the paths which run along the river Salzach and zig-zag through the woods and the grounds of Hellbrunn. The dramatic natural setting of Salzburg means you're never likely to get lost. Rising above the left bank (the Old Town) is the Mönchsberg Mountain and its fortress, the Festung Hohensalzburg, while the right bank (the New Town, this being a relative term) is guarded by the even taller Kapuzinerberg. In the New Town stands the Mozart family home, while the graceful gardens of the Schloss Mirabell draw the right bank crowds. The Altstadt (Old Town) is a UNESCO World Heritage Site and its star turn is its Cathedral. To the east is the quiet Nonntal area overlooked by the Nuns' Mountain.

SALZBURG IN...

→ **ONE DAY**
Festung Hohensalzburg, Museum der Moderne, Cathedral, Residenzplatz.

→ **TWO DAYS**
Mozart's birthplace, Nonntal, Kapuzinerberg, Mirabell Gardens, concert at Mozarteum.

→ **THREE DAYS**
Mozart's residence, Hangar 7, Hellbrunn Palace, concert at Landestheater.

PRACTICAL INFORMATION

ARRIVAL-DEPARTURE

✈Wolfgang Amadeus Mozart Airport is just west of the centre.

🚉The Hauptbahnhof (railway station) is centrally located on the right bank and is served by trains from all Europe's major locations.

Bus no.2 connects the airport with the Hauptbahnhof.

GETTING AROUND

Salzburg boasts a very efficient bus system. There are two main bus departure points on the left bank (Mozartsteg Bridge and Hanuschplatz) and two on the right (Hauptbahnhof and Mirabellplatz). You can buy tickets in three ways: in blocks of five singles; for a day's duration; or for a week. If you take your sightseeing seriously, then get a Salzburg Card for free travel on public transport and reduced admission to many tourist attractions; choose a card for 24, 48 or 72 hours.

CALENDAR HIGHLIGHTS

January/February
Mozartwoche (Mozart Week).

March
Salzburg Raster Festival.

May
Pfingstfestspiele (Whitsun Festival).

June/July
Sommerszene (Performance Festival).

July/August
Festspiele (Salzburg Festival).

October
Kulturtage (Cultural Days).

December
Weihnachtsmarkt (Christmas market).

EATING OUT

Salzburg's cuisine takes much of its influence from the days of the Austro-Hungarian Empire, with Bavarian elements added to the mix. Over the centuries it was characterised by substantial pastry and egg dishes to fill the stomachs of local salt mine workers; it's still hearty and meaty and is typified by dumplings and broths. In the city's top restaurants, a regional emphasis is still very important but the cooking has a lighter, more modern touch. Beyond the city are picturesque inns and tranquil beer gardens, many idyllically set by lakes. Do try the dumplings: Pinzgauer Nocken are made of potato pastry and filled with minced pork; another favourite is Gröstl, a filling meal of 'leftovers', including potatoes, dumplings, sausages and smoked meat roasted in a pan. If you want a snack, then Jausen is for you – cold meals with bread and sausage, cheese, dumplings, bacon etc, followed by an Obstler, made from distilled fruit. Salzburg's sweet tooth is evident in the Salzburger Nockerl, a rich soufflé omelette made with fruit and soft meringue.

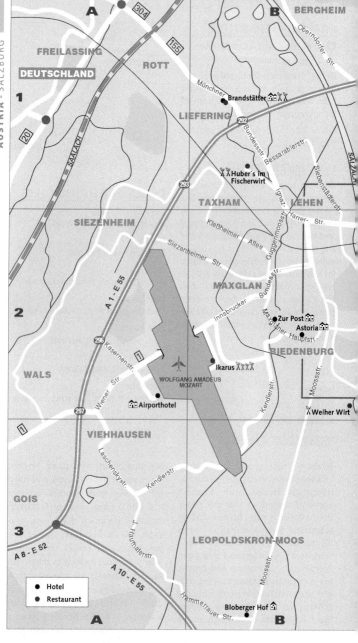

A 304 | **B** BERGHEIM

Oberndorfer Str.

FREILASSING | ROTT

155

DEUTSCHLAND

Münchner Str.

Brandstätter 🏨🏨🍴🍴

1

20

SAALACH

LIEFERING

292

Bundesstr. | Bessarabierstr.

SALZACH

Siebenstädterstr.

293

🍴🍴 **Huber's im Fischerwirt**

TAXHAM | LEHEN

Ignaz- | Harrer- Str.

SIEZENHEIM

Kleßheimer Allee

Guggenmoosstr.

Siezenheimer Str.

MAXGLAN

Bundesstr.

A 1 - E 55

Innsbrucker Str.

Maxglaner

Zur Post 🏨🏨
Astoria 🏨🏨

2

296

Kasernenstr.

1

Hauptstr.

RIEDENBURG

WALS

Wiener Str.

✈
WOLFGANG AMADEUS MOZART

Ikarus 🍴🍴🍴🍴

Kendlerstr.

Moosstr.

297

🏨🏨 **Airporthotel**

🍴 **Weiher Wirt**

1

VIEHHAUSEN

Laschenskystr.

Kendlerstr.

GOIS

J.- Haufnerstr.

3

A 8 - E 52

LEOPOLDSKRON-MOOS

Moosstr.

A 10 - E 55

Hemmetrauer Str.

Bloberger Hof 🏨

● Hotel
● Restaurant

A | **B**

50

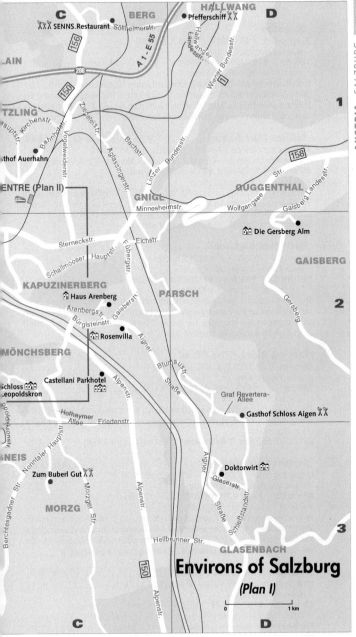

Environs of Salzburg
(Plan I)

C · BERG · HALLWANG · D

XXX SENNS.Restaurant   Söllheimerstr.   ● Pfefferschiff XX

156
41 · E 55
288
150

Hallwanger Landesstr.
Wiener Bundesstr.

AIN
TZLING
Hauptstr. Kirchenstr.
Bahnhofstr.
sthof Auerhahn ●
Zieleisstr.
Vogelweiderstr.
Bachstr.
Aglassingerstr.
Linzer Bundesstr.

158
Str.
Gaisberg Landesstr.

1

ENTRE (Plan II)

GNIGL · GUGGENTHAL
Minnesheimstr.   Wolfgangsee   Gaisberg

Sterneckstr.
Schallmooser Hauptstr.
Eichstr.
Fübergstr.

● Die Gersberg Alm

GAISBERG

KAPUZINERBERG
⌂ Haus Arenberg
Arenbergstr.
Gaisbergstr.
Bürglsteinstr.

PARSCH

Gersberg

2

🏨 Rosenvilla
Aigner Str.

MÖNCHSBERG

Castellani Parkhotel 🏨
Alpenstr.
Blumaustr. Straße

chloss 🏨
eopoldskron

Graf Revertera-
Allee

● Gasthof Schloss Aigen XX

Hofhaymer
Allee   Friedenstr.

eopoldskronstr.

NEIS
Nonntaler Hauptstr.
Berchtesgadner Str.
Morzger Str.

● Zum Buberl Gut XX

MORZG

Aigner
Str.
Glaserstr.
Schießstandstr.

● Doktorwirt 🏨

3

Alpenstr.

Hellbrunner Str.
GLASENBACH

150

0 ——— 1 km

C · D

Sheraton

Auerspergstr. 4 ✉ 5020 – ✆ (0662) 88 99 90 Plan: E1
– www.sheratonsalzburg.com
166 rm – 🚹195/420 € 🚹🚹215/475 € – ☕ 32 € – 14 suites
• Chain hotel • Functional •
This smart hotel with comfortably furnished rooms is situated between the Congress Centre and Mirabelle Gardens. A highlight is the elegant, modern Sky Suite on seventh-floor. Mirabell offers classic cuisine and a garden-facing terrace. Small regional dishes are offered in the bistro.

Schloss Mönchstein

Mönchsberg Park 26 ✉ 5020 – ✆ (0662) 8 48 55 50 Plan: E1
– www.monchstein.at – Closed 1 February-9 March, 1-23 November
24 rm ☕ – 🚹280/460 € 🚹🚹350/520 € – 3 suites
• Historic • Personalised •
This hotel is set in a 14C castle at the "top of Salzburg". It offers rooms decorated in the very best of taste, excellent service and great views over the city. There is also an exclusive spa and an outdoor pool set in 3½ acres of grounds.
Schloss Mönchstein – See restaurant listing

Castellani Parkhotel

Alpenstr. 6 ✉ 5020 – ✆ (0662) 2 06 00 Plan I: C2
– www.hotel-castellani.com
151 rm ☕ – 🚹98/208 € 🚹🚹138/248 € – 2 suites
• Business • Classic • Modern •
The combination of listed mansion house and modern annexe really is a great success. Some of the contemporary rooms boast balconies and the restaurant has a pretty interior courtyard. For events there is the old vicarage and a small chapel, which is a popular wedding venue.

Crowne Plaza - The Pitter

Rainerstr. 6 ✉ 5020 – ✆ (0662) 88 97 80 Plan: F1
– www.imlauer.com
199 rm ☕ – 🚹119/219 € 🚹🚹139/259 € – 9 suites
• Chain hotel • Functional •
This centrally located hotel was built in 1864. It offers comfortable rooms in the classic American style, as well as the exclusive Salzburg Suite. The Pitter Keller offers regional fare.
IMLAUER Sky Bar & Restaurant – See restaurant listing

Schloss Leopoldskron

Leopoldskronstr. 56 ✉ 5020 – ✆ (0662) 83 98 30 Plan I: C1
– www.schloss-leopoldskron.com
67 rm ☕ – 🚹127/157 € 🚹🚹167/262 € – 12 suites
• Rural • Historic • Historic •
With an idyllic setting in 17 acres of grounds, this 18C palace boasts a stunning, almost museum-like hall, the sumptuous Max Reinhardt library and a wonderful stucco-decorated staircase. The main building offers stylish suites, while the adjacent Meierhof annexe is home to attractive, modern guestrooms.

Wolf-Dietrich Altstadthotel

Wolf-Dietrich-Str. 7 ✉ 5020 – ✆ (0662) 87 12 75 Plan: F1
– www.wolf-dietrich.at
40 rm ☕ – 🚹70/136 € 🚹🚹113/238 € – 4 suites
• Townhouse • Cosy •
This hotel in the old town is regularly renovated to ensure everything is in perfect working order. The rooms are well appointed and classic in style. There is also a pretty indoor pool complete with sauna in the former wine cellar.

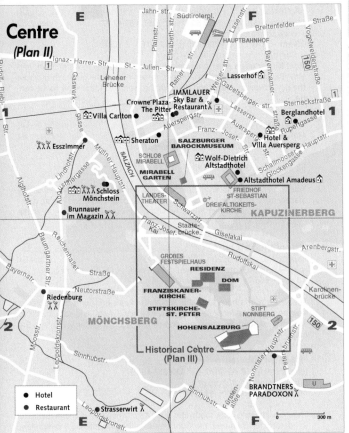

Hotel & Villa Auersperg
♿ 🛉 AC ♨ P

Auerspergstr. 61 ⊠ 5020 – ℰ (0662) 88 94 40
Plan: F1
– www.auersperg.at
55 rm 🖙 **–** †129/180 € ††155/295 € – 1 suite
• **Townhouse** • **Contemporary** • **Elegant** •

A veritable oasis in the city! The hotel offers beautifully appointed and gene-rously sized rooms complete with complimentary fruit and water when you arrive. There is a charming garden, pleasant, attentive staff and a friendly bar that serves snacks. Don't miss the great sauna with its roof terrace!

Villa Carlton
P

Markus-Sittikus-Str. 3 ⊠ 5020 – ℰ (0662) 88 21 91
Plan: E1
– www.villa-carlton.at
39 rm – †87/157 € ††93/195 € – 🖙 15 € – 13 suites
• Townhouse • Modern •

The pretty residence has been completely renovated, and this has not been at the expense of its charming high-ceilinged rooms, which come in various styles. These are all modern and include country house, elegant, traditional and pop art.

AUSTRIA - SALZBURG

Astoria   🅿️

Maxglaner Hauptstr. 7 ✉ 5020 – ☎ (0662) 83 42 77   Plan I: **B2**
– www.salzburgastoria.com
28 rm – 💲70/120 € 💲💲90/150 € – � 10 € – 3 suites
• Family • Functional • Modern •
Josef Illinger offers a personal welcome, modern rooms in warm tones, and everything is nicely cared for. Pastries are served to hotel guests throughout the day, as well as snacks and drinks in the evenings. 15min walk to the centre.

Zur Post   🏮 🅿️

Maxglaner Hauptstr. 45 ✉ 5020   Plan I: **B2**
– ☎ (0662) 8 32 33 90 – www.hotelzurpost.info
– Closed 20-27 December
38 rm – 💲56/90 € 💲💲70/148 € – ⊡ 12 €
• Inn • Functional •
You will enjoy the lovely rooms, excellent breakfast and dedicated family management here. The hotel's main building and the Georg and Renate guesthouses offer a classic feel. While the Villa Ceconi, some 200m away, is a little more modern.

Berglandhotel   🅿️

Rupertgasse 15 ✉ 5020 – ☎ (0662) 87 23 18   Plan: **F1**
– www.berglandhotel.at – Closed 1-20 February, 14-28 December
18 rm – 💲65/75 € 💲💲85/155 € – ⊡ 7 €
• Family • Personalised • Functional •
The rooms at this hotel are either modern or rustic and some have parquet flooring or antique furniture. The breakfast room is warm and cosy thanks to its tiled wood-burning stove and modern red decor. Small terrace behind the hotel.

Haus Arenberg   🛁 ≼ 🛗 🚗

Blumensteinstr. 8 ✉ 5020 – ☎ (0662) 64 00 97   Plan I: **C2**
– www.arenberg-salzburg.at
16 rm ⊡ – 💲85/108 € 💲💲129/159 €
• Family • Cosy •
Though a little long in the tooth now, the hotel retains a certain charm thanks to its adorable female owner, the slightly elevated location offering a lovely view, and breakfast being served on the terrace overlooking the pretty garden.

Altstadthotel Amadeus

Linzer Gasse 43 ✉ 5020 – ☎ (0662) 87 14 01   Plan: **F1**
– www.hotelamadeus.at
20 rm – 💲80/120 € 💲💲135/200 € – ⊡ 12 €
• Historic • Townhouse • Personalised •
The centuries' old Altstadt Hotel Amadeus offers a central location coupled with a contemporary and tasteful interior. The pretty breakfast room with its white vaulted ceiling also serves a small selection of dishes throughout the day.

Lasserhof   🆎

Lasserstr. 47 ✉ 5020 – ☎ (0662) 87 33 88   Plan: **F1**
– www.lasserhof.com
30 rm ⊡ – 💲59/99 € 💲💲75/159 €
• Townhouse • Personalised •
This hotel offers contemporary rooms decorated in homely colours, with breakfast served in the vaulted Panorama room. Guests can park in the underground car park opposite for a reduced fee.

XxX   **Esszimmer** (Andreas Kaiblinger)   🍴 AK
😋   *Müllner Hauptstr. 33 ⊠ 5020 – ℰ (0662) 87 08 99*   Plan: **E1**
     – www.esszimmer.com – Closed 1 week February, 2 weeks September and
     Sunday–Monday
     Menu 68 € (Vegetarian)/118 € – Carte 59/100 € – *(booking advisable)*
     • Creative • Fashionable • Elegant •
     Transforming high quality produce into four menus (including one vegetarian
     and one fish menu), Andreas Kaiblinger offers creative cuisine without losing
     his connection to the local area. Attentive service complete with suggestions
     from the good Austrian wine list. Pretty terrace behind the restaurant.
     → Jakobsmuschel mit Champignons, Zwiebel, Speck und Topinambur.
     Hirschkalbsrücken mit Kürbis, Trauben und Walnüssen. Zwetschgentört-
     chen mit Zwetschgen-Cognac-Eis.

XxX   **Schloss Mönchstein** – Hotel Schloss Mönchstein   ⩽ 🍴 ⅃ AK
     Mönchsberg Park 26 ⊠ 5020 – ℰ (0662) 8 48 55 50   P
     – www.monchstein.at – Closed 1 February-9 March, 1-   Plan: **E1**
     23 November and Tuesday lunch except festival period
     Menu 55/145 € – Carte 52/106 €
     • Classic • Elegant • Classic •
     An exceptional place serving ambitious cuisine, in addition to its idyllic location.
     It offers a classically elegant interior and an elaborate and sophisticated 9-
     course menu from which to pick and choose. There is also an excellent choice
     of steaks.

XX   **Brunnauer im Magazin**   🍴 ✿
     Augustinergasse 13 a ⊠ 5020 – ℰ (0662) 84 15 84 20   Plan: **E1**
     – www.brunnauer.co.at – Closed Sunday-Monday, except festival period
     Menu 63/89 € (dinner) – Carte 52/78 € – *(booking advisable)*
     • Classic • Fashionable • Minimalist •
     Classic food served in a cellar room hewn out of the rock combines successfully
     with a delicatessen, wine shop and events venue. Richard Brunnauer, well known
     in Salzburg, offers seasonal cuisine alongside classics such as Wiener schnitzel.

XX   **Riedenburg**   🍴 P
     Neutorstr. 31 ⊠ 5020 – ℰ (0662) 83 08 15   Plan: **E2**
     – www.riedenburg.at – Closed Sunday-Monday, except festival period
     Menu 43/65 € (dinner) – Carte 35/63 € – *(booking advisable)*
     • Classic • Cosy •
     Nicole and Helmut Schinwald offer classic Austrian cuisine. Wiener schnitzel, Tauern
     lamb and sea bass are served in comfortable yet elegant dining rooms (light wood,
     warm colours, modern pictures...). Wonderful garden with chestnut trees.

XX   **Gasthof Auerhahn**   ⇦ 🍴 ✿ P
😊   *Bahnhofstr. 15 ⊠ 5020 – ℰ (0662) 45 10 52*   Plan I: **C1**
     – www.auerhahn-salzburg.at – Closed 2 weeks early January, 2 weeks
     June, 1 week September and Sunday dinner-Tuesday, festival period:
     Sunday dinner-Monday
     12 rm ⌑ – ♦59/65 € ♦♦96/106 €
     Menu 28 € (Vegetarian)/54 € – Carte 26/52 €
     • Regional/country • Friendly • Cosy •
     Try Topfenknödel, or curd cheese dumplings, and classic dishes such as boiled
     beef with apple and horseradish sauce or medallions of venison with port
     sauce. If you like the warm and friendly dining rooms, you will love the guest-
     rooms, which although not huge, are pretty and well kept.

X   **Strasserwirt**   🍴 P
😊   *Leopoldskronstr. 39 ⊠ 5020 – ℰ (0662) 82 63 91*   Plan: **E2**
     – www.zumstrasserwirt.at – Closed Monday, September-April: Monday-Tuesday
     Menu 39/69 € (dinner) – Carte 31/61 €
     • Traditional • Rurally •
     This guesthouse from 1856 houses a classically decorated restaurant with high
     quality cherry wood-panelling and a conservatory on the terrace. It serves a
     regional city menu.

AUSTRIA - SALZBURG

AUSTRIA - SALZBURG

✗ **Weiher Wirt**

König Ludwig Str. 2 ✉ *5020 –* ✆ *(0662) 82 93 24*   Plan I: **B2**
– www.weiherwirt.com – Closed mid January-mid February and Monday
Menu 35 € (dinner) – Carte 25/43 €
• Austrian • Inn •

The restaurant is wonderfully located on the banks of Leopoldskroner Lake. It serves regional dishes such as Szegediner pork goulash with boiled potatoes. Warm colours and modern notes provide a pleasant feel; outside is a lovely garden.

✗ **IMLAUER Sky Bar & Restaurant** – Hotel Crowne Plaza - The Pitter

Rainerstr. 6 (6th floor) ✉ *5020 –* ✆ *(0662) 88 97 80*
– www.imlauer.com   Plan: **F1**
Carte 21/65 €
• International • Fashionable •

This centrally located hotel was built in 1864. It offers comfortable rooms in the classic American style, as well as the exclusive Salzburg Suite. The Pitter Keller offers regional fare.

Sacher

Schwarzstr. 5 ✉ *5020 –* ✆ *(0662) 88 97 70*   Plan: **G1**
– www.sacher.com
113 rm – 🛏255/365 € 🛏🛏271/846 € – ☕ 34 € – 5 suites
• Traditional • Historic • Classic •

The flagship of the Salzburghotel world, Sacher really is a top international hotel. It offers classically designed, tasteful and luxurious rooms and suites. Alongside the Grill restaurant, don't miss the Café Sacher, the epitome of Vienna coffee house-style.
Zirbelzimmer – See restaurant listing

Bristol

Makartplatz 4 ✉ *5020 –* ✆ *(0662) 87 35 57*   Plan: **G1**
– www.bristol-salzburg.at – Closed 1 February-17 March
53 rm ☕ – 🛏185/235 € 🛏🛏260/420 € – 7 suites
• Traditional • Classic •

The stylish decor in the high-ceilinged rooms hint at the history of this hotel, built in 1619 and run as a hotel since 1892. Individually designed rooms with stucco work, crystal chandeliers, antiques, sumptuous fabrics and paintings. The restaurant serves classic cuisine with traditional influences.

Goldener Hirsch

Getreidegasse 37 ✉ *5020 –* ✆ *(0662) 8 08 40*   Plan: **G1**
– www.goldenerhirsch.com
70 rm – 🛏225/630 € 🛏🛏255/630 € – ☕ 33 € – 5 suites
• Townhouse • Historic • Personalised •

This patrician house built in 1407 stands out not only for its service but also for its thoughtfully retained, traditional style. The attractive rooms boast some lovely wooden furniture including a number of antique pieces. The restaurant offers international cuisine with classic and Austrian influences.
Herz'l – See restaurant listing

Altstadt Radisson BLU

Rudolfskai 28 (Judengasse 15) ✉ *5020 –* ✆ *(0662)*   Plan: **H1**
8 48 57 10 – www.austria-trend.at/ass
62 rm – 🛏110/1500 € 🛏🛏110/1500 € – ☕ 26 € – 13 suites
• Townhouse • Elegant • Classic •

Behind historical walls, not far from Mozartplatz, find the beautiful rooms of this hotel with their classic, elegant style. The executive room and suites are spacious. This international restaurant has a conservatory on the Salzach river, and a terrace in the interior court.

 arthotel Blaue Gans   🏠 ⒶⒸ
Getreidegasse 41 ✉ *5020*   Plan: **G1**
– ☎ *(0662) 8 42 49 10*
– *www.blauegans.at*
35 rm ☐ – ♥150/220 € ♥♥165/360 € – 3 suites
• Townhouse • Modern • Personalised •
At 650 years-old, the centrally located arthotel Blaue Gans is the oldest hotel in Salzburg. It offers light, modern rooms including some smart 'Artelier' rooms, as well as contemporary art.
Blaue Gans – See restaurant listing

🏠 **Goldgasse**   🏠
Goldgasse 10 ✉ *5020*   Plan: **H1**
– ☎ *(0662) 84 56 22*
– *www.hotelgoldgasse.at*
16 rm – ♥130/180 € ♥♥220/280 € – ☐ 12 €
• Townhouse • Historic • Personalised •
This is a real picture-postcard boutique hotel dating back 700 years. Goldgasse simply oozes history, though the rooms (mostly junior suites) are modern and individually designed. The restaurant serves traditional Austrian cuisine.

57

AUSTRIA - SALZBURG

Boutiquehotel am Dom 🏠 · AC

Goldgasse 17 ✉ *5020* – ☎ *(0662) 84 27 65*   Plan: **H2**
– *www.hotelamdom.at*
15 rm – ♦109/219 € ♦♦119/359 € – ☑ 10 €
• Townhouse • Contemporary •

It is hard to imagine that this out of the way little hotel would conceal such generous rooms. They offer smart modern design, beautifully appointed bathrooms and immaculate cleanliness. Use the underground car park in the old town.

XX Zirbelzimmer – Hotel Sacher 🎋 ⅃ AC 🚗

Schwarzstr. 5 ✉ *5020* – ☎ *(0662) 88 97 70*   Plan: **G1**
– *www.sacher.com*
Menu 52/66 € – Carte 44/83 €
• International • Elegant •

Sacher's culinary flagship offers a wide and varied menu ranging from poached langoustine to Styrian fried chicken, all served in a warm, friendly and typically Austrian setting. There is also an attractive balcony overlooking the River Salzach.

XX Carpe Diem ❀ AC

Getreidegasse 50 (1st floor) ✉ *5020* – ☎ *(0662)*   Plan: **G1**
84 88 00 – *www.carpediem.com* – *Closed 2 weeks February and Sunday*
Menu 22 € (lunch)/105 € – Carte 62/82 €
• Creative • Fashionable • Design •

A fashionable restaurant in the famous Getreidegasse. It serves a regional and international menu on the first floor. There is also a terrace at the entrance, a basement bar serving finger food in cones, and homemade patisseries.
→ Cone mit Beef Tatar. Lammrücken und Schulter, Artischocke und Birne. Schwarzbeernocken, Schwarzbeerröster und Sorbert.

XX Pan e Vin

Gstättengasse 1 (1st floor) ✉ *5020* – ☎ *(0662) 84 46 66*   Plan: **G1**
– *www.panevin.at* – *Closed 1-10 September and Sunday, except festival period*
Menu 38/85 € (dinner) – Carte 29/73 €
• Mediterranean • Cosy •

Mediterranean flavoured cuisine awaits guests in this 600 year-old building comfortably decorated in warm tones. The wine menu offers a good international selection. On the ground floor, the Trattoria serves pure Italian cuisine with a starter buffet.

X Maier's

Steingasse 61 ✉ *5020* – ☎ *(0662) 87 93 79*   Plan: **H1**
– *www.maiers-salzburg.at* – *Closed Sunday-Monday*
Carte 30/51 € – *(dinner only) (booking advisable)*
• International • Friendly • Cosy •

Many regulars visit this restaurant in an old alleyway to enjoy classic fare including steaks and Szegediner goulash. The feel is welcoming, the service friendly and you can park in the multi-storey car park right opposite the restaurant.

X Blaue Gans – arthotel Blaue Gans 🎋 AC

Getreidegasse 41 ✉ *5020* – ☎ *(0662) 84 24 91 54*   Plan: **G1**
– *www.blauegans.at* – *Closed Sunday, except festival period*
Menu 39/65 € (dinner) – Carte 34/52 €
• Regional/country • Friendly •

The restaurant is light and friendly with a pretty vaulted ceiling and a lovely terrace. The menu boasts a range of regional dishes with evocative names such as 'Mountain and valley', 'Field and meadow' and 'Stream and sea'.

X Herz'l – Hotel Goldener Hirsch 🎋

Getreidegasse 37 (access via Herbert von Karajan Platz 7)   Plan: **G1**
✉ *5020* – ☎ *(0662) 8 08 48 89* – *www.goldenerhirsch.com*
Carte 25/42 €
• Austrian • Rustic • Cosy •

If you prefer to eat in simpler surroundings, then you will no doubt appreciate the country charm of the wood-panelled Herz'l. Good, regional food is served.

BRANDTNERS PARADOXON

Zugallistr. 7 ✉ *5020 –* ℰ *(0664) 1 61 61 91* — Plan: **F2**
– www.facebook.com/brandtnersparadoxon – closed Sunday-Monday
Carte 36/59 € *– (dinner only)*
• International • Individual •

This is probably the only `permanent' pop-up restaurant in German-speaking Europe! The decor and cuisine change every three months - from Chinese-inspired to workshop-industrial, from dim sum to burgers or spare ribs. One that doesn't change however is the excellent cuisine. Not to be missed!

ENVIRONS OF SALZBURG AND AIRPORT PLAN I

 ### Rosenvilla ▣

Höfelgasse 4 ✉ *5020 –* ℰ *(0662) 62 17 65* — Plan: **C2**
– www.rosenvilla.com – Closed February
15 rm ⌂ – ♦79/108 € ♦♦138/199 €
• Family • Modern • Cosy •

Stefanie Fleischhaker is a born hostess and you are always sure of a warm welcome. Enjoy the great service, tasteful decor and lovely terrace, as well as the excellent breakfast which is popular even with non-residents. Small single rooms.

 ### Die Gersberg Alm

Gersberg 37 ✉ *5020 –* ℰ *(0662) 64 12 57* — Plan: **D2**
– www.gersbergalm.at
44 rm ⌂ – ♦106/150 € ♦♦143/315 € – 4 suites
• Inn • Rustic •

This isolated mountain guesthouse dating back to 1832 has kept its friendly, rustic charm. This is also reflected in the cosy restaurant, which serves seasonal cuisine. The guestrooms also have a rustic charm, although there are a number of elegant, modern rooms. The garden offers an idyllic country setting.

 ### Doktorwirt

Glaser Str. 9 ✉ *5026 –* ℰ *(0662) 6 22 97 30* — Plan: **D3**
– www.doktorwirt.at – Closed 3 weeks February, mid October-end November
41 rm ⌂ – ♦78/125 € ♦♦125/195 €
• Inn • Rustic • Cosy •

The Schnöll family run this cosy 12C tavern. There is a spacious spa area and a lovely garden, as well as beautiful tower rooms with small bay windows. Regional cuisine is served in very comfortable rooms or on the terraces in front and behind of the building. There is a wine cellar.

 ### Brandstätter

Münchner Bundesstr. 69 ✉ *5020 –* ℰ *(0662) 43 45 35* — Plan: **B1**
– www.hotel-brandstaetter.com – Closed 23-26 December
35 rm ⌂ – ♦93/125 € ♦♦140/165 €
• Family • Cosy •

The hotel's proximity to the main street and the motorway is more than compensated for by the hospitality of the Brandstätter family and their staff. Some of the lovely country house-style rooms face out onto the garden.
🕀 **Brandstätter** – See restaurant listing

 ### Airporthotel

Dr.-Matthias-Laireiter-Str. 9 ✉ *5020 Salzburg-Loig* — Plan: **A2**
– ℰ *(0662) 85 00 20 – www.airporthotel.at*
36 rm ⌂ – ♦105/165 € ♦♦135/195 €
• Inn • Cosy •

This hotel is across from the airport, and consists of two connected hotel buildings, which are typical of the region. Functional rooms, some with air-conditioning.

Bloberger Hof

Hammerauerstr. 4 ⊠ 5020 – ℰ (0662) 83 02 27   Plan: **B3**
– www.bloberergerhof.at – Closed 6 January-21 February
22 rm ⌂ – **†**75/90 € **††**90/120 €
• Inn • Cosy •

The Keuschnigg family offers everything you need when you are on the road. Comfortable rooms (book one in the more spacious 'superior' category), a good breakfast with homemade jam, warm, friendly service and parking right outside the door. Some rooms have a view of the Untersberg and others have balconies.

🕸🕸🕸 Ikarus

Wilhelm-Spazier-Str. 7a (Hangar-7, 1st floor) ⊠ 5020   Plan: **B2**
– ℰ (0662) 2 19 70 – www.hangar-7.com – Closed end December - 8 January
Menu 52 € (lunch)/170 € – Carte 93/112 € – *(booking essential)*
• Creative • Fashionable • Elegant •

An unusual concept, the architecturally impressive Hangar-7 is both a Red Bull exhibition space and an ultra-modern luxury restaurant serving top quality creative cuisine. Choose from a menu devised by the international guest chef of the month or the restaurant's own Ikarus selection.
→ Bärenkrebs mit Haselnuss, Pata Negra und schwarzem Trüffel. Rochenflügel mit Tomate, Salatherzen und Bergamotte. Petit Suisse mit Gurke, Kürbiskernen und Vanille.

🕸🕸🕸 SENNS.Restaurant

Söllheimerstr. 16 (at Gusswerk - Object 6c) ⊠ 5020   Plan: **C1**
– ℰ (0664) 4 54 02 32 – www.senns.restaurant.at – Closed 2 weeks mid July, 4-13 September, 24 December-3 January and Sunday-Monday, except festival period
Menu 68/145 € – Carte 66/94 € – *(dinner only) (booking advisable)*
• Creative • Fashionable • Friendly •

Expressive, artful and meticulous are all words you could use to describe Andreas Senn's top quality international cuisine, which is made using the very best produce. This fashionable, modern restaurant is the chef's summer residence; during the winter months he cooks in Kitzbühel. Simple lunchtime menu.
→ Langostino, Kaffir-Limette, Avocado, Kohlrabi, Quinoa. Black Cod, Aubergine, Dashi, Maniok. Bison "a la Stroganoff", Rote Rübe, Champignons, Crème fraîche.

🕸🕸 Zum Buberl Gut

Gneiser Str. 31 ⊠ 5020 – ℰ (0662) 82 68 66   Plan: **C3**
– Closed Tuesday-Wednesday lunch, festival period: Tuesday lunch
Menu 26 € (lunch) – Carte 50/74 € – *(booking advisable)*
• Traditional • Cosy • Rustic •

The Mediterranean cuisine and lovely setting make Zum Buberl Gut an enjoyable dining experience. The elegant dining rooms of this fine 17C manor house have a homely feel. In summer, the tables outside in the attractive garden are a delight.

🕸🕸 Brandstätter

Münchner Bundesstr. 69 ⊠ 5020 – ℰ (0662) 43 45 35   Plan: **B1**
– www.hotel-brandstaetter.com – Closed Sunday, except festival period
Carte 26/74 € – *(booking advisable)*
• Regional/country • Cosy •

Taste the creamy veal goulash and the local venison, and dont' miss the Mohr im Hemd, or chocolate hazelnut pudding (with an exquisite chocolate sauce)! Pretty, cosy dining rooms – the Swiss pine room with its tiled oven has its own charm.

🕸🕸 Gasthof Schloss Aigen

Schwarzenbergpromenade 37 ⊠ 5026 – ℰ (0662) 62 12 84   Plan: **D2**
– www.schloss-aigen.at – Closed Monday-Wednesday, except festival period
Carte 21/76 €
• Austrian • Inn • Friendly •

Highly prized, traditional experience! The pretty rooms exude country charm and the restaurant is well-known for its speciality, boiled beef. The interior courtyard with its sweet chestnut trees is every bit as pleasant as the dining room.

AUSTRIA - SALZBURG

XX · ⊕ **Huber's im Fischerwirt** 🛖
Peter Pfenninger Str. 8 ⊠ 5020 – ℰ (0662) 42 40 59   Plan: **B1**
– www.fischerwirt-liefering.at – Closed 8-25 February, 6-29 June and
September-June: Tuesday-Wednesday
Menu 39/59 € – Carte 28/76 €
· Austrian · Cosy · Rurally ·

The Hubers serve regional classics and international fare in their charming restaurant. Dishes include Viennese fried chicken with lamb's lettuce and potato
salad, and game stew with bread dumplings. There is also a small shop selling
jams, chocolate and caviar.

AT ELIXHAUSEN   North: 7,5 km by Vogelweiderstraße C1

🏠 **Gmachl** 🦌 🛋 🎧 💆 ⊕ 🀄 ⌘ 🔲 ❄ 🆔 🛅 🚗
Dorfstr. 14 ⊠ 5161 – ℰ (0662) 48 02 12 – www.gmachl.com
73 rm ⊑ – 🛏115/202 € 🛏🛏188/324 €
· Country house · Family · Cosy ·

Do you want to escape the hustle and bustle of the city but remain within easy travelling distance of Salzburg? The Hirnböck-Gmachl family has run this country
hotel since 1334. The spa in the cloistered courtyard offers a wonderful view.
Gmachl – See restaurant listing

XX **Gmachl** – Hotel Gmachl 🛋 🎧 ❄ ♿ 🚗
Dorfstr. 14 ⊠ 5161 – ℰ (0662) 48 02 12 – www.gmachl.com
Menu 59/75 € (dinner) – Carte 26/64 €
· Regional/country · Inn · Elegant ·

Fresh, regional cuisine made of high quality ingredients, including sausage and
meat from the restaurant's own butchery. The feel is warm and friendly - Kaiser-
zimmer and Ahnenstube are elegant yet homely, the Gaststube is more rustic.

AT HALLWANG

XX · ❀ **Pfefferschiff** (Jürgen Vigné)
Söllheim 3 ⊠ 5300 – ℰ (0662) 66 12 42   Plan: **D1**
– www.pfefferschiff.at – Closed 2 weeks end February-early March,
2 weeks end June-early July and Sunday-Monday , except festival period
Menu 84 € (Vegetarian)/115 € (dinner)
– Carte 68/94 € – (Tuesday - Friday dinner only, except festival period)
(booking essential)
· Classic · Elegant · Cosy ·

Iris and Jürgen Vigne make the perfect hosts in this wonderful 17C former vica-
rage. Charming dining rooms, elegant yet homely, and a lovely terrace shaded
by trees. The traditionally clad, all-female waiting staff are attentive and friendly.
They serve modern cuisine with classic roots.
→ Jakobsmuschel und Garnele, Avocado, Mango, Koriander. Hirschkalb,
Kerbelwurzel, Apfel, süßer Striezel. Topfenschmarrn.

AT HOF BEI SALZBURG   North-East: 18 km by Wolfgangsee Straße D1

🏰 **Schloss Fuschl** 🦌 🛶 ⪡ 🛋 💆 ⊕ 🎧 🔲 🆔 🛅 🚗
Schloss Str. 19 ⊠ 5322 – ℰ (06229) 2 25 30
– www.schlossfuschlsalzburg.com
110 rm ⊑ – 🛏195/695 € 🛏🛏235/795 € – 13 suites
· Luxury · Classic ·

This 'grand' hotel is set on a small peninsular projecting out into the lake. The
rooms are stylishly elegant, and a remarkable collection of paintings pays tribute to the castle's history. There is even a Rolls Royce at your disposal. Private
bathing beach, a summer restaurant for hotel guests, motorboats...
Schloss Restaurant – See restaurant listing

XxX **Schloss Restaurant** – Hotel Schloss Fuschl

Schloss Str. 19 ✉ *5322* – ☎ *(06229) 2 25 30*
– *www.schlossfuschlsalzburg.com*
Menu 115 € – Carte 56/83 € – *(dinner only)*
• Classic • Romantic •

Ambitious food is served in this classically elegant setting with its stunning view of the Fuschlsee Lake. Dishes range from a traditional *tafelspitz* (boiled topside of veal) to turbot pan-fried in brown butter. Fantastic terrace!

BELGIUM
BELGIË - BELGIQUE

Antwerp

BRUSSELS ●

→ **AREA:**
30 528 km² (11 781 sq mi)

→ **POPULATION:**
11 209 044 inhabitants.
Density = 367 per km².

→ **CAPITAL:**
Brussels.

→ **CURRENCY:**
Euro (€).

→ **GOVERNMENT:**
Constitutional parliamentary monarchy (since 1830) and a federal state (since 1994). Member of European Union since 1957 (one of the 6 founding countries).

→ **LANGUAGES:**
Dutch (in Flanders and Brussels), French (in Wallonia and Brussels), German (Eastern cantons); most Belgians also speak English.

→ **PUBLIC HOLIDAYS:**
New Year's Day (1 Jan); Easter Monday (late Mar/Apr); Labor Day (1 May); Ascension Day (May); Whit Monday (late May/June); Independence Day (21 July); Assumption of the Virgin Mary (15 Aug); All Saints' Day (1 Nov); Armistice Day 1918 (11 Nov); Christmas Day (25 Dec); Boxing Day (26 Dec).

→ **LOCAL TIME:**
GMT+1 hour in winter and GMT+2 hours in summer.

→ **CLIMATE:**
Temperate maritime with cool winters and mild summers (Brussels: January 2°C; July 18°C); more continental towards the Ardennes. Rainfall evenly distributed throughout the year.

→ **EMERGENCY:**
Police ℘ **101**; Medical Assistance and Fire Brigade ℘ **100**. (Dialling **112** within any EU country will redirect your call and contact the emergency services.

→ **ELECTRICITY:**
230 volts AC, 50Hz; 2 round pin sockets.

→ **FORMALITIES:**
Travellers from the European Union (EU), Switzerland, Norway, Iceland and the main countries of North and South America need a national identity card or passport (America: passport required) to visit Belgium for less than three months (tourism or business purpose). For visitors from other countries a visa may be required, in addition to a passport, especially for those wishing to stay for longer than three months. We advise you to check with your embassy before travelling.

BRUSSELS
BRUXELLES/BRUSSEL

Population: 1 175 173

Guitain/Fotolia.com

There aren't many cities where you can use a 16C century map and accurately navigate your way around; or where there are enough restaurants to dine somewhere different every day for five years; or where you'll find a museum dedicated to the comic strip – but then every city isn't Brussels. It was tagged a 'grey' capital because of its EU associations but those who've spent time here know it to be, by contrast, a buzzing town. It's the home of art nouveau, it features a wonderful maze of medieval alleys and places to eat, and it's warm and friendly, with an outgoing, cosmopolitan feel – due in no small part to its turbulent history, which has seen it under frequent occupation. Generally speaking, the Bruxellois believe that you shouldn't take things too seriously: they have a soft spot for puppets and Tintin, street music and majorettes; and they do their laundry in communal places like the Wash Club.

BRUSSELS IN...

➜ ONE DAY
Grand Place, Musées Royaux des Beaux-Arts, Place Ste-Catherine.

➜ TWO DAYS
Marolles, Place du Grand Sablon, Musical Instrument Museum, concert at Palais des Beaux-Arts.

➜ THREE DAYS
Parc du Cinquantenaire, Horta's house, tour St Gilles and Ixelles.

The area where all visitors wend is the Lower Town and the Grand Place but the northwest and southern quarters (Ste-Catherine and The Marolles) are also of particular interest. To the east, higher up an escarpment, lies the Upper Town – this is the traditional home of the aristocracy and encircles the landmark Parc de Bruxelles. Two suburbs of interest are St Gilles, to the southwest, and Ixelles, to the southeast, where trendy bars and art nouveau are the order of the day.

PRACTICAL INFORMATION

ARRIVAL-DEPARTURE

 Brussels Airport is 14km northeast. Trains to and from the airport run every 15min and take 20min.

🚆 **Eurostar** - Brussels Midi Train Station is 2km southwest; high speed Thalys trains also operate from here. Take Metro Line 2, 3, 4 or 6.

GETTING AROUND

Buses, trams and metro all run efficiently. You can buy 1, 5 or 10 trip cards and 1, 2 or 3 day travel cards. These are available from metro stations, travel authority offices (BOOTIK and KIOSK), tourist information centres and newsagents. Remember to stamp your ticket before each journey; red machines are on every metro station concourse and on every tram and bus. Single tickets are valid for an hour and you can hop on and off all forms of public transport. (Roving inspectors impose heavy on-the-spot fines for anyone caught without a valid ticket.)

EATING OUT

As long as your appetite hasn't been sated at the chocolatiers, or with a cone of frites from a street stall, you'll relish the dining experience in Brussels. As long as you stay off the main tourist drag (i.e. Rue des Bouchers), you're guaranteed somewhere good to eat within a short strolling distance. There are lots of places to enjoy Belgian dishes such as moules frites, Ostend lobster, eels with green herbs, or waterzooi (chicken or fish stew with vegetables). Wherever you're eating, at whatever price range, food is invariably well cooked and often bursting with innovative touches. As a rule of thumb, the Lower Town has the best places, with the Ste-Catherine quarter's fish and seafood establishments the pick of the bunch; you'll also find a mini Chinatown here. Because of the city's cosmopolitan character there are dozens of international restaurants - ranging from French and Italian to more unusual Moroccan, Tunisian and Congolese destinations. Belgium beers are famous the world over and are served in specially designed glasses.

CALENDAR HIGHLIGHTS

January
Brussels Jazz Festival.

February
Brussels Book Fair.

May
Kunsten Festival des Arts, Queen Elisabeth Music Contest.

June
Brussels Film Festival.

July
Ommegang (Renaissance Procession).

August
Brussels Summer Festival, Fiesta Latina.

July-August
Foire du Midi Funfair.

September
International Comic Strip and Cartoon Festival.

November
Ars Musica.

BELGIUM - BRUSSELS

The Hotel
bd de Waterloo 38 ⊠ *1000 – ℰ 0 2 504 11 11* Plan: **N3**
– www.thehotel.be
417 rm – ♦125/280 € ♦♦125/280 € – ☲ 25 € – 4 suites
• Townhouse • Grand Luxury • Design •
Enjoy the breathtaking view of Brussels and the hidden charms of the city in this well-preserved district. This establishment is also ideal for exploring the shops along Avenue Louise. Shopaholics take note!

Amigo
r. de l'Amigo 1 ⊠ *1000 – ℰ 0 2 547 47 47* Plan: **M2**
– www.roccofortehotels.com
154 rm – ♦219/660 € ♦♦219/660 € – ☲ 19 € – 19 suites
• Grand Luxury • Townhouse • Personalised •
A real institution, and one of the best hotels in Brussels! Its assets? Its central location (behind the Grand-Place), luxurious rooms, impeccable service and refined charm. You may even run into a celebrity here.
Bocconi – See restaurant listing

Radisson Blu Royal
r. du Fossé aux Loups 47 ⊠ *1000 – ℰ 0 2 219 28 28* Plan: **N1**
– www.radissonblu.com/royalhotel-brussels
269 rm – ♦149/400 € ♦♦149/400 € – ☲ 29 € – 12 suites
• Luxury • Chain hotel • Contemporary •
Impressive modern glass atrium, remains of the city's fortifications, and extremely comfortable suites and guestrooms. Breakfast room adorned with wooden railway sleepers. A contemporary style brasserie illuminated by natural light through the glass roof.

Le Plaza
bd A. Max 118 ⊠ *1000 – ℰ 0 2 278 01 00* Plan: **F1**
– www.leplaza-brussels.be
184 rm – ♦120/495 € ♦♦140/495 € – ☲ 29 € – 6 suites
• Palace • Elegant •
A 1930s building imitating the George V hotel in Paris. Classic public areas, large cosy guestrooms and a superb Baroque theatre used for receptions and events. An elegant bar and restaurant beneath an attractive dome painted with a trompe l'œil sky.

Métropole
pl. de Brouckère 31 ⊠ *1000 – ℰ 0 2 217 23 00* Plan: **M1**
– www.metropolehotel.com
283 rm ☲ – ♦102/475 € ♦♦102/525 € – 5 suites
• Grand Luxury • Historic • Personalised •
This lavish hotel, dating back to 1895, is an institution in Brussels. It has preserved its historic legacy with the added bonus of contemporary luxury. The terrace of the Café Métropole, one of the capital's most illustrious establishments on Place de Brouckère, must not be missed.

Royal Windsor
r. Duquesnoy 5 ⊠ *1000 – ℰ 0 2 505 55 55* Plan: **M2**
– www.royalwindsorbrussels.com
260 rm – ♦99/555 € ♦♦99/555 € – ☲ 30 € – 7 suites
• Luxury • Personalised •
Luxury, comfort and refinement are the hallmarks of this hotel, which has undergone recent refurbishment. Superb service.

Marriott

☆ Ⅰ🖦 🕅 ఈ AC 🙌 🚗

r. A. Orts 7 (opposite stock exchange) ✉ *1000*
– ℰ *0 2 516 90 90 – www.marriottbrussels.com*
Plan: **M1**
214 rm – 🛉169/210 € 🛉🛉169/210 € – ☕ 25 € – 5 suites
• Luxury • Business • Contemporary •
A famous piece of local folklore (The Marriage of Mademoiselle Beulemans) was
conceived behind the 1900 façade adjoining the Stock Exchange. Chic public
areas and bedrooms boasting every creature comfort.

 ### The Dominican

☆ Ⅰ🖦 🕅 ఈ AC 🙌

r. Léopold 9 ✉ *1000* – ℰ *0 2 203 08 08*
– *www.thedominican.be*
Plan: **M1**
147 rm – 🛉140/450 € 🛉🛉140/450 € – ☕ 27 € – 3 suites
• Luxury • Business • Personalised •
A designer-inspired luxury hotel on the site of a former Dominican convent.
Open spaces, elegant furniture and modern comforts which benefit from maximum attention to detail. The Grand Lounge takes full advantage of the natural
light from the patio. A modern menu and non-stop service.

 ### Pillows

ఈ AC 🙌

pl. Rouppe 17 ✉ *1000* – ℰ *0 2 204 00 40*
– *www.sandton.eu/pillowsbrussels*
Plan: **L2**
45 rm – 🛉69/369 € 🛉🛉69/369 € – ☕ 25 €
• Luxury • Modern •
Black and white dominate this handsome manor house on Place Rouppe, a few
steps from the town centre. The warm, inviting rooms offer all the facilities one
has come to expect from a good hotel.

 ### Le Dixseptième

AC 🙌

r. de la Madeleine 25 ✉ *1000* – ℰ *0 2 517 17 17*
– *www.ledixseptieme.be*
Plan: **M2**
37 rm ☕ – 🛉160/430 € 🛉🛉180/450 € – 2 suites
• Luxury • Stylish •
This townhouse dating from the 17C was once the official residence of the Spanish ambassador in the city. Elegant lounges, attractive inner courtyard, and
guestrooms embellished with furniture of varying styles.

Hôtel des Galeries

☆

r. des Bouchers 38 ✉ *1000* – ℰ *0 2 213 74 70*
– *www.hoteldesgaleries.be*
Plan: **M1**
23 rm – 🛉135/350 € 🛉🛉135/350 € – ☕ 17 € – 3 suites
• Luxury • Modern • Elegant •
This boutique hotel in a classical edifice enjoys a premium location on the corner of Rue des Bouchers and the King's Gallery. The luxury setting combines vintage touches with a contemporary interior, whose attention to detail extends as
far as the ceramic tiles in the washrooms. Perfectly located for a stay in Brussels.
Comptoir des Galeries – See restaurant listing

Sandton

ఈ AC 🙌 🚗

r. Paroissiens 15 ✉ *1000* – ℰ *0 2 274 08 10*
– *www.sandton.eu*
Plan: **N2**
67 rm – 🛉69/369 € 🛉🛉69/369 € – ☕ 22 € – 3 suites
• Business • Modern •
If location is your prime criteria, this hotel, located only 5min from the station
and bang in the heart of the city, is perfect. The rooms are brand new and well
looked after, and all have reasonable rates.

 ### Atlas

🗟 ఈ 🙌 🚗

r. Vieux Marché-aux-Grains 30 ✉ *1000* – ℰ *0 2 502 60 06*
– *www.atlas.be*
Plan: **L1**
88 rm ☕ – 🛉85/345 € 🛉🛉99/399 €
• Family • Functional •
This extensively modernised 18C townhouse is situated in a lively part of the
city renowned for its Belgian fashion boutiques. The majority of the hotel's
rooms overlook the courtyard.

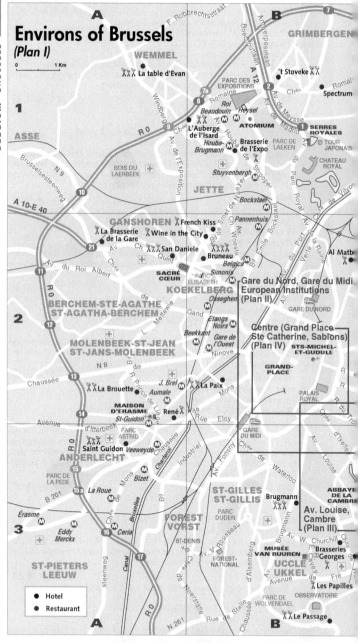

Environs of Brussels
(Plan I)

0   1 Km

A

WEMMEL

✗✗✗ La table d'Evan

F. Robbrechtsstraat

GRIMBERGEN

B

7

A 12

't Stoveke ✗✗

Romai

Spectrum

Boechoutlaan

Antwerpselaan

PARC DES
EXPOSITIONS

7a

8

Roi
Beaudouin

Heysel

ATOMIUM

Chée de Madrid

Av. de Meysse

2

Chée de la Meysse

1   SERRES
ROYALES

TOUR
JAPONAIS

ASSE

9

L'Auberge
de l'Isard

Houba-
Brugmann

✗✗
Brasserie
de l'Expo

PARC DE
LAEKEN

CHATEAU
ROYAL

N 9

Brusselsesteenweg

A 10-E 40

10

BOIS DU
LAERBEEK

Av. de l'Exposition

Houba de Strooper

Stuyvenbergh

JETTE

Bockstael

Av. de Vilvor

GANSHOREN ✗ French Kiss

Pannenhuis

21

✗ La Brasserie
de la Gare

✗ Wine in the City

Av.   du Roi Albert

Ch. ✗✗✗ San Daniele

Quint

SACRÉ
CŒUR

Bruneau

✗✗✗

Belgica

van Woeste

Simonis

Emile Bockstael

Verte a la Reine

Al Matb ✗

11

PARC
ELISABETH

KOEKELBERG

Gare du Nord, Gare du Midi
European Institutions
(Plan II)

BERCHEM-STE-AGATHE
ST-AGATHA-BERCHEM

Osseghem

de   Metewie

GARE DU NORD

Centre (Grand Place
Ste Catherine, Sablons)
(Plan IV)

12

L.

Gand

Etangs
Noirs

STS-MICHEL-
ET-GUDULE

MOLENBEEK-ST-JEAN
ST-JANS-MOLENBEEK

Beekkant

Gare de
l'Ouest

GRAND-
PLACE

N 8

Chaussée

de

R. Prince de Liège

Ninove

J. Brel

PALAIS
ROYAL

13

✗✗ La Brouette

Aumale

✗✗ La Paix

Mons

R.

R.

MAISON
D'ERASME

René ✗

de   Rue   Eloy

GARE
DU MIDI

Chée de Tro

d'ixelles

14

Avenue

d'Itterbeek

St-Guidon

PARC
ASTRID

Veeweyde

Chaussée

Industriel

Av. Fonsny

Av. de Waterloo

Louise

✗✗✗
Saint Guidon

ANDERLECHT

Charleroi

ABBAYE
DE LA
CAMBRE

15

PARC DE
LA PEDE

Mons

Bizet

ST-GILLES
ST-GILLIS

Brugmann

Av. Louise,
Cambre
(Plan III)

15a   La Roue

de

Bruxelles

PARC
DUDEN

✗✗✗

Av. W. Churchill

B 201

Érasme

Chée

Ceria

FOREST
VORST

16

Eddy
Merckx

ST-DENIS

Av. V. Rousseau

FOREST-
NATIONAL

MUSÉE
VAN BUUREN

Brasseries
Georges

ST-PIETERS
LEEUW

17

steenweg

Canal

Chée de Neerstalle

d'Alsemberg

PARC DE
WOLVENDAEL

Cavell

UCCLE
UKKEL

✗ Les Papilles

Fré

OBSERVATOIRE

Av.

● Hotel
● Restaurant

Rue   de Stalle

Chaussée

N 261

✗✗ Le Passage

A

B

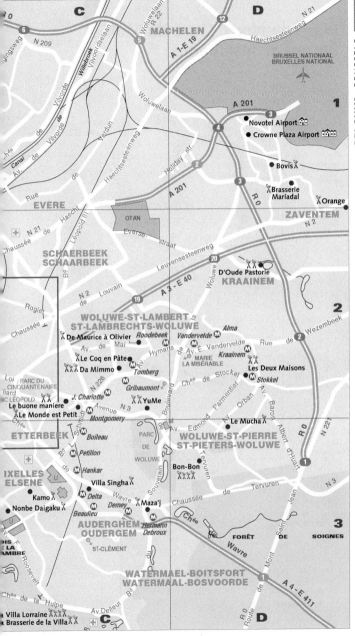

C D

N 21

6 N 209

MACHELEN

A 1-E 19

5 Woluwelaan R 22

Haechtsesteenweg

12

BRUSSEL NATIONAAL
BRUXELLES NATIONAL

1

de Vilvorde

Woluwelaan

Canal de Vilvorde

A 201

Av. de Vilvorde

Holiday str.

Haechtsesteenweg

Veldun

3 Novotel Airport

4 Crowne Plaza Airport

2

3 Bovis

Rue de Haecht

N 21 de Léopold III

EVERE

Brasserie
Mariadal

Orange

Chaussée

OTAN

Eversestraat

SCHAERBEEK
SCHAARBEEK

ZAVENTEM
N 2

Bd N 2 de Louvain

Leuvensesteenweg

A 3 - E 40

20 Woluwe

D'Oude Pastorie

KRAAINEM

Rogier

Chaussée

19

WOLUWE-ST-LAMBERT
ST-LAMBRECHTS-WOLUWE

Alma

Wezembeek

2 Wezembeek

De Maurice à Olivier

Roodebeek

Vandervelde

Rue de

2

Loi

Av. E. Vandervelde

Av. de Mai

Hymans

Kraainem

PARC DU
CINQUANTENAIRE
PC LEOPOLD
liard

Le Coq en Pâte

N 226

MARIE
LA MISÉRABLE

Les Deux Maisons

Da Mimmo

Tomberg

Chée de Stockel

Stokkel

Gribaumont

J. Charlotte

Le buone maniere

N 3

YuMe

Boulevard

Av. d'Orban

Av. Baron Albert d'Huart

R 0

N 22

Le Monde est Petit

Avenue

Montgomery

Av. Edmond Parmentier

ETTERBEEK

Chée

Schmitz

PARC
DE
WOLUWE

Av.

Le Mucha

1

Boileau

Souverain

WOLUWE-ST-PIERRE
ST-PIETERS-WOLUWE

Petillon

Bon-Bon

Bd

IXELLES
ELSENE

Hankar

de

Tervuren

Villa Singha

Saint Jean

Tervuren

N 3

Kamo

Delta

Wavre

Demey

Maza'j

Chaussée

de

Nonbe Daigaku

Beaulieu

AUDERGHEM
OUDERGEM

Hermann
Debroux

Chée

FORÊT

DE

3
SOIGNES

ST-CLÉMENT

Wavre

DIS
LA
AMBRE

Roosevelt

WATERMAEL-BOITSFORT
WATERMAAL-BOSVOORDE

1 A 4 - E 411

Chée de la Hulpe

Av. Delleur

Villa Lorraine

Brasserie de la Villa

C

R 0 Route de

Wavre

D

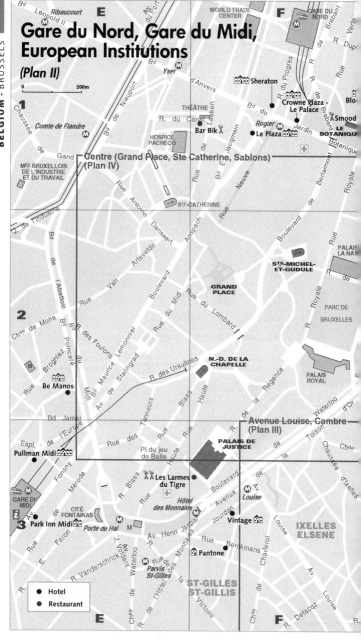

BELGIUM - BRUSSELS

Gare du Nord, Gare du Midi, European Institutions

(Plan II)

0 _____ 200m

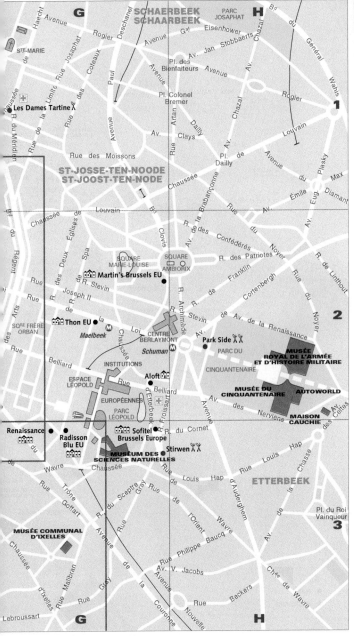

SCHAERBEEK
SCHAARBEEK

PARC
JOSAPHAT

Ste-MARIE

Les Dames Tartine ⚓

Pl. des
Bienfaiteurs

Pl. Colonel
Bremer

Rue des Moissons

ST-JOSSE-TEN-NOODE
ST-JOOST-TEN-NODE

SQUARE
MARIE-LOUISE

SQUARE
AMBIORIX

Martin's Brussels EU

Thon EU

Maelbeek

Park Side

CENTRE
BERLAYMONT

Schuman

PARC DU
CINQUANTENAIRE

MUSÉE
ROYAL DE L'ARMÉE
ET D'HISTOIRE MILITAIRE

INSTITUTIONS

ESPACE
LÉOPOLD

Aloft

MUSÉE DU
CINQUANTENAIRE

AUTOWORLD

EUROPÉENNES

PARC
LÉOPOLD

MAISON
CAUCHIE

Renaissance

Radisson
Blu EU

Sofitel
Brussels Europe

Stirwen

MUSÉUM DES
SCIENCES NATURELLES

ETTERBEEK

MUSÉE COMMUNAL
D'IXELLES

Pl. du Roi
Vainqueur

Lebroussart

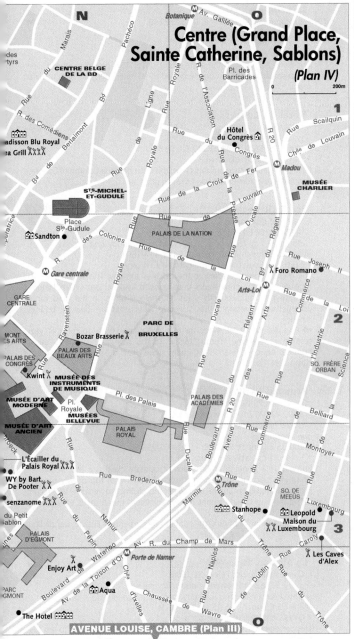

Centre (Grand Place, Sainte Catherine, Sablons)
(Plan IV)

0   200m

N O

Botanique
Av. Galilée

CENTRE BELGE
DE LA BD

Pl. des
Barricades

Hôtel
du Congrès

Scailquin

Chée de Louvain

Madou

adisson Blu Royal
ea Grill XXXX

MUSÉE
CHARLIER

STS-MICHEL-
ET-GUDULE

Rue de la Croix de Fer

Louvain

Place
Ste-Gudule

Sandton

PALAIS DE LA NATION

Gare centrale

Foro Romano

Rue Joseph II

GARE
CENTRALE

Loi

Arts-Loi

Rue de la Loi

MONT
ES ARTS

Bozar Brasserie X

PARC DE
BRUXELLES

PALAIS DES
BEAUX ARTS

SQ. FRÈRE
ORBAN

PALAIS DES
CONGRÈS

Kwint

MUSÉE DES
INSTRUMENTS
DE MUSIQUE

PALAIS DES
ACADÉMIES

MUSÉE D'ART
MODERNE

Pl. des Palais

Pl.
Royale

MUSÉES
BELLEVUE

MUSÉE D'ART
ANCIEN

PALAIS
ROYAL

Belliard

L'Écailler du
Palais Royal XXX

Montoyer

WY by Bart
De Pooter XX

Brederode

senzanome XXX

Stanhope

Trône

SQ. DE
MEEÛS

Leopold

Maison du
X X Luxembourg

PALAIS
D'EGMONT

R. du Champ de Mars

Les Caves
d'Alex

Enjoy Art

Porte de Namur

PARC
GMONT

Aqua

The Hotel

AVENUE LOUISE, CAMBRE (Plan III)

O

La Légende
r. Lombard 35 ✉ *1000 –* ☎ *0 2 512 82 90*　　　Plan: **M2**
– www.hotellalegende.com
27 rm ⌷ – ♦75/205 € ♦♦85/265 €
• Family • Functional •

This hotel has been in the same family since 1957, providing simple, clean rooms spread over two wings separated by an inner courtyard. Nice breakfast room.

Hôtel du Congrès　　　　　　　　　　🛴
r. Congrès 42 ✉ *1000 –* ☎ *0 2 217 18 90*
– www.hotelducongres.be　　　　　　　Plan: **O1**
67 rm – ♦55/250 € ♦♦70/280 € – ⌷ 8 €
• Family • Functional •

Four 19th century style buildings form this hotel near the Column of Congress. Period décor in some rooms and the reception area.

🗙🗙🗙 Sea Grill (Yves Mattagne) – Hôtel Radisson Blu Royal　🕸 🕭 🆑 ⇔ 🍴
❀❀ *r. du Fossé aux Loups 47* ✉ *1000*
– ☎ *0 2 212 08 00 – www.seagrill.be*　　　Plan: **N1**
– closed 23 July-15 August, Bank Holidays, Saturday and Sunday
Menu 65 € (lunch), 120/185 € – Carte 117/180 €
• Fish and seafood • Elegant • Luxury •

The menu varies according to the catch of the day. The sea supplies the treasures and the crew steers the ship with flying colours! A challenging, first-rate performance with some prestigious wines in the hold for an unforgettable crossing. It has secluded tables that are ideal for business lunches.

→ Anguille fumée et gyoza au foie gras, consommé au miso et yuzu, sésame et wakamé. Turbot rôti à l'arête, béarnaise d'huîtres ou de homard. Abricots caramélisés, champagne, fleur de sureau, meringue et citron vert.

🗙🗙🗙 Bruneau (Jean-Pierre Bruneau)　　　🕸 🕭 🆑 ⇔ 🍴 (dinner)
❀ *av. Broustin 75* ✉ *1083*　　　　　　　Plan: **B2**
– ☎ *0 2 421 70 70 – www.bruneau.be*
– closed first 3 weeks July, first 2 weeks January, Tuesday
and Wednesday
Menu 55 € (lunch), 70/90 € – Carte 67/258 €
• French creative • Elegant •

Bruneau is a genuine ambassador of culinary classicism and something of an institution in the region. The chef works with top quality produce, preferably local, to create succulent and distinctive recipes. We recommend the menu. An elegant restaurant where the client is truly pampered.

→ Rosace de homard aux truffes noires de Carpentras. Filet de bar de ligne au caviar. Croustillant au café.

🗙🗙 La Maison du Cygne　　　　　　🆑 ⇔ 🍴 🅿
r. Charles Buls 2 (1st Floor) ✉ *1000*　　　Plan: **M2**
– ☎ *0 2 511 82 44 – www.lamaisonducygne.be*
– closed Bank Holidays, Saturday lunch and Sunday
Menu 25 € (lunch), 65/173 € ▼ – Carte 71/94 €
• Classic cuisine • Elegant •

This prestigious 17C building on the Grand-Place was once home to the city's butchers' guild. Varied traditional cuisine and an opulent decor.
L'Ommegang – See restaurant listing

XxX
🕸🕸

Comme Chez Soi (Lionel Rigolet)   🕸 AC ⇔ 🍴

pl. Rouppe 23 ✉ *1000 –* ✆ *0 2 512 29 21*   Plan: **L2**
– www.commechezsoi.be – closed 29 and 30 March, 5 April, 17 July-
16 August, 1 November, 20 December-4 January, Tuesday
lunch, Wednesday lunch, Sunday and Monday
Menu 60 € (lunch), 94/199 € – Carte 96/233 € – *(pre-book)*
• French creative • Elegant •
This Brussels institution was founded in 1926. The menu features specialities
that have held their own over four generations, complemented by new creations by Lionel Rigolet. It has all the comfort of a bistro, Horta-inspired decor
and comfortable tables in the kitchen itself, from where you can watch the
chefs in action.
➜ Gamberi rossi aux asperges, pourpier, estragon et pomme verte. Carré
et ris de veau au thym, farandole de primeurs champêtres. Dentelle caramélisée aux fraises des bois et au kirsch, sorbet de fruits rouges au citron
vert.

XxX

Bocconi – Hôtel Amigo   ᪰ AC ⇔ 🍴

r. de l'Amigo 1 ✉ *1000 –* ✆ *0 2 547 47 15*   Plan: **M2**
– www.roccofortehotels.com
Menu 18 € (lunch), 42/55 € – Carte 43/67 €
• Italian • Elegant •
This renowned Italian restaurant occupies a luxury hotel near the Grand-Place.
Modern brasserie-style decor provides the backdrop for enticing Italian cuisine.

XxX
🕸

San Daniele (Franco Spinelli)   🕸 AC ⇔

av. Charles-Quint 6 ✉ *1083*   Plan: **A2**
– ✆ *0 2 426 79 23 – www.san-daniele.be*
– closed 1 week Easter, mid July-mid August, late December,
Bank Holidays, Sunday and Monday
Menu 60 € (lunch)/90 € – Carte 59/93 €
• Italian • Intimate •
An attractive dining room serving typical Italian cuisine accompanied by an ent-
icing Italian wine list. Friendly, attentive service from the Spinelli family.
➜ Carpaccio de thon rouge, citron confit, foie gras et sorbet au basilic.
Carré d'agneau en croûte d'olives. Raviolis d'ananas, crème de citron et sor-
bet à l'orange sanguine.

XxX

L'Écailler du Palais Royal   AC ⇔

r. Bodenbroek 18 ✉ *1000 –* ✆ *0 2 512 87 51*   Plan: **N3**
– www.lecaillerdupalaisroyal.be – closed August, late December, Bank
Holidays and Sunday
Carte 70/126 €
• Fish and seafood • Traditional •
An elegant and cosy oyster bar frequented by diplomats and top business exe-
cutives for the past 40 years. Choose from banquette seating and a convivial
counter-bar downstairs or round tables upstairs. Refined fish and seafood.

XxX
🕸

senzanome (Giovanni Bruno)   🕸 AC 🍴

pl. du Petit Sablon 1 ✉ *1000 –* ✆ *0 2 223 16 17*   Plan: **N3**
– www.senzanome.be – closed mid July-mid August, Christmas-New Year,
Bank Holidays, Saturday and Sunday
Menu 45 € (lunch), 95/125 € – Carte 77/99 €
• Italian • Design •
All the flavours and aromas of rich Italian, particularly Sicilian, culinary traditions
are showcased at senzanome. The talented chef rustles up beautifully prepared
and presented dishes of flawless harmony. A prestigious establishment, entirely
in keeping with the neighbourhood.
➜ Burratina à l'huile d'olive, sorbet de tomate et basilic. Bar de ligne cuit
au four aux tomates, câpres et herbes à l'huile d'olive. Gaufre aux amandes,
crème de ricotta à la vanille, pistaches et coulis d'orange.

XX Aux Armes de Bruxelles

r. des Bouchers 13 ✉ *1000 – ℰ 0 2 511 55 50*   Plan: **M1**
– www.auxarmesdebruxelles.com
Menu 23 € (lunch), 40 € ☙/93 € ☙ – Carte 34/109 €
• **Belgian** • **Brasserie** • **Elegant** •
This veritable Brussels institution in the Ilot Sacré district has been honouring Belgian culinary traditions since 1921. Contrasting dining rooms and a lively atmosphere.

XX Lola   📧

pl. du Grand Sablon 33 ✉ *1000 – ℰ 0 2 514 24 60*   Plan: **M3**
– www.restolola.be – closed 2 weeks in August and 24 and 31 December
Carte 41/68 €
• **Mediterranean** • **Brasserie** •
Friendly brasserie with a contemporary decor serving Italian dishes based on the freshest ingredients. The pleasant counter is perfect for a meal on the hoof.

XX Les Brigittines Aux Marches de la Chapelle   ⇔ 🍴

pl. de la Chapelle 5 ✉ *1000 – ℰ 0 2 512 68 91*   Plan: **M3**
– www.lesbrigittines.com – closed 25 December, Saturday lunch and Sunday
Menu 35 € (lunch)/55 € – Carte 38/71 €
• **Traditional cuisine** • **Retro** •
This lavish Art Nouveau brasserie will first and foremost delight the eye! Afterwards you will also find it impossible to resist the mouthwatering recipes rustled up by chef Dirk Myny. He is a genuine Brusseler, whose exuberant personality gives character to his traditional market fresh dishes.

XX La Belle Maraîchère   📧 ⇔ 🅿

pl. Ste-Catherine 11 ✉ *1000 – ℰ 0 2 512 97 59*   Plan: **L1**
– www.labellemaraichere.com – closed late July-early August, 1 week at Carnival, Wednesday and Thursday
Menu 40/64 € – Carte 53/111 € – (booking advisable)
• **Fish and seafood** • **Friendly** • **Elegant** •
This welcoming, family-run restaurant is a popular choice for locals with charmingly nostalgic decor in the dining room. Enticing traditional cuisine, including fish, seafood and game depending on the season, as well as high quality sauces. Attractive set menus.

XX François

quai aux Briques 2 ✉ *1000 – ℰ 0 2 511 60 89*   Plan: **L1**
– www.restaurantfrancois.be – closed 18 August-7 September, Sunday and Monday
Menu 27 € (lunch)/48 € – Carte 47/106 €
• **Fish and seafood** • **Traditional** • **Bistro** •
Fish and seafood take pride of place in this restaurant run by the same family since the 1930s. Maritime-inspired decor including photos from the past. Fishmonger's next door.

XX ⸨ WY by Bart De Pooter

r. Bodenbroek 22 ✉ *1000 – ℰ 0 2 400 42 63*   Plan: **N3**
– www.wybrussels.be – closed 28 March-5 April, 1-23 August, late December-early January, Bank Holidays and Sunday
Menu 32 € (lunch), 44/75 € – Carte 68/82 €
• **Creative** • **Fashionable** •
This haven of fine food nestles in the heart of Brussels' 'Mercedes House'. Once past the car showroom, you will be greeted by a luminous, contemporary restaurant and tasty cuisine. Enjoy fine produce, creative menus and sophisticated service. Flat screens showcase the chefs at work.
➔ Lard et chou blanc croquant au beurre blanc, baies de genévrier et noisettes. Côte à l'os aux artichauts, pomme de terre Opperdoezer et brocoli. A Star is Born : dessert au chocolat et à la vanille.

BELGIUM - BRUSSELS

XX **Comptoir des Galeries** – Hôtel des Galeries
Galerie du Roi 6 ✉ *1000* – ☎ *0 2 213 74 74* Plan: M1
– *www.comptoirdesgaleries.be* – *closed Sunday and Monday*
Menu 26 € (lunch) – Carte 35/76 €
• **French classic** • **Brasserie** • **Friendly** •
Vintage accents add character to this contemporary brasserie, in the heart of which stands a somewhat incongruous medal press! Pleasant establishment, ideal to savour brasserie classics made with good quality ingredients, or just for a glass of good wine.

XX **Alexandre**
✿ *r. du Midi 164* ✉ *1000* – ☎ *0 2 502 40 55* Plan: L2
– *www.restaurant-alexandre.be* – *closed last week August-first week September, first week January, Tuesday lunch, Saturday lunch, Sunday and Monday*
Menu 34 € (lunch), 75/130 €
• **Modern cuisine** • **Intimate** • **Fashionable** •
The restaurant's name gives no hint to the restaurant's feminine character. The charming manageress greets and takes care of patrons, while in the kitchen Isabelle Arpin supervises the subtle cuisine. Her compositions are modern, delicate and elegant with a deliciously feminine touch.
➜ Turbot aux coques et variation sur la carotte, sauce au cumin. Poitrine de canard aux cerises et structures de betterave rouge. Crème vanillée aux fraises des bois et crumble de speculoos.

XX **Les Larmes du Tigre**
r. Wynants 21 ✉ *1000* – ☎ *0 2 512 18 77* Plan: F3
– *www.leslarmesdutigre.be* – *closed Saturday lunch and Monday*
Menu 16 € 🍷 (lunch), 34 € 🍷/45 € – Carte 36/47 €
• **Thai** • **Exotic** •
A real voyage for the taste buds! They have been serving authentic Thai food here for over 30 years, and the enjoyment for money ratio is excellent. Buffet at lunch and Sunday evenings.

XX **JB**
☺ *r. Grand Cerf 24* ✉ *1000* – ☎ *0 2 512 04 84* Plan: M3
– *www.restaurantjb.com* – *closed August, 24-27 December, Bank Holidays, Monday lunch, Saturday lunch and Sunday*
Menu 37/50 € – Carte 47/73 €
• **Classic cuisine** • **Friendly** • **Family** •
Despite being located close to the Place Louise, this family-run restaurant remains discreet. The regulars all have their favourites, be it Flemish asparagus or grilled veal sweetbreads. Flavours are pronounced and the menu represents good value for money.

X **Kwint**
Mont des Arts 1 ✉ *1000* – ☎ *0 2 505 95 95* Plan: N2
– *www.kwintbrussels.com*
Menu 19 € (lunch), 35/46 € – Carte 25/65 € – *(open until 11pm)*
• **French modern** • **Brasserie** •
An amazing sculpture by artist Arne Quinze adds cachet to this elegant brasserie. It serves a tasty up-to-the-minute menu in which fine quality produce takes pride of place. The view of the city from the Mont des Arts is breathtaking. A great way to see another side of Brussels.

X **La Manufacture**
r. Notre-Dame du Sommeil 12 ✉ *1000* – ☎ *0 2 502 25 25* Plan: L1
– *www.manufacture.be* – *closed 27 July-10 August, 24 December-1 January, Bank Holidays, Saturday lunch and Sunday*
Menu 16 € (lunch), 28/50 € – Carte 37/57 €
• **Belgian** • **Brasserie** • **Trendy** •
Metals, wood, leather and granite provide the decor in this lively, trendy brasserie in the former workshop of a famous Belgian luggage maker. Contemporary cuisine.

Bozar Brasserie

ᵐ̃ ✿

r. Baron Horta 3 ⊠ *1000 –* ✆ *0 2 503 00 00*   Plan: **N2**
*– www.bozarbrasserie.be – closed late July-August, 1 week at Carnival,
Sunday and Monday*
Menu 29 € (lunch), 39/60 € – Carte 57/88 €
• **Creative** • **Fashionable** •
If you know the chef at La Paix - the benefactor of this restaurant - you'll recognise his touch right away. Refinement and presentation are the strongpoints of the original brasserie food here. An establishment that's well worth a try!

L'Ommegang

ᴬᶜ 🅿

Grand-Place 9 ⊠ *1000 –* ✆ *0 2 511 82 44*   Plan: **M2**
*– www.brasseriedelommegang.be – closed Bank Holidays, Saturday lunch
and Sunday*
Carte 33/60 €
• **Traditional cuisine** • **Classic** • **Elegant** •
You will enjoy the classic, copious Belgian cuisine served at this brasserie, which is the little sister of the famous Maison du Cygne. It is surrounded by the ambience of "the most beautiful square in the world", as Victor Hugo once said. The affable staff display typical Brussels humour.

De l'Ogenblik

ᵐ̃ ✿

Galerie des Princes 1 ⊠ *1000 –* ✆ *0 2 511 61 51*   Plan: **M1**
*– www.ogenblik.be – closed 1-15 August, lunch on Bank Holidays and
Sunday*
Menu 48 € ▼/60 € – Carte 50/70 € – *(open until midnight)*
• **Classic cuisine** • **Bistro** • **Simple** •
This restaurant, popular with the city's business crowd, has the appearance of an old café. Traditional cuisine including typical bistro dishes.

Little Asia

ᴬᶜ ✿

r. Ste-Catherine 8 ⊠ *1000*   Plan: **L1**
– ✆ *0 2 502 88 36 – www.littleasia.be*
– closed 15 July-15 August, Wednesday and Sunday
Menu 25 € (lunch), 45/69 € – Carte 46/70 €
• **Vietnamese** • **Fashionable** • **Exotic** •
A restaurant known for its well-prepared Vietnamese specialities, modern decor and smiling waitresses, overseen by a charming female owner.

Selecto

r. Flandre 95 ⊠ *1000 –* ✆ *0 2 511 40 95*   Plan: **L1**
*– www.le-selecto.com – closed late December-early January, Sunday and
Monday*
Menu 20 € (lunch), 36/42 €
• **French modern** • **Friendly** •
In the heart of the lively Ste-Catherine neighbourhood, the Selecto leads Belgium's vanguard of bistronomic (bistro + gastronomic) culture. Good food, a great atmosphere and reasonable prices!

Enjoy Art

ᴬᶜ ✿

bd de Waterloo 22 ⊠ *1000 –* ✆ *0 2 641 57 90*   Plan: **N3**
– www.enjoybrussels.be – closed Bank Holidays and Sunday
Menu 21 € (lunch)/39 € – Carte 37/60 €
• **French creative** • **Fashionable** •
Diners can choose from the BMW showroom on the left or the trendy restaurant on the right, which serves brasserie fare amidst modern art. The fresh, flavourful ingredients are a hit with gourmets.

X   **Samourai**   AC ⟷

r. du Fossé aux Loups 28 ✉ *1000 –* 𝒞 *0 2 217 56 39*   Plan: **M1**
– www.samourai-restaurant.be – closed 1-21 August, 24 December-
6 January, Sunday and Monday
Menu 27 € (lunch), 69/99 € – Carte 59/74 €
• **Japanese • Intimate • Minimalist •**
A Japanese restaurant which opened in 1975 near the Théâtre de la Monnaie.
Dining rooms on three floors with a Japanese decorative theme. Top-notch cuisine based around quality products and adapted to Western tastes.

X   **Henri**   🍴

r. Flandre 113 ✉ *1000 –* 𝒞 *0 2 218 00 08*   Plan: **L1**
– www.restohenri.be – closed Saturday lunch, Sunday and Monday
Carte 39/62 €
• **French modern • Friendly •**
Who would not dream of having such a brasserie just down the street? Henri
has been delighting the locals of this Flemish-speaking neighbourhood with
its good food. It is an ideal marriage between flawlessly prepared French dishes
and a laidback ambience. The minute you leave, you will want to return, just like
the many regulars.

X   **Taverne du Passage**

😊   *Galerie de la Reine 30* ✉ *1000 –* 𝒞 *0 2 512 37 31*   Plan: **M2**
– www.taverne-du-passage.be
Menu 26 € (lunch)/37 € – Carte 41/93 €
• **Classic cuisine • Retro •**
An old-fashioned portrait of Brussels in the delightful Galerie de la Reine with its
nostalgic charm and Art Deco features. There are a variety of Belgian delicacies
including croquette de crevettes (shrimp) and eels in sorrel sauce.

X   **Les Petits Oignons**   AC ⟷

😊   *r. Régence 25* ✉ *1000 –* 𝒞 *0 2 511 76 15*   Plan: **M3**
– www.lespetitsoignons.be
Menu 15 € (lunch)/35 € – Carte 40/56 € – *(open until 11pm)*
• **Classic cuisine • Brasserie •**
The visitor is of course charmed by the timeless decor and the lively atmosphere in this restaurant, but the delicious brasserie dishes are the real hit!
Good quality produce, carefully prepared and simply presented dishes and an
excellent wine list – you are in for VIP treatment!

X   **Le Wine Bar des Marolles**   🍴

😊   *r. Haute 198* ✉ *1000 –* 𝒞 *0 2 503 62 50*   Plan: **M3**
– www.winebarsablon.be – closed 22 July-18 August, 25 December-
7 January, Sunday evening, Monday and Tuesday
Menu 15 € (lunch)
– Carte 32/79 € – (dinner only except Saturday and Sunday and until
11pm)
• **Regional • Wine bar •**
Are you a fan of dishes that draw on local specialities, redolent of the terroir? If
so, don't miss Le Wine Bar! Known only to insiders, this restaurant installed in
the heart of the Marolles offers hearty cuisine and a good choice of wines.

X   **La Roue d'Or**

r. Chapeliers 26 ✉ *1000 –* 𝒞 *0 2 514 25 54*   Plan: **M2**
– closed 20 July-20 August
Menu 15 € (lunch), 40/75 € 🍷 – Carte 36/55 € – *(open until 11.30pm)*
• **Regional • Bistro •**
This typical old Brussels café with a friendly atmosphere mixes traditional brasserie-style dishes with a handful of Belgian specialities. Decor includes Magritte-style murals and a superb clock in the dining room.

BELGIUM - BRUSSELS

Viva M'Boma

r. Flandre 17 ✉ 1000 – ☏ 02 512 15 93 – closed first   Plan: **L1**
week April, 27 July-10 August, first week January, Bank Holidays and
Sunday
Menu 19 € (lunch) – Carte 29/40 €
• **Regional** • **Bistro** •
This elegant canteen-style restaurant has closely packed tables and tiled walls reminiscent of a Parisian métro station. It is popular with fans of offal and old Brussels specialities (cow's udder, *choesels* (sweetbreads), marrowbone, ox cheek).

Scheltema

r. Dominicains 7 ✉ 1000 – ☏ 02 512 20 84   Plan: **M1**
– www.scheltema.be – closed 24 and 25 December and Sunday
Menu 19 € (lunch), 32/43 € – Carte 45/96 € – *(open until 11pm)*
• **Fish and seafood** • **Brasserie** •
An attractive old brasserie located in the city's Ilot Sacré district. Traditional dishes and daily specials with fish and seafood specialities. A lively atmosphere and a pleasant retro-style wooden decor.

Bar Bik

quai aux Pierres de Taille 3 ✉ 1000 – ☏ 02 219 75 00   Plan: **F1**
– closed late December-early January, Bank Holidays, Saturday and
Sunday
Carte 33/58 € – *(booking advisable)*
• **Traditional cuisine** • **Friendly** • **Minimalist** •
The Bar Bik (Brussels International Kitchen) features a slate menu with dishes from near and far. Friendly, laidback atmosphere and a minimalist decor.

Peï & Meï

r. Rollebeek 15 ✉ 1000 – ☏ 02 880 53 39   Plan: **M3**
– www.peietmei.be – closed Sunday and Monday
Menu 21 € (lunch), 45/60 €
• **Classic cuisine** • **Friendly** • **Minimalist** •
Peï & Meï means 'man' and 'woman' in the Brussels dialect. Gauthier creates dishes as generous as they are subtle, mingling a consummate blend of classicism and originality, while Mélissa oversees the attentive service. All of which is in a modern, somewhat rough around the edges decor, which further adds to the appeal of the establishment.

Le Fourneau Ibérique

pl. Ste-Catherine 8 ✉ 1000 – ☏ 02 513 10 02   Plan: **L1**
– www.lefourneauiberique.be – closed Sunday and Monday
Menu 20 € (lunch)/47 € – Carte 37/57 €
• **Spanish** • **Design** • **Fashionable** •
We recommend venturing over the threshold of this 'Iberian oven' to feast and make merry on tapas and other Spanish inspired recipes. At the same time admire the kitchen staff wielding knives and spoons in a show worthy of a Broadway stage. A splendid opportunity to hop over to Spain.

Strofilia

r. Marché-aux-Porcs 11 ✉ 1000 – ☏ 02 512 32 93   Plan: **L1**
– www.strofilia.be – closed 21 July-15 August, Saturday lunch and Sunday
Carte 22/41 € – *(open until 11.30pm)*
• **Greek** • **Trendy** •
Located close to the trendy Dansaert district, this typical "ouzeri" serves guests in its large loft-style dining rooms and vaulted cellar. A choice of Greek mezze, main courses and wines. The name comes from the attractive grape press on display ("strofilia" in Greek).

In 't Spinnekopke

pl. du Jardin aux Fleurs 1 ⊠ 1000 – ℰ 0 2 511 86 95

Plan: **L1**

– www.spinnekopke.be – closed Saturday lunch and Sunday

Carte 30/55 € – (open until 11pm)

• Belgian • Bistro •

A charming inn so typical of Brussels, with a bistro-style ambience and a menu that pays homage to the traditions of Belgian brasseries. Terrace on the square.

QUARTIER LOUISE-CAMBRE

Steigenberger Wiltcher's

av. Louise 71 ⊠ 1050 – ℰ 0 2 542 42 42

Plan: **J1**

– www.wiltchers.com

253 rm – †169/599 € ††199/599 € – � 32 € – 14 suites

• Chain hotel • Palace • Classic •

The Steigenberger offers modern luxury within the walls of an historic building dating from 1918. Attractive and stylish guestrooms, excellent leisure and spa options, as well as extensive conference facilities.

Bristol Stephanie

av. Louise 91 ⊠ 1050 – ℰ 0 2 543 33 11

Plan: **J1**

– www.thonhotels.com/bristolstephanie

142 rm – †130/350 € ††140/360 € – � 27 € – 1 suite

• Luxury • Business • Personalised •

A luxury hotel with attractive guestrooms spread between two interconnecting buildings. Superb suites. A modern brasserie with the typical decor of a leading hotel.

Sofitel Le Louise

av. de la Toison d'Or 40 ⊠ 1050 – ℰ 0 2 514 22 00

Plan: **J1**

– www.sofitel.com

159 rm – †150/450 € ††150/450 € – � 28 € – 10 suites

• Chain hotel • Business • Modern •

An escalator skirting an unusual lace mural leads to the chandelier crowned lobby of this hotel. It has been refurbished by interior designer Antoine Pinto and has attractive guestrooms.

Le Châtelain

r. Châtelain 17 ⊠ 1000 – ℰ 0 2 646 00 55

Plan: **J2**

– www.le-chatelain.com

91 rm – †149/420 € ††179/450 € – � 29 € – 16 suites

• Luxury • Business • Personalised •

An opulent hotel offering well-appointed large guestrooms with an Internet connection, satellite TV and air-conditioning. Meeting rooms and a fitness centre. Belgian and French gastronomy influenced by Asian cuisine is to the fore in the restaurant.

Warwick Barsey

av. Louise 381 ⊠ 1050 – ℰ 0 2 641 51 11

Plan: **K3**

– www.warwickbarsey.com

94 rm – †89/475 € ††89/475 € – � 24 € – 5 suites

• Luxury • Business • Stylish •

This magnificent Second Empire-style hotel is home to characterful guestrooms, making it the darling of artists and cinema crews. Meals are served in a neo-Classical, extravagantly glamorous restaurant and lounge, signed by Jacques Garcia. A real gem.

Avenue Louise, Cambre
(Plan III)

CENTRE (Plan IV)

BELGIUM - BRUSSELS

Porte de Namur

● Sofitel Le Louise

✗ Saint
Boniface

● Colonel ✗

● Steigenberger Wiltcher's

● Manos Stephanie

Bristol Stephanie

MUSÉUM DES
SCIENCES NATURELLES

Wavre

PARC
LÉOPOLD

MAISON COMMUNALE
D'IXELLES

Sq.
Sans Souci

MUSÉE COMMUNAL
D'IXELLES

IXELLES
ELSENE

Notos ✗ ✗

Kolya ✗ ✗
Manos Premier

✗ ✗ Rouge Tomate

Lesbroussart

✗ Chez Oki

Le Châtelain

Pl. E.
Flagey

ST-GILLES
ST-GILLIS

STE-TRINITÉ

MUSÉE
HORTA

La Quincaillerie ✗

Sq. de
Biarritz

Lanfray

Kokuban ✗
Rue Vilain XIV

La Canne en Ville ✗
✗ Toucan   Maru ✗
✗ Toucan
sur Mer

Sq. H.
Michaux

MUSÉE
CONSTANTIN
MEUNIER

Warwick Barsey

✗ ✗ La Villa
Emily

ABBAYE
DE LA CAMBRE

✗ ✗ La Villa in the sky

Chez ✗
Montaigne

Pl. Guy
d'Arezzo

✗ ✗ ✗ La Truffe Noire

Av. Lloyd Georges

● Hotel
● Restaurant

0   100 m

Manos Premier

chaussée de Charleroi 102 ⊠ 1060 – ☏ 0 2 537 96 82   Plan: **J2**
– www.manoshotel.com
47 rm ☲ – ♦100/225 € ♦♦150/250 € – 3 suites
• Luxury • Business • Stylish •
The Manos Premier has the grace of a late-19C townhouse with its rich Louis XV and Louis XVI furnishings. If possible, book a room overlooking the garden. Authentic oriental hammam in the basement. Stylish restaurant, veranda and lounge bar. Chic and elegant decor, plus a charming patio.
Kolya – See restaurant listing

Manos Stéphanie
chaussée de Charleroi 28 ⊠ 1060 – ☏ 0 2 539 02 50   Plan: **J1**
– www.manosstephanie.com
55 rm ☲ – ♦100/225 € ♦♦150/250 €
• Luxury • Stylish •
A townhouse with warm, classically styled guestrooms with a contemporary feel and light wood furnishings. Cupola above the breakfast room.

Aqua
r. Stassart 43 ⊠ 1050 – ☏ 0 2 213 01 01   Plan: **N3**
– www.aqua-hotel-brussels.com
97 rm ☲ – ♦85/250 € ♦♦95/250 €
• Business • Modern •
Minimalist decor embellished with a blue wood "wave" sculpture, created by contemporary artist Arne Quinze. It offers pared-down rooms with walls painted white and blue and parquet flooring. A calm environment.

Le Chalet de la Forêt (Pascal Devalkeneer)

Drève de Lorraine 43 ⊠ 1180 – ☏ 0 2 374 54 16
– www.lechaletdelaforet.be – closed last week December-first
week January, Saturday and Sunday
Menu 45 € (lunch), 119/145 € – Carte 107/153 €
• Creative • Elegant •
This chalet with a lovely terrace on the edge of the Forest de Soignes combines elegance and sophistication. The food is particularly stylish with a consummate combination of classicism, creativity, subtlety and generosity. The guarantee of intense sensations.
➔ Tartare d'huîtres au caviar et fleurs de brocolis en parmentier. Ris de veau croustillant, côtes et feuilles de blette, sauce à la réglisse. Chaud-froid au chocolat : sorbet et mousse cuite.

La Villa Lorraine

av. du Vivier d'Oie 75 ⊠ 1000 – ☏ 0 2 374 31 63   Plan: **C3**
– www.villalorraine.be – closed 27 March-4 April, 31 July-15 August,
1 January, Sunday except 14 February and Monday
Menu 48 € (lunch), 115/155 € – Carte 95/192 €
• Creative • Elegant •
Since 1953 this grande dame of the Brussels gastronomic scene has been a popular meeting place for gourmets. The grand, luxurious interior commands respect, as does the cooking. Classical dishes come with modern touches and are packed with flavour. There's also a charming terrace for warmer days.
➔ Langoustines servies nacrées, salées au caviar, mosaïque de céleri et jus à la verveine citronnée. Filet pur de veau de lait aux asperges, girolles, févettes et condiment fenouil-citron. La fraise et la rhubarbe : marmelade de rhubarbe pochée à l'hibiscus, fraises des bois et sorbet de fraises.
⊛ **La Brasserie de la Villa** – See restaurant listing

BELGIUM - BRUSSELS

La Truffe Noire

bd de la Cambre 12 ⊠ *1000 –* ✆ *0 2 640 44 22*   Plan: **K3**
– www.truffenoire.com – closed 1 week Easter, first 2 weeks August,
Christmas-New Year, Saturday lunch and Sunday
Menu 50/225 € – Carte 77/144 €
• Italian • Elegant •
As you might expect, The Black Truffle serves the famous *Tuber Melanosporum*
in all manner of dishes. An elegant decor with a patio-terrace. Charismatic
owner. Splendid choice of wines... some at staggering prices!
→ Carpaccio à la truffe à la façon de Luigi. Saint-pierre farci à la truffe et
son néctar truffé. Souffé chaud aux noisette grillées et sabayon à la vanille
et liqueur de noisettes.

Brugmann

av. Brugmann 52 ⊠ *1190 –* ✆ *0 2 880 55 54*   Plan: **B3**
– www.brugmann.com
Menu 24 € (lunch) – Carte 45/63 € – *(open until 11pm)*
• Modern cuisine • Elegant •
Brugmann is a picture of elegance. The interior is adorned with fine modern art
and the rear terrace is superb. What is more the chef's cuisine is equally stylish,
combining ingredients and techniques in dishes that are as modern as the
decor. A first-class establishment.

La Brasserie de la Villa

av. du Vivier d'Oie 75 ⊠ *1000 –* ✆ *0 2 374 31 63*   Plan: **C3**
– www.villalorraine.be – closed 5-8 Mai, 31 July-15 August, 1 January,
Sunday except 14 February and Monday
Menu 37 € – Carte 42/84 €
• Classic cuisine • Elegant •
The little sister of the Villa Lorraine where you can soak up the atmosphere of
that prestigious establishment at more affordable prices. Classic brasserie
dishes and appetising light meals.

Rouge Tomate

av. Louise 190 ⊠ *1050 –* ✆ *0 2 647 70 44*   Plan: **J2**
– www.rougetomate.com – closed Bank Holidays, Saturday lunch and Sunday
Menu 32 € (lunch), 50/90 € – Carte 54/80 €
• Creative • Trendy •
A healthy mind in a healthy body – such could be the motto of this minimalist
restaurant. The recipes are all designed with the help of nutritionists, so tuck in
without fear of blushing tomato red!

Le Passage (Rocky Renaud)

av. J. et P. Carsoel 17 ⊠ *1180 –* ✆ *0 2 374 66 94*   Plan: **B3**
– www.lepassage.be – closed 2 weeks in July, Saturday lunch and Sunday
Menu 35 € (lunch), 55/75 € – Carte 52/82 €
• Classic cuisine • Cosy •
Rocky has found a ring big enough to demonstrate his striking personal interpretation of classic gastronomy. His flavours have a lot of punch! The wine cellar
is visible from the dining area.
→ Millefeuille de crabe et tartare de thon. Ris de veau aux morilles. Café
glacé.

La Villa Emily

r. Abbaye 4 ⊠ *1000 –* ✆ *0 2 318 18 58*   Plan: **K3**
– www.lavillaemily.be – closed first 2 weeks August, Bank Holidays,
Sunday and Monday
Menu 38 € (lunch)/55 € – Carte approx. 70 €
• Mediterranean • Elegant • Intimate •
The Degand fashion house has designed a tailor-made jewel for discerning
palates. It is as elegant and intimate as a boudoir, with the occasional designer
touch and a huge chandelier. Enjoy the traditional Mediterranean cuisine with a
zest of originality and its subtle and powerful flavours. Taste is the key word of
this place!

BELGIUM - BRUSSELS

XX **Kolya** – Hôtel Manos Premier   🔆 📶 ⟳ 🍴 (dinner) 🚗
chaussée de Charleroi 102 ⊠ 1060 – ℰ 02 533 18 30   Plan: **J2**
– www.kolya.be – closed Saturday lunch and Sunday
Menu 20 € (lunch), 35/55 € – Carte 48/74 €
• **Mediterranean** • **Cosy** •
Enjoy contemporary French cuisine with a Mediterranean accent in the refined setting at Kolya. The veranda and patio are amazing, and the dining room is just as nice.

XX **La Villa in the sky** (Alexandre Dionisio)   🦋 < 🔆 🍴
❁❁ *av. Louise 480 (25th floor) ⊠ 1050 – ℰ 02 644 69 14*   Plan: **K3**
– www.lavillainthesky.be – closed 27 March-4 April, 31 July-22 August, 24-30 December, 1 January, lunch on Bank Holidays, Saturday lunch, Sunday and Monday
Menu 85 € (lunch), 145/175 € – *(booking essential)*
• **Creative** • **Design** • **Minimalist** •
Imagine yourself 102m above avenue Louise, inside a glass edifice that boasts one of the finest views of Brussels. You are now ready to sample the creative cuisine of chef Alexandre Dionisio and his team in a setting worthy of his talent.
➔ King crab à l'avocat, betterave et nori. Bœuf Simmental maturé sur l'os aux asperges, crémeux de pomme de terre et riz soufflé. La fraise dans tous ses états : nougatine, pain de Gênes et glace au lait d'amande.

XX **Notos**   🔆 ⟳
r. Livourne 154 ⊠ 1000 – ℰ 02 513 29 59   Plan: **J2**
– www.notos.be – closed first 3 weeks August, 1 week late December, Saturday lunch, Sunday and Monday
Menu 22 € (lunch), 42/70 € – Carte 51/70 €
• **Greek** • **Minimalist** •
A 'new generation' Greek restaurant located in what used to be a garage. Restrained contemporary setting, authentic Greek dishes with a modern touch, and a good selection of Hellenic wines.

X **Brasseries Georges**   🔆 📶 🍴
av. Winston Churchill 259 ⊠ 1180 – ℰ 02 347 21 00   Plan: **B3**
– www.brasseriesgeorges.be
Menu 14 € (lunch), 33/52 € – Carte approx. 73 € – *(open until 0.30am)*
• **Fish and seafood** • **Brasserie** •
One of the greatest oyster bar/brasseries in Brussels, decorated in Parisian style. A short counter menu at lunchtime. Friendly atmosphere and service with a handy car parking service.

X **Colonel**   🔆
r. Jean Stas 24 ⊠ 1060 – ℰ 02 538 57 36   Plan: **J1**
– www.colonelbrussels.com – closed Sunday and Monday
Carte 38/70 €
• **Meats** • **Brasserie** • **Fashionable** •
Generous cuts of meat greet you as you enter this brasserie, making the house specialty blatantly clear. The quality of the charcuterie, perfectly cooked red meat, French fries and delicious sauces are quite stunning. Paradise for carnivores!

X **Toucan**   🔆 ⟳ 🍴
av. Louis Lepoutre 1 ⊠ 1050 – ℰ 02 345 30 17   Plan: **J3**
– www.toucanbrasserie.com – closed dinner 24 and 31 December
Menu 18 € (lunch)/37 €
– Carte 32/60 € – *(open until 11pm) (booking advisable)*
• **Modern cuisine** • **Bistro** • **Design** •
The inviting nest of this toucan has a striking resemblance to a vintage brasserie, albeit with a few designer touches. The flavoursome dishes (oysters, confit of duck) are washed down with a glass of good wine.

X **La Quincaillerie**　　　　　　　　　　🛜 🄰🄲 ♿ 🐾 🅿

r. Page 45 ✉ *1050 –* ☎ *0 2 533 98 33*　　　　　Plan: **J2**
– www.quincaillerie.be – closed Sunday lunch
Menu 18 € (lunch)/37 € – Carte 37/67 € – *(open until midnight)*
• Classic cuisine • Brasserie •
Shiny and majestic brasserie occupying a former Art Deco hardware store. Daily specials and fresh oysters. Very professional service. Doorman.

X **Chez Oki**　　　　　　　　　　　　　　　🄰🄲

r. Lesbroussart 62 ✉ *1050 –* ☎ *0 2 644 45 76*　　Plan: **K2**
– www.chez-oki.com – closed 3 weeks in August, Monday lunch, Saturday lunch and Sunday
Menu 30 € – Carte 51/82 € – *(pre-book)*
• Japanese • Minimalist •
An inventive restaurant where the chef, Oki, prepares traditional French and Japanese cuisine before your eyes. The surprise menus here are particularly popular. Modern atmosphere and a small zen-inspired patio.

X **Maza'j**　　　　　　　　　　　　　　　　　🛜
😀

bd du Souverain 145 ✉ *1160 –* ☎ *0 2 675 55 10*　　Plan: **C3**
– www.mazaj.be – closed Saturday and Sunday
Menu 20 € (lunch), 35/50 € – Carte 29/55 € – *(bar lunch)*
• Lebanese • Friendly •
If you feel like exploring a new culinary horizon, why not book a table at Maza'j? Don't be misled by the bright contemporary interior, this establishment is the champion of traditional Lebanese cuisine and culture. All the dishes are laid on the table for everyone to sample, in a friendly, relaxed atmosphere.

X **Kokuban**
😀

r. Vilain XIIII 53 ✉ *1000 –* ☎ *0 2 611 06 22*　　Plan: **K2**
– www.kokuban.be – closed Sunday
Menu 12 € (lunch) – Carte 21/36 €
• Japanese • Minimalist •
Japanese classics served in a minimalist decor are the secret of success at the Kokuban. Thanks to its authenticity, rich flavours and moderate prices, the establishment has conquered both the hearts of the local inhabitants, as well as those of the Japanese expats who claim to feel at home here – what more can we say?

X **Les Papilles**　　　　　　　　　　　　　　🛜

chausée de Waterloo 782 ✉ *1180 –* ☎ *0 2 374 69 66*　Plan: **B3**
– www.lespapilles.be – closed Saturday lunch and Sunday
Menu 19 € (lunch), 39/64 € – Carte 43/76 €
• Traditional cuisine • Wine bar •
Your taste buds will definitely start tingling when you enter this delightful establishment. It specialises in distinctive and characteristic brasserie fare, and has a sushi bar in the evening. Before sitting down for your meal, pick yourself a bottle of wine directly from the shelves. Friendly and relaxed.

X **Kamo** (Kamo Tomoyasu)
❀

chaussée de Waterloo 550a ✉ *1050 –* ☎ *0 2 648 78 48*　Plan: **C3**
– www.restaurant-kamo.be – closed Saturday and Sunday
Menu 20 € (lunch), 65/85 € – Carte 65/95 € – *(booking essential)*
• Japanese • Trendy •
Wood, a large bar and an open kitchen: the stage is set! Kamo is resolutely playing the Tokyoite. The menu continues to showcase outstanding, fresh produce revealed in creations as pure as they are balanced. Every mouthful is a discovery, and every dish a memory.
➜ Sashimi et tempura de homard. Teriyaki de ris de veau. Mousse au sésame noir et crème brûlée au thé matcha.

La Canne en Ville

r. Réforme 22 ✉ *1050 –* ☎ *0 2 347 29 26*   Plan: **J3**
– www.lacanneenville.be – closed early Septembre, Christmas, New Year,
Saturday lunch, Sunday and Monday
Carte 48/58 €
• Classic cuisine • Family •
This friendly bistro has taken up abode in a former butchers since 1983, as the
tiles and the occasional decorative feature bear witness. The chef treats diners
to a succulent repertory of classical dishes, while the lady of the house gra-
ciously welcomes diners.

Saint Boniface

r. St-Boniface 9 ✉ *1050 –* ☎ *0 2 511 53 66*   Plan: **J1**
– www.saintboniface.be – closed Bank Holidays, Saturday lunch, Sunday
and Monday
Carte 37/52 €
• Cuisine from the South West • Bistro •
Tightly packed tables, posters on the walls and a collection of biscuit tins depict
this extremely welcoming bistro. The locals from Brussels flock here to sample
its Basque, Lyons and Southwest France specialities. Generous and delicious!

Les Caves d'Alex

r. Caroly 37 ✉ *1050 –* ☎ *0 2 540 89 37*   Plan: **N3**
– www.lescavesdalex.be – closed 27 July-17 August, 24 December-
2 January, Saturday and Sunday
Menu 18 € (lunch)/38 € – Carte 41/78 €
• French classic • Bistro • Neighbourhood •
Most of the wines in the cellar of Alex Cardoso, the owner, come from the Côtes
du Rhône and Languedoc regions of France. The food is free of unnecessary
frills offering classical dishes prepared with enthusiasm and know-how – a
genuine treat!

Maru

chaussée de Waterloo 510 ✉ *1050 –* ☎ *0 2 346 11 11*   Plan: **J3**
– closed Monday
Menu 16 € (lunch) – Carte 32/74 €
• Korean • Minimalist • Neighbourhood •
If your mouth is already watering at the prospect of crunchy deep-fried pancakes or sweet and sour tangsuyuk, head straight for this 'urban-style' Korean restaurant whose fresh ingredients are equalled by the authentic cooking
methods. Even better, the wine list is full of pleasant surprises.

Nonbe Daigaku

av. Adolphe Buyl 31 ✉ *1050 –* ☎ *0 2 649 21 49 – closed*   Plan: **C3**
Bank Holidays, Sunday and Monday
Menu 16 € (lunch) – Carte 31/107 € – *(bookings advisable at dinner)*
• Japanese • Family •
Japanese restaurant established in 2007 by a veteran of Japanese cuisine in
Brussels. Sushi bar stormed at lunchtimes, specialities cooked in the evening.
Admire the chef's dexterity.

Chez Montaigne

pl. G. Brugmann 27 ✉ *1050 –* ☎ *0 2 345 65 23*   Plan: **J3**
– www.chezmontaigne.com – closed Sunday dinner and Monday
Menu 22 € (lunch) – Carte 39/57 €
• Modern cuisine • Bistro • Fashionable •
Artwork by Jean-Luc Moerman sets the scene in the unusual, contemporary
decor of this brasserie, which also doubles as a delicatessen and grocery store.
The chef creates a fine modern repertory that skilfully combines quality ingre-
dients.

✗ Toucan sur Mer

av. Louis Lepoutre 17 ✉ *1050 –* ☎ *02 340 07 40* — Plan: **J3**
– www.toucanbrasserie.com – closed dinner 24 and 31 December
Menu 18 € (lunch)
– Carte 34/62 € – (open until 11pm) (booking advisable)
• **Fish and seafood** • Bistro •

The impeccable quality and freshness of the fish and seafood of the Toucan sur Mer are more than comparable with seafood restaurants on the coast. We will take a bet that this pleasant bistro will appeal to seafood lovers.

✗ Villa Singha 🏧

r. Trois Ponts 22 ✉ *1160 –* ☎ *02 675 67 34* — Plan: **C3**
– www.singha.be – closed 4-30 July, 25 December-2 January, Bank Holidays, Saturday lunch and Sunday
Menu 11 € (lunch)/25 € ☆ *– Carte approx. 35 €*
• **Thai** • Exotic •

Singha, the mythological lion, watches over this pleasant Thai restaurant, where fresh produce and authentic flavours enhance the traditional Thai cuisine. One such dish is Kha Nom Jeep, delicious steamed raviolis of chopped pork and Thai spices. The welcome and service are equally charming.

EUROPEAN INSTITUTIONS

🏨 Renaissance

r. Parnasse 19 ✉ *1050 –* ☎ *02 505 29 29* — Plan: **G3**
– www.renaissancebrussels.com
256 rm – ♦80/500 € ♦♦80/500 € – ☕ 25 € – 6 suites
• **Chain hotel** • Business • Modern •

A modern chain hotel adjoining the European institutions district. Well-appointed bedrooms, studios in the annexe, conference rooms, business facilities, and a 'health academy'. Traditional cuisine and a three-course lunch menu provided at the brasserie.

🏨 Radisson Blu EU

r. Idalie 35 ✉ *1050 –* ☎ *02 626 81 11* — Plan: **G3**
– www.radissonblu.com/euhotel-brussels
145 rm – ♦89/458 € ♦♦185/458 € – 4 suites
• **Chain hotel** • Business • Modern •

An ultra-contemporary hotel offering three types of rooms: Fresh, Chic and Fashion. Popular with a business clientele and European civil servants. Classic, modern cuisine served at your table or at the large, designer bar. Trendy, contemporary decor.

🏨 Sofitel Brussels Europe

pl. Jourdan 1 ✉ *1040 –* ☎ *02 235 51 00* — Plan: **G3**
– www.sofitel-brussels-europe.com
137 rm – ♦140/450 € ♦♦160/450 € – ☕ 28 € – 12 suites
• **Palace** • Luxury • Modern •

A modern luxury hotel overlooking a busy square at the heart of the European institutions district. Glass hall-atrium, leisure facilities, and fully equipped rooms, junior suites and suites. The smart restaurant has a relaxed feel and trendy decor.

🏨 Stanhope

r. Commerce 9 ✉ *1000 –* ☎ *02 506 91 11* — Plan: **N3**
– www.stanhope.be
125 rm – ♦85/530 € ♦♦105/530 € – ☕ 30 € – 9 suites
• **Grand Luxury** • Traditional • Stylish •

The splendours of the Victorian era are brought to life in this British-style townhouse. It offers varying categories of rooms, including superb suites and duplexes. Elegant and classic dining room in line with the menu. Pretty courtyard-terrace.

Martin's Brussels EU   ⚐ ⅃♿ ⌂ AC ♨ ⇔

bd Charlemagne 80 ✉ *1000* – ☎ *0 2 230 85 55*   Plan: **G2**
– www.martinshotels.com
97 rm – ♦79/350 € ♦♦79/350 € – ☲ 23 € – 3 suites
• Chain hotel • Modern •
A modern hotel near the Berlaymont building with three categories of guest-rooms and excellent business and seminar facilities. Designer public areas adorned with snapshots of Hollywood stars. Trendy brasserie with a decor and special effects inspired by the world of film. Lounge bar.

 ### Thon EU   ⚐ ⅃♿ ♿ AC ♨ ⇔

r. Loi 75 ✉ *1040* – ☎ *0 2 204 39 11*   Plan: **G2**
– www.thonhotels.com/eu
405 rm – ♦90/382 € ♦♦105/410 € – ☲ 28 € – 7 suites
• Chain hotel • Contemporary •
Brightly coloured, well-proportioned and comfortable rooms. This hotel, part of the Thon chain, is popular with Eurocrats and others.

 ### Leopold   ⚐ AC ♨ ⇔

r. Luxembourg 35 ✉ *1050* – ☎ *0 2 511 18 28*   Plan: **N3**
– www.hotel-leopold.be
105 rm ☲ – ♦70/350 € ♦♦80/360 €
• Family • Contemporary •
In the heart of the European district of Brussels, this warm, family hotel offers comfortable, regularly renovated guestrooms. The generous breakfasts are served in the spacious winter garden or on the terrace.

 ### Aloft   ⅃♿ ♿ AC ♨

pl. Jean Rey ✉ *1040* – ☎ *0 2 800 08 88*   Plan: **G2**
– www.aloftbrussels.com
150 rm ☲ – ♦65/350 € ♦♦65/350 €
• Business • Functional •
On the doorstep of Europe's institutions, a loft spirit and design reign throughout this hotel. The spacious, comfortable and practical rooms are equally popular with business travellers and civil servants.

 ### Bon-Bon (Christophe Hardiquest)   ♨ 🥢

av. de Tervueren 453 ✉ *1150* – ☎ *0 2 346 66 15*   Plan: **D3**
– www.bon-bon.be – closed 26 March-10 April, 18 July-9 August,
19 December-3 January, Bank Holidays, Monday lunch, Saturday and
Sunday
Menu 85/220 € – Carte 90/230 €
• Creative • Elegant •
Bon-Bon deserves its name: this is one of the best restaurants in Belgium! The chef creates refined dishes with top quality ingredients. The popular surprise menu always boasts lots of new finds.
→ Carpaccio de coquilles Saint-Jacques, gazpacho d'huîtres. Mafé d'agneau "retour du Sénégal". Fontainebleau du jardin.

Da Mimmo   ⅋ ♨ AC

av. du Roi Chevalier 24 ✉ *1200* – ☎ *0 2 771 58 60*   Plan: **D2**
– www.da-mimmo.be – closed 20 July-10 August, late December-early
January, Saturday lunch and Sunday
Menu 43 € (lunch), 85/105 € – Carte 70/92 €
• Italian • Elegant •
This elegant Italian restaurant speaks only one language: that of fine produce! Don't expect fussy, sophisticated dishes, the flavours are frank, generous and precise. The best of Italian cuisine, accompanied by fine vintages!
→ Duo d'asperges à la crème de parmesan, œuf de ferme sur le plat et langoustine. Bar de ligne au gros sel et artichauts violets. Crème de rhubarbe et crumble, fruits rouges et sorbet au yuzu.

BELGIUM - BRUSSELS

XX
🐸 **Park Side** 🍽 🔥 AK ↔

av. de la Joyeuse Entrée 24 ✉ *1040 –* ☎ *0 2 238 08 08*   Plan: **H2**
– www.restoparkside.be – closed Bank Holidays, Saturday and Sunday
Menu 35 € – Carte 39/59 €
• Modern cuisine • Fashionable • Brasserie •

English speakers will get the reference right away, since this establishment abuts the Jubilee Park (parc du Cinquantenaire). A great location for an equally attractive and chic decor with an ultra-modern design – the main ceiling light in particular attracts a lot of stares! New-style brasserie specialities on the à la carte menu.

XX
YuMe 🍽 ↔

av. de Tervueren 292 ✉ *1150 –* ☎ *0 2 773 00 80*   Plan: **D2**
– www.yume.be – closed Saturday and Sunday
Menu 25 € (lunch) – Carte 42/66 €
• Fusion • Fashionable •

YuMe blends East and West. On the Yu side: sushi, gyoza, dim sum and many Japanese specialities; on the Me side, nice little dishes from the Franco-Belgian tradition and a nice variety of meats. A fine blend, in a chic contemporary decor.

XX
🐸 **Les Deux Maisons**

Val des Seigneurs 81 ✉ *1150 –* ☎ *0 2 771 14 47*   Plan: **D2**
– www.lesdeuxmaisons.be – closed 1 week Easter, first 3 weeks August,
late December, Bank Holidays, Sunday and Monday
Menu 19 € (lunch), 37/60 € – Carte 51/77 €
• French classic • Classic •

Two houses have merged to create this elegant restaurant, where a classically trained chef rustles up tempting dishes using excellent ingredients. The 'tradition' menu with its luscious selection of desserts is highly recommended. Fine wine cellar.

XX
Stirwen ↔

chaussée St-Pierre 15 ✉ *1040 –* ☎ *0 2 640 85 41*   Plan: **G3**
– www.restaurant-stirwen.be – closed 30 and 31 March, 6 Mai, 25 July-
16 August, 2 November, 24 and 25 December, Bank Holidays, Saturday
and Sunday
Menu 35 € (lunch), 60/80 € – Carte 60/75 €
• French classic • Retro •

This renowned restaurant, adorned in wood, is today in the capable hands of an ambitious duo. David is in charge of the service, while François-Xavier takes a new look at French classics. First-class ingredients are used such as: Noirmoutier sole, Lozère lamb and Corrèze veal.

XX
Le buone maniere 🍽 ↔

av. de Tervueren 59 ✉ *1040 –* ☎ *0 2 762 61 05*   Plan: **D2**
– www.buonemaniere.be – closed 20 July-20 August, 23 December-
3 January, Saturday lunch and Sunday
Menu 35 € (lunch), 55/75 € – Carte 56/99 €
• Italian • Classic •

Le buone maniere occupies a mansion along a busy road. Authentic Italian-Mediterranean cuisine served to a backdrop of contemporary decor or on the front terrace.

XX
🐸 **Maison du Luxembourg**

r. Luxembourg 37 ✉ *1050 –* ☎ *0 2 511 99 95*   Plan: **N3**
– www.maisonduluxembourg.be – closed 1-21 August, 22 December-
4 January, Bank Holidays, Friday dinner, Saturday and Sunday
Menu 32 € (lunch)/37 € – Carte 46/65 €
• Regional • Fashionable •

Country cooking from the Luxembourg region moves to Brussels. This contemporary restaurant offers well-presented classical fare, highlighting produce sourced from the French-speaking province of Luxembourg. The ingredients are superlatively fresh and the vegetable side dishes are delicious. A great advertisement for the region.

Le Monde est Petit (Loïc Villers)

r. Bataves 65 ✉ *1040*
Plan: **D2**
– ☎ 0 2 732 44 34 – www.lemondeestpetit.be
– closed last week July-first 2 weeks August, 1 week late December, Bank Holidays, Saturday and Sunday
Menu 25 € (lunch) – Carte 51/72 €
• **French creative** • **Friendly** • **Family** •
The world is a small place (Le Monde est Petit) as this friendly restaurant confirms! The chef sources his produce from all over the planet, determined to seek out the best ingredients from the most far-flung, exotic places to the most local and authentic. All of which are then masterfully transformed into rich, flavoursome dishes.
→ Langoustine rôtie à la burrata, gazpacho de chou rouge et huile de moutarde. Échine de porc laqué et betterave, condiment mostarda et poivre sancho. Espuma de crème brûlée et salade de fraises, compote de rhubarbe et poudre de crumble.

Le Coq en Pâte

Tomberg 259 ✉ *1200*
Plan: **C2**
– ☎ 0 2 762 19 71 – www.lecoqenpate.be
– closed Monday
Menu 18 € (lunch), 32/49 € ♟ – Carte 36/49 €
• **Italian** • **Fashionable** •
This family-run restaurant has been regaling diners since 1972. Its secret lies first and foremost in the owner-chef's know-how, born out of his experience, creativity and dedication to Italian cuisine. However, the excellent value for money and comfortable decor are also much appreciated.

De Maurice à Olivier

chaussée de Roodebeek 246 ✉ *1200*
Plan: **C2**
– ☎ 0 2 771 33 98 – www.demauriceaolivier.be
– closed 28 March-8 April, 18 July-16 August, Bank Holidays, Monday dinner and Sunday
Menu 22 € (lunch), 33/55 € – Carte 38/51 €
• **Classic cuisine** • **Retro** •
Maurice, the father, has passed the business onto his son Olivier. He has also bequeathed a rich culinary heritage of French cuisine enriched in Mediterranean influences; the dishes are beautifully presented. Amusingly, the restaurant is also a newsagents.

Le Mucha

av. J. Du Jardin 23 ✉ *1150*
Plan: **D3**
– ☎ 0 2 770 24 14 – www.lemucha.be
– closed last week August-first week September, Sunday dinner and Monday
Menu 17 € (lunch), 33/50 € ♟ – Carte 31/58 €
• **Classic cuisine** • **Retro** •
The interior of the Mucha is reminiscent of Parisian brasseries in the 1900s, even down to the waiters! Ideal to sample traditional French cuisine from a fine choice of classical dishes, without forgetting a few Italian favourites!

Foro Romano

r. Joseph II 19 ✉ *1000* – ☎ *0 2 280 29 76*
Plan: **N2**
– closed Bank Holidays, Monday dinner, Saturday and Sunday
Menu 35 € (lunch)/50 € – Carte 39/49 €
• **Italian** • **Neighbourhood** •
This enoteca offers hearty Italian cuisine, created with its international clientele firmly in mind, and gets very busy at lunchtime.

Sheraton
☆ ↳ ⋒ ▣ ໕ 亜 ໕ ⇔ ☞ **P**

pl. Rogier 3 ⊠ *1210* – ℰ *0 2 224 31 11* Plan: **F1**
– *www.sheratonbrussels.com*
505 rm – ♦89/439 € ♦♦89/439 € – ⊑ 25 € – 6 suites
• Chain hotel • Business • Modern •
Imposing tower hotel with superb facilities for a mainly international business
and conference clientele. Spacious standard and club rooms, as well as numerous suites. Attractive contemporary bar. Traditional cuisine in the restaurant
facing Place Rogier. Lunch buffet.

Crowne Plaza - Le Palace
☆ ↳ ⋒ ໕ 亜 ໕

r. Gineste 3 ⊠ *1210* – ℰ *0 2 203 62 00* Plan: **F1**
– *www.crowneplazabrussels.com*
346 rm – ♦89/399 € ♦♦89/399 € – ⊑ 28 € – 8 suites
• Chain hotel • Business • Classic •
This Belle Époque palace, dating back to 1908, has rediscovered its former glory.
Impressively elegant public areas, a brand-new bar, neo-retro-style guestrooms
and new suites. Cosmopolitan cuisine to a backdrop of chic and trendy decor.

Bloom!
☆ ↳ ໕ 亜 ໕ ⇜

r. Royale 250 ⊠ *1210* – ℰ *0 2 220 66 11* Plan: **F1**
– *www.hotelbloom.com*
304 rm – ♦75/330 € ♦♦75/330 € – ⊑ 19 € – 4 suites
• Business • Design • Personalised •
This fashionable business hotel has made quite an impression with its breathtaking design. Bright, art-inspired bedrooms, each embellished with a modern
fresco. Meeting rooms and fitness area.
SmoodS – See restaurant listing

SmoodS – Hôtel Bloom!
໕ 亜 ⇔

r. Royale 250 ⊠ *1210* – ℰ *0 2 220 66 66* Plan: **F1**
– *www.hotelbloom.com* – *closed July-August, late December-early
January, Bank Holidays, Saturday lunch and Sunday*
Menu 24 € (lunch) – Carte 26/54 €
• Modern cuisine • Fashionable •
Are you in a 'flower power' or a 'safari' mood? Have a seat in one of the 'mood
islands', depending on how you are feeling at that moment. The food is adap-
table too – ranging from snacks to copious meals – so there is something for
everyone.

Al Matbakh

pl. Colignon 8 ⊠ *1030* – ℰ *0 2 248 23 29* Plan: **B2**
– *www.almatbakh.be* – *closed 2nd and 4th Saturday of each month and
Sunday*
Menu 14 € (lunch) – Carte 30/48 €
• Middle Eastern cuisine • Friendly •
With a name like Al Matbakh ("the kitchen" in Arabic), you would be right to
expect an authentic culinary experience of North African origins. This pleasant,
colourful restaurant specialises in dishes that combine North African with Lebanese origins. The menu is as varied as it is delicious.

Les Dames Tartine

chaussée de Haecht 58 ⊠ *1210* – ℰ *0 2 218 45 49* Plan: **G1**
– *closed first 3 weeks August, Saturday lunch, Sunday and Monday*
Menu 20 € (lunch), 36/49 € – Carte 43/53 €
• Classic cuisine • Intimate • Family •
Two women run this restaurant with great panache. Excellent seasonal cuisine,
an intimate atmosphere and an impressive wine list.

Pullman Midi

pl. Victor Horta 1 ✉ *1060 –* ☎ *0 2 528 98 00* — Plan: **E3**
– www.pullmanhotels.com/7431
237 rm – 🛏99/349 € 🛏🛏99/349 € – ☕ 20 € – 2 suites
• Business • Stylish •
Just a stone's throw from Brussels-South railway station, this hotel transports you to another world. Trendy decor and modern comforts go hand in hand with elegant, designer inspired guestrooms. Alternatively, you can drop in and enjoy a good meal.

Be Manos

Square de l'Aviation 23 ✉ *1070 –* ☎ *0 2 520 65 65* — Plan: **E2**
– www.bemanos.com
59 rm ☕ – 🛏100/225 € 🛏🛏150/250 € – 1 suite
• Luxury • Design •
Ultra trendy and high on design, superlatives barely do justice to this hotel in a fashionable district of Anderlecht. Attractive terraces and a spa. The very trendy restaurant serves both Belgian and Mediterranean specialities.

Park Inn Midi

pl. Marcel Broodthaers 3 ✉ *1060 –* ☎ *0 2 535 14 00* — Plan: **E3**
– www.parkinn.com/hotel-brussels
142 rm – 🛏75/275 € 🛏🛏90/295 € – ☕ 17 €
• Business • Functional •
Next to Brussels South (Midi) station, this establishment offers practical, well-kept rooms that are perfect for business travellers.

Vintage

♿

r. Dejoncker 45 ✉ *1060 –* ☎ *0 2 533 99 80* — Plan: **F3**
– www.vintagehotel.be
30 rm ☕ – 🛏55/150 € 🛏🛏70/160 €
• Family • Retro •
Furnished with 1960s fixtures and fittings, complete with psychedelic wallpaper – fans of Sixties memorabilia will love the Vintage. What's more, the hotel is well located, just off the smart, trendy Avenue Louise.

Pantone

pl. Loix 1 ✉ *1060 –* ☎ *0 2 541 48 98 – www.pantonehotel.com* — Plan: **F3**
61 rm – 🛏49/499 € 🛏🛏49/499 € – ☕ 15 €
• Family • Design • Minimalist •
Pantone is something of a household name in the field of colour charts, of which it is one of the world's leading manufacturers. Accordingly, the hotel's motto 'Live in colour, dream in colour' is brought to technicolour life in this design interior.

XxX Saint Guidon

av. Théo Verbeeck 2 ✉ *1070 –* ☎ *0 2 520 55 36* — Plan: **A3**
– www.saint-guidon.be – closed Saturday, Sunday and Club's home match days
Menu 36/75 € 🍷 – Carte 55/95 € – *(lunch only)*
• French classic • Elegant •
Anderlecht Football Club does more than play a good game of football because the ground's Tribune 2 is home to Saint Guidon – a fine classical restaurant. Good produce, consummate preparation and refined flavours: the chef is clearly worthy of the Premiere League.

XX **La Paix** (David Martin)

🌼

r. Ropsy-Chaudron 49 (opposite abattoirs) ✉ *1070* Plan: **B2**
– ✆ 0 2 523 09 58 – www.lapaix.eu – closed July, Christmas – New Year,
Bank Holidays, Saturday and Sunday
Menu 65/95 € – Carte 81/124 € – *(lunch only except Friday)*
• Creative • Brasserie •
This characterful brasserie is a fine example of multicultural Brussels. In the kitchen David Martin creatively and masterfully prepares food that mingles influences from Japan and Belgium. He seeks to enhance excellent produce, among which is red meat in particular. A genuine experience.
➜ Black cod sake-kasu, dashi au laurier et black sésame. Volaille de Bresse shio-koji, cuite en portefeuille. Pain perdu caramélisé.

XX **La Brouette** 🍸 🏠 AK

😊

bd Prince de Liège 61 ✉ *1070 – ✆ 0 2 522 51 69* Plan: **A2**
– www.labrouette.be – closed 1 week Easter, August, 19 and
20 September, 8-10 January, Carnival holiday, Saturday lunch, Sunday
dinner and Monday
Menu 30 € (lunch), 37/55 € – Carte 51/71 €
• French creative • Friendly •
Herman Dedapper isn't afraid of thinking outside the box. Omnipresent in the dining room, he always wore his chef's hat until passing it onto his right hand man. He is still the owner, and nowadays also the sommelier! Don't miss the 'Brouette' menu, which you can put together yourself.

X **René** 🏠 AK

pl. de la Résistance 14 ✉ *1070 – ✆ 0 2 523 28 76* Plan: **A2**
– closed mid June-late July, Monday and Tuesday
Carte 24/62 €
• Belgian • Family •
This former chippy has been turned into a delightful vintage-style bistro by René who takes us back in time to an era when cooking was simple and unfussy. Mussels, steak and nourishing stews are all served with generous portions of French fries – a treat for lovers of down-to-earth, wholesome food.

ATOMIUM QUARTER

XXX **La table d'Evan** 🏠 ♻ **P**

Brusselsesteenweg 21 ✉ *1780 Wemmel* Plan: **A1**
– www.evanrestaurants.be – closed Monday in July and August, Saturday
lunch and Sunday
Menu 50/110 € – Carte approx. 75 €
• Mediterranean • Brasserie • Trendy •
Modern, comfortable and free of unnecessary frills: such is the setting of chef Evan. On a constant quest for fine produce, he deploys his talent and experience to create delicious dishes. Quality before all else is his motto – to the delight of our taste buds!

XX **L'Auberge de l'Isard** 🏠 ♻ **P**

😊

Romeinsesteenweg 964 ✉ *1780 Wemmel* Plan: **B1**
– ✆ 0 2 479 85 64 – www.isard.be – closed dinner on Bank Holidays,
Sunday dinner, Monday and Tuesday
Menu 26 € (lunch), 37/55 € – Carte 39/68 €
• French classic • Formal •
To escape the bustle of Heysel and Brussels' ring road, head for the elegant villa of Roland Taildeman, who has been at the stove for over 25 years. Guests are particularly taken with the establishment's formula… There is a wide and varied choice with one constant byword – taste.

XX
✿

't Stoveke (Daniel Antuna)

Jetsestraat 52 ⊠ 1853 Strombeek-Bever   Plan: **B1**
– ℰ 0 2 267 67 25 – www.tstoveke.be – closed late July-early August, late December-early January, Saturday lunch, Sunday dinner, Tuesday and Wednesday
Menu 35 € (lunch)/65 €
– Carte 72/124 € – (number of covers limited, pre-book)
• Modern cuisine • Minimalist • Design •
The chef of 't Stoveke follows in the footsteps of some of the best-known chefs in the world, including Escoffier, but has added his own creative touch. This has ensured that his cuisine remains resolutely up to date. The dishes reveal an explosion of flavours that are as much a delight to the eye as to the palate.
→ Krokant gebakken kalfszwezerik met jonge bladspinazie, spaghetti van koolrabi en een jus met kokos, gember en citroengras. Patrijs klassiek bereid in druivenblad, gebraiseerd witloof, wilde boschampignons en kweepeer. Roomijs van bosaardbeien en mascarpone, heldere bouillon met aardbeien, munt en gezouten crumble.

X
☺

Brasserie de l'Expo

av. Houba de Strooper 188 ⊠ 1020   Plan: **B1**
– ℰ 0 2 476 99 70 – www.brasseriedelexpo.be
– closed dinner 24 and 31 December
Menu 17 € (lunch)/37 € – Carte 31/56 €
• Fish and seafood • Brasserie •
The memory of the 1958 Expo continues to linger in this delightful vintage brasserie opposite Heysel stadium. Right from the word go, the seafood bar leaves you in no doubt that fresh, quality ingredients take pride of place in the chef's cuisine. Brasserie fare at its best!

X
☺

French Kiss

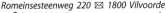

r. Léopold Ier 470 ⊠ 1090 – ℰ 0 2 425 22 93   Plan: **B2**
– www.restaurantfrenchkiss.com – closed 25 July-17 August, 24 and 31 December, 1 January and Monday
Menu 28/38 € – Carte 38/63 €
• Meats • Friendly •
A pleasant restaurant renowned for its excellent grilled dishes and impressive wine list. Dining area with a low ceiling and bright paintings adding colour to the brick walls.

X
☺

Spectrum

Romeinsesteenweg 220 ⊠ 1800 Vilvoorde   Plan: **B1**
– ℰ 0 2 267 00 45 – www.restospectrum.be – closed Monday dinner, Saturday lunch and Sunday
Menu 36 € – Carte 36/56 €
• Classic cuisine • Brasserie •
Good food lovers pay heed! The Spectrum offers one of the best value for money deals in the region of Brussels. Generous, traditional dishes.

X
☺

Wine in the City

pl. Reine Astrid 34 ⊠ 1090 – ℰ 0 2 420 09 20   Plan: **B2**
– www.wineinthecity.be – closed Sunday and Monday
Menu 35/60 €
– Carte 49/74 € – (lunch only except Friday) (booking essential)
• Modern cuisine • Wine bar •
Paradise for wine lovers. This wine bar-cum-restaurant seeks to regale epicureans with tasty bistro cuisine and a setting worthy of some of the most prestigious wine cellars. All the more so as it isn't just for show!

La Brasserie de la Gare

chaussée de Gand 1430 ✉ *1082 –* ✆ *0 2 469 10 09*   Plan: **A2**
– www.brasseriedelagare.be – closed Saturday lunch and Sunday
Menu 13 € (lunch)/35 € – Carte 32/56 €
• Belgian • Brasserie • Neighbourhood •
A whistle-stop from the station, this wood-panelled brasserie bustles. Naive mural on a railroading theme. Traditional dishes and exciting wine list.

AIRPORT & NATO

Crowne Plaza Airport

Da Vincilaan 4 ✉ *1831 Diegem –* ✆ *0 2 416 33 33*   Plan: **D1**
– www.crowneplaza.com/cpbrusselsarpt
312 rm – ♦99/495 € ♦♦99/495 € – ☑ 24 € – 3 suites
• Chain hotel • Business • Modern •
This upmarket chain hotel is located in a business district close to the airport. Central atrium, well-appointed guestrooms, a full range of conference facilities, fitness room and sauna. Club floor with a private lounge. Restaurant with an adjoining lounge bar. Buffet lunch midweek. Terrace overlooking a public park.

Novotel Airport

Da Vincilaan 25 ✉ *1831 Diegem –* ✆ *0 2 725 30 50*   Plan: **D1**
– www.novotel.com
209 rm – ♦89/219 € ♦♦89/219 € – ☑ 20 €
• Chain hotel • Business • Functional •
Convenient for stopover or business travellers, this Novotel is being gradually upgraded in line with the rest of the chain. Fitness centre and meeting rooms. Modern brasserie.

D'Oude Pastorie

Pastoorkesweg 1 ✉ *1950 Kraainem –* ✆ *0 2 720 63 46*   Plan: **D2**
– www.doudepastorie-jaloa.com – closed last 2 weeks September, Monday and Tuesday
Menu 19 € (lunch), 35/40 €
• Classic cuisine • Romantic • Friendly •
The gardens of Jourdain Castle represent a genuine haven of tranquillity, including a superb terrace by a large water feature. The menu will appeal to fans of classical fare, but those with more adventurous tastes will probably want to taste some of the more unusual dishes, such as chicken moambe, a Congolese speciality.

Orange

Leuvensesteenweg 614 ✉ *1930 Nossegem*   Plan: **D1**
– ✆ *0 2 757 05 59 – www.orangerestaurant.be – closed Saturday lunch, Sunday and Monday*
Menu 27 € (lunch)/38 € – Carte 37/72 €
• Modern cuisine • Friendly •
A modern take on good old brasserie cooking, served in an inviting setting: terracotta and chocolate tones, banquettes with fake crocodile-skin upholstery, and designer lighting. Pretty terrace surrounded by greenery.

Brasserie Mariadal

Kouterweg 2 ✉ *1930 Zaventem –* ✆ *0 2 720 59 30*   Plan: **D1**
– www.brasseriemariadal.be
Menu 27 € (lunch)/37 € – Carte 28/63 €
• Classic cuisine • Brasserie •
This modern brasserie occupies an attractive manor house in a public park with a lake. Find an uncluttered, stylish decor, an orangerie, reception rooms and play area. A good value for money menu.

X   **Bovis**   AC

Heldenplein 16 ⊠ 1930 Zaventem – ℰ 0 2 308 83 43   Plan: **D1**
– www.bovis-zaventem.be – closed Bank Holidays, Saturday lunch
and Sunday
Carte 40/71 €

• Meats • Brasserie •

The strapline of this restaurant is 'simply meat', where it uses only the very best quality and ensures that each carcass is aged until it reaches perfect maturity. All is served with handcut chips that are fried in beef fat, along with equally authentic wines.

ANTWERP
ANTWERPEN/ANVERS

Population: 513 570

Nimbus/Fotolia.com

Antwerp calls itself the pocketsize metropolis, and with good reason. Although it's Europe's second largest port, it still retains a compact intimacy, defined by bustling squares and narrow streets. It's a place with many facets, not least its marked link to Rubens, the diamond trade and, in later years, the fashion collective The Antwerp Six.

The city's centre teems with ornate gabled guildhouses, and in summer, open-air cafés line the area beneath the towering cathedral, giving the place a festive, almost bohemian air. It's a fantastic place to shop: besides clothing boutiques, there are antiques emporiums and diamond stores – to say nothing of the chocolate shops with their appealing window displays. Bold regeneration projects have transformed the skyline and the waterfront's decrepit warehouses have started new lives as ritzy storerooms of 21C commerce. The nightlife here is the best in Belgium, while the beer is savoured the way others might treat a vintage wine. The Old Town is defined by Grote Markt, Groenplaats and The Meir shopping street – these are a kind of dividing line between Antwerp's north and south. North of the centre is Het Eilandje, the hip former warehouse area; to the east is the Diamond District. Antique and bric-a-brac shops are in abundance in the 'designer heart' Het Zuid, south of the centre, which is also home to the best museums and art galleries.

ANTWERP IN...

→ **ONE DAY**
Grote Markt, Our Lady's Cathedral, MoMu, Het Zuid.

→ **TWO DAYS**
Rubens' House, Royal Museum of Fine Arts, a stroll to the Left Bank via the Sint-Anna tunnel.

→ **THREE DAYS**
Het Eilandje and MAS, a river trip, Kloosterstraat, Nationalestraat.

PRACTICAL INFORMATION

ARRIVAL-DEPARTURE

✈ Brussels Airport is 40km south. The Airport Express train takes 35min. The Antwerp-Brussels Airport Express shuttle bus to Central Station takes 45min.

✈ Antwerp Airport is 7km southeast. Buses Number 51, 52 and 53 go to the Central Station.

GETTING AROUND

Antwerp has an efficient network of buses, trams and premetro (trams which run underground at some stage of their journey). Invest in a Dagpas - a day pass - which gives unlimited travel on the whole of the city's public transport system; it's obtainable on board buses and trams and from De Lijn kiosks. On many occasions you'll find it quicker to walk around, as this is a compact city ideal for pedestrians. If you'd rather get about by bike, head to Tourism Antwerp on Grote Markt for more information.

CALENDAR HIGHLIGHTS

May
Sinksenfoor Funfair.

May-September
Free carillon concerts.

June
Beer Passion Weekend.

Summer
Zomer van Antwerpen (music, theatre, film).

August
Rubens Market, Festival of Flanders, Jazzfestival Middelheim.

September
Laundry Day, Open Monument Day.

EATING OUT

The menus of Flanders are heavily influenced by the lush meadows, the canals swarming with eels and the proximity of the North Sea – but the eating culture in Antwerp offers more than just seafood. With its centuries old connection to more exotic climes, there's no shortage of fragrant spices such as cinnamon in their dishes, especially in the rich stews so beloved by the locals. If you want to eat with the chic, hang around the Het Eilandje dockside or the rejuvenated ancient warehouses south of Grote Markt. For early risers, the grand cafés are a popular port of call, ideal for a slow coffee and a trawl through the papers. Overall the city boasts the same tempting Belgian specialities as Brussels (stewed eel in chervil sauce; mussels; dishes containing rabbit; beef stew and chicory), but also with a focus on more contemporary cuisine. Don't miss out on the local chocolate (shaped like a hand in keeping with the legend which gave Antwerp its name), and be sure to try their De Koninck beer, served in a glass designed like an open bowl.

CENTRE (Old Town and Main Station)

Hilton Old Town

Groenplaats 32 ✉ *2000* – ℰ *03 204 12 12*
Plan: **D2**
– *www.antwerp.hilton.com*
210 rm – †140/250 € ††140/250 € – ☲ 25 € – 12 suites
• **Chain hotel** • **Luxury** • **Classic** •

A luxury hotel established in 1994 within the walls of the superb, early-20C Grand Bazar building. Sumptuous Belle Époque ballroom. Suites facing the city, standard guestrooms overlooking the courtyard. Views of the cathedral and busy Groenplaats from the Terrace Café's veranda.

Radisson Blu Astrid

Koningin Astridplein 7 ✉ *2018* – ℰ *03 203 12 34*
Plan: **F2**
– *www.radissonblu.com/astridhotel-antwerp*
247 rm – †119/439 € ††119/439 € – ☲ 23 € – 3 suites
• **Chain hotel** • **Luxury** • **Modern** •

This modern, elegant hotel caters admirably for guests in the city on business or for pleasure. The Aquatopia oceanarium inside the hotel is home to 10,000 fish and reptiles. The bright and trendy canteen-style brasserie has a distinctly urban atmosphere.

Lindner

Lange Kievitstraat 125 ✉ *2018* – ℰ *03 227 77 00*
Plan: **F2**
– *www.lindnerhotels.be*
173 rm – †99/189 € ††99/189 € – ☲ 20 € – 4 suites
• **Business** • **Modern** •

This modern, almost futuristic hotel was cleverly built near the new station. A good starting point for your trip, whether it is for business or pleasure. Spacious rooms.

De Witte Lelie

Keizerstraat 16 ✉ *2000* – ℰ *03 226 19 66*
Plan: **D1**
– *www.dewittelelie.be*
10 rm – †245 € ††295 € – ☲ 30 € – 1 suite
• **Historic** • **Personalised** •

This historic abode fully justifies its reputation for poised sophistication and graceful hospitality. The 17C walls, tasteful decor down to the tiniest detail, and its precious peace and quiet in the city centre explain the appeal of this luxury boutique hotel.

Julien

Korte Nieuwstraat 24 ✉ *2000* – ℰ *03 229 06 00*
Plan: **D2**
– *www.hotel-julien.com*
21 rm – †150/259 € ††150/259 € – ☲ 18 €
• **Luxury** • **Stylish** • **Design** •

Hidden behind its carriage entrance this hotel is a real gem. It boasts a warm welcome, cosy atmosphere and very refined Scandinavian-style rooms. Don't miss the spa built in the 16C cellar. From the roof terrace there is a breathtaking view of the cathedral.

't Sandt

Zand 17 ✉ *2000* – ℰ *03 232 93 90* – *www.hotel-sandt.be*
Plan: **C2**
28 rm ☲ – †130/290 € ††150/310 € – 1 suite
• **Luxury** • **Classic** •

This establishment is in an attractive building with a fine Rococo façade near the banks of the Escaut. It offers attentive service, bedrooms full of character, meeting rooms, a patio and a roof terrace.

Les Nuits

Lange Gasthuisstraat 12 ✉ *2000* – ℰ *03 225 02 04*
Plan: **D2**
– *www.hotellesnuits.be*
25 rm – †129/149 € ††139/159 € – ☲ 19 €
• **Luxury** • **Cosy** • **Modern** •

Looking for a hip place in town? This boutique hotel offers a nice contrast between the dark colours of the night (la nuit) and lighter shades, its interior design is really charming.

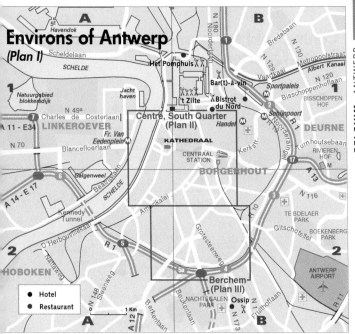

Hyllit
De Keyserlei 28 ✉ *2018 –* ☎ *0 3 202 68 00*
– www.hyllit.com
Plan: **E2**
197 rm – ♦109/190 € ♦♦115/215 € – ☲ 20 € – 3 suites
• Business • Contemporary •
This hotel on a busy shopping street has obliging staff. There are large and well-appointed rooms, suites and junior suites, as well as an extensive breakfast buffet, meeting rooms, lounge and leisure facilities.

The Plaza
Charlottalei 49 ✉ *2018 –* ☎ *0 3 287 28 70*
– www.plaza.be
Plan: **F3**
81 rm ☲ – ♦89/249 € ♦♦89/249 €
• Business • Classic •
A family-run hotel perfect for a good night's sleep. Spacious bedrooms and cosy suites, a lounge with Chesterfield chairs, plus a pleasant breakfast area and bar.

Rubens
Oude Beurs 29 ✉ *2000 –* ☎ *0 3 222 48 48*
– www.hotelrubensantwerp.be
Plan: **D1**
35 rm – ♦150/350 € ♦♦150/350 € – ☲ 20 € – 1 suite
• Family • Classic •
The Rubens occupies a stately building near the Grand Place, in which some of the guestrooms have a terrace overlooking the garden. Welcoming breakfast room and lounge, as well as a colonnaded courtyard filled with flowers. Peace and quiet guaranteed.

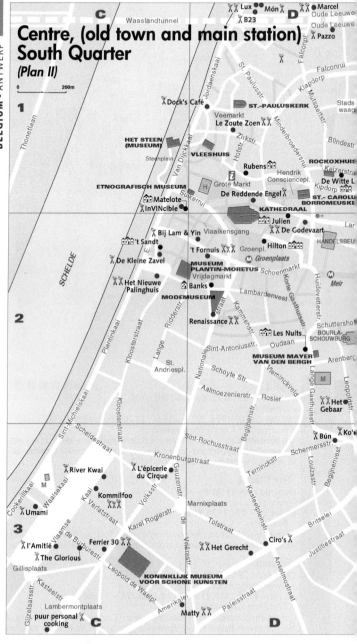

Centre, (old town and main station) South Quarter
(Plan II)

BELGIUM - ANTWERP

Waaslandtunnel

0   200m

1

2

3

SCHELDE

Thonetlaan

Lux · · Món
· B23
Marcel
Oude Leeuwe
Oude Leeuwe
· Pazzo

Falconpl.
Falconrui
St.-Paulusstr.
Klapdorp
Musaertstr.
Stads waag
Blindestr

Dock's Café
ST.-PAULUSKERK
Veemarkt
Le Zoute Zoen
Zirkstr.
Holstr.
Minderbroedersrui

HET STEEN (MUSEUM)
Steenplein
VLEESHUIS
Rubens
Hendrik Consciencepl.
ROCKOXHUIS
Keizerstra
De Witte L
Kipdorp

ETNOGRAFISCH MUSEUM
Grote Markt
De Reddende Engel
ST.- CAROLU
BORROMEUSKE
Matelote
InVINcible
KATHEDRAAL
Julien
Lar

Bij Lam & Yin
Vlaaikensgang
De Godevaart
Hilton
HANDELSBEU

't Sandt
't Fornuis
Groenpl.
Groenplaats
Meir

De Kleine Zavel
MUSEUM PLANTIN-MORETUS
Vrijdagmarkt
Schoenmarkt
Korte Gasthuisstr

Het Nieuwe Palinghuis
Banks
Lambardenvest
Huidevettersstr.
Schuttershof
BOURLA-SCHOUWBURG

MODEMUSEUM
Renaissance
Les Nuits
Oudaan

Plantinkaai
Kloosterstraat
Lange Ridderstraat
Sint-Antoniusstr.
Kammenstr.
Nationalestraat
MUSEUM MAYER VAN DEN BERGH
Lange Gasthuisstr.
Arenberg

St. Andriespl.
Schoyte Str.
Vleminckveld
Het Gebaar
Leopoldstr.

Sint-Michielskaai
Scheldestraat
Aalmoezenierstr.
Rosier
Begijnenstr.

Bún
Ko'

Kronenburgstraat
Sint-Rochusstraat
Schermersstr.

River Kwai
L'épicerie du Cirque
Geuzenstr.
Terninckstr.
Louizastr.
Begijnenvest

Cockerillkaai
Kommilfoo
Volkstr.
Marnixplaats
Kasteelpleinstr.
Britselei

Umami
Waalsekaai
Verlatstraat
Karel Rogierstr.
Tolstraat

l'Amitié
Vlaamse Kaai
de Burburestr.
Ferrier 30
Vlaamse
Ciro's
Het Gerecht
Justitiestraat

The Glorious
Gillisplaats
Kasteelstr.
Leopold de Waelpl.
KONINKLIJK MUSEUM VOOR SCHONE KUNSTEN
Anselmostraat

Gijzelaarsstr.
Lambermontplaats
puur personal cooking
Amerikalei
Matty
Paleisstraat
Paleisstraat

C
D

102

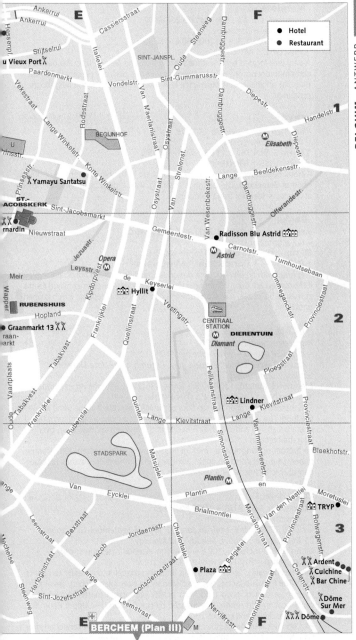

Ankerrui
Ankerrui
Hessenpl.
u Vieux Port
Stijtselrui
Paardenmarkt
Vekestraat
Lange Winkelstr.
Ittalei
Cassiersstraat
Oude
Steenweg
Dambruggestr.
SINT-JANSPL.
Vondelstr.
Sint-Gummarusstr.
Diepestr.
Handelstr.
Rodstraat
Van Maerlanstraat
Prinsesstr.
Hnsstr.
Innsstr.
U
BEGIJNHOF
Korte Winkelstr.
Osystraat
Stralenstr.
Elisabeth
Beeldekensstr.
Diepestr.
Yamayu Santatsu
ST.-
ACOBSKERK
rnardin
Sint-Jacobsmarkt
Nieuwstraat
Jezusstr.
Lange
Van
Van Wesenbeekstr.
Van Dambruggestr.
Offerandestr.
Gemeentestr.
Radisson Blu Astrid
Astrid
Carnotstr.
Turnhoutsebaan
Opera
Leysstr.
Meir
Wapper
Kipdorpvest
de
Keyserlei
Hyllit
Vestingstr.
Frankrijklei
Quellinstraat
Ommeganckstr.
Provinciestraat
RUBENSHUIS
Hopland
Graanmarkt 13
raan-
markt
Tabakvest
CENTRAAL
STATION
DIERENTUIN
Diamant
Ploegstraat
Oude Tabakvest
Vaarplaats
Frankrijklei
Rubenslei
Lange
Kievitstraat
Lindner
Lange
Kievitstraat
Van Immerseelstr.
Provinciestraat
Bleekhofstr.
STADSPARK
Quinten
Matsijslei
Van
Eycklei
Simonsstraat
Plantin
Plantin
en
Moretuslei
TRYP
Rolwagenstr.
ange
Leemstraat
Biexstraat
Jacob
Lange
Hertoginstraat
Mechelse
Steenweg
Sint-Jozefsstraat
Jordaensstr.
Charlottalei
Brialmontlei
Conscienciestraat
Mercatorstraat
Van den Nestlei
Provinciestraat
Ardent
Cuichine
Bar Chine
Coslenstr.
Plaza
Belgiëlei
Lamorinière straat
Nerviërsstr.
Dôme
Sur Mer
Dôme

- ● Hotel
- ● Restaurant

Matelote

Haarstraat 11a ☒ 2000 – ℰ 03 201 88 00   Plan: **C1**
– www.hotel-matelote.be
10 rm – †100/130 € ††100/130 € – ☐ 12 €
• Historic • Modern •

A very well-located hotel a stone's throw from the Grand Place. The decidedly contemporary decor fits in marvellously with the perfectly preserved 16C building. An original luxury experience in Antwerp. Breakfast at the neighbouring restaurant.

TRYP   ও ☒ ঌ ➣

Plantin en Moretuslei 136 ☒ 2018 – ℰ 03 271 07 00   Plan: **F3**
– www.trypantwerp.com
176 rm – †69/189 € ††69/189 € – ☐ 15 €
• Business • Modern •

A hotel perfect for soaking up the atmosphere in the hip Antwerp neighbourhood of Zurenborg. The design is stunning, with a particularly unusual decor and colours. Ideal for trend followers.

Banks   ☒

Steenhouwersvest 55 ☒ 2000 – ℰ 03 232 40 02   Plan: **D2**
– www.hotelbanks.com
68 rm – †80/115 € ††90/155 € – ☐ 15 €
• Business • Functional • Minimalist •

This hotel with an ultra-modern design exemplifies Antwerp hospitality – even if the owners are Dutch. Right near the city centre, it features streamlined rooms at reasonable prices. A welcome drink is offered at the reception, which is open until 8pm.

't Zilte (Viki Geunes)   ৪৪ ≤ ঌ
❄❄
Hanzestedenplaats 5 ☒ 2000   Plan: **B1**
– ℰ 03 283 40 40 – www.tzilte.be
– closed 1 week Easter, 2 weeks July, Autumn break, late December, Saturday and Sunday
Menu 68 € (lunch), 130/180 € – Carte 136/211 € – *(booking essential)*
• Creative • Design • Fashionable •

This establishment is on the top floor of the MAS, a location at the same level as the food! The urban gastronomy here is indeed top flight, a magnificent blend of craftsmanship and creativity – in one of the loveliest spots in town overlooking the harbour.

➜ Bretoense langoustine met gevogeltelever, kumquat en Jamaicaanse peper. Duif met miso en spelt, warmoes en cantharellen. Ananas met bergamot, witte chocolade en limoncello.

The Jane (Nick Bril)   ৪৪ ঌ ☒ ↔ 🅿
❄❄
Paradeplein 1 ☒ 2018 – ℰ 03 808 44 65   Plan: **H1**
– www.thejaneantwerp.com
– closed 27 March-4 April, 26 June-11 July, 25 September-10 October, 25 December-8 January, Sunday and Monday
Menu 65 € (lunch), 75/100 € – *(booking essential) (set menu only)*
• Creative • Fashionable • Design •

Jane has managed to transform this imposing chapel into a trendy temple of food! The former altar has been replaced by an open-plan kitchen, devoted to the preparation of good food from quality produce. A masterful mixture of sophistication and simplicity, enhanced by rich flavours. The Upper Room Bar is ideal for drinks and snacks.

➜ Coquilles met bergamot en knolselderij. Dorade met zeevenkel en dragon. Kamperlam met spinazie, polenta en salie. Cannelé met framboos en basilicum.

XxX
⸙⸙

't Fornuis (Johan Segers)   ⁜ ⇦

Reyndersstraat 24 ⊠ 2000 – ℰ 0 3 233 62 70   Plan: **D2**
– closed 16 July-15 August, late December, Saturday
and Sunday
Carte 75/120 €
• **Classic cuisine** • **Rustic** •
Fine classic cuisine and quality wines are served in this rustic restaurant housed
in an old building. The owner/chef has been running the show since 1976 and
was awarded his first Michelin star in 1986. Miniature stoves exhibited downstairs.
→ Op lage temperatuur gegaard spek en gerookte paling. Mousseline van
aardappel met griet, eitje en kaviaar. Parfait met hazelnoten.

XxX
⸙⸙

Dôme (Julien Burlat)   ⁜ 🆎

Grote Hondstraat 2 ⊠ 2018   Plan: **F3**
– ℰ 0 3 239 90 03 – www.domeweb.be
– closed 2 weeks August, 24 December-5 January, Saturday lunch, Sunday
and Monday
Menu 42 € (lunch), 85/104 € – Carte 82/98 €
• **French creative** • **Elegant** •
Chef Julien Burlat is obsessed with quality and constantly on the lookout for the
finest ingredients. The menu changes according to his latest discoveries and
features dishes that are always authentic without being fussy. Organic and sul-
fite-free wines figure prominently on the excellent wine list.
→ Gebakken coquilles met een salade van belugalinzen, brunoise van eekhoorntjesbrood en algen. Pladijs op de graat gepocheerd met rode kool,
cranberries en boterjus met azijn. Hindefilet met een puree van rode biet
met sinaaszeste, spätzle en champignons.

XX

Het Pomphuis   ⇐ 🏠 ⇦ 🅿

Siberiastraat ⊠ 2030 – ℰ 0 3 770 86 25   Plan: **B1**
– www.hetpomphuis.be
– closed 24 December and Saturday lunch
Menu 29 € (lunch)/49 € – Carte 53/78 €
• **Modern cuisine** • **Retro** •
This extraordinary restaurant occupies a huge warehouse dating from 1920,
where the decor includes three enormous bilge pumps. Enjoy the sophisticated,
contemporary menu and views of the docks from the terrace.

XX

Het Nieuwe Palinghuis   🆎

Sint-Jansvliet 14 ⊠ 2000 – ℰ 0 3 231 74 45   Plan: **C2**
– www.hetnieuwepalinghuis.be
– closed June, Monday and Tuesday
Menu 42/125 € 🍷 – Carte 57/125 €
• **Fish and seafood** • **Friendly** •
Eel is king at this fish restaurant, only dethroned by Escaut lobster in season.
The dining room and veranda are decorated with seascapes and old photo-
graphs of Antwerp. The perfect place to enjoy the pleasures of the North
Sea.

XX

Graanmarkt 13   🏠 🆎 ⇦

Graanmarkt 13 ⊠ 2000 – ℰ 0 3 337 79 91   Plan: **E2**
– www.graanmarkt13.be
– closed Sunday and Monday
Menu 29 € (lunch)/39 €
• **Modern cuisine** • **Minimalist** • **Trendy** •
This trendy, minimalist loft in the mezzanine of a bourgeois house lies in the
heart of Antwerp, behind the Bourla Theatre. Tasty and originally presented
dishes.

XX Het Gebaar (Roger van Damme) 🛍

⚙️

Leopoldstraat 24 ⊠ 2000 – ☎ 0 3 232 37 10 — Plan: **D2**
– www.hetgebaar.be – closed Bank Holidays, Sunday and Monday
Carte 83/93 € – *(lunch only) (booking essential)*
• Creative • Cosy •

This restaurant is located in an elegant building on the edge of the botanical park. Luxury tea room cuisine, which the chef enriches with modern twists; mouthwatering desserts! Non-stop service until 6pm.

→ Gekonfijt kalfsvlees met zomertruffel, verse frietjes met mayonaise en kalfskop met cress-kruiden. Black Jack : combinatie van speculaas en appel, eetbaar kaartenspel en citrustoetsen. Botanique : een "zoete tuin" met melkchocolade, hazelnoten, passievrucht, mango en limoen.

XX De Godevaart

Sint-Katelijnevest 23 ⊠ 2000 – ☎ 0 3 231 89 94 — Plan: **D2**
– www.degodevaart.be – closed first 2 weeks September, 2nd week January, Sunday, Monday and after 8.30pm
Menu 70/110 € – Carte 53/74 € – *(dinner only) (booking essential)*
• Creative • Classic •

The chef lets his creativity run riot in the kitchen of this old house that has retained some of its original architectural features (stucco, fireplace, etc.). His cuisine, in which authentic produce takes pride of place, frequently surprises diners with unexpected mixtures and techniques.

XX Bernardin

Sint-Jacobstraat 17 ⊠ 2000 – ☎ 0 3 213 07 00 — Plan: **E2**
– www.bernardin-antwerpen.be – closed 1 week Easter, last 2 weeks August, Spring break, Thursday dinner, Saturday lunch, Sunday and Monday
Menu 33 € (lunch), 45/51 € – Carte 51/78 €
• Modern cuisine • Fashionable •

This 17C house has been renovated inside and out. Depending on the season and the weather, choose between the modern, sober decor of the dining room or the delightful courtyard in the shadow of St Jacob's church.

XX Marcel

Van Schoonbekeplein 13 ⊠ 2000 – ☎ 0 3 336 33 02 — Plan: **D1**
– www.restaurantmarcel.be – closed Saturday lunch and Sunday
Menu 30 € (lunch), 37/70 € – Carte 47/72 €
• Regional • Brasserie • Retro •

Welcome to Marcel's – a vintage bistro with a distinctly French feel. The culinary repertory mingles traditional recipes with touches of modernity, resulting in cuisine steeped in wholesome flavours. Terrace overlooking the MAS.

XX Lux

Adriaan Brouwerstraat 13 ⊠ 2000 – ☎ 0 3 233 30 30 — Plan: **D1**
– www.luxantwerp.com – closed 1 Januari, lunch on Bank Holidays, Saturday lunch, Sunday and Monday
Menu 29 € (lunch), 45/75 € – Carte 64/78 €
• Classic cuisine • Brasserie •

This restaurant occupies the house of a former ship owner, and has a terrace that overlooks the port. There is a profusion of marble (columns, fireplaces), a wine and cocktail bar, à la carte options, plus an attractive lunch menu.

XX Le Zoute Zoen

Zirkstraat 23 ⊠ 2000 – ☎ 0 3 226 92 20 — Plan: **D1**
– www.lezoutezoen.be – closed Saturday lunch and Monday
Menu 22 € (lunch), 37/80 € ♟ – Carte 46/71 €
• Classic cuisine • Bistro •

This is an intimate and cosy bistro. The culinary emphasis of the chefs is placed as much as possible on Belgian dishes and produce, including the set 'Zoen-menu'.

XX Ardent

Dageraadplaats 3 ⊠ 2018 – ✆ 0 3 336 32 99   Plan: **F3**
*– www.resto-ardent.be – closed 28 March-5 April, 4-19 July, 1-5 January,
Monday and Tuesday*
Menu 25 € (lunch), 45/65 € – Carte 52/66 €
• **Modern cuisine** • **Minimalist** •
Passion is often said to be the distinctive character trait of great chefs. Wouter Van Steenwinkel is no exception to this rule and his tasteful restaurant will give you an insight into his many talents. You can expect well-thought out and balanced meals with perfectly blended flavours. The French fries are to die for!

XX Renaissance

Nationalestraat 32 ⊠ 2000 – ✆ 0 3 233 93 90   Plan: **D2**
– www.resto-renaissance.be – closed Sunday
Carte 38/59 €
• **Italian** • **Design** • **Elegant** •
What a brilliant idea to locate an Italian restaurant in the same building as the fashion museum! This splendid establishment sports an all-white, minimalist interior. The menu, rich in southern sunshine, is authentic and classical in its origins.

X Dock's Café

Jordaenskaai 7 ⊠ 2000 – ✆ 0 3 226 63 30   Plan: **D1**
– www.docks.be – closed Sunday
Menu 18 € (lunch), 28/44 € – Carte 32/81 € – (open until 11pm)
• **Fish and seafood** • **Fashionable** • **Brasserie** •
Set in the post-industrial landscape of the docks, this brasserie encapsulates contemporary taste: Jules Verne decor, trendy clientele and tasty "terre-mer" cuisine (oyster bar). Booking advisable.

X InVINcible

Haarstraat 9 ⊠ 2000 – ✆ 0 3 231 32 07   Plan: **C1**
– www.invincible.be – closed 1-11 January, Bank Holidays, Saturday and Sunday
Menu 25 € (lunch)/37 €
• **Modern cuisine** • **Trendy** • **Fashionable** •
Kenny and Wendy's restaurant really is InVINcible! The food, which is of French inspiration, has the starring role. The vol-au-vent, for instance, plays off sweetbreads! All paired with excellent wines of course. The story always ends happily with a cup of coffee – Kenny being a well-known barista.

X Cuichine

Draakstraat 13 ⊠ 2018 – ✆ 0 3 289 92 45   Plan: **F3**
– www.cuichine.be – closed first 2 weeks September, 24, 25 and 31 December-1 January, Saturday lunch and Monday
Menu 20 € (lunch)/37 € – Carte 37/57 €
• **Chinese** • **Friendly** •
Traditional Chinese flavours, including some of the finest Cantonese dishes, take pride of place in this restaurant, which also calls upon French culinary know-how. A welcoming setting, and special mention for the lunch menu.

X Bistrot du Nord (Michael Rewers)

Lange Dijkstraat 36 ⊠ 2060 – ✆ 0 3 233 45 49   Plan: **B1**
– www.bistrotdunord.be – closed 18 July-15 August, Bank Holidays, Saturday and Sunday
Carte 47/83 €
• **Traditional cuisine** • **Bistro** •
A lesson in tradition! The chef, an authentic craftsman, knows how to enhance fine produce to its best. He admits to a weakness for tripe, but diners need have no fears, whatever your choice, your taste buds will be delighted.
➜ Filet d'Anvers met ganzenlever en morieljes. Gegrilde kalfsnier Helder. Clafoutis van krieken met vers gedraaid vanilleroomijs.

De Reddende Engel

Torfburg 3 ✉ 2000 – ℰ 0 3 233 66 30 Plan: **D1**
– www.de-reddende-engel.be – closed 26 and 27 April, 18 August-15 September, 3, 4 and 5 January, 15-25 February, Saturday lunch, Tuesday and Wednesday
Menu 19 € (lunch), 27/37 € – Carte 37/59 €
• Regional • Rustic •
Provence and Gascony come together in this rustic house near the cathedral. Enjoy dishes such as bouillabaisse from Marseille, brandade from Nîmes, duck liver from the Landes, cassoulet, etc.

De Kleine Zavel

Stoofstraat 2 ✉ 2000 – ℰ 0 3 231 96 91 Plan: **C1**
– www.kleinezavel.be – closed late December, Saturday lunch, Monday and Tuesday
Menu 55 € – Carte 54/72 €
• Modern cuisine • Bistro •
Don't be fooled by the vintage floor, retro counter, little bare tables, wine shelves and old wooden beer racks. The food served at this typical Antwerp bistro is as up-to-the-minute as it gets!

Dôme Sur Mer

Arendstraat 1 ✉ 2018 – ℰ 0 3 281 74 33 Plan: **F3**
– www.domeweb.be – closed 2 weeks in August, 24 December-5 January and Saturday lunch
Carte 39/81 €
• Fish and seafood • Bistro •
Goldfish swimming in a huge aquarium set the scene in this trendy bistro devoted to the sea. The simply prepared, flawlessly fresh fish and seafood in this restaurant are regularly cooked à la plancha. The bread and desserts are all homemade and wickedly appetising!

Pazzo

Oude Leeuwenrui 12 ✉ 2000 – ℰ 0 3 232 86 82 Plan: **D1**
– www.pazzo.be – closed 15 July-15 August, late December-early January, Bank Holidays, Saturday and Sunday
Menu 22 € (lunch) – Carte 36/70 € – (open until 11pm)
• Modern cuisine • Friendly • Fashionable •
This trendy brasserie with a lively atmosphere occupies a former warehouse near the docks. Enjoy Mediterranean- and Asian-inspired bistro cuisine and excellent wines.

B 23

Brouwersvliet 23 ✉ 2000 – ℰ 0 3 345 15 14 Plan: **D1**
– www.brouwersvliet23.be – closed 25 July-24 August, 1-10 January, Saturday lunch and Sunday
Menu 15 € (lunch), 37/45 € – Carte 45/96 €
• Modern cuisine • Brasserie • Wine bar •
Step into this wine bar at N°23 Brouwersvliet and you will find a lively brasserie to the rear. The menu can hold its own with the best, and the fine produce is enhanced by modern techniques and combinations. B 23 brings the promise of an explosion of flavours.

Au Vieux Port

Napelsstraat 130 ✉ 2000 – ℰ 0 3 290 77 11 – closed Plan: **E1**
25 July-15 August, 27 December-2 January, Saturday and Sunday
Carte 50/85 € – (booking essential)
• Classic cuisine • Bistro •
This brasserie is worth keeping in mind for its simple, rustic and tasty cuisine, its gently nostalgic air, and its ritualised service (flambés and carving at guests' tables). Busy atmosphere at lunchtime.

X
✿ **Bij Lam & Yin** (Lap Yee Lam)   AC

Reynderstraat 17 ✉ 2000 – ℰ 0 3 232 88 38 – closed   Plan: **D2**
Easter holiday, Monday and Tuesday
Carte 46/67 € – *(dinner only) (booking essential)*
• Chinese • Minimalist • Exotic •
This Chinese restaurant goes against the grain, challenging preconceived ideas
about Asian cuisine. It has a minimalist decor and a small menu placing the
onus on fresh ingredients, originality and flavour. Be sure to book a table!
→ Stoommandje met dimsum. Gestoomde zeebaars met gember en pijpa-
juin. Gebakken lamslapjes met szechuanpeper.

X **Yamayu Santatsu**   AC ⇔

Ossenmarkt 19 ✉ 2000 – ℰ 0 3 234 09 49   Plan: **E1**
– www.santatsu.be – closed Sunday lunch and Monday
Menu 23 € (lunch), 45/55 € – Carte 37/62 €
• Japanese • Simple •
A lively and authentic Japanese restaurant that only uses the best hand picked
ingredients, and prepares sushi in full view of diners. Assorted à la carte options
with four different menus for two people.

X **Bar(t)-à-vin**

Lange Slachterijstraat 3 ✉ 2060 – ℰ 0 474 94 17 86   Plan: **B1**
– www.bartavin.info – closed 2 weeks July, Bank Holidays, Saturday,
Sunday and after 8.30pm
Carte 42/52 €
• Classic cuisine • Bistro •
Bart, the proprietor, converted his wine bar into a bistro in this attractive former
butcher shop. Everything has gone smoothly thanks to the food with a focus on
ingredients, classic recipes and the limited but varied selections.

X **Ko'uzi**

Leopoldplaats 12 ✉ 2000 – ℰ 0 3 232 24 88   Plan: **D3**
– www.kouzi.be – closed 2 weeks July, Bank Holidays, Sunday, Monday
and after 8pm
Carte 23/59 €
• Japanese • Minimalist • Design •
The minimalist, designer decor is reflected in the cuisine. Classical sushi and sashimi preparations rub shoulders with creative variations. The tea, which can be
sampled in the tea room, is equally delicious.

X
 Bún

Sint-Jorispoort 22 ✉ 2000 – ℰ 0 3 234 04 16   Plan: **D3**
– www.bunantwerp.be – closed Wednesday and Sunday
Carte 26/36 € – *(booking essential)*
• Vietnamese • Simple •
A fresco on the wall depicts a cockerel fight, transporting you right to the midst
of a Vietnamese street! This modest bistro will take you on an amazing gourmet
journey from East to West. Vietnamese cooking at its best.

X **Bar Chine**   ⇑ ⇔

Draakplaats 3 ✉ 2018 – ℰ 0 3 501 28 11   Plan: **F3**
– www.barchine.be – closed 2 weeks September, 24, 25 and 31 December,
Saturday lunch, Sunday lunch and Tuesday
Carte 29/45 €
• Chinese • Fashionable •
The paper lanterns are entirely in keeping with the simple, intimate setting. The
fuss-free menu includes a mouthwatering array of Asian influenced tapas. Per-
fect to share with friends or family.

SOUTH QUARTER AND BERCHEM

X **Món**

Sint-Aldegondiskaai 30 ⊠ *2000 –* ℰ *0 3 345 67 89*
– www.monantwerp.com   Plan: **D1**
Carte 34/59 €
• **Meats** • **Brasserie** • **Trendy** •
The sculpture of a bull's head immediately gives you a foretaste of the menu, in which red meat takes pride of place. In fact, not just any meat but home raised Limousin beef prepared in a Josper charcoal fire. The cooking and accompaniments are a treat for your taste buds.

SOUTH QUARTER AND BERCHEM

 Crowne Plaza

Gerard Le Grellelaan 10 ⊠ *2020 –* ℰ *0 3 259 75 00*
– www.crowneplaza-antwerpen.be   Plan: **G1**
262 rm � – †99/199 € ††109/209 €
• **Business** • **Functional** •
Located close to the ring road and a main road into the city. This huge chain hotel has 262 guestrooms on 16 floors, which are being renovated in stages. Numerous meeting rooms. A relaxed gastro-lounge in which to enjoy a meal or meet with friends or business colleagues.

 Firean

Karel Oomsstraat 6 ⊠ *2018 –* ℰ *0 3 237 02 60*
– www.hotelfirean.com   Plan: **G1**
9 rm – †155/217 € ††155/217 € – ⊑ 18 €
• **Luxury** • **Personalised** •
This property full of charm occupies an Art Deco-style building (1929). It features public rooms in the style of the period, a flower-filled patio, and personalised guestrooms with antique furnishings. Impeccable service.
Minerva – See restaurant listing

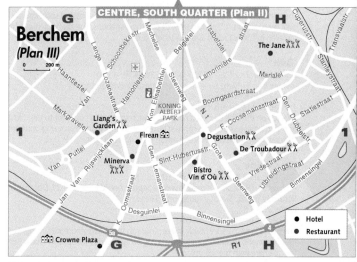

Berchem *(Plan III)*

0   200 m

CENTRE, SOUTH QUARTER (Plan II)

The Jane XXX

Liang's Garden XX

Firean

Degustation XX

De Troubadour XX

Minerva XXX

Bistro Vin d'Où XX

Crowne Plaza

● Hotel
● Restaurant

BELGIUM - ANTWERP

XxX ✿ **Kommilfoo** (Olivier de Vinck de Winnezeele) 🗚 🅿

Vlaamse Kaai 17 ✉ 2000 – 𝒞 03 237 30 00   Plan: **C3**
– www.restaurantkommilfoo.be – closed first 2 weeks July, 25 December,
Saturday lunch, Sunday and Monday
Menu 43 € (lunch), 80/95 € – Carte 83/122 €
• Creative • Cosy •
A comfortable, modern dining room is the setting for the culinary creations of this innovative chef who alternates ever-evolving recipes with molecular experimentation. Pyrenean goat is an ever-present dish on the menu here!
➜ Langoustines, gebakken en in carpaccio, gesmolten paksoi, sushirijst met witte soja en heldere jus van pandanblad. Twee bereidingen van melkgeit, het ribstuk rosé gebraden, de schouder 17 uur gegaard en gekaramelliseerd. Fantasie van chocolade.

XxX **Minerva** – Hotel Firean   🗚

Karel Oomsstraat 36 ✉ 2018 – 𝒞 03 216 00 55   Plan: **G1**
– www.restaurantminerva.be – closed late July-first 2 weeks August, late
December-early January, Saturday and Sunday
Menu 39/65 € – Carte 59/104 €
• Classic cuisine • Elegant •
Minerva was also the name of the legendary Belgian luxury car, the repair workshops of which were located here. The site is now that of a well-oiled restaurant, serving good quality, traditional fare. You might be interested to know that all the meat is sliced in front of you!

XX **Bistro Vin d'Où**   🍴 ↔ 🅿

Terlinckstraat 2 ✉ 2600 Berchem – 𝒞 03 230 55 99   Plan: **H1**
– www.vindou.be – closed 28 March-7 April, 20 July-9 August,
24 December-5 January, Monday dinner, Tuesday dinner, Wednesday
dinner, Saturday lunch and Sunday
Menu 60/80 € – Carte 63/102 €
• Modern cuisine • Bistro •
This smart, contemporary bistro has taken up abode in an attractive bourgeois home. The chef is a genuine craftsman with a distinct taste for the best produce: what more can we say? The patio is heaven in summertime and you may even be forgiven for thinking you are in Italy as you sample a grappa from the house's transalpine distillery!

XX ☺ **De Troubadour**   🗚 ↔ 🅿

Driekoningenstraat 72 ✉ 2600 Berchem   Plan: **H1**
– 𝒞 03 239 39 16 – www.detroubadour.be – closed first 3 weeks August,
Sunday and Monday
Menu 23 € (lunch), 37/49 € – Carte 43/73 €
• Modern cuisine • Trendy •
A modern, cosy dining room where the gregarious owner fosters a warm and friendly atmosphere. Classic, creative à la carte options, as well as appetising menus and daily specials announced at your table. Parking available (prior booking required).

XX **Ferrier 30**   🍴 🗚 ↔

Leopold de Waelplaats 30 ✉ 2000 – 𝒞 03 216 50 62   Plan: **C3**
– www.ferrier-30.be – closed Wednesday
Carte 38/63 €
• Italian • Design •
The best Italian restaurant of the area is doubtless Ferrier 30. The meat, fish and pasta dishes (lasagne al ragu, taglioni con prosciutto) are all steeped in authentic Italian flavours. All of which are further enhanced by wines brought back by the owner in person.

BELGIUM - ANTWERP

XX Het Gerecht

Amerikalei 20 ⊠ 2000   Plan: **D3**
– ℰ 03 248 79 28 – www.hetgerecht.be
– *closed Spring break, Easter holiday, 15 July-5 August, Autumn break, Christmas holiday, Wednesday dinner, Saturday lunch, Sunday and Monday*
Menu 29 € (lunch), 55/98 € ♈ – Carte 70/80 €
• Modern cuisine • Cosy •

This restaurant is full of character. Peggy pampers her customers while Wim treats their taste buds to his talented creations. The photos adorning the walls are Wim's handiwork, as is the French inspired cuisine, which follows the seasons.

XX Matty

Brederodestraat 23 ⊠ 2018   Plan: **C3**
– ℰ 03 293 54 41 – www.restaurantmatty.be
– *closed last 2 weeks July-early August, Saturday lunch, Sunday and Monday*
Menu 30 € (lunch)/58 € – Carte 68/77 €
– *(booking essential)*
• Modern cuisine • Design •

Contemporary cuisine prepared by a chef who can be seen at work from one of the two dining rooms. Modern, startlingly white decor and an outdoor terrace for summer dining.

XX Degustation

Frederik de Merodeplein 6 ⊠ 2600 Berchem   Plan: **H1**
– ℰ 0 495 63 04 97 – www.degustation-restaurant.be
– *closed Saturday lunch, Sunday, Monday and Tuesday*
Menu 25/55 € – Carte 37/68 €
• French modern • Fashionable •

The menu boasts many delights, such as turbot with summer truffles and quinoa with sage. The chef selects the finest ingredients in preparing his flavourful dishes, which are offered at reasonable prices.

XX Liang's Garden

Generaal Lemanstraat 54 ⊠ 2000 – ℰ 03 237 22 22   Plan: **G1**
– *closed 11 July-7 August and Sunday*
Menu 27 € (lunch), 35/72 € – Carte 35/96 €
• Chinese • Traditional • Classic •

A stalwart of Chinese cuisine in the city! A spacious restaurant where the authentic menu covers specialities from Canton (dim sum), Peking (duck) and Szechuan (fondue).

X The Glorious

De Burburestraat 4a ⊠ 2000 – ℰ 03 237 06 13   Plan: **C3**
– www.theglorious.be
– *closed 3 weeks July, Sunday and Monday*
Menu 35 € ♈ (lunch), 65/95 € – Carte 65/86 € – *(set menu only)*
• Classic cuisine • Wine bar • Formal •

This former warehouse now houses a chic, well-designed restaurant. The owner, Jurgen, is in charge of the renowned wine selection and the chef, Johan, tempts you with his cooking, which elevates classic dishes to a whole new level. Enjoy this glorious adventure surrounded by original baroque and art deco features.

→ Carpaccio van Chianina rund, crème van parmezaan, arbequina olijfolie met notensla. Zomerreebok met mirabellen, eekhoorntjesbrood, pomme dauphine en poivrade met wilde tijm. Chocolademousse met gepofte rijst, citrussmaken en een sorbet van Summer Forest dry gin.

BELGIUM - ANTWERP

X ✿ **L'épicerie du Cirque** (Dennis Broeckx)   `AC`
Volkstraat 23 ⊠ 2000 – ✆ 03 238 05 71   Plan: **C3**
– www.lepicerieducirque.be – closed 1 May, 24 and 25 December,
1 week January, Sunday and Monday
Menu 33 € (lunch), 49/69 € – Carte 60/74 €
• French modern • Fashionable • Bistro •
Treat yourself to a simply delicious meal without any unnecessary fuss. The chef focuses on good produce and classical techniques, adding the occasional unusual twist. The dishes sparkle with enticing flavours. The delicatessen shop, which is decked in the same Scandinavian style, is full of tempting delicacies.
→ Salmon delight. Zeebaars met kingkrab en spinazie. Crémeux van chocolade met framboos en gebakken witte chocolade.

X **Umami**   `☶ &`
Luikstraat 6 ⊠ 2000 – ✆ 03 237 39 78   Plan: **C3**
– www.umami-antwerp.be – closed Monday and Tuesday
Menu 55 € – Carte 26/47 € – *(dinner only except Sunday)*
• Asian • Exotic • Fashionable •
Asian wood and lounge furniture happily rub shoulders beneath a well of light in this handsome establishment. The menu respects the house's motto - contemporary Asian cuisine. Oriental traditions with an ingenious modern twist.

X **puur personal cooking**   `☶`
Edward Pecherstraat 51 ⊠ 2000 – ✆ 0 495 83 24 87   Plan: **C3**
– www.puurpersonalcooking.be – closed Saturday, Sunday and Monday
Menu 38 € (lunch)/58 € – *(booking essential)*
• Modern cuisine • Bistro • Intimate •
One man and his AGA oven occupy the heart of this cosy bistro. The chef develops a personal version of contemporary cuisine, focused on unadulterated flavour. A menu in which quality and passion take pride of place.

X ✿ **Ciro's**   `☶ AC`
Amerikalei 6 ⊠ 2018 – ✆ 03 238 11 47 – www.ciros.be   Plan: **D3**
– closed Monday
Carte 35/62 €
• Belgian • Neighbourhood • Traditional •
The nostalgic interior, working class atmosphere and traditional Belgian fare will provide the opportunity to turn a meal at Ciro's into a taste of Antwerp's past. Steak and chips with six sauces is the star of the show. Book ahead – you won't be disappointed!

X **l'Amitié**   `☶`
Vlaamse Kaai 43 ⊠ 2000 – ✆ 03 257 50 05   Plan: **C3**
– www.lamitie.net – closed 2 weeks August, 1 January, Saturday lunch,
Sunday and Monday
Menu 30 € (lunch), 60/70 € – Carte 49/74 €
• Modern cuisine • Bistro •
This welcoming address, located in one of the city's liveliest districts, dedicates itself to the concept of bistronomy (traditional dishes with an inventive twist). On fine sunny days take advantage of the Mediterranean-style terrace.

X **River Kwai**   `☶ AC ⟷`
Vlaamse Kaai 14 ⊠ 2000 – ✆ 03 237 46 51   Plan: **C3**
– www.riverkwai.be – closed Wednesday
Menu 25/49 € ☖ – Carte 32/45 € – *(dinner only)*
• Thai • Exotic •
This reliable restaurant has been serving authentic Thai cuisine for over 20 years. Find an attractive retro façade, dining rooms on separate floors with a typical decor, an elegant lounge and a front terrace.

✗ **Ossip**

Schomstraat 49 ⊠ 2600 Berchem – ✆ 0 3 344 36 26   Plan: **B2**
– www.ossip-berchem.be – closed Tuesday dinner, Saturday lunch, Sunday and Monday
Menu 29 € (lunch) – Carte 30/65 €
• Regional • Bistro •

A minimalist local bistro provides the simple setting for a festival of flavours. At the helm is a woman who creates fresh, natural cuisine in which vegetables take pride of place. Fans of natural wines will be spoilt for choice.

CZECH REPUBLIC
ČESKÁ REPUBLIKA

● PRAGUE

→ **AREA:**
78 864 km² (30 449 sq mi).

→ **POPULATION:**
10 627 448 inhabitants.
Density = 135 per km².

→ **CAPITAL:**
Prague.

→ **CURRENCY:**
Czech crown (Kč).

→ **GOVERNMENT:**
Parliamentary republic (since 1993).
Member of European Union since 2004.

→ **LANGUAGE:**
Czech; also German and English.

→ **PUBLIC HOLIDAYS:**
New Year's Day (1 Jan); Easter Monday (late Mar/Apr); Labor Day (1 May); Liberation Day (8 May); St Cyril and St Methodius Day (5 July); Martyrdom of Jan Hus (6 July); Czech Statehood Day (28 Sept); Independence Day (28 Oct); Freedom and Democracy Day (17 Nov); Christmas Eve (24 Dec – Half Day); Christmas Day (25 Dec); 2nd Day of Christmas (26 Dec).

→ **LOCAL TIME:**
GMT + 1 hour in winter and GMT + 2 hours in summer.

→ **CLIMATE:**
Temperate continental with cold winters and warm summers (Prague: January 0°C; July 20°C).

→ **EMERGENCY:**
Police ☎ **158**;
Medical Assistance ☎ **155**;
Fire Brigade ☎ **150**.
(Dialling **112** within any EU country will redirect your call and contact the emergency services.)

→ **ELECTRICITY:**
230 volts AC, 50Hz; 2 round pin sockets.

→ **FORMALITIES:**
Travellers from the European Union (EU), Switzerland, Iceland and the main countries of North and South America need a national identity card or passport (America: passport required) to visit Czech Republic for less than three months (tourism or business purpose). For visitors from other countries a visa may be required, in addition to a passport, especially for those wishing to stay for longer than three months. We advise you to check with your embassy before travelling.

PRAGUE
PRAHA

Population: 1 272 690

Courtyardpix/Fotolia.com

Prague's history stretches back to the Dark Ages. In the ninth century a princely seat comprising a simple walled-in compound was built where the castle now stands; in the tenth century the first bridge over the Vltava arrived; and by the 13C the enchanting cobbled alleyways below the castle were complete. But Prague has come of age and Europe's most perfectly preserved capital now proffers consumer choice as well as medieval marvels. Its state-of-the-art shopping malls and pulsing nightlife bear testament to its popularity with tourists – the iron glove of communism long since having given way to western consumerism. These days there are practically two versions of Prague: the lively, youthful, 'stag party capital', and the sedate, enchanting 'city of a hundred spires'.

The four main zones of Prague were originally independent towns in their own right. The river Vltava winds its way through their heart and is spanned by the iconic Charles Bridge. On the west side lie Hradčany – the castle quarter, built on a rock spur – and Malá Strana, Prague's most perfectly preserved district, located at the bottom of the castle hill. Over the river are Staré Město, the old town with its vibrant medieval square and outer boulevards, and Nové Město, the new town, which is the city's commercial heart and where you'll find Wenceslas Square and Prague's young partygoers.

PRAGUE IN...

→ **ONE DAY**
Old Town Square, the astronomical clock, Charles Bridge, Prague Castle, Petřín Hill.

→ **TWO DAYS**
Josefov, the National Theatre, Golden Lane.

→ **THREE DAYS**
Wenceslas Square, the National Museum, cross the bridge to look round Malá Strana.

PRACTICAL INFORMATION

ARRIVAL-DEPARTURE

✈ Václav Havel Airport (20km west). The shuttle bus leaves every 30min. Only use a taxi displaying an 'Airport Cars' sign. International trains stop at Hlavní nádraží.

GETTING AROUND

Trams and buses are frequent and run from early morning to past midnight; there's also a metro covering much of the city. All three are invariably cheap and a short-term (tourist) pass allows unlimited travel on bus, tram, metro and Petrin funicular. Be wary of taxis; although regulations specify rates, it's always best to use a designated rank and avoid flagging down a cab on the street.

CALENDAR HIGHLIGHTS

January
Winter Festival.

May
Spring Music Festival, World Roma Festival.

June
Dance Prague, Many visit Kafka's burial place.

September
Autumn Music Festival.

November
St Martin's Young Wine Celebrations

December
Celebrate Christmas and New Year with various events in the Old Town Square.

EATING OUT

Since the late 1980s, Prague has undergone a bit of a foodie revolution. Global menus have become common currency and the heavy, traditional Czech cuisine is now often served – in the better establishments – with a creative flair and an international touch. Lunch is the main meal of the Czech day and many restaurants close well before midnight. Prague was and still is, to an extent, famous for its infinite variety of dumplings – these were the glutinous staple that saw locals through the long years of stark Communist rule. The favoured local dish is still pork, pickled cabbage and dumplings, and those on a budget can also mix the likes of schnitzel, beer and ginger cake for a ridiculously cheap outlay. Some restaurants include a tip in your final bill, so check closely to make sure you don't tip twice. Czechs consume more beer than anyone else in the world and there are some excellent microbrewery tipples to be had.

CZECH REPUBLIC - PRAGUE

Four Seasons

Veleslavínova 1098/2A ✉ *110 00* – ⓜ *Staroměstská*   Plan: **G2**
– ✆ *221 427 000* – *www.fourseasons.com/prague*
161 rm – 🛏7600/24000 CZK 🛏🛏7600/24000 CZK – ⌑ 750 CZK – 20 suites
• Grand Luxury • Modern •

This characterful riverside hotel has an understated elegance which sits well with its baroque and Renaissance features. Bedrooms are designed by Pierre-Yves Rochon; the best are duplex suites with river and castle views.

Boscolo Prague

Senovážné Nám. 13 ✉ *110 00* – ⓜ *Náměsti Republiky*   Plan: **H2**
– ✆ *224 593 111* – *www.prague.boscolohotels.com*
152 rm – 🛏3100/13500 CZK 🛏🛏3100/13500 CZK – ⌑ 750 CZK – 2 suites
• Grand Luxury • Stylish •

This impressive former bank features neo-Renaissance style pillars, a stunning marble lobby and a smart Roman spa and pool. Each of the luxurious bedrooms is unique in shape and style; those in the old building are the most spacious. The elegant restaurant serves a mix of Czech and international dishes.

The Mark

Hybernská 12 ✉ *110 00* – ⓜ *Náměsti Republiky*   Plan: **H2**
– ✆ *226 226 111* – *www.themark.cz*
75 rm – 🛏6915/27755 CZK 🛏🛏6915/27755 CZK – ⌑ 750 CZK – 61 suites
• Historic • Stylish •

A striking 200 year old listed building with a glass-topped atrium, a baroque archway and lovely courtyard gardens. Pass the top-hatted doorman into the sleek, modern interior filled with contemporary art. Many of the bedrooms are suites with kitchenettes. Le Grill has a cool, elegant feel and a modern menu.

Radisson Blu Alcron

Štepánská 40 ✉ *110 00* – ⓜ *Muzeum* – ✆ *222 820 000*   Plan: **H2**
– *www.radissonblu.com/hotel-prague*
206 rm – 🛏4025/13800 CZK 🛏🛏4830/14605 CZK – ⌑ 805 CZK – 12 suites
• Luxury • Business • Modern •

The art deco features of this imposing 1930s building are superb and the original white and green marble floor has been meticulously maintained. Bedrooms are warmly decorated and well-equipped. La Rotonde has a pleasant summer terrace and serves international and Czech cuisine; Alcron offers modern tasting dishes.

❀ **Alcron** – See restaurant listing

Le Palais

U Zvonarky 1 ✉ *120 00* – ⓜ *I. P. Pavlova*   Plan: **H3**
– ✆ *234 634 111* – *www.lepalaishotel.eu*
72 rm ⌑ – 🛏4240/7700 CZK 🛏🛏4240/7700 CZK – 8 suites
• Luxury • Classic •

The stylish bedrooms of this 19C mansion come with luxurious pink marble bathrooms and the terrace of the classical dining room has a wonderful outlook. The hotel has one of the largest private collections of Le Corbusier lithographs, along with works by Czech artists Miloš Reindl and Pavel Skalnik.

Marriott

V Celnici 8 ✉ *110 00* – ⓜ *Náměsti Republiky*   Plan: **H1**
– ✆ *222 888 888* – *www.marriottprague.com*
293 rm – 🛏3450/7475 CZK 🛏🛏6900/10925 CZK – ⌑ 670 CZK – 28 suites
• Business • Classic •

This business hotel's draws are its first class conference facilities and its excellent leisure club. It has a classical feel, from its marble lobby to its spacious bedrooms, which are decorated in red and gold. Choose between steaks and seafood in the restaurant, then kick-back in the Bourbon Bar.

CZECH REPUBLIC - PRAGUE

 ### Hilton Old Town

V Celnici 7 ⊠ *110 00* – ⓜ *Náměstí Republiky*   Plan: **H1**
– ℰ *221 822 100 –* www.prague-oldtown.hilton.com
303 rm – †3000/7500 CZK ††3000/7500 CZK – ☑ 660 CZK – 19 suites
• Business • Modern •

Soft, contemporary colour schemes permeate the bedrooms of this heart-of-the-city hotel. In the art deco lobby, black and white marble is picked out with gold features, while in the restaurant, modern European dishes with Asian influences are served under a shimmering zinc ceiling.

 ### Sheraton

Zitna 8 ⊠ *111 21* – ⓜ *Karlovo Náměstí*   Plan: **G3**
– ℰ *225 999 999 –* www.sheratonprague.com
160 rm – †2200/3800 CZK ††2200/8000 CZK – ☑ 675 CZK – 38 suites
• Townhouse • Business • Stylish •

Convenience and comfort are key at this corporate hotel, which is made up of four 19C buildings. The suites come with terraces or balconies; ask for one of the newer rooms at the back. The rooftop terrace has impressive views over the city and the restaurant offers a choice of three different rooms.

 ### Art Nouveau Palace

Panská 12 ⊠ *111 21* – ⓜ *Můstek* – ℰ *224 093 111*   Plan: **H2**
– www.palacehotel.cz
127 rm ☑ – †2500/10000 CZK ††2500/10000 CZK – 2 suites
• Traditional • Classic •

It's a fitting name: the Viennese art nouveau façade dates from its opening in 1909 and the interior is elegant, with smart wood panelling on display in the lobby and Carrara marble featuring in the bathrooms. Enjoy classic French dishes and a piano accompaniment in the intimate restaurant.

 ### Imperial

Na Porící 15 ⊠ *110 00* – ⓜ *Náměsti Republiky*   Plan: **H1**
– ℰ *246 011 600 –* www.hotel-imperial.cz
126 rm ☑ – †4005/10880 CZK ††4005/10880 CZK – 1 suite
• Business • Retro • Historic •

The cubist-style façade dates from 1914 and the characterful interior features exquisite art deco mosaics (the building is a listed Czech National Monument). Dark wood furnished bedrooms combine retro styling with modern comforts.
Café Imperial – See restaurant listing

 ### Paris

U Obecního domu 1 ⊠ *110 00* – ⓜ *Náměsti Republiky*   Plan: **H1**
– ℰ *222 195 195 –* www.hotel-paris.cz
86 rm ☑ – †4540/5685 CZK ††6440/8080 CZK – 3 suites
• Traditional • Classic •

The bright corridors of this charming townhouse are hung with pieces from the owner's art collection and the characterful bedrooms come in soft hues. Corner rooms have great city views and the duplex Tower Suite offers a fantastic 360° vista. Dine in the Parisian café or more formal art nouveau restaurant.

 ### Kings Court

U Obecního domu 3 ⊠ *110 00* – ⓜ *Náměsti Republiky*   Plan: **H1**
– ℰ *224 222 888 –* www.hotelkingscourt.cz
137 rm ☑ – †8105 CZK ††14865 CZK – 5 suites
• Business • Stylish • Modern •

This grand building near the Obecni Dum was formerly the Chamber of Commerce. Marble and crystal chandeliers feature in the lobby and the ballroom still boasts its original stained glass windows. Relax in the spa then head for dinner on the terrace before retiring to one of the contemporary bedrooms.

Environs of Prague
(Plan I)

0   1 km

A   B

1

Podbabská

Horoměřická

DEJVICE

BUBENEČ

U

Korunovační

Evropská

Milady

Hotákově

nábřeží Edvar

VOKOVICE

Evropská

7

PRAŽSKÝ HRAD

Křižovnická

STŘEŠOVICE

Karmelit-ská

KARLŮV MOST

BŘEVNOV

Patočkova

Masarykovo nábřeží

2

BŘEVNOVSKÝ KLÁŠTER

přejíň

Rašínovo nábřeží

Bělohorská

Pod stadiony

Prague Centre (Plan II)

RUZYNĚ

Kukulova

Radlická

MOTOL

SMÍCHOV

KOŠÍŘE

Smíchovské nádraží

Radlická

Radlická

Na Kopci

Kutvirtova

M

Jinonice

Radlická

M

RADLICE

5

Bucharova

JINONICE

Nové Butovice

Radlická

3

STODŮLKY

Hůrka

M

Jeremiášova

● Hotel
● Restaurant

HLUBOČEPY

A   B

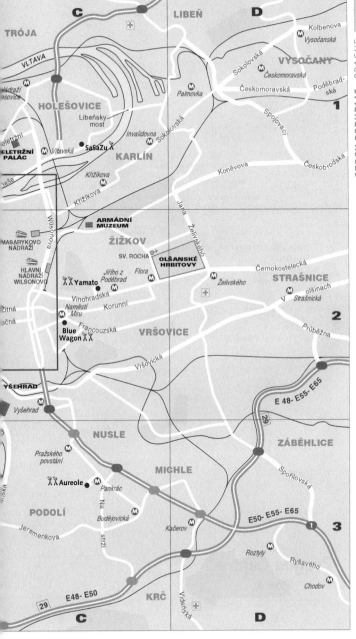

TRÓJA

C

LIBEŇ

D

Kolbenova

Vysočanská

VLTAVA

VYSOČANY

Nádraží
sovice

Sokolovská

Českomoravská

Poděbrad-
ská

HOLEŠOVICE

Palmovka

Českomoravská

1

eletržní

Libeňský
most

Spojovací

ELETRŽNÍ
PALÁC

Vltavská

Invalidovna

SaŠaZu

Sokolovská

KARLÍN

Českobrodská

Koněvova

iéše

Křižíkova

Křižíkova

ARMÁDNÍ
MUZEUM

Jana Želivského

Wilsonova

ŽIŽKOV

MASARYKOVO
NÁDRAŽÍ

SV. ROCHA

OLŠANSKÉ
HŘBITOVY

Černokostelecká

STRAŠNICE

HLAVNÍ
NÁDRAŽÍ
WILSONOVO

Yamato

Jiřího z
Poděbrad

Flora

Želivského

olšinach

Strašnická

Vinohradská

Korunní

2

Žitná

Náměstí
Míru

Průběžná

ečná

Blue
Wagon

Francouzská

VRŠOVICE

Vršovická

VYŠEHRAD

E 48- E55- E65

29

Vyšehrad

NUSLE

ZÁBĚHLICE

Pražského
povstání

MICHLE

Spořilovská

Aureole

Pankrác

PODOLÍ

Na
Budějovická

E50- E55- E65

1

3

Jeremenkova

střži

Kačerov

Roztyly

Ryšavého

Chodov

E48- E50

KRČ

Vídeňská

29

C

D

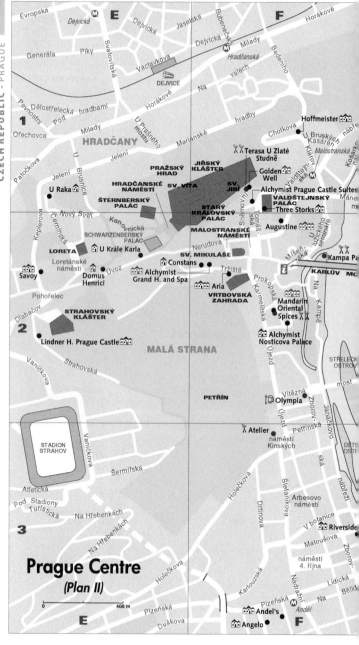

Prague Centre
(Plan II)

0   400 m

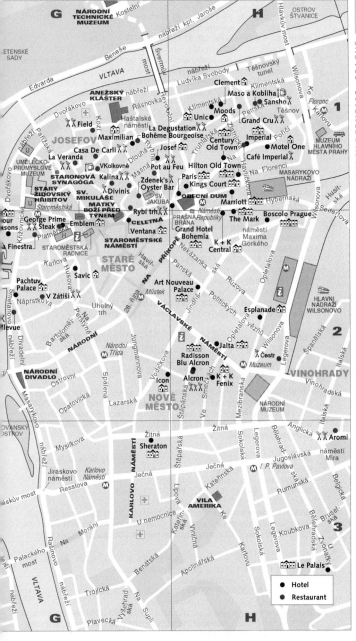

G | H

NÁRODNÍ
TECHNICKÉ
MUZEUM

OSTROV
ŠTVANICE

BELETENSKÉ
SADY

nábřeží kpt. Jaroše

Kostelní

Hlavkův most

Edvarda

VLTAVA

Benešo

Švermůvmost

nábřeží Ludvíka Svobody

Těšnovský
tunel

Wilsonova

Ke
Florenc

Klimentská

Dvořákovo

Rásnovka

Revoluční

Clement

Maso a Kobliha

Sansho

Klimentská

Petrská

Těšnov

Karlova

1

ANEŽSKÝ
KLÁŠTER

nábřeží

Haštalské
náměstí

Klimentská

Moods

Grand Cru

Na
Poříčí

MUZEUM
HLAVNÍHO
MĚSTA PRAHY

Parížská

JOSEFOV

Kozí

Maximilian

La Degustation
Bohême Bourgeoise

Unic

Century
Old Town

Imperial

Motel One

MASARYKOVO
NÁDRAŽÍ

Casa De Carli

Rybná

Josef

Tuhlařská

Café Imperial

Na. Florenci

La Veranda

Masná

Pot au Feu

Hilton Old Town

UMĚLECKO
PRŮMYSLOVÉ
MUZEUM

VKolkovné

Dvořákovo

STARONOVÁ
SYNAGÓGA

Kalina

Zdenek's
Oyster Bar

Paris

Kings Court

Husit-
ská

STARÝ
ŽIDOVSKÝ
HŘBITOV

SV.
MIKULÁŠE

Divinis

SV.
JAKUBA

OBECNÍ DŮM

Marriott

Hybernská

Seifertova

Staroměstská

MATKY
BOŽÍ PŘED
TÝNEM

Rybí trh

Náměstí
Republiky

The Mark

Boscolo Prague

our
sons

George Prime
Steak

Emblem

PRAŠNÁ
BRÁNA

náměstí
Maxima
Gorkého

Finestra

Platnéřská

STAROMĚSTSKÁ
RADNICE

Ventana

CELETNÁ

Grand Hotel
Bohemia

K + K
Central

Karlova

STARÉ
MĚSTO

STAROMĚSTSKÉ
NÁMĚSTÍ

Havel-
ská

PŘÍKOPĚ

Nekázanka

Opletalova

Křížovní

Husova

Pachtuv
Palace

Savic

Panská

M

Art Nouveau
Palace

Rúžova

Náprstkova

V Zátiší

Uhelný
trh

Můstek

VÁCLAVSKÉ

Politických

Esplanade

HLAVNÍ
NÁDRAŽÍ
WILSONOVO

llevue

Bartolomějská

Na Perštýně

Jindřiš

Opletalova věznič

2

Divadelní
nábřeží

NÁRODNÍ

Národní
Třída

Jungmannova

NÁMĚSTÍ

Jalta

Španělská

Italská

NÁRODNÍ
DIVADLO

Ostrovní

Spálená

Vodičkova

Radisson
Blu Alcron

Čestr

Muzeum

VINOHRADY

Masarykovo

Opatovická

Lazarská

Icon

Alcron

K + K
Fenix

Vinohradská

NOVÉ
MĚSTO

Štěpánská

Ve Smečkách

Mezibranská

NÁRODNÍ
MUZEUM

Italská

OVANSKÝ
OSTROV

Myslíkova

NÁMĚSTÍ

Žitná

Sheraton

Žitná

Legerova

Bělehrad

Anglická

Aromi

náměstí
Míra

Jiráskovo
náměstí

Karlovo
Náměstí

Ječná

Štěpánská

Sokolská

Ječná

I. P. Pavlova

Jugoslávská

Belgická

Bruselská

Resslova

KARLOVO

Kateřinská

Rumunská

Palackého
most

Na Moráni

U nemocnice

VILA
AMERIKA

Kateřinská

Viničná

Koubkova

Bělehradská

Sokolská

Legerova

3

VLTAVA

Benátská

Apolinářská

Karlovu

U
Zvonařky

Le Palais

Rašínovo

Na
Slupi

Vyšehrad-
ská

Trojická

ský most

Na Bojišti

● Hotel

● Restaurant

G | H

nábřeží

Plavecká

CZECH REPUBLIC - PRAGUE

 Jalta ⚐ ᙁ 🆎 ⇆ 🔥

Václavské Nám. 45 ✉ *110 00* – Ⓜ *Muzeum* — Plan: **H2**
– ☏ *222 822 111* – *www.hoteljalta.com*
94 rm ⚏ – 🛏3500/8400 CZK 🛏🛏3500/8400 CZK – 5 suites
• Business • Traditional • Stylish •
There's a real sense of history here, from the opal light fixtures and original doors leading out onto the balcony which overlooks Wenceslas Square to the UNESCO listed façade and the nuclear bunker in the basement! The chic restaurant unusually blends Czech, Mediterranean and Japanese influences.

 Century Old Town ⚐ ᙁ 🆎 ⇆ 🔥

Na Porící 7 ✉ *110 00* – Ⓜ *Námesti Republiky* — Plan: **H1**
– ☏ *221 800 800* – *www.centuryoldtown.com*
174 rm – 🛏2600/6580 CZK 🛏🛏2600/6580 CZK – ⚏ 440 CZK – 1 suite
• Business • Functional •
Franz Kafka's spirit can be felt throughout this appealing business hotel, which was formerly the Workmen's Accident Insurance Institute HQ – Kafka's place of work from 1908 to 1922. Contemporary bedrooms have compact, shower-only bathrooms. Dine in the courtyard terrace from an international menu.

 Grand Hotel Bohemia ⚐ ᙁ 🆎 ⇆ 🔥

Královdorská 4 ✉ *110 00* – Ⓜ *Námesti Republiky* — Plan: **H1**
– ☏ *234 608 111* – *www.grandhotelbohemia.cz*
79 rm ⚏ – 🛏3780/9460 CZK 🛏🛏4325/10810 CZK – 1 suite
• Traditional • Modern •
Weekly Mozart dinners are held in the stunningly restored neo-baroque ballroom, which really is the highlight of this classic 1920s hotel. Sleek, modern bedrooms have good facilities, including underfloor heating in the bathrooms. Modern touches are added to Czech dishes in the bistro.

 Emblem ⚐ 🛗 🌐 💬 ᙁ 🆎 ⇆

Platnéřská 19 ✉ *111 00* – Ⓜ *Staroměstská* — Plan: **G2**
– ☏ *226 202 500* – *www.emblemprague.com*
57 rm – 🛏5600/17120 CZK 🛏🛏6230/18055 CZK – ⚏ 500 CZK – 2 suites
• Townhouse • Design • Contemporary •
It might be housed within a 1907 property but inside you'll find a stylish designer hotel with a private members club in the basement. Head to the lounge to check in, then up to one of the sleek, modern bedrooms with oak flooring and walnut desks. Specially commissioned abstract art hangs in the hallways.
George Prime Steak – See restaurant listing

 Josef 🛗 💬 ᙁ 🆎 ⇆ 🔥 🚗

Rybná 20 ✉ *110 00* – Ⓜ *Námesti Republiky* — Plan: **G1**
– ☏ *221 700 111* – *www.hoteljosef.com*
109 rm ⚏ – 🛏4540/16090 CZK 🛏🛏4950/18520 CZK
• Townhouse • Design • Minimalist •
Modern boutique hotel comprising two buildings linked by a delightful courtyard garden. Bedrooms are smart and design-led; ask for one with a view on the 7th or 8th floor. The in-house bakery means that breakfast is a real treat.

 Unic ⚐ ᙁ 🆎 ⇆

Soukenická 25 ✉ *110 00* – Ⓜ *Námesti Republiky* — Plan: **H1**
– ☏ *222 312 521* – *www.hotel-unic.cz*
90 rm ⚏ – 🛏2000/4600 CZK 🛏🛏2000/4600 CZK – 8 suites
• Business • Contemporary • Stylish •
This 19C townhouse conceals a stylish design hotel with subtle Spanish influences. Relax in the library lounge or in the bright, laid-back bar, then head for dinner in the spacious restaurant with its global menu and traditional Czech specialities. Clean-lined contemporary bedrooms have good facilities.

Pachtuv Palace

Karolíny Svetlé 34 ✉ *110 00* – **Ⓜ** *Staroměstská*   Plan: **G2**
– ☎ *234 705 111* – *www.pachtuvpalace.com*
48 rm – ♦4345/8150 CZK ♦♦4345/8150 CZK – ☲ 540 CZK – 29 suites
• Traditional • Personalised • Historic •

This beautiful 18C residence by the river has been charmingly renovated in a baroque style. Most of the spacious, elegant bedrooms are suites with antique furnishings, kitchenettes and mosaic-tiled bathrooms; ask for one with a view. In the pillared restaurant, market produce features in French fusion dishes.

K + K Central

Hybernská 10 ✉ *110 00* – **Ⓜ** *Námesti Republiky*   Plan: **H2**
– ☎ *225 022 000* – *www.kkhotels.com*
127 rm ☲ – ♦3000/7750 CZK ♦♦3500/8250 CZK – 1 suite
• Business • Modern • Historic •

The wonderful art nouveau façade dates back to the hotel's opening in 1901; the glass cube conference room sits within what was once a theatre; and the spa features bas-relief Asian-themed imagery, as it now occupies the theatre's old Orient Bar. The modern bar-bistro offers a range of light dishes.

Maximilian

Haštalská 14 ✉ *110 00* – **Ⓜ** *Námesti Republiky*   Plan: **G1**
– ☎ *225 303 111* – *www.maximilianhotel.com*
71 rm ☲ – ♦2980/6320 CZK ♦♦3310/6655 CZK – 1 suite
• Business • Modern • Minimalist •

Maximilian is set in a peaceful area and comes with a Thai massage studio, comfy, contemporary bedrooms and two brightly furnished lounges – one with an honesty bar. Unusually, you can request a goldfish for the duration of your stay!

Icon

V Jámé 6 ✉ *110 00 Praha* – **Ⓜ** *Můstek*   Plan: **G2**
– ☎ *221 634 100* – *www.iconhotel.eu*
31 rm ☲ – ♦2000/6620 CZK ♦♦2000/6620 CZK – 2 suites
• Business • Modern • Design •

This centrally located hotel has a relaxed feel and is run by a friendly, helpful team. The 'chill-out' lounge is hung with contemporary Czech art and stylish bedrooms feature Hästens beds and biometric safes. An international vibe comes courtesy of a tapas bar and a small Thai massage centre.

Ventana

Celetná 7 (Entrance from 2 Stuparska Street) ✉ *110 00*   Plan: **G2**
– **Ⓜ** *Námesti Republiky* – ☎ *221 776 600* – *www.ventana-hotel.net*
29 rm ☲ – ♦3120/5700 CZK ♦♦3660/6240 CZK – 2 suites
• Traditional • Classic •

Once a residential house, Ventana is a hit with tourists, courtesy of its proximity to the Old Town Square and its spacious bedrooms. The loft rooms have separate lounge areas and the top suite has a balcony with Square views.

K + K Fenix

Ve Smeckách 30 ✉ *110 00* – **Ⓜ** *Muzeum*   Plan: **H2**
– ☎ *225 012 000* – *www.kkhotels.com*
128 rm ☲ – ♦2570/8515 CZK ♦♦2700/9055 CZK
• Business • Modern •

If you want to be close to the nightlife, this bright, business-focussed hotel is the place to be (electric car owners are now catered for too!) A classic façade masks a modern interior; ask for one of the refurbished bedrooms to the rear. Light, international dishes are offered in the modern bar-restaurant.

CZECH REPUBLIC - PRAGUE

CZECH REPUBLIC - PRAGUE

Esplanade   🌂 📺 ⇘ ⚎

Washingtonova 1600-19 ⊠ 110 00 – Ⓜ Muzeum   Plan: **H2**
– ☎ 224 501 111 – www.esplanade.cz
68 rm 🖵 – ✝2675/6190 CZK ✝✝2945/8080 CZK – 6 suites
· Traditional · Classic · Historic ·

This charming, atmospheric hotel sits on a peaceful tree-lined street near Wenceslas Square and is something of an architectural gem. Original features abound, from the marble floor of the lobby and the wallpapers in the 'Historical Suites' to the Murano chandelier and stained glass cupola in the restaurant.

Savic   🌂 📺 ⇘

Jilská 7 ⊠ 110 00 – Ⓜ Staroměstská – ☎ 224 248 555   Plan: **G2**
– www.savic.eu
27 rm 🖵 – ✝2170/3255 CZK ✝✝3255/6775 CZK – 1 suite
· Historic · Rustic · Classic ·

Just around the corner from the Astronomical Clock is this charming 14C monastery, which is surprisingly peaceful considering its setting. Glittering crystal lights are juxtaposed with exposed stone, beams and 15C frescoes. Start your day with breakfast in the conservatory and end it on the brasserie's terrace.

Clement   ⎧ 📺 ⇘ ⚎ ⊜

Klimentská 30 ⊠ 110 00 – Ⓜ Náměsti Republiky   Plan: **H1**
– ☎ 222 314 350 – www.hotelclement.cz
76 rm 🖵 – ✝1900/4070 CZK ✝✝2170/4340 CZK
· Business · Functional ·

This former office building is close to both the river and the city centre. Bedrooms are modern and functional; the Superior rooms are worth the extra, with their bold red and black colour schemes – some also have panoramic windows.

Moods   🔵 ⎧ 📺 ⇘ ⚎

Klimentská 28 ⊠ 110 00 – Ⓜ Náměsti Republiky   Plan: **H1**
– ☎ 222 330 100 – www.hotelmoods.com
51 rm 🖵 – ✝2261/12750 CZK ✝✝2261/12750 CZK
· Business · Design ·

This bright, boutique hotel makes interesting use of natural materials like bamboo and moss. The colourful bedrooms feature Hästens beds and Apple technology, and quotes from Peter Sis's 'The Three Golden Keys' feature throughout.

Motel One   ⎧ ⚎

Na Poříčí 1048/30 ⊠ 110 00 Prague – Ⓜ Florenc   Plan: **H1**
– ☎ (222) 334 500 – www.motel-one.com
141 rm – ✝1870 CZK ✝✝2571/3115 CZK
· Chain hotel · Functional · Minimalist ·

For those who like a boutique feel at a budget price, there's Motel One. Their signature colour, turquoise, features throughout, alongside pictures of old Prague. To keep prices down there are no phones, safes or minibars in the rooms.

❀❀❀ Alcron – Radisson Blu Alcron Hotel   📺 ⇘ 🅿
❀

Štepánská 40 ⊠ 110 00 – Ⓜ Muzeum – ☎ 222 820 000   Plan: **H2**
– www.alcron.cz – Closed 25-31 July, 22-28 February, Saturday lunch and Sunday
Menu 1100/2300 CZK – *(booking essential)*
· Modern · Intimate · Retro ·

An intimate, semi-circular restaurant dominated by an art deco mural of dancing Manhattan couples by Tamara de Lempicka. Choose 'hot' or 'cold' tasting dishes from an international menu; well-presented, creative, contemporary cooking uses top ingredients. There's a good choice of wines and staff are attentive.
→ Redcurrant marinated foie gras with peanut butter biscuit. Octopus with chorizo emulsion, tapenade and crispy capers. Muscat pumpkin cheesecake.

XX   **Field** (Radek Kašpárek)
☆   *U Milosrdných 12 ⊠ 110 00 – Ⓜ Staroměstská*   Plan: **G1**
     – ℰ 222 316 999 – www.fieldrestaurant.cz – Closed 24-26 December
     Menu 400 CZK (lunch) – Carte 850/1070 CZK
     • Innovative • Intimate • Fashionable •
     Two friends run this chic restaurant, which has a warm, intimate feel. An eye-catching mural by artist Jakub Matuška is projected overhead and the Scandinavian style cooking is equally contemporary. Alongside wine pairings they offer non-alcoholic drinks matches such as tomato, cucumber and chilli juice.
     → Snails with pumpkin, marrow and dried apples. Duck with cabbage, mustard and brioche. Plum, chokeberries and almond.

XX   **La Degustation Bohême Bourgeoise** (Oldřich Sahajdák)
☆   *Haštalská 18 ⊠ 110 00 – Ⓜ Náměsti Republiky*   ✸ AC ⇖
     – ℰ 222 311 234 – www.ladegustation.cz – Closed   Plan: **G1**
     1 week January and 24 December
     Menu 2450/3350 CZK – *(dinner only)*
     • Innovative • Intimate • Fashionable •
     This intimate L-shaped restaurant is hidden away in a historic building, down narrow lanes. Choose between two tasting menus: the 6 course option is inspired by the refined Czech cuisine of Marie B Svobodová's 19C cookery school. Cooking is precise, innovative and flavourful, and the service is charming.
     → Trout from Třeboň with buttermilk, dill and egg yolk. Smoked beef tongue with yellow peas and apple. Rhubarb, hazelnuts and crumb.

XX   **Bellevue**   ⇐ 🏠 AC ⇖ ⇔
     Smetanovo Nábreží 18 ⊠ 110 00 – Ⓜ Staroměstská   Plan: **G2**
     – ℰ 222 221 443 – www.zatisigroup.cz – Closed 24 December
     Menu 1190/1490 CZK
     • Modern • Formal • Classic •
     Sit on the pleasant terrace or in the contemporary, pastel-hued dining room of this elegant 19C townhouse and take in views over Charles Bridge and the river. Ambitious, original modern dishes consist of many different elements.

XX   **Aureole**   ⇐ 🏠 AC ⇖
⊛   *Tower (27th floor), Hvězdova 1716/2b ⊠ 140 00*   Plan I: **C3**
     – ⓂPankrác – ℰ 222 755 380 – www.aureole.cz – Closed 25-26 December
     and 1 January
     Menu 490/1550 CZK – Carte 670/1880 CZK
     • International • Design • Trendy •
     Have a drink in the chic cocktail bar of this hip 27th floor restaurant before making for the moody red and black dining room or out onto the fantastic panoramic terrace. Refined, original modern cooking cleverly blends East and West; the degustation menu best showcases the kitchen's talent.

XX   **Grand Cru**   ✸ 🏠 ⅃ AC ⇔
     Lodecká 4 ⊠ 110 00 – ⓂFlorenc – ℰ 775 044 076   Plan: **H1**
     – www.grand-cru.cz – Closed Christmas, New Year, Saturday lunch and
     Sunday
     Menu 400 CZK (weekday lunch) – Carte 945/1160 CZK
     • Modern • Fashionable • Elegant •
     Choose from homemade pâtés, charcuterie and smokehouse cheeses in the charming wine bar with its Enomatic machine or cross the cobbled courtyard to the elegant orangery-style room for attractive modern dishes with innovative touches.

XX   **V Zátiši**   AC ⇖
     Liliová 1, Betlémské Nám. ⊠ 130 00 – ⓂMůstek   Plan: **G2**
     – ℰ 222 221 155 – www.zatisi.cz – Closed 24 December
     Menu 1090 CZK – Carte 1035/1325 CZK – *(booking essential at dinner)*
     • Modern • Cosy • Elegant •
     This modern city centre restaurant is a popular spot. Its name means 'timeless' and with its clever blend of modern Czech and Indian dishes, well-judged spicing and attractive presentation, it looks set to stand up to its name.

XX **George Prime Steak** – Emblem Hotel 🕸 🕭 🅰🅲 ⇕

Platnéřská 19 ✉ *110 00* – Ⓜ *Staroměstská* Plan: **G2**
– ✆ *226 202 599* – *www.georgeprimesteak.com*
Menu 490 CZK (weekday lunch)/1600 CZK – Carte 1160/1685 CZK
• Meats and grills • Fashionable •

The dining room of the Emblem hotel is an authentic feeling American steak-house decorated in black and grey. The USDA Prime steak comes from the Mid-west and is best washed down with something from the impressive Californian wine list.

XX **Casa De Carli** 🕋 🅰🅲 ↩ ⇕

Vezenskská 5 ✉ *11 000* – Ⓜ *Staromestská* Plan: **G1**
– ✆ *224 816 688* – *www.casadecarli.com*
Carte 515/1045 CZK
• Italian • Friendly • Neighbourhood •

Contemporary family-run restaurant with bold artwork and tables on the cobbled street. Flavoursome cooking has a subtle Northern Italian bias; the breads, pastas and ice creams are all homemade – go for one of the daily specials.

XX **Pot au Feu** 🅰🅲 ↩

Rybná 1065/13 ✉ *110 00* – Ⓜ *Náměsti Republiky* Plan: **G1**
– ✆ *739 654 884* – *www.potaufeu.cz* – *Closed Christmas, Saturday lunch and Sunday*
Menu 495 CZK (weekday lunch)/695 CZK – Carte 615/1135 CZK – *(bookings advisable at dinner)*
• French • Intimate • Individual •

The chef-owner's travels inform his cooking – which is inspired largely by the French classics. The intimate interior comes with striking artwork and shelves packed with French wines (sourced directly). Service is relaxed yet clued-up.

XX **Kalina** 🅰🅲 ↩

Dlouhá 12 ✉ *110 00* – Ⓜ *Staromestská* Plan: **G1**
– ✆ *222 317 715* – *www.kalinarestaurant.cz* – *Closed 25 December and 1 January*
Menu 390/450 CZK – Carte 640/1565 CZK
• Modern • Intimate • Individual •

The eponymous chef-owner's cooking is gutsy yet refined and blends both modern and classic Czech and French influences. The atmospheric interior comprises two 16C vaulted rooms; ask for the front room, as that's where the action is.

XX **Rybí trh** 🕋 🅰🅲 ↩

Týnský dvůr 5 ✉ *110 00* – Ⓜ *Náměsti Republiky* Plan: **G1**
– ✆ *602 295 911* – *www.rybitrh.cz*
Carte 900/2000 CZK
• Fish and seafood • Friendly • Intimate •

The aptly named 'Fish Market' is tucked away on a small square. Sit at the front of the vaulted room to watch the chefs at work. Cooking has a Mediterranean edge – the simplest dishes, including the seafood platters, are the best.

XX **Aromi** 🕸 🕋 🅰🅲

Náměstí Míru 6 ✉ *120 00 Praha* – Ⓜ *Náměstí Míru* Plan: **H3**
– ✆ *222 713 222* – *www.aromi.cz*
Carte 865/1065 CZK
• Italian • Minimalist • Friendly •

A friendly team welcome you to this bright modern restaurant. Simply prepared, classically based Italian dishes display modern touches; the fresh fish display demonstrates the owners' commitment to sourcing good quality produce.

XX **Blue Wagon**   🍴 AC ⇔

Uruguayská 19 ✉ *120 00* – **Ⓜ** *Náměstí Míru*   Plan I: **C2**
– 𝒞 *222 561 378 – www.bluewagon.cz – Closed 25 December, Easter,*
Sunday lunch and Sunday dinner July-August
Carte 545/895 CZK
• Modern • Friendly • Elegant •
A very warmly run restaurant with a sleek modern style. The cooking is a blend
of classic Czech and Mediterranean and comes with a refreshing simplicity.
Breads and ice creams are homemade and the wine list is strong in claret.

XX **La Veranda**   AC ⇔

Elišky Krásnohorské 2 ✉ *110 00* – **Ⓜ** *Staroměstská*   Plan: **G1**
– 𝒞 *224 814 733 – www.laveranda.cz – Closed 24 December and Sunday*
Carte 535/1045 CZK
• Mediterranean • Cosy • Friendly •
Sit amongst books and bric-a-brac in the colourfully decorated main room or
head down to the intimate modern basement. Cooking takes its inspiration
from the Med, with Italy playing a big part. Staff are friendly and welcoming.

XX **Yamato**   🍴 AC ⇔

U Kanálky 14 ✉ *120 00 Prague* – **Ⓜ** *Jiřího z Poděbrad*   Plan I: **C2**
– 𝒞 *222 212 617 – www.yamato.cz – Closed Christmas, Saturday lunch*
and Sunday
Menu 250/1090 CZK – Carte 310/1060 CZK
• Japanese • Elegant • Friendly •
The chef might be a local but he trained in Japan and the room has an authentic Japanese feel. The menus focus on sushi, with the beer-marinated tuna a signature dish. A selection of Japanese beers and whiskies complement the cooking.

X **Divinis**   AC ⇔
🍴

Týnská 21 ✉ *110 00* – **Ⓜ** *Náměsti Republiky*   Plan: **G1**
– 𝒞 *222 325 440 – www.divinis.cz – Closed Sunday*
Carte 745/1075 CZK – *(dinner only) (booking essential)*
• Italian • Friendly • Individual •
You'll find this intimate, homely restaurant tucked away on a side street; it's run
with great passion and has a friendly feel. Rustic, seasonal Italian dishes have
original touches and are cooked with flair. The perfect accompaniment comes
in the form of a large collection of wines from Italian growers.

X **Sansho**   🍴 AC
🍴

Petrská 25 ✉ *110 00* – **Ⓜ** *Florenc* – 𝒞 *222 317 425*   Plan: **H1**
– www.sansho.cz – Closed 2 weeks August, 2 weeks Christmas-New Year,
Saturday lunch, Sunday and Monday
Menu 900/1200 CZK (dinner) – Carte lunch 419/588 CZK – *(booking*
essential at dinner)
• Asian • Friendly • Simple •
Homely restaurant set in a small square, with simple styling and a house party
type atmosphere. The owner once kept a butcher's shop, so you'll find rare
breeds hung for long periods and top class husbandry. Asian cooking has an
emphasis on the south-east and dinner offers a set, family-style sharing menu.

X **Zdenek's Oyster Bar**   🍴 AC

Malá Štupartská 7 ✉ *110 00* – **Ⓜ** *Náměsti Republiky*   Plan: **G1**
– 𝒞 *725 946 250 – www.oysterbar.cz – Closed 24-25 December*
Carte 1185/1985 CZK
• Fish and seafood • Bistro • Wine bar •
Deep in the heart of the city is this romantic, dimly lit restaurant with a pretty
pavement terrace. Choose from tapas, caviar, elaborate seafood platters, dishes
from the Josper grill and, of course, 8 different types of oyster.

CZECH REPUBLIC - PRAGUE

129

CZECH REPUBLIC - PRAGUE

La Finestra

𝄪 ▥ ⟺

Platnérská 13 ✉ *110 00 –* Ⓜ *Staroměstská* Plan: **G2**
– ℰ 222 325 325 – www.lafinestra.cz
Menu 425 CZK (weekday lunch) – Carte 965/1165 CZK – *(booking essential)*
• Italian • Rustic • Cosy •

You'd never guess but from 1918-1945 this lovely restaurant – with its red-brick vaulted ceiling – was an Alfa Romeo showroom. Expect rustic Italian dishes and fine Italian wines, and be sure to stop-off at their neighbouring shop.

Café Imperial – Hotel Imperial

▥ ⟿ 🍴

Na Poříčí 15 ✉ *110 00 –* Ⓜ *Náměsti Republiky* Plan: **H1**
– ℰ 246 011 440 – www.cafeimperial.cz
Menu 650 CZK – Carte 397/772 CZK – *(booking essential)*
• International • Brasserie • Retro •

The Imperial hotel's restaurant is an impressive room, with a high ceiling and colourful mosaic-tiled walls and pillars. Global menus follow the seasons. It was the place to be seen in the 1920's and, as they say, Kafka's spirit lives on...

Čestr

🍴 ▥ ⟿

Legerova 57/75 ✉ *110 00 –* Ⓜ *Muzeum* Plan: **H2**
– ℰ 222 727 851 – www.ambi.cz – Closed 24 December
Carte 318/1011 CZK
• Meats and grills • Friendly • Design •

Its name refers to the Czech spotted cattle and the focus is on meat: butchered in-house and hung for 60+ days, then braised, spit-roasted or chargrilled. The large open kitchen takes centre stage in the buzzy canteen-style room.

Maso A Kobliha

🍴

Petrská 23 ✉ *110 00 –* Ⓜ *Florenc – ℰ 224 815 056* Plan: **H1**
– www.masoakobliha.cz – Closed Sunday, Monday, Dinner Tuesday and Saturday
Carte 335/460 CZK
• Traditional • Neighbourhood • Pub •

Behind the butcher's counter of "Meat and Doughnuts" is a bright, fashionable bar. Try a local beer from the 'kegerator' alongside a gutsy, classical dish smoked on-site; the scotch eggs and custard-filled doughnuts are must-tries. Stop off at the counter on your way out to buy some fresh free range meat.

VKolkovně

🍴 ⟿

V Kolkovně 8 ✉ *110 00 –* Ⓜ *Staroměstská* Plan: **G1**
– ℰ 224 819 701 – www.vkolkovne.cz
Carte 373/886 CZK
• Traditional • Traditional • Pub •

An authentic pub with a pavement terrace, a copper bar and a lively atmosphere. Traditional Czech cooking comes in generous portions – the goulash and the smoked sausages are favourites; try them with a Velkopopovický Koze (dark beer).

Mandarin Oriental

⌂ ⟿ 🛋 ⊛ 👤 ▥ ⟿ 🍴 🚗

Nebovidská 459/1 ✉ *118 00 –* Ⓜ *Malostranská* Plan: **F2**
– ℰ 233 088 888 – www.mandarinoriental.com/prague
99 rm ⌂ – 🛏10400/14150 CZK 🛏🛏11650/15380 CZK – 20 suites
• Luxury • Stylish •

A former monastery dating from the 14C provides the charming setting for this luxurious hotel. Chic, tastefully decorated bedrooms have goose down bedding and an Asian feel courtesy of silk bedspreads and potted orchids. Relax on the terraces or in the delightful spa which occupies the old chapel.
Spices – See restaurant listing

CZECH REPUBLIC - PRAGUE

Augustine

Letenská 12/33 ✉ *118 00 –* Ⓜ *Malostranská*
– ☎ 266 112 233 – www.augustinehotel.com
101 rm ⌸ **– †**8235/15580 CZK **††**8856/16155 CZK **– 11 suites**
Plan: F2
• Historic • Design • Stylish •

An impressive hotel set over 7 different buildings, including the 13C monastery after which it is named. Original frescoes and vaulted ceilings remain, yet it has contemporary look and feel; the spa is fittingly luxurious. The bar occupies the old refectory and serves a custom microbrew based on the monks' original recipe. The chic restaurant serves a modern menu.

Aria

Tržiště 9 ✉ *118 00 –* Ⓜ *Malostranská – ☎ 225 334 111*
– www.ariahotel.net
Plan: F2
51 rm ⌸ **– †**6325/10350 CZK **††**6325/10350 CZK **– 7 suites**
• Luxury • Design •

A musical motif features throughout, from the mosaic music notes in the lobby and the collection of 5,000 CDs and DVDs in the music room, to the bedrooms, which are themed around composers or styles of music. The restaurant boasts a superb rooftop terrace with castle views and the piano is played nightly.

Alchymist Grand H. and Spa

Tržiště 19 ✉ *118 00 –* Ⓜ *Malostranská – ☎ 257 286 011*
– www.alchymistgroup.com
Plan: F2
45 rm ⌸ **– †**5775/16700 CZK **††**5775/16700 CZK **– 5 suites**
• Luxury • Historic • Personalised •

The Alchymist is a magnificent baroque townhouse characterised by sumptuous gilt furnishings and over-the-top styling. Bedrooms come in rich reds or blues, picked out with gold. Cross the bridge over the koi carp pond to access the atmospheric Indonesian spa with its Turkish bath and mosaic-tiled pool; then enjoy modern international dishes on the restaurant's terrace.

Lindner H. Prague Castle

Strahovská 128 ✉ *118 00 – ☎ 226 080 000*
– www.lindnerhotels.cz
Plan: E2
138 rm – †1440/4625 CZK **††**1440/4625 CZK **–** ⌸ **485 CZK – 3 suites**
• Business • Historic • Elegant •

This modern hotel is set within the UNESCO protected grounds of the Strahov Monastery and its spacious lobby-lounge was once the stables. Bedrooms feature art deco paintings; those located in the 16C part have characterful timbered ceilings. Summer BBQs use seasonings made from herbs grown in the grounds.

Andel's

Stroupežnického 21 ✉ *150 00 –* Ⓜ *Anděl*
– ☎ 296 889 688 – www.andelshotel.com
Plan: F3
290 rm ⌸ **– †**1900/5700 CZK **††**2300/6100 CZK **– 31 suites**
• Business • Modern • Minimalist •

A stylish business hotel close to the Nový Smíchov shopping centre. Its white marble lobby is punctuated by black leather furnishings; the modern, minimalist bedrooms are warmly furnished and the suites with kitchenettes are ideal for longer stays. Dine from an international menu in the small brasserie.

Savoy

Keplerova 6 ✉ *118 00 – ☎ 224 302 430*
– www.hotelsavoyprague.com
Plan: E2
56 rm ⌸ **– †**4660/5470 CZK **††**5335/6150 CZK **– 7 suites**
• Business • Classic •

Set at the top of the hill, this former cinema complex is now under independent ownership. The elegant restaurant has a retractable roof which is opened on warm summer evenings. The hotel is currently undergoing a refurbishment and is due to reopen in May 2016. The new bedrooms will have a subtle art deco style.

Hoffmeister

Pod Bruskou 7 ⊠ *118 00* – **Ⓜ** *Malostranská* Plan: **F1**
– *𝒞 251 017 111* – *www.hoffmeister.cz* – *Closed 10-25 January*
49 rm ⬚ – ♦2000/5400 CZK ♦♦2000/5400 CZK – 5 suites
• Traditional • Classic •

The classical Hoffmeister hotel is set in a busy corner spot. Images of Old Prague hang on the walls in the modern restaurant and menus mix Czech and French influences. Bedrooms vary in shape and size and many are picked out with reds, golds or blues. Be sure to pay a visit to the steam bath in the old cave!

Golden Well

U Zlaté Studně 166/4 ⊠ *118 00* – **Ⓜ** *Malostranská* Plan: **F1**
– *𝒞 257 011 213* – *www.goldenwell.cz*
19 rm – ♦5290/7705 CZK ♦♦5290/13970 CZK – ⬚ 600 CZK – 2 suites
• Historic • Classic •

A charming, intimate hotel, tucked away in a quiet cobbled street close to the Royal Gardens and Charles Bridge. Understated bedrooms have a classical style and come with antique furnishings, modern touches and fresh fruit. The roof terrace offers outstanding views over the castle and city.
Terasa U Zlaté Studně – See restaurant listing

Alchymist Nosticova Palace

Nosticova 1, Malá Strana ⊠ *118 00* – **Ⓜ** *Malostranská* Plan: **F2**
– *𝒞 257 312 513* – *www.nosticova.com*
19 rm ⬚ – ♦3850/6200 CZK ♦♦3850/6200 CZK – 3 suites
• Townhouse • Classic • Personalised •

An intimate 17C residence which is inspired by the period of Emperor Rudolf II. The opulently decorated interior features antiques and Louis XIV style furniture; the Imperial Suite is nestled amongst the beams and even boasts a piano!

Riverside

Janáckovo Nábreži 15 ⊠ *150 00* – **Ⓜ** *Andĕl* Plan: **F3**
– *𝒞 225 994 611* – *www.mamaison.com*
80 rm – ♦2030/6765 CZK ♦♦2300/7310 CZK – ⬚ 405 CZK – 3 suites
• Business • Modern •

Charming riverside townhouse with a cosy bar and a mix of modern and traditional bedrooms – the latter feature mosaic-tiled bathrooms. Those at the front have the view; the most peaceful are to the rear, overlooking the courtyard.

Three Storks

Valdstejnske Nám 8 ⊠ *118 00* – **Ⓜ** *Malostranská* Plan: **F1**
– *𝒞 257 210 779* – *www.hotelthreestorks.cz*
21 rm ⬚ – ♦2750/8250 CZK ♦♦3300/11000 CZK
• Townhouse • Modern • Minimalist •

It might have a 19C façade but the Three Storks actually dates from the 17C. Take the glass lift up from the pebble-effect lobby to the contemporary bedrooms; many have original features, including vaulted ceilings and exposed beams. The bright restaurant offers a mix of Czech and international dishes.

Angelo

Radlická 1g ⊠ *150 00* – **Ⓜ** *Andĕl* – *𝒞 234 801 111* Plan: **F3**
– *www.vihotels.com/en/angelo-prague*
168 rm ⬚ – ♦1890/4995 CZK ♦♦2295/5400 CZK
• Business • Modern •

Younger sister to Andel's, the Angelo is a chic hotel with a bold red, yellow and black colour scheme running throughout. Bedrooms are spread over 7 floors and have spacious bathrooms with glass-enclosed showers. The lobby-lounge has a jazz motif and the bright restaurant and terrace offer a global menu.

Alchymist Prague Castle Suites

Sněmovní 8 ⌧ 118 00 – **Ⓜ** Malostranská
Plan: **F1**
– ☎ 257 286 960 – www.alchymistpraguecastle.com
8 rm ⌂ – ♦5640/16700 CZK ♦♦5640/16700 CZK
• Townhouse • Personalised • Stylish •

A delightfully restored 15C house in a quiet square beneath the castle; its former owners include the painter Brandl and architect Fanta. Its lavish decoration takes in chandeliers, gilt furnishings and hand-painted wallpapers. All 8 bedrooms have butler service and dinner can be taken at the Alchymist Grand.

U Krále Karla

Nerudova-Úvoz 4 ⌧ 118 00 – ☎ 257 531 211
Plan: **E2**
– www.ukralekarla.cz
19 rm ⌂ – ♦5180/6550 CZK ♦♦7650/9010 CZK
• Historic • Classic • Cosy •

Close to the castle is this Gothic-style townhouse, which was once home to a Benedictine order. Antique-furnished bedrooms are reached via an impressive stone staircase; many feature ornately painted ceilings and stained glass windows.

U Raka

Cernínská 10 ⌧ 118 00 – ☎ 220 511 100
Plan: **E1**
– www.hoteluraka.cz
6 rm ⌂ – ♦2600/3000 CZK ♦♦3700/7000 CZK
• Family • Cosy • Rustic •

You enter through this peaceful hotel's charming cobbled terrace – which is a great spot for summer breakfasts. Rustic bedrooms feature exposed stone, tile and wood and are decorated with old millstones; one even has its own well!

Domus Henrici

Loretánská 11 ⌧ 118 00 – ☎ 220 511 369
Plan: **E2**
– www.hidden-places.com
8 rm ⌂ – ♦2300/3100 CZK ♦♦2700/3500 CZK
• Townhouse • Minimalist •

A privately run townhouse dating back to 1372, perched on a hill in a tranquil location close to the castle. Bedrooms are furnished with art deco pieces and are accessed via the rear terrace, which looks out towards Petřín Hill.

Constans

Bretislavova 309 ⌧ 110 00 – **Ⓜ** Malostranská
Plan: **F2**
– ☎ 234 091 818 – www.hotelconstans.cz
31 rm ⌂ – ♦2035/5300 CZK ♦♦2035/5600 CZK – 2 suites
• Townhouse • Classic •

A warm welcome awaits at this hotel, which has a charmingly traditional feel throughout. It comprises three converted townhouses on a quiet street below the castle. Spacious bedrooms boast parquet floors, period furnishings and marble bathrooms and the intimate restaurant serves modern Czech business lunches.

XX **Terasa U Zlaté Studně** – Golden Well Hotel

U Zlaté Studně 166/4 ⌧ 118 00 – **Ⓜ** Malostranská
Plan: **F1**
– ☎ 257 533 322 – www.terasauzlatestudne.cz
Menu 890 CZK (lunch) – Carte 950/5010 CZK – (booking essential)
• Modern • Cosy • Classic •

This long-standing restaurant opened in 1901 and, in fact, predates the hotel it sits atop. The intimate room has blue and gold walls and a picture window, while above is a heated terrace with a stunning panoramic view. The modern international menu displays influences ranging from the Med through to Asia.

CZECH REPUBLIC - PRAGUE

XX Kampa Park

Na Kampe 8b, Malá Strana ✉ *118 00*   Plan: **F2**
– Ⓜ *Malostranská – ℰ 296 826 102 – www.kampagroup.com*
Carte 735/1785 CZK *– (booking essential at dinner)*
• International • Fashionable • Design •

Kampa Park is stunningly located by the water's edge, next to Charles Bridge.
Choose from several dining areas: the best spots are in the Winter Garden and
on the riverside terrace. The décor is contemporary, as is the global menu.

XX Spices *– Mandarin Oriental Hotel*

Nebovidská 459/1 ✉ *118 00 –* Ⓜ *Malostranská*   Plan: **F2**
– ℰ 233 088 777 – www.mandarinoriental.com/prague
Carte 635/1395 CZK *– (dinner only)*
• Asian • Intimate • Fashionable •

Softly backlit dark wood panels and decorative Chinoiserie items set the tone in
this chic hotel restaurant. The pan-Asian menu is divided into three regions
– Northeast, Southeast and Southwest – and there's a separate sushi list too.

X SaSaZu

Bubenské nábr. 306 ✉ *170 04 –* Ⓜ *Vltavská*   Plan I: **C1**
*– ℰ 284 097 455 – www.sasazu.com – Closed 24-25 December and lunch
1 January*
Menu 600/1250 CZK – Carte 615/960 CZK
• Asian • Exotic • Fashionable •

You'll find this stylish restaurant and bar within Prague Market. It's a cavernous
place with low-level mood lighting and an open kitchen where you can watch
the chefs at work. Innovative, flavoursome Southeast Asian dishes are the focus.
You can even have a Thai massage before you leave!

X Na Kopci

K Kávěrce 2774/20 ✉ *150 00 –* Ⓜ *Smíchovské Nádraží*   Plan I: **B3**
– ℰ 251 553 102 – www.nakopci.com – Closed Christmas
Carte 485/845 CZK *– (booking essential at dinner)*
• Traditional • Bistro • Simple •

Leave the city behind and escape to this busy, buzzy bistro, whose name means
'on the hill'. Expect a warm welcome, an unpretentious atmosphere and great
value, flavoursome Czech classics – along with a few French dishes too. Be sure
to try the local unfiltered beer, which is made just 3km away.

X Atelier

Rošickýh 4 ✉ *150 00 –* Ⓜ *Anděl – ℰ 257 218 277*   Plan: **F3**
– www.atelieratelier.cz – Closed Monday lunch and Sunday
Carte 480/761 CZK
• Modern • Wine bar • Friendly •

This bright, keenly run bistro-cum-wine bar is hidden away off the beaten track.
Wines play a key role – with over 130 on offer – and the unfussy, fiercely seasonal cooking comes with clearly defined flavours and modern twists.

Olympia

Vítezná 7 ✉ *110 00 –* Ⓜ *Národni Třída*   Plan: **F2**
– ℰ 251 511 080 – www.kolkovna.cz
Menu 138 CZK (weekday lunch)/252 CZK – Carte 294/787 CZK
• Traditional • Retro • Pub •

This converted bank is now a lively, friendly pub-cum-brasserie. The bar offers a
good range of local beers and the wood-panelled dining room behind is charming. Go for the home-smoked sausages or one of the tasty Czech dishes.

DENMARK
DANMARK

Aarhus

COPENHAGEN

→ **AREA:**
43 069 km² (16 629 sq mi) excluding the Faroe Islands and Greenland.

→ **POPULATION:**
5 627 235 inhabitants. Density = 131 per km².

→ **CAPITAL:**
Copenhagen.

→ **CURRENCY:**
Danish Krone (DKK).

→ **GOVERNMENT:**
Constitutional parliamentary (single chamber) monarchy (since 1849). Member of European Union since 1973.

→ **LANGUAGES:**
Danish; many Danes also understand and speak English.

→ **PUBLIC HOLIDAYS:**
New Year's Day (1 Jan); Maundy Thursday (late Mar/Apr); Good Friday (late Mar/Apr); Easter Monday (late Mar/Apr); Prayer Day (late Apr/May); Ascension Day (May); Whit Monday (late May/June); Constitution Day (5 June); Christmas Eve (24 Dec – Half Day); Christmas Day (25 Dec); 2nd Day of Christmas (26 Dec).

→ **LOCAL TIME:**
GMT + 1 hour in winter and GMT + 2 hours in summer.

→ **CLIMATE:**
Temperate northern maritime with cold winters and mild summers (Copenhagen: January 1°C, July 18°C).

→ **EMERGENCY:**
Police, Medical Assistance and Fire Brigade ✆ **112**.

→ **ELECTRICITY:**
230 volts AC, 50Hz; 2 round pin sockets.

→ **FORMALITIES:**
Travellers from the European Union (EU), Switzerland, Norway, Iceland and the main countries of North and South America need a national identity card or passport (America: passport required) to visit Denmark for less than three months (tourism or business purpose). For visitors from other countries a visa may be required, in addition to a passport, especially for those wishing to stay for longer than three months. If you plan to visit Greenland or Faroe Islands while in Denmark, you must purchase a visa in advance in your own country. We advise you to check with your embassy before travelling.

COPENHAGEN
KØBENHAVN

Population: 580 184

HaPu99/Fotolia.com

Some cities overwhelm you, and give the impression that there's too much of them to take in. Not Copenhagen. Most of its key sights are neatly compressed within its central Slotsholmen 'island', an area that enjoyed its first golden age in the early seventeenth century in the reign of Christian IV, when it became a harbour of great consequence. It has canals on three sides and opposite the harbour is the area of Christianshavn, home of the legendary freewheeling 'free-town' community of Christiania. Further up from the centre are Nyhavn, the much-photographed canalside with brightly coloured buildings where the sightseeing cruises leave from, and the elegant Frederiksstaden, whose wide streets contain palaces and museums. West of the centre is where Copenhageners love to hang out: the Tivoli Gardens, a kind of magical fairyland. Slightly more down-to-earth

are the western suburbs of Vesterbro and Nørrebro, which were run-down areas given a street credible spit and polish for the 21C, and are now two of the trendiest districts.

Once you've idled away some time in the Danish capital, you'll wonder why anyone might ever want to leave. With its waterfronts, quirky shops and cafés, the city presents a modern, user-friendly ambience – but it also boasts world class art collections, museums, and impressive parks, gardens and lakes, all of which bear the mark of an earlier time.

COPENHAGEN IN...

→ **ONE DAY**
Walk along Strøget, National Museum, Ny Carlsberg Glyptotek, Black Diamond, boat watching at Nyhavn.

→ **TWO DAYS**
Tivoli Gardens, Vesterbro, Opera House, Christiania.

→ **THREE DAYS**
Royal palaces at Frederiksstaden, train ride along the coast.

PRACTICAL INFORMATION

ARRIVAL-DEPARTURE

✈ Copenhagen Airport is located in Kastrup, 9km southeast of the city. The metro will take you to the centre in 15min. A taxi will take 25min.

GETTING AROUND

The metro is a triumph of sleek, smooth efficiency which runs 24 hours a day. If you want to see as much of the city as possible, get a Copenhagen Card, which gives free entry to all museums and galleries, as well as free bus, train and metro travel. They can be purchased from the main tourist office just across the road from the central railway station. Hiring a bicycle is a good way to see the city; it takes about two hours to circumnavigate the major attractions. It's also possible to see the city by kayak. Kajak Ole can get you paddling round the central harbour area for a very different perspective.

CALENDAR HIGHLIGHTS

February
Fashion Festival.

April
Queen Margrethe's birthday.

May
May Day Festival, Copenhagen Beer Festival, Copenhagen Carnival, Copenhagen Marathon.

June
Sankt Hans Eve Festival, Roskilde Music Festival.

July
Jazz Festival.

August
Ballet Festival, Historic Grand Prix, Cooking Festival.

November/December
Tivoli's Special Christmas Market.

EATING OUT

Fresh regional ingredients have revolutionized the menus of Copenhagen's hip restaurants and its reputation for food just keeps getting bigger. The city's dining establishments manage to marry Danish dining traditions such as herring or frikkadeller meatballs with global influences to impressive effect. So impressive that in recent times the city has earned itself more Michelin stars, for its crisp and precise cooking, than any other in Scandinavia. Many good restaurants blend French methods and dishes with regional ingredients and innovative touches and there is a trend towards fixed price, no choice menus involving several courses, which means that dinner can be a pleasingly drawn-out affair, stretching over three or four hours. There's no need to tip, as it should be included in the cost of the meal. Danes, though, have a very good reputation as cheerful, helpful waiting staff, so you might feel like adding a bit extra. But be warned, many restaurants – and even hotels – charge between 2.5% and 5% for using a foreign credit card.

D'Angleterre   ☆ 𝄕 ☺ 𝄞 ☒ ⅃ 🅰 ♨

Kongens Nytorv 34 ☒ *1050 K* – Ⓜ *Kongens Nytorv*   Plan: **C2**
– ☎ 33 12 00 95 – www.dangleterre.com
90 rm – 🛏3500/7000 DKK 🛏🛏3500/7000 DKK – ☲ 285 DKK – 30 suites
• Luxury • Historic • Contemporary •

Smartly refurbished landmark hotel dating back over 250 years. Well-equipped bedrooms come in various shapes and sizes; it's worth paying the extra for a Royal Square view. Unwind in the basement spa or the chic champagne bar.
❀ **Marchal** – See restaurant listing

Copenhagen Marriott   ☆ ≼ 𝄕 𝄞 ⅃ 🅰 ♨ 🅿

Kalvebod Brygge 5 ☒ *1560 V* – ☎ *88 33 99 00*   Plan: **C3**
– www.copenhagenmarriott.dk
402 rm – 🛏1299/5000 DKK 🛏🛏1299/5000 DKK – ☲ 220 DKK – 9 suites
• Luxury • Business • Modern •

Striking waterfront hotel; take in the views from the terrace or from the floor to ceiling windows in the large lounge-bar. Bright, spacious bedrooms are handsomely appointed and afford canal or city views. The popular American grill restaurant offers steaks, chops and seafood, and has a lively open kitchen.

Nimb   ☆ 𝄕 🅰 ♨

Bernstorffsgade 5 ☒ *1577 V*   Plan: **B3**
– Ⓜ København Hovedbane Gård – ☎ 88 70 00 00 – www.nimb.dk
17 rm – 🛏2600/3000 DKK 🛏🛏3900/6400 DKK – ☲ 195 DKK
• Luxury • Design • Stylish •

A Moorish-style building dating from 1909. Smart, stylish bedrooms are sympathetically designed and well-equipped – most overlook Tivoli Gardens. Eat in the lively bar and grill, the formal French brasserie or the chic restaurant. The rustic wine bar offers over 2,000 bottles – and you can enjoy Danish open sandwiches and schnapps in Fru Nimb.
Nimb Terrasse – See restaurant listing

Radisson Blu Royal   ☆ ≼ 𝄕 𝄞 ⅃ 🅰 ♨ 🚗

Hammerichsgade 1 ☒ *1611 V*   Plan: **B3**
– Ⓜ København Hovedbane Gård – ☎ 33 42 60 00
– www.radissonblu.com/royalhotel-copenhagen
260 rm – 🛏1445/3495 DKK 🛏🛏1645/3695 DKK – ☲ 195 DKK – 2 suites
• Business • Design •

Spacious hotel designed by Arne Jacobson, with extensive conference and fitness facilities. Bedrooms have a typical Scandinavian style – the largest are the double-aspect corner rooms; Number 606 still has its original furnishings. Dine informally in all-day Café Royal or enjoy panoramic views from Alberto K.
Alberto K – See restaurant listing

Island   ☆ ≼ 𝄕 𝄞 🅰 ♨ 🅿

Kalvebod Brygge 53 (via Kalvebod Brygge C3) ☒ *1560 V* – ☎ *33 38 96 00*
– www.copenhagenisland.dk
326 rm – 🛏850/2625 DKK 🛏🛏950/2825 DKK – ☲ 170 DKK
• Business • Chain hotel • Modern •

Contemporary glass and steel hotel set just outside the city, on a man-made island in the harbour. Bedrooms are well-equipped – some are allergy friendly and some have balconies; choose a water view over a city view. The stylish multi-level lounge-bar and restaurant serves a wide-ranging international menu.

Admiral   ☆ ≼ 𝄞 ♨ 🅿

Toldbodgade 24-28 ☒ *1253 K* – Ⓜ *Kongens Nytorv*   Plan: **D2**
– ☎ 33 74 14 14 – www.admiralhotel.dk
366 rm – 🛏990/2145 DKK 🛏🛏1935/3145 DKK – ☲ 145 DKK
• Business • Historic • Modern •

An impressive 1787 former grain-drying warehouse, with an appealing maritime theme running throughout. Bedrooms feature vintage beams and bespoke wood furniture and have city or harbour views; opt for one of the duplex suites.
Salt – See restaurant listing

Imperial 🏠 ᴋ 📺 ♨ 🚗

Vester Farimagsgade 9 ✉ *1606 V* — Plan: **B3**
– **Ⓜ** *København Hovedbane Gård* – ✆ *33 12 80 00*
– *www.imperialhotel.dk*
304 rm ⌂ – ♦1300/2300 DKK ♦♦1600/2800 DKK – 1 suite
• Business • Traditional • Modern •

A well-known hotel, geared up for conferences and centrally located on a wide city thoroughfare. Bedrooms are particularly spacious and have a subtle Danish style. The contemporary restaurant features a brightly coloured Italian theme wall and serves Italian dishes to match.

 Kong Arthur ᴋᴋ ⊕ 🛁 ♨ **P**

Nørre Søgade 11 ✉ *1370 K* – **Ⓜ** *Nørreport* Plan: **B2**
– ✆ *33 11 12 12* – *www.arthurhotels.dk*
155 rm ⌂ – ♦1080/2670 DKK ♦♦1455/3045 DKK
• Townhouse • Traditional • Classic •

Four 1882 buildings set around a courtyard, in an elegant residential avenue close to Peblinge Lake. Well-equipped bedrooms have a high level of facilities. Relax in the smart Thai spa and enjoy complimentary drinks from 5-6pm.

 Absalon ♨

Helgolandsgade 15 ✉ *1653 V* Plan: **B3**
– **Ⓜ** *København Hovedbane Gård* – ✆ *33 24 22 11*
– *www.absalon-hotel.dk*
162 rm ⌂ – ♦1000/3000 DKK ♦♦1200/3200 DKK – 2 suites
• Family • Design • Stylish •

A family-run hotel located close to the railway station and furnished with vibrantly coloured fabrics. Elegant, comfortable bedrooms feature an 'artbox' on the wall which celebrates an aspect of Danish design such as Lego or porcelain.

 Andersen

Helgolandsgade 12 ✉ *1653* Plan: **B3**
– **Ⓜ** *København Hovedbane Gård* – ✆ *33 31 46 10*
– *www.andersen-hotel.dk*
77 rm ⌂ – ♦1000/3000 DKK ♦♦1200/3200 DKK
• Family • Design • Contemporary •

Bright and funky boutique styling is the hallmark of this hotel, where the individually furnished bedrooms are classified as 'Cool', 'Brilliant', 'Wonderful' and 'Amazing'. Honesty bar in reception; complimentary glass of wine, 5–6pm.

 Avenue ♨ **P**

Åboulevard 29 ✉ *1960 C* – **Ⓜ** *Forum* – ✆ *35 37 31 11* Plan: **A2**
– *www.avenuehotel.dk* – *Closed Christmas*
68 rm ⌂ – ♦850/1250 DKK ♦♦1050/1650 DKK
• Business • Family • Modern •

Well-maintained, family-run hotel dating back to 1899. Relax around the central bar in the smart modern lounge or out on the courtyard patio. Bedrooms have a bright, crisp style and feature eye-catching Philippe Starck lights.

 Alexandra

H.C. Andersens Boulevard 8 ✉ *1553 V* Plan: **B3**
– **Ⓜ** *København Hovedbane Gård* – ✆ *33 74 44 44*
– *www.hotelalexandra.dk* – *Closed Christmas*
61 rm – ♦1120/2240 DKK ♦♦1120/2430 DKK – ⌂ 150 DKK
• Traditional • Townhouse • Personalised •

A well-run, late Victorian hotel in the city centre, with a contrastingly modern interior. Bedrooms are individually styled and there's an entire 'allergy friendly' floor; the 12 'Design' rooms are styled by famous Danish designers.

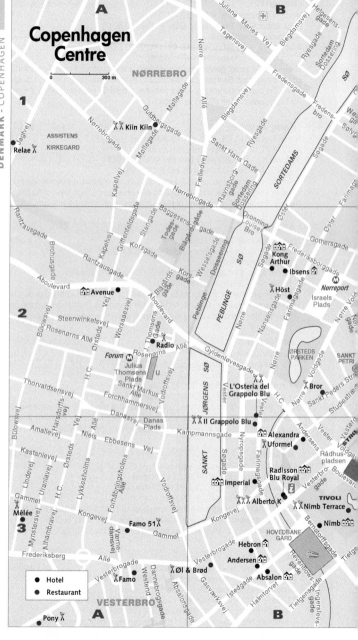

Copenhagen Centre

NØRREBRO

0 — 300 m

A

1

ASSISTENS
KIRKEGARD

Relae ✗

✗✗ Kiin Kiin

2

Avenue

Radio

Forum Ⓜ
Julius
Thomsens
Plads
Sankt Markus
Allé

Kong
Arthur
Ibsens

Höst

Nørreport Ⓜ
Israels
Plads

ØRSTEDS
PARKEN

SANKT
PETRI

L'Osteria del
Grappolo Blu

Bror

Il Grappolo Blu

Alexandra
Uformel

Rådhus
pladsen

Imperial

Radisson
Blu Royal

3

Mêlée ✗

Famo 51 ✗

Alberto K

Nimb Terrace

Nimb

TIVOLI

HOVEDBANE
GÅRD

Hebron

Andersen

ØI & Brød

Famo ✗

Absalon

● Hotel
● Restaurant

VESTERBRO

Pony ✗

B

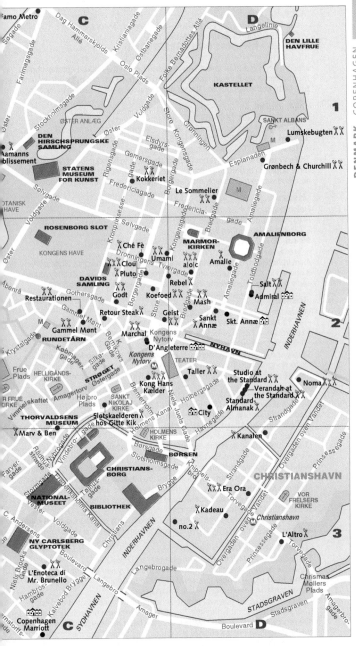

amo Metro

Spgade

Farimagsgade

C

Dag Hammarskjölds Allé

Kristianiagade

Osloanegade

Oslo Plads

Stockholmsgade

ØSTER ANLÆG

Øster

Elsdyrsgade

Gemersgade

Rigensgade

Gade

Fredericiagade

Sølvgade

Voldgade

Stockholmsgade

D

Folke Bernadottes Allé

Langelinie

DEN LILLE HAVFRUE

KASTELLET

1

Grönningen

SANKT ALBANS

M

Lumskebugten ✂

Esplanaden

Grønbech & Churchill ✂ ✂

DEN HIRSCHSPRUNGSKE SAMLING

✗ amanns blissement

STATENS MUSEUM FOR KUNST

Kokkeriet

Le Sommelier ✂

Store Kongensgade

Bredgade

Amaliegade

Fredericia-gade

M

OTANISK HAVE

Voldgade

Øster

Abenrå

ROSENBORG SLOT

KONGENS HAVE

Sølvgade

Kronprinsesse

Kronprinsensgade

Dronningens Tværgade

✗ Ché Fè

Umami

✗✗ Clou

✗ Pluto

MARMOR-KIRKEN

aloc

Rebel ✗

AMALIENBORG

Toldbodgade

Amalie

Amaliegade

Salt ✗✗

Admiral 🏠🏠

DAVIDS SAMLING

Gothersgade

Restaurationen

Godt

Koefoed ✗✗

Mash

✗✗

Gammel Mønt

M

Gammel Mønt ✗✗

RUNDETÅRN

Retour Steak ✗

Store

Geist ✗✗

Sankt ✗ Annæ

Skt. Annæ 🏠🏠

Marchal

Kongens Nytorv

NYHAVN

INDERHAVNEN

2

Krystalgade

Købmager-gade

Silke-gade

Bennikows

D'Angleterre 🏠🏠

Kongens Nytorv

M

TEATER

Frue Plads

HELLIGÅNDS-KIRKE

STRØGET

Østergade

Højbro

Amagertorv

Taller ✗✗

Studio at the Standard ✗✗

Noma ✗✗✗

Strandgade

R FRUE KIRKE

Vimmelskaftet

Kong Hans Kælder

Holbergsgade

Verandah at the Standard ✗

THORVALDSENS MUSEUM

✗ Marv & Ben

Højbro Plads

SANKT NIKOLAJ KIRKE

Niels Juels Gade

Standard Almanak ✗

🏠🏠 City

Slotskælderen hos Gitte Kik

Holmens Kanal

Havnegade

✗ Kanalen

Overgaden oven Vandet

Prinsessegade

Farver-gade

Vindebro

HOLMENS KIRKE

Børsgade

BØRSEN

Slotsholmsgade

Brygge

Strandgade

CHRISTIANSHAVN

Stormgade

CHRISTIANS-BORG

Frederiksholms Kanal

BIBLIOTEK

Torvegade

Overgaden oven Vandet

✗✗✗ Era Ora

VOR FRELSERS KIRKE

NATIONAL-MUSEET

Vester Voldgade

C. Andersens

Christians

✗ Kadeau

M Christianshavn

Overgaden oven Vandet

3

NY CARLSBERG GLYPTOTEK

Niels Brocks Gade

Boulevard

✗✗ L'Enoteca di Mr. Brunello

Hambros-gade

Langebro

INDERHAVNEN

no.2 ✗

Langebrogade

Amager

L'Altro ✗

Torvegade

Amagerbro-gade

Christmas Møllers Plads

🏠🏠

rnstorffs

Copenhagen Marriott

C

SYDHAVNEN

Kalvebod Brygge

STADSGRAVEN

Stadsgraven

Boulevard

D

DENMARK - COPENHAGEN

City

Peder Skrams Gade 24 ⊠ 1054 K – Ⓜ Kongens Nytorv — Plan: **D2**
– ℰ 33 13 06 66 – www.hotelcity.dk
81 rm 🖵 – †895/1995 DKK ††1195/2295 DKK
• Business • Traditional • Stylish •

Modern hotel in a quiet street between the city and the docks. Bedrooms boast monochrome Jan Persson jazz photos and Jacobsen armchairs. Designer furniture features throughout and there's an eye-catching water feature in the lobby.

Skt. Annæ

Sankt Annæ Plads 18-20 ⊠ 1250 V — Plan: **D2**
– Ⓜ Kongens Nytorv – ℰ 33 96 20 00 – www.hotelsanktannae.dk
154 rm – †1045/1945 DKK ††1295/2295 DKK – 🖵 155 DKK – 1 suite
• Business • Townhouse • Cosy •

Three Victorian townhouses not far from the bustling harbourside of Nyhavn. Ask for a 'Superior' bedroom for more space and quiet; Room 601 is the best – it's accessed via the roof terrace and has its own balcony overlooking the rooftops.

Hebron

Helgolandsgade 4 ⊠ 1653 V — Plan: **B3**
– Ⓜ København Hovedbane Gård – ℰ 33 31 69 06 – www.hebron.dk
– Closed 22 December-3 January
99 rm 🖵 – †700/1700 DKK ††900/1900 DKK – 2 suites
• Traditional • Family • Functional •

A smart hotel behind a Victorian façade – this was one of the city's biggest when it opened in 1899 and some original features still remain. There's a comfy lounge and a grand breakfast room; well-kept bedrooms range in shape and size.

Ibsens

Vendersgade 23 ⊠ 1363 K – Ⓜ Nørreport — Plan: **B2**
– ℰ 33 13 19 13 – www.arthurhotels.dk
118 rm 🖵 – †880/2445 DKK ††1230/2820 DKK
• Historic • Family • Personalised •

Simply and brightly furnished hotel with a relaxed, bohemian feel: the little sister to Kong Arthur. The small bar serves breakfast, as well as complimentary drinks from 5-6pm. Bedrooms are well-kept – 'Tiny' really are compact.

Geranium (Rasmus Kofoed)

Per Henrik Lings Allé 4 (8th Fl), Parken National Stadium (Parken National Stadium) (3 km via Dag Hammarask jölds Allé C1) ⊠ 2100
– ℰ 69 96 00 20 – www.geranium.dk – Closed 2 weeks Christmas, Sunday-Tuesday and lunch Wednesday
Menu 1800 DKK – *(booking essential) (surprise menu only)*
• Innovative • Design • Elegant •

With its panoramic park views, this luxurious restaurant feels as if it is inviting the outside in, yet it's unusually located on the 8th floor of the National Football Stadium. Modern techniques and the finest organic and biodynamic ingredients are used to create beautiful, pure and balanced dishes. The chefs invite you into the kitchen for one of the courses.
→ Dill stones with horseradish cream. Chicken with cabbage, pickled pine and chicken skin sauce. Wood sorrel and sweet woodruff crème.

Noma (René Redzepi)

Strandgade 93 ⊠ 1401 K – Ⓜ Christianshavn – ℰ 32 96 32 97 — Plan: **D2**
– www.noma.dk – Closed Christmas-New Year, Sunday and Monday
Menu 1700 DKK – *(booking essential) (set menu only)*
• Innovative • Design • Fashionable •

A converted harbourside warehouse is home to this understated and supremely stylish restaurant where the 75+ staff provide charming and highly attentive service. Innovation and creativity is at the heart of everything they do and the 17 beautifully crafted courses are stimulating, original and memorable. It is closing at the end of 2016 and moving to an urban farm.
→ Flower tart. Cabbage and bone marrow. Rhubarb and sheep's milk yoghurt.

XxX **a|o|c**

罍 ⇔

Plan: **D2**

Dronningens Tvaergade 2 ✉ *1302 K*
– ⓜ *Kongens Nytorv* – ℰ *33 11 11 45* – *www.restaurantaoc.dk*
– *Closed July, Christmas, Easter, Sunday and Monday*
Menu 1000/1400 DKK – *(dinner only) (set menu only)*
• Modern • Elegant • Romantic •

A spacious, simply decorated restaurant in the vaults of an eye-catching 17C former seafarers building close to Nyhavn harbour and the Royal Palace; owned and run by an experienced sommelier. Skilful, well-judged and, at times, playful cooking has a Danish heart and shows great originality as well as a keen eye for detail, flavour and texture.
→ Baked onion with elderflower and caviar. Breast of pigeon with cherries and marrow sauce. Burnt Jerusalem artichoke, brown butter ice cream and malt.

XxX **Kong Hans Kælder**

罍 ⇔

Plan: **C2**

Vingaardsstræde 6 ✉ *1070 K* – ⓜ *Kongens Nytorv*
– ℰ *33 11 68 68* – *www.konghans.dk* – *Closed 18 July-15 August,*
15 February-1 March, 24-26 December, Sunday and Monday
Menu 1400 DKK – Carte 1040/2510 DKK – *(dinner only) (booking essential)*
• French classic • Elegant • Intimate •

An intimate, historic restaurant in a beautiful vaulted Gothic cellar in the heart of the city. Classic French cooking uses luxury ingredients and has rich flavours, with signature dishes like Danish Black lobster. There's a 7 course tasting menu and Gueridon trolleys add a theatrical element to proceedings.
→ Lobster with fava beans and sauce nage. Veal sweetbreads, hazelnuts and brown butter. Blueberry sorbet, white chocolate and liquorice.

XxX **Era Ora**

罍 ⬚

Plan: **D3**

Overgaden neden Vandet 33B ✉ *1414 K*
– ⓜ *Christianshavn* – ℰ *32 54 06 93* – *www.era-ora.dk* – *Closed 24-26 December, 1 January, Easter Monday and Sunday*
Menu 498/950 DKK – *(booking essential) (set menu only)*
• Italian • Elegant • Intimate •

A passionately run restaurant on a quaint cobbled street next to the canal; inside it's grand, with high ceilings, a deep red colour scheme and an air of formality. The set menu covers all regions of Italy and the well-presented, modern dishes use top quality Italian produce in vibrant flavour combinations.
→ Lobster with watermelon and mint. Quail with beets, truffle and polenta. Vin Santo cream with almonds and apricots.

XxX **Clou** (Jonathan Berntsen)

ㅤ ㅤ ㅤㅤㅤㅤ ㅤㅤ ㅤ ㅤ ㅤ ㅤ ㅤ ㅤ &

Plan: **C2**

Borgergade 16 ✉ *1300 K* – ⓜ *Kongens Nytorv*
– ℰ *36 16 30 00* – *www.restaurant-clou.dk* – *Closed first 2 weeks August,*
2 weeks late December-early January, Sunday and Monday
Menu 900/1700 DKK – Carte 450/585 DKK – *(dinner only) (booking essential)*
• Modern • Intimate • Neighbourhood •

A comfortable, intimate restaurant set over three converted shops, with views into the kitchen from the street. Choose between 3, 5 or 7 course set menus and an à la carte: dishes are modern, attractive and inventive, with interesting textures and flavours, and accompanying wine matches. Service is assured.
→ Scallops with caviar. Lobster with veal sweetbreads, morels and coffee. Sweet tomato salad with black olives, basil and goat's milk mozzarella.

XxX **Mielcke & Hurtigkarl**

Runddel 1 (2 km via Veseterbrogade and Frederiksberg Allé A 3) ✉ *2000 C*
– ℰ *38 34 84 36* – *www.mhcph.com* – *Closed Christmas-New Year, Sunday and Monday*
Menu 800/950 DKK – *(dinner only) (booking essential)*
• Innovative • Elegant • Exotic •

Charming 1744 orangery with a fire-lit terrace, set in a delightful spot in Frederiksberg Gardens. The walls are painted with garden scenes and there are backing tracks of birdsong. The ambitious, modern set menus use lots of herbs and vegetables from the gardens. Service is wonderfully attentive.

DENMARK - COPENHAGEN

XxX **Alberto K** – Radisson Blu Royal Hotel ← 🖭 **P**

Hammerichsgade 1 ⊠ 1611 V Plan: **B3**
– 🅜 København Hovedbane Gård – 𝒞 33 42 61 61 – www.alberto-k.dk
– Closed 18 July-8 August, Easter, Christmas, Sunday and bank holidays
Menu 750/950 DKK *– (dinner only) (set menu only)*
• Modern • Formal • Elegant •

Located on the 20th floor of the Radisson Blu Royal and named after its first GM. It has a 1960s inspired, designer interior and offers stunning city views. Monthly set menus offer modern interpretations of classic dishes.

XX **Kiin Kiin** 🖭 ⇔ 🕼

⌘ *Guldbergsgade 21 ⊠ 2200 N – 𝒞 35 35 75 55* Plan: **A1**
– www.kiin.dk – Closed 24-27 December
Menu 495/925 DKK *– (dinner only) (booking essential) (set menu only)*
• Thai • Exotic • Intimate •

A charming restaurant, whose name means 'come and eat'. Start with refined versions of street food in the atmospheric lounge, then head for the tasteful dining room decorated with golden Buddhas and fresh flowers. Menus offer modern, personal interpretations of Thai dishes with vibrant flavour combinations.
→ Red curry with lobster. Beef with oyster sauce and ginger. "Flowers of Thailand".

XX **Studio at the Standard** (Torsten Vildgaard) 🖭

⌘ *Havnegade 44 ⊠ 1058 K – 🅜 Kongens Nytorv* Plan: **D2**
– 𝒞 72 14 88 08 – www.thestandardcph.dk – Closed 11 July-2 August,
19 December-2 January, Monday and Sunday
Menu 450/1050 DKK *– (dinner only and lunch Thursday-Friday) (booking essential) (set menu only)*
• Creative • Fashionable • Design •

A showcase restaurant on the top floor of The Standard; sit at the counter to watch the team at work. Dishes are brought to the table by both the charming serving team and the passionate chefs. Classic flavours and modern techniques intertwine in creative, often playful dishes – and ingredients are top notch.
→ Poached turbot, grilled peas and elderflower sabayon. Glazed deer with beetroot and truffle. Green strawberries with woodruff and sweet spiced bread.

XX **formel B** (Kristian Møller) 🐝 🖭 ⇔

⌘ *Vesterbrogade 182-184, Frederiksberg (2 km on Vesterbrogade A3)*
⊠ 1800 C – 𝒞 33 25 10 66 – www.formelb.dk – Closed 21 December-
5 January and Sunday
Menu 390/780 DKK *– (dinner only) (booking essential)*
• Modern • Fashionable • Design •

Friendly staff create a relaxed environment at this appealing, modern restaurant with its tree pictures and stark dark wood branches; ask for a table by the kitchen on the lower level if you want to get close to the action. Complex and original small plates are created with an assured and confident touch.
→ Langoustines with carrot purée and Danish vegetables. Turbot with parsley, garlic sauce and braised veal tails. Sea buckthorn "en surprise".

XX **Kokkeriet** ⇔

⌘ *Kronprinsessegade 64 ⊠ 1306 K – 𝒞 33 15 27 77* Plan: **C1**
– www.kokkeriet.dk – Closed 24-26 December, 1 January and Sunday
Menu 800/1200 DKK *– (dinner only) (booking essential) (set menu only)*
• Modern • Intimate • Design •

Discreet corner restaurant with two narrow, atmospheric rooms decorated in grey and black, and a collection of contemporary Danish artwork on display. Confidently executed, original cooking offers flavoursome, modern interpretations of classic Danish dishes. Service is smooth and unobtrusive.
→ Fricassee of scallops. Pigeon with beets, mushroom purée and liquorice. Dehydrated carrots with carrot cake crumble and carrot & orange sorbet.

« SEULEMENT LE MEILLEUR »

GEORGES H.MUMM

G.H.MUMM

CHAMPAGNE

PLEASE DRINK RESPONSIBLY

DENMARK - COPENHAGEN

XX £3 **Marchal** – D'Angleterre Hotel
Kongens Nytorv 34 ⊠ 1050 K – Ⓜ Kongens Nytorv
– ☏ 33 12 00 95 – www.marchal.com
Menu 375 DKK (lunch) – Carte 440/820 DKK
Plan: **C2**
• Modern • Elegant • Romantic •
Stylish hotel restaurant overlooking the square and named after the man
who founded the hotel in 1755. Refined Nordic-style cooking has a classical
French base; menus offer a range of small plates – 3 is about the right amount,
or 4 if you're really hungry. Dinner also includes an extensive caviar collection.
➜ Sweetbreads with fermented rhubarb. Lobster with pickled butternut
squash and vanilla. Roasted cocoa powder ice cream with sheep's yoghurt
and lemon.

XX £3 **Grønbech & Churchill** (Rasmus Grønbech)
Esplanden 48/Amaliegade 49 ⊠ 1256 – ☏ 32213230
– www.gronbech-churchill.dk – Closed 3 weeks July-August, Christmas,
Easter and Sunday
Plan: **D1**
Menu 500/900 DKK – (dinner only and lunch March-December) (bookings
advisable at lunch)
• Modern • Intimate • Neighbourhood •
Set below pavement level in a lovely 19C building, this ultra-chic restaurant
comes with crisp linen, fine china, minimalist styling and views of the chefs in
the designer kitchen. Two set menus offer cleanly and confidently prepared
dishes with bold flavours. Relaxed service is courtesy of a young team.
➜ Lemon and grape spiced yellow beets with salted cod. Poussin with
peas, gooseberries, chervil and curry sauce. Rhubarb with hibiscus and
liquorice.

XX **Verandah at the Standard**
Havnegade 44 ⊠ 1058 K – Ⓜ Kongens Nytorv
– ☏ 72 14 88 08 – www.thestandardcph.dk – Closed 24-25 December, 1-
2 January, Sunday and Monday
Plan: **D2**
Menu 225/595 DKK – Carte 320/440 DKK – (booking advisable)
• Indian • Individual • Minimalist •
On the ground floor of an old harbourside customs house; dishes offer a vibrant
modern slant on authentic Indian recipes. If the weather is good then a table on
the terrace is a must – they even have a tandoor oven outside!

XX **Amass**
Refshalevej 153 (3 km via Torvgade and Prinsessgade D3) ⊠ 1432
– ☏ 43 58 43 30 – www.amassrestaurant.com – Closed February, 26 June-
4 July, 21-25 December,1-5 January, Sunday and Monday
Menu 395/795 DKK – (dinner only and lunch Friday-Saturday) (booking
essential)
• Danish • Minimalist • Individual •
Large restaurant just outside the city. It has an urban, industrial feel courtesy of
high graffitied concrete walls and huge windows overlooking the old docks. Prices and the authenticity of ingredients are key; cooking is modern Danish.

XX **Taller**
Tordenskjoldsgade 11 ⊠ 1055 K – Ⓜ Kongens Nytorv
– ☏ 72 14 08 71 – www.restaurant-taller.dk – Closed 20 December-
13 January and Sunday-Tuesday
Plan: **D2**
Menu 575 DKK (lunch)/875 DKK – (dinner only and lunch Friday-Saturday)
(booking essential)
• Other world kitchens • Individual •
Colourful and creative modern interpretations of Venezuelan dishes are served
at this stylish restaurant, whose name translates as 'workshop' in Spanish – get a
seat at the open kitchen counter to see the chef-owner at work close up.

XX

Frederiks Have

Smallegade 41, (entrance on Virginiavej) (1.5 km. via Gammel Kongevej A3) ✉ 2000 F – Ⓜ Frederiksberg – ✆ 38 88 33 35 – www.frederikshave.dk – Closed Christmas, Easter and Sunday
Menu 295/395 DKK – Carte 330/545 DKK
• Danish • Neighbourhood • Family •

Sweet neighbourhood restaurant hidden just off the main street in a residential area. Sit inside – surrounded by flowers and vivid local art – or outside, on the terrace. Well-presented, modern Danish dishes have a classical base; tasty sweet and sour combinations feature. The set lunches are great value.

XX

Umami

Store Kongensgade 59 ✉ 1264 – Ⓜ Kongens Nytorv Plan: **C/D2**
– ✆ 33 38 75 00 – www.restaurantumami.dk – Closed 24 December-2 January, Easter Monday and Sunday
Menu 650 DKK – Carte 350/480 DKK – *(dinner only)*
• Asian • Fashionable • Design •

Attractive building with a large cocktail bar and lounge on the ground floor, and an elegant upper level boasting a stylish, atmospheric dining room, a sushi counter and an open kitchen. Cooking is Japanese, with a European slant.

XX

Geist

Kongens Nytorv 8 ✉ 1050 K – Ⓜ Kongens Nytorv Plan: **C2**
– ✆ 33133713 – www.restaurantgeist.dk – Closed 23-26 December and 1 July
Carte 340/455 DKK – *(dinner only)*
• Modern • Design • Trendy •

A lively, fashionable restaurant with an open kitchen and a sexy nightclub vibe, set in a striking red-brick property with floor to ceiling windows – in a superb spot overlooking the square. Cleverly crafted dishes display a light touch; 4 should suffice.

XX

Restaurationen

Møntergade 19 ✉ 1116 K – Ⓜ Kongens Nytorv Plan: **C2**
– ✆ 33 14 94 95 – www.restaurationen.com – Closed 3 July-29 August, 20 December-4 January, 20-28 March, Sunday and Monday
Menu 515 DKK – *(dinner only)*
• Classic • Formal • Romantic •

Celebrating 25 years in 2016, this restaurant is run by a well-known chef who also owns the next door wine bar. Modern Danish dishes are created with quality local produce. The dining room displays some impressive vibrant modern art.

XX

Koefoed

Landgreven 3 ✉ 1301 K – Ⓜ Kongens Nytorv Plan: **C2**
– ✆ 56 48 22 24 – www.restaurant-koefoed.dk – Closed 22 December-6 January, Sunday and Monday
Menu 300/600 DKK – Carte 450/540 DKK – *(booking essential at dinner)*
• Innovative • Intimate • Romantic •

An intimate collection of rooms in a former coal cellar, where everything from the produce to the glassware celebrates the island of Bornholm. Modern Danish cooking with deconstructed smørrebrød at lunch and an impressive range of bordeaux.

XX

Godt

Gothersgade 38 ✉ 1123 K – Ⓜ Kongens Nytorv Plan: **C2**
– ✆ 33 15 21 22 – www.restaurant-godt.dk – Closed mid-July to mid-August, Christmas-New Year, Easter, Sunday, Monday and bank holidays
Menu 520/680 DKK – *(dinner only) (set menu only)*
• Classic • Friendly • Family •

Stylish restaurant seating just 20, where old WWII shells act as candle holders. Traditional French and European daily menus – of 3, 4 and 5 courses – are formed around the latest market produce. Service is particularly friendly.

XX **Nimb Terrasse**   ☆ ⇔

Vesterbrogade 3 ✉ 1630 V   Plan: **B3**
– **Ⓜ** *København Hovedbane Gård – ☏ 33 75 07 50 – www.nimb.dk*
*– Closed 3 January-1 April, 20 September-9 October, 1-14 November and
Saturday-Sunday lunch*
Menu 385 DKK – Carte 385/465 DKK
• Modern • Elegant • Romantic •

Set close to the Nimb hotel, in the beautiful Tivoli Gardens, with a lovely terrace
and an outdoor BBQ area. The split-level interior is light and airy with a chic,
contemporary feel. Ambitious modern dishes use Scandinavian produce.

XX **Salt** – at Admiral Hotel   ☆ **P**

Toldbodgade 24-28 ✉ 1253 K – **Ⓜ** *Kongens Nytorv*   Plan: **D2**
– ☏ 33 74 14 44 – www.salt.dk
Menu 325 DKK – Carte 265/655 DKK
• Modern • Design • Fashionable •

A bright and airy hotel restaurant; its vast old timber beams a reminder of the
building's previous life as a granary and its harbourside terrace, a great spot in
the summer months. Extensive menus offer interesting modern cooking.

XX **L' Enoteca di Mr. Brunello**   🕸

Rysensteensgade 16 ✉ 1564 K – ☏ 33 114 720   Plan: **C3**
*– www.lenoteca.dk – Closed 10 July-15 August, Easter, Christmas, Sunday,
Monday and bank holidays*
Menu 450 DKK – Carte 405/490 DKK – *(dinner only)*
• Italian • Elegant • Neighbourhood •

Tucked away near the Tivoli Gardens and run by passionate, experienced
owners. Refined, classic Italian cooking uses good quality produce imported
from Italy. Good value all-Italian wine list with over 150 different Brunello di
Montalcinos.

XX **Gammel Mønt**

Gammel Mønt 41 ✉ 1117 K – **Ⓜ** *Kongens Nytorv*   Plan: **C2**
*– ☏ 33 15 10 60 – www.glmoent.dk – Closed July, 22 December-8 January,
Easter, Sunday, Monday and bank holidays*
Menu 395/565 DKK – Carte 355/855 DKK – *(lunch only and dinner Wed-
nesday-Friday)*
• Traditional • Cosy •

A part-timbered house in the heart of the city; dating back to 1739, it sports a
striking shade of deep terracotta. The menu celebrates Danish classics and
dishes are hearty, gutsy and reassuringly traditional; try the pickled herrings.

XX **Lumskebugten**   ☆ ⇔

Esplanaden 21 ✉ 1263 K – ☏ 33 15 60 29   Plan: **D1**
*– www.lumskebugten.dk – Closed 3 weeks July, Christmas, Easter, Sunday,
dinner Monday, Tuesday and bank holidays*
Menu 400/450 DKK – Carte 330/650 DKK
• Traditional • Cosy • Classic •

A restored quayside pavilion dating from 1854; the Royal Family occasionally
dine here. A series of small rooms are adorned with maritime memorabilia and
paintings. Local menus offer a wide selection of traditional fish dishes.

XX **Le Sommelier**   🕸 ⇔

Bredgade 63-65 ✉ 1260 K – ☏ 33 11 45 15   Plan: **D1**
*– www.lesommelier.dk – Closed Christmas and 31 December, Saturday
lunch and Sunday*
Menu 295/435 DKK – Carte 410/620 DKK
• French • Brasserie • Traditional •

Attractively refurbished brasserie in the heart of the Old Town, where French
wine posters and a superb wine list hint at their passion. The small à la carte
features classic French dishes and is supplemented by a daily set menu.

DENMARK - COPENHAGEN

XX **Alchemist** AC

Århusgade 22 (3.5 km via Dag Hammerskjölds Allé off Østerbrogade C1)
✉ 2100 – ℰ 31 26 76 02
– www.restaurant-alchemist.dk – Closed 19 December-6 January,
July-3 August and Sunday-Tuesday
Menu 2500 DKK – *(dinner only) (booking essential)*
• Innovative • Trendy • Individual •
The ambitious chef transports diners to another world in this all-encompassing culinary experience. Attentive staff, counter seating and dramatic music provide the setting. The exciting, highly original 45 course menu includes wines.

XX **Mash** 🕸 AC ⇔

Bredgade 20 ✉ *1260 K –* Ⓜ *Kongens Nytorv* Plan: **D2**
– ℰ 33 13 93 00 – www.mashsteak.dk – Closed Christmas and lunch
Saturday and Sunday
Carte 345/820 DKK – *(booking essential at dinner)*
• Meats and grills • Brasserie •
A smart, lively, American-style steakhouse with a trendy cocktail bar and aged meats on display; sit in the rear room with its red leather booths. Classic steak dishes come with a choice of sides and sauces. French and American wine list.

XX **Il Grappolo Blu**

Vester Farimagsgade 35 ✉ *1606 V* Plan: **B3**
– Ⓜ *Nørreport – ℰ 33 11 57 20 – www.igb.com*
– Closed July, Easter, Christmas, Sunday and Monday
Menu 450/750 DKK – Carte 380/445 DKK – *(dinner only)*
• Italian • Rustic • Elegant •
Cosy restaurant with dark panelling and ornate carvings. 8 & 14 course tasting menus: well-prepared, authentic Italian dishes include appealing antipasti and tasty pastas. Wine list features over 200 different Brunello di Montalcino's.

XX **L' Osteria del Grappolo Blu**

Vester Farimagsgade 37 ✉ *1606 V –* Ⓜ *Nørreport* Plan: **B2/3**
– ℰ 33 12 57 20 – www.osteria.dk – Closed July, Easter, Christmas, Sunday
and Monday
Menu 450/750 DKK – Carte 380/445 DKK – *(dinner only)*
• Italian • Friendly • Traditional •
The more informal counterpart to Il Grappolo Blu; a laid-back restaurant with smart 'osteria' styling. Authentic homemade dishes have their roots in southern Italy; breads, pastas and ice creams are made on the premises daily.

X **Relæ** (Christian Puglisi)
ⴥ
Jægersborggade 41 ✉ *2200 N* Plan: **A1**
– ℰ 36 96 66 09 – www.restaurant-relae.dk
– Closed January and Sunday-Tuesday
Menu 450/725 DKK – *(dinner only and lunch Friday- Saturday) (booking*
essential)
• Modern • Minimalist • Fashionable •
Book well in advance for a table at this simply styled restaurant, or grab a counter seat to watch the talented team in the open kitchen. There are 2 daily menus: one features meat and fish and one is vegetarian. Unfussy, flavourful dishes come in original combinations and make innovative use of vegetables.
→ Cod, kohlrabi and horseradish. Pork from Hindsholm, rye and buckwheat. Chanterelles, apples and granité.

X **Kadeau** (Nicolai Nørregaard)   ✧

Wildersgade 10B ✉ *1408 K –* Ⓜ *Christianshavn*   Plan: **D3**
– ✆ 33 25 22 23 – www.kadeau.dk – Closed 5 weeks July-August, 2 weeks
Christmas, 1 week Easter, Sunday and Monday
Menu 1500 DKK – *(dinner only and lunch Saturday) (booking essential)*
(set menu only)
• Modern • Design • Individual •
Intimate restaurant showcasing cuisine and ingredients from Bornholm island
(set just to the east of the mainland and from where the passionate owners ori-
ginate). Cooking is honest and interesting, with light, modern dishes featuring
well-balanced, flavoursome combinations and many texture variations. The
neighbouring bistro, Eldorado, offers a menu inspired by the owners' travels.
→ Kale and cabbage with fermented peas. Pork-neck with black garlic &
blackcurrant emulsion. Caramelised buttermilk and elderflower frozen pie.

X **Kanalen**   ⟨ 🏡 ✧ Ⓟ

Wilders Plads 2 ✉ *1403 K –* Ⓜ *Christianshavn*   Plan: **D3**
– ✆ 32 95 13 30 – www.restaurant-kanalen.dk – Closed 23-30 December,
1 January, Easter, Sunday and bank holidays
Menu 295/400 DKK – Carte 315/595 DKK – *(booking essential)*
• Danish • Bistro • Cosy •
Former Harbour Police office with a lovely terrace, in a delightful canalside setting. The dining room has a contemporary edge and French windows facing the
water. The chefs in the tiny open kitchen prepare a well-balanced Danish menu
with light French and Asian touches, which is served by a charming team.

X **Øl & Brød**

Viktoriagade 6 ✉ *1655*   Plan: **B3**
– Ⓜ *København Hovedbane Gård – ✆ 33 31 44 22 – www.ologbrod.com*
– Closed Monday
Menu 400/600 DKK (dinner) – Carte lunch 250/400 DKK – *(lunch only and*
dinner Thursday-Saturday) (booking essential)
• Modern • Neighbourhood • Cosy •
A cosy, hip neighbourhood restaurant where the emphasis is as much on aqua-
vit and craft beers as it is on the refined and flavourful modern food. Lunch sees
smørrebrød taken to a new level, while dinner offers a choice of 3 or 6 courses.

X **Rebel**

Store Kongensgade 52 ✉ *1264 K*   Plan: **C/D2**
– Ⓜ *Kongens Nytorv – ✆ 33 32 32 09 – www.restaurantrebel.dk – Closed*
Christmas-New Year, Sunday and Monday
Menu 300 DKK – *(dinner only)*
• Modern • Bistro • Fashionable •
Located in a busy part of the city; a simply decorated, split-level restaurant with
closely set tables and a buzzy vibe – sit on the more atmospheric ground floor,
which looks into the kitchen. Choose 3 or 4 dishes from the list of 11; cooking is
modern, refined and relies on Danish produce.

X **Standard - Almanak**   🏡

Havnegade 44 ✉ *1058 K –* Ⓜ *Kongens Nytorv*   Plan: **D2**
– ✆ 72 14 88 08 – www.thestandardcph.dk – Closed Christmas and New
Year
Menu 155/350 DKK – Carte approx. 400 DKK – *(bookings advisable at*
dinner)
• Modern • Fashionable •
On the ground floor of an impressive art deco former customs building, in a
waterfront setting. At lunch, the emphasis is on smørrebrød, while dinner sees
a concise menu of updated Danish classics. An open kitchen adds to the
theatre.
  ⛛ **Studio at the Standard • Verandah at the Standard** – See restaurant listing

✗ Radio

Plan: **A2**

*Julius Thomsens Gade 12 ☒ 1632 V – ☻ Forum
– ☏ 25102733 – www.restaurantradio.dk – Closed 3 weeks summer,
2 weeks Christmas-New Year, Sunday and Monday*
Menu 300/400 DKK – *(dinner only and lunch Friday-Saturday) (booking
essential) (set menu only)*
• Modern • Minimalist • Neighbourhood •

An informal restaurant with an unfussy urban style, wood-clad walls and cool
anglepoise lighting. Oft-changing set menus feature full-flavoured, good value
dishes and use organic ingredients grown in the chefs' nearby fields.

✗ 56°

*Krudtløbsvej 8 (2.5 km. via Torvgade, Prinsessgade and Refshalevej D3)
☒ 1439 K – ☏ 31 16 32 05 – www.restaurant56grader.dk – Closed
Christmas, Sunday dinner and Monday*
Menu 295/900 DKK
• Danish • Rustic • Romantic •

Sweet, rustic restaurant, unusually set within the 1.5m thick walls of a 17C gunpowder store. Flavoursome Danish cooking mixes modern and traditional elements and keeps Nordic produce to the fore. The large garden is a hit.

✗ L'Altro

Plan: **D3**

*Torvegade 62 ☒ 1400 K – ☻ Christianshavn
– ☏ 32 54 54 06 – www.laltro.dk – Closed 24 December and Sunday*
Menu 398/438 DKK – *(dinner only) (booking essential) (set menu only)*
• Italian • Intimate • Traditional •

The cosy sister of Era Ora, with a warm, rustic style; it celebrates 'la cucina de la
casa' – the homely Italian spirit of 'mama's kitchen'. Regularly changing set
menus feature tasty family recipes from Umbria and Tuscany; dishes are appealing and rely on good quality ingredients imported from Italy.

✗ Marv & Ben

Plan: **C2/3**

*Snaregade 4 ☒ 1205 K – ☻ Kongens Nytorv
– ☏ 33 91 01 91 – www.marvogben.dk – Closed Christmas, Sunday and Monday*
Menu 350 DKK – Carte 300/500 DKK – *(dinner only) (booking advisable)*
• Modern • Friendly • Bistro •

A simple, two-floored restaurant set down a cobbled street off the main tourist
track. Styling is stark and modern, with the kitchen on display behind a glass
wall. Gutsy, flavourful, well-crafted dishes focus on produce from the chefs'
own fields. Service is friendly and is sometimes by the chefs themselves.

✗ Enomania

*Vesterbrogade 187 (2.5 km via Vesterbrogade A3) ☒ 1800 C
– ☏ 33 23 60 80 – www.enomania.dk – Closed 9 July-
8 August, 23 December-2 January, 15-24 October, 11-20 February,
24-28 March, Saturday-Monday and bank holidays*
Menu 375 DKK – Carte 230/360 DKK – *(dinner only and lunch Thursday-
Friday) (booking essential)*
• Italian • Wine bar • Simple •

Simple, bistro-style restaurant near Frederiksberg Park – its name means 'Wine
Mania'. The wine cellar comes with a table for tasting and there's an excellent
list of over 600 bins, mostly from Piedmont and Burgundy. These are complemented by straightforward, tasty Italian dishes from a daily 4 course menu.

✗ Mêlée

Plan: **A3**

*Martensens Allé 16 ☒ 1828 C – ☻ Frederiksberg
– ☏ 35 13 11 34 – www.melee.dk – Closed 3 weeks July, 2 weeks
Christmas-New Year, Easter, Sunday and Monday*
Menu 395 DKK – Carte 305/430 DKK – *(dinner only) (booking essential)*
• French • Friendly • Bistro •

A bustling neighbourhood bistro with a friendly, laid-back atmosphere; run by
an experienced team. Modern, country-style cooking is French-based but has
Danish influences; menus might be concise but portions are generous and flavours are bold. An excellent range of wines from the Rhône Valley accompany.

mbox**DENMARK - COPENHAGEN**

✗ **Famo 51** ⚕
Gammel Kongevej 51 ✉ *1610 V –* ☎ *33 22 22 50*   Plan: **A3**
– www.famo.dk – Closed 2 weeks summer, Christmas and Sunday
Menu 400 DKK *– (dinner only) (booking essential)*
• Italian • Minimalist •
Laid-back restaurant with a modern bistro style and an intimate, two-tabled cellar. The extensive daily set menu offers rustic Italian dishes and relies on seasonal ingredients; on Fridays they only serve fish and shellfish.

✗ **Retour Steak**
Ny Østergade 21 ✉ *1101 –* Ⓜ *Kongens Nytorv*   Plan: **C2**
– ☎ *33 16 17 19 – www.retoursteak.dk*
Carte 240/595 DKK *– (dinner only) (booking essential)*
• Meats and grills • Bistro • Friendly •
A relaxed, informal restaurant with a stark white interior and contrasting black furnishings. A small menu offers simply prepared grills, good quality American rib-eye steaks and an affordable selection of wines.

✗ **Famo**
Saxogade 3 ✉ *1662 –* ☎ *33 23 22 50 – www.famo.dk*   Plan: **A3**
– Closed Christmas and early January
Menu 350 DKK *– (dinner only) (booking essential) (set menu only)*
• Italian • Bistro • Neighbourhood •
A modern, simply styled Italian restaurant serving rustic cooking. Extensive daily menus are presented orally: they offer a choice of 8 antipasti, followed by tasty homemade pastas, generous main courses and authentic desserts.

✗ **Ché Fè**
Borgergade 17a ✉ *1300 –* Ⓜ *Kongens Nytorv*   Plan: **C2**
– ☎ *33 11 17 21 – www.chefe.dk – Closed 21-27 December, 1 January, Easter Monday and 16 May*
Carte 395/445 DKK *– (dinner only) (booking essential)*
• Italian • Simple • Neighbourhood •
An unassuming façade conceals an appealing trattoria with pastel hues and coffee sack curtains. Menus offer authentic Italian classics, including homemade pastas; virtually all ingredients are imported from small, organic producers.

✗ **Aamanns Etablissement**
Øster Farimagsgade 12 ✉ *2100 Ø –* Ⓜ *Nørreport*   Plan: **C1**
– ☎ *35 55 33 10 – www.aamanns.dk – Closed last 2 weeks July, Christmas-New Year and dinner Sunday-Tuesday*
Menu 345/445 DKK – Carte 375/435 DKK *– (booking advisable)*
• Danish • Bistro •
Cosy, contemporary restaurant with cheery service and an informal atmosphere. Concise, seasonal menus blend traditional smørrebrød with more modern 'small plates'. The 4 and 6 course dinner menus come with wine pairings.

✗ **Kødbyens Fiskebar** 🛜 **P**
🈂 *Den Hvide Kødby, Flæsketorvet 100 (1 km via Halmtorvet B3)* ✉ *1711 V*
– ☎ *32 15 56 56 – www.fiskebaren.dk – Closed 24-26 December and 1 January*
Carte 305/540 DKK *– (dinner only)*
• Fish and seafood • Simple • Fashionable •
This buzzy, industrial-style restaurant is set, somewhat incongruously, in a former butcher's shop in a commercial meat market. Concise menus feature fresh, simply prepared seafood dishes which are based around the latest catch; oysters are a speciality. The terrace is a popular spot come summer.

151

X
(☺) **Pluto**   🏠

Borgergade 16 ✉ 1300 K – ⓂKongensNytorv   Plan: **C2**
– ℰ 33 16 00 16 – www.restaurantpluto.dk – Closed Sunday
Menu 450 DKK – Carte 350/545 DKK – *(dinner only)*
• Mediterranean • Bistro • Rustic •
An appealing restaurant in a residential area, with concrete pillars and an inten-
tionally 'unfinished' feel – sit at wooden tables, at the long metal bar or at com-
munal marble-topped tables. An enticing menu of small plates includes 'cheese'
and 'sweets' sections; cooking is rustic, unfussy and flavoursome.

X **Uformel**   🅰️🅲 ↔

Studiestraede 69 ✉ 1554 K   Plan: **B3**
– Ⓜ København Hovedbane Gård – ℰ 70 99 91 11 – www.uformel.dk
– Closed 23-26 December and 1 January
Carte approx. 500 DKK – *(dinner only) (booking essential)*
• Modern • Fashionable • Trendy •
The informal sister of Formel B, with gold table-tops, black cutlery, a smart open
kitchen and a cocktail bar (a lively spot at the weekend!) Dishes are tasting pla-
tes and all are the same price; 4-6 is about the right amount.

X **Pony**

Vesterbrogade 135 ✉ 1620 V – ℰ 33 22 10 00   Plan: **A3**
– www.ponykbh.dk – Closed 24-28 December and Monday
Menu 500 DKK – Carte 360/430 DKK – *(dinner only) (booking essential)*
• Danish • Bistro • Neighbourhood •
Neighbourhood restaurant with chatty service and a buzzy vibe: sit at high
tables opposite the kitchen or on retro seats in the small dining room. Choose
4 of the tasty, original dishes; refined, modern cooking has a 'nose-to-tail'
approach.

X **no.2**   ⇐ 🏠 🅰️🅲

Nicolai Eigtveds Gade 32 ✉ 1402 C   Plan: **D3**
– Ⓜ Christianshaven – ℰ 33 11 11 68 – www.nummer2.dk – Closed
Christmas, Easter and Sunday
Menu 250 DKK (weekday lunch)/450 DKK – Carte 245/405 DKK
• Modern • Design • Fashionable •
Set among smart offices and apartments on the edge of the dock, is this elegant
restaurant; the sister to a|o|c. Fresh, flavoursome small plates focus on quality
Danish ingredients – be sure to try the cheeses and cured hams.

X **Höst**   ↔

Nørre Farimagsgade 41 ✉ 1364 K – Ⓜ Nørreport   Plan: **B2**
– ℰ 89 93 84 09 – www.cofoco.dk/en/restaurants/hoest – Closed
24 December and 1 January
Menu 295/395 DKK – Carte 375/465 DKK – *(dinner only)*
• Modern • Friendly • Rustic •
Busy neighbourhood bistro with fun staff and a lively atmosphere; sit in the Gar-
den Room. The great value monthly set menu comprises 3 courses but comes
with lots of extras. Cooking is modern Nordic, seasonal and boldly flavoured.

X **Bror**   🅰️🅲
(☺)
Skt Peders Strade 24A ✉ 1453 K – Ⓜ Nørreport   Plan: **B2**
– ℰ 32 17 59 99 – www.restaurantbror.dk – Closed 1-22 January, 23-
26 December, Monday and Tuesday
Menu 375/575 DKK – *(dinner only) (booking essential) (set menu only)*
• Regional/country • Bistro • Rustic •
Set on a narrow street in an older part of the city, this simple split-level bistro is
run by two keen young chefs and a friendly team. Set 4 course menu of rustic
bistro dishes; extra courses can be added as desired. Alternatively plump for the
no-choice 5 course menu, which comes with additional snacks.

X **Famo Metro**　　　　　　　　　　　　　　　　　　　　　　　　AC

Øster Søgade 114 ✉ *2100 Ø*　　　　　　　　　　　　Plan: C1
– ℰ 35 55 66 30 – www.famo.dk
– Closed 3 weeks summer, Christmas and Sunday
Menu 400 DKK – *(dinner only)*
• Italian • Bistro • Simple •
A neighbourhood restaurant with floor to ceiling windows, overlooking Sor-
tedams Lake. Daily menu comprises antipasti, primi piatti, il secondo and
dolce; classic Italian dishes are authentic and full of flavour. Helpful, friendly
service.

X **Gorilla**　　　　　　　　　　　　　　　　　　　　　　　　　　🛋

Flæsketorvet 63 (1 km via Halmtorvet B3) ✉ *1711 V – ℰ 33 33 83 30*
*– www.restaurantgorilla.dk – Closed 23-25 December, Sunday and bank
holidays*
Carte 160/610 DKK – *(dinner only)*
• Modern • Brasserie • Simple •
A buzzy, canteen-style restaurant in the meatpacking district; the stone floor,
zinc ducting and large windows create an industrial feel. The menu offers
something for everyone; dishes are well-presented, tasty and designed for
sharing.

SMØRREBRØD *The following list of simpler restaurants and
cafés/bars specialise in Danish open sandwiches and are generally open
from 10.00am to 4.00pm.*

X **Sankt Annæ**　　　　　　　　　　　　　　　　　　　　　🛋 ⬚

Sankt Annæ Plads 12 ✉ *1250 K –* Ⓜ *Kongens Nytorv*　　Plan: D2
– ℰ 33 12 54 97 – www.restaurantsanktannae.dk
*– Closed 18 July - 7 August, Christmas-New Year, Sunday
and bank holidays*
Carte 224/368 DKK – *(lunch only) (booking essential)*
• Smørrebrød • Cosy •
An attractive terraced building with a traditional, rather quaint interior. Seasonal
à la carte and a daily blackboard menu: prices can vary so check before orde-
ring. The lobster and shrimp – fresh from the local fjords – are a hit.

X **Amalie**

Amaliegade 11 ✉ *1256 –* Ⓜ *Kongens Nytorv*　　　　Plan: D2
*– ℰ 33 12 88 10 – www.restaurantamalie.dk – Closed 2 weeks July,
24 December-4 January and Sunday*
Menu 258 DKK – Carte 173/285 DKK – *(lunch only) (booking essential)*
• Smørrebrød • Intimate • Rustic •
Charming 18C townhouse by Amalienborg Palace, with two tiny, cosy rooms
filled with old paintings and elegant porcelain. The authentic Danish menu
offers a large choice of herring, salmon and salads. Service is warm and welcoming.

X **Slotskælderen hos Gitte Kik**

Fortunstræ 4 ✉ *1065 K –* Ⓜ *Kongens Nytorv*　　　　Plan: C2
*– ℰ 33 11 15 37 – www.slotskaelderen.dk – Closed July, 24-26 December,
Sunday, Monday and bank holidays*
Menu 200 DKK – Carte 206/310 DKK – *(lunch only) (booking essential)*
• Smørrebrød • Family • Traditional •
Set in a 1797 building and family-run since 1910; this established restaurant sets
the benchmark for this type of cuisine. The rustic inner is filled with portraits and
city scenes. Go to the counter to see the full selection of smørrebrød.

AT NORDHAVN North : 3 km by Østbanegade and Road 2

XX Paustian ← 🏠 **P**

Kalkbrænderiløbskaj 2 ☒ 2100 Ø – ℰ 39 18 55 01
– www.restaurantpaustian.dk – Closed Christmas and New Year
Carte 345/418 DKK – *(lunch only) (booking advisable)*
• Danish • Fashionable • Design •

A modern restaurant with an open kitchen and an airy, stylish feel, set in an impressive harbourside building designed by renowned architect Jørn Utzon. Fresh, tasty, traditional Danish cooking, with brunch available at weekends.

AT KLAMPENBORG North : 13 km by Østanegade and Road 2

XX Den Røde Cottage (Anita Klemensen and Lars Thomsen) 🏠

ॐ *Strandvejen 550 ☒ 2930 – ℰ 39 90 46 14* ⇔
– www.denroedecottage.dk – Closed 25 December-22 February and Sunday October-May
Menu 525/875 DKK – *(dinner only) (booking essential)*
• Danish • Design •

Attractive former Forestry Officer's house dating back to 1881; built on the site of an old plantation. The small, romantic dining room is set with Royal Copenhagen porcelain and a lovely terrace offers partial sea views. The talented team offer monthly Nordic menus, which are informed by top seasonal produce.
→ Danish oysters with cabbage and horseradish. Veal sweetbread with potato, salted cucumber and watercress. Wild strawberries, rhubarb and vanilla.

X Den Gule Cottage ← 🏠

Strandvejen 506 ☒ 2930 – ℰ 39 64 06 91 – www.dengulecottage.dk
– Closed Christmas-22 February and Monday-Wednesday October-May
Menu 350 DKK – Carte 300/375 DKK – *(booking advisable)*
• Danish • Inn • Minimalist •

Lovely 1844 cottage facing the beach; from the same team as Den Røde. Sit in one of two tiny, simply decorated rooms or on the large terrace with sea views. Choose from an unfussy menu of five main dishes, salads and cheese plates.

AT SØLLERØD North : 20 km by Tagensvej (take the train to Holte then taxi)
- ☒ 2840 Holte

XxX Søllerød Kro 🕸 🏠 ⇔ **P**

ॐ *Søllerødvej 35 ☒ 2840 – ℰ 45 80 25 05 – www.soelleroed-kro.dk – Closed 3 weeks July, 1 week February, Easter, Sunday dinner, Monday and Tuesday*
Menu 375/995 DKK – Carte 715/1015 DKK
• Modern • Inn • Individual •

Characterful 17C thatched inn, in a truly picturesque setting, with three small but stylish dining rooms and a delightful courtyard terrace. The superb wine list features plenty of burgundy and champagne. Choose from an array of menus which offer classically based dishes with deep, clear flavours.
→ Caviar 'en surprise'. Lobster ragout with new onions and stuffed morels. Gourmandise desserts.

AT KASTRUP AIRPORT Southeast : 10 km by Amager Boulevard

Hilton Copenhagen Airport ☆ ← ℩₆ ⓢ 🖥 & 🅼 🏋 🚗

Ellehammersvej 20 ☒ 2770 – Ⓜ København Lufthavn – ℰ 32 50 15 01
– www.copenhagen.hilton.com
378 rm – ♦1295/2995 DKK ♦♦1295/2995 DKK – ☲ 225 DKK – 5 suites
• Business • Luxury • Modern •

A smart, modern business hotel accessed from the airport via a glass walkway. Spacious, well-maintained bedrooms have excellent sound-proofing and offer good views from the higher floors. Relax in the Asian-inspired Ni'mat Spa. Horizon offers everything from sandwiches and grills to Nordic specialities.

AARHUS

AARHUS

Population: 324 000

WeEm/Westend61 RM/age fotostock

Known as the world's smallest big city, Denmark's second city is a vibrant, versatile place, yet has the charm of a small town. It was originally founded by the Vikings in the 8th century and has been an important trading centre ever since. It's set on the Eastern edge of Jutland and is the country's main port; lush forests surround it, and there are beautiful beaches to the north and south. It's easy to enjoy the great outdoors, while also benefiting from the advantages of urban life.

There's plenty to see and do, and most of it is within walking distance: the city centre is awash with shops – from big chains to quirky boutiques – as well as museums, bars and restaurants, and the student population contributes to its youthful feel. The most buzzing area is Aboulevarden; a pedestrianized street which runs alongside the river, lined with clubs and cafés. Cultural activities are also high on the agenda of the European Capital of Culture 2017: visit the 12th century Cathedral and the ARoS Art Museum with its colourful rooftop panorama; witness the 2000 year old Grauballe man on display at the Moesgaard prehistoric museum; or step back in time at Den Gamle By. This is not a place that stands still and bold redevelopment projects are reshaping the cityscape, with shiny new apartment and office blocks springing up around the harbour.

AARHUS IN...

➜ **ONE DAY**
ARoS Art Museum, the Viking Museum, Aarhus Cathedral, stroll around the Latin Quarter.

➜ **TWO DAYS**
Den Gamle By (open air 'living' museum), hire a bike and ride into the country.

➜ **THREE DAYS**
Marselisborg Palace (summer residence of the Royal family), Moesgaard Museum.

PRACTICAL INFORMATION

ARRIVAL-DEPARTURE

✈ Aarhus Airport is 45km northeast of the city in Tirstrup. Airport Bus Number 925X to the city centre takes 50min.

GETTING AROUND

Aarhus city centre is fairly small and all the main sights are easily accessible on foot. Another good way to get around is by bike, using the network of bicycle paths which connect the city. City Bikes are available from April-October and are free of charge; a 20 kroner coin is required to unlock them from the rack. If you're catching a yellow city bus, enter by any door and buy a 1-2, 3 or 4 zone ticket from the machine; for the blue regional buses, enter at the front and buy a ticket from the driver. A multi-ride 'klippekort' is valid for 10 journeys and a 24/48hr AarhusCard allows free travel in zones 1 and 2, as well as free or discounted entry to numerous city attractions.

CALENDAR HIGHLIGHTS

May
Classic Car Race, Spot Music Festival.

May-September
Sand Sculpture Festival.

June
Northside Alternative Music Festival.

July
Viking Moot, International Jazz Festival.

September
Aarhus Festival, with concerts, theatre and outdoor shows, Food Festival.

October
International Guitar Festival.

December
Christmas in the Old Town.

EATING OUT

Being a student city, Aarhus hums with café culture all year round; you'll find cosy coffee shops on almost every street, offering breakfasts, cakes, sandwiches and light lunches – some are also popular places to enjoy an evening drink, especially in the lively Aboulevarden area. Eating out is something the Danes excel at and restaurants range from friendly bistros to elegant fine dining establishments; most offer food with a Danish heart but influences come from around the globe. Local produce includes freshly caught fish landed at the harbour and vegetables from the island of Samso; restaurants tend to offer set menus of between 3 and 7 courses and these are great way to sample a varied selection of dishes. They tend to open early – at around 6pm – while the bars and clubs stay open late, and often offer live music. Not to be overlooked are the city's classic Danish smørrebørd restaurants, where satisfying and wonderfully tasty open sandwiches are served, often along with a tempting selection of cakes and pastries. Tipping is not expected, but obviously greatly appreciated.

DENMARK - AARHUS

Comwell Aarhus
🏝 ⬅ Lß ⅙ 🎰 🛋 🚗

Værkmestergade 2 ✉ *8000* – ℰ *86 72 80 00*   Plan: **B2**
– www.comwellaarhus.dk – Closed Chrismas-New Year
240 rm 🖃 – ♦798/1598 DKK ♦♦998/2798 DKK
• Business • Conference hotel • Modern •

A stylish, modern hotel set over 12 floors of a tower block. Aimed at business-people, with 19 meeting rooms; the largest with space for 475. Bedrooms are bright and contemporary with monsoon showers; choose a corner business class room for super city views. Guest areas include a bar and buzzy bistro.

Scandic Aarhus City
🏝 Lß ⅙ 🎰 🛋 🚗

Østergade 10 ✉ *8000* – ℰ *89 31 81 00*   Plan: **B2**
– www.scandichotels.com
228 rm 🖃 – ♦895/2695 DKK ♦♦995/2895 DKK – 8 suites
• Business • Chain hotel • Modern •

Behind the 19C façade of a Viennese Renaissance café lies a smart, modern hotel with an open-plan lounge, lobby, bar and reception. Bright bedrooms feature photos of city scenes; suites have balconies. Solar panels supply electricity and rooftop hives provide honey. Grill restaurant with an open kitchen.

Radisson Blu Scandinavia
🏝 Lß ⅙ 🎰 🛋 🚗

Margrethepladsen 1 ✉ *8000* – ℰ *86 12 86 65*   Plan: **A2**
– www.radissonblu.com/hotel-aarhus
234 rm 🖃 – ♦995/1795 DKK ♦♦995/1795 DKK – 5 suites
• Conference hotel • Chain hotel • Modern •

A conference-orientated hotel close to the ARoS Museum. Spacious, contemporary bedrooms offer all the facilities a modern traveller would expect. Business class rooms and suites on the top two floors offer the best views along with extra touches. International dishes served in informal, open-plan restaurant.

Villa Provence
🌿 🅿

Fredens Torv 10-12 ✉ *8000* – ℰ *86 18 24 00*   Plan: **B2**
– www.villaprovence.dk – Closed 20 December-5 January
39 rm 🖃 – ♦1295/1895 DKK ♦♦1395/3000 DKK
• Townhouse • Traditional • Personalised •

A little piece of Provence in Aarhus – a charming and elegant townhouse proudly run by an amiable couple; enter through an archway into a lovely cobbled terrace garden. Individual bedrooms; some with antique four-posters. Comfy, traditional lounge full of books and cases of wine which guests can buy.

Hotel Royal
🏝 Lß 🎵 🎰 🛋

Store Torv 4 ✉ *8000* – ℰ *86 12 00 11*   Plan: **B2**
– www.hotelroyal.dk
63 rm 🖃 – ♦995/1695 DKK ♦♦1095/1895 DKK – 5 suites
• Historic • Traditional • Classic •

Beside the cathedral is the city's oldest hotel; open for around 175 years and with a wonderfully classic feel – enhanced by paintings depicting the Kings and Queens of Denmark. Very spacious bedrooms combine antique furniture and modern facilities. The informal restaurant serves international dishes.

Hotel Ritz Aarhus City

Banegårdspladsen 12 ✉ *8000* – ℰ *86 13 44 44*   Plan: **A2**
– www.hotelritz.dk – Closed 24-25 December
67 rm – ♦795/1595 DKK ♦♦845/1895 DKK
• Historic • Traditional • Art Deco •

Iconic 1932 hotel in distinctive yellow brick, situated opposite the railway station. Friendly and welcoming with an appealing art deco style and neatly refurbished, modern bedrooms in warm colours. Showers only in most rooms.

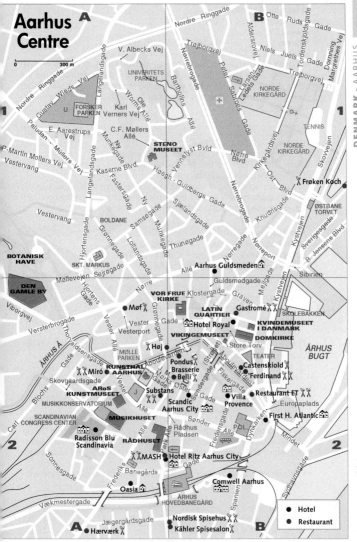

Aarhus A
Centre

0 ___ 300 m

Nordre Ringgade

Otte Ruds Gade

Aldersrovej

Niels Juels Gade

Trøjborgvej

NORDE KIRKEGÅRD

V. Albecks Vej

Nørrebrogade

Trøjborgvej

Langelandsgade

Bartholins Allé

Peter Sabrœs Gade

Larsen Leds Gade

Tordenskjoldsgade

Dorning Margrethes Vej

UNIVERITETS PARKEN

Nordre Ringgade

Gustav Wieds Vej

Worms Allé

Ole Allé

Karl Verners Vej

C.F. Møllers Allé

U **FORSKER PARKEN**

E. Aarestrups Vej

Paludan - Müllers Vej

Munkegade

Ny Munkegade

STENO MUSEET

Nørre Blvd

Skovvejen

TENNIS

NORDE KIRKEGÅRD

P-Martin Mollers Vej

Vestervang

Kaserne Blvd.

Høegh - Guldbergs Gade

Nørrebrogade

Kirkegårdsvej

Øst - Blvd

Frøken Koch

Langelandsgade

Hertensgade

Fastersgade

Ny Sjœlandsgade

Samsøgade

Munkegade

Knudrisgade

Sveriges Gade

B. Jensens Blvd

Vestervang

BOLDANE

Grønnegade

Lollandsgade

Thunøgade

Nørregade

Nørreport

Kystvejen

Sibirien

ØSTBANE TORVET

BOTANISK HAVE

DEN GAMLE BY

SKT. MARKUS

Møllevejen Sejrøgade

Nørre

Allé **Aarhus Guldsmeden**

Guldsmedgade

Graven

Melgade

Kystvejen

Viborgvej

Hjorts Gade

Thorvaldsensgade

Versterbrogade

VOR FRUE KIRKE Klostergade

Møf

Vester Gade

Vester Vesterport

Grønnegade

Vester Gade

LATIN QUARTIER

Gastromé

SKOLEBAKKEN

Hotel Royal

KVINDEMUSEET I DANMARK

VIKINGEMUSEET

Store Torv

DOMKIRKE

ÅRHUS BUGT

Høj

MØLLE PARKEN

Abouleværet

Pondus

Brasserie

Belli

Store

Mølle Østergade

Abouleværet

Fiskergade

Castenskiold

Ferdinand

Restaurant ET

ÅRHUS Å

Thorvaldsensgade

KUNSTHAL AARHUS

Miró

AROS KUNSTMUSEET

J

Substans

Blochs

Skovgaardsgade

MUSIKKONSERVATORIUM

Allé

Scandic Aarhus City

Villa Provence

Europaplads

First H. Atlantic

SCANDINAVIAN CONGRESS CENTER

MUSIKHUSET

Søndre

Rådhus Pladsen

Frederiks Allé

Fredensgade

Spanien

Dynkarken

POL

Mindet

Radisson Blu Scandinavia

RÅDHUSET

Carl

Sønnesgade

MASH

Hotel Ritz Aarhus City

Park Allé

M.P. Bruns Gade

Sydhavnsgade

Oasia

Frederiks

Banegårds Gade

Comwell Aarhus

Væhmestergade

ÅRHUS HOVEDBANEGÅRD

Jægergårdsgade

Nordisk Spisehus

Hærværk

Kähler Spisesalon

| ● | Hotel |
| ● | Restaurant |

159

First H. Atlantic

Europaplads 10 ✉ *8000* – ✆ *86 13 11 11*   Plan: **B2**
– *www.firsthotels.dk*
102 rm �²² – ♥795/1495 DKK ♥♥895/2195 DKK
• Business • Chain hotel • Modern •

Although its exterior can hardly be deemed charming, its rooms are spacious and modern with good facilities, a balcony and a vista of either the city or the sea. Breakfast with a view on the top floor. Classic Italian dishes served in the smart restaurant. Gym membership available at adjacent fitness club.

Oasia   **P**

Kriegersvej 27-31 ✉ *8000* – ✆ *87 32 37 15*   Plan: **A2**
– *www.hoteloasia.com* – *Closed 24-25 December*
65 rm �²² – ♥795/1595 DKK ♥♥845/1695 DKK
• Townhouse • Traditional • Design •

After a day's sightseeing or shopping, you will be happy to head back to this hotel in a quieter area of the city. Bright, uncluttered bedrooms offer good facilities; go for one of the suites with their modern four posters.

Aarhus Guldsmeden

Guldsmedgade 40 ✉ *8000* – ✆ *86 13 45 50*   Plan: **B1**
– *www.guldsmedenhotels.com* – *Closed New Year*
22 rm �²² – ♥825/1325 DKK ♥♥925/1825 DKK
• Townhouse • Traditional • Personalised •

A relaxed hotel with an eco/organic ethos and a friendly atmosphere. Simply decorated bedrooms vary in shape and size; some feature antique furniture and the larger rooms have four posters. Complimentary tea, coffee and juice.

Frederikshøj (Wassim Hallal)
❀

Oddervej 19 (South: 3.5 km by Spanien and Strandvejen) ✉ *8000*
– ✆ *86 14 22 80* – *www.frederikshoj.com*
– *Closed 3 weeks midsummer, 2 weeks Christmas-New Year*
and Sunday-Tuesday
Menu 655/895 DKK – *(dinner only) (booking essential) (set menu only)*
• Innovative • Elegant • Luxury •

Set in the former staff lodge to the Royal Palace, this restaurant is smart, luxurious and contemporary with edgy artwork, iPad menus and floor to ceiling windows affording views over the gardens and out to sea. Dishes are elaborate, creative and visually impressive. Service is professional and knowledgeable.

→ Lobster with quail and onions. Beef, corn and chanterelles. Apple with caramel and vanilla.

Gastromé (William Jørgensen)
❀

Rosensgade 28 ✉ *8000*   Plan: **B2**
– ✆ *28 78 16 17* – *www.gastrome.dk*
– *Closed July, 21 December-5 January, Sunday and Monday*
Menu 498/798 DKK – *(dinner only) (set menu only)*
• Modern • Design • Intimate •

This attractive Latin Quarter restaurant features a semi open plan kitchen and stark white walls punctuated with contemporary art. The concise menu offers carefully cooked, innovative modern dishes made with the best quality produce, and the wine list concentrates on lesser-known wines. Informative service.

→ Norwegian lobster with cauliflower and beach herbs. Veal with peas, wild chanterelles and veal jus. Berries with water mint and soured cream.

XX ✿

Substans (René Mammen)

A/C

Frederiksgade 74 ✉ 8000 – ✆ 86 23 04 01 Plan: **A2**
– www.restaurantsubstans.dk – Closed Christmas, Sunday and Monday
Menu 650/950 DKK – *(dinner only)*
• Modern • Friendly • Simple •

Classically Scandic in style, with an uncluttered, fresh feel, Pondus' older, more adventurous sister is run by the same experienced husband and wife team. Creative, contemporary cooking uses top quality, mostly organic, ingredients. Dishes have original touches, distinct flavours and stimulating combinations.
→ Scallop with cauliflower, almond and buttermilk. Organic pork with brown butter. Raspberries, milk and 'crunch'.

XX

Miró

Marstrandsgade 2 ✉ 8000 – ✆ 86 13 87 00 Plan: **A2**
– www.restaurant-miro.dk – Closed mid July-mid August, 22 December-4 January, Easter, Sunday and Monday
Menu 398/698 DKK – *(dinner only) (set menu only)*
• Traditional • Neighbourhood • Friendly •

A long-standing restaurant with an excellent reputation; owner Toni runs the place with pride, greeting his guests warmly, and passionately explaining the dishes and their matching wines. Set menu of 3-7 courses; traditional cooking.

XX

Restaurant ET

A/C

Åboulevarden 7 ✉ 8000 – ✆ 86 13 88 00 Plan: **B2**
– www.restaurant-et.dk – Closed Christmas and Sunday
Menu 358 DKK – Carte 374/514 DKK
• French • Design • Fashionable •

You'll find charming service, modern brasserie styling and a central kitchen at this well-run restaurant. Classic French dishes have a Danish twist: think moules marinière and crème brûlée. Superb wine choice, particularly from France.

XX

Nordisk Spisehus

A/C

M.P.Bruuns Gade 31 ✉ 8000 – ✆ 86 17 70 99 Plan: **A/B2**
– www.nordiskspisehus.dk – Closed 23-26 December, 1 January and Sunday except December
Menu 499 DKK (dinner) – Carte lunch approx. 237 DKK
• Modern • Individual • Fashionable •

A smart, intimate restaurant with a unique concept: four themed menus a year offering their own versions of dishes from Michelin Starred restaurants around the globe. Décor changes along with the theme: perhaps Japanese, Spanish or Nordic.

XX

Ferdinand

A/C

Åboulevarden 28 ✉ 8000 – ✆ 87 32 14 44 Plan: **B2**
– www.hotelferdinand.dk – Closed 22 December-5 January
19 rm – †950/1150 DKK ††1150/1350 DKK – ☕ 110 DKK – 8 suites
Menu 165/445 DKK – Carte 345/435 DKK
• French • Brasserie • Fashionable •

Red-canopied Ferdinand stands out from neighbouring bars and restaurants on the liveliest street in the city. Classic brasserie-style menus offer a good mix of French and Danish influenced dishes, with small plates in the evening and a great value set lunch. Friendly staff. Spacious, comfortable bedrooms.

XX

MASH

A/C

Banegaardspladsen 12 ✉ 8000 – ✆ 33 13 93 00 Plan: **A2**
– www.mashsteak.dk – Closed 24-26 December, 1 January and lunch Saturday-Sunday
Carte 345/820 DKK
• Meats and grills • Fashionable • Friendly •

This Modern American Steak House (MASH) is bright and smart, with colourful cow ornaments and red leather banquettes; sit in one of the booths. Top quality beef is perfectly cooked and complemented by various sides.

X

(⊛)

Hærværk   ☒ AC

Frederiks Allé 105 ⊠ 8000 – ☏ 50 51 26 51   Plan: **A2**
– www.restaurant-haervaerk.dk – Closed Christmas-New Year and Sunday-Tuesday
Menu 350 DKK – *(dinner only) (set menu only)*
• Danish • Individual • Fashionable •

A lively, keenly run place set in two converted shops; owned and run by four friends, three of whom are chefs. Industrial-chic styling with a concrete floor and stark white décor. Well-crafted, flavoursome dishes have a rustic style but a refined touch. Great value daily changing set menu; enthusiastic service.

X

Castenskiold   ᗱ ☒ AC

Åboulevarden 32 ⊠ 8000 – ☏ 86 18 90 90   Plan: **B2**
– www.castenskiold.net – Closed Sunday-Monday and lunch November-February
Menu 345/700 DKK – Carte 335/605 DKK
• Modern • Fashionable • Trendy •

Something a little different: set by the river on a busy pedestrianized street, this trendy restaurant morphs into a bar and club as the day goes on. Creative modern cooking relies on top quality produce and the flavours shine through.

X

Brasserie Belli   ᗱ

Frederiksgade 54 ⊠ 8000 – ☏ 86 12 07 60   Plan: **B2**
– www.belli.dk – Closed 25 July-8 August, Easter, Christmas and Sunday
Menu 200/380 DKK
• French classic • Brasserie • Traditional •

Celebrating its 22nd year is this intimate, family-owned restaurant with smoked mirrors and colourful Belli Circus themed posters. Satisfying, good value, French brasserie classics and polite, friendly service.

X

(⊛)

Pondus

Åboulevarden 51 ⊠ 8000 – ☏ 28 77 18 50   Plan: **B2**
– www.restaurantpondus.dk – Closed Christmas, Sunday and Monday
Menu 260 DKK – *(dinner only) (booking advisable)*
• Danish • Bistro • Rustic •

Set by the narrow city centre canal, this little sister to Substans is a small, rustic bistro with a friendly vibe and a stripped back style. The blackboard menu offers great value, flavoursome cooking which uses organic Danish produce. Dishes are bright and colourful and represent great value.

X

Møf

Vesterport 10 ⊠ 8000 – ☏ 61 73 33 33   Plan: **A2**
– www.restaurantmoef.com – Closed 1-14 January, Tuesday and Wednesday
Menu 295 DKK – Carte 367/503 DKK – *(dinner only) (booking essential)*
• Danish • Neighbourhood • Trendy •

Owned and run by an experienced young couple, this place is contemporary with monochrome décor and counter dining. Daily 3 course set menu and a concise à la carte; dishes are modern in style but Danish at heart and made with local produce.

X

Frøken Koch   ᗱ AC

Kystpromenaden 5 ⊠ 8000 – ☏ 87 48 01 23   Plan: **B1**
– www.kocherier.dk – Closed Christmas-New Year and Monday-Wednesday
Menu 300 DKK – Carte 325/400 DKK
• Danish • Bistro • Design •

This bistro overlooks the marina, has a delightful raised terrace and is open all day for hearty, homely Danish classics which are full of flavour. Dishes like potato soup with smoked trout evoke memories of family meals in childhood.

SMØRREBRØD *The following simpler restaurants and cafés specialize in Danish open sandwiches*

X **Høj**

Grønnegade 2 ✉ *8000 – www.fhoj.dk – Closed 3 weeks* Plan: **A2**
midsummer, Christmas-New Year, Sunday, Monday and bank holidays
Carte 185/195 DKK – *(lunch only) (bookings not accepted)*
• Smørrebrød • Neighbourhood • Friendly •

A bright, busy café with a pavement terrace; fridges and cabinets have a tempting selection of desserts, cakes, biscuits and drinks. Six choices of fresh, flavoursome classics on the smørrebrød menu; two plus a light dessert should suffice.

X **Kähler Spisesalon**

M.P. Bruuns Gade 33 ✉ *8000 –* ✆ *86 12 20 53* Plan: **A/B2**
– www.spisesalon.dk – Closed 23-26 December and 1 January
Menu 279 DKK *(dinner)* – Carte approx. 321 DKK – *(bookings not accepted)*
• Smørrebrød • Neighbourhood • Traditional •

An informal smørrebrød café, popular with shoppers and open in the evening. They offer soups, salads, smørrebrød and pastries, as well as organic juices and top notch teas and coffees. Monochrome pictures of Aarhus add to the charm.

FINLAND
SUOMI

→ **Area:**
338 145 km² (130 558 sq mi).

→ **Population:**
5 465 000 inhabitants.
Density = 16 per km².

→ **Capital:** Helsinki.

→ **Currency:** Euro (€).

→ **Government:**
Parliamentary republic (since 1917).
Member of European Union since 1995.

→ **Languages:**
Finnish (a Finno-Ugric language related to Estonian) spoken by 92% of Finns, Swedish (6%) and Sami (some 7 000 native speakers). English is widely spoken.

→ **Public holidays:**
New Year's Day (1 Jan); Epiphany (6 Jan); Good Friday (late Mar/Apr); Easter Monday (late Mar/Apr); May Day (1 May); Ascension Day (May); Epiphany (6 Jan); Midsummer (mid June); All Saints' Day (1 Nov); Independence Day (6 Dec); Christmas Day (25 Dec); Boxing Day (26 Dec).

→ **Local time:**
GMT+2 hours in winter and GMT +3 hours in summer.

→ **Climate:**
Temperate continental with very cold winters and mild summers (Helsinki: January -7°C; July 17°C). Midnight sun: for several weeks around Midsummer, the sun never sets in the north. Snow settles from early Dec-Apr in the south and centre of the country.
Northern Lights (Aurora Borealis) visible in the north on clear, dark nights; highest frequency in Feb-Mar and Sep-Oct.

HELSINKI

→ **Emergency:**
Police, Medical Assistance and Fire Brigade: ✆ **112**

→ **Electricity:**
230 volts AC, 50Hz; 2 round pin sockets.

→ **Formalities:**
Travellers from the European Union (EU), Switzerland, Iceland and the main countries of North and South America need a national identity card or passport (America: passport required) to visit Finland for less than three months (tourism or business purposes). For visitors from other countries a visa may be required, in addition to a passport, especially for those wishing to stay for longer than three months. If you plan to visit Russia while in Finland, you must purchase an appropriate visa in advance in your own country. We advise you to check with your embassy before travelling.

HELSINKI
HELSINGFORS

Population: 620 982

Ph. Robic/MICHELIN

Cool, clean and chic, the 'Daughter of the Baltic' sits prettily on a peninsula, jutting out between the landmasses of its historical overlords, Sweden and Russia. Surrounded on three sides by water, Helsinki is a busy port, but that only tells a small part of the story: forests grow in abundance around here and trees reach down to the lapping shores. This is a striking city to look at: it was rebuilt in the 19C after a fire, and many of the buildings have a handsome neoclassical or art nouveau façade. Shoppers can browse the picturesque outdoor food and tourist markets stretching along the main harbour, where island-hopping ferries ply their trade.

In a country with over 200,000 lakes it would be pretty hard to escape a green sensibility, and the Finnish capital has made sure that concrete and stone have never taken priority over its distinctive features of trees, water and open space. There are bridges at every turn connecting the city's varied array of small islands, and a ten kilometre strip of parkland acts as a spine running vertically up from the centre. Renowned as a city of cool, it's somewhere that also revels in a hot nightlife and even hotter saunas – this is where they were invented. And if your blast of dry heat has left you wanting a refreshing dip, there's always a freezing lake close at hand.

HELSINKI IN...

→ **ONE DAY**
Harbour market place, Uspensky Cathedral, Lutheran Cathedral, Katajanokka, Mannerheimintie.

→ **TWO DAYS**
A ferry to Suomenlinna, Church in the Rock, the nightlife of Fredrikinkatu.

→ **THREE DAYS**
Central Park, the Sibelius monument, Esplanadi.

PRACTICAL INFORMATION

ARRIVAL-DEPARTURE

✈ Helsinki-Vantaa Airport is 19km north of the city.

A taxi will take 20-30min to the centre. Buses to the Central Bus Station take 40min.

GETTING AROUND

Getting across Helsinki is fast and easy: trams and buses whizz you round efficiently. A single ticket is cheap and good for any transfers you make within an hour; buy them from the driver, ticket machines, kiosks, metro stations or the ferry terminal. If you need to make several journeys during one day or several days, a day ticket is a good choice. You can choose a ticket valid for 1 to 7 days. The Helsinki Card is valid for one, two or three days with a sliding scale of prices, and allows you unlimited transport plus free admission to museums and attractions. There are regular ferries from the harbour to Suomenlinna; they sail a little less frequently to the other main islands.

CALENDAR HIGHLIGHTS

June
Helsinki Day (the city's birthday), Juhannus (midsummer).

June-July
Helsinki Cup (international youth football tournament).

August
Helsinki Festival.

October
Baltic Herring Festival.

December
Traditional Christmas Markets, Lucia Parade to the Lutheran Cathedral.

EATING OUT

Local - and we mean local - ingredients are very much to the fore in the kitchens of Helsinki's restaurants. Produce is sourced from the country's abundant lakes, forests and seas, so your menu will assuredly be laden with the likes of reindeer, smoked reindeer, reindeer's tongue, elk in aspic, lampreys, Arctic char, Baltic herring, snow grouse and cloudberries. Generally speaking, complicated, fussy preparations are overlooked for those that let the natural flavours shine through. In the autumn, markets are piled high with woodland mushrooms, often from Lapland, and chefs make the most of this bounty. Local alcoholic drinks include schnapps, vodka and liqueurs made from local berries, while lakka (made from cloudberries) and mesimarja (brambleberries) are definitely worth discovering – you may not find them in any other European city. You'd find coffee anywhere in Europe, but not to the same extent as here: Finns are among the world's biggest coffee drinkers. In the gastronomic restaurants, lunch is a simpler affair, often with limited choice.

Kämp

Pohjoisesplanadi 29 ✉ *00100* – **Ⓜ** *Kaisaniemi* – *𝒞 (09)*   Plan: **C2**
576 111 – *www.hotelkamp.fi*
179 rm – ♥199/350 € ♥♥249/400 € – 8 suites
• Grand Luxury • Classic •
The grand façade, columned interior and impressive staircase point back to this luxurious hotel's 19C roots and the classically furnished bedrooms follow suit; the superb spa, meanwhile, adds a modern touch. The chic bar offers an excellent selection of champagne and cocktails, while for dining, there's Asian-inspired 'Yume' or a bustling brasserie with a global menu.
Yume – See restaurant listing

Crowne Plaza Helsinki

Mannerheimintie 50 ✉ *00260* – *𝒞 (09) 2521 0000*   Plan: **A1**
– *www.crowneplaza-helsinki.fi*
349 rm ⌁ – ♥180/230 € ♥♥180/230 € – 4 suites
• Business • Contemporary •
Spacious hotel specialising in conferences. Comfy, up-to-date bedrooms have good facilities and city or lake views; the higher the floor, the better the grade. Make for the huge basement fitness club and spa, then kick-back in the pub or the warm, welcoming restaurant which serves Mediterranean cuisine.

Hilton Helsinki Strand

John Stenbergin Ranta 4 ✉ *00530* – **Ⓜ** *Hakaniemi*   Plan: **C1**
– *𝒞 (09) 393 51* – *www.hilton.com*
190 rm – ♥129/360 € ♥♥165/395 € – ⌁ 27 € – 7 suites
• Business • Luxury • Classic •
This spacious waterfront hotel has a classical 1980s design, an impressive atrium and an 8th floor fitness and relaxation centre; take in the view from the gym or pool. Smartly kept bedrooms boast marble bathrooms – ask for a room overlooking the water. Bridges offers global classics and local specialities.

Haven

Unioninkatu 17 ✉ *00130* – *𝒞 (09) 681930*   Plan: **C2**
– *www.hotelhaven.fi*
77 rm ⌁ – ♥169/329 € ♥♥199/359 €
• Luxury • Business • Stylish •
Centrally located office block conversion with an elegant townhouse-style interior and a warm, clubby bar. Chic bedrooms have top quality beds, fabrics and furniture; 'Lux' offer water views. The smart, marble-decked bathrooms come with TVs, Elemis spa toiletries and Egyptian cotton bathrobes.
Havis – See restaurant listing

Lilla Roberts

Pieni Roobertinkatu 1-3 ✉ *00130* – *𝒞 (09) 689 9880*   Plan: **C2**
– *www.lillaroberts.fi*
130 rm ⌁ – ♥169/299 € ♥♥199/389 € – 1 suite
• Business • Design • Stylish •
The building was designed in 1908 by one of Finland's top architects and was originally head office for the city's energy works. The smart, designer interior uses dark colours and is centred around the concept of 'hygge' (enjoying the simple things in life). The elegant restaurant serves an appealing menu.

Klaus K

Bulevardi 2/4 ✉ *00120* – **Ⓜ** *Rautatientori* – *𝒞 (020)*   Plan: **C2**
770 4700 – *www.klauskhotel.com*
171 rm ⌁ – ♥120/320 € ♥♥140/640 €
• Luxury • Design •
A landmark building with a funky, laid-back vibe and a striking interior designed to reflect the themes of The Kalevala. Bedrooms styles include 'Passion', 'Mystical', 'Desire' and 'Envy'; the top floor 'Sky Lofts' are particularly sumptuous. Modern Tuscan cuisine is served under an embossed metal ceiling.

FINLAND - HELSINKI

GLO Hotel Kluuvi ✿ ⅃ᚷ 🌐 ⋒ 🖧 & AC ↔ ⅍ ⟡
Kluuvikatu 4 ⊠ 00100 – Ⓜ Kaisaniemi – ℰ (010) Plan: **C2**
3444 400 – www.glohotels.fi
184 rm � – ♦125/370 € ♦♦135/380 € – 6 suites
• Luxury • Modern • Design •
Stylish, central hotel; a boutique sister to next door Kämp, whose spa it shares.
Spacious bedrooms have a contemporary look and come with smart glass shower rooms and an impressive range of hi-tech extras. There's also a lively bar-
lounge and a fashionable restaurant serving cuisine from around the globe.

Radisson Blu Plaza ✿ ⅃ᚷ ⋒ & AC ↔ ⅍
Mikonkatu 23 ⊠ 00100 – Ⓜ Kaisaniemi – ℰ (020) Plan: **C2**
1234 703 – www.radissonblu.com/plazahotel-helsinki
302 rm ⊻ – ♦119/449 € ♦♦134/464 € – 1 suite
• Business • Stylish •
Elegant 20C building set close to the station and completed by a more modern
wing. Bright, contemporary bedrooms feature impressive mod cons; some have
3D TVs and saunas. The bar is a fashionable spot and the large, unusual restaurant offers five different types of cuisine listed on digital tablet menus.

Torni ✿ ⋒ AC ↔ ⅍
Yrjönkatu 26 ⊠ 00100 – Ⓜ Rautatientori – ℰ (020) Plan: **B2**
1234 604 – www.sokoshoteltorni.fi
152 rm ⊻ – ♦89/270 € ♦♦104/285 € – 6 suites
• Business • Art Deco •
Charming early 20C hotel with a palpable sense of history. Bedrooms come in
'Art Deco', 'Art Nouveau' and 'Functionalist' styles – the latter, in the 11 storey
tower, have glass-walled bathrooms. The top floor bar has a terrace and superb
city views; the restaurant offers traditional Finnish cuisine.

Holiday Inn Helsinki West Ruoholahti ✿ ⅃ᚷ ⋒ & AC
Sulhasenkuja 3 ⊠ 00180 – Ⓜ Ruoholahti – ℰ (09) ↔ ⅍
4152 1000 – www.holidayinn.com Plan: **A3**
256 rm ⊻ – ♦69/200 € ♦♦84/215 €
• Business • Functional •
Set outside the city on a business park but close to a metro station. Modern
bedrooms display touches of colour and come with compact shower rooms
and excellent soundproofing; the higher, west-facing rooms have pleasant
water and city views. The light, bright restaurant serves international cuisine.

Fabian & AC ↔
Fabiankatu 7 ⊠ 00130 – ℰ (09) 6128 2000 Plan: **C2**
– www.hotelfabian.fi
58 rm ⊻ – ♦139/259 € ♦♦169/289 €
• Townhouse • Stylish • Modern •
Charming boutique hotel close to the harbour. Bedrooms have stylish black &
white themes and smart bathrooms with heated floors. Have breakfast in the
central courtyard in summer – ingredients are organic or from small producers.

Katajanokka ✿ ⅃ᚷ ⋒ & AC ↔ ⅍ Ⓟ
Merikasarminkatu 1 ⊠ 00160 – ℰ (09) 686 450 Plan: **D2**
– www.bwkatajanokka.fi
106 rm ⊻ – ♦99/219 € ♦♦199/319 €
• Historic • Stylish •
A pleasantly restored, late 19C prison with its original staircases and high ceilinged corridors still on display. The old cells are now comfortable, well-equipped
bedrooms with modern bathrooms. The traditional cellar restaurant features a
preserved prison cell and serves traditional Finnish cuisine.

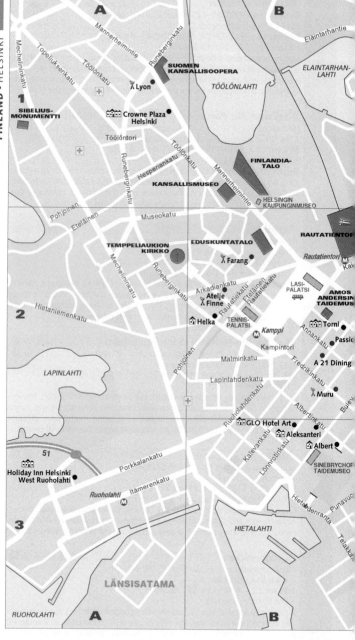

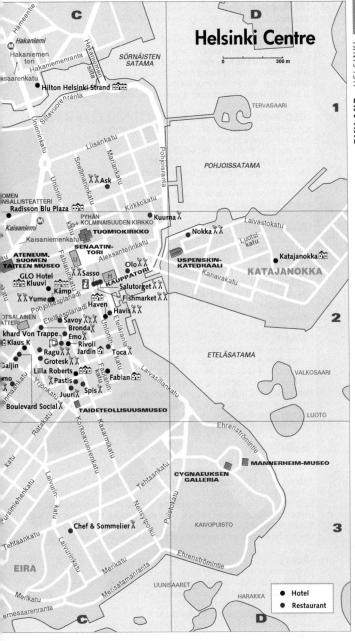

Helsinki Centre

0 — 300 m

C **D**

Hämeentie

Ⓜ *Hakaniemi*

Hakaniemen tori

Hakaniemenranta

Hakaniemen silta

SÖRNÄISTEN SATAMA

saarenkatu

● **Hilton Helsinki Strand** 🏨

Sillavuorenranta

Unioninkatu

TERVASAARI

1

Liisankatu

Mariankatu

Snellmaninkatu

Pohjoisranta

POHJOISSATAMA

Unioninkatu

X X **Ask**

SUOMEN KANSALLISTEATTERI

🏨 **Radisson Blu Plaza**

Kirkkokatu

PYHÄN KOLMINAISUUDEN KIRKKO

Kaisaniemi

● **Kuurna** X

● **Nokka** X X

Laivastokatu

TUOMIOKIRKKO

Kaisaniemenkatu

SENAATIN-TORI

Fabianinkatu

Aleksanterinkatu

Luotsikatu

● **Katajanokka** 🏨

ATENEUM, SUOMEN TAITEEN MUSEO

USPENSKIN-KATEDRAALI

Kanavakatu

KATAJANOKKA

Olo X X

● **GLO Hotel Kluuvi** 🏨

X X **Sasso**

H

🏨

KAUPPATORI

i

● **Kämp**

X X **Yume**

Pohjoisesplanadi

Salutorget X X

Haven

Fishmarket X X

Eteläesplanadi

Unioninkatu

Havis X X

RUOTSALAINEN TEATTERI

● **Savoy** X X X

Bronda X

Emo X

ETELÄSATAMA

khard **Von Trappe** ●

Eteläranta

🏨 **Klaus K** ●

● **Rivoli**

Jardin 🏨

Toca X

VALKOSAARI

Ragu X X

Gaijin

Grotesk X X

Yrjönkatu

Lilla Roberts ● 🏨

Fabianinkatu

Laivasillankatu

mo ●

● **Pastis** X

Fabian 🏨

● **Boulevard Social** X

Juuri X

Spis X

LUOTO

TAIDETEOLLISUUSMUSEO

Ehrenströmintie

Ratakatu

Korkeavuorenkatu

Kasarmikatu

sihenkatu

Laivurin- katu

Tehtaankatu

Neitsytpolku

Puistokatu

CYGNAEUKSEN GALLERIA

■ **MANNERHEIM-MUSEO**

3

Tehtaankatu

● **Chef & Sommelier** X

KAIVOPUISTO

Ehrenströmintie

Laivurinkatu

EIRA

Merikatu

Merisatamanranta

UUNISAARET

HARAKKA

Merikatu

ernesaarenranta

● Hotel

● Restaurant

C **D**

Aleksanteri
☆ ⅃♨ ⋔ ⅍ Ⓐ ⅏   Plan: **B3**

Albertinkatu 34 ⊠ 00180 – Ⓜ Kamppi – ℰ (020)
1234 643 – www.sokoshotels.fi
151 rm ⌂ – ♟85/239 € ♟♟105/300 €
• Business • Contemporary •

Two renovated buildings close to the Alexander Theatre. The 1920s building offers modern, well-equipped 'Neo Classical' bedrooms; the 1880s building boasts larger 'Neo Renaissance' rooms – there are six themed rooms too. The individually styled restaurant has a menu of unfussy international dishes.

GLO Hotel Art
☆ ⋔ ⅍ Ⓐ ⅏ ⅍ ⇔   Plan: **B3**

Lönnrotinkatu 29 ⊠ 00180 – Ⓜ Kamppi – ℰ (010)
3444 100 – www.glohotels.fi
171 rm ⌂ – ♟90/109 € ♟♟164/364 €
• Townhouse • Business • Modern •

Sited in the heart of the lively Design District, a 1903 art nouveau castle with modern extensions and its own art collection. Chic bedrooms were styled by Finnish designers and come in three sizes. You can borrow everything from bicycles to paints & brushes. A Nordic grill menu is served in the old cellars.

Rivoli Jardin
⋔ ⅍ ⅏   Plan: **C2**

Kasarmikatu 40 ⊠ 00130 – ℰ (09) 681 500
– www.rivoli.fi – Closed Christmas
55 rm ⌂ – ♟100/220 € ♟♟120/350 €
• Townhouse • Homely •

Small, city centre oasis hidden away off a courtyard, with an intimate conservatory lounge, and a sauna and meeting room tucked away in the cellar. Bedrooms are cosy and individually decorated; those on the top floor have terraces.

Albert
☆ ⋔ ⅍ Ⓐ ⅏   Plan: **B3**

Albertinkatu 30 ⊠ 00120 – ℰ (020) 1234 638
– www.sokoshotels.fi – Closed Christmas
95 rm ⌂ – ♟129/185 € ♟♟144/195 €
• Business • Contemporary •

Unassuming 19C building with a contrastingly cosy interior. Good-sized contemporary bedrooms are well-equipped and come with Nordic furniture and up-to-date bathrooms. Have drinks in the welcoming open-plan lounge-bar, then head to the trattoria-style restaurant for a selection of Italian classics.

Helka
☆ ⋔ ⅍ Ⓐ ⅏ ⅍   Plan: **B2**

Pohjoinen Rautatiekatu 23 ⊠ 00100 – Ⓜ Kamppi
– ℰ (09) 613 580 – www.helka.fi – Closed 23-27 December
150 rm ⌂ – ♟86/170 € ♟♟90/190 € – 3 suites
• Townhouse • Stylish •

Early 20C building redesigned around the concept of 'nature'. Well-kept, contemporary bedrooms have white walls, stylish wooden furnishings and huge feature photos of plants or flowers on the ceilings. In the restaurant, Finnish cuisine can be enjoyed among real tree trunks and large forest prints.

XxX Savoy
❀ ≼ ⅌ ⅍ Ⓐ ⅏ ⇔   Plan: **C2**

Eteläesplanadi 14 (8th floor) ⊠ 00130 – Ⓜ Kaisaniemi
– ℰ (09) 6128 5300 – www.royalravintolat.com/savoy – Closed Easter,
Christmas, Saturday lunch and Sunday
Menu 63 € (lunch) – Carte 79/94 €
• Modern • Elegant • Individual •

The city's most famous restaurant opened in 1937 and offers impressive views from its 8th floor setting. Choose from updated versions of old favourites or a seasonal 4 course menu of refined, attractively presented modern dishes.

XX
&

Olo (Jari Vesivalo)   ← AK ↤ ⇦

Pohjoisesplanadi 5 ✉ 00170 – ⓜ *Kaisaneimi –* ☏ *(010)*   Plan: **C2**
3206 250 – www.olo-ravintola.fi – Closed Easter, midsummer, Christmas,
Saturday lunch, Sunday and Monday
Menu 46/98 € – *(booking essential) (set menu only)*
• Innovative • Design •
Modern, minimalist restaurant within an attractive 19C townhouse on the harbourside. Cooking is exciting and innovative and uses stimulating ingredient
combinations with contrasting tastes and textures. Relaxed yet professional service heightens the experience. The 18 course dinner menu is called 'The Journey'.
➜ Semolina porridge with mushroom, malt and brown butter. Pike-Perch
with cauliflower and lemon verbena. Sea buckthorn berries with dill and
sour milk.

XX
&

Demo (Tommi Tuominen)   ↤

Uudenmaankatu 9-11 ✉ 00120 – ⓜ *Rautatientori*   Plan: **C2**
– ☏ *(09) 228 90 840 – www.restaurantdemo.fi – Closed 3 weeks July,*
Christmas-New Year, Easter, midsummer, Sunday and Monday
Menu 62/102 € – *(dinner only) (booking essential) (set menu only)*
• Modern • Intimate •
An unassuming-looking restaurant decorated in neutral tones and hung with
huge cotton pendant lights. Classically based cooking combines French and
Finnish influences to produce robust, satisfying dishes with a subtle modern
edge. Choose 4-7 courses; the menu is presented verbally and changes almost
daily.
➜ Braised pork cheek with malt pudding. Wild pike with fermented courgettes and cream cheese sauce. Liquorice and milk chocolate with tobacco
ice cream.

XX
&

Ask (Filip Langhoff)   ↤

Vironkatu 8 ✉ 00170 – ⓜ *Kaisaniemi –* ☏ *(040)*   Plan: **C1**
581 8100 – www.restaurantask.com – Closed 3 weeks July-August, Easter,
Christmas, Sunday, Monday and bank holidays
Menu 49/89 € – *(dinner only and lunch Friday-Saturday) (set menu only)*
• Modern • Intimate •
It may be hidden away but this welcoming restaurant is well-known. It's a charming place, run by a delightful, experienced couple, who offer modern Nordic
cooking crafted almost entirely from organic ingredients. Dishes are light and
original, produce is top quality and flavours are clearly defined.
➜ Beans with butter and mint. Pike-Perch, cucumber and smoke. Parsnip
and caramel.

XX

Sasso   ⌂ AK ↤ ⇦

Pohjoisesplanadi 17 ✉ 00170 – ⓜ *Kaisaniemi –* ☏ *(09)*   Plan: **C2**
6128 5150 – www.royalravintolat.com – Closed Christmas, Easter
and midsummer
Menu 32/59 € – Carte 40/68 €
• Italian • Fashionable •
Start with a drink in the smart bar-lounge of this chic harbourside restaurant
then head on into the stylish dining room. The well-run kitchen uses Scandinavian ingredients to create north Italian dishes with a modern touch.

XX

FishMarket   ← AK ↤ ⇦

Pohjoisesplanadi 17 ✉ 00170 – ⓜ *Kaisaniemi –* ☏ *(09)*   Plan: **C2**
6128 5250 – www.royalravintolat.com – Closed Easter,Christmas,
midsummer and Sunday
Menu 34/63 € – Carte 44/160 €
• Fish and seafood • Fashionable •
This smart, bright basement is divided into several different areas and decorated with contemporary, fish-related art. Try oysters or crustacean platters from
the bar or accomplished modern seafood dishes from the main kitchen.

FINLAND - HELSINKI

XX **Yume** – Kämp Hotel   🛜 🕭 🎦 ↔
Kluuvikatu 2 ⊠ 00100 – 🅜 *Kaisaniemi –* 𝒞 *(09)*   Plan: **C2**
57611718 – www.hotelkamp.fi – Closed Christmas, Easter, Sunday and
Monday
Menu 54/62 € – Carte 27/60 € – *(dinner only)*
• Asian • Design •

Sit on the large heated terrace or head for the comfy modern dining room, which is divided up by ornate wooden frames. Alongside Asian-inspired dishes with a Californian twist, you'll find a selection of sushi, sashimi and nigiri.

XX **Havis** – Haven Hotel   🛜 🎦 ↔ ↻
Eteläranta 16 ⊠ 00130 – 𝒞 *(09) 6819 3116*   Plan: **C2**
– www.ravintolahavis.fi
Menu 40 € – Carte 43/59 €
• Fish and seafood • Elegant •

19C harbourside restaurant serving carefully crafted seafood dishes. Various dining rooms – one with an elegant vaulted ceiling and maritime murals; another with a contemporary open kitchen – are set around a courtyard terrace.

XX **Grotesk**   🛜 🎦 ↔ ↻
Ludviginkatu 10 ⊠ 00130 – 🅜 *Rautatientori –* 𝒞 *(010)*   Plan: **C2**
470 2100 – www.grotesk.fi – Closed Easter, Christmas, midsummer,
Saturday lunch, Sunday and Monday
Carte 33/62 €
• Meats and grills • Fashionable • Brasserie •

Smart, buzzy restaurant behind an impressive 19C façade; which comprises a fashionable cocktail bar, a wine bar serving interesting small plates, and a chic dining room decorated in black, white and red, that specialises in steaks.

XX **Ragu**   🕭 🎦 ↻
Ludviginkatu 3-5 ⊠ 00130 – 🅜 *Rautatientori –* 𝒞 *(09)*   Plan: **C2**
596 659 – www.ragu.fi – Closed July, Easter, midsummer, Christmas and
Sunday
Menu 45 € – Carte 52/54 € – *(dinner only) (booking advisable)*
• Modern • Design • Formal •

Finland's famed seasonal ingredients are used in unfussy Italian recipes and the welcoming service and lively atmosphere also have something of an Italian feel. Choose the weekly 'House' menu to sample the latest produce to arrive.

XX **Nokka**   🛜 🎦 ↔ ↻
Kanavaranta 7F ⊠ 00160 – 𝒞 *(09) 6128 5600*   Plan: **D2**
– www.ravintolanokka.fi – Closed Christmas-New Year, Easter Saturday
lunch and Sunday
Menu 49 € (weekday lunch)/64 € – Carte 46/72 €
• Modern • Elegant •

Converted harbourside warehouse with a nautical feel – look out for the huge anchor and propeller. There's a cookery school, a wine cellar and a smart glass-walled kitchen. Modern Finnish cooking relies on small farm producers.

XX **Salutorget**   🕭 🎦 ↔
Pohjoisesplanadi 15 ⊠ 00170 – 🅜 *Kaisaniemi –* 𝒞 *(09)*   Plan: **C2**
6128 5950 – www.salutorget.fi – Closed Easter, Christmas, Sunday dinner
and lunch Sunday midsummer-mid August
Menu 27 € (weekday lunch)/45 € – Carte 34/72 €
• International • Brasserie • Elegant •

An old bank, located on the esplanade; now an elegant restaurant with impressive columns and attractive stained glass. The classic, brasserie-style menu has global influences. Have afternoon tea or Sunday brunch in the plush cocktail bar.

Chef & Sommelier (Sasu Laukkonen)

Huvilakatu 28A ⊠ 00150 – 𝒸 (400) 959 440 Plan: **C3**
– www.chefsommelier.fi – Closed late June-late July, 10 days Christmas-New Year, 1 week February, Easter, Sunday and Monday
Menu 46/76 € – *(dinner only) (booking essential) (set menu only)*
• Modern • Neighbourhood •

Tiny, simply decorated restaurant with a friendly atmosphere, secreted amongst residential apartment blocks. The open kitchen uses carefully chosen organic and wild ingredients in modern, original Finnish cooking. The passionate chefs deliver dishes to the tables themselves and explain the techniques used.
→ Salmon from river Teno. Lamb and beetroot. Tomato and rose.

Muru

Fredrikinkatu 41 ⊠ 00120 – ⓜ Kamppi – 𝒸 (10) Plan: **B2**
2928 999 – www.murudining.fi – Closed Christmas, New Year, Easter, midsummer, Sunday, Monday and bank holidays
Menu 52 € – Carte 46/52 € – *(dinner only) (booking essential)*
• Modern • Neighbourhood • Trendy •

Three passionate young owners and a charming, chatty team have created a vibrant, welcoming spot. It's cosy and rustic with a contemporary edge, displaying quirky wine-themed lighting and a bar made from old wine boxes. Cooking is refined yet gutsy; there are two sittings for dinner and booking is a must.

Spis

Kasarmikatu 26 ⊠ 00130 – 𝒸 (045) 305 1211 Plan: **C2**
– www.spis.fi – Closed Sunday, Monday and bank holidays
Menu 50/77 € – *(dinner only) (booking essential) (set menu only)*
• Modern • Individual •

Intimate restaurant seating just 18; the décor is 'faux derelict', with exposed brick and plaster walls. Creative, flavoursome cooking features Nordic flavours in attractive, imaginative combinations. Most dishes are vegetable-based.

Toca

Unioninkatu 18 ⊠ 00130 – 𝒸 (044) 5922222 Plan: **C2**
– www.toca.fi – Closed July, 23 December-7 January, Sunday and Monday
Menu 45/65 € – *(dinner only and lunch Tuesday-Thursday-set menu only at dinner) (booking essential)*
• Modern • Trendy • Individual •

Modest little bistro with an unfinished look. At lunch they serve just two dishes – aimed at local workers – while dinner offers a 3 or 5 set course menu. Cooking is an original mix of Italian simplicity and Finnish modernity.

Ateljé Finne

Arkadiankatu 14 ⊠ 00100 – ⓜ Kamppi – 𝒸 (010) Plan: **B2**
2818242 – www.ateljefinne.fi – Closed 22 December-2 January, Sunday and Monday
Menu 45 € – Carte 53/68 € – *(dinner only) (booking advisable)*
• Modern • Bistro •

The old studio of Finnish sculptor Gunnar Finne, who worked here for over 30 years. Local art decorates the small bistro-style dining rooms, set on three levels. Regional dishes are given subtle modern and international twists.

Lyon

Mannerheimintie 56 ⊠ 00260 – 𝒸 (010) 328 1560 Plan: **A1**
– www.ravintolalyon.fi – Closed July, Easter, Christmas, midsummer, Sunday and Monday
Menu 54 € – Carte 66/76 € – *(dinner only)*
• French • Bistro •

Well-established restaurant with a traditional bistro feel, set across from the Opera House. Wide-ranging menus offer seasonal French dishes crafted from Finnish ingredients. These are accompanied by a small French wine selection.

FINLAND - HELSINKI

Emo
🗙 ⊛

Kasarmikatu 44 ✉ 00130 – Ⓜ *Rautatientori* – ☏ (010) Plan: **C2**
505 0900 – www.emo-ravintola.fi – Closed 2 weeks July, Christmas,
Sunday, lunch Saturday and Monday
Menu 27 € (weekday lunch)/49 € – Carte 33/45 €
• **Modern** • **Fashionable** •
Laid-back restaurant with an adjoining bar and a friendly team. The menu is
easy-going too, offering around 10 regularly changing dishes that can be
taken either as starters or main courses. Quality ingredients feature in flavoursome, unfussy preparations, which are good value and come with a contemporary touch.

Farang
🗙 ⊛

Ainonkatu 3 (inside the Kunsthalle) ✉ 00100 Plan: **B2**
– Ⓜ *Kamppi* – ☏ (010) 322 9380 – www.farang.fi – Closed 3 weeks July,
Christmas, Easter, Sunday, Monday and lunch Saturday
Menu 25 € (lunch) – Carte dinner 38/44 €
• **South-East Asian** • **Individual** •
This stylish, modern restaurant is housed in the Kunsthalle art centre. One room
is decorated with large photos of Thai scenes; the other is furnished in red, black
and grey, with transparent curtains separating black tables. Zesty, harmonious
dishes take their influences from Vietnam, Thailand and Malaysia.

Gaijin
🗙 ⊛

Bulevardi 6 ✉ 00120 – Ⓜ *Rautatientori* – ☏ (010) Plan: **C2**
3229386 – www.gaijin.fi
Menu 37 € (lunch) – Carte 37/48 € – *(booking essential)*
• **Asian** • **Fashionable** •
Gaijin comes with dark, contemporary décor, a buzzing atmosphere, attentive
service and an emphasis on sharing. Its experienced owners offer boldly flavoured, skilfully presented modern takes on Japanese, Korean and Northern Chinese recipes. The tasting menus are a great way to sample the different cuisines.

Boulevard Social
🗙 ⊛

Bulevardi 6 ✉ 00120 – Ⓜ *Rautatientori* – ☏ (010) Plan: **C2**
3229382 – www.boulevardsocial.fi – Closed Christmas, Saturday lunch and
Sunday
Menu 29 € (lunch) – Carte 34/51 €
• **Mediterranean** • **Fashionable** •
Owned by the same people as next door Gaijin, this lively, informal restaurant
offers an accessible range of authentic North African, Turkish and Eastern Mediterranean dishes; try the set or tasting menus to experience a cross-section of
them all. If they're fully booked, ask for a seat at the counter.

Bronda
🗙

Eteläesplanadi 20 ✉ 00130 – Ⓜ *Rautatientori* Plan: **C2**
– ☏ (010) 322 9388 – www.ravintolabronda.fi – Closed 3 weeks
July, Christmas and Sunday
Menu 29 € (lunch) – Carte 40/49 €
• **Modern** • **Fashionable** • **Brasserie** •
The floor to ceiling windows of this old furniture showroom flood it with light.
Have cocktails and snacks at the bar or comforting, boldly flavoured Mediterra-
nean sharing plates in the brasserie. Each dish arrives as it's ready.

Pastis
🗙

Pieni Roobertinkatu 2 ✉ 00130 – ☏ (010) 29 28 990 Plan: **C2**
– www.pastis.fi – Closed Easter, Christmas, New Year's Eve, Saturday and
Monday lunch and Sunday
Menu 25/48 € – Carte dinner 40/54 € – *(booking essential)*
• **French classic** • **Bistro** • **Neighbourhood** •
The clue is in the name: they serve classical French dishes, alongside several dif-
ferent brands of pastis. It's a popular place, so there's always a lively atmo-
sphere. Lunch sees a smaller menu but service is suitably swift.

X **Passio** AC

Kalevankatu 13 ⊠ 00100 – Ⓜ Kamppi – ✆ (020) Plan: **B2**
7352 040 – www.passiodining.fi – Closed Christmas and midsummer
Menu 49/69 € – *(dinner only) (booking advisable) (surprise menu only)*
• **Modern** • **Friendly** • **Neighbourhood** •
With its exposed ducts, dimly lit lamps and leather-topped tables, Passio has a
faux industrial look. 3 or 5 course 'Surprise' menus feature regional ingredients.
It's run by a local brewer, so be sure to try the artisan beers.

X **Kuurna** ⇔

Meritullinkatu 6 ⊠ 00170 – Ⓜ Kaisaniemi – ✆ (010) Plan: **C2**
2818241 – www.kuurna.fi – Closed 2 weeks Christmas, Easter and Sunday
Menu 42 € – Carte 42/54 € – *(dinner only) (booking essential)*
• **Traditional** • **Neighbourhood** •
Small but very popular restaurant with a lived-in feel and seating for just twenty
guests. The set menu offers three choices per course and is supplemented by
blackboard specials; cooking is Finnish and follows the seasons.

X **A21 Dining** ⅋ AC ⇔ ⇔

Kalevankatu 17 ⊠ 00100 – Ⓜ Kamppi – ✆ (040) Plan: **B2**
1711117 – www.a21.fi – Closed Christmas, midsummer, Sunday and
Monday
Menu 78 € – Carte 50/78 € – *(dinner only)*
• **Modern** • **Trendy** • **Individual** •
Fashionable spot known as much for its cocktails as for its food. It's minimalist in
style, with one room all in white and another all in black. The décor, along with
the understated modern menu, follows a 'forest journey' theme.

X **Juuri** ⇔

Korkeavuorenkatu 27 ⊠ 00130 – ✆ (09) 635 732 Plan: **C2**
– www.juuri.fi – Closed midsummer and 24-26 December
Carte 35/52 €
• **Traditional** • **Bistro** •
A small bistro close to the Design Museum, with friendly service and a rustic
style. Menus offer a few main dishes along with 'Sapas' – small, tapas-style plates of organic produce. Traditional Finnish recipes are brought up-to-date.

I◻ **Rikhard von Trappe** ⅋ AC

Rikhardinkatu 4 ⊠ 00120 – Ⓜ Rautatientori – ✆ (010) Plan: **C2**
4233 256 – www.ravintola.fi/ravintola/rikhard-von-trappe/ – Closed July,
Easter, Christmas, Sunday and Monday
Carte 39/56 € – *(dinner only)*
• **Traditional** • **Pub** • **Rustic** •
This Finnish take on a gastropub comes with exposed brickwork, low lighting
and clubby banquettes. The appealing menu lists Belgian favourites, with the
likes of mussels, escargots, entrecote and waffles; both savoury and sweet.

🏨 **Hilton Helsinki Airport** ⅋ ⅃⅃ ⟰ ⅋ AC ⅋ ⅍ 🅿

Lentäjänkuja 1 ⊠ 01530 – ✆ (09) 732 20 – www.hilton.com
330 rm – †99/370 € ††109/400 € – ⊑ 27 € – 5 suites
• **Business** • **Modern** • **Stylish** •
3min from the international terminal (T2); a spacious glass hotel with a relaxed
ambience and a large conference capacity. Well-soundproofed bedrooms boast
locally designed furniture, good facilities and large bathrooms – some have saunas. The stylish restaurant serves Finnish and international cuisine.

FRANCE

FRANCE

→ **AREA:**
551 500 km²
(212 934 sq mi).

→ **POPULATION:**
66 735 726 inhabitants.
Density = 121 per km².

→ **CAPITAL:**
Paris.

→ **CURRENCY:**
Euro (€).

→ **GOVERNMENT:**
Parliamentary republic
(since 1946). Member of
European Union since 1957
(one of the 6 founding countries).

→ **LANGUAGE:**
French.

→ **PUBLIC HOLIDAYS:**
New Year's Day (1 Jan); Easter
Monday (late Mar/Apr); Labor Day
(1 May); Victory Day 1945 (8 May);
Ascension Day (late Apr/May); Whit
Monday (late May/June); Bastille
Day (14 July); Assumption of the
Virgin Mary (15 Aug); All Saints' Day
(1 Nov); Armistice Day 1918
(11 Nov); Christmas Day (25 Dec).

→ **LOCAL TIME:**
GMT+1 hour in winter and GMT
+2 hours in summer.

→ **CLIMATE:**
Temperate with cool winters and
warm summers (Paris: January 3°C;
July 20°C). Mediterranean climate
in the south (mild winters, hot and
sunny summers, occasional strong
wind called the mistral).

→ **EMERGENCY:**
Police ☏ **17**; Medical Assistance
☏ **15**; Fire Brigade ☏ **18**.
(Dialling **112** within any EU country
will redirect your call and contact
the emergency services.)

→ **ELECTRICITY:**
230 volts AC, 50Hz; 2 round pin
sockets.

→ **FORMALITIES:**
Travellers from the European Union
(EU), Switzerland, Iceland and
the main countries of North and
South America need a national
identity card or passport (America:
passport required) to visit France
for less than three months (tourism
or business purpose). For visitors
from other countries a visa may be
required, in addition to a passport,
especially for those wishing to
stay for longer than three months.
We advise you to check with your
embassy before travelling.

179

PARIS
PARIS

Population 2 240 621

Cyrille Lips/Fotolia.com

The French capital is one of the truly great cities of the world, a metropolis that eternally satisfies the desires of its beguiled visitors. With its harmonious layout, typified by the grand geometric boulevards radiating from the Arc de Triomphe like the spokes of a wheel, Paris is designed to enrapture. Despite its ever-widening tentacles, most of the things worth seeing are contained within the city's ring road. Paris wouldn't be Paris sans its Left and Right Banks: the Right Bank comprises the north and west; the Left Bank takes in the city south of the Seine. A stroll along the Left Bank conjures images of Doisneau's magical monochrome photographs, while the narrow, cobbled streets of Montmartre vividly call up the colourful cool of Toulouse-Lautrec.

The Ile de la Cité is the nucleus around which the city grew and the oldest quarters around this site are the 1st, 2nd, 3rd, 4th arrondissements on the Right Bank and 5th and 6th on the Left Bank. Landmarks are universally known: the Eiffel Tower and the Arc de Triomphe to the west, the Sacré-Coeur to the north, Montparnasse Tower to the south, and, of course, Notre-Dame Cathedral in the middle. But Paris is not resting on its laurels. New buildings and new cultural sensations are never far away: Les Grands Travaux are forever in the wings, waiting to inspire.

PARIS IN...

→ **ONE DAY**
Eiffel Tower, Notre-Dame Cathedral, a café on Boulevard St Germain, Musée d'Orsay, Montmartre.

→ **TWO DAYS**
The Louvre, Musée du Quai Branly.

→ **THREE DAYS**
Canal Saint-Martin, Centre Pompidou, Picasso Museum and the Marais.

PRACTICAL INFORMATION

ARRIVAL-DEPARTURE

✈ Paris Charles de Gaulle Airport is 23km northeast of Paris. Air France Bus to Montparnasse or Porte Maillot runs every 15min.

✈ Orly Airport is 14km south. Air France Bus runs to Invalides or Montparnasse. Eurostar runs from Gare du Nord, on the Rue de Dunkerque.

GETTING AROUND

A single bus or metro ticket has a flat fare however far you travel; a carnet (book of ten) works out at good value. There are three travel cards: Paris Visite is a 1-day pass for three zones or a 5-day pass for five zones; Mobilis is a 1-day pass giving unlimited travel in either zones 1-2 or zones 1-5; Pass Navigo is a weekly or monthly pass (you'll need a photo). Or try the Velib, the bicycle system; pick up one of the 15,000 bikes at any of the 1,800 points, swipe a travel card to release your bike – then it's just you versus the Parisian traffic...

CALENDAR HIGHLIGHTS

February: Paris Fashion Week.

March: Salon du Livre Paris.

April: Banlieues Bleues.

May: La Nuit des Musées, Foire du Trône funfair.

June: French Open Tennis.

August: Paris Plages.

September: The Autumn Festival, Jazz à la Villette.

October: Nuit Blanche, International Contemporary Art Fair.

November: Great Wines Fair.

EATING OUT

Food plays such an important role in Gallic life that eating well is deemed a citizen's birth-right. Parisians are intensely knowledgeable about their food and wine - simply stroll around any part of the capital and you'll come across lavish looking shops offering perfectly presented treats. Restaurants, bistros and brasseries too can call on the best available bounty around: there are close to a hundred city-wide markets teeming with fresh produce. As Charles De Gaulle said: "How can you govern a country which has 246 varieties of cheese?" Whether you want to linger in a legendary café or dine in a grand salon, you'll find the choice is endless. The city's respect for its proud culinary heritage is palpable but it is not resting on its laurels. Just as other European cities with vibrant restaurant scenes have started to play catch-up, so have young chefs here taken up the cudgels. By breaking away from formulaic regimes and adopting more contemporary styles of cooking, they have ensured that the reputation of the city remains undimmed.

FRANCE – PARIS

RESTAURANTS FROM A TO Z

OPEN SATURDAY AND SUNDAY

A

Aida	✗ ❀	231
Alcazar	✗✗	241
L'Ambroisie	✗x✗✗ ❀❀❀	250
L'Atelier de Joël Robuchon - Étoile	✗ ❀	207
L'Atelier de Joël Robuchon - St-Germain	✗ ❀❀❀	241
Atelier Maître Albert	✗✗	240
Aux Prés	✗	242

B

Benkay	✗x✗	255
Benoit	✗✗ ❀	239
Bofinger	✗✗	250
Brasserie Gallopin	✗✗	220

C-D

Café Constant	✗ ⊛	233
Café de la Paix	✗✗	219
Les Cailloux	✗	259
Camélia	✗✗	218
Les 110 de Taillevent	✗✗	203
114, Faubourg	✗✗ ❀	203
Chamarré Montmartre	✗✗	251
Le Cinq	✗x✗x✗ ❀❀❀	196
Le Cinq Codet	✗✗	230
Clamato	✗ ⊛	258
Les Cocottes - Tour Eiffel	✗ ⊛	232
Le Comptoir du Relais	✗	244
Le Dali	✗✗	218
La Dame de Pic	✗✗ ❀	239
D'Chez Eux	✗✗	231
Le Dôme	✗x✗	246
Drouant	✗x✗	217

E-F-G

Eclectic	✗	257
Épicure	✗x✗x✗ ❀❀❀	196
Les Fables de La Fontaine	✗ ❀	231
Le First	✗✗	219
Fish La Boissonnerie	✗	244
Fogón	✗✗	241
Fouquet's	✗x✗	200
Le Gabriel	✗x✗ ❀❀	198
La Gauloise	✗✗	231
Le George	✗x✗	200
La Grande Cascade	✗x✗ ❀	255

I-J-K-L

Impérial Choisy	✗ ⊛	260
Le Jules Verne	✗x✗ ❀	228
Kunitoraya	✗	223
Lili	✗x✗	199
Le Lumière	✗✗	219

M-N-O

Maison Blanche	✗x✗	200
La Marée Passy	✗	258
Marius et Janette	✗✗	204
La Marlotte	✗ ⊛	242
Mathieu Pacaud - Histoires	✗x✗ ❀❀	197
Mini Palais	✗✗	204
Mirama	✗	245
Mon Vieil Ami	✗	242
Nolita	✗✗	205
L'Oiseau Blanc	✗✗	203
Okuda	✗✗ ❀	204
L'Oriental	✗	252

P-R

Pavillon Elysée Lenôtre	✗	207
Pho Tai	✗ ⊛	260
Pramil	✗	259
Pur' - Jean-François Rouquette	✗x✗ ❀	216
Qui plume la Lune	✗ ❀	250
La Régalade Conservatoire	✗	221
Le Relais Plaza	✗✗	203
La Rotonde	✗✗	247

S-T

Shang Palace	✗x✗ ❀	199
STAY Faubourg	✗x✗	218
Suan Thaï	✗	244
Le Sushi Okuda	✗	208
Les Tablettes de Jean-Louis Nomicos	✗x✗ ❀	201
Taokan	✗	243
Timgad	✗✗	204
Tsé Yang	✗x✗	202

U-V-Z

Un Dimanche à Paris	✗✗	241
Vaudeville	✗✗	220
Le Violon d'Ingres	✗✗ ❀	229
Zen	✗ ⊛	223

Plaza Athénée

25 av. Montaigne (8th) – *Alma Marceau*
– ☎ 01 53 67 66 65   Plan: **G3**
– www.dorchestercollection.com/en/paris/hotel-plaza-athenee
154 rm – †995 € ††1295 € – ☳ 90 € – 54 suites
• Palace • Grand Luxury • Stylish •
Parisian luxury hotel par excellence, the Plaza Athénée, inaugurated in 1911, was given a new lease of life in 2014, thanks to many months of refurbishment. The institution thus confirms its position as the real summit of French-style luxury and elegance. Brilliant classicism, exceptional amenities… The legend lives on.
❀❀❀ **Alain Ducasse au Plaza Athénée** • **Le Relais Plaza** – See restaurant listing

Le Bristol

112 r. du Faubourg-St-Honoré (8th) –  *Miromesnil*
– ☎ 01 53 43 43 00 – www.lebristolparis.com   Plan: **H2**
152 rm – †950/1600 € ††950/1600 € – ☳ 45 € – 36 suites
• Palace • Grand Luxury • Stylish •
This luxury hotel, built in 1925 around a magnificent garden, has retained all its glory. Sumptuous guestrooms decorated in Louis XV or Louis XVI style, as well as impressively-sized suites (Honeymoon, Imperial etc...). Stunning swimming pool on the top floor.
❀❀❀ **Épicure** • ❀ **114, Faubourg** – See restaurant listing

Shangri-La

10 av. d'Iéna (16th) ✉ *75116* –  *Iéna*
– ☎ 01 53 67 19 98 – www.shangri-la.com   Plan: **F3**
75 rm – †695/1375 € ††695/1375 € – ☳ 58 € – 25 suites
• Palace • Historic • Stylish •
The hallmark of this palatial hotel opened in 2011 is its fusion of French Empire and Asian styles. Occupying the former home of Prince Roland Bonaparte (1896), its classic architecture encompasses grandiose lounges, opulent luxury and dining options for every taste. A true sense of exclusivity!
❀❀ **L'Abeille** • ❀ **Shang Palace** – See restaurant listing

Peninsula

19 av. Kléber (16th) ✉ *75116* – **Ⓜ** *Kléber*
– ☎ 01 58 12 28 88 – http://paris.peninsula.com/fr/   Plan: **F2**
166 rm – †850/1250 € ††850/1250 € – ☳ 55 € – 34 suites
• Palace • Historic • Elegant •
So it is with this hotel that the Hong Kong Peninsula group arrived in Paris in 2014. A master stroke! Just minutes from the Arc de Triomphe, in a beautiful Belle Epoque building, the hotel has the greatest of everything. Find luxurious interiors, high-tech equipment and top of the range amenities.
L'Oiseau Blanc • **Lili** – See restaurant listing

Four Seasons George V

31 av. George V (8th) – **Ⓜ** *George V* – ☎ 01 49 52 71 54
– www.fourseasons.com/paris   Plan: **G3**
185 rm – †990/1350 € ††990/1350 € – ☳ 55 € – 59 suites
• Palace • Historic • Elegant •
This mythical luxury hotel, founded in 1928, has an interior design that reflects the splendours and refinement of the 18C. Its sumptuous and spacious guest-rooms, art collections, superb spa and lovely interior courtyard – not to mention its gastronomic history – make this a truly exceptional place!
❀❀❀ **Le Cinq** • **Le George** – See restaurant listing

FRANCE - PARIS

Le Royal Monceau

⇪ ⅃⌂ ⊛ 🖥 ⅄ ℀ 🛁

37 av. Hoche (8th) – **Ⓜ** *Charles de Gaulle-Etoile*
Plan: **G2**
– ✆ 01 42 99 88 00 – www.leroyalmonceau.com
108 rm – 🛏†780/1700 € 🛏†780/1700 € – ⌸ 58 € – 41 suites
• Palace • Grand Luxury • Design •

This 21st-century luxury hotel, decorated by Philippe Starck, plays with current expectations. There is an art gallery, bookshop, high-tech cinema and superb spa. Since 2016, it has a new restaurant: Matsuhisa, the brainchild of emblematic chef Nobu Matsuhisa.
❀ **Il Carpaccio** – See restaurant listing

Raphael

⇪ ⅃⌂ 🛋 ⅄ ℀ 🛁

17 av. Kléber (16th) ⊠ *75116* – **Ⓜ** *Kléber*
Plan: **F2**
– ✆ 01 53 64 32 00 – www.raphael-hotel.com
83 rm – 🛏†650/950 € 🛏†650/950 € – ⌸ 40 € – 37 suites
• Luxury • Classic •

A magnificent entrance gallery with woodwork, very elegant rooms (some with views over Paris), a gourmet restaurant and an undeniably elegant English bar: such are the treasures of the Raphael. Founded in 1925, and a stone's throw from the Arc de Triomphe, it is a legend among Parisian hotels.

Prince de Galles

⇪ ⅃⌂ ⅄ ℀ 🛁

33 av. Georges-V (8th) – **Ⓜ** *George V*
Plan: **G3**
– ✆ 01 53 23 77 77 – www.hotelprincedegalles.fr
115 rm – 🛏†670/1020 € 🛏†670/1020 € – ⌸ 39 € – 44 suites
• Grand Luxury • Art Deco • Stylish •

After two years of refurbishment works, this legendary jewel of Parisian Art Deco, presiding over Avenue George V, reopened its doors in May 2013. Suffused with a new freshness, the charm of the place remains intact, notably in the luxurious and refined guestrooms. The timeless good taste of the Belle Epoque!
❀ **La Scène** – See restaurant listing

La Réserve

⇪ ⅃⌂ ⊛ 🖥 ⅄ ℀

42 av. Gabriel (8th) – **Ⓜ** *Champs Elysées Clémenceau*
Plan: **H3**
– ✆ 01 58 36 60 60 – www.lareserve-paris.com
14 rm ⌸ – 🛏†750/13500 € 🛏†750/13500 € – 26 suites
• Grand Luxury • Palace • Elegant •

Handsome wooden floors, inviting sofas and gold-plated cornices are a few of the exclusive details that set the Belle Epoque scene in this handsome Parisian 19C mansion, revamped by Jacques Garcia. The suites enjoy views over the Elysée palace gardens, Grand Palais or the Eiffel Tower. The quintessence of luxury.
❀❀ **Le Gabriel** – See restaurant listing

Fouquet's Barrière

⇪ ⅃⌂ ⊛ 🖥 ⅄ ℀ 🛁 🚗

46 av. George-V (8th) – **Ⓜ** *George V* – ✆ 01 40 69 60 00
Plan: **G2**
– www.fouquets-barriere.com
48 rm – 🛏†800/1500 € 🛏†800/1500 € – ⌸ 49 € – 33 suites
• Grand Luxury • Townhouse • Modern •

This luxury hotel follows in the tradition of mythical Parisian brasseries. Founded in 2006, its interior was designed by Jacques Garcia and blends French Empire-style with Art Deco. There is plenty of mahogany, silk, and velvet combined with high-tech facilities and a superb spa.
❀ **Le Diane** – See restaurant listing

Champs-Élysées Plaza

⇪ ⅃⌂ ⅄ ℀

35 r. de Berri (8th) – **Ⓜ** *George V* – ✆ 01 53 53 20 20
Plan: **G2**
– www.champselyseesplaza.com
35 rm – 🛏†290/890 € 🛏†290/890 € – ⌸ 32 € – 10 suites
• Luxury • Townhouse • Personalised •

With its elegance, space, harmony of colours, fusion of styles and attentive service, this hotel is the epitome of opulent and cosy luxury. Fitness centre.

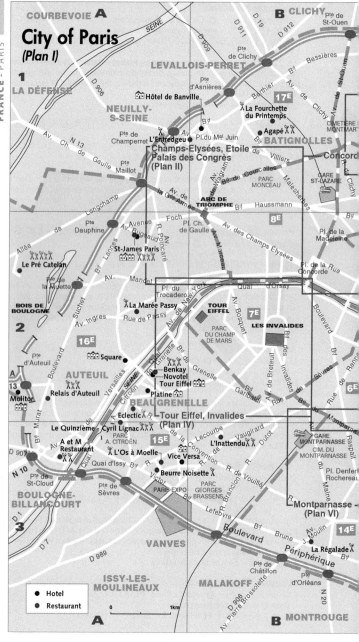

City of Paris
(Plan I)

ST-OUEN **C** ST-DENIS **D**

ulevard Périphérique

Pte de la Villette

PARIS-CHARLES DE GAULLE

A 1

N 2

PANTIN

Pte de Clignancourt Bd

Ney

Pte de la Chapelle

Bd Macdonald

CITÉ DES SCIENCES ET DE L'INDUSTRIE

18E

R. de la Chapelle

R. d'Aubervilliers

Rue

Flandre

PARC DE LA VILLETTE

N 3

Pte de Pantin

1

LE PRÉ-ST-GERVAIS

ontmartre, Pigalle (Plan VIII)

Barbès

R. M. Dormoy

A Q. de Seine

Av.

Crimée

Jean Jaurès

Bd d'Indochine

Pte de la Villette

SACRÉ-CŒUR

Kube

Bd de la Chapelle

GARE DU NORD

19E

Holiday Inn Express Canal de la Villette

LES LILAS

éra, Gare du Nord (Plan III)

Fayette

PARC DES BUTTES CHAUMONT

Botzaris

Bd Sérurier

D 117

9E

Hor

R. de Maubeuge

La

GARE DE L'EST

Chez Marie-Louise

R.

R.

Bichat

de la Villette

Belleville

Pte des Lilas

BELLEVILLE

Haussmann

de Sébastopol

2E

Pl. de la République

10E

Rue

Mortier

Pte de Bagnolet

A 3

ER

Pramil

Av. de la République

Le 20 Prieuré Hôtel

Av. Gambetta

Rue Belgrand

20E

MONTREUIL BAGNOLET

OUVRE

de

3E

Bon Kushikatsu

Fabric

Villaret

R. Lenoir

Voltaire

CIMETIÈRE DU PÈRE LACHAISE

Bd

11E

Yard

Mama Shelter

Davout

2

NOTRE-DAME

4E

Rivoli

Pl. de la Bastille

Henri IV

(Plan VII)

Marais, Bastille Gare de Lyon

Septime

Clamato

Bistrot Paul Bert

aint

St-Michel

Germain

Bd Bourdon

Bd Henri IV

R.

St-Antoine

Mansouria

Tintilou

Pl. de la Nation

Crs de Vincennes

Pte de Vincennes

N 34

JARDIN DU UXEMBOURG

5E

JARDIN DES PLANTES

Q. de la Rapée

Bd de Lyon

Diderot

Table-Bruno Verjus

Pl. de la Nation

ST-MANDÉ

St-Germain-des-Prés, Quartier Latin, Hôtel de Ville (Plan V)

GARE D'AUSTERLITZ

GARE DE LYON

12E

Pl. Félix Éboué

Bd de Bercy

Pl. de Reuilly

Daumesnil

Pte Dorée

BOIS DE VINCENNES

Bs de Port Royal

Auberge du 15

L'Ourcine

Av. Vincent Auriol

Tempero

Quai de Bercy

BERCY

Au Trou Gascon

Charenton

Pullman Paris Centre-Bercy

3

St-Jacques

Pl. d'Italie

Av. d'A. Blanqui

Avenue

BIBLIOTHÈQUE F. MITTERRAND

Quai de

Tolbiac

Pte de Bercy

Les Cailloux

Alésia

Rue

de Choisy

13E

Bd Kellermann

SEINE

Quai d'Ivry

CHARENTON-LE-PONT

A 4

PARC ONTSOURIS

Pho Tai

Imperial Choisy

Bd d'Italie

Masséna

Jourdan

Pte de entilly

Pte de Choisy

Pte d'Italie

IVRY-S-SEINE

N 19

A 6a

GENTILLY

C

D

PARIS-ORLY

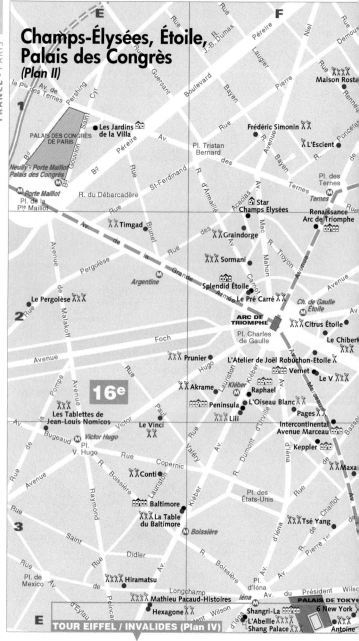

Champs-Élysées, Étoile, Palais des Congrès
(Plan II)

FRANCE - PARIS

PALAIS DES CONGRÈS DE PARIS

Neuilly - Porte Maillot
Palais des Congrès

Ⓜ Porte Maillot
Pl. de la
Pte Maillot
R. du Débarcadère

Les Jardins
de la Villa

Pl. Tristan
Bernard

Maison Rosta

Frédéric Simonin ✕✕

✕ L'Escient

Pl. des
Ternes

Ternes

Renaissance
Arc de Triomphe

Star
Champs Elysées

Timgad ✕✕

Graindorge ✕✕

Sormani ✕✕✕

Splendid Étoile

Le Pergolèse ✕✕✕

Argentine Ⓜ

Le Pré Carré ✕✕

ARC DE
TRIOMPHE

Pl. Charles
de Gaulle

Ch. de Gaulle
Étoile Ⓜ

Citrus Étoile ✕✕✕

Le Chibert
✕✕✕

16e

Prunier ✕✕✕

L'Atelier de Joël Robuchon-Etoile ✕

Vernet

Le V ✕✕✕

Akrame ✕✕

Raphael

L'Oiseau Blanc ✕✕

Les Tablettes de
Jean-Louis Nomicos ✕✕✕

Peninsula

Lili ✕✕✕

Pages ✕✕

Le Vinci
✕✕

Intercontinental
Avenue Marceau

Ⓜ Victor Hugo
Pl.
V. Hugo

Keppler

Maxa ✕✕

Conti ✕✕

Baltimore

La Table
du Baltimore ✕✕✕

Pl. des
États-Unis

Ⓜ Boissière

Tsé Yang ✕✕✕

Hiramatsu ✕✕✕✕

Pl. de
Mexico

Mathieu Pacaud-Histoires ✕✕✕✕

Hexagone ✕✕

Shangri-La

6 New York

L'Abeille ✕✕✕

Shang Palace ✕✕

Antoine ✕✕✕

PALAIS DE TOKYO

TOUR EIFFEL / INVALIDES (Plan IV)

192

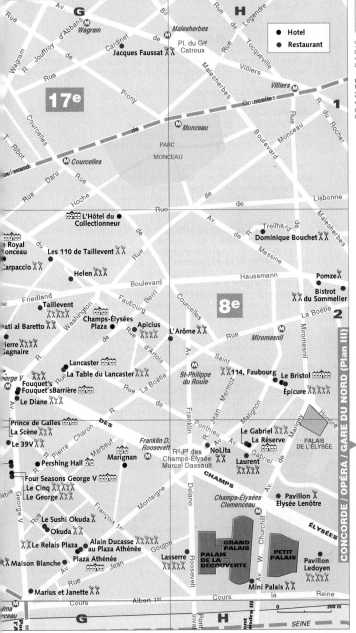

17e

8e

Hotel
Restaurant

Av. G d'Abbans

Wagram

Cardinet

Jacques Faussat

Pl. du Gal Catroux

Malesherbes

Villiers

Villiers

Courcelles

Monceau

PARC MONCEAU

Courcelles

Lisbonne

L'Hôtel du Collectionneur

Treilhard

Dominique Bouchet

Messine

Le Royal Monceau

Les 110 de Taillevent

Carpaccio

Helen

Pomze

Bistrot du Sommelier

Taillevent

Faubourg

Champs-Élysées Plaza

Apicius

L'Arôme

La Boétie

Rati al Baretto

Washington

Pierre Gagnaire

Lancaster

La Table du Lancaster

St-Philippe du Roule

114, Faubourg

Le Bristol

Épicure

Fouquet's
Fouquet's Barrière

Le Diane

Prince de Galles

La Scène

Le 39V

Pershing Hall

Marignan

Franklin D. Roosevelt

Rd-Pt des Champs-Élysée Marcel Dassault

NoLita

Le Gabriel

La Réserve

Laurent

PALAIS DE L'ELYSÉE

Four Seasons George V
Le Cinq
Le George

Le Sushi Okuda

Okuda

Le Relais Plaza

Alain Ducasse au Plaza Athénée

Plaza Athénée

Lasserre

Pavillon Élysée Lenôtre

Maison Blanche

Marius et Janette

CHAMPS

Champs-Élysées Clemenceau

GRAND PALAIS

PALAIS DE LA DÉCOUVERTE

PETIT PALAIS

ÉLYSÉES

Pavillon Ledoyen

Mini Palais

Cours

Albert 1er

la

Reine

SEINE

0   200 m

193

Lancaster

7 r. de Berri (8th) – Ⓜ *George V* – ✆ *01 40 76 40 76* — Plan: **G2**
– *www.hotel-lancaster.com*
45 rm – ♦350/530 € ♦♦450/730 € – ⌷ 42 € – 11 suites
• Luxury • Townhouse • Classic •

Marlene Dietrich loved the discreet luxury of this property built in 1889 just a stone's throw from the Champs-Élysées. Pleasant lobby and lounges filled with antique furniture.

❀❀ **La Table du Lancaster** – See restaurant listing

Vernet

25 r. Vernet (8th) – Ⓜ *Charles de Gaulle-Etoile* — Plan: **F2**
– ✆ *01 44 31 98 00* – *www.hotelvernet.com*
41 rm – ♦269/690 € ♦♦269/690 € – ⌷ 35 € – 9 suites
• Luxury • Townhouse • Elegant •

This building dating back to the Roaring Twenties is in a small street set slightly back from the Champs-Élysées and is home to a brand new hotel. It has been completely refurbished and exudes a very Parisian je ne sais quoi, from the bright lobby to the elegant and refined guestrooms.

Le V – See restaurant listing

L'Hôtel du Collectionneur

51 r. de Courcelles (8th) – Ⓜ *Courcelles* — Plan: **G2**
– ✆ *01 58 36 67 00* – *www.hotelducollectionneur.com*
443 rm – ♦220/789 € ♦♦220/789 € – ⌷ 25 € – 35 suites
• Luxury • Chain hotel • Elegant •

Inspired by the cruise liners of the 1930s, this hotel has revived their luxurious and refined spirit, with its elegant Art Deco bedrooms designed by Jacques Garcia – those facing the patio are particularly quiet. Fitness centre. The brasserie-style menu at the Safran is adapted to international tastes.

Baltimore

88 bis av. Kléber (16th) ✉ *75116* – Ⓜ *Boissière* — Plan: **E3**
– ✆ *01 44 34 54 54* – *www.hotel-baltimore-paris.com*
103 rm – ♦200/690 € ♦♦200/690 € – ⌷ 30 € – 1 suite
• Historic • Elegant • Cosy •

The contemporary decor of elegant furniture and trendy fabrics in the guest-rooms contrasts with the building's 19C Haussmann architecture. The overall feel is warm and welcoming. The bar is worth a special mention and is appreciated by business travellers in particular.

La Table du Baltimore – See restaurant listing

Renaissance Arc de Triomphe

39 av. Wagram (17th) – Ⓜ *Ternes* – ✆ *01 55 37 55 37* — Plan: **F2**
– *www.marriott.fr*
118 rm ⌷ – ♦299/799 € ♦♦299/799 € – 5 suites
• Luxury • Chain hotel • Design •

You cannot miss the impressive façade of this hotel designed by Christian de Portzamparc, which is very close to the Place de l'Etoile and the Arc de Triomphe. The originality and contemporary style also extends to the inside, from the elegant guestrooms to the spacious lobby. A success!

Keppler

10 r. Keppler (16th) ✉ *75116* – Ⓜ *George V* — Plan: **F3**
– ✆ *01 47 20 65 05* – *www.keppler.fr*
34 rm – ♦300/500 € ♦♦300/1200 € – ⌷ 22 € – 5 suites
• Luxury • Personalised • Cosy •

The Keppler's luxurious and refined decor bears the hallmark of Pierre-Yves Rochon. There is a sense of magic pervading the lounges, library and guest-rooms. A hammam, sauna and fitness room complete the picture at one of the city's most elegant addresses.

Intercontinental Avenue Marceau

64 av. Marceau (8th) – Ⓜ *George V*
– ℰ *01 44 43 36 36* – *www.ic-marceau.com*
55 rm – ♦350/1600 € ♦♦550/1600 € – ⌁ 30 €

Plan: **F2-3**

• Luxury • Business • Modern •

This luxury designer hotel is close to the Arc de Triomphe. The decor is a blend of high technology, contemporary furnishings and replicas of Italian Renaissance frescoes and sketches.

Marignan

12 r. de Marignan (8th) – Ⓜ *Franklin D. Roosevelt*
– ℰ *01 40 76 34 56* – *www.hotelmarignanelyseesparis.com*
45 rm – ♦310/580 € ♦♦360/680 € – ⌁ 29 € – 5 suites

Plan: **G3**

• Luxury • Townhouse • Modern •

This hotel in a former townhouse, just off the Champs-Élysées, offers a discreet take on luxury. All of the guestrooms are done out in an elegant and sleek style with oak floorboards, chic 1950s and 1960s furniture and large beds. Style and subtlety.

Splendid Étoile

1bis av. Carnot (17th) – Ⓜ *Charles de Gaulle-Etoile*
– ℰ *01 45 72 72 00* – *www.hsplendid.com*
55 rm – ♦220/420 € ♦♦220/750 € – ⌁ 25 € – 2 suites

Plan: **F2**

• Traditional • Personalised •

The Splendid Étoile is recognisable by its attractive stone façade and wrought-iron balconies. It offers large guestrooms (some with views of the Arc de Triomphe), which owe their character to the Louis XV inspired furniture and heavy drapes. Overall, a very pleasant, elegant style.
Le Pré Carré – See restaurant listing

Pershing Hall

49 r. Pierre-Charron (8th) – Ⓜ *George V*
– ℰ *01 58 36 58 00* – *www.pershinghall.com*
20 rm ⌁ – ♦324/590 € ♦♦324/890 € – 6 suites

Plan: **G3**

• Luxury • Townhouse • Modern •

This townhouse was the residence of General Pershing during the Great War, it was then a veterans' club, and since 2001 it has been home to this luxury hotel styled by designer Andrée Putman. A veritable page in Parisian history with a chic and discreet ambience.

Les Jardins de la Villa

5 r. Bélidor (17th) – Ⓜ *Porte Maillot* – ℰ *01 53 81 01 10*
– *www.jardinsdelavilla.com*
33 rm – ♦155/400 € ♦♦155/400 € – ⌁ 22 €

Plan: **E1**

• Luxury • Business • Design •

Fashion addicts will be bowled over by this small hotel which is big on couture. With its black and shocking pink decor, the references to the world of fashion are numerous. Original, chic and comfortable.

Star Champs Élysées

18 r. de l'Arc-de-Triomphe (17th)
– Ⓜ *Charles de Gaulle-Etoile* – ℰ *01 43 80 27 69*
– *www.hotelstarchampselysees.com*
62 rm – ♦100/290 € ♦♦120/390 € – ⌁ 13 €

Plan: **F2**

• Townhouse • Modern •

This hotel is in a quiet street near the Place de l'Étoile and the Arc de Triomphe. It offers guestrooms which, although small, are functional and well maintained. The reception area with its medieval decoration makes for an original detail! A good bet for both business travellers and tourists.

FRANCE - PARIS

XxXxX   **Le Cinq** – Hôtel Four Seasons George V   🏖 🆔 ⇄ 🐟

🌼🌼🌼   *31 av. George V (8th) –* Ⓜ *George V – ℰ 01 49 52 71 54*   Plan: **G3**
– www.fourseasons.com/paris
Menu 145 € (lunch), 210/310 € – Carte 175/300 €
• Modern cuisine • Luxury • Elegant •
After the magnificent years spent at Ledoyen, Christian Le Squer has moved to
this prestigious address. The majesty of the Grand Trianon inspired decor
remains intact, waiters in uniform still perform their dizzying ballet, and the
expertise of the chef does the rest, keeping the finest tradition alive!
➔ Gratinée d'oignons à la parisienne. Bar de ligne au caviar et lait ribot.
Croquant de pamplemousse confit cru et cuit.

XxXxX   **Alain Ducasse au Plaza Athénée** – Hôtel Plaza Athénée

🌼🌼🌼   *25 av. Montaigne (8th) –* Ⓜ *Alma Marceau*   🏖 🆔 🐟
– ℰ 01 53 67 65 00 – www.alain-ducasse.com – Closed   Plan: **G3**
*August, 19 to 29 December, Monday lunch, Tuesday lunch, Wednesday
lunch, Saturday and Sunday*
Menu 210 € 🍷 (lunch)/380 € – Carte 230/380 €
• Creative • Luxury •
After the Plaza Athénée's recent facelift, the magnificence of the dining room
is breathtaking! Alain Ducasse has rethought his entire restaurant along the
lines of 'naturality' – his culinary Holy Grail is to uncover the truth of each
ingredient. Based on the trilogy fish-vegetables-cereals (here too, a respect
for nature prevails), some of the dishes are really outstanding, and the quest
seems infinite.
➔ Légumes des jardins du château de Versailles, pousses de moutarde pilées. Rouget de l'Île d'Yeu en écailles, jus civet lié au foin, tian. Citron et algues kombu à l'estragon.

XxXxX   **Alléno Paris – Pavillon Ledoyen**   🆔 ⇄ 🐟 🅿

🌼🌼🌼   *8 av. Dutuit (carré Champs-Élysées) (8th)*   Plan: **H3**
– Ⓜ *Champs-Elysées Clemenceau – ℰ 01 53 05 10 01*
*– www.yannick-alleno.com – Closed 6 to 22 August, 23 to 26 December,
Saturday lunch and Sunday*
Menu 135 € (lunch), 295/380 € – Carte 150/320 €
• Modern cuisine • Luxury •
Taken over by Yannick Alléno, this Parisian institution – in an elegant Second
Empire pavilion in the Jardins des Champs Elysées – is embarking on a new
chapter in its history. The chef produces a tour de force, immediately stamping
his hallmark on dishes. He manages with all his mastery to put a new spin on
haute cuisine, magnifying for example jus and sauces through clever extra-
ctions. Prepare to be impressed!
➔ Tarte friande de langoustine au caviar osciètre. Timbale de coquillages,
feuille et chair de seiche, grenailles de Camargue fondantes au piment
d'Espelette. Charlotte norvégienne moderne aux mirabelles.

XxXxX   **Épicure** – Hôtel Bristol   🏖 🍴 🆔 🐟

🌼🌼🌼   *112 r. du Faubourg-St-Honoré (8th) –* Ⓜ *Miromesnil*   Plan: **H2**
– ℰ 01 53 43 43 40 – www.lebristolparis.com
Menu 145 € (lunch)/320 € – Carte 165/315 €
• Modern cuisine • Luxury • Intimate •
An exceptional experience in the heart of the Bristol. The bright dining room
overlooking the garden boasts a restrained, distinguished elegance for which
the French are famous. The virtuosity of Éric Fréchon's classic cuisine bears wit-
ness to his freedom of expression with regard to great tradition. He creates
dishes that are fresh and endowed with the finest flavours!
➔ Macaronis farcis à la truffe noire, artichaut et foie gras de canard grati-
nés au vieux parmesan. Poularde de Bresse en vessie, écrevisses et girolles.
Chocolat du Pérou en cabosse, mousseux et croquant, sorbet chocolat.

XxXxX ★★

Le Taillevent

15 r. Lamennais (8th) – Ⓜ Charles de Gaulle-Etoile   Plan: **G2**
– ✆ 01 44 95 15 01 – www.taillevent.com – Closed 30 July-29 August,
Saturday, Sunday and Bank Holidays
Menu 88 € (lunch), 218/278 € – Carte 155/295 € – *(booking advisable)*
• Classic cuisine • Luxury • Elegant •

Wainscoting and works of art adorn this former private residence dating from
the 19C. It was once home to the Duke of Morny, and is now a guardian of
French haute cuisine. Exquisite cuisine and magnificent wine list.
➔ Boudin de homard bleu tradition Taillevent". Bar de ligne, poireau,
champagne et caviar osciètre. Crêpes Suzette."

XxXxX ★

Lasserre

17 av. F.-D.-Roosevelt (8th) – Ⓜ Franklin D. Roosevelt   Plan: **H3**
– ✆ 01 43 59 02 13 – www.restaurant-lasserre.com – Closed August,
Tuesday lunch, Wednesday lunch, Saturday lunch, Sunday and Monday
Menu 90 € (lunch), 195/375 € Ⓨ – Carte 170/240 €
• Classic cuisine • Luxury • Formal •

One of the temples of Parisian gastronomy. The elegance of the interior (columns,
draperies, tassels etc), the tableware, the quality of the service – it all comes together to magnify haute cuisine! Fashions come and go, Lasserre remains.
➔ Macaroni, truffe noire et foie gras de canard. Bœuf Rossini, pommes
soufflées. Crêpes Suzette.

XxXxX ★

Laurent

41 av. Gabriel (8th) – Ⓜ Champs Elysées Clemenceau   Plan: **H3**
– ✆ 01 42 25 00 39 – www.le-laurent.com – Closed 23 December-
2 January, Saturday lunch, Sunday and Bank Holidays
Menu 95 € (lunch)/180 € – Carte 165/250 €
• Classic cuisine • Elegant • Luxury •

A stone's throw from the Champs Élysées, this former hunting lodge belonging
to Louis XIV with its elegant shaded terraces has a loyal following. Traditional
cuisine and a good wine list.
➔ Araignée de mer dans ses sucs en gelée, crème de fenouil. Turbot nacré
à l'huile d'olive, bardes et légumes verts dans une fleurette iodée. Glace
vanille minute.

XxXX ★★

L'Abeille – Hôtel Shangri-La

10 av. d'Iéna (16th) ✉ 75116 – Ⓜ Iéna   Plan: **F3**
– ✆ 01 53 67 19 90 – www.shangri-la.com – Closed August, 20 to
30 December, Tuesday lunch, Wednesday lunch, Saturday lunch, Sunday
and Monday
Menu 88 € (lunch), 195/230 € Ⓨ – Carte 165/195 €
• Modern cuisine • Luxury • Elegant •

The Shangri-La Hotel's French restaurant has a name that gives a nod to the
Napoleonic emblem of the bee. As you might expect, the grand culinary tradition is honoured here under the auspices of chef Christophe Moret. The menu
promotes fine classicism and noble ingredients.
➔ Oursin et caviar en délicate royale. Homard rôti, primeurs au sautoir,
sucs savoureux. Citron de pays confit, perles du Japon au thé matcha d'Uji.

XxXX ★★

Mathieu Pacaud - Histoires

85 av. Kléber (16th) ✉ 75016 – Ⓜ Trocadéro   Plan: **E3**
– ✆ 01 70 98 16 35 – www.histoires-paris.fr – Closed 27 February-7 March,
1 to 29 August, Tuesday lunch, Sunday and Monday
Menu 95 € (lunch), 195/250 € – Carte 220/290 € – *(booking advisable)*
• Creative • Elegant • Cosy •

Mathieu Pacaud and his team took many months to explore countless combinations and hatch an original and well-crafted menu. The chef draws on numerous techniques – infusion, maceration, deglazing, marinades – and produces
innovative dishes: each one is an experience in itself!
➔ Écrevisses pattes rouges, gaspacho de cerise burlat et dernière russe
rouge. Volaille de Bresse déglacée au xérès, gnocchis à la sauge. Chocolat
madong, croquant chocolat blanc et glace mascarpone.

XxXX Apicius (Jean-Pierre Vigato)

20 r. d'Artois (8th) – **M** St-Philippe du Roule   Plan: **G2**
– *C* 01 43 80 19 66 – www.restaurant-apicius.com – *Closed August,*
Saturday, Sunday and Bank Holidays
Menu 180/200 € – Carte 135/215 €
• Classic cuisine • Elegant •

In the setting of a 18th century listed town house, a succession of fine rooms in a
chic mix of classic, rococo and modern styles. Up-to-date cuisine by Jean-Pierre
Vigato, based around excellent produce. Superb wine list.

➜ Huîtres et crustacés rafraîchis d'eau de mer, cresson. Ris et côte de veau
au sautoir, purée de pomme de terre. Soufflé chocolat.

XxXX Pierre Gagnaire

6 r. Balzac (8th) – **M** George V – *C* 01 58 36 12 50   Plan: **G2**
– www.pierregagnaire.com – *Closed 3 weeks in August, 1 week Christmas*
Holidays, Saturday and Sunday
Menu 155/310 € – Carte 325/405 €
• Creative • Elegant •

The restaurant's chic contemporary decor is in sober contrast to this renowned
chef's creativity, curiosity and open-mindedness...A passionate amateur of jazz
and art, Pierre Gagnaire makes flavours, colours and textures sing. A festival for
the senses!

➜ Gambas de Palamos coraillées, raidies au four, pistes, casserons et poul-
pitos à l'omiza. Saint-pierre pimenté saisi à la poêle, compote de concombre, tomate et txistorra. Le grand dessert de Pierre Gagnaire.

XxxX Hiramatsu

52 r. Longchamp (16th) ✉ 75116 – **M** Trocadéro   Plan: **E3**
– *C* 01 56 81 08 80 – www.hiramatsu.co.jp – *Closed August, 24 December-*
2 January, Saturday and Sunday
Menu 48 € (lunch), 75/115 € – *(booking advisable)*
• Modern cuisine • Elegant • Luxury •

Despite its Japanese name, Hiramatsu honours French cuisine with both inventiveness and talent. In this very elegant setting, high gastronomy is expressed in
the form of a single 'carte blanche' menu in the evening, which changes in line
with market availability.

➜ Cuisine du marché.

XxxX Maison Rostang

20 r. Rennequin (17th) – **M** Ternes – *C* 01 47 63 40 77   Plan: **F1**
– www.maisonrostang.com – *Closed 2 weeks in August, Saturday lunch*
and Sunday
Menu 80 € (lunch), 185/225 € – Carte 150/215 €
• Classic cuisine • Elegant • Luxury •

Wood panelling, Robj statuettes, Lalique glass and Art Deco stained glass combine to give this restaurant a luxurious and original look. Exquisite classic cuisine
and an equally outstanding wine list.

➜ Homard bleu confit, risotto d'artichaut et jus de presse au Condrieu. Ris
de veau croustillant, pâtes farcies de champignons et écrevisses au vin
jaune. Cigare croustillant au tabac Havane et mousseline Cognac.

XxX Le Gabriel – Hôtel La Réserve

42 av. Gabriel (8th) – **M** Champs Elysées Clemenceau   Plan: **H3**
– *C* 01 58 36 60 60 – www.lareserve-paris.com
Menu 67 € (lunch)/115 € – Carte 90/150 €
• Modern cuisine • Elegant • Luxury •

The restaurant is nestled in the elegant setting of La Réserve and features Versailles wooden flooring and *cuir de Cordoue* with a gold patina. Chef Jérôme
Bancel, no stranger to Paris' *grandes maisons*, cooks his own superb take on
the classics, with a smattering of Asian touches and executed in the proper
way. A success!

➜ Saumon miso, raviole de daïkon, aubergines fumées et pâte de citron.
Cochon de lait croustillant, carrotes maraîchères au cumin. Soufflé au chocolat, cœur coulant au safran, sorbet cacao.

FRANCE - PARIS

ⅩⅩⅩ
🕸 ⭐

La Scène – Hôtel Prince de Galles   🕸 ⭐ Ⓐ ⇔ 🍽

33 av. George-V (8th) – Ⓜ George V – ℰ 01 53 23 78 50   Plan: **G3**
– www.restaurant-la-scene.fr – Closed August, Satruday lunch and Sunday
Menu 65 € (lunch), 95/195 € – Carte 95/190 €
• Modern cuisine • Elegant • Luxury •

Within the elegant Prince de Galles Hotel, La Scène shines the spotlight on the
kitchens, which are separated from the dining area by just a white marble counter. They are the realm of Stéphanie Le Quellec, no stranger to the limelight
since winning France's 'Top Chef' TV show in 2011. Imaginative, harmonious
and precise dishes.
➔ Œuf fermier d'Île-de-France, jaune tiède acidulé, asperges vertes
et morilles. Ris de veau doré au jus, compression de romaine, salicornes
et olives noires. Vanille en cinq feuilles, crème onctueuse.

ⅩⅩⅩ
🕸 ⭐

Shang Palace – Hôtel Shangri-La   ⭐ Ⓐ ⇔ 🍽

10 av. d'Iéna (16th) ✉ 75116 – Ⓜ Iéna   Plan: **F3**
– ℰ 01 53 67 19 92 – www.shangri-la.com – Closed 12 July-3 August,
Tuesday and Wednesday
Menu 52 € 🍷 (lunch), 78/128 € – Carte 60/280 €
• Chinese • Exotic •

The Shang Palace occupies one of the basement floors at the Shangri-La hotel.
It gracefully recreates the decor of a luxury Chinese restaurant with its jade
columns, sculpted screens and crystal chandeliers. The menu pays homage to
the full flavours and authenticity of Cantonese gastronomy.
➔ Saumon Lo Hei. Canard laqué façon pékinoise en deux services. Crème
de mangue, pomélo et perles de sagou.

ⅩⅩⅩ

Lili – Hôtel Peninsula   ⭐ Ⓐ ⇔

19 av. Kléber (16th) ✉ 75116 – Ⓜ Kléber   Plan: **F2**
– ℰ 01 58 12 67 50 – http://paris.peninsula.com/fr/ – Closed 22 to
29 February and 13 to 30 August
Menu 68 € (lunch), 115/160 € – Carte 70/250 €
• Chinese • Elegant • Exotic •

Opened by the Hong Kong luxury hotel group of the same name, the already
famous Peninsula Hotel is the rightful home of an Asian restaurant, Lili. It is
named after a famous Chinese singer of the 1920s. In a very theatrical setting,
the long menu unveils a wide range of Chinese specialties. A real embassy!

ⅩⅩⅩ

Prunier   🍴 Ⓐ ⇔ 🍽

16 av. Victor-Hugo (16th) ✉ 75116   Plan: **F2**
– Ⓜ Charles de Gaulle-Etoile – ℰ 01 44 17 35 85 – www.prunier.com
– Closed August, Saturday lunch, Sunday and Bank Holidays
Menu 47 € (lunch), 65/155 € – Carte 69/204 €
• Fish and seafood • Classic • Cosy •

A culinary institution created in 1925 by the architect Boileau. It has a superb,
listed Art Deco interior of black marble, mosaics and stained-glass windows. In
addition to enjoying excellent fish and seafood, mark the occasion by tasting
the house caviar from southwest France.

ⅩⅩⅩ
🕸 🕸

La Table du Lancaster – Hôtel Lancaster   🕸 🍴 Ⓐ ⇔ 🍽

7 r. de Berri (8th) – Ⓜ George V – ℰ 01 40 76 40 18   Plan: **G2**
– www.hotel-lancaster.fr – Closed 3 weeks in August, Saturday, Sunday
and Bank Holidays
Menu 65 € (lunch), 115/205 € – Carte 135/155 €
• Modern cuisine • Elegant •

All the exclusive and confidential atmosphere of a grand hotel restaurant, especially as it is the Lancaster... The moment is all the more special in that the
young chef, Julien Roucheteau, creates brilliant cuisine. Impeccable in its display
of technique, subtle in the way it interweaves textures and flavours, to show off
the exceptional ingredients. Elegance personified.
➔ Fricassée d'escargots de Bourgogne aux herbes folles. Côte de veau de
tradition française. Fraîcheur de mangue pimentée de curry.

XxX 🏵️ **Le Diane** – Hôtel Fouquet's Barrière 🏠 ♿ 🅰️ 🐷 🚗

46 av. George-V (8th) – Ⓜ *George V – ℰ 01 40 69 60 60*   Plan: **G2**
– www.fouquets-barriere.com – Closed August, 1 to 7 January, Saturday lunch, Sunday and Monday
Menu 62 € (lunch), 90/210 € 🍷 – Carte 115/165 €
• Modern cuisine • Luxury •
Tucked away inside the Hotel Fouquet's Barrière, Le Diane is the epitome of elegance and discretion. The dining area is housed in a rotunda, all done out in golden browns and opening onto a lovely patio. Beautifully prepared gourmet cuisine.
➜ Ormeaux, effiloché de tourteau et condiment gingembre. Ris de veau braisé, oignons de Roscoff et arroche rouge. Soufflé chocolat et poire, glace au miel.

XxX **Le George** – Hôtel Four Seasons George V   🏵️ ♿ 🅰️ 🐷

31 av. George-V (8th) – Ⓜ *George V – ℰ 01 49 52 70 00*   Plan: **G3**
– www.legeorge.com
Menu 110 € – Carte 75/90 €
• Mediterranean • Luxury • Elegant •
Remarkable Baccarat chandelier, a decor of immaculate white, delicate flower arrangements – there is no doubt about it, we can only be at the Four Seasons Hotel George V! The food, with pleasing Mediterranean notes, is all about lightness and sharing portions. Be sure to sample the delicious desserts.

XxX **Fouquet's**   🏠 🔄

99 av. Champs-Élysées (8th) – Ⓜ *George V*   Plan: **G2**
– ℰ 01 40 69 60 50 – www.lucienbarriere.com
Menu 89 € – Carte 84/186 €
• Classic cuisine • Elegant •
Since its creation in 1899, this mythical brasserie on "the world's most beautiful avenue" has catered to the Paris jet set. It offers a lovely listed interior, a packed terrace, and brasserie fare.

XxX **Le V** – Hôtel Vernet   🅰️ 🐷

25 r. Vernet (8th) – Ⓜ *Charles de Gaulle-Etoile*   Plan: **F2**
– ℰ 01 44 31 98 00 – www.hotelvernet.com – Closed August, Saturday lunch and Sunday
Carte 51/81 €
• Modern cuisine • Elegant •
The stunning dining room of the Hôtel Vernet is crowned by a large Eiffel designed glass canopy and embellished with pilasters and drapes. The perfect setting for a special occasion, where the refined cuisine encompasses a classic repertoire with new combinations of flavours.

XxX **Maison Blanche**   ⬅️ 🏠 🅰️ 🐷

15 av. Montaigne (8th) – Ⓜ *Alma Marceau*   Plan: **G3**
– ℰ 01 47 23 55 99 – www.maison-blanche.fr – Closed 2 weeks in August and lunch Saturday and Sunday
Menu 69 € (lunch), 95/125 € – Carte 78/209 €
• Modern cuisine • Fashionable •
Majestically located on the rooftop of the Champs Elysées Theatre, this immense two-floor loft overlooks the Eiffel Tower and a big chunk of Paris! The contemporary cuisine with Mediterranean accents bears witness to the chef's international background.

XxX **La Table du Baltimore** – Hôtel Baltimore   🅰️ 🔄 🐷

1 r. Léo-Delibes (16th) ✉️ *75016 –* Ⓜ *Boissière*   Plan: **E3**
– ℰ 01 44 34 54 34 – www.hotel-baltimore-paris.com – Closed August, Saturday, Sunday and Bank Holidays
Menu 95 € – Carte 81/102 €
• Modern cuisine • Cosy •
The Hotel Baltimore is also home to this chic restaurant boasting old wood panelling, contemporary furniture and artwork. An elegant setting for cuisine in keeping with the times.

XxX

£3

Le Chiberta   🖾 ⇔ 🍴

3 r. Arsène-Houssaye (8th) – ⓜ Charles de Gaulle-Etoile   Plan: **F2**
– ☏ 01 53 53 42 00 – www.lechiberta.com – Closed 3 weeks in August,
Saturday lunch and Sunday
Menu 110/165 € ⏱ – Carte 90/135 €
• Creative • Design •

Soft lighting and chic decor designed by J M Wilmotte (dark colours and
unusual wine bottle walls) provide the setting for inventive cuisine overseen
by chef Guy Savoy.
→ Cœur de saumon mariné aux agrumes, pastèque et concombre au
pomélo. Filet de saint-pierre à la plancha, risotto verde et jus vert à
l'amande douce. Sablé au citron, meringue croquante et sorbet citron.

XxX

Sormani   🍷 🖾 ⇔ 🍴

4 r. Gén.-Lanrezac (17th) – ⓜ Charles de Gaulle-Etoile   Plan: **F2**
– ☏ 01 43 80 13 91 – www.restaurantsormani.fr – Closed 3 weeks in
August, Saturday, Sunday and Bank Holidays
Carte 65/145 €
• Italian • Romantic •

All the elegance of Italy finds expression in this chic and intimate restaurant
with its sumptuous fabrics, Murano glass chandeliers, mouldings and mirrors.
Pascal Fayet's cooking pays a fine tribute to Italian cuisine, and to truffles in season: fried eggs with truffle, or lasagne with black truffle and pan-fried foie gras.

XxX

£3

Les Tablettes de Jean-Louis Nomicos   🔥 🖾 🍴

16 av. Bugeaud (16th) ✉ 75116 – ⓜ Victor Hugo   Plan: **E3**
– ☏ 01 56 28 16 16 – www.lestablettesjeanlouisnomicos.com
Menu 58 € ⏱ (lunch), 80 € ⏱/145 € – Carte 100/145 €
• Modern cuisine • Elegant •

Having manned the kitchens at Lasserre, Jean-Louis Nomicos is now pursuing
his solo career on the premises formerly occupied by Joël Robuchon's La
Table. Savour his fine, Mediterranean inspired cuisine to a backdrop of original
and contemporary decor.
→ Macaroni, truffe noire, foie gras de canard, céleri et jus de veau. Rouget
croustillant, marjolaine, pulpe d'olives noires et oignon doux. Tarte soufflée
chocolat grand cru, sorbet cacao et émulsion mascarpone.

XxX

£3

Antoine   🖾 ⇔ 🍴

10 av. de New-York (16th) ✉ 75116 – ⓜ Alma Marceau   Plan: **F3**
– ☏ 01 40 70 19 28 – www.antoine-paris.fr – Closed 3 weeks in August,
1 week Christmas Holidays, Sunday and Monday
Menu 48 € (lunch), 86/138 € – Carte 110/160 €
• Fish and seafood • Elegant •

With chef Thibault Sombardier at the helm, this restaurant is a sure bet for seafood in Paris. Delivered directly from the ports of Brittany, the Basque region or
the Mediterranean, the quality ingredients are handled with expertise and inspiration. Elegant contemporary decor.
→ Carpaccio de mulet noir, huile d'olive parfumée aux feuilles de citron-
nier. Turbot laqué aux sucs de volaille, girolles et purée d'ail noir. Galet chocolat ivoire et algue, compotée de cédrat et sorbet citron.

XxX

£3

Le Pergolèse (Stéphane Gaborieau)   🍷 🖾 ⇔ 🍴

40 r. Pergolèse (16th) ✉ 75116 – ⓜ Porte Maillot   Plan: **E2**
– ☏ 01 45 00 21 40 – www.lepergolese.com – Closed 3 weeks in August,
25 December-1 January, Saturday lunch and Sunday
Menu 58 € ⏱ (lunch), 110/125 € – Carte 80/145 €
• Modern cuisine • Elegant •

A successful reinterpretation of southern cuisine with a smattering of Japanese
touches by a chef awarded the 'Meilleur Ouvrier de France'. It is served in a
decor that is at once pared down and elegant.
→ Moelleux de filets de sardines marinés aux épices, poivron à la basquaise
et sorbet tomate. Sole meunière. Soufflé chaud aux saveurs de saison.

FRANCE - PARIS

XxX Tsé Yang 🄰 ⇔

25 av. Pierre-1er-de-Serbie (16th) ✉ *75016 –* Ⓜ *Iéna* Plan: **F3**
– ✆ *01 47 20 70 22*
Menu 39 € (lunch), 49/59 € – Carte 50/100 €
• Chinese • Exotic •

Elegant dining rooms (gilded ceilings and dominant black colour scheme) provide the setting for traditional Chinese cuisine from Peking, Shanghai and
Sichuan. An exotic location in which guests will also appreciate the attentive
and stylish service.

XxX Citrus Étoile ♿ 🄰 🍴

6 r. Arsène-Houssaye (8th) – Ⓜ *Charles de Gaulle-Étoile* Plan: **F2**
– ✆ *01 42 89 15 51 – www.citrusetoile.com – Closed Christmas Holidays,*
Saturday, Sunday and Bank Holidays
Menu 49/69 € – Carte 50/95 €
• Modern cuisine • Elegant •

In a restaurant decorated with flair by his wife Élisabeth, Gilles Épié creates original and skilfully prepared cuisine. It is testament as much to his solid classical
training as it is to the experience he clocked up in the USA (the couple lived in
California for 10 years) and Asia. Friendly and professional service.

XxX Helen 🄰 ⇔
❀
3 r. Berryer (8th) – Ⓜ *George V –* ✆ *01 40 76 01 40* Plan: **G2**
– www.helenrestaurant.com – Closed 3 weeks in August, 24 December-
4 January, Saturday lunch, Sunday and Monday
Menu 48 € (lunch)/130 € – Carte 80/170 €
• Fish and seafood • Elegant • Design •

Founded in 2012, Helen has made its mark among the fish restaurants of Paris'
chic neighbourhoods. If you love fish, you will be bowled over: from the quality
of the ingredients (only wild fish sourced from fishermen who bring in the catch
of the day on small boats) to the care taken over the recipes. Sober and elegant
decor.
➜ Carpaccio de daurade royale au citron caviar. Bar de ligne aux olives
taggiasche. Saint-honoré.

XX Hexagone 🄰 🍴
❀
85 av. Kléber (16th) ✉ *75116 –* Ⓜ *Trocadéro* Plan: **E3**
– ✆ *01 42 25 98 85 – www.hexagone-paris.fr – Closed Sunday*
Menu 49 € (lunch), 125/175 € – Carte 75/95 €
• Modern cuisine • Trendy • Design •

After many years working with his father Bernard at L'Ambroisie, Mathieu
Pacaud has embarked on his own gourmet adventure. He brilliantly concocts
his own version of French culinary classics, whilst preserving a unity of technique, flavour and sauce. Inspiring!
➜ Velouté de cèpes et jaune d'œuf bio coulant. Noix de ris de veau braisée, émulsion d'estragon, sauce diable. Blanc d'œuf en neige, crème anglaise à la vanille, Melba de brioche et pralin rose.

XX Le 39V (Frédéric Vardon) 🄰 🍴 (dinner)
❀
39 av. George-V (6th floor - entrance at 17 r. Quentin- Plan: **G3**
Bauchart) (8th) – Ⓜ *George V –* ✆ *01 56 62 39 05 – www.le39v.com*
– Closed August, Saturday and Sunday
Menu 50 € (lunch), 95/195 € ▼ – Carte 95/138 €
• Modern cuisine • Design •

The temperature is rising at 39, avenue George V! On the 6th floor of this
impressive Haussmann-style building overlooking the rooftops of Paris, diners
can enjoy the chef's refined cuisine in a stylish setting. Dishes are based around
a classic repertoire, top quality ingredients and fine flavours.
➜ Œuf bio cuit mollet aux petits pois, mousserons des prés. Turbot sauvage aux girolles et pommes de terre de Noirmoutier en cocotte lutée, jus
perlé. Fraises et fraises des bois, crémeux sansho et vanille.

XX
ॐ

114, Faubourg – Hôtel Bristol   [AC]
114 r. du Faubourg-St-Honoré (8th) – Ⓜ Miromesnil   Plan: **H2**
– ☏ 01 53 43 44 44 – www.lebristolparis.com – Closed 1 to 21 August and lunch Saturday and Sunday
Carte 80/150 €
• Modern cuisine • Brasserie • Luxury •
This chic brasserie within the premises of Le Bristol has a lavish interior with gilded columns, floral motifs and a grand staircase. Savour dishes from the menu of fine brasserie classics cooked with care and lots of taste.
➔ Pâté en croûte de canard et légumes aux vinaigres. Sole, pousse d'épinard, huile vierge aux câpres. Millefeuille à la vanille Bourbon, caramel au beurre demi-sel.

XX
ॐ

Il Carpaccio – Hôtel Le Royal Monceau   爺 余 & [AC] ⇔ 爹
37 av. Hoche (8th) – Ⓜ Charles de Gaulle-Etoile   Plan: **G2**
– ☏ 01 42 99 88 00 – www.leroyalmonceau.com – Closed August, Sunday and Monday
Menu 150/200 € – Carte 75/130 €
• Italian • Elegant •
You reach the restaurant via a remarkable baroque-inspired corridor decorated with thousands of shells. The conservatory-style dining room is equally splendid, the setting for a sun-drenched cuisine based on fine produce and bold flavours.
➔ Salade de poulpe de roche grillé, olives taggiasche et fenouil sauvage. Ventrèche de thon rôtie, céleri, tomate verte, olives et câpres. Biscuit cuillère imbibé au café et à l'amaretto, crème de mascarpone.

XX

Le Relais Plaza – Hôtel Plaza Athénée   [AC]
21 av. Montaigne (8th) – Ⓜ Alma Marceau   Plan: **G3**
– ☏ 01 53 67 64 00
– www.dorchestercollection.com/fr/paris/hotel-plaza-athenee/ – Closed mid-July to late August
Menu 58 € – Carte 75/140 €
• Classic cuisine • Elegant • Brasserie •
Within the Plaza Athénée is this chic and exclusive brasserie, popular with regulars from the fashion houses nearby. It is impossible to resist the charm of its lovely 1930s decor inspired by the liner SS Normandie. A unique atmosphere for food that has a pronounced sense of tradition. As Parisian as it gets.

XX

Les 110 de Taillevent   爺 & [AC] 爹
195 r. du Faubourg-St-Honoré (8th)   Plan: **G2**
– Ⓜ Charles de Gaulle-Etoile – ☏ 01 40 74 20 20
– www.taillevent.com/les-110-de-taillevent-brasserie.com – Closed 3 to 24 August
Menu 44 € – Carte 45/120 €
• Traditional cuisine • Elegant •
Under the aegis of the prestigious Taillevent name, this ultra-chic brasserie puts the onus on food and wine pairings. The concept is a success, with its remarkable choice of 110 wines by the glass, and nicely done traditional food (pâté en croûte, bavette steak with a peppercorn sauce etc). Elegant and inviting decor.

XX

L'Oiseau Blanc – Hôtel Peninsula   余 & [AC]
19 av. Kléber (16th) ✉ 75116 – Ⓜ Kléber   Plan: **F2**
– ☏ 01 58 12 67 30 – http://paris.peninsula.com/fr/
Menu 69 € (lunch), 99/109 €
• Modern cuisine • Design • Elegant •
This is the Peninsula's rooftop restaurant for 'contemporary French gastronomy'. Part of the luxury hotel that opened in 2014 near the Arc de Triomphe, the restaurant is presided over by a replica of the White Bird (in homage to the plane in which Nungesser and Coli attempted to cross the Atlantic in 1927) and offers stunning views.

Okuda

   🔥 🅰️ ✨ 🍴

7 r. de la Trémoille (8th) – 🅜 *Alma Marceau*   Plan: **G3**
– ☎ *01 40 70 19 19* – *www.okuda.fr* – *Closed 2 weeks in August, Tuesday lunch and Monday*
Menu 85 € (lunch), 158/198 € – *(booking advisable)*
• Japanese • Elegant • Traditional •

A sober and elegant decor, 23 seats, hostesses in traditional kimonos and golden silence. It is in this setting that since 2013 diners have been tasting the 'kaiseki' creations of the famous Japanese chef Toru Okuda, crowned with multiple Michelin stars back in Tokyo. Harmonious flavours, subtle sauces, delicate textures – this is great art.
➜ Menu omakase.

Timgad

   🅰️ 🍴

21 r. Brunel (17th) – 🅜 *Argentine* – ☎ *01 45 74 23 70*   Plan: **E2**
– *www.timgad.fr*
Menu 79 € 🍷/125 € 🍷 – Carte 45/90 €
• North-African • Exotic • Elegant •

Experience the historic splendour of the city of Timgad in this elegant Moroccan restaurant adorned with fine stuccowork. Fragrant North African cuisine, including couscous and tagines.

Frédéric Simonin

   🅰️

25 r. Bayen (17th) – 🅜 *Ternes* – ☎ *01 45 74 74 74*   Plan: **F1**
– *www.fredericsimonin.com* – *Closed 31 July-24 August, Sunday and Monday*
Menu 49 € (lunch), 86/139 € – Carte 95/155 €
• Modern cuisine • Cosy • Elegant •

A white-and-black decor forms the backdrop to this chic restaurant close to Place des Ternes. Fine, delicate cuisine from a chef with quite a career behind him already.
➜ Tourteau, gelée de tomate, onctuosité d'avocat légèrement épicé. Veau de Normandie en cocotte, lard de colonnata, polenta de Savoie et condiments citronnés. Dessert tout chocolat, biscuit Oreo et sorbet cacao.

Marius et Janette

   📶 🅰️ 🍴

4 av. George V (8th) – 🅜 *Alma Marceau*   Plan: **G3**
– ☎ *01 47 23 41 88* – *www.mariusjanette.com*
Menu 48 € (weekday lunch) – Carte 85/130 €
• Fish and seafood • Mediterranean • Friendly •

This seafood restaurant's name recalls Marseille's Estaque district. It has an elegant nautical decor and a pleasant street terrace in summertime.

L'Arôme

   🎐 🅰️ ✦ 🍴

3 r. St-Philippe-du-Roule (8th)   Plan: **G-H2**
– 🅜 *St-Philippe-du-Roule* – ☎ *01 42 25 55 98* – *www.larome.fr* – *Closed 1 to 23 August, 20 to 28 December, Saturday and Sunday*
Menu 59 € (lunch), 99/155 € – Carte 85/110 €
• Modern cuisine • Friendly •

Attractive restaurant run by Eric Martins (front of house) and Thomas Boullault (in the kitchen). Comfortable dining room with a warm atmosphere and open kitchen. Modern cuisine.
➜ Tourteau, tartare de pêche et concombre, vinaigrette de homard au yuzu. Côte de veau et encornets, cèpes poêlés aux figues et jus à la mûre. Vacherin aux fruits exotiques, meringue au citron vert et sorbet noix de coco.

Mini Palais

   📶 🔥

Au Grand Palais - 3 av. Winston Churchill (8th)   Plan: **H3**
– 🅜 *Champs-Elysées Clemenceau* – ☎ *01 42 56 42 42* – *www.minipalais.com*
Menu 29 € (weekday lunch) – Carte 35/75 €
• Modern cuisine • Friendly •

Concealed within the Grand Palais, the Mini Palace is dedicated to the full pleasures of the palate, with a focus on generosity, abundance and the finest ingredients. The snack menu is available from midday to midnight. Tea room and an exquisite terrace.

FRANCE - PARIS

XX **Conti** ⒶⒸ 🍴

72 r. Lauriston (16th) ✉ *75116 –* Ⓜ *Boissière* Plan: **E3**
– ℰ 01 47 27 74 67 – www.leconti.fr – Closed 1 to 21 August,
24 December-2 January, Saturday, Sunday and Bank Holidays
Menu 38 € – Carte 56/78 €
• Italian • Intimate • Cosy •

The intimate decor of this restaurant brings to mind a private club or an Italian theatre with its red velvet, crystal mirrors and chandeliers. The many regulars are drawn here by the excellent, classic Italian cuisine.

XX **Maxan** ⒶⒸ ⇔

3 r. Quentin-Bauchart (8th) – Ⓜ *George V* Plan: **F3**
– ℰ 01 40 70 04 78 – www.rest-maxan.com – Closed Saturday lunch and
Sunday
Menu 40 € – Carte 46/82 €
• Modern cuisine • Friendly •

This is the new location – a stone's throw from avenue George V – of Maxan, which used to be near Miromesnil. In the elegant and discreet decor, done out in a palette of greys, it is a pleasure to rediscover tasty market cooking. The lunch set menu is a good deal.

XX **Nolita** ⒷⒷ ⒶⒸ

1 av. Matignon (Motor Village - 2nd floor) (8th) Plan: **H3**
– Ⓜ *Franklin D. Roosevelt – ℰ 01 53 75 78 78 – www.nolitaparis.fr*
– Closed 2 weeks in August, Saturday lunch and Sunday dinner
Carte 58/85 €
• Italian • Design •

A chic restaurant inside the MotorVillage (the showroom of a major Italian car manufacturer). Authentic Italian cuisine with flavours to match.

XX **Penati al Baretto** (Alberico Penati) ⒷⒷ ⒶⒸ
🏵

9 r. Balzac (8th) – Ⓜ *George V – ℰ 01 42 99 80 00* Plan: **G2**
– www.penatialbaretto.eu – Closed August, Saturday lunch and Sunday
Menu 45 € (lunch), 115/180 € 🍷 – Carte 75/120 €
• Italian • Classic • Elegant •

Alberico Penati's Italian restaurant, opened mid-2014, right away imposed itself as one of the best in the city! In accordance with the finest Italian tradition, generosity and refinement distinguish each recipe. The dishes are brimming with flavour as they explore all the regions of the peninsula. A succulent voyage...
→ Jambon de Parme et melon cantaloup. Spaghettis di Verrigni aux sardines à la sicilienne. Pannacotta à la vanille de Tahiti et aux fruits rouges.

XX **Dominique Bouchet** ⒷⒷ ⇔
🏵

11 r. Treilhard (8th) – Ⓜ *Miromesnil – ℰ 01 45 61 09 46* Plan: **H2**
– www.dominique-bouchet.com – Closed 2 weeks in August, Saturday and
Sunday
Carte 75/115 € – (booking advisable)
• Modern cuisine • Elegant •

This is the kind of place you will want to recommend to all your friends. It has an intimate, contemporary atmosphere, attentive service, and beautifully prepared dishes based around fresh and tasty market ingredients.
→ Raviole de fromage de chèvre, émulsion de crème au pineau des Charentes. Gigot d'agneau de sept heures à la cuillère, sauce au vin et fèves de cacao. Millefeuille à la vanille Bourbon.

XX **Le Pré Carré** – Hôtel Splendid Étoile ⒶⒸ

1 bis av. Carnot (17th) – Ⓜ *Charles de Gaulle-Etoile* Plan: **F2**
– ℰ 01 46 22 57 35 – www.restaurant-le-pre-carre.com – Closed 3 weeks in
August, 1 week Christmas Holidays, Saturday lunch and Sunday
Menu 39 € (dinner) – Carte 45/75 €
• Traditional cuisine • Elegant •

In the dining room, two mirrors facing each other reflect Le Pré Carré's infinite elegance and welcoming decor. Aromatic herbs and spices add a gentle touch to the gourmet cuisine, which is very much in keeping with the times.

205

Agapé

51 r. Jouffroy-d'Abbans (17th) – Ⓜ Wagram
Plan I: **B1**
– ✆ 01 42 27 20 18 – www.agape-paris.fr
– Closed Saturday and Sunday
Menu 39 € (lunch), 99/129 € – Carte 90/150 €
• Modern cuisine • Elegant •
This smart restaurant, whose name means love in Greek, sports a minimalist decor. Concise, enticing menu. Extremely popular with gourmets.
→ Œuf florentine, parmesan et jambon de Paris. Pêche côtière de Noirmoutier. Arabica du Brésil, whisky pur malt et chocolat grand cru.

Jacques Faussat

54 r. Cardinet (17th) – Ⓜ Malesherbes
Plan: **G1**
– ✆ 01 47 63 40 37 – www.jacquesfaussat.com
– Closed August, 24 December-2 January, Saturday except dinner from October-April, Sunday and Bank Holidays
Menu 40 € (lunch), 98/138 € – Carte 75/90 €
• Traditional cuisine • Elegant •
Comfortable, modern restaurant decorated in a tasteful restrained style. The menu is influenced by the cuisine of southwest France, changes with the seasons and the chef's whims.
→ Soupe de langoustines au lait de coco. Écrevisses pattes rouges mariées à l'aileron de poulet laqué au poivre du Sichuan. Soufflé chaud aux fruits de saison.

Graindorge

15 r. Arc-de-Triomphe (17th)
Plan: **F2**
– Ⓜ Charles de Gaulle-Étoile
– ✆ 01 47 54 00 28 – www.le-graindorge.fr
– Closed 2 weeks in August, Saturday lunch and Sunday
Menu 30 € (lunch), 36/59 € – Carte 45/65 €
• Flemish • Retro • Individual •
Potjevlesch (potted meat), bintje farcie (stuffed potatoes), waterzoï (a stew with Ostend grey prawns) and kippers from Boulogne are just some of the hearty Northern dishes on offer in the Graindorge's attractive Art Deco setting, washed down with some delicious traditional beers.

Bistrot du Sommelier

97 bd Haussmann (8th) – Ⓜ St-Augustin
Plan: **H2**
– ✆ 01 42 65 24 85 – www.bistrotdusommelier.com – Closed 3 to 24 August, Saturday and Sunday
Menu 39 € (lunch), 70 € ♈/118 € ♈ – Carte 50/70 €
• Traditional cuisine • Friendly • Elegant •
This bistro is run by Philippe Faure-Brac – winner of the 1992 world champion sommelier award. It offers market-based cuisine and a pleasant wine tasting cellar, which is the setting for weekly tasting events (Fridays).

Akrame (Akrame Benallal)

19 r. Lauriston (16th) ⊠ 75016 – Ⓜ Kléber
Plan: **F2**
– ✆ 01 40 67 11 16 – www.akrame.com
– Closed 16 April-1 May, August, 23 December-2 January, Saturday and Sunday
Menu 60 € (lunch), 100/130 € – (booking advisable)
• Creative • Design • Trendy •
Having worked, most notably, at Gagnaire and Adrià, the young and sprightly Akrame Benallal creates a very personal and uninhibited cuisine. He dares to try unexpected marriages of flavours but always with finesse. The very trendy interior suits these single set menus that change on a monthly basis. A place to discover!
→ Cuisine du marché.

XX **Pages**
❀ *4 r. Auguste-Vacquerie (16th)* ✉ *75016*   Plan: **F2**
– Ⓜ *Charles de Gaulle-Etoile* – ✆ *01 47 20 74 94* – *www.restaurantpages.fr*
– *Closed 2 weeks in August, Sunday and Monday*
Menu 40 € (lunch), 65/80 € – *(booking advisable)*
• Creative • Minimalist • Trendy •
Veal tartare meets lemon zest, botarga and anchovy cream, and celeriac comes
with lobster and Saint Nectaire cheese; explosive marriages of flavours at this
restaurant run by a young Japanese chef with a passion for French cuisine. The
sleek decor is also up to the minute.
➜ Cuisine du marché.

XX **6 New York**   🕮 🍽
6 av. de New-York (16th) ✉ *75016* – Ⓜ *Alma Marceau*   Plan: **F3**
– ✆ *01 40 70 03 30* – *www.6newyork.fr* – *Closed August, Saturday lunch
and Sunday*
Menu 38 € (lunch), 70 € 🍷/90 € 🍷 – Carte 45/80 €
• Modern cuisine • Design •
The name gives away the address – on Avenue de New York – but the cooking
is not that of a typical North-American restaurant. Marked flavours and a respect
for the seasons underpin cuisine in perfect harmony with the elegant and contemporary setting.

XX **Le Vinci**   🕮 🍽
23 r. Paul-Valéry (16th) ✉ *75116* – Ⓜ *Victor Hugo*   Plan: **E2-3**
– ✆ *01 45 01 68 18* – *www.restaurantlevinci.fr* – *Closed 1 to 21 August,
Saturday and Sunday*
Menu 35 € – Carte 46/81 €
• Italian • Elegant • Friendly •
The sympathetic interior design and friendly service make Le Vinci a very popular choice a stone's throw from the avenue Victor-Hugo. The impressive selection of pastas and risottos, as well as the à la carte meat and fish dishes vary
according to the seasons.

X **L'Atelier de Joël Robuchon - Étoile**   🕮 ♿ 🍽
❀ *133 av. des Champs-Élysées (Publicis Drugstore*   Plan: **F2**
basement) (8th) – Ⓜ *Charles de Gaulle-Étoile* – ✆ *01 47 23 75 75*
– *www.joel-robuchon.com*
Menu 44 € (lunch)/179 € – Carte 95/185 €
• Creative • Design • Minimalist •
Paris, London, Las Vegas, Tokyo, Taipei, Hong Kong, Singapore and back to
Paris: the destiny of these Ateliers, in tune with the times, has been an international one. The chef has come up with a great concept: serving dishes drawing
on France, Spain and Asia cooked with precision, on a long counter with bar
stools and a red and black colour scheme.
➜ Langoustine en ravioli truffé à l'étuvée de chou vert. Caille caramélisée
au foie gras, pomme purée. Chocolat tendance, crémeux onctueux au chocolat araguani, sorbet cacao et biscuit Oréo.

X **Pavillon Elysée Lenôtre**   🍴 ♿ 🕮 ♿ 🍽 🅿
10 av. des Champs-Elysées (8th)   Plan: **H3**
– Ⓜ *Champs Elysées Clemenceau* – ✆ *01 42 65 85 10* – *www.lenotre.fr*
– *Closed 20 to 27 February, 3 weeks in August, Sunday except lunch from
April-October and Monday from November-March*
Carte 48/70 €
• Modern cuisine • Friendly •
Built for the 1900 Universal Exhibition, this pavilion exudes unpretentious eleg-
ance. Appealing lunch suggestions, best enjoyed in the sun on the lovely ter-
race. Boutique dedicated to the culinary arts and cookery school.

FRANCE - PARIS

Le Sushi Okuda

18 r. Boccador (8th) – Ⓜ *Alma Marceau*　　　　　Plan: **G3**
*– ☎ 01 47 20 17 18 – www.sushiokuda.com – Closed 2 weeks in August,
Tuesday lunch and Monday*
Menu 95 € ⏶ (lunch), 125 € ⏶/155 € ⏶ *– (booking advisable)*
• Japanese • Minimalist • Simple •
This sushi bar, next door to Okuda restaurant, is reminiscent of Japanese izakaya
bars. This is as much because of the Japanese cedar on the walls and the narrow
layout as by the matchless freshness of the fish, worked according to the ike-
jime method. Remarkable and exotic.

Pomze

109 bd Haussmann (1st floor) (8th) – Ⓜ *St -Augustin*　　　Plan: **H2**
*– ☎ 01 42 65 65 83 – www.pomze.com – Closed 22 December-2 January,
Saturday except dinner from September-June and Sunday*
Menu 35/58 € – Carte 47/67 €
• Modern cuisine • Minimalist •
The unusual concept behind Pomze is to take the humble apple as a starting
point for a culinary voyage! From the food shop (where you will find cider and
calvados) to the restaurant, the "forbidden fruit" provides the central theme.
Creative and globe-trotting dishes that offer excellent value for money.

L'Escient

28 r. Poncelet (17th) – Ⓜ *Ternes – ☎ 01 47 64 49 13*　　　Plan: **F1**
*– www.restaurantescient.fr – Closed 6 to 17 August, Sunday and Bank
Holidays*
Menu 37/55 € – Carte approx. 47 €
• Modern cuisine • Friendly •
King prawns, taramasalata, daikon, lime and ginger; fresh cod, dried fig crust,
chorizo and preserved lemon etc. The father and daughter team at L'Escient
offers a menu with plenty of original associations, but always judicious! A very
tasty fusion, in an understated decor.

L'Entredgeu

83 r. Laugier (17th) – Ⓜ *Porte de Champerret*　　　Plan I: **AB1**
*– ☎ 01 40 54 97 24 – Closed 2 weeks in August,
1 week Christmas Holidays and Sunday*
Menu 36 €
• Traditional cuisine • Bistro •
Friendly service, a lively atmosphere, a decor that is reminiscent of southwest
France, and delicious seasonally based cuisine are the hallmarks of this restau-
rant with a tongue-twisting name.

Le Meurice

228 r. de Rivoli (1st) – Ⓜ *Tuileries – ☎ 01 44 58 10 10*　　Plan: **J-K3**
– www.lemeurice.com
120 rm *–* ☗695/1850 € ☗☗1550/2050 € *–* ☐ 46 € *– 40 suites*
• Palace • Grand Luxury • Historic •
This luxury hotel opposite the Tuileries was founded at the start of the 19C,
making it one of the first to be built in Paris. It has opulent guestrooms and a
superb suite on the top floor that has breathtaking panoramic views. The hotel
now also bears the contemporary touch of Philippe Starck. A truly fabulous
place to stay.
❀❀ **Le Meurice Alain Ducasse • Le Dali** – See restaurant listing

Mandarin Oriental ☆ ﯼ ⑩ ⬚ ₺ 🆎 ⅏

251 r. St-Honoré (1st) – Ⓜ *Concorde*
– ☎ *01 70 98 78 88*   Plan: **J3**
– *www.mandarinoriental.fr/paris/*
98 rm – ♦975/1395 € ♦♦975/1395 € – ☲ 47 € – 40 suites
• Palace • Elegant • Personalised •

Among all the major new hotels in Paris, the opening of the Mandarin Oriental in mid-2011 made quite an impact. Faithful to the principles of this Hong Kong group, the property is the height of refinement. It combines French elegance with the delicate touches of Asia and features sleek lines, lots of space and peace and quiet. A capital address in the heart of the French capital!

❀❀ **Sur Mesure par Thierry Marx • Camélia**
– See restaurant listing

Park Hyatt ☆ ﯼ ⑩ ₺ 🆎 ⅏ 🚗

5 r. de la Paix (2nd) – Ⓜ *Opéra* – ☎ *01 58 71 12 34*
– *www.paris.vendome.hyatt.fr*   Plan: **K3**
110 rm – ♦890 € ♦♦1280 € – ☲ 44 € – 43 suites
• Luxury • Elegant •

Ed Tuttle designed his dream hotel, which stands on the famous rue de la Paix. It has a collection of contemporary art and French-style classicism with a subtle blend of Louis XVI-style and 1930s furnishings. There is a spa and high-tech equipment, as well as restaurants for all tastes. An authentic palace.

❀ **Pur' - Jean-François Rouquette** – See restaurant listing

Intercontinental Le Grand ☆ ﯼ ⑩ ₺ 🆎 ⅏ 🚗

2 r. Scribe (9th) – Ⓜ *Opéra* – ☎ *01 40 07 32 32*
– *www.paris.intercontinental.com*   Plan: **K2**
442 rm – ♦335/950 € ♦♦335/950 € – ☲ 45 € – 28 suites
• Historic • Stylish • Historic •

Opened in 1862, this hotel celebrated its 150th anniversary in 2012. A true grand hotel typical of the 19C, the Intercontinental stands on the Place de l'Opéra in the heart of Haussmann's Paris. With its superbly decorated Café de la Paix, interior courtyard with a Proustian ambience and its Second Empire-style guestrooms this is a real Parisian landmark.

Café de la Paix – See restaurant listing

Costes ☆ ﯼ ⬚ ₺ 🆎

239 r. St-Honoré (1st) – Ⓜ *Concorde* – ☎ *01 42 44 50 00*
– *www.hotelcostes.com*   Plan: **K3**
80 rm – ♦500/1500 € ♦♦600/1500 € – ☲ 35 € – 2 suites
• Luxury • Personalised • Cosy •

This extremely chic and plush palace remains a firm favourite with the jet set. Intimate lounges with designer furnishings, guestrooms refined down to the smallest details (monogrammed linen, fine artworks, antiques etc.), and a Jacques Garcia-designed restaurant.

Le Burgundy ☆ ﯼ ⑩ ⅏ ⬚ ₺ 🆎

6-8 r. Duphot (1st) – Ⓜ *Madeleine*
– ☎ *01 42 60 34 12*   Plan: **J3**
– *www.leburgundy.com*
51 rm ☲ – ♦455/750 € ♦♦660/1100 € – 8 suites
• Grand Luxury • Design • Personalised •

In this luxury hotel, the wood panelling combines harmoniously with the coloured fabrics, designer furniture and contemporary art to provide a hushed, arty atmosphere.

❀ **Le Baudelaire** – See restaurant listing

FRANCE - PARIS

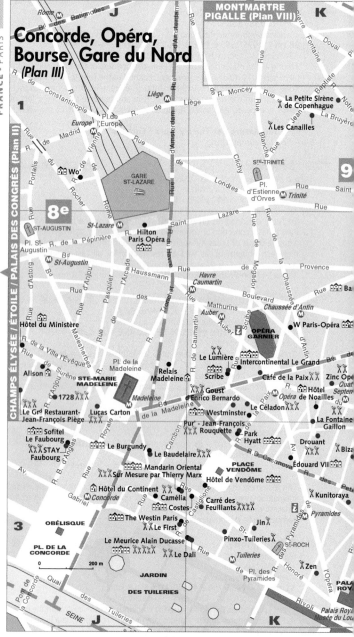

Concorde, Opéra, Bourse, Gare du Nord
(Plan III)

GARE ST-LAZARE

La Petite Sirène de Copenhague
Les Canailles
STE-TRINITÉ
Pl. d'Estienne d'Orves
Trinité
Wo'
ST-AUGUSTIN
St-Lazare
Hilton Paris Opéra
St-Augustin
Pl. St-Augustin
Hôtel du Ministère
Havre Caumartin
Provence
W Paris-Opéra
Alison
1728
Pl. de la Madeleine
STE-MARIE MADELEINE
Relais Madeleine
Scribe
Le Lumière
OPÉRA GARNIER
Intercontinental Le Grand
Café de la Paix
Zinc Opé
Goust d'Enrico Bernardo
Opéra de Noailles
Le Céladon
Le Grd Restaurant-Jean-François Piège
Lucas Carton
Westminster
La Fontaine Gaillon
Hôtel du Ministère
Pur - Jean-François Rouquette
Park Hyatt
Drouant
Biza
Sofitel Le Faubourg
STAY Faubourg
Le Burgundy
Le Baudelaire
PLACE VENDÔME
Édouard VII
Mandarin Oriental
Sur Mesure par Thierry Marx
Hôtel de Vendôme
Kunitoraya
Hôtel du Continent
Concorde
Camélia
Costes
Carré des Feuillants
Jin
Pyramides
OBÉLISQUE
The Westin Paris
Le First
Pinxo-Tuileries
ST-ROCH
PL. DE LA CONCORDE
Le Meurice Alain Ducasse
Le Dali
Tuileries
Pl. des Pyramides
Zen
0   200 m
JARDIN
DES TUILERIES
SEINE
PALA ROY
Palais Roya Musée du Lou

210

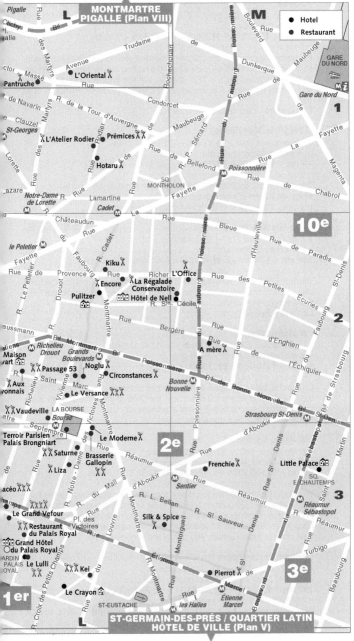

MONTMARTRE
PIGALLE (Plan VIII)

● Hotel
● Restaurant

GARE DU NORD

Gare du Nord

1

10e

2

3

2e

3e

1er

Scribe

1 r. Scribe (9th) – **Ⓜ** *Opéra* – *✆ 01 44 71 24 24* — Plan: **K2**
– *www.hotel-scribe.com*
204 rm – ♦300/910 € ♦♦300/910 € – ☲ 35 € – 9 suites
• Luxury • Personalised • Classic •

Fall under the charm of this chic, very Parisian hotel occupying a Haussmann-style building close to the Opéra, where the hushed atmosphere is almost secretive in feel. It was here, in 1895, that the Lumière brothers hosted their very first cinema screening. A legendary address with a discreet elegance all of its own.
Le Lumière – See restaurant listing

Hôtel de Vendôme

1 pl. Vendôme (1st) – **Ⓜ** *Opéra* – *✆ 01 55 04 55 00* — Plan: **K3**
– *www.hoteldevendome.com*
19 rm – ♦390/590 € ♦♦750/920 € – ☲ 39 € – 10 suites
• Luxury • Palace • Stylish •

The other hotel on Place Vendôme! Antique furniture and marble sit easily alongside state-of-the-art facilities in this fine 18C building. A sense of elegance pervades, and is found in the tiniest details. A real gem.

The Westin Paris

3 r. de Castiglione (1st) – **Ⓜ** *Tuileries* – *✆ 01 44 77 11 11* — Plan: **J3**
– *www.thewestinparis.fr*
394 rm – ♦295/840 € ♦♦395/840 € – ☲ 39 € – 34 suites
• Luxury • Personalised •

This hotel built in 1878 combines old-world charm (Napoleon III lounges) and elegant contemporary touches. Some guestrooms boast views across the Tuileries gardens. Pleasant spa.
Le First – See restaurant listing

Westminster

13 r. de la Paix (2nd) – **Ⓜ** *Opéra* – *✆ 01 42 61 57 46* — Plan: **K2**
– *www.hotel-westminster-opera-paris.fr*
85 rm – ♦250/550 € ♦♦250/550 € – ☲ 30 € – 17 suites
• Luxury • Classic • Retro •

Founded in 1809 – it has celebrated its 200th birthday! –, it was in 1846 that it took the name of its most faithful client, the Duke of Westminster, who had a taste for that distinctly French brand of refinement!
❀ **Le Céladon** – See restaurant listing

W Paris Opéra

4 r. Meyerbeer (9th) – **Ⓜ** *Chaussée d'Antin* — Plan: **K2**
– *✆ 01 77 48 94 94* – *www.wparisopera.fr*
89 rm – ♦750/3200 € ♦♦750/3200 € – ☲ 38 € – 2 suites
• Luxury • Contemporary • Design •

You would be hard-pushed to get any closer to the heart of Haussmann's Paris than in this fine 1870 building adjacent to the Opéra. This hotel, which opened in 2012, may plump for a "Paris-chic" decor, but it is in a resolutely designer vein. Luxury is combined with a laid-back attitude (for example, a circular bed and a view over the Palais Garnier). Very trendy and very enticing.

Hilton Paris Opéra

108 r. St-Lazare (8th) – **Ⓜ** *Saint-Lazare* — Plan: **J2**
– *✆ 01 40 08 44 44* – *www.parisopera.hilton.com*
257 rm – ♦269/999 € ♦♦269/999 € – ☲ 29 € – 11 suites
• Luxury • Townhouse • Elegant •

Completely refurbished in 2015, this hotel is in touch with its Belle Époque past: lobby with marble columns and ceiling crafted with gold leaf, a large majestic lounge, with a glass roof and frescoes... the bright and contemporary guestrooms are very comfortable.

FRANCE - PARIS

Sofitel le Faubourg

15 r. Boissy-d'Anglas (8th) – Ⓜ *Concorde*
– ☎ *01 44 94 14 14* – *www.sofitel-paris-lefaubourg.com*
Plan: **J3**
118 rm – ♦380/1150 € ♦♦380/1300 € – ☷ 36 € – 29 suites
• Luxury • Modern • Personalised •
This elegant hotel occupies two 18C and 19C residences. It offers attractive suites in a contemporary style, as well as elegant guestrooms. There is also a lounge crowned with a glass roof, a fitness centre and a hammam.
STAY Faubourg – See restaurant listing

Hôtel de Nell

7-9 r. du Conservatoire (9th) – Ⓜ *Bonne Nouvelle*
– ☎ *01 44 83 83 60* – *www.charmandmore.com*
Plan: **M2**
33 rm – ♦250/450 € ♦♦250/1200 € – ☷ 21 €
• Luxury • Townhouse • Design •
A very fine hotel, housed in a Haussmann building next to the Conservatoire National Supérieur d'Art Dramatique. You can't find fault with its fittings, in a confident style designed by Jean-Michel Wilmotte. Untreated wood, pale tones, clean lines... in keeping with the spirit of contemporary luxury.
La Régalade Conservatoire – See restaurant listing

Banke

20 r. Lafayette (9th) – Ⓜ *Chaussée d'Antin*
– ☎ *01 55 33 22 22* – *www.derbyhotels.com*
Plan: **K2**
94 rm – ♦250/530 € ♦♦300/705 € – ☷ 29 € – 11 suites
• Luxury • Design •
Situated in the heart of the Belle Epoque business district between the Bourse and the Opera, this former bank building was converted into a unique luxury hotel in 2009. The opulent lobby, crowned by a glass ceiling, is highly striking, while the guestrooms have a warm, welcoming feel.

Édouard VII

39 av. de l'Opéra (2nd) – Ⓜ *Opéra* – ☎ *01 42 61 86 11*
– *www.edouard7hotel.com*
Plan: **K3**
69 rm – ♦209/550 € ♦♦229/790 € – ☷ 35 € – 10 suites
• Luxury • Personalised • Cosy •
Shimmering fabrics and refined decor in the Couture rooms, while the mood in the Edouard VII rooms is more understated. The hotel exudes elegance and the suites are superb. Cosy bar and light meals in a very pleasant contemporary setting.

Grand Hôtel du Palais Royal

4 r. de Valois (1st) – Ⓜ *Palais Royal* – ☎ *01 42 96 15 35*
– *www.grandhoteldupalaisroyal.com*
Plan: **L3**
64 rm – ♦415/790 € ♦♦415/790 € – ☷ 38 € – 4 suites
• Historic • Luxury • Modern •
Next to the Palais Royal, the Ministry of Culture and the Conseil d'État, this 18C building boasts an impeccable location! Inside, the place is elegant but without pomp. The guestrooms are sober and decorated with contemporary furnishings and white walls. Although very central, the neighbourhood is quiet.
Le Lulli – See restaurant listing

Hôtel du Ministère

31 r. de Surène (8th) – Ⓜ *Madeleine* – ☎ *01 42 66 21 43*
– *www.ministerehotel.com*
Plan: **J2**
43 rm ☷ – ♦245/900 € ♦♦280/900 €
• Townhouse • Luxury • Personalised •
This hotel is a stone's throw from the French Interior Ministry, the Palais de l'Élysée and Faubourg St Honoré. The comfortable and very functional guestrooms pay tribute to the 1970s, which won't fail to please fans of the era, nor those who are feeling nostalgic. Charming service.

La Maison Favart

5 r. Marivaux (2nd) – Ⓜ Richelieu Drouot – ✆ 01 42 97 59 83 – www.lamaisonfavart.com Plan: **L2**

36 rm – †260/590 € ††260/590 € – ☕ 24 € – 3 suites

• Luxury • Townhouse • Elegant •

A timeless atmosphere reigns in this hotel (1824), where painter Francisco de Goya once stayed. The guestrooms – some facing the Opéra Comique – are very pleasant. This is a charming hotel, full of romanticism and poetry.

Hôtel de Noailles

9 r. de la Michodière (2nd) – Ⓜ Quatre Septembre – ✆ 01 47 42 92 90 – www.hotelnoailles.com Plan: **K2**

56 rm – †205/425 € ††225/455 € – ☕ 18 €

• Townhouse • Modern • Cosy •

Hip, contemporary elegance behind a pretty 1900 façade. Sleek, minimalist rooms, most of which open on to the patio (with a balcony on the 5th and 6th floors).

WO'

10 r. de Stockholm (8th) – Ⓜ St-Lazare – ✆ 01 45 22 10 85 – www.hotelwo.com Plan: **J1**

30 rm – †149/349 € ††149/530 € – ☕ 15 €

• Townhouse • Business • Design •

WO' as in Wilson Opéra! In a quiet street, close to Gare St Lazare and the *grands magasins*, this hotel offers guestrooms which, although small, are designer and cosy. Some of them come with a balcony offering views over the city. It is like being in a cocoon, right in the heart of Paris. Competitive rates.

Little Palace

4 r. Salomon-de-Caus (3rd) – Ⓜ Réaumur-Sébastopol – ✆ 01 42 72 08 15 – www.littlepalacehotel.com Plan: **M3**

49 rm – †240/370 € ††265/490 € – ☕ 16 € – 4 suites

• Townhouse • Elegant •

The charming Little Palace is a successful fusion of Belle Époque and contemporary styles. Welcoming guestrooms with those on the 6th and 7th floors (with a balcony and views of Paris) preferable.

Pulitzer

23 r. du Faubourg-Montmartre (9th) – Ⓜ Grands Boulevards – ✆ 01 53 34 98 10 – www.hotelpulitzer.com Plan: **L2**

44 rm – †150/550 € ††160/550 € – ☕ 18 €

• Business • Personalised •

The charm of a British library (comfy Chesterfield armchairs) and the contemporary elegance of industrial-style come together at this hotel. It is located in the midst of the city's theatres and department stores. This Pulitzer would be a worthy winner of a prize for originality.

Relais Madeleine

11 bis r. Godot-de-Mauroy (9th) – Ⓜ Havre Caumartin – ✆ 01 47 42 22 40 – www.relaismadeleine.fr Plan: **J2**

23 rm – †155/359 € ††185/359 € – ☕ 15 €

• Traditional • Personalised • Classic •

Staying at this small hotel is a bit like spending time in a family home, but right in the centre of Paris! It has undeniable charm with carefully chosen furniture, sparkling colours and delightful fabrics. Not to mention the attentive service.

Hôtel du Continent

30 r.du Mont-Thabor (1st) – Ⓜ Tuileries – ✆ 01 42 60 75 32 – www.hotelcontinent.com Plan: **J3**

25 rm – †200/400 € ††200/400 € – ☕ 10 €

• Traditional • Townhouse • Elegant •

Near the Tuileries, this hotel run with a personal touch was completely redesigned by Christian Lacroix. The six continents are the theme for the decor. Elegance, interplay of colours and overall character – it is a pleasure to venture into this new territory.

Le Crayon

25 r. du Bouloi (1st) – ⓜ *Palais Royal*   Plan: **L3**
– ℰ *01 42 36 54 19 – www.hotelcrayon.com*
26 rm – 🛏149/347 € 🛏🛏149/347 € – ☲ 12 €
• Townhouse • Personalised •

This far from banal hotel is halfway between an artist's residence and a family home, featuring an explosive mix of colours, contrasts and vintage decor. Each bedroom is its own original creation, adorned with furniture tracked down personally by the hotel's designer.

Alison

21 r. de Surène (8th) – ⓜ *Madeleine –* ℰ *01 42 65 54 00*   Plan: **J2**
– www.hotelalison.com
34 rm – 🛏110/192 € 🛏🛏135/212 € – ☲ 12 €
• Family • Townhouse • Functional •

This small hotel in a quiet street near the Théâtre de la Madeleine offers good value for money. Functional guestrooms offering high levels of comfort.

Le Meurice Alain Ducasse – Hôtel Le Meurice

228 r. de Rivoli (1st) – ⓜ *Tuileries –* ℰ *01 44 58 10 55*   Plan: **J-K3**
– www.alainducasse-meurice.com/fr – Closed 22 February-7 March, 1 to 29 August, Saturday and Sunday
Menu 110 € (lunch)/380 € – Carte 225/280 €
• Modern cuisine • Luxury • Romantic •

In the heart of the famous palace, this is the very embodiment of the grand French restaurant. It has a highly luxurious decor, inspired by the royal apartments at Versailles, and perfectly orchestrated service. Under the aegis of Alain Ducasse since autumn 2013, the food magnifies the finest ingredients, cultivates excellence and puts a new spin on the classics. What style!
→ Pâté chaud de pintade. Bar, fenouil et citron. Chocolat de notre manufacture.

Le Grand Véfour (Guy Martin)

17 r. de Beaujolais (1st) – ⓜ *Palais Royal*   Plan: **L3**
– ℰ 01 42 96 56 27 – www.grand-vefour.com – Closed 3 weeks in August, Saturday and Sunday
Menu 115 € (lunch)/315 € – Carte 215/285 €
• Creative • Classic •

Bonaparte and Joséphine, Lamartine, Hugo, Sartre… For more than two centuries, the former Café de Chartres has been cultivating the legend. Nowadays it is Guy Martin who maintains the aura. Influenced by travel and painting – colours, shapes, textures – the chef 'sketches' his dishes like an artist… between invention and history.
→ Ravioles de foie gras, crème foisonnée truffée. Parmentier de queue de bœuf aux truffes. Palet noisette et chocolat au lait, glace au caramel brun et sel de Guérande.

Carré des Feuillants (Alain Dutournier)

14 r. de Castiglione (1st) – ⓜ *Tuileries*   Plan: **K3**
– ℰ 01 42 86 82 82 – www.carredesfeuillants.fr – Closed August, Saturday lunch and Sunday
Menu 60 € (lunch)/188 € – Carte 130/180 €
• Modern cuisine • Elegant •

Elegant and minimalist contemporary restaurant on the site of the old Feuillants convent. Modern menu with strong Gascony influences. Superb wines and Armagnacs.
→ Huîtres perles de l'impératrice" en nage infusée et rafraîchie, caviar. Agneau de lait des Pyrénées rôti, confit dans l'argile. Framboises en croquembouche, cédrat en zigzag et caillé de brebis."

FRANCE - PARIS

XXX ❀❀ **Le Grand Restaurant - Jean-François Piège** 🍴 ⟷ AC

7 r. d'Aguesseau (8th) – **Ⓜ** *Madeleine* — Plan: **J2**
*– 𝒞 01 53 05 00 00 – www.jeanfrancoispiege.com – Closed 1 to 22 August,
Saturday and Sunday*
Menu 80 € (weekday lunch)/245 €
– Carte 155/205 € – (booking advisable)
• Modern cuisine • Elegant • Design •
Jean-François Piège has found the perfect setting to showcase the great labora-
tory kitchen he had been dreaming of for so long. The lucky few to get a seat
(25 maximum) can sample delicate, light dishes whose emotion can both be
tasted and experienced. The quintessence of talent!
➜ Gâteau de foie blond baigné d'une sauce aux écrevisses selon Lucien
Tendret. Homard bleu de Bretagne mijoté en feuille de figuier. Blanc à
manger, noisettes, lait d'amande glacé et gelée de citron.

XXX ❀❀ **Sur Mesure par Thierry Marx** – Hôtel Mandarin Oriental

251 r. St-Honoré (1st) – **Ⓜ** *Concorde – 𝒞 01 70 98 73 00* — 🍴 ⟷ AC
– www.mandarinoriental.fr/paris/ – Closed August, — Plan: **J3**
Sunday and Monday
Menu 85 € (weekday lunch), 180/210 €
• Creative • Design • Elegant •
Precise 'tailor-made' (sur mesure) cuisine is the hallmark of Thierry Marx, who
confirms his talent as a master culinary craftsman at the Mandarin Oriental's
showcase restaurant. Every dish reveals his tireless scientific approach, which is
sometimes teasing but always exacting. An experience in itself, aided by the
stunning, immaculate and ethereal decor.
➜ Risotto de soja aux huîtres. Bœuf charbon, aubergine confite et herbes
potagères. Sweet bento.

XXX ❀ **Lucas Carton** 🍴 AC ⟷

9 pl. de la Madeleine (8th) – **Ⓜ** *Madeleine* — Plan: **J2**
*– 𝒞 01 42 65 22 90 – www.lucascarton.com – Closed 3 weeks in August,
Sunday and Monday*
Menu 89 € (weekdays), 99 € 🍷/179 € 🍷 – Carte 105/170 €
• Modern cuisine • Elegant •
A new chapter in the story of Lucas Carton's famous address on the Place de la
Madeleine. The young chef, Julien Dumas, excels in balanced Mediterranean-
influenced cuisine using top-notch ingredients.
➜ Foie gras de canard laqué. Agneau de lait des Pyrénées. Paris-reims.

XXX **1728** 🍴 AC ⟷ ♨

8 r. d'Anjou (8th) – **Ⓜ** *Madeleine – 𝒞 01 40 17 04 77* — Plan: **J2**
*– www.1728-paris.com – Closed 3 weeks in August, Sunday, Monday and
Bank Holidays*
Menu 52 € (weekday lunch), 65 € 🍷/165 € 🍷 – Carte 80/118 €
• Creative • Romantic • Elegant •
A restaurant that is full of history! Built by Antoine Mazin in 1728, this mansion
was the residence of La Fayette from 1827 until his death. The dishes cooked by
chef Nicolas Roudier are a happy blend of eastern and western flavours and an
opportunity to travel the world. Very fine wine list.

XXX ❀ **Pur' - Jean-François Rouquette** – Hôtel Park Hyatt ⟷ AC

5 r. de la Paix (2nd) – **Ⓜ** *Opéra – 𝒞 01 58 71 10 60* — ♨
– www.paris-restaurant-pur.fr — Plan: **K3**
– Closed August and lunch
Menu 135/255 € – Carte 115/225 €
• Creative • Elegant •
Enjoy a sense of pure enjoyment as you dine in this restaurant. The highly elegant contemporary decor and creative dishes are carefully conjured by the chef
using the finest ingredients. Attractive, delicious and refined.
➜ Fricassée de girolles, mûres acidulées et crumble de noisettes. Bar de
nos côtes, voile de seiche, courgette et jus de persil. Lait ribot glacé,
crémeux vanille, pomme verte et caramel de lait au gingembre.

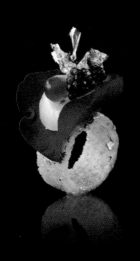

THE HALLMARK
FOR DISTINCTIVE
RECEPTIONS

POTEL & CHABOT

PARIS

Partenaire en France du lancement du

3, rue de Chaillot - 75116 Paris - Tél. : +33(0)1 53 23 15 15
www.poteletchabot.fr

XxX **Le Céladon** – Hôtel Westminster   🄰🄲 ⇔ 🕭

🕄 *15 r. Daunou (2nd)* – Ⓜ *Opéra* – ℰ *01 42 61 77 42*   Plan: **K2**
– www.leceladon.com – Closed August, Saturday, Sunday and Bank
Holidays
Menu 53 € (lunch)/69 € – Carte 85/120 €
• Modern cuisine • Elegant •
A sophisticated decor that combines Regency-style furniture, old paintings and
a collection of pale green Chinese porcelain and celadon vases. Contemporary-
style cuisine with its roots in classic dishes.
➜ Fleur de courgette farcie à l'araignée de mer, émulsion de crustacés.
Noix de ris de veau croustillante en voile de truffe blanche. Framboise tula-
meen crue et cuite à la mélisse, biscuit sablé au gingembre.

XxX **Goust d'Enrico Bernardo**   🕾 🄰🄲 ⇔ 🕭

🕄 *10 r. Volney (2nd)* – Ⓜ *Opéra* – ℰ *01 40 15 20 30*   Plan: **K2**
– www.enricobernardo.com – Closed Saturday lunch, Sunday and Monday
Menu 45 € (lunch) – Carte 80/95 €
• Modern cuisine • Elegant • Intimate •
Within Éléphant Paname, an arts and dance centre set in a lovely mansion next
to the Opera house, this restaurant is all about elegance. Enrico Bernardo,
World's Best Sommelier 2004, leads the dance and the Spanish chef enhances
the French cuisine with Mediterranean influences. The food and wine make a
sweet duo!
➜ Légumes de saison et sabayon aux truffes. Jarret de veau confit, jus de
veau et topinambour. Millefeuille aux noisettes et chocolat.

XxX **Drouant**   🕾 🕼 🄰🄲 ⇔ 🕭

16 pl. Gaillon (2nd) – Ⓜ *Quatre Septembre*   Plan: **K3**
– ℰ 01 42 65 15 16 – www.drouant.com
Menu 45 € (weekday lunch)/59 € – Carte 64/90 €
• Traditional cuisine • Brasserie • Elegant •
A legendary restaurant where the Prix Goncourt has been awarded since 1914.
With Antoine Westermann at the helm, it serves traditional cuisine with a
modern touch. Elegant, richly decorated interior.

XxX **Le Baudelaire** – Hôtel Le Burgundy   🄰🄲 🕭

🕄 *6-8 r. Duphot (1st)* – Ⓜ *Madeleine* – ℰ *01 71 19 49 11*   Plan: **J3**
– www.leburgundy.com – Closed Saturday lunch, Sunday and lunch in
August
Menu 54 € (lunch)/105 € – Carte 90/130 €
• Modern cuisine • Elegant •
This restaurant is within the luxurious Hotel Burgundy. It is a quality, gourmet
establishment, where the food reveals finesse and lightness. There is a lovely
atmosphere around the inner patio.
➜ Saint-Jacques de plongée, sésame noir, mouron des oiseaux et marmelade de citron. Filet de bœuf de Galice, grosse frite, condiment d'échalote
et olives taggiasche. Crémeux chocolat guanaja, sphère caramel et biscuit
cacao.

XxX **Macéo**   🕾 🄰🄲 ⇔

15 r. Petits-Champs (1st) – Ⓜ *Bourse* – ℰ *01 42 97 53 85*   Plan: **L3**
– www.maceorestaurant.com – Closed Saturday lunch, Sunday and Bank
Holidays
Menu 30 € (lunch)/40 € – Carte 50/56 €
• Modern cuisine • Classic •
A Second Empire interior with mouldings, parquet flooring and beautiful mir-
rors is the setting for modern cuisine showcasing seasonal produce. Vegetarian
menu and international wine list.

FRANCE - PARIS

XxX **Le Versance**   AC

16 r. Feydeau (2nd) – 🚇 *Bourse –* ☏ *01 45 08 00 08*   Plan: **L2**
*– www.leversance.fr – Closed 1 to 22 August, 22 December-4 January,
Saturday lunch, Sunday and Monday*
Menu 38 € (lunch) – Carte 70/87 €
• Modern cuisine • Elegant •

A sleek interior with a winning combination of exposed beams, stained-glass
windows and modern furniture. Equally as impressive is the globetrotting
chef's cuisine: think lobster curry, calf's sweetbreads and spiced pears.

XxX **Kei** (Kei Kobayashi)   AC
❀

5 r. du Coq-Héron (1st) – 🚇 *Louvre Rivoli*   Plan: **L3**
*– ☏ 01 42 33 14 74 – www.restaurant-kei.fr – Closed Easter Holidays,
3 weeks in August, Christmas Holidays, Thursday lunch, Sunday and Monday*
Menu 52 € (lunch), 99/188 €
• Modern cuisine • Elegant • Minimalist •

Japanese-born chef Kei Kobayashi's discovery of French gastronomy on TV was a
revelation to him. So much so that as soon as he was old enough he headed
to France to train in some of the country's best restaurants. Here he offers fine
cuisine that reflects his twin influences and his passion.
➜ Jardin de légumes croquants. Bar de ligne rôti et son écaille croustillante. Vacherin fraise, miso et sésame.

XxX **STAY Faubourg** – Hôtel Sofitel le Faubourg   🍴 ⅗ AC ✧ 🐾 P

15 r. Boissy-d'Anglas (8th) – 🚇 *Concorde*   Plan: **J3**
– ☏ 01 44 94 14 14 – www.stay-faubourg.com – Closed 2 weeks in August
Menu 68 € 🍷 (weekday lunch) – Carte 54/104 €
• Modern cuisine • Elegant •

STAY can also be deciphered as 'Simple Table Alléno Yannick', in tribute to its
top chef. The classically inspired menu offers the occasional international twist,
brought back by the chef from his travels. There is also the added bonus of 'last
minute' desserts whipped up before your eyes in the library-cum-pastry kitchen
in the centre.

XX **Le Dali** – Hôtel Le Meurice   AC

228 r. de Rivoli (1st) – 🚇 *Tuileries –* ☏ *01 44 58 10 44*   Plan: **J-K3**
– www.lemeurice.com
Carte 80/124 €
• Modern cuisine • Trendy • Formal •

Le Meurice's 'second' restaurant is located in the thick of it at the luxury hotel. It
is at once a place of transit, a meeting point, and a meticulous, chic and fashionable eatery. The beautiful, classic decor (pillars and mirrors) has a touch of Sur-
realism about it, in homage to Dalí.

XX **Camélia** – Hôtel Mandarin Oriental   🍴 ⅗ AC

251 r. St-Honoré (1st) – 🚇 *Concorde –* ☏ *01 70 98 74 00*   Plan: **J3**
– www.mandarinoriental.fr/paris/
Carte 72/120 €
• Modern cuisine • Elegant • Design •

Keep it simple, concentrate on top quality produce full of flavour, take inspiration from classic French cuisine and add a touch of Asia. These are the aims of
Thierry Marx in this elegant, restful and minimalist-style restaurant.

XX **Le Lulli** – Grand Hôtel du Palais Royal   AC

4 r. de Valois (1st) – 🚇 *Palais Royal –* ☏ *01 42 96 15 35*   Plan: **L3**
*– www.grandhoteldupalaisroyal.com – Closed 31 July-28 August,
Saturday, Sunday and Bank Holidays*
Menu 38 € (weekday lunch) – Carte 52/80 €
• Modern cuisine • Design • Elegant •

The lovely interior design invites you to enjoy the moment with its plant-inspi-
red decoration and contemporary paintings. In the kitchen, chef Jean-Yves
Bournot uses good ingredients to create simple and light meals that have a
meticulous aesthetic. With friendly and professional service to boot, Le Lulli
will win you over!

XX **Restaurant du Palais Royal**

110 Galerie de Valois (1st) – Ⓜ *Palais Royal*   Plan: **L3**
– ☏ *01 40 20 00 27 – www.restaurantdupalaisroyal.com – Closed Sunday and Monday*
Menu 48/140 € – Carte 70/96 €
• Creative • Elegant •

Magnificently located beneath the arcades of the Palais Royal, this elegant restaurant is now the playground of young chef Philip Chronopoulos, formerly of the Atelier Etoile de Joël Robuchon. Philip concocts creative, striking meals, such as flash-fried scampi with girolle mushrooms and fresh almonds.

XX **Café de la Paix** – Hôtel Intercontinental Le Grand

12 bd des Capucines (9th) – Ⓜ *Opéra*   Plan: **K2**
– ☏ *01 40 07 36 36 – www.cafedelapaix.fr*
Menu 43 € (lunch)/82 € – Carte 70/110 €
• Modern cuisine • Elegant • Formal •

Frescoes, gilded panelling and Napoleon III-inspired furniture provide the backdrop for this luxurious and legendary brasserie. Open from 7am to midnight, it is still the place to meet in Paris.

XX **Passage 53** (Shinichi Sato)
❀❀

53 passage des Panoramas (2nd)   Plan: **L2**
– Ⓜ *Grands Boulevards –* ☏ *01 42 33 04 35 – www.passage53.com*
– Closed 2 weeks in August, Sunday and Monday
Menu 60 € (weekday lunch), 140/180 € – *(booking advisable)*
• Creative • Intimate • Design •

In an authentic covered passage, this restaurant has a minimalist decor and offers a fine panorama of contemporary cuisine. Using market-fresh produce, the young Japanese chef – trained at L'Astrance – turns out irrefutably precise compositions that are cooked to perfection.
➜ Calamars et chou-fleur, huître, mousse de haddock et pomme. Pigeonneau, sauce hydromel et mousse de carotte. Dessert autour du citron, crème brûlée au sureau, glace acacia et sorbet miel.

XX **Le Lumière** – Hôtel Scribe

1 r. Scribe (9th) – Ⓜ *Opéra –* ☏ *01 44 71 24 24*   Plan: **K2**
– www.hotel-scribe.com
Menu 95 € – Carte 60/80 €
• Modern cuisine • Elegant •

The Lumière brothers presented their first film to the public in this very setting. The dining room, crowned by a superb glass roof, evokes the elegance of the Belle Epoque period. This image is continued in the kitchen, directed to perfection by a chef who embraces both vivacity and sparkle in his cooking. Simpler à la carte choices at weekends.

XX **La Fontaine Gaillon**

pl. Gaillon (2nd) – Ⓜ *Quatre Septembre*   Plan: **K2-3**
– ☏ *01 47 42 63 22 – www.restaurant-la-fontaine-gaillon.com – Closed 3 weeks in August, Saturday and Sunday*
Menu 58/140 € ⚑ – Carte 65/91 €
• Fish and seafood • Elegant •

Beautiful 17C townhouse owned by Gérard Depardieu. Comfortable setting and terrace around a fountain. Spotlight on seafood, accompanied by a pleasant selection of wines.

XX **Le First** – Hôtel The Westin Paris

234 r. de Rivoli (1st) – Ⓜ *Tuileries –* ☏ *01 44 77 10 40*   Plan: **J3**
– www.lefirstrestaurant.com/fr/
Carte 60/70 €
• Modern cuisine • Elegant • Retro •

Inside the Westin, a stone's throw from the Tuileries, a veritable boudoir designed by Jacques Garcia. The cuisine puts a new spin on traditional dishes (young rabbit with sage). In summer, head for the peaceful terrace in the courtyard.

FRANCE - PARIS

XX **Prémices**

24 r. Rodier (9th) – Ⓜ *Cadet*   Plan: **L1**
– *℘ 01 45 26 86 26*
– *Closed 1 week in May, 3 weeks in August, 1 week Christmas Holidays,*
Monday lunch, Sunday and Monday
Menu 36 € (lunch) – Carte 52/90 € – *(booking advisable)*
• Modern cuisine • Friendly •

Financier in a merchant bank, Alexandre Weill left that behind, started from scratch to indulge his passion for food, and learnt how to cook – so much the better! In his restaurant with a tasteful decor he serves flavoursome dishes, which are lucid, unfussy and made with choice ingredients. And this is just the beginning.

XX **Saturne** (Sven Chartier)   ❀
❀   *17 r. N.-D.-des-Victoires (2nd)* – Ⓜ *Bourse*   Plan: **L3**
– *℘ 01 42 60 31 90* – *www.saturne-paris.fr*
– *Closed 2 weeks in August, Christmas Holidays, Saturday and Sunday*
Menu 45 € (lunch)/75 € – Carte approx. 60 €
• Creative • Trendy •

Saturn (the god of agriculture) and anagram of Natures (in French). The credo of chef Sven Chartier : creative cuisine based on excellent produce in a single menu. Fashionable Scandinavian-style decor (pale wood furniture, polished concrete) and "natural" wines.
➜ Cuisine du marché.

XX **Brasserie Gallopin**   🆎 ⇦

40 r. N.-D.-des-Victoires (2nd) – Ⓜ *Bourse*   Plan: **L3**
– *℘ 01 42 36 45 38* – *www.brasseriegallopin.com*
Menu 29 € – Carte 40/85 €
• Traditional cuisine • Brasserie •

A real institution located opposite the Palais Brongniart, founded in 1876 by a certain Monsieur Gallopin. Once the haunt of Arletty and Raimu, now Parisians and tourists alike head here for the beautiful Victorian decor (mahogany panelling, Belle Époque glass partition etc) and the tasty classic dishes: tartare, rum baba, *Paris-Brest* etc.

XX **Vaudeville**   🌿

29 r. Vivienne (2nd) – Ⓜ *Bourse* – *℘ 01 40 20 04 62*   Plan: **L2**
– *www.vaudevilleparis.com*
Menu 35/42 € – Carte 35/65 €
• Traditional cuisine • Brasserie • Retro •

A grand Art Deco brasserie in the pure Parisian tradition. Seafood, fresh tagliatelle with morels and Beaufort, calf's head with ravigote sauce, andouillette and choucroute are on the menu. By day, a regular lunchtime spot for journalists and in the evening, a haunt for theatre-goers after the show.

XX **Zinc Opéra**

8 r. de Hanovre (2nd) – Ⓜ *Opéra*   Plan: **K2**
– *℘ 01 42 65 58 95* – *www.zinc-opera.com*
– *Closed August, Saturday and Sunday*
Menu 32 € (lunch)/35 € – Carte 37/54 €
• Traditional cuisine • Friendly •

The flavours call the tune at the Zinc Opéra! This chic and cosy bistro is run by a very competent team; the carefully prepared yet simple dishes let the ingredients do the talking. *Confit de canard* with fried potatoes, cherry clafoutis etc: classic dishes that are full of flavour.

FRANCE - PARIS

Jin
▣ ⇿

6 r. de la Sourdière (1st) – ⚫ Tuileries — Plan: **K3**
– ☎ 01 42 61 60 71
– Closed 2 weeks in August, Christmas Holidays, Monday lunch, Tuesday lunch and Sunday
Menu 65 € (lunch)/145 € – (booking advisable)
• Japanese • Elegant • Design •
A new showcase for Japanese cuisine, right in the heart of Paris! Jin is first and foremost about the know-how of Takuya Watanabe, the chef, who comes from Sapporo. Before your eyes, he creates delicious sushi and sashimi, using fish sourced from Brittany, Oléron and Spain. The whole menu is a treat.
➔ Cuisine du marché.

La Régalade Conservatoire – Hôtel de Nell
♿ ▣ ⇿ 🥤

7-9 r. du Conservatoire (9th) – ⚫ Bonne Nouvelle — Plan: **M2**
– ☎ 01 44 83 83 60
– www.charmandmore.com
Menu 37 € – (booking advisable)
• Modern cuisine • Fashionable • Friendly •
After his Régalades in the 14th and 1st arrondissements, Bruno Doucet opened a third, this time close to Grands Boulevards inside the luxurious Hôtel de Nell. Here bistro-style goes chic, and the chef's cooking is as well-executed, generous and tasty as ever.

Terroir Parisien - Palais Brongniart
🛁 ▣ ⇿

28 pl. de la Bourse (2nd) – ⚫ Bourse — Plan: **L3**
– ☎ 01 83 92 20 30 – www.yannick-alleno.com
– Closed 2 weeks in August, Saturday lunch and Sunday
Menu 60 € – Carte 35/60 €
• Traditional cuisine • Bistro •
After the success of his Terroir Parisien in the 5th arrondissement, Yannick Alléno opened this second restaurant in the Palais Brongniart, formerly the Paris stock exchange. It features an inviting decor, rediscovered recipes from the Paris region, and superb charcuterie (prepared by a Meilleur Ouvrier de France). Satisfaction guaranteed!

Atelier Rodier

17 r. Rodier (9th) – ⚫ Notre-Dame de Lorette — Plan: **L1**
– ☎ 09 67 19 94 90 – www.latelier-rodier.com – Closed August, 1 week Christmas Holidays, Tuesday lunch, Wednesday lunch, Saturday lunch, Sunday and Monday
Menu 41/80 €
• Modern cuisine • Fashionable •
Visible from the dining area, the kitchens are proudly on display and reveal a certain flair for the art of cooking. Santiago Torrijos is a young chef who has done stints in some stellar establishments and is quite at ease in his role here as head 'bistronome'. His recipes are creative, inspired and full of surprises.

La Petite Sirène de Copenhague

47 r. Notre-Dame-de-Lorette (9th) – ⚫ St-Georges — Plan: **K1**
– ☎ 01 45 26 66 66 – www.lapetitesireneparis.com
– Closed August, 23 December-2 January, Saturday lunch, Sunday and Monday
Menu 35 € (lunch)/41 € – Carte 50/82 € – (booking advisable)
• Danish • Individual •
The Danish flag flying above the entrance provides a strong clue to the gourmet offerings inside. There is a daily menu chalked up on a slate board, as well as a more expensive à la carte, from which guests can feast on Danish specialities such as herrings.

FRANCE - PARIS

X Le Moderne AC

40 r. N.-D.-des-Victoires (2nd) – ⓜ *Bourse*   Plan: **L3**
– ℰ 01 53 40 84 10 – Closed 1 to 29 August, Saturday
and Sunday
Menu 38/49 €
• Modern cuisine • Fashionable •
Close to the Palais Brongniart, now stripped of its vocation as the Bourse de
Paris, the Café Moderne plunges you into the still bustling atmosphere of the
neighbourhood. At lunchtime, the place is packed to the rafters, while in the
evening it has an intimate feel. On the menu are fresh ingredients, tastefully
prepared.

X Liza AC

14 r. de la Banque (2nd) – ⓜ *Bourse – ℰ 01 55 35 00 66*   Plan: **L3**
– www.restaurant-liza.com – Closed Saturday lunch and Sunday dinner
Menu 38 € (dinner)/53 € – Carte 34/63 €
• Lebanese • Individual •
Originally from Beirut, Liza Asseily gives pride of place to her country's cuisine.
In a contemporary interior dotted with Middle Eastern touches, opt for the shish
taouk or mechoui kafta (lamb, hummus and slow-cooked tomato). Dishes are
meticulously prepared using fresh ingredients. A real treat!

X Bizan ⟷

56 r. Ste-Anne (2nd) – ⓜ *Quatre Septembre*   Plan: **K3**
– ℰ 01 42 96 67 76 – Closed Sunday, Monday and Bank
Holidays
Carte 32/53 €
• Japanese • Minimalist •
Popular address (the name refers to a Japanese mountain) in minimalist style.
Sushi counter, upstairs dining room and fine sake list.

X Aux Lyonnais AC ⟷

32 r. St-Marc (2nd) – ⓜ *Richelieu Drouot*   Plan: **L2**
– ℰ 01 42 96 65 04 – www.auxlyonnais.com – Closed August, Saturday
lunch, Sunday and Monday
Menu 34 € (lunch) – Carte 45/76 € – *(booking advisable)*
• Lyonnaise • Bistro • Retro •
This bistro founded in 1890 serves delicious cuisine which explores the gastro-
nomic history of Lyon. Deliciously retro decor, featuring a zinc counter, ban-
quettes, bevelled mirrors and moulded fixtures and fittings.

X Le Pantruche

3 r. Victor-Massé (9th) – ⓜ *Pigalle – ℰ 01 48 78 55 60*   Plan: **L1**
– www.lepantruche.com – Closed 1 week Easter Holidays, 3 weeks in
August, 24 December-5 January, Saturday and Sunday
Menu 35 € – Carte 42/50 € – *(booking advisable)*
• Modern cuisine • Bistro •
'Pantruche' is slang for Paris... An apt name for this bistro with a chic retro decor,
which happily cultivates a 1940s-1950s 'canaille' atmosphere. As for the food,
the chef and his small team put together lovely seasonal dishes in keeping
with current culinary trends.

X Hotaru

18 r. Rodier (9th) – ⓜ *Notre-Dame de Lorette*   Plan: **L1**
– ℰ 01 48 78 33 74 – Closed 3 weeks in August, 2 weeks
in Winter, Sunday and Monday
Menu 24 € (lunch) – Carte 25/60 €
• Japanese • Rustic • Simple •
A welcoming Japanese restaurant with a young chef who produces traditional,
family cuisine with an emphasis on fish. Enjoy sushi, maki and sashimi, as well as
a selection of cooked and fried dishes.

X

Encore &

43 r. Richer (9th) – **Ⓜ** *Le Peletier –* ℰ *01 72 60 97 72*   Plan: **L2**
– www.encore-restaurant.fr – Closed 2 weeks in August, Christmas Holidays, Saturday and Sunday
Menu 30 € (lunch)/42 € – Carte 40/60 €
• Modern cuisine • Trendy • Friendly •
Yet 'another' trendy bistro? There is nothing copycat here! The Japanese chef creates inventive, enticing dishes that bring out the full flavour of their ingredients. For example, squid from Ile d'Yeu served with 30-month matured ham and Piedmont hazelnuts. Encore!

X

Kunitoraya 🔲 ⇦

5 r. Villedo (1st) – **Ⓜ** *Pyramides –* ℰ *01 47 03 07 74*   Plan: **K3**
– www.kunitoraya.com – Closed 2 weeks in August, Christmas Holidays, Sunday dinner and Monday
Menu 32 € (weekday lunch), 70/100 € – Carte approx. 40 €
• Japanese • Retro • Minimalist •
With its old zinc counter, mirrors and Métro-style tiling, Kunitoraya has the feel of a late-night Parisian restaurant from the early 1900s. Refined Japanese cuisine based around "udon", a thick homemade noodle made with wholemeal flour imported from Japan.

X

Pinxo - Tuileries 🔲

9 r. d'Alger (1st) – **Ⓜ** *Tuileries –* ℰ *01 40 20 72 00*   Plan: **K3**
– www.pinxo.fr – Closed August, Saturday lunch and Sunday
Carte 35/59 €
• Modern cuisine • Fashionable • Friendly •
It was Alain Dutournier – of Carré des Feuillants – who dreamed up this restaurant. You can come and 'pinxer' (nibble with your fingers) delicious tapas-style creations such as sautéed chipirones or beef tartare Rossini. An innovative concept and a delicious way to share and sample a lot of new foods at once.

X
☺

À mère

49 r. de l'Échiquier (10th) – **Ⓜ** *Bonne Nouvelle*   Plan: **M2**
– ℰ 01 73 20 24 52 – www.amere.fr – Closed 2 weeks in August, Saturday and Sunday
Menu 39/57 € – Carte 36/41 €
• Creative • Bistro • Trendy •
Maurizio Zillo, an Italian-Brazilian chef who has had a dazzling career (Bocuse, Alléno, Atala in São Paulo...), has put together a dream team (including a sommelier from the George V) to create this trendy bistro. His dishes are packed with flavour, and his inventiveness hits the nail on the head every time. What a lovely surprise!

X
☺

Zen 🔲

8 r. de L'Échelle (1st) – **Ⓜ** *Palais Royal*   Plan: **K3**
– ℰ 01 42 61 93 99 – Closed 8 to 22 August,
31 December-5 January and Monday dinner
Menu 20 € (weekday lunch), 32/60 € – Carte 20/46 €
• Japanese • Minimalist •
This enticing restaurant combines a refreshing contemporary interior design and authentic Japanese cooking. The menu is well-rounded and faithful to the classic sushi, grilled dishes and tempura, with house specialities of gyoza and chirashi. Ideal for a quick lunch or a relaxing 'zen' dinner.

X

Silk & Spice 🔲 ⇦

6 r. Mandar (2nd) – **Ⓜ** *Sentier –* ℰ *01 44 88 21 91*   Plan: **L3**
– www.silkandspice.fr – Closed Saturday lunch and Sunday
Menu 25 € (lunch), 35/42 € – Carte 34/49 €
• Thai • Exotic •
Low-key atmosphere and delicious Thai-inspired cuisine. The signature dishes here are king prawns and shrimps in a lemon grass reduction, and green beef curry.

FRANCE - PARIS

X **Kiku**   AC ⚌

56 r. Richer (9th) – Ⓜ Cadet – ℰ 01 44 83 02 30 – Closed   Plan: **L2**
1 week in August and in December, Saturday, Sunday and dinner
Menu 17 € – Carte 17/26 €
• Japanese • Intimate •
In Japan, they are called 'izakaya': sake bars serving small tasting dishes. The
concept is original but totally convincing. Very flavoursome and distinct, this
delicious Japanese food is a treat – and just a stone's throw from Les Folies Bergère.

X **Les Canailles**
⊛
25 r. La Bruyère (9th) – Ⓜ St-Georges   Plan: **K1**
– ℰ 01 48 74 10 48 – www.restaurantlescanailles.fr – Closed 3 weeks in
August, Saturday and Sunday
Menu 35 € – Carte 44/72 € – (booking advisable)
• Modern cuisine • Bistro • Friendly •
This pleasant restaurant was created in 2012 by two Bretons with impressive
culinary backgrounds. They slip into the *bistronomy* (gastro bistro), serving
bistro and seasonal dishes. Specialities: ox tongue carpaccio and sauce ravigote,
and rum baba with vanilla whipped cream... Tuck in!

X **L'Office**   AC
⊛
3 r. Richer (9th) – Ⓜ Poissonnière – ℰ 01 47 70 67 31   Plan: **M2**
– www.office-resto.com – Closed 3 weeks in August, Christmas Holidays,
Saturday and Sunday
Menu 22 € (lunch), 28/39 € – (booking advisable)
• Modern cuisine • Bistro • Friendly •
A tiny bistro a stone's throw from Les Folies Bergère. Seated at tightly packed
tables, diners dig into food that changes with the seasons. Precise, flavoursome
dishes accompanied by a well-selected wine list. All at reasonable prices.

X **Pierrot**   ⌂ AC 🍴 (dinner)

18 r. Étienne-Marcel (2nd) – Ⓜ Etienne Marcel   Plan: **M3**
– ℰ 01 45 08 00 10 – Closed Sunday
Menu 50 € ☗ – Carte 40/55 €
• Traditional cuisine • Bistro •
The ideal place to sample the flavours and fine ingredients that the Aveyron
area has to offer. Free-range meat from Aubrac, confit de canard, homemade
foie gras, roast loin of lamb with herbs, veal kidneys with mustard seed sauce...
Simple, hearty, bold dishes served quickly and with a smile!

X **Frenchie**   AC

5 r. du Nil (2nd) – Ⓜ Sentier – ℰ 01 40 39 96 19   Plan: **M3**
– www.frenchie-restaurant.com – Closed 22 July-23 August, 24 December-
4 January, Saturday, Sunday and lunch
Menu 68 € – Carte 45/76 € – (booking advisable)
• Modern cuisine • Friendly •
Near the Sentier metro station, this small, loft-style restaurant has exposed
brickwork, stones and beams. It specialises in contemporary-style cuisine created by a young chef who has worked abroad.

X **Circonstances**   🍴 (dinner)
⊛
174 r. Montmartre (2nd) – Ⓜ Grands Boulevards   Plan: **L2**
– ℰ 01 42 36 17 05 – www.circonstances.fr – Closed 3 weeks in August,
Monday dinner, Tuesday dinner, Saturday and Sunday
Menu 35/45 € – Carte lunch approx. 36 €
• Traditional cuisine • Fashionable • Friendly •
Just next to Grands Boulevards metro station, this bistro was set up by two
experienced partners with a simple mission: to produce good food using first-
rate market ingredients. Diners can savour tasty and well-executed dishes ran-
ging from pan-fried foie gras with lobster emulsion, to pressé de lapin façon
chasseur.

✗ **Noglu**

16 passage des Panoramas (2nd)   Plan: **L2**
*– Ⓜ Grands Boulevards – ✆ 01 40 26 41 24 – www.noglu.fr – Closed
Monday dinner and Sunday*
Menu 37 € (dinner) – Carte 35/50 €
• Modern cuisine • Simple • Trendy •

As its name suggests, Noglu offers an array of carefully prepared dishes certified
gluten-free. Try the white asparagus and smoked trout, sautéed veal with mushrooms or chocolate parfait with preserved orange. Convivial atmosphere, and
for those in a hurry, you can even take it away!

TOUR EIFFEL – INVALIDES   PLAN IV

 Le Cinq Codet   ✗ ⅃ 渝 ᵹ 🆎

5 r. Louis-Codet (7th) – Ⓜ Ecole-Militaire   Plan: **P2**
– ✆ 01 53 85 15 60 – www.le5codet.com
59 rm – ♦259/3000 € ♦♦259/3000 € – ☐ 29 € – 8 suites
• Luxury • Design • Elegant •

A stone's throw from the Invalides, this striking, exclusive hotel is full of attractions. It has an unbeatable location, and rooms with smart, comfortable furnishings and hi-tech fixtures and fittings. There are over 400 contemporary artworks, a stylish restaurant, a well-being centre and a lovely patio terrace.
Concierge and valet parking.
Le Cinq Codet – See restaurant listing

 Juliana   ⅃ 渝 ᵹ 🆎

10-12 r. Cognacq-Jay (7th) – Ⓜ Alma-Marceau   Plan: **P1**
– ✆ 01 44 05 70 00 – www.hoteljuliana.paris
35 rm – ♦450/900 € ♦♦450/900 € – ☐ 29 € – 5 suites
• Luxury • Elegant • Modern •

The superlative elegance of this brand new hotel is undeniable. Find chandeliers, extravagant mirrors, ethnic sculptures and mother-of-pearl furnishings. The rooms satisfy the two-fold demand for good taste and optimum
comfort (Japanese toilets). Attractive, flower-decked façade come summertime.

 Sezz   ᵹ 🆎 🏊 🚗

6 av. Frémiet (16th) ✉ 75016 – Ⓜ Passy   Plan: **N2**
– ✆ 01 56 75 26 26 – www.paris.hotelsezz.com
19 rm – ♦269/484 € ♦♦269/587 € – ☐ 30 € – 7 suites
• Luxury • Design •

Behind the beautiful and elaborately sculpted façade of this building dating
from 1913, the interior has adopted an ultra-design style. It features grey
stone, original furniture, high-tech gadgetry and a sauna. Every guest is also
assigned an individual assistant for the duration of his or her stay.

 Platine   ᵹ 🆎 🏊

20 r. de l'Ingénieur-Robert-Keller (15th)   Plan I: **A2**
– Ⓜ Charles Michels
– ✆ 01 45 71 15 15 – www.platinehotel.fr
46 rm – ♦129/315 € ♦♦149/415 € – ☐ 15 €
• Townhouse • Personalised •

Platine or platinum blonde – like Marilyn Monroe – to whom this hotel pays
homage. The guestrooms are comfortable and well kept. Go for one of those
with a round bed for optimum glamour and to channel your inner star! There
is a pleasant relaxation suite in the basement.

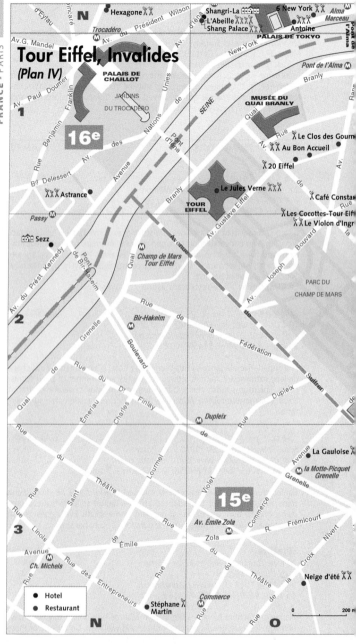

Tour Eiffel, Invalides
(Plan IV)

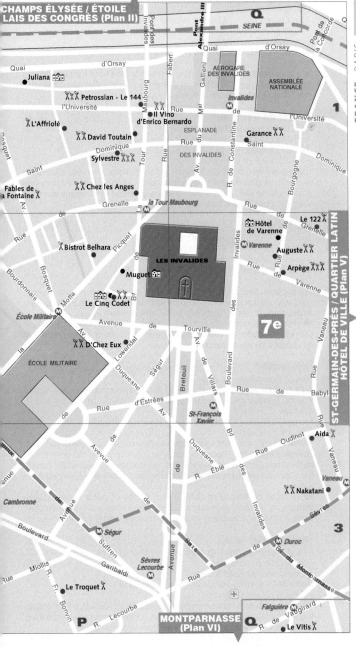

CHAMPS ÉLYSÉE / ÉTOILE
LAIS DES CONGRÈS (Plan II)

SEINE

Quai d'Orsay

d'Orsay

Quai

Juliana

Petrossian - Le 144

l'Université

L'Affriolé

Il Vino
d'Enrico Bernardo

David Toutain

Dominique
Sylvestre

Fables de
a Fontaine

Chez les Anges

Grenelle

la Tour Maubourg

AÉROGARE
DES INVALIDES

Invalides

ESPLANADE

Rue du

DES INVALIDES

Garance

Saint

ASSEMBLÉE
NATIONALE

l'Université

Dominique

1

Bistrot Belhara

LES INVALIDES

Muguet

Le Cinq Codet

École Militaire

ÉCOLE MILITAIRE

D'Chez Eux

Avenue de

Tourville

Hôtel
de Varenne

Le 122

Grenelle

Varenne

Auguste

Arpège

Varenne

7e

ST-GERMAIN-DES-PRÉS / QUARTIER LATIN
HÔTEL DE VILLE (Plan VI)

Boulevard

Rue de

Babyl.

d'Estrées

St-François
Xavier

Aida

Cambronne

Ségur

Boulevard

Miollis

Le Troquet

Suffren

Garibaldi

Sèvres
Lecourbe

Rue

Duquesne

Éblé

Duroc

Bd du Montparnasse

Vaneau

Nakatani

Sèvras

3

Falguière

Vaugirard

Le Vitis

MONTPARNASSE
(Plan VI)

FRANCE - PARIS

Muguet AC

11 r. Chevert (7th) – Ⓜ *École Militaire* — Plan: **P2**
– 𝄞 01 47 05 05 93 – www.hotelparismuguet.com – opening scheduled early May 2016 after renovation
43 rm – ♦120/220 € ♦♦120/220 € – ☲ 14 €
• Family • Classic •

In a quiet street a stone's throw from Les Invalides, this hotel has been refurbished in a classic style. Attractively maintained guestrooms; those overlooking the small flower-decked garden are generally quieter.

Hôtel de Varenne ☷ AC

44 r. de Bourgogne (7th) – Ⓜ *Varenne* — Plan: **Q2**
– 𝄞 01 45 51 45 55 – www.hoteldevarenne.com
24 rm – ♦169/319 € ♦♦169/319 € – ☲ 15 € – 2 suites
• Family • Cosy •

Located between the Rodin Museum and the National Assembly, this hotel is nestled in an attractive and tranquil small courtyard. The overall feel is very classical (Louis XVI and Empire-style) – a look appreciated by the many tourists in search of a true Parisian bolt hole.

Le Jules Verne ❀ ≤ AC ⊠
❀

2nd floor Tour Eiffel (private lift, South pillar) (7th) — Plan: **O1**
– Ⓜ Bir-Hakeim – 𝄞 01 45 55 61 44
– www.lejulesverne-paris.com
Menu 108 € (weekday lunch), 190/230 €
• Modern cuisine • Design • Formal •

The designer decor on the second floor of the Eiffel Tower lives up to expectations, with a magical view as a bonus! French culinary heritage is the focus here, where classic dishes are accompanied by some excellent wines.
➔ Homard, céleri et truffe noire comme une rémoulade, salade de pomme sauvage. Grenadin de veau rôti, pomme de terre Anna. Écrou croustillant au chocolat de notre manufacture à Paris.

Sylvestre ❀ AC ⇔
❀ ❀

79 r. St-Dominique (1st floor) (7th) — Plan: **P1**
– Ⓜ La Tour Maubourg – 𝄞 01 47 05 79 00 – www.thoumieux.fr – Closed August, Tuesday lunch, Wednesday lunch, Saturday lunch, Sunday and Monday
Menu 120/210 € – Carte 130/170 € – *(booking advisable)*
• Modern cuisine • Elegant • Intimate •

It took aplomb, and even courage, to step into the shoes of media star Jean-François Piège at the Thoumieux Hotel. Yet Sylvestre Wahid has done it! This multicultural chef concocts magical, and above all seasonal recipes like cucumber water and vegetable cannelloni or three preparations of cèpes in tribute to autumn.
➔ Tourteau de Roscoff rafraîchi, avocat, brocoli et caviar osciètre. Saint-Jacques de plongée, jus-vinaigrette tiède des barbes, courge butternut et truffe d'Alba. Tarte au citron soufflée au chocolat, sorbet aux agrumes.

Arpège (Alain Passard) AC ⇔
❀ ❀ ❀

84 r. de Varenne (7th) – Ⓜ *Varenne* – 𝄞 01 47 05 09 06 — Plan: **Q2**
– www.alain-passard.com
– Closed Saturday and Sunday
Menu 140 € (lunch), 260/340 € – Carte 185/295 €
• Creative • Elegant •

Precious woods and a Lalique crystal decor provide the backdrop for the dazzling vegetable inspired cuisine of this culinary genius. He creates his astonishing dishes from organic produce grown in his three vegetable gardens!
➔ Fines ravioles potagères multicolores, consommé aux légumes. Corps-à-corps de volaille haute couture. Tarte aux pommes bouquet de roses.

FRANCE - PARIS

XxX **Astrance** (Pascal Barbot)   ⬅ AC
🏵🏵🏵 *4 r. Beethoven (16th)* ✉ *75016 –* Ⓜ *Passy*   Plan: **N1**
*– ℰ 01 40 50 84 40 – www.astrancerestaurant.com – Closed 25 July-
26 August, 1 week in November, Christmas Holidays, Saturday, Sunday,
Monday and Bank Holidays*
Menu 70 € (lunch), 150/230 € *– (booking advisable)*
• Creative • Minimalist • Elegant •
No menu or à la carte choices in this restaurant, where chef Pascal Barbot produces a different 'surprise menu' at each sitting. Sample the inventive cuisine of
a chef at the height of his art, who focuses on excellent ingredients and creative
flair. An unforgettable culinary experience.
➔ Ravioles de butternut, amande amère et chair de crabe épicée. Turbot
vapeur, beurre noisette et miso blanc, jeunes poireaux. Tartelette aux agrumes, streusel au sucre muscovado.

XxX **Petrossian - Le 144**   AC ⇔ 🍴
144 r. de l'Université (7th) – Ⓜ *Invalides*   Plan: **P1**
*– ℰ 01 44 11 32 32 – www.petrossian.fr – Closed August, Sunday and
Monday*
Menu 35 € (lunch), 66/98 € – Carte 80/123 €
• Fish and seafood • Formal • Elegant •
The Petrossians have been serving Parisians with caviar from the Caspian Sea
since 1920. Enjoy fish and seafood in the elegant dining room above the bou-
tique.

XX **Il Vino d'Enrico Bernardo**   ⬅ AC 🍴
🏵 *13 bd La Tour-Maubourg (7th) –* Ⓜ *Invalides*   Plan: **P1**
*– ℰ 01 44 11 72 00 – www.enricobernardo.com – Closed Saturday lunch,
Sunday and Monday*
Menu 35 € (weekday lunch)/70 € – Carte 50/70 €
• Modern cuisine • Elegant • Cosy •
The themed menus 'On the roads of the world' and 'On the roads of France and
Italy' enable Enrico Bernardo, a leading sommelier, to introduce diners to his
favourite wines of the moment, as an accompaniment to the delicious dishes.
The decor, with its vine shoots and wine cabinet, is in tune with the rest!
➔ Menu surprise.

XX **David Toutain**   AC ⇔
🏵 *29 r. Surcouf (7th) –* Ⓜ *Invalides – ℰ 01 45 50 11 10*   Plan: **P1**
*– www.davidtoutain.com – Closed 3 weeks in August, Saturday and
Sunday*
Menu 45 € (lunch), 72/105 €
• Modern cuisine • Design •
Having made a name for himself at some renowned establishments (L'Arpège,
Agapé Substance), David Toutain has opened his own restaurant. All this expe-
rience is channelled into his cooking. While riding the wave of culinary trends,
its finesse, creativity and palette of expressions reveal insight and singularity – a
great balance!
➔ Cuisine du marché.

XX **Le Violon d'Ingres** (Christian Constant)   AC
🏵 *135 r. St-Dominique (7th) –* Ⓜ *École Militaire*   Plan: **O1**
– ℰ 01 45 55 15 05 – www.maisonconstant.com
Menu 45 € (weekday lunch) – Carte 65/85 €
• Traditional cuisine • Elegant •
Diners are fighting each other off for a spot at Christian Constant's restaurant!
His recipes reveal the soul of an authentic cook, firmly in line with the finest tra-
dition. Their execution shows off the know-how of a talented team.
➔ Œuf de poule mollet roulé à la mie de pain, toast de beurre truffé. Véri-
table cassoulet montalbanais. Millefeuille traditionnel à la vanille Bourbon.

XX
❀ **Neige d'Été** (Hideki Nishi)

12 r. de l'Amiral-Roussin (15th) – **Ⓜ** Avenue Émile Zola   Plan: **O3**
– ℰ 01 42 73 66 66 – www.neigedete.fr
– Closed 2 weeks in August, 1 week Christmas Holidays, Sunday and
Monday
Menu 40 € (lunch), 70/100 € – (booking advisable)
• Modern cuisine • Minimalist •
The name (meaning 'Summer Snow') has a very Japanese poetry about it, and
that is no coincidence. This restaurant was opened in mid-2014 by a young
Japanese chef, Hideki Nishi, who used to be at the George V. It also hints at
the contrasts and minimalism that are the hallmarks of his cooking, which is
always spot-on.
→ Cuisine du marché.

XX **Le Cinq Codet** – Hôtel Le Cinq Codet   ⌂ 🅰 ＡＣ

5 r. Louis-Codet (7th) – **Ⓜ** Ecole-Militaire   Plan: **P2**
– ℰ 01 53 85 15 60 – www.le5codet.com
Carte 50/78 €
• Modern cuisine • Elegant •
An enticingly concise menu, with the likes of tuna tataki, orange and sesame
vinaigrette, or marinated meagre (fish) carpaccio with young salad leaves, ser-
ved in a warm designer decor. Comfortable patio.

XX **Chez les Anges**   🏦 ＡＣ ⇔ 🛋

54 bd de la Tour-Maubourg (7th)   Plan: **P1**
– **Ⓜ** La Tour Maubourg – ℰ 01 47 05 89 86 – www.chezlesanges.com
– Closed 3 weeks in August, Saturday and Sunday
Menu 36/55 € – Carte 70/85 €
• Classic cuisine • Fashionable • Elegant •
A stylish interior provides the setting for authentic, appetising food, poised bet-
ween tradition and modernity. Joël Thiébault vegetables in lemon sauce, free-
range guinea fowl, aubergines in orange and spelt curry or Venezuelan dark
chocolate tart. Splendid wine and whisky list.

XX
❀ **Auguste** (Gaël Orieux)   ＡＣ

54 r. de Bourgogne (7th) – **Ⓜ** Varenne   Plan: **Q2**
– ℰ 01 45 51 61 09 – www.restaurantauguste.fr – Closed 1 to 14 August,
Saturday and Sunday
Menu 37 € (lunch), 88/154 € 🍷 – Carte 80/110 € – (booking advisable)
• Modern cuisine • Elegant •
Intimate atmosphere, mirrors, white walls and pretty armchairs... Auguste is per-
fectly tailored to the cuisine of Gaël Orieux, a chef who is passionate about food
and ingredients. His dishes? A quest for harmony and inventiveness, finely wea-
ving together ingredients from land and sea. Affordable prices at lunch; all the
stops are pulled out at dinner.
→ Croustillant de langoustine à la verveine, bavarois de betterave jaune et
kumquat. Ris de veau croustillant, girolles aux abricots secs et vin du Jura.
Soufflé au chocolat Caraïbes, glace au miel.

XX
❀ **Nakatani** (Shinsuke Nakatani)   ＡＣ

27 r. Pierre-Leroux (7th) – **Ⓜ** Vaneau – ℰ 01 47 34 94 14   Plan: **Q3**
– Closed 3 weeks in August, Sunday and Monday
Menu 40 € (lunch), 68/80 € – (set menu only)
• Modern cuisine • Intimate • Romantic •
Japanese chef Shinsuke Nakatani (formerly at Hélène Darroze) is now standing
on his own two feet. With a keen sense of seasoning, technique and the aesthe-
tics of the dishes, he cooks fabulous French cuisine using seasonal ingredients.
All this is served by discreet and efficient staff. Impeccable!
→ Cuisine du marché.

XX
ॐ
Garance (Guillaume Iskandar)   ॐ AC ⇔

34 r. St-Dominique (7th) – Ⓜ Invalides – ℰ 01 45 55 27 56   Plan: **Q1**
– www.garance-saintdominique.fr – Closed Saturday and Sunday
Menu 39 € (lunch)/88 € – Carte 75/105 € – (booking advisable)
• Creative • Design • Elegant •

Guillaume Muller and Guillaume Iskandar (both formerly of L'Arpège) have tea-
med up to open this contemporary bistro in an old building near the Invalides.
The recipes are very contemporary and always highlight the ingredients (celery
cooked in hay and Italian bacon, lamb two ways). Success guaranteed!
→ Cuisine du marché.

XX
D'Chez Eux   ॐ AC

2 av. Lowendal (7th) – Ⓜ École Militaire   Plan: **P2**
– ℰ 01 47 05 52 55 – www.chezeux.com
Menu 34 € (weekday lunch) – Carte 54/108 €
• Cuisine from the South West • Rustic • Friendly •

This restaurant has had a winning formula for over 40 years – and the place
shows no sign of ageing! Sample the generous portions of dishes inspired by
the southwest of France. These are made with quality ingredients and served
by waiters in old-fashioned aprons in a provincial inn ambience.

XX
☺
Au Bon Accueil   AC

14 r. Monttessuy (7th) – Ⓜ Pont de l'Alma   Plan: **O1**
– ℰ 01 47 05 46 11 – www.aubonaccueilparis.com – Closed 3 weeks in
August, Saturday and Sunday
Menu 36/55 € – Carte 65/85 €
• Modern cuisine • Bistro • Cosy •

In the shadow of the Eiffel Tower, this chic and discreet restaurant serves appetising cuisine based around seasonal produce. Excellent value.

XX
La Gauloise   ॐ ⇔

59 av. La Motte-Picquet (15th)   Plan: **O3**
– Ⓜ La Motte Picquet Grenelle – ℰ 01 47 34 11 64
Menu 30 € – Carte 38/72 €
• Traditional cuisine • Elegant • Retro •

This Belle Epoque brasserie boasts the delightful air of Parisian life from yesteryear. It has a menu that features dishes such as poached eggs and vegetable
pot-au-feu, pork crepinettes, turbot with a Béarnaise sauce, and onion soup. La
Gauloise's attractive terrace is also much appreciated by diners.

X
ॐ
Aida (Koji Aida)   ॐ AC ⇔

1 r. Pierre-Leroux (7th) – Ⓜ Vaneau – ℰ 01 43 06 14 18   Plan: **Q3**
– www.aida-paris.net – Closed 1 week in March, 3 weeks in August,
Monday and lunch
Menu 160 € – (booking advisable)
• Japanese • Elegant • Minimalist •

Be transported to the Land of the Rising Sun in this restaurant. It breathes
authenticity and purity through its delicious Japanese cuisine full of finesse.
The fish, presented alive and then prepared in front of you, couldn't be fresher.
The art of simplicity and transparency at its best!
→ Sashimi. Teppanyaki. Wagashi.

X
ॐ
Les Fables de La Fontaine   ॐ AC

131 r. St-Dominique (7th) – Ⓜ École Militaire   Plan: **P1**
– ℰ 01 44 18 37 55 – www.lesfablesdelafontaine.net
Menu 70 € – Carte 45/60 € – (booking advisable)
• Modern cuisine • Bistro • Friendly •

The restaurant's former sous-chef now dons the chef's hat – at barely 21 years
of age! She composes resolutely modern cuisine that is flavoursome and colourful, and demonstrates an impressive degree of maturity in her work. To be
savoured in the elegant setting of a bright, pared-down bistro decor.
→ Jaune d'œuf croustillant, betterave jaune en carpaccio, rouge à l'huile de
noix et mousse de chèvre. Aïoli de lieu, légumes de saison et huile d'olive.
Soufflé litchi, cœur coulant aux fruits rouges, sorbet thym-framboise.

Stéphane Martin   AC ⇔

67 r. des Entrepreneurs (15th) – **M** *Charles Michels*   Plan: **N3**
– ℰ 01 45 79 03 31 – www.stephanemartin.com – Closed 24 April-2 May,
31 July-22 August, 24 December-4 January, Sunday and Monday
Menu 30 € (weekday lunch)/38 € – Carte 49/75 €
• Modern cuisine • Friendly •

This Left Bank address is well known to gourmets. The cosy setting and tasteful decor provide the backdrop for appetising traditional fare with a modern twist. Enjoy the pleasure of dishes such as veal liver meunière or knuckle of pork braised in spiced honey.

Le Clos des Gourmets   ⅏ ⇔

16 av. Rapp (7th) – **M** *Alma Marceau*   Plan: **O1**
– ℰ 01 45 51 75 61 – www.closdesgourmets.com – Closed 1 to 25 August,
Sunday and Monday
Menu 30 € (lunch), 35/39 € – Carte lunch 39/60 €
• Modern cuisine • Fashionable •

Sleek and welcoming modern bistro where the chef loves good food and cares enough to do it well. Asparagus crème brûlée, fennel slow cooked with mellow spices: the cuisine is honest and full of delicious flavours.

Les Cocottes - Tour Eiffel

135 r. St-Dominique (7th) – **M** *École Militaire*   Plan: **O1**
– ℰ 01 45 50 10 28 – www.maisonconstant.com
Menu 28 € (weekday lunch) – Carte 25/57 €
• Traditional cuisine • Fashionable •

The concept in this friendly eatery is based around bistro cuisine with a modern touch cooked in cast-iron casserole pots (cocottes), including popular dishes such as country paté, roast veal etc. No advance booking.

Le 122   AC ⇔

122 r. de Grenelle (7th) – **M** *Solférino*   Plan: **Q2**
– ℰ 01 45 56 07 42 – www.le122.fr – Closed 25 July-25 August, Saturday
and Sunday
Menu 29 € (lunch), 37/65 € – Carte 50/60 €
• Modern cuisine • Design •

A stone's throw from the town hall of the 7th *arrondissement*, this pleasant restaurant draws in numerous politicians at every mealtime. The chef produces flavoursome and skilfully done cuisine such as: pan-fried scallops, black rice risotto, bottarga, as well as fillet of John Dory, quince and grape condiments, celeriac mash...

Bistrot Belhara

23 r. Duvivier (7th) – **M** *École Militaire*   Plan: **P2**
– ℰ 01 45 51 41 77 – www.bistrotbelhara.com – Closed 31 July-25 August,
24 to 29 December, Sunday and Monday
Menu 34 € (lunch), 38/52 € – Carte 43/51 €
• Traditional cuisine • Bistro •

Belhara is a site that is famous for its superb waves on the Basque coast. This is the chef's nod to his origins. It is a tough call to summarise his impressive career path (Guérard, Loiseau, Ducasse etc). A convert to the bistro mode, Thierry Dufroux works wonders as he revisits the classics – the chef is definitely on the crest of the wave!

L'Affriolé   AC

17 r. Malar (7th) – **M** *Invalides –* ℰ *01 44 18 31 33*   Plan: **P1**
– www.laffriole.fr – Closed 3 weeks in August, Sunday and Monday
Menu 30 € (weekday lunch)/39 €
• Modern cuisine • Fashionable •

With his daily specials board and monthly menu, the chef closely follows seasonal market availability. The contemporary designer decor adds a certain charm to the overall feel. A 'bento' menu is also available for those in a hurry.

FRANCE - PARIS

X | **20 Eiffel** | AC

20 r. de Monttessuy (7th) – Ⓜ *Alma Marceau* — Plan: **O1**
– 𝒞 01 47 05 14 20 – Closed August and Sunday
Menu 29 € – Carte 45/55 €
• Traditional cuisine • Classic •

In a quiet street a stone's throw from the Eiffel Tower, this restaurant offers a understated interior full of light. On the menu, you can choose from a range of updated dishes, prepared by two chefs, all of which place the focus on flavour and taste. For example, a delicious fillet of wild pollack with squash.

X | **Le Troquet**

21 r. François-Bonvin (15th) – Ⓜ *Cambronne* — Plan: **P3**
– 𝒞 01 45 66 89 00 – Closed 1 week in May, 3 weeks in
August, 1 week in December, Sunday and Monday
Menu 32 € (lunch), 34/40 € – Carte lunch approx. 35 €
• Traditional cuisine • Retro • Bistro •

A typical Parisian 'troquet' (café-bar) in all its splendour! Although Christian Etchebest is no longer at the helm, a young promising chef is working with the same team. The culinary focus on southwest France remains, as does the commitment to ultra-fresh ingredients.

X | **Café Constant** | AC

139 r. St-Dominique (7th) – Ⓜ *École Militaire* — Plan: **O1**
– 𝒞 01 47 53 73 34 – www.maisonconstant.com
Menu 23 € (weekday lunch) – Carte 34/54 €
• Traditional cuisine • Bistro • Friendly •

This unpretentious and friendly brasserie run by Christian Constant occupies an old café. The gourmet bistro cuisine includes classics such as eggs mimosa, oyster tartare, roast lamb, rice pudding etc. No advance booking.

SAINT-GERMAIN DES PRES – QUARTIER LATIN – HOTEL DE VILLE   **PLAN V**

🏨 | **Victoria Palace** | ⬇ AC ⚐ 🚗

6 r. Blaise-Desgoffe (6th) – Ⓜ *St-Placide* — Plan: **R3**
– 𝒞 01 45 49 70 00 – www.victoriapalace.com
58 rm � – ♥285/402 € ♥♥285/402 € – 4 suites
• Historic • Luxury • Stylish •

A hotel with a great tradition, featuring luxurious fabrics, Louis XVI furniture and marble bathrooms in the guestrooms. The spaciously appointed junior suites are particularly recommended for a relaxing stay. The Victorian style lounge is equally restful.

🏨 | **Duc de St-Simon** | AC

14 r. St-Simon (7th) – Ⓜ *Rue du Bac* – 𝒞 01 44 39 20 20 — Plan: **R1**
– www.hotelducdesaintsimon.com
29 rm – ♥295/395 € ♥♥295/395 € – ⊊ 19 € – 5 suites
• Luxury • Personalised •

The small paved courtyard comes into view as you pass through the entrance, revealing the full beauty of this fine 18C townhouse. The fabrics, panelling, old prints and antique furniture enhance the sense of an aristocratic property from bygone days. The charm here is on an equal par with the peace and quiet.

🏨 | **L'Hôtel** | ⚒ 🐾 AC

13 r. des Beaux-Arts (6th) – Ⓜ *St-Germain des Prés* — Plan: **S1**
– 𝒞 01 44 41 99 00 – www.l-hotel.com
20 rm ⊊ – ♥305/1150 € ♥♥305/1150 €
• Luxury • Historic • Personalised •

It was at L'Hôtel that the great Oscar Wilde died in 1900. The atypical, aesthetic decor, updated by Jacques Garcia, still manages to pay homage to artistic pomp and splendour. There is a nod to Baroque, Empire and Oriental styles.
    ✳ **Le Restaurant** – See restaurant listing

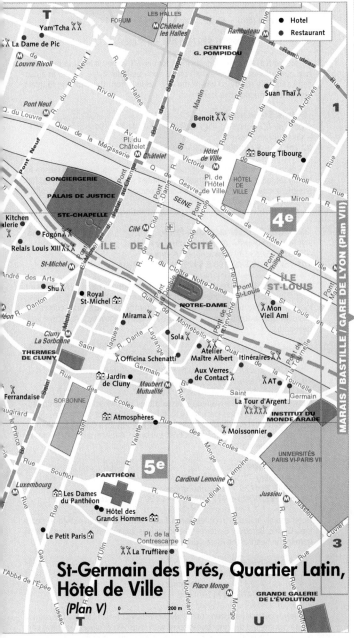

- ● Hotel
- ● Restaurant

Yam'Tcha 🗡🗡

La Dame de Pic 🗡

LES HALLES
FORUM

Châtelet
les Halles Ⓜ

Rambuteau

CENTRE
G. POMPIDOU

Ⓜ de
Louvre Rivoli

Rue du Pont Neuf

R. des Halles

Rivoli

Av.
Martin

Renard

Rambuteau

Temple

Rue des Archives

Rue

1

Pont Neuf

Q. du Louvre

Quai de la Mégisserie

Pl. du
Châtelet

Ⓜ Châtelet

Rue

St

Hôtel
de Ville
Victoria

Suan Thaï 🗡

Benoit 🗡🗡 ●

🏨 Bourg Tibourg

Rue des

CONCIERGERIE

PALAIS DE JUSTICE

STE-CHAPELLE

Pont Neuf

SEINE

Pl. de
l'Hôtel
de Ville

HÔTEL
DE
VILLE

Rue F. Miron

Rivoli

R.

Kitchen
alerie ●

● Fogón 🗡

Relais Louis XIII 🗡🗡

Cité Ⓜ

ÎLE DE LA CITÉ

Quai aux Fleurs

ÎLE
ST-LOUIS

4e

de
l'Hôtel
de
Ville

R.
Philippe

Andrés
des Arts

St-Michel Ⓜ

Shu 🗡

● Royal
St-Michel 🏨

Danton

Quai de

NOTRE-DAME

🗡 Mon
Vieil Ami

St
Louis en

Cluny
La Sorbonne Ⓜ

Saint

Mirama 🗡

THERMES
DE CLUNY

Rue

🗡 Officina Schenatti

Sola 🗡

Atelier
Maître Albert

Itinéraires 🗡🗡

R. Dante

Montebello

Pont de l'Archevêché

Quai de

la

Pont de la Tournelle

🗡 AT ●

Ferrandaise

Saint

🏨 Jardin
de Cluny

Germain

SORBONNE

Maubert
Mutualité Ⓜ

Aux Verres
de Contact 🗡

Bd

Saint

La Tour d'Argent

🗡🗡🗡🗡🗡

Germain

INSTITUT DU
MONDE ARABE

augirard

Rue

● Atmosphères

des

Écoles

🗡 Moissonnier ●

5e

Luxembourg Ⓜ

PANTHÉON

R.

Clovis

Cardinal Lemoine Ⓜ

Monge

Lemoine

UNIVERSITÉS
PARIS VI-PARIS VII

Jussieu Ⓜ Jussieu

R.

3

🏨 Les Dames
du Panthéon

● Hôtel des
Grands Hommes 🏨

Le Petit Paris 🏨

Pl. de la
Contrescarpe

🗡🗡 La Truffière ●

Cardinal

du

Rue

Linné

R. Cuvier

l'Abbé de l'Épée

Lussac

St-Germain des Prés, Quartier Latin,
Hôtel de Ville
(Plan V)

0   200 m

T

Mouffetard

Place Monge

Monge Ⓜ

Monge

GRANDE GALERIE
DE L'ÉVOLUTION

Geoffroy

U

FRANCE - PARIS

L'Abbaye
10 r. Cassette (6th) – Ⓜ *St-Sulpice* – ☎ *01 45 44 38 11*
– www.hotel-abbaye.com
40 rm ☲ – **†**275/640 € **††**275/640 € – 4 suites
• Luxury • Historic • Personalised •
A hotel with a rare charm occupying a former 17C abbey. It features highly refined guestrooms, which are both bright and classically styled, as well as a peaceful and leafy courtyard where the only noise is from the bubbling fountain. Thoughtful and attentive staff.

Relais St-Germain
9 carr. de l'Odéon (6th) – Ⓜ *Odéon* – ☎ *01 44 27 07 97*
– www.hotelrsg.com
22 rm ☲ – **†**230/460 € **††**295/460 €
• Traditional • Townhouse • Personalised •
Life never seems to stand still at the Carrefour de l'Odéon – a good reason for taking refuge in this refined hotel. The painted wood beams, shimmering fabrics and antique furniture bestow a unique character on the guestrooms, which are perfect for literary inspiration!
Le Comptoir du Relais – See restaurant listing

Bel Ami St-Germain des Prés
7 r. St-Benoit (6th) – Ⓜ *St-Germain des Prés*
– ☎ 01 42 61 53 53 – www.hotel-bel-ami.com
108 rm ☲ – **†**270/1190 € **††**290/1190 € – 7 suites
• Townhouse • Contemporary •
The name of this hotel has nothing to do with the famous novel by Maupassant, even if it is located in the literary district of St Germain. The hotel will suit guests looking for a chic, urban ambience. It has a trendy bar and simple, contemporary-style guestrooms, some of which have been renovated. Attractive well-being area.

Montalembert
3 r. Montalembert (7th) – Ⓜ *Rue du Bac*
– ☎ 01 45 49 68 68 – www.hotelmontalembert-paris.fr
49 rm – **†**220/685 € **††**220/685 € – ☲ 26 € – 5 suites
• Historic • Personalised • Design •
Located between St-Germain-des-Prés and the Orsay Museum, this particularly attractive building dates back to 1926. It has very pleasant guestrooms. Some are decorated in Louis-Philippe style, and the majority, in a chic and contemporary style bearing the hallmark of Christian Liaigre. A few even boast an attractive view of the city's rooftops.

Bourg Tibourg
19 r. du Bourg-Tibourg (4th) – Ⓜ *Hôtel de Ville*
– ☎ 01 42 78 47 39 – www.bourgtibourg.com
30 rm – **†**220/320 € **††**290/400 € – ☲ 20 € – 1 suite
• Luxury • Townhouse • Design •
Hotel entirely styled by Jacques Garcia. Each room has its own individual decor (neo-Gothic, Baroque, Eastern etc) and exudes luxury and refinement. A little gem in the heart of the Marais district.

Le Bellechasse
8 r. de Bellechasse (7th) – Ⓜ *Musée d'Orsay*
– ☎ 01 45 50 22 31 – www.lebellechasse.com
33 rm – **†**179/470 € **††**179/470 € – ☲ 21 €
• Luxury • Personalised • Design •
A lovely hotel that has been entirely decorated by Christian Lacroix. The *couture* house has created designer guestrooms with splashes of colour. They have contemporary details that often have a dreamlike quality. It makes for a 'journey within a journey' – fashionable and full of character!

FRANCE - PARIS

La Belle Juliette

92 r. du Cherche-Midi (6th) – Ⓜ *Vaneau*
– ☎ *01 42 22 97 40* – *www.labellejuliette.com*   Plan: **R3**
39 rm – †250/800 € ††350/800 € – ☷ 20 € – 6 suites
• Townhouse • Elegant • Personalised •

Each floor of the hotel is decorated on a different theme. Madame Récamier on
the first floor (the famous Juliette), Italy on the second, Chateaubriand on the
third etc. A decor that combines old and new, and remains inviting. A place
with character.

Les Dames du Panthéon

19 pl. du Panthéon (5th) – Ⓜ *Luxembourg*   Plan: **T3**
– ☎ *01 43 54 32 95* – *www.hotellesdamesdupantheon.com*
35 rm – †200/450 € ††200/450 € – ☷ 18 €
• Luxury • Traditional • Cosy •

The Panthéon, the Sorbonne, the Luxembourg Gardens... no doubt about it, we
are in the heart of the Latin Quarter! Facing the Panthéon, this hotel has guestrooms with decor inspired by French women who have left their mark on
history: Marguerite Duras, Juliette Gréco, George Sand and Édith Piaf. A romantic and elegant hotel.

Atmosphères

31 r. des Écoles (5th) – Ⓜ *Maubert Mutualité*   Plan: **T2-3**
– ☎ *01 43 26 56 02* – *www.hotelatmospheres.com*
56 rm – †160/340 € ††160/720 € – ☷ 16 €
• Business • Luxury • Design •

A hotel with sleek lines and the latest in designer furnishings. In the lobby, there
is a fine exhibition of Thierry des Ouches photographs. From the lounge to the
relaxation area (with sauna and hammam) and the guestrooms, the comfort is
total. A success.

Hôtel des Grands Hommes

17 pl. du Panthéon (5th) – Ⓜ *Luxembourg*   Plan: **T3**
– ☎ *01 46 34 19 60* – *www.hoteldesgrandshommes.com*
30 rm – †250/340 € ††300/470 € – ☷ 14 €
• Traditional • Townhouse • Historic •

This charming hotel enjoys a fine location near the Panthéon. The well-maintained guestrooms are furnished in Directoire-style and have plenty of character.
Superb views from the balconies and terraces on the fifth and sixth floors.

Royal St-Michel

3 bd St-Michel (5th) – Ⓜ *St-Michel* – ☎ *01 44 07 06 06*   Plan: **T2**
– *www.hotelroyalsaintmichel.com*
39 rm ☷ – †190/310 € ††190/340 €
• Business • Townhouse • Modern •

The full atmosphere of the Latin Quarter is right on the doorstep of this welcoming hotel just opposite the St-Michel fountain. Fortunately, the cosy and contemporary guestrooms are well-soundproofed, which is a detail not to be overlooked in this lively district.

Jardin de Cluny

9 r. du Sommerard (5th) – Ⓜ *Maubert Mutualité*   Plan: **T2**
– ☎ *01 43 54 22 66* – *www.hoteljardindecluny.com*
39 rm – †140/250 € ††210/360 € – ☷ 17 €
• Business • Townhouse • Personalised •

Environmentally conscious travellers will enjoy staying at this Écolabel-certified
hotel. The elegance and comfort in the guestrooms has not been sacrificed one
bit. The vaulted room where breakfast is served has lots of charm.

FRANCE - PARIS

Le Petit Paris   ⚠ AC

214 r. St-Jacques (5th) – Ⓜ *Luxembourg*   Plan: **T3**
– ℰ 01 53 10 29 29 – www.hotelpetitparis.com
20 rm – ♦195/350 € ♦♦200/450 € – ⌑ 15 €
• Townhouse • Design • Contemporary •

With their elegant yet fun and colourful decor, the guestrooms in this hotel evoke the style of the Middle Ages, the 1920s, 1970s, or the Louis VX and Napoleon III periods.

✗✗✗✗   La Tour d'Argent   🌣 ⩽ AC ⇔ 🥢
✿

15 quai de la Tournelle (5th) – Ⓜ *Maubert Mutualité*   Plan: **U2**
– ℰ 01 43 54 23 31 – www.tourdargent.com – Closed August, Sunday and Monday
Menu 85 € (lunch) – Carte 165/330 €
• Classic cuisine • Luxury • Elegant •

An unforgettable view of Notre-Dame cathedral and a quintessentially traditional restaurant serving classic dishes from the gastronomic hall of fame, including legendary Challans duck. Formal, elegant service, like in the old days. Superb wine list.
→ Quenelles de brochet André Terrail". Caneton "Tour d'Argent". Crêpes "Belle Époque"."

✗✗✗   Guy Savoy   🌣 ⚠ AC ⇔ 🥢
✿✿✿

11 quai de Conti (6th) – Ⓜ *St-Michel – ℰ 01 43 80 40 61*   Plan: **S1**
– www.guysavoy.com – Closed August, Christmas Holidays, Saturday lunch, Sunday and Monday
Menu 110 € (lunch), 360/530 € ▾ – Carte 205/335 €
• Creative • Luxury • Romantic •

Guy Savoy: the second act! In 2015, the chef set up shop in the Hôtel de la Monnaie, on the banks of the Seine. The setting is sumptuous with six rooms decorated with contemporary artworks, on loan from François Pinault. The host is true to form, injecting the place with sincerity and enthusiasm, inventiveness without excess, and unfailing generosity. Irresistible!
→ Huîtres en nage glacée et deux nouvelles préparations. Saumon figé sur la glace, consommé brûlant et perles de citron. Millefeuille à la gousse de vanille.

✗✗✗   Relais Louis XIII (Manuel Martinez)   🌣 AC ⇔ 🥢
✿

8 r. des Grands-Augustins (6th) – Ⓜ *Odéon*   Plan: **T2**
– ℰ 01 43 26 75 96 – www.relaislouis13.com – Closed 3 weeks in August, 1 week in January, Sunday, Monday and Bank Holidays
Menu 60 € (weekday lunch), 90/140 € – Carte 130/140 €
• Classic cuisine • Rustic • Elegant •

Very close to the Seine, this old house located in historical Paris takes us back to Louis XIII's day. The decor is full of character with exposed beams, stonework and stained-glass windows. This forms an elegant backdrop for Manuel Martinez's cooking, which is in line with French culinary classicism. Good value lunch.
→ Quenelle de bar, mousseline de champignons, glaçage au champagne. Canard challandais rôti aux épices. Millefeuille, crème légère à la vanille Bourbon.

✗✗✗   Hélène Darroze   AC ⇔ 🥢
✿

4 r. d'Assas (6th) – Ⓜ *Sèvres Babylone*   Plan: **R2**
– ℰ 01 42 22 00 11 – www.helenedarroze.com – Closed Sunday and Monday
Menu 58 € (lunch), 98/185 €
• Modern cuisine • Cosy •

Hélène Darroze, the descendent of a family of cooks from southwest France (Aquitaine, Landes, Basque country), finds the raw ingredients for her cuisine in her homeland. To this heritage, she has added her experience, insatiable curiosity and own distinctive blend of talent and intuition.
→ Huître, caviar d'Aquitaine et haricots maïs du Béarn. Homard tandoori, carotte, agrumes et coriandre. Chocolat araguani, fève tonka, caramel et yaourt grec.

XX
❀

Le Restaurant – Hôtel L'Hôtel   AC

13 r. des Beaux-Arts (6th) – Ⓜ St-Germain des Prés   Plan: **S1**
– ℰ 01 44 41 99 01
– www.l-hotel.com
– Closed August, 22 to 28 December, Sunday and Monday
Menu 55 € (lunch), 85 € 🍷/115 € – Carte 118/145 €
• Modern cuisine • Elegant • Luxury •
Le Restaurant is part of L'Hôtel, with a decor also created by Jacques Garcia. The chef revisits classic French gastronomy with creative dishes based around evocative flavours and superb ingredients.
➜ Tourteau de Loctudy, avocat et yuzu. Ris de veau crousti-moelleux", jus aux herbes. Chocolat au parfum de poivre long, poudre de meringue."

XX
❀

La Dame de Pic   ♿ AC ⇔

20 r. du Louvre (1st) – Ⓜ Louvre Rivoli   Plan: **T1**
– ℰ 01 42 60 40 40
– www.ladamedepic.fr
Menu 59 € (weekday lunch), 95/125 €
• Creative • Design • Elegant •
Anne-Sophie Pic's Parisian restaurant is a stone's throw from the Louvre. The Valence-born chef's feeling for flavours is easily recognisable, as is the precision of her creations and her ability to combine unexpected ingredients. Enjoy variations based on the leitmotiv of flavours and aromas.
➜ Berlingots de chèvre fumés, tomates de toutes les couleurs en marinade. Agneau de l'Aveyron mariné à la vodka et bourgeon de sapin, asperges vertes et lard de Colonnata. Palet de chocolat illanka, premières cerises.

XX
❀

Les Climats   🐾 🍴 AC ⇝ 🍽 (dinner)

41 r. de Lille (7th) – Ⓜ Rue du Bac   Plan: **R1**
– ℰ 01 58 62 10 08 – www.lesclimats.fr
– Closed 28 February-7 March, 3 weeks in August, 24 to 28 December, Sunday and Monday
Menu 42 € (lunch) – Carte 80/120 €
• Modern cuisine • Retro • Elegant •
A restaurant in the unusual setting of the former Maison des Dames des Postes, which housed postal and telecommunications service operators from 1905. The French cuisine is spiced up with modern touches. The mosaic floors, antique brass light fittings and vert d'Estours marble give character to the decor.
➜ Homard, bouillon de carapace à la verveine fraîche, fricassée de girolles et d'abricots. Canard de Challans rôti, sauce aux cerises, raviole de cuisse et d'abattis. Crème onctueuse au citron, calisson et parfait aux olives.

XX
❀

Benoit   🐾 AC ⇔

20 r. St-Martin (4th) – Ⓜ Châtelet-Les Halles   Plan: **U1**
– ℰ 01 42 72 25 76 – www.benoit-paris.com
– Closed August
Menu 42 € (lunch) – Carte 70/100 €
• Classic cuisine • Bistro • Retro •
Alain Ducasse supervises this chic and lively bistro, one of the oldest in Paris: Benoit celebrated its 100th anniversary in 2012! The classic food is prepared in time-honoured tradition, and respects the soul of this authentic and fine establishment.
➜ Pâté en croûte, cœur de laitue à l'huile de noix et chapons aillés. Filet de sole Nantua, épinards à peine crémés. Profiteroles Benoit, sauce au chocolat chaud.

FRANCE - PARIS

239

FRANCE - PARIS

La Truffière

4 r. Blainville (5th) – **M** Place Monge – ℰ 01 46 33 29 82   Plan: **T3**
– www.latruffiere.com – Closed 17 to 26 December, Tuesday lunch in July-
August, Sunday and Monday
Menu 40 € (lunch), 65/135 € – Carte 115/155 €
• Modern cuisine • Intimate • Neighbourhood •
The standards are consistently high in this attractive 17C house. Enjoy recipes
full of finesse created with traditional produce and enhanced, in season, by
the exquisite flavours of black or white truffles. The wine list, featuring vintages
from around the world, is remarkable.
➔ Déclinaison de légumes de saison, vinaigrette à la truffe blanche. Parmentier de queue de bœuf à la truffe noire. Soufflé chaud à la truffe
noire, glace truffe et bière blanche.

Itinéraires (Sylvain Sendra)

5 r. de Pontoise (5th) – **M** Maubert Mutualité   Plan: **U2**
– ℰ 01 46 33 60 11 – www.restaurant-itineraires.com – Closed 9 to
24 August, 21 to 28 December, Saturday lunch, Sunday and Monday
Menu 50 € (lunch), 65/105 € – Carte 55/95 € – (booking advisable)
• Modern cuisine • Fashionable •
Chef Sylvain Sendra didn't wait long to install his attractive restaurant – very
light and bright – among the capital's top tables. Finesse, flavours, originality
and quality ingredients: you won't regret including a meal here on your itine-
rary.
➔ Tarte à l'oignon doux des Cévennes, champignons de Paris et noix de
muscade. Carré d'agneau de Lozère, cèpes, noisettes, mousseline de
pomme de terre. Tartelette mûre-framboise et basilic, parfum litchi et rose.

ES (Takayuki Honjo)

91 r. de Grenelle (7th) – **M** Solférino – ℰ 01 45 51 25 74   Plan: **R1**
– Closed 3 weeks in August, Tuesday lunch, Sunday and Monday
Menu 42 € (weekday lunch)/105 € – (booking advisable)
• Modern cuisine • Minimalist •
Restaurant run by Takayuki Honjo, a young Japanese chef who is an adept of
French cuisine. From the first mouthful, his talent strikes a chord with your
taste buds. Foie gras and sea urchin, pigeon and cocoa... all the associations
work a treat. He masters flavours and never forgets the harmony of the whole.
➔ Foie gras, jus de navet et oursin. Pigeon rôti, sauce cacao, pomme de
terre grenaille et herbes de saison. Déclinaison autour de la fraise gari-
guette, crème mascarpone et vieux balsamique.

Yam'Tcha (Adeline Grattard)

121 r. St-Honoré (1st) – **M** Louvre Rivoli   Plan: **T1**
– ℰ 01 40 26 08 07 – www.yamtcha.com – Closed August, Christmas
Holidays, Tuesday lunch, Sunday and Monday
Menu 60 € (weekday lunch)/120 € – (booking advisable)
• Creative • Elegant •
Adeline Grattard has moved to the Rue St Honoré, 50m from her previous add-
ress. This young chef, trained at L'Astrance and in Hong Kong, has a remarkable
feel for ingredients with simple and striking associations – influences of France
and Asia – devised to be paired with a selection of excellent teas.
➔ Cuisine du marché.

Atelier Maître Albert

1 r. Maître-Albert (5th) – **M** Maubert Mutualité   Plan: **U2**
– ℰ 01 56 81 30 01 – www.ateliermaitrealbert.com – Closed lunch
Saturday and Sunday
Menu 31 € (lunch), 36/70 € – Carte 40/70 €
• Traditional cuisine • Cosy • Friendly •
An attractive medieval fireplace and roasting spits take pride of place in this
handsome interior designed by Jean-Michel Wilmotte. Guy Savoy is responsible
for the mouthwatering menu.

XX **Un Dimanche à Paris**   🕭 🅰🅲 ⇔

4 cours du Commerce-St-André (6th) – Ⓜ *Odéon*   Plan: **S2**
– 𝄐 01 56 81 18 18 – www.un-dimanche-a-paris.com
– Closed 1 to 22 August, Tuesday lunch, Sunday dinner and Monday
Menu 31 € (weekday lunch), 39/62 € – Carte 45/65 €
• Modern cuisine • Friendly •

Chocolate is king in this concept store! In the restaurant, the spicy hint of the cocoa bean can even be detected in the meat and fish dishes. The delicious desserts are a particular highlight. An elegant setting, which is equally perfect for a mid- afternoon hot chocolate.

XX **Alcazar**   🕭 🅰🅲 ⇔

62 r. Mazarine (6th) – Ⓜ *Odéon – 𝄐 01 53 10 19 99*   Plan: **S2**
– www.alcazar.fr
Menu 22 € (lunch) – Carte 55/65 €
• Modern cuisine • Trendy • Brasserie •

This former cabaret was given a makeover in autumn 2015, under the direction of architect and decorator Lola Gonzalez. With its plant-filled decor, the whole place exudes the timeless elegance of a large winter garden. As for the food, you can still enjoy an appetising contemporary brasserie menu.

XX **Fogón**   🅰🅲 🍴 (dinner)

45 quai des Grands-Augustins (6th) – Ⓜ *St-Michel*   Plan: **T2**
– 𝄐 01 43 54 31 33 – www.restaurantfogon.com – Closed 3 weeks in August and Monday
Menu 51 € – Carte 45/70 €
• Spanish • Friendly •

A taste of Spain on the banks of the Seine. Spanish cuisine is served in a trendy dining room with a chic, designer-style decor. Note that the set menus and paella rice dishes are only served for a minimum of two people.

X   **Gaya Rive Gauche par Pierre Gagnaire**   🅰🅲
❀

44 r. du Bac (7th) – Ⓜ *Rue du Bac*   Plan: **R1**
– 𝄐 01 45 44 73 73 – www.pierre-gagnaire.com
– Closed 1 week in August, Christmas Holidays, Sunday and Monday
Menu 65 € 🍷 (lunch) – Carte 60/95 €
• Fish and seafood • Cosy • Elegant •

Under the impulsion of designer Violaine Jeantet, this restaurant (Pierre Gagnaire's second in Paris) has become cosier and more refined, thanks in particular to the sapele wall panelling. As for the food, it still celebrates fish and seafood in original ways but without excess. Delicious!
→ Tartare de thon rouge et maquereau aux algues, riquette et salicornes. Gambas au curcuma, risotto rose et côtes de blette. Biscuit roulé de poivrons rouges confits au safran.

X   **L'Atelier de Joël Robuchon - St-Germain**   🕸 🅰🅲 ⇔ 🍴
❀ ❀

5 r. de Montalembert (7th) – Ⓜ *Rue du Bac*   Plan: **R1**
– 𝄐 01 42 22 56 56 – www.joel-robuchon.net
– Open from 11.30am to 3.30pm and 6.30pm to midnight. Reservations possible for certain times only: please enquire
Menu 169 € – Carte 80/175 €
• Creative • Design • Minimalist •

This contemporary Atelier by Joël Robuchon – the first in a long line – is a must! Find the long counter flanked by high stools, a small intimate dining area, and a red and black colour scheme. The studied half-light is all directed onto the shiny plates, chiselled with a jeweller's precision.
→ Caviar sur un œuf de poule mollet, friand au saumon fumé. Merlan frit Colbert, beurre aux herbes. Ganache onctueuse au chocolat araguani, glace au grué de cacao.

FRANCE - PARIS

FRANCE - PARIS

Sola 🗚 ⇔
🕸 *12 r. de l'Hôtel-Colbert (5th) – Ⓜ Maubert Mutualité*   Plan: **T-U2**
– ℰ 01 43 29 59 04 – www.restaurant-sola.com – Closed 2 weeks in August, 30 December-7 January, Sunday and Monday
Menu 48 € (lunch), 78/98 €
• Modern cuisine • Exotic • Elegant •
This restaurant is just a few yards from the banks of the Seine overlooking Notre Dame and yet you'd be forgiven for thinking you were already in Japan! The young Japanese chef is living proof that the cuisine of his home and adopted countries can combine to create harmonious and gracefully presented culinary creations. Ingredients sourced from France are transformed with traditional Far Eastern flavours.
➔ Cuisine du marché.

Ze Kitchen Galerie (William Ledeuil) 🗚 🍴
🕸 *4 r. des Grands-Augustins (6th) – Ⓜ St-Michel*   Plan: **T2**
– ℰ 01 44 32 00 32 – www.zekitchengalerie.fr – Closed 2 weeks in August, 1 week late December, Saturday lunch and Sunday
Menu 48 € (lunch), 85/98 €
• Creative • Friendly •
Attractive fusion cuisine with a hint of Asia, a minimalist, loft-style decor, contemporary paintings on the walls and a view of the open kitchens. For over 10 years, Ze Kitchen has been one of the unmissable restaurants on the Left Bank.
➔ Coquillages, jus de wasabi et pomme verte. Thon blanc, vitello tonnato, sauce vierge. Reines-claudes et mirabelles, sablé et glace gingembre.

Mon Vieil Ami
69 r. St-Louis-en-l'Île (4th) – Ⓜ Pont Marie   Plan: **U2**
– ℰ 01 40 46 01 35 – www.mon-vieil-ami.com
Menu 48 € (dinner)/55 € – Carte 36/56 €
• Traditional cuisine • Inn • Elegant •
Old wooden beams and contemporary decor characterise this trendy, auberge-style restaurant. Delicious traditional recipes with a lovely modern touch and Alsace influences.

Moissonnier ⇔
28 r. des Fossés-St-Bernard (5th) – Ⓜ Jussieu   Plan: **U3**
– ℰ 01 43 29 87 65 – Closed Sunday and Monday
Carte 35/68 €
• Lyonnaise • Bistro • Minimalist •
The decor in this bistro has resisted every passing trend with its gleaming zinc counter, walls showing the patina of age, and comfy banquettes. Veal sweetbread turnovers and oxtail terrine are just two examples of the specialities of the skilful chef.

Aux Prés 🗚
27 r. du Dragon (6th) – Ⓜ St-Germain des Prés   Plan: **S2**
– ℰ 01 45 48 29 68 – www.restaurantauxpres.com
Menu 45/52 €
• Modern cuisine • Retro • Friendly •
Cyril Lignac is clearly not short of a project or two! After changing the name and concept of his St Germain establishment, he now serves international, decidedly creative and spontaneous cuisine, without losing sight of French country roots. The Sunday brunch is a great success.

La Marlotte 🏠
😊 *55 r. du Cherche-Midi (6th) – Ⓜ St-Placide*   Plan: **R2**
– ℰ 01 45 48 86 79 – www.lamarlotte.com – Closed 13 to 21 August
Menu 28 € (weekday lunch)/33 € – Carte 32/51 €
• Traditional cuisine • Rustic •
This modern take on a provincial-style inn is not far from the Bon Marché department store and is a popular haunt for publishers and politicians. The copious and seasonal cuisine honours tradition with dishes such as herring and potatoes in oil, chicken liver terrine, and Grenoble-style skate.

X **L'Épi Dupin**

11 r. Dupin (6th) – Ⓜ Sèvres Babylone   Plan: **R2**
– ✆ 01 42 22 64 56 – www.epidupin.com – Closed 1 to 24 August, Monday lunch, Saturday and Sunday
Menu 39/52 € – *(booking advisable)*
• Modern cuisine • Friendly •

True to his beliefs, chef François Pasteau runs an eco-friendly establishment. He buys his fruit and vegetables locally, recycles organic waste, filters the drinking water on site, etc. This respect for the health of our planet and bodies can be tasted in his recipes, which provide an appetising tribute to French country traditions.

X **La Maison du Jardin**   AC

27 r. Vaugirard (6th) – Ⓜ Rennes – ✆ 01 45 48 22 31   Plan: **S3**
– Closed 1 to 23 August, Saturday lunch and Sunday
Menu 35 € – *(booking advisable)*
• Traditional cuisine • Bistro •

This bistro a stone's throw from the Luxembourg palace explores the flavours and simplicity of traditional cuisine. Try dishes such as homemade terrines, seasonal soups, lamb pastilla, cod with courgette polenta, and the chocolate dessert selection... all accompanied by sensibly priced wines.

X **Yen**   AC

22 r. St-Benoît (6th) – Ⓜ St-Germain-des-Prés   Plan: **S2**
– ✆ 01 45 44 11 18 – www.yen-paris.fr – Closed 2 weeks in August and Sunday
Menu 69 € (dinner) – Carte 32/68 €
• Japanese • Friendly •

The highly refined Japanese decor in this restaurant will appeal to fans of the minimalist look. The menu showcases the chef's speciality, soba – buckwheat noodles served hot or cold and prepared in front of you.

X **La Ferrandaise**   AC ⇔

8 r. de Vaugirard (6th) – Ⓜ Odéon – ✆ 01 43 26 36 36   Plan: **T2**
– www.laferrandaise.com – Closed 3 weeks in August, Monday lunch, Saturday lunch and Sunday
Menu 16 € (lunch), 37/55 €
• Traditional cuisine • Bistro • Friendly •

This pretty restaurant close to the Luxembourg gardens pays homage to the cuisine of the Auvergne and the Puy-de-Dôme. The owner has even developed a partnership with breeders of the traditional 'Ferrandaise' cattle from his homeland, while the Breton chef creates cuisine that is both honest and tasty. A winning combination.

X **Taokan**   AC

8 r. du Sabot (6th) – Ⓜ St-Germain des Prés   Plan: **S2**
– ✆ 01 42 84 18 36 – www.taokan.fr – Closed 1 to 15 August and Sunday lunch
Menu 22 € (lunch), 29/37 € – Carte 35/60 €
• Chinese • Friendly •

In the heart of St-Germain des Prés, come inside this pretty restaurant to enjoy Chinese cuisine. Cantonese specialities feature, for example, dim sum, steamed fish, duck breast with honey, and caramelised sliced chicken. Beautiful presentation and good ingredients: this is a real ambassador for Chinese food!

X **Shu**

8 r. Suger (6th) – Ⓜ St-Michel – ✆ 01 46 34 25 88   Plan: **T2**
– www.restaurant-shu.com – Closed Easter Holidays, 3 weeks in August, Sunday and lunch
Menu 38 € (dinner), 48/63 € – *(booking advisable)*
• Japanese • Minimalist • Friendly •

You will need to duck to get through the door that leads to this 17C cellar. To a backdrop of minimalist decor, discover authentic and impressively crafted Japanese cuisine here. The freshness of the ingredients is showcased to the full in dishes such as kushiage, sushi and sashimi.

FRANCE - PARIS

Fish La Boissonnerie

69 r. de Seine (6th) – Ⓜ Odéon – ℰ 01 43 54 34 69 — Plan: **S2**
– Closed 1 week in August and 23 December-2 January
Carte 36/46 €
• Traditional cuisine • Bistro • Friendly •

It is worth coming to this restaurant just to admire the mosaic façade! For the past 10 years this convivial restaurant has been paying homage to Bacchus, fish and seafood. The menu features dishes such as oyster vichyssoise, scallops with Paimpol beans, and sea bream with barigoule-style artichokes.

Atelier Vivanda - Cherche Midi

20 r. du Cherche-Midi (6th) – Ⓜ Sèvres Babylone — Plan: **R2**
– ℰ 01 45 44 50 44 – www.ateliervivanda.com – Closed 2 weeks in August, 1 week Christmas Holidays, Sunday and Monday
Menu 35 € – Carte 50/70 €
• Meats • Bistro • Friendly •

Welcome to the new bistrot à viande run by Akrame Benallal. Superb pieces of meat are of course on the menu: Black Angus beef (flank and marbled cuts), chicken supreme and Iberian pork chop, all lovingly prepared and accompanied by gratin dauphinois or homemade fries. Wildly good.

Le Bon Saint-Pourçain

10 bis r. Servandoni (6th) – Ⓜ Mabillon — Plan: **S2**
– ℰ 01 42 01 78 24 – Closed Sunday and Monday
Carte 40/52 € – *(booking advisable)*
• Traditional cuisine • Bistro • Neighbourhood •

Tucked away behind St Sulpice church in the heart of the Saint Germain des Prés district, this former restaurant reopened in the spring of 2015. Bistro traditions with a modern twist depict the delicious food – doubtless due to the high quality fresh produce. Booking advisable!

Le Comptoir du Relais – Hôtel Relais St-Germain

5 carr. de l'Odéon (6th) – Ⓜ Odéon – ℰ 01 44 27 07 50 — Plan: **S2**
– www.hotelrsg.com
Carte 35/60 € – *(booking advisable)*
• Traditional cuisine • Bistro • Friendly •

In this pocket-sized 1930s bistro, chef Yves Camdeborde delights customers with his copious traditional cuisine. Brasserie dishes are to the fore at lunchtime, with a more refined single menu available in the evening.

Suan Thaï

35 r. Temple (4th) – Ⓜ Rambuteau – ℰ 01 42 77 10 20 — Plan: **U1**
– www.suanthai.fr
Menu 19 € (lunch) – Carte 30/55 €
• Thai • Exotic •

From the street, a long dining room comes into focus, at the end of which you can make out a green wall, like a promise of freshness. This is fitting for a menu that offers authentic Thai food, cooked by chefs who hail from the country. Enjoy dishes such as seared beef salad with lemongrass or jackfruit soup with coconut milk.

Officina Schenatti

15 r. Frédéric-Sauton (5th) – Ⓜ Maubert Mutualité — Plan: **U2**
– ℰ 01 46 34 08 91 – www.officinaschenatti.com – Closed 3 weeks in August, 24 to 27 December, Monday lunch and Sunday
Menu 35 € – Carte 48/74 €
• Italian • Trendy •

Ivan Schenatti, who comes from Lombardy, chose this street near the Seine to set up his 'officina' (studio) with a decor blending stone and designer furniture. He creates tasty dishes from Italy's regions, such as homemade ravioli stuffed with chanterelles, and pairs them with good Italian wines.

✗ AT   🄰🄲 ⟷

4 r. Cardinal-Lemoine (5th) Paris 05   Plan: **U2**
– Ⓜ Cardinal Lemoine – ℰ 01 56 81 94 08 – www.atushitanaka.com
– Closed August, Sunday and Monday
Menu 35 € (weekday lunch)/95 €
• Creative • Design • Minimalist •

A stone's throw from the banks of the Seine and the Tour d'Argent, the minimalist interior of this small restaurant embodies the quintessence of Japan. Chef
Tanaka, formerly with Pierre Gagnaire, loves fresh ingredients and precise cooking and is forever surprising us with his creative recipes. Vaulted basement.

✗ Aux Verres de Contact   ⅄

33 r. de Bièvre (corner of bd St-Germain) (5th)   Plan: **U2**
– Ⓜ Maubert Mutualité – ℰ 01 46 34 58 02
– www.auxverresdecontact.com – Closed Saturday lunch and Sunday
Menu 35 € – Carte 33/49 €
• Traditional cuisine • Bistro • Friendly •

The team from Le Jadis in the 15th arrondissement runs this pleasant and
colourful contemporary bistro. The food is generous, market-based, accompanied by good wine.

✗ Mirama   🄰🄲

17 r. St Jacques (5th) – Ⓜ Cluny La Sorbonne   Plan: **T2**
– ℰ 01 43 54 71 77
Carte 20/30 €
• Chinese • Simple • Friendly •

A stone's throw from Boulevard St Michel, just behind the Eglise St Séverin
church, Mirama is for those who love authentic Chinese food. Make sure you
try the soups and the Peking duck, the house specialities.

MONTPARNASSE – DENFERT   PLAN VI

Pullman Montparnasse   ⤭ ⟨ ⫫ ⌖ 🄰🄲 ⌿

19 r. du Cdt-Mouchotte (14th)   Plan: **V1**
– Ⓜ Montparnasse Bienvenüe – ℰ 01 44 36 44 36
– www.pullmanhotels.com
926 rm – ♦159/517 € ♦♦159/517 € – ⌷ 26 € – 31 suites
• Business • Modern •

This is one of the largest business hotels in the capital with its 957 guestrooms
and suites, and some 50 meeting rooms. Almost half of the rooms boast panoramic views of Paris and all are very comfortable.

Concorde Montparnasse   ⤭ ⌖ 🄰🄲 ⌿ 🚗

40 r. du Cdt-Mouchotte (14th) – Ⓜ Gaîté   Plan: **V1**
– ℰ 01 56 54 84 00 – http://montparnasse.concorde-hotels.fr
354 rm – ♦125/500 € ♦♦129/500 € – ⌷ 19 €
• Business • Modern •

Situated on Place de Catalogne, this hotel offers functional guestrooms that are
ideal for business travellers. Guests can relax in the trendy bar or enjoy a meal in
the 'salad bar' or on the outdoor patio.

Delambre   ⌖ 🄰🄲

35 r. Delambre (14th) – Ⓜ Edgar Quinet   Plan: **W1**
– ℰ 01 43 20 66 31 – www.hoteldelambreparis.com
30 rm – ♦99/185 € ♦♦99/199 € – ⌷ 13 €
• Traditional • Functional •

The memory of André Breton and Paul Gauguin is still alive in this hotel situated
near Montparnasse railway station. Relax in one of the simple, functional guestrooms before taking a stroll through this lively district.

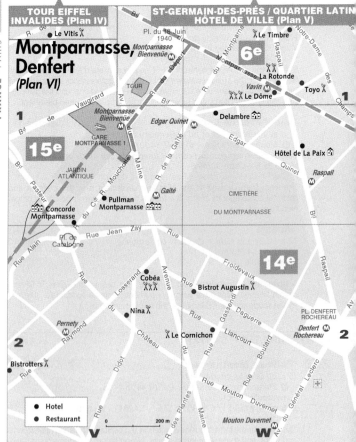

TOUR EIFFEL
INVALIDES (Plan IV)

ST-GERMAIN-DES-PRÉS / QUARTIER LATIN
HÔTEL DE VILLE (Plan V)

Montparnasse, Denfert
(Plan VI)

- ● Hotel
- ● Restaurant

0   200 m

Plan: W1

🏠 Hôtel de la Paix   ⏳

225 bd Raspail (14th) – Ⓜ *Raspail –* ✆ *01 43 20 35 82*
– www.paris-montparnasse-hotel.com
40 rm – ♦90/138 € ♦♦195/220 € – ☐ 10 €
• **Traditional • Personalised •**

Don't be fooled by the façade: this hotel has real charm. The owners have decorated the building with enthusiasm, using carefully chosen objects and old furniture. The guestrooms are bright, pretty and simple in style.

XxX Le Dôme   ⏳ ⏳

108 bd Montparnasse (14th) – Ⓜ *Vavin*
– ✆ *01 43 35 25 81*
Carte 75/140 €
• **Fish and seafood • Brasserie •**

One of the temples of literary and artistic bohemia from the Roaring Twenties with a legendary Art Deco setting. Le Dôme continues to serve the freshest fish and seafood in the best time-honoured fashion.

❀❀❀   **Cobéa** (Philippe Bélissent)   🕸 AC
❀   *11 r. Raymond-Losserand (14th) – Ⓜ Gaité*   Plan: **V2**
– ✆ 01 43 20 21 39 – www.cobea.fr – Closed 1 week Easter Holidays,
August, 1 week Christmas Holidays, Sunday and Monday
Menu 50 € (lunch), 70/120 € *– (booking advisable)*
• Modern cuisine • Elegant •
Co, as in Jérôme Cobou, in the restaurant, Bé, as in Philippe Bélissent, in the kitchens, and A for Associates. Cobéa is the venture of two passionate young pro-
fessionals, who have created a place in their image, that is, guided by the taste
for good things! A feel for ingredients, harmony and strength of flavours, and
finesse. A delicious restaurant.
➜ Couteaux de plongée, concombre et céleri du bassin parisien. Lotte en
kadaïf, carotte et orange. Fraises et meringue.

❀❀   **La Rotonde**   🖼 AC
  105 bd Montparnasse (6th) – Ⓜ Vavin   Plan: **W1**
– ✆ 01 43 26 68 84 – www.rotondemontparnasse.com
Menu 44 € – Carte 31/77 €
• Traditional cuisine • Brasserie • Friendly •
A stone's throw from theatres of the Rue de la Gaîté, La Rotonde has been the
incarnation of the very essence of the Parisian brasserie for over a century. The
decor is typical – very 1930s – all brass fittings and red banquettes, and the
dishes are classic brasserie, such as Salers beef and oyster platters. Plus, it is
open until 2am!

❀   **Le Vitis**   AC 🔄
🕲   *8 r. Falguière (15th) – Ⓜ Falguière – ✆ 01 42 73 07 02*   Plan: **V1**
– www.levitis.fr – Closed 2 weeks in August, 24 December-3 January,
Sunday and Monday
Carte 32/47 € *– (booking advisable)*
• Traditional cuisine • Bistro •
The Delacourcelle brothers, whom we last saw at the Pré Verre in the 5th *arrondissement*, are back with this new pocket-handkerchief bistro. Their tempting
selection of skilfully prepared, distinctive dishes include pig's head with date
purée and melting suckling pig with sweet spices. Superb wine list.

❀   **Le Timbre**
🕲   *3 r. Ste-Beuve (6th) – Ⓜ Notre-Dame des Champs*   Plan: **W1**
– ✆ 01 45 49 10 40 – www.restaurantletimbre.com – Closed August, 1 to
6 January, Sunday and Monday
Menu 26 € (lunch), 36/49 € *– (booking advisable)*
• Traditional cuisine • Bistro • Friendly •
The young chef of this bistro, no bigger than a postage stamp, has preserved all
the charm of the establishment. Find wooden tables, benches and a simple,
unpretentious ambience. He serves unusual, appetising, market-fresh cuisine
and Agnès, his partner, will happily guide your choice of wine.

❀   **Nina**
🕲   *139 r. du Château (14th) – Ⓜ Mouton Duvernet*   Plan: **V2**
– ✆ 09 83 01 88 40 – www.nina-restaurant.fr – Closed Sunday and
Monday
Menu 20 € (weekday lunch)/38 € – Carte 25/44 €
• Creative • Bistro • Trendy •
The impressive choice of flawlessly cooked, fine produce (meagre and scorpion
fish, beef from Galicia) will already have set your taste buds tingling but Nina's
real specialty is vegetables, in all forms, shapes, sizes, colours and textures. A
genuine culinary exploit – well done Nina!

Bistrotters

9 r. Decrès (14th) – Ⓜ *Plaisance* – ☏ *01 45 45 58 59*
– *www.bistrotters.com – Closed Sunday and Monday*
Menu 29 € (weekday lunch)/36 €
• Classic cuisine • Bistro • Simple •
A very lovely find in the southern reaches of the 14th *arrondissement*, close to
Métro Plaisance. The values of *bistronomie* and Epicureanism are at the fore
with hearty, elaborate fare made from fine ingredients (small producers from
the Île-de-France area where possible). Bistro interior and laid-back service.

Plan: **V2**

Le Cornichon

34 r. Gassendi (14th) – Ⓜ *Denfert Rochereau*
– ☏ *01 43 20 40 19 – www.lecornichon.fr – Closed August, 1 week
Christmas Holidays, Saturday and Sunday*
Menu 35/50 € – Carte 45/86 €
• Modern cuisine • Bistro • Friendly •
This business is run by two real food lovers: the first is a computer engineer who
has always wanted to get into the restaurant trade and the second is a well-trai-
ned young chef. They came together to create this bistro with a very modern
feel. With its fine ingredients, appealing dishes, rich flavours etc, Le Cornichon
is sure to win you over!

Plan: **W2**

Bistrot Augustin

79 r. Daguerre (14th) – Ⓜ *Gaîté* – ☏ *01 43 21 92 29*
– *www.augustin-bistrot.fr – Closed Sunday*
Menu 38 € – Carte 40/65 €
• Traditional cuisine • Bistro • Friendly •
This chic bistro with an intimate interior proposes market (and seasonal) cui-
sine with southern influences to whet the appetite. An example: the superb
Périgord pork chop... Ingredients take pride of place here, and our taste buds
aren't complaining!

Plan: **W2**

Toyo

17 r. Jules-Chaplain (6th) – Ⓜ *Vavin* – ☏ *01 43 54 28 03*
– *www.restaurant-toyo.com – Closed 2 weeks in August, Christmas
Holidays, Monday lunch and Sunday*
Menu 39 € (lunch), 95/125 €
• Creative • Design • Minimalist •
In a former life, Toyomitsu Nakayama was the private chef for the couturier
Kenzo. Nowadays, he excels in the art of fusing flavours and textures from
France and Asia to create dishes that are both fresh and delicate.

Plan: **W1**

Pavillon de la Reine

28 pl. des Vosges (3rd) – Ⓜ *Bastille* – ☏ *01 40 29 19 19*
– *www.pavillon-de-la-reine.com*
51 rm – ♟350/510 € ♟♟350/510 € – ⌂ 35 € – 3 suites
• Luxury • Historic • Personalised •
The elegance and noble discretion of historical Paris. Beyond the vaults of the
Place des Vosges, the first flash of inspiration comes at the sight of the beautiful
leafy courtyard, and the hushed and refined guestrooms are cause for further
delight. Luxury without ostentation!

Plan: **Y2**

Le Petit Moulin

29 r. du Poitou (3rd) – Ⓜ *St-Sébastien Froissart*
– ☏ *01 42 74 10 10 – www.hoteldupetitmoulin.com*
17 rm – ♟195/490 € ♟♟195/490 € – ⌂ 16 €
• Luxury • Personalised •
Christian Lacroix is behind the unique and refined decor in this hotel in the
Marais, which plays on the contrasts between the traditional and the modern.
Every bedroom is a delight, with vibrant tones and free-standing bathtubs.

Plan: **X1**

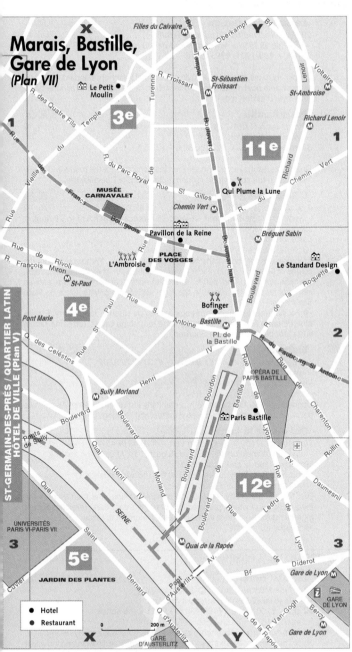

Marais, Bastille, Gare de Lyon
(Plan VII)

Le Petit Moulin

3e

MUSÉE CARNAVALET

Pavillon de la Reine

PLACE DES VOSGES

L'Ambroisie

St-Paul

4e

Pont Marie

Q. des Célestins

Sully Morland

Pont de Sully

Bofinger

Bastille

Pl. de la Bastille

OPÉRA DE PARIS BASTILLE

Paris Bastille

UNIVERSITÉS PARIS VI-PARIS VII

JARDIN DES PLANTES

5e

SEINE

Quai de la Rapée

Pont d'Austerlitz

GARE D'AUSTERLITZ

Filles du Calvaire

St-Sébastien Froissart

St-Ambroise

Richard Lenoir

11e

Qui Plume la Lune

Bréguet Sabin

Le Standard Design

12e

Gare de Lyon

GARE DE LYON

Gare de Lyon

● Hotel
● Restaurant

0   200 m

ST-GERMAIN-DES-PRÉS / QUARTIER LATIN / HÔTEL DE VILLE (Plan V)

FRANCE - PARIS

Le Standard Design

29 r. des Taillandiers (11th) – Ⓜ *Bastille* — Plan: **Y2**
– *℘ 01 48 05 30 97* – *www.standard-design-hotel-paris.com*
37 rm – †90/190 € ††95/200 € – ☲ 15 €
• Traditional • Cosy • Design •
Despite its name, the designer style of this hotel is far from standard. The decor is stylish with bold motifs adorning the fabrics in the guestrooms and the lobby. Attic-style breakfast room.

Paris Bastille

67 r. de Lyon (12th) – Ⓜ *Bastille* – *℘ 01 40 01 07 17* — Plan: **Y2**
– *www.hotelparisbastille.com*
37 rm – †214/332 € ††228/332 € – ☲ 15 €
• Business • Townhouse • Functional •
Fine fabrics, exotic woods and selected hues characterise the rooms and breakfast room in this comfortable modern hotel opposite Opera Bastille.

XXXX L'Ambroisie (Bernard Pacaud)

✿✿✿ *9 pl. des Vosges (4th)* – Ⓜ *St-Paul* – *℘ 01 42 78 51 45* — Plan: **X2**
– *www.ambroisie-paris.com* – *Closed 23 February-8 March, 3 to 24 August, Sunday and Monday*
Carte 210/330 €
• Classic cuisine • Luxury • Elegant •
Ambrosia was the food of the gods on Mount Olympus. Without question, the cuisine of Bernard Pacaud reaches similar heights with its explosion of flavours, scientific approach and perfect execution. Incomparable classicism and an immortal feast for the senses in the regal setting of a private house on Place des Vosges.
➜ Feuillantine de langoustines aux graines de sésame, sauce curry. Escalopine de bar à l'émincé d'artichaut, nage réduite au caviar. Tarte fine sablée au cacao, glace à la vanille Bourbon.

XX Bofinger

(dinner)

5 r. de la Bastille (4th) – Ⓜ *Bastille* – *℘ 01 42 72 87 82* — Plan: **Y2**
– *www.bofingerparis.com*
Menu 38/60 € – Carte 40/81 €
• Traditional cuisine • Retro • Brasserie •
Opened in 1864, this brasserie is a real Paris institution. Striking, Alsace-style decor, including a dome, marquetry, mirrors and paintings by Hansi.

X Qui plume la Lune (Jacky Ribault)

✿ *50 r. Amelot (11th)* – Ⓜ *Chemin Vert* – *℘ 01 48 07 45 48* — Plan: **Y1**
– *www.quiplumelalune.fr* – *Closed August, 1 to 11 January, Sunday, Monday, Tuesday and Bank Holidays*
Menu 60 € (weekday lunch), 85/120 € – *(booking advisable)*
• Modern cuisine • Cosy •
First there is the pretty, inviting and romantic setting. And then there is the food: fresh, full of vitality, prepared by a passionate cook using carefully selected ingredients (organic, great vegetables etc). A moment to savour.
➜ Cuisine du marché.

Terrass' Hôtel

12 r. J.-de-Maistre (18th) – Ⓜ *Place de Clichy* — Plan: **Z1**
– *℘ 01 46 06 72 85* – *www.terrass-hotel.com*
92 rm – †160/380 € ††180/450 € – ☲ 25 € – 6 suites
• Traditional • Business • Personalised •
A few minutes from Montmartre cemetery, this hotel was entirely revamped in 2015. The interior now sports an eclectic mixture of Scandinavian and industrial influences, while the rooms echo the neighbourhood's bohemian artistic spirit. A fine hotel.

FRANCE - PARIS

Relais Montmartre

6 r. Constance (18th) – Ⓜ *Abbesses* – 𝒞 *01 70 64 25 25*   Plan: **Z2**
– www.relaismontmartre.fr
26 rm – ♥119/259 € ♥♥119/259 € – ⬛ 15 €
• Business • Traditional • Cosy •
Not far from the shops on rue Lepic, this small hotel is a somewhat unexpected
find in such a lively district. It is full of character and has all the charm of a bourgeois house. Guestrooms embellished with period furniture, not to mention the
welcome peace and quiet.

Chamarré Montmartre

52 r. Lamarck (18th) – Ⓜ *Lamarck Caulaincourt*
– 𝒞 01 42 55 05 42 – www.chamarre-montmartre.com   Plan: **AA1**
Menu 32 € (lunch), 39/70 € – Carte 61/71 €
• Creative • Friendly •
This contemporary restaurant on Montmartre hill serves creative cuisine with a
blend of culinary influences. Dishes include Seychelles-style sea bass, lobster in
a calamansi sauce and rum baba, all of which can be enjoyed on the attractive
terrace.

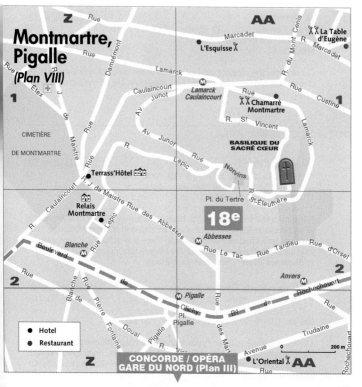

FRANCE - PARIS

XX 🌸 **La Table d'Eugène** (Geoffroy Maillard)

18 r. Eugène-Sue (18th) – **Ⓜ** *Jules Joffrin*   Plan: **AA 1**
– *☎ 01 42 55 61 64* – *www.latabledeugene.com* – *Closed August, 1 week
Christmas Holidays, Sunday and Monday*
Menu 38 € (lunch), 79/99 € – *(booking advisable)*
• Modern cuisine • Design •

Without any difficulty, Geoffroy Maillard – who already had a stint at Frechon
behind him – has propelled his charming Table d'Eugène to rank among the
best. Good news for the 18th arrondissement, and all foodies! He creates very
fresh food, bursting with flavours and colour, which is hearty even in its subtlety.
Power and finesse.
→ Calamars de ligne "black and white". Pigeon en croûte de noisettes.
Sphère chocolat et fève tonka.

X 🌸 **L'Esquisse**

151 bis r. Marcadet (18th) – **Ⓜ** *Lamarck-Caulaincourt*   Plan: **AA1**
– *☎ 01 53 41 63 04* – *Closed 3 weeks in August,
Sunday and Monday*
Menu 22 € (weekday lunch) – Carte 35/42 €
• Modern cuisine • Bistro •

Two young enthusiastic food lovers have pooled their talents to create this inviting vintage bistro with solid wooden floors and benches. The eye-catching, no-
frills dishes pay tribute to the high quality produce. Flawlessly cooked with contrasting seasonings. Delicious!

X **L'Oriental**   🏠 🅰 ♻

47 av. Trudaine (9th) – **Ⓜ** *Pigalle* – *☎ 01 42 64 39 80*   Plan: **AA2**
– *www.loriental-restaurant.com*
Menu 35 € – Carte 32/52 €
• North-African • Exotic •

Choose from the pleasant outdoor terrace or the welcoming and comfortable
dining room with its oriental decor. Evocatively flavoured Moroccan cuisine, including signature couscous dishes.

OUTSIDE CENTRAL AREA   PLAN I

🏨 **St-James Paris**   ☆ 🌸 🛁 ⅃♨ 🅰 🏋 🅿

43 av. Bugeaud (16th) ✉ 75116 – **Ⓜ** *Porte Dauphine*   Plan: **A2**
– *☎ 01 44 05 81 81* – *www.saint-james-paris.com*
17 rm – 🛏380/1680 € 🛏🛏435/1680 € – 🖵 36 € – 32 suites
• Historic • Luxury • Personalised •

This superb late-19C mansion has been given a new look by designer Bambi
Sloan. Napoleon-III style flirts with a very British brand of originality and includes
lovely materials and shimmering prints. There is a delightful library, majestic
staircase and harmonious volumes. The blueprint for a unique place.
🌸 **St-James Paris** – See restaurant listing

🏨 **Pullman Paris Centre-Bercy**   ☆ ⅃♨ ♿ 🅰 🏋

1 r. de Libourne (12th) – **Ⓜ** *Cour St-Émilion*   Plan: **D3**
– *☎ 01 44 67 34 00* – *www.pullmanhotels.com*
396 rm 🖵 – 🛏110/705 € 🛏🛏110/705 € – 20 suites
• Business • Design •

A building that is readily recognisable on account of its imposing glazed façade.
The rooms, some of which have fine views over Paris, are contemporary in style.
The restaurant epitomises the pleasant 'village' atmosphere of the Bercy district.
Brunch on Sundays.

FRANCE - PARIS

 Square 🏠 ⚙ ⚶ 🅰 🄰 🚗

3 r. Boulainvilliers (16th) ✉ *75016 –* Ⓜ *Mirabeau*   Plan: **A2**
– 𝒞 01 44 14 91 90 – www.hotelsquare.com
22 rm – †250/840 € ††250/840 € – ⌒ 25 €
• Luxury • Design •
This contemporary hotel is just opposite the Maison de la Radio. It has guest-rooms that are spacious and quiet, thanks to the excellent soundproofing. The high-tech facilities and modern art collection underline the Square's boutique hotel image.

 Molitor 🏠 ⚙ ⚶ 🄰 🚗

2 av. de la Porte-Molitor (16th) ✉ *75016*   Plan: **A2**
– Ⓜ *Michel Ange Molitor – 𝒞 01 56 07 08 50 – www.mltr.fr*
117 rm – †260/450 € ††260/450 € – ⌒ 26 € – 7 suites
• Luxury • Townhouse • Design •
A true emblem of western Paris since the 1920s, the Piscine Molitor was trans-formed in 2014 into a gorgeous luxury hotel. There are nods to its history with the blue and yellow façade around the pool and the restaurant's decoration, along with ultra-modern minimalism in the guestrooms.

 Kube 🏠 🛗 ⚶ 🄰 🚗

1-5 passage Ruelle (18th) – Ⓜ *La Chapelle*   Plan: **C1**
– 𝒞 01 42 05 20 00 – www.kubehotel-paris.com
40 rm – †169/429 € ††169/829 € – ⌒ 21 €
• Luxury • Design • Minimalist •
Although not located in one of the city's most attractive districts, this resolutely 21C hotel with its designer look and high-tech gadgetry, will appeal to a more contemporary clientele. Glass, clean white lines and loft-style guestrooms set the tone. It has a restaurant, as well as two bars, including the Ice Kube (-10°C, warm clothing provided!).

 Novotel Tour Eiffel

61 quai de Grenelle (15th) – Ⓜ *Bir-Hakeim*   Plan: **A2**
– 𝒞 01 40 58 20 00 – www.restaurant-benkay.com
758 rm – †149/430 € ††149/860 € – ⌒ 20 € – 6 suites
• Chain hotel • Business • Modern •
This contemporary-style Novotel overlooking the Seine and surrounded by 1970s high-rise buildings boasts a high-tech conference centre. The main bonus is that nearly all the guestrooms enjoy views of the river.
Benkay – See restaurant listing

 Hôtel de Banville 🄰

166 bd Berthier (17th) – Ⓜ *Porte de Champerret*   Plan: **B1**
– 𝒞 01 42 67 70 16 – www.hotelbanville.fr
38 rm ⌒ – †159/350 € ††159/600 €
• Townhouse • Personalised •
This charming boutique hotel is decorated with great taste, with guestrooms embellished with shiny wood and opulent detail. Jazz evenings in the piano-bar every Tuesday.

 Vice Versa ⚶ 🄰

213 r. de la Croix-Nivert (15th) – Ⓜ *Porte de Versailles*   Plan: **A3**
– 𝒞 01 55 76 55 55 – www.viceversahotel.com
37 rm – †115/365 € ††115/365 € – ⌒ 15 €
• Townhouse • Personalised • Design •
Greed, gluttony, pride, lust, wrath, sloth and envy: the guestrooms of this hotel decorated by Chantal Thomass illustrate the seven deadly sins! To get here, cross the hall with its heavenly feel. However, if you go down to the basement to visit the hammam, you will find yourself in hell... Diabolically inspired!

FRANCE - PARIS

 Fabric   🔊 ⓖ 🄰🄲

31 r. de la Folie-Méricourt (11th) – Ⓜ Saint-Ambroise   Plan: **C2**
– ☎ 01 43 57 27 00 – www.hotelfabric.com
33 rm – ♦240/360 € ♦♦240/360 € – ☑ 17 €
• Townhouse • Design • Modern •
In a former textile factory, lying halfway between République and Bastille, this beautiful hotel has retained some of its industrial heritage. Find elegant, designer guestrooms, as well as iron light fixtures, beams, antique furniture and a palette of grey tones.

 Mama Shelter   ⚡ ⓖ 🄰🄲 🔊 🚗

109 r. de Bagnolet (20th) – Ⓜ Gambetta   Plan: **D2**
– ☎ 01 43 48 48 48 – www.mamashelter.com
171 rm – ♦79/249 € ♦♦89/249 € – ☑ 16 € – 1 suite
• Townhouse • Design •
Philippe Starck is behind the refined, fantasy decor in this large hotel, which is at the cutting edge of contemporary design. It is characterised by a young and slightly bohemian atmosphere in keeping with this district enjoying an urban revival.

 Hor   ⓖ 🄰🄲

160 r. La Fayette (10th) – Ⓜ Gare du Nord   Plan: **C1**
– ☎ 01 40 05 18 05 – www.hotel-hor.com
47 rm – ♦169/399 € ♦♦169/399 € – ☑ 15 €
• Business • Modern • Functional •
A recent hotel (2012) between the Gare du Nord and Gare de l'Est train stations. The guestrooms are contemporary and functional, and some even have a private terrace. In the morning, breakfast is served in a pretty room that opens onto a patio.

 Holiday Inn Express Canal de la Villette   ≤ ⓖ 🄰🄲 🔊

68 quai de Seine (19th) – Ⓜ Crimée – ☎ 01 44 65 01 01   🚗
– www.holidayinnexpress.com/paris-canal   Plan: **D1**
144 rm ☑ – ♦110/360 € ♦♦110/360 €
• Business • Chain hotel • Modern •
Those who enjoy a stroll around the Bassin de la Villette know this building well: its twin (a warehouse dating from 1853) still stands on the opposite bank. The hotel, rebuilt in 2008, is striking for its unusual metal cladding and has a warm, friendly atmosphere. Some of the spacious guestrooms overlook the water.

 Le 20 Prieuré Hôtel   ⓖ 🄰🄲

20 r. Grand-Prieuré (11th) – Ⓜ Oberkampf   Plan: **C2**
– ☎ 01 47 00 74 14 – www.hotel20prieure.com
32 rm – ♦99/199 € ♦♦109/249 € – ☑ 13 €
• Traditional • Design •
This hotel subscribes to the urban contemporary look and offers small yet agreeable rooms with shades of white, designer furniture, and huge photos of Paris.

XxXxX **Le Pré Catelan**   🍴 🔉 ⓖ 🄰🄲 ⇔ 🛥 🄿
❀❀❀
in Bois de Boulogne - rte de Suresnes (16th) ✉ 75016   Plan: **A2**
– ☎ 01 44 14 41 14 – www.precatelanparis.com – Closed 21 February-
7 March, 31 July-22 August, 23 to 31 October, Sunday and Monday
Menu 130 € (lunch), 220/280 € – Carte 250/300 €
• Creative • Luxury • Elegant •
Based on classic recipes that pay homage to the local produce, Frédéric Anton's inventive cuisine is perfectly accomplished. Each dish is a masterpiece, to be enjoyed to the full amid a magnificent decor of white and silver in the heart of the Bois de Boulogne.
➜ Langoustine en ravioli, bouillon à l'huile d'olive et en nem frit. Crabe parfumé au curry, crème légère au caviar, saveur thaïe. Pomme soufflée croustillante, crème glacée au caramel.

XxxX **La Grande Cascade**

in Bois de Boulogne - allée de Longchamp (16th) ✉ *75016*
– ☎ 01 45 27 33 51 – www.restaurantsparisiens.com
– Closed 19 December-9 January
Menu 79/192 € – Carte 140/190 €
• Modern cuisine • Classic • Elegant •

A charming pavilion (1850) just a stone's throw from the large waterfall (Grande Cascade) in the Bois de Boulogne. To savour the refined cuisine here beneath the majestic rotunda or on the delightful terrace is a rare and elegant treat.
→ Tourteau au naturel, fine gelée iodée, chou-fleur, caviar d'Aquitaine. Carré d'agneau de Lozère au piment d'Espelette, épaule en pastilla et aubergine Riviera. Chocolat grand cru de République Dominicaine, sorbet cacao.

XxxX **St-James Paris** – Hôtel St-James Paris

43 av. Bugeaud (16th) ✉ *75116 –* Ⓜ *Porte Dauphine*   Plan: **A2**
– ☎ 01 44 05 81 81
– www.saint-james-paris.com
– Closed lunch and Sunday dinner
Menu 135 € – Carte 106/155 €
• Modern cuisine • Classic • Elegant •

An exclusive hotel with the atmosphere of an English member's-only club. The setting is superb, as chic as it is elegant with its wood panelling, golden brown fabrics, high, trompe-l'oeil ceiling and very secret garden. The food is in keeping with the rest: delicate, precise and nicely composed. A place with plenty of good taste!
→ Tartare de bar et huîtres, crème légère au citron et caviar. Dos de cabillaud cuit au plat, légumes de saison, beurre citron-mélisse. Café moka d'Éthiopie en crème légère, fines feuilles de chocolat dulcey, crème glacée à la fève tonka.

XxX **Relais d'Auteuil** (Patrick Pignol)

31 bd Murat (16th) ✉ *75016 –* Ⓜ *Michel Ange Molitor*   Plan: **A2**
– ☎ 01 46 51 09 54
– www.relaisdauteuil-pignol.fr
*– Closed August, Christmas Holidays, Saturday lunch, Sunday
and Monday*
Menu 100 € ♈ (lunch), 125/145 € – Carte 90/125 €
• Modern cuisine • Intimate •

This restaurant's intimate setting highlights the numerous modern paintings and sculptures on display. The fine contemporary cuisine is inspired by top quality produce, including game in season. Superb wine list, as well as an impressive choice of champagnes.
→ Amandine de foie gras. Épais filet de bar de ligne cuit au four, peau croustillante au poivre et vinaigre balsamique. Profiteroles, glace à la vanille Bourbon et sauce au chocolat de St-Domingue.

XxX **Benkay** – Novotel Tour Eiffel

61 quai de Grenelle (15th) – Ⓜ *Bir-Hakeim*   Plan: **A2**
– ☎ 01 40 58 21 26 – www.restaurant-benkay.com
– Closed 24 July-24 August
Menu 59 € (lunch), 130/160 € – Carte 93/190 €
• Japanese • Elegant •

On the banks of the Seine, with a view over the river, the elegant Benkay artfully honours Japanese gastronomy. You can opt for the teppanyaki (the hot plate where the dishes are cooked in front of you) or the 'washoku' (table service). Not to mention the sushi counter, which is simply divine.

XXX Le Quinzième - Cyril Lignac 🏠 AC ⇔ 🕿

☺ 14 r. Cauchy (15th) – Ⓜ Javel – ☎ 01 45 54 43 43   Plan: **A2-3**
– www.restaurantlequinzieme.com – Closed 2 weeks in August, Saturday and Sunday
Menu 60 € (lunch), 120/150 €
• Modern cuisine • Elegant •

Cyril Lignac has definitely perfected the art of creating a distinctive cuisine. Not only are the dishes visually striking, the combination of unusual, complimentary flavours is heavenly. An example: three super-fresh, juicy scallops served with a purée of carrot and Corsican clementines.
➔ Foie gras de canard des Landes poêlé, vinaigrette aigre-douce. Homard au beurre de corail, petits pois et framboise, crème de homard à la menthe. Crémeux chocolat Caraïbes et fruits exotiques, sorbet litchi et streusel.

XX Au Trou Gascon 🐾 AC

☺ 40 r. Taine (12th) – Ⓜ Daumesnil – ☎ 01 43 44 34 26   Plan: **D3**
– www.autrougascon.fr – Closed August, 1 to 10 January, Saturday and Sunday
Menu 42 € (lunch)/78 € – Carte 65/80 €
• Cuisine from the South West • Elegant •

This institution dedicated to the cuisine of Southwest France transports diners to the area between the River Adour and the ocean. It has earned the loyalty of many long-standing regulars with its pâté en croûte with duck foie gras, lièvre à la royale (hare), warm and crusty tourtière, not to mention the ever-popular cassoulet.
➔ Pâté en croûte au foie gras de canard des Landes. Caneton croisé rôti, escalope de foie gras, escaoutoun de maïs aux cèpes. Russe pistaché et framboises craquantes, crème glacée à la pistache.

XX Mansouria AC

☺ 11 r. Faidherbe (11th) – Ⓜ Faidherbe-Chaligny   Plan: **D2**
– ☎ 01 43 71 00 16 – www.mansouria.fr – Closed Monday lunch and Sunday
Menu 28/36 € – Carte 32/50 € – (booking advisable)
• North-African • Exotic •

Tajines, couscous, and crème à la fleur d'oranger are among the aromatic dishes prepared by the talented female chefs here under the supervision of Fatema Hal, an ethnologist, writer and leading figure in North African gastronomy.

XX A et M Restaurant 🏠 🕿

136 bd. Murat (16th) ✉ 75016 – Ⓜ Porte de St-Cloud   Plan: **A3**
– ☎ 01 45 27 39 60 – www.am-restaurant.com – Closed August, Saturday lunch and Sunday
Menu 38 € – Carte 40/50 €
• Modern cuisine • Elegant • Friendly •

A true chef's bistro in a chic and welcoming setting. The menu includes dishes such as calf's head with a ravigote sauce, and velouté of Paimpol beans with haddock. The set menu offers excellent value for money.

XX L'Inattendu AC

99 r. Blomet (15th) – Ⓜ Vaugirard – ☎ 01 55 76 93 12   Plan: **B3**
– www.restaurant-inattendu.fr – Closed Sunday and Monday
Menu 37/50 €
• Traditional cuisine • Cosy •

This small restaurant has elegant decor. It is run by two experienced partners who have just opened a fishmonger's next door – a real guarantee of fresh produce! Reliable, well-presented cuisine with the occasional surprise.

XX

L'Auberge du 15

15 r. de la Santé (13th) – Ⓜ Glacière – ✆ 01 47 07 07 45 – www.laubergedu15.com – Closed August, Christmas Holidays, Sunday and Monday

Plan: C3

Menu 39 € (lunch), 68/89 €

• Modern cuisine • Elegant • Cosy •

Radical change is afoot in L'Auberge du 15, yesterday known for celebrating the flavours of Aubrac, today led by a Japanese chef with a love of innovation. In his dishes, he enhances tradition with modern and creative touches, always using choice ingredients.

X

Eclectic

7 r. Linois (15th) – Ⓜ Charles Michel – ✆ 01 77 36 70 00 – www.restauranteclectic.fr

Plan: A2

Menu 37 € 🍷 (weekday lunch) – Carte 35/70 €

• Modern cuisine • Design •

Housed in the new Beaugrenelle shopping centre, this chic brasserie stands out as much for its original decor that revisits the 1970s (designed by Tom Dixon) as for its cuisine. This cleverly juggles cultures and flavours, as in the "new-style" salmon with yuzupon sauce. Beautiful terrace overlooking the waterfront.

X

Bon Kushikatsu

24 r. Jean-Pierre Timbaud (11th) – Ⓜ Oberkampf – ✆ 01 43 38 82 27 – http://kushikatsubon.fr – Closed Sunday

Plan: C2

Menu 30 € (weekday lunch)/60 € – *(booking advisable)*

• Japanese • Intimate • Elegant •

This restaurant is an express trip to Osaka to discover the city's culinary speciality of *kushikatsu* (meat, vegetables or seafood skewers coated with breadcrumbs and deep-fried). Dish after dish reveals fine flavours, such as: beef sancho, peppered foie gras, and shiitake mushrooms. The courteous service transports you to Japan.

X

Table - Bruno Verjus

3 r. de Prague (12th) – Ⓜ Ledru Rollin – ✆ 01 43 43 12 26 – www.tablerestaurant.fr – Closed 3 weeks in August, Saturday lunch and Sunday

Plan: C2

Menu 25 € (lunch), 39/99 € – Carte 72/82 € – *(booking advisable)*

• Modern cuisine • Design • Bistro •

Choosing the finest ingredients and cooking them humbly is the way of Bruno Verjus – a remarkable character, entrepreneur, blogger and food critic... turned chef! His dishes are full of energy and flavour, and reveal a rich interplay of textures, hinting at the chef's sincere and contagious passion.

X ✿

Septime (Bertrand Grébaut)

80 r. de Charonne (11th) – Ⓜ Charonne – ✆ 01 43 67 38 29 – www.septime-charonne.fr – Closed 3 weeks in August, Monday lunch, Saturday and Sunday

Plan: D2

Menu 30 € (lunch)/65 € – *(booking advisable)*

• Modern cuisine • Bistro • Trendy •

Since May 2011, when this restaurant first opened, word of mouth has spread quickly through the local neighbourhood. The key to its success? The neo-industrial decor, resolutely seasonal cuisine and high quality ingredients. Professionalism and simplicity all in one!

→ Cuisine du marché.

X

La Régalade

49 av. Jean-Moulin (14th) – Ⓜ Porte d'Orléans – ✆ 01 45 45 68 58 – Closed 1 to 21 August, 1 to 10 January, Monday lunch, Saturday and Sunday

Plan: B3

Menu 37 € – *(booking advisable)*

• Traditional cuisine • Friendly •

A friendly and relaxed bistro serving well-presented and copious seasonal cuisine accompanied by an astutely compiled choice of wines. La Régalade is always full and it is easy to see why. Make sure you book ahead!

FRANCE - PARIS

La Marée Passy

71 av. Paul-Doumer (16th) ⊠ *75016* – **Ⓜ** *La Muette*   Plan: **A2**
– ℰ 01 45 04 12 81 – www.lamareepassy.com
Carte 45/60 €
• Fish and seafood • Friendly •
With its wood panelling, red tones and maritime inspired backdrop, the decor is
in perfect harmony with the cuisine, which focuses on fish and seafood. The
daily specials board changes according to deliveries from the Atlantic coast.

Beurre Noisette

68 r. Vasco-de-Gama (15th) – **Ⓜ** *Lourmel*   Plan: **A3**
– ℰ 01 48 56 82 49 – Closed 7 to 15 August, Sunday and
Monday
Menu 32 € (lunch), 36/55 € – *(booking advisable)*
• Traditional cuisine • Friendly •
A cosy bistro serving delicious food. Thierry Blanqui draws inspiration from the
local markets with dishes such as duck and foie gras *pâté en croûte*, and slow-
cooked shoulder of suckling lamb with seasonal vegetables. Even the humblest
ingredients are transformed in a happy marriage of tradition and innovation.

Yard

6 r. Mont-Louis (11th) – **Ⓜ** *Philippe Auguste*   Plan: **D2**
– ℰ 01 40 09 70 30 – Closed August, 24 to 31 December,
Saturday and Sunday
Menu 18 € (lunch) – Carte 24/43 € – *(booking advisable)*
• Modern cuisine • Bistro •
This establishment is firmly anchored in its period. It has an engaging façade, a
warm bistro interior of wooden floors, an old fireplace, metal light fixtures and a
relaxed atmosphere. A young British chef skilfully concocts fuss-free, tasty
dishes that are proving irresistible to locals, tourists and other restaurant
owners!

Clamato

80 r. de Charonne (11th) – **Ⓜ** *Charonne*   Plan: **D2**
– ℰ 01 43 72 74 53 – www.clamato-charonne.fr – Closed 3 weeks in
August, Wednesday lunch, Thursday lunch, Friday lunch, Monday and
Tuesday
Carte 28/50 € – *(bookings not accepted)*
• Fish and seafood • Bistro • Design •
The Septime's little sister is becoming something of a bistronomic hit, thanks to
its fashionable interior and concise menu focused on seafood and vegetables.
Each ingredient is selected carefully and meals are served in a genuinely
friendly atmosphere. Bookings impossible – first in, first served!

Tintilou

37 bis r. de Montreuil (11th) – **Ⓜ** *Faidherbe-Chaligny*   Plan: **D2**
– ℰ 01 43 72 42 32 – www.letintilou.fr – Closed 1 week in February,
3 weeks in August, Monday lunch, Saturday lunch and Sunday
Menu 36/49 € – Carte 52/58 €
• Modern cuisine • Friendly •
This 16C former *relais de mousquetaires* – frequented by Louis XIII's guards – is
elegant and original. The flavoursome cuisine served here evokes travel. The
menu is short and changes every month, presenting the dishes by enigmatic
marriages: salmon, pumpkin, fennel, botargo; wild duck and cocoa.

Bistrot Paul Bert

18 r. Paul-Bert (11th) – **Ⓜ** *Faidherbe Chaligny*   Plan: **D2**
– ℰ 01 43 72 24 01 – Closed Sunday and Monday
Menu 19 € (weekday lunch)/41 € – Carte approx. 50 € – *(booking advi-*
sable)
• Traditional cuisine • Retro • Bistro •
Home cooking is very much to the fore in this friendly bistro, with dishes such as
beef parmentier and steak on the menu. Make sure you save space for the rum
baba!

FRANCE - PARIS

✗
⊛
Villaret
⊞ ⓐⓒ ⓓ (dinner)

13 r. Ternaux (11th) – Ⓜ *Parmentier* – ☏ *01 43 57 75 56* — Plan: **C2**
– Closed 2 weeks in August, Saturday lunch and Sunday
Menu 27 € (lunch)/34 € – Carte 45/59 €
• Traditional cuisine • Friendly • Bistro •

From the moment of arrival, something smells unmistakably delicious! This convivial bistro serves appealing seasonal fare: baked eggs with foie gras, salted monkfish, and chocolate biscuits. Good choice of wines.

✗
Pramil

9 r. Vertbois (3rd) – Ⓜ *Temple* – ☏ *01 42 72 03 60* — Plan: **C2**
– www.pramilrestaurant.fr – Closed 25 April-2 May, 15 to 28 August, 19 to 26 December, Sunday lunch and Monday
Menu 33 € – Carte 38/48 €
• Modern cuisine • Bistro •

The elegant yet restrained decor helps focus the senses on the attractive and honest seasonal cuisine conjured up by Alain Pramil. He is a self-taught chef passionate about food who, in another life, was a physics teacher!

✗
⊛
La Fourchette du Printemps (Nicolas Mouton)
ⓐⓒ ⓓ

30 r. du Printemps (17th) – Ⓜ *Wagram* — Plan: **B1**
– ☏ 01 42 27 26 97 – www.lafourchetteduprintemps.com – Closed August, 24 December-2 January, Sunday and Monday
Menu 55/75 € – Carte approx. 60 € – *(booking advisable)*
• Modern cuisine • Bistro • Friendly •

Whatever the season, this contemporary bistro stands out from the crowd. At the controls, the young chef, an alumnus of some top restaurants, hones the frank taste of ingredients to reveal lovely flavours. All in an unpretentious decor that matches the laid-back service.

→ Gambas croustillantes, tête de veau et sauce gribiche. Merlan de ligne rôti dans une pomme darphin, sauce choron. Tarte au chocolat, sablé chocolat craquant, brownie, ganache légère aux chocolats noir et lait.

✗
Les Cailloux

58 r. des Cinq Diamants (13th) – Ⓜ *Corvisart* — Plan: **C3**
– ☏ 01 45 80 15 08 – www.lescailloux.fr – Closed 1 week in August
Carte 34/49 €
• Italian • Bistro • Friendly •

The Butte-aux-Cailles district is home to many restaurants, including this informal Italian bistro that serves delicious sun-kissed food at reasonable prices.

✗
L'Ourcine

92 r. Broca (13th) – Ⓜ *Les Gobelins* – ☏ *01 47 07 13 65* — Plan: **C3**
– www.restaurant-lourcine.fr – Closed 3 weeks in August, Sunday and Monday
Menu 38 €
• Traditional cuisine • Bistro • Friendly •

Quality and modesty summarise nicely the spirit of L'Ourcine, a pleasant little bistro which offers inspired, seasonal cuisine. The menu du jour and 'coups de cœur' set menu on the blackboard offer an array of great suggestions.

✗
⊛
Chez Marie-Louise

11 r. Marie-et-Louise (10th) – Ⓜ *Goncourt* — Plan: **C2**
– ☏ 01 53 19 02 04 – www.chezmarielouise.com – Closed August, 24 December-2 January, Sunday and Monday
Carte 29/38 €
• Traditional cuisine • Bistro •

You will eat well in this small neo-bistro just a stone's throw from the St Martin canal. The simple, delicious dishes on the blackboard include salmon ceviche, shoulder of lamb with cumin, black pudding with herbs and spices, and a selection of tasty desserts.

X L'Os à Moelle

3 r. Vasco-de-Gama (15th) – Ⓜ *Lourmel*   Plan: **A3**
– ℰ 01 45 57 27 27 – Closed 3 weeks in August, Sunday
and Monday
Menu 32/60 € – Carte approx. 35 €
• Traditional cuisine • Friendly • Bistro •
After relinquishing the reins for a few years (so as to focus on his Barbezingue restaurant in Châtillon), Thierry Faucher is back at L'Os à Moelle, where he was one of bistronomie's forerunners. The perfect opportunity to catch up and get to grips with his philosophy that involves restoring bistro cuisine to its rightful place!

X Tempero

5 r. Clisson (13th) – Ⓜ *Chevaleret* – ℰ *09 54 17 48 88*   Plan: **C3**
*– www.tempero.fr – Closed August, 1 week Christmas Holidays, Monday
dinner, Tuesday dinner, Wednesday dinner, Saturday and Sunday*
Menu 20 € (lunch) – Carte dinner 33/44 € – *(booking advisable)*
• Creative • Bistro • Friendly •
A friendly little bistro, which is rather like its chef, Alessandra Montagne. Originally from Brazil, she worked at some fine Parisian establishments before opening her own place. Here she cooks with market-fresh ingredients, creating invigorating and reasonably priced dishes that draw on French, Brazilian and Asian cooking. A lovely fusion!

X Impérial Choisy   🄰🄲

32 av. de Choisy (13th) – Ⓜ *Porte de Choisy*   Plan: **C3**
– ℰ 01 45 86 42 40
Carte 18/54 €
• Chinese • Simple •
A genuine Chinese restaurant frequented by many local Chinese who use it as their lunchtime canteen. Hardly surprising given the delicious Cantonese specials on offer!

X Pho Tai   🄰🄲 ⌁

13 r. Philibert-Lucot (13th) – Ⓜ *Maison Blanche*   Plan: **C3**
*– ℰ 01 45 85 97 36 – Closed 2 weeks in August,
Christmas Holidays and Wednesday*
Carte 20/30 €
• Vietnamese • Simple •
In a quiet street in the Asian quarter, this small Vietnamese restaurant stands out from the crowd. All credit to the chef, Mr Te, who arrived in France in 1968 and is a magnificent ambassador of Vietnamese cuisine. Dumplings, crispy chicken with fresh ginger, bo bun and phô soups: everything is full of flavour.

LA DÉFENSE   PLAN I

 Pullman La Défense   ⛲ 𝑓ð ᶜᵏ 🄰🄲 ⚒ 🚗

11 av. de l'Arche (exit La Défense 6) ✉ *92081* – Ⓜ *La Défense*
– ℰ 01 47 17 50 00 – www.pullmanhotels.com
382 rm – ♦150/550 € ♦♦150/550 € – ☱ 26 € – 31 suites
• Chain hotel • Business • Design •
Beautiful architecture, resembling a ship's hull, a combination of glass and ochre stonework. Spacious, elegant rooms, lounges and very well-equipped auditorium (with simultaneous translation booths). Quality designer décor and spit-roast dishes at the restaurant.

FRANCE - PARIS

 ### Hilton La Défense ⚐ ♨ & ⯐ ⚙

2 pl. de la Défense ✉ *92053 –* Ⓜ *La Défense –* ☎ *01 46 92 10 10*
– www.hiltonparisladefense.com
153 rm – 🛏169/450 € 🛏🛏469/600 € – ☕ 26 € – 4 suites
• Business • Chain hotel • Modern •

Hotel situated within the CNIT complex. Some of the rooms have been particularly designed with the business traveller in mind: work, rest, relaxation and Jacuzzi tubs in the bathrooms. At the restaurant, modern cuisine and a fine view of the Arch of La Défense.

 ### Sofitel Paris La Défense ⚐ & ⯐ ⚙ 🚗

34 cours Michelet (on the ring road, exit La Défense 4) ✉ *92060 Puteaux*
– Ⓜ *Esplanade de la Défense –* ☎ *01 47 76 44 43*
– www.sofitel-paris-ladefense.com
151 rm – 🛏144/1082 € 🛏🛏144/1082 € – ☕ 27 €
• Luxury • Chain hotel • Personalised •

This business hotel not far from the CNIT and Grande Arche blends in perfectly with the high-rise buildings of the Défense district. Spacious, well-equipped guestrooms, as well as a restaurant (Mediterranean cuisine) and small fitness suite.

PARIS AIRPORT ROISSY

AT TERMINAL N° 2

 ### Sheraton ⚐ ≤ ♨ & ⯐ ⚙ 🅿

Aérogare n°2 – ☎ *01 49 19 70 70*
– www.sheraton.com/parisairport
252 rm – 🛏164/650 € 🛏🛏164/650 € – ☕ 33 €
• Chain hotel • Business • Modern •

This is the only hotel in Roissy directly connected with Terminal 2 and is opposite the TGV railway station. A pleasant stay and top-class comfort await you in this building with futuristic lines. In the guestrooms, there is a cosy atmosphere and views over the runways!
Les Étoiles – See restaurant listing

XXX ### Les Étoiles – Hôtel Sheraton & ⯐ 🅿

Aérogare n°2 Roissy-en-France – ☎ *01 49 19 70 70*
– www.sheraton.com/parisairport – Closed August, Christmas Holidays, Saturday, Sunday and Bank Holidays
Menu 63 € – Carte 64/79 €
• Modern cuisine • Elegant • Individual •

This restaurant inside the Sheraton Hotel (Terminal 2) stands out from the crowd on the airport site. The place opts to combine an intimate atmosphere with classic French cuisine and the result is a success. The '100% local' set menu is made exclusively with ingredients sourced from around Paris.

AT ROISSYPOLE

 ### Hilton ⚐ ♨ ▨ & ⯐ ⚙ 🚗

Roissypôle – ☎ *01 49 19 77 77 – www.hiltonhotels.com/fr_fr*
392 rm – 🛏179/809 € 🛏🛏179/809 € – ☕ 25 €
• Chain hotel • Business • Personalised •

A top-class hotel, a veritable modern town within the airport perimeter. It has a huge lobby with a vertiginous glass roof, particularly spacious guestrooms, and many amenities including restaurants, a swimming pool, meeting rooms etc.

Marriott

allée du Verger – ℰ 01 34 38 53 53 – www.parismarriottcharlesdegaulle.fr
297 rm – ♦119/529 € ♦♦129/529 € – ☐ 29 € – 3 suites
• Chain hotel • Business • Classic •
Ideal for business travellers staying overnight in Paris who appreciate the good things in life. This establishment is both classic in style (colonnades, period furniture) and in comfort (fitness area, sauna, brasserie).

Novotel Convention et Wellness

10 allée du Verger – ℰ 01 30 18 20 00
– www.novotel.com/5418
288 rm ☐ – ♦95/529 € ♦♦95/529 € – 7 suites
• Chain hotel • Business • Modern •
This hotel, which is used to receiving travellers and business clients, has perfectly oiled wheels. Its amenities are at the forefront when it comes to seminar organisation (large space dedicated to equipped meeting rooms) and relaxation (spa, Novotel Café etc).

Mercure Roissy

3 allée du Verger – ℰ 01 34 29 40 00
– www.mercure-paris-roissy-charles-de-gaulle.com
194 rm – ♦99/399 € ♦♦99/399 € – ☐ 18 € – 8 suites
• Chain hotel • Business • Functional •
It is worth stressing that this hotel aims to cater to the individual customer, as well as welcoming seminars and groups. The guestrooms are spacious and decorated in soothing tones. The restaurant is also noteworthy, with its traditional menu and reasonable prices.

LYONS
LYON

Population: 496 343

Calzada/Fotolia.com

Lyons is a city that needs a second look, because the first one may be to its disadvantage: from the outlying autoroute, drivers get a vision of the petrochemical industry. But strip away that industrial façade and look what lies within: the gastronomic epicentre of France; a wonderfully characterful old town of medieval and Renaissance buildings with a World Heritage Site stamp of approval; and the peaceful flow of two mighty rivers. Lyons largely came of age in the 16C thanks to its silk industry; many of the city's finest buildings were erected by Italian merchants who flocked here at the time. What they left behind was the largest Renaissance quarter in France, with glorious architecture and an imposing cathedral.

Nowadays it's an energised city whose modern industries give it a 21C feel but that hasn't pervaded the three-hour lunch ethos of the older quarters. The rivers Saône and Rhône provide the liquid heart of the city. Modern Lyons in the shape of the new Villeurbanne and La Part Dieu districts are to the east of the Rhône. The medieval sector, the old town, is west of the Saône. Between the two rivers is a peninsula, the Presqu'ile, which is indeed almost an island. This area is renowned for its red-roofed 16C and 17C houses. Just north of here on a hill is the old silk-weavers' district, La Croix-Rousse.

LYONS IN...

→ **ONE DAY**
Old town including funicular up Fourvière hill, Musée des Beaux-Arts.

→ **TWO DAYS**
Musée des Tissus, La Croix-Rousse, evening river trip, Opera House.

→ **THREE DAYS**
Traboule hunting (map in hand), antique shops in rue Auguste Comte.

ARRIVAL-DEPARTURE

✈ Lyon Saint Exupéry Airport is 27km east of the city centre.
The Express Bus takes around 45min and runs every 20min.

GETTING AROUND

The transport system in the city includes the funicular, as well as the bus, tram and metro. The 'Liberty' ticket is valid for one day's travel on the network; you can also buy single tickets and a carnet of ten tickets. The Lyons City Card is available for 1, 2 or 3 days, and grants unlimited access to the transport network, plus many museums (including the Roman ruins in St-Romain-en-Gal), short river trips and guided city tours. The card is available from the tourist office and major public transport offices. Lyons boasts one of Europe's biggest 'swipe a bike' schemes: using a smart card, you can help yourself to a bicycle at one of two hundred places around town.

CALENDAR HIGHLIGHTS

March
International Fair.

May
Nuits Sonores (Electronic music).

June
Fête de la Musique, Fourvière Festival .

July
Bastille Day celebrations.

September
Lyons Dance Biennial.

October
Red Carpet Antiques Festival.

November
Baroque Music Festival.

December
Festival of Lights.

EATING OUT

Lyons is a great place for food. In the old town virtually every square metre is occupied by a restaurant but if you want a real encounter with the city, step inside a Lyonnais bouchon. These provide the true gastronomic heartbeat of the city - authentic little establishments where the cuisine revolves around the sort of thing the silk workers ate all those years ago: tripe, pigs' trotters, calf's head; fish lovers go for quenelles. For the most atmospheric example of the bouchon, try one in a tunnel-like recess inside a medieval building in the old town. Lyons also has plenty of restaurants serving dishes from every region in France and is a city that loves its wine: it's said that Lyons is kept afloat on three rivers: the Saône, the Rhône and the Beaujolais. Furthermore, the locals still enthusiastically embrace the true concept of lunch and so, unlike in many cities, you can enjoy a midday meal that continues for quite a few hours. With the reputation the city has for its restaurants, it's usually advisable to book ahead.

FRANCE - LYONS

Sofitel Lyon Bellecour   ⚓ ⬿ 🛋 ☆ ❄ AC ⚑ 🚗
20 quai Gailleton ⊠ *69002* – **Ⓜ** *Bellecour*   Plan: **F3**
– ℰ *04 72 41 20 20* – *www.sofitel.com*
135 rm – ✝185/400 € ✝✝350/550 € – ⌂ 26 € – 29 suites
• Business • Luxury • Modern •
A luxurious and elegant Sofitel in a contemporary building with futuristic facilities. Bill Clinton stayed in the presidential suite here. There are two options for
dinner: the beautiful Trois Dômes restaurant (see restaurants) or Le Silk restaurant (international menu, sleek setting).
❀ **Les Trois Dômes** – See restaurant listing

Le Royal   ⚓ ⬿ AC 🚗
20 pl. Bellecour ⊠ *69002* – **Ⓜ** *Bellecour*   Plan: **F2**
– ℰ *04 78 37 57 31* – *www.mgallery.com*
72 rm – ✝160/500 € ✝✝160/500 € – ⌂ 25 € – 5 suites
• Luxury • Traditional • Elegant •
Established in 1912, Le Royal wins over hotel guests with its blend of comfort
and refinement. A century on, the institution has lost none of its charm and
style. Mouldings, Toiles de Jouy fabrics, traditional old furniture… it is quite
simply elegant.
L'Institut – See restaurant listing

Carlton   🛋 ⚑ AC ⚑
4 r. Jussieu ⊠ *69002* – **Ⓜ** *Cordeliers* – ℰ *04 78 42 56 51*   Plan: **F2**
– *www.mgallery.com*
80 rm – ✝165/530 € ✝✝185/530 € – ⌂ 25 €
• Business • Traditional • Art Deco •
This illustrious establishment was completely refurbished in 2013. It transports
guests back in time to a 1930s ambience with an interior in predominantly red
tones. The guestrooms are spacious and well appointed, and the period lift is
magnificent. A marriage of comfort and charm.

Globe et Cécil   ⚑ AC ⚑
21 r. Gasparin ⊠ *69002* – **Ⓜ** *Bellecour*   Plan: **F2**
– ℰ *04 78 42 58 95* – *www.globeetcecilhotel.com*
60 rm – ✝112/200 € ✝✝123/280 € – ⌂ 18 €
• Traditional • Classic • Personalised •
This hotel dating back to the end of the 19C is located a stone's throw from
Place Bellecour. It has pretty and immaculately kept guestrooms (some have
floorboards and fireplaces). The foyer and lounge offer first-rate amenities.

Grand Hôtel des Terreaux   ▣ AC
16 r. Lanterne ⊠ *69001* – **Ⓜ** *Hôtel de Ville*   Plan: **F1**
– ℰ *04 78 27 04 10* – *www.hotel-lyon-grandhoteldesterreaux.fr*
53 rm – ✝85/130 € ✝✝120/295 € – ⌂ 16 €
• Traditional • Classic •
This 19C post house is conducive to relaxing in the centre of town. Find tastefully decorated rooms, a small indoor pool and attentive service.

Mercure Plaza République   ⚑ AC
5 r. Stella ⊠ *69002* – **Ⓜ** *Cordeliers* – ℰ *04 78 37 50 50*   Plan: **F2**
– *www.mercure.com*
82 rm – ✝109/215 € ✝✝109/245 € – ⌂ 19 €
• Business • Chain hotel • Functional •
This pleasant chain hotel is located next to the Rhône. Recently renovated
guestrooms in a contemporary style.

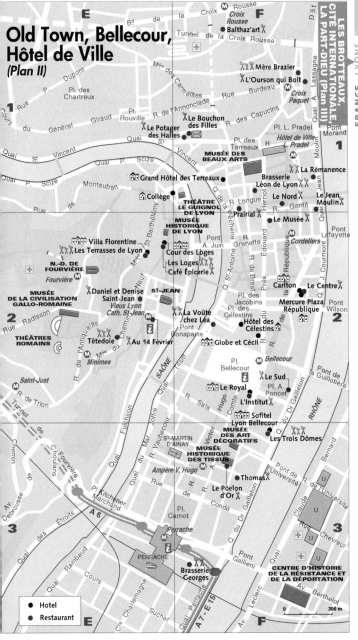

Old Town, Bellecour, Hôtel de Ville
(Plan II)

Bd de la Croix Rousse
Tunnel de la Croix Rousse
Croix Rousse
Balthaz'art

Mée des Carmélites
Mère Brazier
L'Ourson qui Boit
Croix Paquet
Rue Burdeau

P. Dupont
Pl. des Chartreux
Pl. Rouville
R. de l'Annonciade
R. des Capucins
Pl. L. Pradel
Pont Morand

Cours du Général Giraud
Le Potager des Halles
Le Bouchon des Filles
Hôtel de Ville-Pradel

Quai St Vincent
Quai P. Scize
Pl. des Terreaux
MUSÉE DES BEAUX ARTS

Quai P. Scize
Montauban
Grand Hôtel des Terreaux
Brasserie Léon de Lyon
La Rémanence

Rue de
Collège
THÉÂTRE LE GUIGNOL DE LYON
R. Longue
Le Nord
Le Jean Moulin

MUSÉE HISTORIQUE DE LYON
R. de la Pêcherie
Prairial
Le Musée

Villa Florentine
Les Terrasses de Lyon
Pont A. Juin
Cour des Loges
Les Loges
Café Épicerie

N.-D. DE FOURVIÈRE
Fourvière
ST-JEAN
R. St-Antoine
R. Grenette
R. Édouard Herriot
Cordeliers
Pont Lafayette

MUSÉE DE LA CIVILISATION GALLO-ROMAINE
Daniel et Denise Saint-Jean
Vieux Lyon Cath. St-Jean
La Voûte chez Léa
Pl. des Jacobins
Pl. des Célestins
Carlton
Le Centre

Rue Radisson
THÉÂTRES ROMAINS
Têtedoie
Mée du Chemin
Au 14 Février
Pont Bonaparte
Hôtel des Célestins
Mercure Plaza République
Pont Wilson

Minimes
Globe et Cécil

Saint-Just
R. de Trion
Tunnel de Fourvière
SAÔNE
Bellecour
Le Sud
Pl. A. Poncet
Pont de la Guillotière

Le Royal
L'Institut
RHÔNE

Chemin des Choulans
Sofitel Lyon Bellecour
MUSÉE DES ART DÉCORATIFS
Les Trois Dômes

ST-MARTIN D'AINAY
MUSÉE HISTORIQUE DES TISSUS
Pont de l'Université

Av. Debrousse
Ampère V. Hugo
Thomas
Rue Claude
U

Quai des Étroits
Pl. Kitchener Marchand
Le Pôelon d'Or
Rue Chevreul
U

A6
Pl. Carnot
Pont du Dr Gailleton
U

Quai Rambaud
Perrache
Pont Galliéni
U

PERRACHE
CENTRE D'HISTOIRE DE LA RÉSISTANCE ET DE LA DÉPORTATION

Cours Charlemagne
Brasserie Georges
Av. Berthelot

Cours Suchet
A7 - E15
0   300 m

● Hotel
● Restaurant

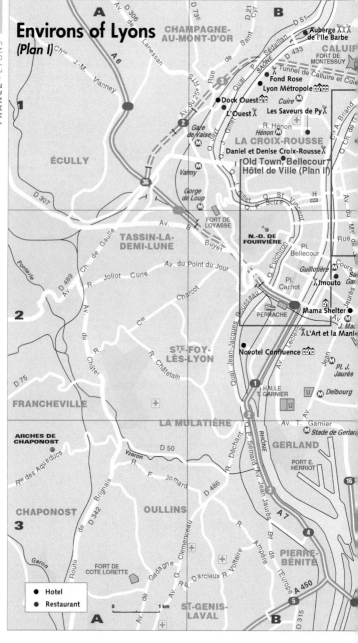

Environs of Lyons
(Plan I)

CHAMPAGNE-AU-MONT-D'OR

CALUIF
FORT DE MONTESSUY

Auberge de l'Île Barbe

Fond Rose
Lyon Métropole
Dock Ouest
Cuire
L'Ouest
Les Saveurs de Py

R. Hénon
Hénon
LA CROIX-ROUSSE

Daniel et Denise Croix-Rousse
Old Town Bellecour
Hôtel de Ville (Plan II)

ÉCULLY

Gare de Vaise

Valmy

Gorge de Loup

FORT DE LOYASSE

N.-D. DE FOURVIÈRE

Pl. Bellecour

TASSIN-LA-DEMI-LUNE

Av. du Point du Jour

Guillotière

Pl. Carnot

Imouto

PERRACHE

Mama Shelter

L'Art et la Mani

Novotel Confluence

STE-FOY-LÈS-LYON

HALLE T. GARNIER

Delbourg

Pl. J. Jaurès

FRANCHEVILLE

LA MULATIÈRE

Av. T. Garnier

Stade de Gerlar

GERLAND

ARCHES DE CHAPONOST

D 50

PORT E. HERRIOT

CHAPONOST

OULLINS

PIERRE-BÉNITÉ

FORT DE COTE LORETTE

ST-GENIS-LAVAL

● Hotel
● Restaurant

0   1 km

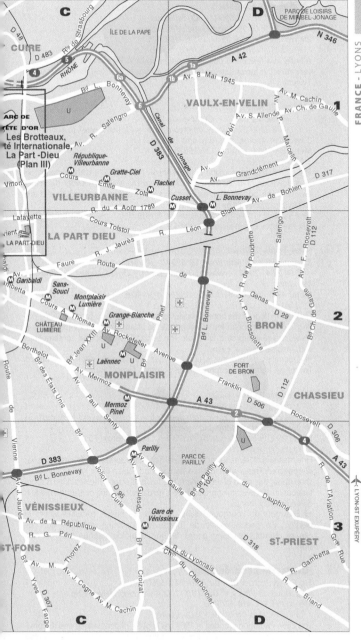

Hôtel des Célestins   🏠   AC

4 r. des Archers ⊠ 69002 – Ⓜ Bellecour   Plan: **F2**
– ℰ 04 72 56 08 98 – www.hotelcelestins.com
29 rm – †87/195 € ††87/195 € – ⌑ 10 €

• Traditional • Family • Functional •

A hotel in a residential building is rather unusual. Pleasant rooms including a very attractive junior suite on the fifth floor (large Italian-style shower, flat screen TV, etc).

Mère Brazier (Mathieu Viannay)   XxX   🕸 AC ⇄ 🍽

❀❀   *12 r. Royale ⊠ 69001 – Ⓜ Hôtel de Ville*   Plan: **F1**
– ℰ 04 78 23 17 20 – www.lamerebrazier.fr – Closed 1 week in February, 3 weeks in August, Saturday and Sunday
Menu 98/155 € – Carte 120/155 €

• Modern cuisine • Elegant • Formal •

The guardian of Lyon cuisine, Eugénie Brazier (1895-1977) is without doubt looking down on Mathieu Viannay – winner of the Meilleur Ouvrier de France award – with pride. Emblematic restaurant where high-powered classics and creativity continue to be served.

→ Artichaut et foie gras. Poularde de Bresse demi-deuil. Paris-brest, glace aux noisettes caramélisées et pralin.

Les Trois Dômes – Hôtel Sofitel Lyon Bellecour   XxX   🕸 ≤ AC 🍽

❀   *20 quai Gailleton (8th floor) ⊠ 69002 – Ⓜ Bellecour*   Plan: **F3**
– ℰ 04 72 41 20 97 – www.les-3-domes.com – Closed August, Sunday and Monday
Menu 47 € (lunch), 81/125 € – Carte 100/140 €

• Modern cuisine • Fashionable •

On the top floor of the hotel, delicious cuisine with brilliant food and wine pairings. Terrine de pot-au-feu with foie gras, leg of lamb from the Limousin-classic dishes are re-interpreted with flair. The setting is elegant and contemporary with magical views of Lyon.

→ Quenelles de brochet, sauce écrevisse, fricassée de pousses d'épinard. Tourte de homard. Compression de pommes façon Tatin.

La Rémanence (Fabien Blanc)   XX   �& AC ⇄

❀   *31 r. du Bât-d'Argent ⊠ 69001 – Ⓜ Hôtel de Ville*   Plan: **F1**
– ℰ 04 72 00 08 08 – www.laremanence.fr – Closed 3 weeks in August, 23 to 26 december, Sunday and Monday
Menu 29 € (weekday lunch), 41/78 € – Carte approx. 75 €

• Modern cuisine • Elegant •

One meaning of 'rémanence' is the persistence of a sensation after its cause has disappeared. This is what inspired Nathalie and Fabien Blanc when they set up shop under the vaults of this elegant 16C Jesuit refectory. Their cooking is spontaneous, instinctive, striking, and there is no danger of tiring of it, as the menu is different every month.

→ Escargots de Bourgogne dans une côte de blette, coquilles aillées et pectine de persil. Poulet de Bresse en ballotine de foie gras de canard, crumble de champignons des bois. Boule de mangue et sorbet passion.

Brasserie Léon de Lyon   XX   🕸 🌭 AC ⇄

1 r. Pleney (corner of r. du Plâtre) ⊠ 69001   Plan: **F1**
– Ⓜ Hôtel de Ville – ℰ 04 72 10 11 12 – www.leondelyon.com
Menu 26 € – Carte 42/51 €

• Traditional cuisine • Brasserie •

This Lyon institution founded in 1904 has kept its affluent setting and its convivial atmosphere. Excellent ingredients combine to produce hearty gourmet dishes.

FRANCE - LYONS

XX **La Voûte - Chez Léa**   AC

11 pl. A.-Gourju ⊠ *69002* – Ⓜ *Bellecour*   Plan: F2
*– ℰ 04 78 42 01 33 – www.lavoutechezlea.com – Closed 2 weeks in August
and Sunday*
Menu 30/42 € – Carte 32/53 €
• Traditional cuisine • Friendly •
One of the oldest restaurants in Lyon. In a welcoming atmosphere, tradition carries on with verve. Fine menu with tasty regional dishes and game in autumn.

XX **Brasserie Georges**   ☐ ঙ ⇔

30 cours de Verdun ⊠ *69002* – Ⓜ *Perrache*   Plan: F3
– ℰ 04 72 56 54 54 – www.brasseriegeorges.com
Menu 23/28 € – Carte 28/54 €
• Traditional cuisine • Brasserie • Retro •
'Good beer and good cheer since 1836' in the jealously guarded Art Deco setting of this brasserie that is a veritable institution. Lively atmosphere.

X **Balthaz'art**   ⇔
☺
7 r. des Pierres-Plantées ⊠ *69001* – Ⓜ *Croix-Rousse*   Plan: F1
*– ℰ 04 72 07 08 88 – www.restaurantbalthazart.com – Closed 12 to
21 August, 24 December-2 January, Tuesday lunch, Wednesday lunch,
Sunday and Monday*
Menu 17 € (weekday lunch), 29/34 € – Carte 35/44 €
• Modern cuisine • Bistro • Friendly •
You have to earn your meal at this restaurant located near the top of La Croix-Rousse! Housed in the former French Communist Party HQ, red dominates the interior, and Picasso and Modigliani prints hang on the walls. The imagination and beauty found in the decoration are also present in the dishes, which are paired with well-chosen wines.

X **L'Institut** – Hôtel Le Royal   ঙ AC ⇔

20 pl. Bellecour ⊠ *69002* – Ⓜ *Bellecour*   Plan: F2
*– ℰ 04 78 37 23 02 – www.institutpaulbocuse.com – Closed 8 to
28 August, 20 December-5 January, Sunday and Monday*
Carte 45/58 € – *(booking advisable)*
• Traditional cuisine • Elegant • Design •
On Place Bellecour, the training restaurant of the Paul Bocuse Institute feels nothing like a school! In a contemporary decor designed by Pierre-Yves Rochon, with open kitchens giving onto the restaurant, the students deliver a high standard of service. The dishes are extremely well made and deserve a high mark.

X **Prairial** (Gaëtan Gentil)   AC
☺
11 r. Chavanne ⊠ *69001* – Ⓜ *Cordeliers*   Plan: F1
*– ℰ 04 78 27 86 93 – www.prairial-restaurant.com – Closed Sunday and
Monday*
Menu 28 € (weekday lunch), 42/76 €
• Modern cuisine • Design • Trendy •
In spring 2015 Gaëtan Gentil took over this restaurant on the Presqu'île that boasts a designer decor (white tables, hanging lamps) and a living wall. He offers diners what he terms "uninhibited gastronomy": creative and contemporary dishes in which vegetables take pride of place.
➜ Cuisine du marché.

X **L'Ourson qui Boit**
☺
23 r. Royale ⊠ *69001* – Ⓜ *Croix-Paquet*   Plan: F1
*– ℰ 04 78 27 23 37 – Closed 4 weeks in July-August,
2 weeks in December, Wednesday, Sunday and Bank Holidays*
Menu 18 € (lunch)/32 €
• Modern cuisine • Friendly • Bistro •
Chef Akira Nishigaki has worked in some of France's finest restaurants. At this contemporary bistro, his cuisine blends traditional regional recipes with Japanese excellence, all at reasonable prices. Not to be missed!

271

Le Jean Moulin [AC]
22 r. Gentil ✉ *69002* – Ⓜ *Cordeliers* – ☏ *04 78 37 37 97*   Plan: **F1**
– www.lejeanmoulin-lyon.com – Closed 2 weeks in August, Sunday and Monday
Menu 27 €
• Modern cuisine • Friendly • Elegant •
Find great value at this elegant, welcoming bistro, run by a chef who trained at some of the top establishments (Bocuse, Viannay, Pic). The cooking is not so different from the man himself: lively, serious, tasteful, colourful and generous. Good enough to whet any appetite!

Le Sud
11 pl. Antonin-Poncet ✉ *69002* – Ⓜ *Bellecour*   Plan: **F2**
– ☏ 04 72 77 80 00 – www.nordsudbrasseries.com
Menu 27 € (weekdays) – Carte 37/55 €
• Mediterranean • Brasserie •
There is a kind of Greek elegance about this Bocuse brasserie located a stone's throw from the Place Bellecour. And it is not by chance as it is all about the Mediterranean here with the Italian-style penne rigate, the soupe Marseillaise and the tajine à l'orientale... all the more so in summer, on the terrace.

Le Centre
14 r. Grolée ✉ *69002* – ⓂCordeliers – ☏ *04 72 04 44 44*   Plan: **F2**
– www.lespritblanc.com
Menu 29 € – Carte 43/73 €
• Meats • Friendly •
Georges Blanc, the famous chef from the restaurant in Vonnas, is the mastermind behind this contemporary brasserie dedicated to meat – and fine meats at that. Find Charolais, Wagyu beef, Aveyron lamb and Bresse chicken served with a large choice of accompaniments and sauces. Calling all carnivores!

Le Nord
18 r. Neuve ✉ *69002* – ⓂHôtel de Ville   Plan: **F1**
– ☏ 04 72 10 69 69 – www.nordsudbrasseries.com
Menu 27 € (weekdays)/33 € – Carte 36/62 €
• Traditional cuisine • Retro • Brasserie •
The smallest (or least large!) brasserie in Bocuse's collection is organised into several areas, including a street-level conservatory and private dining rooms upstairs. The team working in the kitchens has clearly been schooled by the best. Freshness of ingredients is central here, and tradition goes hand-in-hand with generosity and flavour. A sure-fire dining option.

Le Potager des Halles [AC]
3 r. de la Martinière ✉ *69001* – ⓂHôtel de Ville   Plan: **F1**
– ☏ 04 72 00 24 84 – www.lepotagerdeshalles.com – Closed 2 weeks in August, 1 week Christmas Holidays, Sunday and Monday
Menu 19 € (weekday lunch), 39/48 € – Carte approx. 46 €
• Traditional cuisine • Bistro • Friendly •
This pleasant restaurant is between the Quais de la Saône and the Halles de la Martinière. It serves dishes like pan-fried foie gras with turnip, orange and spices, or breast of Basque pork with salsify, cranberry and pomegranate. Organic ingredients and fresh market produce take pride of place.

Thomas [AC]
6 r. Laurencin ✉ *69002* – ⓂBellecour   Plan: **F3**
– ☏ 04 72 56 04 76 – www.restaurant-thomas.com – Closed 3 weeks in August, 24 December-2 January, Saturday and Sunday
Menu 21 € (lunch), 33/45 € – Carte approx. 45 €
• Modern cuisine • Bistro • Friendly •
This cosy, modern bistro is under the auspices of a young chef who communicates his passion for delicious, refined cuisine. Monthly changing menu featuring game during the season along with a signature pain perdu.

BOUCHONS *Regional wine tasting and local cuisine in a typical lyonnaise atmosphere*

Ⅹ
🕙

Daniel et Denise Saint-Jean
AC ⇔

32 r. Tramassac ⊠ 69005 – Ⓜ Vieux Lyon
Plan: **E2**
– ℰ 04 78 42 24 62
– www.danieletdenise-stjean.com
– Closed 31 december-5 january, Sunday and Monday
Menu 30/50 € – Carte 35/53 €
• Lyonnaise • Friendly •

A stone's throw from Cathédrale St-Jean, La Machonnerie – emblematic bouchon of Lyon's Old Town – has been taken over by chef Joseph Viola (Meilleur Ouvrier de France). He is already known for his Daniel et Denise near Part-Dieu train station. The menu offers Lyon cuisine that is hearty and tasty!

Ⅹ
🕙

Daniel et Denise Créqui
🛜 AC

156 r. de Créqui ⊠ 69003 – Ⓜ Place Guichard
Plan: **G3**
– ℰ 04 78 60 66 53 – www.daniel-et-denise.fr
– Closed 23 December-2 January, Saturday, Sunday and Bank Holidays
Menu 30 € – Carte 25/53 € – (booking advisable)
• Lyonnaise • Bistro • Friendly •

A dyed-in-the-wool 'bouchon', smooth with the patina of age, serving tasty, generous cuisine with excellent ingredients. Unsurprisingly, typical dishes take pride of place.

Ⅹ
🕙

Daniel et Denise Croix-Rousse
🛜 AC

8 r. de Cuire – Ⓜ Croix-Rousse
Plan: **F1**
– ℰ 04 78 28 27 44 – www.daniel-et-denise.fr
– Closed Sunday and Monday
Menu 21/30 € – Carte 27/34 €
• Lyonnaise • Bistro • Neighbourhood •

There is no doubt that this Daniel and Denise (the third opening, after Rue de Créqui and St Jean) is certain to enjoy the same success as its elder sisters. It must be said that Joseph Viola is unparalleled in the art of fresh, tasty Lyon classics. There is also a delicious vintage decor.

Ⅹ

Le Bouchon des Filles

20 r. Sergent-Blandan ⊠ 69001 – Ⓜ Hôtel de Ville
Plan: **F1**
– ℰ 04 78 30 40 44 – Closed Christmas Holidays and lunch except Saturday and Sunday
Menu 26 €
• Lyonnaise • Bistro • Cosy •

Next to the charming Place Sathonay, in a little cobbled street, is this picture-postcard bouchon, which is as sweet looking as it is inviting. Run by a pair of Filles, the food consists of lighter versions of Lyon's traditional dishes. It is simple, fresh, tasty and generous.

Ⅹ

Le Musée

2 r. des Forces ⊠ 69002 – Ⓜ Cordeliers
Plan: **F2**
– ℰ 04 78 37 71 54
– Closed August, 24 December-2 January, Sunday and Monday
Menu 23 € (lunch)/28 € – (booking advisable)
• Lyonnaise • Bistro • Rustic •

A sincere and authentic bouchon with a decor of checked tablecloths, closely packed tables and a buzzing atmosphere. In the kitchen, the young chef delivers the classics (brioche-wrapped sausage, lamb's tongue with ravigote sauce...) with real know-how.

✗ Le Poêlon d'or ⚐ ⇔

29 r. des Remparts-d'Ainay ⊠ *69002 –* **Ⓜ** *Ampère*   Plan: **F3**
– ☎ 04 78 37 65 60 – www.lepoelondor-restaurant.fr
*– Closed 6 to 21 August, Saturday except dinner from November-February
and Sunday*
Menu 18 € (lunch), 26/32 € – Carte 30/48 € – *(booking advisable)*
• Lyonnaise • Bistro • Retro •

Difficult to say if the chef does indeed use a golden saucepan (poêlon d'or), but
he must have a secret weapon – he revisits Lyon's terroir so well and proposes
food that is as tasty as it is perfectly put together. From the gâteau de foie de
volaille (chicken liver) with tomato coulis, to the pike quenelle gratin with
béchamel sauce. A must!

OLD TOWN   PLAN II

🏨 Villa Florentine   ♔ ⊜ ← 🛏 🖪 🕷 ⊐ ⭭ 🅰 🛗 🚗

25 montée St-Barthélémy ⊠ *69005 –* **Ⓜ** *Fourvière*   Plan: **E2**
– ☎ 04 72 56 56 56 – www.villaflorentine.com
24 rm – †195/510 € ††195/510 € – ⊡ 25 € – 4 suites
• Luxury • Traditional • Classic •

On the Fourvière hill, this 18C Renaissance inspired residence enjoys an incomparable view of the town. In the guestrooms, refinement and classic styling are
the watchwords.
❀ **Les Terrasses de Lyon** – See restaurant listing

🏨 Cour des Loges   ♔ ⊜ 🖪 🖼 ⭐ 🅰 🛗 🅿

6 r. du Bœuf ⊠ *69005 –* **Ⓜ** *Vieux Lyon*   Plan: **E2**
– ☎ 04 72 77 44 44 – www.courdesloges.com
56 rm – †190/485 € ††370/655 € – ⊡ 27 € – 4 suites
• Luxury • Historic • Personalised •

Vaults, galleries, passages... this magical place has all the character of the Renaissance in the middle of Vieux-Lyon with design and contemporary elegance as a
bonus. Trendy bistro ambience at the Café-Épicerie and daily changing dishes.
At the Loges, the atmosphere is romantic and the cuisine creative.
❀ **Les Loges • Café-Épicerie** – See restaurant listing

🏠 Collège   ⭭ 🅰 🛗 🚗

5 pl. St-Paul ⊠ *69005 –* **Ⓜ** *Vieux Lyon*   Plan: **E-F1**
– ☎ 04 72 10 05 05 – www.college-hotel.com
40 rm – †130/160 € ††130/160 € – ⊡ 14 €
• Business • Townhouse • Personalised •

Desks, a pommel horse, geography maps: everything here evokes the schools
of yesteryear, and all in a designer style. Immaculately white rooms with balcony or terrace and pleasant bar serving 'gôneries' – Lyonnais tapas!

✗✗✗ Têtedoie (Christian Têtedoie)   🎋 ← ⭭ 🅰 ⇔ 🍽 🅿
❀❀

montée du Chemin-Neuf ⊠ *69005 –* **Ⓜ** *Minimes*   Plan: **E2**
– ☎ 04 78 29 40 10 – www.tetedoie.com – Closed Sunday
Menu 37 € (weekday lunch), 62/120 € – Carte 90/150 €
• Creative • Design • Formal •

On the Fourvière hill, this elegant and designer restaurant dominates Lyon.
Christian Têtedoie explores French tradition with talent. The cellar is substantial
and the cocktail bar is the place to be. Find a more relaxed atmosphere on the
Terrasse, serving fine Mediterranean flavours and la plancha cuisine.
➔ Foie gras de canard poêlé et légumes racines, tuile de noix et jus au
savagnin. Homard cuit en cocotte et cromesquis de tête de veau. Soufflé
à la poire, espuma Williamine, glace à la pâte d'amande de Provence.

XXX ✿

Les Terrasses de Lyon – Hôtel Villa Florentine

25 montée St-Barthélémy ✉ 69005 – Ⓜ Fourvière – ✆ 04 72 56 56 02 – www.villaflorentine.com – Closed Sunday and Monday

Plan: **E2**

Menu 49 € (lunch)/112 € – Carte 110/135 €

• Modern cuisine • Elegant • Luxury •

In the heights of Fourvière, these "Terraces" really are charming: from the dining room, the panoramic view of the city is truly splendid... As for the cooking, it is delicious and creative, with local produce given top-billing.

➜ Tartelette soufflée aux cèpes et écrevisses, sauce Nantua. Médaillon de homard bleu fumé au sarment de vigne, pommes de terre charlotte confite. Savarin à la framboise, mousseux au fromage blanc des monts du Lyonnais.

XXX ✿

Les Loges – Hôtel Cour des Loges

6 r. du Bœuf ✉ 69005 – Ⓜ Vieux Lyon – ✆ 04 72 77 44 44 – www.courdesloges.com – Closed August, Monday and lunch except Sunday

Plan: **E2**

Menu 105/115 € – Carte 85/110 € – *(booking advisable)*

• Modern cuisine • Romantic • Elegant •

Time seems to have stood still in this enchanting and romantic setting. Find a Florentine courtyard ringed by three floors of galleries and crowned by a contemporary glass ceiling. Savour the refined and inventive cuisine with flickering candlelight adding a final touch.

➜ Écrevisses de Camargue. Petit épeautre et homard. Dessert au cacao grand cru.

X ✿

Au 14 Février

6 r. Mourguet ✉ 69005 – Ⓜ Vieux Lyon – ✆ 04 78 92 91 39 – www.au14fevrier.com – Closed 2 weeks in August and in January, Sunday, Monday and lunch except Saturday

Plan: **E2**

Menu 85 € – *(booking advisable) (set menu only)*

• Creative • Intimate • Cosy •

The gastronomic worlds of France and Japan are currently enjoying a great romance... and this eatery, named after Valentine's Day, is one of the finest examples of the trend. Under the direction of a talented Japanese chef, the meal is a revelation with its variety of textures, sweet-and-sour contrasts etc. A remarkably well done 'surprise' set menu.

➜ Coulis de tomate verte, concombre, céleri, poulpe, glace avocat et yaourt. Pigeonneau de Bresse rôti, courgette grisette de Provence, condiment figue et datte. Noix de coco, gelée de jasmin et sorbet litchi.

X

Café-Épicerie – Hôtel Cour des Loges

2 r. du Bœuf ✉ 69005 – Ⓜ Vieux Lyon – ✆ 04 72 77 44 44 – www.courdesloges.com

Plan: **E2**

Carte 45/65 €

• Modern cuisine • Trendy • Friendly •

In the marvellous setting of the Cour des Loges, this Café-Épicerie boasts a trendy bistro-style ambience. The locals come to enjoy unpretentious yet well-prepared dishes that change daily.

LES BROTTEAUX – CITÉ INTERNATIONALE – LA PART-DIEU PLAN III

Marriott Cité Internationale

70 quai Charles-de-Gaulle ✉ 69006 – ✆ 04 78 17 50 50 – www.marriottlyon.com

Plan: **H1**

192 rm – †90/565 € ††90/565 € – ☕ 24 € – 5 suites

• Chain hotel • Business • Modern •

Between the Rhône and the Tête d'Or park, an impressive red-brick and glass structure. The rooms are well equipped, spacious and contemporary in style. Guests also appreciate the conference and fitness facilities.

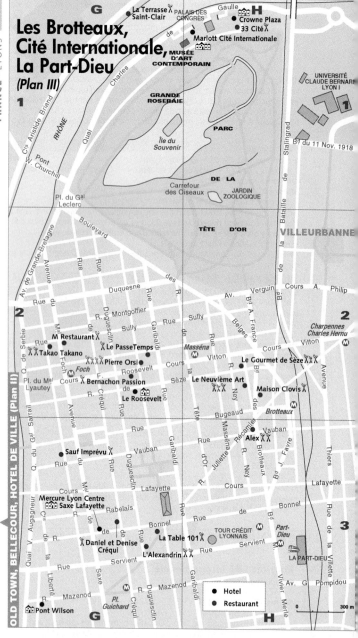

Les Brotteaux, Cité Internationale, La Part-Dieu
(Plan III)

La Terrasse Saint-Clair
PALAIS DES CONGRÈS
Crowne Plaza
33 Cité
Marriott Cité Internationale
MUSÉE D'ART CONTEMPORAIN
UNIVERSITÉ CLAUDE BERNARD LYON I
RHÔNE
Crs Aristide Briand
Quai
Pont W. Churchill
GRANDE ROSERAIE
Île du Souvenir
PARC
Bd du 11 Nov. 1918
Pl. du Gal Leclerc
Carrefour des Oiseaux
DE LA
JARDIN ZOOLOGIQUE
Boulevard
TÊTE D'OR
VILLEURBANNE
Av. de Grande-Bretagne
Avenue
Rue
Rue
Duquesne
Rue
R.
Rue
Cours A. Philip
Av. Verguin
Bd A. France
Charpennes Charles Hernu
R. Duguesclin
Montgolfier
Sully
Rue
Sully
Garibaldi
de
Masséna
Vitton
Belges
Cours
Vitton
M Restaurant
Le PasseTemps
Takao Takano
Pierre Orsi
Le Gourmet de Sèze
Q. de Serbie
Rue
Mal
Foch
Pl. du Mal Lyautey
M Foch
F. Roosevelt
Cours
Bernachon Passion
de
Sèze
Rue
Ney
la
Le Neuvième Art
Tête
Maison Clovis
des
Brotteaux
M
Le Roosevelt
R. Créqui
Bugeaud
Avenue
Q. du Gal Sarrail
Rue
Rue
Masséna
R.
d'Or
Juliette
Récamier
Ney
Rue
Brotteaux
Bd B. Favre
Vauban
Alex
Thiers
Sauf Imprévu
Duguesclin
Vauban
Garibaldi
Cours
Lafayette
Lafayette
Cours
Mercure Lyon Centre
Saxe Lafayette
Rabelais
Rue
de
Bonnel
M
Part-Dieu
Bonnel
Rue de la Villette
Qai V. Augagneur
Crs de
R.
de
Daniel et Denise Créqui
Bonnel
La Table 101
TOUR CRÉDIT LYONNAIS
M
LA PART-DIEU
L'Alexandrin
Rue
Servient
Servient
Rue
Saxe
Mazenod
Garibaldi
Av. G. Pompidou
Pont Wilson
M Pl. Guichard
R. Créqui
R. Duguesclin
Mazenod
Vivier Merle
R. Liberté
G
H

●	Hotel
●	Restaurant

0   300 m

276

FRANCE - LYONS

Crowne Plaza 🏯 👤 AC 🛁 🚗

22 quai Charles-de-Gaulle ✉ 69006 – ℰ 04 78 17 86 86
– www.crownplaza.com/lyonciteintl   Plan: **H1**
156 rm – ♦105/420 € ♦♦105/420 € – ☐ 22 € – 5 suites
• Chain hotel • Business • Modern •
A modern construction designed by Renzo Piano. It has bright guestrooms
overlooking the Tête-d'Or park or the Rhône. Traditional French cuisine and
regional ingredients in the restaurant, as well as a pleasant terrace.

Mercure Lyon Centre Saxe Lafayette 🏯 ₤ 👤 AC 🛁 🚗

29 r. Bonnel ✉ 69003 – ⓜ Place Guichard
– ℰ 04 72 61 90 90   Plan: **G3**
– www.mercure-lyon-saxe-lafayette.com
156 rm – ♦95/300 € ♦♦95/300 € – ☐ 19 €
• Chain hotel • Business • Contemporary •
This former garage built in 1932 is conveniently located between the Gare de la
Part-Dieu (railway station) neighbourhood and the quays of the Rhône. The
guestrooms are spacious and elegant. There is a small indoor pool and fitness
facilities in the basement.

Le Roosevelt 👤 AC 🚗

48 r. de Sèze ✉ 69006 – ⓜ Foch – ℰ 04 78 52 35 67   Plan: **G2**
– www.hotel-roosevelt.com
48 rm – ♦90/235 € ♦♦90/235 € – ☐ 18 €
• Traditional • Cosy •
Pleasant and comfortable hotel. On the courtyard side the rooms are more spacious and quiet. They overlook the famous Bernachon chocolate shop – only a
few steps away for a delicious treat!

Pont Wilson AC 🚗

6 r. Mazenod ✉ 69003 – ⓜ Guillotière   Plan: **G3**
– ℰ 04 78 60 94 94 – www.hotelwilson-lyon.com
54 rm – ♦83/250 € ♦♦93/260 € – ☐ 16 €
• Business • Functional •
This hotel is well located near the quayside and Wilson bridge and is suitable for
business travellers. Quite spacious guestrooms.

🅇🅇🅇🅇 Pierre Orsi 🍴 ⌂ 👤 AC ↔ 🍷
❀

3 pl. Kléber ✉ 69006 – ⓜ Masséna – ℰ 04 78 89 57 68   Plan: **G2**
– www.pierreorsi.com – Closed Sunday and Monday except Bank Holidays
Menu 60 € (weekday lunch), 110/130 € – Carte 90/130 €
• Classic cuisine • Formal • Luxury •
First, you come face to face with the lovely ochre Florentine façade, then, on
entering, you discover the elegance and luxurious comfort of an opulent bourgeois house. As for the food: the cuisine is fine and precise, of the moment,
based on top-notch ingredients and accompanied by superb wines.
➜ Ravioles de foie gras de canard au jus de porto et truffes. Pigeonneau
en cocotte, gousses d'ail confites en chemise. Crêpes Suzette à l'orange.

🅇🅇🅇 Le Neuvième Art (Christophe Roure) 👤 AC
❀ ❀

173 r. Cuvier ✉ 69006 – ⓜ Brotteaux   Plan: **H2**
– ℰ 04 72 74 12 74 – www.leneuviemeart.com – Closed 15 February-
1 March, 7 to 30 August, Sunday and Monday
Menu 85/145 € – Carte approx. 110 €
• Creative • Design •
In a chic, minimalist setting, Christophe Roure (formerly at St-Just-Saint-Ram-
bert) cooks with inventiveness, precision and intelligence, his dishes a pitch-per-
fect harmony of flavours and textures. Exquisite!
➜ Dentelles de saint-pierre sur crème de haddock, dulce et cœur de pal-
mier frais. Pie" de caille aux prunes, quetsches et mirabelles, marinés à l'eau
de noix. Promenade en sous-bois autour de la myrtille."

FRANCE - LYONS

XxX ❀

Le Gourmet de Sèze (Bernard Mariller)　　 ሌ 🅰🅲 ⇄

125 r. de Sèze ✉ *69006 –* Ⓜ *Masséna*　　Plan: **H2**
*– 𝒞 04 78 24 23 42 – www.le-gourmet-de-seze.com – Closed 15 to
18 February, 29 July-24 August, Sunday, Monday and Bank Holidays*
Menu 39 € (weekday lunch), 55/120 € *– (booking advisable)*
• Classic cuisine • Elegant • Cosy •

A new location – a short hop along the rue de Sèze – is thankfully the only real
change at this restaurant! In a spacious yet cosy interior, diners can still enjoy
dishes that show off chef Bernard Mariller's inventiveness and attention to
detail. He continues to pay a fitting tribute to his mentors, who include Joël
Robuchon and Philippe Chavent.
➜ Cannellonis de langoustines de Loctudy, jus de crustacés, girolles et bet-
teraves potagères. Veau de lait rôti en cocotte, pommes nouvelles, artichauts et jus à la sauge. Grand dessert du gourmet.

XX ❀

Takao Takano　　 ሌ 🅰🅲

33 r. Malesherbes ✉ *69006 –* Ⓜ *Foch*　　Plan: **G2**
*– 𝒞 04 82 31 43 39 – www.takaotakano.com – Closed 3 weeks in August,
Sunday and Monday*
Menu 33 € (lunch), 53/83 € *– (booking advisable)*
• Creative • Design •

Takao Takano is back, much to our delight! For this Japanese chef, already
renowned for his sleight of hand, this new eatery – the epitome of minimalist – is
the icing on the cake. How can you fail to be won over by his eye for precision,
sense for flavours, and the subtlety of his compositions? A fine homage to
French cuisine.
➜ Langoustine pochée, condiment concombre, rhubarbe et oseille. Rouget
barbet de petit bateau, jus de tête au saté. Riz au lait crémeux, caramel au
beurre demi-sel et sauge.

XX ❀

L'Alexandrin (Laurent Rigal)　　 🕸 🅰🅲

83 r. Moncey ✉ *69003 –* Ⓜ *Place Guichard*　　Plan: **G3**
*– 𝒞 04 72 61 15 69 – www.lalexandrin.fr – Closed 2 to 24 August, Sunday
and Monday*
Menu 38 € (weekday lunch), 60/115 €
• Modern cuisine • Cosy •

In an elegant setting, Laurent Rigal uses the fine produce of the region to create
inventive, generous cuisine. Vegetarian, Lyon-style revisited or a riff on a single
top-quality ingredient, each menu provides a poetic moment.
➜ Langoustines rôties, millefeuille de guacamole d'avocat et chorizo.
Volaille de Bresse au vinaigre, petits légumes de saison et poêlée de girolles. Madeleines au chocolat guanaja et marmelade d'orange au Grand Marnier.

XX ☻

Alex　　 ሌ 🅰🅲

44 bd des Brotteaux ✉ *69006 –* Ⓜ *Brotteaux*　　Plan: **H3**
*– 𝒞 04 78 52 30 11 – Closed August, Sunday and
Monday*
Menu 24 € (weekday lunch), 28/38 € – Carte 45/55 €
• Traditional cuisine • Cosy • Elegant •

Alex is the chef (and owner) of this chic and simple restaurant. He concocts well-
crafted cuisine with beautifully fresh ingredients picked up at market.

X ❀

Maison Clovis (Clovis Khoury)　　 🅰🅲

19 bd Brotteaux ✉ *69006 –* Ⓜ *Brotteaux*　　Plan: **H2**
*– 𝒞 04 72 74 44 61 – www.maisonclovis.com – Closed 1 to 9 May, 7 to
29 August, 1 to 10 January, Sunday and Monday*
Menu 49/79 € – Carte 60/90 €
• Modern cuisine • Design •

This designer restaurant is elegant without being uptight. Clovis Khoury prepares delicious seasonal cuisine using fine ingredients. The menu is short, but the
choice is nevertheless impossible.
➜ Oursin d'Islande. Pigeon de Bresse. Soufflé au chocolat et menthe poiv-
rée.

Le Passe Temps (Younghoon Lee) · 🅰🄲

52 r. Tronchet ✉ *69006 –* Ⓜ *Masséna* Plan: **G2**
– 𝒞 04 72 82 90 14 – Closed August, Sunday, Monday
and lunch Bank Holidays
Menu 25 € (weekday lunch), 38/60 € – *(booking advisable)*
• Creative • Minimalist • Design •
Mr Lee, originally from Seoul, has brought a little of his native country to the Brotteaux neighbourhood. With a sharp sense of aestheticism and flavours, he reinterprets French cuisine by adding Korean touches. His speciality, foie gras with root and other vegetables in a soya broth, is quite simply delicious!
→ Cuisine du marché.

M Restaurant 🖔 🄲

47 av. Foch ✉ *69006 –* Ⓜ *Foch – 𝒞 04 78 89 55 19* Plan: **G2**
– www.mrestaurant.fr – Closed 20 to 28 February, 1 to 23 August,
Saturday and Sunday
Menu 26/36 € – Carte approx. 43 €
• Modern cuisine • Trendy • Friendly •
Orange-painted wall, designer chairs, bare oak tables-the décor is warm and cheerful. As for the cooking, the chef hails from city institution Léon de Lyon, and here offers an up-to-date repertoire with a particularly enticing daily menu.

33 Cité 🖔 🖔 ♿ 🄲 ⇔

33 quai Charles-de-Gaulle ✉ *69006 – 𝒞 04 37 45 45 45* Plan: **H1**
– www.33cite.com – Closed 3 weeks in August
Menu 27 € – Carte 33/63 €
• Traditional cuisine • Brasserie •
Three talented chefs – Mathieu Viannay (Meilleur Ouvrier de France), Christophe Marguin and Frédéric Berthod (alumnus of Bocuse) – joined forces to create this chic, tasty brasserie. It opens onto the Tête-d'Or Park. On the menu find the great brasserie specialities.

La Table 101 🖔 🄲 ⇔

101 r. Moncey ✉ *69003 –* Ⓜ *Place Guichard* Plan: **G3**
– 𝒞 04 78 60 90 23 – www.latable101.fr – Closed 1 to 22 August, Saturday,
Sunday and Bank Holidays
Menu 26 € (lunch), 31/46 € – Carte 45/56 €
• French modern • Friendly •
Next to the Halles Paul Bocuse, the chef doesn't have to go far to find market fresh ingredients. You can't argue with the results on the plate: tasty food with a skilfully creative edge. Right until the last mouthful the meal will arouse your enthusiasm, and the bill, which is very reasonable, dispels any remaining doubt!

Sauf Imprévu ⇔

40 r. Pierre-Corneille ✉ *69006 –* Ⓜ *Foch* Plan: **G3**
– 𝒞 04 78 52 16 35 – Closed Saturday, Sunday and
dinner except Thursday
Menu 25/30 € – Carte 34/43 €
• Traditional cuisine • Simple • Family •
"Marguerite" terrine in homage to his great-grandmother, coco de Paimpol beans with shellfish, grilled prime rib of beef with homemade chips... With his focus firmly on tradition, Félix Gagnaire proposes delicious and copious dishes. Everything is fresh, homemade and spot on, and the prices are also fair!

Bernachon Passion 🄲

42 cours Franklin-Roosevelt ✉ *69006 –* Ⓜ *Foch* Plan: **G2**
– 𝒞 04 78 52 23 65 – www.bernachon.com – Closed 23 July-24 August,
Sunday, Monday, Bank Holidays and dinner
Menu 29 € – Carte 34/51 € – *(booking advisable)*
• Traditional cuisine • Simple •
A restaurant run by the daughter and grandchildren of Paul Bocuse, owners of the famous chocolate shop next door. Traditional French recipes and lunchtime daily specials. Tea room.

✗ **La Terrasse St-Clair** 🛖
2 Grande-Rue-St-Clair ✉ *69300 Caluire-et-Cuire* — Plan: **G1**
– 𝒞 04 72 27 37 37 – www.terrasse-saint-clair.com – Closed 5 to
22 August, 23 December-7 January, Sunday and Monday
Menu 28 €
• Traditional cuisine • Bistro • Friendly •
Restaurant with the air of an old-fashioned French café serving good, traditional cuisine. Terrace shaded by plane trees and a petanque ground!

AROUND THE CENTER

 Lyon Métropole　⚹ ₤♿ ⊕ ☒ ☒ ❀ ⇥ ♿ Ⓐ🅒 ♨ 🚗
85 quai J.-Gillet ✉ *69004 – 𝒞 04 72 10 44 44* — Plan: **B1**
– www.lyonmetropole.com
174 rm – †99/310 € ††99/310 € – ☲ 20 €
• Business • Spa hotel • Functional •
Hotel popular for its Olympic size swimming pool and sports facilities: superb spa, gym, tennis and squash courts, etc. In the restaurant, seafood and fish are to the fore.

 Novotel Confluence　⚹ ₤♿ ♿ Ⓐ🅒 ♨ 🚗
3 r. Paul-Montrochet ✉ *69002 – Ⓜ Perrache* — Plan: **B2**
– 𝒞 04 37 23 64 00 – www.accorhotel.com/7325
150 rm – †91/250 € ††91/250 € – ☲ 17 € – 3 suites
• Chain hotel • Modern •
In this brand new neighbourhood on the banks of the Saône, you cannot miss this hotel with its resolutely contemporary architecture. It has a large and inviting lobby, a restaurant with a designer look and a terrace on the river. The lovely guestrooms have all the latest mod cons.

🏠 **Dock Ouest**　♿ Ⓐ🅒 🚗
39 r. des Docks ✉ *69009 – Ⓜ Gare de Vaise* — Plan: **B1**
– 𝒞 04 78 22 34 34 – www.dockouest.com
43 rm – †72/242 € ††72/242 € – ☲ 13 €
• Townhouse • Business • Contemporary •
Dock Ouest is located in an up-and-coming district of Lyon, just opposite Paul Bocuse's fast food outlet. The guestrooms are comfortable and decorated in a restrained style, with the added bonus of a kitchenette. Gourmet breakfast.

🏠 **Mama Shelter**　⚹ ♿ Ⓐ🅒 ♨ 🚗
13 r. Domer ✉ *69007 – Ⓜ Jean Macé* — Plan: **B2**
– 𝒞 04 78 02 58 58 – www.mamashelter.com
156 rm – †69/169 € ††79/269 € – ☲ 16 €
• Business • Townhouse • Design •
Like the sister hotels in Paris and Marseille, the decor is as trendy as ever (bare concrete, designer flourishes, offbeat touches), guestrooms are modern and public transport is close by. Splendid.

✗✗✗ **Auberge de l'Île Barbe** (Jean-Christophe Ansanay-Alex) 🍴
🕸 *pl. Notre-Dame (on Barbe Island)* ✉ *69009* ⇔ 🍽 (dinner) 🅿
– 𝒞 04 78 83 99 49 – www.aubergedelile.com – Closed — Plan: **B1**
Sunday dinner and Monday
Menu 48 € (weekday lunch), 95/145 €
• Classic cuisine • Romantic • Elegant •
A country feel in the heart of the leafy île Barbe, an island in the Saône. The walls date from 1601 and there is a softly intimate atmosphere. Classical cuisine based on quality produce.
→ Velouté de cèpe comme un cappuccino. Selle d'agneau dîner de gala de l'Unesco". Soufflé chaud."

Les Saveurs de Py

8 r. Pailleron ⊠ 69004 – Ⓜ Hénon – ℰ 04 78 28 80 86
Plan: **B1**
– www.saveursdepy.fr – Closed August, Sunday and Monday
Menu 16 € (weekday lunch), 30/39 €
• Modern cuisine • Friendly • Bistro •
Right in the heart of the lively Croix-Rousse neighbourhood, this is one of those lovely, contemporary, convivial and colourful little bistros. In the kitchens is a chef who demonstrates talent in his use of market ingredients, daring to throw in wonderful Japanese touches. Bold flavours and excellent value.

L'Art et la Manière

102 Gde-Rue de la Guillotière ⊠ 69007
Plan: **B-C2**
– Ⓜ Saxe-Gambetta – ℰ 04 37 27 05 83 – www.art-et-la-maniere.fr
– Closed 3 weeks in August, Saturday and Sunday
Menu 23 € (lunch)/32 € – Carte approx. 41 € – (booking advisable)
• Traditional cuisine • Bistro • Friendly •
A contemporary bistro that champions conviviality, seasonal cuisine and enticing, reasonably priced wines. It is also a great excuse for discovering the La Guillotière district. As it has a loyal local following, you are best advised to book ahead.

Imouto

21 r. Pasteur ⊠ 69007 – Ⓜ Guillotière
Plan: **B2**
– ℰ 04 72 76 99 53
Menu 19 € (lunch)/32 € – (booking advisable)
• Fusion • Design • Simple •
Originally from Vietnam, Gaby Didonna opened Imouto ('little sister' in Japanese) in a working-class neighbourhood of Lyon. He cooks in tandem with a Japanese chef, Junko Matsunaga, who has some great experience to her name. The result is delicious fusion food, taking in French tradition, Japanese influences and Vietnamese touches. Wow!

L'Ouest

1 quai du Commerce (North via the banks of the Saône,
Plan: **B1**
D51) ⊠ 69009 – Ⓜ Gare de Vaise – ℰ 04 37 64 64 64
– www.nordsudbrasseries.com
Menu 27 € (weekdays)/33 € – Carte 31/69 €
• Traditional cuisine • Brasserie •
The largest of the Bocuse brasseries, with a designer décor and terrace facing the Saône. The menu is eclectic but the great specialities (spit-roast Bresse chicken notably) remain.

Fond Rose

23 chemin de Fond-Rose ⊠ 69300 Caluire-et-Cuire
Plan: **B1**
– ℰ 04 78 29 34 61 – www.nordsudbrasseries.com
Menu 29 € (weekdays) – Carte 37/54 €
• Classic cuisine • Brasserie • Elegant •
A 1920s mansion transformed into a chic brasserie by the Bocuse group. With its terrace surrounded by 100 year-old trees, it is the epitome of peace and quiet. The food is tasty and generous and squarely in the tradition of the region: frogs' legs, quenelles etc.

COLLONGES-AU-MONT-D'OR

Paul Bocuse

40 quai de la Plage – ℰ 04 72 42 90 90 – www.bocuse.fr
Menu 165/255 € – Carte 140/235 €
• Classic cuisine • Elegant • Luxury •
A high temple of tradition and old-style service, which is oblivious to passing culinary trends. Paul Bocuse is still offering the same "presidential" truffle soup first served in 1975, and has had three Michelin stars since 1965!
→ Soupe aux truffes noires V.G.E. Rouget en écailles de pommes de terre. Gâteau Président Maurice Bernachon"."

Charbonnières-les-Bains

Le Pavillon de la Rotonde

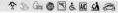

3 av. Georges-Bassinet – ✆ 04 78 87 79 79 – www.restaurant-rotonde.com – Closed 26 July-25 August and 1 to 5 January

16 rm – 170/370 € 170/570 € – 22 €

• Luxury • Spa hotel • Contemporary •

A stone's throw from the casino and set in wooded parkland, this luxury hotel blends the modern with discreet touches of Art Deco. Some of the guestrooms have a hammam and a terrace. A very fine establishment on the outskirts of Lyons.

La Rotonde – See restaurant listing

La Rotonde – Hôtel Le Pavillon de la Rotonde

20 av. du Casino (Domaine du Lyon Vert) ✉ 69260 La Tour de Salvagny – ✆ 04 78 87 00 97 – www.restaurant-rotonde.com – Closed 27 July-27 August, 2 to 6 January, Tuesday lunch, Saturday lunch, Sunday and Monday

Menu 45 € (lunch), 69/135 € – Carte 115/125 €

• Modern cuisine • Elegant • Luxury •

In this beautiful area on the outskirts of town is a moment of true gastronomy. It is set above the casino Le Lyon Vert, which is a fine legacy of the Art Deco period. The menu is in a classic French vein. It combines timeless dishes, with new influences but does not forget the great repertoire of Lyon cuisine.

→ Pâté en croûte "Champion du Monde 2013". Turbot confit et escargots, pomme charlotte, céleri et sauce cresson. Cannellonis de chocolat amer, glace crème brûlée.

STRASBOURG
STRASBOURG

Population: 274 394

DX/Fotolia.com

Would it be stretching things to call Strasbourg the ultimate European city? It can make an impressive claim. Although in France, it sits just across the Rhine from Germany; it's home to the Court of Human Rights and the Council of Europe; its stunning cathedral is the highest medieval building on the continent; and it's a major communications hub as it connects the Mediterranean with the Rhineland, Central Europe, the North Sea and the Baltic. Oh, and the Old Town is a UNESCO World Heritage Site. What's more, there's a real cosmopolitan buzz here. A large student population, courtesy of the city's ancient university, helps generate a year-round feeling of liveliness.

The name 'Strasbourg' translates as 'crossroads', and the city bounced back and forth between France and Germany for over three hundred years. Its unique geographical position also lends the city a great gastronomic tradition, with two cuisine cultures colliding head on and hungry visitors reaping the benefits. Meanwhile, street signs in both French and Alsatian add to a gently teasing schizophrenia, enhanced by distinct areas of medieval French and German architecture. The final brushwork of this striking picture is the handsome waterway that completely encircles the Old Town; the ideal setting for a lingering boat journey on a summer's afternoon.

STRASBOURG IN...

→ **ONE DAY**
Old Town, Notre-Dame Cathedral, Petite France.

→ **TWO DAYS**
Boat trip on the Ill, Museum of Modern and Contemporary Art, meal in a winstub.

→ **THREE DAYS**
Alsatian Museum (or Rohan Palace museum), European Parliament, Orangerie.

PRACTICAL INFORMATION

ARRIVAL-DEPARTURE

✈ Strasbourg Entzheim International Airport is 12km southwest of the city. The train to Central Station runs from Entzheim Station (a 5min walk from the terminal) and takes 15min.

GETTING AROUND

Strasbourg is covered by a bus and tram service. You can buy a single ticket or carnets (multipasses). There's also a Tour Pass which gives unlimited travel for 24hr. The city has impressive green credentials: buses run on natural gas, trams are slick and efficient, and there are 130,000 cyclists and 270 miles of cycle paths – hiring a bike is a great way of getting about here. If you're staying longer, invest in a Strasbourg Pass. This is a three-day pass which offers free travel, plus free admission or discounts to many city-wide monuments and visitor attractions.

CALENDAR HIGHLIGHTS

May
Les Nuits de Musées.

June
Festival de Musique.

July
Les Nuits de Strasbourg, L'Ill aux Lumieres.

August
Route Romane Festival.

September
European Days of Heritage.

November
St-Art Contemporary Art Fair, Jazz d'Or.

December
Christmas Markets.

EATING OUT

Strasbourg is generally considered one of the best cities in France for great food. There's the attention to quality and detail that's the epitome of the French gourmet philosophy, allied to bold and hearty Alsatian fare with its roots firmly set across the Rhine. A favourite of the region is choucroute (or sauerkraut if you're leaning towards Germany), which is a rumbustious mixture of cabbage, potatoes, pork, sausage and ham; then there's baeckoffe, a tasty Alsace stew, which translates as 'ovenbake' and blends pieces of stewing lamb, beef and pork with liberal splashes of Riesling. Talking of which, the fragrant wines of the area have a distinct character of their own: they're white, spicy and floral. The local fruit liquor, eau de vie, has a definite Alsatian kick, too – it's sweetened entirely by fruit without a hint of sugar. A good place to try the local specialities is a typical Strasbourg winstub. Most of the city's smarter restaurants are around the cathedral, in the Petite France quarter, and along the canal and river banks.

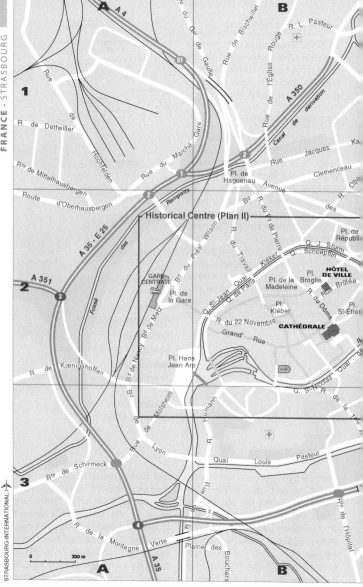

Historical Centre (Plan II)

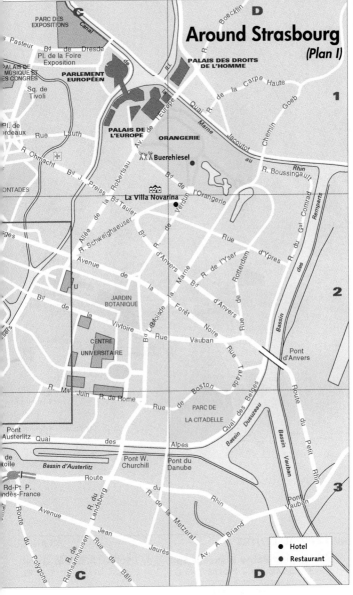

Around Strasbourg
(Plan I)

PARC DES
EXPOSITIONS

Bd de Dresde
Pl. de la Foire
Exposition

PALAIS DES DROITS
DE L'HOMME

PARLEMENT
EUROPÉEN

PALAIS DE MUSIQUE ET
DES CONGRÈS

Sq. de
Tivoli

R. de la Carpe Haute

Goeb

Pl. de
Bordeaux

Rue

Léauth

PALAIS DE
L'EUROPE

ORANGERIE

Chemin

au

Jacoutot

R. Ohmacht

Bd J. Preiss

R. Robertsau

ᚷ Buerehiesel

R. Boussingault

Rhin

CONTADES

La Villa Novarina

Bd de l'Orangerie

Allée de la Bd Tauler

R. Schweighaeuser

Bd d'Anvers

Rue

d'Ypres

R. du Gal Conrad

Remparts

des

Avenue

de

la

Bd

de

JARDIN
BOTANIQUE

la

Victoire

Bd Leblois

Rue

R. de l'Yser

Rotterdam

de

Rue

Bassin

Pont
d'Anvers

Forêt

Noire

d'Anvers

Rue Tarade

CENTRE
UNIVERSITAIRE

Vauban

Rue

R. Mal Juin

R. de Home

Rue

de

Boston

PARC DE
LA CITADELLE

Quai des Belges

Route

du

Petit

Pont
Austerlitz

Quai

des

Alpes

Bassin Dusuzeau

Bassin Vauban

Rhin

de
l'Étoile

Bassin d'Austerlitz

Pont W.
Churchill

Pont du
Danube

Rd-Pt P.
Mendès-France

Route

du

R. de la Metzeral

Pont
Vauban

Avenue

Jean

Rhin

Av. A. Briand

Route

du

Polygone

R. de
Ratisamnhausen

Rue de Bâle

Jaurès

R. du
Landsberg

- ● Hotel
- ● Restaurant

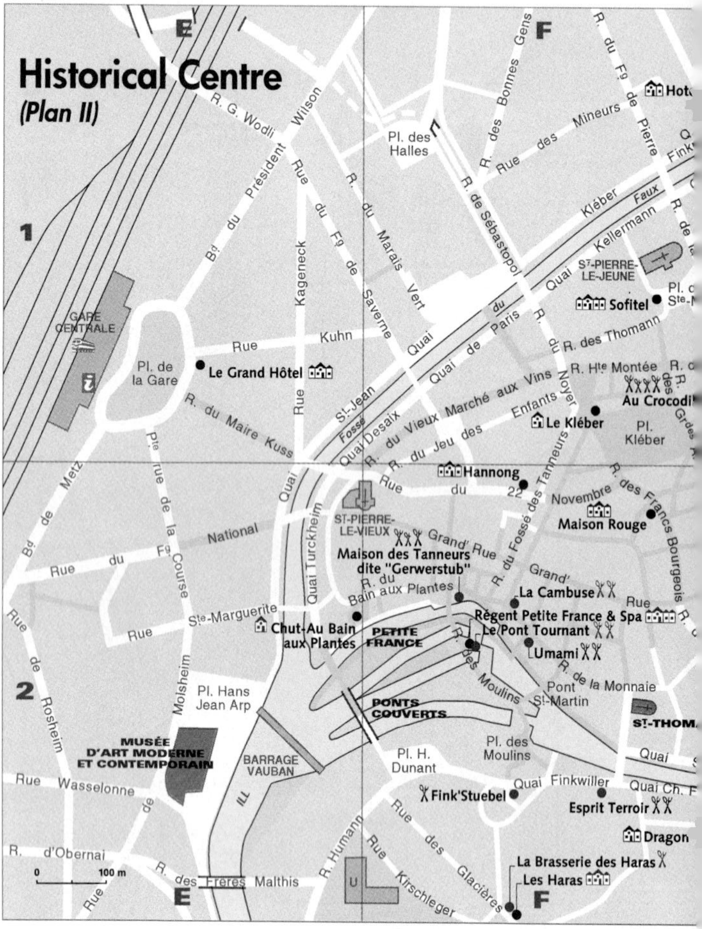
Historical Centre
(Plan II)
E
F
1
2
R. G. Wodli
Wilson
Bd du Président
Rue du Fg de Saverne
R. du Marais Vert
Pl. des Halles
R. des Bonnes Gens
Rue des Mineurs
R. du Fg de Pierre
R. de Sébastopol
Kléber
Faux
Kellermann
ST-PIERRE-LE-JEUNE
Sofitel
Pl.
Ste-
Quai
Finkw
Rue Kageneck
Rue Kuhn
GARE CENTRALE
Pl. de la Gare
Le Grand Hôtel
R. du Maire Kuss
St-Jean
Fossé
Quai Desaix
Quai de Paris
R. du Noyer
R. des Thomann
R. Hte Montée
Au Crocodi
R. du Vieux Marché aux Vins
Enfants
R. du Jeu des
Le Kléber
Pl. Kléber
R. des Grdes
Bd de Metz
Pte rue de la Course
Hannong
Rue du 22 Novembre
R. des Francs Bourgeois
Maison Rouge
Rue du Fg National
ST-PIERRE-LE-VIEUX
Maison des Tanneurs dite "Gerwerstub"
Grand' Rue
R. du Fossé des Tanneurs
R. du Bain aux Plantes
La Cambuse
Quai Turckheim
Rue Ste-Marguerite
Chut-Au Bain aux Plantes
PETITE FRANCE
Régent Petite France & Spa
Le Pont Tournant
Umami
R. des Moulins
R. de la Monnaie
Pont St-Martin
ST-THOM
Rue de Rosheim
Moisheim
Pl. Hans Jean Arp
PONTS COUVERTS
MUSÉE D'ART MODERNE ET CONTEMPORAIN
BARRAGE VAUBAN
Pl. H. Dunant
Pl. des Moulins
Quai Finkwiller
Quai Ch. F
Rue Wasselonne
Fink'Stuebel
Esprit Terroir
ILL
Dragon
Rue des Glacières
R. Humann
Rue Kirschleger
La Brasserie des Haras
Les Haras
R. d'Obernai
0
100 m
R. des Frères
Malthis

HISTORICAL CENTRE

PLAN II

Régent Petite France & Spa

5 r. des Moulins – ✆ 03 88 76 43 43
– www.regent-petite-france.com

Plan: **F2**

63 rm – 🚹190/680 € 🚹🚹190/680 € – ☕ 24 € – 9 suites

• Luxury • Personalised • Modern •

An imposing former ice-making factory on the banks of the river Ill in the historic Petite France district. Modern and stylish interior with comfortable rooms, 17 newly created in the "Pavillon", a 15th century building just opposite.
Le Pont Tournant – See restaurant listing

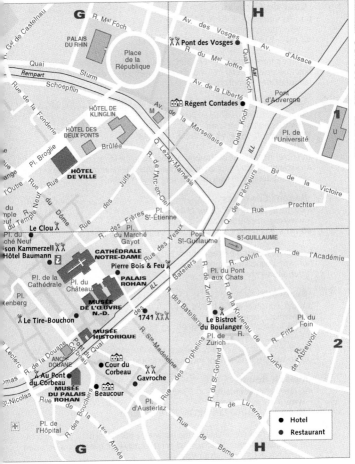

FRANCE - STRASBOURG

 Sofitel

4 pl. St-Pierre-le-Jeune
– ☎ 03 88 15 49 00
– www.sofitel-strasbourg.com
150 rm – 140/396 € 140/396 €
– ☐ 26 € – 4 suites
• Townhouse • Modern •

Space and contemporary design at this modern hotel located in a quiet neigh-bourhood to the north of the cathedral, 15 minutes walk from the station. The pleasant rooms are ideal for a relaxing break.

Plan: **F1**

FRANCE - STRASBOURG

Cour du Corbeau

6 r. des Couples – ℰ 03 90 00 26 26
Plan: **G2**
– www.cour-corbeau.com
63 rm – ♦169/605 € ♦♦169/605 € – ⌑ 24 €
• Historic • Luxury • Elegant •

A stone's throw from the Pont du Corbeau and the cathedral, this attractive hotel occupies several 16C buildings. Contemporary decor and top of the range facilities. Friendly service.

Les Haras

23 r. des Glacières – ℰ 03 90 20 50 00
Plan: **F2**
– www.les-haras-hotel.com
55 rm – ♦150/565 € ♦♦150/565 € – ⌑ 24 €
• Historic • Luxury • Design •

This hotel in the centre of Strasbourg is located in the former national stud farm! An exceptional setting for an exceptional hotel. The guestrooms, done out in a minimalist design, are fairly, or even very, large (17-35m2).

Régent Contades

8 av. de la Liberté – ℰ 03 88 15 05 05
Plan: **H1**
– www.regent-contades.com
46 rm – ♦113/590 € ♦♦113/590 € – ⌑ 21 € – 2 suites
• Luxury • Classic •

Behind the handsome façade of this 19C townhouse is a refined, classical interior (wood panelling, paintings, chandeliers...). Spacious guestrooms with character, and service to match.

Beaucour

5 r. des Bouchers – ℰ 03 88 76 72 00
Plan: **G2**
– www.hotel-beaucour.com
49 rm – ♦96/132 € ♦♦209/249 € – ⌑ 14 €
• Family • Personalised • Cosy •

Two fine 18C Alsatian houses built around a charming flower-filled patio. Very comfortable regional-style or more contemporary guestrooms.

Maison Rouge

4 r. des Francs-Bourgeois – ℰ 03 88 32 08 60
Plan: **F2**
– www.maison-rouge.com
139 rm ⌑ – ♦101/223 € ♦♦111/233 € – 3 suites
• Traditional • Classic •

In the city centre, convenient for the tramway, a traditional hotel offering comfort and quality service. Spacious and immaculately-kept guestrooms, accessed via landings decorated with artworks.

Hannong

15 r. du 22-Novembre – ℰ 03 88 32 16 22
Plan: **F2**
– www.hotel-hannong.com – Closed 1 to 11 January
72 rm – ♦79/239 € ♦♦89/299 € – ⌑ 16 €
• Traditional • Functional •

A family-run hotel full of character, built on the site of the Hannong earthenware factory (18C). Neo-classical façade, glass-roofed lounge, quality materials and meticulous housekeeping. Pleasant terrace area.

Le Grand Hôtel

12 pl. de la Gare – ℰ 03 88 52 84 84
Plan: **E1**
– www.le-grand-hotel.com
90 rm ⌑ – ♦76/375 € ♦♦76/375 €
• Business • Modern •

This hotel opposite the TGV station is definitely on a modern track with its minimalist contemporary decor, understated yet comfortable furnishings, and meticulously maintained guestrooms. Five minutes from the city centre.

FRANCE - STRASBOURG

La Villa Novarina

11 r. Westercamp – ℰ 03 90 41 18 28
– www.villanovarina.com
Plan I: **D2**
24 rm – †147/500 € ††147/900 € – ⟿ 22 €
• Business • Design • Contemporary •

Near the Parc de l'Orangerie in the well-heeled embassy district, this large 1950s building was designed by architect Maurice Novarina (1907-2002). The lobby pays homage to Modernism (furnishings by Eames, Knoll and Le Corbusier). Minimalist guestrooms, lovely pool and tranquil garden.

Hotel.D

15 r. du Fossé-des-Treize – ℰ 03 88 15 13 67
– www.hoteld.fr
Plan: **F1**
37 rm – †109/485 € ††109/485 € – ⟿ 18 €
• Business • Townhouse • Contemporary •

This contemporary hotel is close to the waterfront and the city centre. It has a unique, eye-catching and colourful interior. The comfortable guestrooms (large bed, designer bathrooms) and good breakfast (locally-sourced yogurts and fruit juices) make this a pleasant place to stay.

Dragon

12 r. du Dragon – ℰ 03 88 35 79 80
– www.dragon.fr
Plan: **F2**
32 rm – †79/145 € ††79/179 € – ⟿ 13 €
• Family • Modern •

Two 17C houses built around a flower-filled patio garden (where breakfast is served in summer) in a quiet area of the city. Comfortable, modern rooms, built into the eaves on the top floor.

Chut - Au Bain aux Plantes

4 r. Bain-aux-Plantes – ℰ 03 88 32 05 06
– www.hote-strasbourg.fr
Plan: **E2**
8 rm – †95/168 € ††95/205 € – ⟿ 12 € – 1 suite
• Townhouse • Personalised • Design •

In a picturesque street of Strasbourg's La Petite France quarter, a hotel with more of a guesthouse feel, charm included. Decoration incorporating designer and salvaged objects and furnishings, "zen" atmosphere: it will come as no surprise to hear that the owner is an architect!

Le Kléber

29 pl. Kléber – ℰ 03 88 32 09 53
– www.hotel-kleber.com
Plan: **F1**
37 rm – †85/120 € ††85/120 € – ⟿ 10 €
• Family • Contemporary • Personalised •

All the rooms here have a colourful, sweet and savoury theme (names include Meringue, Fraise and Cannelle). Unbeatable location on the famous Place Kléber.

Au Crocodile

10 r. de l'Outre – ℰ 03 88 32 13 02
– www.au-crocodile.com – Closed Sunday and Monday except in December
Plan: **F1**
Menu 39 € (lunch), 68/120 € – Carte 95/110 €
• Classic cuisine • Elegant •

Under new ownership since 2015 (Cédric Moulot, also behind 1741), the Crocodile has had a welcome return to form. First-class ingredients, subtle flavours and skilful preparation make for cooking that is quite simply delicious, and the professional service is a perfect match.

→ Carpaccio de langoustines au citron vert, émietté de tourteau et huître végétale. Dos de chevreuil doré, mousseline de potimarron au gingembre, sauce réglisse. Vacherin litchi-rose et framboise.

FRANCE - STRASBOURG

XXX 1741 ⁂

22 quai des Bateliers
Plan: **G2**
– ℰ *03 88 35 50 50 – www.1741.fr*
– *Closed 2 weeks in January, Tuesday and Wednesday except in December*
Menu 58 € ♈ (weekday lunch), 92/133 € – Carte 90/105 €
• **Modern cuisine** • **Elegant** •

This townhouse faces the Palais Rohan, a classical masterpiece that dates from 1741. In an elegant boudoir-style decor, discover flavoursome and finely-prepared cuisine accompanied by an interesting selection of wines from Alsace (grand cru, organic etc.).

→ Langoustines royales raidies, émulsion aux agrumes et persil. Entrecôte Simmental cuite au sautoir, petits pois et beurre de ciboulette. Blanc-manger au citron vert, eau de fruits rouges et sorbet fromage blanc.

XXX **Buerehiesel** (Eric Westermann) ⁂

in the parc de l'Orangerie
Plan I: **D1**
– ℰ *03 88 45 56 65 – www.buerehiesel.fr*
– *Closed 7 to 17 February, 31 July-22 August, 24 December-5 January, Sunday and Monday*
Menu 39 € (weekday lunch), 70/98 € – Carte 70/100 €
• **Modern cuisine** • **Individual** • **Elegant** •

An exquisite restaurant housed in a beautiful half-timbered 17C farmhouse that was dismantled from its original location and rebuilt in the Parc de l'Orangerie (bucolic views from the conservatory dining room and terrace). Refined cuisine with regional touches and top-notch produce.

→ Cuisses de grenouilles poêlées au cerfeuil et schniederspaetle. Pillette de Bresse cuite entière comme un baeckeofe. Brioche caramélisée à la bière, glace à la bière et poire rôtie.

XXX **Maison des Tanneurs dite Gerwerstub**

42 r. Bain-aux-Plantes – ℰ *03 88 32 79 70*
Plan: **F2**
– *www.maison-des-tanneurs.com – Closed 1 to 8 August, 2 to 23 January, Sunday and Monday*
Menu 21 € (weekday lunch) – Carte 41/62 €
• **Traditional cuisine** • **Elegant** • **Retro** •

This typical Alsatian house with lots of character (1572) overlooking the river Ill in the historic Petite France district is an institution for choucroute and other famous regional specialities.

XX **La Cambuse**

1 r. des Dentelles – ℰ *03 88 22 10 22 – Closed 1 to*
Plan: **F2**
16 May, 3 July-22 August, 23 December-9 January, Sunday and Monday
Carte 52/63 € – *(booking advisable)*
• **Fish and seafood** • **Cosy** • **Intimate** •

Close to the waterside, a local institution whose intimate dining room is decorated in the style of a yacht cabin. Fish and seafood are the draw here, with Far-Eastern touches and precise cooking.

XX **Le Pont Tournant** – Hôtel Régent Petite France & Spa

5 r. des Moulins – ℰ *03 88 76 43 43*
– *www.regent-petite-france.com – Closed Sunday,*
Plan: **F2**
Monday and lunch
Menu 60/80 € – Carte 47/75 €
• **Modern cuisine** • **Fashionable** •

The canalside location is extremely attractive and the food, composed with talent, harmoniously marries good fresh ingredients. *Pissaladière* (a tart from Provence) with mackerel; roast fillet of hake, tomato and feta tempura; and poached apricots, pistachio cream and Gewurztraminer jelly.

XX ✿

Gavroche (Benoit Fuchs)

A/C

Plan: G2

4 r. Klein – ✆ 03 88 36 82 89 – www.restaurant-gavroche.com – Closed 23 July-16 August, 23 December-3 January, Saturday and Sunday

Menu 58/86 € – Carte 85/90 € – *(booking advisable)*

• Modern cuisine • Fashionable •

You can feel the desire to make the customer happy here, both in the restaurant and the kitchens. Spend a pleasant time over the course of your meal, which has plenty of finesse and character. The dishes concentrate on good ingredients and the result is a treat!

➜ Foie gras de canard cuit au torchon et fumé aux sarments de vigne, marmelade d'églantine. Turbot sauvage, risotto d'épeautre et coquillages, émulsion à l'ail doux. Douceur café et caramel.

XX ✿

Umami (René Fieger)

A/C

Plan: F2

8 r. des Dentelles – ✆ 03 88 32 80 53 – www.restaurant-umami.com – Closed 1 week in May, 3 weeks in September, 1 week in January, Monday lunch, Tuesday lunch, Friday lunch, Wednesday and Thursday

Menu 50/95 € 🍷 – Carte 60/80 € – *(booking advisable)*

• Creative • Cosy •

Sweet, salty, sour, bitter and… "umami" (savoury), the fifth taste in Japanese cuisine and the hallmark of the cooking here, which blends flavours from around the world. Attractive modern decor.

➜ Cuisine du marché.

XX ✿

Esprit Terroir (Joël Philipps)

A/C

Plan: F2

2 quai Finkwiller – ✆ 03 88 37 32 34 – www.esprit-terroir.fr – Closed 3 to 9 May, 26 July-8 August, 1 to 11 January, Sunday and Monday

Menu 29 € (weekday lunch), 61/81 € – Carte 60/70 €

• Creative • Intimate •

This tiny restaurant in an old house on the waterfront is run by a young couple with some great references (Auberge de l'Ill, Le Cerf at Marlenheim). Fine seasonal dishes grace the menu.

➜ Carpaccio de langoustines marinées au yuzu et au gingembre. Médaillon de lotte et de homard en habit de nori, fenouil et sauce au vin jaune. Finger à l'ananas, dacquoise et crème chiboust, sorbet citron et menthe.

XX

Le Violon d'Ingres

1 r. Chevalier-Robert (at La Robertsau) – ✆ 03 88 31 39 50 – Closed 2 weeks in August, 1 week in October and in January, Saturday lunch, Sunday dinner and Monday

Menu 36 € (weekday lunch), 58/62 € – Carte 58/69 €

• Classic cuisine • Rustic •

This historic Alsatian house in the Robertsau district, near the European Parliament, serves impeccably prepared classical cuisine in an elegant dining room or on the shady terrace.

XX

Maison Kammerzell et Hôtel Baumann

A/C

Plan: G2

16 pl. de la Cathédrale – ✆ 03 88 32 42 14 – www.maison-kammerzell.com

9 rm – †110/210 € ††150/210 € – ☕ 10 €

Menu 30/48 € – Carte 36/55 €

• Traditional cuisine • Friendly • Traditional •

A medieval ambiance at this authentic 16C building near the cathedral, with stained-glass windows, paintings, wood carvings and Gothic vaulting. Regional cuisine (choucroute is a speciality) and brasserie-style dishes. Plainly decorated guestrooms.

XX **Pont des Vosges**   Plan: **H1**
15 quai Koch – ℰ 03 88 36 47 75
– www.lepontdesvosges.fr – Closed Sunday
Carte 38/65 €
• Traditional cuisine • Brasserie • Friendly •
Located on the corner of an old building, this brasserie is renowned for its
copious, traditional cuisine. Vintage advertising posters and mirrors decorate
the dining room.

X **La Brasserie des Haras**   Plan: **F2**
23 r. des Glacières – ℰ 03 88 24 00 00
– www.les-haras-hotel.com
Menu 34/71 € – Carte 34/59 €
• Modern cuisine • Design •
In the former national stud farm built in the reign of Louis XV, an elegant and
refined restaurant run by starred chef Marc Haeberlin. Contemporary decor,
open kitchens, fine traditional dishes and local specialities.

X **Le Bistrot du Boulanger**   Plan: **H2**
42 r. de Zürich – ℰ 03 88 37 95 95
– www.aupaindemongrandpere.com – Closed 8 to 15 August,
23 December-3 January and Sunday dinner
Menu 15 € (weekday lunch)/29 € – Carte 27/46 €
• Traditional cuisine • Bistro • Friendly •
In the Krutenau quarter, a business-man-turned-master-baker has joined forces
with his son to give diners their take on bistro cuisine. Mission accomplished!
The traditional dishes on offer are generous and tasty.

X **Pierre Bois & Feu**   Plan: **G2**
6 r. du Bain-aux-Roses – ℰ 03 88 36 25 59
– www.pierreboisetfeu.fr – Closed 1 week in February, 2 weeks in August,
Sunday and lunch
Menu 44/150 € – Carte 55/232 €
• Traditional cuisine • Bistro •
In a narrow street near the waterfront, this contemporary bistro is housed in a
building dating from the 17C. Inside, bare wood tables, open kitchens, seasonal
dishes and fine local produce, with a speciality that begs to be tried: Salers beef
cooked with an iron!

WINSTUBS *Regional specialities and wine tasting in a typical
Alsatian atmosphere*

X **Au Pont du Corbeau**   Plan: **G2**
21 quai St-Nicolas – ℰ 03 88 35 60 68 – Closed 1 week
February Holidays, 25 July-22 August, Sunday lunch and Saturday except
in December
Menu 31 € – Carte 31/52 €
• Alsatian • Traditional • Friendly •
Experience local gastronomic specialities and traditional decor (Renaissance
features, posters) in this restaurant next door to the Musée Alsacien, with its displays of popular art.

X **Le Clou**   Plan: **G1-2**
3 r. du Chaudron – ℰ 03 88 32 11 67
– www.le-clou.com – Closed Sunday
Menu 19 € (weekday lunch) – Carte 28/56 €
• Alsatian • Rustic • Friendly •
Located a short distance from the cathedral, this authentic winstub (typical
Alsace bistro) is packed with olde worlde objects and scenes from yesteryear
(beautiful marquetry). Typical cuisine which pays homage to the region.

Le Tire-Bouchon ⌂ 🅰🅒 ⇔

5 r. des Tailleurs-de-Pierre – ☏ 03 88 22 16 32 Plan: **G2**
– www.letirebouchon.fr
Menu 14 € (weekday lunch), 24/29 € – Carte 27/47 €
• Traditional cuisine • Friendly • Traditional •
In a picturesque little street a stone's throw from the cathedral, don't pass by this winstub, which represents Alsace-style good living! An inviting decor (wood panelling, low lighting), lovely regional cooking and local wines: what more could you ask for?

Fink'Stuebel

26 r. Finkwiller – ☏ 03 88 25 07 57 Plan: **F2**
– www.restaurant-finkstuebel.com – Closed 3 weeks in August, Saturday and Sunday
Carte 33/65 €
• Alsatian • Family • Inn •
Half-timbering, wooden floorboards, painted woodwork, regional furniture and floral tablecloths provide the decor in the Fink'Stuebel, the epitome of a traditional winstub. Local cuisine predominates here, of course, with foie gras to the fore.

GERMANY
DEUTSCHLAND

→ **AREA:**
357 111 km·(137 735 sq mi).

→ **POPULATION:**
80 761 060 inhabitants.
Density = 226 per km².

→ **CAPITAL:**
Berlin.

→ **CURRENCY:**
Euro (€).

→ **GOVERNMENT:**
Parliamentary federal
republic, comprising 16 states
(Länder) since 1990. Member
of European Union since 1957
(one of the 6 founding countries).

→ **LANGUAGE:**
German.

→ **PUBLIC HOLIDAYS:**
New Year's Day (1 Jan); Epiphany
(6 Jan - certain regions only); Good
Friday (late Mar/Apr); Easter Monday
(late Mar/Apr); Labor Day (1 May);
Ascension Day (May); Whit Monday
(late May/June); Corpus Christi (late
May/June – certain regions only);
Assumption of the Virgin Mary
(15 Aug); Day of German Unity
(3 Oct); Reformation Day (31 Oct -
new Federal States only);
All Saints' Day (1 Nov); Day of Prayer
& Repentance (21 Nov, certain
regions only); Christmas Day (25
Dec); Boxing Day (26 Dec).

→ **LOCAL TIME:**
GMT+1 hour in winter and GMT
+2 hours in summer.

→ **CLIMATE:**
Temperate continental, with cold
winters and warm summers (Berlin:
January 0°C; July 20°C).

● Hamburg

BERLIN ●

Cologne
●

● Frankfurt

Munich
●

→ **EMERGENCY:**
Police ☏ 110; Medical Assistance
and Fire Brigade ☏ 112.
(Dialling 112 within any EU country
will redirect your call and contact
the emergency services.)

→ **ELECTRICITY:**
230 volts AC, 50Hz; 2 round pin
sockets.

→ **FORMALITIES**
Travellers from the European Union
(EU), Switzerland, Iceland and the
main countries of North and South
America need a national identity
card or passport (America: passport
required) to visit Germany for
less than three months (tourism
or business purpose). For visitors
from other countries a visa may be
required, in addition to a passport,
especially for those wishing to
stay for longer than three months.
We advise you to check with your
embassy before travelling.

BERLIN
BERLIN

Population: 3 501 880

S. Guillot/MICHELIN

Berlin's parliament faces an intriguing dilemma when it comes to where to call its heart, as, although they are homogeneous in many other ways, the east and the west of the city still lay claim to separate centres after 40 years of partition. Following the tempestuous 1990s, Berlin sought to resolve its new identity, and it now stands proud as one of the most dynamic and forward thinking cities in the world. Alongside its idea of tomorrow, it's never lost sight of its bohemian past, and many parts of the city retain the arty sense of adventure that characterised downtown Berlin during the 1920s: turn any corner and you might find a modernist art gallery, a tiny cinema or a cutting-edge club.

The eastern side of the River Spree, around Nikolaiviertel, is the historic heart of the city, dating back to the 13C. Meanwhile, way over to the west of the centre lie Kurfürstendamm and Charlottenburg; smart districts which came to the fore after World War II as the heart of West Berlin. Between the two lie imposing areas which swarm with visitors: Tiergarten is the green lung of the city, and just to its east is the great boulevard of Unter den Linden. Continuing eastward, the self-explanatory Museum Island sits snugly and securely in the tributaries of the Spree. The most southerly of Berlin's sprawling districts is Kreuzberg, renowned for its bohemian, alternative character.

BERLIN IN...

→ **ONE DAY**
Unter den Linden, Museum Island, Nikolaiviertel, coffee at TV Tower.

→ **TWO DAYS**
Potsdamer Platz, Reichstag, Regierungsviertel including the Gemäldegalerie, concert at Philharmonie.

→ **THREE DAYS**
KaDeWe, Kurfürstendamm, Charlottenburg Palace.

PRACTICAL INFORMATION

ARRIVAL-DEPARTURE

✈ Berlin Tegel Airport lies 12km northwest.

✈ Berlin Schönefeld is 21km southeast.

U-Bahn and S-Bahn trains operate from both.

GETTING AROUND

The U- and S-Bahn trains are quick and efficient but the bus is another good alternative; routes 100 and 200 incorporate most of the top attractions. Trams operate mainly within East Berlin. There are various ticketing options - check with a tourist information office or simply invest in a Berlin Welcome Card, which provides unlimited travel on the S-Bahn, and discounts for selected theatres, museums, attractions and city tours; buy one from a public transport ticket desk, a tourist information office or one of many hotels. Cyclists are well looked after here; there are many cycling routes and most of the main roads have separate cycle lanes and special traffic lights at intersections.

CALENDAR HIGHLIGHTS

January
International Green Week.

February
Berlin Film Festival (Berlinale).

May
Karneval der Kulturen.

July
Classic Open Air Festival.

August
Biennale.

September
Berlin Music Week, International Literary Festival.

October
Berlin Festival of Lights.

EATING OUT

Many of Berlin's best restaurants are found within the grand hotels and you only have to go to Savignyplatz near Ku'damm to realise how smart dining has taken off. Dinner is the most popular meal and you can invariably eat late, as lots of places stay open until 2 or 3am. Berlin also has a reputation for simple, hearty dishes, inspired by the long, hard winter and, when temperatures drop, the city's comfort food has an irresistible allure – there's pork knuckle, Schnitzel, Bratwurst in mustard, chunky dumplings... and the real Berlin favourite, Currywurst. Bread and potatoes are ubiquitous but since reunification, many dishes have also incorporated a more global influence, so produce from the local forests, rivers and lakes may well be given an Asian or Mediterranean twist (Berlin now claims a wider range of restaurants than any other German city). Service is included in the price of your meal but it's customary to round up the bill. Be sure to try the local 'Berliner Weisse mit Schuss' – a light beer with a dash of raspberry or woodruff.

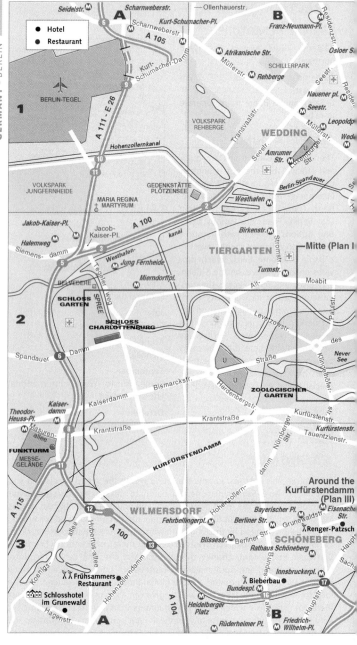

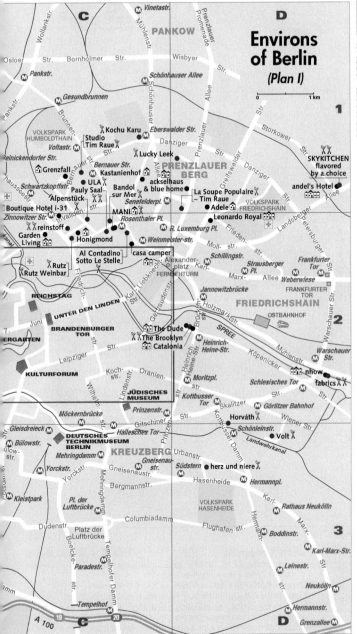

Environs
of Berlin
(Plan I)

0   1 km

PANKOW

Vinetastr.
Prenzlauer Promenade
Wisbyer Str.
Schönhauser Allee
Mühlenstr.
Wollankstr.
Osloer Str.
Bornholmer Str.
Pankstr.
Gesundbrunnen
Storkower Str.
Eberswalder Str.
Danziger
VOLKSPARK HUMBOLDTHAIN
Reinickendorfer Str.
Voltastr.
Kochu Karu
Studio Tim Raue
Bernauer Str.
Grenzfall
Lucky Leek
SKYKITCHEN flavored by a.choice
andel's Hotel
Schwartzkopffstr.
ULA
Pauly Saal
Alpenstück
Kastanienhof
Bandol sur Mer
ackselhaus & blue home
PRENZLAUER BERG
Greifswalder Str.
Danziger Str.
Prenzlauer Allee
Boutique Hotel i-31
Zinnowitzer Str.
Invalidenstr.
MANI
Senefelderpl.
Rosenthaler Pl.
La Soupe Populaire — Tim Raue
Adele
VOLKSPARK FRIEDRICHSHAIN
Landsberger Allee
Petersburger Str.
reinstoff
Garden Living
Honigmond
Weinmeister-str.
R. Luxemburg Pl.
Leonardo Royal
Al Contadino Sotto Le Stelle
casa camper
Karl-Liebknecht-Str.
Alexander-platz
Moll- str.
Schillingstr.
Strausberger Pl.
Frankfurter Tor
Weberwiese
Rutz
Rutz Weinbar
Friedrichstr.
FERNSEHTURM
Marx- Allee
FRANKFURTER TOR
FRIEDRICHSHAIN
REICHSTAG
UNTER DEN LINDEN
Grenadierstr.
Jannowitzbrücke
Holzmarktstr.
OSTBAHNHOF
Warschauer Str.
Juni
BRANDENBURGER TOR
The Dude
The Brooklyn
Catalonia
SPREE
Köpenicker Str.
Mühlenstr.
Warschauer Str.
ERGARTEN
Leipziger Str.
Oranien- str.
Heinrich-Heine-Str.
nhow
fabrics
KULTURFORUM
Koch- str.
Wilhelm- str.
Lindenstr.
JÜDISCHES MUSEUM
Moritzpl.
Kottbusser Tor
Schlesisches Tor
Görlitzer Bahnhof
Möckernbrücke
Prinzenstr.
Skalitzer Str.
Wiener Str.
Gleisdreieck
Bülowstr.
Hallesches Tor
Gitschiner Str.
Horváth
Schönleinstr.
Volt
DEUTSCHES TECHNIKMUSEUM BERLIN
Mehringdamm
Gneisenau- str.
KREUZBERG
Urbanstr.
Landwehrkanal
Bülow- str.
Yorckstr.
Yorckstr.
Gneisenaustr.
Südstern
herz und niere
Hermannpl.
Kleistpark
Pl. der Luftbrücke
Bergmannstr.
Hasenheide
VOLKSPARK HASENHEIDE
Karl- Marx- Str.
Rathaus Neukölln
Dudenstr.
Columbiadamm
Flughafen-str.
Boddinstr.
Platz der Luftbrücke
Tempelhofer Damm
Karl-Marx-Str.
Paradestr.
Leinestr.
Neukölln
Hermannstr.
Tempelhof
A 100
19
C
20
Grenzallee
D

301

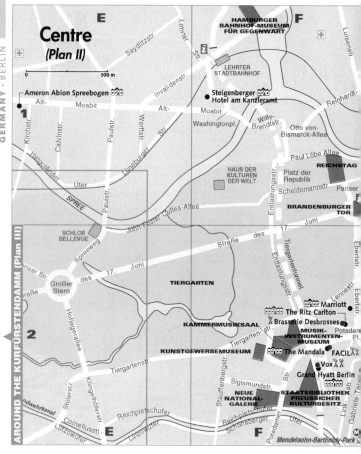

Centre
(Plan II)

0   500 m

Ameron Abion Spreebogen

HAMBURGER BAHNHOF-MUSEUM FÜR GEGENWART

LEHRTER STADTBAHNHOF

Steigenberger Hotel am Kanzleramt

Alt-Moabit

Washingtonpl.

Willy-Brandtstr.

Otto von-Bismarck-Allee

Paul Löbe Allee

REICHSTAG

Platz der Republik

Scheidemannstr.

Pariser

HAUS DER KULTUREN DER WELT

BRANDENBURGER TOR

John-Foster-Dulles-Allee

SCHLOß BELLEVUE

Straße des 17. Juni

Großer Stern

TIERGARTEN

Tiergartentunnel

Marriott
The Ritz Carlton
Brasserie Desbrosses

MUSIK-INSTRUMENTEN-MUSEUM

KAMMERMUSIKSAAL

KUNSTGEWERBEMUSEUM

The Mandala   FACIL

Vox

Grand Hyatt Berlin

NEUE NATIONAL-GALERIE

STAATSBIBLIOTHEK PREUSSICHER KULTURBESITZ

Sigismundstr.

Reichpietschufer

Schöneberger Ufer

Mendelsohn-Bartholdy-Park

Adlon Kempinski

Unter den Linden 77 ⊠ 10117 – Ⓜ Brandenburger Tor   Plan: **G1**
– 𝒞 (030) 2 26 10 – www.hotel-adlon.de
337 rm – ♦240/720 € ♦♦240/720 € – 🖵 42 € – 45 suites
· Grand Luxury · Historic · Classic ·

Situated in the capital, this imposing grand hotel, which has hosted a list of crowned heads far too long to cite here, is synonymous with glitz and glamour. Magical, luxurious ambience, plus presidential suites with limousine and butler service.

✿✿ **Lorenz Adlon Esszimmer · Quarré** – See restaurant listing

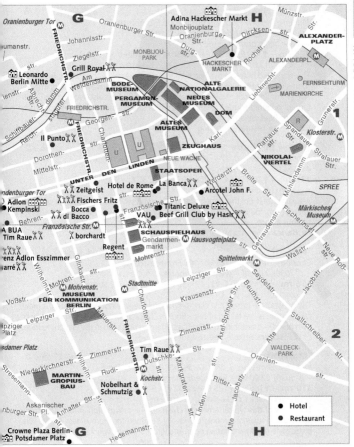

The Ritz-Carlton

Potsdamer Platz 3 ⊠ *10785 –* Ⓜ *Potsdamer Platz*
– ℰ *(030) 33 77 77 – www.ritzcarlton.de/berlin*

Plan: **F2**

263 rm – ♦195/450 € ♦♦195/450 € – ☐ 38 € – 40 suites
• Grand Luxury • Chain hotel • Classic •

One of the most exclusive hotel addresses in Germany. The elegant lobby with
its cantilevered marble staircase is home to a stylish lounge where guests
gather for classic 'teatime' treats.

Brasserie Desbrosses – See restaurant listing

303

Grand Hyatt Berlin
✿ ⅃๓ ⊕ ⌂ ⌶ ⅟ Ⓐ⏨ ⅀

Marlene-Dietrich-Platz 2 (Entrance on Eichhornstraße)   Plan: **F2**
✉ *10785* – **Ⓜ** *Potsdamer Platz* – ✆ *(030) 25 53 12 34*
– www.berlin.grand.hyatt.com
326 rm – ✝199 € ✝✝199 € – ⌓ 36 € – 16 suites
• Grand Luxury • Chain hotel • Design •

This trapezoid hotel on the Potsdamer Platz impresses with modern, high-tech rooms decorated in a minimalist style. The Club Olympus Spa with its impressive swimming pool and views over the roofs of Berlin is also worth a look. Restaurant options include Vox and Mesa which serves a range of dishes from curry wurst to beef roulade.
Vox – See restaurant listing

Hotel de Rome
✿ ⅃๓ ๓ ⌶ ⅟ Ⓐ⏨ ⅀ ⊕

Behrenstr. 37 ✉ *10117* – **Ⓜ** *Französische Str.* – ✆ *(030)*   Plan: **G1**
4 60 60 90 – www.hotelderome.de
136 rm – ✝260/595 € ✝✝260/595 € – ⌓ 35 € – 9 suites
• Grand Luxury • Classic •

A luxury hotel on the Bebelplatz in the impressive framework of a building dating from 1889, formerly used by the Dresdner Bank. Today, the old strongroom is a pool.
La Banca – See restaurant listing

Regent
✿ ⅃๓ ๓ ⌶ ⅟ Ⓐ⏨ ⅀ ⊕

Charlottenstr. 49 ✉ *10117* – **Ⓜ** *Französische Str.*   Plan: **G1**
– ✆ (030) 2 03 38 – www.regenthotels.com/berlin
156 rm – ✝249/850 € ✝✝249/850 € – ⌓ 35 € – 39 suites
• Grand Luxury • Classic •

The guests here expect first class service and they are not disappointed. A pleasant custom is the taking of tea – English-, Russian- or Saxony-style (the hotel's own blend) – on nothing but the finest Meissen porcelain in the elegant lounge.
✿✿ **Fischers Fritz** – See restaurant listing

Marriott
✿ ⅃๓ ๓ ⌶ ⅟ Ⓐ⏨ ⅀ ⊕

Inge-Beisheim-Platz 1 ✉ *10785* – **Ⓜ** *Potsdamer Platz*   Plan: **F2**
– ✆ (030) 22 00 00 – www.berlinmarriott.de
370 rm – ✝185 € ✝✝185 € – ⌓ 32 € – 9 suites
• Chain hotel • Luxury • Contemporary •

The lobby of this typical American chain hotel is a 40m high atrium. The comfortable and luxurious rooms are ideally designed for the business guest. This bistro-style restaurant has an open kitchen and a large window façade.

The Mandala
✿ ⅃๓ ⊕ ๓ Ⓐ⏨ ⅀

Potsdamer Str. 3 ✉ *10785* – **Ⓜ** *Potsdamer Platz*   Plan: **F2**
– ✆ (030) 5 90 05 00 00 – www.themandala.de
131 rm – ✝170/270 € ✝✝170/300 € – ⌓ 29 € – 26 suites
• Business • Luxury • Design •

This hotel in the Potsdamer Platz opposite the Sony Center with its range of spacious and simple yet luxurious rooms and suites boasts an unusual spa. The trendy Bar Qiu serves business lunches.
✿✿ **FACIL** – See restaurant listing

Titanic Deluxe
✿ ⅃๓ ๓ ⅟ Ⓐ⏨ ⅀ ⊕

Französische Str. 30 ✉ *10117* – **Ⓜ** *Hausvogteiplatz*   Plan: **G1**
– ✆ (030) 20 14 37 00 – www.titanic-hotels.de
200 rm – ✝160/290 € ✝✝160/290 € – ⌓ 28 € – 8 suites
• Townhouse • Business • Modern •

Despite its city centre location, the Titanic Deluxe – set in the former costume department of the Berlin State Opera – really is a little world of its own. The design is chic, from the bright, marble lobby to the stylishly modern rooms and the large hammam. Café Parisienne.
Beef Grill Club by Hasir – See restaurant listing

GERMANY - BERLIN

Steigenberger Hotel am Kanzleramt

Ella-Trebe-Str. 5 ✉ *10557 –* Ⓜ *Hauptbahnhof –* ℰ *(030)*
7 40 74 30 – www.kanzleramt-berlin.steigenberger.com   Plan: **F1**
328 rm – ✝119/299 € ✝✝119/299 € – ☑ 25 € – 11 suites
• Business • Modern •

A modern, minimalist style hotel with a spacious lobby and an attractive leisure area with a view of Berlin's Government Quarter. Breakfast is served in a light and airy room on the first floor and meals at No. 5 (restaurant and bar). Convenient location next to the main railway station.

Ameron Abion Spreebogen

Alt-Moabit 99 ✉ *10559 –* Ⓜ *Turmstr. –* ℰ *(030)*   Plan: **E1**
39 92 00 – www.abion-hotel.de
234 rm – ✝80/100 € ✝✝80/100 € – ☑ 19 € – 9 suites
• Business • Contemporary •

You won't find a more attractive location than the one enjoyed by this comfortable, contemporary hotel overlooking the River Spree and its elegantly luxurious Abion Villa, a sort of hotel within a hotel next door. The Lanninger restaurant with its pretty terrace serves regional fare. Another exclusive feature: from April to October you can organise events for up to 20 people on the hotel's 1930s yacht, Aida.

Crowne Plaza Berlin - Potsdamer Platz

Hallesche Str. 10 ✉ *10963 –* Ⓜ *Potsdamer Platz*   Plan: **G2**
– ℰ (030) 8 01 06 60 – www.crowneplaza.com/potsdamerplatz
237 rm – ✝109/344 € ✝✝119/354 € – ☑ 19 € – 19 suites
• Chain hotel • Historic • Modern •

Set in a listed 1930s postal sorting office next to the Tempodrom, this hotel is both comfortable and modern. It offers a wide range of smart guestrooms decorated in warm colours, as well as good events facilities. The Post restaurant serves regional vegetarian and international cuisine.

Boutique Hotel i-31

Invalidenstr. 31 ✉ *10115 –* Ⓜ *Naturkundemuseum*   Plan I: **C1**
– ℰ (030) 3 38 40 00 – www.hotel-i31.de
117 rm – ✝107/999 € ✝✝107/999 € – ☑ 17 €
• Business • Personalised • Modern •

This boutique hotel with its designer interior stands in the heart of Berlin-Mitte, still one of the trendiest parts of Berlin. The fresh, comfortable rooms – categorised as 'Pure', 'White' and 'Brown' – all come with a free mini-bar and the latest in modern technology.

nhow

Stralauer Allee 3 ✉ *10245 –* Ⓜ *Warschauer Str.*   Plan I: **D2**
– ℰ (030) 2 90 29 90 – www.nhow-hotels.com/berlin
303 rm – ✝95/155 € ✝✝95/155 € – ☑ 24 € – 1 suite
• Business • Design • Minimalist •

No other hotel in Berlin combines music and lifestyle in such an unconventional and cosmopolitan manner. Clean lines and functional architecture outside; upbeat design, curved forms and young, fresh colours inside. And with its recording studio looking out over the city, it really is one of a kind!
fabrics – See restaurant listing

Leonardo Royal

Otto-Braun-Str. 90 ✉ *10249 –* Ⓜ *Alexanderplatz*   Plan I: **D2**
– ℰ (030) 7 55 43 00 – www.leonardo-hotels.com
343 rm – ✝79/299 € ✝✝79/299 € – ☑ 19 € – 3 suites
• Business • Modern •

This modern business hotel near Friedrichshain Park offers good transport links and smart rooms including special "Ladies Rooms". It also has conference facilities for up to 700 participants. This spacious restaurant serves international cuisine.

GERMANY - BERLIN

Adina Hackescher Markt

An der Spandauer Brücke 11 ✉ *10178*   Plan: **H1**
– **M** *Alexanderplatz* – ℰ *(030) 2 09 69 80* – *www.adina.eu*
90 rm – ♦109/179 € ♦♦109/179 € – ☱ 19 € – 55 suites
• Business • Modern •

This hotel is resolutely fashionable. From the lobby and bar serving international snacks, through to the guestrooms, each with its own cowhide cube stool. The small fitness and sauna area has two indoor Jacuzzis crowned by a starlit ceiling.

Arcotel John F

Werderscher Markt 11 ✉ *10117* – **M** *Französische Str.*   Plan: **H1**
– ℰ *(030) 4 05 04 60* – *www.arcotelhotels.com/de/john_f_hotel_berlin*
187 rm – ♦89/325 € ♦♦89/325 € – ☱ 22 € – 3 suites
• Business • Modern •

This designer hotel located next to the German Foreign Office is dedicated to John F. Kennedy and offers attractive, modern rooms with rocking chairs, including themed 'Kennedy' and 'International Style' rooms. This restaurant serves international dishes.

The Dude

Köpenicker Str. 92 ✉ *10179* – **M** *Heinrich-Heine-Str.*   Plan I: **D2**
– ℰ *(030) 4 11 98 81 77* – *www.thedudeberlin.com*
27 rm – ♦109/199 € ♦♦149/239 € – ☱ 18 €
• Townhouse • Historic • Personalised •

This is design in its purest form. The mix of historical detail (the building dates back to 1822) and modern style is reminiscent of a mansion house. If you are in search of a snack, the Deli serves sandwiches at lunchtime. Breakfast is also available.

The Brooklyn – See restaurant listing

Garden Living

Invalidenstr.101 ✉ *10115* – **M** *Zinnowitzer Straße*   Plan I: **C2**
– ℰ *(030) 2 84 45 59 00* – *www.gardenliving.de*
30 rm – ♦99/124 € ♦♦119/139 € – ☱ 8 €
• Townhouse • Personalised •

Part of the ethos at the Garden Living is to make you feel as if you are 'staying at home'. This is indeed the impression you get in this pretty group of three old townhouses with their generously sized and tastefully appointed apartments, each with their own small kitchen. The attractive interior courtyard or 'Green Oasis' makes the ideal place for breakfast on a lovely summer's morning.

casa camper

Weinmeisterstr. 1 ✉ *10178* – **M** *Weinmeisterstr.*   Plan I: **C2**
– ℰ *(030) 20 00 34 10* – *www.casacamper.com*
48 rm ☱ – ♦152/278 € ♦♦193/319 € – 3 suites
• Business • Design • Functional •

Fernando Amat and Jordi Tio are behind the design of this high quality interior. The room are decorated in striking red and warm wood. Free snacks in "Tentempié" on the seventh floor.

Leonardo Berlin Mitte

Bertolt Brecht Platz 4 ✉ *10117* – **M** *Friedrichstr.*   Plan: **G2**
– ℰ *(030) 3 74 40 50 00* – *www.leonardo-hotels.com*
308 rm – ♦89/139 € ♦♦89/139 € – ☱ 20 € – 1 suite
• Townhouse • Business • Contemporary •

Boasting a stylish interior from the lobby through to the functional guestrooms, the Leonardo also enjoys a central yet quiet location. After exploring the city you can relax in the small leisure area on the ninth floor.

Catalonia
🏆 👤 AC 🛎

Köpenicker Str. 80 ✉ 10178 – Ⓜ Märk. Museum
– 𝒞 (030) 24 08 47 70 – www.hoteles-catalonia.com
131 rm ⌛ – 📍79/999 € 📍📍89/999 €
Plan I: **D2**
• Chain hotel • Modern • Stylish •
Catalonia is the so-called 'pilot project' of a Catalan hotel group in Germany. The unusual lobby design reflects the variety and changing landscape of Berlin and the landings feature some impressive graffiti. The restaurant serves a mix of Berlin and Spanish cuisine including tapas.

ackselhaus & blue home

Belforter Str. 21 ✉ 10405 – Ⓜ Senefelderplatz
– 𝒞 (030) 44 33 76 33 – www.ackselhaus.de
31 rm ⌛ – 📍110/170 € 📍📍150/360 € – 4 suites
Plan I: **D1**
• Townhouse • Historic • Personalised •
This establishment has a really special historical charm. It is Venetian in style with blue tones. The green inner courtyards with their lounge feel are very pretty.

MANI
🏆 👤 AC

Torstr. 136 ✉ 10119 – Ⓜ Rosenthaler Platz – 𝒞 (030)
53 02 80 80 – www.amanogroup.de
63 rm – 📍70/189 € 📍📍75/189 € – ⌛ 15 €
Plan I: **C2**
• Business • Modern •
This is one of the new stylish boutique hotels in Berlin – chic, fashionable and truly the place to be. The guestrooms are decorated in minimalist-style with dark colours.
MANI – See restaurant listing

Honigmond
🏆 🛎

Tieckstr. 11 ✉ 10115 – Ⓜ Zinnowitzer Str. – 𝒞 (030)
2 84 45 50 – www.honigmond.de
60 rm – 📍89/165 € 📍📍120/209 € – ⌛ 10 €
Plan I: **C2**
• Historic • Classic • Personalised •
Built in 1895 this house in a quiet side street has individually-styled rooms. The Garden Hotel 350m away has a lovely inner courtyard garden. Pleasant coffee shop-cum-restaurant in a classic setting.

Kastanienhof
🛎 🅿

Kastanienallee 65 ✉ 10119 – Ⓜ Senefelderpl.
– 𝒞 (030) 44 30 50 – www.kastanienhof.biz
44 rm – 📍65/149 € 📍📍87/179 € – ⌛ 9 € – 2 suites
Plan I: **C1**
• Townhouse • Functional •
This well-managed hotel offering functional rooms is run by a real Berliner who has decorated it with a vast array of mementos of "his" city.

Grenzfall
🏆 👤 👤 🛎 🚗

Ackerstr. 136 ✉ 13355 – Ⓜ Bernauer Str. – 𝒞 (030)
34 33 33 00 – www.hotel-grenzfall.de
37 rm – 📍63/179 € 📍📍83/199 € – ⌛ 11 €
Plan I: **C1**
• Townhouse • Functional •
The Grenzfall's attractions include a friendly welcome, a 3 000m² garden and its reasonable prices. The hotel, located in a quiet side street close to the site of the former Berlin wall, provides employment opportunities for the disabled. The contemporary feel also extends to the restaurant, which boasts a terrace overlooking the garden.

Adele

Greifswalder Str. 227 ✉ 10405 – Ⓜ Alexanderplatz
– 𝒞 (030) 44 32 43 10 – www.adele-berlin.de
13 rm ⌛ – 📍89/129 € 📍📍109/169 € – 3 suites
Plan I: **D1**
• Townhouse • Design •
This small and very exclusive boutique hotel is furnished in Art Deco-style. It has comfortable, pretty guestrooms and a very modern breakfast room.

XxXxX **Lorenz Adlon Esszimmer** – Hotel Adlon Kempinski

  🕸 ₺ AC

£3 £3 *Unter den Linden 77* ✉ *10117 –* Ⓜ *Brandenburger Tor*
– ℰ (030) 22 61 19 60 – www.lorenzadlon-esszimmer.de   Plan: **G1**
– Closed 1-12 January, 27 March-5 April, 24 July-23 August, 23 October-
1 November and Sunday-Monday
Menu 140/195 € – Carte 136/166 € – *(dinner only)*
• Creative • Luxury • Elegant •
Eminently elegant and luxurious, this restaurant pays tribute to the hotel's foun-
der Lorenz Adlon. You can eat in the dining room with its fine wood panelling
and open fire, or in the library. Sample either of Hendrik Otto's two menus to
find out just how skilfully he combines classic dishes and contemporary ele-
ments.
➔ Kohlrabi, Krustentierfond, Jakobsmuschel, junger Lauch, Meerrettich.
Taube, Pfeffersauce, Sellerie, Spinat, Petersilie, Curry, Koriander. Erdbeere,
Erbsen, Schokolade, Holunder, Minze, Rosmarin.

XxXX **Fischers Fritz** – Hotel Regent   🕸 ₺ AC ⇦ 🚗

£3 £3 *Charlottenstr. 49* ✉ *10117 –* Ⓜ *Französische Str.*   Plan: **G1**
– ℰ (030) 20 33 63 63 – www.fischersfritzberlin.com – Closed end July
- mid August
Menu 105/180 € – Carte 105/154 € – *(dinner only) (booking advisable)*
• Classic cuisine • Elegant •
The elegant wood panelling, open fire and fine chandeliers at Fischers Fritz are
somewhat reminiscent of the classic English style. While Christian Lohse's fish
inspired cuisine, unforgettable for its use of high quality produce and painsta-
king preparation, clearly shares equally classic roots. It is not for nothing that the
restaurant has been awarded two Michelin stars for the past nine years!
➔ Gebackenes Demeter Onsenei mit Spitzmorcheln, Kopfsalatcrème und
Bärlauch. Bretonischer Hummer geröstet mit Salz, Chili und Koriander.
Gebratener Seeteufel, karamellisierter Chicorée und Japanrettich, Jus von
Spätburgunder.

XxX **FACIL** – Hotel The Mandala   🕸 🛋 ₺ AC 🚗

£3 £3 *Potsdamer Str. 3 (5th floor)* ✉ *10785*   Plan: **F2**
– Ⓜ *Potsdamer Platz – ℰ (030) 5 90 05 12 34 – www.facil.de – Closed*
2 weeks January, 3 weeks July - August and Saturday-Sunday
Menu 45 € (weekday lunch)/185 €
– Carte 104/127 € – (booking advisable)
• Creative • Minimalist •
It's hard to imagine a more pleasant place to eat – not even outside in a leafy
courtyard. When the glass frontage and roof are opened up in the summer this
already light and airy restaurant almost becomes a terrace – and it's hard to
believe that you're up on the fifth floor! The main attraction here, however, is
Michael Kempf's excellent cuisine. Its classic roots provide vigour and intensity,
while his modern interpretations make for exciting dishes rich in contrast in
which vegetables play an increasingly important role.
➔ Rochenflügel, Marinda-Tomate und Limonenseitling. Taube, Sauerampf-
fer, Mohn und Karotte. Lammrücken, grüner Anis, Rettich und Roggenbrot.

XxX **VAU** (Kolja Kleeberg)   🕸 🛋 AC ⇦

£3 *Jägerstr. 54* ✉ *10117 –* Ⓜ *Französische Str. – ℰ (030)*   Plan: **G1**
2 02 97 30 – www.vau-berlin.de – Closed Sunday
Menu 120/160 €
• Creative • Fashionable •
The well-practised kitchen team at this restaurant produces two set evening
menus full of flavour and aromas. 'Improvisation' is modern and creative, while
'Komposition' is more classic. There is a simpler menu at lunchtimes. As for the
interior, the hand of star architect Meinrad von Gerkan is clear for all to see.
➔ Temperierter Kalmar, Mandeln, Liebstöckel. Versängter Schweinebauch,
Apfel, Rettich, Frankfurter grüne Kräuter. Zander, saure Rüben, Brunnen-
kresse, junger Knoblauch.

XX
£3 £3   **reinstoff** (Daniel Achilles)   &. AC
Schlegelstr. 26c (Edison Höfe) ⊠ 10115   Plan I: **C2**
– ⓂZinnowitzerstr.
– ℰ (030) 30 88 12 14 – www.reinstoff.eu
– Closed Sunday-Monday
Menu 110/198 € – *(dinner only) (booking advisable)*
• Creative • Fashionable • Intimate •
This really is a very special restaurant. It is set in an old factory building with an
unusual minimalist-style room-in-a-room design. It has a discreet atmo-
sphere, first class service and one of the most interesting and exciting kitchens
in Berlin. With his 'ganz nah' (close to home) and 'weiter draußen' (further afield)
menus, Daniel Achilles shows that top-flight cuisine doesn't need luxury products. German and Spanish wines.
→ Muscheln, Fenchel von der Knospe bis zur Wurzel, würziger Sud. Regen-
bogenforelle, Feldmohn, Kapuzinerkresse und Radieschen. Querrippe vom
Rind mit Ochsenmark und Maistortilla.

XX
£3 £3   **Tim Raue**   &. AC
Rudi-Dutschke-Str. 26 ⊠ 10969 – Ⓜ Kochstr.   Plan: **G2**
– ℰ (030) 25 93 79 30
– www.tim-raue.com
– Closed 24-26 December and Sunday-Monday
Menu 38 € (lunch)/188 € – Carte 100/158 €
• Asian • Friendly • Fashionable •
Tim Raue's pared down Southeast Asian cuisine uses a small number of
high quality ingredients to great advantage. Sweet and savoury, mild and
sharp, soft and crispy – his dishes are a riot of contrasting textures and fla-
vours, always combined to perfection. The lunchtime menu is particularly
popular.
→ Jakobsmuschel, Holunderblüte und Zitronengras. Schweinekinn,
Papaya und Thai Basilikum. Gedämpfter Steinbutt mit Lauch und Ingwer.

XX
£3   **Pauly Saal**   🛖
Auguststr. 11 ⊠ 10117 – Ⓜ Rosenthaler Pl.   Plan I: **C2**
– ℰ (030) 33 00 60 70
– www.paulysaal.com
– Closed Sunday-Monday
Menu 45 € (lunch)/120 € – *(booking advisable)*
• Modern cuisine • Fashionable •
If you are looking for somewhere elegant yet relaxed to eat, this is the place for
you. The high-ceilinged hall in this former Jewish girls' school boasts some stri-
king decorative rockets above the window into the kitchen, as well as stylish
Murano glass chandeliers. The classic cuisine, based on high quality produce,
comes without frills. Smaller lunchtime menu.
→ Kalbstatar, Quinoa, Radieschen, Basilikum. Rote Garnele, Graupen,
Navetten. Erdbeere, Waldmeister, Vanille, Meringue.

XX   **SRA BUA by Tim Raue** – Hotel Adlon Kempinski   🍸 &. AC
Behrenstr. 72 ⊠ 10117 – Ⓜ Brandenburger Tor   🚗
– ℰ (030) 22 61 15 90   Plan: **G1**
– www.srabua-adlon.de
– Closed 2 weeks July and Sunday-Monday
Menu 59/126 € – Carte 50/74 € – *(dinner only)*
• Asian • Elegant • Exotic •
SRA BUA, the latest hotspot at the Hotel Adlon, is well worth a visit, offering
ambitious pan-Asian cuisine. It combines Thai and Japanese influences and is
made using top quality ingredients. The truly unusual, elegant decor provides
the perfect foil to the slightly exotic food. The charming front-of-house team
completes the picture with its professional and attentive service.

GERMANY - BERLIN

XX **Richard**
🕸
Köpenicker Str. 174 (by Köpenicker Straße D2) ✉ *10997*
– Ⓜ *Schlesisches Tor* – ☎ *(030) 49 20 72 42* – *www.restaurant-richard.de*
– *Closed Sunday - Monday*
Menu 46/98 € – *(dinner only)*
• French classic • Fashionable • Trendy •
Yes, this really is it, but don't be put off by the somewhat lacklustre exterior. Inside
the former Köpenicker Hof, built in 1900, the fine interior has an ornate ceiling,
designer lighting and artworks (the owner Hans Richard is also a painter). It provi-
des the perfect setting for an excellent, artful and reasonably priced set menu.
➔ Artischocken à la Barigoule mit Sommertrüffel. Onglet vom Black Angus
mit Auberginencrème und Pimientos de Padron. Mille-feuille mit Himbee-
ren und Pistazien.

XX **Bocca di Bacco**   🕸 🄰🄲 ⇔
Friedrichstr. 167 ✉ *10117* – Ⓜ *Französische Str.*   Plan: **G1**
– ☎ *(030) 20 67 28 28* – *www.boccadibacco.de* – *Closed Sunday lunch and
Bank Holidays lunch*
Menu 20 € (weekday lunch) – Carte 42/62 €
• Italian • Fashionable •
This restaurant with a modern design has a bar and lounge area where good
Italian cuisine is served. Very friendly atmosphere. Beautiful function room on the
first-floor.

XX **Grill Royal**   🕸 🏠
Friedrichstr. 105b ✉ *10117* – Ⓜ *Oranienburger Tor*   Plan: **G1**
– ☎ *(030) 28 87 92 88* – *www.grillroyal.com*
Carte 43/118 € – *(dinner only) (booking advisable)*
• Barbecued • Trendy • Fashionable •
The place to eat on the River Spree, known for its grilled meats. Diners select the
cuts themselves from a glass chiller cabinet! Great selection of Bordeaux and
Italian wines.

XX **Il Punto**   🏠 ♿ 🄰🄲 ⇔
Neustädtische Kirchstr. 6 ✉ *10117* – Ⓜ *Friedrichstr.*   Plan: **G1**
– ☎ *(030) 20 60 55 40* – *www.ilpunto.net* – *Closed Saturday lunch and Sunday*
Menu 30 € (lunch)/80 € – Carte 43/55 €
• Italian • Elegant •
Popular with fans of Italian cuisine, Guiseppe Perna's Il Punto has a healthy fol-
lowing of regulars. His "paccheri alla Ciampi" owe their existence to a visit to
Germany by former Italian premier Dr. A. Ciampi. The tables in the glass-roofed
interior courtyard are particularly attractive.

XX **Zeitgeist**   🄰🄲
Friedrichstr. 84 / corner Unter den Linden (1st floor)   Plan: **G1**
✉ *10177* – Ⓜ *Französische Str.* – ☎ *(030) 20 92 13 13*
– *www.drive-volkswagen-group.com* – *Closed Saturday lunch and Sunday-
Monday*
Menu 34 € (lunch)/105 € – Carte 73/95 €
• Modern cuisine • Design • Trendy •
This latest dining hotspot is located within DRIVE, the VW Group Forum. Set on
the first floor, it offers stylish design and equally modern, ambitious cuisine,
which is upmarket in the evenings and a little simpler at lunchtimes. Try the
pigeon with lardon, celery and gooseberries.

XX **Quarré** – Hotel Adlon Kempinski   ⇐ 🏠 ♿ 🄰🄲 🚗
Unter den Linden 77 ✉ *10117* – Ⓜ *Brandenburger Tor*   Plan: **G1**
– ☎ *(030) 22 61 15 55* – *www.hotel-adlon.de*
Carte 43/89 €
• International • Brasserie •
A hotel like the Adlon naturally takes great pains to provide its guests with a
suitably stylish setting for their stay. Here at Quarré, for example, they have suc-
ceeded in creating an elegant dining environment and cosmopolitan meeting
place for a business lunch, dinner or Sunday brunch.

XX **Vox** – Hotel Grand Hyatt 🛋 👤 🅰🅲 ⇦
Marlene-Dietrich-Platz 2 (Entrance on Eichhornstraße) Plan: **F2**
✉ *10785* – 🔴 *Potsdamer Platz* – 𝒞 *(030) 25 53 17 72*
– *www.vox-restaurant.de* – *Closed Saturday lunch, Sunday lunch*
Menu 46/66 € (dinner) – Carte 48/77 €
• Modern cuisine • Brasserie • Design •
The decor at Vox is bright and modern. The large show kitchen offers guests the chance to watch the team, including the sushi chefs, at work.

XX **The Brooklyn** – Hotel The Dude
Köpenicker Str. 92 ✉ *10179* – 🔴 *Heinrich-Heine-Str.* Plan I: **D2**
– 𝒞 *(030) 20 21 58 20* – *www.thebrooklyn.de* – *Closed Sunday*
Carte 50/180 € – *(dinner only)*
• Barbecued • Individual •
The Brooklyn Beef Club provides the necessary New York-style to make sure you really enjoy your American steak from the grill. It is worth taking a look at the bar, where some 160 different whiskies are available by the glass.

XX **fabrics** – Hotel nhow 👤 🅰🅲 🚗
Stralauer Allee 3 ✉ *10245* – 🔴 *Warschauer Str.* Plan I: **D2**
– 𝒞 *(030) 2 90 29 90* – *www.nhow-hotels.com/berlin* – *Closed Sunday*
Menu 35 € – Carte 26/40 €
• Modern cuisine • Minimalist •
Cool design throughout in white, pink and a trendy green, giving a light and airy feel. The top quality produce in the kitchen is used to create house specials including classics such as steak Chateaubriand. Small lunchtime menu.

XX **La Banca** – Hotel de Rome 🛋 👤 🅰🅲 ⇦ 🚗
Behrenstr. 37 ✉ *10117* – 🔴 *Französische Str.* – 𝒞 *(030)* Plan: **G1**
46 06 09 12 01 – *www.hotelderome.de*
Menu 26 € (lunch)/72 € (dinner) – Carte 31/72 €
• Mediterranean • Cosy • Design •
A casual and yet classy restaurant which offers Mediterrenean cuisine made using fresh products. There is a terrace in the beautiful interior courtyard. Lunch menu with good value for money.

XX **Beef Grill Club by Hasir** – Hotel Titanic Deluxe 🛋 🅰🅲
Französische Str. 30 ✉ *10117* – 🔴 *Hausvogteiplatz* Plan: **G1**
– 𝒞 *(030) 20 14 37 08 60* – *www.titanic-hotels.de*
Menu 20/50 € – Carte 40/165 €
• International • Friendly •
This stylish grill/restaurant with its open show kitchen is a great place to sample some really excellent steak. Take a look in the meat maturing cabinet – this is where the excellent dry aged beef comes from.

X **Rutz** 🕸 🛋 🅰🅲
⸙ *Chausseestr. 8 (1st floor)* ✉ *10115*
– 🔴 *Oranienburger Tor* – 𝒞 *(030) 24 62 87 60* – *www.rutz-restaurant.de*
– *Closed 2 weeks early January and Sunday-Monday*
Menu 98/170 € – *(dinner only)*
• Modern cuisine • Trendy •
A friendly, modern restaurant, Rutz is the ideal place to enjoy a really good meal, and that is exactly what you can expect. Beautifully prepared food based on carefully selected, top-of-the-range ingredients in its own individual style. The set menu comes with four to ten courses.
➜ Verbenesud, Seezunge, Erbsen, Enten Aroma. Saure Beete, Hamachi und Sonnenblumenkerne, Koriander. Deichlamm, Senfkarotte, wilder Brokkoli, junger Knoblauch.
Rutz Weinbar – See restaurant listing

311

GERMANY - BERLIN

✗ Horváth 🍴 ♿

ⓢ ⓢ *Paul-Lincke-Ufer 44a* ✉ *10999* – Ⓜ *Schönleinstr.* Plan I: **D2**
– ℰ *(030) 61 28 99 92* – *www.restaurant-horvath.de* – *Closed Monday*
- Tuesday
Menu 63/119 € – Carte 64/91 € – *(dinner only) (booking advisable)*
• Creative • Minimalist •

With a choice of 12 dishes (including vegetarian options), which you can select in any combination to make four, eight or even the full twelve courses, you will soon be persuaded of the talent of Austrian-born chef Sebastian Frank. Passion, consummate skill, a great kitchen team and excellent produce are the ingredients that go to make up his uncomplicated yet creative cuisine.
→ Forelle, Melanzani, Schweinegoder. Kalbstafelspitz, Suppengemüse, Kerbel. Mispel, Röstgemüse, weiße Schokolade.

✗ Nobelhart & Schmutzig 🐜 AC

ⓢ *Friedrichstr. 218* ✉ *10969* – Ⓜ *Kochstr.* – ℰ *(030)* Plan: **G2**
25 94 06 10 – *www.nobelhartundschmutzig.com* – *Closed 2 weeks early*
January, mid July - mid August and Sunday-Monday
Menu 80 € – *(dinner only) (booking essential)*
• Creative • Trendy • Friendly •

This 'food bar' offers its own special mix of trendy, urban chic and relaxed but professional service. The cuisine also has its own particular style, consciously eschewing any hint of luxury or chichi. The powerful and creative food is made using predominantly regional Brandenburg produce. All in all, it is a real pleasure to eat here.
→ Müritz Saibling, Fenchel. Radieschen, Blutwurst, Petersilie. Kirschen, Hefe, Wacholder.

✗ Studio Tim Raue

Rheinsbergerstr. 76/77 ✉ *10115* – Ⓜ *Bernauer Str.* Plan I: **C1**
– ℰ *(030) 44 31 09 50* – *www.factoryberlin.com/studio* – *Closed Sunday-*
Monday
Menu 36 € (lunch)/108 € – Carte 42/66 €
• Modern cuisine • Fashionable • Friendly •

This restaurant is located right on the line of the former border between East and West. Diners at the chef's table find themselves sitting on what used to be the Berlin wall.

✗ La Soupe Populaire - Tim Raue 🅿

🍴 *Prenzlauer Allee 242* ✉ *10405* – ℰ *(030) 44 31 96 80* Plan I: **D1**
– *www.lasoupepopulaire.de* – *Closed 2 weeks January, 3 weeks August*
and Sunday-Wednesday
Carte 35/50 €
• Regional • Individual • Trendy •

The raw industrial architecture of the former Bötzow brewery provides a great backdrop for eating authentic Berlin food surrounded by art, steel girders and "shabby chic" furniture in this workshop building. In the kitchen, of course, Michael Jaeger brings a little of Raue's finesse to the good, plain food.

✗ Al Contadino Sotto Le Stelle 🍴 AC

Auguststr. 36 ✉ *10119* – Ⓜ *Rosenthaler Platz* Plan I: **C2**
– ℰ *(030) 2 81 90 23* – *www.alcontadino.eu* – *Closed Tuesday*
Menu 36/55 € – Carte 39/51 € – *(dinner only)*
• Italian • Cosy •

Located in the centre of Berlin-Mitte, close to the Marienkirche, Lucio Massaro has been running this friendly trattoria successfully for a number of years. It is popular for both its lively atmosphere and its flavoursome Italian fare. Try the ravioli with sea bass or the ossobuco. Two doors down you will find a delicatessen and snacks in the Mozzarella-Bar.

X **ULA** [AC]

Anklamer Str. 8 ⊠ 10178 Berlin – ⓂBernauer Str.   Plan I: **C1**
– ℰ (030) 89 37 95 70 – www.ulaberlin.jimdo.com – Closed Monday
Menu 35/65 € – Carte 16/45 € – *(dinner only)*
• Japanese • Minimalist •

ULA marks the meeting of Japanese art and cuisine. Based in the same building
as the gallery of the same name, the restaurant offers authentic Japanese cuisine including vegetarian options. The repertoire of chef Daisuke Nakashima
goes well beyond sushi and sashimi. Don't miss the two daily set menus.

X **Lucky Leek** 🈺

Kollwitzstr. 54 ⊠ 10178 – ⓂSenefelderplatz – ℰ (030)   Plan I: **D1**
66 40 87 10 – www.lucky-leek.com – Closed Monday-Tuesday
Menu 32/49 € – Carte 28/52 € – *(dinner only)*
• Vegetarian • Neighbourhood • Trendy •

Lucky Leek is a genuinely modern restaurant with a friendly, personal note. Josita
Hartanto cooks vegan cuisine including vegetable consommé with potato and
cress ravioli, pear and chilli risotto with tandoori cabbage and nori tempeh rolls.

X **Alpenstück** 🈺 ⵁ ⵛ

Gartenstr. 9 ⊠ 10115 – ⓂRosenthaler Platz – ℰ (030)   Plan I: **C1**
21 75 16 46 – www.alpenstueck.de
Menu 35/48 € – Carte 34/45 € – *(dinner only) (booking advisable)*
• Regional • Fashionable •

This relaxed and friendly restaurant uses regional produce in dishes such as
pan-fried fillet of trout with beetroot, yellow turnip and fondant potatoes. At
lunchtimes the restaurant's own bakery over the road sells fine pastries and
small snacks. In the delicatessen you can buy Maultaschen (Swabian pasta squares) and fond (caramelised meat dripping for making gravy) to take home.

X **Kochu Karu** 🈺
🈂️

Eberswalder Str. 35 ⊠ 10437 – ⓂEberswalder Str.   Plan I: **C1**
– ℰ (030) 80 93 81 91 – www.kochukaru.de
Menu 28/38 € – Carte 25/37 € – *(dinner only) (booking advisable)*
• Korean • Minimalist • Neighbourhood •

Korea meets Spain in this small, minimalist-style restaurant. Bin-Lee Zauner (a
famous Korean opera singer) and José Miranda Morillo (a Düsseldorfer of Spanish origin) combine the culinary traditions of the two countries. The menu includes gogi dumplings and octopus with chorizo. Don't miss their 'Musical Meal'.

X **MANI** – Hotel MANI 🈺 ⵛ [AC]

Torstr. 136 ⊠ 10119 – ⓂRosenthaler Platz – ℰ (030)   Plan I: **C2**
53 02 80 80 – www.hotel-mani.com
Menu 50 € (dinner)
– Carte 29/69 € – *(August: Monday-Saturday dinner only)*
• Modern cuisine • Trendy •

MANI is one of Berlin's 'places to be' at the moment. Its open kitchen, minimalist-style and the rich dark tones lend the place a slightly oriental feel, which chi-
mes perfectly with the spirit of the times. Try the interesting evening menu or, if
you prefer, sample the simpler lunchtime offerings.

X **Bandol sur Mer**
❀

Torstr. 167 ⊠ 10115 – ⓂRosenthaler Platz – ℰ (030)   Plan I: **C2**
67 30 20 51 – www.bandolsurmer.de – Closed Tuesday-Wednesday
Menu 69/118 € – Carte 62/72 € – *(dinner only) (booking essential)*
• French modern • Minimalist •

This little restaurant is simple and casual, verging on the rough and ready. By
contrast, the food prepared by Andreas Saul and his small team in the open kitchen is modern, excellent and French-based. The two set menus chalked up on
the blackboard include such intriguing options as 'veal sweetbreads/egg yolk/
coffee/onions'.

➜ Felsenoktopus und Wildgarnele, Essenz, Avocado und Rettich. Reh aus
der Schorfheide, Süßkartoffel, Schmorgurke und Pfifferlinge. Knusperkir-
schen, Joghurt, weiße Schokolade, Petersilie und Rosenblütensorbet.

GERMANY - BERLIN

X **Rutz Weinbar** – Restaurant Rutz

Chausseestr. 8 (1st floor) ⊠ *10115* Plan I: **C2**
– **Ⓜ** *Oranienburger Tor* – ℰ *(030) 24 62 87 60* – *www.rutz-restaurant.de*
– *Closed 2 weeks early January and Sunday-Monday*
Menu 44/54 € – Carte 33/63 € – *(dinner only open from 4pm)*
• Regional • Wine bar •
This genuinely German restaurant has a regionally inspired menu. It offers traditional specialities such as, smoked Neuköllner Rauchknacker sausage and Mangalitza ham hock, which provides a contrast to the more sophisticated Rutz.

X **Brasserie Desbrosses** – Hotel The Ritz-Carlton

Potsdamer Platz 3 ⊠ *10785* – **Ⓜ** *Potsdamer Platz* Plan: **F2**
– ℰ *(030) 3 37 77 54 02* – *www.ritzcarlton.de/berlin*
Carte 45/68 €
• French • Brasserie •
An eclectic group of diners meets here every day to savour the typically French bistro dishes on offer. The original 1875 interior comes from a brasserie in southern Burgundy.

X **herz und niere**

Fichtestr. 31 ⊠ *10967* – **Ⓜ** *Südstern* – ℰ *(030)* Plan I: **D3**
69 00 15 22 – *www.herzundniere.berlin* – *Closed Monday*
Menu 38/83 € – Carte 31/46 € – *(dinner only)*
• Regional • Friendly • Cosy •
The flavoursome food at this restaurant is made from locally sourced produce and served in warm and welcoming surroundings with friendly service and good wine recommendations. Try the ox muzzle salad or perhaps one of the vegetarian dishes.

X **Volt**

Paul-Lincke-Ufer 20 ⊠ *10999* – **Ⓜ** *Schönleinstr.* Plan I: **D3**
– ℰ *(030) 3 38 40 23 20* – *www.restaurant-volt.de*
– *Closed 1 week end December-early January, 2 weeks June-July and Sunday*
Menu 58/76 € – Carte 54/63 € – *(dinner only)*
• Regional • Fashionable •
Matthias Gleiß's restaurant is very popular and for good reason. With its well-chosen industrial design features and good food – including vegetables sourced from local farmers – this former electricity substation built in 1928 fits perfectly into Kreuzberg's lively gastro scene.

AROUND THE KURFÜRSTENDAMM **PLAN III**

 Waldorf Astoria

Hardenbergstr. 28 ⊠ *10623* – **Ⓜ** *Zoologischer Garten* Plan: **K2**
– ℰ *(030) 8 14 00 00* – *www.waldorfastoria.com/berlin*
202 rm – **†**210 € **††**238 € – ⊑ 36 € – 30 suites
• Grand Luxury • Elegant • Classic •
It is truly impressive how the modern, elegant interior of this upmarket hotel captures the style of the 1920s. Wherever you look, the design is a triumph of perfectly matched form and colour. Of course, the Waldorf Astoria just wouldn't be the Waldorf Astoria without Peacock Alley to bring a little bit of New York hotel tradition to Berlin. The Romanische Café on the other hand revives the Berlin coffee house culture of this former artists' meeting place… and the cakes are to die for!
❀ **Les Solistes by Pierre Gagnaire** – See restaurant listing

Sofitel Berlin Kurfürstendamm

Augsburger Str. 41 ✉ *10789 –* Ⓜ *Kurfürstendamm*   Plan: **K2**
– ℰ (030) 8 00 99 90 – www.sofitel-berlin-kurfuerstendamm.com
291 rm – ♦149/1000 € ♦♦169/1000 € – ☑ 30 € – 20 suites
• Business • Grand Luxury • Modern •

This modern luxury hotel stands in the middle of the lively city centre. It has spacious public areas and generously sized rooms. It also offers individual suites, some of which have beautiful views. There is art throughout the hotel. The Brasserie Le Faubourg is elegant and modern.

Palace

Budapester Str. 45 ✉ *10787 –* Ⓜ *Zoologischer Garten*   Plan: **K2**
– ℰ (030) 2 50 20 – www.palace.de
259 rm – ♦129/495 € ♦♦129/495 € – ☑ 26 € – 19 suites
• Grand Luxury • Classic •

This luxurious hotel is at the Europa Center. It offers a large lobby, attentive service and rooms in a classical or modern style, as well as elegant suites. It also provides an 800 m² Mediterranean spa area.

InterContinental

Budapester Str. 2 ✉ *10787 –* Ⓜ *Zoologischer Garten*   Plan: **L2**
– ℰ (030) 2 60 20 – www.berlin.intercontinental.com
545 rm – ♦135/199 € ♦♦135/199 € – ☑ 32 € – 13 suites
• Chain hotel • Luxury • Classic •

The InterContinental is smart and upmarket throughout. Elegant, contemporary guestrooms equipped with the latest technology, tasteful Vitality Club, plus conference and events facilities.
❀ **Hugos** – See restaurant listing

Swissôtel

Augsburger Str. 44 ✉ *10789 –* Ⓜ *Kurfürstendamm*   Plan: **K2**
– ℰ (030) 22 01 00 – www.swissotel.com/berlin
316 rm – ♦140/340 € ♦♦140/340 € – ☑ 23 €
• Business • Modern •

This modern town hotel with its glass façade welcomes its guests with a spacious atrium hall. It has comfortable guestrooms, including business and executive rooms.
 44 – See restaurant listing

Steigenberger

Los-Angeles-Platz 1 ✉ *10789 –* Ⓜ *Augsburger Str.*   Plan: **K2**
– ℰ (030) 2 12 70 – www.berlin.steigenberger.com
387 rm – ♦130/295 € ♦♦150/315 € – ☑ 25 € – 11 suites
• Conference hotel • Business • Modern •

This hotel has an attractive lobby area with bar and smokers' lounge and beautiful, modern rooms decorated in earth tones with clean lines. Executive suites are located on the sixth floor with access to a private lounge. This friendly Berliner Stube has a traditional touch.

Zoo Berlin

Kurfürstendamm 25 ✉ *10179 –* Ⓜ *Uhlandstr. – ℰ (030)*   Plan: **K2**
88 43 70 – www.hotelzoo.de
131 rm – ♦180/1200 € ♦♦180/1200 € – ☑ 27 €
• Luxury • Design • Elegant •

Well-known designer Dayna Lee has brought a bit of Berlin hotel history back to life at Zoo Berlin. She has successfully combined the elegance and class of the old hotel with a new, modern feel. The rooms are tasteful and upmarket, opulent yet functional, with all the atmosphere of a real 'grand hotel'.
Grace – See restaurant listing

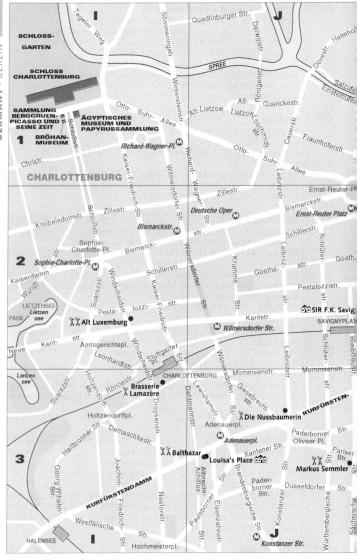

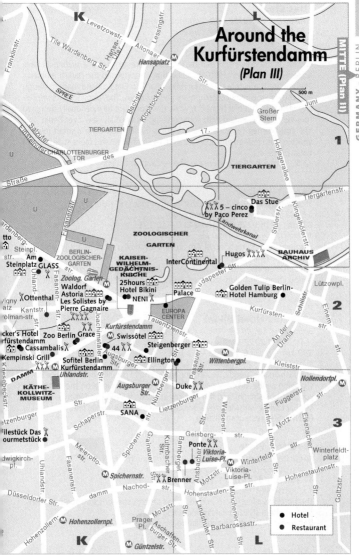

Around the Kurfürstendamm
(Plan III)

K

L

Levetzowstr.

Tile Wardenberg Str.

Hansa

Altonaer

Lessingstr.

Franklinstr.

Hansaplatz

Bachstr.

Klopstockstr.

Str.

SPREE

Juni

0   500 m

Salzufer

Großer
Stern

TIERGARTEN

Lüneburger

CHARLOTTENBURGER
TOR

des

17.

Straße

U

Hofjägerallee

Fasanenstr.

TIERGARTEN

1

Landwehrkanal

Klingelhöferstr.

Tiergartenstr.

Das Stue

ЖЖЖ 5 – cinco
by Paco Perez

otto

Steinpl.

ZOOLOGISCHER

GARTEN

BAUHAUS
ARCHIV

str.   Am
Steinplatz
GLASS

BERLIN-
ZOOLOGISCHER-
GARTEN

KAISER-
WILHELM-
GEDÄCHTNIS-
KIRCHE

Hugos ЖЖЖ

Stülerstr.

Lützowpl.

vigny

Zoolog. Garten

InterContinental

Kantstr.

Ottenthal

Waldorf
Astoria
Les Solistes by
Pierre Gagnaire
ЖЖЖЖ

Fasanenstr.

25hours
Hotel Bikini

NENI Ж

EUROPA
CENTER

Golden Tulip Berlin-
Hotel Hamburg

Einem

str.

Budapester

Palace

atz

colman-str.

Joachimstaler

Kurfürsten-

Kurfürstendamm

An der
Urania

Schillstr.

cker's Hotel
rfürstendamm

Zoo Berlin Grace

Swissôtel

Tauentzienstr.

Steigenberger

str.

Cassambalis Ж

44 ЖЖ

Patsauer Str.

Kempinski Grill
ЖЖЖ

Sofitel Berlin
Kurfürstendamm

Augsburger

Ellington

Wittenbergpl.

Str.

Kleiststr.

DAMM

Uhlandstr.

Str.

Duke ЖЖ

Nürnberger

Noilendorfpl.

KÄTHE-
KOLLWITZ-
MUSEUM

Augsburger
Str.

Fuggerstr.

Motz

tzenburger

Schaperstr.

Str.

Lietzenburger

Str.

Weiserstr.

Martin-Luther-

Elsenacher

Str.

3

Filestück Das Ж
ourmetstück

SANA

Meierotto-

Str.

Geisberg-
str.

Winterfeldt-
platz

ludwigkirch-
pl.

Uhlandstr.

Fasanenstr.

Spichern-

Str.

Gainauer

Bamberger

Kulmbacher

Ponte ЖЖ

Viktoria-
Luise-Pl.

Winterfeldt-

Str.

Hohenstaufenstr.

Goltzstr.

Düsseldorfer Str.

damm

Nachod-

Str.

Motz

Viktoria-
Luise-Pl.

Münchener

Spichernstr.

Brenner ЖЖ

Hohenstaufen-

str.

Landshuter

Hohenzoller-

Hohenzollernpl.

Prager
Pl.

Motzstr.

Aschaffen-
burger Str.

Barbarossastr.

Str.

K

Güntzelstr.

L

● Hotel

● Restaurant

317

GERMANY - BERLIN

 Das Stue

Drakestr. 1 ✉ *10787 –* Ⓜ *Wittenbergplatz –* ✆ *(030)* Plan: **L2**
3 11 72 20 – www.das-stue.com
78 rm – 🛏210/380 € 🛏🛏240/380 € – ☕ 35 €
• Luxury • Design • Elegant •

'Stylish' is the only word that really does justice to what the architects have achieved in this listed 1930's building that once housed the Danish embassy. The interior is a highly successful mixture of neo-Classical and modern design and the decor is ultra-contemporary and luxurious. The lobby with its impressive staircases is a real highlight, while the rooms are all individually designed to a very high standard with some offering an unusual view over Berlin Zoo. The aptly named restaurant, Casual, offers friendly service in a smart interior, which is both relaxed and sophisticated. The menu features tapas-style international dishes.
❀ **5 - cinco by Paco Pérez** – See restaurant listing

 Am Steinplatz

Steinplatz 4 ✉ *10623 –* Ⓜ *Ernst-Reuter-Platz –* ✆ *(030)* Plan: **K2**
5 54 44 40 – www.hotelsteinplatz.com
87 rm – 🛏165/225 € 🛏🛏180/240 € – ☕ 35 €
• Luxury • Townhouse • Elegant •

Formerly Berlin's artists' hotel, Am Steinplatz is now a small, exclusive boutique hotel in the heart of Charlottenburg. The rooms are upmarket, chic and comfortable, the service attentive and personal, and the decor is characterised by period charm and high, stuccoed ceilings. Regionally inspired restaurant concept.

 25hours Hotel Bikini

Budapester Str. 40 ✉ *10787 –* Ⓜ *Zoologischer Garten* Plan: **K2**
– ✆ *(030) 1 20 22 10 – www.25hours-hotels.com*
149 rm – 🛏120 € 🛏🛏120 € – ☕ 14 €
• Business • Personalised • Stylish •

This fashionable, trendy, 'urban jungle' style hotel is built onto the Bikini Berlin shopping centre. It offers views of the zoo (from the sauna on the ninth floor you can look straight into the monkey enclosure!). Woodfire Bakery and Monkey Bar lounge with views over the city. Free bicycle and Mini hire.
NENI – See restaurant listing

 Louisa's Place

Kurfürstendamm 160 ✉ *10709 –* Ⓜ *Adenauerplatz* Plan: **J3**
– ✆ *(030) 63 10 30 – www.louisas-place.de*
47 suites – 🛏145/625 € 🛏🛏145/625 € – ☕ 26 €
• Business • Personalised • Cosy •

This hotel has a friendly service and offers tasteful, spacious suites with kitchens. There is also a stylish breakfast room and library.
Balthazar – See restaurant listing

 Ellington

Nürnberger Str. 50 ✉ *10789 –* Ⓜ *Wittenbergplatz* Plan: **L2**
– ✆ *(030) 68 31 50 – www.ellington-hotel.com*
280 rm – 🛏118/208 € 🛏🛏128/228 € – ☕ 20 € – 5 suites
• Business • Modern • Minimalist •

Numerous photographs of the Duke Ellington, after whom the hotel is named, adorn this simply furnished hotel. It has a beautiful lobby area and a lounge-style interior courtyard. Many details preserve its historic charm. A restaurant with a straightforward style
Duke – See restaurant listing

SANA
🏠 ⛵ 🐾 📺 🕭 🖺 🅰🅒 ♨ 🚗

Nürnberger Str. 33 ✉ 10777 – ⓜ Augsburger Str. Plan: **K3**
– ℰ (030) 20 05 15 10 – www.berlin.sanahotels.com
166 rm – †105/180 € ††105/180 € – ⌂ 18 € – 42 suites
• Business • Modern •

Minimalist, urban design from top to toe, with a lounge in the interior courtyard.
The top floor houses a small fitness suite with great views, while the hotel bar, the
'F8 – feight', has a terrace. In the restaurant the accent is on Portuguese cuisine.

Golden Tulip Berlin - Hotel Hamburg
🏠 🕭 🅰🅒 ♨ 🚗

Landgrafenstr. 4 ✉ 10787 – ⓜ Wittenbergplatz Plan: **L2**
– ℰ (030) 26 47 70 – www.goldentulipberlin.de
186 rm – †89/389 € ††99/399 € – ⌂ 15 € – 3 suites
• Business • Contemporary •

The Golden Tulip is contemporary and businesslike with comfortable rooms
and a daytime bar, all decorated in warm earth tones. The conference room is
cleverly located on the 11th floor so that participants can enjoy peace, quiet
and panoramic views over Berlin as they work.

Hecker's Hotel Kurfürstendamm
🏠 🕭 ♨ 🚗

Grolmanstr. 35 ✉ 10623 – ⓜ Uhlandstr. – ℰ (030) Plan: **K2**
8 89 00 – www.heckers-hotel.de
69 rm – †85/290 € ††95/310 € – ⌂ 16 €
• Business • Design •

This establishment offers contemporary living just a few steps from the Kurfürstendamm. The Bauhaus, Toskana and Colonial themed rooms are tastefully
done out. There is a quiet sun terrace on the fourth-floor, and a modern breakfast room. The Cassambalis offers Mediterranean cuisine in a warm and charming atmosphere.
Cassambalis – See restaurant listing

SIR F.K. Savigny
🅰🅒

Kantstr. 144 ✉ 10623 – ⓜ Uhlandstr. – ℰ (030) Plan: **J2**
3 23 01 56 00 – www.hotel-sirsavigny.de
44 rm – †99/139 € ††99/139 € – ⌂ 18 €
• Townhouse • Modern • Design •

The smart black and white design is particularly striking and the many paintings
are a little reminiscent of an English country house. Tapas and snacks available
in the bar. The rear courtyard offers a small oasis of green.

Otto
🅿

Knesebeckstr. 10 ✉ 10623 – ⓜ Ernst-Reuter-Platz Plan: **K2**
– ℰ (030) 54 71 00 80 – www.hotelotto.com
46 rm – †80/120 € ††100/140 € – ⌂ 15 €
• Business • Modern •

A really friendly, modern hotel with its own clear, functional design. Some of the
guestrooms have kitchenettes. The top floor boasts a bright and airy breakfast
room and a terrace – the perfect place for afternoon tea and cakes.

Les Solistes by Pierre Gagnaire – Hotel Waldorf Astoria
🕭 🅰🅒 ⇄ 🚗

Hardenbergstr. 27 ✉ 10623 Plan: **K2**
– ⓜ Zoologischer Garten – ℰ (030) 81 40 00 24 50
– www.waldorfastoriaberlin.de – Closed 25 July-28 August and Sunday-
Monday
Menu 85/140 € – Carte 87/129 € – (dinner only) (booking advisable)
• Creative • Elegant • Design •

Famous French chef Pierre Gagnaire is now taking the German capital by storm
with his own inimitable style of ambitious, sophisticated and creative cuisine. As
everywhere else at the Waldorf Astoria, the decor in the restaurant ranges from
original New York to Berlin contemporary.
➜ Großer Raviolo vom Taschenkrebs und Staudensellerie mit Velouté und
Spitzen von grünen Spargel. Maibock mit Wacholder, Sauce "Violine", Rote
Bete-Gnocchi. Tarte mit Schokolade aus Ecuador, karamellisierte Mandeln
und Haselnüsse.

GERMANY - BERLIN

XXXX ❀ **Hugos** – Hotel InterContinental   🕸 ⤋ AC ⬦ 🚗
Budapester Str. 2 (14th floor) ✉ *10787*   Plan: **L2**
– Ⓜ *Zoologischer Garten* – ✆ *(030) 26 02 12 63*
– *www.hugos-restaurant.de*
– *Closed Sunday-Monday*
Menu 100/150 € – *(dinner only) (booking advisable)*
• Modern cuisine • Fashionable • Elegant •
It is true that the view from the 14th floor is fantastic but this elegant, minima-list-style restaurant is known first and foremost for its classic, modern cuisine, which is both beautifully crafted and delicious.
➜ Königskrabbe sanft gegart, Tatar, Rhabarber, Vanille, Ingwer. Bar de Ligne gebraten, Sellerie, Liebstöckel. Limousin Lamm und Purple Curry, Brunnenkresse, gegrillte Zwiebel.

XXX ❀ **5 - cinco by Paco Pérez** – Hotel Das Stue   🕸 ♿ AC
Drakestr. 1 ✉ *10787* – Ⓜ *Wittenbergplatz* – ✆ *(030)*   Plan: **L2**
3 11 72 20 – *www.5-cinco.com* – *Closed 2 weeks early January, 2 weeks early August and Sunday-Monday*
Menu 165 € – Carte 97/125 € – *(dinner only) (booking advisable)*
• Creative • Individual • Design •
Paco Pérez has brought the creative seafood cuisine of his two-star Miramar res-taurant in Spain (where he incidentally has several renowned restaurants) to Berlin. How better to sample his precise, elegant and uncomplicated style than with the 25 courses of his Experience menu? If that sounds like too much of a good thing, you can always opt for the à la carte option. Thanks to designer Pat-ricia Urquiola the distinctive interior – featuring 86 copper pans hanging from the centre of the ceiling – has the same Spanish roots as the cooking.
➜ Jakobsmuscheln, Parmentier, Schinken und Pedro Ximénez. Kaisergranat vom Grill. Iberico Schweinerippchen und Garnelen.

XXX **Kempinski Grill**   🍴 ♿ 🚗
Kurfürstendamm 27 ✉ *10719* – Ⓜ *Uhlandstr.* – ✆ *(030)*   Plan: **K2**
88 43 47 67 – *www.kempinski.com/berlinbristol* – *Closed 4 weeks July-August*
Menu 55/75 € – Carte 44/77 €
• French classic • Elegant •
A veritable institution on the Ku'Damm since 1952. Kempinski's classic period elegance remains (despite various refurbishments over the years), providing the restaurant with its unique charm.

XX **Grace** – Hotel Zoo Berlin   🍴 ♿ AC
Kurfürstendamm 25 ✉ *10719* – Ⓜ *Uhlandstr.* – ✆ *(030)*   Plan: **K2**
88 43 77 50 70 – *Closed Sunday-Monday*
Menu 50/90 € – Carte 45/85 € – *(dinner only)*
• International • Elegant • Design •
Combining stylish, modern design and vintage flair, Grace is a really smart place to eat. The food is modern and international and includes such delights as creamy rock shrimps with cucumber, coriander, peanuts and chilli.

XX ❀ **Markus Semmler**   🍴
Sächsische Str. 7 ✉ *10707* – Ⓜ *Hohenzollernpl.*   Plan: **J3**
– ✆ *(030) 89 06 82 90* – *www.kochkunst-ereignisse.de* – *Closed July-August and Sunday-Tuesday*
Menu 85/130 € – Carte 75/105 € – *(dinner only) (booking essential)*
• Classic cuisine • Fashionable •
Markus Semmler cooks fresh classic cuisine including delicacies such as peppe-red tuna with tomato and bread salad, and turbot with oxtail praline. The star-ters and desserts are prepared in the open kitchen before your eyes.
➜ Thunfisch, Radieschen, Bärlauch, Spargel, Kresse. Atlantik Steinbutt, karamellisierter Romana, Kerbel-Beurre blanc. Rhabarber, Erdbeere, grüner Pfeffer, weiße Schokolade.

XX **Balthazar** – Hotel Louisa's Place 🕯 ᴙ ⒶⒸ ⇔

Kurfürstendamm 160 ✉ *10709 –* Ⓜ *Adenauerplatz* Plan: **J3**
– ℰ (030) 89 40 84 77 – www.balthazar-restaurant.de
Menu 44 € – Carte 40/65 € – *(dinner only)*
• International • Fashionable • Trendy •
Holger Zurbrüggen's restaurant offers great food right on the Ku'damm. His
own particular brand of cooking, which he dubs 'Metropolitan Cuisine', is hea-
vily influenced by South-East Asian and Mediterranean styles.

XX **Duke** – Hotel Ellington 🕯 ᴙ ⒶⒸ ⌕

Nürnberger Str. 50 ✉ *10789 –* Ⓜ *Wittenbergplatz* Plan: **L2**
– ℰ (030) 6 83 15 40 00 – www.duke-restaurant.com – Closed Sunday
Menu 22 € (weekday lunch)/68 € (dinner) – Carte 34/94 €
• French modern • Fashionable • Trendy •
This trendy, modern restaurant comes with a guarantee of good food. The
dishes emerging from the open kitchen include ossobuco, fillet of grass-fed
veal with a saffron and fennel risotto and gremolata jus, as well as a delicious
moelleux au chocolat.

XX **Alt Luxemburg** ⒶⒸ ⇔

Windscheidstr. 31 ✉ *10627 –* Ⓜ *Wilmersdorfer Str.* Plan: **I2**
– ℰ (030) 3 23 87 30 – www.altluxemburg.de – Closed Sunday
Menu 52/79 € – Carte 53/73 € – *(dinner only) (booking advisable)*
• French classic • Family •
Attractive, friendly colours contribute to the atmosphere of this restaurant. It
offers classic cuisine, and has been traditionally run by the Wannemacher family
since 1982.

XX **Brenner** ⅋ ᴙ ⇔

Regensburger Str. 7 ✉ *10777 –* Ⓜ *Viktoria-Luise-Platz* Plan: **L3**
*– ℰ (030) 23 62 44 70 – www.restaurant-brenner.de – closed Sunday-
Monday*
Menu 44/69 € – Carte 35/58 € – *(dinner only)*
• International • Cosy •
Back at the Brenner (which he previously managed as the Berlin-Sankt Moritz),
Anton Stefanov and his kitchen team are offering an international menu in this
friendly, rustic yet elegant restaurant. Fine selection of over 350 wines. Try one
of the by-the-glass recommendations with the set menus.

XX **44** – Hotel Swissôtel 🕯 ᴙ ⒶⒸ ⌕
ⓐ
Augsburger Str. 44 ✉ *10789 –* Ⓜ *Kurfürstendamm* Plan: **K2**
– ℰ (030) 2 20 10 22 88 – www.restaurant44.de – Closed Sunday
Menu 44 € – Carte 35/63 €
• Swiss • Fashionable •
This simple, modern and elegant restaurant serves imaginative food in the form
of a tasting menu. Glass frontage and terrace overlooking the Kurfurstendamm.

XX **Ponte** ᴙ

Regensburger Str. 5 ✉ *10777 –* Ⓜ *Viktoria-Luise-Platz* Plan: **L3**
*– ℰ (030) 21 91 24 10 – www.ponte-ristorante.de – Closed 2 weeks
January, 2 weeks July and Tuesday*
Carte 33/56 € – *(dinner only)*
• Italian • Neighbourhood • Friendly •
Valter Mazza, long since an established member of the Berlin culinary family,
has found himself a new culinary home in Schöneberg. The menu includes
fresh, classic Italian dishes such as courgette flowers with ricotta and braised
veal shanks with vegetables, as well as fish and seafood. Some excellent Italian
wines.

GERMANY - BERLIN

GERMANY - BERLIN

X ⌂ ⊞
⬡ **Bieberbau** (Stephan Garkisch)

Durlacher Str. 15 ⊠ *10715 –* Ⓜ *Bundesplatz –* ✆ *(030)* Plan I: **B3**
8 53 23 90 – www.bieberbau-berlin.de – Closed Sunday-Monday
Menu 44/65 € – *(dinner only) (booking advisable)*
• Modern cuisine • Cosy •

This wonderful example of the stucco plasterer's art was created by Richard Bie-
ber in the 19C. The food prepared at the Molteni ranges is based on regional
products and fine herbs. So try not to fill up too much on the homemade
bread and flavoured butters!
➜ Büffelmozzarella und Aprikose, Lakritz, Oliven und Pinien. Linumer Wie-
senkalb, Bohnen, Strandschnecken und Vogelwicke. Erdbeeren, Zitronen-
melisse und Macadamia.

X **Brasserie Lamazère**
☺

Stuttgarter Platz 18 ⊠ *10178 –* Ⓜ *Wilmersdorfer Str.* Plan: **I3**
– ✆ *(030) 31 80 07 12 – www.lamazere.de – Closed 1-4 January and Monday*
Menu 35/45 € – *(dinner only)*
• French • Brasserie • Neighbourhood •

Paris-born Régis Lamazère has brought a little piece of France to Charlottenburg in his charming and lively Parisian-style bistro. The food is very good and
thoroughly unpretentious. It includes dishes such as duo of lamb with honeyed
carrots and riz au lait with salted caramel.

X **GLASS** ♿

Uhlandstr. 195 ⊠ *10623 –* Ⓜ *Zoologischer Garten* Plan: **K2**
– ✆ *(030) 54 71 08 61 – www.glassberlin.de – Closed 2 weeks early*
January, 2 weeks early August and Sunday-Monday
Menu 75/95 € – *(dinner only) (booking advisable)*
• Creative • Minimalist •

The glass, metal and minimalist-style decor in black give a resolutely urban feel
here, creating the ideal setting for Israeli-born Gal Ben Moshe's creative cuisine.
The set menus, which he presents personally at your table (in English), always
include a vegan option while the witty Candy Box dessert is presented in picnic
form. The whole wine selection is available by the glass.

X **Cassambalis** – Hecker's Hotel ⌂ Ⓐ🄲 ⌂

Grolmanstr. 35 ⊠ *10623 –* Ⓜ *Uhlandstr. –* ✆ *(030)* Plan: **K2**
8 85 47 47 – www.cassambalis.de
Menu 35 € (lunch)/90 € – Carte 31/58 €
• Mediterranean • Friendly •

You can't get any closer to the action than this. Close to the Ku'Damm, this restaurant is reminiscent of a bright, friendly brasserie with lots of art on the walls,
open wine shelves and bright colours. Mediterranean cuisine.

X **Filetstück Das Gourmetstück** ⌂

Uhlandstr. 156 ⊠ *10719 –* Ⓜ *Uhlandstr. –* ✆ *(030)* Plan: **K3**
54 46 96 40 – www.filetstueck.de – Closed Sunday
Menu 75/105 € (dinner) – Carte 56/99 €
• Modern cuisine • Brasserie •

This little restaurant close to the Kurfürstendamm is all about meat. Alongside a
variety of steaks, in the evenings it also serves a gourmet set menu with up to seven
creative courses including 'Klosterschwein pork / Büsum crabs / turnip-root parsley /
green asparagus' – all served in a relaxed atmosphere. Try and book table 21.

X **Ottenthal**
☺

Kantstr. 153 ⊠ *10623 –* Ⓜ *Uhlandstr. –* ✆ *(030)* Plan: **K2**
3 13 31 62 – www.ottenthal.com – Closed 1 week July-August
Menu 29/65 € – Carte 33/57 € – *(dinner only) (booking advisable)*
• Austrian • Classic •

Ottenthal's popularity speaks for itself. Its typically Austrian tavern fare is a great
success. In his friendly bistro-style restaurant (named after his home town in
Lower Austria) chef Arthur Schneller produces unfussy dishes including Wiener
Tafelspitz (boiled rump of beef Viennese style) and apple strudel. Good wine
selection.

X

Renger-Patzsch

Wartburgstr. 54 ✉ *10823 –* Ⓜ *Eisenacher Str.*   Plan I: **B3**
– ℰ (030) 7 84 20 59 – www.renger-patzsch.com
Menu 29/34 € – Carte 31/41 € – *(dinner only) (booking advisable)*
• Traditional cuisine • Inn • Cosy •

Renger-Patzsch serves up traditional, tasty and well-executed dishes that provide excellent value for money. Try the Alsatian sauerkraut with shoulder of pork or the flammekueche. The restaurant owes its name to one of the pioneers of landscape photography and a number of his black and white photos adorn the walls of this warm and friendly restaurant. It is a great place to eat and a very popular one to boot, so don't be surprised if you have to squeeze up on the long wooden benches. There is also a wonderful terrace.

X

Jungbluth

Lepsius Str. 63 (by Hauptstraße B3) ✉ *12163 –* Ⓜ *Steglitzer Rathaus*
– ℰ (030) 79 78 96 05 – www.jungbluth-restaurant.de – Closed Monday
Menu 35/70 € – Carte 34/42 €
• Regional • Neighbourhood • Friendly •

The young team that runs Jungbluth have created a pleasant little restaurant serving tasty food at reasonable prices. Try the delicious roast shoulder of beef with cima di rapa and creamed garlic and celery.

X

Die Nussbaumerin

Leibnizstr. 55 ✉ *10629 –* Ⓜ *Adenauerpl. – ℰ (030)*   Plan: **J3**
50 17 80 33 – www.nussbaumerin.de – Closed Sunday
Carte 24/45 € – *(dinner only) (booking advisable)*
• Traditional cuisine • Cosy •

This restaurant serves delicious home-cooked food of the sort you would like to eat more often. The owner herself serves up the freshly cooked Austrian classics including Wiener Schnitzel, boiled rump of beef and Marillenknödel apricot pastries. Unfortunately the good Austrian wines to accompany them are only available by the bottle.

X
NENI – 25hours Hotel Bikini

Budapester Str. 40 (10th floor) ✉ *10787*   Plan: **K2**
– Ⓜ *Zoologischer Garten – ℰ (030) 1 20 22 10 – www.25hours-hotels.com*
Carte 24/46 € – *(booking advisable)*
• Mediterranean • Trendy •

With its glasshouse decor and stunning view, Neni is a restaurant with a difference. The food coming out of the open kitchens is an eclectic mix of Mediterranean, Oriental and local cuisines, including houmous with chicken liver, baba ghanoush and Eifel lamb. The ideas come courtesy of Haya Molcho. Spectacular terrace!

ENVIRONS OF BERLIN   PLAN I

AT **BERLIN-GRUNEWALD**

Schlosshotel im Grunewald

Brahmsstr. 10 ✉ *14193 – ℰ (030) 89 58 40*   Plan: **A3**
– www.schlosshotelberlin.com
43 rm – †262/460 € ††367/460 € – ⌑ 29 € – 10 suites
• Rural • Luxury • Design •

This unique building, formerly part of a large chain, has reverted to a private hotel. It has of course retained its tasteful 1914 palace interior full of pretty period details, its lovely grounds and its attractive leisure area. All this in a quiet location just a short 10min walk from the Kurfürstendamm.

XX Frühsammers Restaurant

Flinsberger Platz 8 ✉ *14193 –* ☎ *(030) 89 73 86 28*   Plan: **A3**
– www.fruehsammers-restaurant.de – Closed 1-6 February, 21 March-
2 April and Saturday lunch, Sunday-Tuesday lunch, Wednesday lunch
Menu 69/94 € *– (booking advisable)*
• Classic cuisine • Friendly •

Here in the grounds of the tennis club, the Frühsammers whisk you away into
their own little gourmet world where chef Sonja creates fine food with Mediterranean and south-east Asian notes using the very best ingredients. If you have a
little time on your hands, try the (all inclusive) lunchtime or evening surprise
menu.

➔ Kalb, Thunfisch, Rucola. Lamm, Gurke, Joghurt, Queller. Pfirsich, weiße
Schokolade, Minze.

AT **B**ERLIN-**L**ICHTENBERG

andel's Hotel

Landsberger Allee 106 ✉ *10369 –* ☎ *(030) 4 53 05 30*   Plan: **D1**
– www.andelsberlin.com
534 rm ➖ – ♦94/120 € ♦♦219/245 € – 23 suites
• Conference hotel • Modern •

This remarkable building is an events and conference hotel. It has a modern
design, very large lobby, and an excellent events area. Executive floors with
free W-LAN. The restaurant decor is elegant with clean lines.

🌼 **SKYKITCHEN flavored by a.choice** – See restaurant listing

XX SKYKITCHEN flavored by a.choice – andel's Hotel

Landsberger Allee 106 ✉ *10369 –* ☎ *(030) 45 3053 26 21*
– www.skykitchen.berlin – Closed Sunday-Monday   Plan: **D1**
Menu 43 € (Vegetarian)/102 € *– (dinner only) (booking advisable)*
• Modern cuisine • Fashionable •

It is hardly surprising that the window tables at this restaurant on the 12th floor
are highly sought after – the view is amazing! Inside, the restaurant's vintage
look is every bit as popular as the modern cuisine, which promises interesting
interpretations of German favourites.

➔ St. Pierre und Pancetta, Fave Bohnen, Radicchio, Safran. Nordsee Hummer, Chicorée, Bio Zitrone, Fenchel. Wachtel, Pfifferlinge, Erbsen.

COLOGNE
KÖLN

Population: 1 030 450

F. Jürgen/Fotolia.com

Cologne is one of Germany's oldest cities and its name was instigated by the Romans, who set up a 'colony' to fend off the Barbarians. It became a Free City, and later fell under the rule of Napoleon and then the Prussians; all of which has given the locals a cosmopolitan, laid-back and sociable outlook. Although it may never be described as Europe's prettiest city, it has an eye-catching old town (largely rebuilt after World War II) and some world-class museums. It also boasts one of the finest collections of medieval churches in Europe, and ploughs its own furrow by celebrating Carnival like it's Rio. Most famously, it has its Cathedral, a massive structure that took over half a millennium to build, stood tall during the War and remains one of the biggest tourist attractions in Germany to this day.

The River Rhine cuts a swathe right through the heart of Cologne, with four central bridges allowing plentiful passage from east to west. The main hub of the city is on the west bank, with the Altstadt (old town) practically on the river bank itself. Out to the west, the old medieval walls are now a ring road which neatly encircles the city centre and just northwest of the ring road is Mediapark, a brash modern development. To the east of the Rhine is the massive Trade Fair Centre, with its 80m-high tower, while to its north is Cologne's biggest and most popular park, Rheinpark.

COLOGNE IN...

→ **ONE DAY**
Altstadt, Dom, Romanesque churches.

→ **TWO DAYS**
Museum Ludwig, Wallraf-Richartz Museum (or Chocolate Museum), Stadtgarten (or Opera House).

→ **THREE DAYS**
Romano-Germanic Museum, Rheinpark.

PRACTICAL INFORMATION

ARRIVAL-DEPARTURE

✈ Cologne / Bonn Airport lies 17km southeast of the city centre. The S13 train takes about 15min.

GETTING AROUND

You can get around Cologne by bus, tram or metro. Validate your ticket by stamping it each time you board. Single and day tickets for Cologne not only take you from one side of the city to the other but are also valid for a journey to nearby Bonn. If you're in the city for a while, invest in a Köln Welcome Card, available from tourist information offices and many hotels. As well as providing free travel on the public transport network, it offers almost ninety deals and discounts at venues ranging from galleries and museums to shops, leisure facilities and eateries.

CALENDAR HIGHLIGHTS

February/March
Crazy Days (carnival).

March
lit.cologne (international literature festival).

July
Cologne Lights, Christopher Street Day (gay pride celebration), Summerjam.

August
Ringfest (two miles of rock stages along the Ringstrassen ring road).

October
Long Night of Cologne Museums, Cologne International Comedy Festival.

November
Carnival begins.

EATING OUT

Cologne is known throughout Germany for its Kölsch. It's the name of the local people and it's the name of their brew, a light beer with the yeast risen to the top rather than sunk to the bottom of the glass. 20 local breweries produce their own versions and you can try them out in an old town brauhaus – atmospheric, dark wood-panelled places where buzzy waiters continuously refill your empty stangen (0.2 litre glass). After that, make the most of the city's ethnic diversity by selecting a restaurant from an impressive global range; pick of the bunch are the fine Italian, Japanese and Turkish establishments. If your preference is for something local, favoured dishes include Himmel un Äad (bloodsausage and mash), Sauerbraten vom Pferd (braised horse) or Töttchen (ragout of brains and calf's head, cooked with herbs). Bars, cafés and restaurants all stay open late, many until 11pm or midnight. Service charge is generally included but most people round up the bill. In summer, seek out an ice-cream parlour, sit under a parasol and tuck into a full-on sundae.

C

FLITTARD

DÜNNWALD

Stadtautobahn

A 3-E 35

Berliner Str.

Mülheime Str.

Odenthaler Str.

MEHL

RHEIN

Industriestr.

friedrich-Karl-Str.

Amsterdamerstr.

Boltensternstr.

STAMMHEIM

HÖHENHAUS

Dünnwalder Mausplad

Höhenfelder Hausplad

Niehler Gürtel

25

Mülheimer Zubringer

Clevischer Str.

Berliner Str.

Str.

Delbrücker

1

RIEHL

Mülheimer Brücke

MÜLHEIM

26

Gladbacher-

Mausplad

NIPPES

Kanalstr.

Niederländer Ufer

Zoobrücke

Bergischer Ring

Frankfurter Ring

Bergisch-

BUCHHEIM

HOLWEIDE

A 4-E 40

D

OM

Platzischer Ring

BUCHFORST

KALK

Str.

MERHEIM

17

Olpener

Str.

2

Kalker Hauptstr.

Olpener

Str.

VINGST

Neubrücker Ring

Deutzer

Zülpischer Str.

Ostheimer Str.

Frankfurter

Rösrather Str.

A 3-E 35

Siegburger Str.

Ring

A 4-E 40

A 4-E 40

Str.

Exhibition Centre
(Plan III)

POLL

13

A 559

A 59

Bonner Str.

Gustav-Heinemann-Ufer

Oberländer Ufer

Kölner Str.

ENSEN

GREMBERG-HOVEN

3

ST. MARIA
KÖNIGIN

Militärringstr.

Hauptstr.

RHEIN

Str.

PORZ

AURA by
Louis Dias

Weißer Str.

Grüngürtelstr.

Frankfurter Str.

RODENKIRCHEN

A 555

Industriestr.

WEISS

Kaiserstr.

Hauptstr.

C

D

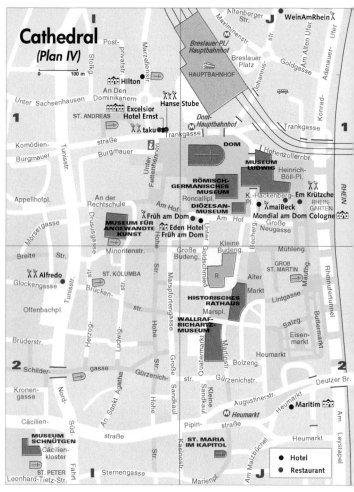

Cathedral
(Plan IV)

0   100 m

Excelsior Hotel Ernst ⚘ ₺₆ ⅏ ⅍ 🖧 ⌂

Domplatz/Trankgasse 1 ✉ *50667*   Plan: I1
– Ⓜ *Dom-Hauptbahnhof* – ☏ *(0221) 27 01*
– *www.excelsior-hotel-ernst.de*
114 rm – 🛏250/350 € 🛏🛏390/490 € – ⌣ 32 € – 26 suites
· Grand Luxury · Traditional · Classic ·
Traditional and modern elements have been combined with style and taste in
this grand hotel by the cathedral. Exclusive reception area, elegant rooms. Particularly luxurious are the rooms in the Hanseflügel wing.
❀ **taku · Hanse Stube** – See restaurant listing

Mondial Am Dom Cologne   🍴 🕸 ⅺ AC 🛁 🚗

Kurt-Hackenberg-Platz 1 ✉ *50667*   Plan: **J1**
– Ⓜ *Dom-Hauptbahnhof* – ✆ *(0221) 2 06 30*
– *www.hotel-mondial-am-dom-cologne.com*
203 rm – 🛏115/455 € 🛏🛏135/475 € – � 28 €
• Business • Modern •

This hotel is in a prime central location by the cathedral. It offers modern functional rooms with all mod-cons, including large deluxe rooms. Habana cigar lounge. Restaurant with tapas bar, brasserie and fine dining. The Dom Pub is popular with opera goers.

Hilton   🍴 🛎 🕸 ⅺ AC 🛁 🚗

Marzellenstr. 13 ✉ *50668* – Ⓜ *Dom-Hauptbahnhof*   Plan: **I1**
– ✆ *(0221) 13 07 10* – *www.hilton.de/koeln*
294 rm – 🛏127/239 € 🛏🛏127/239 € – ⊆ 20 € – 2 suites
• Business • Modern •

This business hotel is in the immediate vicinity of the cathedral. It offers contemporary design in the technically well-equipped rooms, in the 'Ice Bar' for smokers, and in the 'Fit & Well Health Club'. Unpretentious atmosphere and open kitchen in the Konrad restaurant.

Maritim   🍴 🛎 🕸 📺 AC 🛁 🚗

Heumarkt 20 ✉ *50667* – Ⓜ *Heumarkt* – ✆ *(0221)*   Plan: **J2**
2 02 70 – *www.maritim.de*
442 rm – 🛏112/348 € 🛏🛏128/404 € – ⊆ 21 € – 12 suites
• Chain hotel • Functional •

This hotel by the Deutzer Bridge on the edge of the old town has been going for 25 years. The light and airy glass-roofed lobby is home to various shops, while the Piano Bar offers fine cigars and a selection of whiskies. The rooms are functional. Bellevue has a roof terrace and a Rhine view.

Eden Hotel Früh am Dom   🍴 🛁

Sporergasse 1 ✉ *50667* – Ⓜ *Dom-Hauptbahnhof*   Plan: **J1**
– ✆ *(0221) 2 61 32 95* – *www.hotel-eden.de*
78 rm ⊆ – 🛏90/270 € 🛏🛏115/295 €
• Townhouse • Modern •

An established hotel close to the cathedral square. The rooms are up to date in terms of style and technology. Some also have a view of the cathedral – which can also be enjoyed while having breakfast. On the first floor the modern Hof 18 restaurant serves international cuisine.

Hanse Stube – Excelsior Hotel Ernst   🥂 🍴 AC ⇄

Domplatz/Trankgasse 1 ✉ *50667*   Plan: **I1**
– Ⓜ *Dom-Hauptbahnhof* – ✆ *(0221) 2701* – *www.excelsiorhotelernst.com*
Menu 95 € (lunch)/155 € – Carte 66/92 €
• Classic cuisine • Classic •

The Hanse Stube is one of the most elegant restaurants in the city and serves good classic cuisine. Many business people come for the fairly priced, daily changing business lunch.

Alfredo (Roberto Carturan)   AC
❀

Tunisstr. 3 ✉ *50667* – ✆ *(0221) 2 57 73 80*   Plan: **I2**
– *www.ristorante-alfredo.com* – *Closed 3 weeks July-August, Saturday-Sunday and Bank Holidays*
Menu 70/105 € – Carte 48/80 € – *(booking advisable)*
• Italian • Friendly •

Roberto Carturan is following unashamedly in the footsteps of this father, Alfredo, and his authentic Italian cuisine. His food is fresh and unfussy, each dish a tribute to high quality ingredients simply combined. Wait for the waiter's suggestions as you take your seat. The service is professional and accomplished with just the right amount of informality.
➜ Jakobsmuscheln, Linsen. Steinbutt, Pfifferlinge. Joghurt, weiße Schokolade.

GERMANY - COLOGNE

GERMANY - COLOGNE

XX 𝄞 **taku** – Excelsior Hotel Ernst 🕸 Ⓐⓚ 🚗
Domplatz/Trankgasse 1 ✉ *50667* Plan: I1
– Ⓜ *Dom-Hauptbahnhof* – ✆ *(0221) 2 70 39 10 – www.taku.de – Closed 1 week during Carnival, 1 week during Easter, 4 weeks July-August and Sunday-Monday, Bank Holidays lunch*
Menu 41 € (lunch)/155 € – Carte 66/92 € – *(booking advisable)*
• Asian • Minimalist • Fashionable •

If you have a taste for high quality Southeast Asian cuisine, you should try the dishes served in this bright, minimalist-style restaurant by a largely Asian kitchen team headed up by chef Mirko Gaul. Interestingly, his European roots are also evident in the chef's authentic Asian fare. Make sure you book 24hr in advance if you want to sample the 6-course Peking Duck menu.
➜ Kaisergranat, Hijiki, Spargel. Wolfsbarsch, Buchweizen, Shimeji. Entenbrust, Sichuanpfeffer, Wintermelone.

XX **Em Krützche** 🏠 ⇔
Am Frankenturm 1 ✉ *50667* – Ⓜ *Dom-Hauptbahnhof* Plan: J1
– ✆ *(0221) 2 58 08 39 – www.em-kruetzche.de – Closed 21-30 March and Monday*
Menu 20 € (lunch)/59 € – Carte 36/58 € – *(bookings advisable at dinner)*
• Classic cuisine • Traditional • Family •

Run for around 40 years by the Fehn family, this historic guesthouse has pretty rooms, ranging from rustic charm to elegant on two floors. Goose is the speciality in winter.

X 𝄞 **maiBeck** (Jan C. Maier und Tobias Becker) 🏠
Am Frankenturm 5 ✉ *50667* – Ⓜ *Dom-Hauptbahnhof* Plan: J1
– ✆ *(0221) 96 26 73 00 – www.maibeck.de – Closed Monday*
Menu 42 € – Carte 38/53 € – *(booking advisable)*
• Modern cuisine • Fashionable • Design •

This restaurant is the brainchild of Jan Maier and Tobias Becker, two ambitious young men with a passion for cooking and a feel for combining tastes and flavours. Their speciality is homemade pasta. The best place to eat in summer is the terrace with its view of the Rhine.
➜ Forellenfilet aus dem Lambachtal, Kartoffelsalat, eingelegte Gürkchen. Sanft geschmortes Schulterscherzel vom Eifelrind, 2-mal Lauch, Champignonjus. Apfeltarte COX, Tonkabohneneis, Rosmarin.

X **WeinAmRhein** 🕸
Johannisstr. 64 ✉ *50668* Plan: J1
– Ⓜ *Breslauer Pl./Hauptbahnhof* – ✆ *(0221) 91 24 88 85*
– *www.weinamrhein.eu – Closed 2 weeks July-August, Saturday lunch, Sunday-Monday and Bank Holidays*
Menu 22 € (lunch)/59 € – Carte 30/66 €
• International • Fashionable •

Rudolf Mützel's tasty cuisine, which includes such dishes such braised breast of veal with bread dumplings and celery, is accompanied by an excellent selection of open wines. If you fancy lunch at this modern restaurant behind the station, follow the example of most of your co-diners and order the attractively priced two-course daily set menu.

X **Früh am Dom**
Am Hof 12 ✉ *50667* – Ⓜ *Dom-Hauptbahnhof* Plan: J1
– ✆ *(0221) 2 61 32 15 – www.frueh-gastronomie.de*
Carte 16/37 €
• Regional • Traditional • Rustic •

Brewery tradition since 1904. In the many rooms, each with its own atmosphere, Kölsch beer and typical dishes are served by the waiters at ancient bare tables.

GERMANY - COLOGNE

Marriott

Plan: **F1-2**

Johannisstr. 76 ✉ *50668*
– Ⓜ *Breslauer Pl. / Hauptbahnhof –* 𝒞 *(0221) 94 22 20*
– www.koelnmarriott.de
355 rm – 🛉149/450 € 🛉🛉159/460 € – � 27 € – 10 suites
• Business • Modern •

This comfortable and modern hotel has a touch of luxury. The Dom Suite is very pleasant with its large roof terrace and fantastic view. Various conference rooms. 'Plüsch-Bar' in the lobby. 'Fou' is the casual French brasserie-stye restaurant.

Pullman

Plan: **E2**

Helenenstr. 14 ✉ *50667 –* Ⓜ *Friesenplatz –* 𝒞 *(0221)*
27 50 – www.pullmanhotels.com
265 rm – 🛉148/221 € 🛉🛉148/241 € – ⊻ 26 € – 10 suites
• Chain hotel • Conference hotel • Modern •

Sleek, modern business and conference hotel in the centre. Rooms with a hint of luxury and lounge-style bar. Second largest ballroom in the city. In the evening the 'george M' restaurant on the 12th floor serves contemporary organic cuisine, and a simpler menu at lunchtime.

Savoy

Plan: **F1**

Turiner Str. 9 ✉ *50668*
– Ⓜ *Breslauer Pl. / Hauptbahnhof –* 𝒞 *(0221) 1 62 30 – www.savoy.de*
152 rm – 🛉147/179 € 🛉🛉194/285 € – ⊻ 18 € – 5 suites
• Business • Personalised •

For guests looking for something special, Gisela and Daniela Ragge have created very high quality and individual rooms with an eye to detail: New York, Venice, Geisha... In the evening dine in the Mythos restaurant and at lunchtime in the bar. Superb roof terrace.

Im Wasserturm

Plan: **F2**

Kaygasse 2 ✉ *50676 –* Ⓜ *Poststr. –* 𝒞 *(0221) 2 00 80*
– www.hotel-im-wasserturm.de
54 rm – 🛉148/280 € 🛉🛉166/380 € – ⊻ 28 € – 34 suites
• Historic • Business • Design •

The imposing architecture of the over 130 year-old water tower is special here. It offers tasteful and contemporary rooms, beauty treatments and massage in the 'Atelier Beaut'. There is also a business centre. Clean-lined design in the 'd/\blju W' restaurant with a regional and international menu.
❀ **Himmel un Äd • d/\blju "W"** – See restaurant listing

THE QVEST hideaway

Plan: **E2**

Gereonskloster 12 ✉ *50670*
– Ⓜ *Christophstr./Mediapark –* 𝒞 *(0221) 2 78 57 80*
– www.qvest-hotel.com
33 rm ⊻ – 🛉140/250 € 🛉🛉170/320 € – 1 suite
• Traditional • Business • Minimalist •

The Qvest is a unique hotel housed in the former city archives and features a chic mix of neo-Gothic, design and art. The atmosphere is relaxed and the service excellent and personal. If you like a piece of furniture or one of the accessories, you can buy it!

art'otel cologne

Plan: **F3**

Holzmarkt 4 ✉ *50676 –* Ⓜ *Severinstr. –* 𝒞 *(0221)*
80 10 30 – www.artotels.com/cologne
217 rm – 🛉79/145 € 🛉🛉89/145 € – ⊻ 20 € – 1 suite
• Business • Design •

Hotel and gallery in one: trendy designer interior, excellent technical facilities with free W-LAN, as well as works by the Korean artist SEO throughout the building. The Chino Latino restaurant serves Asian cuisine and has a terrace with a view of the Rhine port and Chocolate Museum.

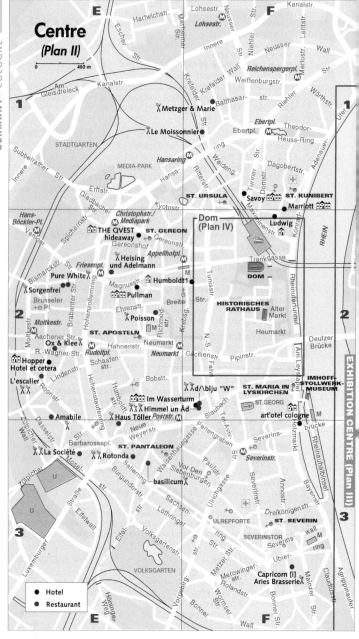

Centre
(Plan II)

0   400 m

GERMANY - COLOGNE

EXHIBITION CENTRE (Plan III)

Metzger & Marie

Le Moissonnier

STADTGARTEN

MEDIA-PARK

Hansaring

ST. URSULA

Savoy

ST. KUNIBERT

Marriott

Dom (Plan IV)

Ludwig

THE QVEST hideaway

ST. GEREON

Heising und Adelmann

Pure White

Humboldt1

Sorgenfrei

Pullman

Poisson

ST. APOSTELN

Neumarkt

DOM

HISTORISCHES RATHAUS

Alter Markt

Heumarkt

Deutzer Brücke

Ox & Klee

Hopper Hotel et cetera

L'escalier

Rudolfpl.

Im Wasserturm

d/\blju "W"

ST. MARIA IN LYSKIRCHEN

IMHOFF-STOLLWERCK-MUSEUM

ST. GEORG

art'otel cologne

Amabile

Himmel un Äd

Haus Töller

ST. PANTALEON

La Société

Rotonda

basilicum

VOLKSGARTEN

ULREPFORTE

ST. SEVERIN

SEVERINSTOR

Capricorn [i]
Aries Brasserie

- ● Hotel
- ● Restaurant

Hopper Hotel et cetera

Brüsseler Str. 26 ✉ *50674 –* Ⓜ *Moltkestr. –* ☎ *(0221)* Plan: **E2**
92 44 00 – www.hopper.de – Closed 20 December-3 January
49 rm ⌷ – 🛉85/250 € 🛉🛉110/310 € – 1 suite
• Townhouse • Personalised •

Former monastery located in the Belgian Quarter. All the rooms have design-orientated furnishings, high quality eucalyptus parquet, marble bathrooms and free W-LAN. The imposing altar painting catches the eye in the cosy restaurant. Inner courtyard terrace under the trees.

Humboldt1

Kupfergasse 10 ✉ *50667 –* Ⓜ *Appellhofpl. –* ☎ *(0221)* Plan: **F2**
27 24 33 87 – www.humboldt1.de
7 rm ⌷ – 🛉160/215 € 🛉🛉259/319 €
• Townhouse • Family • Personalised •

This friendly boutique hotel, which is run with a personal touch, is really a great place to stay. The rooms are individually designed and lavishly furnished. Room 6 – a duplex with bath under the eaves – is particularly attractive.

Ludwig

Brandenburger Str. 24 ✉ *50668*
– Ⓜ *Breslauer Pl. / Hauptbahnhof –* ☎ *(0221) 16 05 40* Plan: **F2**
– www.hotelludwig.de
53 rm ⌷ – 🛉102/115 € 🛉🛉128/145 € – 1 suite
• Townhouse • Functional •

An informally-run hotel close to the old town with bright, cheerful and contemporary guestrooms. The position is ideal for rail travellers and city tourists.

Himmel un Äd – Hotel Im Wasserturm

Kaygasse 2 (11th floor) ✉ *50676 –* Ⓜ *Poststr.* Plan: **F2**
– ☎ *(0221) 2 00 80 – www.hotel-im-wasserturm.de – Closed 1-11 January, 4-11 February, 12 July-9 August and Sunday-Monday*
Menu 89/129 € – Carte 66/83 € – *(dinner only) (booking advisable)*
• Modern cuisine • Fashionable • Elegant •

This impressive building is once again the site of a gourmet restaurant. High up on the 11th floor Mathias Maucher and his team serve modern cuisine with regional accents in an elegant setting with a wonderful view.
→ Hummer, Wasserspinat, Physalis, Kardamomblätter. Felsenrotbarbe, Meeraal-Brandade, Gulaschcrème, Calamaretti. Bergheimer Rehrücken, Sellerie, Waldbeeren, Manjari Schokolade.

Rotonda

Pantaleonswall 27 ✉ *50676 –* Ⓜ *Poststr. –* ☎ *(0221)* Plan: **E3**
9 97 75 11 – www.rotonda-restaurant.de – Closed Saturday-Sunday
Menu 45/65 € – Carte 47/85 € – *(dinner only) (booking advisable)*
• Modern cuisine • Trendy • Fashionable •

During the day a club and in the evenings, a restaurant open to all. The cuisine is modern and international and comes in the form of two set menus, these are `Buddhas Hand', described as "pure and vegan", and `Earth and Water' featuring the finest fish and beef. The design is trendy and urban with a Nordic touch.

d/\blju "W" – Hotel Im Wasserturm

Kaygasse 2 ✉ *50676 –* Ⓜ *Poststr. –* ☎ *(0221) 2 00 80* Plan: **F2**
– www.hotel-im-wasserturm.de – Closed Saturday lunch, Sunday
Menu 54 € – Carte 30/54 €
• International • Fashionable • Elegant •

The interior of this restaurant is light and modern, with the elegant light fittings providing much of the atmosphere. The glass frontage offers a view of the terrace, which boasts an open-air kitchen in fine weather.

XX **L'escalier**   ⌂ ⌂ 🄰🄲

Brüsseler Str. 11 ⊠ 50674 – Ⓜ Moltkestr. – ℰ (0221)   Plan: **E2**
2 05 39 98 – www.lescalier-restaurant.de – Closed 2 weeks early
January, Sunday-Monday except Bank Holidays
Menu 49/98 € – *(dinner only)*
• Modern cuisine • Fashionable • Bistro •

Small, intimate and friendly, L'escalier is everything a really good bistro should be. The classic modern fare comes in the form of two set menus, one traditional and the other more innovative.

XX **La Société**   ⌂
❀ *Kyffhäuser Str. 53 ⊠ 50674 – ℰ (0221) 23 24 64*   Plan: **E3**
– www.lasociete.info – Closed 2 weeks July
Menu 55/109 € – Carte 69/89 € – *(dinner only) (booking advisable)*
• Classic cuisine • Neighbourhood • Intimate •

Jeske's mixture of classic cuisine and creative elements is characterised by its flavour, freshness and vibrancy – and of course by his undisputed talent. Eating here is such a pleasure – thanks not only to the food but also to the friendly service and wine suggestions of the knowledgeable owner Stefan Helfrich – that it hardly seems to matter that the tables in this cosy little restaurant are perhaps a little close together.
→ Tatar vom Limousin-Rind mit gelierter Rauchessenz und Sellerie. Steinbutt mit Kopfsalatrisotto, gebratenem Salatherz, Petersilie und Pariser Karotten. Eifelrehrücken mit Erbse, Lauch und Aprikose.

X **Le Moissonnier**   🄰🄲
❀❀ *Krefelder Str. 25 ⊠ 50670 – ℰ (0221) 72 94 79*   Plan: **F1**
– www.lemoissonnier.de – Closed 1 week Christmas-early January, 1 week
during Easter, 3 weeks July-August and Sunday-Monday except Bank
Holidays
Menu 90 € (weekday lunch)/140 € – Carte 67/113 € – *(booking essential)*
• Creative • Bistro • Friendly •

Liliane and Vincent Moissonnier are French and know all there is to know about French brasserie style. Not surprising then that this lively and uncomplicated restaurant has carved out quite a reputation for itself in Cologne. It serves the creative cuisine of fellow countryman Eric Menchon. The 4-course menu with wine suggestions offers unbeatable value for money.
→ Ris de veau braisé. Loup de mer en bouillabaisse. Pigeonneau rôti.

X **Poisson**   ⌂ 🄰🄲
Wolfsstr. 6 ⊠ 50667 – Ⓜ Neumarkt – ℰ (0221)   Plan: **E2**
27 73 68 83 – www.poisson-restaurant.de – Closed during Carnival,
Sunday-Monday and Bank Holidays
Menu 32 € (weekday lunch)/98 € – Carte 68/99 € – *(booking advisable)*
• Fish and seafood • Bistro • Trendy •

Top quality products are deliciously prepared at this modern bistro with a fish orientated menu. The chef allows Asian, as well as Mediterranean and classic components to influence his food.

X **Capricorn [i] Aries Brasserie**   ⌂ ⌂ ⌂
☺ *Alteburgerstr. 31 ⊠ 50678 – Ⓜ Severinstr. – ℰ (0221)*   Plan: **F3**
3 97 57 10 – www.capricorniaries.com – Closed Saturday lunch, Sunday
and Wednesday
Menu 19 € (weekday lunch)/59 € – Carte 33/54 €
• French classic • Bistro • Cosy •

This street corner brasserie is everything it should be – warm, friendly and down-to-earth. All the food on offer is based on good quality ingredients; try the fish soup with pan-fried scallops or the 'steak frites'. The delicious desserts include crème brûlée with tonka bean ice cream.

GERMANY - COLOGNE

✗ Amabile 🏠

Görrestr. 2 ⊠ 50674 – Ⓜ Moltkestr. – ℰ (0221) 21 91 01　　Plan: **E2**
*– www.restaurant-amabile.de – Closed 2 weeks during Carnival, 2 weeks
September and Sunday-Monday*
Menu 38/70 € – Carte 46/52 € – *(dinner only)*
• International • Friendly • Intimate •

You will find this lovingly decorated restaurant with a rustic touch between the
Millowitsch Theatre and University. The best way to discover the seasonal cuisine is to order the surprise menu.

✗ Heising und Adelmann 🏠 ⇔

Friesenstr. 58 ⊠ 50670 – Ⓜ Friesenplatz – ℰ (0221)　　Plan: **E2**
*1 30 94 24 – www.heising-und-adelmann.de – Closed Sunday-Monday and
Bank Holidays*
Menu 36/56 € – Carte 41/52 € – *(dinner only)*
• International • Bistro • Trendy •

Guests are served modern international cuisine in the relaxed atmosphere of
this lively bistro restaurant with its delightful terrace. Pleasant Lounge and
large bar area.

✗ Ox & Klee 🏠
❀

Richard-Wagner-Str. 20 ⊠ 50674 – Ⓜ Rudolfsplatz　　Plan: **E2**
*– ℰ (0221) 16 95 66 03 – www.oxundklee.de – Closed during Carnival,
2 weeks during Easter, 2 weeks July, Thursday, Sunday and Bank Holidays*
Menu 49/99 € – *(dinner only) (booking advisable)*
• Modern cuisine • Intimate •

A great place to eat fresh modern cuisine, Ox & Klee is an intimate little restaurant run by a friendly, welcoming couple. She takes charge front of house, while
he works in the kitchen preparing ambitious dishes for his à la carte and surprise
menus. The delicious sauces alone will have you coming back for more.
→ Warm gebeizter schottischer Lachs, Topinambur, Muschelgel, Gurke.
Bio-Huhn, Brokkoli, Erdnuss, Zitronengrasjus. Milch und Schokolade in 2
Gängen serviert.

✗ basilicum 🏠
☺

Am Weidenbach 33 ⊠ 50676 – Ⓜ Poststr. – ℰ (0221)　　Plan: **E3**
32 35 55 – www.basilicum.org – Closed 1-9 February and Sunday-Monday
Menu 37/49 € – Carte 33/50 € – *(dinner only) (booking advisable)*
• International • Friendly •

A very dedicatedly and personally-run small establishment with a bistro feel.
Good seasonal and contemporary cuisine. The restaurant also has a lovely
covered inner courtyard terrace.

✗ Metzger & Marie 🏠 ✄
☺

Kasparstr. 19 ⊠ 50670 – Ⓜ Ebertpl. – ℰ (0221)　　Plan: **F1**
99 87 93 53 – www.metzgermarie.de – Closed Tuesday-Wednesday
Menu 25 € – Carte 36/60 € – *(dinner only) (booking advisable)*
• Traditional cuisine • Rustic • Neighbourhood •

A trained butcher and a former dancing girl from the Rhenish carnival serve traditional fare at this restaurant. Wiener schnitzel, marinated pot roast and a vegetarian option are on the menu, all accompanied by good German and Austrian
wines. These are served in an equally traditional setting that offers a pleasant
mix of rustic and modern. Young, relaxed atmosphere.

✗ Sorgenfrei 🎍 🅰

Antwerpenerstr. 15 ⊠ 50672 – Ⓜ Moltkestr. – ℰ (0221)　　Plan: **E2**
*3 55 73 27 – www.sorgenfrei-koeln.com – Closed during Carnival, during
Christmas and Saturday lunch, Sunday*
Menu 17 € (lunch)/35 € – Carte 37/51 €
• International • Friendly • Rustic •

A really appealing and lively address in the Belgian Quarter, next door to which
is a wine dealer with a good European range. No-frills international dishes. The
classic is Argentinean 'Black Ranch' entrecote steak. Simpler lunchtime menu.

GERMANY - COLOGNE

X **Pure White**

Antwerpener Str. 5 ✉ 50667 – ⓜ Rudolfpl. – ℰ (0221)   Plan: **E2**
29 43 65 07 – www.pure-white-food.de – Closed Sunday
Carte 65/119 € – *(dinner only) (booking advisable)*
• Fish and seafood • Neighbourhood • Trendy •
Located close to the Friesenplatz, Pure White serves fresh food based on top quality ingredients in a casual, informal setting. Try the Norwegian king crab, the oysters or the wild halibut. If you prefer meat, you will enjoy the US, Scottish and Japanese dry-aged beef from the Josper grill.

X **Haus Töller**   ⇔ 🍴

Weyerstr. 96 ✉ 50676 – ⓜ Poststr. – ℰ (0221)   Plan: **E3**
2 58 93 16 – www.haus-toeller.de – Closed Christmas-mid January, June-August, Sunday and Bank Holidays
Carte 21/28 € – *(dinner only) (booking advisable)*
• Regional • Traditional • Cosy •
The former 'Steynen Huys' 1343 is really something for connoisseurs with its original wooden tables and floors, coffer ceiling and confession chair. Specialities include pork knuckles, Rhenish marinated roast (horsemeat) and on Friday evenings potato pancakes – all washed down with Päffgen Kölsch draught beer.

AT THE EXHIBITION CENTRE   PLAN III

 Hyatt Regency   🏖 ← ⓕ⒮ 🐾 🖥 ⅃ 🛗 ⅃♨ 🚗

Kennedy-Ufer 2a ✉ 50679 – ⓜ Deutzer Freiheit   Plan: **G2**
– ℰ (0221) 8 28 12 34 – www.cologne.regency.hyatt.de
288 rm – †160/400 € ††160/600 € – ☕ 25 € – 18 suites
• Chain hotel • Luxury • Classic •
Classic business hotel directly by the Rhine at the Hohenzollern bridge. The lobby is large and refined, the rooms sleek, modern, elegant and technically up to date. Even the standard rooms are 36m² in size. International cuisine in the bright Glashaus restaurant on the first floor.

 Stadtpalais   🏖 🐾 ⅃ 🛗 ⅃♨ 🚗

Deutz-Kalker-Str. 52 ✉ 50679 – ⓜ Deutz-Kalker Bad   Plan: **G2**
– ℰ (0221) 88 04 20 – www.hotelstadtpalais.de
115 rm ☕ – †145/329 € ††165/349 €
• Business • Modern •
This attractive group of buildings directly opposite the LANXESS Arena combines historical and modern architecture. Technically well equipped rooms in purist style. Small range of dishes available in menu form.

 Burns Art Hotel   ℗

Adam-Stegerwald-Str. 9 ✉ 51063 – ⓜ Bf. Deutz   Plan: **H1**
– ℰ (0221) 6 71 16 90 – www.hotel-burns.de – Closed 22-30 December
102 rm ☕ – †79/350 € ††99/375 €
• Business • Functional •
This hotel boasts a relatively calm location in a residential area. Guests can choose between contemporary "Fair & More" rooms and the pure lines of its designer "Burns Art" rooms.

🏠 **Inselhotel**

Constantinstr. 96 ✉ 50679 – ⓜ Bf. Deutz – ℰ (0221)   Plan: **G2**
8 80 34 50 – www.inselhotel-koeln.de
42 rm ☕ – †89/225 € ††119/295 €
• Townhouse • Functional •
This corner townhouse opposite Deutz railway station offers its guests friendly service and well-maintained, functional rooms. Close to the Exhibition Centre and LANXESS Arena.

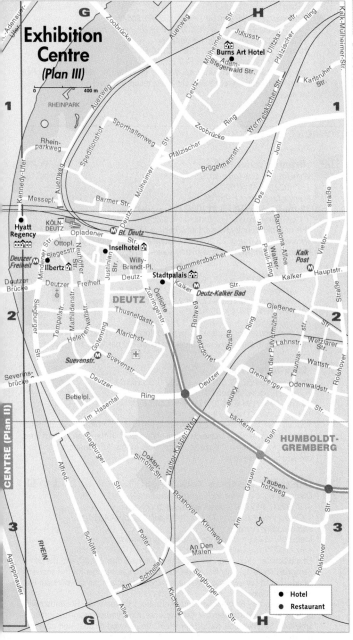

Exhibition
Centre
(Plan III)

0   400 m

RHEINPARK

Rhein-
parkweg

Adenauer-Ufer

Zoobrücke

Auenweg

Mülheimer Str.

Juliusstr.

Burns Art Hotel

Adam-
Stegerwald Str.

Ulitzka

Pfälzischer Ring

Kalk-Mülheimer-Str.

Karlsruher Str.

Speditionshof

Sporthallenweg

Auenweg

Deutz-

Zoobrücke Ring

Pfälzischer Str.

Brügelmannstr.

Des 17. Juni

Wermelskircher Str.

straße

Kennedy-Ufer

Messepl.

Barmer Str.

Auenweg

Mülheimer Str.

KÖLN-
DEUTZ

Bf. Deutz

Str.

Str.

Barcelona-Allee

Walter-
Pauli-Ring

Kalk
Post

Vietor-
straße

Hyatt
Regency

Deutzer
Freiheit

Ilbertz

Ottopl.

Opladener

Mindener Str.

Siegesstr.

Neuhöffer Str.

Justinian
Str.

Inselhotel

Willy-
Brandt-Pl.

Deutz-

Stadtpalais

Gummersbacher

Kalker Str.

Deutz-Kalker Bad

Kalker Hauptstr.

Deutzer
Brücke

Deutzer Freiheit

DEUTZ

Thusneldastr.

Östliche Zubringerstr.

Str.

Rehweg

Betzdorfer Str.

Gießener Str.

An der Pulvermühle

Lahnstr.

Wetzlarer
Str.

Str.

Siegburger Str.

Tempelstr.

Mathildenstr.

Helenenwallstr.

Golenring

Alarichstr.

Suevenstr.

Suevenstr.

Deutzer Ring

Straße

Deutzer

Kanne

Gremberger

Taunus-
str.

Wattstr.

Odenwaldstr.

Rolshover

Str.

Severins-
brücke

Bebelpl.

Im Hasental

Ring

bäckerstr.

Stein

HUMBOLDT-
GREMBERG

Siegburger Str.

Alfred-

Doktor-
Simons-Str.

Walter-Kasper-Weg

Rolshover Kirchweg

Grauen

Am

Tauben-
holzweg

Str.

RHEIN

Schütte-

Poller

An Den Maien

Siegburger Str.

Agrippinauer

Am Schnellert

Allee

Kirchweg

Str.

● Hotel
● Restaurant

339

Ilbertz

🏠 AC 🛁

Mindener Str. 6 (Access by Siegesstr. 6) ✉ *50679*

Plan: **G2**

– **Ⓜ** *Deutzer Freiheit* – ☎ *(0221) 8 29 59 20* – *www.hotel-ilbertz.de*

– *Closed 22-30 December, 1-6 January*

26 rm – ♦92/99 € ♦♦109/125 € – ⌓ 10 €

• Family • Functional •

This immaculate, family-run hotel with its characteristic yellow façade offers functional rooms equipped with the latest technology and a traditional breakfast room.

ENVIRONS OF COLOGNE

Brenner'scher Hof

⌖ 🛁 🚗

Wilhelm-von-Capitaine-Str. 15 ✉ *50858*

Plan: **A2**

– ☎ *(0221) 9 48 60 00*

– *www.brennerscher-hof.de*

38 rm ⌓ – ♦89/255 € ♦♦109/275 € – 2 suites

• Country house • Historic • Cosy •

This beautiful country house dating back to 1754 has been decorated in Mediterranean style. The guest accommodation is in a series of charming and comfortable individually designed rooms, suites and maisonettes.

Garten-Hotel

Königsberger Str. 5 ✉ *50858* – ☎ *(02234) 4 08 70*

Plan: **A2**

– *www.garten-hotel.de* – *Closed 23 December-2 January*

33 rm – ♦89/99 € ♦♦109/139 € – ⌓ 8 €

• Townhouse • Business • Functional •

This guesthouse is in a pleasant, peaceful location and has functional rooms, modern apartments and a nice breakfast room. The garden is very pretty.

EuroNova arthotel

Zollstockgürtel 65 ✉ *50969* – ☎ *(0221) 9 33 33 00*

Plan: **B3**

– *www.euronova-arthotel.de*

73 rm – ♦85/195 € ♦♦100/210 € – ⌓ 15 €

• Business • Design • Modern •

You will find the ultra-modern EuroNova arthotel set amid a maze of office blocks. The owners are architects and it shows: both in the clean straight lines and pure forms and in the spacious, upmarket rooms. As a business guest you can also hire office space.

XxX
❀

Maître im Landhaus Kuckuck (Erhard Schäfer)

Olympiaweg 2 (by Friedrich-Schmitt-Straße) ✉ *50933*

Plan: **A2**

– ☎ *(0221) 48 53 60* – *www.landhaus-kuckuck.de*

– *Closed 1-10 February, 21 March-3 April, 11 July-7 August and Monday-Tuesday*

Menu 99/129 € – *(dinner only) (booking essential)*

• French classic • Elegant • Classic •

Erhard Schäfer offers two menus at this restaurant, one 'classic', and the other 'seasonal'. There are only five tables, exactly the right number for this sophisticated – not to say exclusive – venue. It is located just a stone's throw from the home of FC Cologne.

➜ Geschmorter Bergfenchel mit Anisrahm, bretonische Herzmuscheln, gepuffter Reis. Brust von der Challansente mit Himbeeressig-Honigsauce, Spitzkohl, Selleriepüree, Kartoffelkrusteln. Mousse von Nougat und gerösteten Haselnüssen, Himbeereis mit italienischer Meringue.

Landhaus Kuckuck – See restaurant listing

XX **AURA by Luis Dias**

Wilhelmstr. 35a ✉ 50996 – ✆ (0221) 9 35 23 23 Plan: **C3**
– www.aura-coeln.de – closed 3 weeks July-August and Monday, Saturday lunch
Menu 55/64 € – Carte 44/66 €
• Italian • Elegant • Cosy •
Everyone who finds their way to this pretty, slightly out-of-the-way little restaurant plans to become a regular. This is thanks to Luis Dias' fresh and flavoursome Mediterranean cuisine and the attentive, friendly service. Leave your car in the car park in Maternusplatz.

XX **Landhaus Kuckuck** – Restaurant Maître im Landhaus Kuckuck

Olympiaweg 2 (by Friedrich-Schmitt-Straße)
✉ 50933 – ✆ (0221) 48 53 60 Plan: **A2**
– www.landhaus-kuckuck.de – Closed 1-10 February and Monday
Menu 38 € – Carte 44/63 €
• Regional • Elegant • Luxury •
A real treasure on the outskirts of busy Cologne. This restaurant is the perfect place to relax and unwind with its magnificent countryside location and elegant English country house-style interior.

X **Carls**

Eichendorffstr. 25 ✉ 50823 – ✆ (0221) 58 98 66 56 Plan: **B2**
– www.carlsrestaurant.de – Closed during Carnival, 2 weeks October and Monday except Bank Holidays
Carte 23/42 € – *(dinner only)*
• International • Neighbourhood • Simple •
If you want something friendly and local, you will love the charm of this rustic, down-to-earth eatery. It serves international and regional fare from tuna steak with chicory and lemon risotto to himmel un äd', a local speciality of black pudding, fried onions, mash and apple sauce.

AT THE AIRPORT **South-East: 17 km by A59 D3**

Leonardo Hotel Köln Bonn Airport

Waldstr. 255 (at Köln/Bonn Airport) ✉ 51147 – ✆ (02203) 56 10
– www.leonardo-hotels.com
177 rm – †79/179 € ††99/199 € – ☕ 18 €
• Chain hotel • Business • Elegant •
Ideal for the business traveller, this hotel with its modern reception area and well-appointed contemporary rooms offers a free airport shuttle service. An elegant restaurant serving predominantly international cuisine with a great bar.

FRANKFURT
FRANKFURT AM MAIN

Population: 687 780

Tom Bayer/Fotolia.com

European travellers might feel there's no need to go all the way to New York when they've got Frankfurt. After all, it's earned itself the nickname 'Mainhattan', what with all those slinky, shiny skyscrapers reaching up from the banks of the River Main. This may be a city of big corporations, but you'll also find half-timbered medieval houses (admittedly rebuilt), and an array of museums along the south bank of the river. Located at the crossing point of Germany's north-south and east-west roads, Frankfurt is a city that takes its cultural scene very seriously. It's said that it spends more money on the arts per year than any other European city, and has also become something of a gourmet hotspot with a cuisine range that gets more eclectic by the month.

The centre of Frankfurt is Cathedral Hill, where the cathedral has stood for eight hundred years; it towers over Römerberg, the medieval square, rebuilt following the war. To the west, amongst the mighty skyscrapers of international banks and corporations, lie the main railway station and the Exhibition Centre, while south of the River Main is the famous 'museum embankment' and Frankfurt's oldest area, Sachsenhausen, full of bars, cafés and restaurants. Germany's great poet, novelist and dramatist, Johann Wolfgang von Goethe, was born and bred here; no doubt he wouldn't believe his eyes if he saw Frankfurt today.

FRANKFURT IN...

→ **ONE DAY**
Old Town, Römerberg, the view from Main Tower.

→ **TWO DAYS**
Goethe House, Museum Embankment, an apfelwein lokal restaurant in Sachsenhausen.

→ **THREE DAYS**
Boat trip on the Main, window shopping (Zeil), a concert at the Opera House.

PRACTICAL INFORMATION

ARRIVAL-DEPARTURE

✈ Frankfurt Airport is 9km southeast of the city centre. S-Bahn trains S8 and S9 leave every 15min for Frankfurt station and take just over 10min.

GETTING AROUND

Frankfurt runs an efficient bus, metro and tram system. You can buy a day ticket for one person or for a group (max. 5), which is valid until the last ride of the day. Tickets are available at vending machines and from bus drivers, but cannot be bought on trams, the U-Bahn or S-Bahn. A Frankfurt Card entitles you to free public transport, discounts at a variety of museums and attractions, and reductions of up to thirty per cent on selected boat trips. You can buy the Card at many travel agencies, at tourist information offices and in both terminals at the airport; it's valid for 24 or 48 hours.

EATING OUT

Not so long ago, Frankfurt's gastronomic fame came courtesy of its Apfelwein (a sweet or dry variant of cider), its Handkäs mit Musik (small yellow cheese with vinegar, oil and onions) and its Grüne Sauce (various herbs and sour cream served with boiled eggs). That's not the case now. Head along to the Fressgass (near Opernplatz) – which translates as 'Eatery Alley' or 'Glutton's Lane' – and you've got a pedestrian mile of eateries; choose from a whole range of food to take away or to graze over, all at good prices. Nearly thirty per cent of Frankfurt's citizens have come to the city from overseas,

CALENDAR HIGHLIGHTS

February/March
Carnival.

June
Forest Folk Festival, Rose and Light Festival (music and illuminations in the Palm Garden).

July
Museum Quay Festival.

August
River Main Festival.

September
Autumn Dippe Fair (funfair and fireworks), International Motor Show (odd-numbered years).

October
Book Fair.

so a wealth of eating possibilities has been opened up. It's now easy to 'eat globally' all round the city and foreign communities have added a real touch of spice to the culinary landscape, with the likes of Turkish, Italian and Chinese establishments. Nevertheless, a visit to this city wouldn't be complete without a trip to the äppelwoilokale in Sachsenhausen, the casual but lively cafés where tradition is the key, and Apfelwein is served up in ceramic mugs.

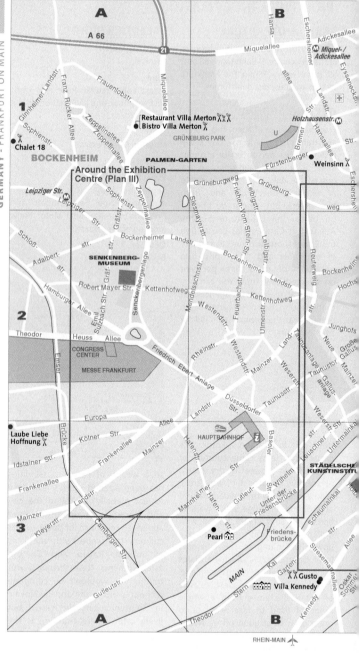

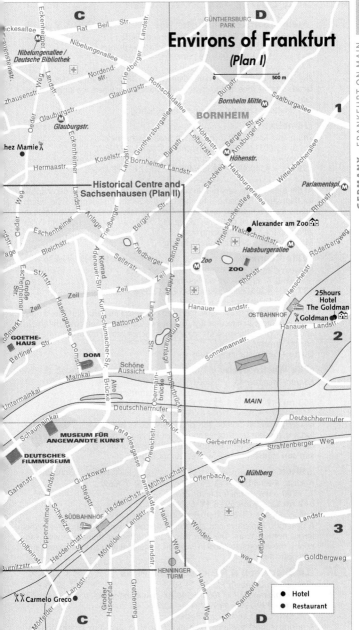

Environs of Frankfurt
(Plan I)

0   500 m

GÜNTHERSBURG PARK

Bornhelm Mitte

BORNHEIM

Höhenstr.

Parlamentspl.

Historical Centre and
Sachsenhausen (Plan II)

Alexander am Zoo

Habsburgerallee

Zoo

ZOO

Hanauer Landstr.

25hours
Hotel
The Goldman

OSTBAHNHOF

Goldman

Hanauer Landstr.

Sonnemannstr.

GOETHE-HAUS

DOM

Schöne
Aussicht

Mainkai

Alte
Brücke

Untermainkai

MAIN

Deutschherrnufer

Deutschherrnufer

**MUSEUM FÜR
ANGEWANDTE KUNST**

Gerbermühlstr.

Strahlenberger Weg

**DEUTSCHES
FILMMUSEUM**

Mühlberg

Offenbacher

SÜDBAHNHOF

Landstr.

Goldbergweg

**HENNINGER
TURM**

Carmelo Greco

| ● | Hotel |
| ● | Restaurant |

345

Steigenberger Frankfurter Hof   🛰 𝓕ᵇ 🌐 🛎 🖔 🖪 🐾 🚗

Am Kaiserplatz ✉ 60311 – ⓜ *Willy-Brandt-Platz*   Plan: **E1**
– 𝒸 (069) 2 15 02 – www.frankfurter-hof.steigenberger.de
261 rm ☷ – †249/699 € ††249/699 € – 42 suites
• Luxury • Traditional • Classic •

The origins of this luxury hotel date back to 1876. The impressive, historic façade sets the tone for the classic atmosphere inside where the lobby is decorated in feudal-style.

❀ **Français • Oscar's** – See restaurant listing

Jumeirah   🛰 🛎 🖔 🖪 🐾 🚗

Thurn-und-Taxis-Platz 2 (access via Große Eschenheimer   Plan: **E1**
Str. 8) ✉ 60313 – ⓜ *Hauptwache – 𝒸 (069) 2 97 23 70*
– www.jumeirah.com/frankfurt
199 rm – †300/480 € ††300/480 € – ☷ 32 € – 18 suites
• Grand Luxury • Modern • Elegant •

At the Jumeirah the very best in comfort, technology and interior decor speak for themselves. No praise is too high for the 220m2 Presidential Suite, which boasts its own massage and beauty facility, a Talise spa and direct access to the adjacent leisure centre. Breakfast and snacks are served in Le Petit Palais adjoining the MyZeil shopping mall.

Max on One – See restaurant listing

Villa Kennedy   🛰 🛥 𝓕ᵇ 🌐 🛎 🖥 🖔 🖪 🐾 🚗

Kennedyallee 70 ✉ 60596 – ⓜ *Schweizer Platz*   Plan I: **B3**
– 𝒸 (069) 71 71 20 – www.villakennedy.com
137 rm – †260/295 € ††260/295 € – ☷ 35 € – 26 suites
• Grand Luxury • Villa • Classic •

The Villa Speyer, built in 1904, has been converted into an impressive luxury hotel with great architectural flair. The interior successfully combines the classic and the modern. The exquisite spa offers Éminence beauty treatments (the only one in Germany).

Gusto – See restaurant listing

The Westin Grand   🛰 𝓕ᵇ 🌐 🛎 🖥 🖔 🖪 🐾 🚗

Konrad-Adenauer-Str. 7 ✉ 60313 – ⓜ *Konstablerwache*   Plan: **F1**
– 𝒸 (069) 2 98 10 – www.westingrandfrankfurt.com
353 rm – †199/699 € ††199/699 € – ☷ 33 € – 18 suites
• Luxury • Chain hotel • Modern •

Enjoying a central location, this large international business hotel boasts comfortable, modern guestrooms and numerous conference areas. Executive club on the first floor. Swimming pool with great views of the city.

san san • Sushimoto – See restaurant listing

Hilton   🛰 𝓕ᵇ 🛎 🖥 🖔 🖪 🐾 🚗

Hochstr. 4 ✉ 60313 – ⓜ *Eschenheimer Tor – 𝒸 (069)*   Plan: **E1**
13 38 00 – www.frankfurt.hilton.com
342 rm ☷ – †169/599 € ††169/599 €
• Business • Chain hotel • Contemporary •

A generous, impressive and airy atrium welcomes you into this hotel at the Bockenheimer centre. The 25m indoor pool, a former municipal swimming pool, is the largest hotel pool in Frankfurt. Restaurant with an international and American menu.

Lindner Hotel & Residence Main Plaza   🛰 ⪡ 𝓕ᵇ 🌐 🛎
🖥 🖪 🐾 🚗

Walther-von-Cronberg Platz 1 ✉ 60594
– ⓜ Lokalbahnhof – 𝒸 (069) 66 40 10 – www.lindner.de   Plan: **F2**
111 rm – †99/799 € ††99/799 € – ☷ 25 € – 7 suites
• Business • Luxury • Modern •

A striking redbrick tower on the banks of the Main. Generous, tasteful and elegant rooms, most with wonderful views over the city. Extensive beauty and spa suite. New Brick serves Californian cuisine from the show kitchen.

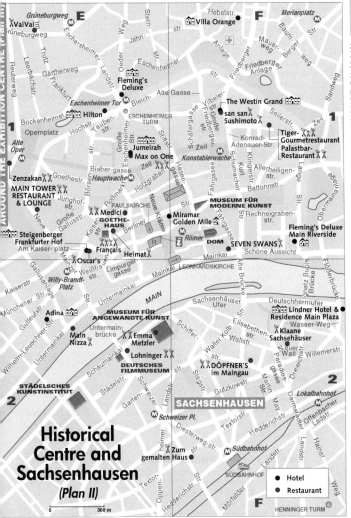

GERMANY - FRANKFURT ON MAIN

 Fleming's Deluxe   ♚ ⪕ 🛁 🛎 🛗 🎬 🚗

Eschenheimer Tor 2 ⊠ 60318 – Ⓜ Eschenheimer Tor   Plan: **E1**
– 𝒞 (069) 4 27 23 20 – www.flemings-hotels.com
206 rm ⌨ – 🚹198/258 € 🚹🚹218/278 € – 4 suites
• Business • Modern •

At the Eschenheimer centre find this listed, former office building from the
1950s with a still operating original Paternoster. It has modern furnishings with
a bar and lounge on the seventh-floor. This roof top restaurant with its show
kitchen offers a view of the Skyline.

GERMANY - FRANKFURT ON MAIN

Adina
Wilhelm-Leuschner-Str. 6 ⊠ *60329*
Plan: **E2**
– **Ⓜ** *Willy-Brandt-Platz*
– *𝒞 (069) 2 47 47 40 – www.adina.eu*
52 rm – **♥**139/399 € **♥♥**139/499 € – � 21 € – 82 suites
• Business • Modern •

Apartment hotel close to the river Main and the city centre, with classic modern furnishings clear cut lines and strong colours. All rooms have a kitchenette. Suites also have a washing machine and dryer. International dishes and tapas.

Alexander am Zoo
Waldschmidtstr. 59 ⊠ *60316* – **Ⓜ** *Habsburgerallee*
Plan I: **D2**
– *𝒞 (069) 94 96 00*
– *www.alexanderamzoo.de*
57 rm � – **♥**69/250 € **♥♥**87/250 € – 9 suites
• Business • Contemporary •

Stay in timelessly styled, spacious rooms in this hotel near the zoo. From the conference floor there is direct access to the roof terrace with a view of the city.

25hours Hotel The Goldman
Hanauer Landstr. 127 ⊠ *60314* – *𝒞 (069) 40 58 68 90*
Plan I: **D2**
– *www.25hours-hotels.com/goldman*
97 rm – **♥**145/405 € **♥♥**145/405 € – � 18 €
• Business • Design • Personalised •

This hotel has all manner of endearing and stylish decor in the form of lamps, fabrics, paints etc. The very pleasant modern rooms could hardly be more individual.
Goldman – See restaurant listing

Villa Orange
Hebelstr. 1 ⊠ *60318* – **Ⓜ** *Merianplatz* – *𝒞 (069)*
Plan: **F1**
40 58 40 – www.villa-orange.de
38 rm � – **♥**95/195 € **♥♥**119/275 €
• Family • Modern • Cosy •

This beautifully appointed villa-style townhouse is one of the Bio Hotels. Modern-style and warm tones from the foyer via the library to the rooms. Organic, quality breakfast.

Fleming's Deluxe Main Riverside
Lange Str. 5 ⊠ *60311* – **Ⓜ** *Römer* – *𝒞 (069) 21 93 00*
Plan: **F1**
– *www.flemings-hotels.com*
145 rm � – **♥**155 € **♥♥**175 € – 4 suites
• Business • Chain hotel • Contemporary •

A business hotel with good rooms in a modern yet elegant style, some – including the wonderful Winter Garden Suite on the top floor – offer a view of the Frankfurt skyline. The view is shared by the conference facilities on the sixth floor. The restaurant boasts a show kitchen serving international food.

Miramar Golden Mile
Berliner Str. 31 ⊠ *60311* – **Ⓜ** *Römer*
Plan: **E-F1**
– *𝒞 (069) 9 20 39 70 – www.miramar-frankfurt.de*
– *Closed 23-31 December*
39 rm � – **♥**80/280 € **♥♥**100/300 €
• Townhouse • Functional •

This well-kept and informally-run hotel is in a central location between Zeil and Römer. The rooms are timeless and functional in style.

XXXX **Français** – Hotel Steigenberger Frankfurter Hof   🦐 🀄 🕭 🏧 🚗

ꑭ *Am Kaiserplatz* ✉ *60311* – Ⓜ *Willy-Brandt-Platz*   Plan: **E1**
– 𝒞 (069) 2 15 83 24 – www.restaurant-francais.de – Closed 1 week
January, 2 weeks during Easter, 4 weeks July-August, Saturday lunch,
Sunday-Monday and Bank Holidays
Menu 59 € (weekday lunch)/104 € (dinner)
– Carte 94/110 € – (booking advisable)
• French classic • Elegant • Classic •

Patrick Bittner and his experienced team continue to hone their skills, bringing
clever modern techniques and interesting textures to their classic cuisine. The
food is served in the suitably elegant dining room complete with fireplace and
winter garden. If you like eating outside, the main courtyard makes a perfect
terrace in the summer.
→ Pochierte Gillardeau Auster Nr. 2, Bohne, Tomate, Chipolata-Wurst. Pacific Black Cod, Miso, Erbse, Spitzmorchel. Französisches Salers Rind "Dry
Aged", Couscous, Rucola, Griechischer Joghurt.

XXX **Tiger-Gourmetrestaurant**   🦐 🏧

ꑭ ꑭ *Heiligkreuzgasse 20* ✉ *60313* – Ⓜ *Konstablerwache*   Plan: **F1**
– 𝒞 (069) 9 20 02 20 – www.tigerpalast.de – Closed 22 December-
10 January, mid May-mid August and Sunday-Monday
Menu 98/135 € – Carte 82/124 € – *(dinner only) (booking essential)*
• French classic • Elegant • Fashionable •

Modern techniques and textures, subtle contrasts and intense aromas: that's
the classically based cuisine on offer here at Tiger. And should the elaborately
and meticulously prepared food make you forget you're sitting in the Variety
Theatre, there are always the historical posters which adorn the walls of this
small, almost intimate restaurant to remind you!
→ Gartengurke in Texturen, Wildkräuter, Radieschen, Rettich. Limousin
Lamm, Rücken, Backe und Bries mit Kreuzkümmeljus. Bio Grand Cru Mada-
gaskar Schokolade, Nusserde, Caramelia Ganache, Kaffirlimetteneis.
Palastbar-Restaurant – See restaurant listing

XXX **Max on One** – Hotel Jumeirah   🕭 🏧

Thurn-und-Taxis-Platz 2 (access via Große Eschenheimer   Plan: **E1**
Str. 8, 1st. floor) ✉ *60313* – Ⓜ *Hauptwache* – 𝒞 *(069) 2 97 23 71 98*
– www.jumeirah.com/frankfurt – Closed Saturday lunch, Sunday
Carte 43/68 € – *(August: Monday-Friday dinner only) (booking advisable)*
• International • Elegant •

Max on One is located on the first floor of an upmarket hotel in the city centre. It
boasts an open show kitchen where you can watch the staff at work surrounded by Japanese interior designer Takashi Sugimoto's smart decor. The cleverly
integrated glass wine cabinet is particularly eye-catching.

XX **Carmelo Greco**   🀃 🏧

ꑭ *Ziegelhüttenweg 1* ✉ *60598* – Ⓜ *Südbahnhof*   Plan I: **C3**
– 𝒞 (069) 60 60 89 67 – www.carmelo-greco.de – Closed Saturday lunch,
Sunday
Menu 37 € (lunch)/139 € – Carte 63/91 €
• Mediterranean • Fashionable •

It is the aromatic Italian cuisine with French influences prepared using fresh,
high quality ingredients by Carmelo Greco that brings the many regulars to
this lovely modern yet elegant restaurant. At lunchtimes you can enjoy his
excellent food in the form of a great value for money lunch menu.
→ Hummer, Taschenkrebs, Kaviar, Gurken-Essigsorbet. Tortelli Carbonara,
Spargel. Bretonische Rotbarbe, Fenchel, Kaffee-Gewürzöl, Krustentiersugo.

XX **Lohninger**   🀃 🏧 ⇔

Schweizer Str. 1 ✉ *60594* – Ⓜ *Schweizer Pl.* – 𝒞 *(069)*   Plan: **E2**
2 47 55 78 60 – www.lohninger.de
Menu 30 € (lunch)/88 € – Carte 45/75 € – *(booking advisable)*
• Austrian • Friendly • Fashionable •

This modern restaurant can be found in the beautiful high-ceilinged rooms of a
classic townhouse. It offers Austrian cuisine with international influences.

XX **MAIN TOWER RESTAURANT & LOUNGE** AC

Neue Mainzer Str. 52 (53rd floor, fee) ⊠ *60311* Plan: **E1**
– ⓜ Alte Oper – ℰ (069) 36 50 47 77 – www.maintower-restaurant.de
– Closed Saturday lunch, Sunday-Monday and Bank Holidays lunch
Menu 79/105 € (dinner) – Carte 37/55 € – *(booking essential)*
• Modern cuisine • Fashionable •
187m above the ground, the Main Tower offers impressive views over Frankfurt, and ambitious, international cuisine in a modern setting. Set menu only in the evenings.

XX **Medici** AC

Weißadlergasse 2 ⊠ *60311 – ⓜ Hauptwache – ℰ (069)* Plan: **E1**
21 99 07 94 – www.restaurantmedici.de – Closed Sunday and Bank Holidays
Menu 39 € (dinner)/64 € – Carte 44/65 €
• International • Friendly •
Two brothers are your hosts in this city centre restaurant. International dishes with a Mediterranean influence are served in a modern atmosphere.

XX **Zenzakan** AC

Taunusanlage 15 ⊠ *60325 – ⓜ Alte Oper – ℰ (069)* Plan: **E1**
97 08 69 08 – www.mook-group.de – Closed Christmas-New Year and Sunday
Menu 100 € – Carte 41/105 € – *(dinner only)*
• Asian • Trendy •
A trendy chic and very international restaurant in striking black with a bar-lounge. Contemporary Asian dishes are served, including modern sushi interpretations.

XX **DÖPFNER'S im Maingau** AC

Schifferstr. 38-40 ⊠ *60594 – ⓜ Lokalbahnhof – ℰ (069)* Plan: **F2**
60 91 42 01 – www.doepfners.de – Closed 3 weeks July-August and Monday-Tuesday
Menu 25 € (lunch)/119 € – Carte 31/61 €
• International • Friendly •
This family-run restaurant located close to the River Main offers a pleasant contemporary atmosphere and serves international and some classic cuisine. Good value lunchtime menu.

XX **Emma Metzler** P

Schaumainkai 17 ⊠ *60594 – ⓜ Schweizer Platz* Plan: **E2**
– ℰ (069) 61 99 59 06 – www.emma-metzler.com – Closed Sunday dinner-Monday except during fairs
Menu 28 € (lunch)/62 € – Carte 54/67 €
• Modern cuisine • Fashionable •
With its bright, modern interior the restaurant in the Frankfurt Museum of Applied Art offers good seasonal cuisine with attentive service. Attractive terrace looking onto the park.

XX **Gusto** – Hotel Villa Kennedy AC

Kennedyallee 70 ⊠ *60596 – ⓜ Schweizer Platz* Plan: **B3**
– ℰ (069) 7 17 12 12 00 – www.villakennedy.com
Menu 28 € (weekday lunch)/75 € – Carte 58/126 €
• International • Elegant •
Find tasteful design with a just hint of fashion and style within the venerable walls of this villa. Enjoy the Italian cuisine and charming setting, particularly in the impressive interior courtyard.

XX **Palastbar-Restaurant** – Tiger-Gourmetrestaurant AC

Heiligkreuzgasse 20 ⊠ *60313 – ⓜ Konstablerwache* Plan: **F1**
– ℰ (069) 92 00 220 – www.tigerpalast.de – Closed mid May-mid August and Monday
Menu 49/54 € – Carte 48/66 € – *(dinner only)*
• International • Cosy • Intimate •
With its comfortable bench seats upholstered in black leather, impressive brick arches and clever lighting, this restaurant is definitely the place to see and be seen.

SEVEN SWANS   🅐🅚

Mainkai 4 ✉ *60311 –* 🅜 *Römer – ℰ (069) 21 99 62 26*   Plan: **F1**
– www.sevenswans.de – Closed Sunday-Monday
Menu 89 € – *(dinner only) (booking essential)*
• Modern cuisine • Design •
Seven Swans is housed in the narrowest building in Frankfurt with one 4 x 10m
dining room on each floor. It offers a private dining club atmosphere and views
of the river through the glass frontage. Personal service from the charming
front-of-house team.
→ Jakobsmuschel mit Kopfsalat, Erdapfel und Schalotte. Ackerbohne mit
Melisse, Erbsen und junger Knoblauch. Ockstädter Kirschen mit Balsames-
sig, Frischkäse und Estragon.

Heimat   🎋 🈐

Berliner Str. 70 ✉ *60311 –* 🅜 *Hauptwache – ℰ (069)*   Plan: **E1**
29 72 59 94 – www.restaurant-heimat.de – Closed 23 December-8 January,
during Easter and during Whitsun
Menu 45/85 € – Carte 48/70 € – *(dinner only) (booking advisable)*
• International • Trendy •
Situated centrally by the Goethe house in a former tram waiting room with
kiosk is this lively and pleasantly relaxed restaurant. A good wine selection
accompanies the delicious seasonal food.

VaiVai

Grüneburgweg 16 ✉ *60322 –* 🅜 *Grüneburgweg*   Plan: **E1**
– ℰ (069) 90 55 93 05 – www.vaivai.de
Carte 31/80 € – *(dinner only) (booking essential)*
• Mediterranean • Trendy •
Try an aperitif in the spacious bar in the lobby before moving onto sample the
simple but flavoursome Mediterranean fare coming out of the open kitchen in
this trendy, casual restaurant. To round things off, how about a cocktail in the
lounge?

MainNizza   🈐 ♻

Untermainkai 17 ✉ *60329 –* 🅜 *Willy-Brandt-Platz*   Plan: **E2**
– ℰ (069) 26 95 29 22 – www.mainnizza.de
Carte 35/48 €
• International • Friendly •
With its excellent location right on the River Main, tables on the terrace are
highly sought after. The restaurant serves flavoursome international cuisine
with regional references, while the Sunday menu is family-oriented with lots of
roast meats. After a trip to the theatre (opposite) you can eat from a small supper menu until midnight.

Goldman – 25hours Hotel The Goldman   🈐

Hanauer Landstr. 127 ✉ *60314 – ℰ (069)*   Plan: **D2**
40 58 68 98 06 – www.goldman-restaurant.com – Closed Saturday lunch,
Sunday and Bank Holidays
Menu 62/99 € – Carte 47/68 €
• Mediterranean • Design •
Comfortable dining in a smart, modern restaurant with an open kitchen and
large glass frontage. Mediterranean dishes with a contemporary interpretation
are served.

Oscar's – Hotel Steigenberger Frankfurter Hof   🈐 ♿ 🅚

Am Kaiserplatz ✉ *60311 –* 🅜 *Willy-Brandt-Platz*   Plan: **E1**
– ℰ (069) 2 15 83 25 – www.frankfurter-hof.steigenberger.de
Carte 43/77 € – *(booking advisable)*
• Traditional cuisine • Bistro • Brasserie •
Informal, just as you would expect from a typical bistro, this is a popular mee-
ting place for bankers and business people, so make sure you book ahead. The
Wiener Schnitzel with cucumber salad and cranberries is particularly recom-
mended.

X **Chez Mamie** 🛱 ⟷

Sömmeringstr. 4 ✉ 60322 – **Ⓜ** *Glauburgstr. – ☏ (069)* Plan I: **C1**
95 20 93 60 – www.chezmamie.de – Closed Saturday lunch, Sunday
Menu 15 € (lunch) – Carte 24/43 €
• French classic • Bistro •
If you have been to Chez Mamie in Wiesbaden, you will recognise the same system here. This friendly bistro and wine bar serves traditional fare from a menu in the form of an Asterix comic, which includes steak tartare and boeuf bourguignon. Simple menu at lunchtimes.

X **san san** – Hotel The Westin Grand 🖔 🆎 🚗

Konrad-Adenauer-Str. 7 ✉ 60313 – **Ⓜ** *Konstablerwache* Plan: **F1**
*– ☏ (069) 91 39 90 50 – www.sansan-restaurant.de – Closed Saturday
lunch*
Carte 29/58 €
• Chinese • Traditional •
A restaurant offering typical Chinese fare in a Chinese setting with a choice of three dining options. The Bamboo Lounge, the Shanghai Suite or an intimate private dining room.

X **Sushimoto** – Hotel The Westin Grand 🖔 🆎 🚗

Konrad-Adenauer-Str. 7 ✉ 60313 – **Ⓜ** *Konstablerwache* Plan: **F1**
*– ☏ (069) 1 31 00 57 – Closed end July-mid August and Monday, Sunday
lunch except during fairs*
Menu 35/138 € – Carte 37/126 € – *(booking advisable)*
• Japanese • Elegant •
The atmosphere is authentic and austere, just as you might expect from a Japanese restaurant. Explore the many facets of Japanese cuisine including sushi and teppanyaki.

X **Klaane Sachsehäuser** 🛱

Neuer Wall 11 (Sachsenhausen) ✉ 60594 Plan: **F2**
– **Ⓜ** *Lokalbahnhof – ☏ (069) 61 59 83 – www.klaanesachsehaeuser.de
– Closed Sunday*
Carte 17/28 € – *(dinner only)*
• Regional • Rustic •
This popular pub-style restaurant reached through an interior courtyard has been serving traditional "Stöffche" brewed on the premises and good Frankfurt fare since 1876. And you'll always find someone to share your evening with!

X **Zum gemalten Haus** 🛱

Schweizer Str. 67 (Sachsenhausen) ✉ 60594 Plan: **F2**
– **Ⓜ** *Schweizer Platz – ☏ (069) 61 45 59 – www.zumgemaltenhaus.de
– Closed 3 weeks July and Monday*
Carte 12/21 €
• Regional • Rustic •
Huddle up, talk shop and chat in the midst of these wall murals and mementoes from bygone days. The main thing is the "Bembel" is always full!

🏨 **Hessischer Hof** 🕴 🖔 🆎 💪 🚗

Friedrich-Ebert-Anlage 40 ✉ 60325 – **Ⓜ** *Hauptbahnhof* Plan: **G2**
– ☏ (069) 7 54 00 – www.hessischer-hof.de
114 rm – **†**249 € **††**279 € – ⊊ 34 € – 7 suites
• Luxury • Classic • Personalised •
Thanks to the excellent service, from the welcome drink, via the free minibar to the good quality breakfast, guests feel very well looked after here. New executive rooms in a classic-elegant style. The exhibition of fine Sèvre porcelain gives the restaurant an exclusive feel.
Sèvres – See restaurant listing

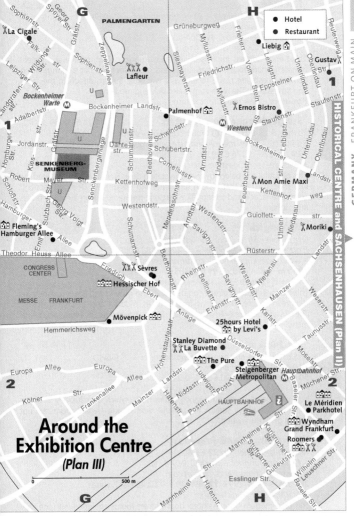

Around the Exhibition Centre
(Plan III)

0 _____ 500 m

 Le Méridien Parkhotel   ☆ ⅃⅌ 🛁 AC 🛗 🚗

Wiesenhüttenplatz 28 ⊠ 60329 – Ⓜ *Hauptbahnhof*   Plan: **H2**
– ℘ (069) 2 69 70 – www.lemeridienparkhotelfrankfurt.com
300 rm – ♦125/659 € ♦♦145/680 € – ☕ 28 €
• **Luxury • Chain hotel • Design •**
In the historic part of this hotel – a stately residence – you will find stylish rooms
and a beautiful staircase. Modern, functional annexe. The Le Parc restaurant is in
a bistro style. Garden bar at the front.

353

Roomers

🍴 ⅃ᵟ 🏛 📠 🚗

Gutleutstr. 85 ✉ *60329* – Ⓜ *Hauptbahnhof* – ℰ *(069)*   Plan: **H2**
2 71 34 20 – www.roomers.eu
116 rm – ♦230/360 € ♦♦230/920 € – ☑ 32 € – 3 suites
• Business • Design • Modern •

This trendy address impresses with its harmonious, high quality and tasteful interior in dark tones. Muted lights and music give the bar a lounge atmosphere. Guests are made to feel very welcome. Superb design in the sauna and fitness area. The restaurant is also chic and modern.
Roomers – See restaurant listing

Steigenberger Metropolitan

🍴 ⅃ᵟ 🏛 ⅃ 📠 ⅃ᵟ 🚗

Poststr. 6 ✉ *60329* – Ⓜ *Hauptbahnhof* – ℰ *(069)*   Plan: **H2**
5 06 07 00 – www.metrolopitan.steigenberger.com
129 rm ☑ – ♦176 € ♦♦196 € – 2 suites
• Business • Contemporary •

This beautiful city palace by the main station dates from the 19C. It is fitted out in a modern style that is both functional and elegant. Art Deco components adorn the façade and interior. The Brasserie restaurant enjoys a contemporary atmosphere.

Mövenpick

🍴 ⅃ᵟ ⅃ 📠 ⅃ᵟ 🚗

Den Haager Str. 5 (near Tor Ost, Halle III) (access by   Plan: **G2**
Platz der Einheit) ✉ *60327* – ℰ *(069) 7 88 07 50*
– www.moevenpick-hotels.com/frankfurt-city
288 rm – ♦145/465 € ♦♦165/485 € – ☑ 24 €
• Chain hotel • Contemporary •

This business hotel is directly on the exhibition ground and has a conspicuous red-green façade. The rooms feature clean, modern and functional design. There is a fitness area with roof terrace. Bistro-style restaurant with international menu.

The Pure

⅃ᵟ 🏛 📠 🚗

Niddastr. 86 ✉ *60329* – Ⓜ *Hauptbahnhof* – ℰ *(069)*   Plan: **H2**
7 10 45 70 – www.the-pure.de
50 rm ☑ – ♦150/190 € ♦♦170/210 €
• Townhouse • Design • Minimalist •

Find minimalist, modern elegance at this hotel, which is exclusively in white. Close to the railway station, the tasteful, modern and elegant rooms are not always generously sized.

Wyndham Grand Frankfurt

🍴 ⅃ᵟ ⅃ 📠

Wilhelm-Leuschner-Str. 32 ✉ *60329*   Plan: **H2**
– Ⓜ *Hauptbahnhof* – ℰ *(069) 9 07 45 90*
– www.wyndhamgrandfrankfurt.com
281 rm – ♦159/199 € ♦♦189/219 € – ☑ 23 € – 7 suites
• Business • Modern •

This ultra-modern business hotel boasts smart rooms equipped with the very latest technology (including the top-of-the-range Sky Deluxe rooms) and an attractive restaurant concept. The Linx is an 'open lobby' serving Mediterranean food, as well as a New York loft-style breakfast in the mornings.

Fleming's Hamburger Allee

🍴 ⅃ᵟ 🏛 📠 🚗

Hamburger Allee 47 ✉ *60486*   Plan: **G1**
– Ⓜ *Bockenheimer Warte* – ℰ *(069) 2 01 74 10*
– www.flemings-hotels.com
59 rm ☑ – ♦91/171 € ♦♦104/184 €
• Business • Townhouse • Modern •

The immediate proximity to the exhibition centre and its sleek modern rooms with open bathrooms distinguish this friendly business hotel. Trams stop right outside the door. Pleasant restaurant in a contemporary, bistro-style.

25hours Hotel by Levi's   ⌂ AC ♨

Niddastr. 58 ✉ *60329 –* Ⓜ *Hauptbahnhof –* ☏ *(069)*   Plan: **H2**
2 56 67 70 – www.25hours-hotels.com/levis
76 rm – 🛏176/426 € 🛏🛏176/426 € – ☕ 18 €
• Townhouse • Design • Modern •

This designer hotel is by the main railway station. The floors have been indivi-dually decorated in the style of the jeans look of the 1930s to 1980s. There is a 'Gibson Music Room' in the basement. The cosy restaurant is colourful, trendy and lively.

 Pearl   AC ♨ 🚗

Gutleutstr. 173 ✉ *60327 –* Ⓜ *Hauptbahnhof –* ☏ *(069)*   Plan I: **B3**
27 13 66 90 – www.pearlhotel.de
55 rm ☕ – 🛏99/344 € 🛏🛏119/349 €
• Business • Design •

This business hotel is slightly outside the centre and not far from the station. Modern rooms in a striking minimalist style.

 Palmenhof

Bockenheimer Landstr. 89 ✉ *60325 –* Ⓜ *Westend*   Plan: **G1**
– ☏ *(069) 7 53 00 60 – www.palmenhof.com – Closed Christmas-2 January*
45 rm – 🛏135/165 € 🛏🛏135/165 € – ☕ 16 €
• Townhouse • Classic •

This privately run hotel in the banking quarter was built in 1890. Behind its Gründerzeit façade it houses pretty rooms furnished with antiques from various periods.

 Liebig   AC

Liebigstr. 45 ✉ *60323 –* Ⓜ *Westend –* ☏ *(069)*   Plan: **H1**
24 18 29 90 – www.hotelliebig.de
19 rm – 🛏135/165 € 🛏🛏165/215 € – ☕ 16 €
• Family • Contemporary • Personalised •

This pretty Art Nouveau-style villa in Frankfurt's West End offers individually designed guestrooms that range from the modern to the classic. Some have a particular charm thanks to their period furniture and antique-style bath fittings. The restored old wooden staircase is also worth a closer look.

𝕏𝕏𝕏 **Lafleur**   ❀ 🍴 ⅃ AC ⇄ 🅿
𝔢𝔢 𝔢𝔢
Palmengartenstr. 11 ✉ *60325 –* Ⓜ *Westend –* ☏ *(069)*   Plan: **G1**
90 02 91 00 – www.restaurant-lafleur.de – Closed 22 December-
12 January, 3 weeks July-August and Saturday lunch, Sunday-Tuesday
lunch
Menu 43 € (weekday lunch)/145 € – Carte 81/120 €
• Classic cuisine • Elegant •

Lafleur serves beautifully presented, classic yet modern cuisine full of masterful aromatic combinations. Set in a glazed, Bauhaus-style annex to the prestigious Palmengarten hospitality complex, it also offers an upmarket, minimalist-style interior and attractive walk-in temperature-controlled wine store.
➜ Lackierter Hamachi, Dashi mit Sudachi, Pak Choi, Reiscrème, Enoki. Filet vom Kabeljau, Champagnersauce, Balsamicoschalotten, Zitronenspinat, Crème von geräucherten Kartoffeln. Delice von Rhabarber und Bio-Topfen mit Basilikum-Pistazieneis.

𝕏𝕏𝕏 **Sèvres** – Hotel Hessischer Hof   ⅃ AC ⇄ 🚗
Friedrich-Ebert-Anlage 40 ✉ *60325 –* Ⓜ *Hauptbahnhof*   Plan: **G2**
– ☏ *(069) 7 54 00 – www.restaurant-sevres.de*
Menu 43/99 € – Carte 53/69 € – (bookings advisable at dinner)
• French classic • Elegant •

A magnificent setting for a magnificent collection! An exhibition of precious Sèvres porcelain has been artfully incorporated into the exquisite interior of the eponymous restaurant. Good value with an 'all-inclusive' menu at lunchti-mes.

GERMANY - FRANKFURT ON MAIN

GERMANY - FRANKFURT ON MAIN

Restaurant Villa Merton

Am Leonhardsbrunn 12 (Corner of Ditmarstraße, at   Plan I: **A1**
Union International Club) ✉ 60487 – ℰ *(069) 70 30 33*
– www.restaurant-villa-merton.de – Closed Saturday-Sunday
Menu 69/128 € – *(dinner only) (booking advisable)*
• Classic cuisine • Fashionable • Elegant •

This listed villa in the diplomatic quarter makes a great place to eat. The decor is elegant and the sophisticated classic cuisine with modern notes comes in the form of three set menus: 'Vegetarian', 'Villa Merton' and 'For Body and Soul'.

→ Variation von Tomate, Mozzarella und Basilikum. Lauwarme Tranche vom Saibling mit Erbsenravioli, Zwiebelchutney, Karottenpüree. Brust und Praline von der Wachtel mit geräuchertem Trauben-Couscous und glacierten Zuckerschoten.

Bistro Villa Merton – See restaurant listing

Roomers – Hotel Roomers

Gutleutstr. 85 ✉ 60329 – Ⓜ *Hauptbahnhof* – ℰ *(069)*   Plan: **H2**
2 71 34 20 – www.roomers.eu – Closed Saturday lunch, Sunday lunch
Carte 30/103 €
• International • Fashionable •

This fashionable address in central 'Mainhattan' has a decor that is simply stunning. It features sand coloured upholstered sofas, indirect lighting and fine materials combined with black accessories.

Stanley Diamond La Buvette

Ottostr. 16 ✉ 60329 – Ⓜ *Hauptbahnhof* – ℰ *(069)*   Plan: **H2**
26 94 28 92 – www.stanleydiamond.com – Closed Saturday lunch, Sunday
Menu 47/69 € – Carte 43/65 €
• Modern cuisine • Trendy • Cosy •

A trendy mix of restaurant and bar, the interior at Stanley Diamond is stylish and upmarket and the service is simple and professional. The ambitious cuisine features reinventions of classic dishes such as jellied oxtail with potato foam and imperial caviar.

Ernos Bistro

Liebigstr. 15 ✉ 60323 – Ⓜ *Westend* – ℰ *(069) 72 19 97*   Plan: **H1**
– www.ernosbistro.de – Closed 2 weeks end December-early
January, 1 week during Easter, 3 weeks August, Saturday-Sunday and
Bank Holidays
Menu 39 € (lunch)/125 € – Carte 66/122 € – *(booking advisable)*
• French classic • Bistro • Cosy •

The decor and service alone make Ernos Bistro a place you will want to come back to. This charming bistro could hardly be more authentic with its wood panelling, pretty decorative lights and wine bottles, friendly staff and of course the ever present owner, Eric Huber. However, it is first and foremost Valéry Mathis' French cuisine, based on great produce, skill and a certain 'je ne sais quoi' that makes the restaurant so popular with so many people.

→ Königskrabbe mit Avocadocreme, Grapefruit und Mango, Wasabieis. Dorade mit Calamaretti und Anchovis, Champagnerrisotto, geräucherte Paparikajus. Milchlammkeule, Fenchelkompott und Artischocken, Lamm-Basilikumjus, Ziegenfrischkäse.

Weinsinn

Fürstenbergerstr. 179 ✉ 60322 – Ⓜ *Holzhausenstr.*   Plan I: **B1**
– ℰ (069) 56 99 80 80 – www.weinsinn.de – Closed 22 March-
2 April, 26 July-13 August, Sunday-Monday and Bank Holidays
Menu 57/79 € – Carte 62/73 € – *(dinner only) (booking essential)*
• International • Minimalist • Retro •

Notwithstanding a wine list boasting over 200 selections, Weinsinn is more than just a treat for wine lovers. It also offers a feast for the eyes in its beautifully judged modern interior, as well as for the taste buds in the form of André Rickert's contemporary, creative yet uncomplicated cuisine.

→ Kalbsbries und Pulpo, Blumenkohl und Petersilie. Iberico Schwein, Erbse, Zwiebel, Sesam. Weiße Schokolade, Erdbeere, Joghurt und Sauerampfer.

X
£3

Gustav

⇗

Reuterweg 57 ⊠ 60323 – ◉ Westend – ℰ (069)   Plan: **H1**
74 74 52 52 – www.restaurant-gustav.de – Closed 22 March-2 April,
26 July-6 August, Saturday lunch, Sunday-Monday and Bank Holidays
Menu 57/79 € – *(bookings advisable at dinner)*
· Creative · Minimalist · Trendy ·

The interior at this restaurant is classy and minimalist and the front-of-house team is young, charming and relaxed. The food is creative, sophisticated and fully flavoured and some of the tables afford a view of the kitchen. Reduced lunchtime menu for diners in a hurry.
➔ Bachforelle, Erbse, Gurke, Dill. Mangold, Olive, Joghurt, Fenchelsaat. Frei-landschwein, Bohnen, Bärlauchknospe, Honig, Senf.

X

Bistro Villa Merton – Restaurant Villa Merton

⇗

Am Leonhardsbrunn 12 (Corner of Ditmarstraße, at   Plan I: **A1**
Union International Club) ⊠ 60487 – ℰ (069) 70 30 33
– www.restaurant-villa-merton.de – Closed Saturday-Sunday
Menu 36 € (lunch) – Carte 39/60 €
· Regional · Elegant ·

The Villa Merton now has an attractive dining alternative in Bistro, in terms of both cuisine and price. It serves fresh and flavoursome food with regional and international influences. Try the Hessen fish and chips or the pan-fried beefsteak with fried onions and potato and chive puree.

X
☺

La Cigale

⇗

Falkstr. 38 ⊠ 60487 – ◉ Bockenheimer Warte   Plan: **G1**
– ℰ (069) 70 41 11 – www.lacigale-restaurant.de – Closed Sunday-Tuesday lunch, Saturday lunch
Menu 64/66 € – Carte 34/48 € – *(bookings advisable at dinner)*
· International · Cosy ·

La Cigale's many regulars are attracted here by the restaurant's friendly, welco-ming atmosphere, as well as the fresh cuisine. This is prepared by chef Martin Kofler, and his braised ox cheeks are a particular favourite.

X

Mon Amie Maxi

⇗

Bockenheimer Landstr. 31 ⊠ 60311 – ◉ Westend   Plan: **H1**
– ℰ (069) 71 40 21 21 – www.mook-group.de – Closed 1 week early January and Saturday lunch
Carte 26/107 € – *(Bank Holidays dinner only)*
· French · Brasserie ·

Take a table in the comfortable, casual interior at Mon Amie Maxi and enjoy the fresh, authentic brasserie-style fare from the open kitchen. The menu ranges from oysters to calves' kidneys and a cheese board, but whatever you do, don't miss the delicious looking seafood buffet.

X

Chalet 18

⌿

Grempstr. 18 ⊠ 60487 – ◉ Leipziger Str. – ℰ (069)   Plan I: **A1**
70 28 14 – www.chalet-18.de – Closed 1 week early January, July and Monday-Tuesday
Menu 61/93 € – Carte 55/67 € – *(dinner only) (booking essential)*
· French creative · Friendly ·

This really charming little restaurant with a French bistro feel is in trendy Bock-enheim. It provides a relaxed setting to sample the young chef's ambitious cui-sine that combines international flavours along classic lines.

X

Moriki

⇗ 🅰🅲

Taunusanlage 12 ⊠ 60325 – ◉ Hauptbahnhof   Plan: **H1**
– ℰ (069) 71 91 30 70 – www.moriki.de
Carte 35/70 € – *(booking advisable)*
· Japanese · Individual · Trendy ·

You will find this stylish, uncomplicated restaurant and sushi bar on the ground floor of Deutsche Bank's headquarters building. The appealing menu – Japanese with Pan-Asian influences – includes crunchy spicy tuna rolls, miso duck and chilli ginger prawn.

🍴 Laube Liebe Hoffnung 🏠 ⇔

Pariser Str. 11 ✉ *60486 –* ☎ *(069) 75 84 77 22* Plan I: **A2**
– www.laubeliebehoffnung.de
Menu 28/50 € (dinner) – Carte 38/57 €
• International • Bistro •

Located in the new European Quarter, this modern wooden building has a charming, relaxed interior. It serves an interesting mix of freshly made food ranging from Laube bratwurst to sea bream served on a bed of olive risotto. There is also a pretty terrace complete with grill.

ENVIRONS OF FRANKFURT

AT THE RHEIN-MAIN AIRPORT **by Kennedy Allee B3**

 ### Kempinski Hotel Gravenbruch 🕯 🦮 🗗 ⅏ 🏊 ⬚ 🍽 ⅙

Graf zu Ysenburg und Büdingen-Platz 1 ✉ *63263* AC 🏋 P
– ☎ *(069) 38 98 80 – www.kempinski.com/gravenbruch*
187 rm – 🛏119/409 € 🛏🛏119/409 € – � 31 € – 37 suites
• Chain hotel • Classic •

Following a programme of investment, the Gravenbruch now offers a choice of bright, modern and more classical guestrooms. You can also relax with a massage or beauty treatment or try a training session in the gym which enjoys a view over the adjacent park. Indeed, the hotel even boasts its own lake. The Torschänke restaurant and beer garden serves traditional Hessen food.
⚜ **Sra Bua by Juan Amador • Torschänke • EssTisch** – See restaurant listing

 ### Hilton 🕯 🗗 ⅏ ⅙ AC 🏋 🚗

Am Flughafen (The Squaire) ✉ *60549 Frankfurt –* ☎ *(069) 26 01 20 00*
– www.frankfurtairport.hilton.com
232 rm ⊒ – 🛏129/569 € 🛏🛏129/569 € – 17 suites
• Business • Modern •

The Frankfurt Hilton offers the very best in urban chic. It is a 625m-long futuristic glass and steel construction, designed as a recumbent skyscraper. The A3 could hardly be closer and there is direct access to both the ICE station and the airport. There is also a ballroom that can accommodate 570 people!

 ### Steigenberger Airport 🕯 🗗 ⅏ 🗗 ⅙ AC 🏋 🚗

Unterschweinstiege 16 ✉ *60549 Frankfurt –* ☎ *(069) 6 97 50*
– www.airporthotel-frankfurt.steigenberger.com
570 rm – 🛏139/229 € 🛏🛏149/239 € – ⊒ 28 € – 10 suites
• Chain hotel • Modern •

This hotel is characterised by its elegant hall, comfortable rooms (in particular the modern Tower room) and the 'Open Sky' leisure area with fantastic views. A cosy atmosphere in the Unterschweinstiege.
Faces – See restaurant listing

🍴🍴 Sra Bua by Juan Amador – Kempinski Hotel Gravenbruch
❀

Graf zu Ysenburg und Büdingen-Platz 1 ✉ *63263 –* ☎ *(069)* 🏠
38 98 80 – www.kempinski.com/gravenbruch – Closed Sunday-Monday
Menu 110/129 € – Carte 71/91 € – *(dinner only) (booking advisable)*
• Fusion • Elegant • Design •

It is not just the elegant, minimalist Sra Bua-style design on a classic Buddha theme that draws the crowds here. The real focal point is the pan-Asian cuisine prepared with precision and a real feel for fusion. The ambitious young kitchen team uses top quality produce.
➜ Thunfisch, Shiitake, Curry Hara. Étouffée Taube, Hanfsamencrème, Rotkohl, Sellerie. Nashi Birne, Salzkaramell, Michel Cluizel Schokolade, Yuzu.

XX **Faces** – Hotel Steigenberger Airport ⛶ ᴴ ᴬᴷ ⇌

Unterschweinstiege 16 ✉ 60549 Frankfurt – ℰ (069) 69 75 24 00
– www.faces.de – Closed Saturday-Sunday and Bank Holidays
Carte 38/66 € – *(dinner only)*
• International • Design •

Behind the glass frontage lies a smart, modern restaurant with original lighting.
It serves contemporary international cuisine focusing on high quality ingredients. Separate bar.

XX **EssTisch** – Kempinski Hotel Gravenbruch ⅋⅋ ⛶

Graf zu Ysenburg und Büdingen-Platz 1 ✉ 63263 – ℰ (069) 38 98 80
– www.kempinski.com/gravenbruch – Closed Friday-Saturday, Sunday
dinner
Carte 38/71 €
• International • Elegant •

The main restaurant in the hotel's new wing is bright and welcoming. You can
choose from an international menu, which also includes a couple of classic
regional dishes, or from the specialities available from the buffet. This feast is
known as the 'Perfume of the Sea' on Fridays when it offers a wide range of
fish and seafood.

X **Torschänke** – Kempinski Hotel Gravenbruch ⛶ ᴬᴷ 🅿

Graf zu Ysenburg und Büdingen-Platz 1 ✉ 63263 – ℰ (069) 38 98 80
– www.kempinski.com/gravenbruch – Closed Monday-Tuesday
Carte 29/47 € – *(dinner only)*
• Regional • Rustic •

Once the starting point for wild boar hunts, Torschänke continues to include
wild boar on its menu, alongside other regional specialities. Pleasant, informal
setting.

HAMBURG
HAMBURG

Population: 1 734 280

Matthias Krüttgen/Fotolia.com

With a maritime role stretching back centuries, Germany's second largest city has a lively and liberal ambience. Hamburg is often described as 'The Gateway to the World', and there's certainly a visceral feel here, particularly around the big, buzzy and bustling port area. Locals enjoy a long-held reputation for their tolerance and outward looking stance, cosmopolitan to the core. Space to breathe is seen as very important in Hamburg: the city authorities have paid much attention to green spaces, and the city can proudly claim an enviable amount of parks, lakes and tree-lined canals.

There's no cathedral here (at least not a standing one, as war-destroyed St Nikolai remains a ruin), so the Town Hall acts as the central landmark. Just north of here are the Binnenalster (inner) and Aussenalster (outer) lakes. The old walls of the city, dating back over eight hundred years, are delineated by a distinct semicircle of boulevards that curve attractively in a wide arc south of the lakes. Further south from here is the port and harbour area, defined by Landungsbrücken to the west and Speicherstadt to the east. The district to the west of the centre is St Pauli, famed for its clubs and bars, particularly along the notorious Reeperbahn, which pierces the district from east to west. The contrastingly smart Altona suburb and delightful Blankenese village are west of St Pauli.

HAMBURG IN...

→ **ONE DAY**
Boat trip from Landungsbrücken, Speicherstadt, Kunsthalle, Fishmarket (Sunday morning).

→ **TWO DAYS**
Steamboat on the Alster, Hamburg History Museum, St Pauli by night.

→ **THREE DAYS**
Arts and Crafts Museum, canal trip, concert at Musikhalle.

PRACTICAL INFORMATION

ARRIVAL-DEPARTURE

Hamburg Airport is 15km north of the city centre. Airport buses leave for Hamburg Hauptbahnhof every 15-20min and Altona Station every 30min; both take 20min.

GETTING AROUND

Hamburg Transport Authority controls all of the bus routes, the overground S-Bahn trains, the U-Bahn underground lines, and several river and ferry services. Tickets are available for single journeys, or for one-day or three-day duration; you can buy them from vending machines or bus drivers. The Hamburg Card is valid for the transport network, and offers discounts in museums, theatres and some restaurants, as well as for tours on land and water. Buy it from Tourist Information offices, vending machines, hotels or travel agents.

CALENDAR HIGHLIGHTS

March, July and November
Dom Festivals (huge funfairs)

April
Long Night of Hamburg Museums.

May
Hafengeburtstag (harbour's birthday celebration), Japanese Cherry Blossom Festival.

July
Duckstein Festival.

August-September
Alster Fair.

September
Hamburg Cruise Days.

October
International Boat Show, Film Festival.

EATING OUT

Being a city immersed in water, it's no surprise to find Hamburg is a good place for fish. Though its fishing industry isn't the powerhouse of old, the city still boasts a giant trawler's worth of seafood places to eat. Eel dishes are mainstays of the traditional restaurant's menu, as is the herring stew with vegetables called Labskaus. Also unsurprisingly, considering it's the country's gateway to the world, this is somewhere that offers a vast range of international dishes. Wherever you eat, the portions are likely to be generous. There's no problem with finding somewhere early: cafés are often open at seven, with the belief that it's never too early for coffee and cake. Bakeries also believe in an early start, and the calorie content here, too, can be pretty high. Bistros and restaurants, usually open by midday, are proud of their local ingredients, so keep your eyes open for Hamburgisch on the menu. Service charges are always included in the bill, so tipping is not compulsory, although most people will round it up and possibly add five to ten per cent.

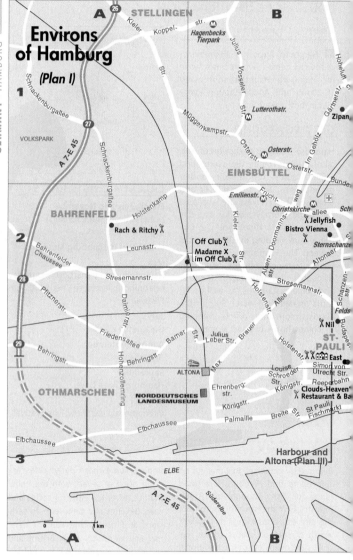

Environs of Hamburg

(Plan I)

STELLINGEN

B

A 26

Kieler

Koppel-

str.

Hagenbecks Tierpark Ⓜ

Julius

Vosseler

Str.

Hoheluft

Garnters tr.

● Zipan

1

Schnackenburgallee

27

VOLKSPARK

A 7-E 45

Schnackenburgallee

Müggenkampstr.

Osterstr.

Lutterothstr.

Osterstr. Ⓜ

Im Gehölz

Osterstr.

Bunde

EIMSBÜTTEL

BAHRENFELD

Holstenkamp

Emilienstr. Ⓜ

Frucht

allee

weg

Christkirche

Doormanns

Kieler

Sch

✚ Sch

✕ Jellyfish

Bistro Vienna

✕

● Sternschanze

Rach & Ritchy ✕

Leunastr.

Off Club ✕

Madame X

Lim Off Club ✕

Str.

2

Bahrenfelder Chaussee

Stresemannstr.

Allen

Holstenstr.

Allee

Stresemannstr.

Schanzen-

str.

Felds

28

Pritznerstr.

Daimler str.

Friedensallee

Barner

Str.

Julius Leber Str.

Brauer

Str.

Holstenstr.

Allee

✕ Nil

Budapest

ST-PAULI

29

Behringstr.

Hohenzollernring

Behringstr.

Max

Str.

ALTONA 🚉

Ehrenberg str.

Louise Schroeder Str.

Königstr.

✕ ✕ 🏨 East

Simon von Utrecht Str.

Reeperbahn

OTHMARSCHEN

NORDDEUTSCHES LANDESMUSEUM

Königstr.

Breite Str.

Palmaille

St Pauli Fischmarkt

Clouds-Heaven Restaurant & Ba ✕

Elbchaussee

Elbchaussee

3

Harbour and Altona (Plan III)

ELBE

A 7-E 45

Süderelbe

0 — 1 km

A

B

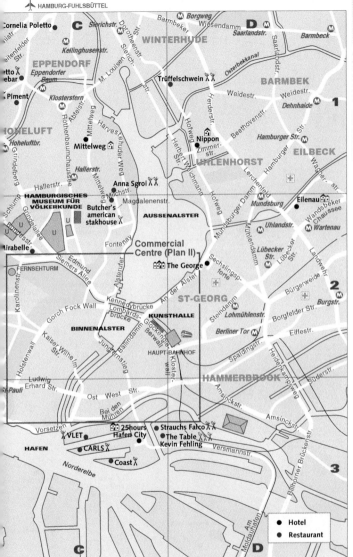

Cornelia Poletto **C** Sierichstr.
Barmbeker **D**
Borgweg
Wiesendamm Saarlandstr.
Barmbeck

Kellinghusenstr.

WINTERHUDE

EPPENDORF
Eppendorfer Baum

etto ✕
ebar

Trüffelschwein ✕✕

BARMBEK

Piment Klosterstern

Weidestr.
Weidestr.
Dehnhaide

1

HOHELUFT
Hoheluftbr.

Mittelweg 🏛

Nippon
Zimmer-
str.
UHLENHORST

EILBECK

Hallerstr.
Anna Sgroi ✕✕

HAMBURGISCHES
MUSEUM FÜR
VÖLKERKUNDE
Butcher's
american
stakhouse ✕

Magdalenenstr.

AUSSENALSTER

Eilenau 🏛
Mundsburg
Wandsbeker
Chaussee
Uhlandstr. Wartenau

Mirabelle

FERNSEHTURM

Fontenay

Commercial
Centre (Plan II)
🏛 The George

Lübecker
Str.

Sechslings-
forte

2
Bürgerweide
Burgstr.

ST-GEORG

Kennedybrücke
Lombards-
brücke

KUNSTHALLE

BINNENALSTER

Steindamm
Lohmühlenstr.
Borgfelder Str.

Berliner Tor
Eiffestr.

HAUPT-BAHNHOF

Ludwig
Erhard Str.

Ost West Str.

Bei den
Mühren

HAMMERBROOK

Vorsetzen
VLET

🏛 25hours
Hafen City

● Strauchs Falco ✕✕
● The Table ✕✕✕
Kevin Fehling

HAFEN

CARLS ✕

● Coast ✕

Norderelbe

Versmannstr.

Amsinckstr.

Amsinckstr.

3

● **Hotel**
● **Restaurant**

C **D**

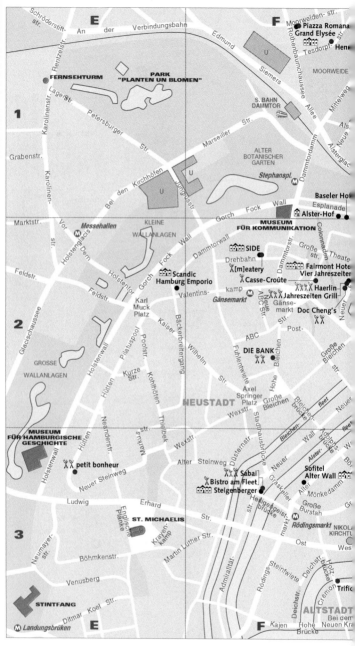

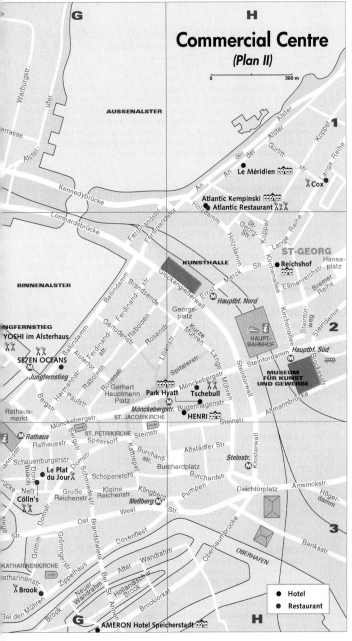

Commercial Centre
(Plan II)

0   300 m

G
H

AUSSENALSTER

1

Le Méridien 🏨
✕ Cox

Atlantic Kempinski 🏨
● Atlantic Restaurant ✕✕

Kennedybrücke

Lombardsbrücke

ST-GEORG

KUNSTHALLE
● Reichshof
Hansaplatz

BINNENALSTER

Hauptbf. Nord

Georgsplatz
Kurze Mühren

2

NGFERNSTIEG
YOSHI im Alsterhaus
✕✕
SE7EN OCEANS
✕
Jungfernstieg

HAUPT-BAHNHOF

Hauptbf. Süd

MUSEUM
FÜR KUNST
UND GEWERBE

Gerhart
Hauptmann
Platz
Park Hyatt 🏨
Tschebull ✕✕

Mönckebergstr.
Bugenhagenstr.
HENRI 🏨

Rathaus-markt

ST. JACOBIKIRCHE

Mönckebergstr.
🅼 Rathaus
Rathausstr.
ST. PETRIKIRCHE
Speersort

Altstädter Str.

Steinstr.
🅼

Le Plat
du Jour

Burchardplatz

Deichtorplatz

3

Cölln's
✕✕

Meßberg 🅼

OBERHAFEN

KATHARINENKIRCHE
✕ Brook

G
H
● AMERON Hotel Speicherstadt 🏨

● Hotel
● Restaurant

GERMANY - HAMBURG

　Fairmont Hotel Vier Jahreszeiten

Neuer Jungfernstieg 9 ⊠ *20354 –* Ⓜ *Jungfernstieg*
– 𝒞 *(040) 3 49 40 – www.fairmont-hvj.de*　　　　　Plan: **F2**
139 rm ☲ *–* ♦295/395 € ♦♦395/495 € *– 17 suites*
• Grand Luxury • Traditional • Classic •

There's surely no more lovely or elegant hotel than the Fairmont anywhere in Hamburg and the service is beyond reproach. The epitome of unobtrusive luxury, it offers tasteful rooms decorated in a classic yet fresh style, an upmarket spa and the stylish Wohnhalle lounge where you can take afternoon tea. Alternatively, try a coffee or a glass of champagne and some nibbles in the trendy Condi Lounge or eat out on the terrace overlooking the Binnenalster.
❀❀ **Haerlin** • **Jahreszeiten Grill** • **Doc Cheng's** – See restaurant listing

　Atlantic Kempinski

An der Alster 72 ⊠ *20099 –* Ⓜ *Jungfernstieg –* 𝒞 *(040)*　　Plan: **H1**
2 88 80 – www.kempinski.com/hamburg
221 rm – ♦199/459 € ♦♦229/489 € *–* ☲ 34 € *– 33 suites*
• Grand Luxury • Classic • Contemporary •

Following extensive renovation work, the Atlantic Kempinski is now even more magnificent than before. It has an elegant, classic lobby, timeless, sumptuously decorated rooms (complete with fine ebony and state-of-the-art technology) and stylish reception and conference facilities.
Atlantic Restaurant – See restaurant listing

　Park Hyatt

Bugenhagenstr. 8 (at Levantehaus) ⊠ *20095*　　　　　Plan: **H2**
– Ⓜ *Mönckebergstr. –* 𝒞 *(040) 33 32 12 34 – www.hamburg.park.hyatt.de*
262 rm – ♦199/550 € ♦♦239/590 € *–* ☲ 34 € *– 21 suites*
• Grand Luxury • Chain hotel • Modern •

This former Hanseatic League trading post welcomes guests on the first floor where they can make themselves comfortable in the tasteful lounge. Combining high quality and modern elegance this is a luxury hotel without equal. The Apples restaurant invites diners to watch the chef working in the show kitchen.

　Le Méridien

An der Alster 52 ⊠ *20099 –* Ⓜ *Hauptbf. Nord*
– 𝒞 *(040) 2 10 00 – www.lemeridienhamburg.com*　　　Plan: **H1**
275 rm – ♦139/369 € ♦♦159/389 € *–* ☲ 30 € *– 14 suites*
• Chain hotel • Luxury • Modern •

This modern hotel has an attractive, clear style extending from the brightly furnished rooms (with specially designed therapeutic beds) to the wellness area. The restaurant on the ninth floor offers a fantastic view over the Außenalster lake.

　Grand Elysée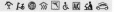

Rothenbaumchaussee 10 ⊠ *20148 –* Ⓜ *Stephanspl.*　　　Plan: **F1**
– 𝒞 *(040) 41 41 20 – www.grand-elysee.com*
494 rm – ♦140/250 € ♦♦160/270 € *–* ☲ 20 € *– 17 suites*
• Luxury • Classic •

The generous hotel lobby with its café greets you in boulevard style. It offers classic, elegant rooms, quiet garden courtyard rooms, and south-facing rooms on the Moorweiden park. Italian cuisine in the Piazza Romana, Brasserie and oyster bar with seafood.
Piazza Romana – See restaurant listing

Sofitel Alter Wall

𝄢 ⅃ᵣ 💿 🕙 🔲 ⅃ 🆔 🐎 🚗

Alter Wall 40 ✉ *20457 –* Ⓜ *Rödingsmarkt –* ℱ *(040)*
36 95 00 – www.sofitel.com

Plan: **F3**

223 rm – ♠150/200 € ♠♠150/200 € – ☐ 30 € – 18 suites
• Chain hotel • Luxury • Design •

The bright, modern style here combines minimalism and luxury. The Alsterfleet canal which runs in front of the hotel is best enjoyed from the terrace just above the water which has its own jetty. Lunch is served in the bistro, dinner in the Ticino.

 ### Steigenberger

𝄢 ⅃ᵣ 💿 🕙 🆔 🐎 🚗

Heiligengeistbrücke 4 ✉ *20459 –* Ⓜ *Rödingsmarkt*
– ℱ *(040) 36 80 60 – www.hamburg.steigenberger.de*

Plan: **F3**

227 rm – ♠129/329 € ♠♠149/349 € – ☐ 29 € – 6 suites
• Luxury • Classic •

Right beside the Alster canal stands this well-run and elegant hotel in the shape of a ship. From the fitness area roof terrace there is a wonderful view over the city. International cuisine in the bistro.

Bistro am Fleet • Sabai – See restaurant listing

 ### SIDE

𝄢 ⅃ᵣ 🕙 🔲 ⅃ 🆔 🐎 🚗

Drehbahn 49 ✉ *20354 –* Ⓜ *Stephanspl. –* ℱ *(040)*
30 99 90 – www.side-hamburg.de

Plan: **F2**

168 rm – ♠160/245 € ♠♠160/245 € – ☐ 26 € – 10 suites
• Luxury • Design •

Behind the natural stone and glass façade lays the impressive 30m high lobby, with a lighting design by Robert Wilson. The hotel has tasteful rooms designed in white and brown by Matteo Thun. The "(m)eatery" is a "high-end steakhouse" and bar.

[m]eatery – See restaurant listing

 ### Scandic Hamburg Emporio

𝄢 ⅃ᵣ 🕙 ⅃ 🆔 🐎 🚗

Dammtorwall 19 (entrance Dragonerstraße) ✉ *20355*
– Ⓜ *Gänsemarkt –* ℱ *(040) 4 32 18 70 – www.scandichotels.de/hamburg*

Plan: **E2**

325 rm – ♠129/219 € ♠♠139/229 € – ☐ 12 €
• Business • Contemporary • Functional •

Water is everywhere here: in the paintings on the walls, the colours and forms… And water stands as the symbol for the principles of sustainability embraced by Scandic Hotels. The rooms are decorated in light wood with warm colours and floor-to-ceiling windows. If you fancy a cycle ride through Hamburg, the hotel will lend you a bike free of charge. The shop is open 24hrs a day.

 ### The George

𝄢 🕙 🆔 🐎 🚗

Barcastr. 3 ✉ *22087 –* Ⓜ *Lohmühlenstr. –* ℱ *(040)*
2 80 03 00 – www.thegeorge-hotel.de

Plan I: **D2**

123 rm – ♠151/182 € ♠♠162/192 € – ☐ 20 € – 2 suites
• Townhouse • Design • Elegant •

Elegant, British-style meets young, modern design throughout this hotel. The library, bar and rooms are decorated in muted tones with feature pictures, furnishing fabrics and wallpapers. Highlights include the roof terrace with its view over Hamburg and the garden behind the hotel. The restaurant serves Mediterranean/Italian cuisine.

Reichshof

𝄢 ⅃ᵣ 🕙 ⅃ 🆔 🐎

Kirchenallee 34 ✉ *20099 –* Ⓜ *Hauptbf. Nord –* ℱ *(040)*
3 70 25 90 – www.reichshof-hamburg.com

Plan: **H2**

278 rm – ♠169/229 € ♠♠169/229 € – ☐ 18 €
• Business • Elegant • Historic •

Built in 1910 as a "grand hotel" and now partly listed, the Reichshof contains many reminders of its heyday – the lobby with its imposing marble columns is particularly impressive – which complement its successful mix of historical flair and modern style which extends to the restaurant. The rooms are contemporary and upmarket.

GERMANY - HAMBURG

 AMERON Hotel Speicherstadt
Am Sandtorkai 4 ✉ *20457 –* Ⓜ *Überseequartier*
Plan: **G3**
– 𝒞 (040) 6 38 58 90 – www.hotel-speicherstadt.de
192 rm – ♦139 € ♦♦139 € – ⌑ 19 €
• Historic • Retro •
This charming hotel is located in the middle of Hamburg's Speicherstadt district.
It boasts a trendy retro decor from the 1950s with warm colours that creates a
friendly and welcoming feel. The restaurant in the modern glass annexe serves
Italian food.

 HENRI
Bugenhagenstr. 21 ✉ *20095 –* Ⓜ *Mönckebergstr.*
Plan: **H2**
– 𝒞 (040) 5 54 35 70 – www.henri-hotel.com
60 rm – ♦98/118 € ♦♦118/148 € – ⌑ 14 € – 5 suites
• Business • Retro • Personalised •
This former office building has been redeveloped with taste, quality and all the
modern facilities you would expect… and with a strong 1950/60s retro feel.
There are charming details such as the homely lounge, a kitchen that serves
snacks and drinks, as well as a daily 'Abendbrod' and German tea and cakes at
the weekend. HENRI provides a sort of hotel home from home.

 25hours Hafen City
Überseeallee 5 ✉ *20457 –* Ⓜ *Überseequartier*
Plan I: **C3**
– 𝒞 (040) 2 57 77 70 – www.25hours-hotels.com
170 rm – ♦125/399 € ♦♦125/399 € – ⌑ 18 €
• Townhouse • Personalised • Design •
One thing is sure, for individuality and originality you can't beat this Hamburg
hotel. Bright, new design meets warm wood and stories of the sea. Old records
cover the walls in the lounge-style Vinyl Room and guests are given a sailors' kit
bag for their personal belongings in the rooftop sauna. It's no surprise in a hotel
full of seafaring references to find that all the rooms have a cabin feel.

 Baseler Hof
Esplanade 11 ✉ *20354 –* Ⓜ *Stephansplatz – 𝒞 (040)*
Plan: **F1**
35 90 60 – www.baselerhof.de
163 rm – ♦79/161 € ♦♦99/181 € – ⌑ 12 € – 9 suites
• Traditional • Functional •
A great hotel located between the Outer Alster Lake and Botanical Gardens. A
number of less grand rooms are available; those in the annexe are the quietest.
Good wine selection in the Kleinhuis restaurant. The annual vintage car rally
draws many aficionados.

 Eilenau
Eilenau 36 ✉ *22089 –* Ⓜ *Mundsburg – 𝒞 (040)*
Plan I: **D2**
2 36 01 30 – www.eilenau.de
17 rm – ♦109/139 € ♦♦119/159 € – ⌑ 15 € – 5 suites
• Townhouse • Personalised • Elegant •
Anything but a typical city hotel, the Eilenau is housed in two carefully renovated buildings dating back to 1890. Antiques, stucco, chandeliers and old parquet flooring mix with stylish modern furniture beneath the high ceilings. There
is also a small, quiet garden where breakfast is served in the summer.

 Alster-Hof
Esplanade 12 ✉ *20354 –* Ⓜ *Stephansplatz – 𝒞 (040)*
Plan: **F1**
35 00 70 – www.alster-hof.de – Closed 23 December-2 January
108 rm ⌑ – ♦90/105 € ♦♦135/160 € – 3 suites
• Traditional • Functional •
This well cared for hotel is in the city centre, near to the Alster. It has functional
guestrooms decorated in homely colours. These include sometimes rather small
single rooms.

XXXXX **Haerlin** – Fairmont Hotel Vier Jahreszeiten 🕸 ≤ 🕭 🔣 ⇧ 🚗

Neuer Jungfernstieg 9 ⊠ 20354 – **Ⓜ** Jungfernstieg   Plan: **F2**
– ℰ (040) 34 94 33 10 – www.fairmont-hvj.de
– Closed Sunday-Monday
Menu 128/168 € – (dinner only) (booking advisable)
• French creative • Luxury • Elegant •
In Christoph Rüffer's sophisticated cuisine every dish is a work of meticulous
preparation culminating in the presentation of a culinary masterpiece. The two
set menus – 'Aromenbehandlung' (flavour treatment) and 'Gaumenparty' (taste
bud treat) – live up to expectations. Great view of the Inner Alster Lake.
→ Jacobsmuschel mit Selleriecrème, Tandoori und Chicorée. Lammrücken
mit Lavendel, Nashi-Birne, violette Aubergine. Himbeere, Douglasie, Sandel-
holz, Sauerteig und Verbene.

XxX **Atlantic Restaurant** – Hotel Atlantic Kempinski ≤ 🕭 🔣 🚗

An der Alster 72 ⊠ 20099 – **Ⓜ** Jungfernstieg   Plan: **H1**
– ℰ (040) 2 88 88 60 – www.kempinski.com/hamburg
Menu 29 € (lunch)/96 € – Carte 58/112 €
• Classic cuisine • Classic • Elegant •
The elegant restaurant in this traditional Hamburg hotel doubles up as a mee-
ting place for significant parts of Hamburg society. The team serve classic cui-
sine of the very highest standard.

XxX **The Table Kevin Fehling**

🕸🕸🕸 Shanghaiallee 15 ⊠ 20457 – ℰ (040) 22 86 74 22   Plan I: **C2**
– www.the-table-hamburg.de
– Closed 24 December-3 January, 7-13 March, 1-21 August
and Sunday-Monday
Menu 180 € – (dinner only) (booking essential)
• Creative • Design •
Probably the most spectacular new restaurant opening, The Table Kevin Fehling
boasts a smart and trendy interior where diners sit at a long, curved table which
seats up to 20 people (private tables also available). Meanwhile, as in his previous culinary incarnation in Travemünde, Fehling's international cuisine continues to top the culinary rankings.
→ Geflämmte Makrele und Tatar mit Rettich, Sojakaviar, Dashi-Sud. Challans Entenbrust mit Reiscrème, Himbeere, Reisessig-Hollandaise und Shiso-
jus. "Wundertüte" mit Lavendel, Blaubeere, Sternanis und Kardamom.

XxX **Sabai** – Hotel Steigenberger 🕭 🔣 🚗

Heiligengeistbrücke 4 ⊠ 20459 – **Ⓜ** Rödingsmarkt   Plan: **F3**
– ℰ (040) 36 80 60 – www.restaurant-sabai.de
– Closed Sunday-Monday
Menu 52/70 € – Carte 60/72 € – (dinner only)
• Fusion • Elegant •
At Sabai, Southeast Asian and European cooking styles blend to create the likes
of turbot, rice, chilli and citrus fruits or apple-fed pig, ras el hanout, asparagus,
apricots and wild garlic. Bright and elegant modern interior.

XxX **Jahreszeiten Grill** – Fairmont Hotel Vier Jahreszeiten ≤ 🕭 🔣

Neuer Jungfernstieg 9 ⊠ 20354 – **Ⓜ** Jungfernstieg – ℰ (040) 🚗
34 94 33 12 – www.fairmont-hvj.de   Plan: **F2**
Menu 30 € (weekday lunch) – Carte 59/106 €
• French classic • Elegant •
The very epitome of elegance, this restaurant pays homage to the Art Deco
style of the 1920s. Its original period pieces provide an upmarket backdrop for
discerning diners.

GERMANY - HAMBURG

XX
⌘
SE7EN OCEANS
Ballindamm 40 (2nd floor) (Europa-Passage) ✉ *20095*   Plan: **G2**
– **Ⓜ** *Jungfernstieg* – ✆ *32 50 79 44* – *www.se7en-oceans.de*
– *Closed 8-14 February, 8-28 August and Sunday, Tuesday*
Menu 43 € (lunch)/129 € – Carte 60/79 €
• International • Fashionable • Design •

If you fancy a good meal after your shopping trip, this modern restaurant in the Europa-Passage shopping centre with its great view over the River Alster is the ideal solution. Refined, classic yet contemporary cuisine.
→ Kalbsbries, Sellerie, Birne, Perigord Trüffel. Steinbutt, Erbsen, Oregano, Rotwein. Bärenkrebs, Grapefruit, Gin Sul, Salbei.

XX
Cölln's
Brodschrangen 1 ✉ *20457* – **Ⓜ** *Rathaus*   Plan: **G3**
– ✆ *(040) 36 41 53* – *www.coellns-restaurant.de*
– *Closed Sunday and Bank Holidays*
Menu 22 € (weekday lunch)/100 € – Carte 45/74 € – *(booking advisable)*
• Fish and seafood • Cosy •

Fish and oysters have been the order of the day here since 1760. Once they were sold over the shop counter, now they appear on the menu alongside other seafood specialities including lobster and caviar. The 13 charming small dining alcoves provide a historical atmosphere.

XX
☺
Tschebull
Mönckebergstr. 7 (1st floor) (at Levantehaus) ✉ *20095*   Plan: **H2**
– **Ⓜ** *Mönckebergstr.* – ✆ *(040) 32 96 47 96* – *www.tschebull.de*
– *Closed Sunday and Bank Holidays*
Menu 30 € (lunch)/65 € (dinner) – Carte 34/62 € – *(booking advisable)*
• Austrian • Cosy • Individual •

In the centre of this exclusive shopping arcade sits a little piece of Austria, courtesy of Carinthian chef Alexander Tschebull. As you would expect, the Austrian classics, such as Tafelspitz (Viennese-style boiled beef) and Fiaker (beef) goulash are excellent, as are the more modern dishes. These include skrei cod with potato and caper champ, radish and pearl onions.

XX
DIE BANK

Hohe Bleichen 17 ✉ *20354* – **Ⓜ** *Gänsemarkt*   Plan: **F2**
– ✆ *(040) 2 38 00 30* – *www.diebank-brasserie.de*
– *Closed Sunday and Bank Holidays*
Menu 29 € (lunch)/75 € – Carte 45/70 € – *(bookings advisable at dinner)*
• International • Brasserie • Trendy •

This brasserie and bar are one of the city's hotspots. The banking hall on the first-floor of this former bank, built in 1897, is an impressive feature of this fashionable venue.

XX
Henriks

Tesdorpfstr. 8 ✉ *20148* – **Ⓜ** *Stephanspl.*   Plan: **F1**
– ✆ *(040) 2 88 08 42 80* – *www.henriks.cc*
Carte 44/102 € – *(booking advisable)*
• International • Design • Elegant •

Whether you prefer the beef tataki with yuzu sauce, squash and truffle or the haddock and fried potatoes with Pommery mustard sauce, the ambitious mix of Asian, Mediterranean and regional cuisine in Claas-Henrik Anklam's chic, designer restaurant provides something for every taste. The large terrace and lounge are particularly popular. Noon diners in a hurry should look out for the great value lunch menu.

XX **YOSHI im Alsterhaus** 🍴 ⚜ 🅰️🅲️

Jungfernstieg 16 (Alsterhaus 4th. floor direct elevator Plan: **G2**
entrance Poststr. 8) ✉ 20354 – Ⓜ *Jungfernstieg –* ☏ *(040) 35 71 44 93*
– www.yoshi-hamburg.de – Closed Sunday and Bank Holidays
Menu 45/95 € – Carte 30/91 €
• Japanese • Fashionable •

Christened 'Gourmet Boulevard', the fourth floor of Hamburg's upmarket Alsterhaus shopping plaza is the location for Ikebana master Yoko Etsuseisai Higashi's meeting place for enthusiasts of Japanese food and culture. The teriyaki and sushi dishes prepared by the Japanese chefs achieve a perfect marriage of the traditional and the modern. Popular roof terrace.

XX **Piazza Romana** – Hotel Grand Elysée ⚜ 🅰️🅲️ 🚗

Rothenbaumchaussee 10 ✉ 20148 – Ⓜ *Stephanspl.* Plan: **F1**
– ☏ *(040) 41 41 27 34 – www.grand-elysee.com*
Carte 32/49 €
• Italian • Classic •

If you fancy carpaccio di vitello, a plate of linguine or tiramisu, then the Italian cuisine on offer at this restaurant is for you.

XX **Strauchs Falco** 🍴

Koreastr. 2 ✉ 20354 – ☏ *(040) 2 26 16 15 11* Plan I: **C3**
– www.falco-hamburg.de
Carte 38/81 €
• International • Fashionable •

Strauchs Falco serves a wide range of good Mediterranean dishes, steaks and classic fare. The restaurant itself is modern in style with an open kitchen and a large terrace in summer. The tapas bar on the first floor doubles up as a café during the day.

XX **Doc Cheng's** – Fairmont Hotel Vier Jahreszeiten ⚜ 🅰️🅲️ 🚗

Neuer Jungfernstieg 9 ✉ 20354 – Ⓜ *Jungfernstieg* Plan: **F2**
– ☏ *(040) 3 49 43 33 – www.fairmont-hvj.de – Closed Sunday*
Menu 56/84 € – Carte 55/71 € – (dinner only)
• Fusion • Individual • Intimate •

The Far East inspires both the design and cuisine of this restaurant. Euro-Asian cuisine is served here.

X **VLET**

Sandtorkai 23 (entrance by Kibbelstegbrücke 1, 1st Plan I: **C3**
floor, Block N) ✉ 20457 – Ⓜ *Baumwall –* ☏ *(040) 3 34 75 37 50*
– www.vlet.de – Closed Saturday lunch and Sunday
Menu 25 € (lunch)/75 € (dinner) – Carte 41/65 €
• Modern cuisine • Trendy •

The deliberate warehouse feel, typical of Hamburg's Speicherstadt area, makes an ideal venue for fashionable cuisine. It is best to park in the Contipark and cross the Kibbelstegbrücke bridge to reach the restaurant.

X **Coast** 🌿 🍴 ⚜

Grosser Grasbrook 14 ✉ 20457 – Ⓜ *Überseequartier* Plan I: **C3**
– ☏ *(040) 30 99 32 30 – www.coast-hamburg.de*
Carte 42/81 €
• Fusion • Friendly • Fashionable •

Occupying a lovely waterside spot on the Marco Polo Terrace on the edge of the port of Hamburg, the location is one of Coast's main attractions. The other is the cuisine: a combination of Euro-Asian dishes and sushi creations. The basement houses a second restaurant, the rustic Sansibar. After 6pm you can park in the Unilever car park next door.

GERMANY - HAMBURG

Brook

Bei den Mühren 91 ✉ *20457* – Ⓜ *Meßberg* – ℰ *(040)* Plan: **G3**
37 50 31 28 – *www.restaurant-brook.de* – *Closed Sunday*
Menu 18 € (weekday lunch)/39 € – Carte 37/50 €
• International • Fashionable •

The most popular dishes at this relaxed modern restaurant include classics such as braised calves' cheeks, but fish fresh from the famous fish market just round the corner are also firm favourites, as is the very reasonable set lunchtime menu. It is worth coming here in the evenings too, when you can enjoy views of the illuminated warehouse district.

CARLS

Am Kaiserkai 69 ✉ *20457* – Ⓜ *Baumwall* – ℰ *(040)* Plan I: **C3**
3 00 32 24 00 – *www.carls-brasserie.de*
Menu 42 € – Carte 34/68 €
• Regional • Brasserie •

This elegant brasserie is at the New Elbe Philharmonic Hall. It serves up French cuisine with a North German slant alongside great views of the port. Savoury tarts and nibbles in the bistro; spices and other gourmet treats in the delicatessen.

La Mirabelle

Bundesstr. 15 ✉ *20146* – Ⓜ *Hallerstr.* – ℰ *(040)* Plan I: **C2**
4 10 75 85 – *www.la-mirabelle-hamburg.de* – *Closed 1-6 January, Sunday-Monday and Bank Holidays*
Menu 33/72 € – Carte 53/68 € – *(dinner only)*
• French classic • Cosy • Family •

What else would a restaurateur with an evocative name like Pierre Moissonnier offer his guests if not impressions of his French home? When he is not at his stove, you will find him front of house.

[m]eatery – Hotel SIDE

Drehbahn 49 ✉ *20354* – Ⓜ *Stephanspl.* – ℰ *(040)* Plan: **F2**
30 99 95 95 – *www.meatery.de*
Menu 75/120 € – Carte 40/150 €
• Meats • Design •

The strong colours may shock some as the furniture and walls in this fashionable restaurant come in various shades of bright green. Steakhouse with glass-fronted meat maturing cabinet.

Bistro am Fleet – Hotel Steigenberger

Heiligengeistbrücke 4 ✉ *20459* – Ⓜ *Rödingsmarkt* Plan: **F3**
– ℰ *(040) 36 80 61 22* – *www.hamburg.steigenberger.de*
Carte 32/68 €
• International • Cosy •

The cool feel of this restaurant is due to the conservatory, which makes the transition from inside to outside almost seamless. A range of international dishes are on offer.

Le Plat du Jour

Dornbusch 4 ✉ *20095* – Ⓜ *Rathaus* – ℰ *(040) 32 14 14* Plan: **G3**
– *www.leplatdujour.de* – *Closed during Christmas*
Menu 33 € (dinner) – Carte 30/44 € – *(booking advisable)*
• French classic • Bistro •

With a reputation forged largely by word of mouth, you will find the lively Le Plat du Jour busy from lunchtime onwards. Both the interior, with its black and white photos and closely packed tables, and the food it serves, are authentic brasserie in style. As an alternative to the dish of the day, try the Mediterranean French fish soup with croutons or the classic 'steak frites'.

GERMANY - HAMBURG

X

Casse-Croûte

Büschstr. 2 ⊠ 20354 – Ⓜ Gänsemarkt – ☏ (040)   Plan: **F2**
*34 33 73 – www.cassecroute.de – Closed during Christmas, Sunday lunch
and Bank Holidays lunch*
Carte 33/49 € – *(booking advisable)*
· French classic · Bistro ·

Casse-Croûte combines French savoir vivre with a certain Hamburg touch to
create a bustling yet pleasantly relaxed feel in a typical bistro setting. Try the
'Northern bouillabaisse', one of the classic dishes from Christian Möllers' repertoire or alternatively the Wiener Schnitzel or whole sole, which also feature on
the menu.

X
Cox

Lange Reihe 68 ⊠ 20099 – Ⓜ Hauptbf. Nord – ☏ (040)   Plan: **H1**
*24 94 22 – www.restaurant-cox.de – Closed Saturday lunch, Sunday lunch
and Bank Holidays lunch*
Menu 28/49 € – Carte 33/52 € – *(mid July-mid August dinner only)*
· International · Bistro · Cosy ·

More casual and urban than chic and elegant, Cox is a bistro in the best sense of
the word. A colourful mix of diners enjoys a varied selection of dishes including
braised lamb shanks, grass-fed beef rissoles and cod. Good value lunchtime
menu.

X

Trific

Holzbrücke 7 ⊠ 20459 – Ⓜ Rödingsmarkt – ☏ (040)   Plan: **F3**
41 91 90 46 – www.trific.de – Closed 10-28 July and Sunday-Monday
Menu 30 € – Carte 31/50 € – *(dinner only) (booking advisable)*
· International · Fashionable · Neighbourhood ·

The location is new but the culinary concept remains the same: guests create
their own menu from a range of delicious dishes including spiny loach, asparagus and potatoes. The restaurant extends over two floors with the floor-to-ceiling windows on the ground floor giving views over the dike.

NORTH OF THE CENTRE   PLAN I

🏠
Mittelweg

Mittelweg 59 ⊠ 20149 – Ⓜ Klosterstern – ☏ (040)   Plan: **C1**
4 14 10 10 – www.hotel-mittelweg-hamburg.de
30 rm � – †95/125 € ††125/220 €
· Villa · Cosy ·

This 1890 villa is full of turn of the century charm. Find it at the staircase,
through to the stucco ceilings in the stylish breakfast room, and in the carefully
selected combinations of colours, motifs and classic furniture in the bedrooms.
Quiet, secluded garden.

XX

Piment (Wahabi Nouri)

Lehmweg 29 ⊠ 20251 – Ⓜ Eppendorfer Baum   Plan: **C1**
*– ☏ (040) 42 93 77 88 – www.restaurant-piment.de – closed Wednesday
and Sunday*
Menu 65/108 € – Carte 58/92 € – *(dinner only) (booking advisable)*
· Creative · Friendly ·

Wahabi Nouri's two set menus – 'Piment' and 'Nouri's' – are the perfect expression of his creative, sophisticated style and ambitious minimalist presentation.
These are both informed by his Moroccan roots, which he uses in a pleasingly
underplayed manner in the form of exotic spices and perfumes – more in one
menu, less in the other.
➔ Couscous mit sieben Gemüsen und Safranglace. Etouffée Taube, B'stilla,
Himbeer-Essigjus. Irischer Lammrücken mit Kardonen und Ras El Hanout.

GERMANY - HAMBURG

XX Anna Sgroi
※
Milchstr. 7 ✉ 20148 – ℰ (040) 28 00 39 30 Plan: **C1**
– www.annasgroi.de
Menu 39 € (lunch)/93 € – Carte 70/78 €
• Italian • Elegant • Cosy •

Anna Sgroi just "fell in love" with this cosy townhouse and its beautiful stucco ceiling. Here in her new restaurant she cooks classic Italian food, continuing to shun modern gimmicks in favour of the more traditional values of good, well-prepared produce.
→ Salat von Flußkrebsen und Gurken mit Mango-Ingwer-Vinaigrette. Ravioli von Felsenaustern und Spinat. Piemonteser Risotto alla Finanziera mit Spitzmorcheln.

XX TrüffelSchwein (Kirill Kinfelt)
※
Mühlenkamp 54 ✉ 22303 – ⓜ Sierichstr. Plan: **D1**
– ℰ (040) 69 65 64 50 – www.trueffelschwein-restaurant.de
– Closed 1-5 January, 7-13 March, 25 July-7 August and Saturday lunch, Sunday-Monday
Menu 49/89 € – *(bookings advisable at dinner)*
• Modern cuisine • Friendly •

This attractive, modern restaurant serves innovative and elaborate dishes. Spring chicken with sweet potatoes, lime and radishes, as well as rhubarb, vanilla, coffee and tonka beans are just two examples. You will find a simpler, good value bistro menu on offer at lunchtimes, though the evening menu is also available on request.
→ Pulpo, Tomate, Bohne. Adlerfisch, Zucchini, Paprika. Ziegenkäse, Estragon, weiße Schokolade.

X Bistrot Vienna
Fettstrasse 2 ✉ 20357 – ⓜ Christkirche – ℰ (040) Plan: **B2**
4 39 91 82 – www.vienna-hamburg.de – Closed Monday
Menu 25 € – Carte 21/53 € – *(dinner only)*
• International • Bistro • Individual •

A small restaurant in a slightly out-of-the-way location, Bistrot Vienna is charming, lively and well frequented. The popular combination of vibrant yet relaxed atmosphere and Sven Bunge's seasonal, international, homemade cuisine means that the tightly packed tables are always in demand. No reservations though.

X Butcher's american steakhouse
Milchstr. 19 ✉ 20148 – ℰ (040) 44 60 82 Plan: **C2**
– www.butchers-steakhouse.de – Closed Saturday lunch, Sunday lunch and Bank Holidays lunch
Carte 57/153 €
• Meats • Family • Cosy •

Here you can taste fine Nebraska beef that the chef presents to the table. A cosy restaurant with a decor dominated by dark wood and warm colours.

X Cornelia Poletto
Eppendorfer Landstr. 80 ✉ 20249 – ⓜ Kellenhusenstr. Plan: **C1**
– ℰ (040) 4 80 21 59 – www.cornelia-poletto.de – Closed 1 week early January, Sunday-Monday and Bank Holidays
Menu 59/98 € – Carte 44/84 € – *(booking advisable)*
• Italian • Friendly • Cosy •

Cornelia Poletto (who Germans will know from the television if not from her previous restaurant) serves Italian specialities in the restaurant and sells them (spices, wine, pasta, cheese) in the shop. Booked out almost daily.

GERMANY - HAMBURG

✗ **Poletto Winebar**   🏵 🏮

Eppendorfer Weg 287 ✉ *20251 –* Ⓜ *Eppendorfer Baum*   Plan: **C1**
– 𝒞 (040) 38 64 47 00 – www.poletto-winebar.de
Menu 39 € (lunch)/69 € (dinner)
– Carte 33/54 € – (bookings advisable at dinner)
• Italian • Cosy •

This lively wine bar is definitely one of the places to be in Eppendorf. The food is flavoursome and Italian in style, including classics such as vitello tonnato and tiramisu served alongside excellent cold meats straight from the Berkel meat slicer. Great wine selection also in the adjacent wine shop.

✗ **Jellyfish**

Weidenallee 12 ✉ *20357 –* Ⓜ *Christkirche – 𝒞 (040)*   Plan: **B2**
4 10 54 14 – www.jellyfish-restaurant.de – Closed 24 December-3 January and Saturday lunch, Sunday lunch, Monday
Menu 35 € (lunch)/99 €
• Fish and seafood • Bistro •

If you are looking for an alternative to Hamburg's established fish restaurants, try Jellyfish. Uncomplicated, urban and minimalist, it serves ambitious food made using excellent produce in the form of a set menu or from the 'Seafood Etagère' – a speciality you will have to order in advance.

✗
🈁 **Zipang**

Eppendorfer Weg 171 ✉ *20253 –* Ⓜ *Eppendorfer Baum*   Plan: **B1**
– 𝒞 (040) 43 28 00 32 – www.zipang.de – Closed Monday, Tuesday lunch, Wednesday lunch, Saturday lunch
Menu 19 € (lunch)/76 € (dinner) – Carte 30/74 €
• Japanese • Minimalist •

The minimalist interior at Zipang has clean lines, muted colours and a smart silver sheen. This makes a perfect match for chef Toshiharu Minami's mix of traditional and modern Japanese cooking styles. The restaurant is popular with Japanese diners – always a good sign.

🏨 **Empire Riverside Hotel**

Bernhard-Nocht-Str. 97 (via Davidstraße) ✉ *20359*   Plan: **J1**
– Ⓜ *Reeperbahn – 𝒞 (040) 31 11 90 – www.empire-riverside.de*
327 rm – ♦129/309 € ♦♦129/309 € – ☲ 22 €
• Business • Conference hotel • Design •

Famous architect David Chipperfield designed this contemporary hotel close to the St Pauli pontoon bridges. Rooms have a view of either the river or the city as does "20", the panoramic bar on the 20th floor. This wharf-side restaurant offers international cuisine in a simple, contemporary setting.

🏨 **East**

Simon-von-Utrecht-Str. 31 ✉ *20359 –* Ⓜ *St. Pauli*   Plan: **B2**
– 𝒞 (040) 30 99 30 – www.east-hamburg.de
120 rm – ♦150/290 € ♦♦160/300 € – ☲ 24 € – 8 suites
• Business • Design •

The design in this former iron foundry is resolutely modern and trendy. It runs from the guestrooms through to the bar-lounge and the leisure and beauty area with its professionally staffed fitness club.
East – See restaurant listing

🏨 **Boston**

Missundestr. 2 ✉ *22769 –* Ⓜ *Feldstr. – 𝒞 (040)*   Plan: **J1**
5 89 66 67 00 – www.boston-hamburg.de
46 rm – ♦130/210 € ♦♦150/230 € – ☲ 18 €
• Business • Design • Modern •

A modern business hotel with tasteful and straightforward fittings. Rooms are available in the categories Design and Business – the latter with a kitchenette This trendy restaurant has an adjoining lounge and bar.

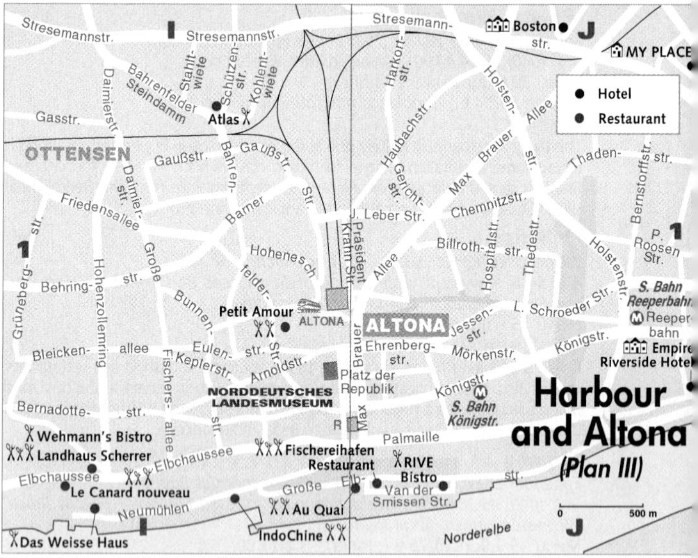

MY PLACE

Lippmannstr. 5 ✉ 22769 – Ⓜ Feldstr. – ✆ (040) 28 57 18 74 – www.myplace-hamburg.de Plan: J1

17 rm – †72/99 € ††89/129 € – ☕ 5 € – 1 suite

• Townhouse • Personalised • Contemporary •

Close to the trendy Schanze district the dedicated hostess runs a small hotel with individually styled, charming modern rooms named after districts of Hamburg.

Landhaus Scherrer (Heinz O. Wehmann)

Elbchaussee 130 ✉ 22763 – ✆ (040) 8 83 07 00 30 – www.landhausscherrer.de – Closed Sunday Plan: I1

Menu 98/128 € – Carte 65/104 €

• French classic • Elegant •

Heinz O. Wehmann has been at the helm at Landhaus Scherrer since 1980. He is still serving classic cuisine in this elegant restaurant where Otto Bachmann's large erotic painting remains the decorative focus. Adding a modern note, the 600 plus wines on the wine list are presented to you on an iPad.

→ Gebratener Steinbutt mit Gartengemüsen und Süßholzaroma. Gefüllter Ochsenschwanz vom Eidertaler Auerochsen mit Kalbskopfgraupen. Geflämmte Knusperschnitte mit Quark aus der Wilstermarsch.

Wehmann's Bistro – See restaurant listing

Le Canard nouveau (Ali Güngörmüs)

Elbchaussee 139 ✉ 22763 – ✆ (040) 88 12 95 31 – www.lecanard-hamburg.de – Closed Sunday-Monday Plan: I1

Menu 51 € (weekday lunch)/139 € – Carte 83/95 € – *(booking advisable)*

• Classic cuisine • Fashionable •

If you find that the name Ali Güngörmüs conjures up images of oriental fare, you would be right. The chef uses the influences of his native Turkey in a pleasingly understated manner to bring out the full flavour of his produce. He is also a stickler for matching the right wine to each dish. To make sure that everyone gets a good view of the port, the dining room is circular with floor-to-ceiling windows!

→ Türkische Morcheln mit Spargel in Sherry à la Crème. Karree vom Salzwiesenlamm mit Artischocken und Gewürzjoghurt. Alis Valrhona Schokoladenkuchen.

XXX **Fischereihafen Restaurant**

Große Elbstr. 143 ⊠ *22767 –* ℰ *(040) 38 18 16* Plan: J1
– www.fischereihafenrestaurant.de
Menu 23 € (lunch)/58 € – Carte 34/80 € – *(booking advisable)*
• Fish and seafood • Classic

This fish restaurant overlooking the port is a veritable Hamburg institution. The service is excellent as is the great value lunchtime menu.

XX **Au Quai**

Große Elbstr. 145 b ⊠ *22767 –* ℰ *(040) 38 03 77 30* Plan: J1
*– www.au-quai.com – Closed during Christmas, 1-15 January and
Saturday lunch, Sunday*
Menu 30/49 € – Carte 42/72 €
• Fish and seafood • Trendy •

This popular establishment is situated close to the harbour and has a terrace facing the water. The modern interior is complemented by designer items and holographs.

XX **Petit Amour**

Spritzenplatz 11 ⊠ *22765 –* ℰ *(040) 30 74 65 56* Plan: I1
*– www.petitamour-hh.com – Closed 1 week January, 2 weeks August and
Sunday-Monday*
Menu 58/120 € – *(dinner only, Thursday also lunch) (booking advisable)*
• Classic cuisine • Elegant • Cosy •

This is a very popular restaurant for a number of reasons… The upmarket design (modern and minimalist yet warm and friendly), the professional service and wine suggestions, and the unfussy, ambitious cuisine with international influences.

XX **IndoChine**

Neumühlen 11 ⊠ *22763 –* ℰ *(040) 39 80 78 80* Plan: I1
– www.indochine.de – Closed Saturday lunch
Menu 43 € (dinner) – Carte 34/64 €
• Asian • Trendy •

The fine view of the Elbe and its container port through the glass frontage, and the interesting style of cuisine, are still drawing the crowds to IndoChine 10 years after it opened. Cambodian, Laotian and Vietnamese influences combine with classic cuisine in this restaurant. A good value two-course à la carte menu is available at lunchtimes.

XX **East** – Hotel East

Simon-von-Utrecht-Str. 31 ⊠ *20359 –* Ⓜ *St. Pauli* Plan: B2
– ℰ *(040) 30 99 33 – www.east-hamburg.de – Closed Saturday lunch and
Sunday lunch*
Menu 49 € (dinner)/99 € – Carte 41/73 €
• Fusion • Design • Fashionable •

The atmosphere in this former factory building draws on many styles and influences. Far Eastern charm combines skilfully with Western industrial heritage. A restaurant not to be missed.

X **RIVE Bistro**
⊛

Van-der-Smissen-Str. 1 (at Kreuzfahrt-Center) ⊠ *22767* Plan: J1
– Ⓜ *Königstr. –* ℰ *(040) 3 80 59 19 – www.rive.de*
Menu 50/55 € – Carte 34/61 € – *(booking advisable)*
• Fish and seafood • Trendy • Bistro •

Find excellent fish and friendly service at this restaurant in Hamburg's famous docks, along with a view of passing ships. The menu boasts local classics such as Hamburger Pannfisch, international fare including yellowfin tuna with pak choi and mango and chilli couscous, along with some meat dishes.

✗ Nil 🛖 �

😊 *Neuer Pferdemarkt 5* ✉ *20359 –* Ⓜ *Feldstr. –* ℰ *(040)* Plan: **B2**
4 39 78 23 – www.restaurant-nil.de – Closed Tuesday except in December
Menu 27/42 € – Carte 30/48 € – *(dinner only)*
• International • Neighbourhood • Friendly •

The casual, trendy atmosphere here is perfectly in keeping with the times. Set over three floors, the tables are a little tightly packed but the feel is friendly and comfortable for all that. The food itself is another reason for Nil's popularity. Try the Mangalitza bratwurst with pumpkin and potato mash and pointed cabbage – the delicious sausages are homemade. In summer the best tables are outside in the garden behind the restaurant. Cookery courses available next door.

✗ Clouds - Heaven's Restaurant & Bar ⩽ 🛖 🆔

Reeperbahn 1 (at 23. floor der Tanzenden Türme) Plan: **B3**
✉ *20359 –* Ⓜ *St. Pauli – ℰ (040) 30 99 32 80 – www.clouds-hamburg.de*
Menu 35 € (weekday lunch) – Carte 49/102 € – *(booking advisable)*
• International • Design •

The view from Hamburg's highest restaurant is simply amazing! High above the River Elbe and St Michael's church you can choose between the ambitious French/Mediterranean cuisine (try the salt-baked turbot for two) or something from the rotisserie. One floor higher up and you will find yourself on the rooftop terrace.

✗ Das Weisse Haus 🛖 ✿

Neumühlen 50 ✉ *22763 – ℰ (040) 3 90 90 16* Plan: **I1**
– www.das-weisse-haus.de – Closed Saturday lunch, Sunday lunch and Monday
Menu 49 € (dinner)/89 € – Carte 35/65 € – *(booking advisable)*
• International • Friendly •

In the little white building on the Elbpromenade your host Patrick Voelz proposes a range of international dishes alongside a now established seasonal surprise menu. The atmosphere is casual and friendly and you can sit outside too.

✗ Wehmann's Bistro – Restaurant Landhaus Scherrer 🕸 🆔 🅿

Elbchaussee 130 ✉ *22763 – ℰ (040) 8 83 07 00 50* Plan: **I1**
– www.wehmanns-bistro.de – Closed Sunday
Menu 40 € – Carte 32/51 €
• Regional • Bistro •

The decor in this lovely bistro gives the impression of classic comfort. Culinary delights are prepared by the owner, Heinz O Wehmann.

🏨 Louis C. Jacob ⚜ ⩽ 🛖 🆔 🐾 🚌

Elbchaussee 401 (by Elbchaussee A3) ✉ *22609 – ℰ (040) 82 25 50*
– www.hotel-jacob.de
66 rm – 🛏205/265 € 🛏🛏265/455 € – ⌑ 32 € – 19 suites
• Luxury • Traditional • Classic •

The successful management and services in this elegant hotel on the Elbe are exemplary. Equally pleasant is the classical furnishing of the rooms, some of which are as spacious as junior suites.
❀❀ **Jacobs Restaurant** • ☺ **Weinwirtschaft Kleines Jacob** – See restaurant listing

🏠 Strandhotel ⩽ 🚪 🛗 🅿

Strandweg 13 (by Elbchaussee A3) ✉ *22587 – ℰ (040) 86 13 44*
– www.strandhotel-blankenese.de – Closed 1-11 January
14 rm – 🛏100/145 € 🛏🛏160/205 € – ⌑ 15 € – 1 suite
• Villa • Classic • Design •

The Strandhotel is the epitome of the lifestyle hotel. Despite its many modern features, the charm of this listed white Art Nouveau villa is omnipresent. Its high-ceilinged, stuccoed rooms match the designer furnishings to perfection. The excellent buffet breakfast comes with a lovely view of the Elbe.

GERMANY - HAMBURG

XXXX **Jacobs Restaurant** – Hotel Louis C. Jacob   😻 ≼ 🏠 🖾 ⇪ 🚗
✿✿ *Elbchaussee 401 (by Elbchaussee A3)* ✉ *22609* – ☏ *(040) 82 25 54 07*
– *www.hotel-jacob.de* – *Closed Monday-Tuesday*
Menu 89/154 € – *(Wednesday-Friday dinner only) (booking advisable)*
• French classic • Elegant •

Without doubt a stylish, classy restaurant with excellent service. This is evident
in the decor from the glittering chandeliers, which hang from the high stuccoed
ceilings, to the fine herringbone parquet. Enjoy Thomas Martin's gourmet 'Tried
and tested', 'Contemporary' and 'Natural' menus. If you want to eat in a more
intimate setting, there are a number of lovely smaller dining rooms. In addition,
when the weather permits there is nothing like eating outside on the lime tree-
shaded terrace overlooking the Elbe.
➜ Roh marinierter Maigre, Avocado, Zitrone, Fenchel. Gebratenes Seezun-
genfilet, Blumenkohl, Curry, Kopfsalat. Kürbiskerne und Joghurt, weiße
Schokolade, Hafer.

XXXX **Süllberg - Seven Seas** (Karlheinz Hauser)   😻 ⇦ ≼ 🏠 ♿ 🖾
✿✿ *Süllbergterrasse 12 (by Elbchaussee A3)* ✉ *22587* – ☏ *(040)*   🚗
8 66 25 20 – *www.suellberg-hamburg.de* – *Closed January-mid February*
and Monday-Tuesday
10 rm – 🛏170/190 € 🛏🛏190/230 € – 🍽 17 € – 1 suite
Menu 74 € (Vegetarian)/175 € – *(dinner only, Sunday also lunch)*
• French modern • Luxury •

The Süllberg is a Blankenese institution and along with the Seven Seas has
become one of Hamburg's top gourmet addresses. It offers a genuinely upmarket dining experience, from the classy interior to Karlheinz Hauser's fragrant,
classic cuisine, as well as the accomplished and attentive service and expert
wine recommendations. The rooms are as attractive and stylish as the restaurant.
➜ Jacobsmuschel, Brunnenkresse, Haselnuss, Imperialkaviar. Schellfisch,
Einkorn, Puntarella, Sanddorn. Limousin Lamm, Pimientos, Schafsjoghurt,
Oliven.
Deck 7 – See restaurant listing

XX **Witthüs**   🏠 🅿
Elbchaussee 499a (access via Mühlenberg) (by Elbchaussee A3) ✉ *22587*
– ☏ *(040) 86 01 73* – *www.witthues.com* – *Closed Monday*
Menu 30/39 € – Carte 38/55 € – *(dinner only)*
• International • Classic •

This historic farmhouse is idyllically located near the Elbe. Enjoy international
cuisine and professional service in a classic, elegant setting with Nordic flair.
Outdoor terrace.

X **Weinwirtschaft Kleines Jacob** – Hotel Louis C. Jacob   😻
🐱 *Elbchaussee 404 (by Elbchaussee A3)* ✉ *22609* – ☏ *(040)*   🏠 🚗
82 25 55 10 – *www.kleines-jacob.de*
Menu 36 € – Carte 36/47 € – *(dinner only) (booking advisable)*
• Classic cuisine • Wine bar • Cosy •

The atmosphere at Kleines Jacob is more casual and relaxed compared to its
stylish gourmet counterpart. The Mediterranean and local fare is simpler here,
though every bit as good. Try the Flammekueche, the cheese fondue or the
veal involtini served on a bed of wild mushroom linguine.

X **Atlas**   🏠 🅿
Schützenstr. 9a (entrance Phoenixhof) ✉ *22761*   Plan: I1
– ☏ *(040) 8 51 78 10* – *www.atlas.at* – *Closed Saturday lunch and Sunday*
dinner
Menu 21 € (lunch)/36 € (dinner) – Carte 20/40 €
• International • Bistro •

This former fish smokery is now a restaurant in the modern bistro style. Shorter
menu available at lunchtimes. Pleasant ivy-covered terrace.

Rach & Ritchy

Holstenkamp 71 ✉ *22525* – ✆ *(040) 89 72 61 70*   Plan: A2
– www.rach-ritchy.de – Closed Saturday lunch, Sunday and Bank Holidays lunch
Carte 32/69 € – *(booking advisable)*
• Meats • Friendly • Fashionable •
TV chef Christian Rach is now a household name. It is the second member of the duo, Richard 'Ritchy' Mayer, who does the cooking in his fashionable, modern grill restaurant. Specialities include succulent steaks from the glass-fronted maturing cabinet.

Deck 7 – Restaurant Süllberg - Seven Seas

Süllbergsterrasse 12 (by Elbchaussee A3) ✉ *22587* – ✆ *(040) 86 62 52 77*
– www.suellberg-hamburg.de
Menu 30 € – Carte 37/82 €
• Regional • Cosy •
In defiance of many a passing trend, this restaurant with its smart, brown leather upholstered chairs and parquet flooring has opted for the versatility of a classic yet modern interior. In summer, eat outside with stunning views of the Elbe.

Off Club

Leverkusenstr. 54 ✉ *22761* – ✆ *(040) 89 01 93 33*   Plan: AB2
– www.offclub.de – Closed Monday-Tuesday
Carte 31/55 €
• Meats • Cosy • Trendy •
One half of a pair of restaurants, Off Club occupies a renovated factory building where it serves flavoursome fare ranging from green asparagus with grapefruit and parmesan to veal shanks with cabbage and roasting juices and excellent sushi. Good value daily menu at lunchtimes.
Madame X im Off Club – See restaurant listing

Madame X im Off Club – Restaurant Off Club

Leverkusenstr. 54 ✉ *22761* – ✆ *(040) 89 01 93 33*   Plan: AB2
– www.offclub.de – Closed Monday-Tuesday
Menu 19 € (dinner)/88 €
– Carte 37/71 € – (dinner only) (booking essential)
• Meats • Cosy • Trendy •
Madame X offers a very special dining experience. Its Carte Blanche set menu features seven 'rounds' served in this intimate, dimly lit restaurant by a relaxed front-of-house team. The chef explains his creations personally to the diners at their tables.

AT THE AIRPORT

Radisson BLU Airport

Flughafenstr. 1 ✉ *22335* – ✆ *(040) 3 00 30 00*
– www.radissonblu.com/hotel-hamburgairport
265 rm – ▪119/256 € ▪▪119/256 € – ☷20 € – 1 suite
• Business • Modern •
Modern circular hotel complex with access to terminals 1 and 2. Purist design throughout, rooms in "Ocean" and "Urban" style, including large business rooms. This bright, stylish restaurant has an integrated bar.

MUNICH
MÜNCHEN

Population: 1 388 310

Lichtblick/Fotolia.com

Situated in a stunning position not far north of the Alps, Munich is a cultural titan. Famously described as the 'village with a million inhabitants', its mix of German organisation and Italian lifestyle makes for a magical mix, with an enviable amount of Italian restaurants to seek out and enjoy. This cultural capital of Southern Germany boasts over forty theatres and dozens of museums; temples of culture that blend charmingly with the Bavarian love of folklore and lederhosen. Perhaps in no other world location – certainly not in Western Europe – is there such an enjoyable abundance of folk festivals and groups dedicated to playing the local music. And there's an abundance of places to see them, too: Munich is awash with Bierhallen, Bierkeller, and Biergarten.

The heart of Munich is the Old Town, with its epicentre the Marienplatz in the south, and Residenz to the north: there are many fine historic buildings around here. Running to the east is the River Isar, flanked by fine urban thoroughfares and green areas for walks. Head north for the area dissected by the Ludwig-strasse and Leopoldstrasse – Schwabing – which is full of students as it's the University district. To the east is the English Garden, a denizen of peace. West of here, the Museums district, dominated by the Pinakothek, is characterised by bookshops, antique stores and galleries.

MUNICH IN...

→ **ONE DAY**
The old town, Frauenkirche, English Garden, Wagner (if possible!) at the National Theatre.

→ **TWO DAYS**
Schwabing, Pinakothek, Hofbräuhaus.

→ **THREE DAYS**
Olympic Park, Schloss Nymphenburg, Deutsches Museum, an evening in a traditional Bavarian inn.

PRACTICAL INFORMATION

ARRIVAL-DEPARTURE

✈ Airport Frank Josef Strauss is 28km northeast of the city. Munich S-Bahn Lines S1 or S8 take 45min to the centre.

GETTING AROUND

The underground network (U-Bahn) operates the same fare system as on Munich's buses and trams: it's divided into 4 ring-shaped price zones; zone 1 (the white zone) is the most important for visitors, as it covers the city centre. Prices rise in accordance with the amount of zones you intend to travel. If you plan to make several journeys, invest in a strip-card (Streifenkarte). You can also buy a 1 or 3-day Tageskarte: good value for tourists and available from tourist information offices, hotel receptions, travel agents and newsagents. The München Welcome Card is available for 1 or 3 days and gives free use of public transport as well as reduced entry to many museums, palaces and sights.

EATING OUT

Munich is a city in which you can eat well - especially if you're a meat-eater – and in large quantities. The local specialities are meat and potatoes, with large dollops of cabbage on the side; you won't have trouble finding roast pork and dumplings or meatloaf and don't forget the local white veal sausage, weisswurst. The meat is invariably succulent, and cabbage is often adorned with the likes of juniper berries. Potatoes, meanwhile, have a tendency to evolve into soft and buttery dumplings. And sausage? Take your pick from over 1,500 recognised species. Other specialities include Schweinshaxe (knuckle of pork) and Leberkäs (meat and offal pâté). Eating out in Munich, or anywhere in Bavaria, is an experience in itself, with the distinctive background din of laughter, singing and the clinking of mugs of Bavarian Weissbier. It's famous for the Brauereigaststätten or brewery inn; be prepared for much noise, and don't be afraid to fall into conversation with fellow diners and drinkers. The many Italian restaurants in the city provide an excellent alternative.

CALENDAR HIGHLIGHTS

March
Starkbierfest (Strong Beer Festival).

May
Biennale (contemporary music).

June/July
Münchner Opernfestspiele (opera and ballet), Summer Tollwood Festival.

July
Sommernachtstraum (concert and fireworks).

August
Theatron Music Summer.

September-October
Oktoberfest.

October
Long Night of Museums, Munich Marathon.

November-December
Winter Tollwood Festival, Christkindlmarkt

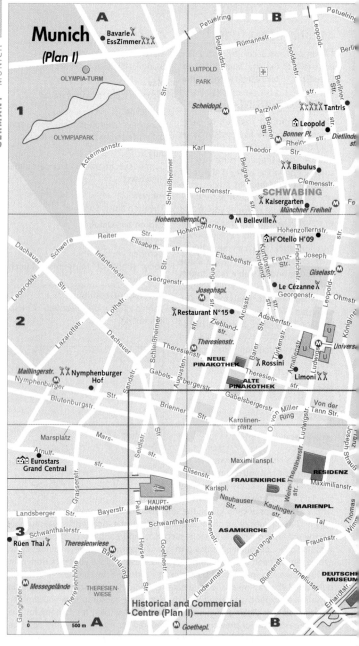

Munich
(Plan I)

A

● Bavarie ✗
EssZimmer ✗✗✗

OLYMPIA-TURM

1

OLYMPIAPARK

Ackermannstr.

Schleißheimer Str.

Karl

B

Petuelring

Belgradstr.

Rümannstr.

Isoldenstr.

Leopold-

Berli

LUITPOLD
PARK

Scheidpl. Ⓜ

Parzival-

Bonner
Str.

Belgrad-

Theodor

Str.

Rhein-
Str.

✗✗✗✗✗ **Tantris**

Berliner
Str.

🏠 **Leopold**

Bonner Pl.

Dietlinde
st.

✗✗ **Bibulus**

Clemensstr.

SCHWABING

Clemensstr.

Clemensstr.

str.

✗ **Kaisergarten**
Münchner Freiheit Ⓜ

Fe

Hohenzollernpl. Ⓜ

Reiter Str.

Elisabeth-

Hohenzollernstr.

● **M Belleville** ✗

Hohenzollernstr.

🏠**H'Otello H'09**

Dachauer Str.

Schwere

Infanteriestr.

Leonrodstr.

Lothstr.

Lazarettstr.

Dachauer

2

Georgenstr.

str.

Ellsabethstr.

Teng-
str.

Kurfürsten-
Nordend.

Franz-
Str.

Joseph

Friedrichstr.

Joseph

Giselastr. Ⓜ

Ohmstr

Josephspl. Ⓜ

Arcisstr.

Georgenstr.

● **Le Cézanne** ✗

Leopold-

Königins

✗ **Restaurant N°15** ●

Schleißheimer

str.

Ziebland-
str.

Adalbertstr.

Barer

Türkenstr.

Amalienstr.

Ⓤ

Ⓤ Ⓜ Ⓤ

Universe

Theresienstr.

Theresienstr.

Augustenstr.

Gabels-

NEUE
PINAKOTHEK

✗ **Rossini**

Theresien-
str.

Limoni ✗✗

Maillingerstr. ✗✗ **Nymphenburger**
Hof

Nymphenburger

Str.

Sandstr.

ALTE
PINAKOTHEK

Blutenburgstr.

Brienner

Str.

Gabelsbergerstr.

Karolinen-
platz

von Miller
Ring

Von der
Tann Str.

Ludwigstr.

Marsplatz

Mars-
str.

Seidlstr.

Arnulf-
str.

🏨 **Eurostars**
Grand Central

Elisenstr.

Maximillanspl.

FRAUENKIRCHE

Wein-Theatinerstr.

RESIDENZ

Maximilianstr.

Franz
Joseph Straul

Landsberger Str.

Bayerstr.

Grasserstr.

Paul

HAUPT-
BAHNHOF

Karlspl.

Neuhauser
Str.

Schwanthalerstr.

Kaufinger-
str.

MARIENPL.

Thomas

Wimm

3

● **Rüen Thai** ✗

str.

Schwanthalerstr.

Theresienwiese

Heysestr.

Goethestr.

Sonnenstr.

ASAMKIRCHE

Oberanger

Tal

Frauenstr.

Blumenstr.

Corneliusstr.

DEUTSCH
MUSEUM

Ganghofer-

Messegelände

Bavariaring

Theresienhöhe

THERESIEN-
WIESE

Str.

Lindwurmstr.

Historical and Commercial
Centre (Plan II)

Erhardtstr.

0   500 m

A

Ⓜ *Goethepl.*

B

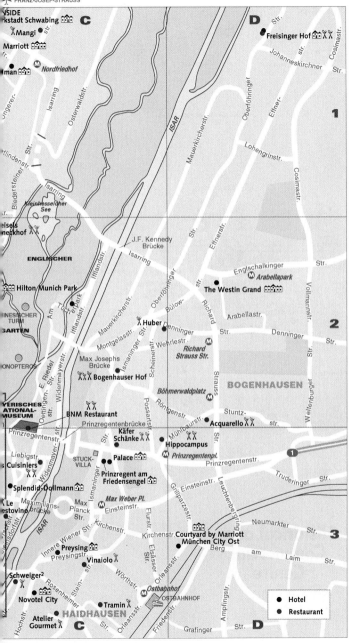

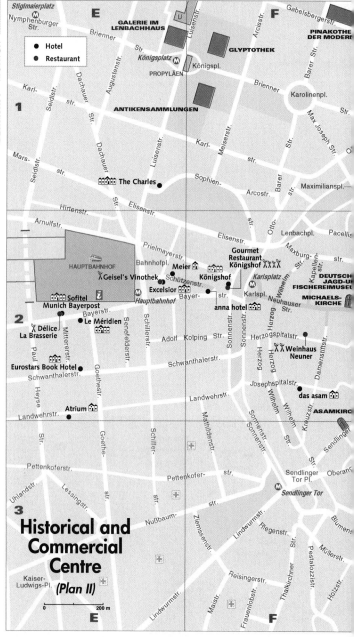

GERMANY - MUNICH

Stiglmaierplatz
Nymphenburger Str.

Gabelsbergerstr.

● Hotel
● Restaurant

GALERIE IM LENBACHHAUS

PINAKOTHE
DER MODERN

Brienner Str.

GLYPTOTHEK

Königsplatz
Königspl.

PROPYLÄEN

Brienner

Karolinenpl.

Karl-

Augustenstr.

Dachauer str.

Seidlstr.

ANTIKENSAMMLUNGEN

Karl-

Meiserstr.

Max Joseph Str.

1

Mars-
Seidlstr.

str.

Dachauer str.

Luisenstr.

str.

Sophien-

Arcostr.

Barer str.

Maximianspl.—

The Charles ●

Hirtenstr.

Arnulfstr.

Elisenstr.

Elisenstr.

Otto-

Lenbachpl.

Pacellis

Prielmayerstr.

HAUPTBAHNHOF

Bahnhofpl.

Geisel's Vinothek

Excelsior
Bayer-

Hauptbahnhof

Sofitel
Munich Bayerpost

Bayerstr.

Le Méridien

Meier

Königshof

Gourmet Restaurant Königshof

Marburg-

str.

Marsstr.

DEUTSCH-
JAGD-UN
FISCHEREIMUSE

Karlsplatz
Karlspl.
Neuhauser

MICHAELS-
KIRCHE

anna hotel

str.

Schützenstr.

Schillerstr.

Senefelderstr.

2

Délice
La Brasserie

Mittererstr.

Paul

Adolf Kolping Str.

Schwanthalerstr.

Sonnenstr.

Herzogspitalstr.

Herzog

Herzog

Weinhaus
Neuner

Damenstiftstr.

Eurostars Book Hotel ●

Schwanthalerstr.

Goethestr.

Heyse

Landwehrstr.

Atrium

Goethe-

Schiller-

Landwehrstr.

Mathildenstr.

Josephspitalstr.

Wilhelm

Sonnenstr.

Sonnenstr.

das asam

Kreuzstr.

ASAMKIRC

Sendlinger

Str.

Pettenkoferstr.

Uhlandstr.

Lessingstr.

str.

Goethe-

Schiller-

str.

Pettenkofer-

str.

Sendlinger
Tor Pl.

Sendlinger Tor

Oberan

3

Historical and
Commercial
Centre

Kaiser-
Ludwigs-Pl.

(Plan II)

Nußbaum-

Ziemssenstr.

Lindwurmstr.

Reisingerstr.

Frauenlobstr.

Maistr.

Thalkirchner Str.

Pestalozzistr.

Müllerstr.

Blumens

Holzstr.

0   200 m

E

F

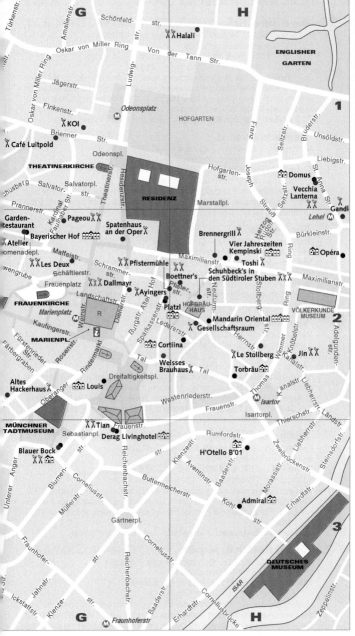

Schönfeld- str.

G

H

Amalienstr.

Oskar von Miller Ring

Von der Tann Str.

✕✕ Halali

ENGLISHER GARTEN

Oskar von Miller Ring

Jägerstr.

Ludwigstr.

Finkenstr.

Odeonsplatz

HOFGARTEN

1

✕ KOI

Brienner

Str.

Franz

Seitzstr.

Bruderstr.

Unsöldstr.

✕ Café Luitpold

Odeonspl.

Hofgarten- str.

Liebigstr.

St. Anna Str.

🏨 Domus

THEATINERKIRCHE

Salvator- str.

Salvatorpl.

Theatinerstr.

Residenzstr.

RESIDENZ

Marstallpl.

Joseph

Straß

Herzog

Vecchia Lanterna

✕✕ Gandl

Prannersr

Kardinal Faulhaber Str.

Lehel 🅼

Garden- restaurant

Pageou ✕✕

Spatenhaus an der Oper ✕

Brennergrill ✕

Vier Jahreszeiten Kempinski 🏨

Bürkleinstr.

Ring

🏨 Opéra

✕ Atelier

Bayerischer Hof 🏨

omenadepl.

Maffeistr.

✕✕ Les Deux

Schäftlerstr.

✕✕ Pfistermühle

Schrammer- str.

Maximilianstr.

Toshi ✕

Schuhbeck's in den Südtiroler Stuben ✕✕✕

Neuturm-

Stollberg

Maximilianstr.

wengrube

Frauenplatz

✕✕✕ Dallmayr

Landschaftstr.

Boettner's

str.

str.

VÖLKERKUNDE MUSEUM

FRAUENKIRCHE

Marienplatz

R

✕ Ayingers

Burgstr.

Alter Hof

Dienerstr.

Platzl 🏨

HOFBRÄU- HAUS

Ledererstr.

Mandarin Oriental 🏨

✕ Gesellschaftsraum

Herrnstr.

Wimmer

Knöbelstr.

2

Adelgunden- str.

Kaufingerstr.

Weinstr.

MARIENPL. 🅼

🏨 Cortiina

Jin ✕✕

Fürstenfrieder Str.

Rosenstr.

Sparkassenstr.

Tal

Weisses Brauhaus ✕

Le Stollberg ✕

Kanalstr.

Färbergraben

Rindermarkt

Tal

Torbräu 🏨

Thomas

Liebherrstr.

Ländstr.

Altes Hackerhaus ✕

Oberanger

Dreifaltigkeitspl.

🏨 Louis

Westenriederstr.

Frauenstr.

🅼 Isartor

Isartorpl.

Thierschstr.

Zweibrückenstr.

Steinsdorfstr.

3

MÜNCHNER STADTMUSEUM

✕✕ Tian

Sebastianpl.

Frauenstr.

Derag Livinghotel 🏨

Rumfordstr.

Klenzestr.

Kanalstr.

Blauer Bock

✕✕ 🏨

str.

Reichenbachstr.

H'Otello B'01 🏨

Aventinstr.

Baaderstr.

Morassistr.

Erhardtstr.

Unterer Anger

Blumenstr.

Corneliusstr.

Müllerstr.

Buttermelcherstr.

Kohl

Admiral 🏨

str.

Erhardtstr.

Fraunhofer-

Gärtnerpl.

Cornelius

DEUTSCHES MUSEUM

Jahnstr.

Klenze-

Reichenbachstr.

Baaderstr.

Erhardtstr.

Corneliusbrücke

ISAR

Zeppelinstr.

ckstattstr.

🅼 Fraunhoferstr

G

H

387

Bayerischer Hof

Promenadeplatz 2 ✉ 80333 – Ⓜ Marienplatz – ✆ (089) 2 12 00 – www.bayerischerhof.de Plan: G2

319 rm – †305/390 € ††380/570 € – ☕ 40 € – 21 suites

• Grand Luxury • Traditional • Classic •

This grand hotel set in a magnificent palace was first opened in 1841. The rooms are exclusively designed in six different styles. The Blue Spa restaurant with its small menu looks out over Munich to the Alps beyond. Other restaurants include Trader Vic's, which serves Polynesian food.

✿✿ **Atelier • Garden-Restaurant** – See restaurant listing

Mandarin Oriental

Neuturmstr. 1 ✉ 80331 – Ⓜ Isartor – ✆ (089) 29 09 80 – www.mandarinoriental.com/munich Plan: H2

67 rm – †525/905 € ††525/905 € – ☕ 45 € – 6 suites

• Grand Luxury • Historic • Classic •

This classy hotel which occupies a beautiful period townhouse is one of the best addresses in Germany. The exemplary service is perfectly complemented by the luxurious but tasteful interior. With a heated pool on the roof.

The Charles

Sophienstr. 28 ✉ 80333 – Ⓜ Hauptbahnhof – ✆ (089) 5 44 55 50 – www.thecharleshotel.com Plan: E1

136 rm – †270/730 € ††270/730 € – ☕ 36 € – 24 suites

• Grand Luxury • Elegant • Modern •

This luxury hotel is situated in the old botanic garden. Its fine decor has a simple, modern and elegant style. There is a high quality spa area, as well as every service you could possibly wish for. Italian food is served at Davvero.

Vier Jahreszeiten Kempinski

Maximilianstr. 17 ✉ 80539 – Ⓜ Lehel – ✆ (089) 2 12 50 – www.kempinski.com/vierjahreszeiten Plan: H2

230 rm – †263 € ††341 € – ☕ 42 € – 67 suites

• Luxury • Traditional • Classic •

Built in 1858, this flagship of Munich's grand hotel scene retains the sort of historical charm seldom found today. Although, a touch of the modern has found its way into its very comfortable guestrooms. Schwarzreiter serves 'Young Bavarian Cuisine' while Tagesbar – overlooking Maximilianstraße – provides more classical regional fare.

Königshof

Karlsplatz 25 ✉ 80335 – Ⓜ Karlsplatz – ✆ (089) 55 13 60 – www.koenigshof-hotel.de Plan: F2

87 rm – †220/520 € ††260/570 € – ☕ 29 € – 8 suites

• Luxury • Traditional • Elegant •

The Geisel family have a long history in the hotel trade stretching back to 1900. It has reached its pinnacle in this classic, luxury hotel in a choice location on the Karlsplatz. The professional front of house team are always on hand to guide and advise.

✿ **Gourmet Restaurant Königshof** – See restaurant listing

Sofitel Munich Bayerpost

Bayerstr. 12 ✉ 80335 – Ⓜ Hauptbahnhof – ✆ (089) 59 94 80 – www.sofitel-munich.com Plan: E2

388 rm – †250 € ††250 € – ☕ 38 € – 8 suites

• Chain hotel • Luxury • Design •

Modern architecture and contemporary design have been incorporated into this imposing listed building dating from the latter part of the 19C with great success as you can see for yourself both in the upmarket spa and the numerous events facilities.

Délice La Brasserie – See restaurant listing

GERMANY - MUNICH

 ### Le Méridien
Bayerstr. 41 ✉ *80335 –* **Ⓜ** *Hauptbahnhof – ℰ (089)*
2 42 20 – www.lemeridienmunich.com
372 rm – ♦159/459 € ♦♦179/459 € – ⌑ 28 € – 9 suites
• Chain hotel • Luxury • Design •
This hotel opposite the main railway station offers modern-style and simple elegance. The restaurant offers a view into the pretty, leafy interior courtyard, which is a small oasis from the bustling city outside. Room prices include entry to some of Munich's museums.

Plan: E2

 ### Hilton Munich Park
Am Tucherpark 7 ✉ *80538 – ℰ (089) 3 84 50*
– www.hilton.de/muenchenpark
481 rm – ♦135/275 € ♦♦135/275 € – ⌑ 20 € – 3 suites
• Chain hotel • Business • Modern •
The Hilton Park's location (in the English Garden) and the comfortable accommodation, which includes business and executive rooms, are both excellent. The restaurant offers an international menu and there is beer garden on the River Eisbach.

Plan I: C2

 ### Eurostars Grand Central
Arnulfstr. 35 ✉ *80636 –* **Ⓜ** *Maillingerstr. – ℰ (089)*
5 16 57 40 – www.eurostarsgrandcentral.com
243 rm ⌑ – ♦99/599 € ♦♦109/629 € – 4 suites
• Business • Modern • Functional •
This business hotel is functional, ultra-modern and just an S-Bahn overground stop from the main railway station. The swimming pool on the roof is a highlight. International cuisine is served in 'Red' and in the lounge bar when the restaurant is closed.

Plan I: A3

Louis
Viktualienmarkt 6 ✉ *80331 –* **Ⓜ** *Marienplatz – ℰ (089)*
41 11 90 80 – www.louis-hotel.com
72 rm – ♦219 € ♦♦269/309 € – ⌑ 27 €
• Townhouse • Elegant • Design •
The Louis enjoys a prime location close to the Viktualienmarkt food market which has the dual benefits of centrality and providing excellent produce for breakfast! Despite their modern lines, the rooms in this designer hotel are both comfortable and individual. And don't forget the additional extras which include a shoe cleaning service, free newspapers and – last but not least – the roof terrace.

Plan: G2

 ### Derag Livinghotel
Frauenstr. 4 ✉ *80469 –* **Ⓜ** *Fraunhoferstr. – ℰ (089)*
8 98 85 65 60 – www.deraghotels.de
83 rm – ♦189/239 € ♦♦219/239 € – ⌑ 20 €
• Business • Design • Functional •
With a great central location on the lively Viktualienmarkt and beautiful designer rooms with all the latest technology, Derag Livinghotel offers a number of apartments with kitchenettes perfect for long-stay guests. There is lots of attention to detail, such as a free mini-bar, Nespresso machine and Wi-Fi. The hotel also boasts the Tian restaurant, which serves vegetarian and vegan cuisine.

Plan: G3

 ### Cortiina
Ledererstr. 8 ✉ *80331 –* **Ⓜ** *Isartor – ℰ (089) 2 42 24 90*
– www.cortiina.com
70 rm – ♦169/409 € ♦♦189/429 € – ⌑ 23 € – 5 suites
• Townhouse • Business • Elegant •
The interior of this hotel in its improbable but nonetheless central location comes as something of a surprise. It has beautiful materials including wood, slate and Jura marble, which are combined perfectly with natural colours. Some of the guestrooms are spacious and include their own kitchenette.

Plan: H2

GERMANY - MUNICH

Eurostars Book Hotel

Schwanthalerstr. 44 ✉ *80336* – ⓜ *Hauptbahnhof*   Plan: **E2**
– 𝒸 (089) 5 99 92 50 – www.eurostarsbookhotel.com
193 rm – ♦99/799 € ♦♦99/799 € – 🍴 14 € – 8 suites
• Business • Design • Modern •

This state-of-the-art business hotel has created a style all of its own with its attractive design and literature inspired decor throughout. The larger than life book that adorns the foyer is a real eye catcher! The furnishings and facilities are in the same vein and the location is excellent. The cuisine has a decidedly Mediterranean/Spanish influence.

anna hotel

Schützenstr. 1 ✉ *80335* – ⓜ *Karlsplatz (Stachus)*   Plan: **F2**
– 𝒸 (089) 5 99 94 40 – www.annahotel.de
75 rm – ♦150/320 € ♦♦165/345 € – 🍴 20 € – 1 suite
• Business • Modern •

The clientele in this modern hotel right on the Karlsplatz – the 'Stachus' as it's known locally – is young or at least young at heart! For a panoramic view take a room on the top floor, and if you feel like some sushi, you need go no further than the hotel's bistro, which also boasts a popular bar.

Excelsior

Schützenstr. 11 ✉ *80335* – ⓜ *Hauptbahnhof – 𝒸 (089)*   Plan: **E2**
55 13 70 – www.excelsior-hotel.de
118 rm – ♦135/315 € ♦♦175/370 € – 🍴 20 € – 8 suites
• Business • Classic •

This hotel, with its individual and cosy rooms, is the sister enterprise of the Königshof. Here you will also find the leisure area. There is a good breakfast buffet in a stylish atmosphere. This pleasant, rustic-style winery shop offers a wide range of wines.

Geisel's Vinothek – See restaurant listing

Platzl

Sparkassenstr. 10 ✉ *80331* – ⓜ *Marienplatz – 𝒸 (089)*   Plan: **G2**
23 70 30 – www.platzl.de
166 rm 🍴 – ♦185/325 € ♦♦215/395 € – 1 suite
• Traditional • Cosy •

This hotel is located in the centre of the old city. It has attractive, classically decorated rooms and a relaxation area in the style of Ludwig II's Moorish pavilion. Ayingers restaurant provides a more relaxed alternative to the formal Pfistermühle.

Pfistermühle • Ayingers – See restaurant listing

Opéra

St.-Anna-Str. 10 ✉ *80538* – ⓜ *Lehel – 𝒸 (089)*   Plan: **H2**
2 10 49 40 – www.hotel-opera.de
22 rm 🍴 – ♦170/210 € ♦♦190/230 € – 3 suites
• Townhouse • Personalised • Classic •

If you are looking for something really special, then this little gem close to the opera might be just what you are after. Opéra boasts individually designed rooms furnished with antique pieces that are skilfully married with modern elements. On warm summer days, breakfast tastes particularly good in the charming inner courtyard. For other meals, the restaurant has its own Mediterranean restaurant, Gandl, which is 200m down the road.

Splendid-Dollmann

Thierschstr. 49 ✉ *80538* – ⓜ *Lehel – 𝒸 (089) 23 80 80*   Plan I: **C3**
– www.hotel-splendid-dollmann.de
36 rm – ♦98/288 € ♦♦128/333 € – 🍴 15 € – 1 suite
• Historic • Personalised •

A haven of peace amid the hustle and bustle of the city, this hotel is set in a stylish old townhouse with a pretty terrace in the rear courtyard. In the evenings, light refreshments are served in the library. Two parking spaces and residents' parking permits are available for guests with cars.

das asam

Josephspitalstr. 3 ✉ *80331 –* Ⓜ *Sendlinger Tor*   Plan: **F2**
– 𝒞 (089) 2 30 97 00 – www.hotel-asam.de – Closed 22 December-
6 January
17 rm – †99/169 € ††139/202 € – ☐ 19 € – 8 suites
• Business • Classic •

Bright, cosy rooms with high quality baths can be found in this hotel in the city centre - some face peacefully onto the interior court. There is a pleasant breakfast area with a small terrace.

 Admiral   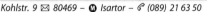

Kohlstr. 9 ✉ *80469 –* Ⓜ *Isartor – 𝒞 (089) 21 63 50*   Plan: **H3**
– www.hotel-admiral.de
31 rm ☐ – †139/299 € ††189/349 € – 1 suite
• Family • Classic • Cosy •

Behind this unprepossessing façade hides a small hotel, which contrary to the current design trend has retained its attractive, classic style. This is evident not only in the neat, comfortable rooms and the charming plush foyer, but also in Kevin Voigt-Masermann's personal management style. You can also rely on an excellent breakfast, served in summer in the small garden.

 Torbräu

Tal 41 ✉ *80331 –* Ⓜ *Isartor – 𝒞 (089) 24 23 40*   Plan: **H2**
– www.torbraeu.de
88 rm ☐ – †162/199 € ††215/310 € – 2 suites
• Traditional • Classic •

The oldest hotel in Munich, Torbräu has been in business since 1490. Now a smart, family-run property it is constantly being upgraded and modernised. Attractive and bright breakfast room on the first floor. Bavarian and Mediterranean food served in the Schapeau.

 Atrium

Landwehrstr. 59 ✉ *80336 –* Ⓜ *Theresienwiese*   Plan: **E2**
– 𝒞 (089) 51 41 90 – www.atrium-hotel.de
161 rm ☐ – †99/359 € ††129/449 €
• Business • Functional •

This hotel is located between the main station and Theresienwiese. It offers practical rooms, a modern breakfast room with a generous buffet, and a beautifully planted interior courtyard with a lounge.

 Domus

St.-Anna-Str. 31 ✉ *80538 –* Ⓜ *Lehel – 𝒞 (089)*   Plan: **H1**
2 17 77 30 – www.domus-hotel.de
45 rm ☐ – †120/185 € ††160/270 €
• Business • Functional •

Aldo Diaco's beautifully kept Domus hotel offers contemporary guestrooms in warm colours with modern bathrooms. In summer you can breakfast outside on the pretty little terrace.
Vecchia Lanterna – See restaurant listing

H'Otello B'01

Baaderstr. 1 ✉ *80469 –* Ⓜ *Isartor – 𝒞 (089) 21 63 10*   Plan: **H3**
– www.hotello.de
56 rm ☐ – †165/175 € ††200/210 €
• Business • Design • Contemporary •

The rooms at this hotel, some of which are a little on the small side, are classily decorated in a minimalist style with shades of beige. The inviting lounge bar on the ground floor and the central location close to the Viktualienmarkt add to the appeal.

Blauer Bock

Sebastiansplatz 9 ✉ *80331* – ⓜ *Marienplatz*   Plan: **G3**
– ℰ (089) 45 22 23 33 – www.restaurant-blauerbock.de
68 rm ☐ – †99/199 € ††155/255 € – 1 suite
• Family • Business • Contemporary •
Just a stone's throw from the Viktualienmarkt, this smart, well-appointed hotel
offers rooms decorated in a variety of different styles. Note that those giving
onto the interior courtyard are a little quieter.
Blauer Bock – See restaurant listing

Meier

Schützenstr. 12 ✉ *80335* – ⓜ *Hauptbahnhof* – ℰ *(089)*   Plan: **E2**
5 49 03 40 – www.hotel-meier.de – Closed during Christmas
50 rm ☐ – †81/115 € ††101/165 €
• Business • Functional •
Ideally for anyone holidaying in the city, this smart and functional multi-storey
hotel is located on a shopping street between the main railway station and the
Karlsplatz or 'Stachus'. The breakfast buffet is both copious and varied.

XxxX
✿

Gourmet Restaurant Königshof – Hotel Königshof

❀ ⩽

Karlsplatz 25 (1st floor) ✉ *80335* – ⓜ *Karlsplatz*   ⒶⒸ ⇳ ⌂
– ℰ (089) 5 51 36 61 42 – www.koenigshof-hotel.de   Plan: **F2**
– Closed 1-12 January, 1 week during Easter, 1 week during Whitsun,
4 weeks August-early September and Sunday-Monday
Menu 115/170 € – Carte 93/123 € – *(booking advisable)*
• French classic • Elegant • Classic •
Stalwarts of the restaurant trade since 1900, the Geisels' choice of chef amply
demonstrates their experience and flair. Martin Fauster, who matches their
dedication and commitment, has been at the helm in the kitchen for many
years. His sophisticated, classic cuisine is accompanied by interesting wines
recommended by an expert team of sommeliers.
→ Roh marinierter Landsberger Saibling mit Caviar, Quinoa und Minze.
Brust und Keule von der Bresse Taube mit Wasserrettich und Blutwurst.
Kokosmilchkonfekt mit dunkler Schokolade und Ananas.

XxX
✿ ✿

Dallmayr

❀ ⒶⒸ

Dienerstr. 14 (1st floor) ✉ *80331* – ⓜ *Marienplatz*   Plan: **G2**
– ℰ (089) 21 35 100 – www.restaurant-dallmayr.de
– Closed 2 weeks end December-early January, 2 weeks during Easter,
3 weeks August, Sunday-Monday and Bank Holidays
Menu 95/175 €
– Carte 82/125 € – (dinner only, Saturday also lunch) (booking advisable)
• French modern • Elegant •
Dallmayr is quite simply the best delicatessen in Munich! If you want to do more
than buy the exquisite products on offer, you can eat in the elegant restaurant on
the top floor. This serves Diethard Urbansky's 'classic modern cuisine', which is art-
ful and full of flavour. Andrej Grunert and his front-of-house team will be on hand
throughout to offer you advice and suggestions, as will the sommelier, ready with
accompanying wines from around the world from the first class wine list.
→ Jakobsmuschel, Karotte, Pinienkerne, Ponzu. Taubenbrust und roter
Shiso, Brioche-Mohncreme, Puntarelle. Birne, Quarkbällchen, Mumbai Curry.

XxX
✿ ✿

Atelier – Hotel Bayerischer Hof

❀ ⒶⒸ ⌂

Promenadeplatz 2 ✉ *80333* – ⓜ *Marienplatz* – ℰ *(089)*   Plan: **G2**
2 12 07 43 – www.bayerischerhof.de – Closed Sunday-Monday
Menu 105/150 € – *(dinner only)*
• French creative • Elegant • Design •
Atelier offers the perfect marriage of Axel Vervoordt's classy, minimalist yet warm
interior, pleasant service and excellent, multifaceted food. This is carefully planned
down to the smallest detail and skilfully executed. Modern elements from Japanese
and other cuisines successfully complement the classic basis.
→ Bayrisches Maishendl vom Gutshof Polting, Petersilie, Mozzarella, Guacamole und Tomatensalat. Wagyu Roastbeef, Süßkartoffel, Shiitake, Zwiebeln
und Rindermark. Erdbeere, Sauerampfer, Milch und Buchweizen.

XXX
£3
Schuhbecks in den Südtiroler Stuben
Platzl 6 ⊠ 80331 – **Ⓜ** *Isartor –* ℰ *(089) 2 16 69 00*
– www.schuhbeck.de – Closed 1-10 January and Sunday
Menu 38 € (weekday lunch)/118 € – *(booking advisable)*
• Regional • Rustic • Elegant •

The food served in the cosy Alpine dining rooms at Alfons Schuhbeck's restaurant is a mix of tried-and-tested fine regional cuisine and more modern offerings, both of which are flavoursome and distinctive. In addition, Platzl offers a delicious range of ice creams, chocolates, spices and wines.
→ Rindertatar handgeschnitten mit Ochsenschwanzgelee, Pfifferlinge, Sauerrahm und Wachtelei. Weißer Heilbutt mit Senfkohl, Kokos und Hummersauce. Tiramisu von der Brombeere mit Cassissorbet.

Plan: **H2**

XX
Pfistermühle – Hotel Platzl
Pfisterstr. 4 ⊠ 80331 – **Ⓜ** *Marienplatz –* ℰ *(089)*
23 70 38 65 – www.pfistermuehle.de – Closed Sunday
Menu 25 € (lunch) – Carte 42/62 €
• Regional • Rustic • Cosy •

A separate entrance leads into this historic hostelry that started life as a ducal mill in 1573. Stylish Bavarian bar crowned by a vaulted ceiling.

Plan: **G2**

XX
Garden-Restaurant – Hotel Bayerischer Hof
Promenadeplatz 2 ⊠ 80333 – **Ⓜ** *Marienplatz –* ℰ *(089)*
2 12 09 93 – www.bayerischerhof.de
Menu 36 € (lunch)/76 € – Carte 49/76 € – *(booking advisable)*
• International • Friendly • Design •

Belgian designer Axel Vervoordt has given this restaurant a very particular look. The industrial-style conservatory design creates a setting reminiscent of an artist's studio.

Plan: **G2**

XX
Limoni
Amalienstr. 38 ⊠ 80799 – **Ⓜ** *Universität –* ℰ *(089)*
28 80 60 29 – www.limoni-ristorante.com
Menu 48/64 € – Carte 42/52 € – *(dinner only)*
• Italian • Elegant • Friendly •

At this restaurant, the decor is minimalist yet welcoming, the service attentive and responsive, and the Italian cuisine fresh and ambitious. Go for a classic such as vitello tonnato or try one of the dishes from the frequently changing menu.

Plan I: **B2**

XX
£3
Les Deux
Maffeistr. 3a (1st floor) ⊠ 80333 – **Ⓜ** *Marienplatz*
– ℰ *(089) 7 10 40 73 73 – www.lesdeux-muc.de – Closed Sunday and Bank Holidays*
Menu 48 € (weekday lunch)/110 € – Carte 71/103 € – *(booking advisable)*
• French modern • Friendly • Fashionable •

Les Deux in question are Fabrice Kieffer and Johann Rappenglück, now running their own brasserie-style restaurant in what used to be the Dukatz. The food on offer downstairs is simple but excellent, while on the first floor you can enjoy fine, modern French cuisine and over 400 different wines. There is also an exemplary front-of-house team. What more could you want?
→ Yellow Fin Thunfisch, Granny Smith-Apfel, Wasabi, Avocado. Heimische Steinpilze, Wildkräuter. Brust und Keule von der Bresse Taube à la Royal, Schwarzer Knoblauch, Trüffeljus.

Plan: **G2**

XX
Blauer Bock – Hotel Blauer Bock
Sebastiansplatz 9 ⊠ 80331 – ℰ *(089) 45 22 23 33*
– www.restaurant-blauerbock.de – Closed Sunday-Monday and Bank Holidays
Menu 35 € (lunch)/85 € (dinner) – Carte 40/71 €
• International • Minimalist • Fashionable •

A chic, modern restaurant with clean lines. It offers an appealing French and regional menu including pan-fried ducks' liver and braised calves' cheeks.

Plan: **K3**

393

XX **Halali**

Schönfeldstr. 22 ✉ *80539* – ⓜ *Odeonsplatz* – ℰ *(089)*   Plan: **H1**
28 59 09 – www.restaurant-halali.de – Closed Saturday lunch, Sunday and
Bank Holidays; October-Christmas: Saturday lunch, Sunday lunch
Menu 25 € (weekday lunch)/66 € – Carte 37/70 € – *(booking advisable)*
• Classic cuisine • Cosy •

The sophisticated restaurant in this 19C guesthouse has almost become an
institution already. The dark wood panelling and lovely decoration has created
a cosy atmosphere.

XX **Boettner's**   🛋 AC

Pfisterstr. 9 ✉ *80331* – ⓜ *Marienplatz* – ℰ *(089)*   Plan: **H2**
22 12 10 – www.boettners.de – Closed Sunday and Bank Holidays
Menu 55/85 € – Carte 41/70 € – *(booking advisable)*
• French classic • Cosy •

This classic Munich restaurant built in 1901 stands next to the Platzl theatre.
Diners appreciate the traditional atmosphere created by Frank Hartung. In addition to the set special menus (which change every month) with accompanying
wines, the bistro also serves dishes such as boiled rump of beef and horseradish
sauce and zander with Savoy cabbage and bacon.

XX **Tian**   🛋

Frauenstr. 4 ✉ *80469* – ⓜ *Isartor* – ℰ *(089)*   Plan: **G3**
8 85 65 67 12 – www.taste-tian.com – Closed Sunday
Menu 24 € (lunch)/62 € (dinner) – Carte 27/49 €
• Vegetarian • Fashionable •

Right on the Viktualienmarkt you will find the first Tian spin-off restaurant in
Germany serving a range of refined and skilfully executed vegetarian dishes.
There is also a trendy bar with a pretty interior courtyard. Reduced lunchtime
menu.

XX **Nymphenburger Hof**   🛋

Nymphenburger Str. 24 ✉ *80335* – ⓜ *Maillingerstr.*   Plan I: **A2**
– ℰ (089) 1 23 38 30 – www.nymphenburgerhof.de – Closed Sunday-
Monday and Bank Holidays
Menu 29 € (weekday lunch)/65 € – Carte 42/73 € – *(booking advisable)*
• International • Friendly •

The Austrian inspired cuisine tastes just as good on the lovely terrace as it does
in the friendly restaurant. Live piano music is also played on some evenings.

XX **BNM Restaurant**   🛋 P

Prinzregentenstr. 3 (at Bayerisches Nationalmuseum)   Plan: **C3**
✉ *80538* – ⓜ *Lehel* – ℰ *(089) 45 22 44 30 – www.bnmrestaurant.de*
– Closed Sunday-Monday
Menu 63/79 € – Carte 46/67 € – *(dinner only)*
• Modern cuisine • Minimalist • Fashionable •

A museum eatery like no other, BNM Restaurant boasts impressive minimalist-
style design and high vaulted ceilings combined with an upmarket culinary
concept all of its own. Evening offerings include ambitious dishes such as Eifel
rare breed lamb with ratatouille and chocolate crème brûlée with ice cream and
cake. The lunch menu promises simpler bistro fare.

XX **Pageou**   🛋

Kardinal-Faulhaber-Str. 10 (1st floor) ✉ *80333*   Plan: **G2**
– ⓜ Marienplatz – ℰ (089) 24 23 13 10 – www.pageou.de – Closed
Sunday-Monday and Bank Holidays
Menu 47 € (lunch)/121 € (dinner) – Carte 67/77 € – *(booking advisable)*
• International • Cosy •

Behind Pageou's magnificent historical façade, the clean lines, beautiful materials and colours of the interior make the perfect setting for its good, modern
cuisine. The quiet courtyard terrace is also very appealing.

XX **Les Cuisiniers**   ⌂

Reitmorstr. 21 ✉ *80538 –* Ⓜ *Lehel –* ℰ *(089) 23 70 98 90*   Plan: **C3**
– www.lescuisiniers.de – Closed Saturday lunch, Sunday and Bank Holidays
Menu 39/93 € (dinner) – Carte 34/49 € – *(booking advisable)*
• French classic • Bistro •

The atmosphere, service and food here are pleasantly uncomplicated – just as you would imagine a French bistro should be. French and half-French respectively, the chef and owner serve authentic French food that is chalked up on a blackboard menu.

XX **Vecchia Lanterna** – Hotel Domus   ⅋⅋ ⌂

St.-Anna-Str. 31 ✉ *80538 –* Ⓜ *Lehel –* ℰ *(089)*   Plan: **H1**
81 89 20 96 – www.vecchia-lanterna.de – Closed 2 weeks end August-mid
September and Saturday lunch, Sunday dinner-Monday
Menu 45/70 € – Carte 48/62 €
• Italian • Elegant • Fashionable •

After years working in Germering, Mirka Otta and Antonio Denami have now moved to the heart of Munich. In this elegantly modern restaurant with its quiet rear courtyard terrace they offer classic Mediterranean cuisine including an interesting lunch menu accompanied by wines mainly from Italy.

XX **Le Barestovino**   ⅋⅋ ⌂ Ⓜ ⟐
☺

Thierschstr. 35 ✉ *80538 –* Ⓜ *Lehel –* ℰ *(089)*   Plan: **C3**
23 70 83 55 – www.barestovino.de – Closed Sunday-Monday
Menu 35/62 € – Carte 31/47 € – *(dinner only)*
• French classic • Bistro •

Owner Joel Bousquet runs a friendly operation here, in both the modern restaurant and the Le Bouchon wine bar. The cuisine is similarly unpretentious – it includes delicious dishes such as mi-cuit salmon with fennel and potato mash, all accompanied by French wines, making this a delightful dining experience.

XX **Jin**   ⌂ ⟐

Kanalstr. 14 ✉ *80538 –* Ⓜ *Isartor –* ℰ *(089) 21 94 99 70*   Plan: **H2**
– www.restaurant-jin.de – Closed Monday
Menu 58/88 € – Carte 43/71 € – *(July-September: Tuesday-Friday dinner only)*
• Asian • Minimalist • Elegant •

Hao Jin combines influences from various South-East Asian countries including China and Japan in his creative cuisine. Guests can choose from two menus, but the chef is always pleased to respond to individual wishes. The contents of the fish tank (including prawns and blue fin tuna) are particularly appetising.

XX **Weinhaus Neuner**   Ⓜ ⟐

Herzogspitalstr. 8 ✉ *80331 –* Ⓜ *Karlsplatz (Stachus) –* ℰ *(089)*   Plan: **F2**
2 60 39 54 – www.weinhaus-neuner.de – Closed Sunday and Bank Holidays
Menu 25 € (lunch)/56 € – Carte 38/64 €
• International • Traditional •

It is worth visiting this 1641 wine house to see the crossed vault 'Tirolian arches'. There is also a beautiful wall painting, old panelling, and the preserved, original carvings.

X **Schweiger²**   ⌂ ⊠
☸

Lilienstr. 6 ✉ *81669 –* Ⓜ *Isartor –* ℰ *(089) 44 42 90 82*   Plan I: **C3**
– www.schweiger2-restaurant.de – Closed 24 December-6 January, 1-
15 August, Saturday-Sunday and Bank Holidays
Menu 99/139 € – *(dinner only) (booking essential)*
• Creative • Friendly • Trendy •

Schweiger² is synonymous with young, uncomplicated but high quality cuisine. This is prepared by the husband and wife team of charming Franziska (from nearby Rosenheim) and Ortenau-born Andreas Schweiger. His fine and varied cuisine made using produce from his father's garden is available in the form of a 5- to 9-course surprise menu.
➜ Epfenhausener Saibling, Lardo, Avocado, Banane. Steinbutt, Rosenheimer Gartengurke, Erbsen, Champagnerschaum, Pimpernelle. Poltinger Lamm, Artischocke, Tomate, Ziegenkäse.

X   ### Le Stollberg
Stollbergstr. 2 ⊠ 80539 – ⓜ Isartor – ℰ (089)   Plan: **H2**
24 24 34 50 – www.lestollberg.de – Closed Sunday
Menu 45 € – Carte 35/63 €
• Classic cuisine • Bistro • Elegant •
After spells at several good restaurants, the charming Anette Huber has started her own venture with this modern restaurant. The classic, French and seasonal cuisine includes offerings such as calves' kidneys in red wine sauce with mashed potato. Good value lunch. Open throughout the day on Saturdays.

X   ### Gesellschaftsraum
Bräuhausstr. 8 ⊠ 80331 – ⓜ Isartor – ℰ (089)   Plan: **H2**
55 07 77 93 – www.der-gesellschaftsraum.de – Closed Saturday lunch and Sunday
Menu 56/85 €
• Creative • Trendy • Fashionable •
If you like things casual, urban and trendy, you will find the atmosphere in this restaurant in the centre of the old town to your taste. The food is creative, modern and ambitious, and the service is pleasantly relaxed.

X   ### Brennergrill
Maximilianstr. 15 ⊠ 80539 – ⓜ Lehel – ℰ (089)   Plan: **H2**
4 52 28 80 – www.brennergrill.de
Menu 48 € (dinner) – Carte 24/53 €
• Meats • Trendy •
A place to see and be seen... The bar, café and restaurant housed in this impressive hall with its high-vaulted ceiling (once the stables of this great residence) are a hot item on the Munich culinary scene. Homemade pasta, as well as meat and fish served hot from the open grill in the centre of the room.

X   ### Toshi
Wurzerstr. 18 ⊠ 80539 – ⓜ Lehel – ℰ (089)   Plan: **H2**
25 54 69 42 – www.restaurant-toshi.de – Closed Saturday lunch, Sunday and Bank Holidays lunch
Menu 80/140 € – Carte 47/110 €
• Japanese • Minimalist •
It is just a short hop from the ritzy Maximilianstraße to this authentic Japanese restaurant. The menu – as characteristic as the minimalist design – offers fresh Far Eastern dishes. These include sushi, teppanyaki and 'pan-Pacific' cuisine.

X   ### KOI
Wittelsbacherplatz 1 ⊠ 80333 – ⓜ Odeonsplatz   Plan: **G1**
– ℰ (089) 89 08 19 26 – www.koi-restaurant.de – Closed during Christmas, Sunday and Bank Holidays lunch
Carte 27/145 €
• Japanese • Friendly • Bistro •
You can look forward to an interesting mix of visual and culinary styles on the two floors at Koi. The kitchens produce a combination of Japanese and European cuisine, including sushi and Robata-grilled meats, all based on fresh produce.

X   ### Gandl
St.-Anna-Platz 1 ⊠ 80538 – ⓜ Lehel – ℰ (089)   Plan: **H1**
29 16 25 25 – www.gandl.de – Closed Sunday
Menu 25 € (lunch)/75 € – Carte 31/54 €
• International • Cosy • Bistro •
Gandl is located in a former colonial goods store, which has retained some of its old shelving and still sells one or two items. The food ranges from classic French to international. If you are here in summer don't miss the terrace overlooking the square.

X **Délice La Brasserie** – Hotel Sofitel Munich Bayerpost   🛜 &

Bayerstr. 12 ✉ *80335 –* Ⓜ *Hauptbahnhof –* ☎ *(089)*   AC 🚗
5 99 48 29 62 – www.sofitel-munich.com   Plan: **E2**
Carte 46/71 €
• International • Friendly • Minimalist •
With its smart decor and incredibly high ceilings, Délice La Brasserie strikes a
perfect balance between casual urban eatery and historic setting. The international cuisine has a distinct French flavour.

X **Geisel's Vinothek** – Hotel Excelsior   🕸 🛜 AC 🚗

Schützenstr. 11 ✉ *80335 –* Ⓜ *Hauptbahnhof –* ☎ *(089)*   Plan: **E2**
*5 51 37 71 40 – www.excelsior-hotel.de – Closed Sunday lunch and Bank
Holidays lunch*
Menu 20 € (lunch)/42 € – Carte 29/63 €
• Regional • Rustic •
The Geisel family offer a great alternative in their Königshof restaurant with the
focus on gourmet cuisine. Perfect for those who prefer a lighter regional or
Mediterranean fare accompanied by a glass of good wine.

X **Cafe Luitpold**   🛜 AC

Brienner Str. 11 ✉ *80333 –* Ⓜ *Odeonsplatz –* ☎ *(089)*   Plan: **G1**
*2 42 87 50 – www.cafe-luitpold.de – Closed Sunday dinner and Monday
dinner except Bank Holidays*
Menu 40/70 € – Carte 23/55 €
• Traditional cuisine • Friendly • Traditional •
Guests can sit in the lively coffee house atmosphere of Cafe Leopold and enjoy
its good, fresh homemade cakes. There is also a museum on the first floor from
which you can see right into the bakery – make sure you try the tarts, pralines
and other delicacies!

X **Ayingers** – Hotel Platzl   🛜 🚗

Sparkassenstr. 10 ✉ *80331 –* ☎ *(089) 23 70 36 66*   Plan: **G2**
– www.ayingers.de
Carte 20/45 €
• Regional • Cosy •
In keeping with its tavern style, classic Bavarian fare is the staple on the menu
here, although you will also find locally hunted game and there is always a pret-
zel to start with! Don't miss the barrel tapping ritual at 5pm every day.

X **Weisses Bräuhaus**   🛜 & ♿

Tal 7 ✉ *80331 –* Ⓜ *Isartor –* ☎ *(089) 2 90 13 80*   Plan: **G2**
– www.weisses-brauhaus.de
Carte 17/54 €
• Regional • Cosy •
This Bavarian hostelry is like something out of a picture book. People from
Munich come here for the 'Kronfleisch' or skirt of beef – just one of the many
specialities from the restaurant's own butchery. Squeezing together in the rustic
dining areas is also traditional!

X **Spatenhaus an der Oper**   🛜

Residenzstr. 12 ✉ *80333 –* Ⓜ *Marienplatz –* ☎ *(089)*   Plan: **G2**
2 90 70 60 – www.kuffler.de
Carte 35/67 €
• Regional • Traditional •
The attractive rooms in this townhouse, opposite the Bavarian State Opera,
exude rural charm. On the ground floor the food is local; on the first-floor the
menu is international.

X **Altes Hackerhaus**   🛜 AC ♿

Sendlinger Str. 14 ✉ *80331 –* Ⓜ *Marienplatz –* ☎ *(089)*   Plan: **G2**
2 60 50 26 – www.hackerhaus.de
Carte 22/52 €
• Regional • Cosy • Romantic •
A very cared-for and well-run rustic restaurant where Bavarian delicacies are ser-
ved in warm and homely rooms. There is a beautiful covered interior courtyard.

Marriott ✿ ⅄ 𝄞 ⌸ ⅋ ⽥ ⅍ 🚗

Berliner Str. 93 ☒ 80805 – ⓜ Nordfriedhof – ✆ (089)   Plan: **C1**
36 00 20 – www.marriott-muenchen.de
345 rm – ♦129/399 € ♦♦129/399 € – ☲ 26 € – 3 suites
• Chain hotel • Contemporary •
A comfortable business hotel in the contemporary style with pleasant, spacious lobby. Massage and beauty treatments available. Modern restaurant serving international cuisine.

The Westin Grand ✿ ⪪ ⅄ 🌐 𝄞 ⌸ ⅋ ⽥ ⅍ 🚗

Arabellastr. 6 ☒ 81925 – ⓜ Arabellapark – ✆ (089)   Plan: **D2**
9 26 40 – www.westingrandmunich.com
599 rm – ♦139/649 € ♦♦139/649 € – ☲ 29 € – 28 suites
• Business • Luxury • Contemporary •
This luxury business hotel and conference venue boasts a wonderful 1500m² spa with adjoining fitness facilities. Great roof lounge for the executive rooms. ZEN offers Asian cuisine cooked in its open kitchen.

Palace ✿ ⅄ 𝄞 ⽥ ⅍ 🚗

Trogerstr. 21 ☒ 81675 – ⓜ Prinzregentenplatz   Plan: **C3**
– ✆ (089) 41 97 10 – www.hotel-muenchen-palace.de
70 rm – ♦220/390 € ♦♦260/540 € – ☲ 28 € – 4 suites
• Business • Classic • Elegant •
This tasteful, impeccably run hotel includes many musicians amongst its regulars. The natural tones and parquet floors combine to create a warm and friendly atmosphere. Pleasant garden and roof terrace. This restaurant serves classic international cuisine.

INNSIDE Parkstadt Schwabing ✿ 𝄞 ⽥ ⅍ 🚗

Mies-van-der-Rohe-Str. 10 ☒ 80807 – ⓜ Nordfriedhof   Plan: **C1**
– ✆ (089) 35 40 80 – www.innside.com
160 rm – ♦98/178 € ♦♦108/191 € – ☲ 22 €
• Business • Functional •
Designed by famous architect Helmut Jahn, this hotel enjoys a convenient location close to the striking HighLight Towers. The whole building is beautifully light, with clean modern lines. This bistro-style restaurant decorated with its modern white interior serves international cuisine.

Pullman ✿ ⅄ 𝄞 ⅋ ⽥ ⅍ 🚗

Theodor-Dombart-Str. 4 (Corner of Berliner Straße)   Plan: **C1**
☒ 80805 – ⓜ Nordfriedhof – ✆ (089) 36 09 90
– www.pullman-hotel-muenchen.de
317 rm – ♦149 € ♦♦169 € – ☲ 24 € – 14 suites
• Chain hotel • Modern •
Previously the Renaissance, the Pullman has been completely refurnished and is now a state-of-the-art business hotel. It features comfortable rooms, a small wellness area and the lively theos restaurant, which has a pleasant interior courtyard terrace serving international cuisine.

Courtyard by Marriott München City Ost ✿ ⅄ ⅋ ⽥

Orleansstr. 83 ☒ 81667 – ⓜ Ostbahnhof – ✆ (089)   ⅍ 🚗
5 58 91 90 – www.courtyardmunich-cityeast.com   Plan: **D3**
227 rm – ♦79/249 € ♦♦79/249 € – ☲ 23 € – 2 suites
• Chain hotel • Modern •
The design concept in this comfortable hotel brings together straight lines, warm colours and all the latest technology. Long-term guests stay in the Residence Inn next door. The options on the international menu include burgers and steaks.

Novotel City 〒 ℔ 🐾 ☒ 🔥 🅰️ 🐾 ⚓

Hochstr. 11 ⊠ 81669 – Ⓜ Ostbahnhof　Plan: **C3**
– ℰ (089) 66 10 70
– www.novotel.com/3280
305 rm – ♥119/219 € ♥♥119/219 € – ☲ 21 € – 2 suites
• Business • Modern •

This business hotel with its modern, well-equipped rooms is located close to the River Isar and the German Museum. The restaurant reflects the light and airy, contemporary design of the hotel.

 Prinzregent am Friedensengel 🐾 🅰️ 🐾 ⚓

Ismaninger Str. 42 ⊠ 81675　Plan: **C3**
– Ⓜ Prinzregentenplatz – ℰ (089) 41 60 50
– www.prinzregent.de
63 rm ☲ – ♥115/159 € ♥♥145/189 € – 2 suites
• Business • Cosy •

This lovely old hotel with its beautiful woodwork is full of Bavarian charm. The cosy, wood-panelled bar offers bar snacks.

 Freisinger Hof 〒 🐾 🐾 ⚓

Oberföhringer Str. 191 ⊠ 81925　Plan: **D1**
– ℰ (089) 95 23 02 – www.freisinger-hof.de
– Closed 28 December - early January
51 rm ☲ – ♥123/133 € ♥♥153/158 €
• Country house • Cosy •

The hotel annexe which has been added to this historical inn offers comfortable country-style rooms. The small lobby is bright and welcoming. Enjoy tasty regional food in this cosy inn dating from 1875. Boiled beef and other classic Austrian dishes served.
🍴 **Freisinger Hof** – See restaurant listing

 Preysing 🅰️ 🐾 ⚓

Preysingstr. 1 / Stubenvollstr. 2 ⊠ 81667　Plan: **C3**
– Ⓜ Max Weber Pl.
– ℰ (089) 45 84 50 – www.hotel-preysing.de
– Closed Christmas-6 January
57 rm ☲ – ♥140/280 € ♥♥186/335 € – 5 suites
• Townhouse • Cosy •

This tip-top furnished hotel has up-to-date guestrooms with granite floors. It is very suited to business travellers.

 H'Otello H'09 🔥 🅰️ ⚓

Hohenzollernstr. 9 ⊠ 80801 – Ⓜ Hohenzollernpl.　Plan: **B2**
– ℰ (089) 3 09 07 70 – www.hotello.de
71 rm ☲ – ♥124/199 € ♥♥159/234 €
• Business • Functional •

Set in the centre of Schwabing, H'Otello H'09 boasts modern, urban-style design and its own very practical underground car park. The hotel is just a 10min drive from the A8 and A96 motorways.

 Leopold 🐾 🐾 ⚓

Leopoldstr. 119 ⊠ 80804 – Ⓜ Dietlindenstr.　Plan: **B1**
– ℰ (089) 36 04 30 – www.hotel-leopold.de
– Closed 23-31 December
57 rm ☲ – ♥89/128 € ♥♥132/175 €
• Family • Contemporary •

This impeccably run, family hotel offers a range of well-appointed rooms furnished in different styles some of which have lovely garden views. Rustic style restaurant, serving international cuisine.

GERMANY - MUNICH

XxxX **Tantris**   🏵 🏠 AC ⇔ P

✿✿ *Johann-Fichte-Str. 7* ✉ *80805 –* Ⓜ *Dietlindenstr.*   Plan: **B1**

– ℰ (089) 3 61 95 90 – www.tantris.de

– Closed 2 weeks early January, Sunday-Monday
and Bank Holidays

Menu 85 € (weekday lunch)/195 € – Carte 95/162 €

– (booking advisable)

• French classic • Retro •

It is hardly surprising that Tantris is so well frequented as Hans Haas has been in charge in the kitchen here for over 20 years and has always demanded the same high standards. His culinary expertise is supported by an excellent front-of-house team and shown off to its advantage by the restaurant's charming retro interior. The wine list contains a few rarities and guarantees the perfect accompaniment to the excellent food.

➜ Ausgelöster Hummer mit weißem Spargel, Krustentierravioli und Curry-Hummersud. Gratinierter Lammrücken mit Bohnen, Artischocken und Tomatenpolenta. Topfensoufflé mit Pistazieneis.

XxX **EssZimmer**   🏵 ♿ AC 🚗

✿✿ *Am Olympiapark 1 (3th floor) (at BMW Welt)* ✉ *80809*   Plan: **A1**

– ℰ (089) 3 58 99 18 14

– www.esszimmer-muenchen.de

– Closed 3 weeks January, August, Sunday-Monday
and Bank Holidays

Menu 90/175 € *– (dinner only) (booking advisable)*

• Modern cuisine • Fashionable • Cosy •

This restaurant on the third floor of BMW Welt is elegant without being overly formal. Admire views of the impressive delivery centre as you enjoy Bobby Bräuer's delicious cuisine. Choose from regional dishes on his set 'Herzstück' menu or international fare on the 'Exkursion' counterpart. Free parking.

➜ Bretonische Langoustine, Wassermelone, Poverade. Salzwiesenlamm, Spitzpaprika, Bronzefenchel. Fichtensprosse, Waldfrüchte, Dulce.

Bavarie – See restaurant listing

XxX **Bogenhauser Hof**   🏠 ⇔

Ismaninger Str. 85 ✉ *81675 –* Ⓜ *Böhmerwaldplatz*   Plan: **C2**

– ℰ (089) 98 55 86

– www.bogenhauser-hof.de

– Closed Christmas-6 January, Sunday and Bank Holidays

Menu 49/119 € – Carte 47/79 €

– (booking advisable)

• Classic cuisine • Traditional • Cosy •

This elegant yet comfortable restaurant housed in a building dating back to 1825 and serving classic cuisine prepared using the finest ingredients has many regulars. Leafy garden complete with mature chestnut trees.

XX **Käfer Schänke**   🏵 🏠 ⇔

Prinzregentenstr. 73 (1st floor) ✉ *81675*   Plan: **C3**

– Ⓜ *Prinzregentenplatz*

– ℰ (089) 4 16 82 47 – www.feinkost-kaefer.de

– Closed Sunday and Bank Holidays

Menu 39 € (lunch)/89 € (dinner)

– Carte 57/98 € – (booking essential at dinner)

• International • Cosy • Individual •

In this popular restaurant with its 12 highly individual dining rooms the international menu is determined by the availability of the best quality produce. The delicatessen sells a range of fine foods.

XX **Geisels Werneckhof**   🏵 AC
&& *Werneckstr. 11* ✉ *80802 –* Ⓜ *Münchner Freiheit*   Plan: **C2**
    – ℰ (089) 38 87 95 68 – www.geisels-werneckhof.de – Closed
    24 December-7 January, end July-mid August and Sunday-Monday
    Menu 95/150 €
    – Carte 90/126 € – (dinner only, Saturday also lunch) (booking essential)
    • Creative • Cosy • Traditional •
    At this restaurant Chef Tohru Nakamura presents classic, modern cuisine. He
    skilfully and subtly integrates a number of Japanese elements to create a
    range of sophisticated and aromatic dishes that are well executed and very per-
    sonal. Choose from the Gaudi set menu (an upgrade to the Omni menu pos-
    sible) and the classic Soli menu.
    → Langoustine, Frühlingsgemüse und Kirschblütendashi. Wagyu Bavette
    gegrillt und Gyoza von der Ochsenbacke, Artischocken, Pfifferlinge. Dunkle
    Schokolade, geräucherte Kokosnuss, Jasminblüte und Pomelo.

XX **Acquarello** (Mario Gamba)   🛋 AC
&& *Mühlbaurstr. 36* ✉ *81677 –* Ⓜ *Böhmerwaldplatz*   Plan: **D2**
    – ℰ (089) 4 70 48 48 – www.acquarello.com – Closed 1-3 January and
    Saturday lunch, Sunday lunch and Bank Holidays lunch
    Menu 49 € (weekday lunch)/110 € – Carte 60/95 €
    • Mediterranean • Friendly • Mediterranean •
    Whether Mario Gamba's cuisine is Italian with a French influence or French with
    Italian roots is largely irrelevant when it comes to tasting his delicious dishes
    made from only the finest quality ingredients. Mario has now been joined by
    his son, Massimiliano, who assists his father as part of the excellent front-of-
    house team.
    → Vitello Tonnato mit zweierlei Thunfischcreme. Gnocchi vom Loup de
    Mer mit Muschelfond. Taubenbrust mit Petersilie souffliert, schwarzen Wal-
    nüssen und kleinen Gemüsen.

XX **Freisinger Hof** – Hotel Freisinger Hof   🛋 ♻ 🚗
☺ *Oberföhringer Str. 189* ✉ *81925 – ℰ (089) 95 23 02*   Plan: **D1**
    – www.freisinger-hof.de – Closed 28 December-early January
    Menu 34/58 € (dinner) – Carte 37/55 €
    • Austrian • Inn •
    This is just what you imagine a traditional Bavarian restaurant to be like. Dating
    back to 1875, it stands just outside the city gates and serves typical Bavarian
    and Austrian cuisine. Dishes include Krosser saddle of suckling pig, and
    Vienna-style beef boiled in broth.

XX **Hippocampus**   🛋
    Mühlbaurstr. 5 ✉ *81677 –* Ⓜ *Prinzregentenplatz*   Plan: **C3**
    – ℰ (089) 47 58 55 – www.hippocampus-restaurant.de – Closed Monday
    and Saturday lunch
    Menu 57/67 € – Carte 45/55 €
    • Italian • Elegant •
    Hippocampus offers friendly service, an informal atmosphere and ambitious
    Italian cuisine. Beautiful fixtures and fittings help create the elegant yet warm
    and welcoming interior.

XX **Bibulus**   🛋
    Siegfriedstr. 11 ✉ *80803 –* Ⓜ *Münchner Freiheit*   Plan: **B1**
    – ℰ (089) 39 64 47 – www.bibulus-ristorante.de – Closed Saturday lunch
    and Sunday
    Menu 20 € (lunch)/72 € – Carte 40/58 €
    • Italian • Elegant •
    It says something when a restaurant is popular with the locals, and the people
    of Schwabing clearly appreciate the uncomplicated and flavoursome Italian
    food. It is especially nice outside in the little square under the plane trees. Char-
    ming service.

GERMANY - MUNICH

GERMANY - MUNICH

X
🕸 **Restaurant N° 15** 🏢 🏠

Neureutherstr. 15 ✉ *80331* – 🚇 *Josephspl. –* 🕾 *(089)* Plan: **B2**
39 99 36 – www.restaurant-n15.com – Closed Saturday lunch and Sunday-Monday
Menu 40 € (lunch)/90 € – Carte 47/90 € – *(booking essential at dinner)*
• Classic cuisine • Elegant • Family •

The Dupuis family, well known in Munich, has made this a veritable mecca of French food and culture, serving flavoursome French country cooking with modern elements made using the highest quality ingredients. Don't miss the great selection of Bordeaux and Burgundy wines.
➔ Kalbskopf, Lauch, Trüffelvinaigrette. Zweierlei Rinderschulter mit Gemüsen. Armer Ritter, Himbeere, Vanillecrème.

X **Acetaia** 🏢 🏠

Nymphenburger Str. 215 (by A2) ✉ *80639* – 🕾 *(089) 13 92 90 77*
– www.restaurant-acetaia.de – Closed Saturday lunch
Menu 29 € (weekday lunch)/61 € – Carte 46/66 €
• Italian • Cosy •

This friendly restaurant with its Art Nouveau decor offers Italian cuisine and the best espresso in the city. The olive oil and balsamic vinegar which gave the place its name are also very good. Attractive terrace.

X **Vinaiolo** 🏠

Steinstr. 42 ✉ *81667* – 🚇 *Ostbahnhof –* 🕾 *(089)* Plan: **C3**
48 95 03 56 – www.vinaiolo.de – Closed Saturday lunch
Menu 27 € (lunch)/52 € – Carte 40/62 € – *(bookings advisable at dinner)*
• Italian • Cosy • Friendly •

Sample a taste of the 'dolce vita' in this restaurant. The service exudes southern charm, the food could not be better, even in Italy, and the lunchtime menu is very reasonably priced. The image of authentic Italy is completed by fixtures and fittings from an old grocer's shop in Trieste.

X **M Belleville** 🏠

Fallmerayerstr. 16 ✉ *80796* – 🚇 *Hohenzollernpl.* Plan: **B2**
– 🕾 *(089) 30 74 76 11 – www.m-belleville.com – Closed Sunday-Monday*
Menu 35/45 € – Carte 39/49 € – *(dinner only)*
• French classic • Bistro • Brasserie •

If you fancy a little bit of Paris in the middle of Munich, this is the place for you. Manina Panzer runs her charming, lively bistro with great dedication. She above all cooks tasty fare including roast shoulder of lamb, braised ox cheeks and riz au lait caramel. Front of house, her father serves unusual natural wines and every second Wednesday there is live music.

X **Mangi** 🏠

Ungererstr. 161 ✉ *80805* – 🚇 *Nordfriedhof –* 🕾 *(089)* Plan: **C1**
36 69 31 – www.mangi.de – Closed 1 week Whitsun, 15 September-1 October and Saturday dinner-Sunday
Menu 22 € (weekday lunch) – Carte 28/43 €
• Italian • Friendly •

It is not just the mix of delicatessen and modern trattoria that impresses here, but also the simple but flavoursome authentic cuisine. Don't miss the homemade organic pasta. Open Mondays to Tuesdays until 4pm and Thursdays and Fridays until 11pm.

X **Atelier Gourmet** 🏠

Rablstr. 37 ✉ *81669* – 🚇 *Ostbahnhof –* 🕾 *(089)* Plan: **C3**
48 72 20 – www.ateliergourmet.de – Closed Sunday
Menu 35/53 € – Carte 42/55 € – *(dinner only) (booking advisable)*
• French classic • Bistro •

Small, intimate, lively and popular, Atelier Gourmet is quite simply a great little restaurant. The food is fresh, delicious and good value for money thanks to chefs Duchardt and Bousquet. It is served in a casual, friendly atmosphere with efficient service and good wine recommendations from the female owner. Try the capon and duck crépinette.

♈ GERMANY - MUNICH

⚚ Le Cézanne
🐌

Konradstr. 1 ✉ *80801* – Ⓜ *Giselastr.* – ✆ *(089) 39 18 05* Plan: **B2**
– www.le-cezanne.de – Closed during Easter, 3 weeks August and Monday
Menu 45 € – Carte 30/52 € – *(dinner only) (booking advisable)*
• French • Family • Friendly •
In this friendly corner restaurant the chef cooks dishes from his French homeland. You can choose from the blackboard or the small menu of classic dishes. In
summer, enjoy your meal outdoors or by the open, glass façade.

⚚ Bavarie – Restaurant Esszimmer

Am Olympiapark 1 (2nd floor) (at BMW Welt) ✉ *80809* Plan: **A1**
– ✆ (089) 3 58 99 18 18 – www.feinkost-kaefer.de – Closed 2 weeks August,
Sunday dinner and Bank Holidays dinner
Menu 32/39 € – Carte 23/57 €
• International • Bistro • Fashionable •
Grounded in the principles of regionality and sustainability, the Bavarie concept
on offer here creates a combination of Bavarian and French cuisine based on
local produce. Dishes include goose liver crème brûlée and Gutshof Polting
lamb. The terrace offers views of the Olympia Park and Tower.

⚚ Tramin
🕸

Lothringer Str. 7 ✉ *81667* – Ⓜ *Ostbahnhof* – ✆ *(089)* Plan: **C3**
44 45 40 90 – www.tramin-restaurant.de – Closed Sunday-Monday
Menu 65/100 € – *(dinner only)*
• Creative • Fashionable • Minimalist •
Tramin is the proof that an informal atmosphere, simple, minimalist-style design
and a young front-of-house team can be the perfect accompaniment to good
food. The service provided by the young jeans- and trainer-clad waiting staff is
particularly attentive.

⚚ Rüen Thai

Kazmairstr. 58 ✉ *80339* – Ⓜ *Messegelände* – ✆ *(089)* Plan: **A3**
50 32 39 – www.rueen-thai.de – Closed 3 weeks August
Menu 49/99 € – Carte 31/54 €
• Thai • Family • Simple •
True to his roots, Anuchit Chetha has dedicated himself to the cuisine of southern Thailand, preparing a range of dishes including gung pla and nüe san
kua, as well as a finger food menu. In addition to specialising in interesting
spice combinations, he is also passionate about wine – the restaurant boasts a
cellar containing a number of real rarities.

⚚ Huber

Newtonstr. 13 ✉ *81679* – Ⓜ *Richard Strauss Str.* Plan: **C2**
– ✆ (089) 98 51 52 – www.huber-restaurant.de – Closed Saturday lunch,
Sunday-Monday
Menu 25 € (lunch)/95 € (dinner) – Carte 51/70 €
• International • Fashionable •
This appealing, modern restaurant offers friendly service and quality contempo-
rary cuisine created by a young chef. The selection of Austrian wines is particu-
larly good. The interior is by a Munich designer.

⚚ Kaisergarten
🌿

Kaiserstr. 34 ✉ *80801* – Ⓜ *Münchner Freiheit* – ✆ *(089)* Plan: **B1**
34 02 02 03 – www.kaisergarten.com
Menu 12 € (weekday lunch) – Carte 31/50 € – *(booking advisable)*
• Regional • Rustic • Neighbourhood •
It is not just the charming mix of modern and rustic elements that draw guests
to the Kaisergarten –now over a century old – its good Bavarian cuisine has also
made a name for itself. The menu includes dishes such as veal tartar with pears
and thyme and organic pork roast with crackling. Unfortunately tables in the
delightful beer garden cannot be reserved in advance.

AT THE EXHIBITION CENTRE

Prinzregent an der Messe

Riemer Str. 350 (Industrialpark-West) ✉ *81829* – ☎ *(089) 94 53 90*
– www.prinzregent.de – Closed 1 week end December
87 rm ⬜ – 🛏124/170 € 🛏🛏164/220 € – 4 suites
• Business • Inn • Cosy •

This lovely hotel, converted from a period inn, offers comfortable rooms in the Bavarian style and a great sauna. Located conveniently close to the exhibition centre. A cosy restaurant with a touch of elegance.

Schreiberhof

Erdinger Str. 2 ✉ *85609* – ☎ *(089) 90 00 60* – *www.schreiberhof.de*
87 rm – 🛏90/300 € 🛏🛏140/420 € – ⬜ 12 €
• Inn • Conference hotel • Functional •

Once a traditional inn, Schreiberhof has been developed into a modern city centre hotel with functional rooms. The light-flooded winter garden makes an unusual conference setting. This restaurant offers a number of dining rooms in different styles ranging from the stylish to the cosy and informal and a beer garden set under mature trees.

AT THE AIRPORT

Novotel München Airport

Nordallee 29 ✉ *85356* – ☎ *(089) 9 70 51 30* – *www.novotel.com/6711*
257 rm – 🛏69/999 € 🛏🛏69/999 € – ⬜ 21 €
• Chain hotel • Contemporary •

Business hotel ideally located at the airport with a large modern lobby and straightforward functional rooms. Restaurant offering international food.

GREECE
ELLÁDA

ATHENS

→ **AREA:**
131 944 km²
(50 944 sq mi).

→ **POPULATION:**
11 120 415 inhabitants.
Density = 84 per km².

→ **CAPITAL:** Athens.

→ **CURRENCY:** Euro (€).

→ **GOVERNMENT:**
Parliamentary republic
(since 1974). Member of European
Union since 1981.

→ **LANGUAGE:** Greek.

→ **PUBLIC HOLIDAYS:**
New Year's Day (1 Jan); Epiphany
(6 Jan); Orthodox Shrove Monday
(late Feb-Mar); Independence Day
(25 Mar); Orthodox Good Friday
(late Mar/Apr); Orthodox Easter
Monday (late Mar/Apr); Labor Day
(1 May); Pentecost Sunday (late
May/June); Orthodox Whit Monday
(late May/June); Assumption of
the Virgin Mary (15 Aug); Ochi Day
(28 Oct); Christmas Day (25 Dec);
Boxing Day (26 Dec).

→ **LOCAL TIME:**
GMT+2 hours in winter and GMT
+3 hours in summer.

→ **CLIMATE:**
Temperate Mediterranean, with
mild winters and hot, sunny
summers (Athens: January 10°C;
July 27°C).

→ **EMERGENCY:**
Police ✆ **100**; Medical Assistance
✆ **166**; Fire Brigade ✆ **199**;
Tourist Police ✆ **171**.
(Dialing **112** within any EU country
will redirect your call and contact
the emergency services.)

→ **ELECTRICITY:**
230 volts AC, 50Hz; 2 round pin
sockets.

→ **FORMALITIES:**
Travellers from the European Union
(EU), Switzerland, Iceland and
the main countries of North and
South America need a national
identity card or passport (America:
passport required) to visit Greece
for less than three months (tourism
or business purpose). For visitors
from other countries a visa may be
required, in addition to a passport,
especially for those wishing to
stay for longer than three months.
We advise you to check with your
embassy before travelling.

ATHENS
ATHÍNA

Population: 664 046

Stefanos Kyriazis/Fotolia.com

Inventing democracy, the theatre and the Olympic Games… and planting the seeds of philosophy and Western Civilisation – Athens was central to all of these, a city that became a byword for glory and learning, a place whose golden reputation could inspire such awe that centuries later just the mention of its name was enough to turn people misty-eyed. It's a magical place, built upon eight hills and plains, with a history stretching back at least 3,000 years. Its short but highly productive golden age resulted in the architectural glory of The Acropolis, while the likes of Plato, Aristotle and Socrates were in the business of changing the mindset of society.

The Acropolis still dominates Athens and can be seen peeking through alleyways and turnings all over the city. Beneath it lies a teeming metropolis, part urban melting pot, part über-buzzy neighbourhood. Plaka, below the Acropolis, is the old quarter, and the most visited, a mixture of great charm and cheap gift shops. North and west, Monastiraki and Psiri have become trendy zones; to the east, Syntagma and Kolonaki are notably modern and smart, home to the Greek parliament and the famous. The most northerly districts of central Athens are Omonia and Exarcheia, distinguished by their rugged appearance and steeped in history; much of the life in these parts is centred round the polytechnic and the central marketplace.

ATHENS IN...

→ **ONE DAY**
Acropolis (Parthenon), Agora and Temple of Hephaestus, Plaka.

→ **TWO DAYS**
Kolonaki, National Archaeological Museum, Filopappou Hill.

→ **THREE DAYS**
Monastiraki flea-market (Sunday), Benaki Museum, Technopolis, National Gardens, Lykavittos Hill.

PRACTICAL INFORMATION

ARRIVAL-DEPARTURE

 Athens International Airport is 33km east of the city. Metro Line 3 takes you to Monastiraki.

 Piraeus Port is the third largest port in the Mediterranean and is 10km southwest of Athens. Metro Line 1 takes you to Monastiraki.

GETTING AROUND

The most sensible way of getting around town is by the metro; buses and trolley-buses run an excellent service but are hampered by traffic. Carnets of 10 tickets are available from newsstands, OASA booths and kiosks, and at metro or subway stations.

Be sure to have some Euros in your wallet when you arrive, as tickets for all forms of public transport can only be paid for in cash; cards are not accepted by either ticket agents or ticket machines.

CALENDAR HIGHLIGHTS

March-April
Candlelit procession up Lykavittos Hill to the chapel of Agios Georgios.

May-September
Greek folk dances at Dora Stratou Theatre.

June
European Music Day, Rockwave Festival (rock music).

June-August
Hellenic Festival.

August
Nights Under The Full Moon (moonlit classical performances at monuments and archaeological sites).

EATING OUT

In recent times, a smart wave of restaurants has hit the city and, with many chefs training abroad before returning home, this is a good time to eat out in the shadow of The Acropolis. If you want the full experience, dine with the locals rather than the tourists and make your reservation for late evening, as Greeks rarely go out for dinner before 10pm. The trend towards a more eclectic restaurant scene now means that you can find everything from classical French and Italian cuisine to Asian and Moroccan dishes, and even sushi. Modern tavernas offer good attention to detail, but this doesn't mean they're replacing the wonderfully traditional favourites. These older tavernas, along with mezedopoleia, are the backbone of Greek dining, and most visitors wouldn't think their trip was complete without eating in one; often the waiter will just tell you what's cooking that day - and you're usually very welcome to go into the kitchen and make your selection. Greece is a country where it is customary to tip good service; ten per cent is the normal rate.

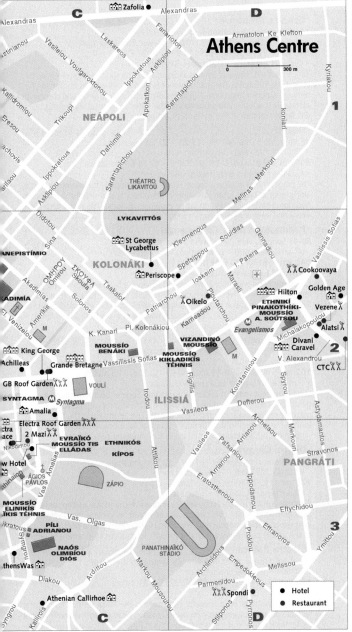

Athens Centre

0   300 m

C **D** **1** **2** **3**

Alexandras
Alexandras
Armatolon Ke Klefton

Ioustinianou
Vasileiou Voulgaroktonou
Laskareos
Fanarioton
Ippokratous
Apokfakon
Askltpiou
Sarantapichou
Konlari
Kyriakou

Kallidromiou
Trikoupi
Dafnimili
NEÁPOLI

Eresou
Machovis
Ippokratous
Sarantapichou

arilisou
Askltpiou
Didotou
Sina
THÉATRO LIKAVITOÚ
Melinas
Merkouri

LYKAVITTÓS

ANEPISTÍMIO
St George Lycabettus
Kleomenous
Souidias
Gennadiou
Vasilissis Sofias

KOLONÁKI
Spetsippou
I. Patera
Cookoovaya

OMHPOY
Ómirou
ΣΚΟΥΦΑ Skoufa
Periscope
Ioakeim
Marasli
Hilton
Golden Age

Akadimias
Tsakalof
Oikeío
Ploutarchou
ETHNIKÍ PINAKOTHÍKI-MOUSSÍO A. SOÚTSOU
Vezene

ADIMÍA
Solonos
Patriarchou
Karneadou
Evangelismos
Alatsi

El. Venizelou
Amerikis
K. Kanari
Pl. Kolonákiou
VIZANDINÓ MOUSSÍO
Michalakopoulou
Divani Caravel

King George
MOUSSÍO BENÁKI
Vassilissis Sofias
MOUSSÍO KIKLADIKÍS TÉHNIS
V. Alexandrou

Achilleas
Grande Bretagne
Rigillis
Konstantinou
Spyrou
CTC

GB Roof Garden
VOULÍ
ILISSIÁ
Irodou
Defterou
Astydamantos

SYNTAGMA Syntagma
Vasileos
Archelaou
Merkouri
Stravonos

Amalia
Vasileos
Patsianiou
Arrianou
Ippodamou
PANGRÁTI

Electra Roof Garden
ctra ace
2 Mazi
EVRAÏKÓ MOUSSÍO TIS ELLÁDAS
ETHNIKÓS KÍPOS
Attikou
Vasileos
Arrianou
Eratosthenous
Eftychidou

Nikodimou
w Hotel
athinaiou
ÁGIOS PAVLOS
ZÁPIO
Prokou
Effranoros
Ymittou

MOUSSÍO ELINIKÍS IKIS TÉHNIS
ikratous
PÍLI ADRIANOU
Vas. Olgas
PANATHINAÏKÓ STÁDIO
Archimidou
Empedokleous
Melissou

Symgrou
NAÓS OLIMBÍOU DIÓS
Ardittou
Markou Mousourou
Parmenidou
Stiponos
Pyrronos

thensWas
Diakou
Athenian Callirhoe
Spondi

Syngrou
Kallirois
C   **D**

● Hotel
● Restaurant

Zafolia

409

Grande Bretagne ✿ ≤ ₤ 🕥 🛖 🔨 🔲 ₺ 🄰🄲 ⇔ 🐟

1 Vas Georgiou A, Constitution Sq ⊠ 105 64   Plan: C2
– Ⓜ Syntagma – ℰ (210) 3330 000 – www.grandebretagne.gr
320 rm – ♦294/509 € ♦♦294/509 € – ☲ 48 suites
• Grand Luxury • Palace • Stylish •
Take in fantastic views of Syntagma Square and the surrounding area from this
impressive 19C hotel. The grand interior is filled with luxurious handmade furnishings. Opulent bedrooms display excellent attention to detail and come with
extremely spacious marble bathrooms; the suites are particularly striking.
GB Roof Garden – See restaurant listing

Hilton ✿ ≤ ₤ 🕥 🛖 🔨 🔲 ₺ 🄰🄲 ⇔ 🐟 ☁

46 Vasilissis Sofias Ave ⊠ 115 28 – Ⓜ Evangelismos   Plan: D2
– ℰ (210) 7281 000 – www.hiltonathens.gr
506 rm – ♦181/320 € ♦♦181/320 € – ☲ 38 € – 34 suites
• Chain hotel • Business • Modern •
The biggest hotel in Athens comes with a well-equipped fitness centre and spa,
along with a huge lobby boasting a bookshop and a hairdresser. Modern
bedrooms have balconies and sea or mountain outlooks. The restaurants serve
Greek and international dishes – rooftop 'Galaxy' offers sea and Acropolis views.

Athenaeum Inter-Continental ✿ ≤ ₤ 🕥 🛖 🔨 ₺ 🄰🄲 ⇔

89-93 Syngrou Ave (Southwest: 2.5 km) ⊠ 117 45   🐟 ☁
– ℰ (210) 9206 000 – www.athens.intercontinental.com
543 rm – ♦190/320 € ♦♦190/320 € – ☲ 40 € – 60 suites
• Grand Luxury • Business • Modern •
Corporate hotel with impressive meeting spaces, a business centre and jewel-
lery and gift shops. The owner is one of the world's top 5 modern art collectors.
Bedrooms are spacious and well-equipped; the Club floors offer dedicated ser-
vices. Eat in the lounge-bar, the casual restaurant or more formal Première.
Première – See restaurant listing

King George ✿ ≤ ₤ 🛖 ₺ 🄰🄲 ⇔ 🐟

3 Vas Georgiou A, Syntagma Sq ⊠ 105 64   Plan: C2
– Ⓜ Syntagma – ℰ (210) 3222 210 – www.kinggeorgeathens.com
102 rm – ♦260/440 € ♦♦260/440 € – ☲ 33 € – 13 suites
• Palace • Grand Luxury • Classic •
Luxuriously converted mansion in Syntagma Square. Bedrooms have an elegant, classical style and come with smart marble bathrooms; the rooftop suite
boasts a private pool and panoramic views. Dine informally in the fashionable
lounge-bar or head to the 7th floor Tudor Hall for a greater sense of occasion
– sit on the terrace and dine from a menu of modern Greek dishes.

Divani Caravel ✿ ≤ ₤ 🛖 🔨 ₺ 🄰🄲 ⇔ 🐟 ☁

2 Vas Alexandrou Ave ⊠ 161 21 – Ⓜ Evelangismos   Plan: D2
– ℰ (210) 7207 000 – www.divanis.com
471 rm – ♦390/500 € ♦♦410/530 € – ☲ 29 € – 44 suites
• Business • Luxury • Classic •
Pass through the marble lobby with its impressive chandelier and up to the elegant bedrooms, which combine classic charm with mod cons. Take in breathtaking views of The Acropolis and Lykavittos Hill from the rooftop pool, then head
to the all-day café-restaurant or chic Brown's for modern Mediterranean fare.

Electra Palace ✿ ≤ 🖑 ₤ 🛖 🔨 🔲 ₺ 🄰🄲 ⇔ 🐟 ☁

18-20 Nikodimou St ⊠ 105 57 – Ⓜ Syntagma – ℰ (210)   Plan: C3
3370 000 – www.electrahotels.gr
155 rm ☲ – ♦120/175 € ♦♦130/225 € – 11 suites
• Luxury • Classic •
An attractive hotel on a peaceful city street in the Plaka district. Its classical
façade conceals an elegantly furnished interior; head up to the rooftop pool
for fantastic panoramic views over downtown Athens and towards The Acropolis. The two restaurants serve traditional Greek and international fare.
Electra Roof Garden – See restaurant listing

Zafolia
🏨 ← ♨ 🐕 ⛱ & 🏧 ⇋ 🛁 🚗

87-89 Alexandras Ave ⊠ *114 74* – **Ⓜ** *Ambelokipi* — Plan: **C1**
– ℰ (210) 6449 002 – www.zafoliahotel.gr
192 rm ☐ – †137/204 € ††144/212 € – 7 suites
• Business • Functional •
You'll find this privately owned business hotel in the north of the city. Bedrooms are modern and well-equipped; the biggest draw here has to be the rooftop terrace, with its pool and bar offering stunning views over Athens and Lykavittos Hill. A Greek and Mediterranean buffet is offered in the dining room.

St George Lycabettus
🏨 ← ♨ 🐕 ⛱ 🏧 ⇋ 🛁 🚗

2 Kleomenous St ⊠ *106 75* – **Ⓜ** *Evangelismos* – ℰ *(210)* — Plan: **C2**
7416000 – www.sgl.gr
154 rm ☐ – †100/180 € ††120/190 € – 10 suites
• Business • Personalised • Modern •
This elegant hotel prides itself on its service. It's set in an exclusive district on the hillside, just a short walk down into town (but you might find you need to take a taxi back up!) Take in the view from the rooftop pool or from the all-day restaurant which offers a modern Mediterranean menu.

Radisson Blu Park H. Athens
🏨 ← ♨ 🐕 ⛱ & 🏧 ⇋ 🛁

10 Alexandras Ave ⊠ *106 82* – **Ⓜ** *Victoria* – ℰ *(210)* — 🚗
8894 500 – www.rbathenspark.com — Plan: **B1**
153 rm ☐ – †110/180 € ††130/260 €
• Business • Contemporary • Personalised •
It's been in the family since 1976 and its elegant tree trunk pillars and colour-changing leaves are inspired by the park opposite. Contemporary bedrooms come in browns and greens and most have park views. The Asian restaurant overlooks The Acropolis and moves up to the rooftop in summer to serve BBQ and pasta dishes. Casual Gallo Nero offers Tuscan-inspired fare.

New Hotel
🏨 ♨ & 🏧 ⇋ 🛁

16 Filellinon St ⊠ *105 57* – **Ⓜ** *Syntagma* – ℰ *(210)* — Plan: **C3**
327 3000 – www.yeshotels.gr
79 rm ☐ – †175/245 € ††195/265 €
• Business • Traditional • Design •
Modern hotel designed by the Campana brothers. The quirky lobby walls feature wood reclaimed from old bedsteads, while the minimalist bedrooms – most with balconies overlooking the city – feature furnishings made from recycled materials. The all-day restaurant uses organic ingredients in Mediterranean dishes.

Athenian Callirhoe
🏨 ♨ 🐕 🏧 ⇋ 🛁

32 Kallirois Ave and Petmeza ⊠ *117 43* – **Ⓜ** *Syngrou-Fix* — Plan: **C3**
– ℰ (210) 9215 353 – www.tac.gr
84 rm – †80/135 € ††80/145 € – ☐ 15 €
• Business • Modern •
This contemporary hotel is located on a road connecting two main avenues. Its elegant lobby is filled with smart design furniture. Comfortable bedrooms come with wooden furnishings and some have balconies and jacuzzis. The 8th floor roof garden restaurant offers international dishes and a panoramic view.

O & B
🏨 🏧 ⇋

7 Leokoriou St ⊠ *105 54* – **Ⓜ** *Thissio* – ℰ *(210)* — Plan: **A2**
331 2940 – www.oandbhotel.com
22 rm ☐ – †170/190 € ††170/190 € – 1 suite
• Townhouse • Design • Minimalist •
Named after its Ochre & Brown colour scheme, this stylish downtown hotel has spacious bedrooms which display good attention to detail, and suites with terraces offering Acropolis views. Have a modern Greek or pasta dish in the all-day restaurant, then head to the lively lounge-bar for music and cocktails.

Amalia

10 Amalias Ave ⊠ *105 57 –* Ⓜ *Syntagma –* ℰ *(210)*
3237 300 – www.amaliahotelathens.gr
97 rm ⌂ – ✦99/350 € ✦✦105/350 € – 1 suite
Plan: **C2**
• Business • Modern • Functional •
Amalia sits on a large avenue near Syntagma Square, close to the Parliament buildings. The modern, minimalist bedrooms have good facilities and a relaxing ambience; those to the front have balconies overlooking the National Garden. The large restaurant serves Mediterranean and local fare.

Periscope

22 Charitos St ⊠ *106 75 –* Ⓜ *Evangelismos –* ℰ *(210)*
7297 200 – www.yeshotels.gr
21 rm ⌂ – ✦135/190 € ✦✦150/205 €
Plan: **D2**
• Business • Modern • Minimalist •
The elegant residential district of Kolonaki is home to Periscope, a small hotel decorated in varying shades of grey. Minimalist bedrooms come with balconies and large aerial photos of Athens – some on the ceiling. The stylish bar features Mini Cooper seating and the all-day restaurant serves global dishes.

Golden Age

57 Michalakopoulou Ave ⊠ *115 28*
Plan: **D2**
– Ⓜ *Megaro Moussikis –* ℰ *(210) 7240 861 – www.hotelgoldenage.com*
122 rm ⌂ – ✦70/140 € ✦✦110/200 €
• Business • Functional •
This business-orientated hotel is located in the city centre, behind a contemporary steel façade, and comes with a cosy lounge and up-to-date facilities. Bedrooms are functional; the Coco-Mat rooms feature natural products and three-layered beds. The restaurant serves Greek and Mediterranean cuisine.

AthensWas

5 Dionysiou Areopagitou St ⊠ *117 42 –* Ⓜ *Acropolis*
Plan: **C3**
– ℰ *(210) 924 9954 – www.athenswas.gr*
21 rm ⌂ – ✦180/1400 € ✦✦180/1400 €
• Townhouse • Stylish • Design •
This stylishly understated hotel sits on a pedestrianised street in a historic part of the city and its ethos is one of relaxation. Dine on modern Mediterranean dishes on the roof terrace. The best bedrooms have large balconies with great views of The Acropolis – no other hotel is this close to the citadel!

Hera

9 Falirou St ⊠ *117 42 –* Ⓜ *Syngrou-Fix –* ℰ *(210)*
923 6682 – www.herahotel.gr
38 rm ⌂ – ✦80/130 € ✦✦90/160 €
Plan: **B3**
• Holiday hotel • Traditional • Modern •
Hera's classical façade is a beautiful match for its location in the historic city centre. Pass through the elegant marbled lobby and up to one of the well-equipped bedrooms. Choose from a mix of Greek and international dishes while taking in stunning views of The Acropolis from the roof terrace.

Acropolis Hill

7 Mousson St ⊠ *117 42 –* Ⓜ *Singrou-Fix –* ℰ *(210)*
9235 151 – www.acropolishill.gr
37 rm ⌂ – ✦65/160 € ✦✦75/170 €
Plan: **B3**
• Traditional • Business • Contemporary •
The bigger sister of Achilleas is set close to the Philoppapos Monument. It has a nice outdoor pool and a contemporary, boutique style. Bedrooms are simple and practical; those at the front have balconies and Acropolis views.

Hermes   `AC`

19 Apollonos St ⊠ 105 57 – Ⓜ Syntagma – ℰ (210)
3235 514 – www.hermeshotel.gr   Plan: **B3**
45 rm ⌂ – ♦55/95 € ♦♦60/105 €
• Family • Functional •

Compact, modern hotel located between Monastiraki and Syntagma Square. Bedrooms are bright and simply furnished; the family rooms have two bedrooms and two bathrooms. Buffet breakfasts are served in the first floor restaurant.

Achilleas   `AC` ⇼

21 Lekka St ⊠ 105 62 – Ⓜ Syntagma – ℰ (210)
3233197 – www.achilleashotel.gr   Plan: **C2**
34 rm ⌂ – ♦60/140 € ♦♦70/160 €
• Family • Functional •

This family-friendly hotel sits in a small street known for its silversmiths, close to Syntagma Square. The spacious, uniform bedrooms can accommodate groups of three and four. Buffet breakfasts are served on the mezzanine level.

Museum   `AC` ⇼ 🛁

16 Bouboulinas St ⊠ 106 82 – Ⓜ Victoria – ℰ (210)
3805 611 – www.hotelsofathens.com   Plan: **B1**
93 rm ⌂ – ♦55/65 € ♦♦60/130 €
• Family • Traditional • Functional •

A small but reasonably priced hotel with a simple, functional style. It's made up of two buildings and overlooks the National Archaeological Museum. Bedrooms in the newer building are larger and more modern; some have roof terraces.

🏵🏵 Spondi   🍴 🌿 `AC` ⇄ `P`

5 Pyronos, off Varnava Sq, Pangrati ⊠ 116 36 – ℰ (210)
7564 021 – www.spondi.gr – Closed Easter   Plan: **D3**
Menu 73/136 € – Carte 99/132 € – *(dinner only)*
• French • Romantic • Elegant •

A discreet, intimate restaurant with two delightful courtyards and two equally charming dining rooms – one in an elegant room built from reclaimed bricks in the style of a vaulted cellar. Top quality seasonal ingredients are used in imaginative, deftly executed and stunningly presented modern French dishes. Greek, French and Italian wines feature on an impressive list.

→ Langoustine with caviar, grapefruit and ground elder. Red mullet, black olive, egg-plant, coffee and orange. Guanaja chocolate with iced nougat, chocolate ice cream and raspberry.

GB Roof Garden – Grande Bretagne Hotel   🍴 ≤ 🌿 `AC`

1 Vas Georgiou A, Constitution Sq ⊠ 105 64
– Ⓜ Syntagma – ℰ (210) 3330 766 – www.gbroofgarden.gr   Plan: **C2**
Carte 39/94 € – *(booking essential)*
• Mediterranean • Fashionable • Elegant •

Set on the 8th floor of the Grande Bretagne hotel, this elegant rooftop restaurant offers spectacular views across Syntagma Square towards The Acropolis. Sunny, modern Mediterranean cooking uses fresh ingredients and is accompanied by an extensive wine list. Service is smooth and efficient.

Première – Athenaeum Inter-Continental Hotel   🍴 🌿 `AC` 🚗

89-93 Syngrou Ave (9th floor) (Southwest: 2.5 km) ⊠ 117 45 – ℰ (210)
9206 981 – www.athens.intercontinental.com – Closed Sunday and Monday
Menu 65/90 € – Carte 55/88 € – *(dinner only)*
• Mediterranean • Friendly • Minimalist •

Start with a drink in the cocktail bar then head through to the elegant restaurant or out onto the terrace to take in views of The Acropolis. Top quality produce features in carefully crafted, delicate Mediterranean dishes.

XXX **Electra Roof Garden** – Electra Palace Hotel ⟨🍴🏠 AC⟩

18-20 Nikodimou St ✉ *105 57* – Ⓜ *Syntagma* – ℰ *(210)*   Plan: **C3**
3370 000 – www.electrahotels.gr
Menu 35 € – Carte 30/54 € – *(dinner only)*
• Mediterranean • Romantic • Elegant •
Set on the top floor of the Electra Palace hotel, this superbly located restaurant
offers unrivalled views of The Acropolis and downtown Athens. Well-made
dishes are a mix of traditional Greek and more international flavours.

XX **Funky Gourmet** (Georgianna Chiliadaki and Nikos Roussos)   AC
❀❀ *13 Paramythias St and Salaminos, Keramikos* ✉ *104 35*   ⟨⟩
– Ⓜ *Keramikós* – ℰ *(210) 5242 727*   Plan: **A2**
– *www.funkygourmet.com* – *Closed August, Sunday and Monday*
Menu 90/130 € – *(dinner only) (booking essential)*
• Innovative • Minimalist • Intimate •
Charming neoclassical house in downtown Athens, off the main tourist track.
The minimalist black, white and grey first floor dining room looks out over the
city. Wonderfully well-crafted, innovative dishes feature unusual but well-
thought-through combinations, and many display a playful, theatrical element.
➔ Sea urchin with sea sponge. The silence of the lamb. Milk skin bracelet.

XX **Hytra**   ⟨🍴 AC⟩
❀ *Onassis Cultural Centre (6th Floor), 107-109 Syngrou Ave C3 (Southwest:
2.5 km)* ✉ *117 45* – ℰ *(210) 3316 767* – *www.hytra.gr*
Menu 58 € (weekdays) – Carte 64/71 € – *(dinner only)*
• Modern • Design • Fashionable •
Take the express lift to the 6th floor of the striking Onassis Cultural Centre; here
you'll find a sultry restaurant and above it, a chic bar and roof terrace which look
out over Syngrou. Classic Greek recipes are executed in a refined modern manner; for something a little different try the cocktail pairings.
➔ Quail with spelt, chestnut and truffle. Pork with cabbage, smoked
cheese and potato & leek cream. Rice pudding with vanilla, orange and
plum & peanut ice cream.

XX **CTC**   AC ⟨⟩
27 Diocharous ✉ *161 21* – Ⓜ *Evangelismos* – ℰ *(210)*   Plan: **D2**
722 8812 – www.ctc-restaurant.com – *Closed August, Sunday and Monday*
Carte 55/71 € – *(dinner only) (booking essential)*
• Modern • Intimate • Fashionable •
Its name is short for "the art of feeding" and the sleek, intimate room seats just
28, with a private table on the mezzanine. The chef has worked in both Greece
and France, so his dishes are a modern blend of Greek and Gallic elements.

XX **Luna Rossa**   ✿
213 Sokratous, Kallithea (Southwest: 4 km) ✉ *176 74* – ℰ *(210) 9423 777*
– *www.lunarossa.gr* – *Closed August, Easter, 25 December and Sunday*
Menu 40 €
– Carte 42/68 € – *(dinner only and lunch by arrangement) (booking
essential)*
• Italian • Family • Elegant •
This intimate, family-run restaurant is unusually located in a residential area.
Two of the three rustic rooms contain just one table each. The Italian cooking
is authentic and the wine list includes some great Tuscan grand crus.

XX **2 Mazi**   🍴 AC
48 Nikis St ✉ *105 58* – Ⓜ *Syntagma* – ℰ *(210) 3222 839*   Plan: **C3**
– *www.2mazi.gr* – *Closed Easter*
Carte 34/55 €
• Greek • Trendy •
Within this neoclassical building you'll find a modern dining room offering a
menu inspired by fresh Greek ingredients and Cretan herbs and vegetables.
They have a good selection of local wines by the glass. Mazi means 'together'.

XX **Cookoovaya** 🛋 & AC

2A Chatzigianni Mexi St ✉ 115 28 – Ⓜ Evangelismos Plan: D2
– ✆ (210) 723 5005 – www.cookoovaya.gr – Closed Easter and 1 week
August
Carte 27/56 € – *(booking advisable)*
• Greek • Friendly • Fashionable •
Five of the city's leading chefs have come together to open this bustling restaurant, where rustic, homely cooking is the order of the day and generous dishes are designed for sharing. The homemade pies from the wood-oven are a hit.

X **Athiri** 🛋
😊
15 Plataion ✉ 104 35 – Ⓜ Keramikós – ✆ (210) Plan: A2
3462 983 – www.athirirestaurant.gr – Closed 2 weeks August, 1 week
Easter, 1-5 January, Sunday dinner and Monday
Menu 25 € – Carte 22/33 € – *(dinner only and Sunday lunch)*
• Greek • Neighbourhood •
In winter, sit inside, surrounded by blue, white and grey hues; in summer, head out to the courtyard and well-spaced tables surrounded by lush green plants. Local, seasonal ingredients are simply prepared in order to reveal their natural flavours. Dishes are generous, good value and have creative touches.

X **Oikeîo** 🛋 AC
😊
15 Ploutarhou St ✉ 106 75 – Ⓜ Evangelismos Plan: D2
– ✆ (210) 7259 216 – Closed Easter, Christmas and Sunday
Carte 15/28 €
• Greek • Rustic • Traditional •
Sweet little restaurant in a chic neighbourhood, with tables on two different levels, as well as outside. The décor is traditional and it has a warm, cosy feel. Menus offer great value family-style cooking made with fresh ingredients and feature the likes of grilled sardines, moussaka and octopus in vinegar.

X **Kuzina** 🛋 AC

9 Adrianou St ✉ 105 55 – Ⓜ Thissio – ✆ (210) 3240 133 Plan: B3
– www.kuzina.gr – Closed Easter, 25 December and 1 January
Menu 19 € (dinner) – Carte 26/50 €
• Mediterranean • Friendly • Bistro •
Lively split-level restaurant in a busy pedestrianised street; its shelves crammed with alcohol and homemade preserves. Cooking makes good use of local produce. Sit on the terrace for a panoramic view which takes in Hephaestus Temple.

X **Vezene** 🛋 AC

Vrasida 11 ✉ 115 28 – ✆ (210) 723 2002 Plan: D2
– www.vezene.gr – Closed Easter, Christmas, New Year and Sunday
Carte 24/64 € – *(dinner only)*
• Meats and grills • Friendly • Minimalist •
Easy-going eatery specialising in wood-fired steaks and seafood. The dark wood interior leads to a glass veranda and terrace. The friendly team guide guests as the menu evolves. Try the mini Wagyu burger and the sliced-to-order salumi.

X **Alatsi** 🛋 AC

Vrasida 13 ✉ 115 28 – Ⓜ Evangelismos – ✆ (210) Plan: D2
7210 501 – www.alatsi.gr – Closed August, 24 December, 1 January and
Sunday
Carte 29/46 €
• Greek • Neighbourhood • Friendly •
Alatsi is the Cretan word for 'salt' and is a clue as to the origin of the tasty dishes. Cooking is fresh and authentic and the service is charming. Choose a seat in the simply decorated mezzanine dining room or out on the terrace.

GREECE - ATHENS

AT KIFISSIA Northeast : 15 km by Vas. Sofias

Kefalari Suites

1 Pentelis and Kolokotroni St, Kefalari ⊠ 145 62 – ⓂKifissia – 𝒞 (210)
6233 333 – www.yeshotels.gr
13 rm � – ♦145/180 € ♦♦160/210 € – 1 suite
• Townhouse • Villa • Elegant •

An elegant 19C villa in a smart residential area a stone's throw from the main square. Elegantly furnished bedrooms come with kitchenettes and are themed around everything from Jaipur to the sea. Have breakfast on the lovely veranda, then take in the view from the jacuzzi on the rooftop terrace.

Semiramis

48 Charilaou Trikoupi St, Kefalari ⊠ 145 62 – ⓂKifissia – 𝒞 (210)
6284 400 – www.yeshotels.gr
51 rm ⊑ – ♦165/200 € ♦♦185/220 € – 1 suite
• Business • Design • Minimalist •

A bold design hotel set on the main plaza of a leafy suburb. Luminous pinks and greens feature inside and out and are complemented by curvaceous modern furnishings. The minimalist bedrooms boast hi-tech facilities and balconies and the Mediterranean restaurant overlooks the pool and sun terrace.

Twenty One

21 Kolokotroni and Mykonou St, Kefalari ⊠ 145 62 – ⓂKifissia – 𝒞 (210)
6233 521 – www.yeshotels.gr
21 rm ⊑ – ♦130/160 € ♦♦145/175 € – 5 suites
• Business • Minimalist • Modern •

This former water mill is building number 21 and it also has 21 bedrooms – 16 are minimalist with feature walls and 5 are stylish loft suites; in each you'll find part of a specially commissioned 70m2 painting by Georgia Sagri. Dine on modern Greek and Mediterranean cuisine in the restaurant or on the terrace.

AT HALANDRI Northeast : 11 km by Vas. Sofias

Botrini's (Ettore Botrini)

24b Vasileos Georgiou ⊠ 104 35 – ⓂHalandri – 𝒞 (210) 6857323
– www.botrinis.com – Closed 10 days August, Sunday and Monday
Menu 40/80 € – Carte 53/66 € – (dinner only)
• Mediterranean • Design • Friendly •

A converted school in a quiet suburb – now a passionately run restaurant with an ultra-modern interior, a sleek glass-fronted kitchen and verdant terraces. Appealing modern menus feature local produce in creative, attractively presented dishes. Many of the oils, salamis and wines are produced by the family.
→ Octopus in its natural environment. Organic veal cheek with potato cream and praline. Sweet 'tzatziki'.

AT MAROUSSI Northeast : 12.5 km by Vas. Sofias

Aneton

Stratigou Lekka 19 ⊠ 151 22 – ⓂMaroussi – 𝒞 (210) 8066 700
– www.aneton.gr – Closed August, Christmas and Easter
Carte 25/51 € – (dinner only and Sunday lunch) (booking essential)
• Greek • Friendly • Intimate •

It's worth travelling into the smart city suburbs to seek out this appealing neighbourhood restaurant. Menus follow the seasons; in summer they have a Mediterranean base and some Middle Eastern spicing, while in winter, hearty stews and casseroles feature. The hands-on owner really brings the place to life.

AT **ATHENS INTERNATIONAL AIRPORT** East : 35 km by Vas. Sofias

Sofitel Athens Airport

Athens International Airport - Spata ⊠ *190 19 –* Ⓜ *Airport*
– ℰ *(210) 3544 000*
– *www.sofitel-athens-airport.com*
332 rm – ♦170/340 € ♦♦170/340 € – ☐ 25 € – 13 suites
• Chain hotel • Business • Contemporary •
Modern business hotel just 50m from the terminal. Bedrooms are spacious and
well-equipped; the 'Luxury Club' rooms have private check-in, panoramic views
and access to a club lounge. 24hr Mesoghaia offers Mediterranean cuisine; intimate Karavi serves French fare in a nautically inspired room.

AT **VOULIAGMENI** South : 18 km by Singrou

Divani Apollon Palace & Thalasso

10 Ag Nikolaou and Iliou St (Kavouri) off
Athinas ⊠ *166 71*
– ℰ *(210) 8911 100 –* *www.divanis.com*
280 rm ☐ – ♦150/320 € ♦♦170/380 € – 7 suites
• Palace • Luxury • Classic •
Chic resort with a particularly impressive spa and thalassotherapy centre, two
outdoor swimming pools and an underground walkway to a private beach.
Luxurious bedrooms boast balconies and gulf views. Dine on fresh seafood in
beachside Mythos, global cuisine in Anemos or all-day snacks in the coffee
lounge.

Apollon Suites

11 Nikolaou St ⊠ *166 71 –* ℰ *(210) 8911 100 –* *www.divanis.com*
– *Closed November-April*
56 rm ☐ – ♦135/220 € ♦♦155/450 €
• Luxury • Contemporary •
The peaceful annexe of the Divani Apollon Palace shares its facilities but has a
more intimate atmosphere. Spacious bedrooms feature hand-chosen fabrics
and terraces (some with sea views). Room service and concierges are available
24/7.

Margi

11 Litous St ⊠ *166 71 –* ℰ *(210) 8929 000*
– *www.themargi.gr*
89 rm ☐ – ♦139/235 € ♦♦149/299 € – 8 suites
• Traditional • Personalised • Mediterranean •
Stylish hotel on the peninsula, just a stone's throw from the beach. The elegant
lobby has a Mediterranean feel, while the bedrooms are furnished in a modern
colonial style – take in a sea or forest view from the balcony. Dishes have international influences and are served on the poolside terrace in summer.

AT **PIRAEUS** Southwest: 8 km by Singrou

Piraeus Theoxenia

23 Karaoli and Dimitriou St ⊠ *185 31 –* Ⓜ *Pireaus*
– ℰ *(210) 4112 550 –* *www.theoxeniapalace.com*
77 rm ☐ – ♦105/114 € ♦♦105/114 € – 1 suite
• Business • Contemporary • Functional •
The Theoxenia is set in the heart of town, close to the bustling local markets
and the harbour. The large marble lobby opens onto a classical restaurant
which serves global dishes with Mediterranean influences. Spacious
bedrooms combine traditional and modern styles and the business centre is
well-equipped.

✗✗ Varoulko ☺

*Akti Koumoundourou 52, Mikrolimano Marina (Southeast: 1.5 km by
coastal road)* ✉ *185 33 –* Ⓜ *Piraeus – ☎ (210) 522 8400
– www.varoulko.gr – Closed Easter and Christmas*
Menu 40/80 € – Carte 38/57 € *– (booking essential)*
• Fish and seafood • Elegant • Fashionable •
Varoulko has relocated to Mikrolimano Marina – the chef's old neighbourhood.
Watch the yachts glide by from the maritime-themed dining room which opens
onto the water. Greek and Mediterranean dishes feature organic vegetables,
Cretan olive oil and the freshest seafood; squid and octopus feature highly.
➜ Sea bass carpaccio with seaweed. Grilled fillets of red mullet with lemon
sauce. Kirsch flavoured vanilla crème with chocolate sauce.

✗ Papaioannou

*Akti Koumoumdourou 42.1, Mikrolimano Marina (Southeast: 1.5 km by
coastal road)* ✉ *185 33 –* Ⓜ *Piraeus – ☎ (210) 4225 059
– www.papaioannoufish.com – Closed 9-19 August, Easter, Christmas and
Sunday dinner*
Carte 25/45 €
• Fish and seafood • Traditional •
A traditional seafood restaurant where diners select the type, weight and cooking style of their fish. Shrimp, mussels and crayfish come 'saganaki' style – in
tomato sauce with feta cheese. Menus evolve as more fresh produce arrives.

HUNGARY
MAGYARORSZÁG

● BUDAPEST

→ **AREA:**
93 032 km²
(35 920 sq mi).

→ **POPULATION:**
9 870 151 inhabitants.
Density = 106 per km².

→ **CAPITAL:**
Budapest.

→ **CURRENCY:**
Hungarian Forint (Ft or HUF).

→ **GOVERNMENT:**
Parliamentary republic (since 1989).
Member of European Union since
2004.

→ **LANGUAGE:**
Hungarian; many Hungarians also
speak English and German.

→ **PUBLIC HOLIDAYS:**
New Year's Day (1 Jan); 1848
Revolution Day (15 Mar); Easter
Monday (late Mar/Apr); Labor Day
(1 May); Whit Monday (late May/
June); St Stephen's Day (20 Aug);
1956 Uprising Remembrance Day
(23 Oct); All Saints' Day (1 Nov);
Christmas Eve (24 Dec); Christmas
Day (25 Dec); Boxing Day (26 Dec).

→ **LOCAL TIME:**
GMT+1 hour in winter and GMT+2
hours in summer.

→ **CLIMATE:**
Temperate continental with
cold winters and warm summers
(Budapest: January -1°C; July 22°C).

→ **EMERGENCY:**
Police ✆ **107**; Medical Assistance
✆ **104**; Fire Brigade ✆ **105**;
Roadside breakdown service
✆ **188**.
(Dialling **112** within any EU country
will redirect your call and contact
the emergency services.)

→ **ELECTRICITY:**
230 volts AC, 50Hz; 2 round pin
sockets.

→ **FORMALITIES:**
Travellers from the European Union
(EU), Switzerland, Iceland and
the main countries of North and
South America need a national
identity card or passport (America:
passport required) to visit Hungary
for less than three months (tourism
or business purpose).
For visitors from other countries a
visa may be required, in addition
to a passport, especially for those
wishing to stay for longer than
three months. We advise you to
check with your embassy before
travelling.

BUDAPEST
BUDAPEST

Population: 1 740 041

Jonathan/Fotolia.com

No one knows quite where the Hungarian language came from: it's not quite Slavic, not quite Turkic, and its closest relatives appear to be in Finland and Siberia. In much the same way, Hungary's capital is a bit of an enigma. A lot of what you see is not as old as it appears. Classical and Gothic buildings are mostly neoclassical and neo-Gothic, and the fabled baroque of the city is of a more recent vintage than in other European capitals. That's because Budapest's frequent invaders and conquerors, from all compass points of the map, left little but rubble behind them when they left; the grand look of today took shape for the most part no earlier than the mid-19C.

It's still a beautiful place to look at, with hilly Buda keeping watch – via eight great bridges – over sprawling Pest on the other side of the lilting, bending Danube. These were formerly two separate towns, united in 1873 to form a capital city. It enjoyed its heyday around that time, a magnificent city that was the hub of the Austro-Hungarian Empire. Defeats in two world wars and fifty years behind the Iron Curtain put paid to the glory, but battered Budapest is used to rising from the ashes and now it's Europe's most earthily beautiful capital, particularly when winter mists rise from the river to shroud it in a thick white cloak. In summer the days can swelter, and the spas are definitely worth a visit.

BUDAPEST IN...

→ **ONE DAY**
Royal Palace, the Parliament Building, a trip on the Danube.

→ **TWO DAYS**
Gellert Baths, a stroll down Váci utca, a concert at the State Opera House.

→ **THREE DAYS**
Museum of Applied Arts, Margaret Island, coffee and cake at Gerbeaud.

PRACTICAL INFORMATION

ARRIVAL-DEPARTURE

 Liszt Ferenc National Airport is 24km southeast of the city. A taxi will take about 45min. Shuttle Minibuses do the rounds of the hotels. A train will take you from Terminal 1 to the Western Railway Station.

GETTING AROUND

Budapest has an extensive public transport system, with a three-line metro, buses, trolley buses and trams. Tickets must be bought in advance and validated in the ticket stampers at the start of the journey. Buy your tickets at metro stations, ticket machines, newsagents or tobacconists.

The Budapest Card includes unlimited travel on public transport; free or reduced price admission to many museums and sights, cultural and folklore programmes; and discounts in some shops, restaurants and thermal baths. Valid for two or three days, it can be bought at the airport, main metro stations, tourist offices and some hotels.

CALENDAR HIGHLIGHTS

April
Spring Festival (classical, opera and folk music).

June-August
Summer Festival (open-air theatre).

August
Sziget Festival (rock music).

October
Contemporary Arts Festival (cutting edge theatre, dance, music and film).

November-December
Winter Festival and Christmas Fair at Vörösmarty tér.

EATING OUT

The city is most famous for its coffee houses so, before you start investigating restaurants, find time to tuck into a cream cake with a double espresso in, say, the Ruszwurm on Castle Hill, the city's oldest, and possibly cosiest, café. In tourist areas, it's not difficult to locate goulash on your menu, and you never have to travel far to find beans, dumplings and cabbage in profusion. Having said that, Budapest's culinary scene has moved on apace since the fall of communism, and Hungarian chefs have become much more inventive with their use of local, seasonal produce. Pest is where you'll find most choice but even in Buda there are plenty of worthy restaurants. Lots of locals like to eat sausage on the run and if you fancy the idea, buy a pocket knife. Sunday brunch is popular in Budapest, especially at the best hotels. Your restaurant bill might well include a service charge; don't feel obliged to pay it, as tipping is entirely at your own discretion – though you may find the persistence of the little folk groups that pop up in many restaurants hard to resist.

Four Seasons Gresham Palace

Szechenyi István tér 5-6 ⊠ 1051 – Ⓜ Vörösmarty tér
– ℰ (01) 268 6000 – www.fourseasons.com/budapest Plan: E2
160 rm – ♦99000/160000 HUF ♦♦99000/160000 HUF – ☲ 12200 HUF
– 19 suites
• Grand Luxury • Palace • Art Deco •
Beautifully renovated art nouveau building constructed in 1906 for the Gresham Life Assurance Company. It boasts a stunning lobby with a mosaic floor and a stained glass cupola, along with an impressive rooftop spa and superb river views. Elegant bedrooms are the ultimate in luxury. The chic brasserie offers a mix of international, Hungarian and rotisserie dishes.

Kempinski H. Corvinus

Erzsébet tér 7-8 ⊠ 1051 – Ⓜ Deák Ferenc tér – ℰ (01)
429 3777 – www.kempinski.com/budapest Plan: E2
349 rm – ♦53795/147935 HUF ♦♦53795/147935 HUF – ☲ 11870 HUF
– 18 suites
• Business • Luxury • Stylish •
Stylish, well-equipped hotel with a striking lobby, lounge and bar; overlooking a central square and named after the charismatic 15C king, Matthias Corvinus. Spacious bedrooms feature Empire-style furniture and boast excellent facilities. The bistro serves modern Hungarian and Viennese cuisine.
Nobu Budapest – See restaurant listing

Corinthia Budapest

Erzsébet krt 43-49 ⊠ 1073 – Ⓜ Oktogon – ℰ (01)
479 4000 – www.corinthia.com/budapest Plan: F1
414 rm – ♦45580/138555 HUF ♦♦45580/138555 HUF – ☲ 10575 HUF
– 28 suites
• Grand Luxury • Historic • Classic •
Superbly restored and comprehensively equipped hotel with a splendid 19C façade and a spectacular atrium, where a marble staircase leads to a rococo-style ballroom. There's a stunning swimming pool and spa, several shops and a patisserie. The Brasserie offers international cuisine; intimate Rickshaw serves wide-ranging Chinese, Thai, Indian and Indonesian dishes.

Aria

Hercegprímás utca 5 ⊠ 1051 – Ⓜ Bajcsy-Zsilinszky út Plan: E2
– ℰ (01) 445 4055 – www.ariahotelbudapest.com
45 rm ☲ – ♦88290/117730 HUF ♦♦88290/117730 HUF – 4 suites
• Luxury • Spa hotel • Personalised •
An 1870s building houses this luxurious hotel, which boasts a stunning glass-enclosed courtyard with views of the sky above. Chic, spacious bedrooms are set in 4 wings and each is themed around a style of music – classical, jazz, opera and contemporary. Modern Hungarian dishes feature in the restaurant. In summer, have a drink in the rooftop bar and take in the view.

Prestige

Vigyázó Ferenc utca 5 ⊠ 1051 – Ⓜ Vörösmarty tér Plan: E1
– ℰ (01) 920 1000 – www.prestigehotelbudapest.com
85 rm – ♦46800/77980 HUF ♦♦46800/77980 HUF – ☲ 8420 HUF – 13 suites
• Luxury • Elegant • Personalised •
In the heart of the city centre you'll find this 19C townhouse designed by neo-classical architect Jozsef Hild. Most of the refined, elegant bedrooms are set around a central atrium; they differ in size and colour but all are equally well equipped with the likes of coffee machines, bathrobes and spa bags.
❀ **Costes Downtown** – See restaurant listing

Around Budapest
(Plan I)

0   1 km

- ● Hotel
- ● Restaurant

VÁSÁHELY-MÚZEUM

ÓBUDA

Szépvölgyi út

DUNA

Forgách u.

ANGYALFÖLD

Árpád Híd

Róbert

Váci

Árpád híd

Károly

Dózsa György út

Lehel Körút

MARGIT-SZIGET

Laci Konyha

Lehel Tér

SZÉCHENYI GYÓGYFÜRDŐ

Mexikói út

Széchenyi Fürdő

SZÉPMŰVÉSZETI MÚZEUM

VAJDAHUNYAD VÁRA

KÖZLEKEDÉSI MÚZEUM

Hősök Tere

MILLENIUMI EMLÉKMŰ

Hősök Tere

Bajza u.

Mamaison H. Andrássy

KIRÁLY GYÓFÜRDŐ

Bem József tér

Margit krt.

Kodály Körönd

VÁROSLIGET

Budapest Centre (Plan II)

NYUGATI PÁLYAUDVAR

RÁTH GYÖRGY MÚZEUM

TERÉZVÁROS

Andrássy

New York Salon

KELETI PÁLYAUDAR

Kerepesi út

SZÉCHENYI LÁNCHID

Continental

Boscolo Budapest

Keleti Pu.

Puskás Ferenc Stadion

DÉLI PU.

BUDAVÁRI PALOTA

BUDA

Rákóczi

Blaha Lujza tér

Palazzo Zichy

JÓZSEFVÁROSI PÁLYAUDAR

PEST

József

Baross

Kőbányai út

Hegyalja

SZABADSÁG HID

IPARMŰVÉSZETI MÚZEUM

Corvin-negyed

Üllői út

Petrus

Klinikák

PLANETÁRIUM

Petőfi Híd

Nagyvárad Tér

Haller

Népliget

DUNA

KELENFÖLD

Rákóczi Hid

Könyves

FERIHEGY

Boscolo Budapest

Erzsébet krt 9-11 ⊠ 1073 – Ⓜ Blaha Lujza tér   Plan I: **B2**
– ℰ (01) 886 6111 – www.boscolohotels.com
185 rm ⌧ – †140000/240000 HUF ††147500/247500 HUF – 7 suites
• Grand Luxury • Historic • Stylish •

Stunning New York Insurance Company building constructed in 1891; set around an impressive five-floor Italian Renaissance style atrium. A feeling of luxury pervades: vast bedrooms feature silk wallpaper, chandeliers and marble bathrooms, and there's an unusual ice-house style spa. The all-day café offers international dishes, while the stunning salon serves modern fare.

New York Salon – See restaurant listing

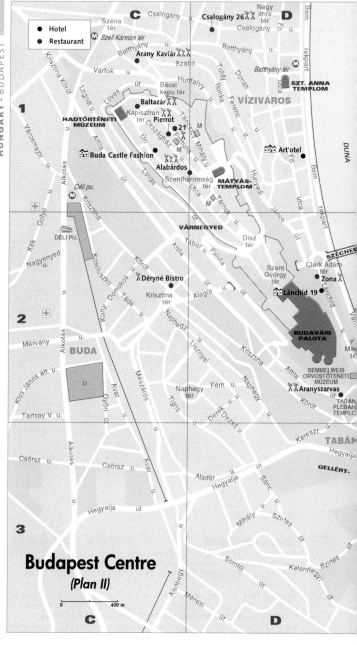

● Hotel
● Restaurant

Csalogány
Széna
tér
Ⓜ Széll Kármán tér
Batthyány
Arany Kaviár
Szabó
Várfok
Bécsi
kapu tér
Baltazár
Kapisztrán
tér **Pierrot**
**HADTÖRTÉNETI
MÚZEUM**
🏠 **Buda Castle Fashion**
Alabárdos
Szentháromság
tér
**MÁTYÁS-
TEMPLOM**

Csalogány 26
Nagy
imre
tér
Csalogány
Batthyány
Batthyány tér Ⓜ
**SZT. ANNA
TEMPLOM**
VÍZIVÁROS

Art'otel 🏠
DUNA

21
Hunfalvy

VÁRNEGYED
Disz
tér

Ⓜ DÉLI PU.
Nagyenyed
u.
✗ **Déryné Bistro**
Krisztina
tér

Szent
György
tér
Clark Ádám
tér **Zona** ✗
🏠 **Lánchíd 19**

BUDA

Ⓤ

**BUDAVÁRI
PALOTA**

**SEMMELWEIS
ORVOSTÖRTÉNETI
MÚZEUM**
✗ ✗ **Aranyszarvas**
**TABÁN
PLÉBÁN
TEMPLC**

TABÁN
Hegyalja

GELLÉRT-

Budapest Centre
(Plan II)

0   400 m

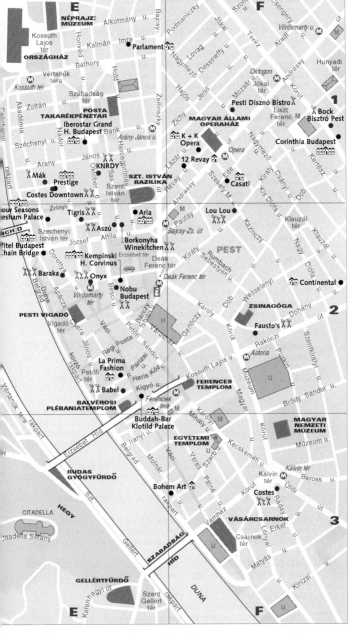

E

NÉPRAJZI MÚZEUM

Kossuth Lajos tér

ORSZÁGHÁZ

Vértanúk tere

Kossuth tér

Zoltán

POSTA TAKARÉKPÉNZTAR

Iberostar Grand H. Budapest

Akadémia

Széchenyi u.

Arany

Mák

Prestige

Costes Downtown

our Seasons esham Palace

ICH'D

fitel Budapest hain Bridge

Széchenyi István tér

Baraka

Onyx

Vörösmarty tér

PESTI VIGADÓ

Vigadó tér

Cserne János

Váci

La Prima Fashion

Petőfi tér

Babel

BALVÉROSI PLÉBANIATEMPLOM

Buddah-Bar Klotild Palace

RUDAS GYÓGYFÜRDŐ

CITADELLA

Citadella Sétány

HEGY

GELLÉRTFÜRDŐ

Kelenhegyi út

Szent Gellért tér

Alkotmány u.

Honvéd

Kálmán

Imre

Parlament

Báthory

Hold

Zrínyi

Zsilinszky

Szabadság tér

Bank

Arany János u.

KNRDY

Sas

Hercegprímás

SZT. ISTVÁN BAZILIKA

Szent István tér

Aria

Aszú

Attila

Borkonyha Winekitchen

Kempinski H. Corvinus

Erzsébet tér

Deák Ferenctér

Deák Ferenc tér

Nobu Budapest

Bécsi u.

Bárczy István u.

Városház

Régi Posta u.

Petőfi Sándor u.

Párizsi u.

Haris Köz.

Kigyó u.

Ferenciek tere

Irányi u.

EGYETEMI TEMPLOM

Veres Pálné

Belgrád

Molnár

SZABADSÁG HÍD

Gellért

DUNA

F

Szondi

Csengery

Podmaniczky

Jókai

Vörösmarty u.

M

Lovag

Nagymező

Dessewffy

Teréz

Aradi

Andrássy

Oktogon

Mozsár

Jókai

Hunyadi tér

1

Pesti Disznó Bistro

Liszt Ferenc tér

Bock Bisztró Pest

MAGYAR ÁLLAMI OPERAHÁZ

K + K Opera

Opera

12 Revay

Casati

Corinthia Budapest

Zichy

Lázár u.

Révay

Andrássy

Székely

Ede

Király

Nagymező

Kis Diófa u.

Dob

Csányi u.

Kertész

Lou Lou

Paulay

Bajcsy-Zs. út

Király

PEST

Rumbach Sebestyén u.

Kazinczy

Klauzál tér

Nagy Diófa

Klauzál

Wesselényi u.

Continental

ZSINAGÓGA

Dohány

Fausto's

Rákóczi

Astoria

Kossuth Lajos u.

Múzeum

FERENCES TEMPLOM

Károly

Mihály u.

MAGYAR NEMZETI MÚZEUM

Múzeum u.

Kecskeméti u.

Szerb

Kálvin tér

Kálvin tér

Baross

Costes

VÁSÁRCSARNOK

Bohem Art

Vámház

Csarnok tér

Mátyás

Kinizsi

Erkel

Üllői

Ráday

2

3

Szentkirály

Piski

Bródy Sándor u.

E

F

Sofitel Budapest Chain Bridge

Széchenyi István tér 2 ✉ *1051* – Ⓜ *Vörösmarty tér*
– ☏ *(01) 235 1234* – *www.sofitel.com* Plan: **E2**
357 rm – †33275/138530 HUF ††33270/138530 HUF – ☑ 7670 HUF
– 34 suites
• Business • Chain hotel • Classic •
Modern hotel with a vast atrium, a stylish lobby-lounge and a pretty terrace
with stunning castle and Danube views. Compact bedrooms boast the latest
mod cons; those on the northwest corner have Buda views. The fashionable restaurant has an unusual open kitchen and blends French and Hungarian cuisine.

Buddha-Bar Klotild Palace

Váci utca 34 ✉ *1052* – Ⓜ *Ferenciek ter* – ☏ *(01)* Plan: **E2**
799 7300 – *www.buddhabarhotel.hu*
102 rm – †43000/156000 HUF ††43000/200000 HUF – ☑ 7400 HUF
• Luxury • Stylish • Oriental •
Chic hotel in a palace built for Princess Klotild of the Habsburg family. It has an
oriental theme, with a Zen garden and bedrooms featuring crimson fabrics, intimate lighting and state-of-the-art facilities. The opulent restaurant with its huge
gold Buddha serves Chinese, Thai and Japanese dishes.

Iberostar Grand H. Budapest

Október 6 utka 26 ✉ *1051* – Ⓜ *Arány Janos utca* Plan: **E1**
– ☏ *(01) 354 3050* – *www.iberostar.com*
50 rm – †32550/102300 HUF ††32550/102300 HUF – ☑ 6100 HUF
• Chain hotel • Modern • Personalised •
A classic-looking hotel with a contrastingly modern interior. The lobby-lounge
features padded silver chairs on a black marble floor, while bright bedrooms
come with good facilities, boldly patterned furnishings and a Spanish edge.
The comfy restaurant serves globally influenced lunches and Hungarian dinners.

Continental

Dohány utca 42-44 ✉ *1074* – Ⓜ *Blaha Lujza tér* Plan I: **B2**
– ☏ *(01) 815 1000* – *www.continentalhotelbudapest.com*
272 rm – †36214/87426 HUF ††39872/91084 HUF – ☑ 5487 HUF
• Business • Art Deco • Functional •
Formerly the public baths; now a stunning art deco hotel with a revolving copper door, spacious modern guest areas and brown-hued bedrooms with padded feature headboards. Relax in the indoor or outdoor pool, or on a sun loun-
ger in the roof garden. The restaurant serves Hungarian and international
dishes.

K + K Opera

Révay utca 24 ✉ *1065* – Ⓜ *Opera* – ☏ *(01) 269 0222* Plan: **F1**
– *www.kkhotels.com*
200 rm ☑ – †25110/59635 HUF ††28250/62770 HUF – 2 suites
• Business • Modern • Functional •
Friendly hotel on a quiet side street behind the Opera House, close to the smart
shops of Andrassy utca. Bedrooms are comfortable, uniform and up-to-date.
Comprehensive continental breakfasts; snacks served in the cool bar-lounge.

Palazzo Zichy

Lörinc pap tér 2 ✉ *1088* – Ⓜ *Kálvin tér* – ☏ *(01)* Plan I: **B2**
235 4000 – *www.hotel-palazzo-zichy.hu*
80 rm ☑ – †34100/69225 HUF ††38420/72370 HUF
• Business • Modern • Functional •
Beautiful rococo building with an impressive 1899 façade; once home to writer
Count Zichy. The glass-roofed atrium has a striking modern design. Bedrooms
are generously sized, well-equipped and have a cool, minimalist style.

Mamaison H. Andrássy
Munkáczy Mihály utca 5-7 ✉ *1063 –* Ⓜ *Bajza utca* — Plan I: **B1**
– ℰ (01) 462 2100 – www.mamaison.com
68 rm – ♦33025/70120 HUF ♦♦33025/70120 HUF – ☐ 5565 HUF – 5 suites
• Business • Townhouse • Stylish •

Classical 1937 Bauhaus building in a superb location on the elegant main street. The modern lobby-lounge features pillars of stainless steel filigree. Light, spacious bedrooms have good facilities and most come with balconies. The stylish monochrome restaurant offers modern international dishes.

La Prima Fashion
Piarista utca 6 ✉ *1052 –* Ⓜ *Ferenciek ter – ℰ (01)* — Plan: **E2**
799 0088 – www.laprimahotelbudapest.com
80 rm ☐ – ♦28000/81400 HUF ♦♦31100/175660 HUF
• Business • Modern • Cosy •

Simple, modern hotel located near Elizabeth Bridge. A beige and turquoise colour scheme runs throughout. The small lobby lounge has deep padded armchairs; bedrooms have velour bedheads, bold feature walls and TVs set into large mirrors.

Parlament
Kálmán Imre utca 19 ✉ *1054 –* Ⓜ *Arany János utca* — Plan: **E1**
– ℰ (01) 374 6000 – www.parlament-hotel.hu
65 rm ☐ – ♦21300 HUF ♦♦24400 HUF
• Townhouse • Business • Modern •

Well-run boutique hotel; its stylish, modern interior a contrast to its classical 19C façade. The splendid open-plan atrium has an unusual display depicting famous Hungarians. Compact bedrooms have a clean, crisp design.

Casati
Paulay Ede utca 31 ✉ *1061 –* Ⓜ *Opera – ℰ (01)* — Plan: **F1**
343 1198 – www.casatibudapesthotel.com
25 rm ☐ – ♦18860/37720 HUF ♦♦22000/44000 HUF
• Townhouse • Personalised • Contemporary •

18C townhouse with an Italian Renaissance style façade. The glass-roofed breakfast room features an old well and leads to a '70s lounge-bar. The gym is in the stone-walled basement. Bedrooms range from bohemian to elegant to minimalist.

Bohem Art
Molnár utca 35 ✉ *1056 –* Ⓜ *Kálvin tér – ℰ (01)* — Plan: **F3**
327 9020 – www.bohemarthotel.hu
60 rm ☐ – ♦18520/62465 HUF ♦♦20405/62465 HUF
• Townhouse • Modern • Stylish •

A trendy hotel in a bohemian area of the city, run by a hip, friendly team. Modern Hungarian art features throughout. Stylish modern bedrooms have large screen prints and are furnished in white; the standard rooms are fairly compact.

12 Revay
Révay utca 12 ✉ *1065 –* Ⓜ *Opera – ℰ (01) 909 1212* — Plan: **F1**
– www.12revayhotel.com
53 rm ☐ – ♦36000/42000 HUF ♦♦40000/46000 HUF – 3 suites
• Business • Modern • Functional •

12 Revay is a bright modern hotel ideally situated between the Basilica and the Opera House. Uniform bedrooms feature large black and white prints of the city's monuments; the 3 apartments have small kitchenettes and wonderful views.

HUNGARY - BUDAPEST

Onyx ❀❀ Ⓐⓚ

Vörösmarty tér 7-8 ✉ 1051 – Ⓜ Vörösmarty tér   Plan: **E2**
– 𝒞 (30) 508 0622 – www.onyxrestaurant.hu – Closed 3 weeks August,
2 weeks January, Saturday lunch, Sunday and Monday
Menu 8990 HUF (lunch)/27900 HUF – Carte dinner 19000/23500 HUF –
(booking essential)
• Modern • Elegant • Intimate •
Right in the heart of the city is this glamorous restaurant, where you sit on gilt
chairs under sparkling chandeliers, surrounded by onyx adornments. Highly
skilled, detailed cooking keeps classical Hungarian flavours to the fore but also
presents some interesting modern twists. On Saturdays, only the tasting menus
are served. Service is assured and formal.
➜ Goose liver with sloes. Venison, asparagus and almond. 21st century
Somló sponge cake.

Costes ❀❀ Ⓐⓚ

Ráday utca 4 ✉ 1092 – Ⓜ Kálvin tér – 𝒞 (01) 219 0696   Plan: **F3**
– www.costes.hu – Closed 2 weeks January, 1 week August, Christmas,
Monday and Tuesday
Menu 23550/34550 HUF – Carte 15390/20730 HUF – *(dinner only) (boo-*
king essential)
• Modern • Design • Elegant •
A sophisticated restaurant with immaculately dressed tables, run by a confident,
experienced service team. The talented chef uses modern techniques and a
deft touch to produce accomplished, innovative dishes with clear flavours.
Most diners choose the 4-7 course set menus and their interesting wine pai-
rings.
➜ Crayfish tails with Ibérico ham. Pigeon, beetroot and coffee. 'Blow Up':
peach, nectarine and apricot.

New York Salon – Boscolo Budapest Hotel Ⓐⓚ

Erzsébet krt. 9-11 ✉ 1073 – Ⓜ Blaha Lujza tér – 𝒞 (01)   Plan I: **B2**
886 6191 – www.boscolohotels.com – Closed 2 weeks August, Sunday and
Monday
Menu 15900 HUF – Carte 12900/17500 HUF – *(dinner only) (booking*
advisable)
• Hungarian • Classic • Luxury •
A stunning baroque salon behind glass doors in a luxurious hotel; admire the
ornate gilding and impressive painted ceiling as you dine. Extensive menus
use the best local ingredients to create attractively presented modern interpretations of Hungarian classics; the 7 course tasting menu is a highlight.

Baraka Ⓐⓚ

Dorottya utca 6 ✉ 1051 – Ⓜ Vörösmarty tér – 𝒞 (01)   Plan: **E2**
200 0817 – www.barakarestaurant.hu – Closed 24-25 December and
Sunday
Menu 4500 HUF (weekday lunch)/21000 HUF – Carte 10550/20800 HUF
• Modern • Elegant • Intimate •
To the front is a beautiful cocktail bar with a cosy lounge and to the rear is an
intimate black and white dining room. Every table has a view of the open kit-
chen, where the chefs prepare creative modern dishes with Asian touches.

Lou Lou ⚹ Ⓐⓚ

Székely Mihály utca 2 ✉ 1061 – Ⓜ Opera – 𝒞 (70)   Plan: **F2**
3335289 – www.lou-lou.hu – Closed Christmas, Saturday lunch, Sunday
and lunch bank holidays
Menu 3950/19900 HUF – Carte 10800/26900 HUF
• Modern • Elegant • Intimate •
A well-known restaurant in an area teeming with life; once inside it's an oasis of
tranquillity and comfort. Two tasteful dining rooms are run by an engaging
team. Dishes have a classic French base but are modern in their execution.

HUNGARY - BUDAPEST

XX ★ **Borkonyha Winekitchen**

Sas utca 3 ✉ 1051 – Ⓜ Bajcsy-Zsilinszky út – ℰ (01)   Plan: **E2**
266 0835 – www.borkonyha.hu – Closed Sunday and bank holidays
Carte 6850/13150 HUF – *(booking essential)*
• Modern • Fashionable • Friendly •

Bustling wine-orientated restaurant close to the Basilica. The fortnightly menu features well-executed dishes with an elaborate modern style and subtle Hungarian influences. Top ingredients are sourced from the surrounding countries. 48 of the 200 wines are offered by the glass; many are from local producers.
→ Crispy duck liver, tomato and spring onion. Mangalica pork belly with buttered vegetables. Dark chocolate and coffee foam.

XX ★ **Costes Downtown** – Prestige Hotel

Vigyázó Ferenc utca 5 ✉ 1051 – Ⓜ Vörösmarty tér   Plan: **E1**
– ℰ (01) 920 1017 – www.costesdowntown.hu
Menu 6900 HUF (lunch) – Carte 10900/15500 HUF
• Modern • Bistro • Cosy •

The more informal sister to Costes sits within the Prestige hotel and has chic bistro styling and a friendly atmosphere; ask to be seated in one of the booths. Refined modern dishes follow the seasons and feature excellent texture and flavour combinations. They offer a good value business lunch.
→ Pan-fried scallops with quinoa salad. Pork with cabbage and chestnuts. Citrus panna cotta with meringue.

XX **Babel**

Piarista Köz 2 ✉ 1052 – Ⓜ Ferenciek ter – ℰ (70)   Plan: **E2**
6000 800 – www.babel-budapest.hu – Closed 24-25 December, Sunday and Monday
Menu 23000 HUF – Carte 11500/17500 HUF – *(dinner only) (booking essential)*
• Modern • Elegant • Design •

You really feel part of proceedings at Babel, thanks to the bread oven located in the restaurant and the hands-on chefs, who often pop out of the kitchen to deliver the dishes themselves. Sophisticated, modern cooking features some original combinations but also shows respect for Hungarian traditions.

XX **Fausto's**

Dohány utca 5 ✉ 1072 – Ⓜ Astoria – ℰ (30) 589 1813   Plan: **F2**
– www.fausto.hu – Closed 2 weeks August, 24-26 December, 1 May, Saturday lunch and Sunday
Menu 6000 HUF (weekday lunch)/21000 HUF – Carte 10500/18900 HUF – *(booking essential)*
• Italian • Cosy • Intimate •

Expect a friendly welcome at this personally run eatery. Dine on sophisticated modern Italian dishes at linen-laid tables in the restaurant or on simpler, more classically based fare in the laid-back, wood-furnished osteria; the daily home-made pasta is a hit. Good quality Hungarian and Italian wines feature.

XX **Tigris**

Mérleg utca 10 ✉ 1051 – Ⓜ Bajcsy-Zsilinszky út   Plan: **E2**
– ℰ (01) 317 3715 – www.tigrisrestaurant.hu – Closed 1 week August, Christmas and Sunday
Carte 7100/12200 HUF – *(booking essential at dinner)*
• Hungarian • Traditional • Neighbourhood •

Traditional bistro in a historic building designed by a Hungarian architect; it exudes a luxurious feel. Classic dishes have an appealing, earthy quality and feature foie gras specialities. The wine list champions up-and-coming producers.

HUNGARY - BUDAPEST

XX **KNRDY** ⒶⒸ

Október 6. utca 15 ✉ *1051 –* Ⓜ *Arány Janos utca*   Plan: **E1**
*– ✆ (01) 788 1685 – www.knrdy.com – Closed 24-26 December and
1 January*
Carte 8600/57100 HUF *– (booking essential at dinner)*
• Meats and grills • Fashionable • Design •
Stylish New York style steakhouse with designer furnishings and a street scene
mural. Choose your steak from the display: they specialise in large cuts, including porterhouse and T-bone. Meat comes from America, Australia and Argentina.

XX **Petrus** 🈺 ⒶⒸ ⇔
⊛
Ferent tér 2-3 ✉ *1094 –* Ⓜ *Klinikák – ✆ (01) 951 2597*   Plan: I: **B2**
*– www.petrusrestaurant.hu – Closed 2 weeks August, 24-26 December,
Sunday and Monday*
Menu 6990 HUF *–* Carte 7580/10900 HUF
• Classic/traditional • Bistro • Neighbourhood •
Friendly neighbourhood bistro where Budapest meets Paris – both in the décor
and the food. The chef-owner's passion is obvious and the cooking is rustic and
authentic, with bold flavours and a homely touch. If you're after something a
little different, ask to dine in the old Citroën 2CV!

XX **Nobu Budapest** – Kempinski H. Corvinus   🅿 ⒶⒸ ⇔
Erzsébet tér 7-8 ✉ *1051 –* Ⓜ *Deák Ferenc tér – ✆ (01)*   Plan: **E2**
429 4242 – www.noburestaurants.com
Menu 5000 HUF *–* Carte 5700/14500 HUF
• Japanese • Minimalist • Fashionable •
Minimalist restaurant in a stylish hotel, with well-spaced wooden tables, Japa-
nese lanterns, fretwork screens and an open kitchen. Numerous menus offer a
huge array of Japanese-inspired dishes; some come with matching wine flights.

XX **Aszú** 🈺 ⒶⒸ
Sas utca 4 ✉ *1051 –* Ⓜ *Bajcsy-Zsilinszky út – ✆ (01)*   Plan: **E2**
328 0360 – www.aszuetterem.hu
Carte 6200/12100 HUF
• Hungarian • Elegant • Design •
As its name suggests, this restaurant celebrates Tokaj and its wines. The kitchen
prepares updated Hungarian classics. The striking room features an ornate mir-
rored wall, a golden-hued vaulted ceiling and handcrafted wooden carvings.

X **Mák** 🅱🅱
Vigyázó Ferenc utca 4 ✉ *1051 –* Ⓜ *Vörösmarty tér*   Plan: **E1**
*– ✆ (30) 723 9383 – www.mak.hu – Closed 16-24 August, 24 December-
4 January, Sunday and Monday*
Menu 3500 HUF *(weekday lunch) –* Carte 8200/13900 HUF *– (bookings
advisable at dinner)*
• Modern • Bistro • Rustic •
Delightfully rustic restaurant with whitewashed bricks and semi-vaulted ceilings: its name means 'poppy seed'. Cooking is delicate and balanced, featuring
well-presented modern interpretations of Hungarian classics. Charming service.

X **Laci Konyha** ⒶⒸ
⊛
Hegedűs Gyula utca 56 ✉ *1134 –* Ⓜ *Lehel Tér*   Plan: I: **A1**
*– ✆ (70) 370 7475 – www.lacikonyha.hu – Closed 24 December-
5 January, Saturday, Sunday and bank holidays*
Carte 5800/9800 HUF
• Modern • Neighbourhood • Individual •
Great value, original modern menus make this edgy restaurant a hit with one
and all; gather your friends and make for a table for 12 – backed by walls of
bold graffiti! Ingredients are well-sourced and accurately cooked, and while
combinations are traditionally based, the techniques and overtones are
modern.

Pesti Disznó Bistro

Nagymező utca 19 ✉ *1065 –* Ⓜ *Oktogon –* ℰ *(01)* Plan: **F1**
951 4061 – www.pestidiszno.hu – Closed 24-25 December
Menu 1190 HUF (lunch) – Carte 4270/8970 HUF
• Meats and grills • Bistro • Wine bar •
A buzzy, easy-going Hungarian bistro; as you cross the threshold, wonderful aromas hint at what is to come. Carefully sourced ingredients feature in authentic recipes and prices are fair; their native Mangalitza pork is a speciality.

Bock Bisztró Pest

Erzsébet krt. 43-49 ✉ *1073 –* Ⓜ *Oktogon –* ℰ *(01)* Plan: **F1**
321 0340 – www.bockbisztro.hu – Closed Sunday and bank holidays
Carte 6200/10500 HUF – *(booking essential)*
• Hungarian • Bistro • Rustic •
Busy, buzzy bistro; its shelves packed with wine. Choose something from the à la carte or try one of the blackboard specials – the friendly, knowledgeable staff will guide you. Cooking is gutsy and traditional with a modern twist.

Art'otel

Bem rkp. 16-19 ✉ *1011 –* Ⓜ *Batthyány tér –* ℰ *(01)* Plan: **D1**
487 9487 – www.artotels.com
165 rm – ♦31000/59000 HUF ♦♦31000/59000 HUF – ☲ 4300 HUF – 10 suites
• Business • Design • Contemporary •
Modern hotel in a stunning waterfront spot. The stylish interior comes in cool shades and features over 700 pieces of art by Donald Sultan. Contemporary bedrooms: some overlook the parliament building; those in the baroque house are the most spacious. Concise menu of international dishes in the bistro-bar.

Lánchíd 19

Lánchíd utca 19 ✉ *1013 –* ℰ *(01) 419 1900* Plan: **D2**
– www.lanchid19hotel.hu
48 rm – ♦23505/62370 HUF ♦♦23505/172365 HUF – ☲ 4075 HUF
• Business • Design • Retro •
Stylish hotel overlooking the river and castle, and featuring a glass-floored lounge looking down to the ruins of a 14C water tower. Bedrooms boast designer chairs, feature walls and modern facilities; those to the front have impressive views. The mezzanine restaurant offers an international menu.

Buda Castle Fashion

Úri utca 39 ✉ *1014 –* Ⓜ *Széll Kármán tér –* ℰ *(01)* Plan: **C1**
224 7900 – www.budacastlehotel.eu
20 rm ☲ – ♦20000/38000 HUF ♦♦24000/43000 HUF – 5 suites
• Townhouse • Functional • Modern •
Lovely 15C merchant's house on a quiet street in the heart of Old Buda; a former HQ of the Hungarian Hunting Association. There's a delightfully peaceful courtyard terrace. Bedrooms are spacious, comfy and pleasantly modern.

Alabárdos

✉ *1014 –* Ⓜ *Széll Kármán tér –* ℰ *(01) 356 0851* Plan: **D1**
– www.alabardos.hu
Menu 11000/18000 HUF – Carte 9700/11600 HUF – *(dinner only and Saturday lunch) (booking essential)*
• Hungarian • Formal • Elegant •
Set in a series of 15C buildings opposite the castle and named after its guards, this professionally run restaurant has stood here for over 50 years. It's formal yet atmospheric, with subtle modern touches and a delightful terrace. Cooking is rich and flavourful and features classic dishes with a modern edge.

HUNGARY - BUDAPEST

XxX **Arany Kaviár**

Ostrom utca 19 ✉ *1015 –* Ⓜ *Moszkva tér – ℰ (01)* Plan: **C1**
*201 6737 – www.aranykaviar.hu – Closed 24-26 December, 20 August,
Monday and bank holidays*
Menu 3900 HUF (weekday lunch) – Carte 11290/36995 HUF
• Russian • Intimate • Elegant •

An elegant winter garden restaurant with a small, opulent side room. French
and Russian influences guide the cooking; Hungarian and Siberian caviar is a
speciality. The impressive wine list offers a great selection of champagne.

XX **Pierrot**

Fortuna utca 14 ✉ *1014 –* Ⓜ *Széll Kármán tér – ℰ (01)* Plan: **C1**
375 6971 – www.pierrot.hu
Carte 7830/18630 HUF
• Hungarian • Elegant • Intimate •

Characterful two-roomed restaurant in a vaulted 13C property within the castle
walls. European and Hungarian classics are prepared with a contemporary
touch; service is efficient. Pierrot themed artwork and live piano music feature.

XX **Csalogány 26**

Csalogány utca 26 ✉ *1015 –* Ⓜ *Batthyány tér – ℰ (01)* Plan: **D1**
*201 7892 – www.csalogany26.hu – Closed 2 weeks summer, 2 weeks
winter, Sunday, Monday and bank holidays*
Menu 9000/18500 HUF – Carte 6100/11000 HUF – *(booking advisable)*
• Modern • Bistro • Friendly •

Homely neighbourhood restaurant with a simple bistro style. A passionate
father and son team offer two daily menus; go for 4 or 8 courses or choose
from the à la carte. Cooking is full of flavour and presented in a modern style.

XX **Baltazár**

Országház utca 31 ✉ *1014 –* Ⓜ *Széll Kármán tér* Plan: **C1**
– ℰ (01) 300 7050 – www.baltazarbudapest.com
11 rm – †40690/71750 HUF ††40690/133150 HUF – ⌑ 4000 HUF
Carte 5890/15030 HUF
• Modern • Design • Bistro •

A hidden gem, tucked away from the crowds in the north of the Old Town.
Relax on the pretty terrace or head for the striking interior, where stage spot-
lights illuminate boldly painted concrete walls. Cooking focuses on tapas dishes
and meats from the Josper grill. The bedrooms are also ultra-modern.

XX **Aranyszarvas**

Szarvas tér 1 ✉ *1013 – ℰ (01) 375 6451* Plan: **D2**
– www.aranyszarvas.hu – Closed 25-26 December
Carte 6000/8400 HUF
• Hungarian • Traditional •

18C marble-floored building that was once a pharmacy – its elevated terrace
looks towards Elizabeth Bridge. The concise menu offers well-presented, stout
Hungarian classics; its name means 'golden deer' and game is a speciality.

X **Tanti**

🕄

Apor Vilmos tér 11-12 (West: 4.25 km by Hegyalja and Jagelló utca)
✉ *1124 – ℰ (20) 243 1565 – www.tanti.hu – Closed 15-23 August and
Sunday*
Menu 3900 HUF (weekday lunch) – Carte 8640/12000 HUF
• Modern • Minimalist • Neighbourhood •

'Auntie' is located in the corner of a pleasant little shopping mall and comes
with an appealing terrace. It's light, bright and simply kitted out and offers a
concise menu of attractively presented, well-balanced dishes. Ingredients
come from Hungary and France and well-chosen native wines accompany.
→ Radish soup with pears and shrimps. Scallops with miso and pineapple.
Raspberry, yoghurt and beetroot.

X **Vendéglő a KisBíróhoz**

Szarvas Gábor utca 8/d (Northwest: 3.5 km by Attila utca, Kristina Körut and Szilágyi Erzsébet off Kutvölgyi utca) ✉ *1125 –* ✆ *(01) 376 6044*
– www.vendegloakisbirohoz.hu – Closed Monday and bank holidays
Carte 6200/11500 HUF
• Hungarian • Bistro • Neighbourhood •
Modern glass and wood building with a large terrace, in a peaceful suburban location. Wine takes centre stage: staff will recommend a match for your dish from the extensive list. Cooking is hearty and classical with a modern edge.

X **Zona**

Lánchíd utca 7-9 ✉ *1013 –* ✆ *(30) 422 5981*   Plan: **D2**
– www.zonabudapest.com – Closed 24-27 December
Menu 2900 HUF (weekday lunch) – Carte 5700/13600 HUF
• Modern • Design • Trendy •
Contemporary restaurant with floor to ceiling windows overlooking the river and a huge shelving unit packed with wines. Gold glass balls illuminate sleek wooden tables. Modern dishes follow the seasons and arrive smartly presented.

X **21**

Fortuna utca 21 ✉ *1014 –* Ⓜ *Széll Kármán tér –* ✆ *(01)*   Plan: **C1**
202 2113 – www.21restaurant.hu
Carte 6130/12660 HUF
• Hungarian • Bistro • Friendly •
Situated within the castle walls; a contemporary take on a traditional bistro. Classic Hungarian dishes are subtly reinvented with an appealing contemporary touch. Sit on the terrace for great views down the cobbled street.

X **Déryné Bistro**

Krisztina tér 3 ✉ *1013 –* Ⓜ *Déli pu. –* ✆ *(01) 225 1407*   Plan: **C2**
– www.bistroderyne.com – Closed 24 December
Carte 3840/10740 HUF
• French classic • Bistro • Traditional •
Wonderfully old bistro-cum-brasserie with a horseshoe bar and lots of old-fashioned charm. French classics sit alongside a few Hungarian dishes. It's open for breakfast, they have their own bakery, and a pianist plays from 3-8pm.

Republic of IRELAND
ÉIRE

DUBLIN ●

→ **AREA:**
70 284 km² (27 137 sq mi).

→ **POPULATION:**
4 595 000 inhabitants.
Density = 65 per km².

→ **CAPITAL:** Dublin.

→ **CURRENCY:** Euro (€).

→ **GOVERNMENT:**
Parliamentary republic
(since 1921). Member of
European Union since 1973.

→ **LANGUAGES:**
Irish and English.

→ **PUBLIC HOLIDAYS:**
New Year's Day (1 Jan);
St Patrick's Day (17 Mar); Easter
Monday (late Mar/Apr); May Bank
Holiday (first Mon in May); June
Bank Holiday (first Mon in June);
August Bank Holiday (first Mon
in Aug); October Bank Holiday (last
Mon in Oct); Christmas Day
(25 Dec); St Stephen's Day (26 Dec).

→ **LOCAL TIME:**
GMT in winter and GMT+1 hour in
summer.

→ **CLIMATE:**
Temperate maritime with cool
winters and mild summers (Dublin:
January 5°C; July 15°C), fairly high
rainfall.

→ **EMERGENCY:**
Police, Medical Assistance, Fire
Brigade ✆ **999** – also used for
Mountain, Cave, Coastguard and
Sea Rescue.
(Dialling **112** within any EU country
will redirect your call and contact
the emergency services.)

→ **ELECTRICITY:**
230 volts AC, 50 H; 3 flat pin
sockets.

→ **FORMALITIES:**
Travellers from the European Union
(EU), Switzerland, Iceland and the
main countries of North and South
America need a national identity
card or passport (except for British
nationals travelling from the UK;
America: passport required) to visit
Ireland for less than three months
(tourism or business purpose).
For visitors from other countries a
visa may be required, in addition
to a passport, especially for those
wishing to stay for longer than
three months. We advise you to
check with your embassy before
travelling.

DUBLIN
BAILE ÁTHA CLIATH

Population: 565 000

Marek Slusarczyk/Fotolia.com

For somewhere touted as the finest Georgian city in the British Isles, Dublin enjoys a very young image. When the 'Celtic Tiger' roared to prominence in the 1990s, Ireland's old capital took on a youthful expression, and for the first time revelled in the epithets 'chic' and 'trendy'. Nowadays it's not just the bastion of Guinness drinkers and those here for the 'craic', but a twenty-first century city with smart restaurants, grand new hotels, modern architecture and impressive galleries. Its handsome squares and façades took shape 250 years ago, designed by the finest architects of the time. Since then, it's gone through uprising, civil war and independence from Britain, and now holds a strong fascination for foreign visitors.

The city can be pretty well divided into three. Southeast of the river is the classiest, defined by the glorious Trinity College, St Stephen's Green, and Grafton Street's smart shops. Just west of here is the second area, dominated by Dublin Castle and Christ Church Cathedral – ancient buildings abound, but it doesn't quite match the sleek aura of the city's Georgian quarter. Across the Liffey, the northern section was the last part to be developed and, although it lacks the glamour of its southern neighbours, it does boast the city's grandest avenue, O'Connell Street, and its most celebrated theatres.

DUBLIN IN...

→ **ONE DAY**
  Trinity College, Grafton Street, St Stephen's Green, Merrion Square, Temple Bar.

→ **TWO DAYS**
  Christ Church Cathedral, Dublin Castle, Chester Beatty Library, the quayside.

→ **THREE DAYS**
  O'Connell Street, Parnell Square, Dublin Writers' Museum, DART train to the coast.

PRACTICAL INFORMATION

ARRIVAL-DEPARTURE

 Dublin Airport is 7 miles north. There are a number of coaches and buses, including Airlink and Aircoach, which take approximately 30mins.

GETTING AROUND

The bus network covers the whole city from the Central Bus Station in Store Street and is cheap and efficient, while the exciting LUAS (meaning 'speed') light rail network will get you to places a little quicker; ticket prices for both relate to the number of stages travelled. If you want to visit the coast, then jump on a DART (Dublin Area Rapid Transport) train. They operate at regular intervals, are amazingly efficient, and leave central Dublin from Connolly, Tara Street and Pearse stations. If you'd rather spend your time in the city, the Dublin Pass provides access to over thirty attractions, and ranges from one to six days.

CALENDAR HIGHLIGHTS

March
St Patrick's Day, Celtic Flame, Temple Bar Fleadh (traditional music)

April
Colours Boat Race, Feis Ceoil (classical music).

June
Bloomsday.

July-August
Diversions (free concerts and open-air theatre).

August
Horse Show.

September
Fringe Theatre Festival.

October
Dublin Theatre Festival.

November
Opera Ireland.

EATING OUT

It's still possible to indulge in Irish stew but nowadays you can also dine on everything from tacos and Thai to Malaysian and Middle Eastern cuisine, particularly in the Temple Bar area. The city makes the most of its bay proximity, so seafood features highly, with smoked salmon and oysters the favourites; the latter washed down with a pint of Guinness. Meat is particularly tasty in Ireland, due to the healthy livestock and a wet climate, and Irish beef is world famous for its fulsome flavour. However, there's never been a better time to be a vegetarian in Dublin, as every type of veg from spinach to seaweed now features, and chefs insist on the best seasonal produce, cooked for just the right amount of time to savour all the taste and goodness. Dinner here is usually served until about 10pm, though many global and city centre restaurants stay open later. If you make your main meal at lunchtime, you'll pay considerably less than in the evening: the menus are often similar, but the bill in the middle of the day will probably be about half the price.

Shelbourne ⌂ 𝆺𝅥 ⊕ 🕸 ▢ & 🄰🄲 🔒 🚗

27 St Stephen's Grn. ✉ *D2* – ☏ *(01) 6634500*   Plan: **E3**
– www.theshelbourne.ie
265 rm 🖵 – 🛏190/750 € 🛏🛏190/750 € – 12 suites
• Grand Luxury • Classic • Elegant •

Famed hotel dating from 1824, overlooking an attractive green; this is where the 1922 Irish Constitution was signed. Elegant guest areas and classical architecture; it even has a tiny museum. The bar and lounge are THE places to go for drinks and afternoon tea. Chic spa and characterful, luxurious bedrooms.
Saddle Room – See restaurant listing

Merrion ⌂ � 𝆺𝅥 ▢ & 🄰🄲 🔒 🚗

Upper Merrion St ✉ *D2* – ☏ *(01) 6030600*   Plan: **F3**
– www.merrionhotel.com
142 rm – 🛏495/635 € 🛏🛏515/655 € – 🖵 29 € – 10 suites
• Townhouse • Luxury • Classic •

A classic Georgian façade conceals this luxury hotel; its opulent drawing rooms filled with antique furniture and fine artwork. Enjoy 'art afternoon tea' with a view of the formal parterre garden. Stylish bedrooms have an understated, classic feel and smart marble bathrooms. Compact spa with impressive pool. Accessible menu in the restaurant and barrel-ceilinged bar.

The Westbury ⌂ 𝆺𝅥 & 🄰🄲 🔒 🚗

Grafton St ✉ *D2* – ☏ *(01) 679 1122*   Plan: **E2**
– www.doylecollection.com/westbury
205 rm – 🛏190/535 € 🛏🛏190/535 € – 🖵 25 € – 8 suites
• Business • Luxury • Contemporary •

Well-run hotel with a stylish bar, a comfy lounge (popular for afternoon tea) and state-of-the-art conference facilities; modern artwork features throughout and service is excellent. Well-equipped, elegant bedrooms come in browns and creams. Dine in the formal Irish restaurant or the Parisian-style brasserie.

Westin ⌂ 𝆺𝅥 & 🄰🄲 🔒

Westmoreland St ✉ *D2* – ☏ *(01) 6451000*   Plan: **E2**
– www.thewestindublin.com
163 rm – 🛏150/600 € 🛏🛏150/600 € – 🖵 22 € – 13 suites
• Luxury • Business • Stylish •

Built in 1860 as a bank; now a smart hotel set over 6 period buildings, with comfy lounges and impressive conference rooms (the old banking hall features ornate plasterwork and chandeliers). Contemporary bedrooms have subtle Celtic touches and media hubs. Atmospheric 'Mint' sits within the old vaults.

Marker ⌂ 𝆺𝅥 ⊕ 🕸 ▢ & 🄰🄲 🔒 🚗

Grand Canal Sq. ✉ *D2* – ☏ *(01) 6875100*   Plan: **B1**
– www.themarkerhoteldublin.com – Closed 25-26 December
187 rm – 🛏199/425 € 🛏🛏199/425 € – 🖵 25 € – 3 suites
• Business • Luxury • Design •

Smart business hotel overlooking the canal basin, with extensive meeting facilities and a well-equipped spa and fitness centre. The striking angular lobby houses a stylish bar and a chic brasserie serving modern Irish cooking. Crisp, contemporary bedrooms have a minimalist style; some overlook the square.

Fitzwilliam ⌂ 𝆺𝅥 🄰🄲 🔒 🚗

St Stephen's Grn ✉ *D2* – ☏ *(01) 478 70 00*   Plan: **E3**
– www.fitzwilliamhotel.com
140 rm – 🛏169/500 € 🛏🛏169/500 € – 🖵 22 € – 3 suites
• Business • Modern •

Stylish, modern hotel set around an impressive roof garden. Contemporary bedrooms display striking bold colours and good facilities; most overlook the roof garden and the best have views over St Stephen's Green. The bright first floor brasserie offers original Mediterranean-influenced menus.
Thornton's – See restaurant listing

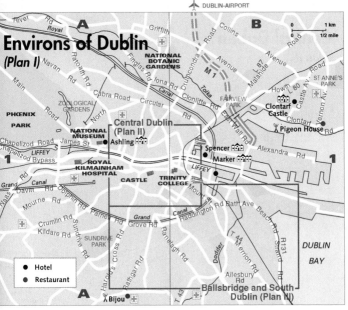

Environs of Dublin
(Plan I)

- Hotel
- Restaurant

DUBLIN BAY

Ballsbridge and South Dublin (Plan III)

Brooks

⇧ 🎿 ⅏ AC ⅏

Drury St ⊠ D2 – ℰ (01) 6704000 – www.brookshotel.ie   Plan: **E2**
98 rm ⊑ – †140/280 € ††140/280 € – 1 suite
• Business • Townhouse • Stylish •
Smart townhouse with a cosy basement lounge, good meeting facilities –including a screening room – and a stylish bar with a collection of over 150 whiskies. Bedrooms vary from traditional 'Classics' to modern 'Executives' with thoughtful extras. Good quality Irish ingredients feature in the restaurant.

Morrison

⇧ ⅃ઙ ⅏ AC ⅏

Ormond Quay ⊠ D1 – ℰ (01) 8872400   Plan: **D2**
– www.morrisonhotel.ie
145 rm – †140/400 € ††140/400 € – ⊑ 15 € – 4 suites
• Business • Luxury • Design •
Modern, centrally located hotel on the banks of the Liffey, opposite Temple Bar. Bright bedrooms with an Irish phrase on the wall, chic white furniture and either pink or blue cube lights and cushions; smart bathrooms. Appealing bar and a stylish restaurant specialising in steaks from the Josper grill.

Clarence

⇧ ⅏ ⅏ ⇩

6-8 Wellington Quay ⊠ D2 – ℰ (01) 4070800   Plan: **D2**
– www.theclarence.ie
51 rm – †109/259 € ††109/259 € – ⊑ 19 € – 5 suites
• Luxury • Design • Contemporary •
Stop for a drink in the famous domed cocktail bar of this old Customs House on the banks of the Liffey. Open fires and wood panelling feature throughout. Understated bedrooms combine Arts and Crafts styling with modern facilities.
Cleaver East – See restaurant listing

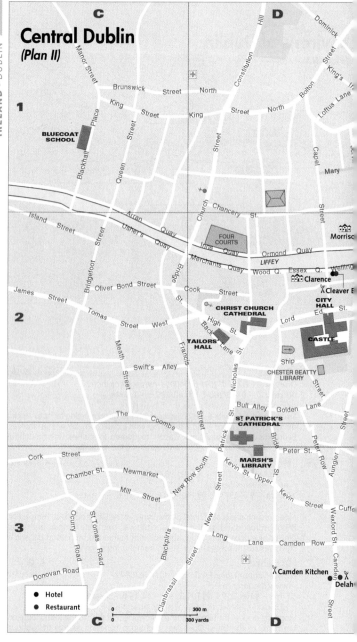

Central Dublin
(Plan II)

IRELAND - DUBLIN

BLUECOAT
SCHOOL

FOUR
COURTS

LIFFEY

Morriso

Clarence

Cleaver E

CHRIST CHURCH
CATHEDRAL

CITY
HALL

TAILORS'
HALL

CASTLE

CHESTER BEATTY
LIBRARY

St PATRICK'S
CATHEDRAL

MARSH'S
LIBRARY

Camden Kitchen

Delah

● Hotel
● Restaurant

0   300 m
0   300 yards

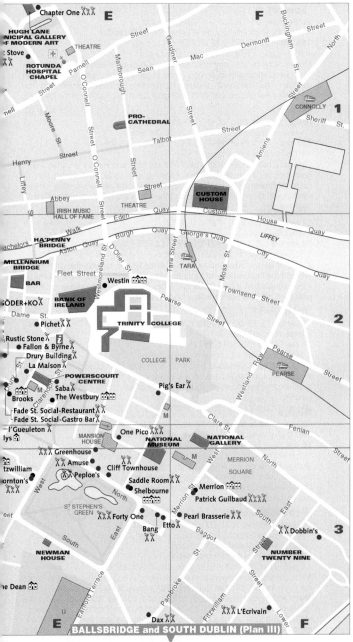

Chapter One ✕✕✕

HUGH LANE
MUNICIPAL GALLERY
OF MODERN ART

Stove ✕✕

THEATRE

ROTUNDA
HOSPITAL
CHAPEL

Dermontt   Street   Mac   Buckingham

E   F

Street   Gardiner

Parnell   O'Connell   Sean   Street

Moore   St.   Marlborough   CONNOLLY   1

Street   Sheriff   St.

PRO-
CATHEDRAL

Henry   Street   Street

Talbot   Street

Amiens

Liffey   O'Connell

Abbey   Street

IRISH MUSIC
HALL OF FAME   THEATRE   Quay   CUSTOM
HOUSE

Eden   Custom   House   Quay

HA'PENNY
BRIDGE   Walk   Burgh   Quay   George's Quay   LIFFEY

Aston Quay   D'Olier St.   City   Quay

MILLENNIUM
BRIDGE   Fleet Street   TARA   Moss St.   Townsend   Street

BAR   Westin 🏨

SÖDER+KO ✕   BANK OF
IRELAND   Pearse   2

Dame   St.   Pichet ✕✕

TRINITY   COLLEGE

Rustic Stone ✕   Pearse

Fallon & Byrne ✕   Street   Row

Drury Building ✕   COLLEGE   PARK   Pearse   Street

La Maison ✕   PEARSE

POWERSCOURT
CENTRE   Pig's Ear ✕

Saba ✕   Westland

Brooks 🏨   The Westbury 🏨

Fade St. Social-Restaurant ✕✕   Clare St.   Fenian

Fade St. Social-Gastro Bar ✕

l'Gueuleton ✕   One Pico ✕✕✕

lys 🏠   MANSION
HOUSE   NATIONAL
MUSEUM   NATIONAL
GALLERY

✕✕✕ Greenhouse   MERRION
SQUARE   North

tzwilliam   ✕✕ Amuse   Cliff Townhouse

ornton's   Peploe's   Saddle Room ✕✕   Merrion 🏨

✕✕✕   Shelbourne   Patrick Guilbaud ✕✕✕

ST STEPHEN'S   🏨

GREEN   ✕✕✕ Forty One   Pearl Brasserie ✕✕

Bang   Etto ✕   ✕✕ Dobbin's   3

✕✕   Baggot   St.

NEWMAN
HOUSE   South   NUMBER
TWENTY
NINE

he Dean 🏨   U

Dax ✕✕   Fitzwilliam   Lower   ✕✕✕ L'Ecrivain

E   **BALLSBRIDGE and SOUTH DUBLIN (Plan III)**   F

441

IRELAND - DUBLIN

Spencer

☆ ┢╅ 🏠 🗔 ₺ 🕵 🖄 🏧

Excise Walk, IFSC ✉ *D1 –* ☏ *(01) 433 8800*   Plan: **B1**
– www.thespencerhotel.com – Closed 24-27 December
166 rm – 🛏125/175 € 🛏🛏140/190 €
• Business • Modern • Minimalist •

Modern hotel by the Convention Centre – its basement leisure facility is a high-light. Sleek, minimalist bedrooms come in muted tones, with floor to ceiling windows and 'rainforest' showers; some have balconies overlooking the river. Enjoy European dishes in the lounge or Asian fusion dishes in the brasserie.

Ashling

☆ ₺ 🖄 🅿

Parkgate St. ✉ *D8 –* ☏ *(01) 677 2324*   Plan: **A1**
– www.ashlinghotel.ie – Closed 24-26 December
225 rm – 🛏89/199 € 🛏🛏97/259 € – ☲ 13 € – 1 suite
• Business • Functional •

Corporate hotel close to the tram and rail links and run by a cheery team. Bedrooms are a mix of classic and contemporary; some overlook the river or Guinness Brewery. The bar-lounge serves all day; the restaurant offers carvery lunches and an evening à la carte; and there are over 100 items at breakfast.

The Dean

☆ ₺ 🕵 🖄

33 Harcourt St ✉ *D2 –* ☏ *(01) 607 8110*   Plan: **E3**
– www.thedean.ie
52 rm – 🛏109/230 € 🛏🛏119/260 € – ☲ 15 € – 3 suites
• Townhouse • Stylish • Design •

A cool, informal, urban boutique. Stylish bedrooms include compact rooms named 'Mod Pods'; suites with record players, amps and guitars; and a penthouse with table football, a poker table and a bar! The moody lobby serves an all-day menu and loft-style Sophie's offers Mediterranean dishes and rooftop views.

Number 31

🖴

31 Leeson Cl. ✉ *D2 –* ☏ *(01) 6765011*   Plan: **H1**
– www.number31.ie
21 rm ☲ **–** 🛏135/240 € 🛏🛏175/240 €
• Townhouse • Design • Stylish •

Unusual and very individual property – once home to architect Sam Stephenson. It's classically styled around the 1960s, with a striking sunken lounge; the most modern bedrooms are found in the Georgian house across the terraced garden.

Kellys

First Floor, 36 South Great George's St ✉ *D2 –* ☏ *(01)*   Plan: **E2**
648 0010 – www.kellysdublin.com – Closed 24-26 December
16 rm ☲ **–** 🛏74/254 € 🛏🛏79/259 €
• Townhouse • Minimalist • Contemporary •

Shabby-chic hotel set among trendy boutiques and bars, in a bustling area. Stripped paint and white emulsioned walls hung with funky artwork; airy, open-plan lounge and bar; spacious, minimalist bedrooms. Breakfast in the restaurant below.

XXXX   **Patrick Guilbaud** (Guillaume Lebrun)   🕸 🕵 ⇔
❀❀   *21 Upper Merrion St* ✉ *D2 –* ☏ *(01) 6764192*   Plan: **F3**
– www.restaurantpatrickguilbaud.ie – Closed 25-31 December, 25 March,
Sunday, Monday and bank holidays
Menu 50/130 € – *(booking essential)*
• French modern • Elegant • Individual •

A truly sumptuous restaurant in an elegant Georgian house; the eponymous owner has run it for over 30 years. Accomplished, original cooking uses luxurious ingredients and mixes classical French cooking with modern techniques. Dishes are well-crafted and visually stunning with a superb balance of textures and flavours.

➔ Red king crab and cucumber maki, lemon croquant, Bombay Sapphire, mint and vanilla oil. Spiced Wicklow lamb, cauliflower two ways, glazed shiitake and crisp sweetbread. Iced caramélia and coffee croquant with Baileys ice cream.

IRELAND - DUBLIN

XxX   **Chapter One** (Ross Lewis)   🕸 ⇔ 🕸

❀   *The Dublin Writers Museum, 18-19 Parnell Sq ✉ D1*   Plan: **E1**
– 𝒞 (01) 8732266 – www.chapteronerestaurant.com – Closed 2 weeks
August, 2 weeks Christmas, Sunday, Monday and bank holidays
Menu 38/95 € *– (booking essential)*
• Modern cuisine • Formal • Design •
Stylish basement restaurant under the Writers Museum, with a modern bar and
several smart dining rooms hung with specially commissioned art. Various set
and tasting menus offer flavoursome, classically based dishes prepared using
modern techniques; the kitchen table has its own special menu. Service is slick.
→ Japanese pearl tapioca with Gabriel cheese, mushrooms and truffle. Turbot with salt baked celeriac, fried cabbage, Morteau sausage and razor
clams. Rose petal and lime jelly with poached rhubarb, white chocolate
ganache and yoghurt mousse.

XxX   **L'Ecrivain** (Derry Clarke)   🕸 🕸 ⇔ 🕸

❀   *109a Lower Baggot St ✉ D2 – 𝒞 (01) 6611919*   Plan: **F3**
– www.lecrivain.com – Closed Sunday and bank holidays
Menu 45/75 €
– Carte 67/78 € – (dinner only and lunch Thursday-Friday) (booking
essential)
• Modern cuisine • Friendly • Individual •
A well-regarded and busy restaurant with a glitzy bar, a whiskey-themed private
dining room and an attractive terrace. The refined, balanced menu has a classical foundation whilst also displaying touches of modernity; the ingredients
used are superlative. Service is structured yet has personality.
→ Scallops with cauliflower, capers, brown butter and vanilla. Suckling pig
with celeriac, langoustine, apple, walnut and celery. Caramelised milk chocolate with dark chocolate and tonka bean cream, white chocolate sorbet.

XxX   **Greenhouse** (Mickael Viljanen)   🕸

❀   *Dawson St ✉ D2 – 𝒞 (01) 676 7015*   Plan: **E3**
– www.thegreenhouserestaurant.ie – Closed 2 weeks July, 2 weeks
Christmas, Sunday and Monday
Menu 32 € (weekday lunch)/60 €
• Modern cuisine • Elegant • Fashionable •
Stylish restaurant with studded chairs, turquoise banquettes and smooth service. A plethora of menus include 3, 5 or 7 course midweek dinners and a 5
course 'Surprise' on Friday and Saturday evening. Accomplished, classically
based cooking has stimulating flavour combinations and subtle modern overtones.
→ Crab and scallop lasagne, cucumber and buttermilk. Roast rump-cap of
beef with winter vegetables and Alsace bacon cream. Passion fruit soufflé
with white chocolate sauce.

XxX   **Thornton's** – Fitzwilliam Hotel   🕸 ♿ 🕸 🕸 🕸 🚗
   128 St Stephen's Grn. ✉ D2 – 𝒞 (01) 4787008   Plan: **E3**
– www.thorntonsrestaurant.com – Closed 24 December-2 January, Sunday
and Monday
Menu 45/75 € *– (dinner only and lunch Friday-Saturday)*
• Modern cuisine • Formal • Intimate •
Elegant first floor restaurant overlooking St Stephen's Green. Eye-catching
photo montages taken by the chef hang on the walls. Choose from a concise à
la carte or a 5 course tasting menu; modern cooking uses classic combinations.

XxX   **Forty One**   ⇔
   41 St. Stephen's Grn. ✉ D2 – 𝒞 (01) 6620000   Plan: **E3**
– www.restaurantfortyone.ie – Closed Good Friday, 2-17 August, 25-
30 December, Sunday and Monday
Menu 35 € (weekday lunch)/75 € *– Carte 60/78 € – (booking advisable)*
• Modern cuisine • Elegant • Intimate •
Intimate, richly furnished restaurant on the first floor of an attractive, creeper-
clad townhouse, in a corner of St Stephen's Green. Accomplished, classical cooking features luxurious Irish ingredients and personal, modern touches.

IRELAND - DUBLIN

XXX **One Pico**   AC ⇔ 🅿🗺
5-6 Molesworth Pl ⌨ D2 – 𝒞 (01) 6760300   Plan: **E3**
– www.onepico.com – Closed bank holidays
Menu 29/45 € – Carte 50/64 €
• French classic • Elegant •

Stylish, modern restaurant tucked away on a back street; a well-regarded place
that's a regular haunt for MPs. Muted colour scheme, mirrors and comfy banquettes; classic French cooking offers plenty of flavour.

XX **Pearl Brasserie**   AC 🗺
20 Merrion St Upper ⌨ D2 – 𝒞 (01) 6613572   Plan: **F3**
– www.pearl-brasserie.com – Closed 25 December and Sunday
Menu 25 € (lunch and early dinner) – Carte 33/60 €
• French classic • Brasserie •

Formal basement restaurant with a small bar-lounge and two surprisingly airy
dining rooms; sit in a stylish booth in one of the old coal bunkers. Intriguing
modern dishes have a classical base and Mediterranean and Asian influences.

XX **Amuse**   AC
22 Dawson St ⌨ D2 – 𝒞 (01) 639 4889 – www.amuse.ie   Plan: **E3**
– Closed 2 weeks Christmas-New Year, last week July, first week August,
Sunday and Monday
Menu 24 € (weekday lunch)/65 € – (booking advisable)
• Modern cuisine • Friendly • Individual •

Modern, understated décor provides the perfect backdrop for the intricate,
innovative cooking. Dishes showcase Asian ingredients – including kombu and
yuzu; which are artfully arranged according to their flavours and textures.

XX **Pichet**   AC 🗺
⊛ 14-15 Trinity St ⌨ D2 – 𝒞 (01) 6771060   Plan: **E2**
– www.pichetrestaurant.ie – Closed 25-26 December
Menu 25 € (lunch and early dinner) – Carte 32/56 € – (booking essential)
• French classic • Fashionable • Bistro •

You can't miss the blue canopies and enamel signs of this buzzy brasserie; bold
blue chairs and an enclosed terrace with a checkerboard floor make it equally
striking inside, too. Modern Mediterranean dishes arrive neatly presented, and a
good selection of wines are available by the glass and 'pichet'.

XX **Hot Stove**   🍴 🗺
38 Parnell Sq West ⌨ D1 – 𝒞 (01) 874 7778   Plan: **E1**
– www.thehotstove.ie – Closed 25 December- 9 January, Sunday and
Monday
Menu 20 € (lunch and early dinner) – Carte dinner 35/58 €
• International • Elegant • Romantic •

A popular pre-theatre spot, in the basement of a Georgian house; it takes its
name from the range in one of the immaculate, elegant dining rooms. Flavoursome cooking showcases seasonal Irish produce in carefully prepared dishes.

XX **Saddle Room** - Shelbourne Hotel   🕭 AC ⇔
27 St Stephen's Grn. ⌨ D2 – 𝒞 (01) 6634500   Plan: **E3**
– www.shelbournedining.ie
Menu 25 € – Carte 35/85 €
• Meats • Elegant • Fashionable •

Renowned restaurant with a history as long as that of the hotel in which it
stands. The warm, inviting room features intimate gold booths and a crustacea
counter. The menu offers classic dishes and grills; West Cork beef is a speciality.

XX **Bang**   AC ⇔ 🗺
11 Merrion Row ⌨ D2 – 𝒞 (01) 4004229   Plan: **E3**
– www.bangrestaurant.com
Menu 25 € – Carte 38/62 € – (dinner only and lunch Wednesday-Friday)
• Modern cuisine • Individual • Fashionable •

Stylish restaurant with an intimate powder blue basement, a bright mezzanine
level and a small, elegant room above. There are good value pre-theatre menus,
a more elaborate à la carte and tasting menus showcasing top Irish produce.

XX **Fade St. Social-Restaurant**   🕭 ⇩ 🍴 🌼

4-6 Fade St ⊠ D2 – ℰ (01) 604 0066   Plan: **E2**
– www.fadestsocial.com – Closed 25-26 December, Good Friday and lunch Saturday and Sunday
Menu 30/50 € – Carte 34/53 €
• Modern cuisine • Brasserie • Fashionable •
Have cocktails on the terrace then head for the big, modern brasserie with its raised open kitchen. Dishes use Irish ingredients but have a Mediterranean feel; they specialise in sharing dishes and large cuts of meat such as chateaubriand.

XX **Cliff Townhouse**   ⇦ ⇩ 🍴

22 St Stephen's Grn ⊠ D2 – ℰ (01) 6383939   Plan: **E3**
– www.theclifftownhouse.com – Closed 17 March, 25 March, 25-29 December and 1 January
9 rm ⌂ – ♦150/200 € ♦♦170/210 €
Menu 28 € (weekdays) – Carte 34/72 € – *(booking advisable)*
• Fish and seafood • Brasserie • Elegant •
Impressive Georgian townhouse overlooking the green. Large dining room with blue leather seating and a marble-topped oyster counter. Seafood-orientated menus offer plenty of choice, from fish and chips to seafood platters or market specials. Bedrooms display contemporary colour schemes and good comforts.

XX **Dax**   🅰🄲

23 Pembroke St Upper ⊠ D2 – ℰ (01) 6761494   Plan: **E3**
– www.dax.ie – Closed 10 days Christmas, Saturday lunch, Sunday and Monday
Menu 25 € (weekday lunch) – Carte 46/61 € – *(booking essential)*
• French • Individual •
Smart, masculine restaurant in the cellar of a Georgian townhouse near Fitzwilliam Square. Tried-and-tested French dishes use top Irish produce and flavours are clearly defined. The Surprise Menu best showcases the kitchen's talent.

XX **Dobbin's**   🍴 🕭 🅰🄲 ⇩

15 Stephen's Ln (via Stephen's Pl off Lower Mount St)   Plan: **F3**
⊠ D2 – ℰ (01) 6619536 – www.dobbins.ie – Closed 24 December-2 January, Saturday lunch, Sunday dinner, Mondays except December and bank holidays
Menu 25/40 € – Carte 39/54 € – *(booking essential)*
• Traditional cuisine • Individual •
Hidden away in a back alley. A small bar leads through to a long, narrow room with cosy leather booths, which opens into a spacious conservatory with a terrace. Good value lunch and early evening menus; cooking is in the classical vein.

XX **Peploe's**   🕭 🅰🄲 🍴

16 St Stephen's Grn. ⊠ D2 – ℰ (01) 6763144   Plan: **E3**
– www.peploes.com – Closed 25-26 December, Good Friday and lunch bank holidays
Menu 26 € (lunch and early dinner) – Carte 41/65 € – *(booking essential)*
• Mediterranean • Cosy • Brasserie •
Atmospheric cellar restaurant – formerly a bank vault – named after the artist. Comfy room with a warm, clubby feel and a large mural depicting the owner. The well-drilled team present Mediterranean dishes and an old world wine list.

X **Delahunt**   🕭 ⇩
🐌
39 Camden Street Lower ⊠ D2 – ℰ (01) 5984880   Plan: **D3**
– www.delahunt.ie – Closed 15 August-1 September, Sunday and Monday
Carte 33/43 € – *(dinner only and lunch Thursday-Saturday) (booking essential)*
• British modern • Bistro • Individual •
A former Victorian grocer's shop, mentioned in James Joyce's 'Ulysses'. The old counter is now a bar and the clerk's snug is a glass-enclosed private dining room. Lunch offer two choices per course and dinner, four. Precisely executed, flavoursome dishes are modern takes of time-honoured recipes.

445

Pig's Ear

4 Nassau St ⊠ D2 – ℰ (01) 6703865   Plan: **E2**
– www.thepigsear.ie – Closed first week January, Sunday and bank
holidays
Menu 22 € (lunch) – Carte 33/50 € – (booking essential)
• Modern cuisine • Bistro • Friendly •

Well-established restaurant in a Georgian townhouse overlooking Trinity College. Floors one and two are bustling bistro-style areas filled with mirrors and porcine-themed memorabilia; floor three is a private room with a Scandinavian feel. Good value menus list hearty dishes with a modern edge.

Etto

18 Merrion Row ⊠ D2 – ℰ (01) 678 8872 – www.etto.ie   Plan: **E3**
– Closed Sunday and bank holidays
Menu 28 € (weekday lunch) – Carte 29/43 € – (booking essential)
• Mediterranean • Rustic • Neighbourhood •

The name of this rustic restaurant means 'little' and it is totally apt! Blackboards announce the daily wines and the lunchtime 'soup and sandwich' special. Flavoursome dishes rely on good ingredients and have Italian influences; the chef understands natural flavours and follows the 'less is more' approach.

Osteria Lucio

The Malting Tower, Clanwilliam Terr ⊠ D2 – ℰ (01)   Plan: **H1**
662 4198 – www.osterialucio.com – Closed Christmas and bank holiday
Mondays
Menu 20 € (dinner) – Carte 24/41 €
• Italian • Intimate • Romantic •

Smart restaurant under the railway arches, run by two experienced chefs. Robust, rustic dishes showcase local produce, alongside ingredients imported from Italy; sit by the bar to watch pizzas being cooked in the oak-burning stove.

Drury Buildings

52-55 Drury St ⊠ D2 – ℰ (01) 960 2095   Plan: **E2**
– www.drurybuildings.com – Closed Good Friday
Menu 24/52 € – Carte 29/59 €
• Italian • Trendy • Brasserie •

A hip, laid-back 'New York loft': its impressive terrace has a retractable roof and reclaimed furniture features in the stylish cocktail bar, which offers cicchetti and sharing boards. The airy restaurant serves rustic Italian dishes.

Fade St. Social-Gastro Bar

4-6 Fade St ⊠ D2 – ℰ (01) 604 0066   Plan: **E2**
– www.fadestreetsocial.com – Closed 25-26 December and Good Friday
Menu 30 € (early dinner)
– Carte 19/40 € – (dinner only and lunch Saturday-Sunday) (booking
essential)
• International • Fashionable • Tapas bar •

Buzzy restaurant with an almost frenzied feel. It's all about a diverse range of original, interesting small plates, from a bacon and cabbage burger to a lobster hot dog. Eat at the kitchen counter or on leather cushioned 'saddle' benches.

La Maison

15 Castlemarket ⊠ D2 – ℰ (01) 672 7258   Plan: **E2**
– www.lamaisonrestaurant.ie – Closed 25-27 December and 1-2 January
Menu 26 € (weekday dinner) – Carte 22/47 €
• French classic • Bistro • Cosy •

Sweet little French bistro with tables on the pavement and original posters advertising French products. The experienced, Breton-born chef-owner offers carefully prepared, seasonal Gallic classics, brought to the table by a personable team.

✗ **SÖDER+KO** [AC]
64 South Great George's St ✉ *D2 –* ✆ *(01) 478 1590* Plan: E2
– www.soderandko.ie – Closed bank holidays
Menu 14/25 € – Carte 17/22 € – *(booking essential)*
• Asian • Musical • Fashionable •

A vast, vibrant bar-cum-bistro in a former nightclub, with numerous rooms and even a chill-out lounge. Skilfully prepared Asian small plates are a mix of the modern and the classic; they are appealing, satisfying and good value.

✗ **Rustic Stone** [icons] & [AC]
17 South Great George's St ✉ *D2 –* ✆ *(01) 707 9596* Plan: E2
– www.rusticstone.ie – Closed 25-26 December and 1 January
Menu 30/50 € – Carte 27/51 €
• Modern cuisine • Bistro • Fashionable •

Split-level restaurant offering something a little different. Good quality ingredients are cooked simply to retain their natural flavours and menus focus on healthy and special dietary options; some meats and fish arrive on a sizzling stone.

✗ **Fallon & Byrne** & [AC]
11-17 Exchequer St ✉ *D2 –* ✆ *(01) 4721000* Plan: E2
– www.fallonandbyrne.com – Closed 25-26 December, 1 January and Good Friday
Menu 25/40 € – Carte 31/57 €
• French classic • Bistro • Friendly •

A former telephone exchange: now a bustling New York style food emporium with a basement wine shop and bar and a first floor Parisian brasserie, where you sit among antique mirrors and dine from a menu of seasonal bistro classics.

✗ **l'Gueuleton** [icons] &
1 Fade St ✉ *D2 –* ✆ *(01) 6753708* Plan: E2
– www.lgueuleton.com – Closed 25-27 December, 1 January and Good Friday
Carte 20/48 €
• French classic • Bistro •

Rustic restaurant with beamed ceilings, Gallic furnishings, a shabby-chic bistro feel and a large pavement terrace. Flavoursome cooking features good value, French country classics which rely on local, seasonal produce. Service is friendly.

✗ **Cleaver East** – Clarence Hotel & [AC] [icon]
6-8 East Essex St ✉ *D2 –* ✆ *(01) 531 3500* Plan: D2
– www.cleavereast.ie – Closed Monday-Tuesday lunch
Menu 22 € (lunch and early dinner) – Carte dinner 33/49 €
• Modern cuisine • Brasserie • Fashionable •

Once the Clarence hotel's ballroom; now an industrial-style restaurant with old railway sleepers hanging from the ceiling and meat cleavers on the walls. Unfussy modern dishes have a Mediterranean edge; steaks are a speciality.

✗ **Camden Kitchen** Plan: D3
3a Camden Mkt, Grantham St ✉ *D8 –* ✆ *(01) 4760125*
– www.camdenkitchen.ie – Closed 24-26 December, Sunday and Monday
Menu 20/32 € – Carte 30/46 €
• Classic cuisine • Bistro • Neighbourhood •

Simple, modern, neighbourhood bistro set over two floors; watch the owner cooking in the open kitchen. Tasty dishes use good quality Irish ingredients prepared in classic combinations. Relaxed, friendly service from a young team.

✗ **Saba** & [AC]
26-28 Clarendon St ✉ *D2 –* ✆ *(01) 679 2000* Plan: E2
– www.sabadublin.com – Closed Good Friday and 25-26 December
Menu 14 € (weekday lunch)/30 € – Carte 24/47 €
• Thai • Fashionable • Simple •

Trendy, buzzy Thai restaurant and cocktail bar. Simple, stylish rooms with refectory tables, banquettes and amusing photos. Fresh, visual, authentic cooking from an all-Thai team, with a few Vietnamese dishes and some fusion cooking too.

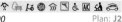

InterContinental Dublin

Simmonscourt Rd. ✉ *D4 – ✆ (01) 665 4000 – www.intercontinental.com/dublin* Plan: **J2**

197 rm ☕ – 🚹200/435 € 🚹🚹220/425 € – 40 suites

• Luxury • Business • Classic •

Imposing hotel bordering the RDS Arena. Elegant guest areas, state-of-the-art meeting rooms and impressive ballrooms boast ornate décor, antique furnishings and Irish artwork. Spacious, classical bedrooms have marble bathrooms and plenty of extras. A wide-ranging menu is served in the bright, airy restaurant.

Dylan

Eastmoreland Pl ✉ *D4 – ✆ (01) 6603000 – www.dylan.ie – Closed 24-26 December* Plan: **H1**

44 rm – 🚹239/395 € 🚹🚹239/395 € – ☕ 25 €

• Townhouse • Stylish • Design •

Red-brick Victorian nurses home with a sympathetically styled extension and a funky, boutique interior. Tasteful, individually decorated bedrooms offer a host of extras; those in the original building are the most spacious. The stylish restaurant offers a menu of modern Mediterranean dishes and comes complete with a zinc-topped bar and a smartly furnished terrace.

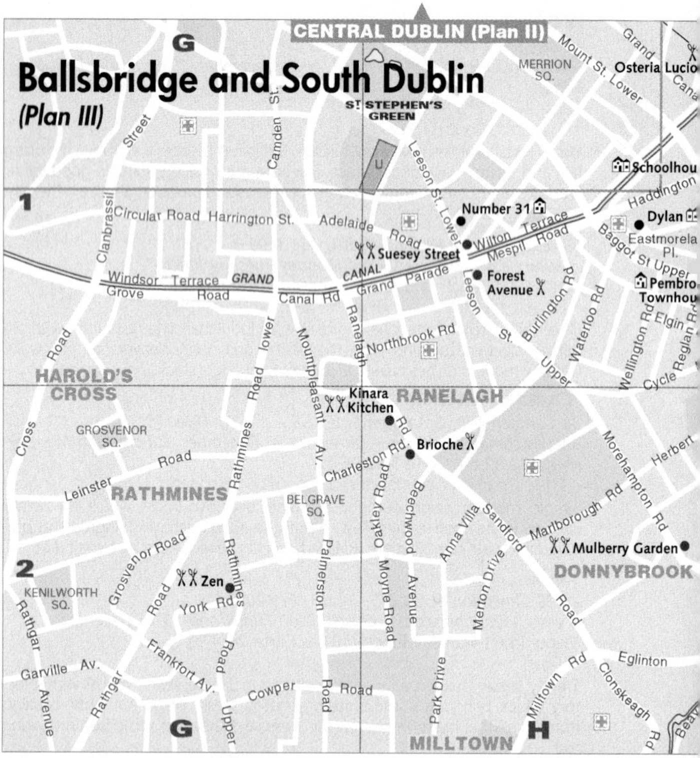

Herbert Park ⭐ 🛁 🅰🅲 🛎 🚗
✉ D4 – ℰ (01) 667 2200   Plan: **J2**
– www.herbertparkhotel.ie
153 rm – 🛏125/400 € 🛏🛏125/600 € – ☕ 22 € – 2 suites
• Business • Luxury • Modern •
Striking modern building with a stark white, open plan, marble-floored lobby
displaying eye-catching art. Comfortable bedrooms with plenty of natural
light; choose an executive room for more luxury. Chic terrace lounge and bar.
The Pavilion restaurant serves classic dishes and has park views.

Schoolhouse ⭐ 🍴 🅰🅲 🅿
2-8 Northumberland Rd ✉ D4   Plan: **H1**
– ℰ (01) 667 5014 – www.schoolhousehotel.com
– Closed 23-26 December
31 rm ☕ – 🛏109/299 € 🛏🛏119/309 €
• Historic • Business • Personalised •
Dating back to 1861 and formerly the St Stephen's Parochial School. Spacious,
well-kept bedrooms – most in the extension – boast William Morris designed
fabrics and locally built Mackintosh-style furniture; some have half-tester beds.
Busy bar with vaulted ceiling; formal restaurant serves classic dishes.

IRELAND - DUBLIN

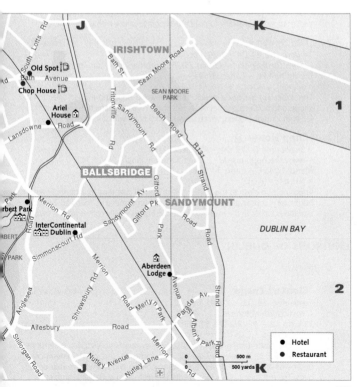

Ariel House

50-54 Lansdowne Rd ⊠ D4 – ℰ (01) 668 5512
Plan: **J1**
– www.ariel-house.net – Closed 22-28 December
37 rm � – †79/290 € ††79/290 €
• Townhouse • Luxury • Classic •

Close to the Aviva Stadium and a DART station; a personally run Victorian townhouse with comfy, traditional guest areas and antique furnishings. Warmly decorated bedrooms have modern facilities and smart bathrooms; some feature four-posters.

Pembroke Townhouse

88 Pembroke Rd ⊠ D4 – ℰ (01) 66 00 277
Plan: **H1**
– www.pembroketownhouse.ie – Closed 2 weeks Christmas-New Year
48 rm – †99/250 € ††99/250 € – ⊇ 15 €
• Townhouse • Traditional • Classic •

Friendly, traditionally styled hotel set in 3 Georgian houses. Small lounge with honesty bar and pantry. Sunny breakfast room offering homemade bread, cakes and biscuits. Variously sized, neutrally hued bedrooms; go for a duplex room.

Aberdeen Lodge

53-55 Park Ave. ⊠ D4 – ℰ (01) 283 8155
Plan: **J2**
– www.aberdeen-lodge.com
16 rm ⊇ – †90/109 € ††129/169 €
• Townhouse • Business • Classic •

Two Edwardian townhouses knocked through into a hotel; set in a smart suburban street, just minutes from the sea. It has a warm, homely atmosphere and well-equipped, classically furnished bedrooms – some with garden views.

Old Spot

14 Bath Ave ⊠ D4 – ℰ (01) 660 5599
Plan: **J1**
– www.theoldspot.ie – Closed 25-26 December and 1 January
Menu 30/40 € – Carte 32/50 €
• Traditional cuisine • Pub • Friendly •

The appealing bar has a stencilled maple-wood floor and a great selection of snacks and bottled craft beers. There's also a relaxed, characterful restaurant filled with vintage posters, which serves pub classics with a modern edge.

Chop House

2 Shelbourne Rd ⊠ D4 – ℰ (01) 6602390
Plan: **J1**
– www.thechophouse.ie – Closed Saturday lunch
Menu 32/45 € – Carte 30/55 €
• Meats • Pub •

Imposing pub close to the stadium, with a small side terrace, a dark bar and a bright, airy conservatory. The relaxed lunchtime menu is followed by more ambitious dishes in the evening, when the kitchen really comes into its own.

ENVIRONS OF DUBLIN

AT CLONTARF

Clontarf Castle

Castle Ave. ⊠ D3 – ℰ (01) 833 2321
Plan: **B1**
– www.clontarfcastle.ie
111 rm ⊇ – †129/249 € ††149/269 €
• Business • Castle • Historic •

A historic castle dating back to 1172, with sympathetic Victorian extensions; well-located in a quiet residential area close to the city. Contemporary bedrooms are decorated with bold, warm colours and many have four-poster beds. The restaurant offers local meats and seafood in a medieval ambience.

X **Pigeon House**

11b Vernon Ave ⊠ D3 – 𝒞 (01) 8057567   Plan: **B1**
– www.pigeonhouse.ie – Closed 25-26 December
Menu 25 € (dinner) – Carte 28/42 €
• Modern cuisine • Neighbourhood • Bistro •

Slickly run neighbourhood bistro that's open for breakfast, lunch and dinner. It's
just off the coast road in an up-and-coming area and has a lovely front terrace
and a lively feel. Cooking is modern and assured. The bar counter is laden with
freshly baked goodies and dishes are full of flavour.

AT **DONNYBROOK**

XX **Mulberry Garden**

Mulberry Ln (off Donnybrook Rd) ⊠ D4 – 𝒞 (01)   Plan: **H2**
269 3300 – www.mulberrygarden.ie – Closed Sunday-Wednesday
Menu 49/65 € – (dinner only and Sunday lunch in summer) (booking
essential)
• Modern cuisine • Individual • Intimate •

Delightful restaurant hidden away in the city suburbs; its interesting L-shaped
dining room set around a small courtyard terrace. Choice of two dishes per
course on the weekly menu; original modern cooking relies on tasty local produce.

AT **DUBLIN AIRPORT**

Radisson Blu H. Dublin Airport

– 𝒞 (01) 844 6000 – www.radissonblu.ie/hotel-dublinairport
229 rm ⊇ – †115/320 € ††160/320 € – 2 suites
• Chain hotel • Modern •

Modern commercial hotel with well-equipped conference rooms and good-
sized bedrooms. They offer 'Grab and Run' breakfasts and run a 24hr shuttle service to both terminals; and have arrival/departure screens and a check-in kiosk
in the lobby. The informal brasserie serves a wide-ranging international menu.

AT **RANELAGH**

XX **Kinara Kitchen**

17 Ranelagh Village ⊠ D6 – 𝒞 (01) 406 0066   Plan: **H2**
– www.kinarakitchen.ie – Closed 25-26 December and Good Friday
Menu 17/22 € (weekdays) – Carte 30/52 €
• Pakistani • Exotic • Neighbourhood •

This smart restaurant has become a destination not just for its cooking but for
its cocktails too. The friendly, professional team serve a menu of homely, well-
spiced Pakistani classics, including a selection from the tandoor oven.

X **Forest Avenue**

8 Sussex Terr. ⊠ D4 – 𝒞 (01) 667 8337   Plan: **H1**
*– www.forestavenuerestaurant.ie – Closed last 2 weeks August,
25 December-10 January, Easter, Monday and Tuesday*
Menu 27 € (weekday lunch)/49 € – (booking essential)
• Modern cuisine • Neighbourhood • Rustic •

This rustic neighbourhood restaurant is named after a street in Queens and has
a fitting 'NY' vibe, with its jam jar and antler light fittings and stags' heads lining
the walls. Top ingredients feature in well-crafted modern dishes.

X **Brioche**

51 Elmwood Ave Lower ⊠ D6 – 𝒞 (01) 4979163   Plan: **H1**
*– www.brioche.ie – Closed 25-27 December, 1 January, Sunday, Monday
and lunch Tuesday-Wednesday*
Menu 23/49 € – Carte 36/55 €
• Modern cuisine • Bistro • Neighbourhood •

As the name suggests, it's all about France at this lovely bistro in this buzzy, village-like district. Attractive modern French-inspired small plates use top Irish
ingredients; three should suffice, followed by cheese or dessert.

IRELAND - DUBLIN

AT RATHGAR

✗ **Bijou** 🛜 ⅙ 🅰🅲 ⇔
46 Highfield Rd ⊠ D6 – 𝒸 (01) 496 1518 Plan: **A1**
– www.bijourathgar.ie – Closed 25-26 December
Menu 20/35 € – Carte 29/42 €
• British modern • Brasserie • Classic •

Friendly restaurant with dining spread over two levels and a clubby heated terrace complete with a gas fire. Local ingredients feature in classically based dishes with modern touches. The experienced owners also run the nearby deli.

AT RATHMINES

✗✗ **Zen** ⅙ 🅰🅲
89 Upper Rathmines Rd ⊠ D6 – 𝒸 (01) 4979428 Plan: **G2**
– www.zenrestaurant.ie – Closed 25-27 December
Menu 24 € – Carte 23/34 € – *(dinner only and Friday lunch)*
• Chinese • Elegant •

Long-standing family-run restaurant, unusually set in an old church hall. At the centre of the elegant interior is a huge sun embellished with gold leaf. Imaginative Chinese cooking centres around Cantonese and spicy Sichuan cuisine.

ITALY
ITALIA

→ **Area:**
301 262 km² (116 317 sq mi).

→ **Population:**
60 795 612 inhabitants.
Density = 201 per km².

→ **Capital:**
Rome.

→ **Currency:**
Euro (€).

→ **Government:**
Parliamentary republic with two chambers (since 1946). Member of European Union since 1957 (one of the 6 founding countries).

→ **Language:**
Italian.

→ **Public holidays:**
New Year's Day (1 Jan); Epiphany (6 Jan); Easter Monday (late Mar/Apr); Liberation Day (25 Apr); Labor Day (1 May); Republic Day (2 June); Assumption of the Virgin Mary (15 Aug); All Saints' Day (1 Nov); Immaculate Conception (8 Dec); Christmas Day (25 Dec); St Stephen's Day (26 Dec).

→ **Local Time:**
GMT+1 hour in winter and GMT +2 hours in summer.

→ **Climate:**
Temperate Mediterranean with mild winters and hot, sunny summers (Rome: January 8°C; July 25°C).

→ **Emergency:**
Police ✆ **112**; Medical Assistance ✆ **118**; Fire Brigade ✆ **115**. (Dialling **112** within any EU country will redirect your call and contact the emergency services.)

→ **Electricity:**
230 volts AC, 50Hz; 2 round pin sockets.

→ **Formalities:**
Travellers from the European Union (EU), Switzerland, Iceland and the main countries of North and South America need a national identity card or passport (America: passport required) to visit Italy for less than three months (tourism or business purpose). For visitors from other countries a visa may be required, in addition to a passport, especially for those wishing to stay for longer than three months. We advise you to check with your embassy before travelling.

ROME
ROMA

Population: 2 872 021

Marie-Louise Detoux/Fotolia.com

Rome wasn't built in a day, and, when visiting, it's pretty hard to do it justice in less than three. The Italian capital is richly layered in Imperial, Renaissance, baroque and modern architecture, and its broad piazzas, hooting traffic and cobbled thoroughfares all lend their part to the heady fare: a theatrical stage cradled within seven famous hills. Being Eternal, Rome never ceases to feel like a lively, living city, while at the same time a scintillating monument to Renaissance power and an epic centre of antiquity. Nowhere else offers such a wealth of classical remains; set alongside palaces and churches, and bathed in the soft, golden light for which it is famous. When Augustus became the first Emperor of Rome, he could hardly have imagined the impact his city's language, laws and calendar would have upon the world.

The River Tiber snakes its way north to south through the heart of Rome. On its west bank lies the characterful and 'independent' neighbourhood of Trastevere, while north of here is Vatican City. Over the river the Piazza di Spagna area to the north has Rome's smartest shopping streets, while the southern boundary is marked by the Aventine and Celian hills, the latter overlooking the Colosseum. Esquiline's teeming quarter is just to the east of the city's heart; that honour goes to The Capitol, which gave its name to the concept of a 'capital' city.

ROME IN...

→ ONE DAY
Capitol, Forum, Colosseum, Pantheon, Trevi Fountain, Spanish Steps.

→ TWO DAYS
Via Condotti, Piazza Navona and surrounding churches, Capitoline museums.

→ THREE DAYS
A day on the west bank of the Tiber at Trastevere, Vatican City.

PRACTICAL INFORMATION

ARRIVAL-DEPARTURE

Leonardo da Vinci Airport at Fiumicino is 32km southwest of Rome. The Fiumicino Leonardo Express train to Stazione Termini runs every 30min and takes 35min. Every 30min the Cotral bus travels to Cornelia Station (Metro Line A).

GETTING AROUND

Rome is served by a metro, bus and tram system. Tickets are available from metro stations, bus terminals, ticket machines, tobacconists, newsagents, cafés and tourist information centres. Choose your ticket type: a single ticket, which must be time stamped on board, or travelcards for one, three or seven days. Rome is best seen on foot, so make sure you have a good pair of walking shoes. Avoid the likes of sleeveless tops, shorts and miniskirts if you want to visit religious sites.

CALENDAR HIGHLIGHTS

February
Carnival.

March
Spring Festival, Independent Film Festival, Cultural Heritage Week, Rome Marathon.

April
Rome's Birthday, Parklife Festival.

June-August
Cinema Isle.

June-September
The Roman Summer.

July
Festa de Noantri, Tevere Expo.

July-August
Secret Passages.

July-September
New Operafestival.

September
White Night.

October
Rome Film Festival.

November
Romaeuropa Festival.

EATING OUT

Despite being Italy's capital, Rome largely favours a local, traditional cuisine, typically found in an unpretentious trattoria or osteria. Although not far from the sea, the city doesn't go in much for fish, and food is often connected to the rural, pastoral life with products coming from the surrounding Lazio hills, which also produce good wines. Pasta, of course, is not to be missed, and lamb is favoured among meats for the main course. So too, the 'quinto quarto': a long-established way of indicating those parts of the beef (tail, tripe, liver, spleen, lungs, heart, kidney) left over after the best bits had gone to the richest families. For international cuisine combined with a more refined setting, head for the elegant hotels: very few other areas of Italy have such an increasing number of good quality restaurants within a hotel setting. Locals like to dine later in Rome than say, Milan, with 1pm, or 8pm the very earliest you'd dream of appearing for lunch or dinner. In the tourist hotspots, owners are, of course, only too pleased to open that bit earlier.

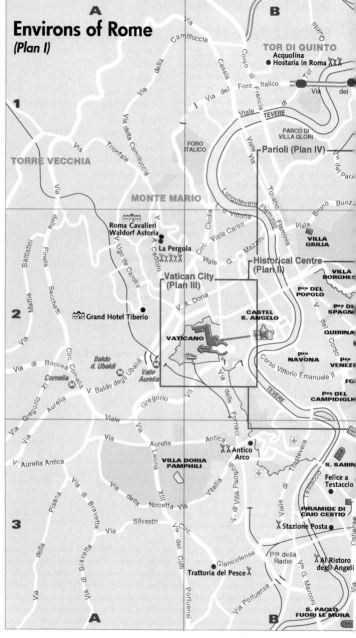

Environs of Rome
(Plan I)

A **B**

TOR DI QUINTO
Acquolina
● Hostaria in Roma

PARCO DI
VILLA GLORI

Parioli (Plan IV)

TORRE VECCHIA

MONTE MARIO

Roma Cavalieri
Waldorf Astoria

La Pergola

**VILLA
GIULIA**

**Historical Centre
(Plan II)**

**VILLA
BORGHES**

Pza DEL
POPOLO

**Vatican City
(Plan III)**

Grand Hotel Tiberio

VATICANO

**CASTEL
S. ANGELO**

Pza DI
SPAGN

QUIRINA

Baldo
d. Ubaldi

Cornelia

Valle
Aurelia

NAVONA

Pza
VENEZI

Corso Vittorio Emanuele II

FO

Pza DEL
CAMPIDIGLI

Antico
Arco

**VILLA DORIA
PAMPHILI**

S. SABIN

Felice a
Testaccio

**PIRAMIDE DI
CAIO CESTIO**

Stazione Posta

Pza della
Radio

Al Ristoro
degli Angeli

Trattoria del Pesce

**S. PAOLO
FUORI LE MURA**

A **B**

456

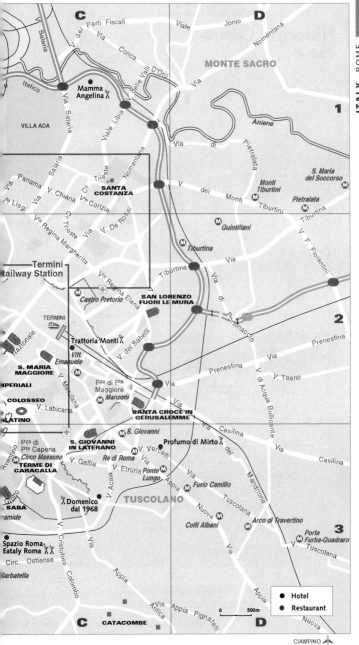

C
Parti Fiscali
Viale
Jonio
del
Via
Conca
Viale Valli D'Oro
Nomentana
D
MONTE SACRO
Salaria

Italico
Via
Salaria
● Mamma
Angelina ✗
Aniene

VILLA ADA

S. Maria
del Soccorso Ⓜ

Via
di
Pietralata

1

Via Salaria
Via
Panama
Ⓜ Liegi
V. Chiana
Co Trieste
V.le Corizia
Trieste
Co
Nomentana
SANTA
COSTANZA
Monti
Tiburtini Ⓜ
V. dei Monti
Pietralata Ⓜ

V.le Regina Margherita
Via
V. De Rossi
Via

Tiburtini
Tiburtina
V. F. Fiorentini

Ⓜ Quintiliani

**Termini
Railway Station**
V.le Regina Elena
Ⓜ Tiburtina

Tiburtina
Via
di
Portonaccio

Ⓜ Castro Pretorio
**SAN LORENZO
FUORI LE MURA**
●

TERMINI
Nazionale

Trattoria Monti ✗
V. dei Sabelli
Prenestina

2

**S. MARIA
MAGGIORE**
Vitt.
Emanuele Ⓜ
V. Merulana
Prenestina
V. di Acqua Bullicante
V. Teano

IMPERIALI

COLOSSEO
V. Labicana
P.za di P.ta
Maggiore
Ⓜ Manzoni
Via
Via
Casilina

LATINO
**SANTA CROCE IN
GERUSALEMME**
Casilina

P.za di
P.ta Capena
Circo Massimo
**S. GIOVANNI
IN LATERANO**
Ⓜ S. Giovanni
Profumo di Mirto ✗
del

**TERME DI
CARACALLA**
Re di Roma Ⓜ
Ⓜ V. Vercelli
V. Gallia
V. Etruria
Ponte
Lungo Ⓜ
Appia
Via
Mandrione

SABA
V. Acaia
Ⓜ Furio Camillo
Arco di Travertino Ⓜ

Piramide
✗ Domenico
dal 1968
TUSCOLANO
Nuova
Ⓜ Colli Albani
Tuscolana

● Spazio Roma-
Eataly Roma ✗✗
Circ. Ostiense
Via
Ⓜ Porta
Furba-Quadraro
V. Tuscolana

3

Barbatella
V. Cristoforo Colombo
Appia
Via
Antica
Appia
Appia Pignatelli
Nuova

●	Hotel
●	Restaurant

0   500m

C
CATACOMBE
D

CIAMPINO ✈

457

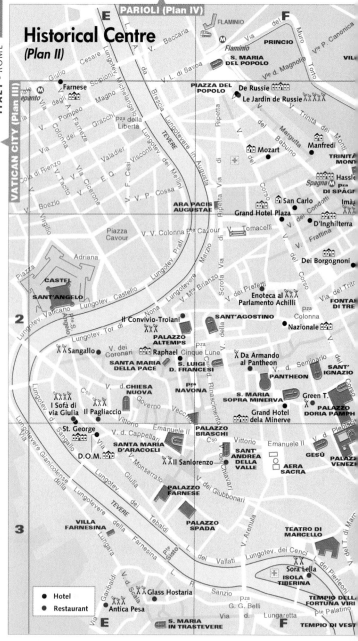

ITALY - ROME

VATICAN CITY (Plan III)

Historical Centre
(Plan II)

PARIOLI (Plan IV)

FLAMINIO

Flaminio

PRINCIO

S. MARIA
DEL POPOLO

Farnese

PIAZZA DEL
POPOLO

De Russie

Le Jardin de Russie

Mozart

Manfredi

TRINITÀ
MONT

Hassle

Spagna

Pza
DI SPAG

San Carlo

Imàg

Grand Hotel Plaza

ARA PACIS
AUGUSTAE

D'Inghilterra

Frattina

Dei Borgognoni

Piazza
Cavour

CASTEL
SANT'ANGELO

Enoteca al
Parlamento Achilli

Pza
Colonna

FONTA
DI TRE

Il Convivio-Troiani

SANT'AGOSTINO

Nazionale

PALAZZO
ALTEMPS

Sangallo

Raphael Cinque Lune

Da Armando
al Pantheon

SANT'
IGNAZIO

SANTA MARIA
DELLA PACE

S. LUIGI
D. FRANCESI

PANTHEON

d. CHIESA
NUOVA

Pza
NAVONA

S. MARIA
SOPRA MINERVA

Green T.

I Sofà di
via Giulia

Il Pagliaccio

Grand Hotel
dela Minerve

PALAZZO
DORIA PAMPH

St. George

PALAZZO
BRASCHI

GESÙ

PALAZZ
VENEZI

D.O.M.

SANTA MARIA
D'ARACOELI

Sanlorenzo

SANT'
ANDREA
DELLA VALLE

AERA
SACRA

PALAZZO
FARNESE

PALAZZO
SPADA

TEATRO DI
MARCELLO

VILLA
FARNESINA

Sora Lella

ISOLA
TIBERINA

TEMPIO DELL
FORTUNA VIRI

Glass Hostaria

Antica Pesa

S. MARIA
IN TRASTEVERE

TEMPIO DI VEST

● Hotel
● Restaurant

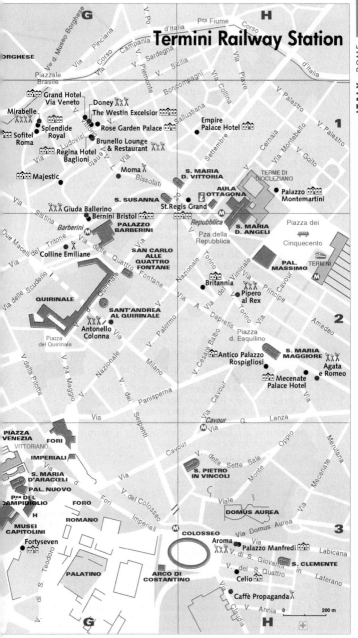

Termini Railway Station

Piazzale Brasile

Grand Hotel Via Veneto

Mirabelle

Doney

The Westin Excelsior

Splendide Royal

Rose Garden Palace

Empire Palace Hotel

Sofitel Roma

Brunello Lounge & Restaurant

Regina Hotel Baglioni

Moma

S. MARIA D. VITTORIA

Majestic

AULA OTTAGONA

TERME DI DIOCLEZIANO

Palazzo Montemartini

S. SUSANNA

Giuda Ballerino

St.Regis Grand

S. MARIA D. ANGELI

Bernini Bristol

Barberini

Repubblica

Piazza dei Cinquecento

PALAZZO BARBERINI

Pza della Repubblica

Colline Emiliane

SAN CARLO ALLE QUATTRO FONTANE

PAL. MASSIMO

TERMINI

QUIRINALE

Britannia

SANT'ANDREA AL QUIRINALE

Pipero al Rex

Antonello Colonna

Piazza del Quirinale

Piazza d. Esquilino

S. MARIA MAGGIORE

Antico Palazzo Rospigliosi

Agata e Romeo

Mecenate Palace Hotel

PIAZZA VENEZIA

FORI

VITTORIANO

IMPERIALI

S. MARIA D'ARACELI

PAL. NUOVO

Cavour

Pza DEL CAMPIDIGLIO

FORO

S. PIETRO IN VINCOLI

MUSEI CAPITOLINI

ROMANO

DOMUS AUREA

Fortyseven

PALATINO

COLOSSEO

Aroma

Palazzo Manfredi

S. CLEMENTE

ARCO DI COSTANTINO

Celio

Caffè Propaganda

0   200 m

ITALY - ROME

Hassler

piazza Trinità dei Monti 6 ✉ *00187 –* Ⓜ *Spagna*
– ☎ *06 699340 – www.hotelhasslerroma.com*   Plan: **F1**
96 rm – ♦295/505 € ♦♦375/920 € – ☕ 38 € – 14 suites
• **Grand Luxury** • **Historic** • **Historic** •
Superbly located at the top of the Spanish Steps, this hotel combines tradition, prestige and elegance. The height of splendour is reached in the magnificent suite that occupies the whole of the eighth floor. It has a private lift, additional accommodation for security staff, two panoramic terraces, modern furnishings and all the latest technology.
❀ **Imàgo** – See restaurant listing

De Russie

via del Babuino 9 ✉ *00187 –* Ⓜ *Flaminio*
– ☎ *06 328881 – www.roccofortehotels.com*   Plan: **F1**
122 rm – ♦385/671 € ♦♦499/869 € – ☕ 38 € – 34 suites
• **Grand Luxury** • **Historic** • **Personalised** •
Designed by Valadier during the early 19C, this hotel is furnished in a simple and harmonious style. It features elegant guestrooms and an attractive 'secret garden' scented with roses and jasmine. One of the best hotels in Rome.
Le Jardin de Russie – See restaurant listing

Indigo Rome St. George

via Giulia 62 ✉ *00186 –* ☎ *06 686611*   Plan: **E2**
– www.hotelindigo.com/romestgeorge
64 rm – ♦250/550 € ♦♦250/550 € – ☕ 25 €
• **Luxury** • **Traditional** • **Personalised** •
This boutique, designer-style hotel is in one of the most beautiful streets in Rome. It offers an elegant ambience and luxurious furnishings in its public areas and spacious guestrooms.
I Sofà di Via Giulia – See restaurant listing

Grand Hotel Plaza

via del Corso 126 ✉ *00186 –* Ⓜ *Spagna –* ☎ *06 67495*   Plan: **F2**
– www.grandhotelplaza.com
196 rm – ♦144/400 € ♦♦159/500 € – ☕ 20 € – 8 suites
• **Grand Luxury** • **Palace** • **Personalised** •
This hotel boasts huge, stunning, late-19C lounges decorated in Art Nouveau-style with coffered ceilings and a profusion of marble, frescoes and glass. The guestrooms are also furnished in period style, as is the atmospheric dining room. Panoramic terrace with a Champagne bar.

Grand Hotel de la Minerve

piazza della Minerva 69 ✉ *00186 –* ☎ *06 695201*   Plan: **F2**
– www.grandhoteldelaminerve.com
123 rm – ♦220/700 € ♦♦270/750 € – ☕ 35 € – 12 suites
• **Luxury** • **Stylish** •
An historic building surrounded by ancient monuments. Elegant atmosphere and an imaginative menu of traditional cuisine. Attractive views from the terrace.

D'Inghilterra

via Bocca di Leone 14 ✉ *00187 –* ☎ *06 699811*   Plan: **F2**
– www.niquesahotels.com
88 rm ☕ **–** ♦315/863 € ♦♦367/946 € – 7 suites
• **Grand Luxury** • **Historic** • **Historic** •
A haven for tourists from around the world since as early as the 17C, this hotel has the charming ambience of an elegant private house with delightful, individual-style guestrooms. Find elegant lounges, an atmospheric bar, and a restaurant serving simple, classic cuisine at lunchtime and more elaborate, ambitious fare in the evening.

Raphaël 👁 🖼 🛗 🛁

largo Febo 2 ✉ *00186 –* ☎ *06 682831*
Plan: **E2**
– www.raphaelhotel.com
49 rm ☲ – ♦180/430 € ♦♦230/605 € – 1 suite
• Palace • Luxury • Personalised •
With its collection of porcelain, antiquarian artefacts and sculptures by famous artists, the entrance to this hotel resembles a museum. The recently renovated guestrooms are modern in style. The menu in this attractive restaurant with a panoramic terrace focuses mainly on Italian cuisine, along with some French dishes.

Dei Borgognoni 🖼 🛁 🚗

via del Bufalo 126 ✉ *00187 –* Ⓜ *Spagna*
Plan: **F2**
– ☎ *06 69941505 – www.hotelborgognoni.it*
51 rm ☲ – ♦205/230 € ♦♦209/295 €
• Luxury • Traditional • Cosy •
Occupying a 19C palazzo, this elegant hotel's spacious, modern public rooms and comfortable guestrooms combine both traditional and modern features.

Nazionale 👁 🖼 🛁 ⇔

piazza Montecitorio 131 ✉ *00186 –* ☎ *06 695001*
Plan: **F2**
– www.hotelnazionale.it
100 rm ☲ – ♦185/290 € ♦♦290/390 € – 1 suite
• Luxury • Traditional • Elegant •
Overlooking Piazza di Montecitorio, this hotel occupies an 18C building with elegant public areas and guestrooms furnished in different styles. In this city so often crowded with visitors, the fact that the restaurant is open non-stop from noon until 7pm will appeal, as will the delicious Mediterranean cuisine.

Grand Hotel Tiberio 👁 🛏 🖼 🛁 🚗

via Lattanzio 51 ✉ *00136 –* Ⓜ *Cipro –* ☎ *06 399629*
Plan: **A2**
– www.ghtiberio.com
91 rm ☲ – ♦♦60/300 € – 5 suites
• Traditional • Elegant •
Hotel located in a quiet residential area that was once an industrial district. Large lobby with floor to ceiling windows, spacious comfortable rooms.

D.O.M. 👁 🖼 🛁

via Giulia 131 ✉ *00186 Roma –* ☎ *06 6832144*
Plan: **E3**
– www.domhotelroma.com
14 rm – ♦240/700 € ♦♦240/700 € – 4 suites
• Luxury • Modern •
The initials of this restaurant stand for Deo Optimo Maximo. The 17C palazzo combines decor from the adjacent church with contemporary furnishings, subtle colours and three works by Andy Warhol. Terrace bar on the top floor.

Grand Hotel del Gianicolo 👁 🛏 🖼 🛁 🚗

viale delle Mura Gianicolensi 107 ✉ *00152*
Plan: **B3**
– Ⓜ *Cipro Musei Vaticani –* ☎ *06 58333405 – www.grandhotelgianicolo.it*
48 rm ☲ – ♦110/475 € ♦♦130/475 €
• Traditional • Classic •
A stylish hotel on the Gianicolo offering comfortable guestrooms and elegant public areas. You also have the illusion of being a guest in a smart country house, thanks to the beautiful outdoor pool – an unusual sight in Rome. Contemporary cuisine is served in the Corte degli Angeli.

Piranesi-Palazzo Nainer 🛁 🛏 🖼

via del Babuino 196 ✉ *00187 –* Ⓜ *Flaminio*
Plan: **F1**
– ☎ *06 328041 – www.hotelpiranesi.com*
32 rm ☲ – ♦80/160 € ♦♦90/250 €
• Luxury • Traditional • Cosy •
The lobby, guestrooms and corridors of this hotel are decorated with marble, elegant furnishings and an unusual exhibition of old fabrics. The hotel also boasts a roof garden and sun terrace.

Manfredi

 AC

via Margutta 61 ✉ *00187 –* Ⓜ *Spagna –* ☎ *06 3207676* Plan: **F1**
– www.hotelmanfredi.it
22 rm ☻ – ♦100/379 € ♦♦120/499 € – 1 suite
• Inn • Traditional • Elegant •

Housed on the third floor of a palazzo on the famous Via Margutta. Elegant, individually furnished guestrooms, all of which boast the latest in modern facilities. Excellent international breakfast of natural products, including yoghurt and homemade pastries.

Mozart

AC

via dei Greci 23/b ✉ *00187 –* Ⓜ *Spagna* Plan: **F1**
– ☎ *06 36001915 – www.hotelmozart.com*
78 rm ☻ – ♦79/299 € ♦♦89/349 €
• Traditional • Family • Cosy •

Housed in a 19C palazzo, this hotel boasts elegant public areas and guestrooms in the same refined style. The Vivaldi Luxury Rooms annexe situated just a stone's throw from the hotel offers slightly larger, modern rooms, as well as its own breakfast room.

Fontanella Borghese

AC

largo Fontanella Borghese 84 ✉ *00186 –* Ⓜ *Spagna* Plan: **F2**
– ☎ *06 68809504*
– www.fontanellaborghese.com
24 rm ☻ – ♦80/135 € ♦♦100/210 €
• Family • Inn • Personalised •

In a central yet peaceful location, on the 2nd and 3rd floors of a historical building looking out over Palazzo Borghese is this distinguished and refined hotel with classy finishings.

San Carlo

AC

via Delle Carrozze 92/93 ✉ *00187 –* Ⓜ *Spagna* Plan: **F1**
– ☎ *06 6784548 – www.hotelsancarloroma.com*
50 rm ☻ – ♦80/125 € ♦♦100/195 €
• Traditional • Cosy •

This inviting hotel is parallel to via Condotti. It offers pleasant guestrooms and a charming breakfast terrace, which is particularly delightful in the summer months.

XxXxX ### Le Jardin de Russie – Hotel De Russie

via del Babuino 9 ✉ *00187 –* Ⓜ *Piazzale Flaminio* Plan: **F1**
– ☎ *06 32888870 – www.roccofortehotels.com*
Menu 39 € (lunch) – Carte 68/126 €
• Mediterranean • Luxury • Formal •

Despite its French name, this restaurant serves creative reinterpretations of distinctly Italian cuisine. This is prepared by Fulvio Pierangelini, one of Italy's great chefs. Extremely elegant atmosphere.

XxxX ### Imàgo – Hotel Hassler

AC

piazza Trinità dei Monti 6 ✉ *00187 –* Ⓜ *Spagna* Plan: **F1**
– ☎ *06 69934726 – www.imagorestaurant.com*
Menu 120/140 € – Carte 97/150 € – *(dinner only)*
• Modern cuisine • Luxury • Friendly •

This restaurant continues to be a perennial favourite, thanks to its large windows and unforgettable views of Rome. Modern cuisine made with high quality ingredients.

→ Cappellotti di parmigiano in brodo freddo di tonno, doppio malto e 7 spezie. Merluzzo carbonaro glassato al sake, verdurine in campo viola. Babà in sospensione al cioccolato e sake, ghiacciato alla banana.

ITALY - ROME

XXXX Hostaria dell'Orso 🕮 🎐 AC ⇄

via dei Soldati 25/c ✉ *00186*   Plan: **E-F2**
– ℰ 06 68301192 – www.hdo.it
– Closed August and Sunday
Carte 116/155 € *– (dinner only) (booking advisable)*
• **Modern cuisine** • **Luxury** • **Traditional** •
Housed in an historic building, this restaurant has intimate, romantic dining
rooms decorated in a simple, elegant style. The elegant cuisine is based around
the highest quality ingredients.

XXX Il Convivio-Troiani *(Angelo Troiani)* 🕮 AC ⇄
❀

vicolo dei Soldati 31 ✉ *00186*   Plan: **E2**
– ℰ 06 6869432 – www.ilconviviotroiani.com
– Closed 1 week in August, 23-26 December and Sunday
Menu 110 € *–* Carte 81/145 € *– (dinner only)*
• **Modern cuisine** • **Luxury** • **Formal** •
This elegant restaurant is in the heart of the historic centre. Amid a decor of fres-
coes, paintings and modern minimalism, enjoy quintessential Italian cuisine.
Choose from risottos and pasta, as well as a selection of specialities from the
Lazio region.
➜ Linguina di farro alla "carbomare". Dall'agnello: quattro differenti prepa-
razioni con le diverse parti del carré. Tiramisù : ieri, oggi e domani.

XXX Il Pagliaccio *(Anthony Genovese)* 🕮 AC
❀❀

via dei Banchi Vecchi 129/a ✉ *00186 – ℰ 06 68809595*   Plan: **E2**
– www.ristoranteilpagliaccio.it
*– Closed 3 weeks in August, 25 January-8 February, Sunday, Monday and
Tuesday lunch*
Menu 75 € (lunch)/155 € *–* Carte 95/135 € *– (booking advisable)*
• **Creative** • **Formal** • **Luxury** •
This restaurant is a breath of modernity in the heart of Renaissance Rome. It is
constantly on the lookout for new products, creating innovative dishes from traditional favourites.
➜ Spaghetti di grano arso con olio, peperoncino, lumache di mare e
gelato di cannolicchi. Faraona con ostrica grigliata, rape, crema di limone
e burrata. Sorbetto di albicocca con soffice alla ricotta e caramello alle
mandorle.

XXX Antica Pesa 🕮 🎐 AC

via Garibaldi 18 ✉ *00153 – ℰ 06 5809236*   Plan: **E3**
– www.anticapesa.it – Closed Sunday
Carte 52/86 € *– (dinner only)*
• **Roman** • **Elegant** • **Cosy** •
Typical Roman dishes made from carefully selected ingredients grace the menu
of this restaurant, which is housed in a grain storehouse that once belonged to
the neighbouring Papal State. Large paintings by contemporary artists hang on
the walls and there is a small lounge with a fireplace near the entrance.

XXX Il Sanlorenzo 🕮 AC ⇄

via dei Chiavari 4/5 ✉ *00186 – ℰ 06 6865097*   Plan: **F3**
*– www.ilsanlorenzo.it – Closed 10-31 August, Sunday, lunch Monday and
Saturday*
Menu 65/85 € *–* Carte 74/144 €
• **Modern cuisine** • **Elegant** • **Trendy** •
Built over the foundations of the Teatro Pompeo, this palazzo now houses an
atmospheric restaurant, which combines a sense of history with contemporary
style. Modern cuisine and fish specialities.

XxX   **Enoteca al Parlamento Achilli**   🕸 🎍 🅰🅲

via dei Prefetti 15 ✉ *00186* – 🅜 *Spagna*   Plan: **F2**
– 🕾 06 6873446 – www.enotecalparlamento.com – Closed 20 days in
August, 10 days in January and Sunday
Menu 120 € – Carte 85/165 €
• **Creative** • **Elegant** •
Although there is little to suggest a restaurant from the exterior, this elegant
wine bar in the city centre leads to two wood-vaulted and interconnecting
dining rooms. The striking individual cuisine is based on bold combinations
and contrasts, perfect for anyone looking for a change from more traditional
fare. A truly delightful and imaginative exploration of culinary flavours!
➔ Rapa, castagne, tartufo e triglia. Lepre stile royal. Gelato al sigaro e
prugne farcite al foie gras.

XxX   **I Sofà di Via Giulia** – Hotel St. George   🎍 ♿ 🅰🅲

via Giulia 62 ✉ *00186* – 🕾 *06 68661245*   Plan: **E2**
– www.isofadiviagiulia.com
Carte 44/77 €
• **Modern cuisine** •
Regional cuisine with a modern twist, and an impressive wine list that more
than meets the high standards of this restaurant. Lively, designer-style decor,
as well as a delightful roof garden for summer dining with panoramic views of
the city centre as a backdrop.

XX   **Sangallo ai Coronari**   🎍 🅰🅲 ♻

via dei Coronari 180 ✉ *00186* – 🕾 *06 68134055*   Plan: **E2**
– www.ristorantesangallo.com – Closed 9-23 August
Menu 50/85 €
– Carte 61/91 € – (dinner only 2 August to 6 September) (booking advi-
sable)
• **Modern cuisine** • **Elegant** • **Traditional** •
A pleasing blend of old and new in a 16C palazzo near San Salvatore in Lauro
church. Various elegant dining rooms act as a stylish setting for the contemporary cuisine.

XX   **Glass Hostaria** (Cristina Bowerman)   🕸 🅰🅲

vicolo del Cinque 58 ✉ *00153* – 🕾 *06 58335903*   Plan: **E3**
– www.glasshostaria.it – Closed 4-26 July, 24-26 December, 11-26 January
and Monday
Menu 75/100 € – Carte 64/100 € – *(dinner only)*
• **Creative** • **Design** • **Fashionable** •
Situated in the heart of Trastevere, this restaurant boasts an ultra-modern
design with an interesting play of light and slightly unsettling atmosphere. The
excellent cuisine also features highly modern touches.
➔ Ravioli di foie gras con mele e amaretto. Astice, mango, yogurt, pepe
rosa e polvere di 'nduja. Zuppetta di caffè, latte condensato, mandorle sab-
biate e gelato al Baileys.

XX   **Sora Lella**   🅰🅲

via di Ponte Quattro Capi 16 (Tiber Island) ✉ *00186*   Plan: **F3**
– 🕾 06 6861601 – www.trattoriasoralella.it – Closed 12-19 August,
Tuesday and Sunday in July-August
Menu 48/55 € – Carte 36/75 €
• **Roman** • **Family** • **Friendly** •
Son and grandchildren of the famous late Sora Lella, perpetuate in a dignified
way the tradition both in the warmth of the welcome and in the typical Roman
elements of the offer.

Felice a Testaccio Ⓚ

via Mastrogiorgio 29 ✉ *00153 –* ☏ *06 5746800* Plan: B3
– www.feliceatestaccio.com – Closed 1 week in August
Carte 34/46 € *– (booking advisable)*
• Roman • Family • Friendly •
One of the standard-bearers of cuisine from Lazio, this simple trattoria with a family atmosphere is now so popular that it is advisable to book your table in advance. Make sure you try the legendary pasta all'amatriciana (bacon and tomato sauce).

Da Armando al Pantheon Ⓚ

salita dè Crescenzi 31 – Ⓜ *Spagna –* ☏ *06 68803034* Plan: F2
– www.armandoalpantheon.it – Closed August, Saturday dinner, Sunday
Carte 34/66 € *– (number of covers limited, pre-book)*
• Roman • Family • Friendly •
Just a few metres from the Pantheon, this small family-run restaurant has been delighting locals and visitors for years with its traditional cuisine. Booking ahead is essential if you want to be sure of a table.

Green T. Ⓚ ⇔

Via del Piè di Marmo 28 ✉ *00186 –* ☏ *06 679 8628* Plan: F2
– www.green-tea.it – Closed 2 weeks in August, Sunday
Menu 9 € (weekday lunch)/17 € – Carte 29/66 €
• Chinese • Minimalist • Friendly •
Owner Yan introduces tea lovers to the 'Tao of Tea' (an introduction and tasting of this ancient beverage) in this original restaurant situated on four floors of a building not far from the Pantheon. Asian cuisine takes pride of place on the menu.

ST-PETER'S BASILICA (Vatican City and Monte Mario) PLAN III

Rome Cavalieri Waldorf Astoria

via Cadlolo 101 ✉ *00136 –* ☏ *06 35091*
– www.romecavalieri.it Plan: A2
345 rm ⌸ – ♦274/925 € ♦♦299/950 € – 25 suites
• Grand Luxury • Classic •
This imposing hotel overlooks the entire city of Rome. The hotel has excellent facilities, including extensive gardens, an outdoor swimming pool, plus a fine art collection. Restaurant with an informal atmosphere by the edge of the swimming pool for dining with live music.
❀❀❀ **La Pergola** – See restaurant listing

Gran Melià Roma

via del Gianicolo 3 ✉ *00165 –* ☏ *06925901*
– www.granmeliarome.com Plan: K2
116 rm – ♦325/725 € ♦♦325/725 € – ⌸ 36 € – 22 suites
• Luxury • Chain hotel • Modern •
This hotel boasts a truly historic setting in an old monastery on the site of the villa that once belonged to Nero's mother, Agrippina. There is an elegant, modern feel to the public areas and guestrooms, some of which feature designer bathtubs that can be seen from the bed. A superb address with a charming atmosphere and an excellent choice of facilities.
Vivavoce – See restaurant listing

Villa Laetitia

lungotevere delle Armi 22/23 ✉ *00195 –* Ⓜ *Lepanto*
– ☏ *0 63 22 67 76 – www.villalaetitia.com* Plan: L2
21 rm ⌸ – ♦90/200 € ♦♦99/400 €
• Luxury • Elegant •
Enjoying a charming location on the banks of the Tiber, this delightful Art Nouveau villa welcomes its guests as if they were visiting a private home - and what a home! The elegant and individual guestrooms all bear the stamp of the famous designer, Anna Fendi.
❀ **Enoteca la Torre** – See restaurant listing

465

Vatican City
(Plan III)
J
K
1
2
Pzale degli Eroi
Cipro-Musei-Vaticani
Alimandi Vaticano
Ottaviano-S. Pietro
Piazza del Risorgimento
MUSEI VATICANI
Sant'Anna
Bramante
PIAZZA S.PIETRO
GIARDINI VATICANI
S. PIETRO
Piazza dei Quiriti
Galleria Principe Amadeo
Gran Melià Roma
Vivavoce
Viale Vaticano
Borgo Angelico
Borgo Pio
Borgo Vittorio
Borgo Santo Spirito
V. d. Conciliazione
Via Aurelia
Viale d. Milizie
Via Cola di Rienzo
Via Crescenzio
V. Germanico
V. degli Scipioni
Via Ottaviano
V. Otranto
V. Vespasiano
Via Leone IV
Via Candia
V. Andrea Doria
V. Trionfale
V. Sebastiano Veniero
Via d. Fornaci
Gianicolo
Hotel
Restaurant
0
200 m
HISTORICAL CENTRE / TERMINI RAILWAY STATION (Plan II)

Farnese

via Alessandro Farnese 30 ✉ *00192 –* Ⓜ *Lepanto* Plan: **E1**
– ✆ 06 3212553 – www.hotelfarnese.com
23 rm ☕ – 🚹99/310 € 🚹🚹99/610 €
• Traditional • Elegant •
Decorated in period style, this hotel has elegant rooms and an attractive lobby housing a 17C polychrome marble frontal. Fine views of St Peter's from the terrace.

Alimandi Vaticano

viale Vaticano 99 ✉ *00165 –* Ⓜ *Ottaviano-San Pietro* Plan: **J1**
– ✆ 06 39745562 – www.alimandi.com
24 rm ☕ – 🚹100/240 € 🚹🚹100/260 €
• Traditional • Elegant •
This pleasant hotel enjoys an excellent location directly opposite the Vatican Museums. The marble and wood decor in the well-appointed guestrooms adds to their elegant atmosphere.

Sant'Anna

borgo Pio 133 ✉ *00193 –* Ⓜ *Ottaviano-San Pietro* Plan: **K1-2**
– ✆ 06 68801602 – www.hotelsantanna.com
20 rm ☕ – 🚹90/150 € 🚹🚹130/250 €
• Traditional • Historic •
An original coffered ceiling and pleasant interior courtyard add a decorative touch to this small, welcoming hotel occupying a 16C building a short distance from St Peter's.

ITALY - ROME

Bramante 🏛 AC

vicolo delle Palline 24 ✉ *00193*   Plan: **K2**
– Ⓜ *Ottaviano-San Pietro* – 𝒞 *06 68806426* – www.hotelbramante.com
16 rm ☕ – †50/160 € ††100/230 €
• Historic • Elegant •
This historic hotel is situated in the heart of the typical, pedestrianised Borgo district. The oldest sections date back to the 15C.

La Pergola – Hotel Rome Cavalieri Waldorf Astoria 🏨 ≤ 🌳 &

𝕏𝕏𝕏𝕏𝕏
🕄🕄🕄   AC ⇄ 🅿
via Cadlolo 101 ✉ *00136* – 𝒞 *06 35092152*   Plan: **A2**
– www.romecavalieri.it – *Closed 2 weeks in*
August, January, Sunday and Monday
Menu 195 € (weekdays)/220 €
– Carte 115/204 € – *(dinner only) (booking essential)*
• Modern cuisine • Classic •
Proverbial Teutonic precision combines with Mediterranean flair at this restaurant to create a whole host of delicious and imaginative dishes. These can be enjoyed in the magnificent setting of a panoramic roof garden, with exquisite fabrics, Sèvres porcelain and an 18C candelabra completing the picture.
→ Ricciola marinata all'aceto balsamico bianco con neve di melograno. Fagottelli "La Pergola". Sfera ghiacciata ai frutti rossi su crema al tè con lamponi cristallizzati.

Vivavoce – Hotel Gran Melià Roma 🍴 & AC

𝕏𝕏𝕏𝕏
via del Gianicolo 3 ✉ *00165* – 𝒞 *06925901* – *Closed*   Plan: **K2**
January and Sunday
Menu 80/95 € – Carte 61/109 € – *(dinner only)*
• Modern cuisine • Elegant • Minimalist •
This restaurant in the Eternal City serves beautifully prepared gourmet dishes inspired by the flavours of the Amalfi Coast.

Enoteca la Torre – Hotel Villa Laetitia 🍴 AC

𝕏𝕏𝕏
🕄
lungotevere delle Armi 22/23 ✉ *00195* – Ⓜ *Lepanto*   Plan: **L2**
– 𝒞 *0645668304* – www.enotecalatorreroma.com – *Closed 10 days in*
August, Sunday, Monday lunch
Menu 55 € (weekday lunch)/120 € – Carte 78/122 €
• Modern cuisine • Elegant •
A stylish restaurant serving superb cuisine. The decor is elegant and refined, with antique furniture, lace tablecloths and marble columns, while the food celebrates creativity with excellent results.
→ Ravioli di ricotta con terrina di fegatini di pollo, cipolla rossa candita e aceto balsamico. Agnello con purè arrostito e la forza delle erbe. Chibouste (crema) al miele e lavanda con mele tatin e sorbetto al cioccolato.

Antico Arco 🏨 AC ⇄

𝕏𝕏
piazzale Aurelio 7 ✉ *00152* – 𝒞 *06 5815274*   Plan: **B3**
– www.anticoarco.it
Menu 38 € (dinner)/78 € – Carte 56/87 €
• Creative • Elegant • Cosy •
The chef at this modern, bright and fashionable restaurant selects the best Italian ingredients to create innovative dishes based on traditional specialities.

Trattoria del Pesce AC

𝕏
via Folco Portinari 27 ✉ *00186* – 𝒞 *349 3352560*   Plan: **B3**
– www.trattoriadelpesce.it – *Closed 11-25 August*
Carte 32/79 €
• Fish and seafood • Bistro • Family •
A good selection of fresh and raw fish dishes served in a welcoming, vaguely bistro-style restaurant with young and competent staff. Parking can be difficult, but your patience is definitely rewarded!

467

ITALY - ROME

Parco dei Principi Grand Hotel & Spa

via Gerolamo Frescobaldi 5 ✉ *00198*
– ✆ *06 854421 – www.robertonaldicollection.com*
Plan: **M2**
179 rm � *–* ♥201/460 € ♥♥281/615 € – 14 suites
• Palace • Elegant •

This hotel is situated in a quiet, residential district not far from the Villa Borghese
gardens. The dome of St Peter's is visible from the top floor rooms. Wood panelling, carpets and reproductions of famous paintings contribute to the luxurious
ambience, while the 2 000m^2 spa offers all the latest treatments and technology.

Lord Byron

via G. De Notaris 5 ✉ *00197 –* ✆ *06 3220404*
– www.lordbyronhotel.com
Plan: **L-M1**
26 rm � *–* ♥183/530 € ♥♥203/630 € – 6 suites
• Palace • Elegant •

Situated just a few metres from the greenery of the Villa Borghese gardens, this
elegant aristocratic hotel is adorned with Art Deco features. The guestrooms
and public areas have been carefully decorated with fabrics and furniture that
bring out the original character of the building.

Sapori del Lord Byron – See restaurant listing

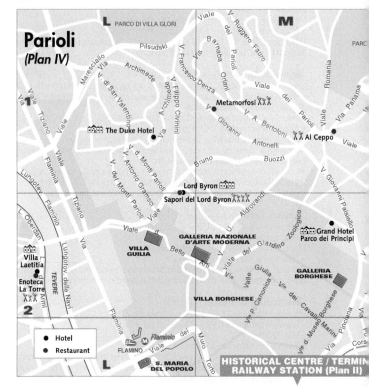

The Duke Hotel

via Archimede 69 ✉ *00197* – ✆ *06 367221*
– *www.thedukehotel.com*
84 rm ⌂ – †84/383 € ††89/646 € – 2 suites
• Traditional • Classic •
Situated in a quiet residential area, this hotel has the discreet, muted atmosphere of an elegant English club. Decorated in typical period style, but with
all the latest modern comforts. Afternoon tea is served in front of the fireplace.
Italian and international dishes are reinterpreted with a creative flair at this restaurant.

Villa Morgagni

via G.B. Morgagni 25 ✉ *00161* – Ⓜ *Policlinico*
– ✆ *06 44202190*
– *www.villamorgagni.it*
34 rm ⌂ – †90/900 € ††120/900 €
• Luxury • Stylish •
Private and quiet in an elegant Art Nouveau setting with comfortable rooms. In
summer or winter, the first meal of the day is prepared in the panoramic roof
garden.

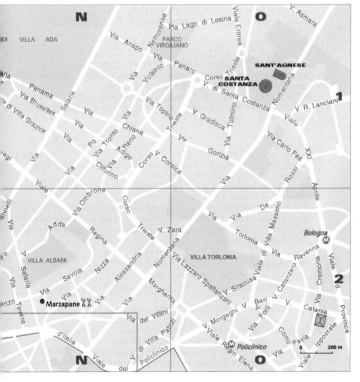

ITALY - ROME

XxxX **Sapori del Lord Byron** – Hotel Lord Byron   🔠 ⇔
via G. De Notaris 5 ⊠ 00197 – ⌀ 06 3220404   Plan: **L-M1**
– www.lordbyronhotel.com – Closed Sunday
Menu 60/100 € – Carte 52/82 € – (dinner only)
• Creative • Elegant •
Be prepared to be stunned by the opulence of this luxury restaurant, which is
adorned with mirrors, paintings and white marble. The skills of the chef combine with a respect for tradition to bring out the very best of Italian cuisine.
The menu includes original dishes such as carpaccio of beetroot with crayfish
and wasabi.

XxX **Metamorfosi** (Roy Caceres)   🔠 ⇔
❀ via Giovanni Antonelli 30/32 ⊠ 00197 – ⌀ 06 8076839   Plan: **M1**
– www.metamorfosiroma.it – Closed Saturday lunch, Sunday
Menu 45 € (weekday lunch)/110 €
– Carte 65/106 € – (dinner only in August)
• Creative • Classic •
Enjoy excellent fusion cuisine with an eclectic and international feel. These are
prepared by a young Colombian chef and his colleagues who hail from all four
corners of the globe. Whether the dishes come from Lazio or South America,
they are all colourful, exciting and full of flavour.
→ Risotto "opercolato" con nocciole e funghi. Piccione con nespole e
camomilla. Mela con pinoli e gelsomino.

XxX **Acquolina Hostaria in Roma**   ❀ 🏠 🔠
❀ via Antonio Serra 60 ⊠ 00191 – ⌀ 06 3337192   Plan: **B1**
– www.acquolinahostaria.it – Closed 10 days in August, Christmas
Holidays, Sunday
Carte 51/118 € – (dinner only) (booking advisable)
• Modern cuisine • Cosy •
Despite an internal change at the helm in 2015, the quality of cuisine at this restaurant remains unchanged. The menu still focuses on classic fare with the
occasional modern twist and an emphasis on fish dishes.
→ Zuppa di mare nuda e cruda. Pappardella ripiena di pecorino con sugo
di totani, asparagi e timo limonato. Ricciola 55°, crema di fagioli cannellini,
porcini, mirtilli e brodo di porri.

XX **Al Ceppo**   ❀ 🔠 ⇔
via Panama 2 ⊠ 00198 – ⌀ 06 8551379   Plan: **M1**
– www.ristorantealceppo.it – Closed 12-25 August, lunch Saturday June-
September, Monday lunch rest of the year
Menu 25 € (weekday lunch) – Carte 42/84 €
• Mediterranean • Traditional •
Elegant bistro-style wood panelling welcomes guests to this rustic yet elegant
restaurant which serves Mediterranean cuisine reinterpreted with a contemporary twist. Specialities include grilled fish and meat dishes prepared in front of
guests in the dining room.

XX **Marzapane**   🔠
via Velletri 39 ⊠ 00198 – ⌀ 06 6478 1692   Plan: **N2**
– www.marzapaneroma.com – Closed 1°-21 August, 2-10 January,
Wednesday
Menu 39/69 € – Carte 40/76 € – (booking advisable)
• Creative • Simple •
A young and informal atmosphere with skill and expertise to the fore in the kitchen. Originally from Spain, the chef has fully adopted the flavours of Roman
cuisine. He serves classic dishes with the occasional Iberian twist and a few
more creative options of excellent quality. Weekday lunchtime dishes are simpler and the service is quicker.

X **Mamma Angelina** 𝔾 🏠 **AC**

viale Arrigo Boito 65 ✉ *00199* – ✆ *06 8608928 – Closed* Plan: **C1**
August and Wednesday
Carte 23/50 €
• Fish and seafood • Simple •
After the antipasto buffet, the cuisine in this restaurant follows two distinct styles – fish and seafood, or Roman specialities. The paccheri pasta with seafood and fresh tomatoes sits in both camps!

ITALY - ROME

 The St. Regis Rome 𝔾 ⅃ 𝔾 🏠 ﹠ **AC** 𝕊

via Vittorio Emanuele Orlando 3 ✉ *00185* Plan: **H1**
– ⓂRepubblica – ✆ *06 47091 – www.stregisrome.com*
138 rm – ♟400/1000 € ♟♟690/1280 € – ⚏ 43 € – 23 suites
• Palace • Elegant •
Frescoes, fine fabrics and Empire-style antique pieces adorn the luxurious guestrooms and lavish lounges of this hotel, which has retained the splendid atmosphere of its early years (1894). The only concession to the modern age is the attractive and well-equipped spa.

The Westin Excelsior 𝔾 ⅃ 🌐 🏠 🔲 **AC** 𝕊

via Vittorio Veneto 125 ✉ *00187* – Ⓜ *Barberini* Plan: **G1**
– ✆ *0647081 – www.westinrome.com*
284 rm – ♟320/650 € ♟♟390/1050 € – ⚏ 38 € – 32 suites
• Grand Luxury • Stylish •
Spoil yourself with a stay in the royal suite (the largest in Europe) or choose one of the luxurious guestrooms, where elegant and comfortable furnishings are complemented by the very latest technology. The "dolce vita" at its best!
Doney – See restaurant listing

Jumeirah Grand Hotel Via Veneto 𝔾 ⅃ 🌐 🏠 ﹠ **AC** 𝕊

via Vittorio Veneto 155 ✉ *00187* – Ⓜ *Barberini* Plan: **G1**
– ✆ *06 487881 – www.jumeirah.com*
106 rm – ♟260/600 € ♟♟260/600 € – ⚏ 33 € – 10 suites
• Luxury • Modern •
Situated on one of Rome's most famous streets, this hotel offers luxury in the true sense of the word, with superb, retro-style guestrooms and a collection of more than 500 original paintings on display. A love of Italian flavours and traditions is clearly evident in the cuisine served in this restaurant. This restaurant serves Italian and international cuisine, as well as a good choice of cocktails.

Regina Hotel Baglioni 𝔾 ⅃ 🏠 ﹠ **AC** 𝕊

via Vittorio Veneto 72 ✉ *00187* – Ⓜ *Barberini* Plan: **G1**
– ✆ *06 421111 – www.baglionihotels.com*
118 rm – ♟285/500 € ♟♟285/500 € – ⚏ 33 € – 9 suites
• Historic • Elegant •
A historic hotel in an Art Nouveau-style building, with an elegant interior decor of stuccowork, period furniture and an imposing bronze and marble staircase. The only concessions to the modern day are the levels of comfort and facilities, as well as the superb guestrooms, some of which are decorated in contemporary designer style.
Brunello Lounge & Restaurant – See restaurant listing

 Majestic 𝔾 ⅃ ﹠ **AC** 𝕊

via Vittorio Veneto 50 ✉ *00187* – Ⓜ *Barberini* Plan: **G1**
– ✆ *06 421441 – www.hotelmajestic.com*
94 rm – ♟190/465 € ♟♟210/640 € – ⚏ 30 € – 4 suites
• Historic • Elegant •
Film-buffs may recognise the backdrop to the famous Italian movie 'La Dolce Vita' at this hotel, which was opened in the late 19C. The Majestic remains one of the bastions of luxury accommodation on the Via Veneto, with its antique furniture, tapestries and frescoes, nowadays accompanied by modern comforts and facilities.
Massimo Riccioli Bistrot – See restaurant listing

ITALY - ROME

Sofitel Rome Villa Borghese

仝 ⅃₅ 阪 ⅍

via Lombardia 47 ✉ *00187 –* Ⓜ *Barberini*　　Plan: **G1**
– ℰ 06 478021 – www.sofitel.com
100 rm ⌑ – �400/660 € ♦♦500/792 € – 4 suites
• Palace • Elegant •

The neo-Classical style dominates in this hotel just a stone's throw from the cosmopolitan Via Veneto. Superb guestrooms and elegant public areas. Situated on the top floor, the panoramic restaurant with its Lounge Bar boasts romantic views of the Villa Medici.

La Terrasse – See restaurant listing

Splendide Royal

仝 ⅃₅ ⅍ 阪 ⅍

via di porta Pinciana 14 ✉ *00187 –* Ⓜ *Barberini*　Plan: **G1**
– ℰ 06 421689 – www.splendideroyal.com
69 rm ⌑ – ♦220/400 € ♦♦250/650 € – 9 suites
• Luxury • Elegant •

Gilded stucco, damask fabrics and sumptuous antique furnishings combine to make this Baroque hotel perfect for those looking for a change from the ubiquitous minimalist style. This ambience of classic luxury continues in the guestrooms, which are decorated in shades of periwinkle blue, golden yellow and cardinal red.

Mirabelle – See restaurant listing

Palazzo Montemartini

仝 ⅃₅ ⊕ ⅍ ▣ ⅍ 阪 ⅍

largo Giovanni Montemartini 20 ✉ *00186 Roma*　Plan: **H1**
– Ⓜ *Termini – ℰ 06 45661 – www.palazzomontemartini.com*
82 rm ⌑ – ♦229/550 € ♦♦249/550 € – 4 suites
• Luxury • Elegant •

The theme of water links this hotel in an aristocratic 19C palazzo with the Roman Baths of Diocletian next door. The hotel's modern interior decor is bright, functional and minimalist.

Bernini Bristol

仝 ⅃₅ ⅍ ⅍ 阪 ⅍

piazza Barberini 23 ✉ *00187 –* Ⓜ *Barberini*　　Plan: **J3**
– ℰ 06 488931 – www.berninibristol.com
127 rm – ♦460/520 € ♦♦590/650 € – ⌑ 33 € – 10 suites
• Luxury • Elegant •

Now an integral part of the famous Piazza Barberini, this elegant hotel offers rooms in either classic or contemporary style – ask for one of the panoramic rooms on the upper floors. At lunchtime, enjoy a "Smart City Lunch" or light à la carte dishes on the rooftop terrace, which in the evening is transformed into the Giuda Ballerino gastronomic restaurant.

❀ **Giuda Ballerino!** – See restaurant listing

Rose Garden Palace

仝 ⅃₅ ⅍ ⅍ 阪 ⅍ ⇔

via Boncompagni 19 ✉ *00187 –* Ⓜ *Barberini*　　Plan: **G1**
– ℰ 06 421741 – www.rosegardenpalace.com
62 rm – ♦130/368 € ♦♦130/385 € – ⌑ 15 € – 3 suites
• Chain hotel • Elegant •

A modern, minimalist design is the inspiration behind the furnishing of this hotel housed in an early-20C palazzo. The building has nonetheless retained some of its original architectural features, such as its high ceilings and marble decor.

Mecenate Palace Hotel

仝 ⅍ 阪 ⅍

via Carlo Alberto 3 ✉ *00185 –* Ⓜ *Vittorio Emanuele*　Plan: **H2**
– ℰ 06 44702024 – www.mecenatepalace.com
68 rm ⌑ – ♦100/335 € ♦♦140/450 € – 3 suites
• Traditional • Elegant •

The warm and elegant period-style interiors are in perfect keeping with the spirit of the 19C building, which houses this hotel. Fine views of Santa Maria Maggiore from the terrace and some of the guestrooms. The restaurant on the top floor serves typical Italian cuisine.

ITALY - ROME

Palazzo Manfredi

via Labicana 125 ✉ 00184 – **Ⓜ** Colosseo
– *☎* 06 77591380 – www.palazzomanfredi.com
Plan: **H3**

14 rm – ♦400/800 € ♦♦400/800 € – ☲ 30 € – 2 suites
• **Grand Luxury** • **Historic** • **Modern** •

The elegant rooms and superb suites of this hotel overlook the Colosseum and the Domus Aurea. Without a doubt the hotel's most striking feature is its delightful roof-garden terrace, which is perfect for a relaxing breakfast or romantic dinner.

❀ **Aroma** – See restaurant listing

Fortyseven

via Luigi Petroselli 47 ✉ 00186 – *☎* 06 6787816
– www.fortysevenhotel.com
Plan: **G3**

59 rm ☲ – ♦180/300 € ♦♦180/300 € – 2 suites
• **Luxury** • **Traditional** • **Personalised** •

The name of this hotel housed in an austere 1930s palazzo refers to the number of the street which leads down to the Teatro di Marcello. Each of the five floors here is dedicated to a 20C Italian artist (Greco, Quagliata, Mastroianni, Modigliani and Guccione) and the hotel is adorned with a collection of paintings, sculptures and lithographs.

Britannia

AC

via Napoli 64 ✉ 00184 – **Ⓜ** Repubblica
– *☎* 06 4883153 – www.hotelbritannia.it
Plan: **H2**

33 rm ☲ – ♦119/400 € ♦♦139/500 €
• **Traditional** • **Elegant** •

Attentive service and stylish personalised decor are some of the features of this small hotel, which offers comfortable guestrooms, most of which are brightened by a small aquarium.

Empire Palace Hotel

via Aureliana 39 ✉ 00187 – *☎* 06 421281
– www.empirepalacehotel.com
Plan: **H1**

110 rm ☲ – ♦100/325 € ♦♦140/405 € – 5 suites
• **Palace** • **Design** •

Sophisticated combination of elements of the 19C building and contemporary design, with a collection of modern art in the public areas; simple, classic bedrooms. This restaurant features cherry wood decor, tables set close together and red and blue chandeliers. Mediterranean specialities take pride of place on the menu.

Celio

Ⅰ₅ **AC** 🛁

via dei Santi Quattro 35/c ✉ 00184 – **Ⓜ** Colosseo
– *☎* 06 70495333 – www.hotelcelio.com
Plan: **H3**

19 rm ☲ – ♦110/180 € ♦♦130/260 € – 1 suite
• **Family** • **Traditional** • **Personalised** •

Delightful artistic touches create an elegant atmosphere in this hotel situated opposite the Colosseum. Stylish guestrooms with individual touches, as well as a hammam and relaxation zone.

Antico Palazzo Rospigliosi

 AC 🛁 **P**

via Liberiana 21 ✉ 00185 – **Ⓜ** Cavour
– *☎* 06 48930495 – www.hotelrospigliosi.com
Plan: **G2**

39 rm ☲ – ♦115/165 € ♦♦149/220 €
• **Historic** • **Elegant** •

This 16C mansion has retained much of its period elegance in its large lounges, as well as in the fine detail of its beautiful bedrooms. The cloister-garden, with its bubbling fountain and splendid 17C chapel, is particularly delightful.

ITALY - ROME

XxxX   **Mirabelle** – Hotel Splendide Royal   ← 🏠 ৬ 🆊 ⇔

via di porta Pinciana 14 ✉ *00187* – ⓜ *Barberini*   Plan: **G1**
– ☏ *06 42168838* – *www.mirabelle.it*
Menu 85 € (lunch)/160 € – Carte 92/200 €
• Modern cuisine • Elegant •
Mirabelle means `beautiful sight' and the view doesn't disappoint - you can
even pick out Villa Borghese in the magical skyline of the historic city centre.
Enjoy classical Italian fare in the luxurious dining room; cooking ranges from
regional specialities right through to dishes with a more international touch.

XxxX   **Massimo Riccioli Bistrot** – Hotel Majestic   🏠 ৬ 🆊 ⇔

via Vittorio Veneto 50 ✉ *00187* – ⓜ *Barberini*   Plan: **G1**
– ☏ *06 42144715* – *www.hotelmajestic.com*
– *Closed Sunday*
Menu 35 € (weekday lunch)/80 € – Carte 46/153 €
• Modern cuisine • Elegant •
The chef of the renowned La Rosetta restaurant has opened a 'Bistrot' in the
stylish and elegant dining rooms of the Hotel Majestic. The menu focuses on
fish and seafood, yet also pays tribute to the more meat-based specialities of
Roman cuisine.

XxX   **Antonello Colonna**

ॐ   *scalinata di via Milano 9/a* ✉ *00184* – ⓜ *Termini*   Plan: **G2**
– ☏ *06 47822641* – *www.antonellocolonna.it* – *Closed August, Sunday and
Monday*
Menu 95 € – Carte 79/114 € – *(dinner only) (booking advisable)*
• Creative • Traditional •
This open-plan, glass-walled restaurant is within the imposing Palazzo delle
Esposizioni. It serves inventive cuisine inspired by traditional dishes, which will
please the most discerning guests.
→ "Negativo" di carbonara. Maialino croccante con patate affumicate e
mostarda. Diplomatico con crema, cioccolato e caramello al sale.

XxX   **Giuda Ballerino!** (Andrea Fusco) – Hotel Bernini Bristol   🕸 🏠

ॐ   *piazza Barberini 23* ✉ *00187* – ☏ *06 42010469*   🆊
– *www.giudaballerino.com* – *Closed Sunday*   Plan: **G2**
Menu 95 € – Carte 70/94 € – *(dinner only)*
• Modern cuisine • Elegant •
In mid 2015, the roof garden on the eighth floor of the historic Hotel Bernini
became the panoramic and elegant setting for the modern cuisine of the
Giuda Ballerino restaurant, which moved from its old premises in the southern
outskirts of the Eternal City to its fashionable centre. Creative dishes and an
excellent wine list.
→ Ricciola con porcini, nocciole e crema di zafferano. Spaghetti cacio e
pepe con polvere di cozze e menta. Biscotto al cocco con crema, foie gras
e cacao.

XxX   **Aroma** – Hotel Palazzo Manfredi   ← 🏠 🆊

ॐ   *via Labicana 125* ✉ *00184* – ⓜ *Colosseo*   Plan: **H3**
– ☏ *06 97615109* – *www.aromarestaurant.it*
Menu 100/140 € – Carte 100/148 € – *(bookings advisable at dinner)*
• Mediterranean • Luxury • Romantic •
The name of this restaurant pays tribute both to the city of Rome and to the
aromas of Mediterranean cuisine. Situated on the top floor of the Palazzo Manf-
redi hotel, the restaurant boasts breathtaking views of Ancient Rome, from the
Colosseum to the dome of St Peter's.
→ Busiate di grano duro con guanciale di Sauris, favette e piselli freschi.
Filetti di spigola in guazzetto con cozze e vongole e pistilli di zafferano.
Soufflé al cacao con cremoso fondente e gelato alla vaniglia Bourbon.

ITALY - ROME

XxX **Brunello Lounge & Restaurant** – Regina Hotel Baglioni
via Vittorio Veneto 72 ✉ *00187* – Ⓜ *Barberini*   ⌖ 🅰 ⇔
– ☎ *06 421111* – *www.brunellorestaurant.com* – *Closed*   Plan: **G1**
Sunday
Menu 60/70 € – Carte 54/115 €
• **Modern cuisine** • **Intimate** • **Elegant** •
This warm, elegant restaurant has a faintly Oriental feel. It provides the perfect
setting to enjoy superb Mediterranean cuisine, as well as international dishes
that will appeal to foreign visitors to the capital.

XxX **Pipero al Rex**   🅰
❀ *via Torino 149* ✉ *00184* – ☎ *06 4815702*   Plan: **H2**
– *www.alessandropipero.it* – *Closed Sunday*
Menu 80/100 € – Carte 67/95 € – *(number of covers limited, pre-book)*
• **Modern cuisine** • **Elegant** •
You walk through the lobby of the Hotel Rex to get to this elegant and intimate
restaurant with its muted lighting. The superb cuisine is prepared by a young
yet experienced chef, and the wine list features a selection of excellent wines.
➜ Ravioli di zucca, mela e uova di salmone. Agnello, alici e lamponi. Ama-
rene, nocciola e cioccolato bianco.

XxX **Doney** – Hotel The Westin Excelsior   🅰
via Vittorio Veneto 125 ✉ *00187* – Ⓜ *Barberini*   Plan: **G1**
– ☎ *06 47082783* – *www.ristorantedoney.it*
Menu 38 € – Carte 63/75 €
• **Mediterranean** • **Bistro** •
Careful attention to detail is evident in the Café Doney, where a combination of
classic and contemporary style creates a modern version of the typical historic
lounge-bar on the Via Veneto. Italian cuisine takes pride of place on the menu.

XxX **Agata e Romeo**   ⅘ 🅰
via Carlo Alberto 45 ✉ *00185* – Ⓜ *Vittorio Emanuele*   Plan: **H2**
– ☎ *06 4466115* – *www.agataeromeo.it* – *Closed 9-*
31 August, Sunday, lunch Monday and Saturday
Menu 60 € – Carte 55/70 €
• **Regional** • **Formal** •
This restaurant stands out for its elegant and refined ambience in a district that
is becoming more and more multi-ethnic and lively. The owner, who has cooked here for decades, prepares Roman and Italian dishes. One of the capital's
classics!

XxX **La Terrasse** – Hotel Sofitel Rome Villa Borghese   🏛 🅰 ⇔
via Lombardia 47 ✉ *00187* – Ⓜ *Barberini* – ☎ *06 478022944*
– *www.laterrasseroma.com*
Carte 58/122 €
• **Modern cuisine** • **Formal** •
As its name suggests, the jewel in the crown of this restaurant is the splendid
terrace that offers panoramic views of the city. The cuisine, however, is equal
to the view with imaginative Mediterranean dishes featured on the menu, as
well as a simpler choice of fare available at lunchtime.

XX **Spazio Roma-Eataly Roma**   ⌖ 🅰
piazzale XII Ottobre 1492 ✉ *00186* – Ⓜ *Piramide*   Plan: **C3**
– ☎ *0690279240* – *www.nikoromitoformazione.it*
Carte 38/54 € – *(number of covers limited, pre-book)*
• **Modern cuisine** • **Traditional** •
Reasonable prices, high quality produce and contemporary-style cuisine with a
young approach. This 'laboratory' restaurant will appeal to anyone wanting to
explore the different flavours of Italian cuisine and the best of Italian produce.

475

Caffè Propaganda   AC

via Claudia 15 ✉ 00186 – Ⓜ Colosseo   Plan: **H3**
*– ☎ 06 94534255 – www.caffepropaganda.it – Closed 10-
20 August, Monday*
Carte 40/52 €
• **Cuisine from Lazio** • **Simple** • **Cosy** •
This restaurant evokes a Parisian bistro of the early 20C with its zinc bar and
tiles, although its cuisine is resolutely Roman. Cured meats, salads and a few
daily specials are served at lunchtime.

Domenico dal 1968   🏤 AC

via Satrico 21 ✉ 00183 – ☎ 06 70494602   Plan: **C3**
*– www.domenicodal1968.it – Closed 20 days in August, Sunday dinner
and Monday*
Carte 30/49 €
• **Roman** • **Simple** • **Family** •
It is worth heading off the tourist track to experience this authentic Roman trattoria. The fritto (fried seafood and vegetables) and linguine with mullet roe and
clams are the house specialities.

Profumo di Mirto   AC

viale Amelia 8/a ✉ 00181 – ☎ 06 786206   Plan: **C3**
– www.profumodimirto.it – Closed August and Monday
Menu 28 € (weekdays)/55 € – Carte 21/78 €
• **Fish and seafood** • **Family** • **Friendly** •
The name of this restaurant pays tribute to Sardinia, the owner's native region.
Fish from the Mediterranean takes pride of place on the menu. It is prepared in
delicious, home-style dishes such as the excellent octopus ravioli served with a
crayfish sauce.

Colline Emiliane   AC ⇔

via degli Avignonesi 22 ✉ 00187 – Ⓜ Barberini   Plan: **G2**
*– ☎ 06 4817538 – Closed August, Sunday dinner,
Monday*
Carte 35/71 € – (booking advisable)
• **Emilian** • **Traditional** •
Just a stone's throw from Piazza Barberini, this simple, friendly, family-run restaurant has just a few tables arranged close together. It serves typical dishes
from the Emilia region, including fresh pasta stretched by hand in the traditional
way.

Al Ristoro degli Angeli   🏤 AC

via Luigi Orlando 2 ✉ 00154 – ☎ 06 51436020   Plan: **B3**
– www.ristorodegliangeli.it – Closed Sunday
Carte 28/59 € – (dinner only)
• **Roman** • **Simple** • **Retro** •
Housed in premises occupied immediately after the war by the Ente Comunale
di Consumo and then later by a grocery store, this unusual restaurant has a
bistro-style ambience. The cuisine is mainly Roman. There is the occasional
gourmet speciality such as grilled beef steak served in a red wine sauce or
with Himalayan crystal salt.

Stazione di Posta   🔄 AC Ⓟ

largo Dino Frisullo snc ✉ 00153 – Ⓜ Piramide   Plan: **B3**
*– ☎ 06 5743548 – www.stazionediposta.eu – Closed Monday, Tuesday
lunch*
Menu 38 € (lunch)/115 € – Carte 56/80 €
• **Creative** • **Trendy** • **Friendly** •
Part of the 'Città dell'Altra Economia' housed in Rome's old abattoir, this open
space is also used as a cocktail bar and exhibition area. The young chef creates
simple and reasonably priced options at lunchtime and more elaborate fare in
the evenings.
➜ Raviolo al vapore con pollo e brodo di patate. Maialino con patate, mela
e senape. Ricotta pera e cioccolato.

X **Moma** 〔AC〕

via San Basilio 42/43 ✉ *00186 –* Ⓜ *Barberini*   Plan: **G1**
– ℰ 0642011798 – www.ristorantemoma.it – Closed Sunday
Menu 50 € (weekday dinner) – Carte 40/80 €
• Modern cuisine • Trendy •

The versatile nature of this bar-cum-bistro and restaurant makes it well worth a visit. At lunchtime, the ambience is busy and lively, while in the evening the restaurant becomes more intimate and atmospheric. Attractive modern cuisine with some imaginative dishes on the menu.

X **Trattoria Monti** 〔AC〕

via di San Vito 13/a ✉ *00185 –* Ⓜ *Cavour*   Plan: **C2**
– ℰ 06 4466573 – Closed Christmas Holidays, 1 week-
Easter, August, Sunday dinner, Monday
Carte 36/53 € – *(booking advisable)*
• Cuisine from The Marches • Traditional • Family •

As a result of renovation work completed a few years ago, this trattoria is resolutely contemporary in style with wooden chairs, copper piping and low-hanging lamps. Specialities include dishes from Lazio and the Marche, the owner's birthplace.

FLORENCE
FIRENZE

Population: 381 037

Giovanni Simeone/Sime/Photononstop

Florence has always stood for beauty, and represents Italy's greatest contribution to the world of arts: the Renaissance. It is said that Cupid lives in Florence and it's hard to imagine a city more romantic than this; lovers visit from around the world, while those not yet in love are thought to find their match here. Florence is surrounded by a ring of hills, and winding streets flanked with cypress and olive trees lead you to the heart of Dante's beloved hometown. The city centre and many of its monuments lie on the northern side of the Arno, a river closely connected with Florence's history and celebrated by poets throughout the years. The river is crossed by many delightful bridges, Ponte Vecchio being the most famous, but, despite its charm, the Arno has in the past wreaked havoc in the form of regular flooding, which has caused huge amounts of damage.

In each area of Florence, civic and religious powers occupy their own distinct site. Piazza della Signoria is home to the town hall, while the Duomo sits in the piazza of the same name at the end of Via dei Calzaiuoli, the city's most famous shopping street. Cross one of the bridges to the south side of the city for a more relaxed, village-like atmosphere; here you will find the Palazzo Pitti and the Giardino di Boboli. Walking eastwards will bring you to the Piazzale Michelangelo, which boasts probably the best views in Florence.

FLORENCE IN...

→ **ONE DAY**
Piazza della Signoria, Via dei Calzaiuoli, the Duomo, Santa Croce, Ponte Vecchio.

→ **TWO DAYS**
The Uffizi, Santa Maria Novella, San Lorenzo.

→ **THREE DAYS**
Palazzo Pitti/Galleria Palatina, Giardino di Boboli, Santa Maria del Carmine, Piazzale Michelangelo.

PRACTICAL INFORMATION

ARRIVAL-DEPARTURE

Amerigo Vespucci, Florence's airport, lies 5km outside of the city. A bus will take you to the Santa Maria Novella Railway Station.

GETTING AROUND

If you are staying in the city centre, the best and most interesting way to see Florence is by foot, as most of the sights are within easy walking distance. Alternatively, one of the municipal orange buses will take you everywhere you need. There are two main tourist offices in Florence; one is in Piazza Stazione (Santa Maria Novella), 4; the other is in Via Cavour 1/R.

CALENDAR HIGHLIGHTS

January
Pitti Immagine Fashion Fair.

February
Carnival.

April
Easter Sunday Celebration in the Piazza del Duomo, Arts and Crafts exhibition.

May
Trofeo Marzocco (flag-waving competition).

June
Festa di San Giovanni (Feast of St John the Baptist – fireworks and a football match).

August
Festa di San Lorenzo (Feast of St Lawrence).

September
Festa della Rificolona (paper lantern festival).

November
Florence Marathon.

EATING OUT

Tuscan food is one of the most famous and highly regarded of Italy's regional cuisines, and it will come as no surprise to learn that some of the best examples are to be found here in Florence. Soups are particularly renowned; don't miss pappa col pomodoro – made with bread and tomatoes – or ribollita – made from cannellini, a local variety of beans, black cabbage, bread and other vegetables. Pasta can certainly not be ignored; pappardelle con la lepre (with hare) and pici (a sort of spaghetti) are two of the most popular.

Meat is a favourite for second courses: the fiorentina, a grilled T-bone steak which takes its name from the city, has now become a favourite nationwide. Restaurants in tourist areas can be very pricey – for a quick, inexpensive meal you're better off opting for a pizza. Wines are equally important in Florence as the cooking: a Chianti, a Morellino di Scansano or a Nobile di Montepulciano will give you good value for money but, if price is not an issue, opt for the Super Tuscans – Ornellaia, Sassicaia, Solaia or Tignanello.

The Westin Excelsior

piazza Ognissanti 3 ✉ *50123 –* ℰ *055 27151*
– www.westinflorence.com

Plan: **C2**

171 rm – 🛏275/890 € 🛏🛏285/920 € – ☲ 41 € – 16 suites
• Grand Luxury • Classic •

Sumptuous interiors of an old nobleman's dwelling on the Arno, where history and tradition combine with more modern accessories for an exclusive aristocratic stay. The dining hall of this restaurant is princely. Among its features are the boxed ceilings and decor in Carrara marble.
SE.STO – See restaurant listing

Four Seasons Hotel Firenze

borgo Pinti 99 ✉ *50121 –* ℰ *055 26261*
– www.fourseasons.com/florence

Plan: **F2**

116 rm ☲ – 🛏325/695 € 🛏🛏325/695 € – 20 suites
• Grand Luxury • Historic •

The austere walls of a 15C palazzo surround this hotel, which boasts the largest private garden in Florence. Sumptuous guestrooms, classic-style decor and bright, secluded courtyards all contribute to the hotel's exclusive charm. The Conventino annexe is popular with guests looking for privacy and tranquillity. Delicious choice of Tuscan and Italian cuisine in the Atrium restaurant, as well as pizza and summer barbecues in the garden.
❀ **Il Palagio** – See restaurant listing

The St. Regis Florence

piazza Ognissanti 1 ✉ *50123 –* ℰ *055 27163*
– www.stregisflorence.com

Plan: **D2**

83 rm – 🛏320/920 € 🛏🛏350/980 € – ☲ 42 € – 17 suites
• Luxury • Elegant •

This hotel is even more luxurious and exclusive after its recent renovation. It offers spacious guestrooms, where modern accessories provide a contrast with the classic decor of frescoes, Murano glass chandeliers and antique furniture.
❀ **Winter Garden by Caino** – See restaurant listing

Savoy

piazza della Repubblica 7 ✉ *50123 –* ℰ *055 27351*
– www.hotelsavoy.it

Plan: **D2**

102 rm – 🛏225/487 € 🛏🛏290/953 € – ☲ 30 € – 14 suites
• Luxury • Classic •

This elegant, historic hotel is situated near the Duomo, the city's museums and luxury fashion boutiques. It offers spacious, comfortable guestrooms with mosaic adorned bathrooms.

Montebello Splendid

via Garibaldi 14 ✉ *50123 –* ℰ *055 27471*
– www.montebellosplendid.com

Plan: **C2**

58 rm ☲ – 🛏150/390 € 🛏🛏199/600 € – 3 suites
• Luxury • Classic •

This stylishly modern hotel is the much frequented haunt of tourists and business persons; common areas are spacious and attractively furnished and give onto a delightful internal garden.

Relais Santa Croce

via Ghibellina 87 ✉ *50122 –* ℰ *055 2342230*
– www.baglionihotels.com

Plan: **E3**

18 rm – 🛏330/490 € 🛏🛏350/510 € – ☲ 28 € – 6 suites
• Palace • Elegant •

Luxury and elegance in the heart of Florence, where period furnishings blend with designer-style decor and rich fabrics to create a unique blend of the traditional and the modern. Time, experience and passion are the essential ingredients here, combining to create simple, delicious dishes from old Tuscan recipes.

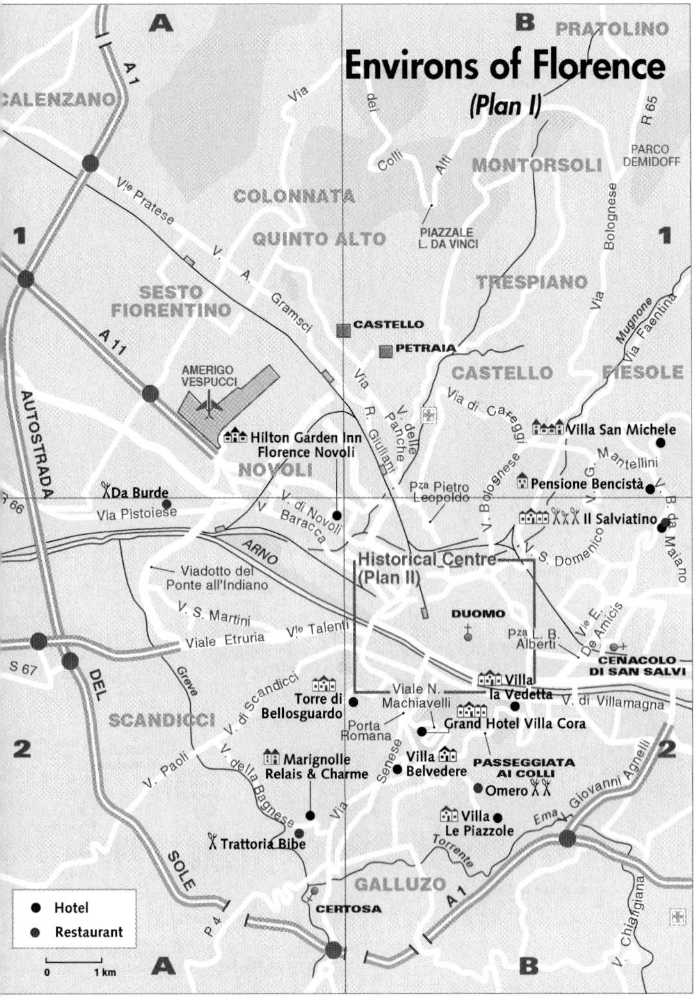

Environs of Florence
(Plan I)
A
B
1
2
PRATOLINO
CALENZANO
A 1
Via dei Colli Alti
MONTORSOLI
PARCO DEMIDOFF
R 65
V.le Pratese
COLONNATA
QUINTO ALTO
PIAZZALE L. DA VINCI
Bolognese
TRESPIANO
SESTO FIORENTINO
V. A. Gramsci
Via
Mugnone
Via Faentina
CASTELLO
PETRAIA
A 11
AMERIGO VESPUCCI
CASTELLO
FIESOLE
AUTOSTRADA
Via R. Giuliani
V. delle Panche
Via di Careggi
Villa San Michele
Hilton Garden Inn Florence Novoli
NOVOLI
V. G. Mantellini
Pensione Bencistà
Da Burde
Via Pistoiese
V. di Novoli
V. Baracca
Pza Pietro Leopoldo
V. Bolognese
Il Salviatino
V. B. da Maiano
ARNO
Historical Centre (Plan II)
V. S. Domenico
Viadotto del Ponte all'Indiano
V. S. Martini
DUOMO
V.le E. De Amicis
Pza L. B. Alberti
Viale Etruria
V.le Talenti
CENACOLO DI SAN SALVI
S 67
DEL
Greve
Villa la Vedetta
Torre di Bellosguardo
Viale N. Machiavelli
V. di Villamagna
V. di Scandicci
SCANDICCI
Grand Hotel Villa Cora
Porta Romana
V. Paoli
V. della Bagnese
Marignolle Relais & Charme
Senese
Villa Belvedere
PASSEGGIATA AI COLLI
Omero
Giovanni Agnelli
Via
Villa Le Piazzole
Ema
Trattoria Bibe
Torrente
SOLE
GALLUZO
A 1
CERTOSA
P 4
V. Chiantigiana
Hotel
Restaurant
0
1 km

Regency

piazza Massimo D'Azeglio 3 ✉ *50121*
– ✆ 055 245247 – www.regency-hotel.com
– Closed 3 January-5 April

Plan: **F2**

29 rm – 183/530 € 203/640 € – 3 suites

• Luxury • Classic •

This elegant hotel was built to offer accommodation for local political figures. It boasts a tranquil, comfortable atmosphere and has retained much of its traditional charm.

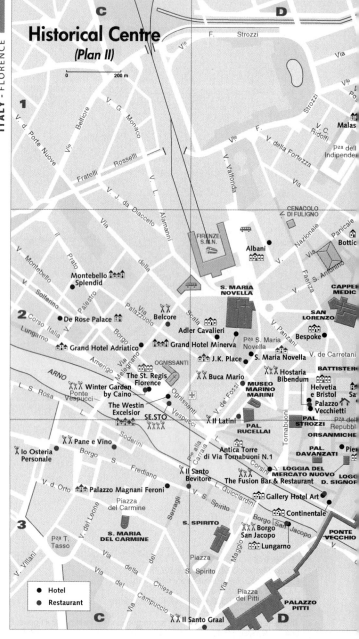

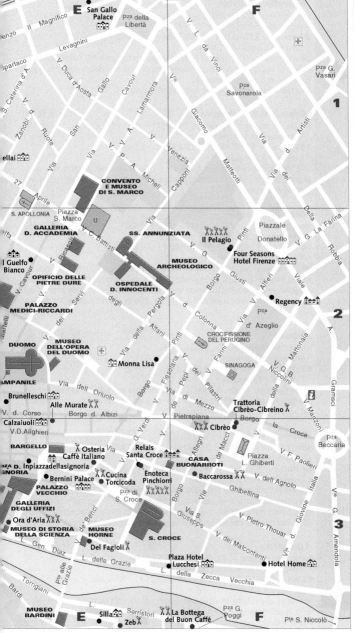

E San Gallo Palace Pza della Libertà

F

Il Magnifico

Levagnini

V. - L. da Vinci

Spartaco

S. Caterina d'A.

Zanobi

V. d. Ruote

V. Duca d'Aosta

V. S. Gallo

Cavour

Lamarmora

Pza G. Vasari

Pza Savonarola

1

Giacomo

V. A. V. P. A. Michell

Venezia

Matteotti

Via d. Artisti

Via dei

ellai

27

Aprile

CONVENTO E MUSEO DI S. MARCO

Capponi

Della Robbia

S. APOLLONIA Piazza S. Marco

U

SS. ANNUNZIATA

Il Pelagio

Piazzale Donatello

V. G. La Farina

GALLERIA D. ACCADEMIA

V. C. Battisti

MUSEO ARCHEOLOGICO

Four Seasons Hotel Firenze

Viale

I Guelfo Bianco

V. Cavour

V. Ricasoli

OPIFICIO DELLE PIETRE DURE

degli Servi

Borgo

Giusti

Alfieri

Regency

2

PALAZZO MEDICI-RICCARDI

Martelli

V. dei

OSPEDALE D. INNOCENTI

Pergola

Colonna

Pza d' Azeglio

Mattonaia

Gramsci

DUOMO

MUSEO DELL'OPERA DEL DUOMO

Via della Alfani

Pinti

CROCIFISSIONE DEL PERUGINO

V. G. B. Niccolini

Monna Lisa

Via dell' Oriuolo

Fiesolana

Farini

SINAGOGA

AMPANILE

Brunelleschi

Via

Borgo

V. dei Pepi

V. di Mezzo

Trattoria Cibrèo-Cibreino

V. Marzoni

i

Calzaiuoli

Alle Murate

Borgo d. Albizi

V. de' Pilastri

Borgo

la

Croce

Pza Beccaria

V. d. Corso

V.D. Alighieri

V. Pietrapiana

Cibrèo

BARGELLO

Osteria

G. Verdi

Relais Santa Croce

V. de' Macci

Piazza L. Ghiberti

V. F. Paolieri

ZA D. Inpiazzadellasignoria SGNORIA

Caffè Italiano

Cucina Torricoda

CASA BUONARROTI

Bernini Palace

Enoteca Pinchiori

Baccarossa

V. dell Agnolo

Via G. Amendola

PALAZZO VECCHIO

Pza di S. Croce

Borgo

Via S Giuseppe

Ghibellina

GALLERIA DEGLI UFFIZI

Ora d'Aria

de' Benci

V. Pietro Thouar

3

MUSEO DI STORIA DELLA SCIENZA

MUSEO HORNE

S. CROCE

V. dei Malcontenti

Del Fagioli

L. Gen. Diaz

L. delle Grazie

Plaza Hotel Lucchesi

Hotel Home

Pte alle Grazie

L. della Zecca Vecchia

Torrigiani

Bardi

MUSEO BARDINI

E Silla

Serristori

La Bottega del Buon Caffè

Pza G. Poggi

F

Zeb

Pte S. Niccolò

ITALY - FLORENCE

Helvetia e Bristol

via dei Pescioni 2 ✉ *50123* – ✆ *055 26651* Plan: **D2**
– www.royaldemeure.com
67 rm ⌂ – ♦270/310 € ♦♦440/510 € – 15 suites
• Grand Luxury • Classic •
Situated near the Duomo and Palazzo Strozzi, this elegant 19C hotel evokes the
charm of bygone days. It has personalised guestrooms decorated with period
paintings and antique furniture.
Hostaria Bibendum – See restaurant listing

Grand Hotel Minerva

piazza Santa Maria Novella 16 ✉ *50123* – ✆ *055 27230* Plan: **D2**
– www.grandhotelminerva.com
101 rm ⌂ – ♦150/300 € ♦♦250/500 € – 5 suites
• Luxury • Elegant •
This hotel is one of the oldest in the city. Elegantly furnished guestrooms, works
of art, a terrace with a swimming pool and fine views all contribute to the welcoming atmosphere.

Bernini Palace

piazza San Firenze 29 ✉ *50122* – ✆ *055 288621* Plan: **E3**
– www.hotelbernini.duetorrihotels.com
74 rm ⌂ – ♦200/400 € ♦♦220/600 € – 11 suites
• Traditional • Elegant •
When Florence was the capital of Italy, members of parliament and senators
would meet in the Sala Parlamento of this hotel. With its spacious corridors,
magnificent guestrooms (those on the Tuscan Floor are particularly impressive),
and an excellent restaurant, this hotel now attracts visitors looking for the highest quality.

Albani

via Fiume 12 ✉ *50123* – ✆ *055 26030* Plan: **D2**
– www.albanihotels.com
95 rm ⌂ – ♦100/420 € ♦♦120/660 € – 2 suites
• Palace • Elegant •
An elegant and imposing early-20C palazzo situated near the railway station,
boasting elegant neo-Classical-style rooms which are full of colour and decorated with artistic and designer touches.

Brunelleschi

piazza Santa Elisabetta 3 ✉ *50122* – ✆ *055 27370* Plan: **E2**
– www.hotelbrunelleschi.it
82 rm ⌂ – ♦209/949 € ♦♦234/1054 € – 14 suites
• Luxury • Personalised •
Housed in the Byzantine Torre della Pagliazza, this hotel with welcoming guestrooms boasts a small museum with Roman remains. A dining room partly enclosed by old walls is home to the gourmet Santa Elisabetta restaurant, while the
hotel also offers bistro dining in the elegant Osteria della Pagliazza.

Lungarno

borgo San Jacopo 14 ✉ *50125* – ✆ *055 27261* Plan: **D3**
– www.lungarnocollection.com
63 rm – ♦225/750 € ♦♦255/850 € – ⌂ 35 € – 10 suites
• Luxury • Personalised •
The name of this hotel situated between Ponte Vecchio and Santa Trinità refers
to its excellent location overlooking the River Arno. Every corner of the hotel is
stylish and elegant. It has numerous terraces and balconies and many of the
guestrooms offer views of the river.
❀ **Borgo San Jacopo** – See restaurant listing

ITALY - FLORENCE

Continentale
👁 ♿ 🅰️

vicolo dell'Oro 6 r ✉ *50123 – ℰ 055 27262*   Plan: **D3**
– www.lungarnocollection.com
43 rm – 🛏155/410 € 🛏🛏200/720 € – ➁ 28 €
• Traditional • Classic •

A modern, elegant hotel built around a medieval tower with a lounge bar over-looking the Arno and the Ponte Vecchio, plus a new White Iris Beauty Spa. The designer-style interior is decorated in bright, warm colours.

Santa Maria Novella
⟨ Ⅰ⑤ 👁 ♿ 🅰️

piazza Santa Maria Novella 1 ✉ *50123 – ℰ 055 271840*   Plan: **D2**
– www.hotelsantamarianovella.it
69 rm ➁ – 🛏150/350 € 🛏🛏185/590 € – 2 suites
• Grand Luxury • Elegant •

Overlooking Piazza Santa Maria Novella, this welcoming hotel offers small lounge areas and elegant guestrooms, all of which have different decor and fur-nishings. Enjoy superb views of this magical city from the hotel's delightful panoramic terrace.

Gallery Hotel Art
🐾 ♿ 🅰️

vicolo dell'Oro 5 ✉ *50123 – ℰ 055 27263*   Plan: **D3**
– www.lungarnocollection.com
71 rm – 🛏190/440 € 🛏🛏190/440 € – ➁ 28 € – 3 suites
• Luxury • Personalised •

African wood in the guestrooms, bathrooms furnished with stone from the Mid-dle East and views of Florence on the walls – the cosmopolitan art in this museum-like hotel creates a strikingly modern ambience.
The Fusion Bar & Restaurant – See restaurant listing

Adler Cavalieri
Ⅰ⑤ 👁 ♿ 🅰️ ♨

via della Scala 40 ✉ *50123 – ℰ 055 277810*   Plan: **D2**
– www.hoteladlercavalieri.com
60 rm ➁ – 🛏115/325 € 🛏🛏145/410 €
• Traditional • Cosy •

This pleasant hotel is located in the immediate vicinity of the station. The soundproofing is excellent and wood has been used to very good effect. The management is youthful and competent.

Grand Hotel Adriatico
🐾 🚑 Ⅰ⑤ ♿ 🅰️ ♨ 🅿️

via Maso Finiguerra 9 ✉ *50123 – ℰ 055 27931*   Plan: **C2**
– www.hoteladriatico.it
126 rm ➁ – 🛏90/270 € 🛏🛏100/410 € – 3 suites
• Traditional • Cosy •

Conveniently situated in the city centre, this hotel has a large lobby and modern guestrooms decorated in simple, yet elegant style. Tuscan and Italian cuisine is served in the quiet, recently renovated dining room, as well as in the attractive garden.

Il Guelfo Bianco
🐾 ♿ 🅰️

via Cavour 29 ✉ *50129 – ℰ 055 288330*   Plan: **E2**
– www.ilguelfobianco.it
40 rm ➁ – 🛏90/160 € 🛏🛏100/260 €
• Traditional • Personalised • Historic •

Situated in the heart of Medici Florence, this hotel offers contemporary-style public areas and spacious guestrooms, some of which have frescoes on the cei-lings. Small bistro selling hot food from 12-3pm.

San Gallo Palace
Ⅰ⑤ ♿ 🅰️ ♨

via Lorenzo il Magnifico 2 ✉ *50129 – ℰ 055 463871*   Plan: **E1**
– www.sangallopalace.it
54 rm ➁ – 🛏79/350 € 🛏🛏99/350 € – 2 suites
• Traditional • Elegant •

This establishment has recently been opened in a two-storey building. Comfort is the keynote both of the public rooms and spacious guest rooms, all of which are double.

Palazzo Magnani Feroni

borgo San Frediano 5 ✉ *50124*
– ℰ 055 2399544
– www.palazzomagnaniferoni.it
13 suites ☲ – 🛉200/960 € 🛉🛉200/960 €
• Grand Luxury • Historic •
Located in the Oltrarno, inside a 17C building, centring on a small internal courtyard. Offering terraces with an all-round panoramic view of the city.

Plan: **C3**

Cellai

via 27 Aprile 14 ✉ *50129 – ℰ 055 489291*
– www.hotelcellai.it
68 rm ☲ – 🛉120/169 € 🛉🛉150/295 €
• Luxury • Personalised •
This luxurious hotel in Florence offers a welcoming atmosphere, period furnishings and antique prints of plants and animals. The top floor is home to an attractive terrace decked with jasmine, which acts as an open-air lounge in which to relax and enjoy views of the city.

Plan: **E1**

Calzaiuoli

via Calzaiuoli 6 ✉ *50122 – ℰ 055 212456*
– www.calzaiuoli.it
52 rm ☲ – 🛉120/500 € 🛉🛉150/650 € – 1 suite
• Luxury • Elegant •
In the pedestrian street between Piazza del Duomo and Piazza della Signoria lies a hotel which has a restricted number of public areas but comfortable and welcoming bedrooms, and recently renovated bathrooms.

Plan: **E3**

Pierre

via Dè Lamberti 5 ✉ *50123 – ℰ 055 216218*
– www.remarhotels.com
49 rm ☲ – 🛉150/330 € 🛉🛉180/410 € – 1 suite
• Traditional • Elegant •
This elegant hotel in the city centre has comfortable, stylishly furnnished rooms and modern amenities. You can see the Duomo from some of the tables in the breakfast room.

Plan: **D3**

Bespoke Number Nine

via dei Conti 9/31r ✉ *50123 – ℰ 055293777*
– www.firenzenumbernine.com
42 rm ☲ – 🛉99/199 € 🛉🛉149/499 €
• Luxury • Design •
Soft, subtle colours add a hint of contemporary style to the traditional Florentine decor in this smart hotel (room 107 is particularly stylish). Friendly service, as well as an excellent gym for fitness enthusiasts.

Plan: **D2**

J.K. Place Firenze

piazza Santa Maria Novella 7 ✉ *50123*
– ℰ 055 2645181
– www.jkplace.com
18 rm ☲ – 🛉380/600 € 🛉🛉380/600 € – 2 suites
• Luxury • Elegant •
Hiding behind the majestic door of a beautiful palazzo in Piazza Santa Maria Novella, this boutique hotel has an elegant yet homely ambience with delightful individual touches, offering contemporary comfort and luxury combined with a traditional historic feel. Situated right in the centre, just a 5-minute walk from the city's main shops and monuments, J.K. Place Firenze is the perfect spot for a relaxing break.

Plan: **G1**

ITALY - FLORENCE

Plaza Hotel Lucchesi   ☆ ≼ AC 🚗

lungarno della Zecca Vecchia 38 ✉ *50122*
– ☏ 05526236 – www.hotelplazalucchesi.it
Plan: **E3**
93 rm ⬚ – ♦150/350 € ♦♦180/700 € – 10 suites
• Luxury • Personalised •

An elegant hotel overlooking the Arno with generously sized public areas and guestrooms decorated with Imperial-style furnishings. There is a 360° view of the monuments and rooftops of Florence from the top floor terrace, which also boasts a bar and a small pool.

Antica Torre di via Tornabuoni 1 – Residenza d'epoca

via Tornabuoni 1 ✉ *50123 – ☏ 055 2658161*
AC
– www.tornabuoni1.com
Plan: **D3**
19 rm ⬚ – ♦200/495 € ♦♦200/495 € – 6 suites
• Luxury • Classic •

The hotel premises include the upper floors of the building. The rooms are spacious and bright and an outstanding feature is the breathtaking view from the two terraces overlooking the entire town.

Home Florence   ɬ & AC ⅏

piazza Piave 3 ✉ *50122 – ☏ 055 243668*
Plan: **F3**
– www.hhflorence.it
39 rm ⬚ – ♦89/230 € ♦♦119/280 €
• Traditional • Homely •

This charming small palazzo with a predominantly white decor has a young, fashionable feel while at the same time – as the name suggests – manages to retain a homely atmosphere. Breakfast is served on three shared tables.

De Rose Palace   AC

via Solferino 5 ✉ *50123 – ☏ 055 2396818*
Plan: **C2**
– www.florencehotelderose.com
18 rm ⬚ – ♦120/350 € ♦♦140/380 €
• Traditional • Cosy •

In a renovated 19th Century building a hotel with a simple, elegant interior, with period style furnishings and beautiful Venetian lamps; pleasant family atmosphere.

Monna Lisa   ⌔ ⌸ ɬ AC ⅏

via Borgo Pinti 27 ✉ *50121 – ☏ 055 2479751*
Plan: **E2**
– www.monnalisa.it
45 rm ⬚ – ♦89/209 € ♦♦139/279 € – 4 suites
• Historic • Classic •

Situated in the historic centre, this hotel occupies an original medieval palazzo with an imposing staircase, brick flooring and coffered ceilings. Rooms and communal areas have Renaissance-style furnishings. The newer rooms, which are just as elegant as the rest of the hotel, can be found in the two annexes in the splendid garden.

Inpiazzadellasignoria – Residenza d'epoca   AC

via de' Magazzini 2 ✉ *50122 – ☏ 055 2399546*
Plan: **E3**
– www.inpiazzadellasignoria.com
10 rm ⬚ – ♦200/250 € ♦♦250/300 € – 2 suites
• Family • Cosy •

As the name implies, this establishment faces the Piazza della Signoria, the political centre of old Florence. It is welcoming and pleasantly elegant.

Malaspina   & AC

piazza dell'Indipendenza 24 ✉ *50129 – ☏ 055 489869*
Plan: **D1**
– www.malaspinahotel.it
31 rm ⬚ – ♦50/175 € ♦♦60/275 €
• Family • Cosy •

In the 13C the Malaspina family received Dante as their guest at the Castello di Fosdinovo. This tradition of hospitality is upheld by the descendants of the Malaspina, who run this 20C hotel decorated in period style. Spacious, well-equipped guestrooms.

ITALY - FLORENCE

Silla

via dei Renai 5 ✉ *50125* – ✆ *055 2342889*
– *www.hotelsilla.it*

Plan: **E3**

36 rm ☕ – ✝90/260 € ✝✝90/320 €

• Family • Classic •

It is pleasant in summer to eat your breakfast or just relax on the wide balcony of this hotel with its family atmosphere, situated as it is on the left bank of the Arno.

Botticelli

via Taddea 8 ✉ *50123* – ✆ *055 290905*
– *www.hotelbotticelli.it*

Plan: **D2**

34 rm ☕ – ✝70/150 € ✝✝100/240 € – 1 suite

• Historic • Classic •

Near to the S.Lorenzo market, in a 16th Century building, is a charming hotel with frescoes in the public areas and a small covered balcony; bedrooms recently refurbished.

Palazzo Vecchietti

via degli Strozzi 4 – ✆ *055 2302802*
– *www.palazzovecchietti.com*

Plan: **D2**

7 rm ☕ – ✝249/559 € ✝✝249/649 € – 5 suites

• Historic • Elegant •

Remains of Florence's 13C walls are still visible in this palazzo, which offers a delightful inner courtyard now transformed into a small lounge. Romantic galleries overlook the courtyard and lead to the luxurious rooms. All of these are decorated in an elegant contemporary style and equipped with a small kitchen.

Enoteca Pinchiorri (Annie Féolde)

via Ghibellina 87 ✉ *50122* – ✆ *055 242777*
– *www.enotecapinchiorri.com* – *Closed 2 weeks in August, 1 week Christmas Holidays, Sunday, Monday*

Plan: **E3**

Menu 175/250 € – Carte 145/270 € – *(dinner only) (booking advisable)*

• Modern cuisine • Elegant • Luxury •

The cuisine at this restaurant is a fine balance of classic and modern, taking the best from both styles to create elegant dishes served in a luxurious and cosmopolitan ambience. The wine list here is legendary.

→ Spaghetti alla chitarra, frutti di mare e briciole di pane con bottarga. Maialino di razza mora romagnola con radicchio, asparagi e fagiolini marinati. Cristallo di pera con caffè e agrumi.

Il Palagio – Four Seasons Hotel Firenze

borgo Pinti 99 ✉ *50121* – ✆ *055 2626450*
– *www.fourseasons.com/florence* – *Closed January-February and Sunday dinner October-May*

Plan: **F2**

Menu 105 € – Carte 88/164 € – *(dinner only)*

• Creative • Elegant •

The magnificent decor of one of the most impressive palazzi in Florence has been given a more contemporary feel in this restaurant. It offers delicious and carefully prepared reinterpretations of traditional Italian cuisine.

→ Cavatelli cacio e pepe, crudo di gamberi rossi e calamaretti spillo. Quaglia ripiena ai fichi di Carmignano con crema di sedano rapa. Cremoso al cioccolato.

SE.STO – Hotel The Westin Excelsior

piazza Ognissanti 3 ✉ *50123* – ✆ *055 27151*
– *www.sestoonarno.com/en/*

Plan: **C2**

Carte 74/111 € – *(booking advisable)*

• Creative • Formal •

This restaurant boasts the highest terrace in Florence, offering stunning views of the Duomo, Giotto's bell tower, the Palazzo della Signoria and Ponte Vecchio. The Mediterranean cuisine, which is reinterpreted with a contemporary twist, provides a real treat for the taste buds.

ITALY - FLORENCE

XXXX ✿ **Winter Garden by Caino** – The St. Regis Florence   🏫 ⅙ 🆎
piazza Ognissanti 1 – ℰ *055 2716*   Plan: **D2**
– www.stregisflorence.com
Menu 95 € – Carte 78/125 € – *(dinner only) (booking advisable)*
• Creative • Luxury •
Horse-drawn carriages once entered the old courtyard of the St Regis hotel, now converted into a winter garden. Enjoy delicious dishes from the Maremma created by Valeria Piccini in the luxurious surroundings of one of Florence's most elegant hotels.
→ Tagliolini con zafferano e astice. Il gioco del galletto. Cioccolato, liquirizia e frutti esotici.

XXX ✿ **Ora D'Aria** (Marco Stabile)   🆎
via de' Georgofili 11/13 r ✉ *50122 –* ℰ *055 2001699*   Plan: **F3**
– www.oradariaristorante.com – Closed 7-28 August, 7-
21 February, Monday lunch and Sunday
Menu 35/85 € – Carte 74/116 € – *(booking advisable)*
• Creative • Elegant •
The dining room at this restaurant faces the open-view kitchen, allowing a continuous exchange of dialogue between chefs and diners. The cuisine focuses on mainly Tuscan produce served in dishes that blend traditional skill with contemporary style.
→ Risotto alla terra e sottobosco: ricordo di mio padre. Piccione con cibreo e mela caramellata al vinsanto. Caramello, latte, sale.

XXX **The Fusion Bar & Restaurant** – Gallery Hotel Art   ⅙ 🆎
vicolo dell'Oro 5 ✉ *50123 –* ℰ *055 27266987*   Plan: **D3**
– www.lungarnocollection.com
Carte 24/65 €
• International • Fashionable •
This bar-cum-restaurant is young and stylish. It offers an interesting choice of cocktails, a simple menu at lunchtime and a good mix of Western and Asian cuisine in the evening, including sushi.

XXX ✿ **Borgo San Jacopo** – Hotel Lungarno   🍴 🆎
borgo San Jacopo 14 ✉ *50125 –* ℰ *055 281661*   Plan: **D3**
– www.borgosanjacopo.com
Menu 90/115 € – Carte 80/153 € – *(dinner only)*
• Creative • Traditional •
The flavours of the region have been given a lighter touch in this restaurant, which also offers an excellent wine list of over 600 labels. In summer, treat yourself to dinner on the delightful small terrace overlooking the Arno, where the candlelight is reflected on the surface of the water.
→ Bottoni di cinghiale con fondo di cinta. Branzino alla piastra, polpo alla brace, melanzane, cetriolo e peperoni. Passione per la nocciola.

XXX **Hostaria Bibendum** – Hotel Helvetia e Bristol   🆎
via dei Pescioni 8/r ✉ *50123 –* ℰ *0552665620*   Plan: **D2**
– www.royaldemeure.com
Carte 28/62 €
• Modern cuisine • Elegant •
The terrace at this restaurant directly overlooks Piazza Strozzi. The dining room is a real melting pot of styles with a mix of warm colours, exotic decor and Art Nouveau details. There is no mistaking the style of the cuisine however, which is resolutely Tuscan in flavour with the occasional imaginative twist.

XXX **Cibrèo**   🍴 ⅙ 🆎 ⇔
via A. Del Verrocchio 8/r ✉ *50122 –* ℰ *055 2341100*   Plan: **F3**
– www.cibreo.com – Closed August, 2 weeks in February, Monday
Menu 77/120 €
• Tuscan • Elegant •
This restaurant has an informal, fashionable atmosphere, with young, confident staff and fine, inventive cuisine inspired by traditional dishes.

XX **Alle Murate** 　　　　　　　　　　　　　　　　🅰️

via del Proconsolo 16 r ✉ *50122* 　　　　　Plan: **E2-3**
– ☎ 055 240618 – www.allemurate.it
– Closed Sunday and lunch
Carte 70/99 € *– (bar lunch Monday-Saturday)*
• **Regional** • **Romantic** •

This restaurant is open to visitors during the day and in the evening (upon request); an audio-guide provides information on the frescoes and archaeological ruins visible here. The menu is also influenced by the past, with its emphasis on traditional, regional cuisine. A unique experience!

XX **Baccarossa** 　　　　　　　　　　　　　　　　🅰️

via Ghibellina 46/r ✉ *50122 – ☎ 055240620* 　　Plan: **F3**
– www.baccarossa.it
Menu 30 € *(weekdays)*
– Carte 37/82 € – (dinner only) (booking advisable)
• **Mediterranean** • **Trendy** •

This elegant, bistro-style, wine bar is decorated in bright colours and furnished with wooden tables. It serves delicious Mediterranean cuisine including fish specialities, homemade pasta and some meat dishes. All the wines available can be ordered by the glass.

XX **Belcore** 　　　　　　　　　　　　　　　　🅰️

via dell'Albero 30r ✉ *50123* 　　　　　　　Plan: **C2**
– ☎ 055 211198 – www.ristorantebelcore.it
– Closed 16-25 August
Menu 30/45 € – Carte 38/58 € *– (dinner only)*
• **Classic cuisine** • **Cosy** •

An excellent selection of wines complement the different types of cuisine served in this restaurant. Taste the fish specialities, traditional favourites from Italy and Tuscany, and more modern dishes.

XX **Buca Mario** 　　　　　　　　　　　　　　🅰️ ↺

piazza Degli Ottaviani 16 r ✉ *50123 – ☎ 055 214179* 　Plan: **D2**
– www.bucamario.it – Closed 9-20 December
Carte 40/111 € *– (dinner only)*
• **Regional** • **Traditional** •

This typical Florentine restaurant opened in 1886. Housed in the cellars of the Palazzo Niccolini in the heart of Florence, it is popular for its excellent, traditional Tuscan cuisine.

XX **Pane e Vino** 　　　　　　　　　　　　　　　🅰️

piazza di Cestello 3 r ✉ *50124 – ☎ 055 2476956* 　Plan: **C3**
– www.ristorantepaneevino.it – Closed 10-20 August and Sunday
Menu 30/45 € – Carte 30/50 € *– (dinner only)*
• **Tuscan** • **Family** •

Friendly, well maintained and furnished with an unusual wooden mezzanine, this pleasant restaurant offers traditional regional cuisine with a creative twist.

XX **Il Santo Graal** 　　　　　　　　　　　　🅰️ ↺

via Romana 70r ✉ *50122 Firenze – ☎ 055 2286533* 　Plan: **D3**
– www.ristorantesantograal.it – Closed 1-7 August, 24-31 January,
Wednesday, Thursday lunch
Menu 35/60 € – Carte 39/61 € *– (dinner only) (booking advisable)*
• **Creative** • **Minimalist** •

An elegant and minimalist ambience pervades the Santo Graal. This gourmet restaurant run by a young chef brings new life to Tuscan traditions with his intense flavours and reinterpretations of local culinary favourites.

ITALY - FLORENCE

XX **Cucina Torcicoda** 🍴 AC

via Torta 5/r – ℰ 055 2654329 – www.cucinatorcicoda.com   Plan: **E3**
Menu 25/55 € – Carte 32/54 €
• Tuscan • Cosy •

An osteria, pizzeria and restaurant (in the evenings) all-in-one. This property has three different options under the same roof, offering informal or more elegant dining depending on your mood. Enjoy traditional Tuscan cuisine at the osteria, Neapolitan-style pizzas at the pizzeria and more refined cuisine at the restaurant. All three serve the house speciality: Florentine steak made from different types of beef.

XX **La Bottega del Buon Caffè** 🍴 AC
❀

lungarno Benvenuto Cellini, 63/r ✉ 50122   Plan: **F3**
– ℰ 055 5535677 – www.borgointhecity.com – Closed November, Monday and dinner Sunday; May to September closed Monday lunch and Sunday
Menu 65 € (lunch)/115 € – Carte 83/107 €
• Creative • Romantic •

La Bottega del Buon Caffè has changed premises for 2015 and is now on the Lungarno, with an outdoor terrace making it perfect for a fine evening. The distinctive creative style of the excellent chef at work in the open-view kitchen remains unchanged.
➔ Crema bruciata di fegato grasso. Cappelletti ripieni di piccione, burro e timo fresco. Filetto di ricciola in crosta di pane nero, sedano e cipolle.

X **Il Santo Bevitore** ✧

via Santo Spirito 64/66 r ✉ 50125 – ℰ 055 211264   Plan: **C3**
– www.ilsantobevitore.com – Closed 10-20 August and Sunday lunch
Carte 28/55 €
• Tuscan • Rustic •

This restaurant offers home-style cooking, such as spelt pappardella pasta with wild boar and bilberries, and duck leg with chicory and foie gras, as well as a touch of creativity in the evening. Good value for money.

X **Io Osteria Personale** ⚫ AC

Borgo San Frediano 167r ✉ 50124 Firenze   Plan: **D2**
– ℰ 055 9331341 – www.io-osteriapersonale.it – Closed 3 weeks in August, 3 weeks in January, Sunday
Menu 40/55 € – Carte 40/62 € – *(dinner only) (booking advisable)*
• Creative • Simple •

The young owner of this restaurant has an interesting background – a former vet with a passion for food. He has opened one of the most fascinating restaurants in Florence, serving original dishes to diners looking for a change from more traditional fare.

X **Osteria Caffè Italiano** AC ✧

via Isola delle Stinche 11 ✉ 50122 – ℰ 055 289368   Plan: **E3**
– www.caffeitaliano.it – Closed Monday (except April-October)
Carte 29/59 €
• Traditional cuisine • Rustic •

These fine premises are part of a historic building. Wood furnishings predominate in the three small dining halls where the cuisine is largely based on Tuscan recipes. There is a fine wine list.

X **Trattoria Cibrèo-Cibreino** AC
☺

via dei Macci 122/r ✉ 50122 – ℰ 0552 341100   Plan: **F3**
– www.edizioniteatrodelsalecibreofirenze.it – Closed August, 10 days in February and Monday
Carte 30/37 €
• Tuscan • Rustic •

This trattoria is named after the famous cibreo, a typical stew from Florence that Catherine of Medici was said to enjoy so much that she even attempted, unsuccessfully, to export it to France. It is often crowded, but there is no point in trying to book a table as they don't take reservations. Roast rack of beef (gran pezzo) is one of the specialities.

491

Il Latini

via dei Palchetti 6 r ✉ 50123 – ✆ 055 210916 – www.illatini.com – Closed 1-15 August, 20 December-2 January, Monday Plan: **D2**

Carte 35/77 €

• Tuscan • Rustic •

Flasks of wine on the walls, hams hanging from the ceiling, friendly informal service and a tradition dating back a hundred years. This famous Florentine trattoria celebrates Tuscan cuisine in all its glory, from ribollita soups to roast meat dishes.

Del Fagioli

corso Tintori 47 r ✉ 50122 – ✆ 055 244285 – Closed August, Saturday and Sunday Plan: **E3**

Carte 26/74 €

• Tuscan • Rustic •

A traditional trattoria that is typical of its genre with an open-view kitchen, lively informal ambience and Tuscan cuisine, including a wide selection of meat dishes and grills. A convivial atmosphere that attracts locals and tourists alike.

Zeb

via San Miniato 2r ✉ 50122 Firenze – ✆ 055 2342864 – www.zebgastronomia.com – Closed 10 days in August, Wednesday and dinner Sunday-Tuesday Plan: **E3**

Carte 21/60 €

• Tuscan • Trendy •

A new take on traditional cuisine in this unique restaurant in the delightful San Niccolò district. Diners sit side-by-side around a central table, as in a sushi bar, enjoying a selection of delicious homemade dishes.

ON THE HILLS — PLAN I

Grand Hotel Villa Cora

viale Machiavelli 18 ✉ 50125 – ✆ 055 228790 – www.villacora.it Plan: **B2**

46 rm – †250/800 € ††270/900 € – ☕ 25 € – 6 suites

• Grand Luxury • Personalised •

This elegant late-19C villa surrounded by century-old gardens offers a profusion of frescoed lounges and marble and stucco decor. Modern well-equipped spa, outdoor swimming pool and refined cuisine in the restaurant, where you can dine on the veranda in summer.

Torre di Bellosguardo

via Roti Michelozzi 2 ✉ 50124 – ✆ 055 2298145 – www.torrebellosguardo.com Plan: **A2**

16 rm – †110/160 € ††260/300 € – ☕ 20 € – 7 suites

• Country house • Historic •

There's a hint of the past in the lounge areas and guestrooms of this simple yet elegant hotel, which has breathtaking views of Florence. It has a magical, fairy tale atmosphere. There is a park with a botanical garden, an aviary and a swimming pool.

Villa La Vedetta

viale Michelangiolo 78 ✉ 50125 – ✆ 055 681631 – www.villalavedettahotel.com Plan: **B2**

11 rm ☕ – †150/980 € ††150/1100 € – 7 suites

• Luxury • Stylish •

Surrounded by mature parkland, this neo-Renaissance-style villa has been transformed into an elegant hotel decorated with a mix of designer-style furnishings and antique pieces. Every guestroom has its own personality, with each boasting charming details, such as bedside tables made from onyx or crocodile, crystal writing desks and precious silk furnishings.

Villa Le Piazzole

via Suor Maria Celeste 28 – ℰ 055 223520 — Plan: **B2**
– www.lepiazzole.com – Closed 20 December-10 January
12 rm ⌂ – ♦150/200 € ♦♦180/265 € – 2 suites
• Traditional • Personalised •
Enjoying a panoramic location overlooking the Ema valley with its old churches and farms, this extensive olive oil and wine estate offers individually decorated rooms with elegant period furnishings. The hotel is surrounded by a delightful Italian-style garden.

 Marignolle Relais & Charme

via di San Quirichino 16, località Marignolle — Plan: **A2**
– ℰ 055 2286910 – www.marignolle.com
8 rm ⌂ – ♦125/235 € ♦♦140/250 € – 1 suite
• Luxury • Personalised •
The pleasant rooms in this rustic dwelling in a holding in the hills are all different from one another and are characterized by refined blends of lively materials; panoramic swimming pool in the greenery.

 Villa Belvedere

via Benedetto Castelli 3 ⊠ 50124 – ℰ 055 222501 — Plan: **B2**
– www.villabelvederefirenze.it – Open 1° March-15 November
26 rm ⌂ – ♦80/207 € ♦♦120/207 €
• Traditional • Cosy •
Villa dating from the 1950s, with a swimming pool in the gardens and a splendid view over the town and the hills, for a quiet stay in a luxury but family orientated environment.

 Omero

via Pian de' Giullari 49 – ℰ 055 220053 — Plan: **B2**
– www.ristoranteomero.it
Carte 31/59 €
• Tuscan • Rustic •
Offering views of the hills, this beautifully kept restaurant has been run by the same family for 30 years. Traditional trattoria ambience and typical regional cuisine. Evening dining on the terrace in summer.

 Trattoria Bibe

via delle Bagnese 15 – ℰ 055 2049085 — Plan: **A2**
– www.trattoriabibe.com – Closed 1 week in November, 2 weeks in February and Wednesday
3 rm – ♦60/120 € ♦♦90/120 € Carte 29/48 € – *(dinner only)*
• Tuscan • Retro •
Immortalised by the Italian writer Montale in his poetry, this trattoria has been run by the same family for almost two centuries. The menu features traditional Tuscan dishes, such as pici pasta with wild boar sauce. Alfresco dining in summer. There are also apartments with kitchens for guests that wish to extend their stay.

 Villa La Massa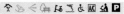

via della Massa 24 – ℰ 055 62611 – www.villalamassa.com – Open 8 April-1° November
23 rm ⌂ – ♦460/620 € ♦♦460/620 € – 14 suites
• Grand Luxury • Historic •
More than just a hotel, this building is an architectural jewel from the Medici period and a bucolic oasis overlooking the River Arno situated just 15min from Florence (easily accessible thanks to the hotel's free shuttle service). Four-poster beds, wood panelling, frescoed ceilings, tapestries and marble bathrooms all combine to provide a warm yet elegant ambience, offering guests a taste of aristocratic Florentine life – with all the comforts of our modern age.
Il Verrocchio – See restaurant listing

ITALY - FLORENCE

🍴🍴🍴 Il Verrocchio – Hotel Villa La Massa

*via della Massa 24 – ☎ 055 62611 – www.villalamassa.com – Open
8 April-1° November*
Menu 55/160 € – Carte 63/120 € – *(dinner only)*
• **Modern cuisine • Classic •**
This restaurant is named after the Florentine artist in whose studio the great
Leonardo da Vinci trained. It boasts an elegant dining room with a vaulted cei-
ling, as well as a delightful terrace overlooking the Arno for alfresco dining.
Regional specialities and traditional Italian favourites are on the menu.

AT FIESOLE   PLAN I

Villa San Michele

via Doccia 4 – ☎ 055 5678201 – www.belmond.com   Plan: **B1**
– Open 1° April-30 October
39 rm 🛏 – ♦550 € ♦♦890/1130 € – 6 suites
• **Luxury • Classic •**
A free shuttle bus takes guests from this hotel to the heart of Florence (10min).
Or you may prefer simply to relax in the tranquil grounds of this elegant 15C
building and enjoy the superb views of the city below.

Il Salviatino

via del Salviatino 21 – ☎ 055 9041111   Plan: **B2**
– www.salviatino.com
45 rm 🛏 – ♦300/1100 € ♦♦330/1100 € – 8 suites
• **Luxury • Historic •**
Luxury is evident not only in the rooms of this 16C villa – which is surrounded
by gardens and boasts fine views of the city – but also in its "service ambassadors", who are on hand to deal with guests' requests 24 hours a day. A truly
idyllic place to stay!
Il Salviatino – See restaurant listing

🏠 Pensione Bencistà

via Benedetto da Maiano 4 – ☎ 055 59163   Plan: **B1**
– www.bencista.com – Open 15 March-15 November
41 rm 🛏 – ♦80/130 € ♦♦130/200 € – 2 suites
• **Family • Retro •**
Situated on the slopes of the hills surrounding Fiesole, this 14C villa offers picture-postcard views of Florence. The interior decor is attractively retro, if occasionally a little dated in style, but full of charm and old-world romance.

🍴🍴🍴 Il Salviatino – Hotel Salviatino

via del Salviatino 21 – ☎ 055 9041111   Plan: **B2**
– www.salviatino.com
Carte 79/125 €
• **Regional • Elegant •**
This restaurant has classic furnishings in shades of white, as well as a beautiful
outdoor terrace overlooking the lovely gardens. The menu focuses on elaborate
dishes made from the best ingredients, which are presented in a simple yet elegant way.

🍴 Tullio a Montebeni

*via Ontignano 48 – ☎ 055 697354 – www.ristorantetullio.it – Closed
August, Monday, Tuesday lunch*
Carte 23/67 € – *(booking advisable)*
• **Tuscan • Simple •**
This restaurant started as a simple grocery shop and in 1958 it began serving
simple meals to locals and hunters in the region. Today the restaurant is enthu-
siastically run by Tullio's children, who continue to offer regional cuisine accom-
panied by their own home produced wine.

AT SAN CASCIANO IN VAL DI PESA

 Villa il Poggiale – Dimora Storica   🕭 ⟨ 🛏 🏠 ㋡ 🆎 🕭 🅿

via Empolese 69 (North-West: 1 km) – 𝒞 *055 828311*
– www.villailpoggiale.it – Closed 7 January-28 February
24 rm ☷ – ♦80/150 € ♦♦90/260 € – 2 suites
• Luxury • Historic •
Situated in the heart of Chianti just a few kilometres from Florence, this Renaissance-style villa is an oasis of peace surrounded by delightful gardens. Guests here are spoilt with a whole host of attentive details which combine to make their stay a truly unforgettable experience, as well as a new spa which offers a range of treatments created exclusively for the hotel. The restaurant serves typical Tuscan cuisine accompanied by a good selection of local wines.

XᵡX **La Tenda Rossa**   🕸 🆎

piazza del Monumento 9/14 – 𝒞 *055 826132* – *www.latendarossa.it*
– Closed 1 week in August, Sunday, Monday lunch
Menu 45 € (lunch)/105 € – Carte 58/111 €
• Creative • Elegant •
Italian restaurants are traditionally family-run, and three families run this one! Its quality of service and the food is three times as good.

AT THE AIRPORT   PLAN I

 Hilton Garden Inn Florence Novoli   🕭 🎞 & 🆎 🚗

via Sandro Pertini 2/9, Novoli ✉ *50127* – 𝒞 *055 42401*   Plan: **A1**
– www.florencenovoli.hgi.com
119 rm ☷ – ♦90/420 € ♦♦90/420 € – 2 suites
• Business • Modern •
This modern hotel near the motorway offers bright and airy public areas, as well as comfortable guestrooms furnished in tasteful modern style and equipped with all the latest facilities.

X **Da Burde**   🆎

via Pistoiese 154 ✉ *50122* – 𝒞 *055 317206*   Plan: **A2**
– www.burde.it – Closed 13-21 August and Bank Holidays
Carte 23/42 € – *(lunch only)*
• Regional • Family •
Opened at the beginning of the 20C as a grocer's shop and trattoria, this historic restaurant is a long way off the usual tourist trail. The two brothers who now run Da Burde have kept everything as it was with cured hams on sale and a bar selling tobacco. To the rear, there is a small dining room in which authentic Tuscan cuisine, such as the famous Florentine steak and pappa al pomodoro soup, is served.

MILAN
MILANO
Population: 1 337 155

If it's the romantic charm of places like Venice, Florence or Rome you're looking for, then best avoid Milan. If you're hankering for a permanent panorama of Renaissance chapels, palazzi, shimmering canals and bastions of fine art, then you're in the wrong place. What Milan does is relentless fashion, churned out with oodles of attitude and style. Italy's second largest city is constantly reinventing itself, and when Milan does a makeover, it invariably does it with flair and panache. That's not to say that Italy's capital of fast money and fast fashion doesn't have an eye for its past. The centrepiece of the whole city is the magnificent gleaming white Duomo, which took five hundred years to complete, while up la via a little way, La Scala is quite simply the world's most famous opera house. But this is a city known primarily for its sleek and modern towers, many housing the very latest threads from the very latest fashion gurus.

Just north of Milan's centre lies Brera, with its much prized old-world charm, and Quadrilatero d'Oro, with no little new-world glitz; the popular Giardini Pubblici are a little further north east from here. South of the centre is the Navigli quarter, home to rejuvenated Middle Age canals, while to the west are the green lungs of the Parco Sempione. For those into art or fashion, the trendy Savona district is also a must.

MILAN IN...

→ ONE DAY
Duomo, Leonardo da Vinci's 'The Last Supper' (remember to book first), Brera, Navigli.

→ TWO DAYS
Pinacoteca Brera, Castello Sforzesco, Parco Sempione, Museo del Novecento, a night at La Scala.

→ THREE DAYS
Giardini Pubblici and its museums, trendy Savona district.

PRACTICAL INFORMATION

ARRIVAL-DEPARTURE

 Malpensa Airport is 48km north-west of the city and Linate Airport, 7km east. A train connects Malpensa with Stazione Cadorna every 30min, which takes 40min. From Linate take the Airport Bus No. 73 to Piazza San Babila metro station (every 10min, it takes 25min).

GETTING AROUND

The best way to get about Milan is by bus, tram or metro. Tickets are valid for one metro ride, or seventy five minutes of travel on buses or trams. You can also purchase books of ten tickets, or unlimited one-day or two-day passes.

Buy them at metro stations, kiosks, bars or tobacconists. The metro provides a fast and efficient service, with frequent trains running on three different lines. Walking is a good alternative: most of Milan's attractions are based in the small and compact centre.

CALENDAR HIGHLIGHTS

February
Milan Fashion Week.

March
MiArt (international modern art fair).

April
Naviglio Grande Flower Market.
International Furniture Fair.

June
Gods of Metal Festival, Festival Latino Americano, Festa del Naviglio, Notte Bianca.

September
September Music, Panoramica (film festival), Milan Fashion Week.
Formula 1 Grand Prix in Monza.

October
Wellness World Exhibition, Celtic New Year celebrations.

December
Opera season at La Scala gets underway.

EATING OUT

For a taste of Italy's regional cuisines, Milan is a great place to be. The city is often the goal of those leaving their home regions in the south or centre of the country; many open trattoria or restaurants, with the result that Milan offers a wide range of provincial menus. Excellent fish restaurants, inspired by recipes from the south, are a big draw despite the fact that the city is a long way from the sea. Going beyond the local borders, the emphasis on really good food continues and the quality of internationally diverse places

to eat is better in Milan than just about anywhere else in Italy, including Rome. You'd expect avant-garde eating destinations to be the thing in this city of fashion and style, and you'd be right: there are some top-notch cutting-edge restaurants, thanks to Milan's famous tendency to reshape and experiment as it goes. For those who want to try out the local gastronomic traditions, risotto allo zafferano is not to be missed, nor is the cotoletta alla Milanese (veal cutlet) or the casoeula (a winter special made with pork and cabbage).

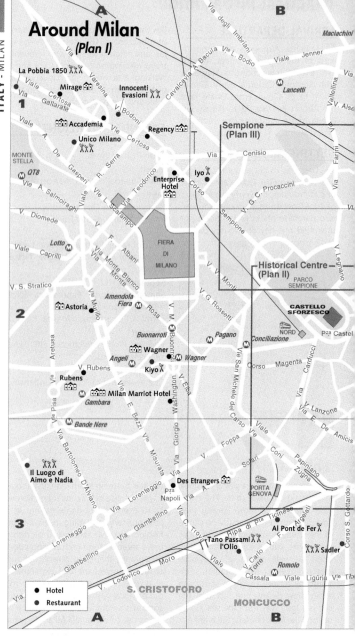

Around Milan
(Plan I)

La Pobbia 1850 ✗✗✗
Mirage 🏨
Innocenti Evasioni ✗✗
Accademia 🏨
Unico Milano ✗✗✗
Regency 🏨
MONTE STELLA
Ⓜ QT8
Enterprise Hotel 🏨
Iyo ✗
Lotto Ⓜ
FIERA DI MILANO
Astoria 🏨
Amendola Fiera Ⓜ
Buonarroti Ⓜ
Wagner 🏨
Angell
Wagner
Kiyo ✗
Rubens 🏨
Ⓜ Milan Marriot Hotel
Gambara Ⓜ
Bande Nere Ⓜ
Il Luogo di Aimo e Nadia ✗✗✗
Des Etrangers 🏨
Pza Napoli
S. CRISTOFORO
Al Pont de Fer ✗
Tano Passami l'Olio ✗✗
✗✗✗ Sadler
Romolo Ⓜ
MONCUCCO

Sempione (Plan III)
Lancetti Ⓜ
Historical Centre (Plan II)
PARCO SEMPIONE
CASTELLO SFORZESCO
NORD
Pza Castel
Conciliazione Ⓜ
Pagano Ⓜ
Corso Magenta
PORTA GENOVA

Maciachini

● Hotel
● Restaurant

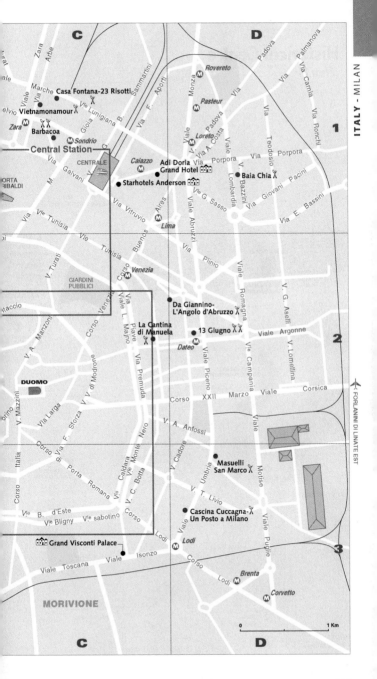

C

D

Via Zara Arbe Aral ale

Via Marche Casa Fontana-23 Risotti

elvio Vietnamonamour X

Zara

Barbacoa

Via Sammartini

Via F. Aporti

B. Gioia

Viale Lunigiana

Roveneto

Monza

Pasteur

Padova

Via Padova

Via Camia

Via Patmanova

Via Ronchi

Sondrio

Central Station

Via Galvani

ORTA RIBALDI

M

Via Vie Tunisia

V. Turati

GIARDINI PUBBLICI

itaccio

CENTRALE

Caiazzo Adi Doria Grand Hotel

Starhotels Anderson

Via Vitruvio

Aires

Lima

Corso Buenos

Via Tunisia

Corso Venezia

Viale L. Majno

Via Plave

Via Premuda

Loreto

Via A. Costa

Vie Porpora

Vle G. Sasso

Viale Abruzzi

Via Plinio

Venezia

Da Giannino-L'Angolo d'Abruzzo

La Cantina di Manuela X

13 Giugno X X

Dateo

Baia Chia X

Via Teodosio

Via Giovanni Pacini

Via E. Bassini

Via Porpora

Bazzini

Via Lombardia

Viale Romagna

V. G. Aselli

Viale Argonne

V. Lomellina

1

2

DUOMO

V. A. Manzoni

V. Mazzini

orino

Via Larga

Corso di Porta Romana

ttalia

Corso

Vle B. d'Este

Vle Bligny

Via F. Sforza

V. V. di Modrone

Vle Caldara

Vle Monte Nero

V. C. Botta

Vle sabotino

Corso

Viale Piceno

Via Campania

Corso XXII Marzo

Viale Corsica

V. A. Anfossi

V. Cadore

Umbria

Masuelli San Marco X

V. T. Livio

Cascina Cuccagna-X Un Posto a Milano

Lodi

Via Morise

Viale Puglie

FORLANINI DI LINATE EST

Grand Visconti Palace

Viale Toscana

Viale Isonzo

Lodi

Corso

Lodi

Brenta

Corvetto

3

MORIVIONE

0   1 Km

C

D

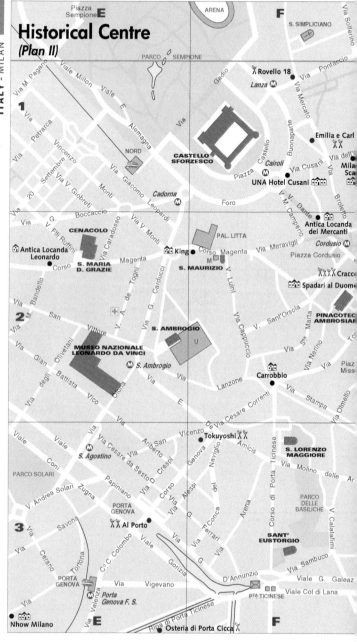

Historical Centre
(Plan II)

Piazza Sempione **E**

ARENA

F

S. SIMPLICIANO

PARCO SEMPIONE

Rovello 18

Lanza Ⓜ

1

NORD

CASTELLO SFORZESCO

Emilia e Carl

Cadorna Ⓜ

Cairoli

UNA Hotel Cusani

Milan Sca

Piazza

Foro

Antica Locanda dei Mercanti

CENACOLO

PAL. LITTA

Cordusio Ⓜ

Antica Locanda Leonardo

S. MARIA D. GRAZIE

King ● Corso Magenta

Via Meravigli

Piazza Cordusio

Magenta

S. MAURIZIO

Cracc

Spadari al Duom

PINACOTEC AMBROSIAN

2

MUSEO NAZIONALE LEONARDO DA VINCI

S. AMBROGIO

Ⓜ S. Ambrogio

Carrobbio

Piaz Miss

PARCO SOLARI

S. Agostino Ⓜ

Tokuyoshi

S. LORENZO MAGGIORE

PORTA GENOVA

Al Porto

PARCO DELLE BASILICHE

3

PORTA GENOVA

SANT'EUSTORGIO

Porta Genova F. S. Ⓜ

D'Annunzio

PTA TICINESE

Viale G. Galeaz

Viale Col di Lana

Nhow Milano

E

Ripa di Porta Ticinese

Osteria di Porta Cicca

F

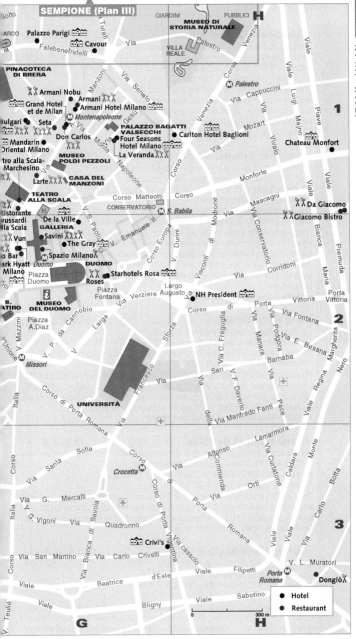

SEMPIONE (Plan III)

GIARDINI
MUSEO DI
STORIA NATURALE
PUBBLICI
VILLA
REALE
Via Turati
Via
Palestro

ARCO
Palazzo Parigi
Cavour
Via Fatebenefratelli

PINACOTECA
DI BRERA
Armani Nobu
Armani
Armani Hotel Milano
Grand Hotel
et de Milan
Bulgari
Seta
Don Carlos
Mandarin
Oriental Milano
MUSEO
POLDI PEZZOLI
tro alla Scala-
Marchesino
Larte
CASA DEL
MANZONI

Via Manzoni
Via Senato
Via Montenapoleone
Gesù
Via Monte
Via Napoleone

PALAZZO BAGATTI
VALSECCHI
Four Seasons
Hotel Milano
La Veranda
Carlton Hotel Baglioni

M Palestro
Via Cappuccini
Via Luigi
Via Mozart
Via Vivaio
Via Majno

M
Chateau Monfort

TEATRO
ALLA SCALA
istorante
russardi
lla Scala
Vun
Bar
ark Hyatt
Milano
De la Ville
GALLERIA
Savini
The Gray
Spazio Milano
DUOMO
Piazza
Duomo

Corso Matteotti
CONSERVATORIO
Corso
M S. Babila
V. S. Paolo
Emanuele II
Corso Europa
V. Durini

Monforte
Via Mascagni
Via Conservatorio
Da Giacomo
Giacomo Bistro

Via Corridoni
Via Bianca
Maria
Via Premuda

DUOMO
Starhotels Rosa
Roses
Piazza
Fontana
Largo
Via Verziere Augusto
NH President

S.
ATIRO
MUSEO
DEL DUOMO
Piazza
A.Diaz
da Cannobio
Larga
Via Storza

Corso di
Porta
di
Corso
Via C. Freguglia
Via Podgora
Via Manara
Porta
Vittoria
Via Fontana
Porta
Vittoria

'Unione
V. Mazzini
M
Missori
V. P.
V.
Via
Francesco
San
V. F. Daverio
Via
Barnaba
Pace
Via E. Besana
Via Regina
Via Margherita
Nero

UNIVERSITÀ
Corso di Porta Romana
Via Manfredo Fanti
Lamarmora
Via Curtatone
Alfonso
Via Caldara
Via Monte
Via Botta

Italia
Corso
Via Santa
Sofia
Crocetta M
Corso
Via
di
Alfonso
Commenda
Orti
Via

Via G. Mercalli
V. G. Vigoni
Via
Quadronno
Porta
Via
Romana
Via Carlo

Via
Corso
Via San Martino
Via Bianca di Savoia
Via Carlo Crivelli
Crivi's
Viale
d'Este
Viale
Filipetti
Porta
Romana M
V. L. Muratori
Dongiò

V. Teulié
Viale
Viale
Beatrice
Bligny
Viale
Sabotino

G   H

• Hotel
• Restaurant

0   300 m

1

2

3

501

ITALY - MILAN

Four Seasons Hotel Milano   ✿ 🖐 ⅃♨ 🌐 🕸 ▣ ⅄ AC ⚑

via Gesù 6/8 ✉ *20121 –* Ⓜ *Montenapoleone –* ☏ *02 77088*   🚗
– www.fourseasons.com/milan   Plan: **G1**
68 rm – 🛉570/1160 € 🛉🛉570/1160 € – ⤋ 35 € – 50 suites
• Luxury • Classic • Personalised •
This evocative hotel has achieved a perfect balance between the original architectural features of the 15C monastery in which it is housed and its elegant contemporary design. Don't be surprised by the highly modern technology available in the superb guestrooms that occupy the former monks' cells.
La Veranda – See restaurant listing

Mandarin Oriental Milano   ✿ ⅃♨ 🌐 🕸 ▣ ⅄ AC ⚑

via Andegari 9 ✉ *20121 Milano –* Ⓜ *Montenapoleone*   Plan: **G1**
– ☏ *02 87318888 – www.mandarinoriental.com*
85 rm – 🛉600/1100 € 🛉🛉700/1200 € – ⤋ 45 € – 19 suites
• Luxury • Contemporary •
This prestigious chain has now opened a hotel in four sober 18C buildings situated in Milan's fashion quarter. Choose between standard rooms (in name only!) and various suites decorated in warm colours and elegant Italian designer style. The attractive spa also features original features, such as the wooden beams that are deliberately arranged asymmetrically, evoking the image of an Asian cane thicket. The ambience is distinctly 1950s in the Mandarin Bar, where guests can choose from a selection of sandwiches, large salads and typical Italian dishes.
❀ **Seta** – See restaurant listing

Park Hyatt Milano   ✿ ⅃♨ 🌐 ⅄ AC ⚑

via Tommaso Grossi 1 ✉ *20121 –* Ⓜ *Duomo*   Plan: **G2**
– ☏ *02 88211234 – www.milan.park.hyatt.com*
90 rm – 🛉630/1220 € 🛉🛉630/1220 € – ⤋ 38 € – 16 suites
• Traditional • Stylish •
Housed in a palazzo dating from 1870, this contemporary-style hotel boasts the best of modern comforts, including spacious guestrooms and equally large bathrooms. Travertine marble covers the building and a splendid work of art by Anish Kapoor "Untitled 2013" can be admired in the lobby.
❀ **Vun • Mio Bar** – See restaurant listing

Grand Hotel et de Milan   ✿ ⅃♨ ⅄ AC ⚑

via Manzoni 29 ✉ *20121 –* Ⓜ *Montenapoleone*   Plan: **G1**
– ☏ *02 723141 – www.grandhoteletdemilan.it*
86 rm – 🛉450/725 € 🛉🛉480/750 € – ⤋ 35 € – 8 suites
• Grand Luxury • Stylish • Historic •
This hotel opened over 150 years ago. Big names in the field of music, theatre and politics have stayed in its elegant rooms that are full of charm. Bright restaurant dedicated to the great tenor, who recorded his first record in this hotel.
Don Carlos – See restaurant listing

Carlton Hotel Baglioni   ✿ ⅃♨ ⅄ AC ⚑ 🚗

via Senato 5 ✉ *20121 –* Ⓜ *San Babila –* ☏ *02 77077*   Plan: **H1**
– www.baglionihotels.com
80 rm ⤋ – 🛉200/650 € 🛉🛉250/850 € – 7 suites
• Luxury • Design • Elegant •
Celebrities and well-known personalities are among the guests who have stayed in this splendid hotel, which describes itself as 'home from home'. It provides luxury in a warm, family atmosphere. Antique pieces and original works of art grace the public areas, while the guestrooms offer stucco decor and modern technology.

Bulgari

via privata Fratelli Gabba 7/b ✉ *20121* Plan: **G1**
– **Ⓜ** *Montenapoleone* – ☎ *02 8058051* – *www.bulgarihotels.com*
47 rm – ♦550/750 € ♦♦550/750 € – ☲ 35 € – 11 suites
• Grand Luxury • Design • Stylish •
Owned by the famous jewellery company, this luxury hotel is decorated in warm colours with fine materials gracing the guestrooms. The hotel boasts one of the best spas in the city with a hammam whose green glass decor evokes an emerald. Exclusive terrace overlooking an unexpected garden.
Bulgari-Il Ristorante – See restaurant listing

Armani Hotel Milano

via Manzoni 31 ✉ *20123* – **Ⓜ** *Montenapoleone* Plan: **G1**
– ☎ *02 8883 8888* – *www.armanihotels.com*
95 rm – ♦500/1600 € ♦♦500/1600 € – ☲ 40 € – 32 suites
• Grand Luxury • Design • Elegant •
This innovative hotel is housed in an austere building dating from 1937, typical of the Armani style. It is run by a 'lifestyle manager' who offers a warm welcome to guests. Luxurious 1 000m² spa and very spacious guestrooms.
❀ **Armani** – See restaurant listing

Starhotels Rosa Grand

piazza Fontana 3 ✉ *20122* – **Ⓜ** *Duomo* – ☎ *02 88311* Plan: **G2**
– *www.starhotels.com*
324 rm ☲ – ♦165/900 € ♦♦300/1300 € – 6 suites
• Palace • Modern • Design •
Situated in the heart of Milan, this hotel has recently undergone a major refurbishment. The interior is arranged around a courtyard, with simple, square shapes creating a naturally elegant look. The guestrooms here are comfortable and stylish, although only a few offer views of the Duomo.
Roses – See restaurant listing

NH President

largo Augusto 10 ✉ *20122* – **Ⓜ** *San Babila* Plan: **H2**
– ☎ *02 77461* – *www.nh-hotels.it*
274 rm – ♦419/1049 € ♦♦439/1069 € – ☲ 25 € – 12 suites
• Chain hotel • Modern • Functional •
An international standard hotel for business travellers or tourists. It has attractive, spacious lounge areas as well as facilities for fashion shows, business lunches and conferences. The restaurant serves specialities from Lombardy, as well as Mediterranean-style dishes.

UNA Hotel Cusani

via Cusani 13 ✉ *20121* – **Ⓜ** *Cairoli* – ☎ *02 85601* Plan: **F1**
– *www.unahotels.it*
87 rm ☲ – ♦200/1100 € ♦♦220/1120 € – 5 suites
• Palace • Modern •
Located in the heart of the historic town centre, this hotel is in an ideal location for business and sightseeing. It has simple and modern, very large attractive rooms. Choose from classic Italian or international dishes at this cosy restaurant.

Château Monfort

corso Concordia 1 ✉ *20129* – ☎ *02 776761* Plan: **H1**
– *www.chateaumonfort.com*
77 rm ☲ – ♦295/990 € ♦♦351/1046 €
• Traditional • Elegant •
Discreet elegance characterises this splendid Art Nouveau-style palazzo that bears the hallmark of the architect Paolo Mezzanotte. The guestrooms are chic and glamorous (those inspired by the opera are truly magical), and there is a small spa in which to rest and relax. Mediterranean cuisine is to the fore in the hotel restaurant.

ITALY - MILAN

The Gray ✿ & 🕮

via San Raffaele 6 ⊠ 20121 – 🕅 *Duomo* Plan: **G2**
– 𝒞 02 7208951 – www.sinahotels.com – Closed August
19 rm – †500/650 € ††550/900 € – � 33 € – 2 suites
• Luxury • Personalised •
All different in style, the rooms in this hotel feature a host of interesting details,
as well as up-to-date technology such as Wi-Fi internet connection and LCD
televisions. 'Gray' in name only (perhaps an ironic reference to Milan's occasional dull weather?), this hotel is one of the most stylish and elegant in the city.

Milano Scala ✿ ₤₅ & 🕮 🔥

via dell'Orso 7 ⊠ 20121 – 🕅 *Cairoli – 𝒞 02 870961* Plan: **F1**
– www.hotelmilanoscala.it
58 rm ⊠ – †150/520 € ††210/680 € – 4 suites
• Luxury • Personalised • Stylish •
A charming hotel built in 2010 with an emphasis on sustainability. The public
areas are fairly small but stylish, while the breakfast room is a real delight, decorated with musical notes on the walls. There is a good choice of dishes in the
restaurant for dinner. At lunchtime the menu is lighter with a focus on snacks.

Grand Visconti Palace ✿ 🍴 ₤₅ 🌐 🛱 🔲 & 🕮 🔥 🚗

viale Isonzo 14 ⊠ 20135 – 🕅 *Lodi TIBB – 𝒞 02 540341* Plan: **C3**
– www.grandviscontipalace.com
166 rm ⊠ – †100/1000 € ††100/1100 € – 6 suites
• Palace • Elegant •
A large old industrial mill has been converted to house this elegant grand hotel
with a welcoming well-being centre, conference rooms and a delightful garden.
Make sure you try the Quinto Piano restaurant, which delights guests with its
refined and imaginative cuisine made with real care and attention.

Nhow Milano ✿ ₤₅ & 🕮 🔥 🄿

via Tortona 35 ⊠ 20144 – 𝒞 02 4898861 Plan: **E3**
– www.nhow-hotels.com
245 rm ⊠ – †89/999 € ††109/1019 € – 1 suite
• Traditional • Stylish •
This designer-style hotel located in a former industrial district has plenty of
charm, and acts as a permanent showcase for artistic and stylistic excellence.
Eclectic guestrooms offering impeccable standards of comfort.

De la Ville ✿ ₤₅ 🛱 🔲 & 🕮 🔥

via Hoepli 6 ⊠ 20121 – 🕅 *Duomo – 𝒞 02 8791311* Plan: **G2**
– www.sinahotels.com
107 rm ⊠ – †250/480 € ††300/500 € – 1 suite
• Traditional • Elegant •
Despite its location in the bustling centre of Milan, there's nothing Milanese
about this hotel, which has a French name and a distinctly British decor. It features wood panelling, fireplaces and attractive prints depicting horses and fox
hunting. The same stylish elegance is evident in the guestrooms.

Spadari al Duomo 🕮

via Spadari 11 ⊠ 20123 – 🕅 *Duomo – 𝒞 02 72002371* Plan: **F2**
– www.spadarihotel.com – Closed 23-27 December
39 rm ⊠ – †198/420 € ††198/420 € – 1 suite
• Traditional • Modern •
This modern hotel has the twin advantage of a central location, as well as a fine
display of contemporary art collected by its art enthusiast owners. Note the Giò
Pomodoro fireplace in the lobby and the careful play of light throughout the
hotel.

Cavour
via Fatebenefratelli 21 ✉ *20121* – Ⓜ *Turati*
– ☎ 02 620001 – www.hotelcavour.it
– Closed 7-20 August
125 rm ⌚ – **♦**115/700 € **♦♦**126/900 € – 7 suites
• Traditional • Elegant •

Plan: **G1**

This simple yet elegant hotel not far from the city's main cultural sights is decorated with high quality materials, from the floors to the wood panelling. The restaurant serves reasonably priced brasserie-style dishes from 11am-7pm.

Crivi's
corso Porta Vigentina 46 ✉ *20122* – Ⓜ *Crocetta*
– ☎ 02 582891 – www.crivis.com
– Closed August and Christmas Holidays
86 rm ⌚ – **♦**120/250 € **♦♦**160/350 €
• Traditional • Classic •

Plan: **G3**

In a convenient location near the metro, this comfortable hotel has pleasant public areas and traditionally furnished, reasonably comfortable and spacious guestrooms.

Antica Locanda dei Mercanti
via San Tomaso 6 ✉ *20121* – Ⓜ *Cordusio*
– ☎ 02 8054080 – www.locanda.it
12 rm ⌚ – **♦**205/325 € **♦♦**225/365 € – 3 suites
• Townhouse • Personalised •

Plan: **F2**

A small, cosy hotel, simple and elegant in style, and furnished with antique furniture. Many of the light and spacious guestrooms have a small terrace.

King
corso Magenta 19 ✉ *20123* – Ⓜ *Cadorna F.N.M.*
– ☎ 02 874432 – www.mokinba.it
48 rm ⌚ – **♦**170/517 € **♦♦**230/670 €
• Traditional • Classic •

Plan: **F2**

This six-floor building not far from the Duomo has been recently refurbished. It boasts some magnificent touches in the public areas and compact but comfortable guestrooms.

Carrobbio
via Medici 3 ✉ *20123* – Ⓜ *Duomo – ☎ 02 89010740*
– www.hotelcarrobbiomilano.com
– Closed August and Christmas Holidays
56 rm ⌚ – **♦**90/180 € **♦♦**120/356 €
• Traditional • Classic •

Plan: **F2**

This recently renovated hotel is in a quiet area and near the historic town centre. It has a small and relaxing winter garden.

Vun – Hotel Park Hyatt Milano
via Silvio Pellico 3 ✉ *20121* – Ⓜ *Duomo*
– ☎ 02 88211234 – www.ristorante-vun.it
– Closed August, Christmas Holidays, Sunday and Monday
Menu 115/150 € – Carte 91/130 € – *(dinner only)*
(booking advisable)
• Modern cuisine • Elegant •

Plan: **G2**

A young Neapolitan chef is at the helm in this restaurant. Enjoy dishes and ingredients from his native region as well as top quality produce from the heel of Italy. Elegant and cosmopolitan ambience.
→ Caprese ...dolce salato. Riso carnaroli riserva, scampi, limone, rosmarino, capperi. Gianduia e lamponi.

XxXX **Seta** – Hotel Mandarin Oriental Milano   🕸 🍴 ⅙ 🆎

⚜️ *via Monte di Pietà 18 ✉ 20121 – Ⓜ Montenapoleone*   Plan: **G1**
– ✆ 02 87318897 – www.mandarinoriental.com – *Closed 7-21 August,
lunch Saturday, Sunday*
Menu 130 € – Carte 85/120 € – *(booking advisable)*
• **Modern cuisine** • **Design** •

One of the characteristics of this restaurant is the sense of connection between
indoors and out created by the large windows. The menu offers fish and meat
dishes, with specialities from northern and southern Italy (the latter is the chef's
native region), as well as desserts with an occasionally exotic twist. A harmonious and successful combination of unusual flavours.
➜ Animelle di vitello, rigaglie di pollo e crema di carote agli agrumi. Spaghetti alla crema di rape rosse e crostacei al lime. Parfait alla liquirizia,
crema di caffè, pera alle spezie e tabacco cristallizzato.

XxXX **Cracco**   🕸 ⅙ 🆎

⚜️⚜️ *via Victor Hugo 4 ✉ 20123 – Ⓜ Duomo – ✆ 02 876774*   Plan: **F2**
– www.ristorantecracco.it – *Closed August, 24 December-7 January,
Saturday lunch, Sunday, Monday lunch*
Menu 120/181 € – Carte 112/150 € – *(booking advisable)*
• **Creative** • **Luxury** • **Formal** •

This restaurant offers traditional dishes from Milan and elsewhere in Italy reinterpreted with a modern twist and playing on contrasts of textures, flavours and
colours. The elegantly discreet ambience is made even more hushed by the
cherrywood panelling on the walls. There is also a "table d'hôte" – a small
table for a maximum of four diners, which offers views of the team at work in
the kitchen.
➜ Musetto di maiale fondente con pomodoro verde e scampi. Risotto allo
zafferano con midollo alla piastra. Cubo di vitello impanato alla milanese,
petalo di pomodoro farcito, agretti e zucchine.

XxXX **Il Ristorante Trussardi alla Scala**   🕸 ⅙ 🆎

piazza della Scala 5 (palazzo Trussardi) ✉ 20121   Plan: **G1**
– Ⓜ Duomo – ✆ 02 80688201 – www.trussardiallascala.com
– *Closed 2 weeks in August, 1-21 January, Saturday lunch, Sunday,*
Menu 150 € – Carte 100/168 € – *(booking advisable)*
• **Modern cuisine** • **Luxury** •

There has been a change in the style of cuisine served at this modern restaurant, which overlooks one of the most famous squares in Milan. A careful selection of produce and imaginative creativity are the hallmarks of the young chef.
Café Trussardi – See restaurant listing

XxXX **Savini**   🕸 ⅙ 🆎 ⇦

galleria Vittorio Emanuele II ✉ 20121 – Ⓜ Duomo   Plan: **G2**
– ✆ 02 72003433 – www.savinimilano.it – *Closed 20 days in August, 10
days in January, Saturday lunch and Sunday*
Menu 110/165 € – Carte 79/172 €
• **Traditional cuisine** • **Luxury** •

The entrance to this restaurant is through the Caffè Savini, which offers a selection of Italy's most famous dishes. A lift takes diners to the first floor, where the
gourmet restaurant has been delighting guests with its mix of Milanese favourites and more creative fare since 1867.

XxX **Larte**   🆎 ⇦

via Manzoni 5 ✉ 20123 – Ⓜ Montenapoleone   Plan: **G1**
– ✆ 0289096950 – www.lartemilano.com – *Closed August, Sunday*
Menu 35 € (lunch) – Carte 60/98 € – *(booking advisable)*
• **Modern cuisine** • **Fashionable** • **Trendy** •

This new Milanese 'salon' showcases the best of Italian culture with a menu featuring a fine selection of meat and fish classics from around the country, as well
as a boutique selling Italian products. Larte is not just a restaurant, but also a
chocolate shop, osteria, café and, last but not least, an art gallery!

ITALY - MILAN

XxX **Don Carlos** – Grand Hotel et de Milan [AC]
via Manzoni 29 ✉ *20121 –* **⊕** *Montenapoleone*   Plan: **G1**
– ☎ 02 72314640 – www.ristorantedoncarlos.it
Menu 75 €
– Carte 77/115 € – (dinner only) (number of covers limited, pre-book)
• **Modern cuisine** • **Romantic** • **Retro** •
Named after one of Verdi's operas, this charming restaurant has a quiet atmosphere and elegant decor, including wood panelling, red appliqué and old photos. The menu focuses on traditional cuisine from Lombardy and Piedmont with a creative touch.

XxX **Armani** – Armani Hotel Milano   ≤ & [AC] ⇔
☸ *via Manzoni 31* ✉ *20123 –* **⊕** *Montenapoleone*   Plan: **G1**
– ☎ 02 8883 8888 – www.armanihotels.com
– Closed Sunday dinner
Menu 120/180 € (dinner) – Carte 75/130 € *– (booking advisable)*
• **Modern cuisine** • **Elegant** • **Design** •
With its black and white tiled floor and large windows offering superb views of Milan, this exclusive restaurant boasts the same stylish design as the rest of the hotel. Delicious, well-prepared dishes - some of which show real technical flair - are typical of contemporary trends, combining Mediterranean ingredients with a hint of creativity and imagination.
→ Riso carnaroli, crescione, spugnole, terriccio alle mandorle, arancia. Scampo gigante, burrata, pesca, 'nduja, pata negra, coriandolo. Ricotta, mango, arachide salata, tartufo nero.

XxX **Teatro alla Scala - Il Marchesino**   & [AC]
via Filodrammatici 2 ✉ *20121 –* **⊕** *Duomo*   Plan: **G1**
– ☎ 02 72094338 – www.ilmarchesino.it
– Closed 1-6 January, Sunday
Menu 39 € (weekday lunch)/150 € – Carte 65/124 € *– (booking advisable)*
• **Modern cuisine** • **Classic** •
Housed within the La Scala opera house, this restaurant with a café and tearoom offers a careful mix of classic columns, modern paintings and designer-style furniture. Fine cuisine presented in the simple yet elegant style that is typical of Gualtiero Marchesi.

XxX **Bulgari-Il Ristorante** – Hotel Bulgari   ⊜ 🛋 & [AC] 🚗
via privata Fratelli Gabba 7/b ✉ *20121*   Plan: **G1**
– **⊕** *Montenapoleone*
– ☎ 02 8058051 – www.bulgarihotels.com
Menu 39 € (lunch), 65/100 € – Carte 67/119 € *– (booking advisable)*
• **Modern cuisine** • **Design** • **Minimalist** •
Overlooking an unexpected yet beautiful garden, this attractive restaurant boasts the same exclusive style as the rest of the hotel. The cuisine showcases top quality Italian produce in dishes that are modern and contemporary in flavour.

XxX **Sadler**   ஃ [AC] ⇔
☸☸ *via Ascanio Sforza 77* ✉ *20141 –* **⊕** *Romolo*   Plan: **B3**
– ☎ 02 58104451 – www.sadler.it
– Closed 2 weeks in August, 1°-8 January and Sunday
Menu 75 € (weekdays)/160 € – Carte 69/154 € *– (dinner only)*
• **Creative** • **Elegant** •
Harmony is the hallmark of this restaurant, with its clean lines, carefully chosen fabrics, large windows and effective lighting. Balance is also evident in the cuisine, which is a fine blend of the traditional and the innovative.
→ Spaghetti trafilati in oro con scampi e pomodoro datterino al peperoncino. Padellata di crostacei, broccoletti e melanzane croccanti con spuma al dragoncello. Insalata di pesche con gelatina di moscato, spuma di latte alle mandorle e biscotto soffice.

ITALY - MILAN

XxX **La Veranda** – Hotel Four Seasons · 🏨 🛱 AC ⟷ 🚗
via Gesù 6/8 ✉ *20121* – Ⓜ *Montenapoleone* Plan: **G1**
– ℰ *02 77081478* – *www.fourseasons.com/milan*
Menu 48/57 € – Carte 73/137 €
• Classic cuisine • Classic • Traditional •
Younger guests will have no problem choosing a dish at this restaurant, thanks
to its special children's menu. While other diners can enjoy Mediterranean cuisine and a wide selection of vegetarian specialities as they admire views of the
cloisters, which are visible through the large windows of the modern dining
room.

XxX **Mio Bar** – Hotel Park Hyatt Milano 🛱 ᶜ AC
via Tommaso Grossi 1 – ℰ *02 88211234* Plan: **G2**
– *www.milan.park.hyatt.com*
Menu 35 € (weekday lunch) – Carte 64/109 €
• Modern cuisine • Trendy •
Both convivial and informal, this restaurant offers a small but exhaustive, selection of traditional Italian dishes as well as classic international cuisine. There is
also a menu "Assaggi" dedicated to small bites. Mio Bar is open from 6 a.m. to
1 a.m.

XX **Armani Nobu** AC ⟷
via Pisoni 1 ✉ *20121* – Ⓜ *Montenapoleone* Plan: **G1**
– ℰ *02 72318645* – *www.armanirestaurants.com* – *Closed Sunday lunch*
Menu 100 € – Carte 47/118 €
• Japanese • Minimalist •
The pure minimalist lines of this restaurant with numerous branches dotted
around the world are not only typical of the Armani style but also distinctly
Japanese in feel. Fusion cuisine takes pride of place with a hint of South Ameri-
can influence.

XX **Roses** – Starhotels Rosa Grand AC 🚗
piazza Fontana 3 ✉ *20122* – Ⓜ *Duomo* – ℰ *02 88311* Plan: **G2**
– *www.starhotels.com*
Menu 55/70 € – Carte 50/66 €
• Modern cuisine • Trendy •
Impeccable service, imaginative cuisine and excellent ingredients all contribute
to the success of this restaurant, which also boasts a delightful atmosphere.
With its flowing spaces and chic decor, this is an ideal venue for a romantic dinner or business lunch.

XX **Emilia e Carlo** 舒 AC
via Sacchi 8 ✉ *20121* – Ⓜ *Cairoli* – ℰ *02 875948* Plan: **F1**
– *www.emiliaecarlo.it* – *Closed August, Saturday lunch, Sunday*
Carte 52/82 €
• Modern cuisine • Rustic •
Housed in an early 19C palazzo, this trattoria has a rustic feel with arches and
wooden beams. Creative contemporary cuisine, and a fine choice of wines.

XX **Al Porto** AC
piazzale Generale Cantore ✉ *20123* Plan: **E3**
– Ⓜ *Porta Genova FS* – ℰ *02 89407425* – *www.alportomilano.it*
– *Closed August, 24 December-3 January, Sunday, Monday lunch*
Carte 48/78 €
• Fish and seafood • Traditional •
There is a definite maritime flavour to this restaurant, which occupies the old
19C Porta Genova toll house. Always busy, Al Porto specialises exclusively in
fresh fish dishes, including raw fish.

ITALY - MILAN

XX **Da Giacomo** 🆎

via P. Sottocorno 6 ⊠ 20129 – ☏ 02 76023313   Plan: **H1**
– www.giacomoristorante.com
Carte 58/106 €
• Fish and seafood • Traditional •
This old Milanese trattoria dates from the early 20C. Seafood enthusiasts will be delighted by the numerous fish specialities on offer. The menu also includes a few meat dishes, as well as Alba truffles, Caesars' mushrooms and cep mushrooms in season.

XX **Giacomo Bistrot** 🆎

via P. Sottocorno 6 ⊠ 20129 – ☏ 0276022653   Plan: **H1**
– www.giacomobistrot.com
Carte 55/102 €
• Modern cuisine • Design •
This restaurant, which stays open until late at night, boasts tables set close together in French-bistro style, while its shelves of leather-bound volumes evoke the distinctly British ambience of a traditional bookshop. The menu features meat dishes, game, oysters and truffles (in season).

X **Rovello 18** 🕸 🆎

via Tivoli 2 ang. Corso Garibaldi ⊠ 20123 – Ⓜ Lanza   Plan: **F1**
– ☏ 02 72093709 – www.rovello18.com – Closed 2 weeks in August,
Sunday lunch
Carte 39/73 €
• Classic cuisine • Retro •
This restaurant has kept its original name and is situated just 300m from its old premises. Nothing else has changed and the ambience is still attractively retro, managing to be both informal and elegant at the same time. The cuisine is Italian in style, with fish and excellent meat dishes on the menu, as well as a carefully selected wine list.

X **Masuelli San Marco** 🆎

viale Umbria 80 ⊠ 20135 – Ⓜ Lodi TIBB   Plan: **D3**
– ☏ 02 55184138 – www.masuellitrattoria.it – Closed 3 weeks in August,
25 December-6 January, Sunday, Monday lunch
Menu 35/45 € – Carte 35/70 €
• Lombardian • Luxury •
A rustic atmosphere with a luxurious feel in a typical trattoria, with the same management since 1921; cuisine strongly linked to traditional Lombardy and Piedmont recipes.

X **Al Pont de Ferr** 🆎

Ripa di Porta Ticinese 55 ⊠ 20143   Plan: **B3**
– Ⓜ Porta Genova FS – ☏ 02 89406277 – www.pontdeferr.it – Closed 9-
24 August, 24 December-6 January
Menu 65/130 € – Carte 60/91 €
• Creative • Trendy •
This rustic osteria is situated near an old wrought-iron bridge alongside an artificial canal designed and built in 1179. This was initially used to irrigate the surrounding fields and is now frequented by boats. The cuisine is seasonal with an equal emphasis on fish and meat dishes.

X **Dongiò** 🆎
😊

via Corio 3 ⊠ 20135 – Ⓜ Porta Romana   Plan: **H3**
– ☏ 02 5511372 – Closed 2 weeks in August, Saturday
lunch, Sunday
Carte 25/42 € – (booking advisable)
• Calabrian • Family •
This family-run restaurant introduces a flavour of traditional Calabria to Milan with a simple, lively atmosphere that is quite rare nowadays. Home cooking based on fresh pasta, 'nduja (spicy sausage) and the ubiquitous peperoncino (chilli pepper).

ITALY - MILAN

✗ **Café Trussardi** – Ristorante Trussardi alla Scala   ⅋ 🅰🅲
piazza della Scala 5 ✉ *20121* – Ⓜ *Duomo*   Plan: **G1**
– ℰ *02 80688295* – *www.cafetrussardi.com* – *Closed 2 weeks in August, 1-7 January, Sunday*
Carte 40/78 €
• **Mediterranean** • **Fashionable** • **Trendy** •
If you are looking for a quick, simple meal with a minimum of fuss, then this is the place for you. There is a lively, cosmopolitan ambience and a menu focusing on delicious Mediterranean flavours.

✗ **Spazio Milano**   🅰🅲
galleria Vittorio Emanuele II (3° piano del Mercato del   Plan: **G2**
Duomo) ✉ *20123* – ℰ *02 878400* – *www.nikoromitoformazione.it/spazio* – *Closed 2 weeks in August and 2 weeks in January*
Carte 39/52 € – *(booking advisable)*
• **Creative** • **Design** •
This restaurant on the top floor of the Mercato del Duomo acts as a training ground for youngsters from the cookery school run by Romito (3-star Michelin restaurant in Abruzzo). Although you would never guess from the food that these chefs are beginners. Three rooms offer views of the kitchen, Galleria and cathedral respectively and the food made from top quality produce is full of flavour.

🏨 **Principe di Savoia**   ⇞ ⅃⅋ ⊕ 🈯 🔲 🅰🅲 ⅍
piazza della Repubblica 17 ✉ *20124* – Ⓜ *Repubblica*   Plan: **M2**
– ℰ *02 62301* – *www.dorchestercollection.com*
257 rm – ♦300/800 € ♦♦350/900 € – ⌂ 45 € – 44 suites
• **Grand Luxury** • **Historic** • **Elegant** •
Overlooking Piazza della Repubblica, this majestic white building dating from the 19C is an imposing sight. With a truly international atmosphere, this luxury hotel boasts superb guestrooms, a well-equipped fitness area and a wellbeing centre. Perfect for a relaxing stay.
Acanto – See restaurant listing

🏨 **Excelsior Hotel Gallia**   ⇞ ⅃⅋ ⊕ 🈯 🔲 🅰🅲 ⅍
piazza Duca d'Aosta 9 ✉ *20124* – Ⓜ *Centrale FS*   Plan: **M1**
– ℰ *02 67851* – *www.excelsiorgallia.com*
182 rm – ♦30/900 € ♦♦30/900 € – ⌂ 40 € – 53 suites
• **Grand Luxury** • **Modern** •
Now boasting a fully restored exterior, the Excelsior Gallia successfully combines the elegance of an early 20C historic building with a contemporary design that is typical of Milan. It has a mix of chrome and marble that comes together to striking effect. Top class leisure options, including a splendid spa where modern facilities and a luxury brand of cosmetics set the scene for moments of sheer indulgence and relaxation.

🏨 **The Westin Palace**   ⇞ ⅃⅋ 🈯 ⅋ 🅰🅲 ⅍ 🚗
piazza della Repubblica 20 ✉ *20124* – Ⓜ *Repubblica*   Plan: **M2**
– ℰ *02 63361* – *www.westinpalacemilan.it*
227 rm – ♦850/1150 € ♦♦850/1150 € – ⌂ 42 € – 5 suites
• **Luxury** • **Elegant** •
The Milanese apotheosis of the Imperial style – a luxury hotel with sober, austere decor. Some of the rooms have views of the Duomo, while all guests can enjoy the roof terrace in summer. Recently refurbished and just as elegant as ever, the restaurant now also offers a private dining area. Mediterranean dishes dominate the menu.

ITALY - MILAN

Palazzo Parigi

corso di Porta Nuova 1 ✉ *20121 –* ✆ *02625625*   Plan: **G1**
– www.palazzoparigi.com
65 rm ⌂ – ♦450/1250 € ♦♦450/1250 € – 33 suites
• Grand Luxury • Elegant •

This extraordinary palazzo has been renovated to provide the highest level of luxury accommodation. It features carefully chosen elegant furnishings, precious marble, plenty of natural light and stunning views of the city from the top floor guestrooms.

Four Points Sheraton Milan Center

via Cardano 1 ✉ *20124 –* Ⓜ *Gioia –* ✆ *02 667461*   Plan: **M1**
– www.fourpointsmilan.com
254 rm ⌂ – ♦120/490 € ♦♦150/530 €
• Business • Modern •

Housed in a modern building in the centre of Milan, this hotel offers relaxing public areas furnished in a simple, elegant style, as well as pleasant and comfortable guestrooms. A bright dining room with tasteful decor.

UNA Hotel Tocq

via A. de Tocqueville 7/D ✉ *20154*   Plan: **L1**
– Ⓜ *Porta Garibaldi FS –* ✆ *02 62071 – www.unahotels.it*
121 rm ⌂ – ♦119/699 € ♦♦119/699 € – 1 suite
• Business • Classic •

This hotel is just a few metres from the metro and Porta Garibaldi station, as well as the restaurants and nightlife of Corso Como. It offers well-maintained guestrooms and traditional hotel decor.

Starhotels Anderson

piazza Luigi di Savoia 20 ✉ *20124 –* Ⓜ *Centrale FS*   Plan: **C1**
– ✆ *02 6690141 – www.starhotels.com*
106 rm ⌂ – ♦99/1500 € ♦♦99/1500 €
• Palace • Elegant •

This hotel has a warm, designer-style atmosphere, with fashionable and intimate public rooms and welcoming guestrooms offering all the usual comforts of a hotel of this standard. The elegant lounge is home to a small restaurant (open only in the evenings) which serves contemporary-style cuisine.

NH Machiavelli

via Lazzaretto 5 ✉ *20124 –* Ⓜ *Repubblica*   Plan: **M2**
– ✆ *02 631141 – www.nh-hotels.com*
100 rm ⌂ – ♦99/799 € ♦♦99/799 € – 3 suites
• Palace • Modern •

A modern hotel with simple, airy guestrooms. There is an open-plan layout that encompasses a number of sitting areas in one large space. Excellent breakfast.

ADI Doria Grand Hotel

viale Andrea Doria 22 ✉ *20124 –* Ⓜ *Caiazzo*   Plan: **C1**
– ✆ *02 67411411 – www.adihotels.com*
124 rm ⌂ – ♦99/400 € ♦♦105/650 €
• Palace • Elegant •

This classical building has an elegant lobby furnished in early 20C-style and large, comfortable guestrooms. Cultural and musical events are occasionally held in the spacious public areas. This elegant restaurant serves fine regional and international cuisine.

Auriga

via Giovanni Battista Pirelli 7 ✉ *20124*   Plan: **M1**
– Ⓜ *Centrale FS –* ✆ *02 66985851 – www.auriga-milano.com – Closed 1-6 January*
52 rm ⌂ – ♦90/320 € ♦♦110/380 €
• Business • Stylish •

The mix of styles, unusual façade and bright colours of this hotel combine to create a striking exterior. Comfortable facilities and efficient service for tourists and business travellers alike.

ITALY - MILAN

XxXX **Acanto** – Hotel Principe di Savoia   AC ⇦

piazza della Repubblica 17 ✉ *20124 –* Ⓜ *Repubblica*   Plan: **M2**
– ℰ 02 62302026 – www.dorchestercollection.com
Menu 29 € (weekday lunch) – Carte 72/137 €
• **Modern cuisine** • **Luxury** •

A modern restaurant with spacious and elegant dining rooms where guests can enjoy attentive service and classic contemporary-style cuisine. The lunchtime buffet and business menu also add to the modern feel, as does the option of enjoying the same dishes at a table in the bar.

XxX **Berton**   🕸 & AC
ॐ
viale della Liberazione 13 ✉ *20123 –* Ⓜ *Gioia*   Plan: **L1**
– ℰ 02 67075801 – www.ristoranteberton.com – Closed 2 weeks in August, Christmas Holidays, Saturday and Monday lunch, Sunday
Menu 45 € (weekday lunch) – Carte 76/140 €
• **Creative** • **Design** • **Minimalist** •

Light, modern and minimalist in style, the restaurant decor echoes the cuisine served here, which uses just a few ingredients to create original and beautifully presented dishes.

→ Risotto con gambero crudo, corallo e crostacei. Spalla d'agnello da latte arrosto, crema di patate fritte e bietoline. Soufflé al cioccolato e gelato al fior di latte.

XxX **Alice-Eataly Smeraldo** (Viviana Varese)   & AC
ॐ
piazza XXV Aprile 10 ✉ *20123 –* Ⓜ *Porta Garibaldi FS*   Plan: **L2**
– ℰ 02 49497340 – www.aliceristorante.it – Closed 24-26 December
Menu 90/100 € – Carte 66/117 € – *(booking advisable)*
• **Creative** • **Design** •

In 2014, the famous Teatro Smeraldo in Milan became the setting for a large Eataly complex, in which the Alice restaurant is certainly one of the highlights. The attractive designer-style decor makes the perfect backdrop for the imaginative cuisine that includes a number of fish dishes.

→ "Superspaghettino" con brodo affumicato, julienne di calamaro, vongole, polvere di tarallo e limone. Pasta e fagioli con polpo, cozze e pasta mista. Sole: rivisitazione della pastiera napoletana.

XxX **Daniel**   & AC

via Castelfidardo 7, angolo via San Marco ✉ *20121*   Plan: **L2**
– ℰ 02 63793837 – www.ristorantedanielmilano.com – Closed August, 1-7 January, Sunday
Menu 60 € (dinner)/80 € – Carte 57/105 €
• **Traditional cuisine** • **Formal** •

One of the first things to strike you in this restaurant is the open-view kitchen, where the young friendly chef happily interacts with diners. His menu focuses on traditional Italian classics, as well as a few more inventive offerings, all of which are prepared using the very best ingredients. Simpler fare available at lunchtime.

XX **Joia** (Pietro Leemann)   🕸 AC ⇦
ॐ
via Panfilo Castaldi 18 ✉ *20124 –* Ⓜ *Repubblica*   Plan: **M2**
– ℰ 02 29522124 – www.joia.it – Closed 3 weeks in August, 25 December-7 January, Saturday lunch, Sunday
Menu 35 € (lunch)/115 € – Carte 70/101 €
• **Vegetarian** • **Formal** •

The cuisine at Joia is firmly vegetarian with beautifully presented dishes that show the occasional hint of Asian influence.

→ Di non solo pane vive l'uomo: panzanella con verdure croccanti e cuore di cannellini al wasabi su letto di zafferano e lampone. Un indovino mi disse: formaggio di soia arrostito con soia e zenzero, rosmarino, letto di pomodoro e balsamico, coste impanate e foglie di rapanelli. Finalmente c'è stata la pioggia: zuppa rinfrescante di albicocca, melone e anguria con sorbetto di prugna.

ITALY - MILAN

XX **I Malavoglia** 　　　　　　　　　　　AC

via Lecco 4 ✉ *20124 –* Ⓜ *Porta Venezia* 　　　　Plan: **M2**
– ℰ 02 29531387 – www.ristorante-imalavoglia.com – Closed August,
25 December-7 January, Sunday, Monday lunch
Menu 48 € – Carte 44/110 €
• Sicilian • Cosy •
The name of this restaurant near the Porta Venezia ramparts hints at its Sicilian
origins. The fish and seafood dishes served here are modern yet inspired by traditional recipes and include delicious specialities such as the beautifully presented swordfish involtini.

XX **13 Giugno** 　　　　　　　　　　　AC ⇔

via Goldoni 44 ang.via Uberti 5 ✉ *20129* 　　　　Plan: **D2**
– ℰ 02 719654 – www.ristorante13giugno.it
Carte 51/92 €
• Sicilian • Cosy •
This lively restaurant boasts a charming winter garden. Pasta with sea urchins,
aubergine caponata, stuffed sardines and couscous are just some of the Sicilian
specialities on the menu.

XX **Il Liberty** 　　　　　　　　　　　AC

viale Monte Grappa 6 ✉ *20124 – ℰ 02 29011439* 　Plan: **L2**
– www.il-liberty.it – Closed 12-18 August, 1°-7 January, Saturday lunch,
Sunday
Menu 50 € – Carte 43/69 €
• Creative • Simple •
Occupying an Art Nouveau-style palazzo, this small restaurant with two rooms
and a loft area has a friendly, welcoming atmosphere. The menu includes a
selection of fish and meat dishes, with a choice of simpler and more reasonably
priced options at lunchtime.

XX **Barbacoa** 　　　　　　　　　　🌿 ₺ AC ⇔

via delle Abbadesse 30 ✉ *20123 –* Ⓜ *Zara* 　　　Plan: **C1**
– ℰ 02 6883883 – www.barbacoa.it – Closed for lunch Saturday, Sunday
and August
Carte 40/75 € *– (dinner only)*
• International • Friendly •
The first European restaurant of a Brazilian chain, Barbacoa is a true celebration
of meat. Beef takes pride of place, although chicken, pork and lamb also feature
on the menu. The traditional caipirinha, a cocktail based on cane sugar and
lime, continues the Brazilian theme, while mixed salads and exotic fruit desserts
complete the picture.

X **Pisacco** 　　　　　　　　　　　　AC

🍃 *via Solferino 48* ✉ *20121 –* Ⓜ *Moscova* 　　　　Plan: **L2**
– ℰ 02 91765472 – www.pisacco.it – Closed 12-19 August, Monday
Menu 12 € *(weekday lunch)* – Carte 30/52 €
• Creative • Design • Trendy •
A modern and informal restaurant with attentive service and reasonable prices.
Excellent selection of creative dishes, as well as some reinterpretations of classic
favourites, such as polenta and baccalà (salted cod) and Caesar salad.

X **Casa Fontana-23 Risotti** 　　　　　　　AC

piazza Carbonari 5 ✉ *20125 –* Ⓜ *Sondrio* 　　　Plan: **C1**
– ℰ 02 6704710 – www.23risotti.it – Closed 2 weeks in August, 1°-
12 January, Monday and Saturday lunch in summer
Menu 30/35 € – Carte 41/63 €
• Lombardian • Traditional •
Despite the obligatory 25min wait for your food, this restaurant is well worth a
visit for its excellent risottos. Attractive pictures of rice fields on the walls.

Serendib   AC

😊 *via Pontida 2* ✉ *20121* – 🚇 *Moscova* – ☎ *02 6592139*   Plan: **K2**
– *www.serendib.it*
Menu 15/23 € – Carte 18/37 €
• **Indian** • **Trendy** •

Serendib, the old name for Sri Lanka, means "to make happy" – an ambitious promise, but one which this restaurant manages to keep! True to its origins, the tempting menu focuses on Indian and Sri Lankan cuisine.

Vietnamonamour   😐 🏠 AC

via Taramelli 67 ✉ *20124 Milano* – 🚇 *Zara*   Plan: **C1**
– ☎ *02 70634614* – *www.vietnamonamour.com* – *Closed August*
4 rm ☕ – 💰80/220 € 👥120/320 €   Carte 29/60 € – *(closed Monday)*
• **Vietnamese** • **Exotic** • **Intimate** •

This Vietnamese restaurant in the Isola district has a twin of the same name in the Città Studi area of the city. Both restaurants offer the same exotic charm and attention to individual detail, as well as delicious cuisine and delightful guest-rooms that are perfect for a relaxing stay.

La Cantina di Manuela   🏠 🏠 AC

via Carlo Poerio 3 ✉ *20129* – ☎ *02 76318892*   Plan: **C2**
– *www.lacantinadimanuela.it*
Carte 33/50 € – *(booking advisable)*
• **Modern cuisine** • **Traditional** •

The dining room in this young, dynamic restaurant is surrounded by bottles of wine. Elaborate dishes feature on the menu, with antipasti available in the evening. At lunchtime these are replaced by various salads aimed at a business clientele in a hurry. Milanese-style cutlets are the house speciality.

Da Giannino-L'Angolo d'Abruzzo   AC

😊 *via Pilo 20* ✉ *20129* – 🚇 *Porta Venezia*   Plan: **D2**
– ☎ *02 29406526*
Carte 29/40 €
• **Cuisine from Abruzzo** • **Traditional** •

A warm welcome combined with a simple but lively atmosphere and typical dishes from the Abruzzo region make this a popular place to eat. Generous portions and excellent roast dishes.

Baia Chia   AC 💬

via Bazzini 37 ✉ *20131* – 🚇 *Piola* – ☎ *02 2361131*   Plan: **D1**
– *www.ristorantesardobaiachia.it* – *Closed 10-25 August, Christmas Holidays*
Carte 31/53 €
• **Sardinian** • **Family** •

This pleasant restaurant with a family atmosphere is divided into two small dining rooms, plus a veranda which can also be used in winter. Excellent fish dishes and Sardinian specialities on the menu. Many of the wines also come from Sardinia.

Un Posto a Milano-Cascina Cuccagna   🏠 AC

via Cuccagna 2 ✉ *20121 Milano* – ☎ *02 5457785*   Plan: **D3**
– *www.unpostoamilano.it* – *Closed 1-6 January, Monday*
Menu 15 € (weekdays)/38 € – Carte 34/56 €
• **Classic cuisine** • **Friendly** •

Occupying an old restored farmhouse in urban Milan, the Cascina Cuccagna is both a restaurant and a cultural centre. It is surrounded by greenery, providing a delightful oasis in the city. At lunchtime, choose from a copious and reasonably priced buffet. The evening menu is more elaborate but still offers good value for money.

FIERA - SEMPIONE - NAVIGLI (viale Fulvio Testi, Niguarda, viale Fermi, viale Certosa, corso Sempione, piazza Carlo Magno, via Monte Rosa, San Siro, via Novara, via Washington, Ripa di porta Ticinese, Corso S. Gottardo)　　**PLAN I**

Hermitage
via Messina 10 ✉ 20154 – Ⓜ Cenisio – ℰ 02 318170　　Plan: **K1**
– www.hotelhermitagemilano.com
– Closed 1-24 August
122 rm ☑ – ♦109/360 € ♦♦129/380 € – 8 suites
• Luxury • Elegant •
Style and comfort are the trademarks of this hotel, which combines the atmosphere of elegant period-style interiors with modern facilities. Situated in a quarter bustling with activity and shops.
Il Giorno Bistrot – See restaurant listing

Milan Marriott Hotel
via Washington 66 ✉ 20146 – Ⓜ Wagner　　Plan: **A2**
– ℰ 02 48521 – www.milanmarriotthotel.com
321 rm – ♦120/590 € ♦♦120/590 € – ☑ 20 €
• Business • Cosy •
Not far from the bustling Corso Vercelli, this hotel combines a modern exterior with a more traditional interior decor. Functional guestrooms. Enjoy regional dishes and Mediterranean cuisine in the La Brasserie de Milan restaurant.

AC Milano
via Tazzoli 2 ✉ 20154 – Ⓜ Monumentale　　Plan: **K1**
– ℰ 02 20424211 – www.ac-hotels.com
156 rm – ♦96/500 € ♦♦106/510 € – 3 suites
• Business • Elegant •
A stone's throw from Corso Como and Milan's nightlife, this modern, designer-style hotel is popular with an upmarket business clientele. Spacious, well-appointed bedrooms in keeping with the high standards of this hotel chain.

Wagner
via Buonarroti 13 ✉ 20149 – Ⓜ Buonarroti　　Plan: **A2**
– ℰ 02 463151 – www.hotelwagnermilano.it – Closed 12-19 August
48 rm ☑ – ♦115/210 € ♦♦150/320 € – 1 suite
• Traditional • Elegant •
This hotel, next to the eponymous metro station, has attractive rooms with marble and modern furnishings.

Mercure Regency Milano
via Arimondi 12 ✉ 20155 – ℰ 02 39216021　　Plan: **A1**
– www.regencymilano.com – Closed 20 December-6 January
71 rm ☑ – ♦290 € ♦♦380 €
• Traditional • Personalised •
This charming and unusual mansion dating from 1925 is built in the style of a small castle. Delightful courtyard and stylish interior furnishings.

Enterprise Hotel
corso Sempione 91 ✉ 20149 – Ⓜ Domodossola　　Plan: **A1**
– ℰ 02318181 – www.enterprisehotel.com
126 rm ☑ – ♦120/514 € ♦♦135/529 € – 2 suites
• Traditional • Elegant •
Attention to detail and design is evident in every aspect of this elegant modern hotel, from the marble and granite exterior to its bespoke furnishings and pleasing geometrical lines. A pleasant and original restaurant for lunch and dinner. Outdoor dining in summer.

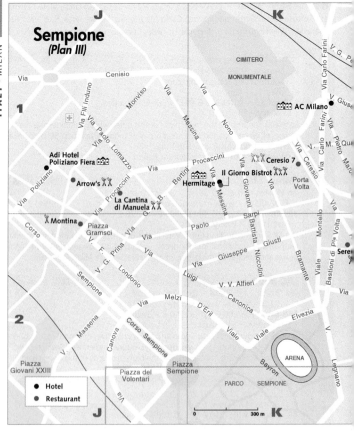

Sempione
(Plan III)

CIMITERO
MONUMENTALE

AC Milano

Adi Hotel
Poliziano Fiera

Arrow's XX

Ceresio 7 XXX

Il Giorno Bistrot XXX

Hermitage

Porta
Volta

La Cantina
di Manuela XX

X Montina

Piazza
Gramsci

ARENA

Piazza
Giovani XXIII

Piazza del
Volontari

Piazza
Sempione

PARCO   SEMPIONE

● Hotel
● Restaurant

0   300 m

ADI Hotel Poliziano Fiera

全 & 瓜 弘
Plan: J1

via Poliziano 11 ✉ *20154* – Ⓜ *Gerusalemme*
– ℰ *02 3191911* – *www.hotelpolizianofiera.it*
98 rm ☲ – ♦73/336 € ♦♦80/397 € – 2 suites
• Business • Elegant •

This modern hotel offers friendly, attentive service and spacious guestrooms
furnished in light green and sand-coloured tones, as well as attractive public
rooms.

Rubens

全 ⅃ゟ 瓜 弘 P
Plan: A2

via Rubens 21 ✉ *20148* – Ⓜ *Gambara* – ℰ *02 40302*
– *www.hotelrubensmilano.com*
87 rm ☲ – ♦95/350 € ♦♦110/450 €
• Business • Elegant •

The spacious, comfortable guestrooms in this elegant hotel are adorned with
frescoes by contemporary artists and furnished in stylish beige, golden and pastel-coloured tones. To get the day off to a good start, enjoy a copious breakfast
in the evocatively named Sala delle Nuvole (Room in the Clouds) on the top
floor.

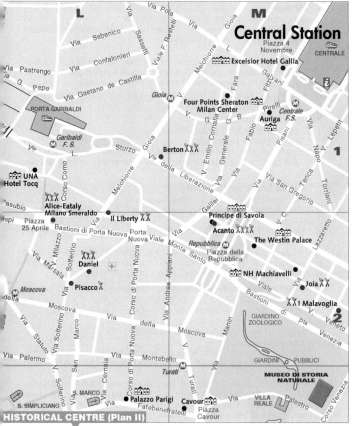

Accademia

☆ Ⅰ☆ 🖼 🏛 ♻ 🚗

viale Certosa 68 ⊠ 20155 – ℰ 02 39211122

Plan: **A1**

– www.hotelaccademiamilano.com

65 rm ☲ – †90/350 € ††99/450 € – 1 suite

• Business • Classic •

Following major renovation work, this hotel features new guestrooms in warm tones with designer-style furnishings and excellent levels of comfort thanks to the careful use of the space available. Note the typical mosaic which frames the lift doors.

Astoria

🖼 🏛

viale Murillo 9 ⊠ 20149 – ⓜ Lotto – ℰ 02 40090095

Plan: **A2**

– www.astoriahotelmilano.com

68 rm ☲ – †80/300 € ††100/400 €

• Business • Homely •

This hotel that caters mostly to business travellers is located along a ring road. The rooms are modern and soundproof.

Mirage ☆ ⌂₆ ₺ AC 🛦 ⌂

viale Certosa 104/106 ☒ *20156 –* ✆ *02 39210471*   Plan: **A1**
– www.hotelmirage-milano.com – Closed August, 24 December-2 January
86 rm ☟ – **♥**99/279 € **♥♥**150/369 €
• Business • Classic •
Thanks to its strategic location near major motorways and not far from the Rho-Pero exhibition complex, this hotel is ideal for business travellers. The guestrooms, some of which have parquet floors, have been renovated in traditional style.

Des Etrangers ₺ AC ⌂⌂ ⌂

via Sirte 9 ☒ *20146 –* ✆ *02 48955325*   Plan: **A3**
– www.hoteldesetrangers.it
94 rm ☟ – **♥**50/350 € **♥♥**60/370 €
• Traditional • Functional •
This well-maintained hotel in a quiet street offers its guests functional and comfortable public areas and guestrooms, as well as convenient underground parking.

Antica Locanda Leonardo ⌂⌂ AC

corso Magenta 78 ☒ *20123 –* Ⓜ *Conciliazione*   Plan: **E2**
– ✆ *02 48014197 – www.anticalocandaleonardo.com – Closed 6-25 August, 2-7 January*
16 rm ☟ – **♥**95/170 € **♥♥**158/395 €
• Family • Cosy •
The luxury atmosphere combines with the family-style welcome in a hotel which overlooks a small inner courtyard, in an ideal location near the place where Leonardo da Vinci's painting of the "Last Supper" is housed.

XxX Il Luogo di Aimo e Nadia *(Aimo Moroni)* ⅏ AC ⌂

❀ ❀ *via Montecuccoli 6* ☒ *20147 –* Ⓜ *Primaticcio*   Plan: **A3**
– ✆ *02 416886 – www.aimoenadia.com – Closed 3 weeks in August, 1-8 January, Saturday lunch, Sunday*
Menu 45 € (weekday lunch)/140 € – Carte 84/173 €
• Creative • Design •
Tuscan cuisine was brought to Milan, and later to other regions. Faithful to this, the selection of Italian products that the restaurant offers today is difficult to equal.
➜ Spaghettoni in salsa di cicale di mare, fave fresche, cozze "pelose" tarantine e cacao venezuelano. Anguilla caramellata alla birra Nora, con cavolfiore all'aspretto e finocchio selvatico. Black lemon: crema ai limoni di Sorrento, spuma al lime e polvere di 'loomi'.

XxX La Pobbia 1850 ₺ AC ⌂

via Gallarate 92 ☒ *20151 –* ✆ *02 38006641*   Plan: **A1**
– www.lapobbia.com – Closed 3 weeks in August, 26 December-6 January, Sunday
Menu 18 € (weekdays) – Carte 40/69 €
• Lombardian • Elegant •
La Pobbia is named after the poplar trees that once stood alongside this road, which ran through open countryside as recently as the late 19C. The old but elegant farmhouse serves a small selection of local dishes (mainly meat) with a focus on the specialities of Milan and Lombardy.

XxX Unico Milano ≼ ₺ AC

❀ *via Achille Papa 30, palazzo World Join Center*   Plan: **A1**
☒ *20149 –* Ⓜ *Portello –* ✆ *02 39214847 – www.unicorestaurant.it*
Menu 100 € (dinner)/130 € – Carte 74/128 €
• Creative • Elegant •
Occupying the 20th floor of a new high-rise in Milan, this restaurant boasts spectacular views of the city. The cuisine is inspired by the regions and produce of Italy, with a range of carefully prepared and imaginative dishes on the menu.
➜ Risotto mantecato al succo di peperone rosso, burro d'arachidi e acciughe affumicate. Merluzzo gratinato alle mandorle con cipollotto e peperone. Granita di fragole e Champagne con semifreddo all'ananas e lime.

XXX **Ceresio 7** ⟨ 🍴 AC

via Ceresio 7 ⊠ 20123 – Ⓜ Monumentale Plan: **K1**
– ✆ 0231039221 – www.ceresio7.com – Closed 5 days in January
Menu 85 € (dinner) – Carte 61/117 € – *(bookings advisable at dinner)*
• **Modern cuisine • Design • Trendy** •

This designer-style restaurant is housed on the fourth floor of the historic ENEL palazzo, remodelled and converted into the Dsquared2 building. It combines the use of brass, marble and wood to create a successful blend of attractive colours and vintage decor. The view of Milan (even better from the long outdoor terrace with its two swimming pools) completes the picture, while the cuisine reinterprets Italian traditional classics with a contemporary twist.

XX **Il Giorno Bistrot** – Hotel Hermitage 🍴 AC 🚗

via Messina 10 ⊠ 20154 – Ⓜ Cenisio – ✆ 02 318170 Plan: **K1**
– www.hotelhermitagemilano.com – Closed August, Saturday, Sunday lunch
Carte 33/56 €
• **Classic cuisine • Cosy** •

The historic restaurant of the Hotel Hermitage demonstrates a real passion for local cuisine, with dishes such as risotto and *cotoletta alla milanese* on the menu. There is also a good choice of gluten-free options.

XX **Innocenti Evasioni** (Arrigoni e Picco) 🛁 🚲 🍴 AC ⟷
❀ *via privata della Bindellina ⊠ 20155 – Ⓜ Portello* Plan: **A1**
– ✆ 02 33001882 – www.innocentievasioni.com – Closed 6-31 August, 1°-10 January and Sunday
Menu 49/68 € – Carte 47/74 € – *(dinner only) (booking advisable)*
• **Creative • Fashionable** •

This pleasant establishment, with large windows facing the garden, offers classic cuisine reinterpreted with imagination. Enjoyable outdoor summer dining.
→ Risotto al brodo di grana padano, coriandolo fresco, bottarga e asparagi. Lombata di maialino iberico con rabarbaro allo zenzero, piselli freschi e cialda al pepe. Meringata alle more, cioccolatoso al 70% e riduzione di panna al dragoncello.

XX **Tano Passami l'Olio** (Gaetano Simonato) AC
❀ *via Villoresi, 16 ⊠ 20143 – ✆ 02 8394139* Plan: **B3**
– www.tanopassamilolio.it – Closed August, 24 December-6 January and Sunday
Menu 70/125 € – Carte 95/140 € – *(dinner only) (booking advisable)*
• **Creative • Traditional** •

The key features here are the soft lighting, romantic atmosphere and creative fish and meat dishes, flavoured with a choice of extra-virgin olive oils on display in the dining room. Smoking lounge with a sofa.
→ Tiramisù di seppia, mascarpone e patata. Piccione laccato, crema di frattaglie, porto e more. Cannoli croccanti con variazioni di mandorla.

XX **Arrow's** 🍴 ὅ AC

via A. Mantegna 17/19 ⊠ 20154 – Ⓜ Gerusalemme Plan: **J1**
– ✆ 02 341533 – www.ristorantearrows.it – Closed 3 weeks in August, Sunday, Monday lunch
Menu 25 € (weekday lunch) – Carte 37/84 €
• **Fish and seafood • Simple** •

Packed, even at midday, the atmosphere becomes cosier in the evening but the seafood cuisine, prepared according to tradition, remains the same.

XX **La Cantina di Manuela** 🛁 ὅ AC
⊛ *via Procaccini 41 ⊠ 20154 – Ⓜ Gerusalemme* Plan: **J1**
– ✆ 02 3452034 – www.lacantinadimanuela.it
Menu 35 € – Carte 31/61 €
• **Modern cuisine • Family** •

Although the chef has changed, the dishes that made the reputation of this restaurant, such as *risotto alla Milanese*, Fassone beef cheek in a Barolo sauce, and tiramisu, are still very much on the menu. Updated traditional cuisine.

XX
☊

Tokuyoshi
♿ AC

via San Calogero 3 ✉ *20123 –* Ⓜ *Sant'Ambrogio*   Plan: **F3**
– ☎ *02 84254626 – www.ristorantetokuyoshi.com – Closed Monday*
Menu 65/100 € – Carte 48/95 € – *(dinner only)*
• Creative • Minimalist •
After gaining experience in a number of major restaurants, Yoji Tokuyoshi is
now the owner and manager of his own establishment. He creates delicious
fusion cuisine, which he describes as "cucina italiana contaminata". With typical
Japanese humility and real attention to detail, Yoji conjures up dishes that are
unique, full of flavour and definitely unforgettable.
→ Insalata di cucurbitacea e salsa al basilico acido. Gli spaghetti nella
patata. Cemento e terra (finto cemento di meringa, gelato di radici).

X
☊

Iyo
🍽 AC

via Piero della Francesca 74 ✉ *20154*   Plan: **B1**
– Ⓜ *Domodossola –* ☎ *02 45476898 – www.iyo.it – Closed 2 weeks in
August, Christmas Holidays, Monday and Tuesday lunch*
Menu 85 € – Carte 44/81 € – *(booking advisable)*
• Japanese • Minimalist •
The "fluctuating world" (ukiyo in Japanese) opens the door to sushi, sashimi and
hot plate cooking. But the selection of desserts on a tempting tray brings us
back to the West.
→ Taiyo: millefoglie di gambero argentino scottato con gambero rosso,
maionese allo yuzu, calamaro e pomodoro. Kobe tataki: tagliata di manzo
giapponese con erbette al burro di soia e crema di asparagi al wasabi
fresco. Sfera esotica.

X

Kiyo
🍽 AC

via Carlo Ravizza 4 ✉ *20121 –* Ⓜ *Wagner*   Plan: **A2**
– ☎ *02 4814295 – www.kiyo.it*
Menu 55 € – Carte 32/52 €
• Japanese • Minimalist •
The manager of this restaurant is Italian and the chef Japanese (the name kiyo
means limpid and pure). Enjoy typical Japanese dishes followed by a choice of
delicious European desserts in the wood-furnished dining rooms.

X

Trattoria Montina
🍽 AC

via Procaccini 54 ✉ *20154 –* Ⓜ *Gerusalemme*   Plan: **J2**
– ☎ *02 3490498 – www.trattoriamontina.it – Closed Easter, 9-
30 August, 26 December-3 January, Sunday, Monday lunch*
Carte 31/63 €
• Traditional cuisine • Simple •
Nice bistro atmosphere, tables close together, defused lighting in the evening
in an establishment managed by twin brothers; seasonal national and Milanese
dishes.

X

Osteria di Porta Cicca
🍽 ♿ AC

ripa di Porta Ticinese 51 ✉ *20143 –* Ⓜ *Porta Genova*   Plan: **E3**
– ☎ *02 8372763 – www.osteriadiportacicca.com – Closed Sunday*
Menu 35/55 €
– Carte 41/86 € – (dinner only except Sunday) (booking advisable)
• Modern cuisine • Romantic • Cosy •
A welcoming, intimate ambience with a hint of Provence in an attractive canal
side setting. The only sign of a traditional osteria is in the name – the cuisine is
modern and innovative in style.

TURIN
TORINO
Population: 896 773

Nimbus/Fotolia.com

Piazza Castello, the square from which some of Turin's most celebrated avenues start, may well be considered the heart of the city; while the city's landmark building has to be the Mole Antonelliana – originally designed as a Jewish synagogue. Named after an ancient Roman settlement, the Quadrilatero Romano is the most fashionable quarter of Turin and boasts some of its most elegant shops; its narrow medieval streets are a fascinating interlude to the city's orthogonal plan. Less fashionable but equally interesting is Borgo Dora, the quarter north of the Piazza della Repubblica – a popular area that has been given a facelift but still retains its old, bohemian atmosphere – and don't miss the Cortile del Maglio, inside the arsenal in Piazza Borgo Dora, with its markets and art.

At the other end of the scale, la Collina provides some of the city's smartest addresses, while crossing the River Po – the longest in Italy – at Piazza Vittorio Veneto will lead you to Turin's luxurious period houses. Those interested in residential architecture can also find some of the city's most beautiful houses – dating back to the 19C – in the Via Galileo Ferraris area of the Crocetta quarter. For a more vibrant atmosphere, head for the embankment between Piazza Vittorio Veneto and Corso Vittorio Emanuele and you will find the 'murazzi', where you will get the best of Turin's nightlife with its bars and clubs.

TURIN IN...

→ ONE DAY
Piazza Castello, Via Roma, Piazza San Carlo, Mole Antonelliana, Piazza Vittorio Veneto, Duomo, Sacra Sindone.

→ TWO DAYS
Egyptian Museum, Sabaudia Gallery, Palazzo Carignano & Madama.

→ THREE DAYS
Valentino Park, Reggia di Venaria, Museum of Cinema.

PRACTICAL INFORMATION

ARRIVAL-DEPARTURE

 Better known as Caselle – after the nearby town – Turin's airport, Sandro Pertini, is 16km north of the city. Trains run every 30min and bring you into Torino Dora Railway Station in 19min. A shuttle bus takes 50min to the centre. A taxi will take about 40min.

GETTING AROUND

Turin has a very efficient public transport network, with buses and trams crossing the city from 5am until midnight. Tickets for buses, trams and the underground can be bought at tobacconists, newsagents and other places exhibiting a special GTT sign, and must be stamped on board. Options range from 90min travel to unlimited daily use, as well as blocks of 5 or 25 tickets.

CALENDAR HIGHLIGHTS

February
CioccolaTò Chocolate Festival.

May
Fiera Internazionale del Libro (International Book Fair).

June
Feast of Patron Saint John the Baptist.

September
Mito (over 200 music events).

October
Salone del Gusto (biennial food fair, organised by the Slow Food Movement).

November
Torino Film Festival.

EATING OUT

Turin can rightly boast of being one of Italy's gastronomic centres. Not to be missed are the fresh egg pastas, and the local braised beef, lamb and pigeons. White truffles deserve a mention, although they've become so rare that prices are often incredibly high; they are usually served with pasta or fonduta (melted cheese, milk and egg yolks). With some of the best Italian chocolate produced in Turin, desserts are a real treat. You might find bonèt (chocolate pudding with almond biscuits), torta di nocciole (hazelnut cake) or panna cotta (cooked cream). Alongside Tuscany, Piedmont's red wines are indisputably the best in Italy; try a local Barbera, a reliable Nebbiolo or a world famous Barbaresco or Barolo. Cafés have a long tradition in Turin; try a bicerin (a drink made from coffee, cream and chocolate) with a gianduiotto (a chocolate made with 'tonda gentile', a famous variety of hazelnut). Look out for the world's biggest food market, 'Eataly': 2,500m² of delicacies brought to you by local producers, who pride themselves on their excellent, often rare, ingredients.

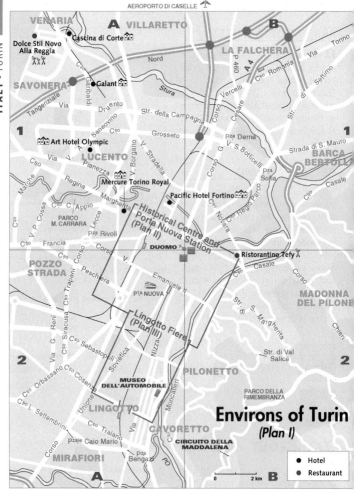

AEROPORTO DI CASELLE ✈

Environs of Turin
(Plan I)

● Hotel
● Restaurant

0 ___ 2 km

HISTORICAL CENTRE　　　　　　　　　　　　　　　**PLAN II**

Golden Palace 　　　　　　　　　　　 ⇗ ⅃⅚ ⊕ ⅏ 🆇 ㊅ 🄰🄲 🆂🄰
via dell'Arcivescovado 18 ⊠ *10121 –* Ⓜ *Re Umberto*　　　Plan: **D2**
– ℰ 011 5512111 – www.allegroitalia.it
182 rm *–* 🛏650 € 🛏🛏650 € *–* ⌒ 25 € *– 13 suites*
• Grand Luxury • Conference hotel • Personalised •
When Palazzo Toro (the present location of this hotel) was built after the Second
World War, the building was cited for its design and structure in some of the
best books on architecture. Half a century later, its Art Deco influence and minimalist style continues to delight guests. A hotel fit for a king!

Grand Hotel Sitea
via Carlo Alberto 35 ✉ *10123 – ℰ 011 5170171*   Plan: **E2**
– www.grandhotelsitea.it
120 rm ⌂ – ♦105/360 € ♦♦168/540 € – 1 suite
• Luxury • Palace • Personalised •
Founded in 1925, this hotel keeps the traditions of elegant hospitality alive. It has a stylish, classic and period decor that contributes to its delightful atmosphere.
Carignano – See restaurant listing

Principi di Piemonte
via Gobetti 15 ✉ *10123 –* Ⓜ *Porta Nuova*   Plan: **E2**
– ℰ 011 55151 – www.atahotels.it/principi-di-piemonte
81 rm ⌂ – ♦155/500 € ♦♦155/500 € – 18 suites
• Luxury • Business • Elegant •
This historic 1930s building is situated just a stone's throw from the centre. It offers spacious guestrooms decorated in marble, an elegant atmosphere and resolutely modern comfort.
Casa Savoia – See restaurant listing

Victoria
via Nino Costa 4 ✉ *10123 – ℰ 011 5611909*   Plan: **E2**
– www.hotelvictoria-torino.com
106 rm ⌂ – ♦180/225 € ♦♦300/350 € – 4 suites
• Luxury • Traditional • Rural •
Antique furniture, symphonies of colours, four poster beds, and exacting attention to details in the personalised environment of an elegant residence with few rivals for fascination and atmosphere.

Art Hotel Boston
via Massena 70 ✉ *10128 – ℰ 011 500359*   Plan: **D3**
– www.hotelbostontorino.it
71 rm ⌂ – ♦90/350 € ♦♦130/550 € – 5 suites
• Luxury • Business • Personalised •
Comfortable guestrooms decorated with contemporary art feature in this designer-style hotel just a stone's throw from the city's main galleries and museums.

Genova
via Sacchi 14/b ✉ *10128 –* Ⓜ *Porta Nuova*   Plan: **E2**
– ℰ 011 5629400 – www.albergogenova.it
88 rm ⌂ – ♦70/200 € ♦♦99/360 € – 3 suites
• Luxury • Historic • Personalised •
This 19C building houses an elegant, beautifully kept hotel which combines modern standards of comfort with a classic ambience. A dozen guestrooms boast frescoes on the ceiling.

Genio
corso Vittorio Emanuele II 47 ✉ *10125*   Plan: **E2**
– Ⓜ *Porta Nuova – ℰ 011 6505771 – www.hotelgenio.it*
119 rm ⌂ – ♦70/150 € ♦♦95/300 €
• Traditional • Spa hotel • Retro •
Occupying an attractive late-19C palazzo, this hotel boasts a retro atmosphere and personalised, vaguely British-style guestrooms. Artistic flooring in the corridors and rooms add a touch of elegance.

Art Hotel Olympic
via Verolengo 19 ✉ *10149 – ℰ 011 39997*   Plan: **A1**
– www.arthotelolympic.com
147 rm ⌂ – ♦100/130 € ♦♦250/350 €
• Business • Traditional • Modern •
Situated in an area which is constantly being embellished, this modern hotel has a young, bright and occasionally futuristic feel.

Map legend:
- ● Hotel
- ● Restaurant

0 ——— 300 m

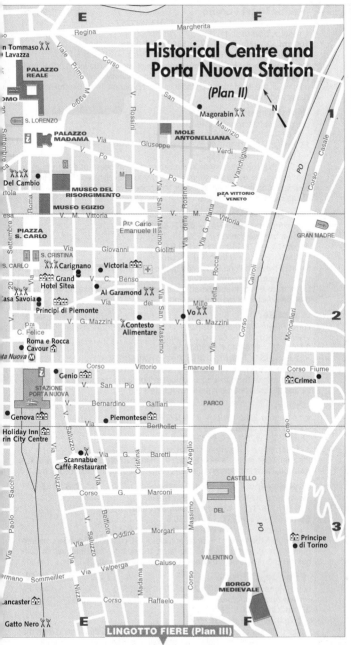

Historical Centre and
Porta Nuova Station
(Plan II)

N

E   F

Margherita

Regina

n Tommaso 🍴🍴
Lavazza

PALAZZO
REALE

OMO

Corso

Viale Primo

Maggio

San

V. Rossini

Magorabin 🍴🍴

Maurizio

1

S. LORENZO

PALAZZO
MADAMA   Via

Giuseppe

MOLE
ANTONELLIANA

Verdi

Settembre

V. Po

V. di

V. Po

Rosine

V. Vanchiglia

PO

Corso

Casale

Del Cambio 🍴🍴🍴🍴

rtola

Roma

MUSEO DEL
RISORGIMENTO

MUSEO EGIZIO

Via San Massimo

Via delle Rosine

pzA VITTORIO
VENETO

V. M. Vittoria

V. M. Vittoria

V. G. Plana

esa

Pza Carlo
Emanuele II

PIAZZA
S. CARLO

S. CRISTINA

Via
Giovanni

Giolitti

GRAN MADRE

Rocca

Cairoli

S. CARLO

🍴🍴 Carignano

Victoria 🏨

Casa Savoia 🍴🍴🍴

Grand
Hotel Sitea 🏨

Al Garamond 🍴🍴

V. C. Benso

Mille

Vo 🍴🍴

delle

Moncalieri

2

Principi di Piemonte 🏨

V. G. Mazzini

Contesto 🍴
Alimentare

Via San Massimo

V. G. Mazzini

Corso

Pza
C. Felice

Roma e Rocca
Cavour 🏨

Via

da Nuova Ⓜ

Corso   Vittorio

Emanuele II

Corso Fiume

🏨 Crimea

Genio 🏨

V. San Pio V

STAZIONE
PORTA NUOVA

Bernardino

Galliari

PARCO

Corso

3

Genova 🏨

Via

Berthollet

Piemontese 🏨

Holiday Inn 🏨
rin City Centre

Sacchi

Nizza

Saluzzo

Scannabue
Caffè Restaurant

Via   G. Cristina

Baretti

d'Azeglio

CASTELLO

Paolo

Via

Corso   G.   Marconi

Massimo

DEL

Po

Bellotta

Oddino

Morgari

🏨 Principe
di Torino

Via

Via

Valperga

Caluso

VALENTINO

ormano   Sommeiller

Nizza

Madama

Corso

BORGO
MEDIEVALE

Lancaster 🏨

Corso   Raffaelo

Gatto Nero 🍴🍴

E   F

LINGOTTO FIERE (Plan III)

Pacific Hotel Fortino 🏠 ⚛ 🆑 🏃 🚗
strada del Fortino 36 ✉ *10152* – ✆ *011 5217757*   Plan: **A1**
– www.pacifichotels.it
100 rm 🖙 – ♦50/900 € ♦♦60/1300 € – 8 suites
• Business • Conference hotel • Personalised •

This modern hotel meets the requirements of business travellers. It has well-equipped conference rooms and welcoming, warmly furnished guestrooms offering all the latest high-tech facilities. The restaurant in the basement serves classic and regional cuisine.

 Hotel Royal Torino 🏠 🆑 🏃 🚗
corso Regina Margherita 249 ✉ *10144*   Plan: **A1**
– ✆ 011 4376777 – www.hotelroyaltorino.it
75 rm 🖙 – ♦65/190 € ♦♦85/240 €
• Traditional • Classic •

The fact that this hotel is not in the centre of town does not detract from its high quality. Renovated in recent years, it works with all types of clientele; fully equipped Conference Centre. Classic atmosphere with clear refinement in the dining room of the restaurant.

 Piemontese 🆑 🆑
via Berthollet 21 ✉ *10125* – ✆ *011 6698101*   Plan: **E2**
– www.hotelpiemontese.it
39 rm 🖙 – ♦70/140 € ♦♦80/160 €
• Business • Traditional • Classic •

Situated between Porta Nuova and the Po river, this hotel offers colourfully furnished guestrooms with individual touches; the attic-style rooms are particularly attractive with their exposed beams and hydro-massage baths. In fine weather, breakfast is served on the veranda.

 Lancaster 🆑 🏃
corso Filippo Turati 8 ✉ *10128* – ✆ *011 5681982*   Plan: **E3**
– www.lancaster.it – Closed 3-23 August
83 rm 🖙 – ♦70/140 € ♦♦90/200 €
• Business • Traditional • Personalised •

Each floor in this hotel is decorated in a different colour. Attractive, personalised furnishings give the public areas a modern look, while the guestrooms are classic and the breakfast room more rustic in feel.

 Crimea 🆑 🏃
via Mentana 3 ✉ *10133* – ✆ *0116604700*   Plan: **F2**
– www.hotelcrimea.it
48 rm 🖙 – ♦79/129 € ♦♦89/169 €
• Business • Family • Functional •

Pleasantly discreet and simply elegant interiors in a hotel in a quiet position in a residential area in the foothills; recently refurbished comfortable bedrooms.

 Holiday Inn Turin City Centre 🏠 ⚛ 🆑 🏃 🚗
via Assietta 3 ✉ *10128* – Ⓜ *Porta Nuova*   Plan: **E2**
– ✆ 011 5167111 – www.holidayinn.com/turin-cityctr
56 rm 🖙 – ♦92/175 € ♦♦118/230 €
• Business • Chain hotel • Functional •

Not far from the station, this hotel occupies a 19C palazzo which offers modern guestrooms equipped with all the latest technology. The hotel has its own garage. This restaurant is modern in both tone and layout.

 Principe di Torino ⚛ 🆑 🅿
corso Moncalieri 85 ✉ *10122* – ✆ *011 19504950*   Plan: **F3**
– www.principeditorino.it
23 rm 🖙 – ♦120 € ♦♦360 €
• Traditional • Modern •

Situated slightly above the Valentino park, this noble building dating from the 1920s has retained its slightly austere exterior. The guestrooms inside are modern and functional with good soundproofing.

ITALY - TURIN

Roma e Rocca Cavour

piazza Carlo Felice 60 ✉ *10121 Torino*　Plan: **E2**
– Ⓜ *Porta Nuova – ℰ 011 5612772 – www.romarocca.it*
85 rm – ♦54/105 € ♦♦75/135 € – ☲ 11 €
• Historic • Historic •
This historic hotel has been run by the same family since 1854. It will appeal to anyone who enjoys a slightly old-fashioned and nostalgic atmosphere, thanks to its period furnishings and location near the elegant arcades and gardens of the square. The Italian writer Cesare Pavese committed suicide in room 346.

Magazzini San Domenico

via San Domenico 21 a ✉ *10122 – ℰ 011 4368341*　Plan: **D1**
– www.magazzinisandomenico.it – Closed 8-30 August
6 rm ☲ – ♦80/90 € ♦♦100/120 €
• Family • Inn • Modern •
In the heart of Italy's former capital city, this contemporary-style hotel offers high quality accommodation. An excellent base for exploring the city centre.

Del Cambio

piazza Carignano 2 ✉ *10123 –* ℰ *011 546690*　Plan: **E1**
– www.delcambio.it – Closed Sunday dinner, Monday
Menu 35 € (weekday lunch)/150 € – Carte 79/121 € – *(booking advisable)*
• Regional • Luxury • Formal •
One of the most elegant historic restaurants in Italy, where you will find unexpected contemporary works of art alongside the more traditional 19C decor and furnishings. Matteo Baronetto is at the helm in the kitchen, creating dishes with a strong individual flavour. The restaurant also serves light lunches, and offers a pleasant outdoor area for alfresco dining, as well as a Chef's Table option.
→ Riso Cavour. Branzino al vapore e coda di bue brasata. Giandujotto e sorbetto alle more.

Vintage 1997 (Pierluigi Consonni)

piazza Solferino 16/h ✉ *10121 –* Ⓜ *Re Umberto*　Plan: **D2**
– ℰ 011 535948 – www.vintage1997.com – Closed 3 weeks in August, 1-6 January, Saturday lunch, Sunday
Menu 40/75 € – Carte 50/106 €
• Italian • Elegant • Traditional •
Scarlet fabrics, lampshades and elegant wood panelling all add to the muted ambience of this elegant restaurant. It serves imaginative cuisine inspired by traditional favourites using carefully selected ingredients. Champagne imported from France.
→ Agnolotti di gallina ai profumi dell'orto. La Torinese (costoletta di fassone con panatura di nocciole e grissini). Selezione di 5 piccoli dolci piemontesi.

Casa Savoia – Hotel Principi di Piemonte

via Gobetti 15 ✉ *10123 –* Ⓜ *Porta Nuova*　Plan: **CY**
– ℰ 011 55152 – www.atahotels.it
Carte 33/88 €
• Mediterranean • Cosy • Luxury •
The splendid decor of the hotel is echoed in the restaurant. No detail is left to chance, ensuring that your gastronomic experience is a memorable one. Mediterranean cuisine.

Carignano – Grand Hotel Sitea

via Carlo Alberto 35 ✉ *10123 – ℰ 011 5170171*　Plan: **CY**
– www.grandhotelsitea.it – Closed August, Sunday
Carte 46/75 € – *(dinner only)*
• Mediterranean • Luxury • Intimate •
Natural light filters through the large windows of this restaurant that overlooks the greenery outside. Mediterranean cuisine and Piedmontese specialities take pride of place on the menu. These are supplemented by tasting menus (Principe Amedeo, Re Umberto, Vittorio Emanuele) for guests who like to be 'guided' in their choice of dishes.

ITALY - TURIN

XX
ξ3
Vo (Stefano Borra)   AC
via Provana 3/d ⊠ *10123 –* ℰ *011 8390288*   Plan: **E2**
– www.ristorantevo.it – Closed 3 weeks in August, Saturday lunch, Sunday
Menu 45/55 € – Carte 45/82 € – *(booking advisable)*
• **Creative • Minimalist • Trendy •**
His culinary expertise may have been acquired in France, but the gastronomic
passion of the young chef at this modern, minimalist restaurant is completely
Piedmontese. Fresh stuffed pastas and the famous Fassone beef are the main
specialities on the menu, which also includes fish dishes.
➜ Agnolotti ai tre arrosti burro e timo. Scaloppa di rombo in crosta di riso
Venere con farinata alle olive. Crostatina di meliga con crema al limone e
sorbetto al bergamotto.

XX
ξ3
Magorabin (Marcello Trentini)   ⅋ ᕼ AC
corso San Maurizio 61/b ⊠ *10124 –* ℰ *011 8126808*   Plan: **F1**
– www.magorabin.com – Closed Monday lunch, Sunday
Menu 30/50 € – Carte 70/90 € – *(booking advisable)*
• **Modern cuisine • Cosy • Simple •**
Forget the noisy, traffic-filled avenue and soak up the atmosphere of this
enchanting restaurant. It serves imaginative, creative cuisine with the occasional
hint of the Piedmont. A real contrast to conservative, traditional Turin.
➜ Spaghetti pane, burro e acciughe. Anatra all'orientale. Nocciola, fichi e
basilico.

XX
Al Garamond   ⅋ AC ⇔
via Pomba 14 ⊠ *10123 –* ℰ *011 8122781*   Plan: **E2**
– www.algaramond.it – Closed August, Saturday lunch, Sunday
Menu 40/80 € – Carte 43/78 €
• **Modern cuisine • Fashionable • Intimate •**
Bearing the name of a lieutenant in Napoleon's Dragoons, this restaurant offers
creative modern cuisine run by young, skilled and enthusiastic management.

XX
Al Gatto Nero   ⅋ AC
corso Filippo Turati 14 ⊠ *10128 –* ℰ *011 590414*   Plan: **E3**
– www.gattonero.it – Closed August and Sunday
Carte 42/75 € – *(pre-book)*
• **Classic cuisine • Retro • Traditional •**
This restaurant has built up a reputation for fine dining, with a focus on Piedmontese and Tuscan dishes, as well as Mediterranean cuisine. Excellent wine
list offering a selection of around 1 000 different wines.

XX
Galante   AC
corso Palestro 15 ⊠ *10122 –* Ⓜ *XVIII Dicembre*   Plan: **E1**
– ℰ *011532163 – www.ristorantegalante.it – Closed 5-31 August,*
26 December-6 January, Saturday lunch, Sunday
Menu 42 € – Carte 29/63 € – *(bookings advisable at dinner)*
• **Fish and seafood • Intimate • Classic •**
Soft shades and padded seating in the small, well-cared for elegant restaurant
with neo classical setting; on the menu with its wide selection there are both
meat and fish dishes.

XX
Porta Rossa   ⅋ AC
via Passalacqua 3/b ⊠ *10122 –* Ⓜ *XVIII Dicembre*   Plan: **C2**
– ℰ *011 530816 – www.laportarossa.it – Closed 26 December-6 January,*
Saturday lunch, Sunday
Menu 30 € (weekday lunch)/70 € – Carte 37/79 €
• **Fish and seafood • Intimate • Elegant •**
A small, modern restaurant with tables set close together, specialising in dishes
made from fish and seasonal produce. Excellent choice of wine and spirits.

ITALY - TURIN

XX **Tre Galline**   🕮 ⬛ ⇔
via Bellezia 37 ⊠ 10122 – ℰ 011 4366553   Plan: **D1**
– www.3galline.it – Closed 3 weeks in July, 1 week in January, Sunday
(except October-May)
Menu 50 € – Carte 37/74 € – *(dinner only)*
• **Regional** • **Classic** • **Traditional** •
Well cared-for rustic environment in the dining rooms, with wooden ceiling
beams characterising this historic city restaurant, where you can sample typical
and tasty Piedmont cuisine.

XX **Solferino**   🍽 ⬛
piazza Solferino 3 ⊠ 10121 – ℰ 011 535851   Plan: **D2**
– www.ristorantesolferino.com
Carte 29/63 €
• **Regional** • **Classic** • **Intimate** •
In a beautiful Turin square, competently managed for almost 30 years you will
find a classic restaurant, renowned and popular - even at lunchtime; traditional
cuisine.

XX **Capriccioli**   ⬛
via San Domenico 40 ⊠ 10122 – ℰ 011 595221   Plan: **C1**
– www.ristorantecapriccioli.it – Closed 3 weeks in August, 1 week in
January, Monday, Tuesday lunch
Carte 40/80 €
• **Modern cuisine** • **Formal** • **Family** •
A tiny corner of Sardinia in northern Italy. The menu at this elegant restaurant
features specialities such as mullet roe and Carloforte tuna, as well as a good
selection of fish and seafood from other parts of the country. The ecru tones
evoke the sandy beach of Capriccioli.

XX **San Tommaso 10 Lavazza**   ⬛
via San Tommaso 10 ⊠ 10122 – ℰ 011 534201   Plan: **E1**
– www.lavazza.it – closed August and Sunday
Carte 33/76 €
• **Classic cuisine** • **Cosy** •
The Lavazza grocery store opened here in 1895 and now you will find a bar with
a restaurant to the rear. Enthusiasts of the brand can admire old adverts and
calendars while enjoying the classic Italian cuisine served here.

X **Consorzio**   🕮 ⬛
ⓐ *via Monte di Pietà 23 ⊠ 10122 – ℰ 011 2767661*   Plan: **D1**
– www.ristoranteconsorzio.com – Closed 3 weeks in August, Saturday
lunch, Sunday
Menu 26/32 € – Carte 32/45 € – *(booking advisable)*
• **Piedmontese** • **Friendly** • **Trendy** •
Two young associates run this simple, informal restaurant that serves delicious
Piedmontese specialities and traditional regional cuisine. This includes a selection of local wines and cheeses. If you want to try something really special, ask
for the Fassone beef casserole cooked in Ruché wine.

X **Taverna delle Rose**   ⬛
via Massena 24 ⊠ 10128 – Ⓜ Re Umberto   Plan: **D3**
– ℰ 011 538345 – Closed August, Saturday lunch,
Sunday
Carte 25/62 €
• **Regional** • **Family** • **Traditional** •
Typical regional cuisine served in a charming, informal atmosphere. The dining
room is particularly romantic in the evening, with its exposed brickwork and
soft lighting.

ITALY - TURIN

Ristorantino Tefy   Ⓚ

corso Belgio 26 ✉ 10153 – ℰ 011 837332 – Closed   Plan: **B1**
1 week June, 3 weeks August, Saturday lunch, Sunday
Menu 30/40 € – Carte 31/59 €
• **Regional** • **Family** • **Intimate** •
Enthusiasm and commitment in the management of this welcoming establishment; for a journey between the flavours of the sea and the land, in particular from Umbria, take the owners advice.

L'Acino   ⅋

via San Domenico 2/a ✉ 10121 – ℰ 011 5217077   Plan: **D1**
– Closed 3 weeks in August, 1 week in January and Sunday
Carte 28/38 € – *(dinner only) (number of covers limited, pre-book)*
• **Piedmontese** • **Rustic** • **Family** •
A small, friendly and family-run trattoria serving strictly Piedmontese cuisine accompanied by an excellent choice of wines. Be warned – if you haven't booked, it is difficult to get a table!

Scannabue Caffè Restaurant   Ⓐ Ⓚ

largo Saluzzo 25/h – Ⓜ – ℰ 011 6696693   Plan: **E3**
– www.scannabue.it – Closed 1 week in August
Menu 30 € – Carte 31/60 € – *(booking advisable)*
• **Piedmontese** • **Retro** •
This lively local trattoria has an old-fashioned feel. All the focus is on excellent Piedmontese dishes, including specialities such as tajarin pasta, Fassone beef and hazelnuts. A few fish options are also available.

Contesto Alimentare   Ⓚ

via Accademia Albertina 21/e ✉ 10123   Plan: **E2**
– Ⓜ Porta Nuova – ℰ 011 8178698 – www.contestoalimentare.it – Closed
2 weeks in August, Monday
Menu 25/35 € – Carte 28/48 € – *(number of covers limited, pre-book)*
• **Piedmontese** • **Simple** •
You will be surprised by the small size of this restaurant, which has just a few tables in a very simply furnished dining room, and even more taken aback by the quality of the cuisine. The chef uses his knowledge of local produce to create dishes that are full of flavour and inspired by classic Piedmontese recipes. Fish is also served on Friday evenings and Saturdays.

LINGOTTO FIERE   PLAN III

NH Lingotto Tech   ☆ ⅃ Ⓚ ⅍ ⇔

via Nizza 230 ✉ 10126 – Ⓜ Lingotto – ℰ 011 6642000   Plan: **C2**
– www.nh-hotels.it/lingotto – Closed August
140 rm ☲ – †119 € ††289 € – 1 suite
• **Business** • **Conference hotel** • **Modern** •
A panoramic lift leads to the guestrooms of this hotel, which are decorated with designer-style furniture. The sister-hotel to the Hotel Lingotto, the Lingotto Tech is more modern in style.

NH Lingotto   ☆ ⇔ ⅃ ⊛ ⅃ Ⓚ ⅍ Ⓟ

via Nizza 262 ✉ 10126 – Ⓜ Lingotto – ℰ 011 6642000   Plan: **H2**
– www.nh-hotels.it
226 rm ☲ – †109 € ††299 € – 14 suites
• **Business** • **Traditional** • **Modern** •
This modern hotel in the Palazzo del Lingotto provides a good example of the successful restoration of an industrial building. Guestrooms designed by Renzo Piano, as well as a tropical garden.
Torpedo – See restaurant listing

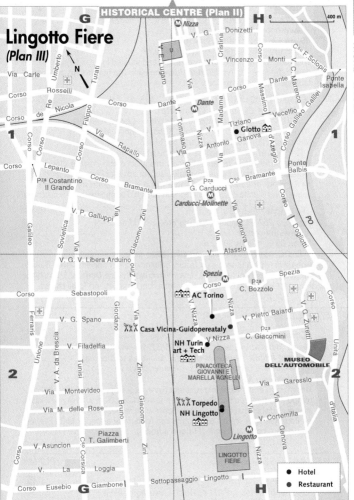

Lingotto Fiere
(Plan III)

MUSEO
DELL'AUTOMOBILE

LINGOTTO
FIERE

● Hotel
● Restaurant

AC Hotel Torino by Marriott

via Bisalta 11 ✉ *10126 –* Ⓜ *Spezia –* ☎ *011 6395091*
– www.hotelactorino.com   Plan: **H2**

86 rm ⌓ – ♦102/400 € ♦♦112/410 € – 3 suites

• **Traditional** • **Modern** •

Once a pasta factory, this early 20th century building in the Lingotto area is now
an up-to-date hotel that offers ideal comfort and completely modern facilities.

Giotto   AC ⚐
via Giotto 27 ⊠ 10126 – Ⓜ Dante – ☏ 011 6637172   Plan: H1
– www.hotelgiottotorino.com
49 rm ⌷ – †55/140 € ††65/160 €
• Family • Business • Functional •
This hotel is run by an experienced family and situated in a residential area bordering the River Po, not far from Valentino park. The guestrooms are comfortable but not overly spacious.

Casa Vicina-Eataly Lingotto (Claudio Vicina)   💆 ৬ AC
via Nizza 224 ⊠ 10126 – Ⓜ Lingotto   Plan: H2
– ☏ 011 19506840 – www.casavicina.com – Closed 7 August-
10 September, Christmas Holidays, Sunday dinner, Monday
Menu 38 € (lunch)/110 € – Carte 55/112 €
• Regional • Minimalist • Elegant •
This minimalist-style restaurant serves imaginative and creative cuisine. It is located inside Eataly, the leading Italian supermarket for niche food products.
→ Agnolotti di Casa Vicina pizzicati a mano al sugo d'arrosto. Rognone à la coque con vellutata di senape ed aglio in camicia. Torrone morbido al cucchiaio.

Torpedo – Hotel NH Lingotto   ⛲ ৬ AC P
via Nizza 262 ⊠ 10126 – Ⓜ Lingotto – ☏ 011 6642714   Plan: H2
– www.nh-hotels.it
Menu 60 € – Carte 30/72 €
• Traditional cuisine • Minimalist • Cosy •
Housed in what was once a car factory belonging to Fiat (the emblem of Turin in the 20C), this elegant restaurant serves high quality cuisine. Don't miss the Vialone Piemontese-style rice with leeks, pancetta ham, potatoes and Toma cheese.

AT RIVOLI

Combal.zero (Davide Scabin)   💆 ◁ AC
piazza Mafalda di Savoia – ☏ 011 9565225 – www.combal.org
– Closed August, Christmas Holidays, Sunday and Monday
Menu 200 € – Carte 100/185 € – (dinner only)
• Creative • Classic •
This modern and minimalist restaurant has a decor inspired by the nearby contemporary art museum in Rivoli castle. It serves classic Piedmontese specialities, as well as dishes that are more imaginative and creative in style.
→ Bombolone di scarola e acciughe con fonduta di grana padano. Fassona impanata e cotta al camino. Fusione a freddo.

AT VENARIA REALE   PLAN I

Galant   AC P
corso Garibaldi 155 – ☏ 011 4551021 – www.hotelgalant.it   Plan: A1
39 rm ⌷ – †39/190 € ††44/259 €
• Business • Family • Classic •
A modern-style structure, ideal for business clientele. Pleasant and rational common areas, comfortable bedrooms with large writing desks. There is also a meeting room.

Cascina di Corte   AC
via Amedeo di Castellamonte 2 – ☏ 011 4593278   Plan: A1
– www.cascinadicorte.it
10 rm ⌷ – †100/220 € ††120/280 € – 2 suites
• Family • Country house • Elegant •
Not far from the famous palace, this 19C farmhouse with adjoining ice-cream parlour has a simple architectural style that is typical of the region. A rustic interior with exposed brickwork in the bedrooms goes hand-in-hand with modern, comfortable furnishings and facilities.

XxX **Dolce Stil Novo alla Reggia** (Alfredo Russo) 🍴 ⅙ 🅰🅲 ⇔
❀ *piazza della Repubblica 4 – ✆ 3462690588*   Plan: A1
– www.dolcestilnovo.com – Closed 2 weeks in August, 2 weeks
in January, Sunday dinner, Monday, Tuesday lunch
Menu 38 € (weekday lunch)/90 €
– Carte 77/117 € – (number of covers limited, pre-book)
• Creative • Elegant • Luxury •
Located inside the Torrione del Garove, this restaurant boasts a pretty terrace
overlooking the Reggia di Venaria garden. There are two ample dining rooms
with spacious tables, which are contrasted by minimalist furnishings. Sample
the welcoming local cuisine with several seafood specialities.
➜ Riso mantecato al gusto di pizza margherita. Il bollito misto del Dolce
Stil Novo. Cremoso di ricotta e gli altri ingredienti della cassata.

ITALY - TURIN

LUXEMBOURG
LËTZEBUERG

LUXEMBOURG

→ **Area:**
2 586 km² (998 sq mi).

→ **Population:**
562 958 inhabitants (nearly 62% nationals, 38% resident foreigners). Density = 218 per km².

→ **Capital:** Luxembourg.

→ **Currency:** Euro (€).

→ **Government:**
Constitutional parliamentary monarchy (since 1868). Member of European Union since 1957 (one of the 6 founding countries).

→ **Languages:**
The national language is Lëtzebuergesch, a variant of German, similar to the Frankish dialect of the Moselle valley; German is used for general purposes and is the first language for teaching; French is the legislative language. Both French and German are used as administrative languages.

→ **Public holidays:**
New Year's Day (1 Jan); Easter Monday (late Mar/21 Apr); Labor Day (1 May); Ascension Day (May); Whit Monday (late May/June); National Day (23 June); Assumption of the Virgin Mary (15 Aug); All Saints' Day (1 Nov); Christmas Day (25 Dec); St Stephen's Day (26 Dec).

→ **Local Time:**
GMT+1 hour in winter and GMT +2 hours in summer.

→ **Climate:**
Temperate continental with cold winters and mild summers (Luxembourg: January 1°C; July 17°C).

→ **Emergency:**
Police ☎ 113; Medical Assistance ☎ 112; Fire Brigade ☎ 118. (Dialling 112 within any EU country will redirect your call and contact the emergency services.)

→ **Electricity:**
230 volts AC, 50Hz; 2 round pin sockets.

→ **Formalities:**
Travellers from the European Union (EU), Switzerland, Norway, Iceland and the main countries of North and South America need a national identity card or passport (America: passport required) to visit the Grand Duchy of Luxembourg for less than three months (tourism or business purpose). For visitors from other countries a visa may be required, in addition to a passport, especially for those wishing to stay for longer than three months. We advise you to check with your embassy before travelling.

LUXEMBOURG
LËTZEBUERG

Population: 111 287

Raymond Thill/Fotolia.com

Luxembourg may be small but it's perfectly formed. Standing high above two rivers on a sandstone bluff, its commanding position over sheer gorges may be a boon to modern visitors, but down the centuries that very setting has rendered it the subject of conquest on many occasions. Its eye-catching geography makes it a city of distinctive districts, linked by spectacular bridges spanning lush green valleys.

The absolute heart of the city is the old town, its most prominent landmarks the cathedral spires and the city squares with their elegant pastel façades – an ideal backdrop to the 'café culture' and a worthy recipient of UNESCO World Heritage Status. Winding its way deep below to the south west is the river Pétrusse, which has its confluence with the river Alzette in the south east. Follow the Chemin de la Corniche, past the old city walls and along the Alzette's narrow valley to discover the ruins of The Bock, the city's first castle, and the Casemates, a labyrinth of rocky 17C and 18C underground defences. Directly to the south of the old town is the railway station quarter, while down at river level to the east is the altogether more attractive Grund district, whose northerly neighbours are Clausen and Pfaffenthal. Up in the north east, connected by the grand sounding Pont Grand-Duchesse Charlotte, is Kirchberg Plateau, a modern hub of activity for the EU.

LUXEMBOURG CITY IN...

→ **ONE DAY**
Place d'Armes, Ducal Grand Palace, National Museum of History and Art, Chemin de la Corniche.

→ **TWO DAYS**
Luxembourg City History Museum, Bock Casemates, the Grund.

→ **THREE DAYS**
Kirchberg Plateau, Museum of Modern Art, concert at Luxembourg Philharmonic Hall.

PRACTICAL INFORMATION

ARRIVAL-DEPARTURE

✈ Luxembourg Findel Airport is 6km northeast of the city centre. City bus Number 16 runs every 10min and takes 25min.

GETTING AROUND

Buses run from 5am to 10pm and there's an additional late night service on Fridays and Saturdays (there's no metro). The most convenient bus stations are at the exit of the Gare Centrale and on Place Hamilius in the old town. The fare system (valid for trains too) is simple enough: for trips of 10km or less you buy a 'short' ticket; for an unlimited day ticket (valid until 8am the next day) you buy a Billet Reseau. Available from Easter-October, the Luxembourg Card offers unlimited travel and free admission to many attractions countrywide. In winter, the Stater Museeskaart offers three days of free admission to important sights in the city.

CALENDAR HIGHLIGHTS

March-May
Printemps Musical.

May
Foire du Printemps (spring festival).

June
National Day Eve - Fireworks over the Pétrusse Valley and partying on Place d'Armes and Place Guillaume II.

June-September
Summer in the City.

August-September
Schueberfouer (One of Europe's biggest funfairs).

November-January
Winterlights Festival.

EATING OUT

The taste buds of Luxembourg have been very much influenced by French classical cuisine, particularly around and about the old town, an area that becomes a smart open-air terrace in summer. Look out for the local speciality Judd mat Gaardebounen, smoked neck of pork with broad beans. The centre of town is an eclectic place to eat as it runs the gauntlet from fast-style pizzeria to expense account restaurants favoured by businessmen. A good bet for atmosphere is the Grund, which offers a wide variety of restaurants and price ranges, and is certainly the area that boasts the most popular cafés and pubs. A few trendy places have sprouted over recent times near the Casemates, and these too are proving to be pretty hot with the younger crowd. A service charge is included in your bill but if you want to tip, ten per cent is reasonable. The Grand Duchy produces its own white and sparkling wines on the borders of the Moselle. Over the last decade it has produced some interesting varieties but you'll rarely find these abroad, as they're eagerly snapped up by the locals.

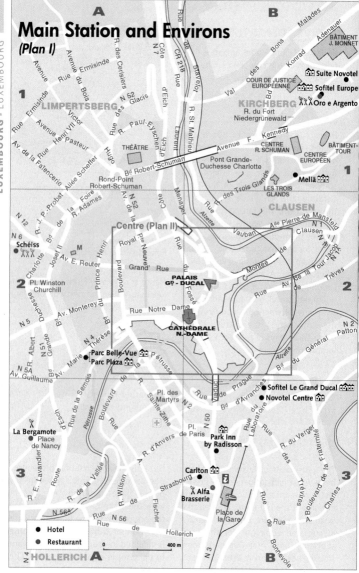

Main Station and Environs
(Plan I)

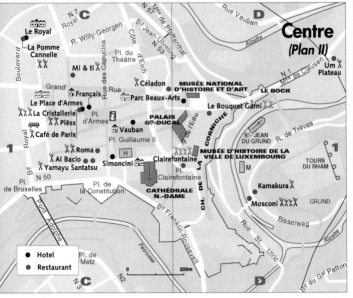

CENTRE

Le Royal
❀ ⓕ⑥ ⓰ ⌧ ⓺ ⒜ ⓢ ⌂

12 bd Royal ✉ *2449 –* ☏ *241 61 61*
Plan: **C1**
– www.leroyalluxembourg.com
190 rm ⌣ – †230/540 € ††250/560 € – 20 suites
• Grand Luxury • Business • Classic •
Nothing in this hotel is left to chance, to such an extent that a king would feel perfectly at home! Guests are waited on hand and foot by an army of staff that are available day and night. It is ideally located in the city's 'Wall Street' neighbourhood.
La Pomme Cannelle – See restaurant listing

Le Place d'Armes
❀ ⓕ ⌧ ⒜ ⌂

18 pl. d'Armes ✉ *1136 –* ☏ *27 47 37*
Plan: **C1**
– www.hotel-leplacedarmes.com
20 rm – †240/400 € ††240/400 € – ⌣ 24 € – 8 suites
• Grand Luxury • Historic • Elegant •
Although on the liveliest square in the town centre, this establishment is a real haven of peace. This former townhouse has been given a complete makeover. It exudes charm and an old Luxembourg atmosphere without feeling stuffy. A must.
❀ **La Cristallerie • Plëss • Café de Paris** – See restaurant listing

Sofitel Le Grand Ducal
❀ ﹤ ⓕ ⓺ ⌧

40 bd d'Avranches ✉ *1160 –* ☏ *24 87 71*
Plan: **B3**
– www.sofitel.com
126 rm – †180/570 € ††180/570 € – ⌣ 29 € – 2 suites
• Business • Luxury • Modern •
This Sofitel has everything you would expect from a top class, international hotel. The plush, understated ambience is set off by an interior that combines designer details with luxurious comfort. It also has a view over the town and the lush gardens of the Pétrusse Valley (from the bathtub of some rooms).

541

Parc Beaux-Arts

1 r. Sigefroi ✉ *2536* Plan: **D1**
– ℰ *26 86 76*
– *www.goeres-group.com*
11 rm – �english170/475 € ♥♥170/475 € – ⌣ 20 € – 1 suite
• Historic • Luxury • Elegant •
This delightful hotel stands right next door to the Museum of Art and History and the Grand Ducal Palace, with whom it shares a taste for beauty and refinement. Each individually appointed spacious room has its own distinctive character. For lovers of sophisticated art de vivre!

Novotel Centre

35 r. Laboratoire ✉ *1911* Plan: **B3**
– ℰ *24 87 81*
– *www.novotel.com*
150 rm – ♥109/285 € ♥♥109/285 € – ⌣ 20 €
• Chain hotel • Contemporary •
This contemporary, highly practical hotel is just a 2min walk from the station and only a few steps from the historic centre.

Parc Plaza et Parc Belle-Vue

5 av. Marie-Thérèse ✉ *2132* – ℰ *45 61 41* Plan: **A2**
– *www.goeres-group.com*
153 rm – ♥79/375 € ♥♥79/375 € – ⌣ 19 €
• Business • Rural • Functional •
A hotel outside the bustling city centre can in fact be a bonus, as this establishment demonstrates by its tranquillity and fine view of the city. Although the concrete structure can hardly be deemed charming, the rooms are spacious.

Simoncini

6 r. Notre-Dame ✉ *2240* – ℰ *22 28 44* Plan: **C1**
– *www.hotelsimoncini.lu*
35 rm ⌣ – ♥125/185 € ♥♥145/190 €
• Business • Townhouse • Design •
This fashionable establishment, which is half hotel, half art gallery, is something of a wild card in Luxembourg's traditional hotel landscape. Well located right in the centre, it is ideal for a city trip and has a public car park nearby.

Français

14 pl. d'Armes ✉ *1136* – ℰ *47 45 34* Plan: **C1**
– *www.hotelfrancais.lu*
22 rm ⌣ – ♥120/160 € ♥♥140/220 €
• Business • Family • Contemporary •
Located on one of the city's most beautiful squares, the Français has been run by the same family since 1970. The owner organises regular art exhibitions on the premises. The café and restaurant (French cuisine and terrace) are similarly representative of the arty ambience.

Vauban

10 pl. Guillaume II ✉ *1648* – ℰ *22 04 93* Plan: **C1**
– *www.hotelvauban.lu*
16 rm ⌣ – ♥70/140 € ♥♥105/160 €
• Townhouse • Traditional • Functional •
Put on your walking shoes: this traditional hotel could not be better located to explore the historic centre. After exploring every avenue and back alley of Luxembourg, take a seat on the hotel's terrace overlooking a lively square and quench your thirst. The breakfast is served in a compact room.

XxxX ✿ **Clairefontaine** (Arnaud Magnier) ⊞ 🍴 🗚 ⇄ 🅿
9 pl. de Clairefontaine ✉ 1341 – ☏ 46 22 11 Plan: **D1**
– www.restaurantclairefontaine.lu – closed 1 week Easter, last
2 weeks August-first week September, Christmas-New Year, first week
January, Bank Holidays, Saturday and Sunday
Menu 57 € (lunch)/99 € – Carte 72/117 €
• French creative • Elegant •
This attractive restaurant with a terrace stands on an elegant square. It has a traditional decor with old wooden panelling and contemporary furnishings. Creative, modern cuisine and astute wine pairings.
→ Millefeuille de langoustines à la tomate mi-confite, pomme verte et
coriandre fraîche, vinaigrette au miel et tarama au chorizo. Pigeon légèrement fumé et petits pois à la française, sauce façon salmis. Tarte au chocolat et au café, glace mascarpone et café en voile de caramel.

XxxX ✿ **Mosconi** (Ilario Mosconi) ⊞ 🍴 ⇄ 🛥
13 r. Münster ✉ 2160 – ☏ 54 69 94 – www.mosconi.lu Plan: **D1**
– closed 1 week Easter, last 3 weeks August, 24 December-early January,
Bank Holidays, Saturday lunch, Sunday and Monday
Menu 44 € (lunch), 74/130 € – Carte 99/129 €
• Italian • Elegant • Luxury •
Ilario and Simonetta Mosconi are an enthusiastic couple that proudly pay
homage to the gastronomic traditions of Italy. Their Italian cuisine is as full of
flair as it is steeped in flavours. The secret of their success no doubt lies in the
infinite care and attention they devote to choosing their suppliers.
→ Linguini di gragnano et tartare de sardines marinées, huile et citron
confit. Il fassone, bœuf piémontais à la truffe blanche d'Alba en saison.
Caramelle à la sicilienne, sauce à l'orange et pistaches.

XxX **Schéiss** 🍴 ⇄ 🅿
142 r. Val Sainte Croix ✉ 1370 – ☏ 24 61 82 Plan: **A2**
– www.scheiss.lu – closed Bank Holidays
Menu 28 € (lunch)/54 € – Carte 49/74 €
• Modern cuisine • Elegant • Fashionable •
Despite the elegant minimalist interior, you need have no fear of the usual hefty
bill associated with such decors. Enjoy the delicious, contemporary cuisine that
is steeped in simplicity.

XxX ✿ **La Cristallerie** – Hôtel Le Place d'Armes 🗚 🛥
18 pl. d'Armes (1st floor) ✉ 1136 – ☏ 274 73 74 21 Plan: **C1**
– www.hotel-leplacedarmes.com – closed Saturday lunch, Sunday and
Monday
Menu 58 € (lunch), 78/175 € – (set menu only)
• French modern • Classic • Elegant •
An elegant dining room surrounded by a superb Art Nouveau glass wall. Contemporary cuisine drawing from classical sources. The chef has a predilection
for fine ingredients, in keeping with the setting.
→ Barbue rôtie, beurre aux algues et salsifis. Poularde de Bresse rôtie, cas-
solette de légumes verts et tomates cerise confites. Baba saké yuzu.

XX **La Pomme Cannelle** – Hôtel Le Royal ⊞ & 🗚 ⇄ 🛥
12 bd Royal ✉ 2449 – ☏ 241 61 67 36 Plan: **C1**
– www.leroyalluxembourg.com – closed August, first week January, Bank
Holidays, Saturday lunch, Sunday and Monday
Menu 46 € (lunch)/89 € – Carte 59/77 €
• Modern cuisine • Romantic •
La Pomme Cannelle represents a culinary marriage between French traditions
and oriental flavours. The Indian Empire interior echoes that of the hotel to
which it belongs.

LUXEMBOURG - LUXEMBOURG

✗✗ Le Bouquet Garni ⌂ ✿ 🥘 (dinner)
32 r. Eau ✉ *1449 –* ☎ *26 20 06 20* Plan: **D1**
*– www.lebouquetgarni.lu – closed Bank Holidays, Saturday lunch
and Sunday*
Menu 30 € (lunch), 42/72 €
• French creative • Classic • Rustic •
As the establishment's name suggests, the dishes are steeped in the aroma of
French cuisine. Chef Thierry Duhr demonstrates his talent by the quality of his
recipes. The dining room, both elegant and rustic, provides the perfect backdrop to the menu.

✗✗ Roma ⌂ ✿
5 r. Louvigny ✉ *1946 –* ☎ *22 36 92 – www.roma.lu* Plan: **C1**
– closed Sunday dinner and Monday
Carte 51/65 €
• Italian • Elegant •
The Roma, Luxembourg's first Italian restaurant, specialises in homemade pasta,
ultra fresh ingredients, and more unusually, theme festivals. All of which have
enabled it to become a firm favourite with the locals. There is a popular range
of daily specials.

✗✗ Plëss – Hôtel Le Place d'Armes ⒶⒸ
18 pl. d'Armes ✉ *1136 –* ☎ *274 73 74 11* Plan: **C1**
– www.hotel-leplacedarmes.com
Menu 39 € (lunch) – Carte 52/88 €
• Classic cuisine • Brasserie • Fashionable •
Plëss means 'square' in Luxembourgish – an obvious reference to the Place
d'Armes. This is where this lovely contemporary brasserie is located, in the
heart of town. Glamorous, urban atmosphere.

✗ Mi & Ti ⌂ ⒶⒸ
🙂 *8 av. de la Porte-Neuve* ✉ *2227 –* ☎ *26 26 22 50* Plan: **C1**
*– closed 1 week Easter, last 3 weeks August, 1 week late December,
Monday dinner, Tuesday dinner and Sunday*
Menu 35 € (lunch) – Carte approx. 45 €
• Italian • Fashionable •
A trendily decorated Italian restaurant occupying the first floor of a modern building. Authentic produce imported directly from Italy. Simplified menu at the
downstairs Bottega. Busy street terrace.

✗ La Bergamote
🙂 *2 pl. de Nancy* ✉ *2212 –* ☎ *26 44 03 79* Plan: **A3**
*– www.labergamote.lu – closed 1 week Easter, last 2 weeks August, late
December, Bank Holidays, Monday dinner, Saturday lunch and Sunday*
Menu 24 € (lunch)/35 € – Carte 54/64 €
• Modern cuisine • Trendy • Friendly •
Have you ever actually tasted bergamot? The subtle, fresh taste of this small
citrus fruit is a recurring ingredient in Philippe Bridard's sun-drenched cuisine.
Vitello tonnato, roast sea bream and shrimp polenta, without forgetting a few
modern, French touches...

✗ Céladon ✿
1 r. Nord ✉ *2229 –* ☎ *47 49 34 – www.thai.lu – closed* Plan: **C1**
Saturday lunch and Sunday
Carte 43/51 €
• Thai • Elegant • Fashionable •
Lovers of Thai cuisine won't be disappointed by the fresh produce and authen-
tic Asian flavours of the Céladon. Vegetarians will no doubt be in seventh hea-
ven with the range that is on offer.

X

Kamakura

4 r. Münster ✉ 2160 – ☎ 47 06 04 – www.kamakura.lu   Plan: **D1**
– closed 2 weeks Easter, last 2 weeks Easter-early September, late
December-early January, Bank Holidays, Saturday lunch and Sunday
Menu 12 € (lunch)/33 € – Carte 34/69 €
• Japanese • Minimalist • Exotic •
The minimalist design of this Japanese restaurant has made no concessions to the West. It is named after the former capital of the Land of the Rising Sun and embodies the essence of Japanese cooking: understated, low-key presentation and virtuoso preparation. Kamakura celebrated its 25th anniversary in 2013.

X

Yamayu Santatsu

26 r. Notre-Dame ✉ 2240 – ☎ 46 12 49 – closed last   Plan: **C1**
week July-first 2 weeks August, late December-early January, Bank
Holidays, Sunday and Monday
Menu 15 € (lunch)/34 € – Carte 26/61 €
• Japanese • Neighbourhood • Exotic •
Yamayu Santatsu's sushi is fully equal to that of Tokyo, explaining the establishment's popularity by gourmets who know how to appreciate the subtlety of Japanese cuisine. It has an understated decor and private rooms for business meetings.

X

Al Bacio   AC

24 r. Notre Dame ✉ 2240 – ☎ 27 99 48 81 – closed last   Plan: **C1**
2 weeks August-first week September, late December-early January, Bank
Holidays, Monday dinner, Tuesday dinner and Sunday
Menu 13 € (lunch) – Carte 32/45 €
• Italian • Bistro • Simple •
Presto, presto! The characteristic liveliness associated with Italian towns forms the backdrop to this popular restaurant. The regulars return for the authentic, super fresh cuisine. Who could resist such a delicious Italian kiss (bacio)?

X

Café de Paris – Hôtel Le Place d'Armes

18 pl. d'Armes ✉ 1136 – ☎ 26 20 37 70   Plan: **C1**
– www.cafedeparis.lu
Carte 38/62 €
• Regional • Bistro • Intimate •
The mood is lively and the decor is cosy in this engaging bistro! The chefs pay tribute to Luxembourg's culinary traditions and tasty country produce. If you fell in love with one of the ingredients you just sampled, pop next door to the shop.

MAIN STATION

Park Inn by Radisson   🖧 AC ⚙ P

45 av. de la Gare ✉ 1611 – ☎ 268 91 81   Plan: **B3**
– www.parkinn.com/hotel-luxembourg
99 rm – ♦89/799 € ♦♦89/899 € – ⏁ 20 €
• Chain hotel • Modern •
Anyone in search of the modernity and comfort of a hotel chain will appreciate the recently created Park Inn.

Carlton   🚗

9 r. Strasbourg ✉ 2561 – ☎ 29 96 60 – www.carlton.lu   Plan: **B3**
50 rm ⏁ – ♦95/185 € ♦♦115/195 €
• Townhouse • Art Deco • Classic •
The Carlton continues to embody a certain image of the Grand Duchy. Behind its fine Art Deco façade the visitor can admire a spacious interior that is steeped in 'turn of the last century' nostalgia. Well located near the station and in a quiet neighbourhood.

✗ **Alfa Brasserie** &. AK

16 pl. de la Gare ✉ *1616 –* ℰ *49 00 11 30 00* Plan: **B3**
– www.alfabrasserie.lu
Menu 25 € (lunch) – Carte 31/50 €
• Classic cuisine • Brasserie • Elegant •
Alfa Brasserie will take you back in time. Copper pots, high ceilings and Art Deco features recreate the authentic setting of a 1930s Parisian brasserie. The menu is deliciously classical, with the occasional Luxembourg specialty.

ENVIRONS OF LUXEMBOURG

 Sofitel Europe ✿ ⌂ ⊾ 🛁 🐾 AK 🛗 🚗

4 r. Fort Niedergrünewald (European Centre) Plan: **B1**
✉ *2015 Kirchberg –* ℰ *43 77 61 – www.sofitel.com*
105 rm – ♦120/450 € ♦♦180/520 € – ☲ 27 € – 4 suites
• Business • Grand Luxury • Elegant •
A bold, oval shaped hotel at the heart of the European Institutions district. Central, oval atrium and spacious, extremely comfortable guestrooms. The attentive, friendly service you would expect from this upmarket chain. Typical restaurant serving regional cuisine, warm atmosphere enhanced by the staff in traditional costume.
Oro e Argento – See restaurant listing

 Meliã ✿ ⌂ ≤ 🛁 🐾 & AK 🛗

1 Park Dräi Eechelen ✉ *1499 Kirchberg –* ℰ *27 33 31* Plan: **B1**
– www.melia-luxembourg.com
160 rm ☲ – ♦90/390 € ♦♦110/410 € – 1 suite
• Business • Modern •
The first hotel of this Spanish chain in Benelux, located next to the conference centre. Rooms are stylish, comfortable and functional. Lovely view of the city.

Suite Novotel 🛁 AK 🛗 🚗

13 av. J.F. Kennedy ✉ *1855 Kirchberg –* ℰ *2 70 40* Plan: **B1**
– www.suitenovotel.com
110 rm – ♦114/280 € ♦♦114/280 € – ☲ 15 €
• Business • Chain hotel • Design •
Seasoned travellers will no doubt appreciate the fixtures and fittings of this trendy hotel, which is 5min from the centre. Music and film are on demand to satisfy the mind, and there are microwave and ready-to-eat dishes for the body.

✗✗✗ **Oro e Argento** – Hôtel Sofitel Europe AK **P**

6 r. Fort Niedergrünewald (European Centre) Plan: **B1**
✉ *2015 Kirchberg –* ℰ *43 77 68 70 – www.sofitel.com*
Menu 39 € (lunch), 62/75 € – Carte 66/77 €
• Italian • Intimate •
An attractive Italian restaurant in a luxury hotel. Contemporary cuisine served to a backdrop of plush interior decor with a Venetian touch. Intimate atmosphere and stylish service.

✗✗ **Mamma Bianca** 🍴 &. AK
🈂

33 av. J.F. Kennedy (Ellipse Kirchberg 2) ✉ *1855 Kirchberg –* ℰ *27 04 54*
– www.mammabianca.lu – closed late December-early January, Bank Holidays, Saturday and Sunday
Menu 27 € (lunch)/37 € – Carte 30/71 €
• Italian • Trendy • Musical •
Mamma mia – what a restaurant! A spacious interior done up in a designer, trendy style, bordering on a lounge ambience. The menu features Italian classics and fresh sushi. The chef rustles up dishes full of generous flavours and devoid of unnecessary frills. A delicious Bib!

Bick Stuff

95 r. Clausen ✉ 1342 Clausen – ℰ 26 09 47 31 – www.bickstuff.lu – closed 2 weeks in August, late December, Bank Holidays, Saturday lunch, Sunday dinner and Monday

Menu 23 € (lunch), 36/46 € – Carte 48/67 €

• Home cooking • Classic •

You will instantly feel at home in this family-run restaurant where everything is homemade. Find classic recipes full of character with the chef's distinctive touch. We recommend the set menu.

Um Plateau

6 Plateau Altmunster ✉ 1123 Clausen – ℰ 26 47 84 26 – www.umplateau.lu – closed Saturday lunch and Sunday

Plan: **D1**

Menu 27 € (lunch)/35 € – Carte 36/56 €

• Modern cuisine • Design • Fashionable •

An elegant neo-bistro with designer chairs, pop lighting, warm colours and, for a retro touch, stained-glass windows. Contemporary cuisine: black rice risotto, salmon tartare with fennel…

NETHERLANDS
NEDERLAND

AMSTERDAM

● The Hague

● Rotterdam

→ **AREA:**
41 543 km² (16 163 sq mi).

→ **POPULATION:**
16 957 605 inhabitants.
Density = 408 per km².

→ **CAPITAL:**
Amsterdam; The Hague
is the seat of government
and Parliament.

→ **CURRENCY:**
Euro (€).

→ **GOVERNMENT:**
Constitutional parliamentary
monarchy (since 1815). Member
of European Union since 1957
(one of the 6 founding countries).

→ **LANGUAGE:**
Dutch; many Dutch people also
speak English.

→ **PUBLIC HOLIDAYS:**
New Year's Day (1 Jan); Easter
Monday (late Mar/Apr); King's Day
(26/27 Apr); Liberation Day (5 May);
Ascension Day (May); Whit Monday
(late May/June); Christmas Day
(25 Dec); St Stephen's Day (26 Dec).

→ **LOCAL TIME:**
GMT+1 hour in winter and GMT
+2 hours in summer.

→ **CLIMATE:**
Temperate maritime with cool
winters and mild summers
(Amsterdam: January 2°C; July
17°C), rainfall evenly distributed
throughout the year.

→ **EMERGENCY:**
Police, Medical Assistance and Fire
Brigade ✆ 112.

→ **ELECTRICITY:**
230 volts AC, 50Hz; 2 round pin
sockets.

→ **FORMALITIES:**
Travellers from the European
Union (EU), Switzerland, Norway,
Iceland and the main countries of
North and South America need a
national identity card or passport
(America: passport required) to
visit the Netherlands for less than
three months (tourism or business
purpose). For visitors from other
countries a visa may be required, in
addition to a passport, especially
for those wishing to stay for longer
than three months. We advise you
to check with your embassy before
travelling.

AMSTERDAM
AMSTERDAM

Population: 812 895

Packshot/Fotolia.com

Once visited, never forgotten; that's Amsterdam's great claim to fame. Its endearing horseshoe shape – defined by 17C canals cut to drain land for a growing population – allied to finely detailed gabled houses, has produced a compact city centre of aesthetically splendid symmetry and matchless consistency. Exploring the city on foot or by bike is the real joy here and visitors rarely need to jump on a tram or bus.

'The world's biggest small city' displays a host of distinctive characteristics, ranging from the world-famous red light district to the cosy and convivial brown cafés, from the wonderful art galleries and museums to the quirky shops, and the medieval churches to the tree-lined waterways with their pretty bridges. There's the feel of a northern Venice, but without the hallowed and revered atmosphere. It exists on a human scale, small enough to walk from one end to the other. Those who might moan that it's just too small should stroll along to the former derelict docklands on the east side and contemplate the shiny new apartments giving the waterfront a sleek, 21C feel. Most people who come here, though, are just happy to cosy up to old Amsterdam's sleepy, relaxed vibe. No European city does snug bars better: this is the place to go for cats kipping on beat-up chairs and candles flickering on wax-encrusted tables…

AMSTERDAM IN...

→ **ONE DAY**
A trip on a canal boat, Rijksmuseum, Anne Frank Museum, Van Gogh Museum.

→ **TWO DAYS**
Begijnhof, shopping in the '9 Straatjes', Vondelpark, evening in a brown café.

→ **THREE DAYS**
The Jordaan, Plantage and Entrepotdok, red light district.

PRACTICAL INFORMATION

ARRIVAL-DEPARTURE

✈ Schiphol International Airport is 18km southwest of the city. Trains run regularly to Amsterdam Central Station, and take 15min.

GETTING AROUND

With its narrow streets and canals, this is a city geared to walking. It's also one of the most bike-friendly capitals in the world, so rent one if you want to experience life as a local. Trams and buses run mostly from the central station; the metro has four short lines, mostly used by commuters. The Amsterdam Card entitles the holder to free public transport, admission to major museums, a canal cruise and discounts in some restaurants. Valid for 24hr, 48hr, or 72hr, it is available from the Tourist Information Office opposite the central station.

CALENDAR HIGHLIGHTS

May
Kunst RAI (modern art exhibition).

June
Holland Festival (theatre, concerts and ballets), Open Garden Days.

July
Roots Festival (music and dance).

August
Uitmarkt (theatrical/musical shows), Gay Pride's Canal Parade, Grachtenfestival (classical concerts).

September
Jordaan Festival (musical shows and fairs).

November
Museumnacht (many museums stay open during the night).

EATING OUT

Amsterdam is a vibrant and multicultural city and, as such, has a wide proliferation of restaurants offering a varied choice of cuisines, where you can eat well without paying too much. Head for an eetcafe and you'll get a satisfying three course meal at a reasonable price. The Dutch consider the evening to be the time to eat your main meal, so some restaurants shut at lunchtime. Aside from the eetcafe, you can top up your middle-of-day fuel levels with simple, home-cooked meals and local beers at a bruin (brown) café, or for something lighter, a café specialising in coffee and cake. If you wish to try local specialities, number one on the hit list could be rijsttafel or 'rice table', as the Dutch have imported much from their former colonies of Indonesia. Fresh raw herring from local waters is another nutritious local favourite, as are apple pies and pancakes of the sweet persuasion; often enjoyed with a hot chocolate. Restaurants are never too big but are certainly atmospheric and busy, so it's worth making reservations.

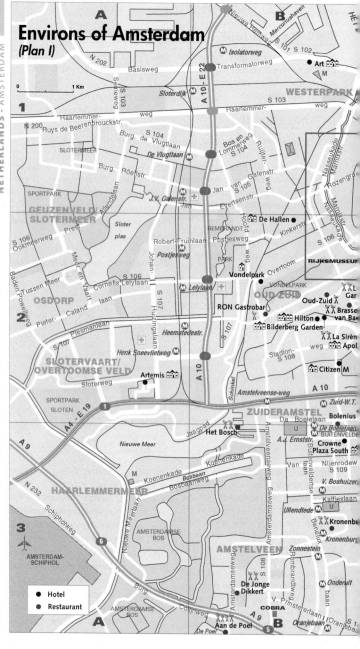

Environs of Amsterdam
(Plan I)

NETHERLANDS - AMSTERDAM

0   1 Km

A

B

N 202

Basisweg

Nieuwe Hemweg

Mercuriushaven

HET I

Isolatorweg

Transformatorweg

Art

M

Senneweg

S 103

Sloterdijk

A 10 - E 22

S 102

S 101

WESTERPARK

1

Haarlemmer-

weg

Haarlemmer-

S 103

weg

N 200

Ruys de Beerenbrouckstr.

Burg. de Vlugtlaan

S 104

Bos en Lommerweg

S 104

Ruiter-

Nassaukade

Marnixstr.

Rozengr

SLOTERMEER

De Vlugtlaan

Jan van Galenstr.

S 105

van

weg

SPORTPARK

Burg. Röettstr.

J.V. Galenstr.

Galenstr.

Jan

Evertsenstr.

Nassaukade

Marnixstr.

GEUZENVELD/
SLOTERMEER

Sloter
plas

REMBRANDT

Jan

Evertsenstr.

De Hallen

Kinkerstr.

S 106

S 106

Ookmeerweg

Prest

Robert-Fruinlaan

Postjesweg

PARK

Overtoom

RIJKSMUSEU

Baden-Powellweg

Meer en Vaart

Postjesweg

Johan-

Huizingalaan

VONDELPARK

Vondelpark

OUD-ZUID

Gar

X L

Tussen Meer

S 106

Cornelis Lelylaan

Lelylaan

RON Gastrobar

Oud-Zuid

Brasse
van Ba

OSDORP

Pieter- Caland

laan

S 107

Hilton

Bilderberg Garden

X X La Sirèn

Plesmanlaan

Heemstedestr.

S 107

weg

Apol

SLOTERVAART/
OVERTOOMSE VELD

Henk Sneevlietweg

Stadion-
S 108

Citizen M

Sloterweg

Artemis

A 10

Schinkel

Amstelveense-weg

A 10

SPORTPARK
SLOTEN

A4 - E 19

1

Jaagpad

ZUIDERAMSTEL

De Boelelaan

Zuid-W.T.

Bolenius

Het Bosch

Amstelveenseweg

U

De Boelelaan

BUITENVELD

Nieuwe Meer

A.J. Ernststr.

Crowne
Plaza South

A 9

N 232

Koenenkade

Bosbaan

Van

Buitenvelderts

laan

Nijenrode
S 109

V. Boshuizer

Koenenkade

Bosbaanweg

M

Kalfjeslaan

Schipholweg

HAARLEMMERMEER

Nieuwe Meerdan

AMSTERDAMSE
BOS

Ullendtede

U

Kronenbu

Benelux

Kronenburg

3

AMSTERDAM-
SCHIPHOL

6

AMSTERDAMSE
BOS

Burg.

AMSTELVEEN

Zonnestein

Rembrandtweg

Nestein

Onderuit

M

V. Prinstererlaan

baan

S 1

De Jonge
Dikkert

S 108

COBRA

Oranjebaan

Oranjeba

Collijnweg

Aan de Poel

A 9

De Poel

B

5

● Hotel

● Restaurant

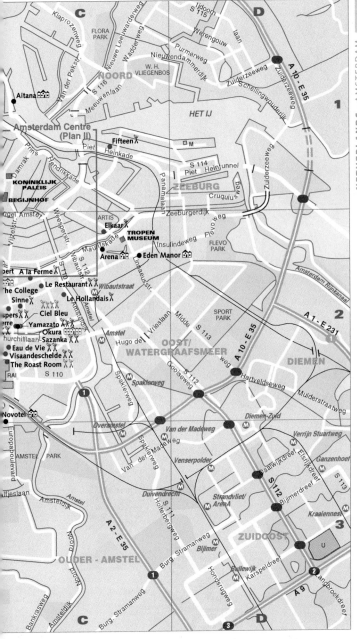

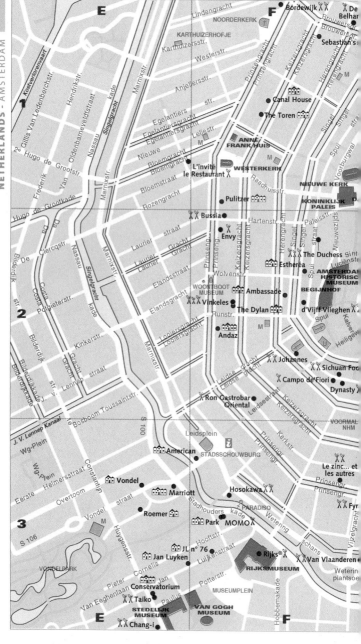

E

F

Bordewijk

De Belhar

Brouwersgr.

Brouwersgr.

Lindengracht

NOORDERKERK

Sebastian's

KARTHUIZERHOFJE

Karthuizersstr.

Westerstr.

Anjeliersstr.

Canal House

The Toren

Egelantiersstr.

Egelantiersgracht

Egelantiersgracht

Nieuwe

Leliestr.

ANNE FRANK HUIS

Bloemgracht

Bloemgracht

L'invité le Restaurant

WESTERKERK

Raadhuisstr.

NIEUWE KERK

Bloemstraat

KONINKLIJK PALEIS

Rozengracht

Pulitzer

Hartenstr.

Bussia

Laurier

straat

Gracht

Envy

The Duchess

Laurier

Gracht

Estherea

AMSTERDAM HISTORISC MUSEUM

Laurier

Elandsstraat

Wolvenstr.

WOONTBOOT

Ambassade

BEGIJNHOF

Elandsgracht

Vinkeles

The Dylan

d'Vijff Vlieghen

Runstr.

Andaz

Looiersgracht

Spui

Johannes

Sichuan Foo

Leidse gracht

Campo de'Fiori

Dynasty

Ron Gastrobar Oriental

Leidsestraat

VOORMAL NHM

Leidseplein

American

STADSSCHOUWBURG

Le zinc... et les autres

Prinsengr.

Prinsengr.

Vondel

Marriott

Hosokawa

Fyr

Roemer

PARADISO

Stadhouders

kade

Weteringschans

Park

MOMO

JL n° 76

Hooftstr.

Jan Luyken

Luijkenstraat

Rijks

Van Vlaanderen

RIJKSMUSEUM

Weterin plantsoe

Conservatorium

Potterstr.

Pieter

Jan

Van Eeghenlaan

Paullus

Taiko

MUSEUMPLEIN

STEDELIJK MUSEUM

VAN GOGH MUSEUM

E

F

Chang-i

VONDELPARK

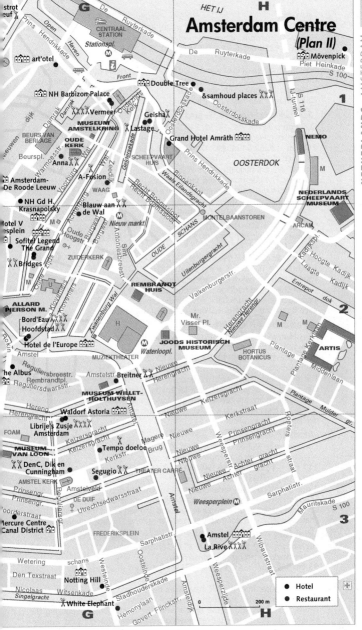

Amsterdam Centre
(Plan II)

HET IJ

De Ruyterkade

Piet Heinkade

Mövenpick

art'otel

CENTRAAL STATION

Stationspl.

Front

Double Tree

&samhoud places

NEMO

NH Barbizon Palace

Oosterdokskade

Vermeer

Geisha

Lastage

MUSEUM AMSTELKRING

OUDE KERK

Grand Hotel Amrâth

Prins Hendrikkade

OOSTERDOK

NEDERLANDS SCHEEPVAART MUSEUM

Beurspl.

Anna

SCHEEPVAART HUIS

Amsterdam-De Roode Leeuw

A-Fusion

WAAG

Recht Boomssloot

Binnenkant

Waals Eilandsgracht

NH Gd H. Krasnapolsky

Blauw aan de Wal

Nieuw markt!

MONTELBAANSTOREN

ARCAM

Hotel V esplein

Sofitel Legend The Grand

Oude Hoogstr.

SCHANS

OUDE

Uilenburgergracht

Hoogte Kadijk

Laagte Kadijk

Bridges

ZUIDERKERK

Sint Antoniesbreestr.

Entrepot dok

ALLARD PIERSON M.

REMBRANDT HUIS

Valkenburgerstr.

Bord'Eau

Hoofdstad

Mr. Visser Pl.

ARTIS

Hotel de l'Europe

MUZIEKTHEATER

Waterloopl.

JOODS HISTORISCH MUSEUM

HORTUS BOTANICUS

Plantage Middenlaan

Amstel

Reguliersbreestr.

he Albus

Rembrandtpl.

Reguliersdwarsstr.

Amstelstr.

Breitner

MUSEUM WILLET-HOLTHUYSEN

Kerkstraat

Waldorf Astoria

Herengr.

Herengracht

Keizersgracht

Nieuwe Keizersgracht

Prinsengracht

Plantage Muider gr.

FOAM

Librije's Zusje Amsterdam

Magere Brug

Nieuwe Prinsengracht

MUSEUM VAN LOON

Tempo doeloe

Kerkstr.

THEATER CARRÉ

Nieuwe Achter gracht

DenC, Dik en Cunningham

Segugio

AMSTEL KERK

Amstelveld

Prinsengr.

DE DUIF

Utrechtsedwarsstraat

Weesperplein

Sarphatistr.

Mauritskade

oorderstraat

Mercure Centre Canal District

FREDERIKSPLEIN

Sarphatistr.

Amstel

La Rive

Wetering schans

Den Texstraat

Notting Hill

Nicolaas Singelgracht

Witsenkade

White Elephant

Stadhouderskade

Hemonylaan

Govert Flinckstr.

Weesperzijde

● Hotel
● Restaurant

0   200 m

555

Amstel

Prof. Tulpplein 1 ⊠ 1018 GX – ℰ (0 20) 622 60 60   Plan: **H3**
– www.amsterdam.intercontinental.com

63 rm – †350/655 € ††350/655 € – ⊑ 35 € – 16 suites
• Grand Luxury • Palace • Personalised •

A veritable haven of luxury and good taste in this grand hotel on the banks of the Amstel. The vast rooms are decorated with attention to detail and stylish furnishings. Complete, efficient service.

✾ **La Rive** – See restaurant listing

Sofitel Legend The Grand

O.Z. Voorburgwal 197 ⊠ 1012 EX – ℰ (0 20) 555 31 11   Plan: **G2**
– www.sofitel-legend-thegrand.com

148 rm – †265/540 € ††295/570 € – ⊑ 38 € – 29 suites
• Grand Luxury • Palace • Historic •

This magnificent building, where William of Orange once stayed, oozes historic grandeur. The guestrooms and public spaces breathe luxury and French elegance – and there is even a butler service. Le Petit Bistro will delight fans of bistro cuisine with its many classic favourites.

✾ **Bridges** – See restaurant listing

Hotel de l'Europe

Nieuwe Doelenstraat 2 ⊠ 1012 CP – ℰ (0 20) 531 17 77   Plan: **G2**
– www.leurope.nl

88 rm – †389/633 € ††389/699 € – ⊑ 36 € – 23 suites
• Luxury • Palace • Personalised •

This luxury hotel, which dates back to the end of the 19C, offers a chic combination of charm and tradition. The rooms are elegant and the junior suites were inspired by the Dutch School. Views of the canals.

✾✾ **Bord'Eau** • ✾ **Hoofdstad** – See restaurant listing

Grand Hotel Amrâth

Prins Hendrikkade 108 ⊠ 1011 AK – ℰ (0 20) 552 00 00   Plan: **G1**
– www.amrathamsterdam.com

165 rm – †199/399 € ††199/399 € – ⊑ 25 € – 7 suites
• Chain hotel • Business • Historic •

The monumental staircase in this imposing Art Nouveau hotel will be your stairway to heaven as you won't want for anything here. The location is nice and central, the rooms are comfortable and the service is very personal and attentive. In the restaurant, you will find a hint of retro in the decor and an international flavour on your plate.

Andaz

Prinsengracht 587 ⊠ 1016 HT – ℰ (0 20) 523 12 34   Plan: **F2**
– www.amsterdam.prinsengracht.andaz.com

117 rm – †350/600 € ††350/600 € – ⊑ 30 € – 5 suites
• Luxury • Business • Design •

A design hotel on the Prinsengracht with an interior decor by Marcel Wanders. This former library lends itself to an experience encapsulating both luxury and style, accompanied by a personal welcome and service. In the restaurant, the charcoal oven is used for freshly cooked dishes served in large or small portions.

Waldorf Astoria

Herengracht 542 ⊠ 1017 CG – ℰ (0 20) 718 46 00   Plan: **G3**
– www.waldorfastoria.com/amsterdam

93 rm – †495/1055 € ††495/1055 € – ⊑ 35 € – 8 suites
• Palace • Stylish •

Six canal houses from the 17C have been transformed into a luxury hotel with stylish decor, marble bathrooms and staff who are ever attentive to guests' needs. The views add to the appeal, with the front rooms overlooking the Herengracht and those to the rear overlooking the beautiful courtyard. Wonderful!

✾✾ **Librije's Zusje Amsterdam** – See restaurant listing

Pulitzer
☆ 🏠 ʦ ⓘ 🅰ℂ 🐾 🚗

Prinsengracht 315 ☒ 1016 GZ – 𝒞 (0 20) 523 52 35
Plan: **F1**
– www.pulitzeramsterdam.com
225 rm – ♦209/459 € ♦♦229/479 € – ☑ 26 € – 8 suites
· Chain hotel · Luxury · Historic ·

A distinctive complex of 25 houses from the 17C and 18C located around a manicured garden. The rooms are tastefully decorated and the public spaces adorned by works of art. In the restaurant, feast on grilled dishes looking out over the canals of Amsterdam.

NH Grand Hotel Krasnapolsky
☆ ʦ 🏯 ⓘ 🅰ℂ 🐾 🚗

Dam 9 ☒ 1012 JS – 𝒞 (0 20) 554 91 11
Plan: **G1**
– www.nh-collection.com
451 rm – ♦249/559 € ♦♦249/559 € – ☑ 30 € – 2 suites
· Luxury · Traditional · Classic ·

Monuments should be cherished, that is why this historic grand hotel dating back to 1855 has been fully renovated. Business people and holidaymakers alike will appreciate the modern luxury and the more classic features. Breakfast in the winter garden and dinner in the stylish Grand Café complete the experience.

Conservatorium
☆ ʦ ⊕ 🏯 ▢ 🅰ℂ 🐾 🚗

Van Baerlestraat 27 ☒ 1071 AN – 𝒞 (0 20) 570 00 00
Plan: **E3**
– www.conservatoriumhotel.com
129 rm – ♦455/775 € ♦♦485/900 € – ☑ 37 €
· Historic · Grand Luxury · Modern ·

The Conservatorium is one of Amsterdam's finest hotels. Neither expense nor effort was spared in the renovation of this neo-Classical jewel that dates back to the end of the 19C. Excellent service, with staff at hand to meet your every need. Pure, unadulterated luxury.
Taiko – See restaurant listing

Marriott
☆ ʦ 🏯 ⓘ 🅰ℂ 🐾 🚗

Stadhouderskade 12 ☒ 1054 ES – 𝒞 (0 20) 607 55 55
Plan: **E3**
– www.amsterdammarriott.com
391 rm ☑ – ♦200/450 € ♦♦220/470 € – 5 suites
· Chain hotel · Business ·

A high-class, American-style hotel on a major thoroughfare. The rooms are vast and well-equipped. A good seminar infrastructure and business centre. Modern steak house specialising in grilled Black Angus Beef.

art'otel
☆ ʦ 🏯 ⓘ ▢ 🅰ℂ 🐾 ↔

Prins Hendrikkade 33 ☒ 1012 TM – 𝒞 (0 20) 719 72 00
Plan: **G1**
– www.artotelamsterdam.com
107 rm – ♦185/559 € ♦♦185/559 € – ☑ 24 €
· Chain hotel · Grand Luxury · Modern ·

From the exhibition in the cellar to the creations in the corridors and bedrooms, art is the theme of this modern hotel. It also exhibits a good grasp of the art of indulgence, from the luxury and comfort of the bedrooms to the exquisite care in the wellness suite. All this with the backdrop of beautiful works of art.

NH Barbizon Palace
☆ ʦ 🏯 ⓘ 🅰ℂ 🐾 🚗

Prins Hendrikkade 59 ☒ 1012 AD – 𝒞 (0 20) 556 45 64
Plan: **G1**
– www.nh-hotels.com
271 rm – ♦199/450 € ♦♦199/450 € – ☑ 25 € – 3 suites
· Chain hotel · Business · Modern ·

This elegant property directly opposite the station has a hint of 17C charm. Renovations are taking place to upgrade the traditional comfort. The famous Amsterdam canals await discovery from the private jetty. At Bar Mar-Dique discover dishes prepared in a modern bistro style, with a penchant for vegetables.
❀ **Vermeer** – See restaurant listing

Ambassade
☆ ⪕ AC

Herengracht 341 ☒ *1016 AZ – ℰ (0 20) 555 02 22*　　　Plan: **F2**
– www.ambassade-hotel.nl
54 rm – ♦185/265 € ♦♦185/285 € – ☐ 20 € – 3 suites
• Luxury • Townhouse • Stylish •

The CoBrA collection and the books in the library signed by authors who have stayed here all testify to the artistic style of this hotel. It is just perfect for art loving Amsterdam!

The Dylan
☆ ₤₅ AC ⅍

Keizersgracht 384 ☒ *1016 GB – ℰ (0 20) 530 20 10*　　　Plan: **F2**
– www.dylanamsterdam.com
40 rm – ♦350/550 € ♦♦495/550 € – ☐ 28 € – 2 suites
• Grand Luxury • Design • Oriental •

Discover the intimate harmony of this 17C boutique hotel with a surprising designer decor. Magnificent guestrooms and personal service make this one of the city's special addresses.
❀ **Vinkeles** – See restaurant listing

American
☆ ₤₅ 📶 ⅙ AC ⅍

Leidsekade 97 ☒ *1017 PN – ℰ (0 20) 556 30 00*　　　Plan: **F3**
– www.hampshire-hotels.com/american
175 rm – ♦120/400 € ♦♦120/400 € – ☐ 20 €
• Palace • Business • Art Deco •

This historic building in a lively square immediately commands your attention with its imposing façade that exudes a certain dignity. The fine brasserie cuisine on offer in the Café Americain is served in a stylish Art Deco pub with a magnificent ceiling.

Mövenpick
☆ ⪕ ₤₅ 📶 ⅙ AC ⅍ ⊟

Piet Heinkade 11 ☒ *1019 BR – ℰ (0 20) 519 12 00*　　　Plan: **H1**
– www.moevenpick-hotels.com/amsterdam
408 rm – ♦159/380 € ♦♦159/380 € – ☐ 25 € – 1 suite
• Chain hotel • Business • Modern •

Modern chain hotel in a modern district. The rooms have panoramic views. Concert hall, jazz club and congress centre next door. Restaurant serving international cuisine.

Canal House
⇦ AC ⅍

Keizersgracht 148 ☒ *1015 CX – ℰ (0 20) 622 51 82*　　　Plan: **F1**
– www.canalhouse.nl
23 rm ☐ – ♦285/700 € ♦♦285/700 € – 1 suite
• Luxury • Personalised •

Canal House is synonymous with luxury and is set alongside one of Amsterdam's canals. Take your pick from guestrooms ranging in category from 'good' to 'better' to 'best', the ultimate treat! The modern character of the rooms fits in perfectly with the historic ambience of this hotel.

Estheréa
AC ⅍ ⊟

Singel 305 ☒ *1012 WJ – ℰ (0 20) 624 51 46*　　　Plan: **F2**
– www.estherea.nl
91 rm – ♦150/450 € ♦♦180/480 € – ☐ 18 € – 2 suites
• Traditional • Family • Personalised •

The Estheréa is a beautiful, elegant hotel full of charm. Its warm, classic interior clad in red velvet will tempt you in, and its excellent breakfast will win you over completely.

The Toren
⇦ AC

Keizersgracht 164 ☒ *1015 CZ – ℰ (0 20) 622 63 52*　　　Plan: **F1**
– www.thetoren.nl
38 rm – ♦80/330 € ♦♦150/600 € – ☐ 14 € – 2 suites
• Traditional • Cosy • Retro •

This romantic boutique hotel can be found just a few steps away from the Anne Frank House. The breakfast room is elegant and the bedrooms are decorated in a warm, neo-Baroque style. The three garden suites will ensure a memorable stay.

Notting Hill 🕏 🅐🅒 🚗

Westeinde 26 ✉ *1017 ZP –* ✆ *(0 20) 523 10 30* — Plan: **G3**
– www.hotelnottinghill.nl
71 rm – 🛏150/400 € 🛏🛏150/400 € – ⭥ 24 €
• Luxury • Design •

A boutique hotel equipped with every type of modern comfort. The rooms not only look sumptuous, they are also finished with top quality materials. The hotel's car park is handy in this location in the city centre. Enjoy international cuisine to a backdrop of designer decor in the restaurant.

 Double Tree 🕏 ≼ 🖪 ⅅ 🔊

Oosterdoksstraat 4 ✉ *1011 DK –* ✆ *(0 20) 530 08 00* — Plan: **H1**
– www.eastwoodamsterdam.com
557 rm ⭥ – 🛏169/425 € 🛏🛏169/425 €
• Chain hotel • Business • Functional •

This hotel with its huge windows boasts dazzling views to tempt the curious traveller, as well as a great location close to the canal IJ and the station. The bedrooms of this rather futuristic hotel are light and airy. Impressive Sky lounge.

 Aitana 🕏 ⊗ ≼ 🖪 🕅 ⅅ 🅐🅒 🔊 🚗

IJdok 6 ✉ *1013 MM –* ✆ *(0 20) 891 48 00* — Plan: **C1**
– www.room-matehotels.com
285 rm – 🛏119/279 € 🛏🛏119/279 € – ⭥ 19 € – 6 suites
• Chain hotel • Business • Design •

Amsterdam has a new design hotel on the canal IJ, and quite an exceptional one too! Lots of light and a minimalist design in the themed rooms and suites create a relaxed 'Zen-like' feel. Breakfast is served until noon, allowing guests a lazy morning in the comfortable beds. A nice extra touch: the hotel has its own marina.

 Park 🕏 🖪 ⅅ 🅐🅒 🔊 🚗

Stadhouderskade 25 ✉ *1071 ZD –* ✆ *(0 20) 671 12 22* — Plan: **F3**
– www.parkhotel.nl
189 rm – 🛏119/459 € 🛏🛏119/459 € – ⭥ 19 €
• Palace • Business • Design •

Fully renovated hi-tech hotel set between Vondelpark and the busy centre. Five types of spacious and pleasant trendy rooms. Meeting and fitness facilities. Stylish service.
MOMO – See restaurant listing

 Amsterdam - De Roode Leeuw 🕏 🅐🅒

Damrak 93 ✉ *1012 LP –* ✆ *(0 20) 555 06 66* — Plan: **G1**
– www.hotelamsterdam.nl
79 rm – 🛏95/410 € 🛏🛏105/420 € – ⭥ 17 €
• Traditional • Classic •

A veteran in the Amsterdam hotel and catering industry with a central location along the busy Damrak. Guestrooms offering good levels of comfort. Choose from a traditional Dutch menu in the restaurant.

 The Albus 🕏

Vijzelstraat 49 ✉ *1017 HE –* ✆ *(0 20) 530 62 00* — Plan: **G2**
– www.albushotel.com
74 rm – 🛏99/369 € 🛏🛏99/369 € – ⭥ 19 €
• Business • Design •

A bright, modern design hotel in the city centre, where the guestrooms have been named 'smart', 'superb' and 'stunning' depending on their size. A useful tip: the rooms at the back are particularly quiet. The Senses restaurant also has a relaxed atmosphere with slow food prepared from top quality produce in a traditional way.

Mercure Centre Canal District

Noorderstraat 46 ✉ 1017 TV – 𝒞 (0 20) 622 03 28   Plan: **G3**
– www.mercure.com/1032
93 rm – ♥99/229 € ♥♥99/229 € – � 20 €

• Townhouse • Chain hotel • Modern •

Breathe in the true atmosphere of Amsterdam in these former weavers' cottages, which have made way for a boutique hotel. It makes an excellent base for visits to the city's museums and the guestrooms are renovated in a modern style. The basement houses a flashy bar.

Hotel V Nesplein

Nes 49 ✉ 1012 KD – 𝒞 (0 20) 662 32 33 – www.hotelv.nl   Plan: **G2**
43 rm – ♥119/349 € ♥♥119/349 € – ⊡ 15 €

• Townhouse • Functional •

This modern, urban hotel has hit the stage in the very heart of the theatre district. The corridors are decorated with old theatre posters, while the guestrooms are imposing yet comfortable. The atmospheric brasserie, which serves delicious cuisine, also plays a leading role here.

Roemer

Roemer Visscherstraat 10 ✉ 1054 EX – 𝒞 (0 20)   Plan: **E3**
589 08 00 – www.hotelroemer.com
38 rm – ♥100/300 € ♥♥120/350 € – ⊡ 18 €

• Business • Design •

An attractive hotel with an elegant, designer-style interior, in an early 20C townhouse situated close to the Vondel Park. Modern interior, immaculate rooms and breakfast served in the garden in summer.

Vondel

Vondelstraat 26 ✉ 1054 GD – 𝒞 (0 20) 612 01 20   Plan: **E3**
– www.hotelvondel.com
86 rm – ♥90/300 € ♥♥120/350 € – ⊡ 18 €

• Business • Luxury • Modern •

This boutique hotel was created out of seven 1900s houses. Communal areas, bedrooms and conference room in a decidedly contemporary style. Breakfasts on the stylish patio when the weather is good. Hip, stylish bistro serving local and international cuisine.

Jan Luyken

Jan Luijkenstraat 58 ✉ 1071 CS – 𝒞 (0 20) 573 07 30   Plan: **E3**
– www.janluyken.nl
62 rm – ♥99/299 € ♥♥129/349 € – ⊡ 20 €

• Townhouse • Cosy •

Three 1900s houses make up this hotel with contemporary interior décor. Modern bedrooms, designer bar with a few period touches and small courtyard terrace.

JL n° 76

Jan Luijkenstraat 76 ✉ 1071 CT – 𝒞 (0 20) 348 55 55   Plan: **F3**
– www.hoteljlno76.com
39 rm – ♥100/300 € ♥♥120/350 € – ⊡ 18 €

• Luxury • Modern •

Two 18C townhouses have been converted into one at Jan Luijkenstraat 76, hence the name. Comfortable accommodation, which might not be the ultimate in luxury but is definitely stylish and elegant. This hotel is situated in the fashion and museum district, so there is plenty to do in the neighbourhood.

De Hallen

Bellamyplein 47 ✉ 1053 AT – 𝒞 (0 20) 820 86 70   Plan: **B2**
– www.hoteldehallen.com
55 rm – ♥150/350 € ♥♥150/350 € – ⊡ 20 €

• Historic • Townhouse • Cosy •

The tram depot near Amsterdam's Foodhallen has been converted into a contemporary hotel. You will discover a combination of retro, industrial, trendy and Scandinavian design elements, all of which result in a warm and charming hotel.

Sebastian's

Keizersgracht 15 ✉ 1055 CC – ✆ (0 20) 423 23 42
– www.hotelsebastians.nl

Plan: **F1**

34 rm – †70/170 € ††100/260 € – ☖ 10 €

• **Traditional** • **Personalised** •

A boutique hotel with an adventurous, yet warm colour scheme. Its convenient location on the Keizersgracht canal, close to the Jordaan area, will suit business travellers and night-owls alike. Trendy bar.

XxxX · Bord'Eau – Hotel de l'Europe &⬠⬝AC⇄🛏P

Nieuwe Doelenstraat 2 ✉ 1012 CP – ✆ (0 20) 531 16 19
Plan: **G2**
– www.bordeau.nl – closed 26 July-18 August, first 2 weeks January,
Saturday lunch, Sunday and Monday
Menu 48 € (lunch), 108/118 € – Carte 75/144 €

• **Creative** • **Elegant** •

Delicious and sophisticated, or deliciously sophisticated is the best way of summing up the hallmarks of this restaurant. The chef makes every effort to please his demanding clientele by serving well-sourced produce in dishes that reflect the spirit of the times completely.

→ Kaluga kaviaar met oesterroomijs, runderwang en ijsgekoelde consommé. Tournedos Rossini met gebraiseerde ui en pommes soufflées. Ballon van bittere chocolade met koffie en praliné.

XxxX · Librije's Zusje Amsterdam – Hotel Waldorf Astoria AC⇄

Herengracht 542 ✉ 1017 CG – ✆ (0 20) 718 46 43
Plan: **G3**
– www.waldorfastoria.com – closed 26-28 April, 3-5 May,
24 July-18 August, 1-20 January, Sunday and Monday
Menu 80/140 €
– Carte 94/230 € – (dinner only except Friday and Saturday)

• **Creative** • **Luxury** •

Extraordinarily beautiful and classy! This refined, classic restaurant offers a true fine dining experience. The food is elegant, with a unique interplay of textures and tastes that is spot on, creating a wonderful harmony where every bite surprises. Definitely worth a visit!

→ Platte oesters met ganzenlever, tomaat, shiso, roos en saké. Gebraden duif met worteltjes, rogge, kardamom en mosterdzaadjes. Sorbet van avocado met komkommer, yoghurt en chocolade.

XxxX · Vermeer – Hotel NH Barbizon Palace &⬠AC⇄🛏P

Prins Hendrikkade 59 ✉ 1012 AD – ✆ (0 20) 556 48 85
Plan: **G1**
– www.restaurantvermeer.nl – closed 17 July-22 August, 25 December-
8 January, Bank Holidays and Sunday
Menu 90/110 € – Carte approx. 100 € – *(dinner only)*

• **Modern cuisine** • **Elegant** • **Individual** •

An elegant restaurant in a top class hotel, where the chef applies a personal style and a touch of daring. Beautiful à la carte menu, extensive wine cellar and an experienced sommelier.

→ Morieljes gestoofd met amandel, bloemkoolzalfje en daslooksaus. Runderribstuk met sjalot- en veenbessenchutney, snijbiet en rodewijnsaus. Chocoladetaart met rumroomijs.

XxxX La Rive – Hotel Amstel &⬠⬝AC⇄🛏P

Prof. Tulpplein 1 ✉ 1018 GX – ✆ (0 20) 520 32 64
Plan: **H3**
– www.restaurantlarive.com – closed 4-21 January
Menu 100/165 € – Carte 125/150 € – *(dinner only)*

• **French modern** • **Formal** •

An intimate ambience, refined decor, sublime comfort and exquisite wines characterise this gastronomic restaurant in the Amstel Hotel. The kitchen is modern, producing dishes that show touches of Asian inspiration. The canal-side tables are particularly sought after.

→ Coquilles met gazpacho, groene appel en kalamansi. Kamperlam met aubergines, sesam en sumak. Creatie met gin tonic, yoghurt, kaneel en komkommer.

✗✗✗ **The Duchess** 〔AC〕

Spuistraat 172 ✉ 1012 VT – 𝒞 (0 20) 811 33 22   Plan: **F2**
– www.the-duchess.com
Carte 60/85 € – *(dinner only)*
• Mediterranean • Elegant •

The Duchess has flair. Once the vault of a bank, this is now a stylish restaurant dominated by dark marble with a Belle Epoque atmosphere. The beautiful Molteni kitchen produces Mediterranean dishes with a modern twist.

✗✗✗ **Vinkeles** – Hotel The Dylan

✿ *Keizersgracht 384 ✉ 1016 GB – 𝒞 (0 20) 530 20 10*   Plan: **F2**
– www.vinkeles.com – closed 1-17 August, 1-20 January, Bank Holidays and Sunday
Menu 90/120 € – Carte 82/262 € – *(dinner only)*
• Creative • Elegant •

Smart restaurant set in a characterful hotel. Creative, tasty cuisine, served stylishly in the former bakery (view of the old ovens) or facing the courtyard.
➔ Geglaceerde kalfszwezerik met ossenstaartbouillon, fregola en groene tomaat. Wilde zeebaars met serranoham, radijs en pijlinktvis. Rabarber met macadamianoten, havermout en vlierbesbloesem.

✗✗✗ **& samhoud places** (Moshik Roth) 〔AC〕 ⇔

✿✿ *Oosterdokskade 5 ✉ 1011 AD – 𝒞 (0 20) 260 20 94*   Plan: **H1**
– www.samhoudplaces.com – closed first 2 weeks August, first 2 weeks January, Monday and Tuesday
Menu 105/169 €
– Carte 120/280 € – (dinner only except Friday and Sunday)
• Creative • Design •

Moshik Roth takes guests on a culinary adventure in his fashionable restaurant, which provides one surprise after another. The chef skilfully combines inventiveness with sophistication and rich flavours. On the ground floor the street food restaurant introduces diners to cuisine from all around the world. A real experience!
➔ Langoustine en kaviaar. Tarbot met citrus. Chocolade, passievrucht en praliné.

✗✗ **Bridges** – Hotel Sofitel The Grand

✿ *O.Z. Voorburgwal 197 ✉ 1012 EX – 𝒞 (0 20) 555 35 60*   Plan: **G2**
– www.bridgesrestaurant.nl – closed Monday
Menu 30 € (lunch), 69/89 € – Carte 51/90 €
• Fish and seafood • Elegant •

The dishes on offer in this beautiful fish restaurant combine refinement, surprise, originality and quality, and are worthy of the utmost praise. Overall, good quality, reasonably priced cuisine.
➔ Oosterscheldekreeft met eendenlevercrème, champignons en asperges. Gebakken heilbot met witte kool, krabslaatje en een appel-komijnjus. Gemarineerde aardbeien met tomaat, amandelchiboust en basilicum.

✗✗ **Dynasty** 〔AC〕 ⇔

Reguliersdwarsstraat 30 ✉ 1017 BM – 𝒞 (0 20)   Plan: **F2**
626 84 00 – www.fer.nl – closed 27 December-2 February and Tuesday
Menu 43/66 € – Carte 39/69 € – *(dinner only until 11pm)*
• Chinese • Exotic •

A pleasant, longstanding restaurant featuring cuisine from around Asia. The trendy exotic décor is warm and colourful. Lovely terrace in the back and attentive service.

✗✗ **Hoofdstad** – Hotel de l'Europe 〔AC〕

Nieuwe Doelenstraat 2 ✉ 1012 CP – 𝒞 (0 20) 531 16 19   Plan: **G2**
– www.hoofdstadbrasserie.nl
Menu 36 € – Carte 55/148 € – *(open until 11pm)*
• Classic cuisine • Cosy • Brasserie •

On the terrace of this luxurious canal-side brasserie, with its views of bridges and passing boats, Amsterdam really comes into its own. The delicious dishes, which are uncomplicated yet always full of flavour, can also be enjoyed indoors. Sole Meunière and charcoal-grilled entrecote are just two of the kitchen's culinary delights.

XX

d'Vijff Vlieghen

Spuistraat 294 (via Vlieghendesteeg 1) ✉ 1012 VX Plan: **F2**
– ✆ (0 20) 530 40 60 – www.vijffvlieghen.nl – closed 27 April, 25 July-7 August, 24 December-3 January
Menu 37/116 € – Carte 45/71 € – *(dinner only)*
• Traditional cuisine • Rustic •

The classic dishes on offer at these charming 17C premises are all prepared with typical Dutch products. A set menu is served in various attractive, country-style dining rooms where original Rembrandt sketches decorate the walls.

XX

Breitner

Amstel 212 ✉ 1017 AH – ✆ (0 20) 627 78 79 Plan: **G2**
– www.restaurant-breitner.nl – closed 20 July-10 August, 25 December-5 January and Sunday
Menu 40/45 € – Carte 53/68 € – *(dinner only)*
• French creative • Formal •

Creative and elaborate meals served in a classical modern setting. There are views over the Amstel with sightseeing boats and monuments (drawbridges, Hermitage museum) in the background.

XX

Blauw aan de Wal

O.Z. Achterburgwal 99 ✉ 1012 DD – ✆ (0 20) 330 22 57 Plan: **G2**
– www.blauwaandewal.com – closed Sunday and Monday
Menu 55/68 € – *(dinner only until 11pm) (booking advisable) (set menu only)*
• Market cuisine • Friendly •

A popular restaurant at the end of a cul-de-sac in the lively red light district. Discreet décor, simple and tasty modern cuisine, good wine selection and a shady terrace.

XX

Le zinc... et les autres

Prinsengracht 999 ✉ 1017 KM – ✆ (0 20) 622 90 44 Plan: **F3**
– www.lezinc.nl – closed 31 December-8 January, Sunday and Monday
Menu 36/54 € – *(dinner only)*
• French modern • Rustic •

This stylish 17C warehouse is on the Prinsengracht canal. The interior has been modernised but the rustic bar and beams have been left just as they were. Diners looking for a quieter meal should choose the lower room. Well-chosen menu and an interesting assortment of wines available by the glass.

XX

Anna

Warmoesstraat 111 ✉ 1012 JA – ✆ (0 20) 428 11 11 Plan: **G1**
– www.restaurantanna.nl – closed Easter Monday, Whit Monday, 25 and 26 December and Sunday
Menu 48/65 € – Carte 46/57 € – *(dinner only)*
• Modern cuisine • Fashionable •

There is no lack of vitality at Anna given its location in the middle of the vibrant red-light district. This cosmopolitan restaurant has a relaxed and informal atmosphere – a choice setting for balanced, modern cooking.

XX

Fyra

Noorderstraat 19 ✉ 1017 TR – ✆ (0 20) 428 36 32 Plan: **F3**
– www.restaurantfyra.nl – closed 27 April, 2 weeks in August and 24 December-2 January
Menu 36 € – Carte 51/61 € – *(dinner only)*
• Mediterranean • Friendly •

The intimate and cosy atmosphere will immediately make customers feel at home. The menu features up-to-the-minute dishes with a Mediterranean twist and an occasional surprise element. A kitchen with ambition.

XX Hosokawa

AC ⇔

Max Euweplein 22 ✉ *1017 MB –* ✆ *(0 20) 638 80 86*   Plan: **F3**
– www.hosokawa.nl
– closed 31 December, 1 January and Tuesday
Menu 50/92 € – Carte 27/91 € – *(dinner only except Friday and weekends)*
• Teppanyaki • Minimalist •

A sober, modern Japanese restaurant with tables and a sushi bar, worth a detour to watch the entertaining show of food rotating past your eyes!

XX Segugio

AC ⇔

Utrechtsestraat 96 ✉ *1017 VS –* ✆ *(0 20) 330 15 03*   Plan: **G3**
– www.segugio.nl – closed 27 April, 24, 25 and 31 December-1January and Sunday
Menu 43/58 € – Carte 54/63 € – *(dinner only)*
• Italian • Friendly •

This establishment with three modern dining rooms on several levels features sunny Italian cuisine made right before your eyes. Good selection of Italian wines.

XX Sichuan Food

AC ⇔

Reguliersdwarsstraat 35 ✉ *1017 BK –* ✆ *(0 20) 626 93 27*   Plan: **F2**
– www.sichuanfood.nl
– closed 31 December
Menu 33 € – Carte 39/104 € – *(dinner only)*
• Chinese • Exotic •

Small Chinese restaurant with good local reputation situated in a lively area. Beijing Duck prepared and served in the dining room.

XX Van Vlaanderen

⌂ AC ⇔

Weteringschans 175 ✉ *1017 XD –* ✆ *(0 20) 622 82 92*   Plan: **F3**
– www.restaurant-vanvlaanderen.nl
– closed 27 December-2 January, Saturday lunch, Sunday and Monday
Menu 30 € (lunch), 36/60 € – Carte 51/62 €
• Modern cuisine • Classic •

Van Vlaanderen has long been recognised as the place to go for the good things in life. It has a pleasant location in the centre of Amsterdam with its own jetty on the patio. The restaurant's success lies in attentive service and a young, spirited team whose enthusiasm is evident in the modern, original versions of the classic dishes served here.

XX DenC, Dik en Cunningham

AC ⇔

Kerkstraat 377 ✉ *1017 HW –* ✆ *(0 20) 422 27 66*   Plan: **G3**
– www.restaurantdenc.nl – closed Saturday lunch and Sunday
Menu 27 € (lunch), 35/90 € ♟ – *(open until 11pm)*
• French creative • Classic •

The deer heads on the walls of this contemporary restaurant hint at chef Dik's hunter-family upbringing and, unsurprisingly, his cooking puts the spotlight firmly on game. Sommelier Cunningham's choice of wines make a good match.

XX Bussia

⇔

Reestraat 28 ✉ *1016 DN –* ✆ *(0 20) 627 87 94*   Plan: **F2**
– www.bussia.nl – closed 19 juli-6 August, 1-7 January, Tuesday lunch, Wednesday lunch and Monday
Menu 36 € (lunch), 49/79 € – Carte 54/72 €
• Italian • Trendy • Mediterranean •

A restrained yet stylish modern restaurant that conjures up Italian cuisine with a French influence. This is accompanied by an impressive choice of fine Italian wines presented by the female owner. As a bonus, the open kitchen enables you to look behind the scenes.

XX **Bordewijk**
Noordermarkt 7 ⊠ 1015 MV – ℰ (0 20) 624 38 99   Plan: **F1**
– www.bordewijk.nl – closed mid July-mid August, 24 December-
2 January, Sunday and Monday
Menu 39 € – Carte 52/71 € – *(dinner only until 11pm)*
• Modern cuisine • Friendly • Neighbourhood •
Popular restaurant due to its modern menu with inventive touches and mini-malist décor: bare floorboards, Formica tables and designer chairs. Noisy atmo-sphere when busy.

XX **Johannes**
Herengracht 413 ⊠ 1017 BP – ℰ (0 20) 626 95 03   Plan: **F2**
– www.restaurantjohannes.nl – closed 27 April, 31 December and
1 January
Menu 49/67 € – *(dinner only) (set menu only)*
• International • Trendy • Brasserie •
Take your place in the pleasant dining room or on the large terrace to the rear, and let Johannes surprise you. All you have to do is choose the number of cour-ses, then sit back and enjoy balanced dishes. These often feature bold and unusual combinations and techniques, as well as distinctive flavours blended together in delicious harmony.

XX **Taiko** – Hotel Conservatorium   🕭 AC
Van Baerlestraat 27 ⊠ 1071 AN – ℰ (0 20) 570 00 00   Plan: **E3**
– www.conservatoriumhotel.com – closed 19 July-17 August and Sunday
Menu 78/115 € – Carte 43/128 € – *(dinner only until 11pm)*
• Asian influences • Intimate • Elegant •
Taiko is an atmospheric, cosmopolitan restaurant and deliciously trendy. The establishment serves a contemporary take on Asian cuisine. It is beautifully pre-sented, diverse and pure in flavour.

X **RIJKS°**   🕭 & 🚗
Museumstraat 2 ⊠ 1077 XX – ℰ (0 20) 674 75 55   Plan: **F3**
– www.rijksrestaurant.nl – closed 27 April, 31 December dinner
and 1 January
Carte 38/62 €
• French modern • Brasserie • Trendy •
The Rijksmuseum has acquired a real showpiece in this lively luxury brasserie. The focus is on accessible quality with modern combinations of ingredients delivering a whole host of more complex flavours.

X **Envy**   AC
😊 *Prinsengracht 381 ⊠ 1016 HL – ℰ (0 20) 344 64 07*   Plan: **F2**
– www.envy.nl
Carte 30/55 € – *(dinner only except Friday, Saturday and Sunday)*
• Mediterranean • Brasserie • Tapas bar •
A new-style brasserie with dining on either side of a long refectory table under low, spherical lights or standing at one of the smaller tables. All the food is on display in glass showcases.

X **MOMO** – Hotel Park   & AC
Hobbemastraat 1 ⊠ 1071 XZ – ℰ (0 20) 671 74 74   Plan: **F3**
– www.momo-amsterdam.com
Menu 22/69 € – *(open until 11pm)*
• Asian • Brasserie • Design •
Momo is still one of the city's hot spots, with fusion cuisine in a fashionable set-ting. Bento (Japanese lunch box) at lunchtime and a menu designed for sha-ring in the evening.

NETHERLANDS - AMSTERDAM

Lastage (Rogier van Dam) 𝔸ℂ
Geldersekade 29 ⊠ *1011 EJ* – 𝒞 *(0 20) 737 08 11*   Plan: **G1**
– www.restaurantlastage.nl – closed 27 and 28 April, 2-22 August,
26 December-4 January and Monday
Menu 43/89 € – *(dinner only)*
• Creative • Bistro • Friendly •

At Lastage you'll find a concise selection of tempting dishes full of character and depth, like vichyssoise or potato with mackerel tartare or veal cheek confit with lobster. The relatively small bill at the end will make the experience even more enjoyable.
→ Tartaar van zeebaars en langoustines met een crème van maïs, groene boontjes en mierikswortel. Gegrilde varkensnek met artisjok, doperwtjes en een barbecuesaus. Parfait van hazelnootjes met rabarber, aardbeien en mousse van tonkabonen.

De Belhamel ⪕ 🕸 𝔸ℂ ⇄
Brouwersgracht 60 ⊠ *1013 GX* – 𝒞 *(0 20) 622 10 95*   Plan: **F1**
– www.belhamel.nl
Menu 35/45 € – Carte 43/52 €
• Classic cuisine • Bistro •

This local brasserie is at the confluence of delightful canals. Small traditional choice plus a blackboard menu (simpler at lunchtimes). Belle Epoque-style dining room with a mezzanine. Terrace near the canals.

Tempo doeloe 𝔸ℂ
Utrechtsestraat 75 ⊠ *1017 VJ* – 𝒞 *(0 20) 625 67 18*   Plan: **G3**
– www.tempodoeloerestaurant.nl – closed 27 April, 25, 26 and
31 December-1 January and Sunday
Menu 35/53 € – Carte 36/63 €
• Indonesian • Exotic •

Regular diners at Tempo doeloe or 'Times Gone By' find it difficult to hide their enthusiasm when they visit this restaurant. They know that an Indonesian feast like no other in Amsterdam awaits them. The food here is authentically Indonesian, with no concessions to Western taste. Selamat makan!

A-Fusion
Zeedijk 130 ⊠ *1012 BC* – 𝒞 *(0 20) 330 40 68*   Plan: **G1**
– www.a-fusion.nl
Menu 18 € (lunch), 33/45 € – Carte 23/41 € – *(open until 11pm)*
• Asian • Bistro •

A fusion of Chinese and Japanese cuisine in the heart of Amsterdam's Chinatown. This restaurant boasts a grill, sushi bar, dim sum and wok kitchen. Be sure to try the prawn dim sum, the beef with a black pepper sauce and the oysters with ginger. Alternatively, give the cooks carte blanche to come up with some surprising choices.

Fifteen 🕸 ⅄ 𝔸ℂ
Jollemanhof 9 ⊠ *1019 GW* – 𝒞 *(0 20) 509 50 15*   Plan: **C1**
– www.fifteen.nl – closed Sunday lunch
Menu 39/50 € – *(bar lunch)*
• Italian • Brasserie •

Jamie Oliver is the driving force behind the concept of this trendy restaurant, which aims to reintegrate unemployed young people. The kitchen is resolutely Italian and the food delicious. Paid parking is available in the car park below the restaurant.

Bistrot Neuf 🎴 𝔸ℂ
Haarlemmerstraat 9 ⊠ *1013 EH* – 𝒞 *(0 20) 400 32 10*   Plan: **G1**
– www.bistrotneuf.nl
Menu 20 € (lunch), 32/45 € – Carte 36/63 € – *(open until 11pm)*
• Classic cuisine • Bistro •

With its clean, modern design, this relaxed bistro is ideally located in a lively area of Amsterdam. Enjoy original Amsterdam flair expressed in traditional French dishes, impeccably cooked to bring out the true flavours of the ingredients. Efficient service.

NETHERLANDS - AMSTERDAM

✗ Geisha
🔼 ⇔

Prins Hendrikkade 106a ✉ *1011 AJ* – ☎ *(0 20) 626 24 10*   Plan: **G1**
– www.restaurantgeisha.nl – closed 30 December-4 January and Sunday
Menu 35/55 € – Carte 25/66 € – *(dinner only until 11pm)*
• Asian • Fashionable •

Run by the Wang sisters, this restaurant decorated in a trendy style specialises in innovative Asian cuisine. The small portions allow diners to sample a variety of dishes.

✗ Ron Gastrobar Oriental
🔼 ⇔

Kerkstraat 23 ✉ *1017 GA* – ☎ *(0 20) 223 53 52*   Plan: **F2**
– www.rongastrobaroriental.nl – closed 27 April, 31 December and 1 January
Carte 38/48 € – *(dinner only until 11pm) (booking advisable)*
• Chinese • Trendy • Exotic •

Subtle lighting, Asian decor and natural materials set the mood at this stylish restaurant, while a renowned bartender shakes cocktails at the extensive bar. Full of flavour, the delicious dishes offer a contemporary take on traditional Chinese cuisine.

✗ L'invité le Restaurant
🏠

Bloemgracht 47 ✉ *1016 KD* – ☎ *(0 20) 570 20 10*   Plan: **E1**
– www.linvitelerestaurant.nl – closed Monday lunch, Tuesday lunch and Wednesday lunch
Menu 29 € (lunch), 45/59 € – Carte 45/73 €
• Modern cuisine • Friendly •

This restaurant invites guests on a stylish trip to France. The smart and elegant dining room acts as the perfect backdrop for contemporary cuisine, which is created with a whole host of exciting flavours and textures. Sit back, relax and accept the invitation!

✗ Campo de' Fiori
🏠

Reguliersdwarsstraat 32 ✉ *1017 BM* – ☎ *(0 20)*   Plan: **F2**
303 95 00 – www.campodefiori.nl – closed Monday lunch, Tuesday lunch and Wednesday lunch
Menu 33 € – Carte 38/58 €
• Italian • Trendy • Friendly •

Close your eyes, savour the cuisine and imagine you are on the Campo de' Fiori in Rome. The chef may include modern features in his dishes but the flavours remain deliciously authentic. Well worth the effort, as is the enclosed garden at this welcoming establishment.

SOUTH and WEST QUARTERS

🏨 Okura
🔼 🛝 ≤ 𝕃ⓕ ⊕ 🛝 ☑ ᠶ 🔼 ᠕ 🚗

Ferdinand Bolstraat 333 ✉ *1072 LH* – ☎ *(0 20)*   Plan: **C2**
678 71 11 – www.okura.nl
291 rm – ✝190/470 € ✝✝190/470 € – ⏛ 33 € – 9 suites
• Palace • Grand Luxury • Elegant •

A luxurious Japanese-style hotel set in a modern tower building. Various types of rooms and suites, superb wellness centre, extensive conference facilities and a full range of services.
🌸🌸 **Ciel Bleu** • 🌸 **Yamazato** • 🌸 **Sazanka** • 🏵 **Serre** – See restaurant listing

🏨 Hilton
🔼 ≤ 🛏 𝕃ⓕ 🛝 ᠶ 🔼 ᠕ 🅿

Apollolaan 138 ✉ *1077 BG* – ☎ *(0 20) 710 60 00*   Plan: **B2**
– www.amsterdam.hilton.com
271 rm – ✝209/509 € ✝✝209/509 € – ⏛ 27 € – 4 suites
• Chain hotel • Business • Modern •

A modern apartment-style building with a waterside garden and several terraces. Contemporary rooms and suites with panoramic views, one of which was the scene of 'John and Yoko's bed-in' in 1969. Restaurant Roberto's is one of the best Italians in the city.

Crowne Plaza South
George Gershwinlaan 101 ✉ *1082 MT –* ✆ *(0 20)* Plan: **B3**
504 36 66 – www.crowneplaza.com/amstsouth
207 rm – ♦100/300 € ♦♦100/300 € – ☐ 23 € – 5 suites
· Chain hotel · Business · Modern ·

This hotel in a rapidly expanding part of Amsterdam is ideal for business travellers. It has a fresh feel and a bright, minimalist decor. The airport and RAI congress centre are only minutes away by public transport.

Bilderberg Garden
Dijsselhofplantsoen 7 ✉ *1077 BJ –* ✆ *(0 20) 570 56 00* Plan: **B2**
– www.bilderberg.nl/hotels/garden-hotel
122 rm – ♦129/499 € ♦♦129/499 € – ☐ 23 € – 2 suites
· Business · Luxury · Contemporary ·

Chain hotel catering mainly to corporate customers in the business district. Inviting interior, spacious and comfortable guestrooms, meeting facilities and valet parking. In restaurant De Kersentuin, the dishes are fresh, original and brimming with flavour.

Art
Spaarndammerdijk 302 ✉ *1013 ZX –* ✆ *(0 20) 410 96 70* Plan: **B1**
– www.westcordhotels.com
187 rm – ♦79/299 € ♦♦79/299 € – ☐ 19 € – 3 suites
· Chain hotel · Business · Functional ·

Near a slip road off the ring, a modern hotel with very contemporary guestrooms, available in two sizes. Exhibition of paintings in the public areas. A la carte meals served in a trendy atmosphere.

The College
Roelof Hartstraat 1 ✉ *1071 VE –* ✆ *(0 20) 571 15 11* Plan: **C2**
– www.thecollegehotel.com
40 rm – ♦129/300 € ♦♦139/320 € – ☐ 20 €
· Grand Luxury · Design ·

This hotel is located in a former 19C "college", redecorated with refinement. Chic and fashionable lounge bar and rooms in the same style. The modern restaurant installed in a former gym serves modern cuisine.

Apollo
Apollolaan 2 ✉ *1077 BA –* ✆ *(0 20) 673 59 22* Plan: **B2**
– www.wyndham.nl
223 rm – ♦99/399 € ♦♦99/499 € – ☐ 23 €
· Chain hotel · Business · Modern ·

An international chain hotel located at the intersection of five canals. Guestrooms designed with the business traveller in mind. Waterside bar, terrace and landing stage.
🕸 **La Sirène** – See restaurant listing

Novotel
Europaboulevard 10 ✉ *1083 AD –* ✆ *(0 20) 541 11 23* Plan: **C2**
– www.novotelamsterdamcity.com
610 rm ☐ – ♦99/499 € ♦♦99/499 €
· Chain hotel · Business · Functional ·

An imposing hotel complex with one of the largest accommodation capacities in Benelux. The interior has been fully refurbished and the rooms are modern and functional. A lounge restaurant serves international dishes.

Citizen M
Prinses Irenestraat 30 ✉ *1077 WX –* ✆ *(0 20) 811 70 90* Plan: **B2**
– www.citizenm.com
215 rm – ♦69/169 € ♦♦69/169 € – ☐ 11 €
· Chain hotel · Functional · Design ·

The M in Citizen M stands for mobile: this slightly eccentric hotel focuses on independent travellers open to new concepts. The guestrooms have been kept bright and functional and the public areas very attractive. CanteenM offers food for those in need of a light snack.

Arena   ♤ ⌂ AC ♨ **P**

's-Gravesandestraat 51 ✉ *1092 AA –* ✆ *(0 20) 850 24 00*   Plan: **C2**
– www.hotelarena.nl
116 rm – ♛89/229 € ♛♛89/229 € – ☕ 19 €
• Business • Design •

Formerly an orphanage (1890), now an ultra-trendy hotel. 3 fantastic old staircases, designer bar and guestrooms of various styles and levels of comfort. Weekend nightclub (separate access). Designer setting and modern cuisine in the restaurant.

 Eden Manor   ♤ ♿ AC ♨

Linnaeusstraat 89 ✉ *1093 EK –* ✆ *(0 20) 700 84 00*   Plan: **C2**
– www.edenamsterdammanorhotel.com
125 rm – ♛150/450 € ♛♛150/450 € – ☕ 18 €
• Chain hotel • Historic • Contemporary •

A former civic hospital that has been transformed into a delightful place to stay. This is thanks to its carefully maintained historic character and the harmonious use of modern, trendy materials. Every comfort is provided for your stay, and you can easily explore the city from the tram that stops nearby.

 Albert   ♤ ♪ AC

Albert Cuypstraat 6 ✉ *1072 CT –* ✆ *(0 20) 305 30 20*   Plan: **C2**
– www.siralberthotel.com
87 rm – ♛160/425 € ♛♛160/425 € – ☕ 24 € – 3 suites
• Townhouse • Business • Design •

Sir Albert receives you with open arms in his boutique hotel. The spirit of the hotel's namesake is kept alive through subtle touches, such as notes on the mirrors and works of art. Design and luxury rule supreme in all the rooms. Enjoy individual flavours influenced by Japanese cuisine at Izakaya.

 Vondelpark   ♿ 🚗

Overtoom 519 ✉ *1054 LH –* ✆ *(0 20) 820 33 33*   Plan: **B2**
– www.conscioushotels.com
81 rm – ♛60/200 € ♛♛60/200 € – ☕ 13 €
• Chain hotel • Functional •

Green and sustainable, that's the innovative philosophy behind this hotel. "So that you can be kind to the planet even when you're away from home" and still want for nothing during your stay. Vondelpark proves that ecology and comfort can go hand in hand.

 Ciel Bleu – Hotel Okura, (23rd floor)   ⅘ ≤ AC ⇄ 🍽 **P**

Ferdinand Bolstraat 333 ✉ *1072 LH –* ✆ *(0 20)*   Plan: **C2**
678 74 50 – www.cielbleu.nl – closed 24 July-14 August, 31 December-
7 January and Sunday
Menu 110/185 € – Carte 125/190 € – *(dinner only)*
• Creative • Elegant • Formal •

A chic restaurant at the top of the Okura Hotel with a superb contemporary décor and a fascinating urban panorama. Experience stylish service, delicious creative cuisine with exotic touches, a fine wine list and sunset views from the lounge.
➜ Langoustines met zilte groenten, combova en gember. Zeetong met kaviaar en beurre blanc. Creatie van cacao, koffie en basilicum.

Yamazato – Hotel Okura   ⅘ AC ⇄ 🍽 **P**

Ferdinand Bolstraat 333 ✉ *1072 LH –* ✆ *(0 20)*   Plan: **C2**
678 74 50 – www.yamazato.nl – closed 13-23 July
Menu 40 € (lunch), 75/115 € – Carte 28/153 €
• Japanese • Minimalist •

Excellent Japanese restaurant featuring authentic Kaiseki cuisine in a Sukiya décor. Sushi bar. Meticulous and friendly service. Simplified lunch menu possible (bentobox).
➜ Omakase en nigiri sushi. Magurosteak, gegrilde tonijn met knoflook. Shabu shabu, dunne plakjes entrecote en groenten in een bouillon.

NETHERLANDS - AMSTERDAM

XX **The Roast Room** 🏠 ⇔

Europaplein 2 ⊠ 1078 GZ – ℰ (0 20) 723 96 14   Plan: **C2**
– www.theroastroom.nl
Menu 40 € (lunch), 45/65 € – Carte 50/77 €
• Meats • Trendy •

An impressive steakhouse. Glass, steel and meat are the dominant features of
the Roast Bar (brasserie on the ground floor) and the Rotisserie (restaurant upstairs). See the meat hanging ready to cook, smell it on the grill and taste the
results when it has been cooked to perfection. Excellent side dishes complete
the picture.

XX **Het Bosch** ⬅ 🏠 **P**

Jollenpad 10 ⊠ 1081 KC – ℰ (0 20) 644 58 00   Plan: **B3**
– www.hetbosch.com – closed 26 December-10 January and Sunday
Menu 40 € (lunch), 50/65 € – Carte 49/73 €
• French creative • Trendy •

The restaurant and patio of this cube-shaped, up-to-the-minute restaurant offer
views of the marina at Nieuwe Meer. Classic dishes with an adventurous twist
feature on the menu. In summer, Het Bosch Waterfront serves cocktails and barbecued choices on – as its name suggests – the waterfront.

XX **Visaandeschelde** 🏠 🅰🅲 🥢 (dinner)

Scheldeplein 4 ⊠ 1078 GR – ℰ (0 20) 675 15 83   Plan: **C2**
– www.visaandeschelde.nl – closed 27 April, 26 and 31 December-
1 January, Saturday lunch and Sunday lunch
Menu 40/65 € – Carte 59/107 € – (open until 11pm)
• Fish and seafood • Fashionable •

Opposite the RAI congress centre, this restaurant is popular with Amsterdam-
mers for its dishes full of the flavours of the sea, contemporary brasserie décor
and lively atmosphere.

XX **Bolenius** 🏠 ⇔

George Gershwinlaan 30 ⊠ 1082 MT – ℰ (0 20)   Plan: **B2**
404 44 11 – www.bolenius-restaurant.nl – closed Easter, 27 April,
Pentecost, 30 July-15 August, 28 December-3 January and Sunday
Menu 35 € (lunch), 69/99 € – Carte 65/74 €
• Creative • Design •

This restaurant has an 'open space' minimalistic design reminiscent of Scandinavia. Bolenius has a vision of being open and transparent and completely in
touch with contemporary gastronomy. Delightful, creative presentations that
are a joy to behold.

XX **Le Garage** 🅰🅲 ⇔ 🥢
🐸

Ruysdaelstraat 54 ⊠ 1071 XE – ℰ (0 20) 679 71 76   Plan: **B2**
– www.restaurantlegarage.nl – closed 25, 26 and 31 December-1 January,
Saturday lunch and Sunday lunch
Menu 27 € (lunch)/37 € – Carte 61/75 € – (open until 11pm)
• French • Fashionable •

Excellent up-to-date establishment with an original décor. The entertainment
and business clientele come to see and be seen as well as to enjoy the great
food.

XX **Serre** – Hotel Okura 🅰🅲 🥢 **P**
🐸

Ferdinand Bolstraat 333 ⊠ 1072 LH – ℰ (0 20)   Plan: **C2**
678 74 50 – www.serrerestaurant.nl – closed 18-29 January
Menu 37/40 € – Carte approx. 54 €
• Modern cuisine • Brasserie • Formal •

Luxurious, French brasserie ambience, select menus, sensible prices and a
young enthusiastic team in the kitchen. A favourite hotel restaurant for locals.

XX **Le Restaurant** (Jan de Wit)   ⅋ AC

🏵 *2e Jan Steenstraat 3* ✉ *1073 VK – ℰ (0 20) 379 22 07*   Plan: **C2**
– www.lerestaurant.nl – closed 24 April-5 Mai, 16 July-16 August,
19 December-6 January, Sunday and Monday
Menu 80 € – *(dinner only until 8.30pm) (number of covers limited, pre-
book) (set menu only)*
• Market cuisine • Individual •
A deliciously small grand restaurant! Appetising market-fresh set menu, poised
between tradition and modernity. Made with sumptuous produce, the dishes
are served in an intimate and distinguished setting. Bookings essential.
→ Noordzeekrab met jonge venkel, appel en dragon. Zacht gegaarde
kabeljauw met miso, aubergine en saus van langoustines. Duo van rabarber
met karnemelkroomijs.

XX **Eau de Vie**   🍴 AC

Maasstraat 20 ✉ *1078 HK – ℰ (0 20) 662 95 88*   Plan: **C2**
– www.restaurant-eaudevie.nl – closed 31 December-1 January
Menu 30 € (lunch), 36/50 € – Carte 46/53 €
• French modern • Friendly •
The elixir of life in this restaurant is its love of modern cuisine. The team at Eau
de Vie serves French cuisine with a distinctly contemporary flavour.

XX **Sazanka** – Hotel Okura   AC 🥢 P

🏵 *Ferdinand Bolstraat 333* ✉ *1072 LH – ℰ (0 20)*   Plan: **C2**
678 74 50 – www.okura.nl
Menu 80/110 € – Carte 67/111 € – *(dinner only)*
• Japanese • Friendly •
Sazanka takes you on an adventure to Japan. The sober interior and waitresses
dressed in kimonos set the tone; then enters the chef, who proudly takes his
place behind the teppan-yaki grill. He confidently demonstrates his skills and
uses excellent ingredients to create flavours which provide contrast but are
always well balanced. What a show!
→ Salade met licht gerookte eend en eendenlever. Sutiyakiroll van Wagyu
rund met tamagosaus. In zeezout gerolde zeebaars met een preisausje.

XX **Brasserie van Baerle**   ⅋ 🍴 ↔

🏵 *Van Baerlestraat 158* ✉ *1071 BG – ℰ (0 20) 679 15 32*   Plan: **B2**
*– www.brasserievanbaerle.nl – closed 27 April, 25, 26 and 31 December-
1 January, Monday lunch and Saturday lunch*
Menu 36 € – Carte 42/58 € – *(open until 11pm)*
• Classic cuisine • Retro • Brasserie •
This retro brasserie attracts regular customers, mainly from the local area
because of its attractive menu, tasty steak tartare and well-matched wines.
Courtyard terrace.

XX **Chang-i**   AC ↔

Jan Willem Brouwersstraat 7 (adjacent to the artists'   Plan: **E3**
entrance to the Concertgebouw) ✉ *1071 LH – ℰ (0 20) 470 17 00*
– www.chang-i.nl
Menu 36/54 € – Carte 34/58 € – *(dinner only) (booking advisable)*
• Chinese • Fashionable •
The 'i' in the name highlights the innovative nature of this chef's Asian cuisine.
Trendy and intimate lounge atmosphere. Near a theatre.

XX **Jaspers**   ↔

Ceintuurbaan 196 ✉ *1072 GC – ℰ (0 20) 471 52 33*   Plan: **C2**
*– www.restaurantjaspers.nl – closed 28 July-21 August, 30 December-
4 January, Sunday and Monday*
Menu 38/78 € – *(dinner only) (set menu only)*
• French creative • Trendy • Minimalist •
Although there is no choice on offer in this restaurant (only a set menu), this is
more than compensated for by the fresh ingredients used. Jaspers' cooking style
demonstrates French roots with a modern twist. Dishes such as poached egg with
asparagus, Comté cheese and hazelnut-truffle tapenade feature on the menu.

XX **La Sirène** – Hotel Apollo

Apollolaan 2 ⊠ 1077 BA – ℰ (0 20) 570 57 24   Plan: **B2**
– www.lasirene.nl – closed 13 July-23 August, 26 December-5 January and
Sunday
Menu 37 € – Carte 40/60 € – (dinner only)
• **Market cuisine** • **Trendy** •

It is not easy finding somewhere for a delicious meal at a reasonable price in
Amsterdam. The chic La Sirène restaurant at Wyndham Apollo Hotel is the answer, offering fresh, contemporary cuisine at attractive prices. The terrace offers
views of Amsterdam's typical wooden yachts.

X **RON Gastrobar** (Ron Blaauw)

Sophialaan 55 ⊠ 1075 BP – ℰ (0 20) 496 19 43   Plan: **B2**
– www.rongastrobar.nl – closed 27 April, 31 December-1 January and
Saturday lunch
Carte approx. 50 €
• **French creative** • **Fashionable** •

Ron Blaauw returns to basics here, creating cuisine that is pure and prepared
with quality ingredients. This urban gastro-bar combines a hip, lively ambience
with top class cuisine without the frills. It also means little formality but original,
delicious food and sensational flavours. Phenomenal value for money, which is
also reflected in the wine list. The reversal in style by this top chef is a great hit
with customers.
→ Tartaar van coquilles met hibiscus, aardappelschuim en belegen kaas.
Wagyu rund met dragon, zuringcrème en krokante aardappel. Appel in
karamel gegaard met calvados en schapenmelkroomijs.

X **Sinne** (Alexander Ioannou)

Ceintuurbaan 342 ⊠ 1072 GP – ℰ (0 20) 682 72 90   Plan: **C2**
– www.restaurantsinne.nl – closed Monday and Tuesday
Menu 35/80 € – (dinner only except Sunday) (booking essential)
• **Modern cuisine** • **Cosy** •

The open kitchen at the back of this warm and friendly restaurant is reminiscent
of a theatre scene. While chef Ioannou plays the lead role, the top quality produce steals the show in the form of modern, meticulously prepared dishes.
Attentive service from hostess Suzanne, as well as reasonable prices.
→ Ceviche van makreel met een ponzuvinaigrette, laos en rettich. Gegrilde
runderentrecote met een rodewijnsaus. Rabarber met yoghurtpannacotta,
rabarberroomijs en meringue.

X **Le Hollandais**

Amsteldijk 41 ⊠ 1074 HV – ℰ (0 20) 679 12 48   Plan: **C2**
– www.lehollandais.nl – closed 26 April, 3 weeks in August, Sunday and
Monday
Menu 36/54 € – Carte 50/61 € – (dinner only)
• **Classic cuisine** • **Fashionable** •

The 1970s furniture and lighting, wooden floors and panelling create a charming setting. The menu features traditional simmered dishes, offal, blood sausage and homemade cold meats.

X **A la Ferme**

Govert Flinckstraat 251 ⊠ 1073 BX – ℰ (0 20) 679 82 40   Plan: **C2**
– www.alaferme.nl – closed 7-22 July, 26 December-6 January, Sunday
and Monday
Menu 35/53 € – Carte 42/59 € – (dinner only)
• **Classic cuisine** • **Friendly** •

Monthly menus feature in the contemporary dining room, in one of the smaller,
more intimate rooms in the back, or under the grape arbour in summer.

White Elephant

Van Woustraat ✉ 1074 AA – ✆ (0 20) 679 55 56 Plan: **G3**
– www.whiteelephant.nl – closed 31 December-1 January
Menu 32/57 € – Carte 35/44 € – *(dinner only)*
• Thai • Exotic •
Thai restaurant with matching décor: panelling, orchids, bar in a traditional "hut", exotic terrace and friendly waiters in traditional costume. Authentic cuisine.

Elkaar

Alexanderplein 6 ✉ 1018 CG – ✆ (0 20) 330 75 59 Plan: **C2**
– www.etenbijelkaar.nl – closed 27 April, 25 and 31 December-1 January, Saturday lunch and Sunday dinner
Menu 30 € (lunch), 36/50 € – Carte approx. 46 €
• French modern • Family • Bistro •
Refined lunches and menus are offered at this restaurant in a large townhouse. Enthusiastic young team, bistro comforts, modern paintings and a teak terrace facing the Tropenmuseum.

Oud-Zuid

Johannes Verhulststraat 64 ✉ 1071 NH – ✆ (0 20) 676 60 58 – www.restaurantoudzuid.nl – closed 27 April, 25, 26 and 31 December-1 January Plan: **B2**
Menu 28 € (lunch)/35 € – Carte 39/54 €
• Classic cuisine • Brasserie • Neighbourhood •
Brasserie-type dining room and servings: this characterful restaurant presents traditional dishes with a modern touch. For music lovers, Oud-Zuid is less than a 10 min walk from the Concertgebouw.

AT SCHIPHOL AIRPORT

Radisson Blu Amsterdam Airport

Boeing Avenue 2 (Rijk) (South: 4 km via N201)
✉ 1119 PB Schiphol – ✆ (0 20) 655 31 31
– www.radissonblu.com/hotel-amsterdamairport
279 rm – †119/339 € ††119/339 € – ☕ 25 €
• Business • Modern •
This hotel is ideal for business trips. It is spacious, close to the airport and motorway, with a cosy bar, meeting rooms and modern guestrooms lacking nothing in comfort. The restaurant menu offers international cuisine, dominated by Mediterranean dishes.

Crowne Plaza Amsterdam-Schiphol

Planeetbaan 2 ✉ 2132 HZ Hoofddorp – ✆ (0 23) 565 00 00
– www.crowneplaza.com/ams-schiphol
238 rm – †139/350 € ††139/350 € – ☕ 22 € – 4 suites
• Business • Functional •
Establishment in a modern building, popular with business and conference clientele. Huge lobby, superb swimming pool, health club, large guestrooms and suites with lounges. "Sleep advantage" programme. Restaurant offering an international menu in several rooms.

Artemis

John M. Keynesplein 2 (exit 1 Sloten) ✉ 1066 EP Plan: **A2**
– ✆ (0 20) 714 10 00 – www.artemisamsterdam.com
256 rm – †99/209 € ††99/209 € – ☕ 20 €
• Luxury • Design •
This modern building of original design in the business district features Dutch designer-style décor. There is an art gallery to explore the subject in more detail. A large restaurant with ultra-modern décor and a big waterside terrace. Contemporary menu.

De Herbergh
Sloterweg 259 ⊠ *1171 CP Badhoevedorp* – ℰ *(0 20) 659 26 00*
– *www.herbergh.nl*
24 rm – ♥70/179 € ♥♥70/179 € – ☑ 15 €
• Inn • Classic •

If you are visiting Amsterdam by car, you will appreciate the easy, free parking. It is perfect for visitors to the Keukenhof, and the shuttle service to Schiphol makes it ideal for holidaymakers who have to catch an early flight. Italian cuisine in Trattoria La Bocca.
Brasserie la Bouche – See restaurant listing

XxxX Aan de Poel (Stefan van Sprang)
Handweg 1 ⊠ *1185 TS Amstelveen* – ℰ *(0 20) 345 17 63*   Plan: **B3**
– *www.aandepoel.nl* – *closed 27 April, 24 July-8 August, 27 December-7 January, Saturday lunch, Sunday and Monday*
Menu 42 € (lunch), 66/99 € – Carte 65/100 €
• Creative • Trendy •

A successful marriage of technical skill and brilliant produce ensures that every dish is a feast for the senses. Here, contemporary cuisine can be savoured in one of its most beautiful and tasteful forms. What's more, this restaurant benefits from a superb lakeside setting, a chic and sophisticated designer interior and a skilled sommelier.
→ Langoustine met mango en tataki van ganzenlever. Zacht gegaard en gebakken kalfssukade met piccalilli en rodewijnjus. Proeverij van aardbeien, witte chocolade en rabarber.

XX Brasserie la Bouche – Hotel De Herbergh
Sloterweg 259 ⊠ *1171 CP Badhoevedorp* – ℰ *(0 20) 659 26 00*
– *www.brasserielabouche.nl* – *closed Sunday*
Menu 30 € – Carte approx. 40 €
• French modern • Family •

French cooking combines with global flavours and exotic ingredients on the menu at Brasserie la Bouche. Ask for the vegetable tempura salad to start; follow it with lamb souvlaki; and for dessert, try a classic tarte Tatin.

XX De Jonge Dikkert
Amsterdamseweg 104a ⊠ *1182 HG Amstelveen*   Plan: **B3**
– ℰ *(0 20) 643 33 33* – *www.jongedikkert.nl* – *closed 1-21 August, 24 and 31 December-4 January, Saturday lunch and Sunday lunch*
Menu 35/70 € – Carte 43/56 €
• Regional • Retro • Classic •

This timber windmill dating back to the 17C feels nice and cosy thanks to the new contemporary interiors. Indulge yourself in this fantastic setting, which is equalled by the superb cuisine featuring local ingredients, beautifully crafted dishes, and modern techniques and combinations. A strong Bib Gourmand.

XX Kronenburg
Prof. E.M. Meijerslaan 6 ⊠ *1183 AV Amstelveen*   Plan: **B3**
– ℰ *(0 20) 345 54 89* – *www.restaurant-kronenburg.nl* – *closed 26 April, 25 July-7 August, 27 December-4 January, Saturday lunch and Sunday*
Menu 29 € (lunch), 35/50 € – Carte approx. 45 €
• Mediterranean • Trendy • Design •

An oasis in the Kronenburg business quarter on the edge of a lake in a verdant setting. Dine on the terrace or behind the glass façade in an elegant, bright interior that is positively sparkling. The dishes have a Mediterranean flair and are inspired by French cuisine.

THE HAGUE
DEN HAAG –'S GRAVENHAGE

Population: 510 909

Iconotec/PHOTONONSTOP

The Hague appears to be a city of anomalies. Although the seat of Dutch government, it's not the capital of the Netherlands (which is Amsterdam); although a city of Europe-wide importance, it's just as famous for its modern seaside resort of Scheveningen; and although populated by hundreds of years by the well-to-do, its canal-side houses share little of Amsterdam's flamboyance. The Hague earned its nickname 'the biggest village in Europe' because of its relatively small population sprawled about a large area: that 'village' is marked by an aristocratic charm, which is why it's rightly obtained another title – Holland's most elegant town.

The Hague is also doffing its neatly tailored cap to the 21C: parts of the centre now shoot skywards courtesy of shiny government high-rises, while a rash of reasonably priced, buzzy restaurants and bars has brightened the streets. An outward-thinking city council has helped loosen the staid image with a lively programme of concerts and events, and there's an enticing range of museums clustered in the centre. A village, however large, wouldn't be a village without its sections of green and pleasant land, and The Hague doesn't disappoint, with a kaleidoscope of leafy lanes and large parks. The air of gentle manners is all-pervasive, and bureaucrats and bankers know that in a few minutes they can be sitting in a deckchair on a sandy beach.

THE HAGUE IN...

→ **ONE DAY**
Binnenhof, Mauritshuis, Panorama Mesdag.

→ **TWO DAYS**
Gemeentemuseum, 'The Fred', a stroll around Noordeinde, a show at Lucent Dans Theater.

→ **THREE DAYS**
A day out by the sea at Scheveningen, Madurodam.

ARRIVAL-DEPARTURE

 Rotterdam The Hague Airport is 16km southeast of The Hague. Bus Number 33 to Central Station takes 45min. The train to Schiphol Airport takes 30min.

GETTING AROUND

Single tickets can be purchased from the bus driver but saver tickets must be bought in advance from the tourist information office, post offices, tobacconists, newsagents and hotels. You can buy good value stripcards in two varieties – as a 15-stripcard or a 45-stripcard – and these are valid throughout the country on buses, trams and metro. A one-day pass is also available; with the price dependent on the amount of zones to be covered. The only rail travel within the city is the line linking the two stations, Den Haag Centraal Station and Den Haag Hollands Spoor, which is a kilometre to the south of the centre.

EATING OUT

Locals like to think that their 'biggest village in Europe' is the result of a lot made from a little; they call it the Hague Bluff. But what's that got to do with food? Well, the Hague Bluff is also a local pudding, a gooseberry fool made with eggs and sugar, representing the idea that something grand can be made from humble ingredients. There's no bluff, though, about the city's restaurant scene. It's first rate in every respect, and although some establishments are targeted full-on at the embassy army, many more are very affordable. With the cuisine

CALENDAR HIGHLIGHTS

April
King's Night Festival.

April-June
International Sand Sculpture Festival.

May
North Sea Regatta.

May-June
Tong Tong Fair (the world's biggest Eurasian fair).

July
De Parade (fairground rides, music, theatre).

August
International Fireworks Festival.

September
Todaysart Festival.

November
Crossing Border Festival (literature, music and visual arts).

of more than 20 nationalities on offer, the choice is broad and pleasingly sophisticated, and the number of exotic restaurants reflects the many cultures found here. Asian influences are everywhere, but in particular, the Indonesian connection is clear. There's a host of top-notch restaurants in the area just beyond Lange Voorhout, around Denneweg and Frederikstraat. If you can't find what you want there, then head to Molenstraat, near the Noordeinde Palace, for another exciting cluster.

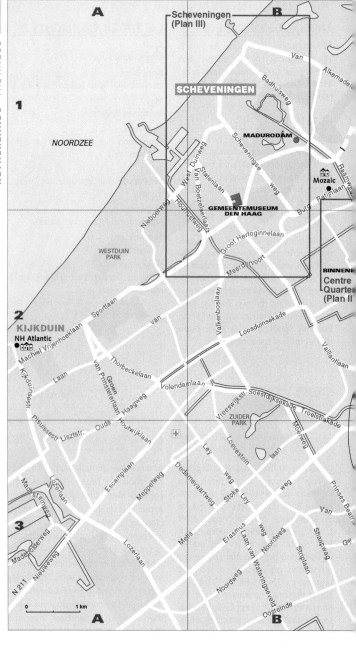

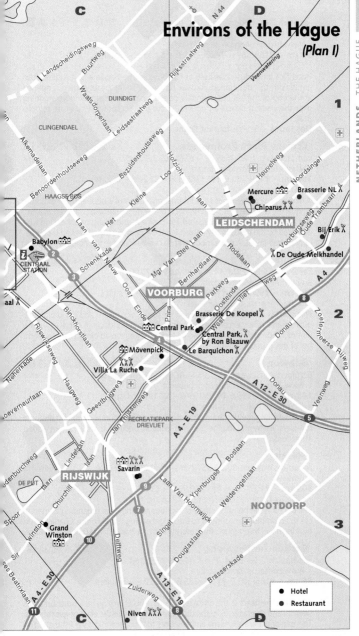

Environs of the Hague
(Plan I)

C

D

N 44

Veenwatering

1

Landscheidingsweg

Buurtweg

Waalsdorperlaan

Rijksstraatweg

DUINDIGT

Leidsestraatweg

CLINGENDAEL

Alkemadelaan

Benoordenhoutseweg

Bezuidenhoutseweg

Loo

Hofzicht

Heuvelweg

Noordsingel

Mercure 🏨 **Brasserie NL** ✗

HAAGSE BOS

Kleine

Het

laan

Chiparus ✗✗

LEIDSCHENDAM

Babylon 🏨

Laan

van

Schenkade

Neuw

Mgr Van Stee Laan

Voorburgseweg Oude Trambaan

Bij Erik ✗

✗ **De Oude Melkhandel**

CENTRAAL STATION

Oost

Einde

Bernhardlaan

Parkweg

Rodelaan

weg

A 4

🏨

8

aal ✗

Rijswijkseweg

Blinckhorstlaan

Prins

VOORBURG

West

Oosteinde

Vliet

Donau

2

Zoetermeerse Rijweg

Brasserie De Koepel ✗

🏨🏨🏨 **Central Park**

Central Park, ✗
by Ron Blaauw

Naherkade

Haagweg

Geestbrugweg

🏨 **Mövenpick**

Le Barquichon ✗

Villa La Ruche ●

🏥

Donau

A 12 - E 30

Veenweg

oeverneurlaan

Jan

Thomsonweg

RECREATIEPARK DRIEVLIET

A 4 - E 19

5

Lindelaan

laan

🏨🏨🏨✗✗✗
Savarin

Laan Van Ypenburgse

Bostaan

Weidevogellaan

NOOTDORP

DE PUT

laan

Churchill

RIJSWIJK

9

Singel

Douglaslaan

🏥

3

edenburchweg

Spoor

Winston

7

Delftweg

Grand Winston 🏨🏨

10

Sir

Beatrixlaan

A 4 - E 30

Zuiderweg

A 13 - E 19

Brasserskade

● Hotel
● Restaurant

11

Niven ✗✗✗

8

C

D

579

Hotel Des Indes 🔧 ⚙ 🏠 🖼 ᖈ 🏋 🅿

Lange Voorhout 54 ✉ *2514 EG – ✆ (0 70) 361 23 45*   Plan: **F1**
– www.luxurycollection.com/desindes
90 rm – ♦169/569 € ♦♦206/569 € – ⌷ 35 € – 2 suites
• Grand Luxury • Palace • Design •

Hotel Des Indes describes itself as the hotel in The Hague and it is difficult to argue with this description. Already renowned for its beauty when it opened at the end of the 19C, this fairytale palace has become simply more stunning over the years. It boasts an opulent decor that is characteristic of its colonial past.
Des Indes – See restaurant listing

Crowne Plaza Promenade 🔧 ≤ 🔧 ⚙ 🏠 🖼 ᖈ 🖼 🏋 ⧫ 🅿

van Stolkweg 1 ✉ *2585 JL – ✆ (0 70) 352 51 61*   Plan: **H2**
– www.crowneplazadenhaag.nl
168 rm – ♦110/180 € ♦♦133/203 € – ⌷ 24 € – 6 suites
• Chain hotel • Functional •

Whether you're here to visit the International Court of Justice and the diplomatic quarter, the beach at Scheveningen or the miniature village at Madurodam, this hotel is conveniently situated for business and pleasure alike. Don't be deceived by the flashy lobby – the interior decor of the main building is comparatively traditional. A more modern style can be found in the new tower.

Hilton 🔧 🔧 ᖈ 🖼 🏋 ⧫

Zeestraat 35 ✉ *2518 AA – ✆ (0 70) 710 70 00*   Plan: **E1**
– www.thehague.hilton.com
195 rm – ♦99/229 € ♦♦99/229 € – ⌷ 27 € – 6 suites
• Business • Luxury • Design •

This hotel is conveniently situated close to the city centre and the diplomatic quarter and offers excellent conference facilities. Its decor is modern with a hint of 1960s' style and the service is just what you would expect from a member of this group of hotels.

Babylon 🔧 🔧 ᖈ 🖼 🏋 ⧫ 🅿

Bezuidenhoutseweg 53 ✉ *2594 AC – ✆ (0 70) 381 49 01*   Plan: **C2**
– www.hampshire-hotels.com/babylon
143 rm – ♦79/199 € ♦♦79/199 € – ⌷ 19 € – 1 suite
• Chain hotel • Business • Design •

Hotel Babylon provides the typical modern hotel comfort so prized by business travellers. Its trendy lounge bar and location close to the station are added attractions.

Bel Air 🔧 ≤ 🍽 🔧 🖼 🏋 ⧫ 🅿

Johan de Wittlaan 30 ✉ *2517 JR – ✆ (0 70) 352 53 54*   Plan: **H3**
– www.worldhotelbelair.com
308 rm – ♦109/199 € ♦♦109/199 € – ⌷ 21 € – 9 suites
• Chain hotel • Business • Classic •

The Bel Air hotel boasts a range of facilities ranging from organising conferences to accommodating visitors to the neighbouring World Forum. Characterised by a fresh feel throughout, the hotel also offers a bar with a jazz-style ambience.

Carlton Ambassador 🔧 🍽 🖼 🏋 🅿

Sophialaan 2 ✉ *2514 JP – ✆ (0 70) 363 03 63*   Plan: **E1**
– www.carlton.nl/ambassador
88 rm – ♦105/305 € ♦♦135/335 € – ⌷ 20 € – 3 suites
• Palace • Classic •

A pearl in the heart of the embassy quarter. This charming little hotel breathes warmth and character, from the distinguished lobby to the elegant guestrooms. The personnel are excellent ambassadors for this splendid establishment and will ensure that you lack nothing during your stay.
Henricus – See restaurant listing

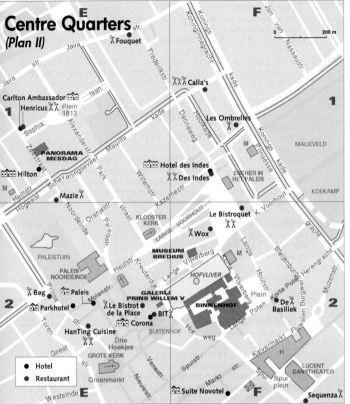

Centre Quarters
(Plan II)

E · F

0 · 200 m

Java str.

✕ Fouquet

Koninginnegracht

Jan van Nassaustr.

Frederikstr.

Kade

✕✕✕ Calla's

Java str.

laan

Carlton Ambassador 🏨

Henricus ✕✕ · Plein 1813

Hoornweg

Denneweg

Les Ombrelles
✕

Koningskade

MALIEVELD

1

Sophia

Alexanderstr.

Maurits

PANORAMA MESDAG

Scheveningseveer

Prinsessegracht

M

🏨 Hilton

Hotel des Indes 🏨

✕✕ Des Indes

ESCHER IN HET PALEIS

KOEKAMP

M

Heinstr.

Hogewal

Park

Willemstr.

Kazernestr.

K. Voorhout

✕ Mazie

Noordeinde

Oranjestraat

Paleisstraat

KLOOSTER KERK

LANGE VOORHOUT

Le Bistroquet
✕✕

gracht

✕ Wox

Bleijenburg

Herengracht

PALEISTUIN

Heulstr.

Kneuterdijk

MUSEUM BREDIUS

Lange Vijverberg

Korte Poten

Muzenstr.

PALEIS NOORDEINDE

PALEIS NOORDEINDE

HOFVIJVER

Lange Vijverberg

Houtstr.

Fluwelen Burgwal

✕ Bøg

🏨 Paleis

Molenstr.

GALERIJ PRINS WILLEM V

BINNENHOF

Plein

De ✕ Basiliek

2

🏨 Parkhotel

Prinse

✕ Le Bistrot de la Place

BIT ●

🏨 Corona

Poten

HanTing Cuisine
✕✕

Toren

Geest

Drie Hoekjes

BUITENHOF

Hofweg

Kalvermarkt

Spui

LUCENT DANSTHEATER

GROTE KERK

Venestr.

Spuistr.

Markt str.

H

● Hotel
● Restaurant

Groenmarkt

Nieuwstr.

Spui plein

Westeinde E

🏨 Suite Novotel ● F

Sequenza ✕

Corona
☆ AC 🛁

Buitenhof 42 ✉ 2513 AH – ℰ (0 70) 363 79 30
– www.corona.nl

Plan: **E2**

36 rm – †75/145 € ††85/175 € – ☲ 18 € – 1 suite

· Palace · Townhouse · Design ·

Corona's rich history gives it an international allure, a reputation upheld by guestrooms that live up to the expectations of today's guests and business people. The location in the heart of the city, opposite the government buildings of the Binnenhof, is a trump card.

BIT – See restaurant listing

Parkhotel
🛏 AC 🛁 🚗

Molenstraat 53 ✉ 2513 BJ – ℰ (0 70) 362 43 71
– www.parkhoteldenhaag.nl

Plan: **E2**

120 rm – †79/109 € ††89/259 € – ☲ 22 €

· Traditional · Functional ·

This hotel offers pleasant accommodation and has been a feature of the hospitality scene in The Hague for over a century. The Berlage-style staircase bears witness to its rich history. The hotel oozes historic charm whilst providing all the comforts you would expect of a modern hotel.

NETHERLANDS - THE HAGUE

Suite Novotel
Grote Marktstraat 46 ✉ *2511 BJ* – ✆ *(0 70) 850 51 80*   Plan: **F2**
– www.suitenovotel.com
118 rm ⌐ – ♦99/219 € ♦♦109/229 €
• Chain hotel • Townhouse • Cosy •

Leave the busy high street, take the lift and enter this new, cosy, functionally furnished hotel. It is worth noting that children under 16 sleeping in the same room as their parents receive bed and breakfast free of charge.

Paleis
Molenstraat 26 ✉ *2513 BL* – ✆ *(0 70) 362 46 21*   Plan: **E2**
– www.paleishotel.nl
20 rm – ♦129/199 € ♦♦129/199 € – ⌐ 17 €
• Luxury • Classic •

A luxury hotel inspired by the Louis XVI-style. Details that make all the difference include fabrics used for the curtains, chairs and bedspreads sourced from Pierre Frey, a renowned French furnishings company, and even a luxurious hassock at the foot of the bed. The royal welcome you will receive is enhanced by the king-size beds.

Mozaic
Laan Copes van Cattenburch 38 ✉ *2585 GB* – ✆ *(0 70)*   Plan: **B1**
352 23 35 – www.mozaic.nl
25 rm – ♦70/100 € ♦♦70/150 € – ⌐ 15 €
• Family • Design •

The team at Mozaic offer their guests that little bit extra. Find a warm personal welcome, a townhouse with a hint of history and a touch of modern design in the bedrooms. An inspired alternative to the usual chain hotels.

Court Garden
Laan van Meerdervoort 96 ✉ *2517 AR* – ✆ *(0 70)*   Plan: **H3**
311 40 00 – www.hotelcourtgarden.nl
70 rm – ♦69/115 € ♦♦79/135 € – ⌐ 13 €
• Business • Functional •

The first sustainable hotel in The Hague stands at the edge of the city centre. It features restrained and simple furnishings. An organic breakfast is available in the morning and free tea and coffee are served all day long in the lounge.

Calla's (Marcel van der Kleijn)
Laan van Roos en Doorn 51a ✉ *2514 BC* – ✆ *(0 70)*   Plan: **F1**
345 58 66 – www.restaurantcallas.nl – closed 25 July-16 August,
25 December-6 January, Saturday lunch, Sunday and Monday
Menu 43/100 € – Carte 87/102 €
• French creative • Elegant •

'Calla' refers to a Mexican lily, which derives its name from the Greek word for beauty. To continue with the international theme, the cuisine is French and the wine list a combination of the Old World and the New. The delicious, simple yet refined cuisine served here provides a truly memorable dining experience.
➜ Tartelette van coquilles, parmezaankaas en zwarte truffel. Gebraden lamsrug met een persillade en voorjaarsgroentjes, jus met papalo. Gelaagde citroenflensjes met aardbeien en rabarberroomijs.

Le Bistroquet
Lange Voorhout 98 ✉ *2514 EJ* – ✆ *(0 70) 360 11 70*   Plan: **F2**
– www.bistroquet.nl – closed 24-31 December, Saturday lunch and Sunday
Menu 28 € (lunch), 35/45 € – Carte 34/59 €
• Market cuisine • Cosy • Formal •

Red booths and designer chairs light up the austere interior of this lively establishment. The traditional dishes will certainly cheer you. These form the foundation of the menu with beautifully combined flavours. A top venue since 1968!

XX **HanTing Cuisine** (Xiaohan Ji)   🄰🅒 ⇔
🕸 *Prinsestraat 33 ⊠ 2513 CA – 𝒞 (0 70) 362 08 28*   Plan: E2
    – www.hantingcuisine.nl – closed Monday
    Menu 37/68 € – Carte approx. 50 € – *(dinner only)*
    • Fusion • Exotic • Friendly •

HanTing Cuisine is certainly the place to discover fusion cooking at its best. Han, the chef, brings all his expertise to bear in balancing the flavours of China with those of the West. He creates cuisine that is delicate and pleasingly harmonious. Not surprisingly, it is also very popular.

→ Rauwe tonijn en zeekwal met komkommer, Chinese kool, rode peper en knoflook. Gegrilde kalfslende met bleekselderij, vijgen en waterkastanjes. Banaan en chocolade met rum, yoghurt, pinda en passievrucht.

XX **Des Indes** – Hotel Des Indes   � ⇔ 🛎 🅿
    Lange Voorhout 54 ⊠ 2514 EG – 𝒞 (0 70) 361 23 45   Plan: F1
    – www.luxurycollection.com/desindes – closed Sunday and Monday
    Menu 30/49 € – Carte 56/68 € – *(open until 11pm)*
    • Modern cuisine • Elegant • Formal •

Fine dining or brasserie? Here you have the choice, but whatever you decide, the stunning backdrop can't fail to charm. Surrounded by classic elegance, what you find on your plate will be thoroughly contemporary. The chef works with excellent ingredients, presenting them in intricate dishes.

XX **Henricus** – Hotel Carlton Ambassador   🄰🅒 ⇔ 🅿
    Sophialaan 2 ⊠ 2514 JP – 𝒞 (0 70) 363 03 63   Plan: E1
    – www.carlton.nl/ambassador
    Menu 35 € – Carte 36/58 €
    • International • Cosy •

The menu at the Henricus takes the form of a 'mood book'. Whatever you are in the mood for – whether it is 'light & easy' or 'delightful' – you will be given suggestions to suit from a range of light meals and international dishes.

X   **Fouquet**   🏠 ⇔
    Javastraat 31a ⊠ 2585 AC – 𝒞 (0 70) 360 62 73   Plan: E1
    – www.fouquet.nl – closed Sunday
    Menu 30/85 € 🍷 – Carte 43/93 € – *(dinner only)*
    • Market cuisine • Brasserie •

This established business still swears by French cuisine. This is the ultimate place for market fresh dishes, prepared with a reverence for tradition. Dine on the enclosed patio terrace in summer.

X   **Wox**   🍸 🄰🅒 ⇔
    Lange Voorhout 51 ⊠ 2514 EC – 𝒞 (0 70) 365 37 54   Plan: F2
    – www.wox.nl – closed Bank Holidays, Saturday lunch, Sunday and Monday
    Menu 32 € (lunch) – Carte 46/85 €
    • Fusion • Tapas bar •

The name gives you an inkling of the ambience here and the interior confirms it: this flashy brasserie is an ultra trendy venue. Fashionable Franco-Asian dishes feature on the menu, as well as phenomenal wines with a good selection available by the glass.

X   **De Basiliek**   🏠 ⇔
    Korte Houtstraat 4a ⊠ 2511 CD – 𝒞 (0 70) 360 61 44   Plan: F2
    – www.debasiliek.nl – closed Sunday
    Menu 28 € (lunch), 38/75 € 🍷 – Carte 39/49 €
    • Modern cuisine • Design •

This is the perfect place to kick off a Saturday night with friends. Friendly bustling ambience, smart contemporary cuisine and an attractive formula allowing you to choose from the entire menu: the tone is set for a great night out.

NETHERLANDS - THE HAGUE

Basaal

Dunne Bierkade 3 ⊠ 2512 BC – ℰ (0 70) 427 68 88 Plan: **C2**
– www.restaurantbasaal.nl – closed 18-26 October, 27 December-
6 January, Sunday from September till April and Monday
Menu 35/56 € – Carte 43/67 € – *(dinner only until 11pm)*
• Modern cuisine • Intimate •

This modern restaurant with its lovely canal terrace proves that smart can also
be relaxed. The hostess Loes creates a casual atmosphere, while her husband
Bastiaan opts for European cuisine with a preference for local delicacies. Whatever you pick, the ingredients will be fresh and the flavours distinctive.

Les Ombrelles

Hooistraat 4a ⊠ 2514 BM – ℰ (0 70) 365 87 89 Plan: **F1**
– www.lesombrelles.nl – closed 25 December-3 January, Saturday lunch
and Sunday
Menu 35/50 € – Carte 46/56 €
• Fish and seafood • Trendy •

You don't need to be an expert in Molière's language to know the meaning of
Ombrelles – just glance at the ceiling full of umbrellas to find the clue. The chef
focuses on fish and shellfish dishes, adding his own original touches to traditional French recipes.

Le Bistrot de la Place

Plaats 27 ⊠ 2513 AD – ℰ (0 70) 364 33 27 Plan: **E2**
– www.bistrotdelaplace.nl – closed Saturday lunch and Sunday
Menu 20 € (lunch), 36/50 € – Carte 44/71 €
• French classic • Bistro • Retro •

The record sleeves on the walls, the French music in the background and the
flavours of archetypal French cuisine: the spirit of France has penetrated every
fibre of this exceptional bistro. On Fridays and Saturdays, the owner performs
French songs.

Sequenza

Spui 224 ⊠ 2511 BX – ℰ (0 70) 345 28 53 – closed Plan: **F2**
Sunday and Monday
Menu 43 € – *(dinner only until 11pm) (set menu only)*
• Market cuisine • Trendy •

The cosy atmosphere of Sequenza has won the hearts of its many regular customers. They return time and time again for the French inspired cuisine made
from fresh, market-sourced produce. The restricted menu may offer only a
small selection of dishes, but the food is full of flavour.

Mazie

Maziestraat 10 ⊠ 2514 GT – ℰ (0 70) 302 02 86 Plan: **E1**
– www.restaurantmazie.nl – closed late December-early January, Tuesday
lunch, Saturday lunch, Sunday and Monday
Menu 33 € (lunch), 43/70 € – Carte approx. 60 €
• Creative • Neighbourhood •

The atmosphere is cosy in this little neighbourhood restaurant; situated in a side
street of het Noordeinde. Dishes arrive in tasty, modern combinations and are
nicely presented. This all comes at a satisfyingly honest price.

Bøg

Prinsestraat 130 ⊠ 2513 CH – ℰ (0 70) 406 90 44 Plan: **E2**
– www.bog.com – closed 27-31 March, 23 July-20 August, 20 December-
5 January, Sunday and Monday
Menu 53 € – *(dinner only)*
• Scandinavian • Design •

Slick Scandinavian design is beautifully executed at Bøg. You have the choice
between a vegetarian menu and a meat/fish menu, both as creative as they
are attractive. The pure flavours drawn from local ingredients are truly delicious.

✗ **BIT** – Hotel Corona
Buitenhof 42 ✉ *2513 AH* – ☎ *(0 70) 790 00 32* Plan: **E2**
– *www.bitgrill.nl*
Carte 29/87 €
• Meats • Brasserie • Trendy •

This urban establishment focuses on quality. BIT stands for Best In Town and they aim to prove that their name is justified with first-rate meat prepared on the Josper grill. Grilling is an art and they clearly understand that here. The restaurant also serves breakfast.

SCHEVENINGEN

🏨 **Kurhaus**
Gevers Deynootplein 30 ✉ *2586 CK* – ☎ *(0 70) 416 26 36* Plan: **G1**
– *www.amrathkurhaus.nl*
253 rm ⬚ – †99/300 € ††119/320 € – 8 suites
• Palace • Conference hotel • Classic •

This grand residence is much more than a hotel; it's an institution. With its superb seaside location, a refined ambience and a restaurant with an impressive terrace, it more than justifies its reputation.

🏨 **Carlton Beach**
Gevers Deynootweg 201 ✉ *2586 HZ* – ☎ *(0 70)* Plan: **H1**
354 14 14 – *www.carlton.nl/beach*
177 rm ⬚ – †105/300 € ††105/300 € – 6 suites
• Holiday hotel • Chain hotel • Modern •

Despite its typical 1980s exterior, the Carlton Beach boasts smart modern rooms with views of the dunes, the beach or the promenade. In summer, experience the added pleasure of feeling the warm sand under your feet as you enjoy breakfast in the beach pavilion. Take your pick from a selection of grilled dishes at the Smuggler's Bar & Grill.

🏨 **Europa**
Zwolsestraat 2 ✉ *2587 VJ* – ☎ *(0 70) 416 95 95* Plan: **H1**
– *www.bilderberg.nl*
174 rm ⬚ – †99/249 € ††99/249 €
• Chain hotel • Functional •

This modern hotel on a busy road stands just 300m from the famous Pier. Good levels of comfort, with the best rooms overlooking the sea and dunes. Mangerie OXO offers contemporary dishes and an attractive à la carte menu.

🏨 **Badhotel**
Gevers Deynootweg 15 ✉ *2586 BB* – ☎ *(0 70) 351 22 21* Plan: **G1**
– *www.badhotelscheveningen.nl*
90 rm ⬚ – †75/150 € ††75/150 €
• Traditional • Classic •

Whether you are travelling for business or pleasure, Badhotel is an excellent choice for visitors looking for a well-maintained, reputable hotel. When you make your booking, remember to enquire about specially arranged events, perhaps treating yourself to an evening out at the theatre or casino.

🏨 **Ibis**
Gevers Deynootweg 63 ✉ *2586 BJ* – ☎ *(0 70) 354 33 00* Plan: **G1**
– *www.ibishotel.com/1153*
88 rm – †79/119 € ††89/169 € – ⬚ 16 €
• Chain hotel • Functional •

This well-maintained chain hotel offers two major trump cards. The sights of Scheveningen seaside resort are nearby, and although the standard rooms are on the small side, all the guestrooms are well equipped.

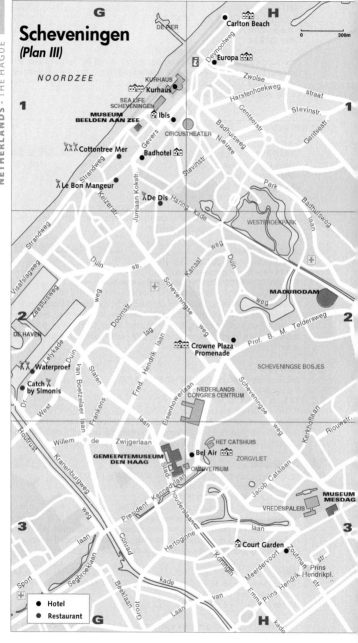

Scheveningen
(Plan III)

NETHERLANDS - THE HAGUE

NOORDZEE

DE PIER

Carlton Beach

Europa

Zwolse straat

Deynootweg

Harstenhoekweg

KURHAUS

Kurhaus

Gentsestr.

Stevinstr.

SEA LIFE
SCHEVENINGEN

Gentsestr.

MUSEUM
BEELDEN AAN ZEE

Ibis

Badhuisweg

Gevers

CIRCUSTHEATER

Nieuwe

Cottontree Mer

Badhotel

Stevinstr.

Park

Le Bon Mangeur

Strandweg

Keizerstr.

Jurriaan Kokstr.

De Dis

Haring

Kade

Badhuisweg

laan

WESTBROEKPARK

weg

Strandweg

Visafslagweg

Duin

str.

Scheveningse

Kanaal

Duin

Zeesluisweg

Doornstr.

weg

MADURODAM

DE HAVEN

Lelykade

Duin

laan

lag

Prof. B. M. Teldersweg

Waterproef

Staten

Van Boetzelaer laan

Fred. Hendrik laan

Crowne Plaza
Promenade

SCHEVENINGSE BOSJES

Catch
by Simonis

Dr. West

Frankens

laan

Eisenhowerlaan

NEDERLANDS
CONGRES CENTRUM

Scheveningse

Kerkhoflaan

Riouwer

weg

Willem

de

Zwijgerlaan

HET CATSHUIS

Kranenburgweg

GEMEENTEMUSEUM
DEN HAAG

Stad.

Bel Air

OMNIVERSUM

ZORGVLIET

Jacob Catslaan

MUSEUM
MESDAG

President Kennedylaan

houderslaan

VREDESPALEIS

laan

Holtrust

weg

Conrad

Hertoginne

Court Garden

Koningin

Meerdervoort

Touman

str.

Prins
Hendrikpl.

Sport

laan

Segbroeklaan

Beeklaan

Groot

kade

van

Emma

Prins Hendrik

str.

Laan

G   **H**

- ● Hotel
- ● Restaurant

0   300m

XXX
£3

Cottontree Mer

Zeekant 60 ⊠ 2586 AD
– 𝒞 (0 70) 355 52 50 – www.cottontree.nl/mer
– closed Bank Holidays, Saturday lunch, Sunday and Monday
Menu 35 € (lunch), 49/69 € – Carte 63/83 €

Plan: **G1**

• Fish and seafood • Elegant • Design •

The market-sourced menus at Cottontree Mer prove that restaurants with stars are not just for the happy few. Meals served are generously portioned, extremely fresh and well presented, and include refined seafood dishes. Along with the spectacular sea view, what more could you wish for?

→ Lauwwarme paling met ui, appel en groene kruiden. Gebakken rode mul met groene asperges, lamsoren en mosseltjes. Rabarbercrumble met pannacotta van geitenmelk en citroentijm- en aardbeiensorbet.

XX

Waterproef

Dr. Lelykade 25 ⊠ 2583 CL – 𝒞 (0 70) 358 87 70
– www.restaurantwaterproef.nl
– closed 26 December-2 January, Saturday lunch, Sunday lunch, Monday lunch and Wednesday
Menu 25 € (lunch), 40/60 € – Carte 48/64 €

Plan: **G2**

• French modern • Fashionable •

A very large restaurant beside the quay, where up to 100 guests can be served in a beautiful combination of old and new. The cuisine is modern (the fixed menus offer best value) and the service informal. The wine list is a real eye-catcher, offering a spectacular choice for diners.

X

Catch by Simonis

Dr. Lelykade 43 ⊠ 2583 CL – 𝒞 (0 70) 338 76 09
– www.catchbysimonis.nl
Carte 34/58 €

Plan: **G2**

• Fish and seafood • Fashionable • Trendy •

No, you are not in New York, although this impressive restaurant wouldn't be out of place there with its fashionable interior, trendy ambience, prestigious bottles adorning the wine wall and delicious food. Fish and seafood steal the show in dishes that are as fresh as they are modern. A great catch!

X

Le Bon Mangeur

Wassenaarsestraat 119 ⊠ 2586 AM – 𝒞 (0 70) 355 92 13
– www.lebonmangeur.nl – closed 24 July-8 August, 31 December-11 January, Sunday and Monday
Menu 33/45 € – Carte 50/63 € – (dinner only)

Plan: **G1**

• French modern • Family • Simple •

Le Bon Mangeur restaurant is run by Theo and Patricia Pronk who aim to introduce their guests to French cuisine with an international flavour. This congenial restaurant opens its doors wide to everyone, making it the perfect place for a friendly, informal dinner.

X

De Dis

Badhuisstraat 6 ⊠ 2584 HK – 𝒞 (0 70) 350 00 45
– www.restaurantdedis.nl
– closed Monday and Tuesday
Menu 42/100 € 🍷 – (dinner only) (surprise menu only)

Plan: **G1**

• Creative • Bistro • Neighbourhood •

This restaurant has a very modest decor and is located in a working class area of Scheveningen. There are plenty of surprises on the plate, ensuring that guests will want to spend time appreciating the cuisine on offer. Top quality seasonal produce that is beautifully flavoured and presented.

NETHERLANDS - THE HAGUE

Grand Winston

Generaal Eisenhowerplein 1 ✉ 2288 AE Rijswijk
– ✆ (0 70) 414 15 00 – www.worldhotelgrandwinston.com
252 rm – ♦69/189 € ♦♦85/225 € – ☑ 20 € – 7 suites

Plan: **C3**

• Business • Modern • Functional •

Sir Winston Churchill stands guard over the reception at this designer hotel adjacent to the station. Two turrets house the guestrooms, which like the public areas, are well-maintained. The restaurant is trendy and serves snacks, as well as classic international dishes.

Savarin

Laan van Hoornwijck 29 ✉ 2289 DG Rijswijk – ✆ (0 70)
307 20 50 – www.savarin.nl
36 rm – ♦109/229 € ♦♦109/229 € – ☑ 22 € – 2 suites

Plan: **C3**

• Business • Luxury • Design •

An oasis between motorways and huge office buildings, where you'll find a winning mix of leisure and wellness facilities and personal service, with guestrooms that are intimate and extremely comfortable. A real delight!
Savarin – See restaurant listing

Mercure

Weigelia 22 ✉ 2262 AB Leidschendam – ✆ (0 70)
320 92 80 – www.mercuredenhaagleidschendam.com
92 rm – ♦69/169 € ♦♦69/169 € – ☑ 15 € – 4 suites

Plan: **D1**

• Chain hotel • Classic •

This lakeside hotel stands on stilts and is close to a large shopping mall. The reception area in the atrium welcomes guests with a lighting feature consisting of no fewer than 2400 LED light bulbs. The best rooms have balconies with views over the water.
Chiparus – See restaurant listing

NH Atlantic

Deltaplein 200 ✉ 2554 EJ Kijkduin – ✆ (0 70) 448 24 82
– www.nh-hotels.com
132 rm – ♦89/159 € ♦♦89/159 € – ☑ 19 € – 20 suites

Plan: **A2**

• Holiday hotel • Chain hotel • Classic •

In this large hotel, pleasure is combined with business. It has some 20 meeting rooms, as well as leisure facilities. Best of all, the views of the sea and surrounding nature are stunning. For many years the same chef has turned out dishes with an international flavour.

Central Park

Oosteinde 14 ✉ 2271 EH Voorburg – ✆ (0 70) 387 20 81
– www.centralparkronblaauw.com
14 rm – ♦98/150 € ♦♦98/350 € – ☑ 13 €

Plan: **D2**

• Luxury • Elegant •

If you are looking for a luxurious and relaxing place to stay, then this boutique hotel is an absolute must. Here you will discover the true meaning of style – just 10min drive from the centre of The Hague.
Central Park, by Ron Blaauw – See restaurant listing

Mövenpick

Stationsplein 8 ✉ 2275 AZ Voorburg – ✆ (0 70)
337 37 37 – www.moevenpick-hotels.com/denhaag-voorburg
125 rm – ♦70/160 € ♦♦70/160 € – ☑ 19 €

Plan: **C2**

• Business • Functional •

A chain hotel in a modern building looking out over the station. The rooms are functional – those at the back are preferable – and easily accessible to wheelchair users. The modern brasserie offers an international menu.

XxX **Savarin** – Hotel Savarin   🍴 🕭 ⇔ **P**

Laan van Hoornwijck 29 ⊠ 2289 DG Rijswijk – ℰ (0 70)   Plan: **C3**
307 20 50 – www.savarin.nl – closed Sunday
Menu 35 € (lunch), 40/75 € – Carte 47/54 €
• Modern cuisine • Trendy •

Serving contemporary cuisine with an international twist, this restaurant occupies a modernised farmhouse that has retained its traditional charm. Original flavours add a fresh touch to the occasionally playfully prepared dishes.

XxX **Niven** (Niven Kunz)   🍴 ⇔ **P**
✿
Delftweg 58a ⊠ 2289 AL Rijswijk – ℰ (0 70) 307 79 70   Plan: **C3**
– www.restaurantniven.nl – closed late December, Sunday and Monday
Menu 35 € (lunch), 50/100 € – Carte approx. 79 € – *(dinner only except Friday and Saturday)*
• Creative • Elegant •

The basic principle of Niven is to ensure that every dish consists of 80% vegetables. With that philosophy in mind and the use of field-fresh produce, the chef succeeds in creating imaginative delicacies. This fresh, modern business exudes a smart ambience, including in the guestrooms, which boast a terrace overlooking a golf course.

→ Tartaar en gebakken langoustines met zure room en komkommer in rijstpannenkoekje. Kabeljauw en oester met aardpeer en hazelnootjes. Chocolademagnum met specerijen.

XxX **Villa la Ruche**   🍴 **AC** ⇔

Prinses Mariannelaan 71 ⊠ 2275 BB Voorburg   Plan: **C2**
*– ℰ (0 70) 386 01 10 – www.villalaruche.nl – closed 27 July-3 August,
Saturday lunch, Sunday and Monday*
Menu 43 € (lunch), 45/85 € – Carte 68/78 €
• French modern • Elegant •

Villa la Ruche is a villa from the 19C with a modernised interior. It treats its guests to up-to-the-minute cuisine, served either in the atmospheric restaurant with a conservatory or on the patio under the shade of the plane trees.

XX **Chiparus** – Hotel Mercure   ≤ 🍴 **AC** ⇔

Weigelia 22 ⊠ 2262 AB Leidschendam – ℰ (0 70)   Plan: **D1**
320 92 80 – www.restaurantchiparus.nl
Menu 20 € (lunch), 35/50 € – Carte 37/56 €
• Creative • Elegant •

This restaurant, treated to a smart, modern makeover, also boasts a lakeside terrace. Seasonal and à la carte menu. A glass of wine is suggested with each dish.

X **Central Park, by Ron Blaauw**   🍴 ⇔

Oosteinde 14 ⊠ 2271 EH Voorburg – ℰ (0 70) 387 20 81   Plan: **D2**
*– www.centralparkronblaauw.com – closed 27 April, 31 December-
1 January, 21-28 February and Saturday lunch*
Carte 39/60 €
• French modern • Trendy •

With a name like Central Park you expect something cosmopolitan, and that is exactly what you will find at this luxury brasserie. Chef Ron Blaauw's concept takes shape beautifully here. For a fixed price of €15 you can enjoy exciting dishes, deliciously combining different preparation methods with quality ingredients.

X **Brasserie De Koepel**   🍴 🍴 ⇔

Oosteinde 1 ⊠ 2271 EA Voorburg – ℰ (0 70) 369 35 72   Plan: **D2**
– www.brasseriedekoepel.nl – closed 27-31 December and Sunday
Menu 35/44 € – Carte 35/52 € – *(dinner only until 11pm)*
• Market cuisine • Brasserie • Classic •

A former orangery located in a park where you can sit and enjoy nature on the terrace. Beneath the dome, with its paintings of scantily clad women, enjoy the house specialities of Caesar salad, lobster and cream soup, hare filet with a spicy sauce and tarte Tatin.

X
☺
Brasserie NL

Neherpark 5 ✉ 2264 ZD Leidschendam – ℰ (0 70)   Plan: **D1**
320 85 50 – www.brasserienl.com – closed 25, 26 and 31 December-
3 January and Sunday
Menu 25 € (lunch), 35/50 €
– Carte 37/87 € – (dinner only except Thursday and Friday)
• Modern cuisine • Brasserie • Retro •

The large, concrete radio tower with its telephone paraphernalia inside is a
reminder of its history as the headquarters of the postal service in the Netherlands. What stands out most about this restaurant is its vintage appeal and the
designer chairs from the sixties. The menu is straightforward: modern, generous
and based on excellent produce.

X
De Oude Melkhandel

Sluiskant 22 ✉ 2265 AB Leidschendam – ℰ (0 70)   Plan: **D2**
317 82 70 – www.deoudemelkhandel.nl – closed late December-early
January and Monday
Menu 20 € (lunch)/33 € – Carte 42/52 €
• Market cuisine • Brasserie • Simple •

A picturesque waterside location with views over the lock. This former dairy is
now home to a contemporary brasserie, where the kitchen follows the rhythms
of the seasons. The up-to-date dishes are based around fresh and authentic
ingredients.

X
Le Barquichon

Kerkstraat 6 ✉ 2271 CS Voorburg – ℰ (0 70) 387 11 81   Plan: **D2**
– www.lebarquichon.nl – closed 25 July-15 August, Saturday lunch,
Sunday lunch, Tuesday and Wednesday
Menu 28 € (lunch)/33 € – Carte 44/54 € – *(bar lunch)*
• Classic cuisine • Bistro •

A young couple breathed new life into this little neighbourhood restaurant.
Given its location along a pedestrian walkway, the pavement terrace is opened
up whenever the weather allows. The menu is short and traditional, the dining
room small but cosy.

X
☺
Bij Erik

Sluisplein 9 ✉ 2266 AV Leidschendam – ℰ (0 70)   Plan: **D2**
301 04 51 – www.bijerik.nl – closed 27 December-11 January, Saturday
lunch, Sunday lunch and Monday
Menu 23 € (lunch), 35/50 € – *(set menu only)*
• French modern • Trendy •

The highly motivated and enthusiastic chef of this cosy establishment, Erik Tas,
works with a single set menu that is sure to impress. The power of his cuisine
lies in the strong, well-balanced flavours that bring out the best in the ingredients. Bij Erik is also excellent value for money.

ROTTERDAM
ROTTERDAM

Population: 619 879

Jérôme Dancette/Fotolia.com

Rotterdam trades on its earthy appeal, on a rough and ready grittiness that ties in with its status as the largest seaport in the world; it handles 350 million tonnes of goods a year, with over half of all the freight that is heading into Europe passing through it. Flattened during the Second World War, Rotterdam was rebuilt on a grand scale, jettisoning the idea of streets full of terraced houses in favour of a modern cityscape of concrete and glass, and there are few places in the world that have such an eclectic range of buildings to keep you entertained (or bewildered): try the Euromast Space Tower, the Groothandelsgebouw (which translates as 'wholesale building'), the 'Cube Houses' or the fabulous sounding Boompjestorens for size. The city is located on the Nieuwe Maas but is centred around a maze of other rivers – most importantly the Rhine and the Maas – and is only a few dozen kilometres inland from the North Sea. It spills over both banks, and is linked by tunnels, bridges and the metro; the most stunning connection across the water is the modern Erasmusbridge, whose graceful, angular lines of silver tubing have earned it the nickname 'The Swan', and whose sleek design has come to embody the Rotterdam of the new millennium. It's mirrored on the southern banks by the development of the previously rundown Kop Van Zuid area into a zone of new build and sleek promise.

ROTTERDAM IN...

→ **ONE DAY**
Blaak area including Kijk-Kubus and Boompjestorens, Oude Haven, Museum Boijmans Van Beuningen.

→ **TWO DAYS**
More Museumpark, Delfshaven, take in the view from Euromast, cruise along the Nieuwe Maas.

→ **THREE DAYS**
Kop Van Zuid, a show at the Luxor Theatre.

PRACTICAL INFORMATION

ARRIVAL-DEPARTURE

 The Airport is 8km northwest of the city. Shuttle bus No. 33 runs every 10min and takes 20min to Centraal Railway Station.

GETTING AROUND

There are a variety of stripcards to ease your way around on metro, bus, tram and train: from two-strip right up to forty-five strip tickets. That could entail a lot of fiddling about and franking. A better bet could be to invest in a one-day, two-day, or three-day card, which gives you unlimited travel on any form of transport. A Rotterdam Card provides unlimited use of the transport network as well as free admission to most attractions and is available for either 24 or 72 hours. You can hire bicycles from the Centraal Station cycle shop. These work out at good value, and can be hired for either a day or a week.

EATING OUT

Rotterdam is a hot place for dining, in the literal and metaphorical sense. There are lots of places to tuck into the flavours of Holland's colonial past, in particular the spicy delicacies of Indonesia and Surinam. The long east/west stretch of Oude and Nieuwe Binnenweg is not only handy for many of the sights, it's also chock-full of good cafés, café-bars and restaurants, and the canal district of Oudehaven has introduced to the city a good selection of places to eat while taking in the relaxed vibe. Along the waterfront, various

CALENDAR HIGHLIGHTS

January-February
International Film Festival.

March
Museum Night.

May
Dance Parade.

June
Poetry International Festival.

July
North Sea Jazz Festival,
Summer Carnival (street parade),
Robin Rotterdam Unlimited (music, dance, art, street theatre).

September
World Port Festival (ship tours, demos and cruises).

warehouses have been transformed into mega-restaurants, particularly around the Noordereiland isle in the middle of the river, while in Kop Van Zuid, the Wilhelminapier Quay offers quality restaurants and tasty views too. Many establishments are closed at lunchtime, except business restaurants and those that set a high gastronomic standard and like to show it off in the middle of the day as well as in the evening. The bill includes a service charge, so tipping is optional: round up the total if you're pleased with the service.

Environs of Rotterdam
(Plan I)

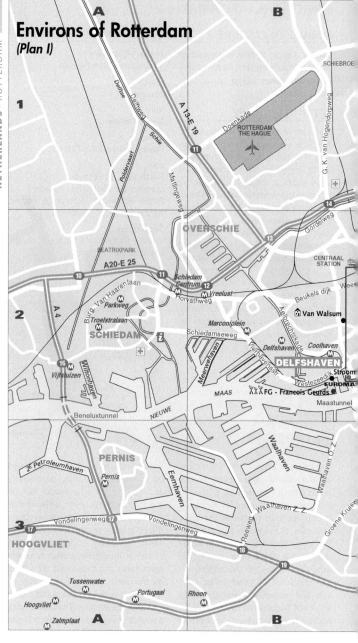

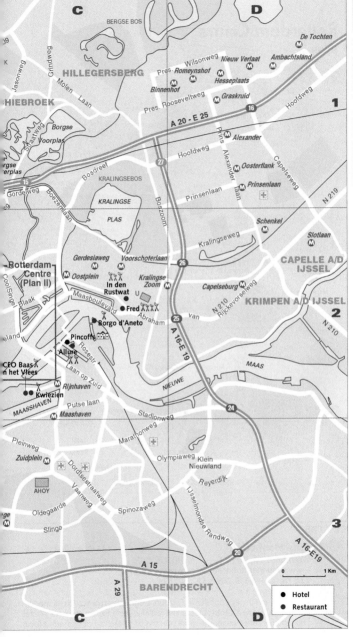

BERGSE BOS

De Tochten

HILLEGERSBERG

Wilsonweg

Pres. Romeynshof

Nieuw Verlaat

Ambachtsland

Binnenhof

Hesseplaats

HIEBROEK

Pres. Rooseveltweg

Graskruid

Grindweg

Jasonweg

Molen Laan

Hoofdweg

1

Straatweg

Borgse

A 20 - E 25

16

Voorplas

Hoofdweg

Alexander

Bosdreef

Prins Alexander

Oosterflank

Capelseweg

Gordelweg

KRALINGSEBOS

Boezemlaan

KRALINGSE

Prinsenlaan

Prinsenlaan

N 219

PLAS

Boszoom

Schenkel

Slotlaan

Kralingseweg

Gerdesiaweg

Voorschoterlaan

CAPELLE A/D
IJSSEL

Rotterdam
Centre
(Plan II)

Oostplein

26

**In den
Rustwat**

Kralingse
Zoom

Capelseburg

KRIMPEN A/D IJSSEL

Coolsingel

Maasboulevard

U

N 210

Rijckevorselweg

Blaak

● **Fred**

Abraham

van

N 210

● **Borgo d'Aneto**

25

eland

Pincoffs

Rossstr.

Allure

Laan op Zuid

MAAS

CFO Baas
n het Vlees

NIEUWE

24

Kwiezien

Rijnhaven

MAASHAVEN

Putse laan

Maashaven

Stadionweg

Pleinweg

Marathonweg

Zuidplein

Olympiaweg

Klein
Nieuwland

Dordsestraatweg

Vaanweg

Reyerdijk

AHOY

Oldegaarde

Spinozaweg

IJsselmonde Randweg

gse

Slinge

3

A 16-E 19

20

A 15

A 29

BARENDRECHT

0   1 Km

● Hotel
● Restaurant

C   **D**

595

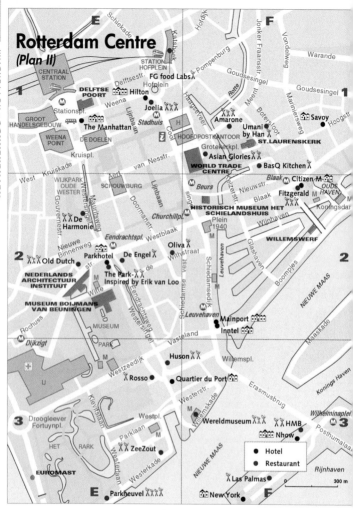

Rotterdam Centre
(Plan II)

CENTRE

 The Manhattan   ☆ ← 🛗 🕙 ⅜ 🅺 🔧 🐾 🚗

Weena 686 ⊠ *3012 CN –* ℰ *(0 10) 430 20 00*   Plan: **E1**
– www.manhattanhotelrotterdam.com
230 rm ⌴ – 👤119/269 € 👤👤139/289 €
• Business • Luxury • Modern •

A colossal skyscraper opposite the station. Large guestrooms with all modern comforts, a business centre, plus all the facilities you'd expect of a luxury hotel. The top floors offer wonderful views over the city. Seasonal cuisine with a focus on fish, served in a restaurant with panoramic windows and a modern décor on the first floor.

596

Hilton   ⚘ ⅃⌂ ᴋ 🆎 🏊 🛁 🚗

Weena 10 ✉ 3012 CM – ℰ (0 10) 710 80 00   Plan: **E1**
– www.rotterdam.hilton.com
246 rm – †99/269 € ††99/269 € – ☲ 25 € – 8 suites
• Chain hotel • Business • Design •

This established business hotel has been fully renovated, with bedrooms and meeting rooms decorated in warm hues, with lots of timber and earthy colours, and modern comfort guaranteed. New additions include the restaurant and the lobby, the biggest in the city.
❀ **Joelia** – See restaurant listing

 Mainport   ⚘ ⋞ ⅃⌂ ⊕ ᴋ 🆎 🛁

Leuvehaven 77 ✉ 3011 EA – ℰ (0 10) 217 57 57   Plan: **F2**
– www.mainporthotel.com
213 rm ☲ – †130/480 € ††150/500 € – 2 suites
• Business • Luxury • Modern •

A prominent hotel on the Rotterdam skyline. It is situated walking distance from the centre and has a magnificent view of the port. Luxurious, stylish accommodation (some rooms have a private sauna) and an attractive restaurant. Not to be missed!

 Nhow   ⚘ ⋞ ⅃⌂ 🆎 🛁 🚗

Wilhelminakade 137 ✉ 3072 AP – ℰ (0 10) 206 76 00   Plan: **F3**
– www.nhow-hotels.com
278 rm – †109/159 € ††109/159 € – ☲ 20 € – 5 suites
• Luxury • Chain hotel • Design •

This imposing building by the River Maas has an impressive view of Rotterdam. The interior has the grandeur to match with minimalist guestrooms that combine designer style and comfort. A hotel offering true luxury.

 Parkhotel   ⚘ ⋞ ⅃⌂ 🛀 🆎 🛁 🅿

Westersingel 70 ✉ 3015 LB – ℰ (0 10) 436 36 11   Plan: **E2**
– www.bilderberg.nl
187 rm – †59/195 € ††79/205 € – ☲ 20 € – 2 suites
• Business • Modern •

A contemporary hotel with a history dating back to 1922, situated in the heart of modern Rotterdam. The two tower blocks built in the 1980s offer panoramic views of the 'Architectural Capital of the Netherlands'.
The Park - Inspired by Erik van Loo – See restaurant listing

 Inntel   ⚘ ⋞ ⅃⌂ 🛀 🔲 🆎 🛁 🅿

Leuvehaven 80 ✉ 3011 EA – ℰ (0 10) 413 41 39   Plan: **F2**
– www.inntelhotelsrotterdamcentre.nl
263 rm ☲ – †100/280 € ††135/300 €
• Chain hotel • Business • Modern •

The only hotel in the city with its own swimming pool, the Inntel also boasts superb views of the Erasmus Bridge and the museum harbour, making this a delightful place to stay. Enjoy a drink in the aptly named 'Water' bar-brasserie.

 Pincoffs   🆎 🛁 🅿

Stieltjesstraat 34 ✉ 3071 JX – ℰ (0 10) 297 45 00   Plan: **C2**
– www.hotelpincoffs.nl – closed 1-16 August
16 rm – †119/129 € ††139/169 € – ☲ 18 € – 1 suite
• Historic • Modern •

This trendy renovated customs office is the place to be for visitors wanting to explore the city and indulge in a little pampering. Bulgari accessories in the bathroom, your favourite music on the iPod docking station and impeccable, friendly service all add to the appeal.

Savoy

Hoogstraat 81 ✉ 3011 PJ
– ☎ (0 10) 413 92 80
– www.hampshire-hotels.com
94 rm ⌑ – ♦80/200 € ♦♦94/214 €

Plan: **F1**

• Business • Functional •

This functional, modern hotel is ideally located for a visit to Rotterdam's famous cube houses and the Markthal (the market hall, a paradise for foodies), making this the perfect choice for visitors to the city.

New York

Koninginnenhoofd 1 (Wilhelminapier) ✉ 3072 AD
– ☎ (0 10) 439 05 00 – www.hotelnewyork.nl
72 rm – ♦99/315 € ♦♦99/315 € – ⌑ 18 €

Plan: **F3**

• Traditional • Retro •

Stay at the New York hotel and experience the excitement of the fortune-seekers who came to buy their tickets here for the ocean crossing to New York. The whole place radiates character and dynamic energy, from the elegant rooms to the large restaurant, which has a pleasant lively ambience.

Citizen M

Gelderseplein 50 ✉ 3011 WZ – ☎ (0 10) 810 81 00
– www.citizenm.com
151 rm – ♦79/169 € ♦♦79/169 € – ⌑ 12 €

Plan: **F2**

• Chain hotel • Townhouse • Contemporary •

Citizen M offers all the facilities you would expect of a modern hotel. Find comfortable and well-equipped designer-style guestrooms, atmospheric public spaces that invite relaxation, and a delicious breakfast – and all at favourable prices.

Quartier du Port

Van Vollenhovenstraat 48 ✉ 3016 BJ
– ☎ (0 10) 240 04 25
– www.quartierduport.nl
20 rm – ♦95/134 € ♦♦95/135 € – ⌑ 17 €

Plan: **E3**

• Townhouse • Retro • Functional •

A boutique hotel with a warm, welcoming atmosphere, a feeling of space and openness in the guestrooms, and just a hint of nostalgia in the reception area. The bread at breakfast is a real treat. The restaurant menu is traditional and changes regularly.

Stroom

Lloydstraat 1 ✉ 3024 EA – ☎ (0 10) 221 40 60
– www.stroomrotterdam.nl
18 rm – ♦89/105 € ♦♦115/145 € – ⌑ 15 € – 3 suites

Plan: **B2**

• Townhouse • Design •

Once energy was generated in this former power station, today it houses a boutique hotel. The interior has a rather austere design, but the personal approach of the managers brings warmth to the place. The effect is truly electric.

Van Walsum

Mathenesserlaan 199 ✉ 3014 HC – ☎ (0 10) 436 32 75
– www.hotelvanwalsum.nl
28 rm ⌑ – ♦70/105 € ♦♦80/130 €

Plan: **B2**

• Family • Classic •

The Van Dam family have been running this hotel for three generations. Renovations take place here on a regular basis, so it is worth asking for a refurbished room when you book.

XxxX **Parkheuvel** (Erik van Loo)   🕃 ⬵ 🏠 ⇔ 🅿
🕄🕄 *Heuvellaan 21* ⬧ *3016 GL* – ℰ *(0 10) 436 07 66*   Plan: **E3**
– www.parkheuvel.nl – closed 27 April, 1-21 August, 27 December-
8 January, 8-11 February, Bank Holidays except Christmas, Saturday lunch
and Sunday
Menu 43 € (lunch), 55/140 € – Carte 89/129 €
• Creative • Elegant • Formal •

A semicircular modern pavillion located on the Maas by a park with bay wind-
ows and a terrace overlooking the harbour. Lovely remodelled art deco interior,
extensive menu and wine list, as well as impeccable service.
➜ Tartaar van wagyu-rund met kaviaar en zacht gekookte kwarteleitjes.
Proeverij van lam met ravioli van niertjes, zwezerik, artisjok en tomaat.
Frambozen gevuld met wittechocolademousse en basilicumsiroop.

XxxX **Fred** (Fred Mustert)   🆎 🍸 (dinner)
🕄🕄 *Honingerdijk 263* ⬧ *3063 AM* – ℰ *(0 10) 212 01 10*   Plan: **C2**
– www.restaurantfred.nl – closed 25 July-7 August, 26 December-
1 January, Saturday lunch and Sunday
Menu 48 € (lunch)/110 € – Carte 82/96 €
• French creative • Elegant • Formal •

'Less is more' is Fred's philosophy. The decor is contemporary and elegant; stunning because of its class and simplicity. And the dishes? They are refined, well
considered creations, where every ingredient has a function. Fred Mustert delivers a personalised experience, where everything matches.
➜ In miso gemarineerde tonijn met avocado, tomaat, haringkaviaar en ker-
rieroomijs. Gebraden eend met karamel, sinaasappel en druivensap. Delice
van karamel, wittechocolademousse en roomijs van chocoladebiscuit.

XxX **Old Dutch**   🏠 ⇔ 🍽 🅿
Rochussenstraat 20 ⬧ *3015 EK* – ℰ *(0 10) 436 03 44*   Plan: **E2**
– www.olddutch.net – closed Bank Holidays, Saturday and Sunday
Menu 38 € (lunch), 43/60 € – Carte 55/93 €
• French modern • Classic •

With its serving staff decked out in suits and bow ties, this traditional restaurant
with an incredibly spacious terrace has the atmosphere of a gentlemen's club.
Familiar produce is given a fresh twist, such as marinated Scottish salmon served
with chicory, walnuts, apple and crème fraîche. Meat is even sliced at your table.

XxX **Wereldmuseum**   ⅙ 🆎
🕃 *Willemskade 25* ⬧ *3016 DM* – ℰ *(0 10) 270 71 85*   Plan: **F3**
– www.wereldmuseum.nl – closed 27 April, 2-22 August, 22 December-
3 January, Saturday lunch and Monday
Menu 30 € (lunch), 40/75 € – Carte 50/71 €
• Modern cuisine • Trendy •

Just like its neighbour, this fashionable restaurant has plenty of draws; starting
with beautiful views over the historic port. The ambitious cooking style of the
chef has evolved and is now an attraction in its own right. Dishes are modern,
without unnecessary frippery, and are full of flavour.
➜ Geroosterde langoustines met rode biet, hibiscus en haringkuit. Gebraden duif met aubergines, bosui, noten en olijf. Geroosterde ananas met
pompoen en yoghurt-limoenroomijs.

XxX **Joelia** (Mario Ridder) – Hotel Hilton   🕃 ⇔
🕃 *Coolsingel 5* ⬧ *3012 AA* – ℰ *(0 10) 710 80 34*   Plan: **E1**
– www.joelia.eu – closed Saturday lunch
Menu 40 € (lunch), 75/80 € – Carte approx. 157 €
• French creative • Trendy •

Joelia proves that refinement does not need to be complex. Her eclectic decor
beautifully combines vintage and design to unique effect. Her cuisine is creative
without being fussy, and serves one aim: to achieve a harmony of subtle perfumes and intense flavours.
➜ Gouden gebak van brioche met ganzenlever en truffel. Tarbot met eekhoorntjesbrood en kruidengnocchi. Vijg met gekaramelliseerde druivensi-
roop en vanilleroomijs.

XxX ❋ Amarone (Gert Blom)

Meent 72a ✉ *3011 JN – ☎ (0 10) 414 84 87*   Plan: **F1**
– www.restaurantamarone.nl – closed 25 July-8 August, 31 December-
1 January and Sunday
Menu 35 € (lunch), 50/80 € – Carte 68/90 €
• Creative • Formal •

This fashionable city restaurant emanates the same elegance and superior quality as the fine wine from which it takes its name. Inventive cuisine made from
the best ingredients.
➜ Carpaccio van coquilles met truffel, hazelnoot en pecorinokaas. Gepocheerde tarbot met nage van tomaat en kaneel, gemarineerde tomaatjes
en een crème van ui. Cilinder met een mousse van vanille en chocoladet-
ruffel, druiven en roomijs van rode wijn.

XxX ☺ In den Rustwat

Honingerdijk 96 ✉ *3062 NX – ☎ (0 10) 413 41 10*   Plan: **C2**
– www.idrw.nl – closed 26 July-15 August, 27 December-9 January,
Saturday lunch, Sunday and Monday
Menu 35/58 € – Carte 50/68 €
• Modern cuisine • Rustic •

In den Rustwat adds an exotic touch to metropolitan Rotterdam with its thatched roof, history dating back to the 16C and an idyllic setting close to an arbo-
retum. The food here is anything but traditional, offering contemporary-style
dishes with an abundance of ingredients and cooking methods.

XxX ❋ ❋ FG - François Geurds

Lloydstraat 204 ✉ *3024 EA – ☎ (0 10) 425 05 20*   Plan: **B2**
– www.fgrestaurant.nl – closed 17 July-10 August, 1-15 January, Sunday
and Monday
Menu 45 € (lunch), 91/151 € – Carte 82/108 €
• Creative • Individual •

This exclusive, spectacular restaurant could hardly be more impressive. The
chef's style of cooking is not only clever and highly innovative, but also features
convincing combination of flavours. It therefore comes as no surprise to learn
that this culinary genius learnt his craft at The Fat Duck. FG could easily stand
for fantastically good!
➜ Gepocheerde eendenlever met aardappelkaantjes en kruidenparfum.
Tarbot en inktvis met eekhoorntjesbrood en saffraan. Wentelteefje
met pompoen, kaas en gepofte rijst.

XxX Fitzgerald

Gelderseplein 49 ✉ *3011 WZ – ☎ (0 10) 268 70 10*   Plan: **F2**
– www.restaurantfitzgerald.nl – closed 25 July-7 August, 25 December-
7 January, Saturday lunch, Sunday and Monday
Menu 25 € (lunch), 40/78 € – Carte 51/68 €
• French modern • Elegant •

Fitzgerald has real allure with its Italian marble, large glass windows, and design
and vintage elements. The same goes for the experienced staff who will introduce you to cuisine that is thoroughly modern, varied and delicious.

XX ☺ Huson

Scheepstimmermanslaan 14 ✉ *3011 BS – ☎ (0 10)*   Plan: **E3**
413 03 71 – www.huson.info – closed 26 December-2 January, Saturday
lunch and Sunday dinner
Menu 34 € – Carte 42/55 €
• Creative • Brasserie •

Huson is a trendy restaurant with class, and like the nearby harbour, there is
always a lively buzz here. Feast on the wondrous marriage of French and creative cuisine in attractive combinations that capture both subtlety and exube-
rance. Fantastic prices too.

XX **De Harmonie**   🏠 ⇔
Westersingel 95 ✉ *3015 LC – ✆ (0 10) 436 36 10*   Plan: **E2**
– www.deharmonierotterdam.nl – closed 25 December-1 January, Bank Holidays, Saturday lunch and Sunday
Menu 35/72 € – Carte approx. 45 €
• Modern cuisine • Trendy •
Having learned his culinary craft from chefs such as Gordon Ramsay (in London's Maze restaurant), Marco Somer is now putting this experience to good use and is making his mark with his own, contemporary cuisine. He offers small dishes of harmonious, authentic flavours at a fixed price.

XX **Zeezout**   🏠 AC
Westerkade 11b ✉ *3016 CL – ✆ (0 10) 436 50 49*   Plan: **E3**
– www.restaurantzeezout.nl – closed Sunday lunch and Monday
Menu 35 € (lunch), 48/58 € – Carte 54/65 €
• Fish and seafood • Design •
The only sensible thing to eat in the skippers' quarter of one of the main ports of the world is fish, fish and... more fish! The dorado in salt crust is a real treat here. Stylish decor with a cosy atmosphere.

XX **The Park - Inspired by Erik van Loo** – Hotel Parkhotel
Westersingel 70 ✉ *3015 LB – ✆ (0 10) 440 81 65*   ⅃ AC ⇔ 🅿
– www.thepark.nl   Plan: **E2**
Menu 36 € – Carte 23/48 €
• Modern cuisine • Trendy •
A refreshing breeze blows through this blue-tinted luxury brasserie. It is a pleasant spot to enjoy carefully prepared and beautifully presented cuisine made from top quality ingredients. The restaurant stands out for signature dishes by top chef Eric van Loo.

XX **HMB**   ⟨ 🏠 ⇔
Holland Amerika Kade 104 ✉ *3072 MC – ✆ (0 10)*   Plan: **F3**
760 06 20 – www.hmb-restaurant.nl – closed 1-15 August, 28 December-11 January, Saturday lunch, Sunday and Monday
Menu 35 € (lunch), 49/71 € – Carte 38/51 € – *(booking advisable)*
• International • Fashionable • Elegant •
HMB stands for hummingbird, and in keeping with its name, the interior of this restaurant is elegantly playful. The large windows also provide a stunning view of the Rotterdam skyline. The delicious, beautifully presented dishes are prepared with care and attention using ingredients from different international culinary traditions.

XX **Allure**   ⟨ 🏠 AC
Cargadoorskade 107 ✉ *3071 AW – ✆ (0 10) 486 65 29*   Plan: **C2**
– www.restaurant-allure.nl – closed 26 December-4 January and Monday
Menu 30 € (lunch), 36/53 € – Carte 48/60 €
• Market cuisine • Design •
This restaurant's purple designer-style interior blends harmoniously with its spectacular view of the marina. The dishes are beautifully presented with a blaze of colour. Attractive, modern cuisine with plenty of appeal.

XX **Asian Glories**   AC ⇔
🍃 *Leeuwenstraat 15* ✉ *3011 AL – ✆ (0 10) 411 71 07*   Plan: **F1**
– www.asianglories.nl – closed Wednesday
Menu 30/49 € – Carte 29/49 €
• Chinese • Family • Friendly •
Asian Glories offers an authentic, high quality Chinese cuisine, which focuses on the culinary traditions of Canton and Szechuan. Specialities on the menu include the Peking duck and the delicious dim sum, a type of Oriental dumpling that is served either boiled or fried.

NETHERLANDS - ROTTERDAM

☓ Las Palmas

Wilhelminakade 330 ✉ *3072 AR –* ☏ *(0 10) 234 51 22* Plan: **F3**
– www.restaurantlaspalmas.nl – closed Saturday lunch
Menu 23 € (lunch), 40/70 € – Carte 59/114 €
• Classic cuisine • Brasserie •

There's always plenty going on at Herman den Blijker's brasserie, which is styled as a loft. You get a sneak preview before your meal arrives: meats age in special cabinets, the shellfish is on display and the open kitchen is on a raised platform. Dishes are recognisable and produce is fresh. The lunch menu is great.

☓ C.E.O baas van het vlees

Sumatraweg 1 ✉ *3072 ZP –* ☏ *(0 10) 290 94 54* Plan: **C2**
– www.ceobaasvanhetvlees.nl – closed Monday
Carte 40/79 € – *(dinner only until 11pm)*
• Meats • Bistro • Trendy •

A lively bistro where prime quality American meat takes pride of place on the menu. All you have to decide is how you would like your meat cooked and whether you would like French fries and homemade mayonnaise to go with your meal.

☓ Oliva

Witte de Withstraat 15a ✉ *3012 BK –* ☏ *(0 10) 412 14 13* Plan: **E2**
– www.restaurantoliva.nl – closed 25 December-1 January
Menu 34/44 € – Carte 29/48 € – *(dinner only)*
• Italian • Bistro •

Enjoy down-to-earth Italian cuisine in this delightful trattoria. The menu changes daily and the dishes are made from ingredients straight from Italy. Authentic and delicious.

☓ FG Food Labs

❀
Katshoek 41 ✉ *3032 AE –* ☏ *(0 10) 425 05 20* Plan: **E1**
– www.fgfoodlabs.nl – closed 17 July-10 August and 1-15 January
Menu 43/110 € – Carte 48/76 €
• Creative • Fashionable •

This 'taste laboratory' housed in a trendy version of a train tunnel is definitely part of the Rotterdam scene. The emphasis is on new flavours and textures and on pushing culinary boundaries. This results in inventive cuisine that is bold and full of character.

→ Japanse pannenkoek. Kabeljauw met tom kha kai-smaken. Aardbeien met meringue.

☓ De Engel

Eendrachtsweg 19 ✉ *3012 LB –* ☏ *(0 10) 413 82 56* Plan: **E2**
– www.restaurant-deengel.nl – closed 27 April, 1 January, Saturday lunch and Sunday
Menu 30 € (lunch), 40/80 €
• Classic cuisine • Friendly •

The relaxed ambience and hint of old-fashioned grandeur in this welcoming townhouse make it the perfect place for an enjoyable meal. Seasonal cuisine with a French flavour and numerous options on the menu.

☓ Umami by Han

☺
Binnenrotte 140 ✉ *3011 HC –* ☏ *(0 10) 433 31 39* Plan: **F1**
– www.umami-restaurant.com – closed Monday
Menu 25/35 € – *(dinner only) (booking advisable)*
• Asian • Fashionable • Minimalist •

The trendy, modern interior with bright colours immediately catches the eye, but the trump card of this restaurant is its rock solid concept… A range of Asian dishes with a French twist from which you can choose your heart's desire. A wonderful journey of discovery at amazing prices!

Rosso 🅰🅲 ⇔

Van Vollenhovenstraat 15 (access via Westerlijk Plan: **E3**
Handelsterrein) ✉ *3016 BE –* ℰ *(0 10) 225 07 05 – www.rossorotterdam.nl*
– closed 27 July-9 August and Sunday
Menu 40/80 € ▼ – Carte 38/66 € – *(dinner only)*
• French creative • Trendy •

Shades of red lend colour to the relaxed and intimate interior of this trendy restaurant. It offers fine wines and a menu that you can put together as you please, choosing from a variety of small dishes prepared with top quality produce. Excellent food and an attractive ambience.

Kwiezien 🀪 🅰🅲

Delistraat 20 ✉ *3072 ZK –* ℰ *(0 10) 215 14 40* Plan: **C2**
– www.kwiezien.nl – closed 25, 26, 27 and 31 December and Monday
Carte approx. 36 € – *(dinner only)*
• Market cuisine • Family •

The concept of cosy Kwiezien is simple: you put together your own meal with little dishes each costing 9,50 euros. Karin and Remco work in their open kitchen, using exclusively fresh ingredients in a continual quest for exciting combinations. A modest price for a rich palette of flavours.

Borgo d'Aneto ← 🀪 🅰🅲

Nijverheidstraat 2 ✉ *3071 GC –* ℰ *(0 10) 290 77 32* Plan: **C2**
– www.borgodaneto.nl – closed Saturday lunch, Sunday, Monday and Tuesday
Menu 35 €
• Italian • Bistro • Traditional •

In a bustling but cosy atmosphere, Faouzi Chihabi dishes up pure Italian cuisine with an emphasis on beautiful and tasty produce. The chef's passion is evidenced by the food, which can be savoured while admiring the fantastic view of the Rotterdam skyline.

BasQ Kitchen

Grote Markt 188 ✉ *3011 PA –* ℰ *(0 10) 414 00 99* Plan: **F1**
– www.basqkitchen.nl
Menu 20 € (lunch)/33 € – Carte approx. 35 €
• Basque • Brasserie • Tapas bar •

Rotterdam's Markthal is a place of delicacies and BasQ fits in perfectly here. In this lively bistro you will discover different aspects of Basque cuisine from traditional to modern. The pintxos and tapas offer an authentic flavour of the Basque Country.

NORWAY
NORGE

→ **Area:**
323 878 km² (125 049 sq mi).

→ **Population:**
5 137 000 inhabitants. Density = 16 per km².

→ **Capital:**
Oslo.

→ **Currency:**
Norwegian Krone (kr or NOK) divided into 100 øre.

→ **Government:**
Constitutional parliamentary monarchy with single-chamber Parliament (since 1945).

→ **Languages:**
Norwegian has two written variants: Bokmål - influenced by Danish and spoken by 80% of the population - and Nynorsk (New Norwegian). Sami is the language of the Sami people in the far north. English is widely spoken.

→ **Public holidays:**
New Year's Day (1 Jan); Maundy Thursday and Good Friday (late Mar/Apr); Easter Monday (late Mar/Apr); Labor Day (1 May); Constitution Day (17 May); Ascension Day (May); Whit Monday (late May/June); Christmas Day (25 Dec); St Stephen's Day (26 Dec).

→ **Local Time:**
GMT+1 hour in winter and GMT +2 hours in summer.

→ **Climate:**
Temperate northern maritime with cold winters and mild summers (Oslo: January -4°C; July 16°C). Colder interior, fairly high precipitation in the coastal regions.

OSLO

→ **Emergency:**
Police ☏ 112; Medical Assistance ☏ 113; Fire Brigade ☏ 110. (Dialling 112 within any EU country will redirect your call and contact the emergency services.)

→ **Electricity:**
230 volts AC, 50Hz; 2 round pin sockets.

→ **Formalities:**
Travellers from the European Union (EU), Switzerland, Iceland and the main countries of North and South America need a national identity card or passport (America: passport required) to visit Norway for less than three months (tourism or business purpose). For visitors from other countries a visa may be required, in addition to a passport, especially for those wishing to stay for longer than three months. We advise you to check with your embassy before travelling.

OSLO

OSLO

Population: 634 400

Sime/PHOTONONSTOP

Oslo has a lot going for it – and one slight downside: it's one of the world's most expensive cities. It also ranks high when it comes to its standard of living, however, and its position at the head of Oslofjord, surrounded by steep forested hills, is hard to match for drama and beauty. It's a charmingly compact place to stroll round, particularly in the summer, when the daylight hours practically abolish the night and, although it may lack the urban cool of some other Scandinavian cities, it boasts its fair share of trendy clubs and a raft of Michelin Starred restaurants. There's a real raft, too: Thor Hyerdahl's famous Kon-Tiki – one of the star turns in a city that loves its museums.

Oslo's uncluttered feel is enhanced by parks and wide streets and, in the winter, there are times when you feel you have the whole place to yourself. Drift into the city by boat and land at the smart harbour of Aker Brygge; to the west lies the charming Bygdøy peninsula, home to museums permeated with the smell of the sea. Northwest is Frogner, with its famous sculpture park, the place where locals hang out on long summer days. The centre of town, the commercial hub, is Karl Johans Gate, bounded at one end by the Royal Palace and at the other by the Cathedral, while further east lie two trendy multi-cultural areas, Grunerlokka and Grønland, the former also home to the Edvard Munch Museum.

OSLO IN...

→ ONE DAY
Aker Brygge, Karl Johans Gate, Oslo Opera House.

→ TWO DAYS
Akershus, Astrup Fearnley Museum, ferry trip to Bygdøy.

→ THREE DAYS
Vigeland Park, Holmenkollen Ski Jump, Grunerlokka, Munch Museum.

PRACTICAL INFORMATION

ARRIVAL-DEPARTURE

✈ Oslo International Airport, Gardermoen, is 47km north of the city. The train station is located beneath the terminal and the Flytoget train takes 19min to Oslo's central station. The Express Bus to Oslo city centre leaves every 20min and takes 45min.

GETTING AROUND

The integrated transport system comprises bus, tram or metro and you can obtain single or day tickets. You can get an electronic 'Tourist Card' for a small deposit from a tourist information centre and hire one of the many free Citybike scheme bicycles parked at different points around the city. You pay a toll if you arrive by car. The Oslo Pass, which covers the transport system and entry to all museums, is valid for one to three days and is available from the Information Centre next to Oslo Central Station.

CALENDAR HIGHLIGHTS

March
By:Larm (music festival), Oslo International Church Music Festival.

May
St Hallvard's Day (concerts and theatre productions).

June
Norwegian Wood Rock Festival.

August
International Jazz Festival.

November
Oslo World Music Festival.

December
Nobel Peace Prize awarded (parades and festivities).

EATING OUT

Oslo has a very vibrant dining scene, albeit one that is somewhat expensive, particularly if you drink wine. The cooking can be quite classical and refined but there are plenty of restaurants offering more innovative menus too. What is in no doubt is the quality of the produce used, whether that's the ever-popular game or the superlative shellfish, which comes from very cold water, giving it a clean, fresh flavour. Classic Norwegian dishes often include fruit, such as lingonberries with venison. Lunch is not a major affair; most prefer just a snack or sandwich at midday while making dinner the main event of the day. You'll find most diners are seated by 7pm and are offered a 6, 7 or 8 course menu which they can reduce at their will, with a paired wine menu alongside. It doesn't have to be expensive, though. Look out for konditoris (bakeries) where you can pick up sandwiches and pastries, and kafeterias which serve substantial meals at reasonable prices. Service is a strength; staff are generally very polite, speak English and are fully versed in the menu.

607

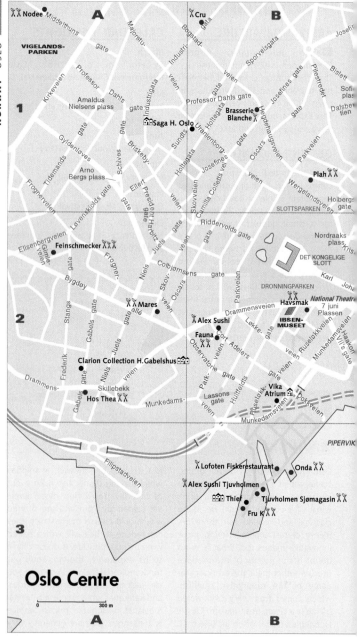

VIGELANDS-PARKEN

Nodee

Cru

Saga H. Oslo

Brasserie Blanche

Plah

Amaldus Nielsens plass

Arno Bergs plass

SLOTTSPARKEN

Nordraaks plass

DET KONGELIGE SLOTT

Feinschmecker

DRONNINGPARKEN

National Theatre
7 juni Plassen

Havsmak

IBSEN-MUSEET

Mares

Alex Sushi

Fauna

Clarion Collection H.Gabelshus

Vika Atrium

Skillebekk

Hos Thea

PIPERVIK

Lofoten Fiskerestaurant

Onda

Alex Sushi Tjuvholmen

Thief

Tjuvholmen Sjømagasin

Fru K

Oslo Centre

0   300 m

608

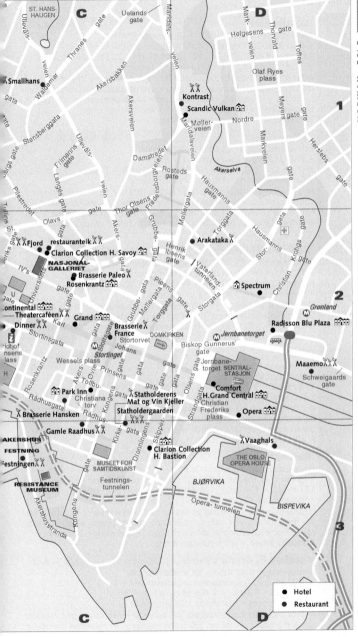

St. Hans-
Haugen

Uelands
gate

Mark-

Helgesens gate

Thorvald gate

Olaf Ryes
plass

Smallhans

Kontrast

Scandic Vulkan

Nordre

Spectrum

Fjord   restauranteik

Arakataka

Clarion Collection H. Savoy

NASJONAL-
GALLERIET

Brasserie Paleo

Rosenkrantz

Continental

Theatercaféen

Grand

Brasserie
France

Dinner

Radisson Blu Plaza

Grønland

Maaemo

DOMKIRKEN

Stortorvet

Jernbanetorget

Slortinget

Biskop Gunnerus'
gate

Schweigaards
gate

Jernbane-
torget

SENTRAL-
STASJON

Park Inn

Christiana
torv

Comfort
H.Grand Central

Statholderens
Mat og Vin Kjeller

Christian
Frederiks
plass

Opera

Brasserie Hansken

Statholdergaarden

Gamle Raadhus

Vaaghals

AKERSHUS
FESTNING

Festningen

Clarion Collection
H. Bastion

MUSEET FOR
SAMTIDSKUNST

THE OSLO
OPERA HOUSE

RESISTANCE
MUSEUM

BJØRVIKA

BISPEVIKA

Festnings-
tunnelen

Opera- tunnelen

● Hotel
● Restaurant

609

NORWAY - OSLO

Continental

Stortingsgaten 24-26 ✉ *0117 –* Ⓜ *National Theatret*
– ✆ *22 82 40 00 – www.hotelcontinental.no – Closed Christmas*
Plan: **C2**
155 rm – ♟1695/2950 NOK ♟♟1935/3600 NOK – ☷ 245 NOK – 3 suites
• **Grand Luxury • Traditional • Classic** •
A classic hotel situated by the National Theatre and run by the 4th generation of the family, who ensure the service remains very personal. Stylish, contemporary bedrooms – deluxe are the biggest and come with bathrobes and sofas. Dine in the grand café or from an inventive daily menu in Annen Etage.
Theatercaféen – See restaurant listing

Grand

Karl Johans Gate 31 ✉ *0159 –* Ⓜ *Stortinget*
– ✆ *23 21 20 00 – www.grand.no*
Plan: **C2**
292 rm ☷ – ♟1425/5495 NOK ♟♟1425/5495 NOK – 7 suites
• **Grand Luxury • Traditional • Classic** •
An imposing, centrally located hotel built in 1874; the guest areas and grand ballrooms reflect this. Bedrooms are charming: some are modern, some are feminine and others are in a belle époque style. The winners of the Nobel Prize are interviewed here! Classical Norwegian cuisine is served in elegant Palmen.

Radisson Blu Plaza

Sonja Henies Plass 3 ✉ *0134 –* Ⓜ *Jernbanetorget*
– ✆ *22 05 80 00 – www.radissonblu.com/plazahotel-oslo*
Plan: **D2**
676 rm ☷ – ♟1195/5745 NOK ♟♟1395/5945 NOK – 19 suites
• **Business • Modern • Functional** •
This is Norway's tallest hotel and it boasts more bedrooms than any other in Oslo; the modern 'Business' rooms are the most comfortable. It has a large marble lobby with a lounge and bar, extensive conference facilities, an Irish pub and a top floor restaurant offering a Norwegian menu and city views.

Thief

Landgangen 1 ✉ *0252 –* ✆ *24 00 40 00*
Plan: **B3**
– www.thethief.com
118 rm ☷ – ♟1640/3890 NOK ♟♟1940/4190 NOK – 11 suites
• **Luxury • Contemporary • Stylish** •
A smart hotel located on a huge development on Thief Island. Works from global artists – including Andy Warhol – feature throughout; facilities are state-of-the-art and a tablet controls all of the technology in the bedrooms. Super spa.
Fru K – See restaurant listing

Rosenkrantz

Rosenkrantz gate 1 ✉ *0159 Oslo*
Ⓜ *National Theatret –* ✆ *23 31 55 00 – www.thonhotels.no*
Plan: **C2**
151 rm ☷ – ♟995/2695 NOK ♟♟1295/3695 NOK
• **Business • Chain hotel • Functional** •
Located in the city centre and perfect for the business traveller. Brightly styled 8th floor guest lounge with complimentary coffee, mineral water, fruit and cakes. Functional bedrooms come with Smart TVs and modern bathrooms.
Brasserie Paleo – See restaurant listing

Comfort H. Grand Central

Jernbanetorget 1 ✉ *0154 –* Ⓜ *Jernbanetorget*
– ✆ *22 98 28 00 – www.comfortgrandcentral.no*
Plan: **D2**
170 rm ☷ – ♟1049/1949 NOK ♟♟1149/2249 NOK
• **Chain hotel • Business • Functional** •
A great choice for businesspeople, this delightful hotel has a superb location above the main train station. 130 of the soundproofed bedrooms have been individually styled and boast coordinating fabrics and colour schemes, as well as feature bathrooms. The restaurant offers a menu of simple Italian dishes.

Opera
❄ ⩽ ⅃♨ ⋒ & 🅰️🅲 ⅄🄰

Dronning Eufemias gate 4 ✉ *0191* – Ⓜ *Jernbanetorget*
Plan: **D2**
– ✆ *24 10 30 00* – *www.thonhotels.no* – *Closed 23 December-4 January*
480 rm ⌾ – ♛1045/2195 NOK ♛♛1345/2595 NOK – 2 suites
• **Business** • **Modern** • **Personalised** •

Imposing light-stone building in front of the Opera House, close to the sea.
Guest areas are spacious; bedrooms are a split of classic and modern styles but
all are equally well-equipped. The restaurant boasts huge windows and panoramic views; watch the chefs at work in the open kitchen.

Clarion Collection H. Bastion
⅃♨ ⋒ 🅰️🅲 ⅄ ⅄🄰

Skippergata 7 ✉ *0152* – Ⓜ *Jernbanetorget*
Plan: **C3**
– ✆ *22 47 77 00* – *www.choicehotels.no* – *Closed Easter and Christmas*
99 rm ⌾ – ♛880/2980 NOK ♛♛1180/3180 NOK – 5 suites
• **Business** • **Modern** • **Stylish** •

Set on the edge of the city, close to the port, this hotel has friendly staff, a cosy
lounge and a charming English-style lobby complete with free snacks.
Bedrooms vary in both their size and furnishings; many have seating areas.

Clarion Collection H. Gabelshus
🐾 ⅃♨ ⋒ ⅄🄰 🅿️

Gabelsgate 16 ✉ *0272* – ✆ *23 27 65 00*
Plan: **A2**
– *www.nordicchoicehotels.no* – *Closed Easter and Christmas*
114 rm ⌾ – ♛680/2240 NOK ♛♛1080/2780 NOK – 1 suite
• **Traditional** • **Business** • **Classic** •

Beautiful ivy-covered house with a peaceful atmosphere, in a smart residential
neighbourhood. The classical wood-furnished lounge has a complimentary all-
day buffet. Charming bedrooms offer a pleasing contrast between old and new.

Saga H. Oslo
❄ ⅄ 🅿️

Eilert Sundstgate 39 ✉ *0259* – ✆ *22 55 44 90*
Plan: **B1**
– *www.sagahoteloslo.no* – *Closed Christmas and Easter*
47 rm ⌾ – ♛795/4295 NOK ♛♛895/4895 NOK
• **Townhouse** • **Historic** • **Stylish** •

A late Victorian townhouse with a smart, contemporary interior, set in a quiet
city suburb. Most of the bedrooms are spacious: they have bold feature walls,
modern facilities – including coffee machines – and small but stylish shower
rooms. There's a small sushi restaurant in the basement.

Scandic Vulkan
❄ ⩽ ⅃♨ & 🅰️🅲 ⅄ ⅄🄰

Maridalsveien 13A ✉ *0178* – ✆ *21 05 71 00*
Plan: **D1**
– *www.scandichotels.no* – *Closed Easter and Christmas*
149 rm ⌾ – ♛840/1890 NOK ♛♛890/2500 NOK
• **Business** • **Chain hotel** • **Design** •

Designer hotel on the site of a former silver mine, next to a great food market.
Modern bedrooms have bold feature walls and good facilities; the external-
facing ones have full length windows. The bright restaurant offers accessible
menus and Norwegian daily specials, and adjoins a trendy bar and deli.

Clarion Collection H. Savoy
❄ ⅄

Universitetsgata 11 ✉ *0164* – Ⓜ *National Theatret*
Plan: **C2**
– ✆ *23 35 42 00* – *www.nordicchoicehotels.no* – *Closed 20-27 December
and Easter*
93 rm ⌾ – ♛980/2440 NOK ♛♛1180/2680 NOK
• **Business** • **Classic** • **Modern** •

Centrally located by the National Gallery, in a building dating back to 1850.
Bedrooms are decorated in a mix of classic and more contemporary styles; the
latter feature 'action photos'. Complimentary breakfast and light evening meal.
🍴 **restauranteik** – See restaurant listing

NORWAY - OSLO

Park Inn

                                                ს ᴀᴄ ᴚ

Øvre Slottsgate 2c ✉ *0157 –* Ⓜ *Stortinget*   Plan: **C2**
– ℰ 22 40 01 00 – www.parkinn.com/hotel-oslo
118 rm ⌂ – †995/2500 NOK ††995/2500 NOK
• **Business** • **Chain hotel** • **Functional** •
A converted apartment block near Karl Johans Gate. Inside it's bright and modern with pleasant guest areas. Good-sized, functional bedrooms have pale wood furniture and modern lighting; the top floor rooms have balconies.

Vika Atrium

               ᖚ ⯑ ⇔ ᴚ ⇔

Munkedamsveien 45 ✉ *0250 –* Ⓜ *National Theatret*   Plan: **B2**
– ℰ 22 83 33 00 – www.thonhotels.no
102 rm ⌂ – †925/2095 NOK ††1095/2295 NOK
• **Conference hotel** • **Functional** • **Modern** •
A busy conference hotel located in a large modern office block in the redeveloped harbour area. Functional bedrooms are set over 7 floors and have contemporary styling and marble bathrooms: some overlook the atrium, others the street.

Spectrum

                                                     ს

Brugata 7 ✉ *0186 –* Ⓜ *Grønland – ℰ 23 36 27 00*   Plan: **D2**
– www.thonhotels.no/spectrum – Closed Christmas
151 rm ⌂ – †700/1400 NOK ††900/1600 NOK
• **Business** • **Functional** • **Minimalist** •
Good value lodge-style hotel in a pedestrianised shopping street, close to the station. An unassuming exterior conceals a modern lobby and spacious breakfast room. Light-hued bedrooms offer basic comforts; some sleep up to four.

𝕏𝕏𝕏
𝔢𝔰𝔢 𝔢𝔰𝔢 𝔢𝔰𝔢

Maaemo (Esben Holmboe Bang)

                                             ᴀᴄ

Schweigaardsgate 15b (entrance via staircase) ✉ *0191*   Plan: **D2**
– Ⓜ *Grønland – ℰ 91 99 48 05 – www.maaemo.no – Closed Christmas, Easter, 1 January, Sunday and Monday*
Menu 2050 NOK – *(dinner only and Saturday lunch) (booking essential) (set menu only)*
• **Innovative** • **Design** • **Fashionable** •
A striking, modern restaurant with an intimate, brightly lit interior and an unusual mezzanine-level kitchen; dishes are finished at the table, with some presented by the chefs themselves. Maaemo means 'Mother Earth' and top quality Norwegian produce guides the 20+ course menu; cooking is intricate, original and visually stimulating with some sublime flavour combinations.
→ Emulsion of Norwegian oysters. Charred onions and quail eggs in bone marrow vinaigrette. Norwegian strawberries with elderflower and grilled rose hip.

𝕏𝕏𝕏
𝔢𝔰𝔢

Statholdergaarden (Bent Stiansen)

Rådhusgate 11 (entrance on Kirkegata) ✉ *0151*   Plan: **C3**
– Ⓜ *Stortinget – ℰ 22 41 88 00 – www.statholdergaarden.no*
– Closed 17 July-7 August, 23 December-3 January, 19-28 March, 1, 5 and 14-17 May, Sunday and Monday
Menu 1095 NOK – Carte 960/1160 NOK – *(dinner only) (booking essential)*
• **Classic** • **Formal** • **Elegant** •
A charming 17C house in the city's heart. Three elegant rooms feature an array of antiques and curios, and have wonderfully ornate stucco ceilings hung with chandeliers. Expertly rendered classical cooking uses seasonal Norwegian ingredients in familiar combinations. Service is well-versed and willing.
→ Langoustines and salmon with tarragon. Entrecôte of veal, Welsh onion sauce. Vanilla and lime bavarois with raspberry, cucumber and elderflower sherbet.
Statholderens Mat og Vin Kjeller – See restaurant listing

NORWAY - OSLO

XXX **Feinschmecker**   88 AK ⇔

Balchensgate 5 ✉ *0265 –* ☎ *22 12 93 80*   Plan: **A2**
– www.feinschmecker.no
– Closed July, Easter, Christmas and Sunday
Menu 875 NOK – Carte 755/925 NOK – *(dinner only)*
• **Traditional** • **Classic** • **Neighbourhood** •
This long-standing restaurant with its cosy, welcoming atmosphere has a loyal
local following and is run by a charming team. The well-presented dishes are
classically based, with French influences. Wine pairings are available.

XX **Fauna** (Bjørn Svensson/Jo Bøe Klakegg)
ॐ *Solligata 2* ✉ *0254 –* Ⓜ *National Theatret*   Plan: **B2**
– ☎ *41 67 45 43 – www.restaurantfauna.no – Closed July, 20 December-*
4 January, Sunday and Monday
Menu 795 NOK – *(dinner only) (booking essential) (set menu only)*
• **Modern** • **Trendy** • **Design** •
More relaxed than its formal façade suggests, this busy place is run by 3 friends.
Dishes are attractively presented and full of flavour; watch the chefs in action in
the open kitchen to fully appreciate their skill. Service flows seamlessly and
wines are top notch. Extra dishes can be added to the set menu.
→ Lobster with celeriac and juniper berries. Norwegian duck, asparagus
and leek. Chocolate, hazelnut and blackcurrant.

XX **Kontrast** (Mikael Svenssen)   & AK ⇔
ॐ *Maridalsveien 15* ✉ *0178 –* ☎ *21 60 01 01*   Plan: **D1**
– www.restaurant-kontrast.no – Closed 20 December-6 January, 9-
19 April, 24 July-10 August, Sunday and Monday
Menu 745 NOK – Carte 420/565 NOK – *(dinner only)*
• **Scandinavian** • **Design** • **Fashionable** •
A modern restaurant with a stark, semi-industrial feel created by the concrete
floor, exposed pipework and open kitchen. Seasonal, organic Norwegian produce is used to create refined, original, full-flavoured dishes whose apparent
simplicity often masks their complex nature. Service is well-paced and professional.
→ Scallop with roe emulsion and nasturtium leaves. Smoked lamb with
carrot and kale. Salted caramel, chocolate and sweetcorn.

XX **Festningen**   88 < 斎 & AK 4⁄ ⇔
Myntgata 9 ✉ *0151 –* ☎ *22 83 31 00*   Plan: **C3**
– www.festningenrestaurant.no – Closed 19 December-6 January except
dinner 31 December, 1 week Easter and Sunday
Menu 315/595 NOK – Carte dinner 630/725 NOK
• **Modern** • **Brasserie** • **Fashionable** •
A smart, contemporary brasserie with a terrace and lovely views over the water
to Aker Brygge; it was once a prison and its name means 'fortress'. The experienced kitchen create unfussy and attractively presented modern Nordic dishes
using fresh local produce. The impressive wine list is strong on Burgundy.

XX **Fru K** – Thief Hotel   & AK 🖤
Landgangen 1 ✉ *0252*   Plan: **B3**
– ☎ *24 00 40 40 – www.thethief.com*
– Closed 28 June-24 August, Christmas and Sunday
Menu 895/1095 NOK – *(dinner only) (set menu only)*
• **Modern** • **Design** • **Fashionable** •
Chic hotel restaurant, named after Fru Krogh who tended animals on the Tjuvholmen peninsula long ago. Set 5 and 7 course menus use fine Norwegian
ingredients to create tasty modern dishes. Rooftop 'Foodbar' in summer with
pleasant views.

XX **restauranteik** – Clarion Collection H. Savoy   🅰🅲 ⟷

Universitetsgata 11 ⊠ 0164 – Ⓜ *National Theatret*   Plan: **C2**
– 𝒞 22 36 07 10 – www.restauranteik.no – Closed July, Easter, Christmas,
Sunday and Monday
Menu 395 NOK – *(dinner only) (set menu only)*
• Modern • Fashionable • Brasserie •

A contemporary L-shaped dining room in a hotel close to the National Gallery.
Minimalist in style, it features colourful artwork, an open kitchen and a glass-
walled wine cellar. Modern, weekly changing 3-5 course set menu of inventive
international cuisine; efficient service and a friendly atmosphere.

XX **Ekeberg**   🍴 ⟷ 🅿

Kongsveien 15 (Southeast: 1 km by Rostockergata, Bispegata amd
Geitabru) ⊠ 0193 – 𝒞 23 24 23 00 – www.ekebergrestauranten.com
– Closed Easter and Christmas
Menu 350/470 NOK – Carte 464/649 NOK
• Fish and seafood • Retro • Design •

A delightfully restored art deco house on the hillside, with charming original fittings, several large terraces and commanding views over the fjords and the city.
Cooking is careful, fresh and seasonal; seafood features highly.

XX **Gamle Raadhus**   🍴

Nedre Slottsgate 1 ⊠ 0157 – Ⓜ *Stortinget*   Plan: **C3**
– 𝒞 22 42 01 07 – www.gamle-raadhus.no – Closed 3 weeks July,
22 December-3 January, Easter and Sunday
Menu 469 NOK (dinner) – Carte 481/725 NOK
• Traditional • Rustic •

Brightly painted house dating from 1641; its charming, antique-filled interior
includes a library and an open-fired lounge. Lunch is served in the bar and classical dinners in the traditional dining room. There's also a lovely terrace.

XX **Fjord**   🅰🅲

Kristian Augusts Gt. 11 ⊠ 0164 – Ⓜ *National Theatret*   Plan: **C2**
– 𝒞 22 98 21 50 – www.restaurantfjord.no – Closed 4 weeks summer,
Christmas, Easter, Sunday and Monday
Menu 445/695 NOK – *(dinner only) (booking essential) (set menu only)*
• Fish and seafood • Design • Fashionable •

A contemporary restaurant opposite the National Gallery. Inside it's dimly lit,
with an open kitchen, unusual cobalt blue walls and buffalo horns set into the
chandeliers. The 3-5 course menu offers flavoursome fish and seafood dishes.

XX **Dinner**   🅰🅲 ⟷

Stortingsgata 22 ⊠ 0161 – Ⓜ *National Theatret*   Plan: **C2**
– 𝒞 23 10 04 66 – www.dinner.no – Closed Christmas, Easter and lunch
Sunday
Menu 248/499 NOK – Carte 445/917 NOK
• Chinese • Design • Elegant •

An intimate restaurant on the central square, close to the National Theatre. A
black frosted-glass façade masks a smart split-level interior. The kitchen focuses
on Sichuan cuisine, with some artfully presented dim sum at lunch.

XX **Onda**   ≤ 🍴 & 🅰🅲 ⟷ ⟷

Stranden 30 ⊠ 0250 – 𝒞 45 50 20 00 – www.onda.no   Plan: **B3**
– Closed Christmas
Menu 349/495 NOK – Carte 573/743 NOK
• Fish and seafood • Fashionable • Design •

Stylish restaurant in an eye-catching sea shell shaped building with a fabulous
terrace and harbour views. Beautifully fresh, simply prepared seafood from local
waters. There's also a small grill restaurant with its own menu (dinner only).

XX **Nodee** 🛱 🗚 🔄
Middelthunsgt 25 ⊠ 0368 – Ⓜ *Majorstuen* Plan: **A1**
*– ℰ 22 93 34 50 – www.nodee.no – Closed Christmas, Easter and lunch
Sunday*
Menu 325/495 NOK – Carte 340/530 NOK
• **Asian** • **Fashionable** • **Trendy** •
A smart, modern restaurant, which is the sister to 'Dinner'. The extensive menu
mixes Chinese, Japanese and Thai dishes; staff are knowledgeable and they also
offer a take away service. The restaurant will be moving premises during 2016.

XX **Tjuvholmen Sjømagasin** 🕸 🛱 🔄
Tjuvholmen Allé 14 ⊠ 0252 – ℰ 23 89 77 77 Plan: **B3**
*– www.sjomagasinet.no – Closed Christmas, Easter, Sunday and bank
holidays*
Menu 355/645 NOK – Carte 565/735 NOK
• **Fish and seafood** • **Design** • **Brasserie** •
Vast restaurant with three dining rooms, a crab and lobster tank, a superb terrace and a wet fish shop. Its name means 'sea store' and menus are fittingly seafood based. Shellfish is from the nearby dock – the langoustines are fantastic.

XX **Mares** 🗚
Skovveien 1 ⊠ 0257 – ℰ 22 54 89 80 – www.mares.no Plan: **A2**
*– Closed 3 July-3 August, 23 December-3 January, 23-29 March and
Sunday*
Menu 495 NOK – Carte 515/665 NOK – *(dinner only) (booking advisable)*
• **French** • **Neighbourhood** • **Brasserie** •
Neighbourhood restaurant with an adjoining deli and fish shop; it's bright and
modern, with white furniture and a slightly industrial feel. Classical French
menus have Spanish and Italian touches; order the fruits de mer 24hrs ahead.

XX **Hos Thea**
Gabelsgate 11 ⊠ 0272 – ℰ 22 44 68 74 Plan: **A2**
– www.hosthea.no – Closed July, Easter and Christmas
Menu 515 NOK – Carte 625/680 NOK – *(dinner only)*
• **Italian** • **Family** • **Neighbourhood** •
A small, well-established restaurant in a charming residential area. It's decorated
in natural hues and hung with beautiful oils. Menus offer a concise selection of
Mediterranean dishes; start with the delicious homemade bread.

XX **Plah** 🛱 🗚 🔄
Hegdehaugsveien 22 ⊠ 0167 Plan: **B1**
– ℰ 22 56 43 00 – www.plah.no
– Closed 2 weeks July, Christmas, Easter, and Sunday
Menu 595/685 NOK – Carte 495/665 NOK – *(dinner only)*
• **Thai** • **Neighbourhood** • **Friendly** •
Well-run restaurant offering tasty Thai dishes; Plah means 'fish' and the produce
is from local waters. The tasting and wine menus are good value; service is
friendly and knowledgeable. Their next door bar serves authentic street food.

XX **Theatercaféen** – Continental Hotel 🕸 丞 🗚 🔄
Stortingsgaten 24-26 ⊠ 0117 – Ⓜ *National Theatret* Plan: **C2**
– ℰ 22 82 40 50 – www.theatercaféen.no
– Closed 6 July-2 August and 24 December-2 January
Menu 655 NOK – Carte 489/700 NOK
• **Traditional** • **Luxury** • **Romantic** •
A prestigious Oslo institution in a grand hotel, this charming Viennese 'grand
café' comes with pillars, black banquettes and art nouveau lighting. Elaborate
lunchtime sandwiches and fresh cakes make way for ambitious dinners.

XX **Havsmak**   🅰 🔲 ⇦

Henrik Ibsens gate 4 ⊠ 0255 – 🅜 National Theatret   Plan: **B2**
– 🕿 24 13 38 00 – www.havsmak.no – Closed Easter, 4 July-
4 August, 21 December-5 January and Sunday
Menu 495 NOK – Carte 420/599 NOK
• **Fish and seafood** • **Elegant** • **Romantic** •
A smart, professionally run restaurant close to the Henrik Ibsen Museum, with a
vast seafaring mosaic on one wall. Fish and seafood based menus keep fresh
local salmon and langoustines to the fore; be sure to try the rich fish soup.

XX **Brasserie Paleo** – Hotel Rosenkrantz   🅰 🔲 ⇦

Rosenkrantz gate 1 ⊠ 0159 – 🅜 National Theatrer   Plan: **C2**
– 🕿 23 31 55 80 – www.brasseriepaleo.no
Menu 495/645 NOK – Carte 535/645 NOK
• **Scandinavian** • **Trendy** • **Trendy** •
With a name which reflects its philosophy, and a contemporary urban style, this
is not your typical hotel restaurant. Watch the chefs prepare attractive modern
Scandinavian dishes in the open kitchen. Service is professional and friendly.

X **Brasserie Blanche**   🖼 🔲 ⇦

Josefenisgate 23 ⊠ 0351 – 🕿 23 20 13 10   Plan: **B1**
– www.blanche.no – Closed 2 weeks July, 23-25 December and Monday
Menu 495/525 NOK – Carte 340/630 NOK – *(dinner only)*
• **French** • **Cosy** • **Brasserie** •
Cosy French restaurant housed in an 18C building which was originally a stable
and later spent time as a garage and then an interior furnishings store. It has a
small front terrace, a bar decorated with wine boxes and a wall made of corks.
The Francophile chef creates flavoursome classic French dishes.

X **Vaaghals**   🖼 🔲 ⇦

Dronning Eufemias gate 8 ⊠ 0151 Oslo   Plan: **D3**
– 🅜 Jernbanetorget – 🕿 92 07 09 99 – www.vaaghals.com – Closed 3 last
weeks July, 22 December-3 January, Easter and Sundays
Menu 590 NOK (dinner) – Carte 425/595 NOK
• **Scandinavian** • **Brasserie** •
A bright, contemporary restaurant with an open kitchen and a terrace, located
on the ground floor of one of the modern 'barcode' buildings near the Opera
House. Scandinavian menus feature dry aged meat and many dishes designed
for sharing.

X **Statholderens Mat og Vin Kjeller** – Statholdergaarden

Rådhusgate 11 (entrance from Kirkegata) ⊠ 0151   Plan: **C3**
– 🅜 Stortinget – 🕿 22 41 88 00 – www.statholdergaarden.no
– Closed 9 July-7 August, 23 December-3 January, 19-28 March, 1, 5 and
14-17 May, Sunday and Monday
Menu 695 NOK – Carte 660/680 NOK – *(dinner only) (booking essential)*
• **Norwegian** • **Rustic** • **Simple** •
The informal sister of Statholdergaarden – set over three rooms in the old vaults
beneath it. One wall of the large entranceway is filled with wine bottles. Choose
from a huge array of small plates or go for the 10 course tasting menu.

X **Brasserie Hansken**   ⇦

Akersgate 2 ⊠ 0158 – 🅜 Stortinget – 🕿 22 42 60 88   Plan: **C2**
– www.brasseriehansken.no – Closed 3 weeks late July-early August,
1 week Easter, 1 week Christmas and Sunday
Menu 495/595 NOK – Carte 435/645 NOK
• **Modern** • **Family** • **Brasserie** •
A delightfully traditional brasserie, centrally located by City Hall, with various
charming dining areas and a fantastic terrace. Classical cooking follows the seasons and mixes French and Scandic influences; ingredients are top quality.

X   ⅏

Cru
Ingelbrecht, Knudsønsgt 1 ✉ *0365 –* ℰ *23 98 98 98*   Plan: **B1**
– www.cru.no – Closed July, 23 December-5 January and Sunday
Menu 485 NOK – Carte 320/420 NOK – *(dinner only)*
• **Norwegian** • **Wine bar** • **Trendy** •
A trendy, informal and well run wine bar which offers two choices: a tapas menu is served in the charming open-fired basement, while a set 3, 5 or 7 course menu of seasonal Scandinavian dishes is served upstairs in the rustic restaurant.

X   🅰🄲 ⇄

Arakataka
Mariboes gate 7 ✉ *0183 –* Ⓜ *Stortinget*   Plan: **D2**
– ℰ *23 32 83 00 – www.arakataka.no – Closed July, Christmas-New Year and Easter*
Menu 495 NOK – Carte 470/675 NOK – *(dinner only) (booking advisable)*
• **Norwegian** • **Fashionable** • **Friendly** •
A smart glass-fronted restaurant with a central food bar, an open kitchen and a buzzy atmosphere. Choose from a concise menu of seasonal Norwegian small plates – they recommend 3 savoury dishes plus a dessert per person.

X   ≤ 🍴 ⇄

Lofoten Fiskerestaurant
Stranden 75 ✉ *0250 –* ℰ *22 83 08 08*   Plan: **B3**
– www.lofotenfiskerestaurant.no – Closed Christmas
Menu 535 NOK (dinner) – Carte 413/695 NOK
• **Fish and seafood** • **Brasserie** • **Simple** •
Traditional fjord-side restaurant decorated in bright maritime colours and offering lovely views from its large windows and charming terrace. Watch as fresh, simply cooked fish and shellfish are prepared in the semi-open kitchen.

X   🍴

Alex Sushi Tjuvholmen
Strandpromenaden 11 ✉ *0252 –* ℰ *2243 99 99*   Plan: **B3**
– www.alexsushi.no – Closed Easter, Christmas and Sunday
Menu 485/950 NOK – Carte lunch 320/425 NOK
• **Sushi** • **Simple** • **Neighbourhood** •
Set in a fantastic harbourside spot, with a great terrace. The skilful, knowledgeable chefs are surrounded by large scuba diver models. Sushi, sashimi and nigiri feature at lunch, followed by 3 set menus at dinner. The tuna is superb.

X   ⇄
🐼

Smalhans
Waldemar Thranes gate 10A ✉ *0171 –* ℰ *22 69 60 00*   Plan: **C1**
– www.smalhans.no – Closed 3 weeks July, Easter, Christmas and Monday
Menu 415 NOK (dinner) – Carte lunch 310/380 NOK
• **Traditional** • **Neighbourhood** • **Simple** •
A sweet neighbourhood café with friendly staff and an urban feel. Coffee and homemade cakes are served in the morning, with a short selection of dishes including soup and a burger on offer between 12pm and 4pm. A daily hot dish is available from 4-6pm, while set menus and sharing plates are served at dinner.

X   🍴 🅰🄲 ⇄

Brasserie France
Øvre Slottsgate 16 ✉ *0157 –* Ⓜ *Stortinget*   Plan: **C2**
– ℰ *23 10 01 65 – www.brasseriefrance.no – Closed 23 December-4 January and Sunday*
Menu 375 NOK – Carte 455/635 NOK – *(dinner only and light lunch Saturday)*
• **French** • **Brasserie** • **Traditional** •
A lively Gallic brasserie in a pedestrianised shopping street, with several private dining rooms above. Brasserie classics from steak frites to bouillabaisse feature; for dessert, choose from the 'eat-as-much-as-you-like' pastry trolley.

X   ⇄

Alex Sushi
Cort Adelers Gate 2 ✉ *0254 –* Ⓜ *National Theatret*   Plan: **B2**
– ℰ *22 43 99 99 – www.alexsushi.no – Closed July, Easter and Christmas*
Menu 485 NOK – Carte 550/745 NOK – *(dinner only)*
• **Japanese** • **Design** • **Minimalist** •
A glass-fronted Japanese restaurant and takeaway, with a bright interior made of wood, steel and glass. Sit at the boat-shaped sushi bar to try top quality local sashimi. Half of customers have the set menus, which offer the best value.

ENVIRONS OF OSLO

AT GREFSEN North : 10 km by Ring 3

XX **Grefsenkollen**

Grefsenkollveien 100 ⌧ 0490 – ℰ 22 79 70 60 – www.grefsenkollen.no
– Closed July, Easter, Christmas and dinner Sunday-Monday
Menu 620/845 NOK (dinner) – Carte lunch 360/550 NOK – *(booking essential at dinner)*
• Norwegian • Romantic • Cosy •
A fairytale chalet in the mountains, with a spacious terrace, a characterful open-fired dining room and lovely views over the city and fjord. Appealing 3 and 5 course dinner menus are well-balanced, intricate and playful – Norwegian ingredients take centre stage. Lunch is light; dinner offers wine pairings.

AT OSLO AIRPORT Northeast : 45 km by E 6 at Gardermoen

filel **Clarion Oslo Airport**

Hans Gaarderveg 15 (West: 6 km) ⌧ 2060 – ℰ 63 94 94 94
– www.clarionosloairport.no
432 rm ⌧ – †652/1350 NOK ††852/1550 NOK
• Business • Functional • Classic •
Typical two-storey Norwegian house, accessed from the airport by a shuttle bus; it has one of the largest conference capacities in the country. Modern Scandinavian bedrooms come in pale hues. Live music features in the bar and open-fired lounges, and buffet meals are served in the traditional restaurant.

AT HOLMENKOLLEN Northwest : 10 km by Bogstadveien, Sørkedalsveien and Holmenkollveien

filel **Holmenkollen Park**

Kongeveien 26 ⌧ 0787 – ⓜ Holmenkollen – ℰ 22 92 20 00
– www.holmenkollenparkhotel.no – Closed 21 December-2 January
336 rm ⌧ – †750/1740 NOK ††990/1990 NOK
• Traditional • Personalised • Alpine •
Impressive 1894 red building (once a sanatorium for TB patients!), located beside a world-class ski resort. The interior displays a curious mix of styles, from the classical to the modern; three of the bedrooms have their own saunas.
De Fem Stuer – See restaurant listing

XxX **De Fem Stuer** – Holmenkollen Park Hotel

Kongeveien 26 ⌧ 0787 – ⓜ Holmenkollen – ℰ 22 92 27 34
– www.holmenkollenparkhotel.no – Closed 21 December-2 January
Menu 325/395 NOK – Carte 655/885 NOK
• Norwegian • Elegant • Romantic •
A series of five elegant dining rooms in an impressive hotel; three with delightful 20C panelling. A buffet lunch is followed by a concise, seasonal à la carte and a daily set menu. Cooking is classical and displays French influences.

AT STABEKK Southwest : 9 km by E18

XX **Strand**

Strandalleén 48 ⌧ 1368 – ℰ 67 53 05 75 – www.strandrestaurant.no
– Closed Chrismas, Easter and Monday
Menu 395/795 NOK – Carte 485/600 NOK
• Scandinavian • Traditional •
18C wooden house with a bakery and café, set in a quiet seaside town. The restaurant is bright and contemporary with an open kitchen and a terrace affording views out over the marina. Classic Scandinavian cooking uses organic produce.

POLAND
POLSKA

WARSAW ●

● Cracow

→ **AREA:**
312 677 km² (120 725 sq mi).

→ **POPULATION:**
38 440 163 inhabitants. Density = 123 per km².

→ **CAPITAL:**
Warsaw.

→ **CURRENCY:**
Polish Złoty (zl or PLN).

→ **GOVERNMENT:**
Parliamentary republic (since 1990). Member of European Union since 2004.

→ **LANGUAGE:**
Polish.

→ **PUBLIC HOLIDAYS:**
New Year's Day (1 Jan); Easter Monday (late Mar/Apr); Labor Day (1 May); Constitution Day (3 May); Pentecost Monday (late May/June); Corpus Christi (late May/June); Assumption of the Virgin Mary (15 Aug); All Saints' Day (1 Nov); Independence Day (11 Nov); Christmas Day (25 Dec); Boxing Day (26 Dec).

→ **LOCAL TIME:**
GMT+1 hour in winter and GMT +2 hours in summer.

→ **CLIMATE:**
Temperate continental with cold winters and warm summers (Warsaw: January -2°C; July 20°C).

→ **EMERGENCY:**
Police ℰ **997**;
Medical Assistance ℰ **999**;
Fire Brigade ℰ **998**.
(Dialling **112** within any EU country will redirect your call and contact the emergency services.)

→ **ELECTRICITY:**
230 volts AC, 50Hz; 2 round pin sockets.

→ **FORMALITIES:**
Travellers from the European Union (EU), Switzerland, Iceland and the main countries of North and South America need a national identity card or passport (America: passport required) to visit Poland for less than three months (tourism or business purpose). For visitors from other countries a visa may be required, in addition to a passport, especially for those wishing to stay for longer than three months. We advise you to check with your embassy before travelling.

WARSAW
WARSZAWA

Population: 1 714 400

Céline Lecardonnel/Fotolia.com

When UNESCO added Warsaw to its World Heritage list, it was a fitting seal of approval for its inspired rebuild, after eighty per cent of the city was destroyed during World War II. Using plans of the old city, architects painstakingly rebuilt the shattered capital throughout the 1950s, until it became an admirable mirror image of its former self. Now grey communist era apartment blocks sit beside pretty, pastel-coloured aristocratic buildings, their architecture ranging from Gothic to baroque, rococo to secession.

Nestling against the River Vistula, the Old Town was established at the end of the 13C, around what is now the Royal Castle, and a century later the New Town, to the north, began to take shape. To the south of the Old Town runs 'The Royal Route', so named because, from the late middle ages, wealthy citizens built summer residences with lush gardens along these rural thoroughfares. Continue southwards and you're in Lazienki Park with its palaces and pavilions, while to the west lie the more commercial areas of Marshal Street and Solidarity Avenue, once the commercial heart of the city. The northwest of Warsaw was traditionally the Jewish district, until it was destroyed during the war; today it has been redeveloped with housing estates and the sobering Monument to the Ghetto Heroes.

WARSAW IN...

→ **ONE DAY**
Royal Castle, Warsaw History Museum, National Museum, Lazienki Park.

→ **TWO DAYS**
Monument to the Ghetto Heroes, Saxon Gardens, concert at Grand Theatre or Philharmonic Hall.

→ **THREE DAYS**
The Royal Route, Marshal Street, Solidarity Avenue, Wilanow.

PRACTICAL INFORMATION

ARRIVAL-DEPARTURE

✈ Warsaw Frederic Chopin Airport is 10km southwest. Bus 175 or 188 takes 20min. Trains run every 10-12min and take 25min. If travelling by taxi, ensure you take one from the rank outside arrivals.

✈ Warsaw Modlin Airport is 40km northwest. Modlinbus operate a regular service to the Central Station that takes 60min.

GETTING AROUND

If you are visiting the central attractions, go on foot; otherwise, hire a City Bike, take the metro, bus or tram. The RUCH kiosks are often closed in the evenings and at weekends, so it's best to buy tickets in a pack of ten. A flat rate fare for all single journeys applies, and one-day, seven-day and family tickets are also available. The Warsaw Tourist Card is available from tourist information offices; it entitles you to free travel on public transport, free admission to 21 museums, and discounts in some shops, restaurants and leisure centres. (All museums offer free entry on a Sunday.)

CALENDAR HIGHLIGHTS

March-April
Beethoven Easter Festival.

May-September
Chopin concerts in Lazienki Park.

June-July
Mozart Festival.

July-August
Summer Jazz Days.

October
International Film Festival (WIFF), Baroque Opera Festival, Jazz Festival.

November
Piano Festival, Jazz Jamboree.

EATING OUT

The centuries-old traditional cuisine of Warsaw was influenced by neighbouring Russia, Ukraine and Germany, while Jewish dishes were also added to the mix. Over the years there has been a growing sophistication to the cooking and a lighter, more contemporary style has become evident, with time-honoured classics - such as the ubiquitous pierogi (dumplings with various fillings) and the ever-popular breaded pork dish 'bigos' - having been updated with flair. These are accompanied, of course, by chilled Polish vodka, which covers a bewildering range of styles. Warsaw also has a more global side, with everything from stalls selling falafel to restaurants serving Vietnamese, and a large Italian business community has ensured there are a good number of Italian restaurants too. Stylised settings are popular, such as a burghers' houses or vaulted cellars; wherever you eat, check that VAT has been included within the prices (it's not always) and add a ten per cent tip. If it's value for money you're after, head for a Milk Bar, a low priced cafeteria selling traditional dairy-based food.

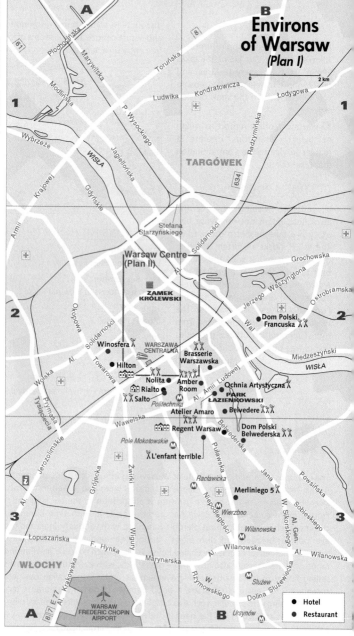

Environs of Warsaw
(Plan I)

0   2 km

TARGÓWEK

Warsaw Centre
(Plan II)

ZAMEK
KRÓLEWSKI

WISŁA

Winosfera

WARSZAWA
CENTRALNA

Brasserie
Warszawska

Dom Polski
Francuska

Hilton

Nolita

Amber
Room

Ochnia Artystyczna

Rialto

PARK
ŁAZIENKOWSKI

Salto

Politechnika

Atelier Amaro

Belvedere

Regent Warsaw

Dom Polski
Belwederska

L'enfant terrible

Racławicka

Merliniego 5

Wierzbno

Wilanowska

WŁOCHY

Służew

Ursynów

● Hotel
● Restaurant

WARSAW
FREDERIC CHOPIN
AIRPORT

POLAND - WARSAW

Intercontinental

ul. Emilii Plater 49 ✉ *00 125* – Ⓜ *Centrum* – ✆ *(022)*   Plan: **C2**
328 8888 – *www.warsaw.intercontinental.com*
414 rm ⚏ – ♦330/1925 PLN ♦♦375/1965 PLN – 21 suites
• Grand Luxury • Business • Modern •
Striking high-rise hotel in a central location. Smart guest areas include a modern lounge and a clubby bar; bedrooms are large and contemporary. The impressive health and leisure club on the 43rd and 44th floors boasts fantastic views. Informal buffet lunches in Downtown, with steaks a speciality in the evening; refined modern cooking in Platter.
Platter by Karol Okrasa – See restaurant listing

Hotel Bristol

ul. Krakowskie Przedmiescie 42-44 ✉ *00 325* – ✆ *(022)*   Plan: **D1**
551 10 00 – *www.hotelbristolwarsaw.pl*
206 rm ⚏ – ♦530/2330 PLN ♦♦635/2440 PLN – 38 suites
• Grand Luxury • Historic • Classic •
Built in 1901 and set next to the Presidential Palace, this grand, art deco hotel boasts an elegant marble-floored reception and an impressive columned bar. Luxurious bedrooms have a high level of facilities. Unwind in the wine bar or on the terrace. The smart restaurant offers a modern Polish menu.

Regent Warsaw

ul. Belwederska 23 ✉ *00 761* – ✆ *(022) 558 12 34*   Plan I: **B3**
– *www.regent-warsaw.com*
246 rm – ♦297/907 PLN ♦♦362/972 PLN – ⚏ 92 PLN – 19 suites
• Luxury • Business • Modern •
Contemporary hotel close to a large park, featuring an impressive open-plan lobby and a glass-roofed lounge-bar. Spacious bedrooms boast top quality furniture, smart bathrooms and a host of cleverly concealed facilities. Split-level Venti Tre offers an extensive Mediterranean menu and wood-fired specialities.

Hilton

ul. Grzybowska 63 ✉ *00 844* – ✆ *(022) 356 55 55*   Plan I: **A2**
– *www.hilton.com*
314 rm – ♦269/1619 PLN ♦♦269/1619 PLN – ⚏ 95 PLN – 10 suites
• Business • Chain hotel • Modern •
Large, corporate hotel in the 'new' business district. The bright atrium houses shops and a lounge-bar; extensive business and leisure facilities include a smart club lounge, a casino and the city's largest event space. Bedrooms are contemporary and well-equipped. Informal dining from an international menu.

Sheraton

ul. Boleslawa Prusa 2 ✉ *00 493* – ✆ *(022) 450 6100*   Plan: **D2**
– *www.sheraton.pl*
350 rm – ♦346/1458 PLN ♦♦346/1458 PLN – ⚏ 107 PLN – 15 suites
• Luxury • Business • Classic •
Spacious hotel on the historic Three Cross Square, with a large open-plan lobby, a smart ballroom, and good conference and leisure facilities. Bedrooms are well-equipped; the top floor Club Rooms are the most contemporary. InAzia offers dishes from China, Thailand, Indonesia, Singapore and Vietnam.

Sofitel Warsaw Victoria

ul. Królewska 11 ✉ *00 065* – Ⓜ *Świętokrzyska*   Plan: **C1**
– ✆ *(022) 657 80 11* – *www.sofitel-victoria-warsaw.com*
343 rm – ♦330/1225 PLN ♦♦330/1525 PLN – ⚏ 95 PLN – 53 suites
• Business • Contemporary • Stylish •
Smartly refurbished hotel by Pilsudski Square, overlooking the Saxon Gardens. Unwind in the lovely spa or reflective-ceilinged pool. Contemporary guest areas pay homage to the 1970s with geometric designs, and bedrooms are bold, sleek and well-equipped. The delightful brasserie mixes Polish and French cuisine.

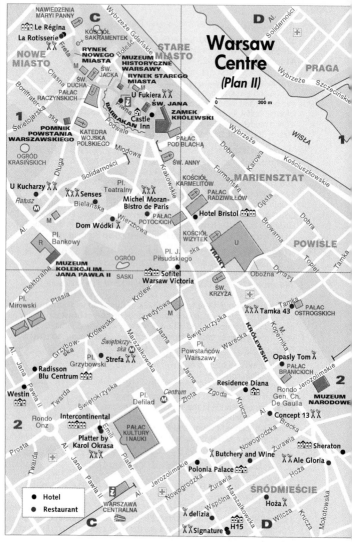

POLAND - WARSAW

NAWIEDZENIA
MARYI PANNY

Le Régina
La Rotisserie

NOWE
MIASTO

KOŚCIÓŁ
SAKRAMENTEK

Wybrzeże Gdańskie

C

RYNEK
NOWEGO
MIASTA

ŚW.
JACKA

SW.
DUCHA
Freta

PAŁAC
RACZYŃSKICH

Clasna

Bonifraterska

Bielska

Świętojerska

POMNIK
POWSTANIA
WARSZAWSKIEGO

OGRÓD
KRASIŃSKICH

Długa

STARE
MIASTO

MUZEUM
HISTORYCZNE
WARSZAWY

RYNEK STAREGO
MIASTA

U Fukiera
ŚW. JANA

BARBAKAN

Piwna

Castle
Inn

Podwale

KATEDRA
WOJSKA
POLSKIEGO

Miodowa

ZAMEK
KRÓLEWSKI

PAŁAC
POD BLACHĄ

ŚW. ANNY

Krakowskie

D

Al. Solidarności

Warsaw
Centre
(Plan II)

0   300 m

Wybrzeże

WISŁA

PRAGA

Szczecińskie

1

Solidarności

U Kucharzy
Ratusz
M

Senses
Bielańska

Pl.
Teatralny

Michel Moran-
Bistro de Paris

Dom Wódki

Wierzbowa

KOŚCIÓŁ
KARMELITÓW

PAŁAC
RADZIWIŁŁÓW

PAŁAC
POTOCKICH

Hotel Bristol

Furmańska

MARIENSZTAT

Karowa

Gęsta

Dobra

Browarna

Kościuszkowskie

POWIŚLE

Elektoralna

M

Pl.
Bankowy

R

MUZEUM
KOLEKCJI IM.
JANA PAWŁA II

OGRÓD
SASKI

Pl. J.
Piłsudskiego

KOŚCIÓŁ
WIZYTEK

ska

U

Sofitel
Warsaw Victoria

TRAKT

Oboźna

Dynasy

Topiel

Tamka

Pl.
Mirowski

Ptasia

Elektoralna

ŚW.
KRZYŻA

ŚW.
KRZYŻA

Tamka 43
PAŁAC
OSTROGSKICH

Al. Jana Pawła II

Grzybow-
ska

Radisson
Blu Centrum

Westin

2
Rondo
Onz

Prosta

Twarda

Intercontinental

Platter by
Karol Okrasa

Królewska

Świętokrzy-
ska
M

Pl.
Grzybowski

Strefa

Świętokrzyska

Twarda

Świętokrzyska

Pl.
Defilad

PAŁAC
KULTURY
I NAUKI

Emilii Plater

Jana Pawła II

Marszałkowska

Kredytowa

Jasna

Jasna

Centrum
M

Złota

Zgoda

Pl.
Powstańców
Warszawy

Warecka

KRÓLEWSKA

Kopernika

Opasly Tom
PAŁAC
BRANICKICH

Residence Diana

Rondo
Gen. Ch.
De Gaulla

Concept 13

Jerozolimskie

Krucza

2

MUZEUM
NARODOWE

Hotel
Restaurant

WARSZAWA
CENTRALNA

C

Jerozolimskie

Nowogrodzka

Butchery and Wine

Polonia Palace

Żurawia

Marszałkowska

Żurawia

Nowogrodzka

Wspólna

delizia

Signature

H15

Bracka

Nowogrodzka

Ale Gloria

Sheraton

Hoża

ŚRÓDMIEŚCIE

Hoża

Wilcza

Krucza

Mokotowska

D

624

POLAND - WARSAW

 Le Régina 　　　　　　　　　　　☆ 🐜 ⅋ 🕹 ↝ 🖧

ul. Koscielna 12 ✉ 00 218 – ☎ (022) 531 60 00 　　　Plan: **C1**
– www.mamaison.com/leregina
61 rm – ♦378/1134 PLN ♦♦378/1134 PLN – ⬛ 115 PLN – 2 suites
• Luxury • Family • Design •
Charming boutique hotel housed in a neo-18C building, on a peaceful cobbled
street close to the castle and Old Town. The décor is cool and understated, with
a Mediterranean feel. Subtle design features include room numbers projected
onto the floor and hand-painted frescoes on the bedheads. Friendly service.
La Rotisserie – See restaurant listing

 Polonia Palace 　　　　　　　　　☆ 🛁 🐜 ⅋ 🕹 ↝ 🖧

al. Jerozolimskie 45 ✉ 00 692 – Ⓜ Centrum – ☎ (022) 　　Plan: **D2**
318 2800 – www.poloniapalace.com
206 rm – ♦260/915 PLN ♦♦260/915 PLN – ⬛ 80 PLN – 3 suites
• Business • Family • Contemporary •
Striking hotel dating from 1913, on a busy central street. The elegant interior
has a lovely glass-roofed lobby, a popular lounge-bar and a beautifully ornate
gilded ballroom. Modern, well-equipped bedrooms come in browns and
creams. Formal Strauss offers a large menu of Polish and European cuisine.

 Westin 　　　　　　　　　☆ ≼ 🛁 🐜 ⅋ 🕹 ↝ 🖧 🚗

al. Jana Pawla II 21 ✉ 00 854 – Ⓜ Świętokrzyska 　　Plan: **C2**
– ☎ (022) 450 80 00 – www.westin.pl
361 rm – ♦205/1458 PLN ♦♦205/1458 PLN – ⬛ 107 PLN – 15 suites
• Luxury • Business • Modern •
Eye-catching modern building on a busy street, featuring an impressive glass
atrium with glass lifts. Smart, contemporary bedrooms have good facilities; the
top floor Club Rooms are the best. There's a wide choice of conference and
events rooms. Worldwide ingredients meet Eastern recipes in the restaurant.

 Radisson Blu Centrum 　　　☆ 🛁 🐜 ⃞ ⅋ 🕹 ↝ 🖧 🚗

ul. Grzybowska 24 ✉ 00 132 – Ⓜ Świętokrzyska 　　Plan: **C2**
– ☎ (022) 321 88 88 – www.radissonblu.com/hotel-warsaw
311 rm ⬛ – ♦270/1080 PLN ♦♦292/1080 PLN – 18 suites
• Business • Modern • Stylish •
Glass-fronted hotel in the business district, boasting state-of-the-art conference
facilities and a well-equipped leisure centre. Smart bedrooms come in a choice
of 'Maritime', 'Scandinavian' or 'Italian' themes. The all-day brasserie offers
modern interpretations of Polish and Mediterranean dishes.

 H15 　　　　　　　　　　　　　☆ ⅋ 🕹 🖧 🚗

ul. Poznańska 15 ✉ 00 680 – Ⓜ Politechnika – ☎ (022) 　　Plan: **D2**
553 87 00 – www.h15ab.com
46 rm – ♦280/750 PLN ♦♦300/800 PLN – ⬛ 65 PLN – 30 suites
• Townhouse • Luxury • Contemporary •
Extended townhouse built around a glass quadrangle; once the Russian
Embassy and later occupied by the Germans during WWII. Most bedrooms are
spacious, bespoke-furnished suites with small kitchenettes and marble-floored
bathrooms.
Signature – See restaurant listing

 Rialto 　　　　　　　　　☆ 🛁 🐜 ⅋ 🕹 ↝ 🖧 🅿

ul. Wilcza 73 ✉ 00 670 – Ⓜ Politechnika – ☎ (022) 　　Plan I: **A2**
584 87 00 – www.rialto.pl
44 rm – ♦280/950 PLN ♦♦300/1090 PLN – ⬛ 80 PLN – 11 suites
• Business • Townhouse • Art Deco •
This delightfully converted townhouse dates back to 1906 and its sympathetically refurbished interior still boasts original art deco and art nouveau features.
Elegant bedrooms come with a host of facilities and boast beautiful marble-
floored bathrooms. There's also a smart bar, a small gym and a sauna.
Salto – See restaurant listing

Residence Diana   ⇧ 🅰🄺 ↳

ul Chmielna 13a ✉ *00 021* – Ⓜ *Centrum* – ✆ *(022)*   Plan: **D2**
505 9100 – *www.mamaison.com*
46 rm – ♦286/362 PLN ♦♦286/362 PLN – ⊆ 56 PLN – 8 suites
• Townhouse • Business • Cosy •

Set in a quiet courtyard off a busy central shopping street, with a spacious lounge and a smart bar furnished in black wood. Large, modern bedrooms have small kitchen areas and good facilities; some are duplex or have jacuzzis. The rustic Italian restaurant specialises in traditional Neapolitan pizzas.

Castle Inn   ≼ ↳

Plac Zamkowy, ul Swietojanska 2 ✉ *00 288* – ✆ *(022)*   Plan: **C1**
4250100 – *www.castleinn.pl*
22 rm – ♦180/350 PLN ♦♦200/650 PLN – ⊆ 35 PLN
• Family • Historic • Historic •

Small 16C property on a cobbled street in the heart of the Old Town, just a stone's throw from the castle. Bedrooms are unique – designed by local artists, they range from bohemian to contemporary and come with quirky touches.

XXXX Amber Room   🕸 ⇦ ♨ ↳ ⇔ 🅿

al Ujazdowskie 13 ✉ *00 567* – ✆ *(022) 523 66 64*   Plan I: **B2**
– *www.amberroom.pl* – *Closed Christmas-New Year, Easter and bank holidays*
Menu 79 PLN (lunch) – Carte 137/254 PLN
• Modern • Formal • Intimate •

Grand dining room in an attractive villa; home to the exclusive 'Round Table of Warsaw'. Modern cooking uses top ingredients and has original touches. Service is attentive and well-paced, and there's a great selection of Krug champagne.

XXX Atelier Amaro (Wojciech Amaro)   ♨ ⅋ 🅰🄺 ↳ 🅿
※

ul. Agrykola 1 ✉ *00 460* – ✆ *(022) 6285747*   Plan I: **B2**
– *www.atelieramaro.pl* – *Closed Easter, Christmas-New Year, 11-16 August,
1 and 11 November, Sunday and lunch Saturday-Tuesday*
Menu 145/320 PLN – *(booking essential)*
• Innovative • Design • Individual •

Chic restaurant with a delightful terrace overlooking the park. Highly original cooking uses carefully sourced and foraged ingredients and the concise menus give little away. Unusual combinations are inspired by the 'calendar of nature' and feature lots of herbs and wild flowers. The Polish spirits are a must.
→ Sterlet with green strawberries and mint. Pigeon, blackberry and sweet millet. Aubergine with blackcurrant and acorn.

XXX Senses   🅰🄺 ⇔
※

ul. Bielanska 12 ✉ *00 085* – Ⓜ *Ratusz* – ✆ *(022)*   Plan: **C1**
331 9697 – *www.sensesrestaurant.pl* – *Closed 2 weeks August,
23 December-7 January, Easter and Sunday*
Menu 170 PLN (weekdays)/370 PLN – *(dinner only) (booking essential) (set
menu only)*
• Innovative • Elegant • Romantic •

As with the historic building in which it is housed, this formal restaurant connects tradition with modernity. Of the 3 set menus, most opt for the 7 course dinner to best experience cooking that is innovative, creative and at times theatrical, but also underpinned by classic Polish flavours.
→ Duck with Jerusalem artichoke and onion. Pork and shellfish goulash. Chocolate, vanilla and quince.

XXX Belvedere   ♨ 🅰🄺 ↳ ⇔ 🅿

Lazienki Park, ul. Agrykoli 1 (entry from ul Parkowa)   Plan I: **B2**
✉ *00 460* – ✆ *(022) 55 86 700* – *www.belvedere.com.pl* – *Closed
23 December-1 January*
Menu 67 PLN (lunch) – Carte 108/195 PLN – *(booking essential)*
• Modern • Formal • Romantic •

Impressive Victorian orangery in Lazienki Park; large arched windows keep it light despite it being packed with shrubs and trees. Dishes are classic both in style and presentation. Smartly uniformed staff provide formal service.

XxX **Michel Moran - Bistro de Paris**   AC ⊬ ⇔
Pl. Pilsudskiego 9 ⊠ 00 078 – Ⓜ Ratusz – Ⓒ (022)   Plan: **C1**
*826 01 07 – www.restaurantbistrodeparis.com – Closed Easter, Christmas
and Sunday*
Menu 70/165 PLN – Carte 157/218 PLN
• French • Elegant • Formal •

Smart, marble-floored restaurant at the rear of the Opera House, with striking
columns and colourful glass panels. The large menu offers reworked Polish
and French dishes, with produce imported from France; the 'Classics' are a hit.

XxX **Tamka 43**   & AC ⊬
ul. Tamka 43 (1st Floor) ⊠ 00 355 – Ⓜ Świętokrzyska   Plan: **D2**
– Ⓒ (022) 441 62 34 – www.tamka43.pl – Closed Christmas-New Year and Easter
Menu 59 PLN (lunch)/250 PLN – Carte 133/206 PLN
• Modern • Design • Fashionable •

Smart, formal, first floor restaurant opposite the Chopin Museum, with bare
brick walls, steel girders and floor to ceiling windows. Concise menus use local
ingredients; flavours are pronounced and combinations, sometimes ambitious.

XxX **Platter by Karol Okrasa** – Intercontinental Hotel   AC ⊬ ⇨
ul. Emilii Plater 49 ⊠ 00 125 – Ⓜ Centrum – Ⓒ (022)   Plan: **C2**
328 8730 – www.platter.pl – Closed Sunday
Menu 108 PLN (lunch) – Carte 162/244 PLN
• Modern • Formal • Intimate •

First floor hotel restaurant with smart red and black décor. Menus change with
the seasons and offer modern Polish dishes and European classics. Cooking is
refined, sophisticated and flavoursome, and relies on native ingredients.

XX **Brasserie Warszawska**   AC ⊬ ⇔
☺ *ul. Górnośląska 24 ⊠ 00 484 – Ⓒ (022) 628 94 23*   Plan I: **B2**
– www.brasseriewarszawska.pl – Closed Christmas and Easter
Menu 35 PLN (weekday lunch) – Carte 62/204 PLN
• Modern • Brasserie • Retro •

Smart brasserie with a zinc-topped bar, a black and white tiled floor and carica-
tures of its regulars on the walls. Modern European dishes are executed with
care and passion. Meats come from their own butcher's shop and mature steaks
are a feature, with a choice of cuts from Poland, Ireland and Australia.

XX **Strefa**   ☆ AC
ul. Próżna 9 ⊠ 00 107 – Ⓜ Świętokrzyska – Ⓒ (022)   Plan: **C2**
255 0850 – www.restauracjastrefa.pl
Carte 99/173 PLN
• Modern • Elegant • Intimate •

Sit in the small bar, the neutrally hued restaurant or out on the delightful terrace
in the shadow of the church. Modern cooking has a traditional Polish heart – the
pierogi in particular are a must-try. Service is professional.

XX **Nolita**   AC ⊬
ul. Wilcza 46 ⊠ 00 679 – Ⓒ (022) 29 20 424   Plan I: **A2**
*– www.nolita.pl – Closed 2 weeks August, Christmas-New Year, Easter,
Saturday lunch, Sunday and bank holidays*
Menu 89 PLN (weekday lunch) – Carte 163/238 PLN – *(booking essential)*
• Modern • Design • Intimate •

Whitewashed stone and black window blinds are matched inside by a smart,
monochrome theme, where an open kitchen takes centre stage. Bold, modern
dishes feature many flavours and take their influences from across the globe.

XX **AleGloria**   ☆ AC ⊬ ⇔
pl. Trzech Krzyzy 3 ⊠ 00 535 – Ⓒ (022) 584 70 80   Plan: **D2**
– www.alegloria.pl – Closed 24-25 and 31 December and Easter
Menu 100 PLN (lunch)/135 PLN – Carte 88/252 PLN
• Polish • Traditional •

Steep steps lead down from a boutique shopping arcade to a spacious restaurant, made up of several charming interconnecting rooms and furnished in
white. Hearty, homemade Polish classics are served by a smartly attired team.

POLAND - WARSAW

627

POLAND - WARSAW

XX **Salto** – Rialto Hotel   �'s AC

ul. Wilcza 73 ✉ 00 670 – ⓜ *Politechnika –* ℰ *(022)*   Plan I: **A2**
584 87 00 – www.rialto.pl
Menu 50 PLN (weekday lunch) – Carte 132/175 PLN
• Modern • Intimate • Brasserie •

This plainly decorated dining room sits within an attractive suburban hotel. The chef hails from Argentina and is a fan of all things modern, so you'll find gels, meats cooked in a waterbath and some unusual flavour combinations.

XX **Signature** – H15 Hotel   �'s AC

ul. Poznańska 15 ✉ 00 680 – ⓜ *Politechnika –* ℰ *(022)*   Plan: **D2**
553 87 55 – www.h15ab.com – Closed Easter, 1-3 May, 24-26 December -
1 January and lunch Saturday-Sunday
Menu 42 PLN (lunch) – Carte 68/188 PLN
• Modern • Intimate • Bistro •

Black and white photos of old Hollywood actors and actresses hang against white walls in this delightful hotel restaurant. Cooking is a modern take on traditional Polish recipes; the puddings are particularly memorable.

XX **Dom Polski Francuska**   ⌂ AC ⇄

ul. Francuska 11 ✉ 03 906 – ℰ *(022) 616 24 32*
– www.restauracjadompolski.pl – Closed 24 December   Plan I: **B2**
Menu 40 PLN (dinner) – Carte 76/169 PLN
• Polish • Classic • Elegant •

Mediterranean-style villa with attractive gardens and a lovely terrace, in a smart residential area. Various small rooms are set over two floors. Extensive menus offer refined yet hearty dishes; duck and goose are the specialities.

XX **Dom Polski Belwederska**   ⌂ ⌂ AC ⇄

ul. Belwederska 18a ✉ 00 762 – ℰ *(022) 840 5060*   Plan I: **B3**
– www.restauracjadompolski.pl – Closed 24 December
Menu 80/120 PLN – Carte 80/174 PLN
• Polish • Romantic • Cosy •

The second Dom Polski was opened following popular demand. The early 19C house has a cosy, traditional feel and there's a lovely garden and terrace. Old favourites such as roast wild boar and catfish are given some modern touches.

XX **U Kucharzy**   ⌂

Państwowego Muzeum Archeologicznego, ul. Długa 52   Plan: **C1**
✉ 00 238 – ⓜ *Ratusz –* ℰ *(022) 826 79 36 – www.gessler.pl – Closed*
Easter and 31 December
Carte 74/171 PLN
• Traditional • Formal • Individual •

'The Cook' is located in a 16C former arsenal and two of the original cannons sit in its large inner courtyard. The day's ingredients are on display in the open kitchen and the chef will often come to the table to carve your meat.

XX **Concept 13**   ⌂ 's AC ⇄

Vitkac (5th Floor), ul. Bracka 9 ✉ 00 501 – ⓜ *Centrum*   Plan: **D2**
– ℰ *(022) 3107373 – www.likusrestauracja.pl – Closed Sunday dinner*
and bank holidays
Menu 55 PLN (lunch) – Carte 93/166 PLN
• Modern • Design • Fashionable •

Huge restaurant on top of a chic department store, with a wine bar and deli below. Black furnishings, a glass-walled kitchen and a smart terrace feature. Dishes are appealing and well-presented; small plates are the focus at lunch.

XX **U Fukiera**   ⌂ AC ⇄

Rynek Starego Miasta 27 ✉ 00 272 – ℰ *(022) 831 10 13*   Plan: **C1**
– www.ufukiera.pl – Closed 24-25 and 31 December
Menu 120/150 PLN – Carte 85/230 PLN
• Polish • Traditional • Individual •

Immaculately kept house in the heart of the Old Town, overlooking a historic cobbled square. The fiercely traditional interior comprises several intimate, homely rooms, including a 17C vaulted cellar. Cooking is hearty and classical.

XX   **La Rotisserie** – Le Régina Hotel   🛋 ᵹ 🄰🄲 ⇜
ul. Koscielna 12 ⊠ *00 218* – ℰ *(022) 531 60 00*   Plan: **C1**
– *www.mamaison.com/leregina* – *Closed dinner 24 December*
Menu 95 PLN (lunch) – Carte 162/205 PLN – *(booking essential)*
• Modern • Formal • Intimate •
Small but stylish hotel restaurant with an arched ceiling, Mediterranean styling
and an intimate feel. Refined modern dishes have Polish origins and arrive
attractively presented; the well-travelled chef sources top ingredients.

X   **Butchery and Wine**   ᵹᵹ 🛋 ⇜
🆎   *ul. Zurawia 22* ⊠ *00 515* – Ⓜ *Centrum* – ℰ *(022)*   Plan: **D2**
5023118 – *www.butcheryandwine.pl* – *Closed Christmas and Easter*
Carte 56/223 PLN – *(booking essential)*
• Meats and grills • Friendly • Trendy •
Keenly run modern bistro in a long, narrow room. The name says it all: staff wear
butcher's aprons, there's a diagram of cuts above the kitchen pass and the
emphasis is on offal and meat – particularly beef – which is served on wooden
boards. Wines from around the world provide the perfect match.

X   **L'enfant terrible**   🄰🄲
ul. Sandomierska 13 (entrance on Rejtana St.)   Plan I: **B3**
⊠ *02 567* – Ⓜ *Pol Mokotowskie* – ℰ *(022) 119 57 05* – *www.eterrible.pl*
– *Closed Christmas, Easter, Sunday and lunch Saturday and Monday*
Menu 83 PLN (lunch) – Carte 140/160 PLN
• Modern • Neighbourhood • Romantic •
This delightfully rustic restaurant is owned by a self-taught chef, who picks up
the day's produce on his 40km drive into work. The atmosphere is welcoming
and dishes are modern and well-presented; the sourdough bread is fantastic.

X   **Opasły Tom**   🛋 🄰🄲
ul. Foksal 17 ⊠ *00 372* – Ⓜ *Centrum* – ℰ *(022)*   Plan: **D2**
621 18 81 – *www.kregliccy.eu/opaslytom* – *Closed 24-26 December,*
1 November and Easter
Menu 115/148 PLN – Carte 70/137 PLN
• Polish • Simple • Neighbourhood •
Head past the outside tables, through the front room and on towards the tables
by the kitchen. Good value menus follow the seasons and come under the hea-
dings of 'cold', 'hot' and 'sweet'. Dishes are fresh, zingy and full of flavour.

X   **Dom Wódki**   🛋 🄰🄲 ⇦
ul. Wierzbowa 9-11 ⊠ *00 094* – Ⓜ *Ratusz* – ℰ *(022)*   Plan: **C1**
828 22 11 – *www.domwodki.pl* – *Closed 24-25 December, 1 January*
and Easter
Carte 80/130 PLN
• Polish • Wine bar • Fashionable •
A smart, very fashionable bar and restaurant is the setting for the marriage of
modern Polish cuisine and top quality vodkas. The likes of local herring, dumplings and beef tartar are paired with over 250 vodkas from around the world.

X   **Hoża**   🄰🄲 ⇦
ul. Hoża 25a ⊠ *00 521* – Ⓜ *Centrum* – ℰ *(515)*   Plan: **D2**
037 001 – *www.hoza.warszawa.pl* – *Closed Good Friday, 11 November*
and 25 December
Carte 66/244 PLN
• Meats and grills • Bistro • Neighbourhood •
The exposed brick walls of this Argentinian steakhouse are painted in striking
colours and its shelves are crammed with red wine. The engaging team offer
good advice and the mature Polish and Argentinian steaks are superbly cooked.

629

X **Winosfera** 🛣 ᴠ 🏤 ⇔
ul. Chlodna 29-31 ✉ *00 867* – ☎ *(022) 526 25 00*   Plan I: **A2**
– *www.winosfera.pl* – *Closed Easter, Christmas, Sunday and bank holidays*
Menu 39 PLN (weekday lunch) – Carte 82/256 PLN
• Modern • Design • Trendy •
Found in a former factory on a site where a famed cinema once stood; an industrial feel remains and they have even incorporated a screening room. Modern European menus focus on Italy. Select your wine from the well-stocked shop.

X **Merliniego 5** 🛣 AC ᴠ
ul. Merliniego 5 ✉ *02 511* – ☎ *(022) 6460849*   Plan I: **B3**
– *www.merliniego5.pl* – *Closed Easter and 25 December*
Menu 205/245 PLN – Carte 90/292 PLN – *(booking essential at dinner)*
• Traditional • Bistro • Neighbourhood •
Passionately run bistro in the suburbs, with low lighting, exposed brick and dark wood furnishings. Wide ranging menus offer carefully prepared European classics. Meat lovers should opt for a Polish steak or the steak tasting menu.

X **delizia** 🛣 AC ᴠ
ul. Hoża 58-60 (entrance on ul. Poznańskiej) ✉ *00 682*   Plan: **D2**
– Ⓜ *Centrum* – ☎ *(022) 622 66 65* – *www.delizia.com.pl* – *Closed Easter, Christmas and Sunday*
Carte 129/246 PLN – *(booking essential at dinner)*
• Italian • Neighbourhood • Friendly •
An unassuming neighbourhood restaurant where fresh flowers sit on chunky tables. It's owned by friends and run with the care of a family business. Menus are concise, with pasta a speciality; fish and cheese are imported from Italy.

X **Qchnia Artystyczna** 🛣 ᴠ
ul. Jazdow 2 ✉ *00 467* – ☎ *(022) 625 76 27*   Plan I: **B2**
– *www.qchnia.pl* – *Closed Easter, Christmas and bank holidays*
Carte 81/141 PLN
• Modern • Fashionable • Simple •
Busy, two-roomed restaurant with simple furnishings, in a contemporary art gallery; the terrace looks over the Royal Park. Short daily menus mix Polish and international influences – dishes are light, seasonal and full of flavour.

CRACOW
KRAKÓW
Population: 757 430

B. Brillion/MICHELIN

Cracow was deservedly included in the very first UNESCO World Heritage List. Unlike much of Poland, this beautiful old city – the country's capital from the 11C to the 17C – was spared Second World War destruction because the German Governor had his HQ here. So Cracow is still able to boast a hugely imposing market square – the biggest medieval square Europe – and a hill that's crowned not just with a castle, but a cathedral too. Not far away there's even a glorious chapel made of salt, one hundred metres under the ground.

Cracow is a city famous for its links with Judaism and its Royal Route, but also for its cultural inheritance. During the Renaissance, it became a centre of new ideas that drew the most outstanding writers, thinkers and musicians of the day. It has thousands of architectural monuments and millions of artefacts displayed in its museums and churches; but it's a modern city too, with an eye on the 21C. The heart and soul of Cracow is its old quarter, which received its charter in 1257. It's dominated by the Market Square and almost completely encircled by the Planty gardens. A short way to the south, briefly interrupted by the curving streets of the Okol neighbourhood, is Wawel Hill, and further south from here is the characterful Jewish quarter of Kazimierz. The smart residential areas of Piasek and Nowy Swiat are to the west.

CRACOW IN...

→ **ONE DAY**
St Mary's Church, Cloth Hall, Wawel, main building of National Museum.

→ **TWO DAYS**
Kazimierz, Oskar Schindler's Factory, 'Footsteps of Pope Jean Paul II' tour.

→ **THREE DAYS**
Auschwitz-Birkenau, Wieliczka salt mine.

PRACTICAL INFORMATION

ARRIVAL-DEPARTURE

John Paul II International Airport is 13km west of the city centre. Bus 292 goes to the central bus station. There's a free shuttle to the train station; trains to the centre take 15min. A taxi takes 20min.

GETTING AROUND

The historic city centre is a largely pedestrian precinct, so getting about on foot here is a traffic-free pleasure; the streets in the old quarter are laid out in a grid pattern, which makes orientation even easier. The public transport system is made up of an extensive network of buses and trams – you can use your tickets on both, and there several types available, from 15-minute timed tickets to 7-day passes. Be sure to stamp your ticket upon boarding. The Cracow Tourist Card includes unlimited free travel, as well as free entry to many museums, offers on excursions, and discounts in shops and restaurants; it's valid for 48 or 72 hours.

CALENDAR HIGHLIGHTS

May-June
Film Festival

June
The Lajkonik Parade, Wianki (flowers floated down the river, music and fireworks).

June-July
Cracow Jewish Culture Festival.

July-August
Festival of Music in Old Cracow.

September
Sacrum Profanum (concerts in post-industrial spaces).

November
Festiwal Muzyki Polskiej (Polish Music Festival)

EATING OUT

Even during the communist era, Cracow had a reputation as a good place to eat. In the 1990s, hundreds of new restaurants opened their doors, often in pretty locations with medieval or Renaissance interiors or in intimate cellars. Many Poles go misty-eyed at the thought of Bigos on a cold winter's day; it's a game, sausage and cabbage stew that comes with sauerkraut, onion, potatoes, herbs and spices, and is reputed to get better with reheating on successive days. Pierogi is another favourite: crescent-shaped dumplings which come in either savoury or sweet style. Barszcz is a lemon and garlic flavoured beetroot soup that's invariably good value, while in Kazimierz, specialities include Jewish dumplings - filled with onion, cheese and potatoes - and Berdytchov soup, which imaginatively mixes honey and cinnamon with beef. There are plenty of restaurants specialising in French, Greek, Vietnamese, Middle Eastern, Indian, Italian and Mexican food too. Most restaurants don't close until around midnight and there's no pressure to rush your drinks and leave.

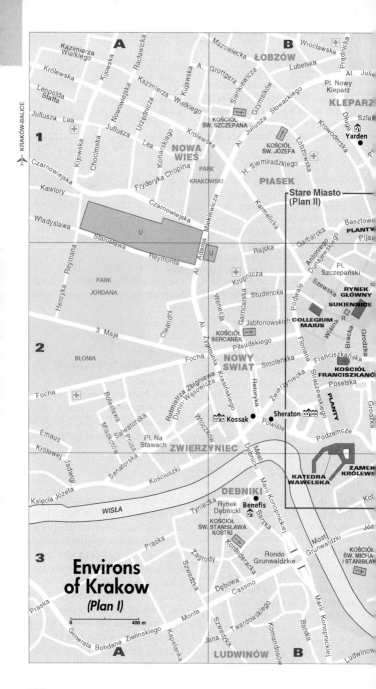

Environs of Krakow
(Plan I)

0 — 400 m

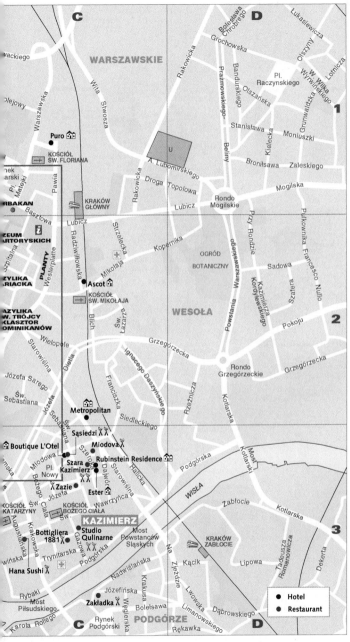

C

D

Łukasiewicza

Bolesława
Chrobrego

Grochowska

W. Wilka
Wyrwińskiego

Olszyny

Lotnicza

wackiego

WARSZAWSKIE

Rakowicka

Pl.
Raczynskiego

Prażmowskiego

Bandurskiego

Olszańska

Grunwaldzka

Moniuszki

1

Wila

Siwosza

Warszawska

olejowy

Stanisława

Bieliny

Kielecka

Bronisława

Zaleskiego

Puro 🏠🏠

KOŚCIÓŁ
✚ SW. FLORIANA

A. Lubomirskiego

Droga Topolowa

Rondo
Mogilskie

Mogilska

nek
arski

Pl.
Matejki

Pawia

Rakowicka

Lubicz

Przy Rondzie

Pułkownika Francesco Nullo

RBAKAN

Basztowa

KRAKÓW
GŁÓWNY

Radziwiłłowska

Lubicz

Strzelecka

Kopernika

OGRÓD
BOTANICZNY

Sadowa

Warszawskiego

Kazimierza
Kordylewskiego

Szafera

ZEUM
ARTORYSKICH

ℹ️

Westerplatte

PLANTY

Mikołaja

Ascot 🏠

KOŚCIÓŁ
✚ SW. MIKOŁAJA

Sw.
Łazarza

WESOŁA

Pokoju

2

ZYLIKA
RIACKA

Szpitalna

AZYLIKA
W. TRÓJCY
KLASZTOR
OMINIKANÓW

Blich

Wielopole

Dietla

Starowiślna

Ignacego Daszyńskiego

Grzegórzecka

Rzeźnicza

Rondo
Grzegórzeckie

Grzegórzecka

Kotlarska

Józefa Sarego

Św.
Sebastiana

Józefa

Św. Sebastiana

Franciszka

Siedleckiego

Metropolitan 🏠🏠

Sąsiedzi ✕ ✕

Miodova ✕

🏠 Boutique L'Otel

Miodowa

Szara
Kazimierz ✕

Starowiślna

Szeroka

Dajwór

Halicka

Podgórska

Most
Kotlarski

Most Kotlarski

Pl.
Nowy

Bożego Ciała

Rubinstein Residence 🏠🏠

Zazie ✕

Ester 🏠

Wawrzyńca

WISŁA

Zabłocie

Kotlarska

KOŚCIÓŁ ŚW.
KATARZYNY

Augustiańska

Św.
Rakowska

KOŚCIÓŁ ŚW.
BOŻEGO CIAŁA

Św. Krakowska

KAZIMIERZ

Studio
Qulinarne ✕

Most
Powstańców
Śląskich

KRAKÓW
ZABŁOCIE

Lipowa

Tadeusza
Romanowicza

Dekerta

3

Bottigliera
1881 ✕

Trynitarska

Podgórska

Nadwiślańska

Na Zjeżdzie

Kącik

Lwowska

wińska

Hana Sushi ✕

Rybaki

Most
Piłsudskiego

Karola Rollego

Józefińska

Zakładka ✕

Rynek
Podgórski

Krakusa

Węgierska

Bolesława

PODGÓRZE

Limanowskiego

Dąbrowskiego

Ręækawka

●	Hotel
●	Restaurant

C

D

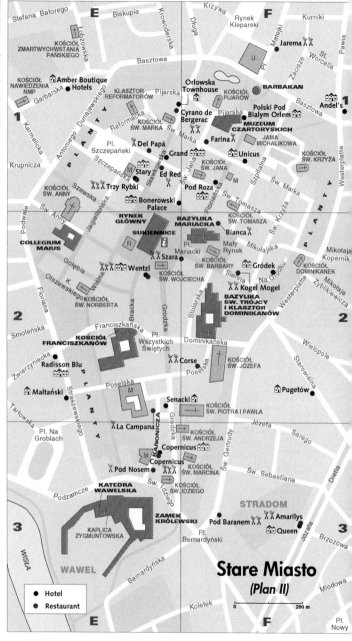

Stare Miasto
(Plan II)

- Hotel
- Restaurant

POLAND - CRACOW

Sheraton

ul. Powisle 7 ✉ *31 101 –* ✆ *(12) 662 10 00* Plan I: **B2**
– *www.sheraton.pl/krakow*
232 rm ☲ – ♦535/1277 PLN ♦♦600/1355 PLN – 3 suites
• Luxury • Business • Modern •

Well-located international hotel with an impressive glass-roofed atrium and extensive event space in the basement. Bedrooms are luxuriously appointed and well-equipped – some boast river and castle views. Olive offers a popular global menu and Polish specialities, while the sports bar serves a range of pub-style dishes. Start with a drink in the rooftop lounge-bar.

Radisson Blu

ul. Straszewskiego 17 ✉ *31 101 –* ✆ *(12) 618 88 88* Plan: **E2**
– *www.radissonblu.com/hotel-krakow*
196 rm ☲ – ♦491/1690 PLN ♦♦561/1760 PLN – 7 suites
• Business • Modern •

Purpose-built business hotel by the Planty, not far from the castle and the main square. Bedrooms are spacious and well-appointed: 'City' come in warm red hues and 'Harmony', in cool blues. There's a smart basement fitness centre and an informal dining room offering global dishes and themed weekend buffets.

Grand

ul. Slawkowska 5/7 ✉ *31 014 –* ✆ *(12) 424 08 00* Plan: **E1**
– *www.grand.pl*
64 rm ☲ – ♦400/1000 PLN ♦♦500/1000 PLN – 9 suites
• Traditional • Luxury • Historic •

Once Duke Czartoryski's palace; now the city's oldest hotel. The classic façade masks a columned lobby and rooms filled with gold leaf, stained glass and antiques. Bedrooms are spacious and the suites are vast, opulent and impressively furnished. The traditional Viennese café offers Polish cuisine.

Stary

ul. Szczepanska 5 ✉ *31 011 –* ✆ *(12) 384 08 08* Plan: **E1**
– *www.stary.hotel.com.pl*
78 rm ☲ – ♦490/950 PLN ♦♦590/1100 PLN – 7 suites
• Luxury • Townhouse • Design •

Behind a traditional townhouse façade, dramatic modern glass and steel structures blend cleverly with 15C features. The contemporary bar and rooftop terrace sit alongside original brick and stonework. Stylish bedrooms boast handmade furniture, impressive marble bathrooms and state-of-the-art lighting.
Trzy Rybki – See restaurant listing

Copernicus

ul. Kanonicza 16 ✉ *31 002 –* ✆ *(12) 424 34 00* Plan: **E3**
– *www.copernicus.hotel.com.pl*
29 rm – ♦800 PLN ♦♦900/980 PLN – ☲ 70 PLN – 4 suites
• Historic • Luxury • Stylish •

Elegant townhouse in the castle's shadow, on one of the city's oldest streets. The central atrium has a lounge and a small patio for breakfast/light lunch. Luxurious beamed bedrooms boast handmade furniture and excellent comforts. There's an intimate pool in the medieval cellars and a lovely rooftop terrace.
Copernicus – See restaurant listing

Bonerowski Palace

ul. Św. Jana 1 ✉ *31 013 –* ✆ *(12) 374 13 09* Plan: **E1**
– *www.palacbonerowski.pl*
16 rm – ♦650/950 PLN ♦♦650/950 PLN – ☲ 75 PLN – 3 suites
• Palace • Historic • Personalised •

A former palace, superbly located on the main square and featuring medieval portals, ornate ceilings, restored polychrome décor and the largest Swarovski chandelier in Europe. Large, antique-furnished bedrooms and chic suites come with marble bathrooms. The restaurant focuses on steaks and fish.

POLAND - CRACOW

Wentzl
☆ ≤ ▥ ⇔

Rynek Główny 19 ✉ *31 008* – ☏ *(12) 430 26 64*   Plan: **E2**
– *www.wentzl.pl*
18 rm – ♦450/860 PLN ♦♦460/870 PLN – ⌣ 60 PLN
• Luxury • Historic • Elegant •

15C tenement house offering fantastic views over the market square towards St Mary's Basilica. Individually furnished bedrooms feature four-posters, antiques and interesting art: those on the top floor are the most modern.
Wentzl – See restaurant listing

Pod Róza
☆ ♨ 🏠 ▥ ⇔ 🏋

ul. Florianska 14 ✉ *31 021* – ☏ *(12) 424 33 00*   Plan: **F1**
– *www.podroza.hotel.com.pl*
57 rm – ♦400/650 PLN ♦♦450/720 PLN – ⌣ 50 PLN – 4 suites
• Historic • Traditional • Classic •

A discreet entrance leads to a surprisingly large glass-covered courtyard, complete with a modern restaurant and a laid-back Italian trattoria. Classically appointed bedrooms feature silhouette artwork and modern bathrooms; many have jacuzzis. The fourth floor rooms are cosiest and boast city skyline panoramas; the top floor fitness suite shares the view.

Kossak
☆ ≤ ♨ ♿ ▥ ⇔ 🏋

Plac Kossaka 1 ✉ *31 106* – ☏ *(12) 379 59 00*   Plan I: **B2**
– *www.hotelkossak.pl*
60 rm ⌣ – ♦750/800 PLN ♦♦800/860 PLN – 5 suites
• Business • Modern • Stylish •

Contemporary business hotel named after the famous Polish painter and offering views over the river towards the castle. Each of its well-equipped, modern bedrooms features a piece of Kossak's art; opt for one of the comfortable corner suites. The ground floor restaurant offers Polish specialities; the 7th floor café and terrace serves a modern international menu.

Andel's
☆ ♨ 🏠 ♿ ▥ ⇔ 🏋 🚗

ul. Pawia 3 ✉ *31 154* – ☏ *(12) 660 01 00*   Plan: **F1**
– *www.andelscracow.com*
159 rm ⌣ – ♦380/845 PLN ♦♦465/930 PLN – 6 suites
• Business • Modern • Stylish •

An eye-catching modern building by the station and the shopping centre. Its spacious interior is decorated in bold colours and all of the well-equipped bedrooms boast floor to ceiling windows. The bright, curvaceous restaurant has a global menu and tables on the square. Live music features in the chic bar.

Gródek
☆ ♨ ♿ ▥ ⇔

ul. Na Gródku 4 ✉ *31 028* – ☏ *(12) 431 90 30*   Plan: **F2**
– *www.donimirski.com*
23 rm ⌣ – ♦350/510 PLN ♦♦390/690 PLN – 2 suites
• Historic • Townhouse • Elegant •

This charming townhouse is hidden in a quiet side street close to the square. If you need to unwind, seek out the pleasant wood-panelled library bar or grab a seat on the roof terrace. Appealing bedrooms come with good facilities; they vary in size and each has its own character. The restaurant is themed around the South Pacific and serves dishes from across Oceania.

Queen
☆ ♨ ♿ ▥ ⇔ 🏋

ul. Józefa Dietla 60 ✉ *31 039* – ☏ *(12) 433 33 33*   Plan: **F3**
– *www.queenhotel.pl*
31 rm ⌣ – ♦280/590 PLN ♦♦330/750 PLN – 1 suite
• Business • Design • Stylish •

This chic boutique hotel sits between the old market square and Kazimierz. Charming bedrooms come in brown and silver and feature the latest mod cons: the 'Sky' rooms look out over the castle and the 3rd floor rooms have balconies.
Amarylis – See restaurant listing

Puro

ul. Ogrodowa 10 ✉ 31 155 – Ⓜ Krakow Glowny — Plan I: **C1**
– ✆ (12) 314 2100 – www.purohotel.pl
138 rm – ♦250/1399 PLN ♦♦250/1399 PLN – ☐ 50 PLN – 6 suites
• Chain hotel • Modern •
Colour-changing lights illuminate the modern façade and the spacious lobby is decked out with vintage furnishings. Up-to-date bedrooms feature yellow Chesterfield-style headboards, tablet-operated controls and glass-walled bathrooms decorated with frosted flowers. The restaurant serves an international menu.

 Unicus

ul Sw. Marka 20 ✉ 31 020 – ✆ (12) 433 71 11 — Plan: **F1**
– www.hotelunicus.pl
35 rm ☐ – ♦380/600 PLN ♦♦440/660 PLN
• Business • Townhouse • Modern •
Stylish boutique hotel converted from a row of old tenement houses. Well-appointed bedrooms range in colour from green to gold and boast state-of-the-art shower rooms; 'Double Deluxe's, overlooking Florianska Street, are the best. The bright, barrel-ceilinged basement restaurant serves a modern menu.

 Polski Pod Bialym Orlem

ul. Pijarska 17 ✉ 31 015 – ✆ (12) 422 11 44 — Plan: **F1**
– www.donimirski.com
60 rm ☐ – ♦240/390 PLN ♦♦320/590 PLN – 3 suites
• Historic • Townhouse • Classic •
A traditional hotel overlooking the city walls, with a cosy brick bar dating from the 16C; it's owned by the family of the Czartoryski Princes. Bedrooms are currently undergoing refurbishment – some are classical while others are more up-to-date.

 Senacki

ul. Grodzka 51 ✉ 31 001 – ✆ (12) 422 76 86 — Plan: **E2**
– www.hotelsenacki.pl
20 rm ☐ – ♦750/800 PLN ♦♦800/860 PLN – 2 suites
• Townhouse • Classic •
Peaceful hotel with an ornate stone façade, opposite a 17C church on the Royal Way. Bedrooms are bright and modern – those on the upper floors have air con and rooftop views. Buffet breakfasts are in the hugely atmospheric 13C cellar.

 Amber Boutique Hotels

ul. Garbarska 10 ✉ 31 131 – ✆ (12) 421 06 06 — Plan: **E1**
– www.hotel-amber.pl
38 rm ☐ – ♦299/514 PLN ♦♦359/529 PLN
• Townhouse • Modern •
Two traditional townhouses in a residential street. Well-equipped contemporary bedrooms come with complimentary cherry vodka: the 'Design' rooms have feature walls and display local artists' work. Smart breakfast and fitness rooms.

 Orlowska Townhouse

ul. Slawkowska 26 ✉ 31 014 – ✆ (12) 429 54 45 — Plan: **E1**
– www.orlowskatownhouse.com
5 rm – ♦360/635 PLN ♦♦360/780 PLN – ☐ 36 PLN
• Historic • Townhouse • Elegant •
17C townhouse on a peaceful central street. Spacious apartment-style bedrooms have small kitchenettes and modern bathrooms – and are furnished in themes including 'Art Deco', 'Poets' and 'Boudoir'. Relax in the intimate piano bar.

 Yarden

ul Długa 35 ✉ 31 147 – ✆ (535) 26 27 54 — Plan I: **B1**
– www.yardenhotel.pl
49 rm ☐ – ♦220/350 PLN ♦♦250/500 PLN – 4 suites
• Townhouse • Classic •
Modern hotel in a traditional townhouse building, with a tranquil garden hidden behind. Good-sized bedrooms have up-to-date facilities and are furnished with heavy, freestanding wooden furniture; ask for a room with a balcony.

🏠 **Pugetów** ⬛ ⇔ 🅿
ul. Starowislna 15a ✉ 31 038 – ℰ (12) 432 49 50 Plan: **F2**
– www.donimirski.com
6 rm ☕ – 🛉250/310 PLN 🛉🛉350/510 PLN – 2 suites
• Historic • Classic • Elegant •

Set in the shadow of Pugetów Palace, in the 19C servants' quarters. With its calm, intimate interior and antique-filled bedrooms, it feels like a private residence. The cosy lounge and breakfast area are in the characterful cellars.

🏠 **Maltanski** ⇔ 🅿
ul. Straszewskiego 14 ✉ 31 101 – ℰ (12) 431 00 10 Plan: **E2**
– www.donimirski.com
16 rm ☕ – 🛉310/410 PLN 🛉🛉350/510 PLN
• Traditional • Personalised •

Lovely little hotel by the Planty, named after its previous owners, The Knights of Malta. With the castle and square just a stroll away, it makes a great base for exploring. Some of the charming, traditional bedrooms have patios.

🏠 **Benefis** ⇪ ⅙ ⇔ 🅿
ul. Barska 2 ✉ 30 307 – ℰ (12) 252 0710 Plan I: **B3**
– www.hotelbenefis.pl
20 rm ☕ – 🛉240/310 PLN 🛉🛉270/370 PLN – 7 suites
• Traditional • Modern • Functional •

Small, purpose-built hotel just over the Wisla River, a short walk from town. Bedrooms are modern and surprisingly spacious – most have balconies; the 4th floor rooms come with air con and distant castle views. The smart basement houses a small bar and a simple restaurant serving Polish and Italian cuisine.

🏠 **Ascot** ⅙ ⬛ ⇔
ul. Radziwillowska 3 ✉ 31 026 – ℰ (12) 384 06 06 Plan I: **C2**
– www.hotelascot.pl
49 rm ☕ – 🛉313/397 PLN 🛉🛉376/501 PLN
• Business • Traditional • Functional •

Modern hotel located in a residential area, just 5 minutes' walk from town. Bold contemporary art lines the lobby walls and there's a small corner bar. Up-to-date bedrooms come in yellows and reds; those at the front are quieter.

XxX **Copernicus** – Copernicus Hotel ⅗ ⬛ ⇔
ul. Kanonicza 16 ✉ 31 002 – ℰ (12) 424 34 21 Plan: **E3**
– www.copernicus.hotel.com.pl
Menu 160/340 PLN – Carte lunch 137/187 PLN – (booking essential)
• Modern • Intimate • Elegant •

Set in the atrium of a charming hotel, an intimate split-level restaurant of less than 10 tables, boasting an ornate hand-painted Renaissance ceiling. 5, 7 and 12 course menus offer well-crafted modern Polish and European dishes.

XxX **Trzy Rybki** – Stary Hotel ⅗ ⅙ ⬛ ⇔ ⟳
ul. Szczepanska 5 ✉ 31 011 – ℰ (12) 384 08 06 Plan: **E1**
– www.hotel.com.pl
Menu 150/200 PLN – Carte 159/199 PLN
• Fish and seafood • Elegant • Design •

Airy two-roomed restaurant in a unique hotel. An impressive vaulted stone ceiling and dramatic flower arrangements dominate. Original modern menus keep seafood to the fore and are accompanied by a superb collection of Italian wines.

XxX **Wentzl** ⟨ 🏠 ⬛ ⇔ ⟳
Rynek Glówny 19 ✉ 31 008 – ℰ (12) 430 26 64 Plan: **E2**
– www.wentzl.pl – Closed 25 December
Carte 80/182 PLN
• Traditional • Elegant • Formal •

A grand, formal restaurant on the first floor of a 17C hotel, boasting polished parquet floors, a stunning 15C ceiling and a belle époque style. The traditional menu mixes French and Polish influences. Below is a more casual bistro.

XX **Szara** 🍽 ⇪
Rynek Główny 6 ✉ *31 042* – ☎ *(12) 421 66 69* Plan: **E/F2**
– www.szara.pl – Closed 1 November and 24 December
Carte 92/161 PLN
• International • Brasserie • Classic •
Well-regarded family-run restaurant on the Grand Square, featuring a lovely terrace, a hand-painted Gothic ceiling and a pleasant brasserie atmosphere. Menus mix Polish, French and Swedish classics; cooking is authentic and hearty.

XX **Kogel Mogel** 🍽 AC ⇪
ul. Sienna 12 ✉ *31 041* – ☎ *(12) 426 49 68* Plan: **F2**
– www.kogel-mogel.pl – Closed Easter and Christmas
Carte 58/118 PLN
• Polish • Brasserie • Fashionable •
Smart, lively brasserie; the wine room with its original painted ceiling is a popular spot, as is the enclosed terrace. Extensive menus offer refined, modern versions of classic Polish and Cracovian dishes. Live music is a feature.

XX **Pod Baranem** AC ⇪
ul. Sw. Gertrudy 21 ✉ *31 049* – ☎ *(12) 429 40 22* Plan: **F3**
– www.podbaranem.com – Closed Easter and Christmas
Carte 47/161 PLN – *(booking essential at dinner)*
• Polish • Neighbourhood • Family •
Traditional family-run restaurant set over 5 rooms, with rug-covered stone floors, homely furnishings and contemporary artwork by Edward Dwurnik. The large menu offers classic Polish cuisine; sharing dishes must be ordered in advance.

XX **Jarema** 🍽 AC ⇪
Pl. Matejki 5 ✉ *31 157* – ☎ *(12) 429 36 69* Plan: **F1**
– www.jarema.pl
Carte 53/148 PLN
• Polish • Musical • Rustic •
Charming restaurant with a homely feel. Hunting trophies fill the walls and there's live violin and piano music every night. Family recipes are handed down through the generations and focus on dishes from the east of the country.

XX **Amarylis** – at Queen Hotel ⅃ AC ⇪
ul. Józefa Dietla 60 ✉ *31 039* – ☎ *(12) 433 33 33* Plan: **F3**
– www.queenhotel.pl
Carte 103/139 PLN
• Modern • Design •
Head down to the hotel's basement and choose from either a traditional brick room or a more modern space furnished in black and white. Cooking is a mix of Polish and global influences and dishes are well presented and full of flavour.

XX **Cyrano de Bergerac** 🍽 ⇪
ul Slawkowska 26 ✉ *31 014* – ☎ *(12) 411 72 88* Plan: **E1**
– www.cyranodebergerac.pl – Closed Easter, Christmas and 1 November
Carte 89/226 PLN
• Polish • Intimate • Rustic •
Atmospheric restaurant in the barrel-ceilinged cellars of a 17C townhouse. Tapestries, antiques and old implements fill the room, and there's a lovely enclosed terrace to the rear. Refined Polish cooking has French touches.

XX **Corse** ⇪
ul Poselska 24 ✉ *31 002* – ☎ *(12) 421 62 73* Plan: **F2**
– www.corserestaurant.pl – Closed Easter and Christmas
Carte 63/165 PLN
• Mediterranean • Traditional • Bistro •
Nautically themed restaurant featuring model ships, paintings of clippers and old ships' lamps. Good-sized menus offer Mediterranean-influenced dishes which use Polish produce; they specialise in seafood but offer more besides.

POLAND - CRACOW

X **Pod Nosem** 🛜 ⇗

ul. Kanonicza 22 ✉ *31 002 –* ☎ *(12) 376 00 14*   Plan: **E3**
– www.podnosem.com
Carte 78/167 PLN *– (Closed Christmas)*
• Polish • Cosy • Romantic •

This cosy, characterful restaurant has a medieval feel. The bright ground floor room is hung with tapestries and the white wooden banquettes have tapestry-style chair backs to match; downstairs is more dimly lit, with a mix of brick and stone walls. Traditional Polish dishes are given a modern touch.

X **Bianca** 🛜

Plac Mariacki 2 ✉ *31 042 –* ☎ *(12) 422 18 71*   Plan: **F2**
– www.biancaristorante.pl – Closed Easter and Christmas
Carte 50/111 PLN
• Italian • Bistro • Intimate •

Sit on the small terrace opposite St Mary's Basilica and watch the world go by. Classical menus cover all regions of Italy and the pasta and ragu are freshly made; be sure to try the delicious saltimbocca with its sharp, lemony tang.

X **La Campana** 🛜 ⇔

ul. Kanonicza 7 ✉ *31 000 –* ☎ *(12) 430 22 32*   Plan: **E2**
– www.lacampana.pl – Closed Easter and 24 December
Carte 54/111 PLN
• Italian • Cosy • Rustic •

Discreetly set under an archway; the charming country interior features pine dressers and an olive branch frieze and there's also a beautiful walled garden. The wide ranging Italian menu features imported produce; the hams are a hit.

X **Farina** 🏧 ⇔

ul. Św. Marka 16 ✉ *31 018 –* ☎ *(12) 422 16 80*   Plan: **F1**
– www.farina.com.pl – Closed Christmas
Carte 59/238 PLN
• Fish and seafood • Cosy • Friendly •

Pretty little restaurant set over three rooms; all of them cosy and candlelit but each with its own character. Seafood is the speciality, with fish arriving from France several times a week and then cooked whole over salt and herbs.

X **Ed Red**

ul. Skawkowska 3 ✉ *31 014 –* ☎ *(690) 900 555*   Plan: **E1**
– www.edred.pl
Carte 49/140 PLN
• Meats and grills • Rustic • Neighbourhood •

It's all about beef at Ed Red, from roast bone marrow and homemade blood pudding to Polish 21 day dry-aged Limousin steak with béarnaise sauce. Three rustic rooms with reclaimed wooden panels on the walls set the scene perfectly.

X **Del Papá** 🛜 🏧 ⇔

ul. Św. Tomasza 6 ✉ *31 014*   Plan: **E1**
– ☎ *(12) 421 83 43 – www.delpapa.pl*
– Closed 24-26 December
Carte 63/90 PLN
• Italian • Bistro •

Simple Italian trattoria; dine in the bistro-style room, the characterful Italian 'street' or on the partially covered rear terrace. Menus echo the seasons, offering a good range of honest Italian classics and a fat free selection.

Metropolitan ⚜ 🛏 & 🆔 ⇇ 🛎

ul Berka Joselewicza 19 ✉ *31 068* – ☎ *(12) 442 75 00* — Plan: **C2**
– www.hotelmetropolitan.pl
59 rm ☒ – 🛏345/795 PLN 🛏🛏385/900 PLN
• Townhouse • Modern • Stylish •

Converted 19C townhouse with a smart lobby and a lounge with a central bar. Bold modern décor features throughout; in summer, have breakfast in the enclosed courtyard. Bedrooms come in neutral hues and have a high level of facilities. The informal restaurant serves international fusion dishes.

Rubinstein Residence ⚜ 🕸 🆔 ⇇ 🛎

ul. Szeroka 12 ✉ *31 053* – ☎ *(12) 384 00 00* — Plan: **C3**
– www.rubinstein.pl – Closed 26-31 July
28 rm ☒ – 🛏330/590 PLN 🛏🛏359/659 PLN – 2 suites
• Historic • Townhouse • Stylish •

This pair of restored townhouses is joined by a bright, glass-roofed restaurant and named after Helena Rubinstein, who lived nearby. Well-equipped, characterful bedrooms come with luxurious marble and alabaster bathrooms. It's located in a pleasant square and the roof terrace affords panoramic city views.

Boutique L'Otel ⚜ 🆔 ⇇

ul. Miodowa 25 ✉ *31 055* – ☎ *(12) 633 34 44* — Plan: **C3**
– www.apartmenty.oberza.pl – Closed 24-27 December
18 rm – 🛏165/225 PLN 🛏🛏195/290 PLN – ☒ 20 PLN – 1 suite
• Townhouse • Design • Stylish •

Delightful former tenement house in the heart of Kazimierz. An impressive staircase leads up to the stylish, individually themed bedrooms which range in design from 'Art Deco' to 'Crystal' and boast smart, modern bathrooms.
Sąsiedzi – See restaurant listing

Ester ⚜ 🕸 & 🆔 ⇇ 🛎

ul. Szeroka 20 ✉ *31 053* – ☎ *(12) 429 11 88* — Plan: **C3**
– www.hotel-ester.krakow.pl – Closed 24 December
32 rm ☒ – 🛏400/590 PLN 🛏🛏440/1400 PLN
• Townhouse • Homely • Cosy •

Cosy little hotel overlooking a pleasant square in the Jewish quarter, with a traditionally furnished interior and bird cages dotted about the place. Comfortable bedrooms are colour themed and boast both baths and showers. The simple café and terrace serves a mix of traditional Polish and Jewish dishes.

XX Studio Qulinarne 🍴 🆔 ⇇

ul. Gazowa 4 ✉ *31 060* – ☎ *(12) 430 69 14* — Plan: **C3**
– www.studioqulinarne.pl – Closed Easter and Christmas
Carte 115/157 PLN
• International • Individual • Neighbourhood •

Passionately run, restyled bus garage with folding glass doors, a cocktail bar and an intimate enclosed terrace. The airy interior features exposed timbers, unusual lighting and black linen. A monthly menu offers well-presented, modern international dishes, and live piano music features later in the week.

XX Szara Kazimierz 🍴 ⇇

ul. Szeroka 39 ✉ *31 053* – ☎ *(12) 429 12 19* — Plan: **C3**
– www.szarakazimierz.pl – Closed 24-25 December
Carte 70/129 PLN
• Polish • Brasserie • Neighbourhood •

Friendly brasserie in a pleasant spot on the square. Sit out the front, on the enclosed rear terrace, or inside, surrounded by photos of Gaultier models. Menus reflect the owners' heritage by mixing Polish and Swedish classics.

✗ **Sąsiedzi** – Boutique L'Otel   🛋 ⅍ ♿

ul. Miodowa 25 ✉ *31 055* – ☎ *(12) 654 83 53*   Plan: **C3**

– *www.oberza.pl* – *Closed 24-27 December*

Carte 59/100 PLN

• Polish • Intimate • Rurally •

With its relaxed, welcoming atmosphere and delightful team, its name, 'Neighbourhood', sums it up well. Dine on the small terrace or in one of several charming cellar rooms. Honest, good value cooking uses old Polish recipes.

✗ **Bottiglieria 1881**   🍷

ul. Bochenska 5 ✉ *31 061* – ☎ *(660) 66 17 56*   Plan: **C3**

– *www.1881.com.pl* – *Closed Christmas, Easter and Monday*

Carte 105/125 PLN

• Creative • Wine bar •

This century old cellar is found in the Jewish district. Old wine boxes decorate the room, hand-crafted wood and stone feature and the large cave offers over 100 different wines. The menu is a concise selection of modern dishes.

✗ **Zazie**

🏮 *ul. Józefa 34* ✉ *32 056* – ☎ *(500) 410 829*   Plan: **C3**

– *www.zaziebistro.pl*

Menu 28 PLN (weekday lunch) – Carte 59/84 PLN – *(Closed 24 December and Good Friday) (booking essential at dinner)*

• French • Bistro •

You'll find this bistro in a corner spot on a pleasant square. Inside it has a lively vibe; ask for a table in the attractive cellar, with its pleasing mix of French memorabilia and brick and stone walls. Great value Gallic dishes range from quiches and gratins to roast duck and beef Bourguignon.

✗ **Miodova**   🛋 ♿

ul. Szeroka 3 ✉ *31 053* – ☎ *(12) 432 5083*   Plan: **C3**

– *www.miodova.pl*

Carte 77/132 PLN – *(Closed 24-25 December, 27 March and 16 April)*

• Polish • Cosy •

Among a strip of lively restaurants you'll find Miodova, a fashionable restaurant owned by two sisters. It's a comfortable place, with soft sofa-style banquettes and colourful cushions. The menu focuses on regional specialities.

✗ **Hana Sushi**

ul Weglowa 4 ✉ *31 063* – ☎ *(538) 20 86 66*   Plan: **C3**

– *www.hanasushikrakow.wix.com/home* – *Closed Monday*

Menu 32/49 PLN – Carte 40/89 PLN

• Japanese • Simple •

Hana Sushi is a simple Japanese-style restaurant set slightly off the beaten track. The chef travelled the world working his way up in sushi restaurants, while the sushi master trained in Tokyo. Good value sushi is prepared with finesse.

---

at PODGÓRZE   **PLAN I**

✗ **Zakladka**   🛋 🅰🅺 ⅍ ♿

ul. Józefińska 2 ✉ *30 529* – ☎ *(12) 442 74 42*   Plan: **C3**

– *www.zakladkabistro.pl* – *Closed 24-25 December and Easter Day*

Carte 73/106 PLN

• French • Bistro • Neighbourhood •

Set over the footbridge in an orange former tenement building and run by a well-known local chef. With their chequered floors and red banquettes, the front rooms have a classic bistro feel; the French dishes are equally traditional.

PORTUGAL

PORTUGAL

→ **AREA:**
92 391 km² (35 521 sq mi).

→ **POPULATION:**
10 459 806. Density = 114 per km².

→ **CAPITAL:**
Lisbon.

→ **CURRENCY:**
Euro (€).

→ **GOVERNMENT:**
Parliamentary republic (since 1976). Member of European Union since 1986.

→ **LANGUAGE:**
Portuguese.

→ **PUBLIC HOLIDAYS:**
New Year's Day (1 Jan); Good Friday (late Mar/Apr); Liberation Day (25 Apr); Labor Day (1 May); Corpus Christi (late May/June – currently suspended); Portugal Day (10 June); Assumption of the Virgin Mary (15 Aug); Republic Day (5 Oct – currently suspended); All Saints' Day (1 Nov – currently suspended); Restoration of Independence Day (1 Dec – currently suspended); Immaculate Conception (8 Dec); Christmas Day (25 Dec).

→ **LOCAL TIME:**
GMT in winter and GMT+1 hour in summer.

→ **CLIMATE:**
Temperate Mediterranean with warm winters and hot summers (Lisbon: January 15°C; July 26°C).

LISBON

→ **EMERGENCY:**
Police, Medical Assistance and Fire Brigade ☏ **112**.

→ **ELECTRICITY:**
230 volts AC, 50Hz; 2 round pin sockets.

→ **FORMALITIES:**
Travellers from the European Union (EU), Switzerland, Iceland and the main countries of North and South America need a national identity card or passport (America: passport required) to visit Portugal for less than three months (tourism or business purpose). For visitors from other countries a visa may be required, in addition to a passport, especially for those wishing to stay for longer than three months. We advise you to check with your embassy before travelling.

LISBON
LISBOA

Population: 547 733

Alain Rapoport/Fotolia.com

Sitting on the north bank of the River Tagus, beneath huge open skies and surrounded by seven hills, Lisbon boasts an atmosphere that few cities can match. An enchanting walk around the streets has an old-time ambience all of its own, matched only by a jaunt on the trams and funiculars that run up and down the steep hills. At first sight Lisbon is all flaky palaces, meandering alleyways and castellated horizon quarried from medieval stone; but there's a 21C element, too. Slinky new developments line the riverside, linking the old and new in a glorious jumble which spills down the slopes to the water's edge. The views of the water from various vantage points all over Lisbon and the vistas of the 'Straw Sea' – so named because of the golden reflections of the sun – reach out to visitors, along with the sounds of fado, the city's alluring folk music, which conjures up a melancholic yearning.

The compact heart of the city is the Baixa, a flat, 18C grid of streets flanked by the hills. To the west is the elegant commercial district of Chiado and the funky hilltop Bairro Alto, while immediately to the east is Alfama, a tightly packed former Moorish quarter with kasbah-like qualities. North of here is the working-class neighbourhood of Graça and way out west lies the spacious riverside suburb of Belém, while up the river to the east can be found the ultra-modern Parque das Nações.

LISBON IN...

→ **ONE DAY**
Alfama, Castelo São Jorge, Bairro Alto.

→ **TWO DAYS**
Baixa, Calouste Gulbenkian Museum, Parque das Nações.

→ **THREE DAYS**
Museu Nacional de Arte Antiga, Belém.

ARRIVAL-DEPARTURE

Lisbon Portela Airport is 7km north of the town centre. The Metro Red Line takes about 20min. The Aerobus runs every 20-30min.

GETTING AROUND

Lisbon is easy to get around. Four metro lines cover much of the central part of the city and there are six main bus routes and three funiculars. Buses and trams operate every 11-15 minutes; tram routes 15 and 28 serve the main sights. Tickets can be bought as a single fare but it might be worthwhile investing in a 7 Colinas or Viva Viagem Card, which can be loaded with various tickets (which give discounts on standard single fares) or with pre-pay credit for 'zapping'. The 24, 48 or 72 hr Lisboa Card is valid for unlimited travel on public transport and for free or reduced admission to most museums and cultural sites.

CALENDAR HIGHLIGHTS

February
Carnaval.

March
Spring Festival.

April
CCB Music Festival.

June
Festas dos Santos Populares (Feast Days of the Popular Saints), National Day, Lisbon Book Fair, Alkantara Festival (17-day jamboree).

July
Super Bock Super Rock Festival, Almada International Theatre Festival.

November
Arte Lisboa.

EATING OUT

Lisboetas love their local agricultural produce and the cuisine of the region can be characterised by its honesty and simplicity. The city has an age-old maritime tradition and there are a number of fishing ports nearby, so ocean-fresh fish and seafood features in a range of dishes. One thing the locals love in particular is bacalhau (cod), and it's said that in Lisbon, there's a different way to prepare it for every day of the year: it may come oven-baked, slow-cooked or cooked in milk, and it can be served wrapped in cabbage, with tocino belly pork or in a myriad of other ways. While eating in either a humble tasca, a casa de pasto or a restaurante, other specialities to keep an eye out for are clams cooked with garlic and coriander, traditional beef, chicken and sausage stew with vegetables and rice, bean casserole with tocino belly pork, and lamprey eel with rice. Enjoy them with a vinho verde, the wine of the region. A service charge will be included on your bill but it's customary to leave a tip of about ten per cent.

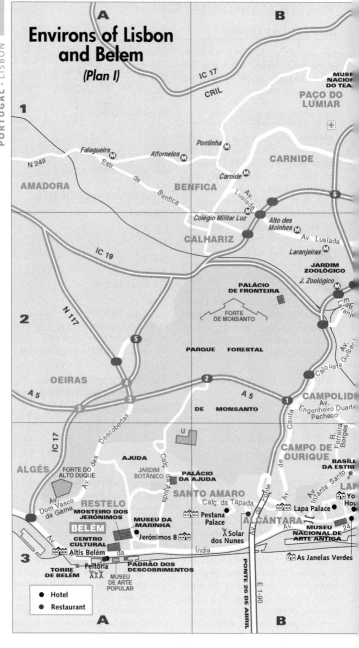

Environs of Lisbon and Belem
(Plan I)

IC 17
CRIL

MUSE NACIONA DO TEA

PAÇO DO LUMIAR

Pontinha

Falagueirs Afforneios

N 249 Estr. de Benfica

AMADORA

BENFICA

Carnide

CARNIDE

Av. Lusíada

Colégio Militar Luz

Alto des Moinhes

Av. Lusíada

IC 19

CALHARIZ

Laranjeiras

JARDIM ZOOLÓGICO

PALÁCIO DE FRONTEIRA

J. Zoológico

FORTE DE MONSANTO

N 117

PARQUE FORESTAL

Estr. Laranje

Av. Gulben

OEIRAS

A 5

DE MONSANTO

A 5

Caula

Calouste Gulbenki

CAMPOLIDE
Av. Engenheiro Duarte Pacheco

IC 17

ALGÉS

Av. das Descobertas

U

AJUDA

Calç. da Ajuda

PALÁCIO DA AJUDA

da Ponte

de

Av. Infante Santo

CAMPO DE OURIQUE

Ferreira Borges

BASÍLI DA ESTRE

LA

FORTE DO ALTO DUQUE

JARDIM BOTÂNICO

SANTO AMARO

Calç. da Tapada

Pestana Palace

Lapa Palace

Yo Hou

Av. Vasco da Gama

RESTELO

MOSTEIRO DOS JERÓNIMOS

MUSEU DA MARINHA

Solar dos Nunes

ALCÂNTARA

MUSEU NACIONAL DE ARTE ANTIGA

24

BELÉM

CENTRO CULTURAL

Jerónimos 8

Av.

Índia

As Janelas Verdes

Altis Belém

TORRE DE BELÉM

Feitoria

da

PADRÃO DOS DESCOBRIMENTOS

MUSEU DE ARTE POPULAR

PONTE 25 DE ABRIL

E 1-90

● Hotel
● Restaurant

648

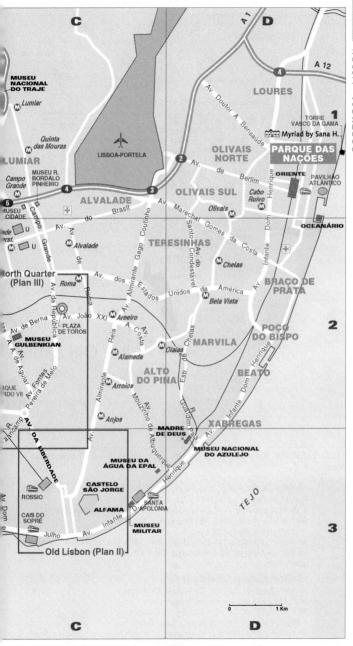

C
D

A 1
D

A 12

MUSEU
NACIONAL
DO TRAJE

Lumiar

LOURES

A 4

TORRE
VASCO DA GAMA

Myriad by Sana H.

Quinta
das Mouras

LISBOA-PORTELA

OLIVAIS
NORTE

Av. de Berlim

PARQUE DAS
NAÇÕES

ORIENTE

PAVILHÃO
ATLÂNTICO

LUMIAR

Campo
Grande

MUSEU R.
BORDALO
PINHEIRO

ALVALADE

OLIVAIS SUL

Cabo
Ruivo

Av. Doutor A. Bensaúde

Av. de Berlim

Henrique

MUSEU
CIDADE

Campo

Av. do Brasil

Av. Marechal Gomes da Costa

Olivais

OCEANÁRIO

Av. Infante Dom

U
U

Av. Alvalade

TERESINHAS

Av. do Condestável

Chelas

BRAÇO DE
PRATA

orth Quarter
(Plan III)

Av. dos Estados

Av. Almirante Gago Coutinho

Unidos

da

América

POÇO
DO BISPO

2

Roma

Av. de Roma

MUSEU
GULBENKIAN

Av. da República

Av. João XXI

Areeiro

PLAZA
DE TOROS

A. Costa

Chelas

Bela Vista

Av. de Berna

Av. A. de Aguiar

Reis

Av. Almirante

Alameda

Olaias

MARVILA

Henrique

BEATO

Av. Infante Dom

ARQUE
RDO VII

Av. Fontes Pereira de Melo

ALTO
DO PINA

Av. Guadim Pais

Estr.

Arroios

Av. Mouzinho de Albuquerque

R.

AV. DA LIBERDADE

Anjos

MADRE
DE DEUS

XABREGAS

MUSEU NACIONAL
DO AZULEJO

ROSSIO

MUSEU DA
ÁGUA DA EPAL

CASTELO
SÃO JORGE

Av. Infante Dom Henrique

CAIS DO
SOPRÉ

ALFAMA

SANTA
APOLÓNIA

TEJO

Av. Dom

Julho

Av. Infante

MUSEU
MILITAR

3

Old Lisbon (Plan II)

0   1 Km

C
D

649

NORTH QUARTER (Plan III)

Old Lisbon
(Plan II)

0   300 m

TEJO

OLD LISBON (Alfama, Castelo de São Jorge, Rossio, Baixa, Chiado, Bairro Alto)
PLAN II

Avenida Palace

Rua 1° de Dezembro 123 ✉ *1200-359*   Plan: **E1**
– **Ⓜ** *Restauradores* – 𝄞 *213 21 81 00* – www.hotelavenidapalace.pt
66 rm ⌁ – 🛉148/194 € 🛉🛉181/228 € – 16 suites
• Historic • Elegant •
An elegant, prestigious building dating from 1892. This hotel has a magnificent lounge area, delightful English-style bar and well-maintained, classical-style guestrooms.

Sofitel Lisbon Liberdade

Av. da Liberdade 127 ✉ *1269-038* – **Ⓜ** *Avenida*   Plan: **E1**
– 𝄞 *213 22 83 00* – www.sofitel-lisboa.com
151 rm – 🛉🛉160/530 € – ⌁ 25 € – 12 suites
• Business • Townhouse • Design •
This hotel is decorated in contemporary-style with numerous designer details. It has fully equipped guestrooms furnished with top-quality materials.
Ad Lib – See restaurant listing

650

PORTUGAL - LISBON

Bairro Alto H
Praça Luis de Camões 2 ✉ *1200-243* – Ⓜ *Baixa-Chiado*
– ☏ *213 40 82 88* – www.bairroaltohotel.com
51 rm ☑ – ♥♥270/440 € – 4 suites
• Luxury • Elegant • Classic •
This hotel in the historic centre of Lisbon gives priority to keeping its guestrooms in pristine condition. Contemporary decor, excellent service and a panoramic rooftop terrace. The simply furnished restaurant overlooks the attractive Luís de Camões square.

Plan: **E2**

Heritage Av Liberdade
Av. da Liberdade 28 ✉ *1250-145* – Ⓜ *Avenida*
– ☏ *213 40 40 40* – www.heritage.pt
42 rm – ♥150/450 € ♥♥163/450 € – ☑ 14 €
• Business • Contemporary •
The Heritage has a classic façade and a multipurpose public area, which also serves as the breakfast room. Well-appointed guestrooms that are contemporary in style.

Plan: **E1**

Internacional Design H.
Rua da Betesga 3 ✉ *1100-090* – Ⓜ *Rossio*
– ☏ *213 240 990* – www.idesignhotel.com
55 rm ☑ – ♥100/400 € ♥♥110/400 €
• Townhouse • Design •
In keeping with the hotel name, the decor here is very much designer focused. The guestrooms are on four floors, each with its own style: urban, tribal, zen and pop.

Plan: **E2**

Do Chiado
Rua Nova do Almada 114 ✉ *1200-290*
– Ⓜ *Baixa-Chiado* – ☏ *213 25 61 00* – www.hoteldochiado.pt
39 rm ☑ – ♥120/240 € ♥♥150/300 €
• Townhouse • Oriental •
A hotel with well-appointed guestrooms in the heart of the Chiado district. Those on the seventh floor have private balconies with splendid views of the city.

Plan: **E2**

The Beautique H. Figueira
Praça da Figueira 16 ✉ *1100-241* – Ⓜ *Rossio*
– ☏ *210 49 29 40* – www.thebeautiquehotels.com
50 rm ☑ – ♥98/420 € ♥♥105/465 €
• Chain hotel • Design •
A hotel occupying a completely remodelled building, which now boasts a distinct designer look. The intimately styled guestrooms (some with a shower, others a bathtub) are superbly appointed. Enjoy traditional Portuguese cuisine in the hotel restaurant.

Plan: **E-F2**

Britania
Rua Rodrigues Sampaio 17 ✉ *1150-278* – Ⓜ *Avenida*
– ☏ *213 15 50 16* – www.heritage.pt
33 rm – ♥130/450 € ♥♥143/450 € – ☑ 14 €
• Townhouse • Art Deco •
A unique property designed by the famous Portuguese architect Cassiano Branco. Stylish lounge-bar and meticulous bedrooms showcasing the spirit of the Art Deco period.

Plan: **E1**

NH Liberdade
Av. da Liberdade 180-B ✉ *1250-146* – Ⓜ *Avenida*
– ☏ *213 51 40 60* – www.nh-hotels.com
83 rm – ♥♥90/255 € – ☑ 14.50 €
• Business • Functional •
A good choice in Lisbon's business district. Highlights include the comfortable guestrooms designed in a contemporary style and the rooftop terrace boasting magnificent views of the old city. The multi-function restaurant offers Portuguese à la carte options alongside a selection of pasta dishes.

Plan: **E1**

Olissippo Castelo

Rua Costa do Castelo 120 ✉ *1100-179 –* Ⓜ *Rossio*
– ☎ *218 82 01 90 – www.olissippohotels.com*   Plan: **F1-2**
24 rm ☟ – 🛏200/220 € 🛏🛏220/240 €
• Family • Classic •

Located on a hill next to the San Jorge castle, part of this hotel is built up against the castle ramparts. Very comfortable guestrooms, a dozen of which have their own garden terrace and magnificent views.

Solar do Castelo

Rua das Cozinhas 2 ✉ *1100-181 –* ☎ *218 80 60 50*
– www.heritage.pt   Plan: **F2**
20 rm – 🛏162/450 € 🛏🛏176/450 € – ☟ 14 €
• Historic • Contemporary •

This hotel partially occupies a small 18C palace. It boasts a pretty paved patio with peacocks and a tiny ceramics museum. The classic yet contemporary guestrooms have seven personalised rooms in the palace itself and these offer greater comfort.

Memmo Alfama H.

Travessa das Merceeiras 27 ✉ *1100-348*   Plan: **F2**
– ☎ *210 49 56 60 – www.memmohotels.com*
42 rm ☟ – 🛏🛏180/450 €
• Townhouse • Design •

Modern, truly unique and with a great location in the heart of the Alfama district, where it occupies three inter-connected buildings. Make sure you spend time enjoying the idyllic views from its sun terraces.

Solar dos Mouros

Rua do Milagre de Santo António 6 ✉ *1100-351*
– ☎ *218 85 49 40 – www.solardosmouroslisboa.com*   Plan: **F2**
13 rm ☟ – 🛏109/199 € 🛏🛏129/299 €
• Holiday hotel • Contemporary •

A traditional-style hotel with an original decor, a somewhat irregular layout and a modern interior. Colourful guestrooms, some enjoying excellent views.

Belcanto (José Avillez)

Largo de São Carlos 10 ✉ *1200-410 –* Ⓜ *Baixa-Chiado*
– ☎ *213 42 06 07 – www.belcanto.pt – Closed 18 Janeiro-2 February, 1-*   Plan: **E2**
16 August, Sunday and Monday
Menu 90/145 € – Carte approx. 98 €
• Creative • Classic •

Behind the Belcanto's discreet façade in the Bairro Alto (a district popular with tourists) guests will be surprised to find elegant dining rooms with a classic yet contemporary feel. Its talented chef conjures up creative cuisine combining technical skill and imaginative flair. The end result is beautifully prepared and presented. It can be enjoyed via various menus, each as enticing as the next.
→ A horta da galinha dos ovos de ouro. Mergulho no mar, robalo com algas e bivalves. Tangerina.

Tágide

Largo da Academia Nacional de Belas Artes 18-20
✉ *1200-005 –* Ⓜ *Baixa-Chiado –* ☎ *213 40 40 10*   Plan: **E2**
– www.restaurantetagide.com – Closed Sunday
Menu 45 € – Carte 38/69 €
• Modern cuisine • Classic •

Climb a few steps to Tágide's elegant dining room embellished with spider lamps and attractive azulejo tilework. Updated traditional cuisine and a tapas bar at the entrance.

XX **Solar dos Presuntos**   🦞 ♿ 🄰🄲 🚗
Rua das Portas de Santo Antão 150 ⊠ 1150-269   Plan: **E1**
*– Ⓜ Avenida – 𝒞 213 42 42 53 – www.solardospresuntos.com – Closed
August, Christmas, Sunday and Bank Holidays*
Menu 47 € – Carte 45/70 €
• Traditional cuisine • Inn •
Run by its owners, this pleasant restaurant has an attractive counter of fresh
produce on display. Large selection of traditional dishes and seafood speciali-
ties, as well as an excellent wine list.

XX **Ad Lib** – Hotel Sofitel Lisbon Liberdade   🄰🄲
Av. da Liberdade 127 ⊠ 1269-038 – Ⓜ Avenida   Plan: **E1**
– 𝒞 213 22 83 50 – www.restauranteadlib.pt
Menu 20/45 € – Carte 43/62 €
• Modern cuisine • Trendy •
Contemporary dining with a colonial touch. Two types of menu are offered
here. The menu at lunchtime combines traditional cuisine with French brasse-
rie-style dining. The menu in the evening is a more elaborate affair.

X **Mini Bar Teatro**   🛜 ♿ 🄰🄲
Rúa António Maria Cardoso 58 ⊠ 1200-027   Plan: **E2**
– Ⓜ Baixa-Chiado – 𝒞 211 30 53 93 – www.minibar.pt
Menu 39/49 € – Carte 30/40 € – *(dinner only)*
• Creative • Bistro •
An informal, enticing and relaxed eatery in the Bairro Alto theatre district. Diners
are in for a pleasant surprise as the dishes on the menu have been created by
José Avillez – Michelin-starred chef at the Belcanto restaurant.

X **100 Maneiras**   🄰🄲
Rua do Teixeira 35 ⊠ 1200-459 – 𝒞 910 30 75 75   Plan: **E1**
– www.restaurante100maneiras.com
Menu 55 € – *(dinner only) (set menu only)*
• Creative • Simple •
A small restaurant in a narrow street in the Barrio Alto district. The young chef
offers a creative tasting menu, which is fresh, light and imaginatively presented.

NORTH QUARTER (Av. da Liberdade, Parque Eduardo VII, Museu
Gulbenkian)   **PLAN III**

🏯🏯 **Four Seasons H. Ritz Lisbon**   🍽 < 🛁 🕸 🖥 ♿ 🄰🄲 🎿 🚗
Rua Rodrigo da Fonseca 88 ⊠ 1099-039   Plan: **G3**
– Ⓜ Marquês de Pombal – 𝒞 213 81 14 00 – www.fourseasons.com
241 rm – ♟390/585 € – � 39 € – 41 suites
• Luxury • Classic • Stylish •
Experience true pleasure at this luxury hotel where the contemporary look of
the building contrasts with the incredibly bright and classically elegant interior.
Spacious lounge areas, highly comfortable guestrooms, and an impressive array
of beauty treatments.
Varanda – See restaurant listing

🏯🏯 **Sheraton Lisboa**   🍽 < 🛁 🕸 🏊 ♿ 🄰🄲 🎿 🚗
Rua Latino Coelho 1 ⊠ 1069-025 – Ⓜ Picoas   Plan: **H2**
– 𝒞 213 120 000 – www.sheratonlisboa.com
369 rm – ♟139/410 € – ⊻ 24 € – 11 suites
• Business • Modern •
Clearly focused towards a business clientele, the Sheraton's main selling points
are its meeting and conference rooms and comfortable guestrooms. The latter
are generally modern in appearance with glass-fronted bathrooms and spectacular views of Lisbon from those on the upper floors.

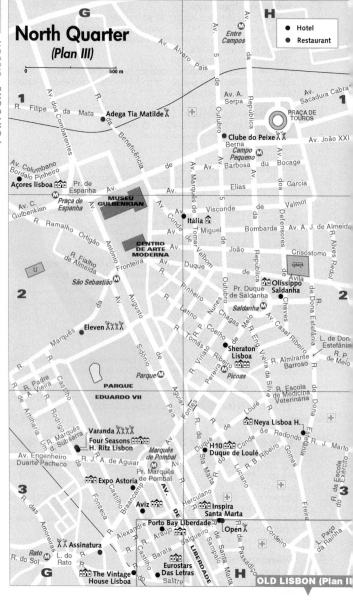

North Quarter
(Plan III)

0   500 m

Hotel
Restaurant

Adega Tia Matilde

Entre Campos

Av. Álvaro Pais

Av. A. Serpa

Av. Sacadura Cabra

PRAÇA DE TOUROS

Av. João XXI

R. Filipe
da Mata
Av. dos Combatentes
Beneficência

Clube do Peixe

Berna

Campo Pequeno

Av. Columbano Bordalo Pinheiro

Açores lisboa

Pr. de Espanha

Praça de Espanha

MUSEU GULBENKIAN

Av. Conde de Tomar

Itália

Av. Barbosa du Bocage

Elias

Garcia

Av. C. Gulbenkian

R. Ramalho Ortigão

Visconde

Miguel

Bombarda

Valmor

Av. A. J. de Almeida

R. Fialho de Almeida

CENTRO DE ARTE MODERNA

António Fronteira

Av. Duque

João

Crisóstomo

São Sebastião

Av. da

Augusto

R. Pinheiro

Pr. Duque de Saldanha

Olissippo Saldanha

Saldanha

R. de Dona Estefânia

Eleven

R. Latino Coelho

R. Tomás

R. Viriato

Eng. Vieira da Silva

Chaves

Av. Casal Ribeiro

L. de Don Estefânia

R. P. de Melo

Marquês

Sidónio

Parque

Sheraton Lisboa

Picoas

R. Almirante Barroso

R. Escola de Medicina Veterinária

PARQUE EDUARDO VII

Aguiar

Fontes

Pais

Loulé

Neya Lisboa H.

R. J. Marto

Varanda
Four Seasons
H. Ritz Lisbon

Marquês de Pombal

H10 Duque de Loulé

de Conde de Redondo

Av. Engenheiro Duarte Pacheco

R. J. A. de Aguiar

Pr. Marquês de Pombal

R. B. Ribeiro

Gomes

R. da Escola do Exército

Expo Astoria

Castilho Braamcamp

AV. DA LIBERDADE

Herculano

Inspira Santa Marta

Aviz

Porto Bay Liberdade

Open

Assinatura

L. do Rato

Barata

Salgueiro

Sampaio

R. de Passadico

L. Paço da Rainha

Rato

R. do Sol

The Vintage House Lisboa

Eurostars Das Letras

Salitre

OLD LISBON (Plan II)

654

Eurostars Das Letras

Rua Castilho 6-12 ✉ *1250-069* – ☏ *213 57 30 94*
– *www.eurostarshotels.com*   Plan: **G3**
107 rm 🖃 – ♦94/300 € ♦♦129/350 € – 6 suites
• Townhouse • Contemporary •

The modern look and designer detail in the hotel's public areas compete with
the crisp aesthetics of its classic guestrooms, which are comfortable and contemporary in style. The multi-function restaurant offers a choice of traditional
cuisine.

 Porto Bay Liberdade

Rua Rosa Araújo 8 ✉ *1250-195* – Ⓜ *Avenida*   Plan: **G3**
– ☏ *210 01 57 00* – *www.portobay.com*
95 rm 🖃 – ♦140/201 € ♦♦158/226 € – 3 suites
• Townhouse • Contemporary •

This establishment occupies a restored palatial property with a delightfully
classic façade and an interior with a contemporary feel. Attractive lobby and
well-appointed bedrooms with a classic-modern look, although the standard
rooms are a little on the small side. A bistro-style menu is on offer in the restaurant.

 The Vintage House Lisboa

Rua Rodrigo da Fonseca 2 ✉ *1250-191* – Ⓜ *Rato*   Plan: **G3**
– ☏ *210 40 54 00* – *www.nauhotels.com*
53 rm 🖃 – ♦♦115/360 € – 3 suites
• Townhouse • Contemporary •

Strong attention to detail has resulted in a look that is both personalised and
welcoming. The guestrooms are classic yet contemporary in style with top quality fixtures and furnishings. The multi-function restaurant is the setting for
breakfast, lunch and dinner.

 Aviz

Rua Duque de Palmela 32 ✉ *1250-098*   Plan: **G3**
– Ⓜ *Marquês de Pombal* – ☏ *210 40 20 00* – *www.hotelaviz.com*
56 rm 🖃 – ♦67/200 € ♦♦97/250 € – 14 suites
• Traditional • Classic •

This classically designed hotel features an elegant lobby and meticulously furnished and equipped guestrooms. Each one is dedicated to a character from
history who has stayed here.

 Açores Lisboa

Av. Columbano Bordalo Pinheiro 3 ✉ *1070-060*   Plan: **G1**
– Ⓜ *Praça de Espanha* – ☏ *217 22 29 20* – *www.bensaudehotels.com*
123 rm 🖃 – ♦69/292 € ♦♦76/299 € – 5 suites
• Business • Contemporary •

A modern and functional chain hotel with friendly and enthusiastic staff. The
limited space in its public areas is compensated by the well-appointed guestrooms and fully equipped bathrooms. The restaurant offers a buffet at midday,
and a traditional menu at night.

 Inspira Santa Marta

Rua Santa Marta 48 ✉ *1150-297*   Plan: **H3**
– Ⓜ *Marqués de Pombal* – ☏ *210 44 09 00* – *www.inspirahotels.com*
89 rm – ♦99/240 € ♦♦109/250 € – 🖃 15 €
• Townhouse • Modern •

A hotel combining designer features, comfort and a spa. Its aim is to be environmentally sustainable and it has rooms arranged according to the Oriental principles of Feng Shui.
Open – See restaurant listing

PORTUGAL - LISBON

H10 Duque de Loulé

Avenida Duque de Loulé 81-83 ✉ 1050-088 Plan: **H3**
– Ⓜ Marqués de Pombal – ☎ 213 18 20 00 – www.h10hotels.com
84 rm – †90/190 € ††100/200 € – ☕ 15 € – 5 suites
• Traditional • Classic • Cosy •

A hotel with lots of personality occupying a former convent from which it has retained the original façade. The splendid interior comes as a delightful surprise with its mix of modernity and traditional Portuguese-style. The focus in the restaurant is very much on the country's gastronomy.

Expo Astoria

Rua Braamcamp 10 ✉ 1250-050 Plan: **G3**
– Ⓜ Marquês de Pombal – ☎ 213 86 13 17 – www.expoastoria.pt
109 rm ☕ – †63/119 € ††73/129 €
• Townhouse • Minimalist •

The hotel's attractive, classical façade leads to a modern interior featuring lots of designer detail. The best rooms are those with a lounge and glass-fronted balcony. The restaurant menu is a little on the unusual side with several dishes featuring prawns as the main ingredient.

Olissippo Saldanha

Av. Praia da Vitória 30 ✉ 1000-248 – Ⓜ Saldanha Plan: **H2**
– ☎ 210 00 66 90 – www.olissippohotels.com
49 rm ☕ – †180/200 € ††200/220 €
• Townhouse • Modern • Minimalist •

A hotel with a distinctly urban feel, in which the lack of public spaces is compensated by particularly comfortable guestrooms. These are bright, contemporary and boast individually designed headboards.

Neya Lisboa H.

Rua Dona Estefânia 71 ✉ 1150-132 – ☎ 213 10 18 01 Plan: **H3**
– www.vivalisboa.pt
72 rm ☕ – †60/180 € ††70/250 € – 4 suites
• Townhouse • Contemporary •

A hotel with a contemporary feel in a residential district close to the city centre, opposite the Dona Estefânia hospital. Small foyer with a lobby bar, up-to-date guestrooms, plus a restaurant offering a concise menu featuring Portuguese and Italian dishes.

Itália

Av. Visconde de Valmor 67 ✉ 1050-239 Plan: **G-H2**
– Ⓜ Saldanha – ☎ 217 61 14 90 – www.hotelitalia.pt
44 rm – †35/250 € ††45/450 € – ☕ 5 €
• Family • Functional •

The attractive patio with its tables, lawn and orange trees comes as a pleasant surprise in the centre of the city. The guestrooms are modern, simple and functional.

Eleven (Joachim Koerper)

Rua Marquês de Fronteira ✉ 1070-051 – Ⓜ São Sebastião Plan: **G2**
– ☎ 213 86 22 11 – www.restauranteleven.com – Closed Sunday
Menu 76 € – Carte 65/98 €
• Creative • Formal •

Housed in a designer-style building above the Amália Rodrigues gardens, this light, airy and modern restaurant boasts splendid views of the Eduardo VII park and the city. Creative gourmet cuisine features on the menu.

➜ Salada de lavagante com raviolis de melancia e vinagrete de hortelã. Carré de cordeiro marinado em saké, alho preto e infusão de nori. Sopa de morangos biológicos com gelado de Grand Marnier.

Varanda – Hotel Four Seasons H. Ritz Lisbon

Rua Rodrigo da Fonseca 88 ✉ 1099-039 Plan: **G3**
– Ⓜ Marquês de Pombal – ☎ 213 81 14 00 – www.fourseasons.com
Carte 50/80 €
• Modern cuisine • Classic •

This restaurant stands out both for its terrace overlooking the Eduardo VII park and for its cuisine, which includes a full buffet and contemporary-style dishes.

PORTUGAL - LISBON

XX **Assinatura** 🔲 ⇔
Plan: **G3**
Rua Vale do Pereiro 19 ✉ *1250-270 –* Ⓜ *Rato*
– ℘ *213 86 76 96 – www.assinatura.com.pt – Closed Saturday lunch,*
Sunday and Monday lunch
Menu 47/56 € – Carte 23/48 €
• Modern cuisine • Formal •

A restaurant with a minimalist atmosphere, a colour scheme focusing on red and white tones, and a private room called 'The Chef's Table'. Updated traditional cuisine.

XX **Clube do Peixe** 🔲
Plan: **H1**
Av. 5 de Outubro 180-A ✉ *1050-063 –* Ⓜ *Campo Pequeno*
– ℘ *217 97 34 34 – www.clube-do-peixe.com – Closed Sunday*
Carte 25/39 €
• Fish and seafood • Classic •

A popular local restaurant with an attractive display of fish and seafood at the entrance. The dining room is classic-contemporary in style with the occasional maritime detail in the decor.

X **Open** – Hotel Inspira Santa Marta 🔲
Plan: **H3**
Rua Santa Marta 48 ✉ *1150-297 –* ℘ *210 44 09 00*
– www.open.com.pt – Closed Saturday lunch, Sunday lunch and Bank
Holidays lunch
Menu 14/35 € – Carte 20/38 €
• Modern cuisine • Design •

A restaurant with a young and relaxed ambience. Healthy, contemporary cooking that endeavours to work with organic products as much as possible. Gluten-free dishes are also available.

X **Adega Tia Matilde** 🔲 ⇔ 🚗
Plan: **G1**
Rua da Beneficéncia 77 ✉ *1600-017*
– Ⓜ *Praça de Espanha –* ℘ *217 97 21 72 – www.adegatiamatilde.com*
– Closed Saturday dinner and Sunday
Menu 27 € – Carte 25/50 €
• Traditional cuisine • Classic •

Family-run restaurant with a good local reputation. Spacious dining rooms and traditional cuisine. The large underground car park makes up for the poor location.

PARQUE DAS NAÇÕES PLAN I

🏨 **Myriad by Sana H.**
Plan: **D1**
Cais das Naus, Lote 2.21.01 (Parque das Naçoes)
✉ *1990-173 –* Ⓜ *Oriente –* ℘ *211 10 76 00 – www.myriad.pt*
186 rm – 🛏210 € 🛏🛏240 € – ☕ 30 €
• Business • Modern •

A hotel with a striking look next to the Vasco de Gama tower. The interior showcases high-level design and functionality with every guestroom overlooking the river and the impressive terrace. The restaurant offers both Portuguese and international cuisine.

WEST PLAN I

🏨 **Pestana Palace** 🛎 🐕 🍴 🏊 🖥 & 🔲 🧖 🚗
Plan: **B3**
Rua Jau 54 ✉ *1300-314 –* ℘ *213 61 56 00*
– www.pestana.com
177 rm ☕ – 🛏🛏199/358 € – 17 suites
• Grand Luxury • Elegant •

A beautiful 19C palace decorated in line with the period with sumptuous lounges, guestrooms featuring an array of decorative detail, and grounds that have the feel of a botanical garden. In the restaurant, choose from several set menus at lunchtime and traditional à la carte choices with a modern flair in the evening. A small private room is also available in the old kitchen.

Lapa Palace

☆ ⌚ ⬳ ⌂ ⌘ ⌸ ⌖ ⌻ ⟁ 🅰 🅺 🚗

Rua do Pau de Bandeira 4 ✉ *1249-021* – **Ⓜ** *Rato* — Plan: **B3**
– 𝒞 *213 94 94 94* – *www.olissippohotels.com*
102 rm ⌚ – ♥♥370/430 € – 7 suites
• Grand Luxury • Classic • Stylish •

A luxurious 19C palace standing on one of the seven hills overlooking Lisbon and boasting stunning views of the Tagus estuary. The elegant and bright restaurant serves pleasantly updated traditional cuisine. The perfect setting for an unforgettable stay!

As Janelas Verdes

⌖ 🅰

Rua das Janelas Verdes 47 ✉ *1200-690* — Plan: **B3**
– 𝒞 *213 96 81 43* – *www.heritage.pt*
29 rm – ♥143/450 € ♥♥157/450 € – ⌚14 €
• Traditional • Classic • Elegant •

This hotel partially occupies an 18C house that is also home to the National Museum of Ancient Art. The hotel has a delightful mix of classic romanticism, warmth, history and personality.

York House

☆ 🅰 🚗

Rua das Janelas Verdes 32 ✉ *1200-691* — Plan: **B3**
– 𝒞 *213 96 24 35* – *www.yorkhouselisboa.com*
33 rm – ♥90/155 € ♥♥120/185 € – ⌚15 €
• Historic • Contemporary • Functional •

This hotel housed in a 17C Carmelite convent has retained much of its original character. Its renovated interior offers modern comfort and decor. It has two types of guestrooms available, one contemporary and the other more classic in design. The restaurant is striking for its old glazed tiles.

Solar dos Nunes

🅰 🥘

Rua dos Lusíadas 68-72 ✉ *1300-372* – 𝒞 *213 64 73 59* — Plan: **B3**
– *www.solardosnunes.pt* – *Closed Sunday*
Menu 30/60 € – Carte 30/58 €
• Traditional cuisine • Rustic •

This welcoming restaurant stands out for the magnificent mosaic-style floor in the main dining room and its walls covered with appreciative newspaper and magazine reviews. Impressive fish display, as well as a live seafood tank. Traditional Portuguese menu and an excellent wine list.

BELÉM — PLAN I

Altis Belém

☆ ⬳ ⌘ 🌐 ⌻ ⌖ 🅰 🚗 🌊

Doca do Bom Sucesso ✉ *1400-038* – 𝒞 *210 400 200* — Plan: **A3**
– *www.altishotels.com*
45 rm ⌚ – ♥350/400 € ♥♥390/500 € – 5 suites
• Luxury • Modern •

Luxury and modernity in equal measure! Facilities here include a rooftop chill-out zone, minimalist café and spacious guestrooms, all decorated around the theme of the country's age of discoveries and its cultural exchanges. Enjoy cuisine with a contemporary flair in the bright and elegant restaurant.
❀ **Feitoria** – See restaurant listing

Jerónimos 8

⌖ 🅰 🚗

Rua dos Jerónimos 8 ✉ *1400-211* – 𝒞 *213 60 09 00* — Plan: **A3**
– *www.themahotels.pt*
65 rm ⌚ – ♥135/250 € ♥♥140/280 €
• Business • Modern •

This comfortable hotel is located next to the Monasterio de Los Jerónimos. It occupies an old building that has been completely renovated with a minimalist feel.

XxX **Feitoria** – Hotel Altis Belém 🕸 📶 ᴧ 🅰 🚗

🕸 *Doca do Bom Sucesso* ✉ *1400-038* – ☏ *210 40 02 08*
– *www.restaurantefeitoria.com* – *Closed Sunday*
Menu 85/145 € – Carte 70/91 € – *(dinner only)*
• Modern cuisine • Inn •

A restaurant of a very high standard featuring a bar for a pre-dinner drink and a dining room arranged in contemporary-style. The chef offers creative, modern cuisine steeped in tradition, with a focus on high quality products and top-notch presentation.

→ Âmbar de sapateira, maçã e wasabi. Carré de vitela de leite com puré de batata e cogumelos silvestres. Chocolate, fava tonka, caramelo e flor de sal.

PORTUGAL - LISBON

SPAIN
ESPAÑA

→ **AREA:**
504 645 km²
(194 595 sq mi).

→ **POPULATION:**
46 439 864 inhabitants.
Density = 92 per km².

→ **CAPITAL:** Madrid.

→ **CURRENCY:**
Euro (€).

→ **GOVERNMENT:**
Constitutional
parliamentary
monarchy (since 1978).
Member of European
Union since 1986.

→ **LANGUAGES:**
Spanish (Castilian) but also Catalan
in Catalonia, Gallego in Galicia,
Euskera in the Basque Country,
Valencian in the Valencian Region
and Mallorquin in the Balearic Isles.

→ **PUBLIC HOLIDAYS:**
New Year's Day (1 Jan); Epiphany
(6 Jan); Good Friday (late Mar/Apr);
Labor Day (1 May); Assumption of
the Virgin Mary (15 Aug);
National Day (12 Oct); All Saints' Day
(1 Nov); Constitution Day
(6 Dec); Immaculate Conception
(8 Dec); Christmas Day (25 Dec).
Autonomous communities may
replace some dates.

→ **LOCAL TIME:**
GMT+1 hour in winter and GMT
+2 hours in summer.

→ **CLIMATE:**
Temperate Mediterranean with
mild winters (colder in interior)
and sunny, hot summers (Madrid:
January 6°C; July 25°C).

→ **EMERGENCY:**
Police ✆ **091**; Medical Assistance
and Fire Brigade ✆ **112.**
(Dialling **112** within any
EU country will redirect your
call and contact the emergency
services.)

→ **ELECTRICITY:**
230 volts AC, 50Hz; 2 round pin
sockets.

→ **FORMALITIES:**
Travellers from the European Union
(EU), Switzerland, Iceland and the
main countries of North and South
America need a national identity
card or passport (America: passport
required) to visit Spain for less than
three months (tourism or business
purpose). For visitors from other
countries a visa may be required,
in addition to a passport, especially
for those wishing to stay for longer
than three months. We advise you
to check with your embassy before
travelling.

MADRID
MADRID

Population: 3 141 991

Aidas Zubkonis/Fotolia.com

The renaissance of Madrid has seen it develop as a big player on the world cultural stage, attracting more international music, theatre and dance than it would have dreamed of a few decades ago. The nightlife in Spain's proud capital is second to none and the superb museums of art which make up the city's 'golden triangle' have all undergone thrilling reinvention in recent years. This is a city that might think it has some catching up to do: it was only made the capital in 1561 on the whim of ruler, Felipe II. But its position was crucial: slap bang in the middle of the Iberian Peninsula. Ruled by Habsburgs and Bourbons, it soon made a mark in Europe, and the contemporary big wigs of Madrid are now having the same effect – this time with a 21C twist.

The central heart of Madrid is compact, defined by the teeming Habsburg hubs of Puerta del Sol and Plaza Mayor, and the mighty Palacio Real – the biggest official royal residence in the world, with a bewildering three thousand rooms. East of here are the grand squares, fountains and fine museums of the Bourbon District, with its easterly boundary, the Retiro park. West of the historical centre are the capacious green acres of Casa de Campo, while the affluent, regimented grid streets of Salamanca are to the east. Modern Madrid is just to the north, embodied in the grand north-south boulevard Paseo de la Castellana.

MADRID IN...

→ **ONE DAY**
Puerta del Sol, Plaza Mayor, Palacio Real, Prado.

→ **TWO DAYS**
Museo Thyssen-Bornemisza, Retiro, Gran Vía, tapas at a traditional taberna.

→ **THREE DAYS**
Chueca, Malasaña, Centro de Arte Reina Sofía.

PRACTICAL INFORMATION

ARRIVAL-DEPARTURE

✈ Adolfo Suárez Madrid-Barajas Airport is 13km east of the city. Metro Line 8 runs every 4-7min and takes 50min. Commuter rail service C-1 connects T4 with Chamartin and Atocha Railway Stations (frequency 30min); Chamartin for services to the north of Spain and France; Atocha for those to the south.

GETTING AROUND

You can buy single journey tickets, but better value for longer visits is a ten-trip Metrobus ticket, valid on both bus and metro networks, and available from underground stations, bus ticket offices, newsstands and tobacconists. The Tourist Travel Pass is valid from one to seven days for unlimited travel on all public transport in either Zone A or Zone T. A Madrid Card, valid for one, two, three or five day periods, entitles you to travel on all forms of public transport, and grants admission to more than fifty museums. It is also valid for discounts in some nightclubs, shops and restaurants.

CALENDAR HIGHLIGHTS

January
Twelfth Night Procession, Fitur (International Tourism Trade Fair).

February
ARCO (contemporary art fair), Carnaval, Madrid Fusion (gastronomic summit).

April
Día de Cervantes (book fair).

May
Dos de Mayo, Fiesta de San Isidro, Madrid Book Fair.

July-August
Los Veranos de la Villa.

September
Festival de Otoño.

EATING OUT

Madrileños know how to pace themselves. Breakfast is around 8am, lunch 2pm or 3pm; the afternoon begins at 5pm and dinner won't be until 10pm or 11pm. Madrid is the European capital which has best managed to absorb the regional cuisine of the country, largely due to massive internal migration to the city, and it claims to have highest number of bars and restaurants per capita than anywhere else in the world. If you want to tuck into local specialities, you'll find them everywhere around the city. Callos a la Madrileña is Madrid-style tripe, dating back to 1559, while sopas de ajo (garlic soup) is a favourite on cold winter days. Another popular soup (also a main course) is cocido Madrileño, hearty and aromatic and comprised of chickpeas, meat, tocino belly pork, potatoes and vegetables, slowly cooked in a rich broth. To experience the real Madrid dining ambience, get to a traditional taberna in the heart of the old neighbourhood: these are distinguished by a large clock, a carved wooden bar with a zinc counter, wine flasks, marble-topped tables and ceramic tiles.

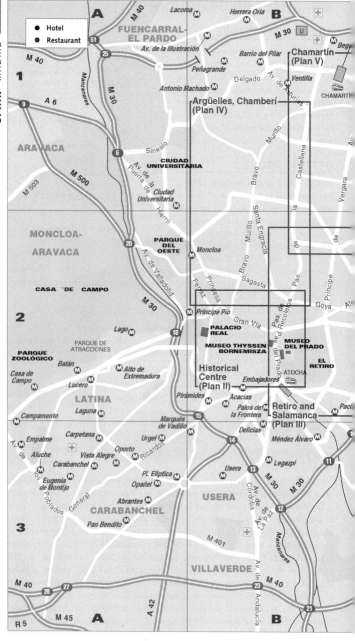

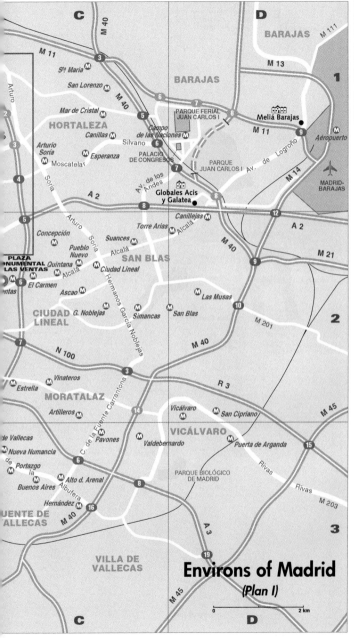

Environs of Madrid

(Plan I)

0   2 km

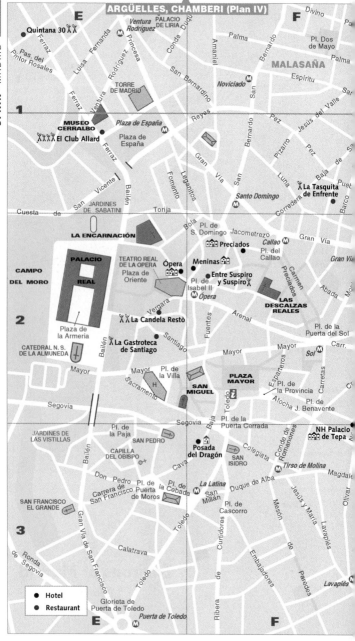

ARGÜELLES, CHAMBERI (Plan IV)

MALASAÑA

Quintana 30

Ventura Rodríguez

PALACIO DE LIRIA

Pas. del Pintor Rosales

Ferraz

Luisa Fernanda

Princesa

Ventura Rodríguez

San Bernardino

TORRE DE MADRID

Plaza de España

MUSEO CERRALBO

El Club Allard

Ferraz

San Vicente

Bailén

Fomento

Leganitos

Gran Vía

San

Bernardo

Luna

Pez

Pizarro

Baja

Santo Domingo

Corredera

La Tasquita de Enfrente

Cuesta de

JARDINES DE SABATINI

Torija

LA ENCARNACIÓN

Pl. de S. Domingo

Jacometrezo

Gran Vía

Callao

Pl. del Callao

Gran Vía

Preciados

Meninas

CAMPO DEL MORO

PALACIO REAL

TEATRO REAL DE LA ÓPERA

Plaza de Oriente

Ópera

Pl. de Isabel II

Ópera

Entre Suspiro y Suspiro

Carmen

Preciados

Abada

LAS DESCALZAS REALES

Plaza de la Armería

La Candela Restò

Vergara

Santiago

Arenal

Pl. de la Puerta del Sol

Sol

CATEDRAL N.S. DE LA ALMUDENA

La Gastroteca de Santiago

Bailén

Mayor

Fuentes

Mayor

Carr.

Mayor

Sacramento

Pl. de la Villa

H

SAN MIGUEL

PLAZA MAYOR

Pl. de la Provincia

Espartero

Carretas

Segovia

Pl. de J. Benavente

Segovia

Baja

Pl. de la Puerta Cerrada

JARDINES DE LAS VISTILLAS

Pl. de la Paja

SAN PEDRO

CAPILLA DEL OBISPO

Posada del Dragón

SAN ISIDRO

Colegiata

Conde de Romanones

NH Palacio de Tepa

Tirso de Molina

Magdale

Bailén

Don Pedro

Cava

Carrera de San Francisco

Pl. de la Cebada

Pl. de Puerta de Moros

La Latina

San Millán

Duque de Alba

Pl. de Cascorro

Mesón

Jesús y María

Olivar

SAN FRANCISCO EL GRANDE

Gran Vía de San Francisco

Toledo

Curtidores

Embajadores

Paredes

Lavapiés

Ronda de Segovia

Calatrava

Toledo

Ribera

● Hotel

● Restaurant

Glorieta de Puerta de Toledo

Puerta de Toledo

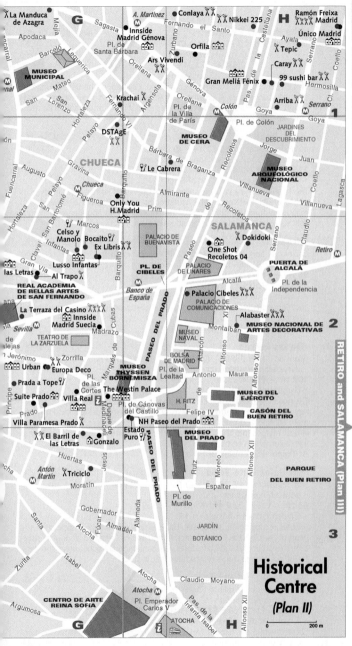

Historical
Centre
(Plan II)

The Westin Palace

pl. de las Cortes 7 ✉ *28014* – Ⓜ *Sevilla*　　　　　　Plan: **G2**
– ℰ *913 60 80 00* – www.westin.com
467 rm – ♥♥750/830 € – ☲ 34 €
• Luxury • Classic • Elegant •

This elegant, historic building is considered a symbol of the Belle Époque. Its unusual lounge area is crowned by an expansive Art Nouveau-style glass atrium. Superb guestrooms furnished in classic-style. Its restaurant, La Rotonda, offers an international menu.

Villa Real

pl. de las Cortes 10 ✉ *28014* – Ⓜ *Sevilla*　　　　　　Plan: **G2**
– ℰ *914 20 37 67* – www.hotelvillareal.com
115 rm – ♥♥140/475 € – ☲ 23 €
• Chain hotel • Personalised •

This hotel displays a valuable collection of Greek and Roman art in many of its public areas. The comfortable guestrooms are attractively decorated with mahogany furniture. This informal restaurant with an abundance of natural light serves cuisine with an international flavour.

Urban

Carrera de San Jerónimo 34 ✉ *28014* – Ⓜ *Sevilla*　　Plan: **G2**
– ℰ *917 87 77 70* – www.hotelurban.com
96 rm – ♥♥175/550 € – ☲ 23 €
• Chain hotel • Design •

An avant-garde hotel with high quality furnishings, attractive lighting effects and numerous works of art on display. Well-equipped guestrooms with real attention to detail.
Europa Decó – See restaurant listing

De las Letras

Gran Vía 11 ✉ *28013* – Ⓜ *Gran Vía* – ℰ *915 23 79 80*　　Plan: **G2**
– www.hoteldelasletras.com
109 rm – ♥♥124/350 € – ☲ 15 €
• Business • Classic •

The hotel's restored façade contrasts sharply with the colourful and contemporary interior. The guestrooms showcase New York-style design, including intimate lighting and even poems on the walls. The modern restaurant, which almost merges into the lounge-bar, offers à la carte choices and set menus with an emphasis on traditional cuisine.
Al Trapo – See restaurant listing

NH Palacio de Tepa

San Sebastián 2 ✉ *28012* – Ⓜ *Sol* – ℰ *913 89 64 90*　　Plan: **F2-3**
– www.nh-hotels.com
83 rm – ♥139/622 € ♥♥149/669 € – ☲ 31 €
• Chain hotel • Modern •

A hotel occupying an aristocratic 18C building with a superb location in the heart of the city's Las Letras district. Although it has retained its original structure, the interior nowadays features very contemporary public areas and minimalist guestrooms, some of which are attic in style.

NH Paseo del Prado

pl. Cánovas del Castillo 4 ✉ *28014*　　　　　　　　　Plan: **G2**
– Ⓜ *Banco de España* – ℰ *913 30 24 00* – www.nh-hotels.com
114 rm – ♥129/289 € ♥♥199/450 € – ☲ 30 €
• Chain hotel • Business • Classic •

Located within the famous "Art Triangle", this chain hotel offers classic-cum-contemporary guestrooms, a café serving traditionally inspired tapas and raciones with a creative touch.

Ópera　　　　　　　　　　　　　　☆ & 🅰🄺 🕍
cuesta de Santo Domingo 2 ✉ *28013 –* Ⓜ *Ópera*　　Plan: **E2**
– ℰ 91 541 28 00 – www.hotelopera.com
79 rm – ♦90/190 € ♦♦100/225 € – ⌿ 12 €
• Chain hotel • Modern •
This hotel has a traditional bar with a lively ambience, one multi-purpose break-fast room and one room for meetings. Modern bedrooms with contemporary furnishings. One of the specific attractions of this restaurant is its live evening performances of opera and zarzuela.

Only You H. Madrid　　　　　　☆ ⌟ & 🅰🄺 🕍 ⇨
Barquillo 21 ✉ *28004 –* Ⓜ *Chueca – ℰ 910 05 22 22*　　Plan: **G1**
– www.onlyyouhotels.com
120 rm – ♦♦165/265 € – ⌿ 22 €
• Business • Design •
A charming hotel occupying a restored 19C palace in the heart of the Chueca district. Considerable work on the inside has resulted in a modern interior featuring myriad decorative details. It has welcoming guest areas, very well-equipped bedrooms, and a pleasant restaurant.

Lusso Infantas　　　　　　　　☆ & 🅰🄺 🕍
Infantas 29 ✉ *28004 –* Ⓜ *Chueca – ℰ 915 21 28 28*　　Plan: **G2**
– www.hotelinfantas.com
40 rm – ♦♦72/248 € – ⌿ 15 €
• Historic • Modern •
The Infantas occupies an old building that has been completely renovated in a contemporary-style. Well-appointed guestrooms and bathrooms.
Ex Libris – See restaurant listing

Preciados　　　　　　　　　　☆ & 🅰🄺 🕍 🍃
Preciados 37 ✉ *28013 –* Ⓜ *Callao – ℰ 914 54 44 00*　　Plan: **F2**
– www.preciadoshotel.com
100 rm – ♦90/225 € ♦♦99/250 € – ⌿ 18 €
• Traditional • Modern •
The plain classic architectural style of this building, dating back to the 19C, contrasts with the modern, fully equipped interior. Smallish, cosy lounge area. This versatile restaurant offers a choice between traditional à la carte dining and two set menus.

Innside Madrid Suecia　　　　　& 🅰🄺 🕍 🍃
Marqués de Casa Riera 4 ✉ *28014*　　　　　　　Plan: **G2**
– Ⓜ *Banco de España – ℰ 912 00 05 70 – www.melia.com*
120 rm – ♦♦125/400 € – ⌿ 20 € – 7 suites
• Chain hotel • Functional •
This hotel is located close to the Círculo de Bellas Artes. It boasts a modern lobby-bar, functional and contemporary guestrooms, as well as a pleasant rooftop terrace with a bar area and superb views.

Suite Prado　　　　　　　　　　　　　🅰🄺
Manuel Fernández y González 10 ✉ *28014*　　　Plan: **G2**
– Ⓜ *Antón Martín – ℰ 914 20 23 18 – www.suiteprado.com*
9 rm – ♦68/220 € ♦♦78/220 € – ⌿ 9 € – 9 suites
• Family • Contemporary •
Behind the classic yet contemporary façade, guests will find this homely hotel which makes up for its limited public areas with reasonably spacious bedrooms, all featuring modern furnishings, and half of which boast a separate lounge area.

One Shot Recoletos 04　　　　　　　& 🅰🄺
Salustiano Olózaga 4 ✉ *28001 –* Ⓜ *Banco de España*　Plan: **H2**
– ℰ 911 82 00 70 – www.oneshothotels.com
61 rm ⌿ – ♦150/300 € ♦♦170/350 €
• Historic • Cosy •
This small hotel with an informal air mixes the old and the new. Although small and on the functional side, the guestrooms are embellished with photos by young contemporary artists.

Meninas   🛇 AC

Campomanes 7 ✉ 28013 – Ⓜ *Ópera – 𝒞 915 41 28 05*   Plan: **F2**
– www.hotelmeninas.com
37 rm – ♦95/165 € ♦♦115/185 € – ⌂ 12 €
• Family • Cosy •

This hotel occupying a residential building is renowned for its friendly and personalised service. It has a welcoming public area with a library, in addition to modern guestrooms.

Gonzalo   AC

Cervantes 34-3ª planta ✉ 28014 – Ⓜ *Antón Martín*   Plan: **G3**
– 𝒞 914 29 27 14 – www.hostalgonzalo.com
11 rm – ♦50 € ♦♦60 €
• Family • Functional •

This typical, family-run guesthouse occupies a residential building in the Las Letras district. Spacious guestrooms with simple, functional furnishings.

Posada del Dragón   ⨂ AC

Cava Baja 14 ✉ 28005 – Ⓜ *La Latina – 𝒞 911 19 14 24*   Plan: **F3**
– www.posadadeldragon.com
27 rm – ♦79/219 € ♦♦89/239 € – ⌂ 12 €
• Historic • Design •

Although it occupies the site of one of the oldest inns in the city, this hotel is a cutting-edge property. It has only retained the framework and 19C courtyard from the original building. The restaurant, which embraces the 'show cooking' concept, occupies what was once the La Antoñita soap factory, from which it takes its name.

XXXX   La Terraza del Casino (Paco Roncero)

❀❀   *Alcalá 15-3° ✉ 28014 –* Ⓜ *Sevilla – 𝒞 915 32 12 75*   Plan: **G2**
– www.casinodemadrid.es – Closed August, Sunday, Monday and Bank Holidays
Menu 69/135 € – Carte 77/93 €
• Creative • Elegant •

A palatial 19C setting for a restaurant that boasts a more contemporary look nowadays. The chef here offers creative à la carte choices, evident from the starters through to the dessert menu, with everything cooked to perfection. Magnificent terrace!
→ Paella con falso arroz de aceite de oliva. Pichón con gelée cru manzana al cassis. Fresas con nata.

XXXX   El Club Allard

❀❀   *Ferraz 2 ✉ 28008 –* Ⓜ *Plaza España – 𝒞 915 59 09 39*   Plan: **E1**
– www.elcluballard.com – Closed August, Sunday and Monday
Menu 86/115 € – *(set menu only)*
• Creative • Classic •

A restaurant housed in a listed modernist building, hence the lack of signage outside. The classically elegant interior provides the backdrop for creative, delicately presented cuisine featuring skilful fusions of ingredients and impressive technical ability.
→ Arroz del mar. Cordero con ñoquis de dátiles y okra. Rocas de chocolate.

XXX   Palacio Cibeles

pl. de Cibeles 1-6° ✉ 28014 – Ⓜ *Banco de España*   Plan: **H2**
– 𝒞 915 23 14 54 – www.adolfo-palaciodecibeles.com
Menu 58/81 € – Carte 58/80 €
• Traditional cuisine • Formal •

The Palacio Cibeles enjoys a marvellous location on the sixth floor of the city's emblematic city hall (Ayuntamiento). In addition to the modern-style dining room, the restaurant has two attractive terraces where guests can dine or simply enjoy a drink. The cooking is of a traditional flavour.

XxX **La Manduca de Azagra**　　　　　　　　　　　AC

Sagasta 14 ⊠ 28014 – **Ⓜ** *Alonso Martínez*　　　　Plan: **G1**
– 𝒞 915 91 01 12 – www.lamanducadeazagra.com – Closed August,
Sunday and Bank Holidays
Carte 35/55 €
• Traditional cuisine • Minimalist •
This spacious, well-located restaurant is decorated in minimalist style with parti-
cular attention paid to the design and lighting. The menu focuses on high qua-
lity produce.

XxX **Alabaster**　　　　　　　　　　　　　　　　&. AC ⇔

Montalbán 9 ⊠ 28014 – **Ⓜ** *Retiro – 𝒞 915 12 11 31*　Plan: **H2**
– www.restaurantealabaster.com – Closed Sunday
Menu 50/70 € – Carte 48/65 €
• Modern cuisine • Fashionable •
A gastro-bar and contemporary interior featuring designer detail and a predominantly white colour scheme. It offers updated traditional cuisine that is devoted to Galician ingredients.

XX **DSTAgE** (Diego Guerrero)　　　　　　　　　　　AC ⇔
ᘓ
Regueros 8 ⊠ 28004 – **Ⓜ** *Alonso Martínez*　　　　Plan: **G1**
– 𝒞 917 02 15 86 – www.dstageconcept.com – Closed Holy Week, 25 July-
14 August, Sunday and Monday
Menu 88/118 € – *(set menu only)*
• Creative • Bistro •
This restaurant has an urban and industrial look and a relaxed feel that reflects
the personality of the chef. The name is an acronym of his core philosophy:
'Days to Smell Taste Amaze Grow & Enjoy'. Discover cuisine that brings dispa-
rate cultures, ingredients and flavours together from Spain, Mexico and Japan.
→ Nigiri de ajoblanco y anguila ahumada. Pichón asado en anticucho de
ají mochero y quinoa negra. La ruta de las especias.

XX **El Barril de las Letras**　　　　　　　　　　　&. AC

Cervantes 28 ⊠ 28014 – **Ⓜ** *Antón Martín*　　　　Plan: **G3**
– 𝒞 91 186 36 32 – www.barrildelasletras.com
Carte 45/55 €
• Traditional cuisine • Friendly •
A restaurant full of contrasts occupying an old stone-built house with a comple-
tely modernised interior, albeit with the occasional exposed brick wall. The tra-
ditional menu includes a fair proportion of fish and seafood dishes.

XX **Ex Libris** – Hotel Lusso Infantas　　　　　　　AC

Infantas 29 ⊠ 28004 – **Ⓜ** *Chueca – 𝒞 915 21 28 28*　Plan: **G2**
– www.restauranteexlibris.com – Closed August
Menu 12 € – Carte 27/40 €
• Traditional cuisine • Elegant •
A restaurant with an attractively maintained contemporary style and an original
decor that features pictures of "ex libris" on the walls. Well-prepared up-to-date
cuisine and a variety of menus.

XX **Europa Decó** – Hotel Urban　　　　　　　　88 AC 🚗

Carrera de San Jerónimo 34 ⊠ 28014 – **Ⓜ** *Sevilla*　Plan: **G2**
– 𝒞 917 87 77 70 – www.hotelurban.com – Closed August, Sunday,
Monday and Bank Holidays
Menu 25 € – Carte 25/62 €
• Mediterranean • Fashionable •
Increasingly popular for its innovative design and excellent service. Mediterra-
nean and ethnic cuisine prepared using fresh and exotic produce.

XX **La Candela Restò** 〔AC〕

Amnistía 10 ⊠ 28013 – Ⓜ Ópera – ℰ 911 73 98 88   Plan: **E2**
– www.lacandelaresto.com – Closed 1-15 August, Sunday and Monday
Menu 53/79 € – *(set menu only)*
• Creative • Friendly •
Both unusual and unique, this restaurant is guaranteed to make an impression!
In the dining room, decorated simply and with a retro touch, the bold cuisine is
a fusion of different culinary cultures.

XX **Quintana 30** 〔AC ⇔ 🎴〕

Quintana 30 ⊠ 28008 – Ⓜ Argüelles – ℰ 915 42 65 20   Plan: **E1**
*– www.restaurantequintana30.com – Closed Holy Week, 15-31 August and
Sunday dinner*
Menu 32/65 € – Carte 40/52 €
• Traditional cuisine • Friendly •
A restaurant with a modern and contemporary look, including a split-level
dining room and a small, glass-fronted private section. Its extensive à la carte
menu of traditional basque and navarra cuisine, particularly rich in cod dishes
and soups and stews, is enhanced by two seasonal set menus.

X **La Tasquita de Enfrente** 〔AC〕

Ballesta 6 ⊠ 28004 – Ⓜ Gran Vía – ℰ 915 32 54 49   Plan: **F1**
– www.latasquitadeenfrente.com – Closed August and Sunday
Menu 50/65 € – Carte 48/75 € – *(booking essential)*
• Traditional cuisine • Family •
Intimate and friendly with a loyal clientele. The chef, who announces the menu
at your table, creates traditional, seasonal cuisine with the occasional contemporary French touch.

X **Entre Suspiro y Suspiro** 〔AC〕

Caños del Peral 3 ⊠ 28013 – Ⓜ Ópera   Plan: **F2**
– ℰ 915 42 06 44 – www.entresuspiroysuspiro.com – Closed Sunday
Menu 35/50 € – Carte 29/52 €
• Mexican • Friendly •
A good option for those looking to try Mexican cuisine. Behind the discreet
façade you will discover this bright, colourful restaurant. It has a bar at the ent-
rance and dining rooms spread across two floors. An impressive collection of
tequilas!

X **Al Trapo** – Hotel De Las Letras 〔& AC〕

Caballero de Gracia 11 ⊠ 28013 – Ⓜ Gran Vía   Plan: **G2**
*– ℰ 915 24 23 05 – www.altraporestaurante.com – Closed August, Sunday
and Monday*
Menu 22 € – Carte 23/40 €
• Modern cuisine • Fashionable •
A bright, modern restaurant with a restrained contemporary decor that includes
bare white tables. The expert knowledge and tutelage of renowned chef Paco
Morales is behind the informal, contemporary cuisine featuring on the enticing
and imaginatively descriptive menu.

X **Krachai** 〔AC〕

Fernando VI-11 ⊠ 28004 – Ⓜ Alonso Martínez   Plan: **G1**
– ℰ 918 33 65 56 – www.krachai.es – Closed August and Sunday dinner
Menu 13/30 € – Carte 21/53 €
• Thai • Simple •
The Krachai is split between two dining rooms, each with attractive lighting and
a contemporary feel. The Thai cuisine on offer is listed on the menu according
to the way it is prepared.

SPAIN - MADRID

X

La Gastroteca de Santiago
☆ AC

pl. Santiago 1 ✉ *28013* – Ⓜ *Ópera* – 𝒞 *915 48 07 07*   Plan: **E2**
– www.lagastrotecadesantiago.es – Closed 15-31 August, Sunday dinner and Monday
Menu 50/87 € – Carte 34/56 €
• **Modern cuisine** • **Cosy** •
A small, cosy restaurant with two large windows and a modern decor. Friendly staff, contemporary cuisine and a kitchen that is partially visible to diners.

X
☺

Triciclo
AC

Santa María 28 ✉ *28014* – Ⓜ *Antón Martin*   Plan: **G3**
– 𝒞 910 24 47 98 – www.eltriciclo.es – Closed 15 days February, 15 days July and Sunday
Carte approx. 35 €
• **Creative** • **Bistro** •
A restaurant that is on everyone's lips! Triciclo's simplicity is compensated by a high degree of culinary expertise. This is showcased in well-prepared and attractively presented dishes that encompass the personal and traditional, as well as Oriental and fusion influences.

X

Villa Paramesa Prado
AC

Prado 15 ✉ *28014* – Ⓜ *Sevilla* – 𝒞 *914 29 03 51*   Plan: **G2**
– www.villaparamesa.com – Closed 15 days August, Sunday dinner and Monday
Menu 18/42 € – Carte 30/45 €
• **Modern cuisine** • **Fashionable** •
Good contemporary cuisine, including surprising tapas options, delicious raciones and dishes that demonstrate real technical skill and creativity. There is also an interesting choice of set menus.

X
☺

Tepic
☆ AC

Ayala 14 ✉ *28001* – Ⓜ *Goya* – 𝒞 *915 22 08 50*   Plan: **H1**
– www.tepic.com
Menu 25 € – Carte 27/36 €
• **Mexican** • **Rustic** •
A Mexican restaurant with its very own character, featuring a rustic yet contemporary space defined by a profusion of wood and a predominance of varying tones of white. High quality cuisine from the homeland alongside an interesting menu of beers, tequila and mezcal.

X

Dokidoki
�& AC ⇄

Villalar 4 ✉ *28001* – Ⓜ *Retiro* – 𝒞 *917 79 36 49*   Plan: **H2**
– www.restaurantedokidoki.es – Closed Holy Week, 15 days August, Sunday dinner and Monday
Menu 14/28 € – Carte 45/55 €
• **Japanese** • **Minimalist** •
Simplicity and design are the hallmarks of this restaurant where the chef, a passionate fan of Japanese cuisine, offers a menu with two options. One features traditional Japanese dishes and the other is adapted to more European tastes.

Y/

Le Cabrera
AC

Bárbara de Braganza 2 ✉ *28004* – Ⓜ *Colón*   Plan: **H1**
– 𝒞 915 77 59 55 – www.lecabrera.com – Closed August and Sunday
Ración approx. 10 € – *(dinner only)*
• **Modern cuisine** • **Design** •
This original restaurant with its trendy decor is divided into two sections. One has access to the chef who prepares dishes behind a counter, and the other, in the basement, is designed primarily for drinks.

SPAIN - MADRID

Estado Puro

pl. Cánovas del Castillo 4 ✉ *28014*   Plan: **G2**
– Ⓜ *Banco de España* – ✆ *917 79 30 36* – *www.estadopuromadrid.com*
Tapa 3 € **Ración** approx. 10 €
• Modern cuisine • Design •

This gastro-bar with a modern design is in a high-end location between the city's museums and art galleries. The menu covers tapas, *tostas* and *raciones*, all adapted from dishes of the highest quality.

Bocaito

Libertad 6 ✉ *28004* – Ⓜ *Chueca* – ✆ *915 32 12 19*   Plan: **G2**
– *www.bocaito.com* – *Closed August and Sunday*
Tapa 4.50 € **Ración** approx. 8 €
• Traditional cuisine • Tapas bar •

This restaurant is split between two premises which are connected to each other. Four dining rooms in total, each furnished in rustic Castilian style with a few bullfighting mementoes as part of the decor. Traditional cuisine.

Prada a Tope

Príncipe 11 ✉ *28012* – Ⓜ *Sevilla* – ✆ *914 29 59 21*   Plan: **G2**
– *www.pradaatope.es* – *Closed 31 July-14 August*
Tapa 5 € **Ración** approx. 10 €
• Traditional cuisine • Tapas bar •

This restaurant follows the typical decor found throughout this chain. A bar, rustic-style tables and a plethora of wood in the dining room, which is adorned with old photos and typical products from the El Bierzo region.

Celso y Manolo

Libertad 1 ✉ *28004* – Ⓜ *Gran Vía* – ✆ *915 31 80 79*   Plan: **G2**
– *www.celsoymanolo.es*
Ración approx. 9 €
• Traditional cuisine • Neighbourhood •

A young and informal eatery occupying the site of an old tavern. Extensive ración based menu with an emphasis on natural and organic ingredients.

RETIRO – SALAMANCA   PLAN III

Ritz

pl. de la Lealtad 5 ✉ *28014* – Ⓜ *Banco de España*   Plan: **I2**
– ✆ *917 01 67 67* – *www.ritzmadrid.com*
137 rm ☏ – 👥275/645 € – 30 suites
• Grand Luxury • Elegant •

This internationally prestigious hotel occupies a palatial property from the early 20C. It features beautiful public spaces and sumptuously decorated guestrooms. In the Goya restaurant, endowed with its own inimitable personality, enjoy well-prepared dishes based around a concept that is classical in style.

Villa Magna

paseo de la Castellana 22 ✉ *28046* – Ⓜ *Rubén Darío*   Plan: **I1**
– ✆ *915 87 12 34* – *www.hotelvillamagna.es*
120 rm – 👤350/730 € – 👥350/800 € – ☏ 42 € – 30 suites
• Luxury • Classic •

This magnificent hotel boasts a classically elegant lounge area and various categories of guestroom, with the suites on the top floor enjoying the added bonus of a terrace. The enticing food choices include lighter lunch options, one gastronomic restaurant, and another dedicated to a mix of Cantonese and Oriental cuisine.

Tsé Yang – See restaurant listing

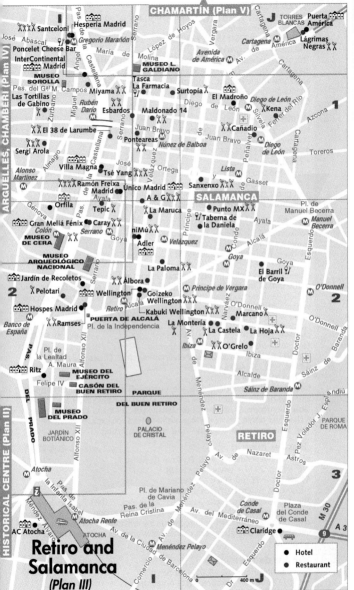

CHAMARTÍN (Plan V)

ARGÜELLES, CHAMBERÍ (Plan IV)

HISTORICAL CENTRE (Plan II)

Santceloni
Hesperia Madrid
José Abascal
Gregorio Marañón
Poncelet Cheese Bar
InterContinental Madrid
MUSEO SOROLLA
Pas. del Gal M. Campos
Las Tortillas de Gabino
Miyama
Tasca La Farmacia
Surtopía
El Madroño
Kena
Esbardos
Maldonado 14
El 38 de Larumbe
Juan Bravo
Cañadio
Sergi Arola
Ponteareas
Núñez de Balboa
Juan Bravo
Diego de León
Villa Magna
Tsé Yang
Lista
Sanxenxo
Ramón Freixa Madrid
Único Madrid
SALAMANCA
A & G
Orfila
Tepic
La Maruca
Punto MX
Gran Meliá Fénix
Caray
niMü
Taberna de la Daniela
MUSEO DE CERA
Adler
Velázquez
MUSEO ARQUEOLÓGICO NACIONAL
La Paloma
El Barril de Goya
Jardín de Recoletos
Álbora
Príncipe de Vergara
O'Donnell
Pelotari
Wellington
Goizeko Wellington
Hospes Madrid
Kabuki Wellington
Marcano
Ramses
PUERTA DE ALCALÁ
Pl. de la Independencia
La Montería
La Castela
La Hoja
O'Grelo
Ritz
MUSEO DEL EJÉRCITO
CASÓN DEL BUEN RETIRO
PARQUE
DEL BUEN RETIRO
MUSEO DEL PRADO
JARDÍN BOTÁNICO
PALACIO DE CRISTAL
RETIRO
Atocha
PARQUE DE ROMA
Atocha
AC Atocha
Atocha Renfe
Claridge

Retiro and Salamanca
(Plan III)

TORRES BLANCAS
Puerta América
Lágrimas Negras

● Hotel
● Restaurant

0   400 m

675

Gran Meliá Fénix

Hermosilla 2 ✉ *28001 –* Ⓜ *Colón – ✆ 914 31 67 00*
– www.gran-melia-fenix.com   Plan: I2
178 rm ☲ – ♥205/535 € ♥♥230/560 € – 20 suites
• Luxury • Elegant •
This distinguished aristocratic hotel boasts spacious facilities. These include an impressive cupola-crowned entrance hall and classically elegant guestrooms appointed to the highest standards. The restaurant, decorated by the famous interior designer Lorenzo Castillo, is complemented by a cocktail bar.
Caray – See restaurant listing

Wellington

Velázquez 8 ✉ *28001 –* Ⓜ *Retiro – ✆ 915 75 44 00*
– www.hotel-wellington.com   Plan: I2
250 rm – ♥♥155/325 € – ☲ 30 € – 26 suites
• Luxury • Classic •
Luxury and tradition go hand-in-hand in this truly emblematic hotel – one that is used by many bullfighters during the city's San Isidro festival. Classically elegant public spaces, a busy English-style bar, plus fully equipped bedrooms.
❀ **Kabuki Wellington** • **Goizeko Wellington** – See restaurant listing

Adler

Velázquez 33 ✉ *28001 –* Ⓜ *Velázquez – ✆ 914 26 32 20*
– www.adlerhotelmadrid.com   Plan: I2
44 rm – ♥200/400 € ♥♥250/495 € – ☲ 27 € – 2 suites
• Luxury • Elegant •
An exclusive and select property with an elegant interior created from materials of the utmost quality. The comfortable guestrooms, all equipped to the very highest level, are worthy of special mention. Small English-style bar, plus a restaurant with its very own character.
niMú – See restaurant listing

Único Madrid

Claudio Coello 67 ✉ *28001 –* Ⓜ *Serrano*
– ✆ 917 81 01 73 – www.unicohotelmadrid.com – Closed 4-24 August   Plan: I2
43 rm – ♥♥231/429 € – ☲ 26 € – 1 suite
• Luxury • Contemporary •
Behind the attractive classical façade, guests will discover a designer-inspired entrance hall, an elegant public area with several small lounges, and comfortable guestrooms, all featuring a combination of classic and avant-garde decor. A chauffeur-driven service is also available to help you explore the city.
❀❀ **Ramón Freixa Madrid** – See restaurant listing

Hospes Madrid

pl. de la Independencia 3 ✉ *28001 –* Ⓜ *Retiro*
– ✆ 914 32 29 11 – www.hospes.com   Plan: I2
41 rm ☲ – ♥♥160/900 € – 1 suite
• Luxury • Contemporary •
The Hospes Madrid occupies a building dating back to 1883. Facilities here include a reception desk located in what was once the carriage entrance, two meeting rooms, and modern guestrooms, many overlooking Alcalá Gate. In the informal restaurant, guests can choose between tapas, raciones and the daily set menu.

Jardín de Recoletos

Gil de Santivañes 6 ✉ *28001 –* Ⓜ *Serrano*
– ✆ 917 81 16 40 – www.recoletos-hotel.com   Plan: I2
43 rm – ♥♥85/350 € – ☲ 18 €
• Traditional • Classic •
Following its refurbishment, this hotel boasts its very own style with Bauhaus and Art Deco influences. It offers spacious guestrooms, each with their own kitchen, and a charming patio-garden. The welcoming restaurant offers a pleasantly surprising choice of fish and meat cooked on a lava rock grill.

SPAIN - MADRID

El Madroño

General Díaz Porlier 101 ✉ *28006 –* Ⓜ *Diego de León*
– ☎ *915 62 52 92 – www.madrono-hotel.com*
66 rm – †††54/309 € – ⏛ 15 €
• Business • Modern •

Plan: J1

Located next to the Hospital Universitario de la Princesa, this hotel is an interesting option for families and longer stays, as many of the generally modern and spacious guestrooms have the bonus of a small kitchen. Landscaped internal patio.

Claridge

pl. Conde de Casal 6 ✉ *28007 –* Ⓜ *Conde de Casal*
– ☎ *915 51 94 00 – www.hotelclaridge.com*
112 rm – †††75/220 € – ⏛ 14 € – 2 suites
• Business • Classic •

Plan: J3

Following a complete renovation, the Claridge now offers a modern setting with a decorative homage to classic British and American images. It has elegant and spacious guestrooms geared towards a business clientele. The restaurant, which includes a private dining room, offers a menu catering to international tastes.

AC Atocha

Delicias 42 ✉ *28045 –* Ⓜ *Atocha –* ☎ *915 06 22 21*
– www.ac-hotels.com
161 rm – †††88/200 € – ⏛ 16 €
• Chain hotel • Modern •

Plan: I3

This hotel is situated right next to Atocha train station. It boasts a modern lounge area typical of the AC chain, as well as contemporary-style rooms and a couple of patios – the one with the olive trees is particularly attractive.

XxxX
❀ ❀
Ramón Freixa Madrid – Hotel Único Madrid

Claudio Coello 67 ✉ *28001 –* Ⓜ *Serrano*
– ☎ *917 81 82 62 – www.ramonfreixamadrid.com – Closed Holy Week, August, Sunday and Monday*
Menu 85/135 € – Carte 103/147 €
• Creative • Design •

Plan: I2

Fronted by a pleasant terrace, this restaurant has a thoroughly modern look and a limited number of tables. In the kitchen, the focus is on impressively consistent cuisine, which is superbly presented and prepared using high quality ingredients.
→ El estudio del tomate 2016 (summer). Paletilla de cordero lechal, remolachas y rabanitos. Momento dulce.

XxX
❀
Kabuki Wellington (Ricardo Sanz) – Hotel Wellington

Velázquez 6 ✉ *28001 –* Ⓜ *Retiro –* ☎ *915 77 78 77*
– www.restaurantekabuki.com – Closed Holy Week, 1-21 August, Saturday lunch, Sunday and Bank Holidays
Menu 93 € – Carte 70/100 €
• Japanese • Design •

Plan: I2

The group's flagship restaurant boasts a large, contemporary-style dining room on two floors, featuring designer detail and a sushi bar. Japanese cuisine skilfully prepared with top-quality ingredients, accompanied by an exclusive sake menu.
→ Huevos rotos con atún picante y papa frita canaria. Costilla de buey de wagyu. Cremoso de yuzu.

XxX
Goizeko Wellington – Hotel Wellington

Villanueva 34 ✉ *28001 –* Ⓜ *Retiro –* ☎ *915 77 01 38*
– www.goizekogaztelupe.com – Closed Sunday
Menu 68 € – Carte 51/77 €
• Modern cuisine • Classic •

Plan: I2

The contemporary-classic dining room and the two private rooms have been exquisitely designed. The cuisine on offer is a fusion of traditional, international and creative cooking, and is enriched with a few Japanese dishes.

SPAIN - MADRID

XxX **A & G**

Ayala 27 ⊠ 28001 – Ⓜ Goya   Plan: I1-2
– 𝒞 917 02 62 62 – www.aygmadrid.com
– Closed Sunday
Menu 45/69 € – Carte 44/65 €
• Peruvian • Minimalist •
A restaurant with an urban feel offering Peruvian cuisine with Japanese touches, in addition to several signature dishes such "ají de gallina", "ceviche del amor" and "beso de moza".

XxX **Sanxenxo**

José Ortega y Gasset 40 ⊠ 28006 – Ⓜ Núñez de Balboa   Plan: J1
– 𝒞 915 77 82 72 – www.sanxenxo.com.es – Closed Holy Week, 15 days August and Sunday dinner
Menu 50 € – Carte 44/65 €
• Fish and seafood • Classic •
This restaurant serves traditional Galician cuisine based on quality fish and seafood. Covering two floors, the superb dining rooms are decorated with a profusion of granite and wood.

XxX **Tsé Yang** – Hotel Villa Magna

paseo de la Castellana 22 ⊠ 28046 – 𝒞 914 31 18 18   Plan: I1
– www.cafesaigon.es
Carte 42/75 €
• Chinese • Exotic •
Enjoy the flavours of authentic Cantonese cuisine at this elegantly appointed Chinese restaurant. It re-creates traditional dishes dating back centuries.

XX **La Paloma**

Jorge Juan 39 ⊠ 28001 – Ⓜ Príncipe de Vergara   Plan: I2
– 𝒞 915 76 86 92 – www.lapalomarestaurante.es – Closed Holy Week, August, Sunday and Bank Holidays
Menu 45 € – Carte 42/77 €
• Classic cuisine • Classic •
A professionally run restaurant in an intimate setting. The extensive menu brings together classic and traditional dishes alongside a selection of daily suggestions and set menus. Signature dishes here include sea urchin, carpaccio of liver and stuffed pigeon.

XX **Ramsés**

pl. de La Independencia 4 ⊠ 28001 – Ⓜ Retiro   Plan: I2
– 𝒞 914 35 16 66 – www.ramseslife.com
– Closed Monday dinner
Carte 44/54 €
• Traditional cuisine • Design •
Thanks to its different sections, this design inspired restaurant, decorated by the famous interior designer Philippe Starck, can turn its hand to numerous events, from dining to cocktails. High-level cuisine both in terms of concept and technical skill.

XX **El 38 de Larumbe**

paseo de la Castellana 38 ⊠ 28006 – Ⓜ Rubén Darío   Plan: I1
– 𝒞 915 75 11 12 – www.larumbe.com – Closed 15 days August, Sunday dinner and Bank Holidays dinner
Menu 63 € – Carte 45/56 €
• Modern cuisine • Classic •
This restaurant has two highly distinct dining areas – one has a gastro-bar feel, and the other has a more refined setting for à la carte dining. Updated traditional cuisine with the option of ordering half-raciones.

SPAIN - MADRID

XX **Caray** – Hotel Gran Meliá Fénix   ⚘ ♿ 🅰️ ⇔ 🚗

Hermosilla 2 ⊠ 28001 – **Ⓜ** *Colón – ℰ 914 85 78 01*   Plan: I2
– www.caraymadrid.com
Carte 45/56 €
• Traditional cuisine • Elegant •
Attractive, elegant and eclectic, Caray's interior design is a true labour of love.
Updated traditional cuisine accompanied by fine wines from Spain and around
the world.

XX **O grelo**   🅰️ ⇔

Menorca 39 ⊠ 28009 – **Ⓜ** *Ibiza – ℰ 914 09 72 04*   Plan: J2
– www.restauranteogrelo.com – Closed Sunday dinner
Carte 32/78 €
• Galician • Classic •
Experience the excellence of traditional Galician cuisine at this restaurant ser-
ving a huge variety of fish and seafood. Having undergone gradual renovation,
O grelo has a more modern look, which includes a reasonably popular gastro-
bar, a main dining room and three private sections.

XX **Maldonado 14**   🅰️

Maldonado 14 ⊠ 28006 – **Ⓜ** *Núñez de Balboa*   Plan: I1
*– ℰ 914 35 50 45 – www.maldonado14.com – Closed Holy Week, 10-
28 August, Sunday and Bank Holidays dinner*
Menu 35/50 € – Carte 38/58 €
• Traditional cuisine • Classic •
A single dining room on two levels, both featuring a classic decor, quality furnis-
hings and wood floors. The à la carte menu has a traditional feel and includes
delicious homely desserts, such as the outstanding apple tart.

XX **Punto MX** (Roberto Ruiz)   🅰️
🏵️ *General Pardiñas 40 ⊠ 28001 –* **Ⓜ** *Goya*   Plan: J2
*– ℰ 914 02 22 26 – www.puntomx.es – Closed 23 December - 4 January,
Holy Week, 15 days August, Saturday lunch and Sunday*
Carte 35/60 € – *(booking essential)*
• Mexican • Minimalist •
A Mexican restaurant that steers clear of stereotypes. Both the decor and cuisine
are thoroughly modern. Traditional recipes are bolstered by a contemporary
technical approach while at the same time adapting to local tastes. Highly inte-
resting combination of Mexican ingredients and others sourced from Spain.
→ Enchilada de carnitas de pato, salsa de pipián verde. Tuétano a las bra-
sas, salsa molcajetada, majado de hierbas. Crêpes de cajeta.

XX **99 sushi bar**   🅰️ ⇔

Hermosilla 4 ⊠ 28001 – **Ⓜ** *Serrano – ℰ 914 31 27 15*   Plan II : **H1**
*– www.99sushibar.com – Closed 1-23 August, Saturday lunch, Sunday and
Bank Holidays*
Menu 75 € – Carte 45/80 €
• Japanese • Minimalist •
A good address in which to discover the flavours and textures of Japanese cuisine. There is a small bar where sushi is prepared in front of diners, an attractive
glass-fronted wine cellar, and a modern dining room featuring typical Japanese
decor and furnishings.

XX **Álbora**   🍽️ 🅰️
🏵️ *Jorge Juan 33 ⊠ 28001 –* **Ⓜ** *Velázquez – ℰ 917 81 61 97*   Plan: I2
– www.restaurantealbora.com – Closed 9-24 August and Sunday
Menu 54/74 € – Carte 49/79 €
• Modern cuisine • Design •
An attractive modern setting with two distinct sections: the gastro-bar on the
ground floor and the gastronomic restaurant upstairs. Enjoy high level cuisine
that makes full use of seasonal ingredients, with some dishes available in smaller half portions.
→ Guisante lágrima de Guetaria con licuado de su vaina. Cocochas de merluza
en nuestra salsa verde. Torrija caramelizada con helado de plátano y canela.

SPAIN - MADRID

XX **Ponteareas**   🕭 🕭 🕭

Claudio Coello 96 ✉ 28005 – Ⓜ Núñez de Balboa   Plan: I1
– 𝒞 915 75 58 73 – www.grupoportonovo.es – Closed 10-29 August,
Sunday dinner and Bank Holidays
Menu 50 € – Carte 45/66 €
• Galician • Classic •
This restaurant with a modern decor offers a tapas bar and an attractive dining
room overlooking a garden. Traditional cuisine with Galician roots, as well as
good quality fish dishes.

XX **Arriba**   🕭
🕭
Goya 5 (Platea Madrid) ✉ 28001 – Ⓜ Serrano   Plan II : H1
– 𝒞 912 19 23 05 – www.restaurantearriba.com
Carte 33/45 €
• Traditional cuisine • Design •
An old cinema is the unique setting for this gourmet food hall that includes this
restaurant. It occupies the movie hall's balcony with staggered dining sections
overlooking the flurry of activity inside the complex. A fun take on traditional
and seasonal cuisine.

XX **Esbardos**   🕭 🕭

Maldonado 4 ✉ 28006 – Ⓜ Núñez de Balboa   Plan: I1
– 𝒞 914 35 08 68 – www.restauranteesbardos.com – Closed Holy Week,
August and Sunday dinner
Menu 35/60 € – Carte 30/44 €
• Asturian • Traditional •
Esbardos takes its name from an Asturian word meaning 'bear cub', which is
appropriate given that the owners own another restaurant called El Oso (The
Bear). Typical Asturian cuisine based around top quality products and traditional
stews.

XX **niMú** – Hotel Adler
Goya 31 ✉ 28001 – Ⓜ Velázquez – 𝒞 914 26 32 25   Plan: I2
– www.nimubistro.com – Closed August
Carte 28/48 €
• Modern cuisine • Design •
This bistro-style restaurant has a striking decor full of charm and character crea-
ted by interior designer Pascua Ortega. Contemporary menu that includes a
choice of raciones.

XX **Cañadío**
Conde Peñalver 86 ✉ 28005 – Ⓜ Diego de León   Plan: J1
– 𝒞 912 81 91 92 – www.restaurantecanadio.com – Closed August and
Sunday dinner
Carte 30/52 €
• Traditional cuisine • Simple •
The name will ring a bell with those familiar with Santander, given the location
of this, the original Cañadío restaurant, on one of the city's most famous squa-
res. Café-bar for tapas, two contemporary dining rooms, and well-prepared tra-
ditional cuisine.

XX **La Hoja**
Doctor Castelo 48 ✉ 28009 – Ⓜ O'Donnell   Plan: J2
– 𝒞 914 09 25 22 – www.lahoja.es – Closed August, Sunday dinner and
Monday
Menu 25/30 € – Carte 42/50 €
• Asturian • Traditional •
A reference for Asturian cuisine in Madrid! Two dining rooms with elaborate
decor, and another more multi-purpose one dedicated to hunting. The menu
features typical bean stews (fabes and verdinas), game and even chicken from
the restaurant's own farm... all delicious and in copious portions.

X **Surtopía**   AC

Núñez de Balboa 106 ✉ *28006 –* Ⓜ *Núñez de Balboa*   Plan: I1
*– ℰ 915 63 03 64 – www.surtopia.es – Closed Holy Week, 8-28 August,
Sunday, Monday dinner and Tuesday dinner*
Menu 38/58 € – Carte 34/42 €
• Andalusian • Trendy •
A modern restaurant impressively run by its owner who keeps a close on eye on
everything. Traditional Andalucian cuisine with clear culinary influences from
the city of Cádiz.

X
☺ **La Maruca**   🍴 AC ⇔ 🍽

Velázquez 54 ✉ *28001 –* Ⓜ *Velázquez – ℰ 917 81 49 69*   Plan: I2
– www.restaurantelamaruca.com
Carte 25/39 €
• Traditional cuisine • Fashionable •
A bright, casual and contemporary restaurant offering high standard, traditional
cuisine. There is a predominance of typical and very reasonably priced Cantab-
rian dishes.

X
☺ **La Montería**   AC

Lope de Rueda 35 ✉ *28009 –* Ⓜ *Ibiza – ℰ 915 74 18 12*   Plan: J2
– www.lamonteria.es – Closed Sunday dinner
Menu 39 € – Carte 25/40 €
• Traditional cuisine • Simple •
This family-run business has a bar and intimate dining room, which are both
contemporary in feel. The chef creates updated traditional cuisine including
game dishes. Don't leave without trying the monterías (stuffed mussels)!

X **Marcano**   AC ⇔

Doctor Castelo 31 ✉ *28009 –* Ⓜ *Ibiza – ℰ 914 09 36 42*   Plan: J2
*– www.restaurantemarcano.com – Closed Holy week, 21 days August and
Sunday*
Carte 37/67 €
• International • Simple •
The cooking here focuses on well-defined flavours. This is demonstrated by the
range of traditional and international dishes, the latter with a European and
Asian twist.

X **Pelotari**   AC ⇔

Recoletos 3 ✉ *28001 –* Ⓜ *Colón – ℰ 915 78 24 97*   Plan: I2
– www.pelotari-asador.com – Closed Sunday
Menu 40/68 € – Carte 25/55 €
• Basque • Rustic •
This typical Basque eatery specialising in roasted meats is run by its owners,
with one in the kitchen and the other front of house. Four regional style dining
rooms, two of which can be used as private rooms.

X **Kena**   AC

Ferrer del Río 7 ✉ *28028 –* Ⓜ *Diego de León*   Plan: J1
*– ℰ 917 25 96 48 – www.kenadeluisarevalo.com – Closed Sunday and
Bank Holidays*
Menu 25/60 € – Carte 22/46 €
• Peruvian • Simple •
An impressive restaurant offering a fusion of Japanese and Peruvian cuisine.
The menus combine the delicate preparation of the former with the typical fla-
vours of the latter.

X
☺ **La Castela**   ⅓ AC

Doctor Castelo 22 ✉ *28009 –* Ⓜ *Ibiza – ℰ 91 574 00 15*   Plan: J2
– www.lacastela.com – closed August and Sunday dinner
Carte 30/41 €
• Traditional cuisine • Traditional •
A traditional Madrid style tavern with a tapas bar at the entrance. The menu in
the traditional dining room is centred on international cuisine.

SPAIN - MADRID

♥/ **Tasca La Farmacia**   🍴 AC
Diego de León 9 ✉ *28006 –* Ⓜ *Núñez de Balboa*   Plan: **I1**
*– ☏ 915 64 86 52 – www.asadordearanda.com – Closed 28 July-17 August
and Sunday*
Tapa 7 € **Ración** approx. 10 €
• Traditional cuisine • Tapas bar •
Traditional style tasca, with a beautifully tiled bar adorned with elegant motifs.
House specialities include cod and 'zancarrón' (meat on the bone) tapas and
snacks.

♥/ **El Barril de Goya**   🍴 AC
Goya 86 ✉ *28009 –* Ⓜ *Goya – ☏ 915 78 39 98*   Plan: **J2**
– www.elbarrildegoya.com – Closed Sunday dinner
Tapa 5 € **Ración** approx. 14 €
• Fish and seafood • Tapas bar •
A highly renowned seafood restaurant thanks to the extraordinary quality of its
ingredients. Away from the sea, its marvellous sliced Iberian ham is equally deli-
cious.

♥/ **Taberna de la Daniela**   AC
General Pardiñas 21 ✉ *28001 –* Ⓜ *Goya*   Plan: **J2**
– ☏ 915 75 23 29 – www.tabernadeladaniela.com
Tapa 5 € **Ración** approx. 12 €
• Traditional cuisine • Tapas bar •
A typical taberna in the Salamanca district, with a tiled façade and various
dining rooms in which to enjoy a range of tapas. The restaurant is particularly
famous for its cocido madrileño (a meat, potato and chickpea stew) that is traditionally eaten in three stages.

ARGÜELLES   PLAN IV

XX **El Barril de Argüelles**   AC
Andrés Mellado 69 ✉ *28015 –* Ⓜ *Islas Filipinas*   Plan: **K2**
– ☏ 915 44 36 15 – www.grupo-oter.com
Menu 40 € – Carte 35/60 €
• Fish and seafood • Mediterranean •
A bar with enticing seafood counters precedes the classic yet contemporary
dining room decorated with a maritime theme. The specialities here are shellfish and octopus, although savoury rice dishes and delicious homemade stews
also feature on the menu.

♥/ **El Barril de Argüelles**   AC
Andrés Mellado 69 ✉ *28015 –* Ⓜ *Islas Filipinas*   Plan: **K2**
– ☏ 915 44 36 15 – www.grupo-oter.com
Tapa 11 € **Ración** approx. 20 €
• Fish and seafood • Tapas bar •
This impressive seafood restaurant has an elegant layout and extremely popular
bar. Superb fish and seafood, including octopus and delicious Andalucian-style
fresh fish, is served.

CHAMBERÍ   PLAN IV

🏨 **InterContinental Madrid**   ✿ ✳ ♿ AC ⚙ 🚗
paseo de la Castellana 49 ✉ *28046 –* Ⓜ *Gregorio Marañón*   Plan: **L3**
– ☏ 917 00 73 00 – www.madrid.intercontinental.com
302 rm – ♗♗200/500 € – ☲ 32 €
• Grand Luxury • Classic •
A luxury hotel with a classically elegant entrance hall crowned by a cupola and
embellished with a profusion of marble, a pleasant inner patio-terrace, and
guestrooms that stand out for their high levels of comfort. In the restaurant
adjoining the entrance hall-bar, the focus is on an attractive international
menu, with an impressive brunch on Sundays.

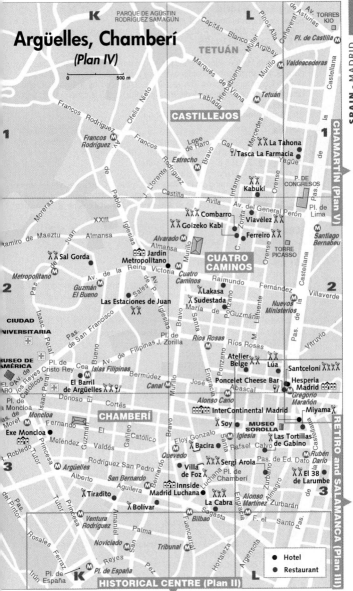

Argüelles, Chamberí
(Plan IV)

PARQUE DE AGUSTÍN
RODRÍGUEZ SAMAGUN

K · L

TETUÁN

CASTILLEJOS

TORRES
KIO

Pl. de Castilla

Valdeacederas

Tetuán

La Tahona
Tasca La Farmacia

Kabuki

P. DE
CONGRESOS

Pl. de
Lima

Combarro
Goizeko Kabi

Viavélez
Ferreiro

Santiago
Bernabéu

Sal Gorda

Jardín
Metropolitano

**CUATRO
CAMINOS**

TORRE
PICASSO

Metropolitano

Guzmán
El Bueno

Las Estaciones de Juan

Cuatro
Caminos

Lakasa

Sudestada

Nuevos
Ministerios

Villaverde

**CIUDAD
UNIVERSITARIA**

Ríos Rosas

MUSEO DE
AMÉRICA

Pl. de
Cristo Rey

Islas Filipinas

Atelier
Belge

Lúa

Santceloni

El Barril
de Argüelles

Poncelet Cheese Bar

Hesperia
Madrid

Pl. de
la Moncloa

Moncloa

CHAMBERÍ

InterContinental Madrid

Gregorio
Marañón

Miyama

Exe Moncloa

Soy

MUSEO
SOROLLA

Las Tortillas
de Gabino

Rubén
Darío

Bacira

Sergi Arola

El 38
de Larumbe

Argüelles

Villa
de Foz

Tiradito

Innside
Madrid Luchana

La Cabra

Bolívar

Ventura
Rodríguez

Noviciado

Tribunal

● Hotel
● Restaurant

Pl. de
España

K · Pl. de España · L

HISTORICAL CENTRE (Plan II)

SPAIN - MADRID

CHAMARTÍN (Plan VI)

RETIRO and SALAMANCA (Plan III)

683

Hesperia Madrid
paseo de la Castellana 57 ✉ *28046* Plan: **L2**
– 🚇 Gregorio Marañón – ✆ 912 10 88 00 – www.hesperia-madrid.com
171 rm ⌱ – ♛♛169/259 €
• Luxury • Elegant •
The Hesperia Madrid enjoys a good location in one of the city's central business districts. The small lobby is compensated by a wide choice of lounges and classically elegant guestrooms. The restaurant, enhanced by a sushi bar, offers diners the choice between Mediterranean-influenced à la carte options and a good set menu.
❀❀ **Santceloni** – See restaurant listing

Orfila
Orfila 6 ✉ *28010 – 🚇 Alonso Martínez* Plan II : **H1**
– ✆ 917 02 77 70 – www.hotelorfila.com – Closed August
29 rm – ♛♛225/355 € – ⌱ 30 € – 3 suites
• Luxury • Luxury • Elegant •
This delightfully charming small palace built in the 19C occupies a quiet street in a central location. It has elegant guestrooms embellished with period furniture. The restaurant has a classic air and serves traditional cuisine as impressive as its welcoming terrace.

Exe Moncloa
Arcipreste de Hita 10 ✉ *28015 – 🚇 Moncloa* Plan: **K3**
– ✆ 917 45 92 99 – www.hotelexemoncloa.com
161 rm – ♛50/150 € ♛♛65/190 € – ⌱ 10 €
• Chain hotel • Functional •
Occupying the same building as Moncloa market, this hotel offers comfortable guestrooms decorated in a functional, contemporary style. Attractive terrace with pleasant views.

Innside Madrid Génova
pl. Alonso Martínez 3 ✉ *28004 – 🚇 Alonso Martínez* Plan II : **G1**
– ✆ 912 06 21 60 – www.melia.com
64 rm – ♛♛125/400 € – ⌱ 20 €
• Chain hotel • Functional •
This hotel occupies a fine Modernist building dating back to 1919. The interior combines a few decorative details synonymous with an aristocratic property, such as period mouldings, with a more contemporary, functional and casual look. Pleasant rooftop terrace.

Innside Madrid Luchana
Luchana 22 ✉ *28010 – 🚇 Bilbao – ✆ 912 92 29 40* Plan: **L3**
– www.melia.com
43 rm – ♛♛125/400 € – ⌱ 20 €
• Chain hotel • Contemporary •
The building known as the Palacio de Luchana now houses a contemporary style hotel behind its neo-Classical façade. Simply decorated lounge areas and modern guestrooms.

Santceloni – Hotel Hesperia Madrid
❀❀
paseo de la Castellana 57 ✉ *28046* Plan: **L2**
– 🚇 Gregorio Marañón – ✆ 912 10 88 40
– www.restaurantesantceloni.com – Closed Holy Week, August, Saturday lunch, Sunday and Bank Holidays
Menu 150/180 € – Carte 117/150 €
• Creative • Elegant •
A great gastronomic experience. This elegant restaurant boasts a superbly arranged classic-contemporary dining room split between two floors. The culinary focus is on updated traditional cuisine that is well presented and comes with a creative touch.
➔ Caballa ahumada, coliflor, jalea de manzana, puré de limón y remolacha. Molleja de ternera, alcachofa, avellana y curry. Granizado de zanahoria, lima, eneldo, avena y jengibre.

XXX **Sergi Arola**   🆎 ⇔
ಬಿ ಬಿ *Zurbano 31 ⊠ 28010 – ⓂRubén Darío*   Plan: **L3**
– 𝒞 913 10 21 69 – www.sergiarola.es – Closed 5-12 January, 1-
15 September, Sunday and Monday
Menu 105/195 € – Carte 92/110 € – *(dinner only except Saturday)*
• Creative • Design •

This inquisitive and dynamic chef offers guests two distinct culinary options.
Upstairs he continues with his gourmet restaurant theme. In the basement
(Sot) choose from bolder, unpretentious fare where diners can share dishes
and enjoy a complete creative experience.
→ Molleja de ternera asada en especias y berenjena a la manera de
Andhra. Lomo de rodaballo cocido a baja temperatura, chutney de coco y
curry casero de naranja. Sopa de cerezas, helado de yogur y haba tonka
con falsas torrijas.

XXX **La Cabra** (Javier Aranda)   🆎 ⇔
ಬಿ *Francisco de Rojas 2 ⊠ 28010 – ⓂBilbao*   Plan: **L3**
– 𝒞 914 45 77 50 – www.restaurantelacabra.com – Closed 1-6 January,
Holy Week, August and Sunday
Menu 77/121 € – Carte 44/67 €
• Modern cuisine • Fashionable •

A modern and informal restaurant with various spaces. These range from the
tapería, a library-cum-lounge in which to relax after work, and a wine cellar
that can also be booked privately. It offers traditional cuisine with a cutting
edge, a high level of technical skill, strong emphasis on top quality, and on the
whole, seasonal ingredients.
→ Albóndigas de anguila. Salmonete con risotto de trigo, kimchi, coco y
albahaca. Chocolate 2.1.

XX **Nikkei 225**   🆎 🍽
paseo de la Castellana 15 (entrance door Fernando El   Plan II : **H1**
Santo St) ⊠ 28046 – ⓂColón – 𝒞 913 19 03 90 – www.nikkei225.es
– Closed August, Sunday and Bank Holidays
Menu 70 € – Carte 35/86 €
• Peruvian • Friendly •

This particularly interesting dining option is set in an elegant, designer inspired
setting. Explore the flavours of Japanese cuisine with a Peruvian influence,
developed by Japanese descendants who emigrated to South America.

XX **Las Estaciones de Juan**   🍴 🆎 ⇔
paseo San Francisco de Sales 41 ⊠ 28003 Madrid   Plan: **K2**
– ⓂGuzmán el Bueno – 𝒞 915 98 86 66
– www.lascuatroestacionesdejuan.com – Closed 24-31 December and
Sunday dinner
Carte 36/57 €
• Traditional cuisine • Classic •

A solid performer preparing traditional cuisine with well-prepared ingredients
in an impeccable setting combining the traditional and modern. One of the signature dishes is fillet of T-bone steak.

XX **Lúa** (Manuel Domínguez)   🆎 ⇔
ಬಿ *Eduardo Dato 5 ⊠ 28003 – ⓂRubén Darío*   Plan: **L2**
– 𝒞 913 95 28 53 – www.restaurantelua.com – Closed Sunday
Menu 56 € – *(set menu only)*
• Modern cuisine • Cosy •

A restaurant that is constantly evolving, with an attractive tapas bar, informal
ambience, and a rustic yet contemporary feel. The chef conjures up modern
cooking with its roots in his native Galicia. The excellent tasting menu showcases his undoubted skill.
→ Arroz de apio, eneldo, menta, albahaca, cilantro, alga wakame y carabinero. Cochinillo confitado a baja temperatura con ciruelas, pasas y orejo-
nes. Brownie de chocolate con helado de turrón y crema de vainilla.

XX **Conlaya** 🔲 ⇔

Zurbano 13 ✉ *28010 –* Ⓜ *Alonso Martínez* Plan II : **H1**
– ℰ 913 19 31 16 – www.conlaya.es – Closed August, Sunday and Monday dinner
Menu 35/68 € – Carte 35/55 €
• Classic cuisine • Classic •

A touch of Cantabria in the heart of Madrid! Impeccable interior with a traditional ambience, where the regional cuisine is centred around fresh fish straight from the market.

XX **Atelier Belge** 🔲

Bretón de los Herreros 39 ✉ *28003 –* Ⓜ *Alonso Cano* Plan: **L2**
– ℰ 915 45 84 48 – www.atelierbelge.es – Closed 8-15 August, Sunday dinner and Monday
Menu 12/52 € – Carte 38/51 €
• Belgian • Classic •

An interesting dining option where you can discover authentic Belgian cuisine with the occasional nod to creativity. Dishes well worth trying include the snails, mussels and the impressive 'Coquelet Brabançonne'!

XX **Ars Vivendi** 🔲 ⇔
😊

Zurbano 6 ✉ *28010 –* Ⓜ *Alonso Martínez* Plan II : **H1**
– ℰ 913 10 31 71 – www.restaurantearsvivendi.es – Closed 10-17 August and Sunday dinner
Menu 45/80 € – Carte 32/49 €
• Italian • Cosy •

The life and soul of this restaurant is provided by the couple that own it, with the husband working front-of-house and his wife in charge of the kitchen. Delicious, Italian inspired cuisine that is both creative and attractively presented. The homemade pasta is a feast for the senses!

X **Las Tortillas de Gabino** 🔲
😊

Rafael Calvo 20 ✉ *28010 –* Ⓜ *Rubén Darío* Plan: **L3**
– ℰ 91 319 75 05 – www.lastortillasdegabino.com – Closed Holy Week, 15 days August, Sunday and Bank Holidays
Carte 24/37 €
• Traditional cuisine • Cosy •

Almost always full every day, this restaurant boasts an entrance hall, two modern dining rooms decorated with wood panelling, and a private dining section. The traditionally inspired menu is complemented by a choice of tortillas which changes through the course of the year.

X **Bolívar** 🔲
😊

Manuela Malasaña 28 ✉ *28004 –* Ⓜ *San Bernardo* Plan: **K3**
– ℰ 914 45 12 74 – www.restaurantebolivar.com – Closed August and Sunday
Menu 25/36 € – Carte 30/43 €
• Traditional cuisine • Family •

A small, family-run restaurant in the city's Malasaña district in which the single dining room is divided into two sections, both with a modern look. Moderately priced traditional cuisine and excellent service.

X **Miyama** 🔲

paseo de la Castellana 45 ✉ *28013* Plan: **L3**
– Ⓜ *Gregorio Marañón – ℰ 913 91 00 26 – www.restaurantemiyama.com – Closed August, Sunday and Bank Holidays*
Menu 23/100 € – Carte 36/75 €
• Japanese • Minimalist •

A Japanese restaurant that is hugely popular in the city, including with Japanese visitors. An extensive sushi bar and simply laid tables share space in the single dining area. High quality, traditional Japanese cuisine.

※ **Sudestada**   ఉ AC

Ponzano 85 ⊠ 28003 – ⓜ *Rios Rosas –* ℰ *915 33 41 54*   Plan: **L2**
– www.sudestada.eu – Closed Sunday and Monday
Menu 35/55 € – Carte 40/55 €
• Asian • Fashionable •
You can't talk about Sudestada without mentioning chef Estanis Carenzo, the
main force behind fashionable ideas such as Street Food. Here Carenzo offers
Asian cuisine with a strong Vietnamese focus.

※ **Villa de Foz**   AC

Gonzálo de Córdoba 10 ⊠ 28010 – ⓜ *Bilbao*   Plan: **L3**
– ℰ *914 46 89 93 – www.villadefoz.es – closed August and Sunday dinner*
Menu 20/46 € – Carte 29/47 €
• Galician • Classic •
The Villa de Foz has two pleasant dining rooms, both decorated in a style that
reflects traditional and contemporary influences. Its à la carte menu of traditio-
nal Galician cuisine is enhanced by a fine choice of raciones and home-made
desserts.

※ **Bacira**   AC

Castillo 16 ⊠ 28005 – ⓜ *Iglesia –* ℰ *918 66 40 30*   Plan: **L3**
– www.bacira.es – Closed Christmas, August, Sunday dinner and Monday
Menu 14/45 € – Carte 30/44 € – *(booking advisable)*
• International • Classic •
An attractive restaurant with hints of vintage decor run by its three young
owner-chefs. Find fusion cuisine with a blend of traditional, seasonal Spanish
fare, Japanese dishes and Peruvian specialities.

※ **Lakasa**   ᝡ ఉ AC

Raimundo Fernández Villaverde 26 ⊠ 28003   Plan: **L2**
– ℰ *915 33 87 15 – www.lakasa.es – Closed Holy Week, 15 days August,*
Sunday dinner and Monday
Carte 29/54 €
• Traditional cuisine • Individual •
A contemporary and informal restaurant serving honest and tasty market-fresh
cuisine. This includes a choice of homemade pizzas and the option of half-racio-
nes.

※ **Soy**   AC

Viriato 58 ⊠ 28010 – ⓜ *Iglesia –* ℰ *914 45 74 47*   Plan: **L3**
– www.soypedroespina.com – Closed 15 days August, Saturday lunch,
Sunday and Monday dinner
Menu 65 € – Carte 40/55 € – *(booking essential)*
• Japanese • Classic •
This restaurant is simple, intimate and contemporary in style – the perfect set-
ting for the delicious, traditional Japanese cuisine served here. It is not so easy
to find, as there is no sign on the building!

※ **Tiradito**   ᝡ AC

Conde Duque 13 ⊠ 28015 – ⓜ *San Bernardo*   Plan: **K3**
– ℰ *915 41 78 76 – www.tiradito.es – Closed 15 days August, Sunday*
dinner and Monday
Menu 25/60 € – Carte 30/40 €
• Peruvian • Fashionable •
A young and easy-going restaurant serving 100% traditional Peruvian cuisine.
Dishes on the menu include ceviches, tiraditos, picoteos and tapas criollas.

⑨/ **Poncelet Cheese Bar**   AC

José Abascal 61 ⊠ 28003 – ⓜ *Gregorio Marañon*   Plan: **L2**
– ℰ *913 99 25 50 – www.ponceletcheesebar.es*
Tapa 4.90 € **Ración** approx. 12.90 €
• Cheese, fondue and raclette • Design •
An innovative designer space in which everything revolves around the world of
cheese. Attractive display cabinets, a bar for tastings, as well as a library specia-
lising in this fine product. Contemporary cuisine and wines by the glass.

SPAIN - MADRID

Jardín Metropolitano
🕍 🛗 🔥 🅰🄲 🛗 🚗

av. Reina Victoria 12 ✉ 28003 – Ⓜ *Cuatro Caminos*
– ☏ 911 83 18 10 – www.metropolitano-hotel.com   Plan: **K-L2**
96 rm – 👫55/260 € – 🍽 15 € – 6 suites
• Business • Classic •

Attractively laid out around a patio, this hotel offers guests well-appointed, classically styled bedrooms, with the suites on the top floor the pick of the bunch.
The restaurant, serving typical cuisine, comprises of a traditional dining area and
an attractive room with the feel of a winter garden.

Combarro
🍽 🄰🄲 ⟷

Reina Mercedes 12 ✉ 28020 – Ⓜ *Nuevos Ministerios*   Plan: **L2**
*– ☏ 915 54 77 84 – www.combarro.com – Closed Holy Week, 15 days
August and Sunday dinner*
Menu 50/120 € – Carte 44/55 €
• Fish and seafood • Classic •

Galician cuisine with an emphasis on fresh quality produce, including live fish
tanks. Public bar, dining on the first floor and a number of rooms in the basement. Classic and elegant in style.

Viavélez
🄰🄲

av. General Perón 10 ✉ 28020 – Ⓜ *Santiago Bernabeu*   Plan: **L2**
*– ☏ 915 79 95 39 – www.restauranteviavelez.com – Closed August, Sunday
and Monday lunch except summer, Sunday dinner and Monday rest of the
year*
Menu 28/52 € – Carte 40/60 €
• Creative • Fashionable •

This tavern-restaurant features a select tapas bar at the entrance and a modern
and intimate dining room in the basement. Its creative cuisine is based on traditional Asturian recipes.

Goizeko Kabi
🍽 🄰🄲 🕹

Comandante Zorita 37 ✉ 28020 – Ⓜ *Alvarado*   Plan: **L2**
– ☏ 915 33 01 85 – www.goizekogaztelupe.es – Closed Sunday dinner
Menu 45/65 € – Carte 43/59 €
• Basque • Trendy •

A fine example of Madrid's more traditional restaurant scene, albeit with a renovated and more contemporary look. Basque cuisine, tapas and dishes perfect
for sharing.

Kabuki
🍽 🔥 🄰🄲
⚬

av. Presidente Carmona 2 ✉ 28020   Plan: **L1-2**
– Ⓜ *Santiago Bernabeu – ☏ 914 17 64 15 – www.restaurantekabuki.com
– Closed Holy Week, 10-31 August, Saturday lunch, Sunday and Bank
Holidays*
Menu 70/90 € – Carte 55/85 €
• Japanese • Minimalist •

An intimate Japanese restaurant with a minimalist feel. Modern terrace, as well
as a kitchen-bar serving a range of dishes including a wide choice of nigiri
sushi. It is best to book ahead as it is often full.
➜ Degustación de atún en sashimi. Selección de niguiris de pescado azul
ahumado. Torrija.

Ferreiro
🄰🄲 ⟷ 🕹

Comandante Zorita 32 ✉ 28020 – Ⓜ *Alvarado*   Plan: **L2**
– ☏ 915 53 93 42 – www.restauranteferreiro.com
Menu 30/60 € – Carte 35/50 €
• Traditional cuisine • Classic •

Classic-contemporary dining rooms act as a backdrop for traditional cuisine
with strong Asturian roots in this restaurant. Extensive menu that is supplemented by a good choice of specials.

SPAIN - **MADRID**

XX **La Tahona** 🔲 🏧 ⟷

Capitán Haya 21 (beside) ✉ *28020 –* Ⓜ *Cuzco*   Plan: **L1**
– 𝒞 915 55 04 41 – www.asadordearanda.com – Closed 3-27 August and
Sunday dinner
Menu 38/50 € – Carte 40/60 €
• Meats • Classic •
Part of the El Asador de Aranda chain. La Tahona's dining rooms have a medie-
val Castillian ambience with a wood fire at the entrance taking pride of place.
The suckling lamb (lechazo) is the star dish here!

XX **Sal Gorda** 🏧

Beatriz de Bobadilla 9 ✉ *28040 –* Ⓜ *Guzmán El Bueno*   Plan: **K2**
– 𝒞 915 53 95 06 – www.restaurantesalgorda.es – Closed Holy Week,
August, Sunday and Monday dinner
Menu 30/50 € – Carte 35/54 €
• Classic cuisine • Classic •
A compact restaurant with a single dining room decorated in a classic yet con-
temporary style. The loin of beef cooked in coarse-grained salt (sal gorda) is the
house speciality, hence the restaurant name, but is just one of an extensive
choice of dishes on the traditional menu.

Y/ **Tasca La Farmacia** 🏧

Capitán Haya 19 ✉ *28020 –* Ⓜ *Cuzco – 𝒞 915 55 81 46*   Plan: **L1**
– www.asadordearanda.com – Closed 10-30 August and Sunday
Tapa 7 € **Ración** approx. 10 €
• Traditional cuisine • Tapas bar •
Delightful restaurant decorated with azulejo tiles, stone arches, exposed brickwork, wrought iron lattice windows and an impressive glass ceiling. La Farmacia
is famous for its cod dishes.

CHAMARTÍN   **PLAN V**

🏨 **Puerta América**

av. de América 41 ✉ *28002 –* Ⓜ *Cartagena*   Plan: **N3**
– 𝒞 917 44 54 00 – www.hotelpuertamerica.com
301 rm ☲ – ♥♥110/160 € – 14 suites
• Business • Business • Design •
This colourful and cosmopolitan hotel has a distinct design feel with each of its
floors reflecting the creativity of a renowned architect or famous interior designer. Highly original guestrooms with an attractive fitness and well-being space
on the top floor.
Lágrimas Negras – See restaurant listing

🏨 **NH Eurobuilding** 🔲 🏧 ⟷

Padre Damián 23 ✉ *28036 –* Ⓜ *Cuzco*   Plan: **M2**
– 𝒞 913 53 73 00 – www.nh-hotels.com
431 rm – ♥♥105/300 € – ☲ 25 €
• Business • Business • Contemporary •
This hotel has a spectacular lobby featuring a high-tech LED inspired barrel-
vaulted ceiling that doubles as the biggest multimedia screen in Europe! Overall, the facilities are spacious with well-equipped contemporary-style guestrooms, a plethora of meeting rooms and myriad lounge areas. The interesting
culinary options add an extra dimension.
❀❀❀ **DiverXO** • **99 sushi bar** – See restaurant listing

🏨 **Don Pío**

av. Pío XII-25 ✉ *28016 –* Ⓜ *Pío XII – 𝒞 913 53 07 80*   Plan: **N2**
– www.hoteldonpio.com
41 rm – ♥77/180 € ♥♥94/230 € – ☲ 17 €
• Family • Traditional • Classic •
This friendly, family-run hotel has an elegant patio-cum-entrance-hall at its centre, crowned by a modern skylight. Classic guestrooms offering good levels of
comfort and, on the whole, impressive dimensions.

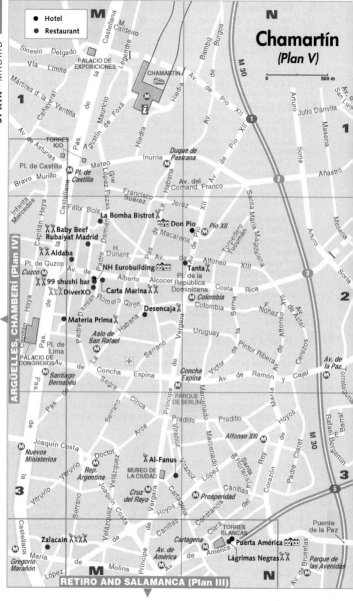

Chamartín
(Plan V)

- Hotel
- Restaurant

SPAIN - MADRID

XxxX **Zalacain** ⬱ AC ⇔ 🝔

Álvarez de Baena 4 ⊠ *28006 –* Ⓜ *Gregorio Marañón*
– ☏ *915 61 48 40 – www.restaurantezalacain.com – closed Holy Week,*
August, Saturday lunch, Sunday and Bank Holidays
Carte 60/113 €

• Classic cuisine • Elegant •

Zalacain is an integral part of Madrid's recent culinary history. It boasts an elegantly classical feel, highly professional service and an extensive à la carte featuring classic Spanish and international cuisine.

XxX **DiverXO** Dabiz Muñoz – Hotel NH Eurobuilding ⬱ AC 🚗
❀❀❀ *Padre Damián 23* ⊠ *28036 –* Ⓜ *Cuzco* Plan: M2
– ☏ *915 70 07 66 – www.diverxo.com – Closed 21 days August, Sunday*
and Monday
Menu 165/220 € *– (booking essential) (set menu only)*

• Creative • Design •

This restaurant is an exciting and groundbreaking culinary wonderland, and a journey into the highly personal world of this chef. To a backdrop of stunning modern design, enjoy world cuisine that will challenge your palate, intensifying sensations and reaching its apogee in presentation worthy of the finest canvas.
→ Maíces con suero de búfala, hongos negroazulados, crestas de gallo y alitas de pollo tandoori. Lienzo vintage, jarrete lechal infusionado con lemongrass y cardamomo con complementos del mundo con alma de Francia. Madriz by Dabiz, violetas, ajo negro y albahaca thai.

XxX **Aldaba** ⬱ ﬦ AC ⇔

av. de Alberto Alcocer 5 ⊠ *28036 –* Ⓜ *Cuzco* Plan: M2
– ☏ *913 45 21 93 – www.restaurantealdaba.es – Closed Holy Week, August*
and Sunday
Menu 60/65 € – Carte 55/80 €

• Traditional cuisine • Design •

This restaurant has an unexpectedly bright and modern interior that is almost minimalist in feel. The menu combines classic house specialities with dishes that are more contemporary in presentation and technique.

XxX **Lágrimas Negras** – Hotel Puerta América ⬱ ﬧ AC ⇔ 🚗

av. de América 41 ⊠ *28002 –* Ⓜ *Cartagena* Plan: N3
– ☏ *917 44 54 05 – www.hotelpuertamerica.com*
Menu 36/55 € – Carte 34/55 €

• Modern cuisine • Fashionable •

Part of a designer hotel, this restaurant boasts a contemporary look, including high ceilings and large windows, plus direct access to the terrace. Contemporary cuisine of a very high standard.

XX **Carta Marina** ﬧ AC

Padre Damián 40 ⊠ *28036 –* Ⓜ *Cuzco* Plan: M2
– ☏ *914 58 68 26 – www.restaurantecartamarina.com – Closed Holy*
Week, August and Sunday
Menu 45 € – Carte 40/70 €

• Galician • Classic •

A true classic! Attractive summer and winter terraces, private bar, and meticulously arranged dining rooms, all featuring a profusion of wood. The menu remains faithful to traditional Galician ingredients, hence the predominance of fish and seafood.

XX **99 sushi bar** – Hotel NH Eurobuilding ﬧ AC

Padre Damián 23 ⊠ *28036 –* Ⓜ *Cuzco* Plan: M2
– ☏ *913 59 38 01 – www.99sushibar.com – Closed Sunday dinner*
Menu 80 € – Carte 55/75 €

• Japanese • Design •

This restaurant is modern and full of decorative detail. The menu combines traditional Japanese dishes alongside other recipes blending elements of Spanish cooking.

SPAIN - MADRID

XX   Baby Beef Rubaiyat Madrid   🕸 🛱 ⚹ 🎴 ⇄ 🐂

Juan Ramón Jiménez 37 ⊠ 28036 – Ⓜ Cuzco   Plan: **M2**
– ℰ 913 59 10 00 – www.rubaiyat.es
– Closed Sunday dinner
Menu 48 € – Carte 42/65 €
• Meats • Brasserie •

The flavours of São Paulo in the Spanish capital. Meat served here includes Brangus and tropical Kobe beef, although traditional Brazilian dishes also feature, such as the famous feijoada on Saturdays.

X   Desencaja   🎴

😊   *paseo de la Habana 84 ⊠ 28036 – Ⓜ Colombia*   Plan: **M2**
– ℰ 914 57 56 68 – www.dsncaja.com – Closed Holy Week, August,
Sunday dinner and Monday
Menu 32/40 € – Carte 25/40 €
• Traditional cuisine • Classic •

An interesting dining option in a resolutely contemporary space with an uncluttered minimalist feel. Trained in some of the country's best restaurants, the chef here creates traditionally inspired seasonal dishes that are only available to diners via set menus.

X   Tanta   🎴

pl. del Perú 1 ⊠ 28016 – Ⓜ Pío XII – ℰ 913 50 26 26   Plan: **M-N2**
– www.tantamadrid.com
Menu 17/35 € – Carte 33/59 €
• Peruvian • Simple •

Enjoy typical Peruvian dishes such as ceviche, tiraditos, makis, causas and anticuchos in this simple restaurant. It takes its name from the Quechua word for bread.

X   La Bomba Bistrot   🛱 🎴 🐂

Pedro Muguruza 5 ⊠ 28036 – Ⓜ Cuzco   Plan: **M2**
– ℰ 913 50 30 47 – www.labombabistrot.com – Closed 1-21 August,
Sunday dinner and Monday
Carte 35/45 €
• Traditional cuisine • Bistro •

A welcoming restaurant that tries to recreate the essence of a typical French bistro. It has an open-view kitchen, pleasing natural light and seasonal home-style cuisine.

X   Materia Prima   🛱 🎴

Doctor Fleming 7 ⊠ 28036 – Ⓜ Santiago Bernabeu   Plan: **M2**
– ℰ 913 44 01 77 – www.materia-prima.es
Carte 25/47 €
• Traditional cuisine • Classic •

A unique culinary concept where products are displayed as they would be in a market, which customers then buy at market rates, before being prepared at a fixed price. Materia Prima's range of fish options is particularly superb.

X   Al-Fanus   🎴

Pechuán 6 ⊠ 28002 – Ⓜ Cruz del Rayo   Plan: **M3**
– ℰ 915 62 77 18 – www.restaurantealfanus.es – Closed Sunday dinner
and Monday dinner
Menu 21/33 € – Carte 27/50 €
• International • Classic •

If you're unfamiliar with Syrian cuisine, Al-Fanus provides an opportunity to enjoy the country's best recipes, which are full of subtlety and always loyal to their Mediterranean roots. Arabian ambience and decor.

PARQUE FERIAL

PLAN I

Globales Acis y Galatea

Galatea 6 ✉ 28042 – Ⓜ Canillejas – ☎ 917 43 49 01
– www.hotelesglobales.com
25 rm – 🛏55/130 € 🛏🛏66/260 € – � 8 €
• Family • Elegant •

Plan: **D1**

Located in a residential district of the city, this hotel boasts a certain charm, with its classic yet contemporary guestrooms, with the three boasting a terrace the pick of the bunch. A dinner option is available to guests staying here, who can make their choice from a concise set menu.

AT BARAJAS AIRPORT

PLAN I

Meliá Barajas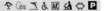

av. de Logroño 305 (A 2, then towards Barajas Town:
15 km) ✉ 28042 – Ⓜ Barajas – ☎ 917 47 77 00 – www.melia-barajas.com
229 rm ⊒ – 🛏🛏75/300 € – 8 suites

Plan: **D1**

• Business • Classic •

Comfortable, classically furnished facilities, including fully equipped guestrooms and a wide choice of meeting rooms arranged around the garden and pool area. International dining with the occasional Asian influence is to the fore in the restaurant.

SPAIN - MADRID

BARCELONA
BARCELONA

Population: 1 602 386

B. Brillion/MICHELIN

It can't be overestimated how important Catalonia is to the locals of Barcelona: pride in their region of Spain runs deep in the blood. Barcelona loves to mix the traditional with the avant-garde, and this exuberant opening of arms has seen it grow into a pulsating city for visitors. Its rash of theatres, museums and concert halls is unmatched by most other European cities, and many artists and architects, including Picasso, Miró, Dalí, Gaudí and Subirachs, have chosen to live here.

The 19C was a golden period in the city's artistic development, with the growth of the great Catalan Modernism movement, but it was knocked back on its heels after the Spanish Civil War and the rise to power of the dictator Franco, who destroyed hopes for an independent Catalonia. After his death, democracy came to Spain and since then, Barcelona has relished its position as the capital of a restored autonomous region. Go up on the Montjuïc to get a great overview of the city below. Barcelona's atmospheric old town is near the harbour and reaches into the teeming streets of the Gothic Quarter, while the newer area is north of this; its elegant avenues in grid formation making up Eixample. The coastal quarter of Barça has been transformed with the development of trendy Barceloneta. For many, though, the epicentre of this bubbling city is Las Ramblas, scything through the centre of town.

BARCELONA IN...

→ ONE DAY
Catedral de Santa Eulalia, Las Ramblas, La Pedrera, Museu Picasso, Sagrada Familia.

→ TWO DAYS
Montjuïc, Parc Güell, Nou Camp Stadium, Barceloneta Waterfront, Tibidabo.

→ THREE DAYS
Barri Gotic and Palau de la Musica Catalana, Via Laietana, Sitges.

PRACTICAL INFORMATION

ARRIVAL-DEPARTURE

🛬 Barcelona-El Prat Airport is located 13km southwest of the city. The Renfe train (Line R2, suburban train) runs every 30min. The Aerobus runs every 5min.

GETTING AROUND

The Barcelona Card offers three to five days of unlimited travel on the metro and buses, discounts on airport buses and cable cars, reduced entry to museums and attractions and discounts in some restaurants, bars and shops; it is sold at the airport, tourist offices and various other venues. The Articket gives free entry to six museums and galleries over six months and is available from tourist offices. Look out for two tourist buses – the Barcelona City Tour and the Bus Turistic.

CALENDAR HIGHLIGHTS

March
Mobile World Congress

May
Ciutat Flamenco, Barcelona Guitar Festival.

June
Bicycle Week, Saint John's Day (concerts, dances and bonfires).

September
Fiesta de la Merce (Feast of Our Lady of Mercy).

October
International Jazz Festival, LIBER International Book Fair

October-July
Classical performances at Gran Teatre del Liceu.

EATING OUT

Barcelona has long had a good gastronomic tradition, and geographically it's been more influenced by France and Italy than other Spanish regions. But these days the sensual enjoyment of food has become something of a mainstream religion here. The city has hundreds of tapas bars; a type of cuisine which is very refreshing knocked back with a draught beer. The city's location brings together produce from the land and the sea, with a firm emphasis on seasonality and quality produce. This explains why there are myriad markets in the city, all in great locations. Specialities to look out for include Pantumaca: slices of toasted bread with tomato and olive oil; Escalibada, which is made with roasted vegetables; Esqueixada, a typically Catalan salad, and Crema Catalana, a light custard. One little known facet of Barcelona life is its exquisite chocolate and sweet shops. Two stand out: Fargas, in the Barri Gothic, is the city's most famous chocolate shop, while Cacao Sampaka is the most elegant chocolate store you could ever wish to find.

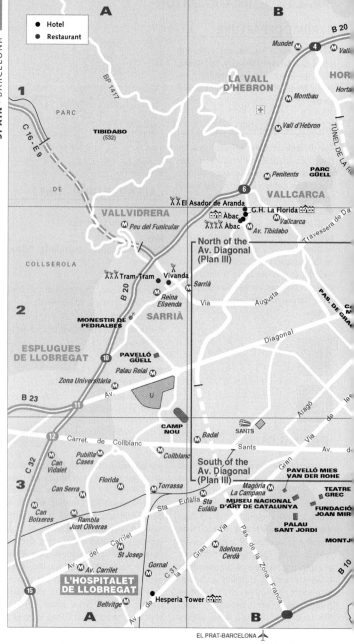

Environs of Barcelona
(Plan I)

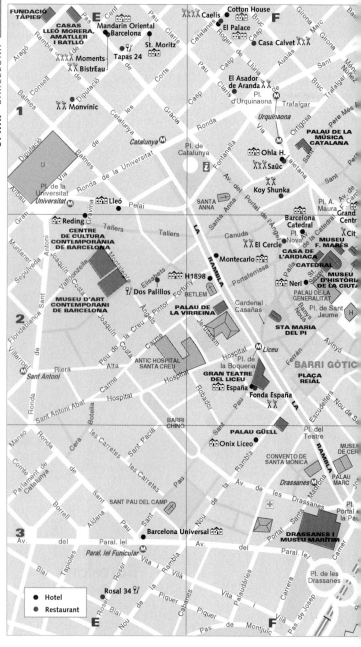

Legend:
- ● Hotel
- ● Restaurant

FUNDACIÓ TÀPIES
CASAS LLEÓ MORERA, AMATLLER I BATLLÓ
Mandarin Oriental Barcelona
St. Moritz
Moments
BistrEau
Tapas 24
Monvínic
Caelis
Cotton House
El Palace
Casa Calvet
El Asador de Aranda
Pl. d'Urquinaona
Urquinaona
PALAU DE LA MÚSICA CATALANA
Ohla H.
Saüc
Koy Shunka
Catalunya
Pl. de Catalunya
SANTA ANNA
Lleó
CENTRE DE CULTURA CONTEMPORÀNIA DE BARCELONA
Reding
Barcelona Catedral
El Cercle
MUSEU F. MARÉS
CASA DE L'ARDIACA
CATEDRAL
Grand Centr
Cit
Montecarlo
H1898
Dos Palillos
MUSEU D'ART CONTEMPORANI DE BARCELONA
BETLEM
PALAU DE LA VIRREINA
MUSEU D'HISTÒRI DE LA CIUT
Neri
PALAU DE LA GENERALITAT
Cardenal Casañas
STA MARIA DEL PI
Pl. de Sant Jaume
ANTIC HOSPITAL SANTA CREU
Liceu
Pl. de la Boqueria
BARRI GÒTIC
GRAN TEATRE DEL LICEU
España
Fonda España
PLAÇA REIAL
BARRI CHINO
PALAU GÜELL
Onix Liceo
Pl. del Teatre
CONVENTO DE SANTA MÒNICA
MUSE DE CER
Drassanes
PALAU MARC
SANT PAU DEL CAMP
Pl. Portal la Pau
Barcelona Universal
DRASSANES I MUSEU MARÍTIM
Paral. lel
Paral. lel Funicular
Rosal 34
Pl. de les Drassanes

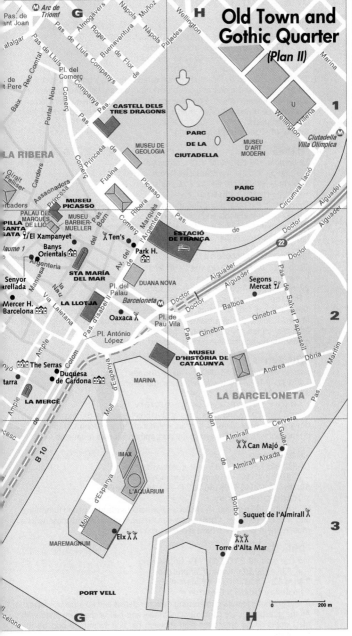

Old Town and Gothic Quarter
(Plan II)

Pas. de ant Joan
M Arc de Triomf

G

H

Wellington

Marina

LA RIBERA

Almogàvers

Nàpols Muñoz

Nàpols Pujades

Pas. de Lluís Companys

Roger de Flor

Buenaventura

Companys

Wellington

Villena

Marina

1

M Ciutadella Vila Olímpica

Pl. del Comerç

Portal Nou

Comerç

Pas.

Comerç

CASTELL DELS TRES DRAGONS

PARC DE LA CIUTADELLA

U

Comtal

Baix

Princesa

Pas. de

de

Pere

MUSEU DE GEOLOGIA

Carders

Giralt

Felisser

Princesa

Fusina

MUSEU D'ART MODERN

Picasso

Assaonadors

MUSEU PICASSO

Ribera

Comerç

Marquès

l'Argentera

PARC ZOOLOGIC

rcaders

Princesa

Circumval lació

Aiguader

Aiguader

PALAU DELS MARQUES DE LLIÓ

MUSEU BARBIER-MUELLER

CAPILLA SANTA AGATA

Y/El Xampanyet

X Ten's

Pas. de

de

ESTACIÓ DE FRANÇA

22

Doctor

Jaume 1

Banys Orientals

Park H.

Aiguader

Aiguader

Doctor

Senyor arellada

Argenteria

Manresa

STA MARÍA DEL MAR

Via

Nau

Pl. del Palau

DUANA NOVA

Segons Mercat Y

Pas. de Salvat Papasseit

Mercer H. Barcelona

Via Laietana

LA LLOTJA

Pas. d'isabel

Barceloneta M

Doctor

Balboa

Ginebra

Doria

2

tarra

Oaxaca X

Pl. de Pau Vila

Ginebra

Andrea

Marítim

Colom

Pl. António López

Doctor

The Serras

d'Espanya

MUSEU D'HISTÒRIA DE CATALUNYA

Ample

Duquesa de Cardona

MARINA

LA BARCELONETA

LA MERCÉ

Moll

Joan

Cervera

de

B 10

cesc

IMAX

Almirall

X X Can Majó

Almirall Aixada

Guitle

Moll d'Espanya

L'AQUÀRIUM

Borbó

Suquet de l'Almirall X

3

MAREMAGNUM

Elx X X

X X X Torre d'Alta Mar

celona

PORT VELL

0   200 m

G

H

W Barcelona

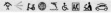

pl. de la Rosa dels Vents 1 (Moll De Llevant) ⊠ 08039   Plan I: **C3**
– ✆ 932 95 28 00 – www.w-barcelona.com
473 rm – ♥♥190/900 € – ⚏ 32 € – 67 suites
• Business • Luxury • Design •
This hotel designed by Ricardo Bofill is located in the city's port area. It comprises of two glass buildings: one a cube, the other a huge sail rising impressively above the Mediterranean. Extensive spa facilities. This contemporary looking gastronomic restaurant offers guests an à la carte menu based around high quality products.
Bravo 24 – See restaurant listing

H1898

La Rambla 109 ⊠ 08002 – **Ⓜ** *Catalunya*   Plan: **F2**
– ✆ 935 52 95 52 – www.hotel1898.com
166 rm – ♥♥180/510 € – ⚏ 24 € – 3 suites
• Chain hotel • Historic •
The decor in this hotel occupying the former Tabacos de Filipinas headquarters is a mix of the traditional and contemporary. Spa area, guestrooms offering the very best amenities, plus a rooftop solarium with views of the city. This resolutely contemporary restaurant offers an à la carte menu of international dishes.

Mercer H. Barcelona

⚲ ⭑ 🆎

Lledó 7 ⊠ 08002 – **Ⓜ** *Jaume I* – ✆ 93 310 74 80   Plan: **G2**
– www.mercerbarcelona.com
27 rm – ♥♥350/600 € – ⚏ 34 € – 1 suite
• Palace • Historic • Contemporary •
This hotel has lots of history and occupies a palace remodelled by Rafael Moneo. It still retains impressive vestiges of the past, such as the original wall from the Roman city of Barcino. Other noteworthy features include a vertical garden, highly comfortable guestrooms and an attractive restaurant.

The Serras

⚲ 🖪 ⭑ 🆎

Passeig de Colom 9 ⊠ 08002 – **Ⓜ** *Drassanes*   Plan: **G2**
– ✆ 931 69 18 68 – www.hoteltheserrasbarcelona.com
28 rm – ♥♥200/400 € – ⚏ 24 €
• Luxury • Elegant • Contemporary •
Luxury, practicality and pure lines at this hotel opposite the gigantic Prawn designed by Javier Mariscal. It offers well-equipped guestrooms, a sun terrace on the roof with superb views of the port, and an informal restaurant.

Montecarlo

⭑ 🆎 🔊 🚗

La Rambla 124 ⊠ 08002 – **Ⓜ** *Catalunya*   Plan: **F2**
– ✆ 934 12 04 04 – www.montecarlobcn.com
50 rm – ♥87/165 € ♥♥106/358 € – ⚏ 14 € – 6 suites
• Traditional • Cosy •
Housed in a 19C mansion, this hotel is a harmonious blend of period furnishings and modern comforts. Choose between classic bedrooms and those with a more modern look which have recently been renovated.

Ohla H.

⚲ 🖪 ⭑ 🆎 🔊 🚗

Vía Laietana 49 ⊠ 08003 – **Ⓜ** *Urquinaona*   Plan: **F1**
– ✆ 933 41 50 50 – www.ohlahotel.com
74 rm ⚏ – ♥231/405 € ♥♥245/430 €
• Holiday hotel • Design •
A modern hotel featuring interesting designer details and an attractive façade. All the guestrooms are contemporary in feel and half of them are fitted with glass doors giving onto open-plan showers. Bar and swimming pool on the roof terrace.
❀ **Saüc** – See restaurant listing

Neri ☆ AC ☼

Sant Sever 5 ✉ *08002 –* Ⓜ *Liceu –* ℰ *933 04 06 55* — Plan: **F2**
– www.hotelneri.com
21 rm – ♥♥250/1200 € – ☑ 20 € – 1 suite
• Historic • Modern •

The modern interior of this hotel occupying an 18C mansion comes as something of a surprise. Library-lounge, designer-inspired guestrooms and a rooftop terrace. In the dining room, embellished with two 12C stone arches, diners can choose from a selection of contemporary Mediterranean cuisine.

España ☆ & AC ⚶

Sant Pau 9 ✉ *08001 –* Ⓜ *Liceu –* ℰ *935 50 00 00* — Plan: **F2**
– www.hotelesespanya.com
83 rm – ♥♥142/347 € – ☑ 17 €
• Chain hotel • Cosy •

Located right in the heart of the old quarter and easy to find since it occupies a 19C building next to the Liceu. Pleasant lounge area with some historical details, plus comfortable, albeit rather small guestrooms with a contemporary design.
⊛ **Fonda España** – See restaurant listing

Grand H. Central ☆ ♬ ⨆ & AC ⚶

Via Laietana 30 ✉ *08003 –* Ⓜ *Jaume I* — Plan: **F2**
– ℰ 932 95 79 00 – www.grandhotelcentral.com
146 rm ☑ – ♥♥210/751 € – 6 suites
• Traditional • Contemporary •

A hotel with a contemporary look and welcoming facilities. Here, guests will find bedrooms with lots of attention to detail, and interesting public spaces such as the rooftop Sky Bar, with a chill- out zone and panoramic pool, the modern City Bar, and the multi-functional The Gallery.
City – See restaurant listing

St. Moritz ☆ & AC ⚶ 🚗

Diputació 264 ✉ *08007 –* Ⓜ *Passeig de Gràcia* — Plan: **E1**
– ℰ 934 12 15 00 – www.hcchotels.es
91 rm – ♥143/260 € ♥♥143/318 € – ☑ 22 €
• Traditional • Classic •

The St Moritz occupies a listed building dating back to 1883 in the centre of the city. Behind the classical façade, you will find a pleasant lobby-reception area with a monumental staircase and contemporary bedrooms that are functional in style. The focus in the simply furnished restaurant is on a set menu.

Duquesa de Cardona & AC ⚶

passeig de Colom 12 ✉ *08002 –* Ⓜ *Drassanes* — Plan: **G2**
– ℰ 932 68 90 90 – www.hduquesadecardona.com
52 rm – ♥180/265 € ♥♥190/275 € – ☑ 18 €
• Holiday hotel • Contemporary •

An aristocratic 19C property with superb guestrooms and a rooftop terrace-solarium. It offers a simple menu in winter and a barbecue-tapas menu in summer.

Barcelona Catedral ☆ ♬ ⨆ & AC ⚶

Dels Capellans 4 ✉ *08002 –* Ⓜ *Catalunya* — Plan: **F2**
– ℰ 933 04 22 55 – www.barcelonacatedral.com
80 rm – ♥♥99/360 € – ☑ 19 €
• Holiday hotel • Modern •

Behind the modern façade is a contemporary hotel that stands out for its high class decor and guestrooms equipped with all mod cons. Impressive terrace on the interior patio. The restaurant, located next to the bar, combines traditional à la carte choices with a good set menu. Guided tours of the Gothic quarter available.

SPAIN - BARCELONA

Barcelona Universal

av. del Paral.lel 80 ✉ *08001 –* Ⓜ *Paral.lel*
Plan: **E3**
– ☎ 935 67 74 47 – www.hotelbarcelonauniversal.com
165 rm – ♥♥100/500 € – ⌴ 15 € – 2 suites
• Chain hotel • Contemporary •
This modern hotel offers spacious, well-appointed guestrooms and a lounge area with bar. Panoramic swimming pool with a solarium on the top floor. A simply furnished restaurant serving a buffet of grilled meats.

Lleó

Pelai 22 ✉ *08001 –* Ⓜ *Universitat – ☎ 933 18 13 12*
Plan: **E1**
– www.hotel-lleo.com
92 rm – ♥100/170 € ♥♥120/250 € – ⌴ 15 €
• Traditional • Functional •
An interesting property, given the elegant façade, spacious public areas and functional, contemporary guestrooms. Small rooftop pool and a café serving meals.

Onix Liceo

Nou de la Rambla 36 ✉ *08001 –* Ⓜ *Liceu*
Plan: **F3**
– ☎ 934 81 64 41 – www.onixhotels.com
45 rm – ♥54/424 € ♥♥59/429 € – ⌴ 9 €
• Traditional • Contemporary • Functional •
This establishment occupies a 19C renovated building, whose façade, light well and original marble staircase have been preserved. It has a modern social area and bedrooms in a functional style.

Park H.

av. Marqués de l'Argentera 11 ✉ *08003*
Plan: **G2**
– Ⓜ *Barceloneta – ☎ 933 19 60 00 – www.parkhotelbarcelona.com*
91 rm – ♥66/188 € ♥♥105/301 € – ⌴ 12 €
• Holiday hotel • Functional •
Occupying a listed building dating back to 1953 with a delightful spiral staircase and a majority of rooms which have been pleasantly updated. Make sure you visit the Ten's gastro-bar.

Reding

Gravina 5-7 ✉ *08001 –* Ⓜ *Universitat*
Plan: **E1-2**
– ☎ 934 12 10 97 – www.hotelreding.com
44 rm – ♥70/350 € ♥♥75/355 € – ⌴ 14 €
• Traditional • Functional •
The Reding is located close to the Plaça de Catalunya. Its attractions include a contemporary-style lobby, a lounge, and functionally furnished guestrooms, as well as a plentiful breakfast buffet.

Banys Orientals

L'Argenteria 37 ✉ *08003 –* Ⓜ *Jaume I*
Plan: **G2**
– ☎ 932 68 84 60 – www.hotelbanysorientals.com
43 rm – ♥97/120 € ♥♥106/153 € – ⌴ 14 €
• Traditional • Functional •
This hotel has comfortable, minimalist-style rooms. They feature plenty of design features, wooden floors and canopies above the beds. No lounge.
🕮 **Senyor Parellada** – See restaurant listing

XxX Torre d'Alta Mar

passeig Joan de Borbó 88 ✉ *08039 –* Ⓜ *Barceloneta*
Plan: **H3**
– ☎ 932 21 00 07 – www.torredealtamar.com – Closed 24-28 December, Sunday and Monday lunch
Menu 39/100 € – Carte 69/91 €
• Modern cuisine • Formal •
A restaurant whose outstanding feature is its location on top of a 75m-high metal tower. Highly contemporary glass-fronted circular dining room with superb views of the sea, port and city. Traditional à la carte menu featuring contemporary touches.

SPAIN - BARCELONA

XxX
ⓔ
Saüc (Xavier Franco) – Hotel Ohla H.   🄰🄲 🚗
Vía Laietana 49 ✉ *08003* – Ⓜ *Urquinaona*   Plan: **F1**
– ☎ *933 21 01 89 – www.saucrestaurant.com*
Menu 82/112 € – Carte 73/86 € – *(dinner only)*
• **Creative** • **Minimalist** •
A restaurant with a good reputation in the city. There is a modern gastro-bar and a contemporary, almost minimalist dining room upstairs. The chef offers innovative cuisine, in addition to several tasting menus, which combine traditional and up-to-date dishes.
→ Terrina de pies de cerdo con cigala, calabacín y clorofila. Pescado de costa a la ginebra, pepino, manzana y limón. Leche de oveja helada, rocío de hierbas y tomillo.

XxX
Bravo 24 – Hotel W Barcelona   🛇 🏤 🖫 🄰🄲
pl. de la Rosa dels Vents 1 (Moll De Llevant) ✉ *08039*   Plan I: **C3**
– ☎ *932 95 26 36 – www.carlesabellan.com*
Carte 58/85 €
• **Modern cuisine** • **Traditional** •
Located on the mezzanine of the W hotel in Barcelona, Bravo 24 has a resolutely contemporary feel, in which wood takes pride of place, plus an attractive summer terrace. Traditionally inspired cuisine enhanced by contemporary touches, plus an impressive array of raciones!

XX
ⓔ
Senyor Parellada – Hotel Banys Orientals   🄰🄲
L'Argenteria 37 ✉ *08003* – Ⓜ *Jaume I*   Plan: **G2**
– ☎ *933 10 50 94 – www.senyorparellada.com*
Menu 36 € – Carte approx. 35 €
• **Regional** • **Cosy** •
An attractive restaurant with a classic-cum-colonial style and various dining rooms in which time seems to have stood still. The highlights are the authentic Catalan cuisine and the small patio with an impressive glass roof.

XX
El Cercle   🖫 🄰🄲 ⟷
dels Arcs 5 (1st floor) ✉ *08002* – Ⓜ *Liceu*   Plan: **F2**
– ☎ *93 624 48 10 – www.elcerclerestaurant.com*
Menu 38 € – Carte 32/55 €
• **Classic cuisine** • **Classic** •
This restaurant is housed in the Reial Cercle Artístic. It offers different types of cuisine in different dining areas. These range from Japanese specialities to modern Catalan fare.

XX
Elx   ⟨ 🏤 🄰🄲
Moll d'Espanya 5-Maremagnum, Local 9 ✉ *08039*   Plan: **G3**
– Ⓜ *Drassanes –* ☎ *932 25 81 17 – www.elxrestaurant.com*
Carte 30/45 €
• **Traditional cuisine** • **Fashionable** •
A restaurant graced with views of the fishing port. Modern dining room and an attractive terrace, where the focus is on fish and a good selection of savoury rice dishes.

XX
ⓔ
Koy Shunka (Hideki Matsuhisa)   🄰🄲
Copons 7 ✉ *08002* – Ⓜ *Urquinaona –* ☎ *934 12 79 39*   Plan: **F1**
– www.koyshunka.com – Closed Christmas, Holy Week, August, Sunday dinner and Monday
Menu 82/128 € – Carte 65/85 €
• **Japanese** • **Fashionable** •
The perfect place to watch delicious nigiri and other types of sushi being prepared in front of you, as one of the dining rooms has an open-view kitchen in the middle of it. Japanese gastronomy created with ingredients from the Mediterranean.
→ Nigiri de anguila del Delta del Ebro. Tataki de bogavante. Tarta de crema de queso.

703

XX Can Majó   🏠 AC

Almirall Aixada 23 ✉ *08003 –* Ⓜ *Barceloneta*   Plan: **H3**
– ☏ 932 21 54 55 – www.canmajo.es – Closed Sunday dinner and Monday
Carte 30/52 €
• Fish and seafood • Cosy •

This family-run restaurant has a contemporary feel. Can Majó's menu specialises in fish, seafood and savoury rice dishes, as witnessed by its enticing display cabinet.

XX Fonda España – Hotel España   & AC
(🙂)
Sant Pau 9 ✉ *08001 –* Ⓜ *Liceu – ☏ 935 50 00 00*   Plan: **F2**
– www.hotelesespanya.com – Closed Sunday dinner and Bank Holidays dinner
Menu 27/65 € – Carte 29/37 € – *(dinner only August)*
• Traditional cuisine • Classic •

This charming address is in a listed building with high ceilings, a Modernist decor and beautiful mosaics created by the renowned Barcelona architect Domènech i Montaner. Updated traditional cuisine.

X Oaxaca   🏠 & AC

Pla del Palau 19 ✉ *08002 –* Ⓜ *Barceloneta*   Plan: **G2**
– ☏ 933 19 00 64 – www.oaxacacuinamexicana.com
Carte 40/61 €
• Mexican • Exotic •

Discover authentic Mexican cuisine in a restaurant with a modern and informal ambience, which nonetheless manages to retain a typical flavour of Mexico. The mezcalería is well worth a visit!

X City – Hotel Grand H. Central   & AC

Pare Galifa 3 ✉ *08003 –* Ⓜ *Jaume I – ☏ 932 95 79 05*   Plan: **F2**
Carte 30/40 € – *(dinner only)*
• Traditional cuisine • Fashionable •

This restaurant has a very distinctive urban and modern feel. Interesting, varied menu offering a selection of salads, organic savoury rice dishes and gourmet hamburgers.

X Pitarra   AC ⟷

Avinyó 56 ✉ *08002 –* Ⓜ *Liceu – ☏ 933 01 16 47*   Plan: **G2**
– www.restaurantpitarra.cat – Closed 9-30 August, Sunday and Bank Holidays dinner
Menu 14/55 € – Carte 27/50 €
• Traditional cuisine • Traditional •

It was in these premises that Frederic Soler, a leading figure from the world of Catalan theatre, once had his watchmaker's shop. Dining rooms with an old-fashioned feel, including two rooms for private parties. Traditional cuisine.

X Suquet de l'Almirall   🏠 AC

passeig Joan de Borbó 65 ✉ *08003 – ☏ 932 21 62 33*   Plan: **H3**
– www.suquetdelalmirall.com – Closed Sunday dinner and Monday
Menu 38 € – Carte 34/52 €
• Fish and seafood • Traditional •

A restaurant boasting a maritime inspired decor and a very pleasant outdoor terrace. Extensive menu of traditional cuisine, including a varied selection of fish and rice dishes.

X Ten's – Hotel Park H.   🏠 AC

av. Marqués de l'Argentera 11 ✉ *08003*   Plan: **G2**
– Ⓜ *Barceloneta – ☏ 93 319 22 22 – www.parkhotelbarcelona.com*
Tapa 3,70 € – Ración approx. 9 €
• Modern cuisine • Fashionable •

A gastro-bar with a thoroughly modern look that is dominated by varying tones of white. Its concise menu, overseen by the TV chef Jordi Cruz, features tapas and half portions. These cleverly combine traditional and more cutting-edge cuisine.

SPAIN - BARCELONA

Dos Palillos 🏠 Ⓚ

Elisabets 9 ⊠ 08001 – Ⓜ *Catalunya* Plan: **E2**
– ℰ 933 04 05 13 – www.dospalillos.com
– Closed 24 December-2 January, 9-31 August, Sunday, Monday, Tuesday lunch and Wednesday lunch
Tapa 7 €
• Fusion • Fashionable •
The chefs work directly in front of diners here, with an end result that is pleasantly surprising, both in terms of the culinary philosophy and cuisine on offer, with a focus on a fusion between Oriental cuisine and Spanish ingredients. Tapas menu and interesting set menus.
→ La sardina que quería ser anchoa. Papada de cerdo ibérico con buey de mar. Kakigori de piel de yuzu.

El Xampanyet

Montcada 22 ⊠ 08003 – Ⓜ *Jaume I – ℰ 933 19 70 03* Plan: **G2**
– Closed 15 days January, August, Sunday dinner and Monday
Tapa 6 € **Ración** approx. 12 €
• Traditional cuisine • Tapas bar •
This old tavern with a long-standing family tradition is decorated with typical azulejo tiles. Varied selection of tapas with an emphasis on cured meats and high-quality canned products.

Rosal 34 Ⓚ

Roser 34 ⊠ 08004 – Ⓜ *Paral.lel* Plan: **E3**
– ℰ 933 24 90 46 – www.rosal34.com
– Closed 1-15 September, Sunday and Monday dinner
Tapa 6 € **Ración** approx. 12 €
• Creative • Rustic •
Rosal 34 is located in an old family wine cellar, where the rustic stonework blends in with the contemporary decor. Seasonal dishes plus interesting tapas with a creative touch.

Segons Mercat 🏠 Ⓚ

Balboa 16 ⊠ 08003 – Ⓜ *Barceloneta – ℰ 933 10 78 80* Plan: **H2**
– www.segonsmercat.com
Tapa 6 € **Ración** approx. 12 €
• Traditional cuisine • Tapas bar •
A contemporary restaurant with a splendid bar featuring an impressive fish and seafood cabinet, and equally attractive dining rooms. Tapas, raciones and daily specials are the order of the day here.

SOUTH of AV. DIAGONAL **PLAN III**

Mandarin Oriental Barcelona ⚐ 𝄐 ⊛ 🖼 ⅋ Ⓚ ✜

passeig de Gràcia 38-40 ⊠ 08007 Plan: **K2**
– Ⓜ *Passeig de Gràcia*
– ℰ 931 51 88 88 – www.mandarinoriental.com
120 rm – †⊨†295/575 € – ⊑ 39 € – 18 suites
• Luxury • Design •
Experience a fusion of luxury, relaxation and pleasure in a building that once served as a bank. Today, the designer interior is highly innovative and cosmopolitan in feel. It features guestrooms offering high levels of comfort, excellent dining options in the lobby, an attractive patio-terrace, and a laid-back rooftop terrace with great views of the city.
❀❀ **Moments** • **BistrEau** – See restaurant listing

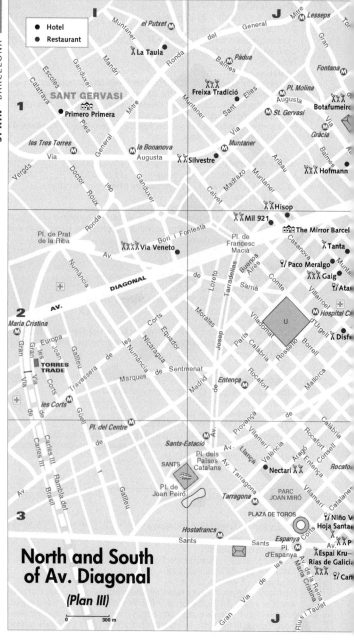

Hotel
Restaurant

Muntaner
el Putxet
General
Mitre
Lesseps

del
General
Tor

X La Taula
Balmes
Pàdua
Gran

Ronda
Mandri
Fontana

Escoles
Ganduxer
Mitre
Elies
Pl. Molina

Calatrava
XXX Freixa Tradició
Augusta
Botafumeiro

SANT GERVASI
Sant
St. Gervasi

Primero Primera
Via
Gràcia

les Tres Torres
la Bonanova
Muntaner
Balmes

Via
Augusta
XX Silvestre
Aribau
Muntaner
XXX Hofmann

Vergós
Doctor Roux
Ganduxer
Calvet
Madrazo
Muntaner

Ronda
XX Hisop

Pl. de Prat
de la Riba
Bori i Fontestà
XX Mil 921
Pl. de
Francesc
Macià
The Mirror Barcel

Numància
XXXX Via Veneto
Casanova
Tanta

DIAGONAL
de
Loreto
Tarradellas
Buenos Aires
Sarrià
Comte
Paco Meralgo
XXX Gaig
Munta
Ata

AV.
Maria Cristina
Morales
Josep
París
Viladomat
Rosselló
Borrell
Hospital Cl
d'Urgell
U
Disf

Europa
Corts
Equador
Nicaragua
de
Catàlria

TORRES
TRADE
Gran
Via
les Corts
Joan
Galileu
de
Numància
de
Sentmenat
Madrid
Entença
Rocafort
Mallorca

Marques

les Corts
de
Güell
Travessera

Pl. del Centre
Provença
Calàbria

Carles III
Rambla del
Brasil
Galileu
Sants-Estació
SANTS
Pl. dels
Països
Catalans
Av.
Vilamarí
Llançà
València
Aragó
Entença
Rocafort
Consell
Rocafo

AV.
de
Pl. de
Joan Peiró
Tarragona
PARC
JOAN MIRÓ
Vilamarí
Catalane

3
Hostafrancs
Sants
PLAZA DE TOROS
Niño V
Hoja Santa
Espanya
Pl.
d'Espanya
Corts
Av. X P
Espai Kru
Rias de Galicia
Can

Nectari XX
Sants
de
les
Av. de la Reina
Maria Cristina
Rius i Taulet

North and South
of Av. Diagonal

(Plan III)

0   300 m

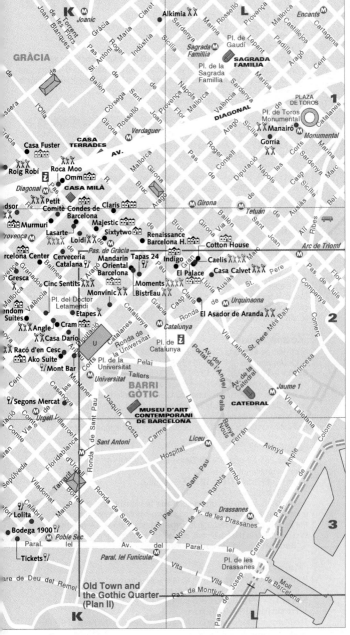

Old Town and
the Gothic Quarter
(Plan II)

SPAIN - BARCELONA

 El Palace 　　　　　　　　　　Plan: **L2**

Gran Via de les Corts Catalanes 668 ✉ *08010*
– Ⓜ *Urquinaona –* ℰ *935 10 11 30 – www.hotelpalacebarcelona.com*
107 rm – ♦♦275/575 € – ☑ 28 € – 18 suites
• Luxury • Classic •
This emblematic hotel occupies a historic building that has been restored to re-create the essence of the golden years of the 1920s. Distinguished lounges and superbly equipped guestrooms, the majority of which are classically elegant in feel with some bathrooms inspired by Roman baths!
❀ **Caelis** – See restaurant listing

 Majestic 　　　　　　　　　　Plan: **K2**

passeig de Gràcia 68 ✉ *08007 –* Ⓜ *Passeig de Gràcia*
– ℰ *934 88 17 17 – www.hotelmajestic.es*
275 rm – ♦♦290/600 € – ☑ 34 € – 41 suites
• Traditional • Classic •
The Majestic is superbly located and boasts an impressive rooftop terrace with a snack bar and delightful views. It combines excellent service with classic guestrooms offering high levels of comfort. The more functional restaurant alternates between a set menu and à la carte dining in the evening.

 Claris 　　　　　　　　　　Plan: **K2**

Pau Claris 150 ✉ *08009 –* Ⓜ *Passeig de Gràcia*
– ℰ *934 87 62 62 – www.hotelclaris.com*
84 rm – ♦♦190/600 € – ☑ 23 € – 40 suites
• Traditional • Modern •
This elegant, stately hotel occupies the former Vedruna palace. It offers a perfect fusion of tradition, cutting-edge design and technology. Impressive archaeological collection. The attractively presented restaurant is decorated in a style that recalls the work of Andy Warhol.

 Cotton House 　　　　　　　　　　Plan: **L2**

Gran Vía de les Corts Catalanes 670 ✉ *08010*
– Ⓜ *Urquinaona –* ℰ *934 50 50 45 – www.hotelcottonhouse.com*
80 rm – ♦♦190/230 € – ☑ 29 € – 3 suites
• Chain hotel • Luxury • Elegant •
As its name suggests, this imposing late-19C building was once the headquarters of the Fundación Textil Algodonera (cotton foundation). Full of character, the hotel offers beautifully kept rooms, albeit some a little on the small side, and creative cuisine based on traditional and international dishes.

 Omm 　　　　　　　　　　Plan: **K1**

Rosselló 265 ✉ *08008 –* Ⓜ *Diagonal –* ℰ *934 45 40 00*
– www.hotelomm.es
87 rm – ♦♦215/450 € – ☑ 26 € – 4 suites
• Business • Design •
A hotel with an urban, cutting-edge and fashionable feel. It features spacious guest areas, modern bedrooms, and a large multi-purpose space with views of the Passeig de Gràcia through its large picture windows. There is the OmmSession nightclub in the basement, as well as a rooftop bar area.
❀ **Roca Moo** – See restaurant listing

 Murmuri 　　　　　　　　　　Plan: **K2**

Rambla de Catalunya 104 ✉ *08008 –* Ⓜ *Diagonal*
– ℰ *935 50 06 00 – www.murmuri.com*
53 rm ☑ – ♦♦210/500 € – 5 suites
• Traditional • Modern •
The Murmuri stands out for its unbeatable location at the heart of the Ramblas. Guests can take advantage of elegant, classically designed rooms, a restaurant inspired by the Mediterranean, and a cocktail bar that is open to non-residents.

SPAIN – BARCELONA

The Mirror Barcelona
Córsega 255 ✉ *08036* – Ⓜ *Provença* – ✆ *932 028 686*
– *www.themirrorbarcelona.com*   Plan: **J2**
63 rm ⌕ – ♦113/328 € ♦♦236/611 €
• Business • Design •
The most striking aspect of this hotel is its design, which will appeal to guests keen on this type of minimalist decor. Everything is dominated by mirrors, the colour white and the use of simple, clean lines.

Condes de Barcelona
passeig de Gràcia 73-75 ✉ *08008*   Plan: **K2**
– Ⓜ *Passeig de Gràcia* – ✆ *934 45 00 00* – *www.condesdebarcelona.com*
124 rm – ♦♦142/347 € – ⌕ 21 € – 2 suites
• Traditional • Classic •
This hotel is housed in an elegant 19C building, which stands out for its location in the heart of the Passeig de Gràcia. It offers well-equipped guestrooms and an attractive sun terrace with a pleasant bar area for an evening drink.
Loidi – See restaurant listing

Barcelona Center
Balmes 103 ✉ *08008* – Ⓜ *Diagonal* – ✆ *932 73 00 00*   Plan: **K2**
– *www.hotelescenter.es*
129 rm – ♦♦88/550 € – ⌕ 17 € – 3 suites
• Business • Classic •
This hotel is hidden behind a striking façade. It boasts an equally impressive lounge area, classically furnished guestrooms with contemporary detail, as well as a huge sun terrace on the roof. The uncluttered, classic yet charming restaurant is arranged around a large central column.

Cram
Aribau 54 ✉ *08011* – Ⓜ *Universitat* – ✆ *932 16 77 00*   Plan: **K2**
– *www.hotelcram.com*
67 rm ⌕ – ♦121/265 € ♦♦139/283 €
• Business • Modern •
The smart look, high-tech facilities and creativity shown by renowned interior designers more than make up for the lack of space here. There is a mini swimming pool with a pleasant rooftop sun terrace, which is also the setting for breakfast.
❀ **Angle** – See restaurant listing

Renaissance Barcelona H.
Pau Claris 122 ✉ *08009* – Ⓜ *Passeig de Gràcia*   Plan: **K2**
– ✆ *932 72 38 10* – *www.renaissancebarcelonahotel.com*
209 rm ⌕ – ♦♦160/500 € – 2 suites
• Business • Chain hotel • Modern •
This hotel is located close to the Passeig de Gràcia. It boasts a modern lobby, pleasant public spaces and comfortable guestrooms. There is also its standout feature: the private chill-out terrace on the roof.

Ako Suite
Diputació 195 ✉ *08011* – Ⓜ *Universitat*   Plan: **K2**
– ✆ *934 53 34 19* – *www.akosuite.com*
28 suites – ♦♦99/499 € – ⌕ 12 €
• Family • Modern •
Located in the city's L'Eixample district, this hotel is a good option for families and couples. High quality apartments, all modern in style and with fully equipped kitchens. Half of the bathrooms are equipped with relaxing rain-type showers.

709

SPAIN - BARCELONA

Indigo
⇗ 🍸 ⅙ 🆎 🛗

Gran Vía de les Corts Catalanes 629 ✉ *08010* Plan: **L2**
– 🖾 *Passeig de Gràcia*
– 𝒞 *936 02 66 90 – www.indigobarcelona.com*
77 rm – †109/327 € ††124/372 € – ⌚ 15 €
• Business • Design •

The Indigo's classic residential façade leads to a modern interior with numerous references to Gaudí. There is an attractive lounge area and themed guestrooms. These are contemporary in style with curved lines and furnished with a personal touch. Traditional daily set menu and a limited choice of international à la carte options.

Sixtytwo
⅙ 🆎

Passeig de Gràcia 62 ✉ *08007* – 🖾 *Passeig de Gràcia* Plan: **K2**
– 𝒞 *932 72 41 80 – www.sixtytwohotel.com*
– *Closed 21-26 February*
45 rm – †109/599 € ††114/599 € – ⌚ 20 €
• Traditional • Modern • Design •

This small hotel, with its attractive façade and modern interior, is situated along the paseo de Gràcia. Well-equipped guestrooms, albeit a little on the small side.

Splendom Suites
🆎

Valencia 194 ✉ *08011* – 🖾 *Universitat* Plan: **K2**
– 𝒞 *934 52 10 30 – www.splendomsuites.com*
11 suites – ††69/250 €
• Family • Contemporary •

Occupying a listed building with a classic Modernist façade in the heart of the Eixample district. Its apartments are spread across six floors, the majority of which have well-equipped kitchens, sitting rooms with sofa beds and comfortable bedrooms.

XxxX   Lasarte
🏵 ⅙ 🆎 ⇔
❀❀

Mallorca 259 ✉ *08008* – 🖾 *Passeig de Gràcia* Plan: **K2**
– 𝒞 *934 45 32 42 – www.restaurantlasarte.com – Closed Holy Week,*
15 August-15 September, Sunday, Monday and Bank Holidays
Menu 145/180 € – Carte 99/114 €
• Creative • Design •

This impeccable contemporary-style restaurant is constantly changing and has the personal stamp of Martín Berasategui and his team. The original and imaginative cuisine bears the innovative hallmark of the chef, whose creativity is evident in the à la carte options and tasting menus alike.
➜ Gamba roja templada sobre un fondo marino, hinojo y mayonesa de su coral. Ventresca de atún a la brasa, cítrico de alcaparra, oliva negra y salsa ahumada. Sorbete de chocolate, crema montada de sésamo, yogur y yuzu.

XxxX   Caelis (Romain Fornell) - Hotel El Palace
⅙ 🆎 ⇔ 🚗
❀

Gran Vía de les Corts Catalanes 668 ✉ *08010* Plan: **L2**
– 🖾 *Urquinaona – 𝒞 935 10 12 05 – www.caelis.com – Closed Sunday,*
Monday and Tuesday lunch
Menu 39/130 € – Carte 85/105 €
• Creative • Elegant •

This restaurant is characterised by its 19C elegance and spacious surroundings. It has separate access to the hotel, one private room, a classic-cum-contemporary main dining room, as well as an attractive cocktail bar open in the evenings. Creative and meticulously presented cuisine of a high standard.
➜ Macarrones en dos servicios, mar y montaña, celery y foie-gras. Solomillo de buey Rossini, cojín de foie-gras y chalota confitada. Canetón "à la presse" en dos servicios.

SPAIN - BARCELONA

XxxX ✿✿ **Moments** – Hotel Mandarin Oriental Barcelona ⊛ ⴺ 🅰

passeig de Gràcia 38-40 ✉ *08007* Plan: **K2**
– Ⓜ *Passeig de Gràcia*
– ✆ *931 51 87 81 – www.mandarinoriental.com – Closed 10 August-10 September, Sunday and Monday*
Menu 65/143 € – Carte 95/119 €
• Creative • Design •
Access to this restaurant, which stands out for its originality and open-view kitchen, is via the hotel reception. The chef prepares skilful and creative cuisine that respects flavours, embraces textures and pays great attention to delicate presentation.
→ Caviar verde (winter-spring). Lomo de cordero lechal del Pirineo, velo crujiente de patata y zanahoria, y cremoso de queso. Nácar de coco, vainilla picante, mango y fruta de la pasión.

XxX ✿ **Angle** – Hotel Cram ⴺ 🅰 ⟺ 🕭

Aragó 214 ✉ *08011* – Ⓜ *Universitat* – ✆ *932 16 77 77* Plan: **K2**
– *www.restaurantangle.com – Closed Sunday and Monday*
Menu 80 € – Carte 58/86 €
• Modern cuisine • Minimalist •
A restaurant with a contemporary look and superb decor. Guests can savour cuisine of the highest level combining the cutting-edge and the traditional, and encompassing fine presentation and carefully selected ingredients.
→ Canelones de jarrete asado con setas, foie, trufa y bechamel con leche de cabra. Rodaballo con tsukandani de shitake thai, vegetales crocantes con limón y aceite de oliva. Chocolate, café, aceituna negra y toffee.

XxX **Casa Calvet** ⴺ 🅰 ⟺

Casp 48 ✉ *08010* – Ⓜ *Urquinaona* – ✆ *934 12 40 12* Plan: **L2**
– *www.casacalvet.es – Closed 7 days August, Sunday, Monday summer and Bank Holidays*
Menu 34/70 € – Carte 46/64 €
• Traditional cuisine • Classic •
This restaurant occupies a Modernist building designed by Gaudí. It once served as a textile factory and the offices have been converted into private dining rooms. A mix of classic Catalan dishes for à la carte dining alongside good set menus.

XxX **Racó d'en Cesc** ⊛ 🍴 ⴺ 🅰 ⟺

Diputació 201 ✉ *08011* – Ⓜ *Universitat* Plan: **K2**
– ✆ *934 51 60 02 – www.elracodencesc.com – Closed Holy Week, August, Sunday and Bank Holidays*
Menu 29/69 € – Carte 40/51 €
• Modern cuisine • Classic •
A restaurant with a small terrace, a bistro-style section and a classic dining room, with a different creative Catalan menu in each. A wide choice of craft beers is also available.

XxX ✿ **Gaig** (Carles Gaig) ⴺ 🅰 ⟺

Còrsega 200 ✉ *08036* – Ⓜ *Hospital Clinic* Plan: **J2**
– ✆ *934 29 10 17 – www.restaurantgaig.com – Closed Holy Week, 7 days August, Sunday dinner, Monday and Bank Holidays dinner*
Menu 65/115 € – Carte 50/90 €
• Modern cuisine • Elegant •
Arranged on two floors, this spacious restaurant exudes elegance and a thoroughly modern feel. The chef here offers a menu divided in two parts, one focusing on traditional dishes, the other on contemporary cuisine. Interesting set menus, select ingredients and superb presentation.
→ Canelones tradicionales con crema de trufa. Arroz de pichón y setas de Burdeos. Nuestra crema catalana.

XxX
✿
Roca Moo – Hotel Omm   🕭 & 🅰🄲 🛆

Rosselló 265 ✉ 08008 – Ⓜ *Diagonal –* ☎ *934 45 40 00*   Plan: **K1**
– www.hotelomm.es – Closed 10 days January, 21 days August, Sunday
and Monday
Menu 45/110 € – Carte 51/77 €
• Creative • Fashionable •

A cosmopolitan ambience pervades the café and bright dining room. Contemporary decor defined by skylights and designer details. Signature cuisine, a good combination of flavours and a very original wine list.
➜ Ravioli de cola de buey con gambas de Palamós. Rodaballo salvaje con crema de lentejas amarillas. La pera limonera.

XxX
Windsor   🕭 🍴 & 🅰🄲 ⇔ 🚗

Còrsega 286 ✉ 08008 – Ⓜ *Diagonal –* ☎ *932 37 75 88*   Plan: **K2**
– www.restaurantwindsor.com – Closed 1-10 January, Holy Week, 1-
27 August, Sunday and Bank Holidays
Menu 30/45 € – Carte 41/69 €
• Modern cuisine • Classic •

This elegant restaurant has a classic feel and features one main glass-fronted dining room, two private sections and a summer terrace. A menu of Catalan cuisine with a few international touches.

XxX
✿
Cinc Sentits (Jordi Artal)   🅰🄲

Aribau 58 ✉ 08011 – Ⓜ *Universitat –* ☎ *933 23 94 90*   Plan: **K2**
– www.cincsentits.com – Closed 15 days August, Sunday, Monday and
Bank Holidays
Menu 100/120 € – *(set menu only)*
• Creative • Minimalist •

An elegant setting matched by an original minimalist look, in the main dominated by dark tones. No à la carte options here, instead, diners can choose from three enticing menus. These feature dishes that change on a regular basis with a focus on invention and select Catalan ingredients.
➜ El huerto ecológico en texturas y temperaturas con yogur de hierbas. Pichón asado con croqueta y falso arroz de su hígado, pera al vino y fruta escabechada. Helado de leche a la parrilla con su crujiente, papel y salsa caliente.

XxX
Rías de Galicia   🕭 🅰🄲

Lleida 7 ✉ 08004 – Ⓜ *Espanya –* ☎ *934 24 81 52*   Plan: **J3**
– www.riasdegalicia.com
Menu 65 € – Carte 70/90 €
• Fish and seafood • Classic •

This restaurant is run by brothers and located close to the city's exhibition area. It boasts an attractive display cabinet at its entrance, a live fish tank, plus a meticulously arranged dining room decorated in a classic yet contemporary style. The extensive à la carte specialises in Galician fish and seafood, which is always of the very highest quality.

XxX
Petit Comitè   & 🅰🄲 ⇔

passatge de la Concepció 13 ✉ 08007 – Ⓜ *Provença*   Plan: **K2**
– ☎ *935 50 06 20 – www.petitcomite.cat*
Menu 52 € – Carte 35/66 €
• Regional • Design •

This contemporary restaurant is decorated with lots of dishes. The focus is on local cuisine prepared using Spanish ingredients, including enticing themed daily specials.

XX
El Asador de Aranda   & 🅰🄲 ⇔

Londres 94 ✉ 08036 – Ⓜ *Hospital Clínic*   Plan: **L2**
– ☎ *934 14 67 90 – www.asadordearanda.com – Closed Sunday dinner*
Menu 32/50 € – Carte 34/46 €
• Meats • Classic •

This spacious restaurant is decorated in Castilian style with a wood oven in full view of the dining room. Traditional cuisine with a particular focus on roast dishes.

XX   **Gorría**   AC ⇔
Diputació 421 ✉ 08013 – **Ⓜ** *Monumental*   Plan: **L1**
– 𝒞 932 45 11 64 – www.restaurantegorria.com – Closed Holy Week,
August, Sunday, Monday dinner and Bank Holidays dinner
Carte 40/65 €
• Basque • Rustic •
A well-established Basque restaurant with rustic style decor. The excellent menu
is complemented by an extensive wine list. Attentive service.

XX   **Pakta**   ⅙ AC
⁂   *Lleida 5 ✉ 08002 –* **Ⓜ** *Espanya – 𝒞 936 24 01 77*   Plan: **J3**
– www.pakta.es – Closed Christmas, Holy Week, 3 weeks August, Sunday
and Monday
Menu 95/130 € *– (dinner only except Saturday) (booking essential) (set*
menu only)
• Peruvian • Design •
A colourful, contemporary and informal restaurant that evokes Peruvian culture.
This is evident both in its name (that means 'together' or 'union' in the Quechua
language) and its decor with walls and ceilings adorned with striking fabrics.
However, the cuisine is very much Japanese, showcasing lots of technical pro-
wess and meticulous presentation. Bookings need to be made online.
→ El ceviche de corvina con leche de tigre de almendra tierna. Lomo alto
de vaca vieja con polvo parrillero. Picarones de boniato con miel de higos
secos.

XX   **Nectari** (Jordi Esteve)   AC ⇔
⁂   *València 28 ✉ 08015 –* **Ⓜ** *Tarragona – 𝒞 932 26 87 18*   Plan: **J3**
– www.nectari.es – Closed 15 days August and Sunday
Menu 35/70 € – Carte 43/67 €
• Modern cuisine • Classic •
A cosy setting for this completely family-run operation with two small contem-
porary-style dining rooms and one private area. The owner-chef has put toge-
ther a menu with a marked Mediterranean bias, enhanced by pleasing creative
and innovative touches.
→ Raviolis de gamba con duxelle de setas y salsa de crustáceos. Pichón de
Bresse con cuscús de verduritas y boniato. Coulant de chocolate con
helado de naranja.

XX   **Casa Darío**   ⅙ AC ⇔
Consell de Cent 256 ✉ 08011 – **Ⓜ** *Universitat*   Plan: **K2**
– 𝒞 934 53 31 35 – www.casadario.com – Closed 21 days August and
Sunday dinner
Menu 25 € – Carte 35/65 €
• Galician • Classic •
A well-established restaurant with a good reputation for the quality of its ingre-
dients. The restaurant has a private bar, three dining rooms and three private
rooms. Galician dishes and seafood are the house specialities.

XX   **Monvínic**   ⅛ ⅙ AC ⇔
Diputació 249 ✉ 08007 – **Ⓜ** *Catalunya*   Plan: **K2**
– 𝒞 932 72 61 87 – www.monvinic.com – Closed August, Saturday lunch,
Sunday and Monday lunch
Menu 20/60 € – Carte 50/65 €
• Modern cuisine • Wine bar •
A highly original, cutting-edge restaurant with the world of wine as its leitmotiv!
Designer inspired tapas bar, a single dining room with two large tables, and an
area reserved for tastings. Updated traditional cuisine and an impressive wine
cellar.

SPAIN - BARCELONA

713

XX **BistrEau** – Hotel Mandarin Oriental Barcelona   ♿ AC

passeig de Gràcia 38-40 ✉ *08007*   Plan: **K2**
– **M** *Passeig de Gràcia* – ☏ *931 51 87 83* – *www.restaurantbistreau.com*
Menu 35/60 € – Carte 40/65 €
• Traditional cuisine • Design •
This is the fiefdom of Ángel León, the so-called 'chef of the sea', in Barcelona. Savour dishes blending the traditional with the creative, and all bearing the stamp of this renowned chef. In the evening, enjoy a unique chef's table experience, limited to just a dozen guests, feasting on a menu faithful to the culinary traditions of his Aponiente restaurant in Andalucia.

XX **Loidi** – Hotel Condes de Barcelona   ♿ AC 🛏

Mallorca 248 ✉ *08008* – **M** *Passeig de Gràcia*   Plan: **K2**
– ☏ *934 92 92 92* – *www.loidi.com* – *Closed August, Sunday dinner and Bank Holidays dinner*
Menu 28/48 € – *(set menu only)*
• Modern cuisine • Friendly •
In this restaurant, the innovative cuisine on offer is light, fast and reasonably priced. Several menus are available, all created under the tutelage of famous chef Martín Berasategui.

XX **Manairó**   AC

Diputació 424 ✉ *08013* – **M** *Monumental*   Plan: **L1**
– ☏ *932 31 00 57* – *www.manairo.com* – *Closed 1-7 January, Sunday and Bank Holidays*
Menu 40/90 € – Carte 55/78 €
• Creative • Classic •
A unique restaurant, both in terms of its modern decor and intimate lighting. Contemporary, meticulously presented cuisine with its roots in Catalan cooking.

X **Hoja Santa**   AC
✿

av. Mistral 54 ✉ *08015* – **M** *Poble Sec* – ☏ *933 48 21 94*   Plan: **J3**
– *www.hojasanta.es* – *Closed 23 December-4 January, 20-28 March, 7-29 August, Sunday and Monday*
Menu 80/110 € – Carte 55/75 € – *(dinner only except Saturday)*
• Mexican • Individual •
Discover gourmet Mexican cuisine at this restaurant, which takes its name from a Mexican plant. The atmosphere is lively and modern, with ethnic and colonial details in the decor.
➜ Ceviche bajo un estanque helado. Chichilo negro con pluma ibérica "Joselito". Margarita con nube de coco.

X **Gresca**   AC

Provença 230 ✉ *08036* – **M** *Diagonal* – ☏ *934 51 61 93*   Plan: **K2**
– *www.gresca.net* – *Closed 7 days Christmas, Holy Week, 15 days August, Saturday lunch and Sunday*
Menu 19/70 € – Carte 31/55 €
• Modern cuisine • Family •
Much talked about in Barcelona thanks to its relaxed atmosphere and friendly service. Find attractive contemporary cuisine including enticing set menus.

X **Disfrutar**   🍽 ♿ AC
✿

Villarroel 163 ✉ *08036* – **M** *Hospital Clinic*   Plan: **J2**
– ☏ *933 48 68 96* – *www.disfrutarbarcelona.com* – *Closed 1-15 August, Sunday and Monday*
Menu 68/98 € – *(set menu only)*
• Creative • Design •
Creativity, high technical skill, fantasy and good taste are the hallmarks of the three chefs here. They conjure up a true gastronomic experience via several tasting menus in a simple, contemporary space with an open-view kitchen. The name of the restaurant, which translates as 'enjoy', says it all!
➜ Galleta de Idiazábal ahumado con manzana. Langostinos al ajillo unilateral. Pimientos de chocolate, aceite y sal.

SPAIN - BARCELONA

✗ **Espai Kru** 🖼 🕸 ⇔
Lleida 7 ✉ *08002 –* Ⓜ *Espanya –* ☎ *934 23 45 70* Plan: **J3**
– www.spaikru.com – Closed 15 days August, Sunday dinner and Monday
Carte 30/50 €
• International • Bistro •
Located on the first floor of a building, Espai Kru boasts an impressive appearance enhanced by its single space featuring an open-view kitchen, private dining room and cocktail bar. Extensive international and fusion menu, featuring both raw and cooked ingredients.

✗
🉐 **Etapes** 🛋 🖼 ⇔
Enrique Granados 10 ✉ *08007* Plan: **K2**
– ☎ *933 23 69 14 – www.restaurantetapes.com*
– Closed Christmas, Sunday dinner January-February, Saturday and Sunday lunch
Menu 16/60 € – Carte 33/40 €
• Modern cuisine • Individual •
An address that is well worth bearing in mind! This small restaurant has a modern yet informal look featuring an elongated dining room with a decor that combines wood, iron and glass. Enjoy contemporary cuisine with an emphasis on meticulous presentation and carefully selected ingredients.

✗ **Tanta** ♿ 🖼
Còrsega 235 ✉ *08036 –* Ⓜ *Hospital Clínic* Plan: **J2**
– ☎ *936 67 43 72 – www.tantabarcelona.com*
Menu 19/45 € – Carte 26/53 €
• International • Friendly •
Roomy, informal and above all offering a culinary concept that is fresh and contemporary. The focus is on modern and highly authentic Peruvian-Japanese cuisine. Charming patio featuring a vertical garden.

🍴 **Cervecería Catalana** 🛋 🖼
Mallorca 236 ✉ *08008 –* Ⓜ *Diagonal* Plan: **K2**
– ☎ *932 16 03 68*
Tapa 4.50 € **Ración** approx. 7.50 €
• Traditional cuisine • Tapas bar •
This popular local pub, decorated with racks full of bottles, serves a comprehensive choice of top quality tapas.

🍴 **Paco Meralgo** 🖼 ⇔
Muntaner 171 ✉ *08036 –* Ⓜ *Hospital Clínic* Plan: **J2**
– ☎ *934 30 90 27 – www.restaurantpacomeralgo.com*
Tapa 7 € **Ración** approx. 15 €
• Traditional cuisine • Mediterranean •
The Paco Meralgo has two bars and two separate entrances. Although its most impressive features are its seafood display cabinets with a varied, fresh and top quality choice of options. A private room is also available.

🍴 **Bodega 1900** 🛋 🖼
Tamarit 91 ✉ *08015 –* Ⓜ *Poble Sec* Plan: **K3**
– ☎ *933 25 26 59 – www.bodega1900.com*
– Closed Christmas, Holy Week, 3 weeks August, Sunday and Monday
Ración approx. 7 €
• Traditional cuisine • Neighbourhood •
This restaurant has all the charm of an old-fashioned grocery store. The small menu features grilled dishes, Iberian specialities and homemade preserves, all of excellent quality.

715

Tickets
⟡ AC

av. del Paral.lel 164 ✉ *08015* – Ⓜ *Espanya*   Plan: **K3**
– *www.ticketsbar.es* – *Closed Christmas, Holy Week, 21 days August,*
Sunday and Monday
Tapa 6 € **Ración** approx. 15 € – *(dinner only except Saturday) (booking*
essential)
• Creative • Friendly •
A unique restaurant with lots of colour and several bar counters. The innovative
cuisine on offer here, prepared in front of diners, plays homage to the legendary
dishes that were once created at El Bulli. Bookings can only be made via its web-
site.
→ Las oliva-S del Tickets. Vaca vieja de Burgos al Josper. Bola de coco nitro
con fruta de la pasión y especies.

Mont Bar
🐾 ⟡ ♿ AC ⇔

Diputació 220 ✉ *08011* – Ⓜ *Universitat*   Plan: **K2**
– ☎ *933 23 95 90* – *www.montbar.com* – *Closed 24-26 December and 10-*
25 January
Tapa 7 € **Ración** approx. 17 €
• Traditional cuisine • Bistro •
This charming and unusual gastro-bar serves traditional cuisine prepared using
top quality ingredients. Friendly and professional service.

Segons Mercat
AC

Gran Via de les Corts Catalanes 552 ✉ *08011*   Plan: **K2**
– Ⓜ *Urgell* – ☎ *934 51 16 98* – *www.segonsmercat.com*
Tapa 6 € **Ración** approx. 12 €
• Traditional cuisine • Mediterranean •
A modern and spacious restaurant with an informal atmosphere. There is a bar
and an elongated dining room decorated with photos and striking wall panels.
Traditional cuisine.

Cañota
⟡ AC

Lleida 7 ✉ *08002* – Ⓜ *Plaza España* – ☎ *933 25 91 71*   Plan: **J3**
– *www.casadetapas.com* – *Closed Sunday dinner and Monday*
Tapa 4 € **Ración** approx. 10 €
• Traditional cuisine • Friendly •
A pleasant and relaxed tapas restaurant that has received the backing of several
famous chefs. Two dining rooms, classically furnished in regional style, and a
terrace, provide the setting for traditional tapas and raciones. Almost everything
on the menu has been designed for sharing!

Tapas 24
⟡ AC

Diputació 269 ✉ *08007* – Ⓜ *Passeig de Gràcia*   Plan: **K2**
– ☎ *934 88 09 77* – *www.carlesabellan.com*
Tapa 5 € **Ración** approx. 14 €
• Traditional cuisine • Tapas bar •
This bar is located in a half-basement. It creates a contemporary atmosphere
with two bars and walls decorated with mosaics. Choose from its delicious
menu of tapas and side dishes.

Lolita
AC

Tamarit 104 ✉ *08015* – Ⓜ *Poble Sec* – ☎ *93 424 52 31*   Plan: **K3**
– *www.lolitataperia.com* – *Closed December, Sunday and Monday*
Tapa 6 € – *(dinner only except Friday and Saturday)*
• Traditional cuisine • Tapas bar •
Situated close to the city's exhibition site, this restaurant stands out for its per-
sonalised decor. Traditional tapas created using top quality ingredients.

🍸/ **Atapa-it**
Muntaner 146 ✉ *08036* – Ⓜ *Hospital Clínic*   Plan: **J2**
– 𝒞 934 52 07 82 – www.atapait.com – Closed 15 days August and Sunday
Tapa 2 € **Ración** approx. 10 €
• Regional • Bistro •
Contemporary-style restaurant with a small bar and two dining rooms, both with an informal feel. It serves modern tapas and small dishes that change depending on market availability.

🍸/ **Niño Viejo**
av. Mistral 54 ✉ *08015* – Ⓜ *Poble Sec* – 𝒞 *933 48 21 94*   Plan: **J3**
– www.ninoviejo.es – Closed 23 December-4 January, 20-28 March, 7-29 August, Sunday and Monday
Tapa 4.80 € **Ración** approx. 12 €
• Mexican • Exotic •
Unusual, lively, colourful and informal – this taco bar with an ethnic feel serves delicious homemade tacos, antojitos and spicy salsas. High quality Mexican cuisine.

SANT MARTÍ   PLAN I

 Arts   ⚐ ⚑ ⮜ 🛗 ⊕ 🛆 ♿ 🄰🄺 🕍 🚗
Marina 19 ✉ *08005* – Ⓜ *Ciutadella-Vila Olímpica*   Plan: **C2**
– 𝒞 932 21 10 00 – www.hotelartsbarcelona.com
397 rm – ♟295/485 € – 🍽 39 € – 114 suites
• Luxury • Contemporary •
Superb in every respect. Occupying one of two glass-fronted towers at the Olympic port, the hotel's many selling points include its magnificent views and a stunning, spacious interior including intimate public areas and top-notch guestrooms high on detail. Extensive lounges adorned with works of art and exquisite dining options complete the picture.
❀❀ **Enoteca • Arola** – See restaurant listing

 Hilton Diagonal Mar Barcelona   ⚐ ⮜ 🛗 🛆 ♿ 🄰🄺 🕍 🚗
passeig del Taulat 262-264 ✉ *08019*   Plan: **D2**
– Ⓜ El Maresme Fòrum – 𝒞 935 07 07 07
– www.hiltondiagonalmarbarcelonahotel.es
413 rm – ♟129/749 € – 🍽 25 € – 20 suites
• Conference hotel • Contemporary •
Located near the Fórum, the Hilton is a popular conference venue. The guestrooms have a clean, contemporary design, with high-quality modern furnishings ensuring a comfortable stay. The functional restaurant doubles as the breakfast buffet room and a dining room offering an international à la carte menu.

Pullman Barcelona Skipper   🛗 🛆 ♿ 🄰🄺 🕍 🚗
av. del Litoral 10 ✉ *08005*   Plan: **C2**
– Ⓜ Ciutadella-Vila Olímpica – 𝒞 932 21 65 65
– www.pullman-barcelona-skipper.com
241 rm 🍽 – ♟130/350 € ♟♟155/375 € – 6 suites
• Business • Modern •
This hotel combines designer detail and technology with a warm and welcoming setting. A varied lounge area, guestrooms offering modern creature comforts, a spa, plus an attractive rooftop terrace with a swimming pool. A bright, contemporary-style restaurant with views of the terrace. International cuisine.

SPAIN - BARCELONA

Meliá Barcelona Sky

Pere IV-272 ✉ *08005* – Ⓜ *Poblenou* – ℰ *933 67 20 50*   Plan: **D2**
– *www.meliahotels.com*
249 rm – †90/425 € †‡112/447 € – ⌚ 22 € – 9 suites
• Business • Design •
The Meliá's main selling points are its modern, designer inspired lobby, lounge bar, and contemporary bedrooms, most enjoying splendid views. The good dining options on offer are complemented by the uniquely decorated restaurant in the lobby with a menu focusing on light and traditional cuisine.
✿ **Dos Cielos** – See restaurant listing

Enoteca – Hotel Arts

Marina 19 ✉ *08005* – Ⓜ *Ciutadella-Vila Olímpica*   Plan: **C2**
– ℰ *934 83 81 08* – *www.hotelartsbarcelona.com* – *Closed 3-10 February and Sunday*
Menu 170 €
– Carte 103/121 € – *(dinner only except Monday and Tuesday)*
• Modern cuisine • Mediterranean •
The Enoteca boasts a very bright dining room, pure Mediterranean in style and with wine racks providing part of the attractive decor. The perfectly crafted contemporary cuisine has its roots in traditional dishes. It is prepared with top quality ingredients and superb attention to detail.
→ Kokotxas a la brasa, tuétano y caviar. Mero con matices del Alt Empordà, huerta, mar y montaña. Selva Negra.

Dos Cielos (Sergio y Javier Torres) – Hotel Meliá Barcelona Sky

Pere IV-272 ✉ *08005* – Ⓜ *Poblenou*   Plan: **D2**
– ℰ *933 67 20 70* – *www.doscielos.com*
– *Closed January-10 February,* Sunday and Monday
Menu 85/110 € – Carte approx. 82 € – *(dinner only except July-15 September)*
• Modern cuisine • Design •
Occupying the 24th floor of the Meliá Barcelona Sky hotel, the restaurant's surprising design includes a kitchen incorporated into the dining room, a steel bar where guests can also eat, as well as a terrace. Innovative cuisine that is constantly striving for new flavours. Superb views of a less-photographed side of Barcelona!
→ Berenjenas blancas, cilantro, comino y verdolagas. Carabinero de Huelva, algas, pepino y estragón. Nuestra versión del gin tonic.

Els Pescadors

pl. Prim 1 ✉ *08005* – Ⓜ *Poblenou* – ℰ *932 25 20 18*   Plan: **D2**
– *www.elspescadors.com* – *Closed 22 December-4 January*
Carte 50/70 €
• Fish and seafood • Fashionable •
This restaurant has three dining rooms, one in early-20C café style and two with a more modern decor. A generous menu based on fish and seafood with rice dishes and cod to the fore.

Arola – Hotel Arts

Marina 19 ✉ *08005* – Ⓜ *Ciutadella-Vila Olímpica*   Plan: **C2**
– ℰ *934 83 80 90* – *www.hotelartsbarcelona.com* – *Closed 2 January-2 February, Monday and Tuesday*
Menu 62/89 € – Carte 65/98 €
• Creative • Friendly •
Modern, urban and informal, including live music sessions with a DJ. Savour a creative tapas- and ración-based menu either in the dining room or on the chill-out terrace.

Casa Fuster

passeig de Gràcia 132 ✉ 08008 Plan: **K1**
– Ⓜ Diagonal – ✆ 932 55 30 00
– www.hotelescenter.es
85 rm – ††176/600 € – ☕ 28 € – 20 suites
• Luxury • Design • Cosy •
Occupying a majestic Modernist building, Casa Fuster boasts top-notch guestrooms, an attractive café-lounge, and a panoramic bar on the rooftop terrace. Its elegant restaurant conjures up traditional and international dishes with a creative touch.

G.H. La Florida

carret. Vallvidrera al Tibidabo 83-93 ✉ 08035 Plan I: **B2**
– ✆ 932 59 30 00
– www.hotellaflorida.com
62 rm – †180/600 € ††200/600 € – ☕ 28 € – 8 suites
• Luxury • Chain hotel • Design •
Find charm and avant-garde design on the top of Tibidabo hill, with an interior created by famous designers and delightful terraces built on different levels. Its biggest attraction is without doubt the spectacular view of the city from both the hotel and restaurant.

ABaC

av. del Tibidabo 1 ✉ 08022 – Ⓜ Av. Tibidabo Plan I: **B2**
– ✆ 933 19 66 00
– www.abacbarcelona.com
15 rm – †225/625 € ††275/800 € – ☕ 31 €
• Luxury • Modern •
Enjoy a stay in superb, highly contemporary guestrooms featuring the latest smart technology and even chromotherapy in the bathrooms. Some spa services are also available.
✿✿ **ABaC** – See restaurant listing

Primero Primera

Doctor Carulla 25-29 ✉ 08017 – Ⓜ Tres Torres Plan: **I1**
– ✆ 934 17 56 00
– www.primeroprimera.com
25 rm ☕ – †155/320 € ††165/330 € – 5 suites
• Traditional • Elegant •
This hotel with considerable charm is accessed via a passageway reminiscent of an old carriage entrance. Guestrooms have a contemporary look, with those under the eaves the pick of the bunch.

Via Veneto

✿

Ganduxer 10 ✉ 08021 – Ⓜ Hospital Clínic Plan: **I2**
– ✆ 932 00 72 44 – www.viavenetorestaurant.com
– Closed August, Saturday lunch and Sunday
Menu 85/125 € – Carte 75/105 €
• Classic cuisine • Retro •
A famous property in attractive Belle Epoque-style with a dining room laid out on several levels and a number of private dining areas. Impressively updated classic menu with game in season and interesting tasting menus. Its wine cellar, featuring around 1 400 labels, is one of the best in Spain.
➜ Gamba roja en tartar y templada, con lima y zanahoria. Salmonetes de roca con "samfaina" y panceta adobada. Sorbete de frutos rojos del Maresme, crema fina Bellini y ensalada de fruta de temporada.

SPAIN - BARCELONA

XXX **ABaC** – Hotel ABaC

⚓ 🏢 AK ⇔ 🚐

av. del Tibidabo 1 ✉ *08022* – Ⓜ *Av. Tibidabo*   Plan I: **B2**
– ℰ 933 19 66 00 – www.abacbarcelona.com
Menu 135/165 € – Carte 105/135 €
• Creative • Design •
A superb culinary experience awaits in the upper reaches of the city. There is a
terrace, designer inspired bar, and a bright, contemporary-style dining room.
ABaC's innovative, technically faultless cuisine is fascinating in its creativity and
pairing of products.
→ Ceviche de lulo con ostras y pisco sour. Ternera con salazones y chalo-
tas de mar. Blanco del cacao con sabores asiáticos y tropicales.

XXX **Hofmann** (Mey Hofmann)

♿ AK ⇔

La Granada del Penedès 14-16 ✉ *08006* – Ⓜ *Diagonal*   Plan: **J1**
*– ℰ 932 18 71 65 – www.hofmann-bcn.com – Closed Christmas, Holy
Week, August, Sunday and Bank Holidays*
Menu 45/70 € – Carte 44/63 €
• Modern cuisine • Classic •
The Hofmann reflects a contemporary gastronomic philosophy with its semi-
private small rooms and an attractive main dining room with views of the kit-
chen via a large window. Creative cuisine that attracts a sizeable business clien-
tele.
→ Canelón de ternera con foie, crema de queso y teja de parmesano.
Bacalao al carbón, su ajoarriero y pil pil. La bola sorpresa.

XXX **Freixa Tradició**

AK

Sant Elíes 22 ✉ *08006* – Ⓜ *Plaça Molina*   Plan: **J1**
*– ℰ 932 09 75 59 – www.freixatradicio.com – Closed Holy Week, 21 days
August, Sunday dinner and Monday*
Menu 25/38 € – Carte approx. 35 €
• Regional • Design •
Run by the couple that owns the restaurant, the Freixa Tradició has, over the
years, established itself as one of the city's culinary institutions. In its minimalist
interior enjoy the high quality and well-prepared traditional Catalan cuisine.

XXX **Roig Robí**

🏢 AK ⇔

Sèneca 20 ✉ *08006* – Ⓜ *Diagonal* – ℰ *932 18 92 22*   Plan: **K1**
*– www.roigrobi.com – Closed 7 days January, 21 days August, Saturday
lunch and Sunday*
Menu 33/59 € – Carte 40/76 €
• Regional • Classic •
A pleasant restaurant in a classic setting that includes a winter garden-style
dining room laid out around a patio-garden. Traditional Catalan à la carte
dining, set menus and an extensive wine list.

XXX **Tram-Tram**

🏢 AK ⇔

Major de Sarrià 121 ✉ *08017* – Ⓜ *Reina Elisenda*   Plan I: **A2**
*– ℰ 932 04 85 18 – www.tram-tram.com – Closed Holy Week, 15 days
August, Sunday dinner, Monday and Bank Holidays*
Menu 28 € – Carte 40/61 €
• Modern cuisine • Family •
This restaurant occupies a house with a classic appearance and offers a choice
of dining rooms, private sections and a patio-terrace. The updated traditional
and international à la carte options are enhanced by various set menus.

XXX **Botafumeiro**

AK ⇔

Gran de Gràcia 81 ✉ *08012* – Ⓜ *Fontana*   Plan: **J1**
– ℰ 932 18 42 30 – www.botafumeiro.es
Carte 60/95 €
• Fish and seafood • Classic •
Adorned with live fish tanks, the entrance to this restaurant leads to an attrac-
tive bar and several classically furnished dining rooms. It serves fish and seafood
of the highest quality, with whole fish dishes a particular speciality.

XX **El Asador de Aranda**　　　🛖 ㅊ 🆎 ⇔ 🅿️

av. del Tibidabo 31 ✉ *08022 – ☎ 934 17 01 15*　　Plan I: **B1-2**
– www.asadordearanda.com – Closed Sunday dinner
Menu 32/50 € – Carte 34/46 €
• Meats • Retro •
This restaurant occupies the incomparable Casa Roviralta, a Modernist building
also known as El Frare Blanc. The culinary focus here is on typical Castilian cuisine, with a house speciality of roast lamb cooked in a clay oven.

XX **Alkimia** (Jordi Vilá)　　　　　　　ㅊ 🆎

🍃 *Indústria 79 (transfer to ronda de Sant Antoni 41-1st*　Plan: **K1**
floor) ✉ *08025 – ⓜ Sagrada Familia – ☎ 932 07 61 15 – www.alkimia.cat*
– Closed Christmas, Holy Week, Sunday and Monday
Menu 39/130 € – Carte 48/88 €
• Creative • Minimalist •
This restaurant is located in a relatively quiet part of the Eixample district and
boasts a minimalist dining room. The concise à la carte and various tasting
menus feature a mix of innovative and more traditional dishes, from which
diners can pick and choose individual dishes.
→ Tartar de pescado con caviar. Pichón curado con ciruelas. Mango con
sorbete de leche de cabra.

XX **Hisop** (Oriol Ivern)　　　　　　　🆎

🍃 *passatge de Marimon 9* ✉ *08021 – ⓜ Hospital Clínic*　Plan: **J2**
– ☎ 932 41 32 33 – www.hisop.com – Closed 1-8 January, Saturday lunch,
Sunday and Bank Holidays
Menu 31/62 € – Carte 55/75 €
• Creative • Minimalist •
Because of its size, this modern restaurant offers guests an intimate dining
experience. Enjoy fresh and creative dishes based around traditional recipes in
the minimalist dining room. Everything is prepared with locally sourced and
seasonal products brought together to produce some interesting combinations.
→ Colmenillas con curry y berberechos. Corzo con romesco de remolacha
y calçots. Fresones con aceitunas negras y pimienta.

XX **Silvestre**　　　　　　　　　　🆎 ⇔

🍃 *Santaló 101* ✉ *08021 – ⓜ Muntaner – ☎ 932 41 40 31*　Plan: **J1**
– www.restaurante-silvestre.com – Closed Holy Week, 21 days August,
Saturday dinner July-August, Saturday lunch, Sunday and Bank Holidays
Menu 22 € – Carte approx. 35 €
• Traditional cuisine • Classic •
This restaurant is cosy and welcoming with various private dining areas that add
an intimate feel. Traditional and international cuisine, including appealing fixed
menus and the option of half-raciones for every dish. Try the pig's trotters filled
with cep mushrooms, or the Catalan sausage (butifarra) with port wine... delicious!

XX **Mil921**　　　　　　　　　　　🛖 🆎

Casanova 211 ✉ *08021 – ⓜ Hospital Clinic*　Plan: **J2**
– ☎ 934 14 34 94 – www.mil921.com – Closed Sunday and Monday dinner
Menu 21/45 € – Carte 37/55 €
• Modern cuisine • Fashionable •
Updated, traditional cuisine based around seasonal, locally sourced ingredients
is served in the two contemporary dining rooms. The menu also includes some
dishes with a resolutely Japanese flavour.

X **Vivanda**　　　　　　　　　　　🛖 ㅊ 🆎 ⇔

🍃 *Major de Sarrià 134* ✉ *08017 – ⓜ Reina Elisenda*　Plan I: **A2**
– ☎ 932 03 19 18 – www.vivanda.cat – Closed Sunday dinner and Monday
Carte 22/35 €
• Traditional cuisine • Cosy •
Somewhat unusual, in that its menu includes lots of smaller dishes served in
half-ración portions. There is an attractive tree-shaded terrace and a modern
interior with a combination of regular restaurant-style tables and taller tables
for tapas, all designed in the same style.

La Taula

🍴
😊

Sant Màrius 8-12 ✉ *08022 –* Ⓜ *El Putxet* — Plan: I1
*– 𝄐 934 17 28 48 – www.lataula.com – Closed Holy Week, August,
Saturday lunch, Sunday and Bank Holidays*
Menu 15/33 € – Carte 25/40 € – *(lunch only except Thursday and Friday)*
• **International** • **Classic** •
A small and cosy restaurant with a unique, classic-contemporary ambience. À la
carte options focus on international cuisine alongside typical home favourites
and a couple of very reasonably priced set menus. The crispy Gruyère cheese
Malakoff is particularly memorable!

AT SANTA COLOMA de GRAMENET

Ca n'Armengol

🔡 ⇧ 🥘
😊

Prat de La Riba 1 ✉ *08921 Santa Coloma de Gramenet
–* Ⓜ *Santa Coloma – 𝄐 933 91 68 55 – www.canarmengol.net – Closed
Holy Week, 2 weeks August, Sunday dinner, Monday and Tuesday dinner*
Menu 11/33 € – Carte 29/46 €
• **Traditional cuisine** • **Classic** •
A family-run restaurant with a classic ambience. There are two entrances: one
directly through to the old bar, where customers can dine from the set menu,
and the other to the dining rooms and private section reserved for à la carte
dining. Traditionally based cuisine with the option of half-raciones (portions).

Lluerna (Víctor Quintillà)

🔡 ⇧
🏵

Rafael Casanovas 31 ✉ *08921 Santa Coloma de Gramenet
–* Ⓜ *Santa Coloma – 𝄐 933 91 08 20 – www.lluernarestaurant.com
– Closed Holy Week, 8-29 August, Sunday and Monday*
Menu 37/72 € – Carte 40/68 €
• **Modern cuisine** • **Trendy** •
A centrally located restaurant well run by the couple that owns it. In the small,
minimalist-style dining room, enjoy updated traditional dishes that can be best
explored via the tasting menus on offer. The perfectly cooked dishes have a
strong emphasis on attention to detail and meticulous presentation.
→ Arroz de gambas de playa. Pichón de la familia Tatjé con anchoas y
aceitunas negras. Coulant de avellana y fruta de la pasión.

AT L'HOSPITALET de LLOBREGAT   PLAN I

Hesperia Tower

🎾 ⟨ 🛗 📺 ⚒ 🔡 ⚖ 🥘

Gran Via 144 ✉ *08907 L'Hospitalet de Llobregat
–* Ⓜ *Hospital de Bellvitge – 𝄐 934 13 50 00 – www.hesperia-tower.com* — Plan: A3
280 rm – ♦♦89/499 € – ⚏ 25 € – 42 suites
• **Chain hotel** • **Modern** •
This hotel occupying a tower block designed by the famous architect Richard
Rogers boasts spacious public areas, a convention centre and contemporary
guestrooms. The emphasis in this first-floor restaurant is on traditional cuisine
prepared using seasonal products.

VALENCIA
VALÈNCIA

Population: 800 469

Gregory Gerault/hemis.fr

Spain's third largest city offers undeniable character and charm, with unspoilt beaches, numerous museums, amazing nightlife and rip roaring fiestas. The city sits in an enviable position on the Mediterranean coast, with its port and its long golden beach to the east. A mile or so inland is the heart of the city, its beautiful old town; a labyrinth of ancient cobbled streets which pay testament to its rich history, with medieval churches, Renaissance halls of trade and baroque mansions layered on top of an earlier Roman city.

Valencia is the home of paella, and a thriving café scene gives you ample opportunity to tuck into it. The sun shines most of the time here, but if you want shelter there are plenty of museums on hand to offer a cool escape. Culturally, the city has been propelled into the major league in the last few decades. What's taken it there is the exciting City of Arts and Sciences complex, a 21C addition to the city's skyline built within the confines of the Turia River Park; the fabulous nine-mile green space created when the river was diverted after flooding in 1957. This futuristic 'city' draws over four million visitors each year, is made up of four stunning buildings and is home to a science museum, an opera house, an aquarium and an Imax cinema with a planetarium and laserium.

VALENCIA IN...

→ **ONE DAY**
Plaza de la Virgen, La Lonja, Central Market, a trip to the beach.

→ **TWO DAYS**
IVAM (Valencian Institute of Modern Art), City of Arts and Sciences, Carmen district nightlife.

→ **THREE DAYS**
A stroll along the Turia River Park.

PRACTICAL INFORMATION

ARRIVAL-DEPARTURE

✈ Valencia Airport is 8km west of the city. Metro trains (lines 3 and 5) take about 25min. The Airport bus Number 150, which runs every 26min, takes around 45min.

GETTING AROUND

Valencia has an integrated transport system with metro, buses and trams. Single tickets for the metro, which has six lines, are cheap and can be purchased from station machines or ticket offices. You can buy a one day pass for the metro, trams and buses or, alternatively, a more cost-effective 10-trip pass. Another useful investment is the Valencia Tourist Card, available from tourist offices, hotels, tobacconists and kiosks. It offers free travel on all forms of public transport, as well as discounts in museums, shops, restaurants and on various leisure activities; the cards last for one, two, or three days.

CALENDAR HIGHLIGHTS

January
Epiphany, St Vincent's Day.

March
Las Fallas (the arrival of spring).

April
Semana Santa Marinera (Holy Week).

May
The Crosses of May, Feast of Our Lady of the Forsaken.

June
Corpus Christi.

July
Feria de Julio (July Fair).

August
La Tomatina (battle of the tomatoes) in the village on Buñol.

EATING OUT

Valencia is the city of paella. It was invented here, and this is the place to try it in infinite varieties. For a gargantuan helping, head off to the Las Arenas beach promenade, which is lined with a whole legion of seafood restaurants. On a hot day, the traditional liquid accompaniment is agua de Valencia, a potentially lethal combination of orange juice, Cava and vodka. Most restaurants remain very Spanish in character, and if you're not eating paella, then you'll probably be enjoying tapas, with an emphasis on the excellent local cured hams and cheeses. A little different is the

local delicacy of all i pebre, a mouth-watering meal of stewed eels from the local wetlands, served in a garlic and red pepper sauce. The drink to cool down with is horchata: it's tigernut milk – a mixture of nuts, cinnamon, sugar and water – and is best enjoyed with a doughy cake. Meal times can throw the unwary visitor: lunch is often not served until two in the afternoon, and dinner, in general, is never eaten before nine at night.

VALENCIA-MANISES

A
GODELLA
Burjassot-Godella
BORBÒTO
B
Palmaret

Llíria
TVV
V. Andrés E.
Càmpus
U
St. Joan
La Granja
BURJASSOT
Burjassot

Ctra del Pla del Pou
Fira
Benimàmet
Les Carolines
Cantereria
Empalme
Juan
XXIII
Av. de Juan XXIII
Montcada
de

CV 31
PATERNA
Campament

CV 31
CV 31
Palau de Congressos
PALACIO DE CONGRESOS
Av.
Av. Florista
de
Palau de
🏠 Sorolla Palace

Camp
Av. del Túria
de
las
Cortes
Garbí
de
Benicalap
Tránsits
Av. Dr. Peset Aleixandre
Marxalenes
Reus
Sag
Sagunto

Beniferri
Safor
Valencianas
Aviiès
Reus

Av.
Maestro
Gil
● Kaymus

Av.
Valencianas
Burjassot
Campanar

Nuevo
Cauce
Ronda
San Antonio
MISLATA
Mislata-Almassil
Mislata
de
CAMPANAR
Rodrigo
9
Pechina
Av. M. de Falla
Paseo
Valencia Centre (Plan II)
Gran Via de Fernando el Católico
CATEDRA

Ronda
Cauce
338
XIRIVELLA
Nou d'Octubre
Av. del Cid
Av. del Cíd
Forques
Av.
Tres
Av. Tres
Av. de Pérez Galdós
Gran Via de Ramón y Cajal
Av.
Giorgeta
ESTACIÓN DEL NORTE
Jesús

Río
Turia
Marginal
de
Picaña
Cruces
Archiduque
Carlos
Hospital
Patraix
Av. de G. Aguilar
San
Vicente
Martir
Av. de F

Nuevo
Marginal
Sant Isidre
San

Camino
València-Sud
V 30
V 30
Av.
Av. del Pianista M. Carrasco

CV 36
Barranc
Ronda
Ronda

3
PICANYA
Picanya
Paiporta
Xiva
BENETÚSSER
Av. del País Valenciano
V 31

PAIPORTA
Sur
V 400
Av. del
Av. Real de Madrid
SEDAVÍ

A
B

●	Hotel
●	Restaurant

**Environs of
Valencia**

(Plan I)

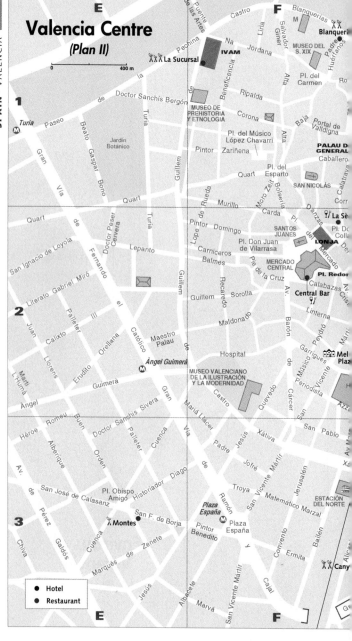

Valencia Centre
(Plan II)

0   400 m

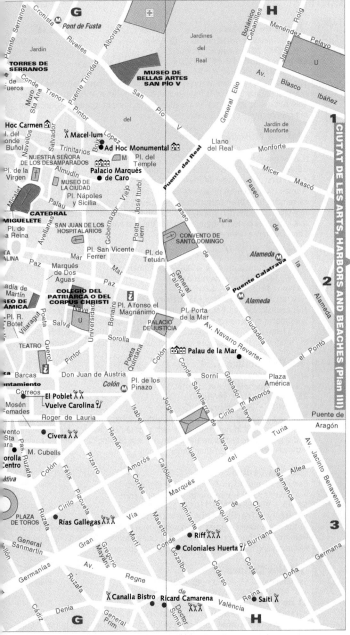

G

Cronista
Puente Serranos
Rivelles
Jardin
Pont de Fusta

TORRES DE SERRANOS

Conde
Muro Sta Ana
de Fueros
Trenor
Puente Trinidad
Pintor

San Pío V

MUSEO DE BELLAS ARTES SAN PÍO V

Hoc Carmen
I. del Conde Buñol
Salvador
Navellos
Macel·lum
Lopez
Trinitarios
Ad Hoc Monumental

NUESTRA SEÑORA DE LOS DESAMPARADOS
Pl. del Temple

Almudín
José Iturbi
Gobernador Viejo
Palacio Marqués de Caro

Pl. de la Virgen
Micalet
Palau
MUSEO DE LA CIUDAD

Pl. Nápoles y Sicilia

CATEDRAL
MIGUELETE
Pl. de la Reina

Avellanas
SAN JUAN DE LOS HOSPITALARIOS

Paz

Pl. San Vicente
Mar Ferrer

Pl. de Tetuán

CONVENTO DE SANTO DOMINGO

Marqués de Dos Aguas

Mar

Paz

COLEGIO DEL PATRIARCA O DEL CORPUS CHRISTI

Nave
Bonaire
Universidad
Pl. Alfonso el Magnánimo

Pl. Porta de la Mar

PALACIO DE JUSTICIA

Salva
Vilaragut
Poeta

Sorolla

Colón

Av. Navarro Reverter

Ciudadela

Palau de la Mar

TEATRO
Querol
Pintor
Poeta Quintana

Barcas

Don Juan de Austria
Colón

Pl. de los Pinazo

Sorní
Grabador Esteve
Conde
Salvatierra

Plaza América

Ayuntamiento
Correos

El Poblet
Vuelve Carolina

Mosén Femades
Roger de Lauria

Isabel la Católica
Jorge

Cirilo
Amorós

Puente de Aragón

Convento Sta Clara
Civera

M. Cubells

Colón
Félix Pizcueta
Pizarro
Hernán Cortés
Amorós

Juan de Mena

Sorolla Centro
Xàtiva

PLAZA DE TOROS

Ruzafa
Cirilo
Via
Maestro
Marqués
Almirante
Joaquín
Ciscar

Rías Gallegas

Riff

Coloniales Huerta

Conde
Gozalbo
Cadarso
Costa

General Sanmartín
Gregorio Mayáns
Marti
Gran Via

Germanías

Ruzafa

Av. Regne

Canalla Bistro
Ricard Camarena
Doctor Sumsi
Reina

Valencia

Saiti

Cádiz
Denia
General Prim

G

H

Botánico Cabanilles
Menéndez
Roig
Pelayo

Av. Blasco Ibáñez

Jaume

Jardín de Monforte

Llano del Real
Monforte
Micer Mascó

1

Turia

Paseo
Alameda

Puente Calatrava
Alameda

2

Av. Jacinto Benavente

Turia
Altea
Salamanca

3

Germana
Doña

de

H

Palau de la Mar

Navarro Reverter 14 ✉ 46004 – Ⓜ Colón Plan: **H2**
– ✆ 963 16 28 84 – www.hospes.com
66 rm – 🚹125/535 € 👥135/550 € – ☕ 22 € – 1 suite
• Business • Palace • Modern •
The 'Sea Palace' partially occupies two 19C mansions. These house the hotel's public areas and most of its fully equipped, minimalist-style rooms. Spa centre. This restaurant specialises in creative Mediterranean cuisine, including an impressive choice of rice dishes.

Palacio Marqués de Caro

Almirante 14 ✉ 46003 – ✆ 963 05 90 00 Plan: **G1**
– www.carohotel.com
25 rm – 👥145/600 € – ☕ 20 € – 1 suite
• Luxury • Palace • Minimalist •
A small 19C palace full of fascinating historical interest. Important archaeological remains have been preserved in almost every guestroom, where contemporary urban style sits in harmony with Roman and Moorish artefacts. The restaurant combines perfectly these vestiges of the past with a more modern setting. Contemporary à la carte menu.

Meliá Plaza

pl. del Ayuntamiento 4 ✉ 46002 – Ⓜ Xàtiva Plan: **F2**
– ✆ 963 52 06 12 – www.melia.com
98 rm – 👥85/300 € – ☕ 18 €
• Business • Classic • Functional •
This centrally located hotel has limited lounge space but its classically styled guestrooms make up for this and offer excellent facilities for the price. There is also a fully equipped fitness centre on the top floor boasting views of the city. In the modern restaurant choose from a set menu or traditional à la carte.

Ad Hoc Monumental

Boix 4 ✉ 46003 – Ⓜ Alameda – ✆ 963 91 91 40 Plan: **G1**
– www.adhochoteles.com
28 rm – 🚹60/110 € 👥68/140 € – ☕ 12 €
• Family • Traditional • Cosy •
This hotel occupies an attractive 19C building. It has a small lounge area and rooms decorated in neo-rustic style with exposed brickwork, wooden beams and clay tiles. The restaurant has a pleasant and relaxing atmosphere, making it the perfect place for an after dinner cocktail.

Sorolla Centro

Convento Santa Clara 5 ✉ 46002 – Ⓜ Xàtiva Plan: **G3**
– ✆ 963 52 33 92 – www.hotelsorollacentro.com
58 rm – 🚹66/88 € 👥77/110 € – ☕ 10 €
• Family • Traditional • Functional •
As the name would suggest, this hotel enjoys a central location a stone's throw from the best shopping areas in the city. Guest facilities include a bright breakfast room and functional, yet well-appointed bedrooms.

Ad Hoc Carmen

Samaniego 20 ✉ 46003 – Ⓜ Alameda Plan: **G1**
– ✆ 960 45 45 45 – www.adhochoteles.com
21 rm – 🚹45/75 € 👥49/99 €
• Traditional • Family • Functional •
The origins of this small hotel close to the cathedral date back to the 15C. It offers a variety of guestrooms that are comfortable on the whole, and those that are duplex in layout are geared towards families.

SPAIN - VALENCIA

La Sucursal ❀ ❀ ⬚ 🅰🅲

Guillém de Castro 118 ✉ *46003 –* Ⓜ *Túria*   Plan: **F1**
– ☎ 963 74 66 65 – www.restaurantelasucursal.com – Closed 15 days
August, Saturday lunch and Sunday
Menu 45/85 € *– (set menu only)*
• Creative • Minimalist •

This restaurant is inside the Instituto Valenciano de Arte Moderno (IVAM). It has
a café on the ground floor and a minimalist dining room upstairs. Various
menus offering a perfect marriage between updated cooking with its roots in
traditional recipes, and dishes that are highly innovative in style.
→ La yema con emulsión de bacalao ahumado y crujiente de ibérico. Arroz
cremoso de col, cocochas de bacalao y suave pil-pil. Toffee de galletas, frutos rojos y helado de yogur.

Ricard Camarena 🅰🅲

Doctor Sumsi 4 ✉ *46005 –* Ⓜ *Xàtiva*   Plan: **G3**
– ☎ 963 35 54 18 – www.ricardcamararestaurant.com
– Closed 28 December-12 January, Sunday and Monday
Menu 75/105 € *– (set menu only)*
• Modern cuisine • Design •

A restaurant boasting a thoroughly modern and meticulous look. There is a
unique private section and highly original table that dominates the room
from its position opposite the open-view kitchen. The concise choice of
daily à la carte choices and the tasting menu demonstrate excellent culinary
skill.
→ Alcachofas baby marinadas con romero, mandarina y ravioli de alcachofas fritas. Pescadilla en salmuera, habitas, cebolletas y jugo de tomates
secos. Ensalada ligeramente picante de naranja, eucalipto y perifollo.

Rías Gallegas 🅰🅲 ⬚

Cirilo Amorós 4 ✉ *46004 –* Ⓜ *Xàtiva – ☎ 963 52 51 11*   Plan: **G3**
– www.riasgallegas.es
– Closed 10-17 August, Sunday dinner and Monday
Menu 35 € – Carte 36/51 €
• Traditional cuisine • Elegant •

A family-run restaurant with an impeccable appearance. The cuisine is focused
on tradition, hence the typical Galician dishes with a contemporary touch.

Riff (Bernd Knöller) ❀ 🅰🅲

Conde de Altea 18 ✉ *46005 –* Ⓜ *Colón*   Plan: **H3**
– ☎ 963 33 53 53 – www.restaurante-riff.com – Closed August, Sunday
and Monday
Menu 30/95 € – Carte 55/74 €
• Creative • Minimalist •

This centrally located restaurant has an attractive layout and a carefully styled
minimalist look. The owner-chef, who is German but considers himself more of
a Valencian, creates innovative cuisine. This is based around seasonal, local
ingredients of the highest quality. Interesting set menus.
→ Arroz negro de aceitunas con papada ibérica. Salmonete con col de
pico agudo. Fresitas del bosque con almendra salada y café.

El Poblet ❀ ❀ 🅰🅲 ⬚

Correos 8-1º ✉ *46002 –* Ⓜ *Colón – ☎ 961 11 11 06*   Plan: **G2**
– www.elpobletrestaurante.com
– Closed Sunday and Tuesday dinner
Menu 39/66 € – Carte 41/61 €
• Creative • Friendly •

In the heart of Valencia, this comfortable restaurant has a contemporary look. It
encapsulates the creativity developed in Dénia by the award-winning chef Qui-
que Dacosta. Its extensive à la carte choices are complemented by two interesting and reasonably priced set menus.
→ Gambas rojas de Denia hervidas y frías. Salmonete con perlas de su
cabeza. Campo de cítricos.

XX **Civera**   🏖 🍴 ♿ ㎞ ⇔
Mosén Femades 10 ⊠ 46002 – Ⓜ Colón   Plan: **G3**
– ℰ 963 52 97 64 – www.marisqueriascivera.com
Menu 36 € – Carte 30/60 €
• Fish and seafood • Mediterranean •
The Civera specialises in fish, seafood and savoury rice dishes. It has a bar with
several tables, enticing display cabinets and a dining room with a maritime
ambience. Interesting glass-fronted wine cellar.

XX **Canyar**   ㎞ ⇔
Segorbe 5 ⊠ 46004 – Ⓜ Bailén – ℰ 963 41 80 82   Plan: **F3**
– www.canyarrestaurante.com
– Closed August and Sunday
Menu 45/73 € – Carte 30/56 €
• Fish and seafood • Classic •
The Canyar is somewhat unusual in that it combines old-style decor with
modernist detail. It features an astutely selected wine list and high quality fish
that arrives daily from Denia.

XX **Blanqueries**   ㎞ ⇔
😊 *Blanqueries 12 (entrance on Padre Huérfanos) ⊠ 46002*   Plan: **F1**
*– ℰ 963 91 22 39 – www.blanquerias.com – Closed Holly Week, Sunday
dinner and Monday*
Menu 19/26 € – Carte 27/36 €
• Modern cuisine • Minimalist •
This restaurant with a thoroughly cosmopolitan feel is located next to the Torres
de Serranos. The interior is dominated by varying tones of white and provides
the backdrop for seasonally influenced cuisine with a creative touch.

X **Saiti**   ㎞
😊 *Reina Doña Germana 4 ⊠ 46005 – ℰ 960 05 41 24*   Plan: **H3**
– www.saiti.es – Closed 15-31 August, Sunday and Monday dinner
Menu 25/45 € – Carte 29/35 €
• Traditional cuisine • Friendly •
A contemporary yet informal bistro-style restaurant in which the kitchen team's
ethic focuses on exciting cuisine, hard work and a desire to please. Delicious
cooking teeming with interesting combinations is presented in a manner that
showcases the quality of ingredients used.

X **Macel·lum**   ㎞ ⇔
Boix 6 ⊠ 46002 – ℰ 963 91 38 15   Plan: **G1**
*– www.restaurantemacellum.com – Closed Holy Week, 7 days August,
Sunday summer and Monday*
Menu 20/55 € – Carte approx. 35 €
• Modern cuisine • Cosy •
An intimate, family-run and welcoming restaurant with a rustic-modern interior
full of character. The menu revolves around highly interesting contemporary
cuisine, which is well presented and full of marked flavours and textures.

X **Montes**   ㎞
😊 *pl. Obispo Amigó 5 ⊠ 46007 – Ⓜ Pl. Espanya*   Plan: **E3**
*– ℰ 963 85 50 25 – Closed Holy Week, August, Sunday
dinner, Monday and Tuesday dinner*
Menu 13/21 € – Carte 27/35 €
• Traditional cuisine • Classic •
A restaurant very much traditional in feel with lots of loyal customers thanks to
its friendly, personalised service. Moderately priced classic cuisine, including
tasty soups, stews and savoury rice dishes.

✗ Canalla Bistro `AC`

Maestro José Serrano 5 ✉ 46003 – 𝒞 963 74 05 09   Plan: **G3**
– www.canallabistro.com
Menu 16/26 € – Carte 26/39 €
• **Modern cuisine • Friendly •**
A fun and informal restaurant with an open-view kitchen and a decor that partly features crates that were once used to transport oranges. It offers world cuisine that is perfect for sharing and prepared using local ingredients.

♈ Vuelve Carolina   ⅋ `AC`

Correos 8 ✉ 46002 – Ⓜ Colón – 𝒞 963 21 86 86   Plan: **G2**
– www.vuelvecarolina.com – Closed Sunday
Tapa 4 € **Ración** approx. 8 €
• **Creative • Fashionable •**
The wood panelling that completely covers the walls and ceilings provides the unique look here. The large room by the entrance is home to the bar, and there is a more sophisticated looking dining room to the rear. Creative à la carte tapas, as well as two set menus.

♈ Coloniales Huerta   🛒 `AC`

Maestro Gozalbo 13 ✉ 46005 – Ⓜ Colón   Plan: **H3**
– 𝒞 963 34 80 09 – www.colonialeshuerta.com – Closed 15 days August and Sunday dinner
Tapa 6 € **Ración** approx. 14 €
• **Traditional cuisine • Wine bar •**
Accessed via a wine shop, this restaurant has maintained the spirit of the grocery store that opened its doors here in 1916. Tapas and raciones for sharing, as well as attractive menus.

♈ La Sènia   🛒 ⅋

Sènia 2 ✉ 46001 – 𝒞 963 15 37 28   Plan: **F2**
– www.tabernalasenia.net
Tapa 7 € **Ración** approx. 12 € – *(dinner only except Friday, Saturday and Sunday)*
• **Mediterranean • Rustic •**
Located right in the heart of Valencia, La Sènia has a very clear culinary philosophy: simplicity and quality. This rustic, informal restaurant is a good option if you are looking for contemporary, Mediterranean-style tapas prepared on the spot.

♈ Central Bar

pl. del Mercado, Central Market, locals 105-131   Plan: **F2**
✉ 46001 – 𝒞 963 82 92 23 – www.centralbar.es – Closed Sunday
Tapa 3.50 € **Ración** approx. 11 € – *(lunch only)*
• **Traditional cuisine • Tapas bar •**
Another property in chef Ricard Camarena's stable, with the added attraction of a location inside the city's impressive central market. Seasonal cuisine, daily suggestions, and delicious baguette-style bocadillos!

CIUDAD DE LAS ARTES – HARBOURS – BEACHES   **PLAN III**

🏨 The Westin València   🕌 🛗 🌐 ▢ & `AC` 🛗 🚗

Amadeo de Saboya 16 ✉ 46010 – Ⓜ Alameda   Plan: **J1**
– 𝒞 963 62 59 00 – www.westinvalencia.com
130 rm – ♦140/400 € ♦♦160/420 € – ☑ 24 € – 5 suites
• **Luxury • Historic • Classic •**
The city's Westin occupies a historic building with an attractive Modernist look. Delightful interior garden, elegant lounges, plus superbly equipped guestrooms, including the spectacular Royal Suite, whose decor is courtesy of the designer Francis Montesinos. Interesting dining options.
Komori – See restaurant listing

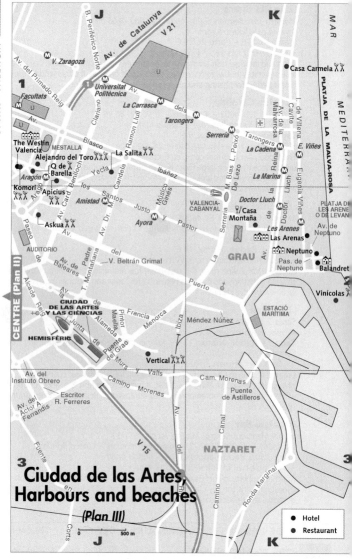

Ciudad de las Artes,
Harbours and beaches
(Plan III)

●	Hotel
●	Restaurant

SPAIN - VALENCIA

Las Arenas

Eugenia Viñes 22 ✉ *46011*
Plan: **K2**
– ⓜ *Marina Real Juan Carlos I –* ☏ *963 12 06 00*
– *www.hotelvalencialasarenas.com*
243 rm – ♥♥140/565 € – ☲ 23 € – 10 suites
• **Luxury** • **Business** • **Classic** •
This luxury hotel, located right on the beach, is divided between three buildings and features welcoming public areas, superb meeting rooms, and well-appointed guestrooms. In the elegant Brasserie Sorolla the focus is very much on creative cuisine.

Neptuno

paseo de Neptuno 2 ✉ *46011*
Plan: **K2**
– ⓜ *Marina Real Juan Carlos I –* ☏ *963 56 77 77*
– *www.hotelneptunovalencia.com*
49 rm ☲ – ♥121/176 € ♥♥138/198 € – 1 suite
• **Family** • **Holiday hotel** • **Modern** •
Well located right by the beach, with guestrooms that are minimalist in design. The overall look here is contemporary, with rooms embellished with a valuable collection of avant-garde works painted by different Valencian artists. The modern and colourful restaurant serves cuisine with a traditional flavour.

Balandret

paseo de Neptuno 20 ✉ *46002 –* ☏ *963 81 11 41*
Plan: **K2**
– *www.balandret.com*
20 rm ☲ – ♥60/180 € ♥♥70/190 € – 1 suite
• **Holiday hotel** • **Functional** •
Half of the guestrooms at this seafront hotel boast sea views. The decor is functional and reasonably attractive, while the restaurant is spacious and contemporary in style. Regional cuisine with a good selection of savoury rice dishes and fideuá specialities.

Alejandro del Toro

Amadeo de Saboya 15 ✉ *46010 –* ⓜ *Aragón*
Plan: **J1**
– ☏ *963 93 40 46 – www.restaurantealejandrodeltoro.com – Closed 1-15 September, 24 December-1 January, Sunday dinner and Monday*
Menu 24/82 € – Carte 35/51 €
• **Creative** • **Elegant** •
The owner-chef here conjures up creative cuisine in a spacious, minimalist-style dining room with a glass-fronted wine cellar with views through to the kitchen. Alternatively, choose from a more informal menu on the bistro-style terrace.

Vertical

Luis García Berlanga 19 ✉ *46023 –* ☏ *963 30 38 00*
Plan: **J2**
– *www.restaurantevertical.com*
Menu 45/90 € – *(set menu only)*
• **Creative** • **Design** •
In addition to its interesting creative cuisine, which is reflected in its gastronomic menus, Vertical stands out for its attractive decor and excellent views from its location on the top floor of the Confortel Aqua 4 hotel. Contemporary look in the dining room, as well as an unusual chill-out terrace.

Kōmori – Hotel The Westin València

General Gil Dolz ✉ *46010 –* ⓜ *Alameda*
Plan: **J1**
– ☏ *961 86 62 90 – www.restaurantekomori.com – Closed Holy Week, 15 days August, Saturday lunch, Sunday and Bank Holidays*
Menu 50/70 € – Carte 40/80 €
• **Japanese** • **Minimalist** •
A Japanese eatery that follows in the footsteps of the famous Kabuki restaurant in Madrid, both in terms of its decor and cuisine. The Japanese charcoal grill here is unique in Spain.

XX **Apicius**   🕃 AC

Eolo 7 ✉ *46021 –* Ⓜ *Aragón –* 𝄐 *963 93 63 01*   Plan: **J1**
*– www.restaurante-apicius.com – Closed Holy Week, August, Saturday
lunch and Sunday*
Menu 28/51 € – Carte 36/49 €
• **Modern cuisine • Minimalist •**
The single dining room is both spacious and contemporary in feel with an
emphasis on modern, seasonal cuisine. The extensive wine cellar has a particularly fine selection of German whites.

XX **Vinícolas**   ⩻ 🕃 AC P

Marina Real Juan Carlos I, Local F2 (Marina Sur)   Plan: **K2**
✉ *46024 –* 𝄐 *961 10 22 44 – www.vinicolasvalencia.com – Closed
Monday except summer and Sunday dinner*
Menu 30/65 € – Carte 50/65 €
• **Traditional cuisine • Design •**
An interesting option, given its setting inside a glass cube with a highly minima-
list look. The à la carte menu offers a pleasantly updated take on traditional cui-
sine with a focus on technique, presentation and intense flavours.

XX **Askua**   🕃 ⴺ AC

Felip María Garín 4 ✉ *46021 –* Ⓜ *Aragón*   Plan: **J2**
– 𝄐 *963 37 55 36 – www.restauranteaskua.com – Closed 2 weeks August,
Sunday, Tuesday dinner and Bank Holidays*
Carte 31/59 €
• **Traditional cuisine • Minimalist •**
A well-respected restaurant thanks to the quality of its ingredients. In the
modern, brightly decorated dining room the focus is on cuisine full of flavour
prepared using high quality ingredients.

XX **La Salita**   AC

Séneca 12 ✉ *46021 –* 𝄐 *963 81 75 16*   Plan: **J1**
– www.lasalitarestaurante.com – Closed Sunday
Menu 44.50 € – *(set menu only)*
• **Creative • Cosy •**
You can't talk about La Salita without mention of Begoña Rodrigo, Spain's top
chef. The single tasting menu is highly creative, well defined and teeming with
intriguing flavours.

XX **Casa Carmela**   🕃 AC ⟷

Isabel de Villena 155 ✉ *46011 –* 𝄐 *963 71 00 73* Plan: **K1**
– www.casa-carmela.com – Closed Monday
Carte 33/52 € – *(lunch only)*
• **Traditional cuisine • Rustic •**
This local institution opened its doors on Malvarrosa beach in 1922. The beautiful glazed Manises tiles provide the perfect backdrop for Casa Carmela's superb
paellas.

X **Q de Barella**   AC
☺
Finlandia 7 ✉ *46010 –* Ⓜ *Alameda –* 𝄐 *963 93 63 00* Plan: **J1**
*– www.qdebarella.com – Closed Holy Week, August, Sunday and Monday
dinner*
Menu 18/40 € – Carte 26/37 €
• **Creative • Trendy •**
This restaurant has two functional and contemporary dining rooms, both featuring designer detail. The chef's clearly defined concept involves creative cuisine
favouring traditional flavours and products, yet enjoying the benefit of up-to-
date techniques and presentation.

℣ **Casa Montaña**   🕸 AC
José Benlliure 69 ✉ *46011 –* Ⓜ *Maritim Serreria*   Plan: **K2**
– 𝒞 963 67 23 14 – www.emilianobodega.com – Closed Sunday dinner
Tapa 3 € **Ración** approx. 9 €
• **Traditional cuisine** • **Tapas bar** •
An old tavern-style eatery decorated in typical style, including large wine barrels. Various private rooms, an impressive tapas menu and a wine list featuring several prestigious labels.

 Sorolla Palace   🌂 ⅃ 🔲 ⅃ 🔲 ✆ 🚗
av. Cortes Valencianas 58 ✉ *46015 –* Ⓜ *Beniferri*   Plan: **B1**
– 𝒞 961 86 87 00 – www.hotelsorollapalace.com
250 rm – ♥♥50/330 € – ⬚ 17 € – 22 suites
• **Business** • **Functional** •
Popular with business travellers thanks to its modern facilities and proximity to the city's conference centre. Guestrooms with a contemporary, functional feel. The restaurant is decorated in a similar style occupying a partitionable dining room complemented by three private dining areas.

XX **Kaymus**   🕸 AC ✆
😊 *av. Maestro Rodrigo 44* ✉ *46015 –* Ⓜ *Beniferri*   Plan: **B2**
– 𝒞 963 48 66 66 – www.kaymus.es – Closed 16-23 August and Monday dinner
Menu 24/58 € – Carte 31/42 €
• **Traditional cuisine** • **Design** •
A modern restaurant known for its high quality cuisine, which is prepared simply yet with great finesse. The wine cellar benefits from similar attention to detail.

SWEDEN
SVERIGE

→ **AREA:**
449 964 km² (173 731 sq mi).

→ **POPULATION:**
9 580 568 inhabitants.
Density = 21 per km².

→ **CAPITAL:**
Stockholm.

→ **CURRENCY:**
Swedish Krona (Skr or SEK).

→ **GOVERNMENT:**
Constitutional parliamentary
monarchy (since 1950).
Member of
European Union since 1995.

→ **LANGUAGE:**
Swedish; many Swedes also speak
good English.

→ **PUBLIC HOLIDAYS:**
New Year's Day (1 Jan); Epiphany
(6 Jan); Good Friday (late Mar/
Apr); Easter Monday (late Mar/Apr);
Labor Day (1 May); Ascension Day
(May); Whit Sunday (late May/June);
National Day (6 June); Midsummer's
Day (Sat between 20-26 June);
All Saints' Day (1 Nov); Christmas
Day (25 Dec); St Stephen's Day
(26 Dec).

→ **LOCAL TIME:**
GMT+1 hour in winter and GMT
+2 hours in summer.

→ **CLIMATE:**
Temperate continental with
cold winters and mild summers
(Stockholm: January -3°C; July 16°C).

→ **EMERGENCY:**
Police, Medical Assistance and Fire
Brigade ☎ **112** – also on-call doctors
and roadside breakdown service.

STOCKHOLM

Gothenburg

Malmö

→ **ELECTRICITY:**
230 volts AC, 50Hz; 2 round pin
sockets.

→ **FORMALITIES:**
Travellers from the European Union
(EU), Switzerland, Iceland and the
main countries of North and South
America need a national identity
card or passport (America: passport
required) to visit Sweden for less
than three months (tourism or
business purpose). For visitors
from other countries a visa may be
required, in addition to a passport,
especially for those wishing to
stay for longer than three months.
We advise you to check with your
embassy before travelling.

STOCKHOLM
STOCKHOLM

Population: 897 124

imagepassion/Fotolia.com

Stockholm is the place to go for clean air, big skies and handsome architecture. And water. One of the great beauties of the city is the amount of water that runs through and around it; it's built on 14 islands, and looks out on 24,000 of them. An astounding two-thirds of the area within the city limits is made up of water, parks and woodland, and there are dozens of little bridges to cross to get from one part of town to another. It's little wonder Swedes appear so calm and relaxed.

It's in Stockholm that the salty waters of the Baltic meet head-on the fresh waters of Lake Mälaren, reflecting the broad boulevards and elegant buildings that shimmer along their edge. Domes, spires and turrets dot a skyline that in the summertime never truly darkens. The heart of the city is the Old Town, Gamla Stan, full of alleyways and lanes little changed from their medieval origins. Just to the north is the modern centre, Norrmalm: a buzzing quarter of shopping malls, restaurants and bars. East of Gamla Stan you reach the small island of Skeppsholmen, which boasts fine views of the waterfront; directly north from here is Östermalm, an area full of grand residences, while southeast you'll find the lovely park island of Djurgården. South and west of Gamla Stan are the two areas where Stockholmers particularly like to hang out, the trendy (and hilly) Södermalm, and Kungsholmen.

STOCKHOLM IN...

→ **ONE DAY**
Gamla Stan, City Hall, Vasa or Skansen museums, an evening in Södermalm.

→ **TWO DAYS**
Coffee in Kungsholmen, museums in Skeppsholmen, a stroll around Djurgården.

→ **THREE DAYS**
Shopping in Norrmalm, boat trip round the archipelago.

PRACTICAL INFORMATION

ARRIVAL-DEPARTURE

 Stockholm Arlanda Airport is 40km north of the city. The Arlanda Express train takes 20min to Centralstation and departs every 15min. The airport bus (Flygbuss) to Cityterminalen takes 40min.

 Bromma Stockholm Airport is 7km northwest of the city.

GETTING AROUND

The efficient metro system offers a more direct route than the buses. The No. 7 tram, which runs throughout the summer, takes in quite a few of the main attractions. You can buy single tickets for the bus, tram and metro, but if you're planning to do lots of travelling about the city, you can also get travelcards which cover one or three days. From April-October, city bikes are a cheap way to travel. Purchase a 3-day card, pick up a bike from any of the stands and it's yours for 3 hours.

CALENDAR HIGHLIGHTS

January/February
The Viking Run (ice skating race).

April
Walpurgis Night.

June
Midsummer's Eve celebrations, Stockholm Marathon.

August
Baltic Sea Festival (classical music).

October
Jazz Festival.

November
International Film Festival.

December
Nobel Prize Day.

EATING OUT

Everyone thinks that eating out in Stockholm is invariably expensive, but with a little forward planning it doesn't have to be. In the middle of the day, most restaurants and cafés offer very good value set menus. Keep in mind that, unlike in Southern Europe, the Swedes like to eat quite early, so lunch can often begin at around 11am and dinner may start from 6pm. Picking wild food is a birthright of Swedes, and there's no law to stop you going into forest or field to pick blueberries, cloudberries, cranberries, strawberries, mushrooms and the like. This love of outdoor, natural fare means that Stockholmers have a special bond with menus which relate to the seasons: keep your eyes open for restaurants that feature husmanskost (traditional Swedish dishes), along with huge buffet-style smörgåsbords. These days, however, you might find that your classic meatball, dumpling, herring or gravlax dish comes with a modern twist.

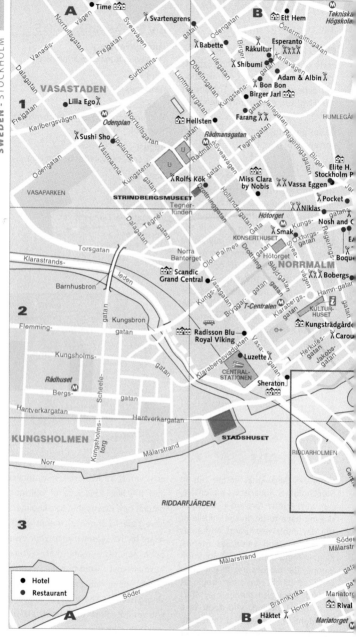

Time

A

Norrtullsgatan

Vanadis-

Dalagatan

Norrtullsgatan

vägen

Sveavägen

Freigatan

Surbrunns-

X Svartengrens

gatan

Odengatan

X Babette

Tulegatan

Birger

Döbeinsgatan

X Shibumi

Lunnmakargatan

VASASTADEN

Lilla Ego X

1

Karlbergsvägen

Freigatan

Odengatan

M Odenplan

Norrtullsgatan

Upplands-

X Sushi Sho

Västmanna-

Kungstens-

gatan

Rådmansgatan

Sveavägen

Höllända-gatan

Tegnérgatan

Hellsten

X Rolfs Kök

Drottninggatan

Rådmans-gatan

Tegnér-lunden

STRINDBERGSMUSEET

Dalagatan

Tegnér gatan

B

Ett Hem

Teknïska

Högskola

Östermalmsgatan

Esperanto XXXX

X Råkultur

Kariavägen

Bon Bon

Adam & Albin X

Birger Jarl

gatan

Jarlsgatan

Regeringsgatan

Farang X X

HUMLEGÅF

Birger

Elite H.

Stockholm P

Miss Clara
by Nobis

X X Vassa Eggen

Jar

X Pocket

X X Niklas

gatan

X

VASAPARKEN

Torsgatan

Klarastrands-

Barnhusbron

Kungsbron

2

Flemming-

Kungsholms-

Scheele-

Rådhuset

Bergs-

Hantverkargatan

KUNGSHOLMEN

Kungsholms-

torg

Norr

Klarabergs-

leden

gatan

gatan

Hötorget

Hötorget

X Smak

KONSERTHUSET

Norra
Bantorget

Olof Palmes

Drottning

gatan

Hötorget

Sloldsgatan

Kungs-gatan

Vasagatan

Bryggar-

gatan

gatan

Scandic
Grand Central

T-Centralen

Radisson Blu
Royal Viking

Klarabergsviadukten

Vasa-gatan

Luzette X

**CENTRAL-
STATIONEN**

Sheraton

Hantverkargatan

STADSHUSET

Mälarstrand

Norr

Nosh and C

E/

X

Boque

NORRMALM

X X Bobergs

Hamn-gatan

KULTUR-
HUSET

Kungsträdgårde

X Carou

Herkules-

gatan

Jakobs-

gatan

RIDDARHOLMEN

Cer

RIDDARFJÄRDEN

3

Mälarstrand

Söder

Söde
Mälarstr

gatan

ga

Mariatorg

Rival

●	Hotel
●	Restaurant

A

Söder

Brännkyrka-

Häktet X Horns-

B

Mariatorget

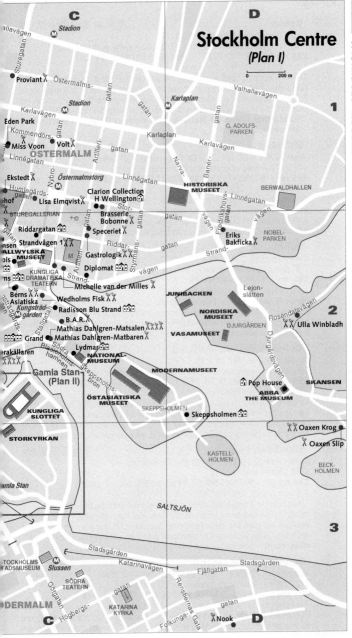

Stockholm Centre
(Plan I)

0   200 m

C
D

Stadion

aliavägen

Sturegatan

Proviant ✕ Östermalms-

Stadion

Karlaplan

Valhallavägen

G. ADOLFS-
PARKEN

1

Karlavägen

Eden Park

Kommendörs-

gatan

Karlaplan

Karlavägen

Miss Voon Volt ✕

ÖSTERMALM

Artilleri-

gatan

BERWALDHALLEN

Linnégatan

Ekstedt ✕

Nybro-

Östermalmstorg

Linnégatan

Narva-

HISTORISKA
MUSEET

Fredrikshovs-

Linnégatan

Humlegårds-
gatan

Lisa Elmqvist ✕

Clarion Collection
H Wellington

Banér-

vägen

hof

STUREGALLERIAN

Stor-

Brasserie
Bobonne ✕

Riddargatan

Speceriet ✕

gatan

Eriks
Bakficka ✕

NOBEL-
PARKEN

Strandvägen 1 ✕✕

Riddar-

Styrmans-

gatan

Strand-

ALLWYLSKA
MUSEET

Gastrologik ✕

vägen

Diplomat

KUNGLIGA
DRAMATISKA
TEATERN

Strand-

Michelle van der Milles ✕

JUNIBACKEN

Lejons-
slätten

Berns ✕✕

Asiatiska

Wedholms Fisk ✕✕

NORDISKA
MUSEET

Rosendalsvägen

Kungsträd-
gården

Radisson Blu Strand

DJURGÅRDEN

✕✕ Ulla Winbladh

B.A.R. ✕

VASAMUSEET

Mathias Dahlgren-Matsalen ✕✕✕✕

Grand Mathias Dahlgren-Matbaren ✕

Djurgårdsvägen

erakällaren

Lydmar

✕✕✕

Gamla Stan
(Plan II)

Blasieholms-
hamnen

Skeppsholms-
bron

NATIONAL-
MUSEUM

MODERNAMUSEET

Pop House

SKANSEN

ÖSTASIATISKA
MUSEET

ABBA
THE MUSEUM

KUNGLIGA
SLOTTET

SKEPPSHOLMEN

Skeppsholmen

STORKYRKAN

KASTELL-
HOLMEN

✕✕ Oaxen Krog

✕ Oaxen Slip

BECK-
HOLMEN

amla Stan

SALTSJÖN

3

Stadsgården

TOCKHOLMS
ADSMUSEUM Slussen

Katarinavägen

Stadsgården

Fjällgatan

Renstiernas

SÖDRA
TEATERN

Göt

KATARINA
KYRKA

Högbergs-

gatan

Folkunga-Gata

gatan

✕ Nook

ODERMALM

C
D

SWEDEN - STOCKHOLM

Grand

Södra Blasieholmshamnen 8 ⊠ *11148*   Plan: **C2**
– ⓜ *Kungsträdgården* – ✆ *(08) 679 35 00* – *www.grandhotel.se*
278 rm ☐ – †2700/5200 SEK ††3300/5800 SEK – 34 suites
• Grand Luxury • Classic •

Classic waterfront hotel made up of 3 buildings; the oldest dating back to 1874.
Good-sized bedrooms are uncluttered and those at the front have great views.
There's a handsome, panelled bar and an impressive spa. Bright Verandan res-
taurant has a pleasant harbour outlook and is renowned for its smörgåsbords.
❀❀ **Mathias Dahlgren-Matsalen** • ❀ **Mathias Dahlgren-Matbaren**
– See restaurant listing

Sheraton

Tegelbacken 6 ⊠ *101 23* – ⓜ *T-Centralen* – ✆ *(08)*   Plan: **B2**
412 34 00 – *www.sheratonstockholm.com*
465 rm – †1300/4195 SEK ††1300/4195 SEK – ☐ 259 SEK – 7 suites
• Business • Chain hotel • Modern •

Well-run hotel: the first Sheraton to open in Europe. Spacious, well-equipped,
modern bedrooms – ask for one with Gamla Stan views or opt for the 7th floor
with its dedicated business lounge. Lively restaurant with central open kitchen
offers international buffet lunches and traditional Swedish dinners.

Nobis

Norrmalmstorg 2-4 ⊠ *111 86* – ⓜ *Östermalmstorg*   Plan: **C2**
– ✆ *(08) 614 10 00* – *www.nobishotel.com*
201 rm – †1790/2190 SEK ††2890/3190 SEK – ☐ 175 SEK – 1 suite
• Historic • Design •

Formerly two 19C Royal Palaces; later the bank where the famous 'Stockholm
Syndrome' robbery took place. Spacious bedrooms offer clean lines, neutral
hues, African wood and Italian marble bathrooms. Rustic Italian menu in basement Caina; informal, all-day Bistro has a pavement terrace.

Radisson Blu Royal Viking

Vasagatan 1 ⊠ *101 24* – ⓜ *T-Centralen* – ✆ *(08)*   Plan: **B2**
506 540 00 – *www.radissonblu.com/royalvikingstockholm*
459 rm – †1625/4375 SEK ††1625/4625 SEK – ☐ 112 SEK – 3 suites
• Business • Chain hotel • Modern •

Large, central hotel boasting good leisure and meeting facilities. Bedroom styles
vary greatly – from classical to newly refurbished with dark wood furnishings
and bright, modern fabrics; one suite even has a jacuzzi and a sauna. Contemporary restaurant focuses on seafood; panoramic sky bar affords city views.

Elite Eden Park
Sturegatan 22 ⊠ *114 36* – ⓜ *Östermalmstorg* – ✆ *(08)*   Plan: **C1**
5556 2700 – *www.elite.se*
124 rm ☐ – †1352/3290 SEK ††1672/3690 SEK – 1 suite
• Business • Contemporary • Stylish •

Smart hotel in a converted office block, designed with the business traveller in
mind. Stylish bedrooms boast comfy beds and large showers – some rooms
overlook the park and some have small balconies. Choose from an Asian-inspired menu in the restaurant or traditional pub-style dishes in their 'British pub'.
Miss Voon – See restaurant listing

Scandic Grand Central

Kungsgatan 70 ⊠ *111 20* – ⓜ *T-Centralen* – ✆ *(08)*   Plan: **B2**
5125 2000 – *www.scandichotels.com/grandcentral*
391 rm ☐ – †890/2990 SEK ††1090/2990 SEK – 4 suites
• Chain hotel • Business • Contemporary •

Contemporary hotel on the site of the first university in Stockholm (1885), next
to the theatres; its décor tying in with the arts theme of the area. Modern
bedrooms range from cabin bunks to well-equipped suites. The coffee shop
offers snacks, the restaurant serves Swedish classics and the bar has live music.

Radisson Blu Strand

⛲ ≤ 🎵 ⑯ 🏋️

Nybrokajen 9 ✉ *103 27* – Ⓜ *Kungsträdgården* – ✆ *(08)* Plan: **C2**
506 640 00 – *www.radissonblu.com/strandhotel-stockholm*
152 rm – ♦1560/2995 SEK ♦♦1595/3995 SEK – ⚌ 170 SEK
• Chain hotel • Contemporary •

A well-run hotel in a lively harbourside setting; part-dating from the 1912 Olympics. Choose a modern or traditional Scandinavian-style bedroom: many have water views and balconies; the impressive Tower Suite has a private roof terrace. The atrium restaurant mixes Swedish and international cuisine.

 ## Diplomat

⛲ ≤ 🎵 🎵 ⑯ 🏋️

Strandvägen 7c ✉ *114 56* – Ⓜ *Kungsträdgården* Plan: **C2**
– ✆ *(08) 459 68 00* – *www.diplomathotel.com*
130 rm – ♦1650/3450 SEK ♦♦1850/3650 SEK – ⚌ 250 SEK – 2 suites
• Traditional • Classic •

Attractive 1911 art nouveau building blending early 20C charm with contemporary furnishings and facilities. Cosy library-lounge and lovely preserved cage lift. Elegant bedrooms in pastel hues: all boast marble bathrooms and some have harbour views. Scandinavian-inspired brasserie dishes in all-day T Bar.

 ## Berns

⛲ 🎵 🏋️

Näckströmsgatan 8, Berzelii Park ✉ *111 47* Plan: **C2**
– Ⓜ *Kungsträdgården* – ✆ *(08) 566 322 00* – *www.berns.se*
82 rm – ♦1399/3199 SEK ♦♦1699/3499 SEK – ⚌ 195 SEK – 3 suites
• Business • Historic • Stylish •

Originally built as a theatre in 1863 by the Royal Family tailor, this was the venue for the first cancan performance in Sweden. Its interior is now modern and minimalist; the newer bedrooms are the largest and most comfortable.
Berns Asiatiska – See restaurant listing

 ## Miss Clara by Nobis

⛲ 🎵 🎵 ⑯ 🏋️

Sveavägen 48 ✉ *111 34* – ✆ *(08) 440 67 00* Plan: **B1**
– Ⓜ *Hötorget* – *www.missclarahotel.com*
94 rm – ♦1490/2690 SEK ♦♦1590/3090 SEK – ⚌ 169 SEK – 2 suites
• Business • Modern •

A fashionable hotel in a great location; it used to be a girls' school and its name is that of the former principal. Surprisingly quiet, dark wood bedrooms offer good facilities. All-day dining in the atmospheric brasserie, where an international menu has an Italian slant and offers Swedish specialities.

 ## Birger Jarl

⛲ 🎵 ⑯ 🏋️ 🚗

Tulegatan 8 ✉ *104 32* – Ⓜ *Rådmansgatan* – ✆ *(08)* Plan: **B1**
674 1800 – *www.birgerjarl.se*
271 rm ⚌ – ♦1090/2790 SEK ♦♦1190/2990 SEK – 7 suites
• Business • Design • Modern •

1970s building set in a residential area and named after the city's founder. An unassuming façade belies its chic interior: the lobby features modern Swedish art and 17 of the chic bedrooms are styled by famous native designers. Regional dishes and express business lunches offered in the bright restaurant.

 ## Time

🎵 🏋️ 🏋️ 🚗

Vanadisvägen 12 ✉ *113 46* – Ⓜ *Odenplan* – ✆ *(08)* Plan: **A1**
54 54 73 00 – *www.timehotel.se*
144 rm ⚌ – ♦950/2050 SEK ♦♦1750/2250 SEK
• Business • Modern •

Spacious, friendly, purpose-built business hotel in a pleasant residential area on the edge of town. High-ceilinged lobby and modern buffet breakfast room. Large, functional bedrooms and studios; some with comfy chairs or balconies.

Ett Hem
🕥 🥢 🖺 🕅

Sköldungagatan 2 ✉ *114 27 –* **Ⓜ** *Tekniska Högskolan*   Plan: **B1**
– 𝒞 (08) 20 05 90 – www.etthem.se
12 rm ⌷ – 🛉3800 SEK 🛉🛉4900 SEK
• Luxury • Design • Classic •
A charming Arts and Crafts townhouse built as a private residence in 1910. It's
elegant and understated and makes good use of wood; its name means 'home'
and that's exactly how it feels. Bedroom No.6 features an old chimney and No.1
has a four-poster and a huge marble bath. Modern set menus use fine seasonal
produce and are served in the kitchen, library or orangery.

Lydmar
🕥 ≤ ㅎ 🆔

Södra Blasieholmshamnen 2 ✉ *103 24*   Plan: **C2**
– **Ⓜ** *Kungsträdgården – 𝒞 (08) 22 31 60 – www.lydmar.com*
46 rm ⌷ – 🛉3600 SEK 🛉🛉3600 SEK – 6 suites
• Townhouse • Stylish • Design •
A charming townhouse, superbly located opposite the Palace; once a store for
the adjacent museum's archives. The gallery entrance sets the scene with eclectic art and unusual décor. Spacious bedrooms boast funky furnishings and stylish bathrooms. Casual lounge and smart roof terrace with a cocktail bar. Attractive restaurant offers modern European brasserie menu.

Riddargatan
🖧

Riddargatan 14 ✉ *11435 –* **Ⓜ** *Östermalmstorg*   Plan: **C2**
– 𝒞 (08) 555 730 00 – www.profilhotels.com
78 rm ⌷ – 🛉895/2799 SEK 🛉🛉1095/2995 SEK – 4 suites
• Business • Modern • Stylish •
Smart hotel close to the shops, restaurants and theatres. Bedrooms in the newer
wing have bright, bold designs and wet rooms; all have exercise DVDs, weights
and maps for joggers. Contemporary breakfast room doubles as a lively bar.

Elite H. Stockholm Plaza
🕥 🕅 ㅎ 🖧

Birger Jarlsgatan 29 ✉ *103 95 –* **Ⓜ** *Östermalmstorg*   Plan: **B1**
– 𝒞 (08) 566 220 00 – www.elite.se
143 rm ⌷ – 🛉1290/3190 SEK 🛉🛉1690/3790 SEK – 12 suites
• Business • Chain hotel • Functional •
The smaller sister of the Elite Eden Park is this attractive, centrally located buil-
ding with a façade dating from 1884. Bright fabrics stand out against neutral
walls in the compact modern bedrooms; go for one of the corner suites.
Vassa Eggen – See restaurant listing

Kungsträdgården
🕥 🖺 🕅 🆔

Västra Trädgårdsgatan 11b ✉ *111 53*   Plan: **B2**
– **Ⓜ** *Kunsträdgården – 𝒞 (08) 440 6650 – www.hotelkungstradgarden.se*
98 rm ⌷ – 🛉1490/2990 SEK 🛉🛉1790/3990 SEK
• Townhouse • Historic • Classic •
Overlooking the park of the same name is this part-18C building with a classical
façade and attractive original features. Bedrooms are individually furnished in a
Gustavian-style – it's worth paying the extra for a bigger one. Buffet lunches and
classical French dinners are served in the covered courtyard.

Hellsten
🖺 🕅 ㅎ 🖧

Luntmakargatan 68 ✉ *113 51 –* **Ⓜ** *Rådmansgatan*   Plan: **B1**
– 𝒞 (08) 661 86 00 – www.hellsten.se
78 rm ⌷ – 🛉890/2090 SEK 🛉🛉1290/2490 SEK
• Townhouse • Personalised • Cosy •
Quirky hotel filled with interesting pieces from the owner's globetrotting
adventures. Choose a large, high-ceilinged bedroom or a smaller, more uniquely styled room. Snacks served in the bar, which features live jazz on Thursdays.

Clarion Collection H. Wellington

Storgatan 6 ✉ *114 51* – Ⓜ *Östermalmstorg* – ℰ *(08)* Plan: **C1**
667 09 10 – *www.wellington.se* – *Closed 21-29 December*
60 rm 🛏 – 🛉*1120/2720 SEK* 🛉🛉*1320/3020 SEK* – *2 suites*
• Business • Functional •

This well-run, centrally located hotel – in a former office block – makes an ideal base for shopping and sightseeing. Simple bedrooms feature bright fabrics and those on the top floor have city views. Buffet dinners are included.

Operakällaren

Operahuset, Karl XII's Torg ✉ *111 86* Plan: **C2**
– Ⓜ *Kungsträdgården* – ℰ *(08) 676 58 01* – *www.operakallaren.se*
– *Closed July, 1-14 January, 25-30 December, Sunday and Monday*
Menu 995/1450 SEK – *(dinner only)*
• Classic • Formal • Luxury •

Sweden's most opulent restaurant is set in the historic Opera House; the stunning high-ceilinged room having 19C wood carvings, original frescoes and elegant chandeliers. Enjoy carefully constructed dishes underpinned by classical techniques, and a wine list boasting extensive vintages of the world's great wines.

→ Mackerel with artichoke, courgette and caviar. Pike-perch with sea urchin butter. Flambéed plums with fudge, roast chocolate and goat's milk ice cream.

Mathias Dahlgren-Matsalen – Grand Hotel

Södra Blasieholmshamnen 6 ✉ *111 48* Plan: **C2**
– Ⓜ *Kungsträdgården* – ℰ *(08) 679 35 84* – *www.mdghs.com* – *Closed 15 July-9 August, 23 December-9 January, Sunday and Monday*
Menu 1900 SEK – *(dinner only) (booking essential) (set menu only)*
• Innovative • Elegant • Luxury •

An elegant waterfront restaurant in the city's top hotel, which blends striking architectural features with contemporary furnishings. From a 5 course menu come dishes that are light and focused on textures and natural flavours. Service is slick and unobtrusive, and natural wines are a feature. Book the 'chef's dining table' for an interactive experience.

→ Grilled carrot with trout roe and smoked sour cream. Chanterelles with truffle and 63° egg. Swedish strawberries with vanilla, champagne and pepper.

Esperanto (Sayan Isaksson)

Kungstensgatan 2 (1st Floor) ✉ *114 25* Plan: **B1**
– Ⓜ *Tekniska Högskolan* – ℰ *(08) 696 23 23*
– *www.esperantorestaurant.se* – *Closed July, Christmas, Easter and Sunday-Tuesday*
Menu 1350/1750 SEK – *(dinner only) (set menu only)*
• Innovative • Formal • Luxury •

Understated, candlelit restaurant on the first floor of a converted theatre, boasting a striking curved ceiling. Expect creative, original yet light cooking where the flavours are well-defined. The 6 and 10 course menus mix Swedish and Asian influences. Service is professional and engaging.

→ Nettle and wild onion porridge with a pullet egg. Pike-perch in kombu with potato dashi broth. Frozen Jerusalem artichoke.

Bobergs

NK, Hamngatan 18-20 (4th floor) ✉ *111 47* Plan: **B2**
– Ⓜ *Kungsträdgården* – ℰ *(08) 762 8161* – *www.bobergsmatsal.se*
– *Closed early July-mid August and Sunday*
Menu 395 SEK – Carte 390/630 SEK – *(lunch only) (booking advisable)*
• Modern • Elegant • Classic •

Head past the canteen in this historic department store to the elegant birch-panelled room and ask for a river view. Choose from the seasonal à la carte or have the set business lunch; classic cooking mixes French and Swedish influences.

SWEDEN - STOCKHOLM

Gastrologik (Jacob Holmström and Anton Bjuhr)

*Artillerigatan 14 ⊠ 11451 – **Ⓜ** Östermalmstorg*   Plan: **C2**
– ℰ (08) 66 23 060 – www.gastrologik.se – Closed Christmas,
31 December, Sunday and Monday
Menu 1295 SEK – *(dinner only) (booking essential) (surprise menu only)*
• Innovative • Design • Individual •
This intimate restaurant is owned by two accomplished young chefs. Cooking is innovative, flavours are pure and each main ingredient is allowed to shine. There's no menu as the dishes constantly evolve with each new delivery. Sit looking into the open kitchen or dine communally in the side room.
→ Scallop, pork fat and scallop broth. Beef with beets and wild beach plants. Goat's yoghurt and elderflower ice cream with goat's whey caramel.

Nosh and Chow

*Norrlandsgatan 24 ⊠ 111 43 – **Ⓜ** Hötorget – ℰ (08)*   Plan: **B2**
503 389 60 – www.noshandchow.se – Closed Sunday and lunch
Saturday and bank holidays
Menu 350 SEK – Carte 368/777 SEK
• International • Brasserie •
Chic townhouse with a cocktail bar on one side and a smart NYC-style brasserie on the other, serving filling American, Swedish and French classics. At the back is a third room with the same menu but more of a 'New England' look.

Strandvägen 1

*Strandvägen 1 ⊠ 114 51 – **Ⓜ** Kungsträdgården*   Plan: **C2**
– ℰ (08) 663 80 00 – www.strandvagen1.se – Closed 24 December
Carte 425/765 SEK
• International • Design • Elegant •
Sit on the terrace of this contemporary restaurant – a former bank – and watch the boats bobbing in the harbour. Seasonal menus offer generous, globally inspired dishes with a focus on bold flavours. Live music two nights a week.

Wedholms Fisk

*Nybrokajen 17 ⊠ 111 48 – **Ⓜ** Kungsträdgården*   Plan: **C2**
– ℰ (08) 611 78 74 – www.wedholmsfisk.se – Closed 27 June-14 August,
Easter, Christmas-New Year, midsummer, Saturday lunch, Sunday and
bank holidays
Carte 403/1092 SEK – *(booking essential)*
• Fish and seafood • Formal •
Set on Stockholm's 'little Wall Street'; an impressive 19C harbourside building with an elegant interior and friendly service. Unfussy seafood menu lists the likes of turbot, halibut, prawns and scallops, prepared in several different ways.

Berns Asiatiska – Berns Hotel

Näckströmsgatan 8, Berzelii Park ⊠ 111 47   Plan: **C2**
*– **Ⓜ** Kungsträdgården – ℰ (08) 566 322 22 – www.berns.se*
Carte 210/815 SEK
• Asian • Fashionable • Elegant •
Stunningly restored rococo ballroom from 1863, with a pleasant terrace overlooking Berzelii Park. Bento boxes at lunch; extensive Asian fusion menu and a wide-ranging sushi selection. An Asian brunch is served at the weekend.

AG

Kronobergsgatan 37 (2nd Floor), Kungsholmen (via Flemminggatan A2)
*⊠ 112 33 – **Ⓜ** Fridshemsplan – ℰ (08) 410 681 00*
– www.restaurangag.se – Closed July, 24-25 and 31 December, 1 January
and Sunday
Carte 205/760 SEK – *(dinner only)*
• Meats and grills • Rustic • Fashionable •
Industrial, New York style eatery on the 2nd floor of an old silver factory. Swedish, American and Scottish beef is displayed in huge cabinets: choose your accompaniments. Expect a great wine list and smooth service.

XX

Niklas

Regeringsgatan 66 ✉ 111 39 – Ⓜ Hötorget – ✆ (08) 20 60 10 – www.niklas.se – Closed 24 December, 1 January, Sunday and lunch Saturday Plan: **B2**

Carte 355/705 SEK

• Modern • Fashionable • Bistro •

Contemporary, industrial-style bistro with large blackboard menus on the walls. The owner's extensive travels guide the menus for the next 6 months. You can also try the 'Punk Gastronomy' dinner menu in the adjoining nightclub Weds-Sat.

XX

Vassa Eggen – Elite H. Stockholm Plaza

A/C

Birger Jarlsgatan 29 ✉ 103 95 – Ⓜ Östermalmstorg – ✆ (08) 21 61 69 – www.vassaeggen.com – Closed midsummer, Christmas, Saturday lunch and Sunday Plan: **B1**

Menu 515 SEK (lunch) – Carte 260/870 SEK

• Meats and grills • Fashionable • Rustic •

A pleasant bar leads through to a dimly lit hotel dining room where bold artwork hangs on the walls. Hearty Swedish cooking relies on age-old recipes, with a particular focus on meat; whole beasts are butchered and hung on-site.

XX

Farang

♿ A/C

Tulegatan 7 ✉ 113 53 – Ⓜ Rådmansgatan – ✆ (08) 673 74 00 – www.farang.se – Closed July, midsummer, Christmas, Sunday and Monday Plan: **B1**

Menu 245/690 SEK – Carte 385/700 SEK

• South-East Asian • Minimalist •

Sister to Farang in Helsinki – a vast restaurant with a fashionable bar. Cooking focuses on southeast Asia and on hot, sweet and sour tastes; dishes are aromatic, zingy and colourful. Sharing is encouraged and there's a family atmosphere.

X ✿

Mathias Dahlgren-Matbaren – Grand Hotel

♿ A/C

Södra Blasieholmshamnen 6 ✉ 103 27 – Ⓜ Kungsträdgården – ✆ (08) 679 35 84 – www.mdghs.com – Closed 15 July-9 August, 23 December-9 January and Sunday Plan: **C2**

Carte 415/1120 SEK – *(booking advisable)*

• Modern • Fashionable • Design •

Vibrant restaurant featuring stylish design furniture, where you can have anything from one course to a full meal. The concise, modern menu changes up to twice a day, featuring carefully crafted, perfectly balanced recipes with a simple yet playful style. Each dish is prepared and delivered within 7 minutes.

→ Squid with juniper-smoked trout roe, garlic and parsley. Beetroot and Jerusalem artichoke with truffle and almond. Berries with yuzu sabayon and rye.

X ✿

Ekstedt

❀ ♿

Humlegårdsgatan 17 ✉ 114 46 – Ⓜ Östermalmstorg – ✆ (08) 611 1210 – www.ekstedt.nu – Closed last 2 weeks July, Christmas, first week January, Sunday and Monday Plan: **C1**

Menu 795/990 SEK – *(dinner only) (booking essential) (set menu only)*

• Meats and grills • Individual • Neighbourhood •

An unassuming façade hides a very relaxed, friendly, yet professionally run brasserie, where ingredients are cooked in a wood-burning oven, over a fire-pit or smoked through a chimney using birch wood. Dishes are inventive but well-balanced – they are given their finishing touches at the stone bar.

→ Langoustine, white asparagus and smoked scallop roe. New potato with truffle and wood-fired onion. Frozen yoghurt with raspberries and pistachio.

Volt (Peter Andersson and Fredrik Johnsson)

Kommendörsgatan 16 ⊠ 114 48 – Ⓜ Stadion – ℰ (08)   Plan: C1
662 34 00 – www.restaurangvolt.se – Closed 4 weeks summer, Christmas,
31 December, Sunday and Monday
Menu 585/735 SEK – (dinner only) (booking essential)
• Innovative • Intimate • Neighbourhood •

Intimate and welcoming restaurant run by a young but experienced team. Cooking is natural in style, with the largely organic produce yielding clear, bold flavours – natural wines also feature. Ingredients are arranged in layers, so that each forkful contains a little of everything; choose 4 or 6 courses.
➜ Carrot, goat's milk and currants. Sirloin of beef with turnip and lovage. Sour milk, elder and vinegar.

Sushi Sho (Carl Ishizaki)

Upplandsgatan 45 ⊠ 113 28 – Ⓜ Odenplan – ℰ (08)   Plan: A1
30 30 30 – www.sushisho.se – Closed Christmas-New Year, July,
midsummer, Sunday and Monday
Menu 295/455 SEK – (dinner only and Saturday lunch)
• Japanese • Neighbourhood • Friendly •

With its white tiled walls and compact counter seating the room couldn't be simpler, but the food is sublime. Meals are served 'omakase' style, with the chef deciding what's best each day and dishes arriving as and when they're ready. Top quality seafood from local waters features alongside some great egg recipes.
➜ Salmon, sea bass and scallop nigri. Tuna with okra, scallions and egg yolk. Razor clam with edamame & pea purée, sake and ginger.

Proviant

Sturegatan 19 ⊠ 114 36 – Ⓜ Stadion – ℰ (08) 22 60 50   Plan: C1
– www.proviant.se – Closed July, Easter, Christmas-New Year and lunch
Saturday-Sunday
Menu 625 SEK (dinner) – Carte 410/625 SEK
• Swedish • Bistro • Intimate •

Lively restaurant boasting smart, contemporary décor, a small counter and an adjoining foodstore; located in a chic residential area by Sture Park. Swedish ingredients feature highly – choose from the rustic, classically based dishes on the blackboard, the French-inspired à la carte or the house specialities.

Brasserie Bobonne

Storgatan 12 ⊠ 114 51 – Ⓜ Östermalmstorg – ℰ (08)   Plan: C1
660 03 18 – www.bobonne.se – Closed 5 weeks July-August, midsummer,
Christmas and Sunday
Menu 225/498 SEK – Carte 355/625 SEK – (booking essential)
• French • Cosy • Bistro •

Sweet little two-roomed restaurant with comfy chairs, period floor tiles and a homely feel. The open-plan kitchen fills the room with pleasant aromas. The blackboard lists tasty, well-balanced dishes crafted from fresh ingredients. Menus are French-inspired, with modern touches and the odd Swedish influence.

Lilla Ego

Västmannag 69 ⊠ 113 26 – Ⓜ Odenplan – ℰ (08)   Plan: A1
27 44 55 – www.lillaego.com – Closed Christmas, Easter, Sunday and
Monday
Carte 390/615 SEK – (dinner only) (booking essential)
• Modern • Friendly • Simple •

One of the hottest tickets in town comes with a pared down look and a buzzy atmosphere; if you haven't booked, try for a counter seat. The two modest chef-owners have created an appealingly priced menu of robust, satisfying, seasonal dishes. The 'wrestling' sausage will challenge even the very hungry.

X **Adam & Albin**

Rådmansgatan 16 ✉ *114 25* – ⓜ *Tekniska Högskolan* Plan: **B1**
– ☎ (08) 411 5535 – www.adamalbin.se – Closed Saturday and Sunday
Menu 225 SEK – *(lunch only)*
• Modern • Friendly • Individual •
Named after its experienced chef-owners, this 'food studio' and cookery school offers superbly prepared noodle dishes at lunchtime and creative, modern gourmet dinners one weekend per month. Dining takes place at communal tables.

X **Luzette** ⚌ ಈ ⓐⓒ

Centralstationen, Centralplan 25 ✉ *111 20* Plan: **B2**
– ⓜ T-Centralen – ☎ 519 316 00 – www.luzette.se
Menu 165/220 SEK – Carte 425/715 SEK
• Swedish • Brasserie • Design •
A modern brasserie and takeaway in the Central train station, inspired by the grand restaurants of old. Its name means 'light' and refers to the 1920s lumin-aire designed by Peter Behrens. Swedish cooking features rotisserie specials.

X **Carousel** ಈ ⓐⓒ

Gustav Adolfs torg 20 ✉ *111 52* – ⓜ *Kungsträdgården* Plan: **B2**
– ☎ (08) 10 27 57 – www.restaurantcarousel.se – Closed Christmas and Sunday
Carte 380/830 SEK
• Swedish • Fashionable • Neighbourhood •
Start with a drink under the impressive original ceiling in the bar then move on to communal tables beneath the carousel. Classic Swedish dishes are skilfully prepared by the experienced chefs – be sure to give the gravadlax a try.

X **Shibumi** ⓐⓒ

Kungstensgatan 2 ✉ *114 25* – ⓜ *Tekniska Högskolan* Plan: **B1**
– ☎ (08) 696 23 10 – www.shibumi.se – Closed Christmas, Easter, Midsummer, Sunday and Monday
Carte 220/380 SEK – *(dinner only) (booking advisable)*
• Japanese • Intimate • Minimalist •
Minimalist, modern and discreet Japanese restaurant, based on an izakaya. It comes with an underground buzz – and that's not just because it's in a base-ment. Expect plenty of original dishes and great cocktails; it's also open late.

X **Michelle van der Milles** ⚌ ⓐⓒ

Strandvägen 1 ✉ *114 51* – ⓜ *Kungsträdgården* Plan: **C2**
– ☎ (08) 663 80 00 – www.mmilles.se – Closed 24 December and Sunday dinner in winter
Carte 425/725 SEK
• International • Bistro • Fashionable •
Known as the bakficka (back pocket) restaurant to its sister Strandvägen 1, this intimate bistro boasts striking artwork from Jesper Waldersten and a great waterfront terrace. A concise menu offers a mix of influences from the Med, Asia and Sweden.

X **Miss Voon** – Elite Eden Park Hotel ಈ ⓐⓒ

Sturegatan 22 ✉ *114 36* – ⓜ *Östermalmstorg* – ☎ *(08)* Plan: **C1**
5052 4470 – www.missvoon.se
Menu 130/250 SEK – Carte 230/410 SEK
• Asian • Trendy • Design •
Smart, Asian-inspired restaurant and large bar, set within a stylish hotel. Bento boxes and a few specials are offered at lunch; the evening à la carte is influen-ced by Japan, Vietnam and Thailand, with dishes designed for sharing.

SWEDEN - STOCKHOLM

X **Svartengrens**

Tulegatan 24 ⊠ 113 53 – ⓜ Tekniska Högskolan Plan: **B1**
– ⓒ (08) 612 65 50 – www.svartengrens.se – Closed 4 weeks July-August,
Christmas and midsummer
Carte 295/845 SEK – *(dinner only) (booking advisable)*
• Meats and grills • Friendly • Neighbourhood •
The eponymous chef-owner has created a friendly, modern bistro specialising
in sustainable meat and veg from producers in the archipelago. Along with
smoking and pickling, the dry-ageing is done in-house, and the cuts change
daily.

X **Babette**

Roslagsgatan 6 ⊠ 113 55 – ⓜ Tekniska Högskolan Plan: **B1**
– ⓒ (08) 5090 2224 – www.babette.se – Closed 23-28 December and
midsummer
Carte 280/550 SEK – *(dinner only)*
• Modern • Neighbourhood • Bistro •
You'll feel at home in this modern neighbourhood bistro. Cooking is rustic and
unfussy and the daily selection of small plates and pizzas makes dining flexible.
They limit their bookings so that they can accommodate for walk-ins.

X **Pocket**

Brunnsgatan 1 ⊠ 111 38 – ⓜ Östermalmstorg – ⓒ (08) Plan: **B1**
545 27300 – www.pontusfrithiof.com – Closed July-mid August, Sunday
and bank holidays
Carte 325/415 SEK – *(bookings not accepted)*
• Traditional • Bistro • Simple •
Grab a table in the window of this casual bistro or sit at the counter to watch the
chefs at work. Menus offer French bistro classics with some Swedish influences;
start with a selection of snacks – three are equal to a starter.

X **Sturehof**

Stureplan 2 ⊠ 114 46 – ⓜ Östermalmstorg – ⓒ (08) Plan: **C1**
440 57 30 – www.sturehof.com
Carte 415/900 SEK
• Fish and seafood • Brasserie • Individual •
A city institution dating back to 1896. The bold interior has a buzzy atmosphere
and consists of several rooms; a large etched Labouret glass screen separates
the bar and the restaurant. Unfussy seafood and a superb selection of wines
from DRC.

X **Eriks Bakficka**

Fredrikshovsgatan 4 ⊠ 115 23 – ⓒ (08) 660 15 99 Plan: **D2**
– www.eriks.se – Closed July, Christmas, Easter, Saturday lunch and
Sunday
Menu 495 SEK (dinner) – Carte 325/750 SEK
• Swedish • Bistro •
Set in a residential area close to Djurgårdsbron Bridge; a favourite with the
locals. Bistro-style interior with wood-panelling and marble-topped tables. Sim-
ple, unpretentious cooking features Swedish classics and a 'dish of the day'.

X **Prinsen**

Mäster Samuelsgatan 4 ⊠ 111 44 – ⓜ Östermalmstorg Plan: **C2**
– ⓒ (08) 611 13 31 – www.restaurangprinsen.se – Closed 24-25 December
and midsummer
Carte 433/729 SEK – *(booking essential)*
• Traditional • Brasserie • Retro •
Characterful and bustling bistro-style eatery with a large basement bar and a
private dining room. Since opening in 1897, it's been frequented by literary
and artistic figures. Menus mix French, Swedish and Mediterranean influences.

X **B.A.R.** [AC]

Blasieholmsgatan 4A ⊠ 111 48 – Ⓜ Kungsträdgården — Plan: **C2**
– ℰ (08) 611 53 35 – www.restaurangbar.se – Closed Christmas-New Year, lunch 4 weeks July-August and lunch Saturday-Sunday
Carte 212/595 SEK
• Fish and seafood • Brasserie • Trendy •

Spacious, canteen-style restaurant with an industrial feel. Wide-ranging menu changes with each season and offers some interesting side dishes. For the daily specials, head to the counter and select your meat or fish from the ice display.

X **EAT** 🛖 �

ⓐ *Jakobsbergsgatan 15 ⊠ 111 44 – Ⓜ Hötorget – ℰ (08)* — Plan: **B2**
50920300 – www.eatrestaurant.se – Closed 4 weeks July-August, 1 week Christmas and Sunday
Menu 210/435 SEK – Carte 235/555 SEK – *(bookings advisable at dinner)*
• Asian • Brasserie • Fashionable •

Pass the EAT 'Market' fast food outlet in this upmarket shopping mall and head for the slick Oriental 'Bistro' with its rich, moody colour scheme and central cocktail bar. The name stands for 'European Asian Taste' and the Chinese dishes are flavoursome, well-executed and designed for sharing.

X **Boqueria** 🛖 ⅆ

Jakobsbergsgatan 17 ⊠ 111 44 – Ⓜ Hötorget – ℰ (08) — Plan: **B2**
307400 – www.boqueria.se – Closed midsummer and 24 December
Carte 370/940 SEK
• Spanish • Tapas bar • Fashionable •

Vibrant, bustling tapas bar with high-level seating, located in a smart shopping mall. Appealing menus offer a range of authentic Spanish dishes and tapas specials. Sangria and pintxos can be enjoyed in their downstairs outlet.

X **Speceriet** [AC]

Artillerigatan 14 ⊠ 114 51 – Ⓜ Östermalmstorg — Plan: **C2**
– ℰ (08) 662 30 60 – www.speceriet.se – Closed Christmas, 31 December, Sunday and lunch Monday
Carte 265/460 SEK – *(bookings not accepted)*
• Classic/traditional • Simple •

From the Gastrologik boys comes this little addendum: just three communal tables and a simple menu – you pay at the counter. At lunch select one of three main courses, which are also available as takeout; at night there's more choice.

X **Råkultur** [AC] ⇔

Kungstensgatan 2 ⊠ 114 25 – Ⓜ Tekniska Högskolan — Plan: **B1**
– ℰ (08) 696 23 25 – www.rakultur.se – Closed Christmas, Easter, midsummer and Sunday
Menu 420 SEK – Carte 207/575 SEK
• Japanese • Trendy •

In the same building and run by the same team as Esperanto. The name means 'raw culture' and the menu reflects this, focusing on sushi, sashimi and maki in the evening, along with contemporary Japanese and Swedish recipes.

X **Gro**

Sankt Eriksgatan 67 (via Odengatan on Sankt Eriksgatan just before bridge A1) ⊠ 113 32 – Ⓜ Sankt Eriksplan – ℰ (08) 643 42 22
– www.grorestaurang.se – Closed July, December 23-mid January, Easter, Sunday and Monday
Menu 500 SEK – Carte 440/565 SEK – *(dinner only)*
• Modern • Simple • Friendly •

Formerly a butcher's shop, this is now a simple, relaxed little eatery. Cooking is the chef-owners' take on Swedish classics and uses both traditional and modern techniques; local ingredients, particularly vegetables, play a key role.

Rolfs Kök

Tegnérgatan 41 ⊠ 111 61 – ⓜ Rådmansgatan   Plan: **B1**
– ℰ (08) 10 16 96 – www.rolfskok.se – Closed July, 24-25 December,
midsummer and lunch Saturday-Sunday
Menu 139 SEK (weekday lunch) – Carte 285/660 SEK – *(booking essential)*
• Modern • Bistro • Rustic •

Popular, buzzy restaurant in a lively commercial district, run by a passionate chef-owner. The contemporary interior was designed by famous Swedish artists. Sit at the counter to watch the chefs in action. Dishes include homely Swedish classics and blackboard specials; every dish has a wine match.

Zink Grill

Biblioteksgatan 5 ⊠ 111 46 – ⓜ Östermalmstorg   Plan: **C2**
– ℰ (08) 611 42 22 – www.zinkgrill.se – Closed Christmas and midsummer
Carte 327/633 SEK
• French • Bistro • Traditional •
This lively, late night bistro is one of Stockholm's oldest restaurants and the purchase of its French zinc bar – dating from 1933 – is how it all began. The Gallic and Italian inspired menu features lots of charcuterie and grills.

Smak

Oxtorgsgatan 14 ⊠ 104 35 – ⓜ Hötorget – ℰ (08)   Plan: **B2**
22 09 52 – www.restaurangentm.com – Closed Christmas, Saturday lunch
and Sunday
Menu 275/400 SEK – *(booking essential)*
• Innovative • Trendy •
Hanging brass lamps and tapestries decorate this large, contemporary restaurant. Express-style light lunches; interesting dinners consist of innovative tasting plates with Asian influences; choose 3, 5 or 7 dishes by 'flavour'.

Bon Bon

Kungstensgatan 9 ⊠ 114 25 – ⓜ Rådmansgatan   Plan: **B1**
– ℰ (08) 20 17 10 – www.restaurangbonbon.se – Closed July, Easter,
Christmas, New Year and Sunday
Carte 220/440 SEK – *(dinner only) (booking advisable)*
• Modern • Simple • Neighbourhood •
Lively, split-level restaurant with a large open kitchen and bar; simply furnished in a modern Scandic style. There's no menu – instead a repertoire of tapas-sized dishes are brought round for you to accept or decline. Go in a group.

Lisa Elmqvist

Östermalmstorg ⊠ 114 39 – ⓜ Östermalmstorg   Plan: **C1**
– ℰ (08) 553 40410 – www.lisaelmqvist.se – Closed Christmas,
midsummer, Sunday and bank holidays
Carte 317/1440 SEK – *(lunch only)*
• Fish and seafood • Minimalist •
While the original 19C market hall is being restored, this established family-run restaurant is operating from the temporary marketplace next door. Top quality seafood from the day's catch features in unfussy, satisfying combinations.

AT GAMLA STAN (OLD STOCKHOLM)   PLAN II

Scandic Gamla Stan

Lilla Nygatan 25 ⊠ 111 28 – ⓜ Gamla Stan   Plan: **F1**
– ℰ (08) 723 72 50 – www.scandichotels.se
52 rm ⊊ – ♥845/1908 SEK ♥♥1424/2108 SEK – 1 suite
• Townhouse • Historic • Cosy •
A historic townhouse dating from the 17C, located on a cobbled street in the heart of the Old Town. Bedrooms are cosy and decorated in a traditional Swedish style; bathrooms are modern. The roof terrace offers great city views.

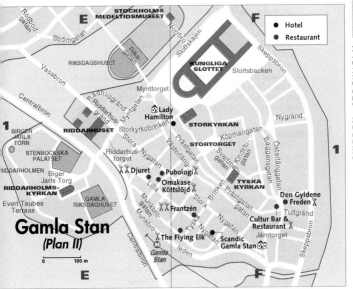

Gamla Stan
(Plan II)

|——————| 100 m
0

🏠 **Lady Hamilton**   🕸 ⚱

Storkyrkobrinken 5 ✉ *111 28* – Ⓜ *Gamla Stan* – ✆ *(08)*   Plan: F1
506 401 00 – www.ladyhamiltonhotel.se
34 rm ⌷ – 🛏1150/2850 SEK 🛏🛏1650/3450 SEK
· Historic · Cosy ·

This 15C building stands in a hugely characterful part of the Old Town. Inside it's packed with antiques and nautical curios, including a figurehead in reception. The sauna is in a vaulted cellar and the plunge pool is in an old well.

XX **Frantzén** (Björn Frantzén)   ✧

❀❀ *Lilla Nygatan 21* ✉ *111 28* – Ⓜ *Gamla Stan* – ✆ *(08)*   Plan: F1
20 85 80 – www.restaurantfrantzen.com – Closed mid July-mid August, 21 December-7 January, Easter, Sunday and Monday
Menu 2300 SEK – *(dinner only) (booking essential) (set menu only)*
· Innovative · Romantic · Fashionable ·

You'll be welcomed into this intimate restaurant by name and seated alongside just 22 other guests. A large counter dominates the room – to really immerse yourself in the preparation process, sit at the bar. The set menu features top quality produce from around the world in some interesting combinations and each new dish is carefully developed in the test kitchen.
➔ Deep-fried langoustine with crispy rice. Kagoshima beef with toasted hay oil. Smoked ice cream with date toffee and hazelnut.

XX **Djuret**   🎋

Lilla Nygatan 5 ✉ *111 28* – Ⓜ *Gamla Stan* – ✆ *(08)*   Plan: E1
506 400 84 – www.djuret.se – Closed midsummer to mid-August, Christmas, New Year and Sunday
Menu 595/750 SEK – *(dinner only and Friday lunch) (booking essential)*
· Meats and grills · Rustic · Neighbourhood ·

It's all about meat here at Djuret. A different beast features on the menu every two weeks – maybe wild boar or reindeer – and there's an excellent selection of wines to accompany. Dine in the 'Meat' room or the 'Trophy' room.

X
🐸
Den Gyldene Freden

Österlånggatan 51 ✉ *10317* – ⓜ *Gamla Stan* – ☎ *(08)*   Plan: **F1**
24 97 60 – *www.gyldenefreden.se* – *Closed Sunday*
Menu 320 SEK (weekdays)/450 SEK – Carte 405/775 SEK – *(booking essential)*
• Traditional • Rustic • Inn •
Dating back to 1722 and reputedly the city's oldest restaurant. The Swedish Academy – who award the Nobel Prize for literature – meet here weekly. Two rustic, café style, candle-filled dining rooms. Good choice of refined Swedish dishes with modern influences, accompanied by a thoughtfully compiled wine list.

X
Pubologi

Stora Nygatan 20 ✉ *111 27* – ⓜ *Gamla Stan* – ☎ *(08)*   Plan: **E1**
506 400 86 – *www.pubologi.se* – *Closed July, Christmas and Sunday*
Menu 495/895 SEK – *(dinner only) (booking advisable)*
• Innovative • Individual • Rustic •
A modern wine-orientated bistro, with one long, communal table and several smaller ones. Cooking is quite elaborate with some original combinations and good use is made of the chargrill. Choose from 5, 6 or 7 courses.

X
The Flying Elk

Mälartorget 15 ✉ *111 27* – ⓜ *Gamla Stan* – ☎ *(08)*   Plan: **F1**
20 85 83 – *www.theflyingelk.se* – *Closed 24 and 31 December and midsummer*
Carte 440/705 SEK – *(dinner only and lunch Saturday and Sunday)*
• Traditional • Inn • Neighbourhood •
A good night out is guaranteed at this lively corner spot, which is modelled on a British pub and features several different bars. Menus offer plenty of choice, with bar snacks, a tasting menu and Scandinavian-style pub dishes with a twist.

X
Cultur Bar & Restaurant

Österlånggatan 34 ✉ *103 17* – ⓜ *Gamla Stan* – ☎ *(08)*   Plan: **F1**
22 66 66 – *www.culturbar.se* – *Closed 24-27 and 31 December, 1-2 January, Easter, midsummer and Sunday*
Menu 135 SEK (weekday lunch) – Carte 150/450 SEK
• Mediterranean • Tapas bar • Simple •
Its Moorish-style tiling is accentuated by the black colour scheme and the terrace is great for people-watching. It comes alive at night when tapas with wide-ranging Mediterranean influences is served. Weekday lunch is more limited.

X
Omakase Köttslöjd

Yxsmedsgränd 12 ✉ *111 28* – ⓜ *Gamla Stan* – ☎ *(08)*   Plan: **E1**
506 400 80 – *www.omakasekottslojd.se* – *Closed July, 2 weeks Christmas and Sunday-Tuesday*
Menu 995 SEK – *(dinner only) (booking essential) (set menu only)*
• Swedish • Cosy • Trendy •
There's plenty of interaction between the chefs and the diners at this small restaurant, which seats 15. The chefs pick up to 20 dishes to serve and cooking is an unusual cross between Japanese sushi and home-cured Swedish charcuterie.

AT DJURGÅRDEN   PLAN I

🏠
Pop House

Djurgårdsvägen 68 ✉ *115 21* – ☎ *(08) 502 541 40*   Plan: **D2**
– *www.pophousehotel.se*
49 rm ⌂ – †1200/2500 SEK ††1400/2700 SEK – 3 suites
• Holiday hotel • Functional •
This simply furnished hotel is ideally placed for visitors to the parks and museums of Djurgården. It's also handily located in the same building as ABBA The Museum and the Swedish Music Hall of Fame. Most of the bedrooms have balconies with pleasant views. The small lounge, bar and restaurant are open-plan.

XX
❀❀ **Oaxen Krog** (Magnus Ek)

Plan: **D3**

Beckholmsvägen 26 (off Djurgårdsvägen) ✉ *115 21*
– ℰ (08) 551 531 05 – www.oaxen.com – Closed Sunday and Monday
Menu 1650/1950 SEK – *(dinner only) (booking essential)*
• Innovative • Design • Friendly •

This rebuilt boat shed sits in a delightful waterside location. Diners are led through a secret door in Oaxen Slip into an oak-furnished room with a natural, slightly nautical feel. Choose 6 or 10 courses of 'New Nordic' cuisine: beautifully constructed dishes are allied to nature and the seasons – they're delicate and balanced but also offer real depth of flavour.
➜ Trout with chive cream and hemp seed mayonnaise. Cod jaw and smoked lard with grilled salad. Strawberry sorbet in salted toffee with elderberry cream.

XX
🏵 **Ulla Winbladh**

Plan: **D2**

Rosendalsvägen 8 ✉ *115 21 – ℰ (08) 534 897 01*
– www.ullawinbladh.se – Closed 24-25 December
Carte 278/755 SEK – *(booking essential)*
• Swedish • Classic • Cosy •

Ulla Winbladh was originally built as a steam bakery for the 1897 Stockholm World Fair and is set in charming parkland beside the Skansen open-air museum. Sit on the terrace or in the older, more characterful part of the building. Traditional, hearty Swedish dishes include sweet and sour herring and fish roe.

X
🏵 **Oaxen Slip**

Plan: **D3**

Beckholmsvägen 26 (off Djurgårdsvägen) ✉ *115 21*
– ℰ (08) 551 53105 – www.oaxen.com – Closed Christmas
Carte 340/625 SEK
• Traditional • Bistro •

A bright, bustling bistro next to the old slipway; try for a spot on the delightful terrace. Light floods the room and boats hang from the girders in a nod to the local shipbuilding industry. The food is wholesome and heartening and features plenty of seafood – whole fish dishes are a speciality.

AT SKEPPSHOLMEN

PLAN I

🏠 **Skeppsholmen**

Plan: **D2**

Grona Gången 1 ✉ *111 86 – ℰ (08) 407 23 00*
– www.hotelskeppsholmen.se
81 rm 🖵 – ♥1495/2995 SEK ♥♥1495/2995 SEK – 1 suite
• Historic • Design • Stylish •

This 17C hotel is perfect for a peaceful stay close to the city. It's set on a small island beside a beautiful park and was built by the king in 1699 for his soldiers (the conference room was once the officers' mess). White bedrooms have a minimalist style and sea or park views. Menus feature Swedish recipes.

AT SÖDERMALM

PLAN I

🏠 **Rival**

Plan: **B3**

Mariatorget 3 ✉ *118 91 – Ⓜ Mariatorget – ℰ (08)*
545 789 00 – www.rival.se
99 rm – ♥1295/3795 SEK ♥♥1495/3995 SEK – 🖵 175 SEK – 2 suites
• Business • Stylish •

The location is delightful: opposite a beautiful square with gardens and a fountain. It's owned by ABBA's Benny Andersson and the stylish bedrooms come with Swedish movie themes and murals of famous scenes. The 700-seater art deco theatre hosts events and shows. Dine on global dishes either in the bistro or on the balcony; the café-bakery is popular for snacks.

SWEDEN - STOCKHOLM

Ⅹ Nook

Åsögatan 176 ✉ *116 32* – 🅜 *Medborgarplatsen*   Plan: **D3**
– ☎ *(08) 702 1222* – *www.nookrestaurang.se* – *Closed July, Sunday and Monday*
Menu 350/500 SEK – *(dinner only) (booking advisable)*
• Modern • Intimate • Friendly •

This modern restaurant offers great value. Drop in for Asian-influenced snacks in the bar or head through to the intimately lit dining room with its checkerboard floor for one of two set menus. Creative cooking blends Swedish ingredients with Korean influences; order 3 days ahead for the suckling pig feast.

Ⅹ Häktet

Hornsgatan 82 ✉ *118 21* – 🅜 *Zinkensdamm* – ☎ *(08)*   Plan: **B3**
84 59 10 – *www.haktet.se*
– *Closed Christmas, midsummer and Sunday*
Menu 390/450 SEK – Carte 390/570 SEK – *(dinner only)*
• Modern • Bistro • Simple •

From 1781-1872 this was a debtors' prison. It has a characterful courtyard terrace and three bars – one in the style of a speakeasy, with a secret door. The simple bistro at the back serves classic Swedish recipes with a modern edge.

AT ARLANDA AIRPORT Northwest : 40 km by Sveavägen and E 4

🏨 Clarion H. Arlanda Airport

Tornvägen 2, Sky City (at Terminals 4-5, 1st floor above street level)
✉ *190 45* – ☎ *(08) 444 18 00* – *www.choice.se/clarion/arlandaairport.se*
414 rm ☲ – †1180/2680 SEK ††1380/2880 SEK – 13 suites
• Business • Conference hotel • Modern •

A sleek, corporate hotel next to Terminals 4 and 5, with sound eco-credentials – they even make honey from their own hives. Relax in the large 'living room' style lounge area or in the outside pool, then have dinner in the bistro which offers a mix of international and Swedish dishes along with runway views.

🏨 Radisson Blu Sky City

Sky City (at Terminals 4-5, 2nd floor above street level) ✉ *190 45* – ☎ *(08) 50 67 4000* – *www.radissonblu.com/skycityhotel-arlanda*
260 rm – †1356/2895 SEK ††1356/2895 SEK – ☲ 165 SEK – 1 suite
• Modern • Functional •

This comfy business hotel enjoys a unique location, looking out over the atrium of the terminal as well as the runway. Well-soundproofed bedrooms come in three different styles; go for 'Business Class' for more space and amenities. The restaurant serves a blend of Swedish classics and more global dishes.

ENVIRONS OF STOCKHOLM

AT NORRTULL North : 2 km by Sveavägen (at beginning of E4)

🏨 Stallmästaregården

Nortull ✉ *113 47* – 🅜 *Karlberg* – ☎ *(08) 610 13 00*
– *www.stallmastaregarden.se* – *Closed 24-30 December*
49 rm ☲ – †1095/2395 SEK ††1095/2395 SEK – 3 suites
• Inn • Cosy •

Enjoy beautiful views over the water to the Royal Park from this brightly painted inn, which dates from the 17C. It comprises several buildings set around a garden courtyard. Cosy bedrooms have a classic style and Oriental touches. Modern Swedish cuisine is influenced by classic Tore Wretman recipes.

AT **LADUGÅRDSGÄRDET** East : 3 km by Strandvägen

 Villa Källhagen ⇧ ⊛ ⩽ 🛏 🐎 AC 🛁 🅿

Djurgårdsbrunnsvägen 10 ⊠ *115 27 –* ℰ *(08) 665 03 00*
– www.kallhagen.se
36 rm ☲ – **†**1195/2795 SEK **††**1395/2995 SEK – 3 suites
• Inn • Business • Modern •

This well-run hotel is a popular place for functions, but with its idyllic waterside
location, it's a hit with leisure guests too. Bedrooms feature four different colour
schemes – inspired by the seasons – and have park or water views. The modern
Swedish menu has a classic edge and comes with wine pairings.

AT **FJÄDERHOLMARNA ISLAND** East: 25 minutes by boat from Södermalm,
or 5 minutes from Nacka Strand

XX **Fjäderholmarnas Krog** ⩽ 🍴 ⛱

Stora Fjäderholmen ⊠ *111 15 –* ℰ *(08) 718 33 55*
– www.fjaderholmarnaskrog.se – Closed 14 November-10 April except
23 November-22 December and restricted opening 9 September-
13 November
Carte 445/725 SEK *– (booking essential)*
• Fish and seafood • Friendly • Rustic •

The location is idyllic and on a sunny day nothing beats a spot on the terrace
watching the ships glide through the archipelago. The airy interior has a boat-
house feel. Classic seafood dishes are replaced by a buffet table at Christmas.

AT **HAMMARBY SJÖSTAD** Southeast : 6,5 km by Centralbron,
Söderledstunnel, Skansbron and Hammarby allé

X **Nya Carnegiebryggeriet** ⩽ ⛱ AC ⇄

Ljusslingan 17 ⊠ *120 64 –* ⓜ *Gullmarsplan –* ℰ *(08) 51 06 50 82*
– www.nyacarnegiebryggeriet.se – Closed Christmas-early January, Easter,
midsummer, Sunday and Monday
Carte 375/575 SEK *– (bookings advisable at dinner)*
• Modern • Bistro • Retro •

The 'New Carnegie Brewery' sits within an impressive 1930s light bulb factory
with thick windows and reinforced beams. Modern interpretations of Nordic
dishes come with beer pairings. Snacks are served in the bar and on the terrace.

AT **NACKA STRAND** Southeast : 10 km by Stadsgården or 20 mins by boat
from Nybrokajen

🏨 **Hotel J** ⇧ ⊛ ⩽ 🛏 AC 🛁 🅿

Ellensviksvägen 1 ⊠ *131 28 –* ℰ *(08) 601 30 00 – www.hotelj.com*
158 rm ☲ – **†**1390/2990 SEK **††**1390/2990 SEK – 4 suites
• Historic • Design •

This was once a summer house belonging to a local politician and a relaxed
atmosphere still pervades. Maritime knick-knacks feature in the charming
guest areas and bedrooms have a quirky New England style; many overlook
the water.
Restaurant J – See restaurant listing

X **Restaurant J** – Hotel J ⩽ 🍴

Ellensviksvägen 1 ⊠ *131 28 –* ℰ *(08) 601 30 25 – www.hotelj.com*
– Closed 25-30 December and 1-10 January
Carte dinner 360/705 SEK
• Swedish • Brasserie •

A short stroll along the waterfront from Hotel J is its long, narrow restaurant.
Huge windows and a lovely terrace make the most of the marina setting (it's
just 20min from the city by boat). Swedish dishes mix with global fare.

SWEDEN - STOCKHOLM

AT LILLA ESSINGEN   West : 5.5 km by Norr Mälarstrand

XX   **Lux Dag för Dag**
Primusgatan 116 ✉ 112 67 – ℰ (08) 619 01 90 – www.luxdagfordag.se
– Closed 4 weeks July-August, Christmas-New Year and Sunday-Monday
Carte 257/645 SEK
• Modern • Brasserie • Neighbourhood •
Bright, modern, brasserie-style restaurant in an old waterside Electrolux factory dating back to 1916. Generously proportioned dishes might look modern but they have a traditional base; sourcing ingredients locally is paramount.

AT BOCKHOLMEN ISLAND   Northwest : 7 km by Sveavägen and E18

XX   **Bockholmen**
Bockholmsvägen ✉ 170 78 – ⓜ Bergshamra – ℰ (08) 624 22 00
– www.bockholmen.com – Closed 20 December-6 January,
midsummer and lunch October-April
Menu 355/655 SEK – Carte 465/599 SEK – *(booking essential)*
• Swedish • Friendly • Cosy •
With charming terraces leading down to the water and an outside bar, this 19C summer house is the perfect place to relax on a summer's day. It's set on a tiny island, so opening times vary. Wide-ranging menus include weekend brunch.

AT EDSVICKEN   Northwest : 8 km by Sveavägen and E 18 towards Norrtälje

XX   **Ulriksdals Wärdshus**
Ulriksdals Slottspark (take first junction for Ulriksdals Slott) ✉ 170 79
– ⓜ Bergshamra – ℰ (08) 85 08 15 – www.ulriksdalswardshus.se
– Closed Monday dinner
Menu 285 SEK (weekday lunch)/485 SEK – Carte 450/745 SEK – *(booking essential)*
• Traditional • Inn •
A charming 19C wooden inn located in the park, with traditional winter garden styling and a lovely wine cellar. Classic Swedish dishes are supplemented by a smörgåsbord at lunch. Start with drinks on the terrace overlooking the lake.

GOTHENBURG
GÖTEBORG

Population: 543 000

Kjell Holmner/Göteborg & Co/www.imagebank.sweden.se

Gothenburg is considered to be one of Sweden's friendliest towns, a throwback to its days as a leading trading centre. This is a compact, pretty city whose roots go back four hundred years. It has trams, broad avenues and canals and its centre is boisterous but never feels tourist heavy or overcrowded. Gothenburgers take life at a more leisurely pace than their Stockholm cousins over on the east coast. The mighty shipyards that once dominated the shoreline are now quiet; go to the centre, though, and you find the good-time ambience of Avenyn, a vivacious thoroughfare full of places in which to shop, eat and drink. But for those still itching for a feel of the heavy industry that once defined the place, there's a Volvo museum sparkling with chrome and shiny steel.

The Old Town is the historic heart of the city: its tight grid of streets has grand façades and a fascinating waterfront. Just west is the Vasastan quarter, full of fine National Romantic buildings. Further west again is Haga, an old working-class district which has been gentrified, its cobbled streets sprawling with trendy cafes and boutiques. Adjacent to Haga is the district of Linné, a vibrant area with its elegantly tall 19th century Dutch-inspired buildings. As this is a maritime town, down along the quayside is as good a place to get your bearings as any.

GOTHENBURG IN...

➜ ONE DAY
The Old Town, Stadsmuseum, The Museum of World Culture.

➜ TWO DAYS
Liseberg amusement park, The Maritiman, Art Museum, a stroll around Linné.

➜ THREE DAYS
A trip on a Paddan boat, a visit to the Opera House.

ARRIVAL-DEPARTURE

 Landvetter Airport is 25km east of the city. There are regular bus connections to the city centre, including FlyBussarna; payment is by card only and journey time is around 25min.

 City Airport is 15km northwest.

GETTING AROUND

The Gothenburg Card gives you unlimited bus, tram and boat travel within the city and is valid for one or two days. It will also guarantee you a sightseeing tour, admission to the Liseberg amusement park, entry to most museums, and discounts in certain shops. Alternatively, buy a 24 or 72 hour credit card style travel pass for unlimited travel on trams, buses and boats. Single tickets are also available. Punts – flat Paddan boats – are a pleasant way to explore this maritime city in summer, gliding past stately canalside buildings.

CALENDAR HIGHLIGHTS

January
International Film Festival.

April
International Science Festival.

June
Match Cup (Sailing),
Midsummer's Eve Celebrations.

July
Gothia Cup (Youth Football).

August
Jazz Festival, Culture Festival.

October
Kulturnatta (Culture Night).

December
Liseberg Christmas Market.

EATING OUT

Gothenburg's oldest food market is called Feskekörka or 'Fish Church'. It does indeed look like a place of worship but its pews are stalls of oysters, prawns and salmon, and where you might expect to find an organ loft, you'll find a restaurant instead. Food – and in particular the piscine variety – is a big reason for visiting Gothenburg. Its restaurants have earned a plethora of Michelin stars, which are dotted all over the compact city. If you're after something a little simpler, head for one of the typical Swedish Konditoris (cafés) – two of the best are Brogyllen and Ahlströms. If you're visiting between December and April, try the traditional cardamom-spiced buns known as 'semla'. The 19C covered food markets, Stora Saluhallen at Kungstorget and Saluhallen Briggen at Nordhemsgatan in Linnestaden, are worth a visit. Also in Kungstorget is the city's most traditional beer hall, Ölhallen 7:an; there are only 6 others in town. Gothenburgers also like the traditional food pairing 'SOS', where herring and cheese are washed down with schnapps.

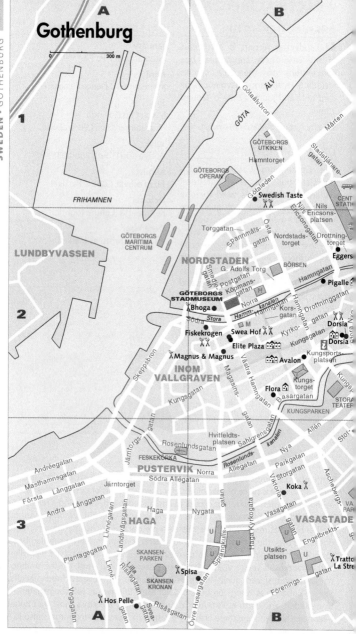

Gothenburg

0   300 m

A

B

1

GÖTA ÄLV

Götaälvbron

Mårten

GÖTEBORGS
UTKIKEN

Stadstjänare-
gatan

Hamntorget

GÖTEBORGS
OPERAN

Götaleden

● **Swedish Taste**
✗✗

FRIHAMNEN

Nils
Ericssons-
platsen

CENT
STATI

Torggatan

GÖTEBORGS
MARITIMA
CENTRUM

Spannmåls-
gatan

Östra

Nordstads-
torget

Nils Ericsonsgatan

Drottning-
torget

LUNDBYVASSEN

NORDSTADEN

BÖRSEN

● **Eggers**

2

G. Adolfs Torg

Smedje-
gatan

Postgatan

Köpmans-
gatan

Hamngatan

● **Pigalle**

**GÖTEBORGS
STADSMUSEUM**

Norra

Hamm-
kanalen

Hamngatan

Drottninggatan

✗**Bhoga** ●

Södra

Stora

Hamngatan

Kors-
gatan

✗✗

Kyrko-

gatan

Dorsia

Drottninggatan

Fiskekrogen ●

● **Swea Hof** ✗✗

Kungsgatan

Dorsia

✗✗
Magnus & Magnus

Elite Plaza

● **Avalon**

Kungsports-
platsen

**INOM
VALLGRAVEN**

Skeppsbron

Magasins-

Västra Hamngatan

Flora

Kungs-
torget

Kungs

Kungsgatan

gatan

Basargatan

KUNGSPARKEN

STORA
TEATER

Hvitfeldts-
platsen

Sahlgrensgatan

Kanalen

Allén

Stor

Rosenlundsgatan

Järntorgs-
gatan

FESKEKÖRKA

Rosenlunds-
Allégatan

Nya

Parkgatan

3

Andréegatan

Masthamnsgatan

Första   Långgatan

Järnvägsgatan

Södra Allégatan

Norra

V. Storgatan

Aschebergs-

● **Koka** ✗

VA
PAR

Andra   Långgatan

Nygata

Viktoria-

gatan

Vasagatan

VASASTADE

HAGA

Haga

Haga Kyrkogata

U

Plantagegatan

Landsvägsgatan

Linné-

SKANSEN-
PARKEN

Sprängkulls-

U

U

Utsikts-
platsen

U

Engelbrekts-

Linné-

Lilla Risåsgatan

✗**Spisa**

SKANSEN
KRONAN

Övre Husargatan

gatan

Föreningsgatan

✗ **Tratto
La Stre**

Vegagatan

✗ **Hos Pelle**

Risåsgatan

Svea-
gatan

A

B

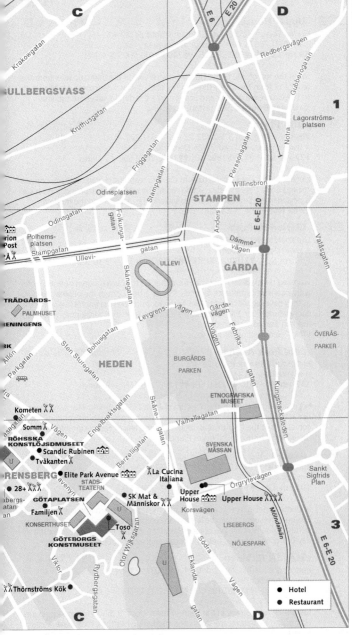

SWEDEN - GOTHENBURG

Upper House   ♨ ≤ ⅄ ⊕ ⋔ ⊒ & AC ▣

Gothia Towers (25th Floor), Mässans Gata 24 ⊠ *402 26*   Plan: **D3**
– ℰ (031) 708 82 00 – www.upperhouse.se
53 rm ⌤ – **♦**1990/5290 SEK **♦♦**2490/5790 SEK – 5 suites
• Conference hotel • Modern •

Set at the top of one of the Gothia Towers; take in the dramatic view from the
terrace or from the lovely three-storey spa. Spacious bedrooms are filled with
top electronic equipment and Scandic art – the duplex suites are sublime.
⊛ **Upper House** – See restaurant listing

Elite Plaza   ♨ ⅄ ⋔ ⊒ ⇌

Västra Hamngatan 3 ⊠ *402 22 – ℰ (031) 720 40 00*   Plan: **B2**
– www.elite.se – Closed 24-26 December
127 rm ⌤ – **♦**1200/1800 SEK **♦♦**1600/2800 SEK – 3 suites
• Luxury • Modern •

Elegant former bank dating back to the 19C, featuring a grand staircase, ornate
ceilings and a Venetian-style sitting room. The team are welcoming and service
is personalised. Bedrooms seamlessly blend the classical and the modern.
Swea Hof – See restaurant listing

Clarion H. Post   ♨ ≤ ⅄ ⊕ ⋔ ⊒ AC ⅍ ⇌

Drottningtorget 10 ⊠ *411 03 – ℰ (031) 61 90 00*   Plan: **C2**
– www.clarionpost.com
500 rm ⌤ – **♦**1180/2580 SEK **♦♦**1280/2880 SEK – 3 suites
• Historic • Business • Modern •

Stunning neoclassical Post Office from the 1920s; now a modern business hotel
with extensive conference facilities. Ask for a bedroom in the original building
as they have higher ceilings. Relax in the rooftop pool, the impressive spa or the
cool ground floor bar. Norda is a slick New York style restaurant; vRÅ offers
modern Japanese cuisine.
vRÅ – See restaurant listing

Elite Park Avenue   ♨ ≤ ⅄ ⊕ ⋔ AC ⅍ ⇌

Kungsportsavenyn 36-38 ⊠ *400 15 – ℰ (031) 727 1000*   Plan: **C3**
– www.elite.se
317 rm ⌤ – **♦**1050/2350 SEK **♦♦**1250/2750 SEK – 9 suites
• Business • Chain hotel • Modern •

Set in a lively location by the Museum of Art, a 1950s building with a stylish interior and spacious, well-equipped bedrooms – the rooftop suites come with balconies. Eat in the English cellar pub; the small Italian eatery-cum-nightclub; or
the informal bistro, which mixes French and Swedish cooking.

Avalon   ♨ ⋔ ⊒ & AC ⅍ ⇌

Kungstorget 9 ⊠ *411 17 – ℰ (031) 751 02 00*   Plan: **B2**
– www.avalonhotel.se
101 rm ⌤ – **♦**1145/2145 SEK **♦♦**1345/2345 SEK – 3 suites
• Business • Modern •

Boutique hotel in a great central location near the shops, harbour and theatres.
Designer bedrooms have the latest mod cons and come with stylish bathrooms;
penthouse suites have balconies. Relax in the rooftop pool then head for the all-
day bistro, which opens onto the piazza and serves international dishes.

Scandic Rubinen   ♨ ⅄ & ⅍

Kungsportsavenyn 24 ⊠ *400 14 – ℰ (031) 751 54 00*   Plan: **C3**
– www.rubybar.se
289 rm ⌤ – **♦**1165/2195 SEK **♦♦**1265/2595 SEK – 3 suites
• Business • Chain hotel • Modern •

Set on the main street, in the heart of town, close to the shops and city sights.
Half of the bedrooms are stylish and modern, while the others have a classic
Scandic style. Relax in the spa or out beside the lovely rooftop bar with some
nibbles or cold meats, then dine overlooking the avenue.

Radisson Blu Riverside

⇧ ≼ 🖪 🕸 ⅙ 🖾 🔬 ⇌

Lindholmspiren 4, Lindholmen Science Park (West: 4 km by Götaälvbron or take free shuttle ferry from Rosenlund 7am-7pm) ✉ 417 56 – ✆ (031) 383 4000 – www.radissonblu.se/riversidehotel-gothenburg.com
265 rm 🖵 – ♦1095/2495 SEK ♦♦1195/2595 SEK – 7 suites
• Business • Modern •

Striking waterfront hotel in the Science Park; a regular shuttle bus operates to the city centre. The rooftop wellness complex has a lovely terrace and hot tub. Some of the modern bedrooms afford great river and city views. The open-plan dining area offers a mix of classical and innovative Swedish cuisine.

Dorsia

⇧ 🖾 🔬

Trädgårdsgatan 6 ✉ 411 08 – ✆ (031) 790 10 00
– www.dorsia.se
Plan: **B2**
37 rm 🖵 – ♦1950 SEK ♦♦2550/6950 SEK
• Townhouse • Family • Art Deco •

Exuberant, eccentric, seductive and possibly a little decadent. This townhouse hotel comes with a theatrical belle époque style, where art from the owner's personal collection, fine fabrics and rich colours add to the joie de vivre. The restaurant is equally vibrant and the atmosphere, suitably relaxed. The Salon serves small plates from Friday-Sunday.
Dorsia – See restaurant listing

Pigalle

⇧

Södra Hamngatan 2A ✉ 411 06 – ✆ (031) 802921
– www.hotelpigalle.se
Plan: **B2**
38 rm 🖵 – ♦1000/2000 SEK ♦♦1400/3000 SEK
• Townhouse • Family • Contemporary •

A top-hatted manager will welcome you to the reception-cum-welcome-bar of this quirky hotel, which is set within the walls of a historic building. The décor is bold and eclectic, with dramatic features and plenty of personality. In the restaurant you can choose to sit at proper tables or on comfy sofas.

Eggers

⇧ 🔬

Drottningtorget ✉ 411 03 – ✆ (031) 333 44 40
– www.hoteleggers.se – Closed 23-28 December
Plan: **B2**
69 rm 🖵 – ♦975/2095 SEK ♦♦1290/2490 SEK
• Traditional • Classic •

Smart 1859 railway hotel that opened with electricity and telephones in every room. The warm, welcoming interior features old wrought iron, stained glass and period furnishings. The characterful restaurant still has its original wallpaper, and offers Swedish classics and international favourites.

Novotel Göteborg

⇧ ≼ 🕸 ⅙ 🔬 🅿

Klippan 1 (Southwest: 3.5 km by Andréeg taking Kiel-Klippan Ö exit, or boat from Rosenlund) ✉ 414 51 – ✆ (031) 720 22 00 – www.novotel.se
151 rm 🖵 – ♦990/1740 SEK ♦♦1090/1840 SEK – 1 suite
• Chain hotel • Business • Functional •

Close to the foot ferry, a converted waterfront brewery where you can still buy some vintage Porter beers. The clean, bright interior affords views of the Göta Älv river. Bedrooms are spacious and have a Scandic style; pay the extra for a water view. The restaurant offers Swedish and international classics.

Flora

Grönsakstorget 2 ✉ 411 17 – ✆ (031) 13 86 16
– www.hotelflora.se – Closed Christmas
Plan: **B2**
65 rm 🖵 – ♦860/1510 SEK ♦♦1190/1890 SEK
• Family • Functional •

This well-located Victorian mid-terrace is nicely run and has a relaxed, funky feel. Bedrooms benefit from high ceilings; ask for one of the newer, designer rooms. The bar-lounge is a popular spot and doubles as a breakfast room.

XxXx ❀ **Upper House** – Upper House Hotel ⌾ ≤ & AC

Gothia Towers (25th Floor), Mässans Gata 24 ✉ *402 26*   Plan: **D3**
– 𝒞 (031) 708 82 00 – www.upperhouse.se – Closed July, Sunday and Monday
Menu 1250 SEK – *(dinner only) (booking essential) (set menu only)*
• Swedish • Elegant • Formal •

Look out from the 25th floor over 360° of twinkling city lights. Start with 'nibbles' in the plush bar then watch your bread being cooked over a hot stone. The set menu offers elaborate, visually pleasing, flavourful dishes made with an abundance of fresh, local ingredients. Service is attentive and professional.

→ Langoustine with fennel and brown butter. Quail with garlic and peas. Strawberries, cream and meringue.

XxX ❀ **Sjömagasinet** (Gustav Trägårdh) ⌾ ≤ 🏠 & ✿ 🅿

Klippans Kulturreservat 5, Adolf Edelsvärds gata 5 (Southwest: 3.5 km by Andréeg taking Kiel-Klippan exit (Stena Line), or boat from Rosenlund. Also evenings and weekends in summer from Lilla Bommens Hamn)
✉ *414 51*
– 𝒞 (031) 775 59 20 – www.sjomagasinet.se
– Closed 24 December-7 January, Saturday lunch and Sunday
Menu 875 SEK (dinner) – Carte 595/1055 SEK – *(booking essential)*
• Swedish • Rustic • Cosy •

An East India Company warehouse dating from 1775; now a charming split-level restaurant with a lovely terrace and harbour views. Seafood is the strength, with classic Swedish dishes on the 'Wagner' menu and modern Nordic choices on the 'Trägårdh' menu. At lunch they offer a buffet and a concise version of the à la carte.

→ Salmon and scallops with ponzu and asparagus. Turbot, lobster béarnaise and almond potatoes. Milk chocolate mousse and dark chocolate sorbet.

XxX ❀ **Thörnströms Kök** (Håkan Thörnström) ⌾ AC ✿

Teknologgatan 3 ✉ *411 32 – 𝒞 (031) 16 20 66*   Plan: **C3**
– www.thornstromskok.com – Closed 4 weeks July-August, 23 December-8 January, Easter and Sunday
Menu 465 SEK – Carte 565/805 SEK – *(dinner only) (booking essential)*
• Classic • Neighbourhood •

An elegant long-standing restaurant with a stunning wine cave; set in a quiet residential area and run by a welcoming, knowledgeable team. There's a good choice of menus, including 3 different tasting options. Precise, confident, classically based cooking uses top quality produce to create pronounced flavours.

→ Quail with duck liver, browned butter and mushrooms. Halibut with tomatoes and oyster broth. Chocolate with Aronia berry meringue and hazelnut crust.

XxX ❀ **28+** (Hans Borén) ⌾ AC ✿

Götabergsgatan 28 ✉ *411 34 – 𝒞 (031) 20 21 61*   Plan: **C3**
– www.28plus.se
– Closed 3 July-24 August, Sunday and bank holidays
Menu 895/995 SEK – Carte 655/715 SEK – *(dinner only)*
• Modern • Formal •

This passionately run basement restaurant has been a Gothenburg institution for over 30 years. The modern cooking showcases prime seasonal ingredients, skilfully blending French and Swedish influences to create intricate, flavourful dishes. There's an exceptional cheese selection and an outstanding wine list.

→ King scallops with warm asparagus mayonnaise. Turbot, ramson gnocchi and elderflower vinegar. Valrhona milk chocolate, liquorice and rhubarb sorbet.

XX ⊗ **SK Mat & Människor** (Stefan Karlsson) &. AC

Plan: **C3**

Johannebergsgatan 24 ⊠ *412 35 – 𝒞 (031) 812 580*
*– www.skmat.se – Closed 8 weeks summer, 2 weeks Christmas, Sunday
and bank holidays.*
Menu 595 SEK – Carte 485/575 SEK – *(dinner only) (booking essential)*
• Swedish • Individual • Cosy •
The main focal point of this cosy restaurant is the completely open kitchen; not
only can you watch the chefs at work but they also deliver your food. The effort
put into sourcing and the reverence with which ingredients are treated is commendable and dishes are exciting and packed with flavour.
→ Langoustine with Jerusalem artichoke. Variations of lamb with roast root
vegetables. Blackcurrant mousse with almond milk sorbet and lemon
meringue.

XX **Dorsia** – Dorsia Hotel ৩ ⌂ AC ⇔

Plan: **B2**

Trädgårdsgatan 6 ⊠ *411 08 – 𝒞 (031) 790 10 00*
– www.dorsia.se – Closed Sunday lunch
Carte 460/845 SEK
• Modern • Exotic • Romantic •
A dramatic hotel dining room split over two levels, with gloriously quirky lighting, striking flower arrangements by the owner and belle époque oil paintings
hanging proudly on the walls. Local fish features highly and puddings are worth
saving room for. Ask for the rare wine book – you'll be impressed!

XX **Fiskekrogen** ৩ AC ⇔

Plan: **B2**

Lilla Torget 1 ⊠ *411 18 – 𝒞 (031) 10 10 05*
*– www.fiskekrogen.se – Closed 4 July-7 August, 22 December-8 January,
midsummer, Easter and Sunday*
Carte 510/815 SEK – *(dinner only)*
• Fish and seafood • Elegant • Cosy •
A charming restaurant in a columned 1920s Grand Café. Top quality seafood
dishes, with extensive buffets Friday early evening and Saturday lunch. 'Bif-
ångst' offers a tasting menu of modern small plates as well as a chef's table.

XX **Swedish Taste** ⇔

Plan: **B1**

Sankt Eriksgatan 6 ⊠ *411 05 – 𝒞 (031) 13 27 80*
*– www.swedishtaste.com – Closed 11 July-8 August, Easter,
Christmas, Saturday lunch and Sunday*
Menu 315/625 SEK – Carte 490/845 SEK
• Modern • Fashionable •
Three-storey venture near the Opera House, consisting of a restaurant, a café, a
deli and a cookery school. Lunch is traditional; more elaborate, contemporary
offerings follow at dinner. Produce is top quality and flavours are authentic.

XX **Kometen** ⌂

Plan: **C2**

Vasagatan 58 ⊠ *411 37 – 𝒞 (031) 137988*
*– www.restaurangkometen.se – Closed midsummer, 23-27 December and
1 January*
Carte 425/705 SEK – *(booking essential)*
• Scandinavian • Family • Neighbourhood •
With its classic façade and its clubby feel, this is the oldest restaurant in town;
opened in 1934, it is now part-owned by celebrated chef, Leif Mannerström.
Sweden's culinary traditions are kept alive here in the generous, tasty dishes.

XX **Swea Hof** – Elite Plaza Hotel AC ⌂

Plan: **B2**

Västra Hamngatan 3 ⊠ *404 22 – 𝒞 (031) 720 40 40*
– www.sweahof.se – Closed 24-26 December
Carte 210/635 SEK
• Modern • Formal •
Striking hotel restaurant in an impressive glass-enclosed courtyard. Start
with drinks in the bar, then head to the spacious dining room. Fresh, modern
cooking combines French and Scandinavian influences; concise business lunches.

SWEDEN - GOTHENBURG

Koka   AC

$\mathbb{X}$
$\mathbb{S}$

Viktoriagatan 12 ✉ *411 25* – ℰ *(031) 701 79 79*   Plan: **B3**
– *www.restaurangkoka.se* – *Closed Christmas, New Year and Sunday*
Menu 480/880 SEK – *(dinner only) (set menu only)*
• Modern • Design • Neighbourhood •

Kock & Vin has been reinvented as Koka, with wooden planks on the floors and walls and wooden furniture to match. Choose 3, 5 or 7 courses from the daily set menu; dishes are light and refreshingly playful in their approach and fish features highly. Well-chosen wines and smooth service complete the picture.
→ Mackerel with salad and seaweed. Pork cheek, beetroot and cherries. Raspberries with walnuts and buttermilk.

$\mathbb{X}$
$\mathbb{S}$

Bhoga (Gustav Knutsson and Niclas Yngvesson)

Norra Hamngatan 10 ✉ *411 14* – ℰ *(031) 13 80 18*   Plan: **B2**
– *www.bhoga.se* – *Closed 20-27 December, Sunday and Monday*
Menu 525/895 SEK – *(dinner only)*
• Innovative • Friendly • Simple •

A chic, contemporary restaurant with an elegant feel, passionately run by two well-travelled chefs and their charmingly attentive team. Top quality seasonal ingredients are used in innovative and imaginative ways, creating provocative yet harmonious texture and flavour combinations. Wine pairings are original.
→ Pickled mackerel, green strawberries and blackcurrant. Turbot with black kale, ramson berries and elderflower. Fennel ice cream, lemon and rosehip.

$\mathbb{X}$
$\textcircled{@}$

Somm $\textcircled{83}$ AC

Lorensbergsgatan 8 ✉ *411 36* – ℰ *(031) 28 28 40*   Plan: **C3**
– *www.somm.se* – *Closed 24-27 December*
Menu 395 SEK – Carte 440/515 SEK – *(dinner only)*
• Modern • Friendly • Cosy •

A simply but warmly decorated neighbourhood bistro, with contemporary artwork and a cosy, friendly feel. Quality seasonal ingredients are used to create tasty modern dishes, with an à la carte and various tasting menus available. The wine list offers great choice and the service is charming and professional.

$\mathbb{X}$
$\textcircled{@}$

Familjen $\textcircled{83}$ ⌂ AC

Arkivgatan 7 ✉ *411 34* – ℰ *(031) 20 79 79*   Plan: **C3**
– *www.restaurangfamiljen.se* – *Closed Christmas, New Year and Sunday*
Menu 355/455 SEK – Carte 334/545 SEK – *(dinner only) (booking essential)*
• Scandinavian • Retro • Design •

A lively, friendly eatery divided into three parts: a bar with bench seating and an open kitchen; a bright red room with a characterful cellar and a glass wine cave; and a superb wrap-around terrace. Cooking is good value and portions are generous; there's an appealing wine, beer and cocktail list too.

$\mathbb{X}$

Toso   AC

Götaplatsen ✉ *412 56* – ℰ *(031) 787 98 00*   Plan: **C3**
– *www.toso.nu* – *Closed 1 week Christmas and bank holidays*
Menu 450 SEK – Carte 352/653 SEK – *(dinner only)*
• Asian • Bistro • Exotic •

There's something for everyone at this modern Asian restaurant, where terracotta warriors stand guard and loud music pumps through the air. Dishes mix Chinese and Japanese influences; start with some of the tempting small plates.

$\mathbb{X}$

Magnus & Magnus   ⌂

Magasinsgatan 8 ✉ *411 18* – ℰ *(031) 13 30 00*   Plan: **B2**
– *www.magnusmagnus.se* – *Closed 24-25 December*
Menu 495 SEK – Carte 585/605 SEK – *(dinner only)*
• Innovative • Intimate • Neighbourhood •

A trendy restaurant with a warm, intimate atmosphere, a central bar, an open kitchen and a bright and well-informed team. Modern Nordic cooking has the occasional Asian twist; most diners plump for the set 4 course menu.

X **Hos Pelle**

Djupedalsgatan 2 ✉ *413 07*   Plan: **A3**
– ℰ (031) 12 10 31 – www.hospelle.com
– Closed 20 June-12 August and Sunday
Menu 215 SEK (weekday lunch)/425 SEK – Carte dinner 255/485 SEK
• Traditional • Neighbourhood •

An established neighbourhood eatery close to the castle; eat in the wine bar or one of the cosy, rustic rooms. Simple bistro selection and a concise set dinner with suggested wine pairings. Cooking is stout, seasonal and satisfying.

X **La Cucina Italiana**

Skånegatan 33 ✉ *412 52*   Plan: **C3**
– ℰ (031) 16 63 07 – www.lacucinaitaliana.nu
– Closed Christmas, Easter, midsummer and Sunday
Menu 399 SEK – Carte 445/675 SEK – *(dinner only) (booking essential)*
• Italian • Friendly •

An intimate and enthusiastically run restaurant consisting of 6 tables. Choose between the à la carte, a 3 course menu and a 6 course surprise tasting 'journey'. The chef-owner regularly travels to Italy to buy cheeses, meats and wine.

X **Tvåkanten**

Kungsportsavenyn 27 ✉ *411 36*   Plan: **C3**
– ℰ (031) 18 21 15 – www.tvakanten.se
– Closed Christmas, Easter, midsummer and bank holidays
Menu 275/470 SEK – Carte 339/615 SEK
• Traditional • Brasserie •

Set in a prime corner position on one of the city's most famous streets. A busy bar leads to a cosy cellar-style dining room. Classical menus range from snacks and brunch to a more ambitious à la carte; there's also a great wine list.

X **Spisa**

Övre Husargatan 3 ✉ *411 22 – ℰ (031) 3860610*   Plan: **B3**
– www.spisamatbar.se
Menu 465 SEK – Carte 305/375 SEK – *(dinner only)*
• Mediterranean • Tapas bar •

Contemporary restaurant set a short walk from the city centre in an up-and-coming area and frequented by a lively, sociable crowd. The menu offers tasty sharing plates with French, Spanish and Italian origins. Try a cocktail too!

X **vRÅ** – Clarion Hotel Post

Drottningtorget 10 ✉ *411 03*   Plan: **C2**
– ℰ (031) 61 90 60 – www.restaurangvra.se
– Closed Sunday, Monday and Friday
Menu 395 SEK – Carte 625/689 SEK – *(dinner only)*
• Japanese • Bistro • Simple •

Modern restaurant in a hotel; run by an attentive, knowledgeable team. Their tagline is 'Swedish ingredients, Japanese flavours' and the produce is top quality. Choose the 8 course set menu or one with 3 core dishes which you add to.

X **Trattoria La Strega**

Aschebergsgatan 23b ✉ *411 25 – ℰ (031) 18 15 01*   Plan: **B3**
– www.trattorialastrega.se
Carte 365/480 SEK – *(dinner only) (booking essential)*
• Italian • Friendly • Bistro •

A lively little trattoria in a quiet residential area; run by a charming owner. Sit at a candlelit table to enjoy authentic, boldly flavoured Italian cooking and well-chosen wines. Signature dishes include pasta with king crab ragout.

771

SWEDEN - GOTHENBURG

AT ERIKSBERG West : 6 km by Götaälvbron and Lundbyleden, or boat from Rosenlund

 Villan

Sjöportsgatan 2 ⊠ *S-417 64 – 𝒞 (31) 725 77 77 – www.hotelvillan.com*
26 rm ⌖ – ▮1100/1600 SEK ▮▮1300/4500 SEK
• Traditional • Modern •

Characterful wood-clad, family-run house; once home to a shipbuilding manager and later floated over to this location. The stylish interior has smart, clean lines. Contemporary bedrooms boast good mod cons – No.31 has a sauna and a TV in the bathroom. The first floor restaurant overlooks the river.

XX **River Restaurant On The Pier**

Dockepiren ⊠ *417 64 – 𝒞 (31) 51 00 00 – www.rivercafe.se*
– Closed 2 weeks January, Christmas, Saturday lunch, Sunday and Monday
Menu 375/575 SEK – Carte 395/795 SEK – *(booking advisable)*
• Modern • Friendly •

Delightful waterfront restaurant overlooking the city and harbour, with a bright, modern ground floor and an elegant upstairs level. Come at lunch for an unfussy set menu or at dinner for a seasonal à la carte of hearty Scandic dishes.

AT LANDVETTER AIRPORT East : 30 km by Rd 40

 Landvetter Airport Hotel

Flygets Hotellväg ⊠ *438 13 – 𝒞 (031) 97 75 50*
– www.landvetterairporthotel.com
186 rm ⌖ – ▮1495 SEK ▮▮1595/1695 SEK – 1 suite
• Business • Modern •

Located just minutes from the airport terminal but in a peaceful setting; unusually, it's family-run. The light, open interior has a calm air and a fresh Scandic style; bedrooms are sleek and modern. The informal restaurant offers a mix of Swedish and global dishes, along with a BBQ and grill menu at dinner.

MALMÖ
MALMÖ

Population: 312 400

Michelin

Malmö was founded in the 13C under Danish rule and it wasn't until 1658 that it entered Swedish possession and subsequently established itself as one of the world's biggest shipyards. The building of the 8km long Oresund Bridge in 2000 reconnected the city with Denmark and a year later, the Turning Torso apartment block was built in the old shipyard district, opening up the city to the waterfront. Once an industrial hub, this 'city of knowledge' has impressively green credentials: buses run on natural gas and there are 400km of bike lanes. There's plenty of green space too; you can picnic in Kungsparken or Slottsparken, sit by the lakes in Pildammsparken or pet the farm animals in 'Folkets'.

At the heart of this vibrant city lie three squares: Gustav Adolfs Torg, Stortorget and Lilla Torg, connected by a pedestrianised shopping street. You'll find some of Malmö's oldest buildings in Lilla Torg, along with bustling open-air brasseries; to the west is Scandinavia's oldest surviving Renaissance castle and its beautiful gardens – and beyond that, the 2km Ribersborg Beach with its open-air baths. North is Gamla Väster with its charming houses and galleries, while south is Davidshall, filled with designer boutiques and chic eateries. Further south is Mollevangstorget, home to a throng of reasonably priced Asian and Middle Eastern shops.

MALMÖ IN...

→ **ONE DAY**
Lilla Torg and the Form/Design Centre, Western Harbour.

→ **TWO DAYS**
Modern Museum, Contemporary Art Exhibition at the Konsthall.

→ **THREE DAYS**
Skt Petri Church, an evening at the Malmö Opera.

PRACTICAL INFORMATION

ARRIVAL-DEPARTURE

 Sweden's Malmö Sturup Airport is 30km east of the city. The airport bus (Flygbussarna) takes 40min to reach the city centre.

 Denmark's Copenhagen Kastrup Airport is 32km northwest of the city. Oresund trains to Malmö Central Station depart every 20min and take 25min.

GETTING AROUND

You must buy your ticket before boarding the bus or train (aside from for the yellow regional buses, where you can pay by card on-board). All ticket machines accept debit/credit cards but very few accept cash. You can buy single, return or 24/72hr tickets; alternatively, purchase a pre-pay reloadable 'jojo' card for a 20% discount on all journeys. Single tickets can also be bought via the Skanetrafiken app and activated upon boarding. 'Around the Sound' tickets offer two days' unlimited travel and discounts for sightseeing, restaurants and hotels. You can complete the circuit in either direction – it includes the train journey over the Oresund Bridge and the ferry crossing from Helsingborg to Helsingor.

CALENDAR HIGHLIGHTS

February
Malmö Games.

March
BUFF Young People's Film Festival.

April
Beer & Whisky Festival, Walpurgis Night.

May
Malmö Garden Show.

June
Sommarscen Malmö (free theatre, concerts and performances).

July
Malmö City Horse Show.

August
Malmö Festival.

September
Malmö Galleries Night, Malmö Chamber Music Festival.

EATING OUT

The gloriously fertile region of Skane puts a wealth of top quality produce on Malmö's doorstep. Dishes rich in dairy and meat – perhaps a little meatier than expected given its waterside proximity – are staple fare and wild herbs and foraged ingredients are the order of the day; wild garlic, asparagus, potatoes and rhubarb are all celebrated here. The locals eat early, so don't be surprised if you're one of just a handful of diners at 1pm or 8pm. The popular social phenomenon 'fika' is a tradition observed by most, preferably several times a day, and involves the drinking of coffee accompanied by something sweet, usually cake or cinnamon buns. Hot meals are popular midday – look out for the great value dagens lunch, which often offers the dish of the day plus salad, bread and water for under 100kr – or for lunch on the run, grab a tunnbrödsrull (sausage and mashed potato in a wrap) from a Korv kiosk. Local delicacies include äggakaka (thick pancakes and bacon), wallenbergare (minced veal patties with mashed potato and peas), marinated herring, eel and goose.

Malmö
(Plan I)

0   400 m

ÖRESUND

Kranplatsen

A

B

Frihamnen

HAMN
PARKEN

Saltimporten-Canteen

Grimsbygatan

Brisgatan

SCANIA
PARKEN

Riggaregatan

Västra

Flaggskeppsgatan

Barometergatan

VARVS
PARKEN

**TURNING
TORSO**

Lilla

Varvsgatan

Varvsgatan

STAPELBÄDDS
PARKEN

Dockan

Kranplan

Marina

Dockgatan

Dockgatan

Isbergs
gata

Hallenborg
gata

Stora

Varvsgatan

Universitetsbron

Hans Michelsensgatan

VÄSTRA HAMNEN

Varvsgatan

Klaffbron

Nordenskiöldsgatan

Inre hamnen

Jörgen
Kocksgatan

Carlsgatan

Rödergatan

Salongsgatan

Västra Varvsgatan

LANKAR
PARKEN

Stora

1

Park Inn
by Radisson Malmö

Södra
Varv-
Bassängen

MALMÖ
CENTRAL

Propellergatan

Västra Skeppsgatan

Norra

Neptunigatan

Neptunigatan

Skeppsbyggaregatan

ÖRESUNDS
PARKEN

Citadellsvägen

Västra hamkanalen

Vallgatan

Centre (Plan II)

Mariedalsvägen

KOMMENDANTHUSET

Malmöhusvägen

Norra

Västergatan

Slottsgatan

Långgårds
gatan

Norra

STORTORGET

MALMÖHUS SLOTT

SLOTTSTRÄDGÅRDEN

GAMLA STADI

Limhamnsvägen

Ola Hanssonsgatan

SLOTTSMÖLLAN

KUNGSPARKEN

**CASINO
COSMOPOL**

GAMLA KYRKOGÅRDEN

Parkkanalen

RIBERSBORG

Tessins väg

Sergels väg

Zollgatan

Kung

Stora
dammen

Lilla
dammen

Södra

Förstadskanal

Kilian

G. Rydbergsgatan

Mariedalsvägen

SLOTTSPARKEN

Ferséns

väg

Regementsgatan

Södra

Drottni
gata

SLOTTSSTADEN

Tessins väg

Erikstorpsgatan

Oscar

väg

Mrs Brown

Storga

Regementsgatan

Carl

Regementsgatan

HÄSTHAGEN

Dahlbergsgatan

väg

Atmosfär

B.A.R.

Davidshallsgatan

Södra Förstadsgatan

LUGNE

Lugne
gatan

Berga
gatan

Lundbergsgatan

Kristinelundsvägen

Erik

**HELGEANDS
KYRKAN**

VÅR FRÄLSARES
KYRKA

Östra

Rönneholmsvägen

OPERA

Pildammsvägen

**SÖDR
FÖRSTAD**

2

RÖNNEHOLMS

Fågelbacksgatan

Västra

Gustafs

FÅGELBACKEN

Rönneholmsvägen

ADVENTKYRKAN

väg

KONSTHALL

Friisg

RÖNNEHOLM

**ST JOHANNES
KYRKA**

PARKEN

**MALMÖ
IDROTTSPLATS**

TRANGELN

Kapellgatan

Köpenhamnsvägen

Korsörvägen

Kronborgs
vägen

Mariedalsvägen

Roskildevägen

Margaretavägen

Kronobergsvägen

Roskildevägen

PILDAMMSPARKEN

Carl

Pildammsvägen

**RÅDMANS
VÄNGEN**

Gustafs

Änglidalavägen

Platevägen

DAMMFRI

Ribevägen

John

Ericssons

KRONOBORG

väg

Roskildevägen

Brittiska

MARGARETA
PAVILJONGEN

PILDAMMARNA

**Bloom
in the Park**

B

UNIVERSITETSSJUKHU
MAS

A

● Hotel
● Restaurant

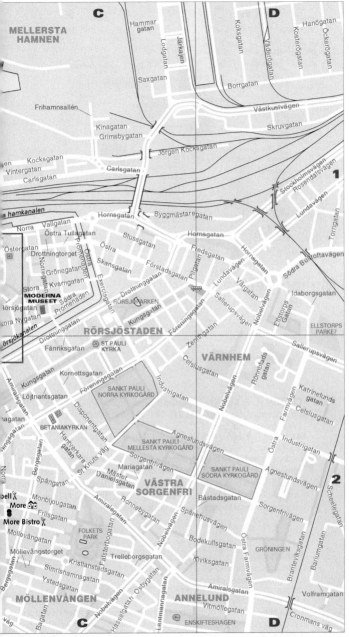

C

D

MELLERSTA
HAMNEN

Hammar
gatan

Järkajen

Lodgatan

Koksgatan

Väderögatan

Hanögatan

Kosterögatan

Öckerögatan

Saxgatan

Borrgatan

Frihamnsallén

Kinagatan

Grimsbygatan

Västkustvägen

Skruvgatan

Jörgen Kocksgatan

Stockholmsvägen

Rosendalsvägen

Kocksgatan

Vintergatan

Carlsgatan

Carlsgatan

1

Lundavägen

a hamkanalen

Norra Vallgatan

Hornsgatan

Byggmästaregatan

Torngatan

Östra Tullgatan

Stussgatan

Hornsgatan

Hornsgatan

Östergatan

Drottningtorget

Promenaden

Östra

Fredsgatan

Lundavägen

Södra Bulltoftavägen

Grönegatan

Östra

Norregatan

Förstadsgatan

Pilgatan

Värgatan

Nobelvägen

Idaborgsgatan

Stora

Kvarngatan

Skansgatan

Drottninggatan

Exercisgatan

RÖRSJÖPARKEN

Sallerupsvägen

Ellstorps Gatan

ELLSTORPS
PARKE?

MODERNA
MUSEET

Södra
Promenaden

Kungsgatan

Föreningsgatan

Rörsjögatan

ora Nygatan

Drottninggatan

RÖRSJÖSTADEN

örsjökanalen

Fänriksgatan

ST PAULI
KYRKA

VÄRNHEM

Sallerupsvägen

Kungsgatan

Kornettsgatan

Celsiusgatan

Rörnblads gatan

Katrinefunds gatan

Amiralsgatan

Löjtnantsgatan

Föreningsgatan

SANKT PAULI
NORRA KYRKOGÅRD

Industrigatan

Nobelvägen

Fariwvägen

Celsiusgatan

nagatan

Disponentgatan

BETANIAKYRKAN

Hantverkare gatan

Agneslundsvägen

Östra Industrigatan

Norra

Bergsgatan

St Knuts väg

SANKT PAULI
MELLESTA KYRKOGÅRD

Sorgenfrivägen

Spångatan

Mäster
Danielsgatan

Mariagatan

VÄSTRA
SORGENFRI

SANKT PAULI
SÖDRA KYRKOGÅRD

Agneslundsvägen

Scheelegatan

2

bell

More

Monbijougatan

Frilsgatan

Ronnebygatan

Amiralsgatan

Båstadsgatan

Spånehusvägen

Sorgenfrivägen

More Bistro

Möllevångsgatan

FOLKETS
PARK

Falsterbogatan

Nobelvägen

Bodekullsgatan

Östra Farmvägen

GRÖNINGEN

Brantevaksgatan

Barumgatan

Möllevångstorget

Kristianstadsgatan

Trelleborgsgatan

Kiviksgatan

Bergsgatan

Simrishamnsgatan

Ystadsgatan

Hasselgatan

Osbygatan

Lantmannagatan

Amiralsgatan

Vitmöllegatan

Volframgatan

MÖLLEVÅNGEN

Bågatan

Nobelvägen

väg

C

ANNELUND

ENSKIFTESHAGEN

Cronmans väg

D

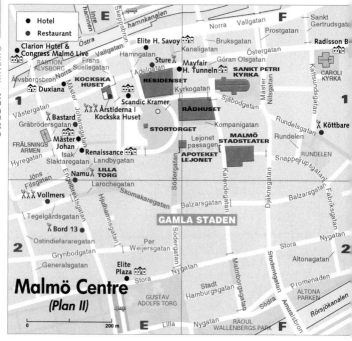

Malmö Centre
(Plan II)

0   200 m

Clarion H. & Congress Malmö Live   余 ≼ ⅙ 斺 ㊅ AC ⅍
Dag Hammarskjölds Torg 2 ✉ *211 18* – *℘ (040) 207500*   🚗
– *www.choicehotels.com*   Plan II : **E1**
444 rm ☲ – 🛉1080/2480 SEK 🛉🛉1180/2780 SEK – 2 suites
• Conference hotel • Modern •
The city's second tallest building affords a superb 360° view of the city; choose a
bedroom on the upper floors for a view of the Oresund Bridge and Denmark.
Kitchen & Table's eclectic menu combines American classics and international
influences; enjoy a cocktail in the adjoining Skybar. The ground floor Eatery
Social is an informal Mexican-themed restaurant and bar.

Renaissance   余 ⅙ 斺 ㊅ AC ⅍ 🚗
Mäster Johansgatan 15 ✉ *211 21* – *℘ (040) 248 500*   Plan II : **E1**
– *www.renaissancemalmo.se*
128 rm ☲ – 🛉895/2395 SEK 🛉🛉895/2395 SEK – 1 suite
• Business • Modern •
A smart hotel on the site of the city's original food market: beamed ceilings and
iron columns bring character to the modern interior. Bright, well-equipped
bedrooms are quiet considering the hotel's location. Spacious, colourful bar
and simply furnished restaurant; modern dishes created with local produce.

Elite Plaza

Gustav Adolfs torg 49 ⊠ 211 39 – 𝒞 (040) 66 44 871
– www.elite.se
Plan II : **E2**

116 rm ⟳ – ♦977/2450 SEK ♦♦1100/2712 SEK – 1 suite
• Business • Chain hotel • Modern •
Behind the wonderful period façade is a smart and up-to-date corporate hotel.
Modern bedrooms are a good size: the best look onto a pretty square; the
quietest look over the inner courtyard. British-themed bar with a pavement
terrace.

Mäster Johan

Mäster Johansgatan 13 ⊠ 211 21 – 𝒞 (040) 664 64 00
– www.masterjohan.com
Plan II : **E1**

68 rm – ♦960/2090 SEK ♦♦1190/2320 SEK – ⟳ 145 SEK – 10 suites
• Business • Modern •
Centrally located hotel, just off the main square, with a relaxed and peaceful air.
Stylish, well-proportioned bedrooms have luxurious touches. Enjoy a locally
sourced organic breakfast under the glass-roofed atrium.

Scandic Kramer

Stortorget 7 ⊠ 211 22 – 𝒞 (040) 693 54 00
– www.scandichotels.com/kramer
Plan II : **E1**

113 rm ⟳ – ♦1000/1700 SEK ♦♦1200/2000 SEK – 1 suite
• Traditional • Chain hotel • Historic •
This grand old dame, built in the 1870s, sits majestically on the main square.
Inside, it has a nostalgic air and an old-fashioned elegance; its charming lobby
replete with marble and stained glass. Half the bedrooms are modern and half
are decorated in a warm classic style. Swedish cooking with a street view.

Radisson Blu

Östergatan 10 ⊠ 211 25 – 𝒞 (040) 698 40 00
– www.radissonblu.com/hotel-malmo
Plan II : **F1**

229 rm ⟳ – ♦990/1875 SEK ♦♦990/1875 SEK – 5 suites
• Chain hotel • Functional •
Set beside the city's newest shopping mall, the Caroli, this smart, friendly hotel
offers some of the most spacious bedrooms in the city: they were originally built
as apartments and the smallest measure 43m² – as an added bonus, many open
out onto a courtyard garden. Traditional Swedish menu in 16C restaurant.

Elite H. Savoy

Norra Vallgatan 62 ⊠ 211 22 – 𝒞 (040) 66 44 800
– www.elite.se
Plan II : **E1**

109 rm ⟳ – ♦977/2450 SEK ♦♦1100/2712 SEK – 3 suites
• Traditional • Classic • Historic •
A grand classic opposite the train station: well run, with an old world elegance.
Bedrooms vary in terms of size and style: some of the top floor front rooms have
far-reaching water views; the quietest look onto the inner courtyard. Watch the
chefs at work in the open kitchen of the Grill restaurant.

More

Norra Skolgatan 24 ⊠ 214 22 – 𝒞 (040) 655 10 00
– www.themorehotel.com
Plan I: **C2**

68 rm ⟳ – ♦695/1545 SEK ♦♦795/1745 SEK
• Townhouse • Modern •
A striking aparthotel converted from a late 19C chocolate factory. The studios
are modern and extremely spacious with kitchenettes, sofa beds and light 'loft
style' living areas. Let on a nightly basis, but ideal for longer stays.
More Bistro – See restaurant listing

SWEDEN - MALMÖ

Duxiana   🕹 Ⓐ🅲

Mäster Johansgatan 1 ✉ *211 21 –* ℰ *(040) 60 77 000*   Plan II : **E1**
– www.hotellinmalmo.com
22 rm – 🛏873/2315 SEK 🛏🛏1130/2315 SEK – ☐ 70 SEK
• Townhouse • Design • Contemporary •

Boutique hotel owned by the Dux bed company, who unusually use part of the lobby to showcase their products! Chic, contemporary bedrooms range from compact singles to elegant junior suites which have a bath in the room.

Mayfair H. Tunneln   🕭 🕹

Adelgatan 4 ✉ *211 22 –* ℰ *(040) 10 16 20*   Plan II : **E1**
– www.mayfairhotel.se
81 rm ☐ – 🛏795/1400 SEK 🛏🛏855/2900 SEK
• Townhouse • Personalised •

An imposing early 18C property steeped in history, with cellars dating back to 1307; enjoy a complimentary coffee in the classical lounge. Bedrooms are spotless and homely; some have a spa bath. Snapphane showcases the latest local, organic ingredients while Malmö Rökeri specialises in smoked produce: both restaurants are overseen by the Vollmer brothers.

Park Inn by Radisson Malmö   🕭 🕹 🕹 🚗

Sjömansgatan 2 ✉ *211 19 –* ℰ *(040) 628 6000*   Plan I : **A1**
– www.parkinn.com/hotel-malmo
231 rm ☐ – 🛏795/1395 SEK 🛏🛏795/1395 SEK
• Chain hotel • Functional • Modern •

A brand new, good value hotel, well-situated in the Western Harbour beside the World Trade Centre and the Västra Hamnen waterfront. Bedrooms are spacious and well-equipped; the business rooms on the higher floors come with robes and boast better views. Easy dining in the bar and grill.

XxX   Vollmers (Mats Vollmer)   Ⓐ🅲 ⇔
❀

Tegelgårdsgatan 5 ✉ *211 33 –* ℰ *(040) 57 97 50*   Plan II : **E2**
– www.vollmers.nu – Closed 3 weeks July, Sunday and bank holidays
Menu 650/950 SEK – *(dinner only) (booking essential) (set menu only)*
• Creative • Elegant • Intimate •

An understatedly elegant restaurant in a pretty 19C townhouse. Here, the eponymous Mats Vollmer showcases some of the area's finest seasonal ingredients in a set menu of intricate and elaborate modern dishes, full of flavour and originality. Choose 4, 6 or 8 courses. Professional service from a charming team.
→ Local tomatoes, marjoram and marrow. Veal with buttermilk and onions. Raspberry with poppy seed fudge and lemon.

XxX   Årstiderna i Kockska Huset   🕭 ⇔

Frans Suellsgatan 3 ✉ *211 22 –* ℰ *(040) 23 09 10*   Plan II : **E1**
– www.arstiderna.se – Closed July, Easter, 24-26 December, Saturday lunch and Sunday
Menu 265/595 SEK – Carte 445/875 SEK
• Traditional • Elegant •

Set in softly lit, vaulted cellars, this elegant, formal restaurant is a city institution. Classic cooking proves a match to its surroundings, with local, seasonal ingredients proudly used to create traditional Swedish dishes.

XX   Bloom in the Park (Titti Qvarnström)   🕭 🕹 Ⓐ🅲
❀

Pildammsvägen 17 ✉ *214 66 –* ℰ *(040) 793 63*   Plan I : **B2**
– www.bloominthepark.se – Closed 24-25 December, Easter and Sunday
Menu 495/695 SEK – *(dinner only) (booking advisable) (surprise menu only)*
• Creative • Design • Individual •

A restaurant with a difference: it has no menu and no wine list – they even make you guess what you are eating! Precisely cooked, boldly flavoured dishes use imaginative and original combinations of top quality ingredients. The pretty lakeside lodge has a cool, ultra-stylish interior and a waterside terrace.
→ Oyster with cucumber, salted lemons and nasturtium. Halibut, cauliflower, walnut and oxalis. Blueberries with mascarpone, lemongrass and hibiscus.

XX **Atmosfär**   ⌂ ⌖ AC ⇔

Fersens väg 4 ✉ 211 42 – ℰ (040) 12 50 77   Plan I: **B2**
– www.atmosfar.com – Closed Christmas, Saturday lunch and Sunday
Menu 125/330 SEK – Carte 295/395 SEK
• Swedish • Neighbourhood •

A formal yet relaxed eatery on the main road; dine at the bar, in the restaurant or on the pavement terrace. The menu consists of small plates, of which three or four should suffice. Fresh Skåne cooking is delivered with a light touch.

X **Ambiance à Vindåkra** (Karim Khouani)   ⌂ ⌖ ⇔ **P**
✿
Vindåkra Gård, Vindåkravägen 3 (South 10.5 km by Trelleborgsvägen E22/
E6) ✉ 218 75 – ℰ (070) 8380472 – www.ambiancerestaurant.se – Closed
2 weeks Christmas, Sunday and Monday
Menu 650 SEK – *(dinner only) (booking essential) (set menu only)*
• French • Friendly • Romantic •

This is a delightful idyll: a romantic 19C farmhouse where beams, candlelight and a lovely log burner mix with modern art and an ultra-stylish open kitchen. It is charmingly run by an experienced chef-owner, and the talented kitchen serve a fixed 5 course menu which offers a blend of French and Scandic dishes, meticulously created using the finest ingredients.
→ Lobster and caviar. Beef cheek with foie gras and truffle. Oxalis, grapefruit and raspberry.

X **Sture**   ⌂ AC
☺
Adelgatan 13 ✉ 211 22 – ℰ (040) 12 12 53   Plan II : **E1**
– www.sture.me – Closed Christmas, Saturday lunch and Sunday
Menu 345/595 SEK – Carte 289/815 SEK
• Traditional • Friendly • Neighbourhood •

A city institution, rejuvenated by the charismatic Anders Vendel. Original features like wood panelling, tall arched windows and an ornate mirrored ceiling add grandeur, while the lively rear area with its open kitchen adds a contemporary edge. Flavourful, carefully prepared Swedish dishes. Friendly service.

X **Bastard**   ⌂ AC
☺
Mäster Johansgatan 11 ✉ 211 21 – ℰ (040) 12 13 18   Plan II : **E1**
– www.bastardrestaurant.se – Closed Christmas, New Year, Easter,
midsummer, Sunday and Monday
Carte 245/355 SEK – *(dinner only) (booking advisable)*
• Modern • Individual • Trendy •

Popular with locals, this is a bustling venue with an edgy, urban vibe. Schoolroom meets old-fashioned butchers style-wise, with vintage wood furniture, tiled walls, moody lighting and an open kitchen. Small plates offer nose-to-tail eating with bold, earthy flavours; start with a Bastard Plank to share.

X **Bord 13**

Engelbrektsg 13 ✉ 211 33 – ℰ (042) 58788   Plan II : **E2**
– www.bord13.se – Closed Christmas, 1 January, Sunday and Monday
Menu 495/645 SEK – *(dinner only) (set menu only)*
• Creative • Wine bar • Individual •

Sister to B.A.R restaurant, is the bright, spacious and stylish 'Table 13', which offers a set 3 or 6 course menu and a diverse selection of biodynamic wines. Original Nordic cooking with some interesting texture and flavour combinations.

X **B.A.R.**   ⌂ ⇔

Erik Dahlbergsgatan 3 ✉ 211 48 – ℰ (040) 17 01 75   Plan I: **B2**
– www.barmalmo.se – Closed Easter, Christmas, Sunday and Monday
Menu 395 SEK – Carte 340/430 SEK – *(dinner only) (booking advisable)*
• Modern • Wine bar • Neighbourhood •

In trendy Davidshall is this lively wine-bar-cum-restaurant named after its owners, Besnick and Robert. The interesting modern menu tends towards the experimental; expect dishes like Jerusalem artichoke ice cream with hazelnut mayo.

X **More Bistro** – More Hotel ⬆ ⛄ &

Norra Skolgatan 24 ✉ *214 22 –* ☎ *(040) 236250*   Plan I: **C2**
– www.themorebistro.com – Closed Saturday lunch, Monday dinner,
Sunday and bank holidays
Menu 95 SEK (lunch) – Carte dinner 245/305 SEK
• Modern • Bistro • Neighbourhood •

A former chocolate factory – now an aparthotel – houses this appealing restaurant with minimalist furnishings, an open kitchen and a pretty terrace. The keen chef showcases seasonal, local produce in modern dishes. Limited lunch menu.

X **Namu** 🔲

Landbygatan 5 ✉ *21134 –* ☎ *(040) 12 14 90*   Plan II : **E1**
– www.namu.nu
Menu 395/595 SEK
• Korean • Friendly • Simple •

Mouth-watering, colourful, zingy food from a past Swedish MasterChef winner blends the authenticity of Korean dishes with a modern Scandinavian touch. Cookbooks line the shelves and friendly service adds to the lively atmosphere.

X **Rebell** ⛄

Friisgatan 8 ✉ *211 46 –* ☎ *(040) 97 97 35*   Plan I: **C2**
– www.restaurantgrebell.se – Closed Christmas, Easter, midsummer and Sunday
Menu 325 SEK (weekday dinner) – Carte 289/444 SEK
• Modern • Trendy • Bistro •

A cool, contemporary bistro with a stark, simple feel, serving vibrant and tasty modern interpretations of local dishes, with ribs the speciality. Surprise set menu called 'The Chef is Always Right'. Locally brewed unfiltered beer.

X **Mrs Brown** ⛄ & 🔲

Storgatan 26 ✉ *211 41 –* ☎ *(040) 97 22 50*   Plan I: **B2**
– www.mrsbrown.nu – Closed 25 December, 1 January and Sunday
Menu 375 SEK – Carte 385/500 SEK *– (dinner only and Saturday lunch)*
• Traditional • Wine bar • Trendy •

This retro brasserie's bar opens at 3pm for drinks and nibbles, while the kitchen opens at 6pm. Make sure you try one of the cocktails! The tasty, unfussy cooking has a modern edge and showcases the region's ingredients.

X **Bistro Stella** ⇔

Linnégatan 25, Limhamn (Southwest: 7 km by Limhamnsvägen: bus 4
from Central station) ✉ *216 12 –* ☎ *(040) 15 60 40 – www.bistrostella.se*
– Closed July, Christmas, New Year, Sunday and Monday
Menu 400 SEK – Carte 335/535 SEK *– (dinner only)*
• Modern • Neighbourhood •

A lively gastropub in a residential area not far from the Oresund Bridge. Its bright, cosy bar sits between two dining rooms and its menu features pub dishes like burgers, fish and chips and charcuterie platters. Tasty rustic cooking.

X **Köttbaren** ⛄ 🔲

Rundelsgatan ✉ *211 26 –* ☎ *(040) 635 89 01*   Plan II : **F1**
– www.kottbaren.se – Closed 15-16 April, 24-25 December, 1 January,
Easter and midsummer
Menu 97/395 SEK – Carte dinner 245/500 SEK
• Meats and grills • Trendy •

A trendy new restaurant in the Caroli shopping centre: also a shop and a deli, where you can order takeaway meals and buy good value, quality Swedish meat. Lunch is a help-yourself buffet; dinner might mean steak, stew or a burger.

X **Saltimporten Canteen** 🅿

Grimsbygatan 24, Hullkajen ✉ *211 20 –* ☎ *(070) 651 8426*   Plan I: **B1**
– www.saltimporten.com – Closed Saturday, Sunday and bank holidays
Menu 95 SEK *– (lunch only) (bookings not accepted)*
• Traditional • Simple • Trendy •

A remote, simply styled dockside canteen, open between 12 and 2pm on weekdays: the place to be for young locals. Queue for the fresh, flavourful dish of the day, eaten at communal tables. No dessert – but great homemade bread.

SWITZERLAND
SUISSE, SCHWEIZ, SVIZZERA

→ **AREA:**
41 285 km² (15 940 sq mi).

→ **CAPITAL:**
Bern (Berne).

→ **POPULATION:**
8 123 880.
Density = 197 per km².

→ **CURRENCY:**
Swiss Franc (CHF).

→ **GOVERNMENT:**
Federation of 26 cantons with 2 assemblies (National Council and Council of State) forming the Federal Assembly.

→ **LANGUAGES:**
German (64% of population), French (20%) and Italian (7%), are spoken in all administrative departments, shops, hotels and restaurants.

→ **PUBLIC HOLIDAYS:**
New Year's Day (1 Jan); Ascension Day (May); Swiss National Day (1 Aug); Christmas Day (25 Dec). All other holidays are decided upon by each canton, the most popular being: St Berchtold's Day (2 Jan); Good Friday (Friday before Easter); Easter Monday (late Mar/Apr); Whit Monday (late May/June); Corpus Christi (late May/June); Assumption of the Virgin Mary (15 Aug); All Saints' Day (1 Nov); Immaculate Conception (8 Dec); St Stephen's Day (26 Dec).

→ **LOCAL TIME:**
GMT+1 hour in winter and GMT +2 hours in summer.

→ **CLIMATE**
Temperate continental, varies with altitude – most of the country has cold winters and warm summers (Bern: January 0°C; July 19°C).

→ **EMERGENCY**
Police ℰ **117**; Medical Assistance ℰ **144**; Fire Brigade ℰ **118**. Anglo-Phone 24hr helpline ℰ **0900 576 444**.
(Dialling **112** within any EU country will redirect your call and contact the emergency services.)

→ **ELECTRICITY:**
230 volts AC, 50Hz; 2 round pin sockets.

→ **FORMALITIES:**
Travellers from the European Union (EU), Iceland and the main countries of North and South America need a national identity card or passport (America: passport required) to visit Switzerland for less than three months (tourism or business purpose). For visitors from other countries a visa may be required, in addition to a passport, especially for those wishing to stay for longer than three months. We advise you to check with your embassy before travelling.

BERN
BERNE

Population: 128 848

N. Parneix/Fotolia.com

To look at Bern, you'd never believe it to be a capital city. Small and beautifully proportioned, it sits sedately on a spur at a point where the River Aare curves gracefully back on itself. The little city is the best preserved medieval centre north of the Alps – a fact recognised by UNESCO when it awarded Bern World Heritage status – and the layout of the streets has barely changed since the Duke of Zahringen chose the superbly defended site to found the city over 800 years ago. Most of the buildings date from between the 14 and 16C – when Bern was at the height of its power – and the cluster of cobbled lanes, surrounded by ornate sandstone arcaded buildings and numerous fountains and wells, give it the feel of a delightfully overgrown village. (Albert Einstein felt so secure here that while ostensibly employed as a clerk in the Bern patent office he managed to find the time to work out his Theory of Relativity.)

BERN IN...

➡ **ONE DAY**
River walk, Old Town (cathedral, clock Tower, arcades), Museum of Fine Arts, cellar fringe theatre.

➡ **TWO DAYS**
Zentrum Paul Klee, Einstein's house, Stadttheater.

➡ **THREE DAYS**
Bern Museum of History, Swiss Alpine Museum, Rose Garden.

The Old Town stretches eastwards over a narrow peninsula, and is surrounded by the arcing River Aare. The eastern limit of the Old Town is the Nydeggbrücke bridge, while the western end is marked out by the Käfigturm tower, once a city gate and prison. On the southern side of the Aare lies the small Kirchenfeld quarter, which houses some impressive museums, while the capital's famous brown bears are back over the river via the Nydeggbrücke.

PRACTICAL INFORMATION

ARRIVAL-DEPARTURE

✈ Bern Belp International Airport is 9km southeast of the city. The shuttle bus leaves every 30min and takes about 20min.

GETTING AROUND

The Bern Card is well worth investing in. It gives unlimited travel, free admission to museums and gardens, and various reductions around the city. It's available from the Tourist Office, museums and hotels, and is valid for 24hr, 48hr or 72hr.

As Bern is small enough to walk around, it requires no more than a super-efficient bus and tram network. A short cable-railway links the Marzili quarter to the Bundeshaus. You can buy your ticket at the bus or tram stop.

EATING OUT

Bern is a great place to sit and enjoy a meal. Pride of place must go to the good range of alfresco venues in the squares of the old town – popular spots to enjoy coffee and cake. Hiding away in the arcades are many delightful dining choices; some of the best for location alone are in vaulted cellars that breathe historic ambience. If you want to feel what a real Swiss restaurant is like, head for a traditional rustic eatery complete with cow-bells and sample the local dishes like the Berner Platte – a heaving plate of hot and cold meats, served with beans and sauerkraut –

CALENDAR HIGHLIGHTS

February
Carnival.

March
Museums Night.

March-May
International Jazz Festival, Bern Grand Prix (Run).

July
Gurtenfestival (rock music).

August-September
Buskers Bern Street Music festival (series of concerts in the old town).

October
Short Film Festival.

November
Onion Market.

or treberwurst, a sausage poached with fermented grape skins. There's no shortage of international restaurants either, and along with Germany, France and Italy also have their country's cuisine well represented here – it's not difficult to go from rösti to risotto. And, of course, there's always cheese – this is the birthplace of raclette - and tempting chocolates waiting in the wings. A fifteen percent service charge is always added but it's customary to round the bill up.

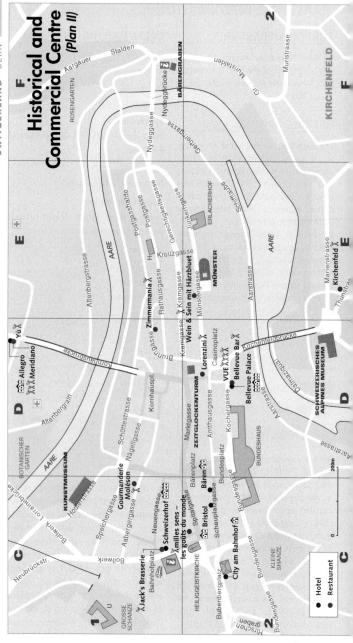

Historical and Commercial Centre
(Plan II)

Bellevue Palace

Kochergasse 3 ⊠ 3000 – ℰ 031 320 45 45
– www.bellevue-palace.ch   Plan: **D2**
128 rm – ♦399/518 CHF ♦♦534/636 CHF – ☲ 40 CHF – 28 suites
• Grand Luxury • Classic •

This exclusive hotel established in 1913 and sited in the heart of Bern offers first-class guestrooms and suites and elegant conference facilities in a truly unique atmosphere. Modern gym with sauna. The comfortable Bellevue Bar serves international cuisine.
VUE · Bellevue Bar – See restaurant listing

Schweizerhof

Bahnhofplatz 11 ⊠ 3001 – ℰ 031 326 80 80
– www.schweizerhof-bern.ch   Plan: **C1**
99 rm – ♦355/435 CHF ♦♦455/535 CHF – ☲ 25 CHF – 5 suites
• Luxury • Elegant •

Behind the beautifully restored historic façade lies a happy marriage of modern and classic chic that looks beautiful and provides all the latest technology for business guests. Those of you in search of charm will love Jack's Brasserie.
Jack's Brasserie – See restaurant listing

Allegro

Kornhausstr. 3 ⊠ 3000 – ℰ 031 339 55 00
– www.allegro-hotel.ch   Plan: **D1**
167 rm – ♦270/330 CHF ♦♦300/390 CHF – ☲ 26 CHF – 4 suites
• Business • Modern •

This lifestyle hotel is ideal for conferences and events, as well as individual guests. Modern rooms in different categories, plus a beautiful penthouse floor with its own lounge. One of the restaurants, Il Giardino, serves Italian food.
❀ **Meridiano · Yù** – See restaurant listing

Bristol

Schauplatzgasse 10 ⊠ 3011 – ℰ 031 311 01 01
– www.bristolbern.ch   Plan: **C2**
92 rm ☲ – ♦135/285 CHF ♦♦180/395 CHF
• Business • Modern •

This townhouse hotel offers contemporary rooms and a small sauna (additional charge payable) which is shared with the adjacent Hotel Bären.

Bären

Schauplatzgasse 4 ⊠ 3011 – ℰ 031 311 33 67
– www.baerenbern.ch   Plan: **C2**
57 rm ☲ – ♦135/285 CHF ♦♦180/355 CHF
• Business • Modern •

Just a stone's throw from the Bundesplatz, this hotel located in a well-maintained townhouse offers individually furnished guestrooms in a contemporary style. A small sauna is available for an additional charge.

City am Bahnhof

Bubenbergplatz 7 ⊠ 3011 – ℰ 031 311 53 77
– www.fassbindhotels.ch   Plan: **C2**
58 rm – ♦120/270 CHF ♦♦155/315 CHF – ☲ 16 CHF
• Business • Functional •

Conveniently located close to the pedestrian zone and opposite the railway station, this hotel offers well-equipped rooms.

XxxX   VUE – Hotel Bellevue Palace

Kochergasse 3 ⊠ 3000 – ℰ 031 320 45 45
– www.bellevue-palace.ch/vue   Plan: **D2**
Menu 66 CHF (weekday lunch) – Carte 64/146 CHF
• Creative • Classic •

Ambitious, contemporary seasonal cuisine with traditional roots is served in this tastefully decorated setting. The terrace affords magnificent views over the Aare.

XxX   **Meridiano** – Hotel Allegro

❀   *Kornhausstr. 3* ✉ *3000 –* ☏ *031 339 52 45*   Plan: **D1**
– www.allegro-hotel.ch – Closed 1-12 January, 11-26 April, 4-26 July and
Saturday lunch, Sunday dinner-Tuesday
Menu 54 CHF (lunch)/165 CHF – Carte 105/125 CHF
• Modern cuisine • Fashionable • Trendy •
You may have to search around a little to find this restaurant, but it's worth it. In
Meridiano's elegant, modern interior – or alternatively on what is undoubtedly
one of the Swiss capital's loveliest terraces – head chef Jan Leimbach serves up
perfectly judged dishes with a distinct Mediterranean flavour.
➜ Gebeizter Thunfisch, lauwarmes vom Milchkalb, Wachtelei, Vitello-
Crème, Salzkapern. Konfierter Steinbutt, Entenleber-Royal, Walliser Apriko-
sen, grüne Mandeln, Blumenkohl. Impressionen vom Weiderind, Karotten,
Wiesenchampignons.

X   **Lorenzini**   🌫 ⬧

Hotelgasse 10 ✉ *3011 –* ☏ *031 318 50 67*   Plan: **D2**
– www.lorenzini.ch
Carte 41/87 CHF
• Italian • Friendly •
This attractive Italian restaurant located in the pedestrian zone is tastefully
decorated with original paintings. It boasts a formal restaurant on the first floor
and a bar, bistro and attractive interior courtyard at ground level.

X   **Bellevue Bar** – Hotel Bellevue Palace   🌫 ੬

Kochergasse 3 ✉ *3000 –* ☏ *031 320 45 45*   Plan: **D2**
– www.bellevue-palace.ch
Carte 49/236 CHF
• International • Traditional •
The sedate charm of this long established grand hotel also extends into the restaurant. Diners, many of whom have travelled from far and wide to get here,
can choose from an international menu.

X   **milles sens - les goûts du monde**

😊   *Spitalgasse 38 (Schweizerhofpassage, 1st floor)* ✉ *3011*   Plan: **C2**
– ☏ *031 329 29 29 – www.millesens.ch*
– Closed end July-early August and Sunday; at summer:
Saturday-Sunday
Menu 59 CHF (weekday lunch)/114 CHF – Carte 58/108 CHF
• International • Fashionable •
This fine Bern restaurant offers seasonal, international cuisine with a Swiss influ-
ence in a modern, minimalist-style interior. To accompany your choice from the
Surpris or Tour Du Monde menus, try a bottle from the Wineflight wine list.
Lunchtime offerings include the Quick Tray and the Menu d'affaires (business
menu).

X   **Kirchenfeld**   🌫 ⬧

😊   *Thunstr. 5* ✉ *3005 –* ☏ *031 351 02 78*   Plan: **E2**
– www.kirchenfeld.ch – Closed Sunday-Monday
Carte 40/96 CHF – *(booking advisable)*
• Regional • Brasserie •
Eating in this loud and lively restaurant is great fun! Try the flavoursome zander fish served on Mediterranean couscous and one of the sweets, which includes lemon tart and chocolate cake, displayed on the dessert trolley. At
lunchtimes the restaurant is full of business people who swear by the daily
set menu.

X **Wein & Sein mit Härzbluet**

Münstergasse 50 (at cellar) ⊠ *3011 –* ℰ *031 311 98 44*   Plan: **E2**
– www.weinundsein.ch – Closed 1 week March, 2 weeks September and Saturday lunch, Sunday-Monday
Menu 39 CHF (weekday lunch)/98 CHF
• Modern cuisine • Trendy • Rustic •

Steep steps lead down into this cosy cellar where you can sample a 4-course menu (changes daily) in the evenings and a lunch menu or a small à la carte selection at lunchtimes. The terrace in the arcade is charming and, of course, very popular.

X **Gourmanderie Moléson**

Aarbergergasse 24 ⊠ *3011 –* ℰ *031 311 44 63*   Plan: **C1**
– www.moleson-bern.ch – Closed Christmas-New Year and Saturday lunch, Sunday
Menu 38 CHF (weekday lunch)/59 CHF – Carte 53/87 CHF
• Traditional cuisine • Brasserie •

Established in 1865, the Moléson is a lively restaurant located in the centre of Bern. It serves a range of traditional-style dishes from Alsatian flammekueche to multi-course meals.

X **Jack's Brasserie** – Hotel Schweizerhof

Bahnhofplatz 11 ⊠ *3001 –* ℰ *031 326 80 80*   Plan: **C1**
– www.schweizerhof-bern.ch
Menu 57 CHF (weekday lunch)/105 CHF – Carte 73/118 CHF
• Traditional cuisine • Brasserie •

The restaurant at the Schweizerhof promises an elegant setting, an attractive decor with pretty alcoves, parquet flooring and stylish lighting. The menu features typical, brasserie-style fare alongside a number of popular classics including the Wiener schnitzel.

X **Yù** – Hotel Allegro

Kornhausstr. 3 ⊠ *3000 –* ℰ *031 339 52 50*   Plan: **D1**
– www.allegro-hotel.ch – Closed 3-31 July and Sunday-Monday
Menu 59 CHF – Carte 51/70 CHF – *(dinner only)*
• Chinese • Minimalist •

This restaurant open to the hotel's atrium is one of the most fashionable addresses in town. It exudes stylish Asian cool and serves modern Chinese cuisine.

X **Zimmermania**

Brunngasse 19 ⊠ *3011 –* ℰ *031 311 15 42*   Plan: **D1**
– www.zimmermania.ch – Closed 4 July-3 August and Sunday-Monday; June-September: Saturday lunch
Menu 65 CHF – Carte 42/95 CHF
• Traditional cuisine • Traditional •

The atmosphere in this cosy, traditionally run restaurant located in a narrow alleyway in the old town is lively and informal.

ENVIRONS OF BERN   **PLAN I**

 Innere Enge

Engestr. 54 ⊠ *3012 –* ℰ *031 309 61 11*   Plan: **A1**
– www.innere-enge.ch
26 rm – †205/295 CHF ††230/330 CHF – ☑ 25 CHF
• Country house • Personalised •

Passionate about jazz, your hosts have created this unique hotel-cum-jazz venue. Many of the rooms are named after famous musicians and decorated with original artefacts. The basement houses a jazz club. Josephine's Brasserie and the historic Park Pavilion offer views over the city.

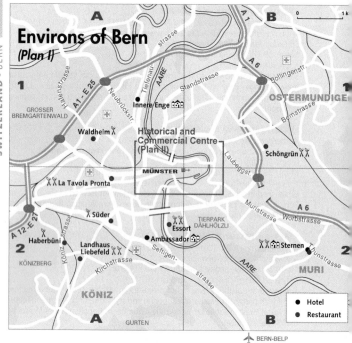

Environs of Bern
(Plan I)

GROSSER
BREMGARTENWALD

Waldheim X

Innere/Enge

Historical and
Commercial Centre
(Plan II)

MÜNSTER

La Tavola Pronta X X

Süder X

Haberbüni

Landhaus
Liebefeld X X

KÖNIZBERG

KÖNIZ

GURTEN

Ambassador

Essort X X

TIERPARK
DÄHLHÖLZLI

OSTERMUNDIGE

Schöngrün X X

Sternen X X

MURI

● Hotel
● Restaurant

BERN-BELP

Sternen

Thunstr. 80 – ℰ 031 950 71 11
Plan: **B2**
– www.sternenmuri.ch
44 rm – ♦135/280 CHF ♦♦190/345 CHF – ☲ 20 CHF
• Traditional • Functional •
This recently extended hotel offers contemporary rooms decorated in shades of yellow, green and blue in the annexe and more traditional rooms, some with exposed beams, in the main building. Good transport connections into the city. Both the Läubli restaurant and residents' dining room serve contemporary cuisine. Attractive private dining rooms are also available.
Sternen – See restaurant listing

Ambassador

Seftigenstr. 99 ✉ 3007 – ℰ 031 370 99 99
Plan: **A2**
– www.fassbindhotels.ch
97 rm – ♦145/360 CHF ♦♦190/405 CHF – ☲ 19 CHF
• Business • Functional •
This business hotel enjoys good transport links on the edge of the city. It boasts modern, functionally designed bedrooms with good facilities and free underground parking. Japanese cuisine in the Taishi, and international dishes in the light and airy conservatory.

XX Landhaus Liebefeld

Schwarzenburgstr. 134 – ℰ 031 971 07 58
Plan: **A2**
– www.landhaus-liebefeld.ch – Closed Sunday
6 rm ☐ – ♦180 CHF ♦♦290 CHF
Menu 60 CHF (weekday lunch)/133 CHF
– Carte 52/114 CHF – (booking advisable)
• Traditional cuisine • Elegant •

Anywhere you can eat this well in such pleasant surroundings as this former 1671 sheriff's house is bound to attract plenty of regulars. Try the fish soup – they've been making it from the same recipe for 25 years! The Gaststube serves simpler fare including meatloaf and German noodle dishes. And if you fancy staying the night, the individually designed rooms are pretty and well furnished.

XX Schöngrün

Monument im Fruchtland 1 (near Paul Klee Centre)
Plan: **B1**
✉ 3006 – ℰ 031 359 02 90 – www.restaurants-schoengruen.ch – closed
21-30 December and Sunday dinner-Tuesday
Menu 55 CHF (weekday lunch)/185 CHF
– Carte 88/122 CHF – (booking advisable)
• Creative • Fashionable •

This lovely historical villa with its smart, light and airy glazed annexe stands next to the Paul Klee Centre. The restaurant offers a minimalist interior and a comfortable terrace. A wide range of dishes from the daily special to a set menu is served. It is just a 23min bus ride from the main railway station.

XX La Tavola Pronta

Laupenstr. 57 ✉ 3008 – ℰ 031 382 66 33
Plan: **A2**
*– www.latavolapronta.ch – Closed 6 weeks July-August and Saturday
lunch, Sunday-Monday*
Menu 78/99 CHF *– (booking advisable)*
• Italian • Cosy •

A pleasant little basement restaurant with modern decor where chef Beat Thomi creates flavoursome Piedmontese food in a number of set menus.

XX Sternen – Hotel Sternen

Thunstr. 80 – ℰ 031 950 71 11 – www.sternenmuri.ch
Plan: **B2**
Menu 25 CHF (weekday lunch)/85 CHF – Carte 39/100 CHF
• Swiss • Cosy •

In the Sternen, guests can take their pick from a number of small, attractive dining rooms – 170 years old with original features to match. On a fun note, to order simply tick the relevant box on the menu and hand it to the waiter.

XX Essort

Jubiläumstrr. 97 ✉ 3000 – ℰ 031 368 11 11
Plan: **A2**
*– www.essort.ch – Closed 1 week early January, 2 weeks early October,
during Christmas*
Menu 61/105 CHF – Carte 55/96 CHF
• International • Friendly •

In the former US embassy the Lüthi family runs a modern restaurant. It produces international fare in its open kitchen, which is inspired by the owners' countless trips abroad. In summer, dine alfresco at one of the lovely tables laid outside under the mature trees.

X Haberbüni

Könizstr. 175 – ℰ 031 972 56 55 – www.haberbueni.ch
Plan: **A2**
– Closed Saturday lunch and Sunday
Menu 61/105 CHF – Carte 57/83 CHF *– (booking advisable)*
• Modern cuisine • Simple • Cosy •

This warm and welcoming restaurant set in the loft of a large renovated farmhouse or Büni offers ambitious contemporary cuisine and a fine selection of wines. Shorter midday menu and good business lunch options.

✕ Waldheim ⇱

Waldheimstr. 40 ✉ 3000 – ✆ 031 305 24 24   Plan: **A1**
– www.waldheim-bern.ch – Closed Saturday lunch, Sunday-Monday
Menu 49 CHF – Carte 43/79 CHF
• Swiss • Neighbourhood •

This pretty restaurant is panelled in light wood and located in a quiet residential area. It boasts a healthy number of regulars thanks to the fresh Swiss cuisine (try the marinated leg of lamb, spit-roasted to a perfect pink) and the friendly service.

✕ Süder ⇱ 🅿

Weissensteinstr. 61 ✉ 3000 – ✆ 031 371 57 67   Plan: **A2**
– www.restaurant-sueder.ch – Closed 1-11 January, 15 July-2 August and Saturday lunch, Sunday-Monday
Menu 68/89 CHF – Carte 51/82 CHF
• Swiss • Simple •

This down-to-earth corner restaurant with its lovely wood panelling has many regulars. They are attracted by the good, honest, fresh Swiss cooking, such as the veal ragout. In the summer it is no surprise that the tables in the garden are particularly popular.

GENEVA
GENEVE

Population: 191 557

Kheng Guan Toh/Fotolia.com

In just about every detail except efficiency, Geneva exudes a distinctly Latin feel. It boasts a proud cosmopolitanism, courtesy of a whole swathe of international organisations (dealing with just about every human concern), and of the fact that roughly one in three residents is non-Swiss. Its renowned savoir-vivre challenges that of swishy Zurich, and along with its manicured city parks, it boasts the world's tallest fountain and the world's longest bench. It enjoys cultural ties with Paris and is often called 'the twenty-first arrondissement' – it's also almost entirely surrounded by France.

The River Rhône snakes through the centre, dividing the city into the southern left bank - the old town - and the northern right bank - the 'international quarter' (home to the largest UN office outside New York). The east is strung around the sparkling shores of Europe's largest alpine lake, while the Jura Mountains dominate the right bank, and the Alps form a backdrop to the left bank. Geneva is renowned for its orderliness: the Reformation was born here under the austere preachings of Calvin, and the city has provided sanctuary for religious dissidents, revolutionaries and elopers for at least five centuries. Nowadays, new arrivals tend to be of a more conservative persuasion, as they go their elegant way balancing international affairs alongside *la belle vie*.

GENEVA IN...

→ **ONE DAY**
St Peter's Cathedral, Maison Tavel, Jet d'Eau, Reformation Wall.

→ **TWO DAYS**
MAMCO (or Art & History Museum), a lakeside stroll, a trip to Carouge.

→ **THREE DAYS**
A day in Paquis, including time relaxing at the Bains des Paquis.

PRACTICAL INFORMATION

ARRIVAL-DEPARTURE

✈ Geneva International Airport is 4km northwest of the city. Trains depart every 15min and take 6min. Bus 10 runs every 10min.

GETTING AROUND

Geneva is served by an efficient public transport network which runs like clockwork. There are various timed cards depending on how much travelling you intend to do: for one hour, one day, or 9am-midnight. A useful alternative: if you're making several trips, pick up a 48hr or 72hr Geneva Transport Card from the tourist office for unlimited use of the city's trams, trains, buses and boats. It also offers free admission to many top museums and attractions, plus reductions in some restaurants and shops. The city encourages cycling and from May to October bikes can be borrowed for free. More information from Geneva Tourism on Rue du Mont-Blanc.

CALENDAR HIGHLIGHTS

February
Fête de la Feuille (arrival of Spring).

March
Salon International de l'Automobile

April
International Exhibition of Inventions.

June-July
Bol d'Or Regatta, Fête de la Musique.

July-August
Fêtes de Genève.

September
Suisse Romande Heritage Days.

December
L'Escalade Procession.

EATING OUT

With the number of international organisations that have set up camp here, this is a place that takes a lot of feeding, so you'll find over 1,000 dining establishments in and around the city. If you're looking for elegance, head to a restaurant overlooking the lake; if your tastes are for home-cooked Sardinian fare, make tracks for the charming Italianate suburb of Carouge; and if you fancy something with an international accent, trendy Paquis has it all at a fair price and on a truly global scale, from Mexican to Moroccan and Jordanian to Japanese. The old town, packed with delightful brasseries and alpine-style chalets, is the place for Swiss staples: you can't go wrong here if you're after a fondue, rustic longeole (pork sausage with cumin and fennel) or a hearty papet vaudois (cream and leek casserole); for a bit of extra atmosphere, head downstairs to a candlelit, vaulted cellar. Although restaurants include a fifteen per cent service charge, it's customary to either round up the bill or give the waiter a five to ten per cent tip.

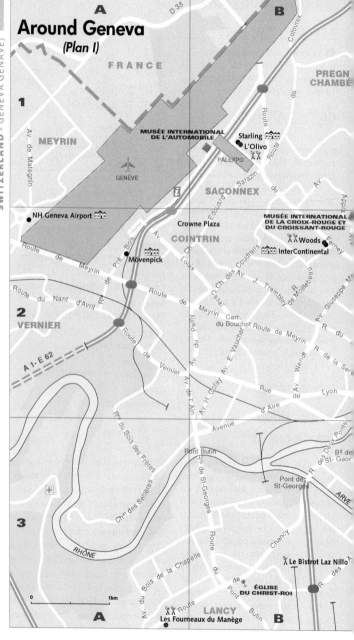

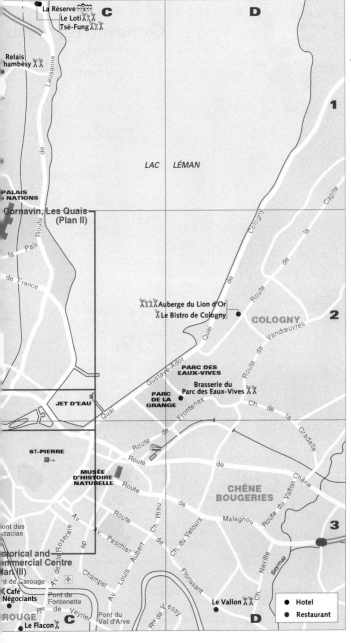

La Réserve 🏨
Le Loti ✕✕
Tsé-Fung ✕✕✕

C

D

Relais
Chambésy ✕✕

Lausanne

de

1

LAC LÉMAN

Capite

PALAIS
S NATIONS

Cornavin, Les Quais
(Plan II)

Cologny

de

la

la Paix

de

Route

de France

✕✕✕✕ Auberge du Lion d'Or
✕ Le Bistro de Cologny

Route

de

Vandœuvres

COLOGNY

2

Quai

Gustave-Ador

**PARC DES
EAUX-VIVES**

Route de

JET D'EAU

Quai

**PARC
DE LA
GRANGE**

Brasserie du
Parc des Eaux-Vives ✕✕

Frontenex

de

Ch. de

la Gradelle

Chêne

ST-PIERRE

Route

Route

de

**CHÊNE
BOUGERIES**

Route du Vallon

MUSÉE
D'HISTOIRE
NATURELLE

Route

Ch. Rieu

de

Malagnou

3

ont des
cacias

Av. de la Roseraie

Av. de

Av. Peschier

Ch. du Velours

de

Naville

Seymaz

storical and
ommercial Centre
lan (II)

Champel

Av. Louis Aubert

Florissant

nt de Carouge

✕ Café
Négociants

Pont de
Fontenette
de

Rte de Vessy

Le Vallon ✕✕ Ch.

● Hotel

ROUGE

C

Veyrier

Pont du
Val d'Arve

D

● Restaurant

Le Flacon ✕

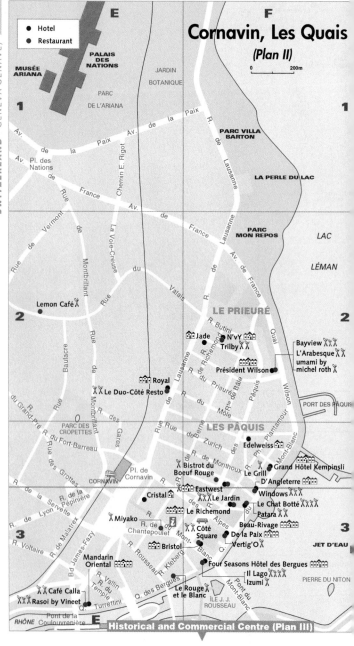

Cornavin, Les Quais
(Plan II)

0   200m

● Hotel
● Restaurant

SWITZERLAND - (GENEVA GENÈVE)

MUSÉE ARIANA

PALAIS DES NATIONS

PARC DE L'ARIANA

JARDIN BOTANIQUE

PARC VILLA BARTON

LA PERLE DU LAC

Av. de la Paix

Av. de la Paix

Pl. des Nations

Rue de France

Chemin E. Rigot

Av. de France

PARC MON REPOS

LAC

LÉMAN

Rue de Vermont

La Voie-Creuse

Rue du Valais

Av. de Lausanne

Av. de France

LE PRIEURÉ

Lemon Café ✗

R. Butini

Jade 🏠   N'vY 🏠
Trilby ✗ 🏠

Bayview ✗✗
L'Arabesque ✗✗
umami by michel roth ✗

Président Wilson 🏠

PORT DES PÂQUIS

Baulacre

Rue du Montbrillant

Rue de Lausanne

R. de Richemont

R. du Prieuré

Quai Wilson

Royal 🏠
✗✗ Le Duo-Côté Resto

PARC DES CROPETTES

Rue des Gares

Rue de Berne

R. du Môle

LES PÂQUIS

du Grand-Pré

R. du Fort-Barreau

R. des Grottes

Rue de Zurich

Edelweiss 🏠

Mont-Blanc

R. de Monthoux

Bistrot du Boeuf Rouge ✗

Le Grill ✗

Grand Hôtel Kempinsli 🏠

CORNAVIN

Pl. de Cornavin

Eastwest ● 🏠
✗✗ Le Jardin

D'Angleterre 🏠
Windows ✗✗✗

R. de Lyon

R. de la Servette

R. de la Pépinière

Cristal ● 🏠

R. des Alpes

Le Richemond 🏠

Le Chat Botté ✗✗✗
Patara ✗✗

R. Voltaire

R. de Malatrex

✗ Miyako

R. de Chantepoulet

Beau-Rivage 🏠
De la Paix 🏠
Vertig'O ✗

Bd James-Fazy

R. Rousseau

Mont-Blanc

Côté Square ●

R. Kléberg

Bristol 🏠

JET D'EAU

Mandarin Oriental 🏠

Four Seasons Hôtel des Bergues 🏠

Il Lago ✗✗✗
Izumi ✗

PIERRE DU NITON

R. du Temple

R. Vallin

Q. Turrettini

✗✗ Café Calla
✗✗✗ Rasoi by Vineet

Q. des Bergues

Pont du Mont-Blanc

ÎLE J. J. ROUSSEAU

RHÔNE

Pont de la Coulouvrenière

Le Rouge ✗
et le Blanc

Historical and Commercial Centre (Plan III)

E   F

1

2

3

Four Seasons Hôtel des Bergues

Quai des Bergues 33 ✉ *1201 –* ☏ *022 908 70 00*
– www.fourseasons.com/geneva
Plan: **F3**
95 rm – ♥715/1200 CHF ♥♥715/1200 CHF – ☕ 55 CHF – 20 suites
• Palace • Stylish •

With a lovely location at the point where the River Rhône rises from the clear waters of Lake Geneva, this was the first of the great Geneva hotels (1834). It is the very essence of the grand hotel with excellent service and a splendid decor (period furniture, marble, fine fabrics, etc). All in all a superb luxury hotel.
❀ **Il Lago • Izumi** – See restaurant listing

Mandarin Oriental

Quai Turrettini 1 ✉ *1201 –* ☏ *022 909 00 00*
– www.mandarinoriental.fr/geneva
Plan: **E3**
189 rm – ♥595/1550 CHF ♥♥695/2400 CHF – ☕ 52 CHF – 27 suites
• Grand Luxury • Art Deco • Elegant •

Shimmering fabrics, precious woods and marble panelling all contribute to the Art Deco style of this luxurious hotel on the banks of the Rhone river. On the seventh floor, the suites have their own private terrace with views of the entire city. Highly comfortable, extremely chic and infinitely elegant.
Rasoi by Vineet • Café Calla – See restaurant listing

Président Wilson

Quai Wilson 47 ✉ *1211 –* ☏ *022 906 66 66*
Plan: **F2**
– www.hotelpresidentwilson.com
180 rm – ♥450/1080 CHF ♥♥450/1080 CHF – ☕ 47 CHF – 48 suites
• Grand Luxury • Stylish •

A large, modern building on the waterfront, the Président Wilson offers every conceivable comfort. This includes wonderful architectural spaces, beautiful materials, a panoramic pool and a range of restaurants. From the upper floors on the Lake Geneva side, the city pales into insignificance before the wonderful green or snow covered scenery beyond.
❀ **Bayview • L'Arabesque • umami by michel roth** – See restaurant listing

Grand Hôtel Kempinski

Quai du Mont-Blanc 19 ✉ *1201 –* ☏ *022 908 90 81*
Plan: **F3**
– www.kempinski.com/geneva
379 rm – ♥490/1500 CHF ♥♥490/1500 CHF – ☕ 50 CHF – 33 suites
• Grand Luxury • Classic •

This contemporary hotel that looks out over the famous fountain and across Lake Geneva offers a wide range of services. The interior is modern but muted. It is full of bars and restaurants, meeting rooms, banqueting suites and shops – offering all the facilities you could ever need!
Le Grill – See restaurant listing

Beau-Rivage

Quai du Mont-Blanc 13 ✉ *1201 –* ☏ *022 716 66 66*
Plan: **F3**
– www.beau-rivage.ch
90 rm – ♥490/1090 CHF ♥♥490/1090 CHF – ☕ 47 CHF – 6 suites
• Grand Luxury • Stylish •

A truly grand hotel established in the mid-19C. The Beau-Rivage entered into the annals of history in 1898 when Empress Elisabeth of Austria passed away in one of its rooms. Its illustrious past is ever present – though never overbearing – in the timeless beauty of its columns and pillars and its marble and stucco work. An elegant refuge from the modern world.
❀ **Le Chat Botté • Patara** – See restaurant listing

SWITZERLAND - GENEVA GENÈVE

Le Richemond

Rue Adhémar-Fabri 8 ✉ *1201* – ✆ *022 715 70 00*   Plan: **F3**
– *www.dorchestercollection.com*
99 rm – ♦485 CHF ♦♦1005 CHF – ⌲ 55 CHF – 10 suites
• Grand Luxury • Historic • Modern •

Opened in 1863, Le Richemond provides the perfect combination of late-19C European style and the international taste of the modern day. Its original rotunda shaped lobby and wrought iron balconies looking out over the city. This contrasts with the luxuriously remodelled areas that are full of refined understatement.
Le Jardin – See restaurant listing

D'Angleterre

Quai du Mont-Blanc 17 ✉ *1201* – ✆ *022 906 55 55*   Plan: **F3**
– *www.hoteldangleterre.ch*
45 rm – ♦400/800 CHF ♦♦400/800 CHF – ⌲ 37 CHF
• Luxury • Townhouse • Classic •

Is it the stone façade reminiscent of Haussmann's Paris that gives the Hotel d'Angleterre its very particular character? Or perhaps the muted London club style of its lounges, or even the carefully chosen decor (classic, Venetian, 'design', etc.) in each of its individually furnished rooms? Whatever the answer, this hotel is without a doubt the epitome of elegance.
Windows – See restaurant listing

De la Paix

Quai du Mont-Blanc 11 ✉ *1211* – ✆ *022 909 60 00*   Plan: **F3**
– *www.hoteldelapaix.ch*
84 rm – ♦570/855 CHF ♦♦570/855 CHF – ⌲ 43 CHF – 2 suites
• Luxury • Classic •

The decorative themes of this hotel, based on drops of water and rose petals, are in perfect harmony with its environment. These themes are evident in all the rooms, whether they face the lake or the garden. It has a tranquil ambience with the sense of service that you would expect from an establishment founded in 1865.
❀ **Vertig'O** – See restaurant listing

InterContinental

Chemin du Petit-Saconnex 7 ✉ *1209*   Plan I: **B2**
– ✆ *022 919 39 39*
– *www.intercontinental-geneva.ch*
333 rm – ♦330/1200 CHF ♦♦330/1200 CHF – ⌲ 46 CHF – 58 suites
• Chain hotel • Luxury • Elegant •

Just behind the United Nations, this hotel perfect for business travellers is housed in the highest building in the city. Spacious, contemporary-style guestrooms with views of the Jura or the lake, a superb spa, a cocktail bar and an elegance that is evident right down to the last detail. Quite simply exceptional!
Woods – See restaurant listing

Bristol

Rue du Mont-Blanc 10 ✉ *1201* – ✆ *022 716 57 00*   Plan: **F3**
– *www.bristol.ch*
100 rm – ♦290/850 CHF ♦♦290/850 CHF – ⌲ 38 CHF – 1 suite
• Business • Classic •

A smart hotel with very comfortable guestrooms decorated in unfussy, classic style. After a hard day's work, take some time to relax in the basement fitness centre which also offers a sauna, hammam and jacuzzi.
Côté Square – See restaurant listing

N'vY   ⇪ ₤₅ 🅰🅲 ₤₄ 🚗

Rue de Richemont 18 ✉ *1202* – ☏ *022 544 66 66*   Plan: **F2**
– www.hotelnvygeneva.com
153 rm – ♦280/650 CHF ♦♦280/650 CHF – ⊑ 30 CHF – 1 suite
• Business • Luxury • Design •

This hotel has enjoyed a major facelift and the result is explosive. Find arty design, super trendy, high-tech fittings wherever you look, and bright guestrooms that owe as much to the writer Jack Kerouac as to street art. The N'vY will take your breath away!
Trilby – See restaurant listing

Royal   ⇪ ₤₅ 🀧 ₺ 🅰🅲 ₤₄ 🚗

Rue de Lausanne 41 ✉ *1201* – ☏ *022 906 14 14*   Plan: **E2**
– www.hotelroyalgeneva.com
202 rm – ♦260/620 CHF ♦♦260/620 CHF – ⊑ 30 CHF – 6 suites
• Business • Classic •

A certain distinction emanates from this neo-Gothic style hotel, whose lounges and cosy guestrooms evoke the atmosphere of a private house. The hotel restaurant, Le Duo, offers two dining options: fine dining at Côté Resto and international cuisine at Côté Bistro.
Le Duo - Côté Resto – See restaurant listing

Eastwest   ⇪ ₤₅ 🀧 🅰🅲 ₤₄

Rue des Pâquis 6 ✉ *1201* – ☏ *022 708 17 17*   Plan: **F3**
– www.eastwesthotel.ch
39 rm – ♦195/440 CHF ♦♦198/560 CHF – ⊑ 32 CHF – 2 suites
• Townhouse • Modern • Cosy •

This pleasant, impeccable hotel is firmly up to date in style with its contemporary furniture, dark tones, occasional splash of colour and open-plan bathrooms. Extremely central location not far from the banks of the river.
Eastwest – See restaurant listing

Jade   🅰🅲

Rue Rothschild 55 ✉ *1202* – ☏ *022 544 38 38*   Plan: **F2**
– www.hoteljadegeneva.com
47 rm – ♦220/440 CHF ♦♦220/440 CHF – ⊑ 18 CHF
• Business • Modern •

This hotel is inspired by the ideas of the famous Chinese philosopher Feng Shui and focuses on the circulation of energy. It is decorated with ethnic objects and has a tranquil, Zen-like ambience. An excellent place to rest both body and mind.

Edelweiss   ⇪ 🅰🅲

Place de la Navigation 2 ✉ *1201* – ☏ *022 544 51 51*   Plan: **F3**
– www.hoteledelweissgeneva.com
42 rm – ♦220/440 CHF ♦♦220/440 CHF – ⊑ 18 CHF
• Business • Cosy • Alpine •

Named after the famous Swiss flower (known as the immortal flower of the snow), this hotel has the typical ambience of a welcoming Swiss chalet. Light wood dominates in the guestrooms, while the restaurant boasts a real ski resort atmosphere, with its live music (every night) and cheese specialities on the menu.

Cristal   ₺ 🅰🅲 ₤₄

Rue Pradier 4 ✉ *1201* – ☏ *022 716 12 21*   Plan: **E3**
– www.fassbindhotels.ch
78 rm – ♦140/250 CHF ♦♦170/300 CHF – ⊑ 19 CHF
• Business • Design • Minimalist •

A stone's throw from the train station, this Cristal shines brightly. This is firstly thanks to its commitment to the environment, as witnessed by its solar panels and heating supplied by water circulation and airflow. And secondly, by its bright, designer layout dominated by silver and glass.

XXXX   **Le Chat Botté** – Hôtel Beau Rivage   ⌚ ≤ 🏠 🅰🅲 ⇄ 🚗

🏵   *Quai du Mont-Blanc 13* ✉ *1201* – ℰ *022 716 69 20*   Plan: **F3**
– *www.beau-rivage.ch* – *Closed 20 March-4 April and Saturday lunch, Sunday*
Menu 70 CHF (lunch)/220 CHF – Carte 125/191 CHF – *(booking advisable)*
• French classic • Elegant •

Cannelloni fondant, Swiss veal filet mignon and apple opaline are just some of the top quality dishes served in this restaurant. The skilful chef perfectly illustrates Le Chat Botté's philosophy that industry and knowledge are worth far more than material possessions. Impeccable service and a magnificent terrace overlooking Lake Geneva.
→ Asperge verte de Provence. St. Pierre de Bretagne. Pintade de Bresse.

XXXX   **Il Lago** – Four Seasons Hôtel des Bergues   ⌚ 🏠 ⅋ 🅰🅲

🏵   *Quai des Bergues 33* ✉ *1201* – ℰ *022 908 71 10*   Plan: **F3**
– *www.fourseasons.com/geneva*
Menu 78 CHF (lunch)/130 CHF – Carte 108/163 CHF
– *(booking essential)*
• Italian • Classic • Elegant •

Offering a taste of Italy on Lake Geneva, this restaurant combines a chic decor (superb pilasters and paintings) with elegant Italian cuisine which is light, subtle and fragant. A delightful dining experience!
→ Langoustines avec haricot coco et consommé d'oignons. Risotto de homard. Filet de bar de ligne rôti, artichaut violet et émulsion au citron.

XXX   **Windows** – Hôtel D'Angleterre   ⌚ ≤ 🅰🅲

Quai du Mont-Blanc 17 ✉ *1201* – ℰ *022 906 55 14*   Plan: **F3**
– *www.hoteldangleterre.ch*
Menu 59 CHF (weekday lunch) – Carte 93/141 CHF
• Creative • Elegant • Friendly •

Housed in the Hôtel d'Angleterre, this restaurant offers superb views of Lake Geneva, the Jet d'eau and the mountains in the distance. The menu features delicacies such as scallop carpaccio with lime, avocado tartare and fleur de sel, and half a baked lobster with little gem lettuce and potatoes.

XXX   **Rasoi by Vineet** – Hôtel Mandarin Oriental   🏠 ⅋ 🅰🅲 ⇄ 🚗

Quai turrettini 1 ✉ *1201* – ℰ *022 909 00 06*   Plan: **E3**
– *www.mandarinoriental.fr/geneva* – *Closed Sunday-Monday*
Menu 65 CHF (lunch)/155 CHF – Carte 103/161 CHF – *(booking advisable)*
• Indian • Design • Fashionable •

All the fragrances and colours of Indian cuisine are interpreted here with incredible refinement. Enjoy the cuisine of the sub-continent at its best in this chic and elegant restaurant where you can imagine yourself as a 21C maharaja!

XXX   **Bayview** – Hôtel Président Wilson   ⌚ ≤ ⅋ 🅰🅲 🚗

🏵   *Quai Wilson 47* ✉ *1211* – ℰ *022 906 65 52*   Plan: **F2**
– *www.hotelpresidentwilson.com* – *Closed 1-18 January, mid July-mid August and Sunday-Monday*
Menu 65 CHF (lunch)/170 CHF – Carte 138/210 CHF
• Creative • Design • Elegant •

Large bay windows facing the lake and a carefully designed, simple yet chic decor – the ideal setting in which to enjoy dishes created by famous and talented chef Michel Roth, who made his name in the Lasserre and Ritz restaurants in Paris. The fine cuisine offers creative and subtle interpretations of French favourites.
→ Foie gras canard en chaud-froid, religieuse et craquant rambouton Calvados. Bar aux coquillages, coulis coriandre, agnolotti à la brousse, tartare d'huître et caviar. Pur Criollo 75% Venezuela, mousseux de yuzu.

SWITZERLAND - GENEVA (GENÈVE)

XxX **Le Jardin** – Hôtel Le Richemond
Rue Adhémar-Fabri 8 ✉ *1201 –* ✆ *022 715 71 00*
– www.dorchestercollection.com   Plan: **F3**
Menu 68/90 CHF – Carte 80/141 CHF
• Classic cuisine • Elegant • Fashionable •
This restaurant faces the lake from inside the Hôtel Le Richemond and has a ter-
race that is a must when the weather allows. Elegantly classical cuisine with a
special devotion to the Italian flavours.

XX **Café Calla** – Hôtel Mandarin Oriental
Quai Turrettini 1 ✉ *1201 –* ✆ *022 909 00 00*
– www.mandarinoriental.fr/geneva   Plan: **E3**
Menu 85 CHF (lunch) – Carte 68/131 CHF
• International • Mediterranean •
Situated on the lakeside, the Mandarin Oriental's chic brasserie specialises in
Mediterranean flavours, offering dishes from all over the Mediterranean,
such as aubergine caviar, chicken and lemon tagine, and Italian-style veal
picatta.

XX **Côté Square** – Hôtel Bristol
Rue du Mont-Blanc 10 ✉ *1201 –* ✆ *022 716 57 58*
– www.bristol.ch – Closed Saturday-Sunday   Plan: **F3**
Menu 55 CHF (weekday lunch)/87 CHF – Carte 73/93 CHF
• International • Classic •
This restaurant has a classic elegance. Wood panelling and paintings add an
aristocratic air, enhanced by the occasional notes emanating from the attractive
black piano near the bar. On tables covered with immaculately white cloths,
enjoy delicious dishes showcasing a variety of textures and flavours.

XX **Patara** – Hôtel Beau-Rivage
Quai du Mont-Blanc 13 ✉ *1201 –* ✆ *022 731 55 66*
– www.patara-geneva.ch   Plan: **F3**
– Closed 2 weeks Christmas-New Year
Menu 49 CHF (lunch)/125 CHF – Carte 67/113 CHF
• Thai • Exotic •
Thai specialities served in one of the most beautiful luxury hotels in Geneva. Sty-
lised gold motifs on the walls evoke the exotic ambience of Thailand, while the
delicious specialities on the menu add to the sense of discovery.

XX **Trilby** – Hôtel N'vY
Rue de Richemont 18 ✉ *1202 –* ✆ *022 544 66 66*
– www.hotelnvygeneva.com   Plan: **F2**
Menu 85 CHF – Carte 54/114 CHF
• International • Fashionable • Elegant •
You might want to doff your own trilby as you enter this elegant and welco-
ming restaurant. The speciality is the outstanding beef, whether it is Scottish
(Black Angus), Japanese (Wagyu Kobe) or Swiss (Simmental), accompanied by
a choice of original sauces.

XX **L'Arabesque** – Hôtel Président Wilson
Quai Wilson 47 ✉ *1211 –* ✆ *022 906 67 63*
– www.hotelpresidentwilson.com   Plan: **F2**
Menu 59 CHF (weekday lunch)/95 CHF – Carte 58/95 CHF
• Lebanese • Elegant •
An attractive decor featuring gold mosaic, white leather and black lacquerware
evoking the magic of the Orient. In particular the Lebanon, from where the
authentic aromas of dishes such as bastorma (dried beef with spices) and houmous (chickpea purée) transport diners to the land of the cedar tree!

SWITZERLAND - GENEVA GENÈVE

XX **Le Duo - Côté Resto** – Hôtel Royal

Rue de Lausanne 41 ⊠ 1201 – ℰ *022 906 14 14* Plan: **E2**
– www.hotelroyalgeneva.com – Closed 2 weeks Christmas-New Year,
3 weeks August and Saturday-Sunday
Menu 75 CHF (weekday lunch)/90 CHF
• French • Elegant • Classic •

This restaurant has an intimate ambience perfect for a romantic dinner. Enjoy the top quality ingredients and carefully prepared dishes, such as skrei cod marinated in kaffir lime and slow-cooked Swiss veal filet mignon. Interesting choice of wines by the glass.

XX **Woods** – Hôtel InterContinental

Chemin du Petit-Saconnex 7 ⊠ 1209 Plan I: **B2**
– ℰ *022 919 33 33 – www.intercontinental-geneva.ch – Closed Saturday*
Menu 59 CHF (weekday lunch)/100 CHF – Carte 76/127 CHF
• Modern cuisine • Friendly •

This attractive, contemporary-style restaurant is in the Inter-Continental Hotel. It boasts an attractive wood decor and serves cuisine that is full of flavour.

X **Vertig'O** – Hôtel de la Paix
🌳
Quai du Mont-Blanc 11 ⊠ 1211 – ℰ *022 909 60 73* Plan: **F3**
– www.concorde-hotels.com/vertigo – Closed Christmas-New-Year, 1 week
during Easter, 4 weeks July-August and Saturday lunch, Sunday-Monday
Menu 69 CHF (weekday lunch)/185 CHF
– Carte 133/164 CHF – (bookings advisable at dinner)
• French modern • Fashionable •

Despite its name, you will experience no Hitchcock-like fear in this restaurant, where the cuisine is the only thing likely to raise your heartbeat. The dishes are beautifully presented and deceptively simple, allowing the flavour of the ingredients to shine through. Trendy decor.
➜ Duo de tourteau et araignée de mer relevé au rougail. Tartare de filet de lapin fermier, quinoa et truffe noire de la Drôme. Le pigeon d'Anjou juste saisi aux morilles, galettes de blé tendre.

X **Miyako**

Rue Chantepoulet 11 ⊠ 1201 – ℰ *022 738 01 20* Plan: **E3**
– www.miyako.ch – Closed Sunday
Menu 34 CHF (weekday lunch)/105 CHF – Carte 56/96 CHF
• Japanese • Simple •

This aptly named restaurant (Miyako is the Japanese for heart) plunges you into the heart of Japan. It has tatami flooring, teppanyaki cuisine, fresh fish and attentive service. Arigato!

X **umami by michel roth** – Hôtel Président Wilson

Quai Wilson 47 ⊠ 1211 – ℰ *022 906 64 52*
– www.hotelpresidentwilson.com – Closed October- Plan: **F2**
December
Menu 65 CHF (lunch)/95 CHF – Carte 64/94 CHF
• Japanese • Exotic • Fashionable •

Dine at this restaurant and you will soon realise that there is far more to Japanese cuisine than sushi and sashimi. Creativity is very much to the fore, with the occasional French influence thrown in for good measure. For example, the maki rolls sautéed with foie gras, green apple and ginger are a delicious combination.

X **Bistrot du Boeuf Rouge**

Rue Dr. Alfred-Vincent 17 ⊠ 1201 – ℰ *022 732 75 37* Plan: **F3**
– www.boeufrouge.ch – Closed Christmas-4 January, 18 July-
16 August, Saturday-Sunday and Bank Holidays
Menu 38 CHF (weekday lunch)/54 CHF
– Carte 51/93 CHF – (booking advisable)
• Traditional cuisine • Brasserie • Retro •

Run by the Farina family for over 20 years, this restaurant serves simple, rustic, yet fresh and tasty cuisine. Dishes include duckling terrine, fera fish from Lake Geneva in a tarragon sauce, and raspberry tart. Attractive, Parisian bistro-style decor.

X
Le Rouge et le Blanc
Quai des Berges 27 ✉ 1201

Plan: **E3**

– ℰ *022 731 15 50*
– *www.lerougeblanc.ch*
– *Closed 23 December-4 January and Saturday lunch, Sunday*
Carte 67/99 CHF – *(dinner only) (booking advisable)*
• Traditional cuisine • Wine bar •

A good wine selection, rib of beef as the house speciality (for two or three people), plates of tapas that vary according to market availability, and a relaxed and convivial atmosphere. This restaurant makes a good choice for an enjoyable meal out. Open evenings only.

X
Lemon Café
Rue du Vidollet 4 ✉ 1202

Plan: **E2**

– ℰ *022 733 60 24*
– *www.lemon-cafe.ch*
– *Closed 2 weeks end December-early January, 2 weeks end July-early August, Saturday-Sunday and Bank Holidays*
Menu 52 CHF – Carte 49/81 CHF
• French modern • Friendly • Simple •

This pleasant Geneva restaurant showcases cuisine that is both fresh and delicate. Try dishes such as Andalucian gazpacho with ricotta quenelles and double crispy fillets of sea bass with a coulis of summer vegetables, panisses and fried basil. Fine, simply prepared cuisine, whether you are eating inside or on the terrace, where tables are highly prized in the summer months.

X
Le Grill – Grand Hôtel Kempinski
Quai du Mont-Blanc 19 ✉ 1201

Plan: **F3**

– ℰ *022 908 92 20*
– *www.kempinski.com/geneva*
Menu 99 CHF (lunch) – Carte 89/134 CHF
• Meats • Fashionable •

A chic and original restaurant. It offers views of Lake Geneva, as well as of the kitchens, rotisserie and cold rooms where the splendid cuts of meat are stored (300g Parisian entrecôte, beef fillet, rack of lamb etc). The meat is cooked to perfection and the formula works well.

X
Eastwest – Hôtel Eastwest
Rue des Pâquis 6 ✉ 1201

Plan: **F3**

– ℰ *022 708 17 07*
– *www.eastwesthotel.ch*
Carte 49/93 CHF – *(booking advisable)*
• International • Design • Cosy •

An attractive Japanese influenced decor and inviting patio contribute to the simple elegance of this restaurant. Provençal vegetables and beef tartare feature on the menu alongside teriyaki sauce and Thai basil.

X
Izumi – Four Seasons Hôtel des Bergues
Quai des Bergues 33 ✉ 1201

Plan: **F3**

– ℰ *022 908 75 22*
– *www.fourseasons.com/geneva*
– *Closed 3 weeks July-August*
Menu 65 CHF (lunch)/130 CHF – Carte 78/125 CHF
• Japanese • Elegant • Trendy •

Situated on the top floor of Geneva's leading hotel, this restaurant is bound to surprise and delight you. The Japanese specialities served here are flavoured with the occasional hint of Peru, providing a whole host of striking contrasts which work extremely well. Enjoy your dinner on the terrace while taking in the lovely views of Geneva and the River Rhône below.

SWITZERLAND - GENEVA GENÈVE)

Swissôtel Métropole
Quai Général-Guisan 34 ✉ *1204 –* ☎ *022 318 32 00* Plan: **H1**
– www.swissotel.com/geneva
118 rm – ♦370/910 CHF ♦♦390/910 CHF – ⌑ 42 CHF – 9 suites
• Luxury • Classic •
Situated in the corner of Lake Geneva opposite the Jardin Anglais, this elongated neo-Classical building (1854) evokes the splendid past of this historic diplomatic capital. A true luxury hotel with a long tradition, the Swissôtel Métropole
offers extremely comfortable rooms in a classic or contemporary style.

Les Armures
Rue du Puits-Saint-Pierre 1 ✉ *1204 –* ☎ *022 310 91 72* Plan: **H2**
– www.hotel-les-armures.ch
32 rm – ♦450/525 CHF ♦♦695/720 CHF – ⌑ 35 CHF
• Traditional • Historic • Modern •
Situated in the heart of the old town, this 17C residence has a certain charm. It
has old stone walls and wooden beams, as well as some superb painted ceilings. It is also intimate, romantic and resolutely contemporary in style. Offering
a completely different atmosphere, the restaurant is an authentic tavern serving
raclettes and fondues.

De la Cigogne
Place Longemalle 17 ✉ *1204 –* ☎ *022 818 40 40* Plan: **H1**
– www.relaischateaux.com/cigogne
46 rm ⌑ – ♦350/540 CHF ♦♦460/650 CHF – 6 suites
• Luxury • Townhouse • Historic •
A cosy, luxurious hotel decorated with pretty prints, antique furniture, paintings
and carpets, all of which create a chic, delicate and classic ambience. The sense
of comfort and well-being makes it very difficult to leave.
De la Cigogne – See restaurant listing

Tiffany
Rue de l'Arquebuse 20 ✉ *1204 –* ☎ *022 708 16 16* Plan: **G2**
– www.tiffanyhotel.ch
65 rm – ♦180/495 CHF ♦♦248/550 CHF – ⌑ 29 CHF
• Traditional • Modern • Cosy •
This small, stylish Belle Époque hotel is situated on the edge of the old town. It
offers Art Nouveau decor in its lobby and restaurant and Art Deco furnishings in
its guestrooms. Pleasant ambience and friendly welcome.

XX Brasserie du Parc des Eaux-Vives
Quai Gustave-Ador 82 ✉ *1211 –* ☎ *022 849 75 75* Plan I: **D2**
– www.parcdeseauxvives.ch
Menu 69/89 CHF – Carte 66/93 CHF
• Modern cuisine • Classic •
Situated in the Parc des Eaux-Vives, this beautiful classic-style restaurant occupies a magical setting with long green lawns running down to the lake. The à la
carte menu features dishes such as octopus with citrus fruit, local pork chops
and veal kidneys in a mustard sauce. Guestrooms with a view of the lake add
to the appeal.

XX De la Cigogne – Hôtel De la Cigogne
Place Longemalle 17 ✉ *1204 –* ☎ *022 818 40 40* Plan: **H1**
– www.relaischateaux.com/cigogne – Closed Christmas-New Year and
Saturday lunch, Sunday
Menu 65/125 CHF – Carte 92/122 CHF
• Modern cuisine • Elegant • Friendly •
This restaurant is sure to please with its intimate atmosphere that is typical of
certain hotel restaurants. The classic cuisine includes dishes such as tomato
and caper tart and crayfish tails with rocket.

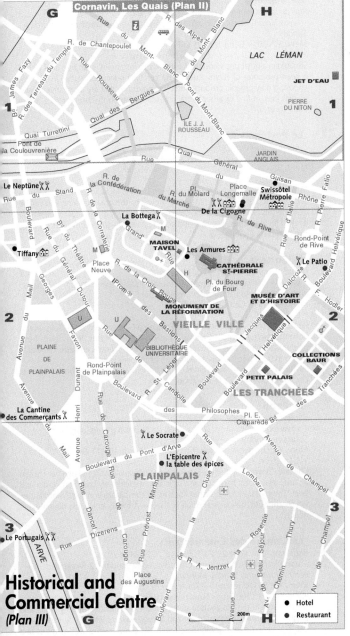

SWITZERLAND - GENEVA GENÈVE

LAC LÉMAN

G

H

Rue du Mont-Blanc

R. de Chantepoulet

R. des Alpes

Q. du Mont-Blanc

Bd James Fazy

R. des Terreaux du Temple

Rue Rousseau

Bergues

JET D'EAU

Pont du Mont-Blanc

PIERRE DU NITON

1

Quai des

ÎLE J. J. ROUSSEAU

Quai Turrettini

Pont de la Couloubrenière

Rue

Quai

JARDIN ANGLAIS

Général

du

Guisan

Le Neptune ✕✕

Stand

R. de la Confédération

Pl. du Molard

Place Longemalle

Swissôtel Métropole

R. Pierre Fatio

Rue

du

Boulevard

R. du Marché

De la Cigogne

Rhône

R. d'Italie

R. de Rive

La Bottega ✕

Grand'

M

MAISON TAVEL

Les Armures

CATHÉDRALE ST-PIERRE

✕ Le Patio

Boulevard Helvétique

Tiffany

Bd du Théâtre

R. de la Corraterie

M

Place Neuve

R. de la Croix-Rouge

H

Pl. du Bourg de Four

MUSÉE D'ART ET D'HISTOIRE

Rond-Point de Rive

R. Pierre Fatio

Rue du Général

Prom

MONUMENT DE LA RÉFORMATION

VIEILLE VILLE

Dalcroze

R. F. Hodler

2

Georges

Avenue

du

Mail

Rue

de

Bastions

BIBLIOTHÈQUE UNIVERSITAIRE

Jacques

Helvétique

COLLECTIONS BAUR

Rue des Tranchées

PLAINE DE PLAINPALAIS

Rond-Point de Plainpalais

Boulevard

R. St-Léger

Candolle

Boulevard

PETIT PALAIS

LES TRANCHÉES

des

La Cantine des Commerçants ✕

Avenue

Henri

Rue de

des

Philosophes

Pl. E. Claparède

Bd

✕ Le Socrate

Dunant

Carouge

Pont d'Arve

Rue

Avenue de

Champel

L'Epicentre ✕ la table des épices

PLAINPALAIS

Rue

Boulevard du Pont

Rue Prévost Martin

Rue de Carouge

Cluse

Lombard

3

ARVE

Le Portugais ✕✕

Rue

Dizerens

Rue

Dancet

de

R. A. Jentzer

la

de

Roseraie

Av. de Beau Séjour

Chemin

Thury

Av. de Champel

Place des Augustins

Boulevard

Historical and Commercial Centre
(Plan III)

G

H

0   200m

● Hotel
● Restaurant

807

SWITZERLAND - GENEVA GENÈVE

XX **Le Neptūne**

Rue de la Coulouvrenière 38 ✉ *1204 –* ℰ *022 320 15 05*   Plan: **G1**
– www.leneptune.ch – Closed 11-24 January, 1-15 August and Saturday-Sunday
Menu 97 CHF – Carte 80/101 CHF
• Modern cuisine • Elegant • Friendly •

Situated in a quiet district on the left bank, this restaurant is run by a chef who is a keen promoter of Alpine cuisine. He carefully selects his suppliers himself, choosing only organic produce and creating dishes that are innovative as well as delicious. In fine weather, enjoy alfresco dining on the small terrace in the inner courtyard.

XX **Le Portugais**   AC

Boulevard du Pont d'Arve 59 ✉ *1205 –* ℰ *022 329 40 98*   Plan: **G3**
– www.leportugais.ch – Closed Sunday-Monday
Menu 45 CHF (lunch)/59 CHF – Carte 51/96 CHF
• Portuguese • Simple •

Many Portuguese have left their mark on history, including famous explorers such as Vasco de Gama and Magellan. However, the only exploring you will be doing in this restaurant is of the culinary variety. Enjoy a choice of excellent fish cooked by an enthusiastic chef and accompanied by good local wine. Friendly, rustic ambience. Obrigado!

X **La Bottega**
☙
Grand Rue 3 ✉ *1204 –* ℰ *022 736 10 00*   Plan: **G2**
– www.labottegatrattoria.com – Closed 23 December-6 January, 2 weeks end July-early August and Saturday-Sunday
Menu 46 CHF – Carte 71/97 CHF
• Italian • Cosy •

Renowned chefs Paulo Airaudo and Francesco Gasbarro are at the helm of this delightful trattoria in old Geneva. Simply prepared organic ingredients, fresh homemade pasta and a minimalist decor. They follow Leonardo da Vinci's motto to the letter: "Simplicity equals absolute perfection."
→ Ravioli, oignon, aubergines et balsamique. Joue de bœuf braisée, carotte et pomme. Tarte au citron.

X **Le Patio**

Boulevard Helvétique 19 ✉ *1207 –* ℰ *022 736 66 75*   Plan: **H2**
– www.lepatiorestaurant.ch – Closed 24 December-4 January and Saturday-Sunday
Menu 45 CHF (weekday lunch)/115 CHF – Carte 48/111 CHF
• Creative • Friendly • Bistro •

Philippe Chevrier (chef at the Domaine de Châteauvieux in Satigny) has chosen an original concept here: cuisine that is almost exclusively based on lobster and beef. The menu includes dishes such as lobster tartare and oxtail parmentier, which are fresh, delicious and full of flavour. A highly enjoyable dining experience!

X **La Cantine des Commerçants**   🕏 &

Boulevard Carl Vogt 29 ✉ *1205 –* ℰ *022 328 16 70*   Plan: **G2**
– www.lacantine.ch – Closed Christmas-early January, 2 weeks end July-early August and Sunday-Monday
Menu 48/65 CHF (dinner) – Carte 53/79 CHF
• French • Design • Fashionable •

A neo-bistro in the old abattoir district of the city characterised by white and bright green walls, a retro decor, and a large counter where you can sit and eat. The varied menu is very much with the times: risotto with gambas and wild herbs, grilled fish and pan-fried fillet of beef.

X **Le Socrate**

Plan: **H3**

Rue Micheli-du-Crest 6 ⊠ 1205 – ℰ 022 320 16 77
– www.lesocrate.ch – Closed Saturday lunch, Sunday
Carte 46/70 CHF
• Traditional cuisine • Retro • Friendly •

A bistro with a delightfully retro dining room adorned with old posters on its walls. Sample simple, honest and delicious dishes at tables set close together. A place where good food and conversation are to the fore, in an atmosphere that a certain Greek philosopher would have appreciated!

X **L'Epicentre, la table des épices**

Plan: **G3**

Rue Prévost-Martin 25 ⊠ 1205 – ℰ 022 328 14 70
– www.lepicentre.ch – Closed 3 weeks end June-mid July and Saturday-Sunday
Menu 37 CHF (weekday lunch)/124 CHF – Carte 64/100 CHF
• Creative • Exotic • Simple •

The two chefs at this aptly named restaurant (table des épices means spice table) create fragrant and well-balanced dishes that are full of flavour. They select one or two spices from the 300 varieties bought either in Geneva or abroad as the foundation for the dish. Excellent wine list featuring mainly natural wines.

 La Réserve

Plan: **C1**

Route de Lausanne 301 ⊠ 1293 Bellevue
– ℰ 022 959 59 59 – www.lareserve.ch
85 rm – †420/995 CHF ††480/995 CHF – ☑ 45 CHF – 17 suites
• Grand Luxury • Elegant • Cosy •

This luxury hotel is a true sanctuary of beauty! Designer Jacques Garcia has used fine materials and dark colours to create guestrooms with an exotic atmosphere and a style that brings to mind an African lodge. Superb spa, access to the lake, boat available for guests – everything seems possible here. Three restaurants offering a vast selection of flavours.
Le Loti • Tsé-Fung – See restaurant listing

 Starling

Plan: **B1**

Route François-Peyrot 34 ⊠ 1218 Grand-Saconnex
– ℰ 022 747 02 02 – www.shgeneva.com
496 rm – †230/360 CHF ††250/380 CHF – ☑ 39 CHF
• Business • Chain hotel • Contemporary •

Situated near the airport and Palexpo, this hotel is worthy of the A380, with almost 500 rooms used mainly by business travellers and conference guests. Despite its size, the hotel is anything but impersonal, with an attentive staff and numerous leisure facilities (fitness room, well-being centre restaurants etc.).
L'Olivo – See restaurant listing

🏨 **Mövenpick**

Plan: **A2**

Route de Pré-Bois 20 ⊠ 1215 – ℰ 022 717 11 11
– www.moevenpick-geneva-airport.com
343 rm – †210/750 CHF ††210/750 CHF – ☑ 40 CHF – 7 suites
• Chain hotel • Townhouse • Modern •

This Mövenpick hotel close to the airport is ideal for business travellers. It offers comfortable, spacious rooms, a choice of bars and restaurants (international cuisine in the Latitude, Japanese in the Kamome), various meeting and conference rooms and even a casino.

NH Geneva Airport

Avenue de Mategnin 21 ⊠ *1217 Meyrin*
– ℰ 022 989 00 00 – www.nh-hotels.com
190 rm – ♦145/205 CHF ♦♦175/235 CHF – ⊡ 34 CHF

Plan: **A2**

• Chain hotel • Traditional • Modern •

Situated near the runways, this typical modern hotel is designed to appeal to an international clientele. Although similar to hotels elsewhere in the world, the hotel has plenty of style and offers a good level of comfort.

Auberge du Lion d'Or (Thomas Byrne et Gilles Dupont)

Place Pierre-Gautier 5 ⊠ *1223 Cologny*
– ℰ 022 736 44 32 – www.dupont-byrne.ch – Closed
24 December-11 January and Saturday-Sunday
Menu 78 CHF (lunch)/190 CHF – Carte 132/206 CHF

Plan: **D2**

• Modern cuisine • Elegant •

Two heads are often better than one and the two chefs at this restaurant certainly combine their talents to good effect. They offer an excellent choice of produce, original food combinations and cuisine that is full of flavour. Not to mention a romantic view of the lake. A good dining option!

→ Ravioles de crabe du Kamtchatka, grosse langoustine Asia. Dos de loup de mer, matelote de poulpes au fumet de calamar, couteau au pesto. Filet de bœuf Angus d'Irlande, chutney d'oignons et raisins de Augustin.

Le Bistro de Cologny – See restaurant listing

Domaine de Châteauvieux (Philippe Chevrier)

Chemin de Châteauvieux 16 (West: 10 km)
⊠ *1242 Satigny – ℰ 022 753 15 11 – www.chateauvieux.ch – Closed*
2 weeks Christmas-New Year, 1 week during Easter, 2 weeks end July-early August
13 rm ⊡ – ♦260/400 CHF ♦♦330/455 CHF
Menu 96 CHF (weekday lunch)/290 CHF
– Carte 192/225 CHF – (booking advisable)

• Creative • Luxury •

Off the beaten track, standing above the Geneva countryside and its vineyards, this large traditional house teeming with cachet and individual charm cultivates a true sense of excellence! A culinary technician as much as he is an artist, Philippe Chevrier follows a unique path to unearth truly natural flavours that reconnect with the basics. Delightful rooms for those wishing to stay the night.

→ Féra du lac Léman en chaud-froid, coulis de persil, cébettes et mousseline aux agrumes. Suprêmes de pigeon des Deux-Sèvres rôtis, tartare de cuisses, panisse frit et tomate confite, jus laqué aux graines de sésame. Sphère au chocolat ivoire, riz soufflé et mousse au fromage blanc, coulis aux fruits exotiques et sorbet à la mangue.

Le Floris (Claude Legras)

Route d'Hermance 287 (North-East: 12 km) ⊠ *1247 Anières*
– ℰ 022 751 20 20 – www.lefloris.com – Closed 24 December-11 January,
27 March-4 April, 6-14 September and Sunday-Monday
Menu 78 CHF (weekday lunch)/250 CHF
– Carte 137/196 CHF – (booking advisable)

• Classic cuisine • Elegant • Mediterranean •

Le Floris serves beautifully presented food that is typical of chef Claude Legras. It is clever, creative and prepared with a light hand and a real feel for flavour. The magnificent view over Lake Geneva from the terrace provides the finishing touch.

→ Bonbons de foie gras aux truffes. Le rouget snacké à la plancha, risotto de boulgour au pamplemousse rose, tombée de choux. Agneau fumé au bois de sapin, cannelloni de poivrons grillés et aubergines.

Café F. – See restaurant listing

XxX **Le Loti** – Hôtel La Réserve
Route de Lausanne 301 ✉ 1293 Bellevue Plan: **C1**
– ✆ 022 959 59 79 – www.lareserve.ch
Menu 55/62 CHF – Carte 68/129 CHF
• Mediterranean • Elegant • Intimate •
Named after the travel writer Pierre Loti, this restaurant with its warm tones and exotic influences, evokes a fascination with other lands. The menu features dishes such as truffle risotto, veal chops, rum baba and chocolate fondant.

XxX **Tsé-Fung** – Hôtel La Réserve
Route de Lausanne 301 ✉ 1293 Bellevue Plan: **C1**
– ✆ 022 959 58 88 – www.lareserve.ch
Menu 100/180 CHF – Carte 68/177 CHF
• Chinese • Exotic •
The La Réserve hotel's restaurants feature cuisine from around the world. At the elegant and original Tsé-Fung, enjoy dim sum, grilled ravioli and an extensive choice of classic Chinese specialities.

XX **Le Cigalon** (Jean-Marc Bessire)
❀ *Route d'Ambilly 39 (South-East: 5 km by Route de Chêne D3)*
✉ 1226 Thônex – ✆ 022 349 97 33 – www.le-cigalon.ch
– Closed 2 weeks end December-early January, Easter, 3 weeks mid July-early August and Sunday-Monday
Menu 54 CHF (weekday lunch)/150 CHF – Carte 90/120 CHF
• Fish and seafood • Elegant •
Judging by the fresh fish on the menu, you would be forgiven for thinking that this restaurant was situated on the Breton or Mediterranean coast. Fish and seafood take pride of place with dishes such as fresh fish soup, scallops and monkfish from Roscoff featuring on the menu. Table d'hôte meals are also served for up to five guests.
→ Paupiette de thon aux algues de Bretagne, parfumée à l'huile de café torréfié. Crevettes gambero rosso sautées, émulsion au citron Yuzu. Légine australe rôtie sur peau, vierge de tomates.

XX **Le Relais de Chambésy**
Place de Chambésy 8 ✉ 1292 Chambésy Plan: **C1**
– ✆ 022 758 11 05 – www.relaisdechambesy.ch
– Closed Christmas, New Year and Sunday, July-August: Saturday lunch, Sunday
Menu 62/82 CHF – Carte 56/101 CHF
• French classic • Rustic • Friendly •
Situated in a quiet village, this old coaching inn continues its tradition of hospitality on the outskirts of Geneva. Classic French cuisine, as well as an attractive terrace surrounded by greenery.

XX **L'Olivo** – Hôtel Starling
Route François-Peyrot 34 ✉ 1218 Grand-Saconnex Plan: **B1**
– ✆ 022 747 04 00 – www.shgeneva.com
– Closed end December-early January, Saturday-Sunday and Bank Holidays
Menu 55 CHF (weekday lunch) – Carte 60/96 CHF
• Italian • Mediterranean • Friendly •
A pleasant restaurant near the airport with a large terrace shaded by olive trees. The flavours of Italy dominate the menu, which features specialities such as pasta, risotto, gnocchi with sweet chestnuts, and veal escalopes in a Milanese sauce.

SWITZERLAND - GENEVA (GENÈVE)

SWITZERLAND - GENEVA (GENÈVE)

XX   Les Fourneaux du Manège

Route de Chancy 127 ✉ *1213 Onex*   Plan: **A3**
– 𝒞 022 870 03 90 – www.fourneauxdumanege.ch
– Closed 21 December-6 January and Saturday lunch, Sunday dinner-Monday
Menu 52 CHF (lunch)/150 CHF – Carte 48/126 CHF
• Traditional cuisine • Cosy • Inn •

In this attractive 19C building in the centre of Onex, enjoy a warm welcome from a dynamic team. They work mainly with regional produce, in particular the famous fish from Lake Geneva: pike, the salmon-like féra, char and perch. It is all served with great enthusiasm in the dining room or on the terrace.

XX   Le Vallon

Route de Florissant 182 ✉ *1231 Conches*   Plan: **D3**
– 𝒞 022 347 11 04 – www.restaurant-vallon.com
– Closed Sunday
Menu 45 CHF (weekday lunch)/84 CHF
– Carte 70/104 CHF – *(booking advisable)*
• French • Bistro •

This restaurant is a delightful place to eat with its pink façade, green shutters, wisteria-entwined sign and tree-shaded terrace. The interior decor is typical of a traditional inn and the menu features classic cuisine.

X   Le Flacon
❀

Rue Vautier 45 ✉ *1227 Carouge –* 𝒞 *022 342 15 20*   Plan: **C3**
– www.leflacon.ch – Closed Saturday lunch and Sunday-Monday
Menu 39 CHF (weekday lunch)/120 CHF – Carte 80/113 CHF
• Modern cuisine • Design • Fashionable •

An enchanting restaurant where the young chef, only just in his 30s, creates delicious cuisine from his open-view kitchen. He demonstrates a fine command of flavour and food combinations, as well as a real eye for detail in his beautifully presented dishes.

→ Dorade marinée et lard de Colonnata, feuille de capucine, combawa et brioche crispy. Agneau de Vessy, artichaut, céleri, sarriette, yaourt grec et concombre. Crème caramel, poivre Timut et spéculoos, sorbet rhubarbe.

X   Café F. – Restaurant Le Floris

Route d'Hermance 287 (North-East: 12 km) ✉ *1247 Anières*
– 𝒞 022 751 20 20 – www.cafe-f.com – Closed 24 December-11 January, 27 March-4 April, 6-14 September and Sunday-Monday
Menu 53 CHF – Carte 68/96 CHF – *(booking advisable)*
• International • Bistro • Friendly •

The Café de Floris has taken on a new lease of life by renaming itself the Café F.! In the kitchen, Claude Legras' dishes will delight guests with their delicious combinations of flavours. Regular visitors will still feel at home – the view of Lake Geneva is still stunning and has not changed at all.

X   Café des Négociants

Rue de la Filature 29 ✉ *1227 Carouge*   Plan: **C3**
– 𝒞 022 300 31 30 – www.negociants.ch – Closed Christmas-4 January and Sunday
Menu 29 CHF (weekday lunch)/74 CHF
– Carte 53/79 CHF – *(booking advisable)*
• French • Bistro • Friendly •

This retro-style bistro offers all the pleasures of flavoursome, seasonal cuisine and a wine cellar of gargantuan proportions accompanied by excellent advice. A combination that has more than proved its worth: the restaurant is often fully booked.

X

Le Bistro de Cologny – Restaurant Auberge du Lion d'Or

Place Pierre-Gautier 5 ⊠ 1223 Cologny
– ✆ 022 736 57 80 – www.dupont-byrne.ch – Closed
24 December-11 January and Saturday-Sunday
Menu 78 CHF – Carte 76/91 CHF

Plan: **D2**

• Traditional cuisine • Bistro • Inn •

An annexe to the gourmet Lion d'Or restaurant, Le Bistro is much more than an add-on. It serves delicious dishes, which proves that the chef here certainly knows how to cook! Informal atmosphere and superb views from the terrace.

X

Le Bistrot Laz Nillo

Route des Acacias 34 ⊠ 1227 Carouge
– ✆ 022 342 34 34 – www.lebistrot.ch – Closed Monday dinner, Tuesday dinner, Saturday-Sunday
Menu 40 CHF (weekday lunch) – Carte 60/82 CHF

Plan: **B3**

• French modern • Bistro • Simple •

Crispy soft-boiled egg and sauté mushrooms with garlic is just one of the delicious dishes on the menu at this restaurant. The fine ingredients (including fish from the lake and Swiss cheeses) are showcased in carefully prepared dishes that are full of flavour. The reasonable prices provide the icing on the cake.

SWITZERLAND - GENEVA (GENÈVE)

ZURICH
ZÜRICH

Population: 402 275

Mirubi/Fotolia.com

Zurich has a lot of things going for it. A lot of history (2,000 years' worth), a lot of water (two rivers and a huge lake), a lot of beauty and, let's face it, a lot of wealth. It's an important financial and commercial centre, and has a well-earned reputation for good living and a rich cultural life. The place strikes a nice balance – it's large enough to boast some world-class facilities but small enough to hold onto its charm and old-world ambience. The window-shopping here sets it apart from many other European cities – from tiny boutiques and specialist emporiums to a shopping boulevard that's famed across the globe. Although it's not Switzerland's political capital, it's the spiritual one because of its pulsing arts scene: for those who might think the Swiss a bit staid, think again – this is where the nihilistic, anti-art Dada movement began. The attractive Lake Zurich flows northwards into the city, which forms a pleasingly symmetrical arc around it. From the lake, the river Limmat bisects Zurich: on its west bank lies the Old Town, the medieval hub, where the stylishly vibrant Bahnhofstrasse shopping street follows the line of the old city walls. Across the Limmat on the east side is the magnificent twin-towered Grossmünster, while just beyond is the charmingly historic district of Niederdorf and way down south, is the city's largest green space, the Zürichhorn Park.

ZURICH IN...

→ **ONE DAY**
Old Town, Bahnhofstrasse, Zurich West, Grossmünster.

→ **TWO DAYS**
Watch chessplayers on Lindenhof, see Chagall's windows at Fraumünster, Kunsthaus, Cabaret Voltaire, Café Odeon.

→ **THREE DAYS**
Utoquai, Zürichhorn Park, night at the Opera House.

PRACTICAL INFORMATION

ARRIVAL-DEPARTURE

 Zurich International Airport (Kloten) is 10km north of the city. Zürich Hauptbahnhof is the main railway station. Trains run every 10-15min and take 10min.

GETTING AROUND

The public transport system runs like clockwork. The city operates an efficient system on bus, tram, metro, train and boat. You can buy a single ticket, a day ticket or a 9 o'clock Pass. Tickets are available from ticket machines and tourist offices. Remember to validate your ticket at the ticket machine or special orange-coloured machine before boarding. The Zurichcard grants unlimited travel on all public transport (including river and lake boats). It also gives admission to more than forty museums and art collections. The card can be purchased for 24 or 72 hours. Cycling is encouraged here; hire bikes for free from beside the main railway station by leaving ID and a deposit.

EATING OUT

Zurich stands out in Switzerland (along with Geneva) for its top-class restaurants serving international cuisine. Zurich, though, takes the prize when it comes to trendy, cutting-edge places to dine, whether restaurant or bar, whether along the lakeside or in the converted loft of an old factory. In the middle of the day, most locals go for the cheaper daily lunchtime menus, saving themselves for the glories of the evening. The city is host to many traditional, longstanding

CALENDAR HIGHLIGHTS

February-March
Art On Ice, Carnival Procession concluding with the Guggen Monster Concert.

June and July
Zurich Festival.

August
Theatre Spectacle.

September
Weltklasse (Athletics).

October
Zurich International Art Fair.

October-November
Jazznojazz (music festival).

December
Silvesterlauf (Festive race through the Old Town).

Italian restaurants, but if you want to try something 'totally Zurcher', you can't do any better than tackle geschnetzeltes with rösti: sliced veal fried in butter, simmered with onions and mushrooms, with a dash of white wine and cream, served with hashed brown potatoes. A good place for simple restaurants and bars is Niederdorf, while Zurich West is coming on strong with its twenty-first century zeitgeist diners. It's customary to round up a small bill or leave up to ten percent on a larger one.

815

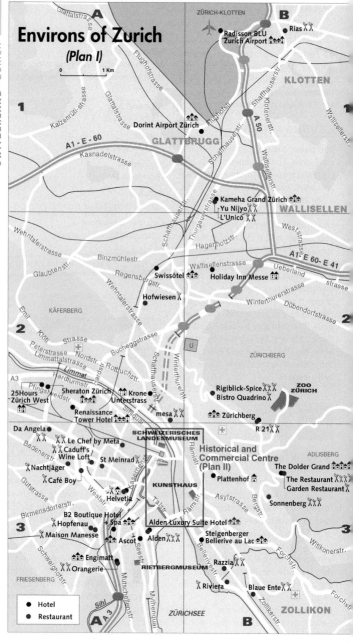

Environs of Zurich
(Plan I)

0   1 Km

ZÜRICH-KLOTTEN   B

Rias ✗✗

Radisson BLU
Zurich Airport ⌂⌂⌂

KLOTTEN

Glattalstrasse

Flughofstrasse

Kalzenrüti-strasse

Glattalstrasse

A1 - E 60

Kasnadelstrasse

Dorint Airport Zürich ⌂⌂

GLATTBRUGG

Schaffhauserstr.

Klotenerstr.

Wallisellerstr.

A 50

Thurgauerstr.

Kameha Grand Zürich ⌂⌂⌂
Yu Nijyo ✗
L'Unico ✗ ✗

WALLISELLEN

West strasse

A1- E 60- E 41

Wehntalerstrasse

Binzmühlestr.

Hagenholzstr.

Wallisellenstrasse

Ueberland

strasse

Glaubtenstr.

Regensbergstr.

Swissôtel ⌂⌂

Holiday Inn Messe ⌂⌂

Winterthurerstrasse

Dübendorfstrasse

Emil

Hofwiesen ✗

KÄFERBERG

Wehntalerstrasse

Bucheggstrasse

Schaffhauserstr.

Winterthurerstr.

Ü

ZÜRICHBERG

Kröt

Strasse

Petersstrasse

Nordstr.

Rottuchstr.

Limmatt

ZOO
ZÜRICH

Rigiblick-Spice ✗✗✗
Bistro Quadrino ✗

Limmattalstrasse

Hardturmstr.

A3

Pfingst

weidstr.

Sheraton Zürich ⌂⌂
Krone
Unterstrass

25Hours
Zürich West
⌂⌂

Renaissance
Tower Hotel ⌂⌂⌂

mesa ✗✗

⌂⌂ Zürichberg

ZÜRICHBERG

R 21✗✗

Da Angela ●
✗✗

✗✗ Le Chef by Meta
✗✗ Caduff's
Wine Loft

SCHWEIZERISCHES
LANDESMUSEUM

ADLISBERG

The Dolder Grand ⌂⌂⌂⌂

Badenerstr.

St Meinrad

Historical and
Commercial Centre
(Plan II)

Plattenhof ⌂

The Restaurant ✗✗✗
Garden Restaurant ✗

✗ Nachtjäger

✗ Café Boy

Gutstrasse

Weststr.

Kalkbreitestr.

Limmatst.

Talstr.

Rämistr.

KUNSTHAUS

Asylstrasse

Bergstr.

Sonnenberg ✗✗✗

✗✗ Helvetia

Birmensdorferstr.

B2 Boutique Hotel
✗ Hopfenau
+ Spa

Alden Luxury Suite Hotel ⌂⌂

✗ Maison Manesse

⌂⌂ Ascot

Alden ✗✗✗

Steigenberger
Bellerive au Lac ⌂⌂

Razzia ✗✗

Seestr.

Bellerivestr.

Forchstr.

Witikonerstr.

⌂⌂ Engimatt
✗✗ Orangerie

RIETBERGMUSEUM

✗ Riviera

Blaue Ente ✗✗

ZOLLIKON

FRIESENBERG

Schweigh.str.

Sihl

Mutschellenstr.

Mythenquai

ZÜRICHSEE

Zollikerstr.

Forchstr.

A 3

● Hotel
● Restaurant

A   B

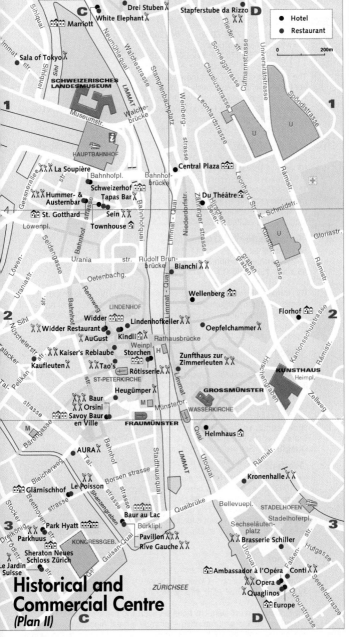

Drei Stuben ✕
White Elephant ✕
Stapferstube da Rizzo ✕✕

● Hotel
● Restaurant

Marriott 🏨

Sala of Tokyo ✕

SCHWEIZERISCHES
LANDESMUSEUM

0   200m

SWITZERLAND - ZURICH

U

U

U

Museumstr.

ℹ️

HAUPTBAHNHOF

Central Plaza 🏨

La Soupière ✕✕✕

Bahnhofpl.
Bahnhof-
brücke

Du Théâtre 🏨

Schweizerhof 🏨
Hummer- & ✕✕✕
Austernbar
Tapas Bar ✕

St. Gotthard 🏨
Sein ✕✕

Townhouse 🏨

Löwenpl.

Urania   str.   Rudolf Brun-
brücke
Bianchi ✕✕

Oetenbachg.

Wellenberg 🏨

LINDENHOF

Widder 🏨
✕✕ Widder Restaurant
AuGust
Kindli 🏨✕
Lindenhofkeller ✕✕

Florhof 🏨

Oepfelchammer ✕

✕✕ Kaiser's Reblaube
Kaufleuten ✕
✕✕ Tao's
Storchen 🏨
Weinpl.
Rathausbrücke

Zunfthaus zur ✕✕
Zimmerleuten ✕✕

KUNSTHAUS
Heimpl.

ST-PETERKIRCHE
Rôtisserie ✕✕
Heugümper ✕

GROSSMÜNSTER

✕✕ Baur
✕✕ Orsini
Savoy Baur 🏨
en Ville

WASSERKIRCHE

FRAUMÜNSTER

Helmhaus 🏨

AURA ✕

Kronenhalle ✕✕

Glärnischhof 🏨
Le Poisson ✕

STADELHOFEN

Baur au Lac 🏨
Bürklipl.

Bellevuepl.
Sechseläuten-
platz

Park Hyatt 🏨
Parkhuus ✕✕

Pavillon ✕✕
Rive Gauche ✕✕

✕✕ Brasserie Schiller

Sheraton Neues
Schloss Zürich 🏨
Le Jardin
Suisse

KONGRESSGEB.

ZÜRICHSEE

Ambassador à l'Opéra 🏨
Opera ✕✕
Quaglinos ✕
Conti ✕✕
Europe 🏨

Historical and
Commercial Centre
(Plan II)

817

SWITZERLAND - ZURICH

 Marriott

Neumühlequai 42 ⊠ *8006 –* ✆ *044 360 70 70*　　　Plan: **C1**
– www.zurichmarriott.com
266 rm – ♦235/470 CHF ♦♦235/470 CHF – ☲ 39 CHF – 4 suites
• Chain hotel • Classic • Modern •
The first skyscraper in Zurich (now a listed building) plays home to this upmarket hotel. Offering a real touch of luxury, it promises tasteful rooms with great views and everything else you would expect from an international hotel. eCHo serves its own particular take on Swiss food in the evenings, while Bar & Lounge 42 serves American-style snacks.
White Elephant – See restaurant listing

 Central Plaza

Central 1 ⊠ *8001 –* ✆ *044 256 56 56 – www.central.ch*　　　Plan: **D1**
97 rm – ♦180/316 CHF ♦♦200/376 CHF – ☲ 24 CHF – 4 suites
• Business • Contemporary •
This 1883 hotel with its classic façade and spacious lobby is located opposite the railway station and beside the Limmat. Although most of the rooms are not very large, they are comfortable and modern. Find the King's Cave grill restaurant in the vaulted cellar, which was formerly part of the UBS Treasury.

 Ambassador à l'Opéra

Falkenstr. 6 ⊠ *8008 –* ✆ *044 258 98 98*　　　Plan: **D3**
– www.ambassadorhotel.ch
45 rm – ♦295/560 CHF ♦♦415/680 CHF – ☲ 33 CHF
• Townhouse • Elegant • Cosy •
This former patrician's house is right next to the opera house. As an extra in the rooms: electrically adjustable beds and espresso machines. The restaurant l'Opéra features murals with operatic scenes. The speciality is fish. A fish menu is also available.
Opera – See restaurant listing

 Europe

Dufourstr. 4 ⊠ *8008 –* ✆ *043 456 86 86*　　　Plan: **D3**
– www.europehotel.ch – Closed 21-26 December
39 rm ☲ – ♦199/395 CHF ♦♦250/495 CHF – 2 suites
• Historic • Townhouse • Cosy •
Hotel directly by the opera house. In keeping with the flair of the old buildings (erected 1898-1900) the rooms are harmoniously appointed with high quality and classically stylish furniture and fabrics. Three of the rooms have a 1950s charm. Brasserie Quaglinos: lively, authentic with French cuisine.
Quaglinos – See restaurant listing

 Wellenberg

Niederdorfstr. 10 (at Hirschenplatz) ⊠ *8001*　　　Plan: **D2**
– ✆ *043 888 44 44 – www.hotel-wellenberg.ch*
42 rm ☲ – ♦199/360 CHF ♦♦240/550 CHF – 3 suites
• Business • Modern •
The location in the old town is ideal for a city break. Most of the rooms are spacious, some particularly stylish. Fitness park close by. Beauty centre directly opposite.

 Florhof

Florhofgasse 4 ⊠ *8001 –* ✆ *044 250 26 26*　　　Plan: **D2**
– www.hotelflorhof.ch – Closed 24 December-2 January
32 rm ☲ – ♦210/319 CHF ♦♦329/389 CHF
• Townhouse • Elegant •
The Florhof is an excellent city hotel set in an 18C patrician house. The rooms – comfortable and well furnished – promise a great night's sleep, while the relaxed and cosy yet stylish restaurant serves seasonal cuisine. In the summer you can eat outside on the lovely terrace by the sculpted stone fountain.

SWITZERLAND - ZURICH

🏠 **Helmhaus** ⚨

Schifflände 30 ⊠ 8001 – ℰ 044 266 95 95   Plan: **D3**
– www.helmhaus.ch
24 rm � – ♦225/320 CHF ♦♦310/470 CHF
• Townhouse • Cosy • Contemporary •

This carefully run hotel is in the city centre near the lake. It will impress with its cosy, good value and up-to-date furnishings. There is a friendly and modern breakfast room.

🏠 **Du Théâtre** ♿

Seilergraben 69 ⊠ 8001 – ℰ 044 267 26 70   Plan: **D1**
– www.hotel-du-theatre.ch
50 rm – ♦130/235 CHF ♦♦170/300 CHF – ⊻ 20 CHF
• Townhouse • Modern •

Today home cinema and radio plays replace the former theatre. Attic rooms with air-conditioning. La Suite Lounge has a roof terrace for breakfast and international dishes. Only a few minutes walk from the main station.

XX **Conti**

Dufourstr. 1 ⊠ 8008 – ℰ 044 251 06 66   Plan: **D3**
– www.bindella.ch – Closed 4 weeks mid July-mid August
Carte 76/130 CHF
• Italian • Mediterranean •

This restaurant is immediately next to the opera. Find an interior of classical dignity with a lovely high stucco ceiling, an exhibition of paintings, and Italian cuisine.

XX **Bianchi** 🍽 ⚨

Limmatquai 82 ⊠ 8001 – ℰ 044 262 98 44   Plan: **D2**
– www.ristorante-bianchi.ch
Carte 52/119 CHF – *(booking advisable)*
• Fish and seafood • Fashionable •

This bright, modern restaurant is located in a quiet spot on the banks of the River Limmat. It serves Mediterranean cuisine and diners are invited to take their pick from the fish and seafood on offer at the generous buffet.

XX **Kronenhalle** ⚨ ⇔

Rämistr. 4 ⊠ 8001 – ℰ 044 262 99 00   Plan: **D3**
– www.kronenhalle.com
Carte 64/124 CHF – *(booking advisable)*
• Traditional cuisine • Classic •

This building, constructed in 1862, is a Zurich institution located on Bellevue Square. Be sure to take a look at the art collection put together over a period of decades. The atmosphere is traditional, as is the cooking.

XX **Brasserie Schiller** 🍽 ♿

Sechseläutenplatz 10 ⊠ 8001 – ℰ 044 222 20 30   Plan: **D3**
– www.brasserie-schiller.ch
Menu 29 CHF (weekday lunch)/69 CHF – Carte 41/104 CHF
• Traditional cuisine • Brasserie •

This lovely historic building used to be the offices of the Zurich newspaper, the Neue Zürcher Zeitung. Nowadays, the modern brasserie serves classic cuisine including an opera menu available until 11pm. Sunday brunch.

XX **Opera** – Hotel Ambassador à l'Opéra ⚨

Falkenstr. 6 ⊠ 8008 – ℰ 044 258 98 98   Plan: **D3**
– www.operarestaurant.ch
Menu 68/120 CHF (dinner) – Carte 51/100 CHF
• French classic • Elegant •

In this modern, elegant restaurant you will find your gaze inevitably wandering to the walls and ceiling to marvel at the opera related decor that fills the room. Fortunately, the food is just as appealing - classic cuisine with an emphasis on fish but also dishes such as saddle of venison and calves' cheeks.

SWITZERLAND - ZURICH

Stapferstube da Rizzo ☆ P

Culmannstr. 45 ✉ 8006 – ☎ 044 350 11 00
– *www.stapferstube.com – Closed Sunday*
Menu 65/110 CHF – Carte 64/119 CHF
• Mediterranean • Rustic •

Plan: **D1**

Southern Italian Giovanni Rizzo has been calling the shots here at Stapferstube, a well-known Zürich eatery, for some time now. As a result the food has a strongly Italian feel as evidenced by the delicious pan-fried squid with garlic, herbs and chilli. The food is served in a friendly, rustic setting and outdoors in summer. Conveniently, the restaurant has its own car park.

Zunfthaus zur Zimmerleuten ⚏ ✿

Limmatquai 40 (1st floor) ✉ 8001 – ☎ 044 250 53 65
– *www.zunfthaus-zimmerleuten.ch*
Carte 72/104 CHF

Plan: **D2**

• Traditional cuisine • Cosy • Traditional •

For over 550 years this Zürich monument on the banks of the River Limmat has belonged to the Guild of Carpenters. Now it serves ambitious, traditional cuisine in a stylish setting on the first floor and with the stunning Zunftsaal function room on the floor above. Simpler fare in the pleasant Küferstube.

Razzia ⚏

Seefeldstr. 82 ✉ 8008 – ☎ 044 296 70 70
– *www.razzia-zuerich.ch – Closed Saturday lunch, Sunday*
Menu 42/58 CHF – Carte 67/125 CHF – *(booking advisable)*
• International • Trendy • Brasserie •

Plan: **B3**

One of Zürich's most fashionable eateries, the small tables arranged in this stylish, high-ceilinged former cinema are much in demand. The menu is considerable, ranging from red chicken curry to pasta, goose liver and grilled meats.

Drei Stuben ⚏ ✿

Beckenhofstr. 5 ✉ 8006 – ☎ 044 350 33 00
– *www.dreistuben-zuerich.ch – Closed during Christmas and Saturday lunch, Sunday*
Menu 114 CHF – Carte 50/119 CHF

Plan: **C1**

• Traditional cuisine • Rustic •

The floors, ceilings and walls here are all done out in rustic wood, lending a comfortable, cosy atmosphere to this restaurant – just what you would expect from a local hostelry with a 300-year-old tradition of serving food. There is also a lovely garden with mature trees. Marco Però and his team cook ambitious traditional but contemporary international food.

White Elephant - Hotel Marriott

Neumühlequai 42 ✉ 8001 – ☎ 044 360 73 18
– *www.whiteelephant.ch – Closed Saturday lunch, Sunday lunch*
Menu 37 CHF (weekday lunch) – Carte 40/99 CHF

Plan: **C1**

• Thai • Exotic •

Right in the heart of the city, visitors will really get their money's worth in this restaurant. It serves Southeast Asian cuisine with a focus on Thailand.

Quaglinos - Hotel Europe

Dufourstr. 4 ✉ 8008 – ☎ 043 456 86 86
– *www.europehotel.ch – Closed 21-26 December*
Carte 54/108 CHF

Plan: **D3**

• French classic • Brasserie •

A lively and authentic Quaglinos brasserie based on the tried and tested bistro formula. It offers typical French savoir vivre and, of course, classic French cuisine including duck foie gras and 'Café de Paris' entrecote.

SWITZERLAND - ZURICH

✗ **Oepfelchammer**

Rindermarkt 12 (1st floor) ⊠ *8001 –* ☎ *044 251 23 36* — Plan: **D2**
– www.oepfelchammer.ch – Closed Sunday-Monday and Bank Holidays
Carte 65/78 CHF
• Traditional cuisine • Rustic • Wine bar •
The poet Gottfried Keller was a regular of the original wine bar. The restaurant serves modern and traditional cuisine in this 19C building.

 Baur au Lac

Talstr. 1 ⊠ *8001 –* ☎ *044 220 50 20 – www.bauraulac.ch* — Plan: **C3**
112 rm – †570 CHF ††870 CHF – ☝ 46 CHF – 8 suites
• Grand Luxury • Elegant • Personalised •
Magnificent 19C architecture with luxurious facilities, conscientious management (the second generation of managers from the same family) and plentiful and attentive staff. Some very lovely newer rooms. A terrace leads to the pretty garden.
❀ **Pavillon • Rive Gauche** – See restaurant listing

 Park Hyatt

Beethoven Str. 21 ⊠ *8002 –* ☎ *043 883 12 34* — Plan: **C3**
– www.zurich.park.hyatt.ch
134 rm – †490/1050 CHF ††640/1200 CHF – ☝ 39 CHF – 4 suites
• Grand Luxury • Modern • Elegant •
The Park Hyatt has a large, elegant hall and a lobby area with an entrance to the striking Onyx Bar. It features stylish and modern rooms with lots of space, and a tasteful little spa. The elegant Parkhuus has a show kitchen and a glazed wine cellar on two floors.
Parkhuus – See restaurant listing

 Widder

Rennweg 7 ⊠ *8001 –* ☎ *044 224 25 26* — Plan: **C2**
– www.widderhotel.ch
42 rm – ☝ †620/820 CHF ††690/1090 CHF – 7 suites
• Luxury • Design • Historic •
Swiss architect Tilla Theus has successfully combined old and new in these nine beautifully restored townhouses in the old city. Historic detail is combined with some lovely one-off decorative pieces. The service is excellent and the Wirtschaft zur Schtund serves tasty Flammkuchen.
❀ **AuGust • Widder Restaurant** – See restaurant listing

 Savoy Baur en Ville

Poststr. 12 (at Paradeplatz) ⊠ *8001 –* ☎ *044 215 25 25* — Plan: **C2**
– www.savoy-zuerich.ch
95 rm – ☝ †400/495 CHF ††690/820 CHF – 9 suites
• Luxury • Classic • Elegant •
The building of this wonderful hotel in 1838 laid the foundations of a long and lasting hotel tradition. Offering first class service in a made-to-measure interior, the upmarket restaurant features unusual Brazilian rock crystal chandeliers and fine table settings. Live piano music in the bar.
Orsini • Baur – See restaurant listing

 Storchen

Weinplatz 2 (access via Storchengasse 16) ⊠ *8001* — Plan: **C2**
– ☎ *044 227 27 27 – www.storchen.ch*
67 rm – ☝ †350/580 CHF ††430/700 CHF – 1 suite
• Traditional • Classic • Elegant •
Right on the banks of the River Limmat, this is one of the oldest hotels in the city. Tasteful toile de Jouy fabrics adorn the elegant guestrooms, while the Storchen suite has a roof terrace and lake view. The restaurant's balcony terrace and the 'Barchetta' café in Weinplatz are wonderful. Sunday brunch.
Rôtisserie – See restaurant listing

XXX   **Pavillon** – Hotel Baur au Lac   🐝 ✿ AC 🚗
✨   *Talstr. 1* ✉ *8001 – ☎ 044 220 50 22*   Plan: **C3**
  – www.aupavillon.ch
  – Closed Saturday lunch, Sunday
  Menu 76 CHF (weekday lunch)/160 CHF – Carte 120/165 CHF
  • French classic • Elegant • Friendly •
  Star architect Pierre-Yves Rochon designed the spatial concept of this elegant
  restaurant. The almost 360° glazed rotunda with its country views is wonderful.
  Good classic cuisine prepared by Laurent Eperon, with dishes that include roast
  sea bass with Périgord truffles.
  → Kaninchenroulade, Erbsen, Limetten und Koriander. Wilder Wolfsbarsch
  auf der Haut gebraten. Kalbshaxe glasiert mit schwarzem Pfeffer.

XXX   **La Soupière** – Hotel Schweizerhof   ✿ AC
  Bahnhofplatz 7 ✉ *8021 – ☎ 044 218 88 40*   Plan: **C1**
  – www.hotelschweizerhof.com – Closed Saturday lunch, Sunday
  Menu 79 CHF (weekday lunch) – Carte 95/114 CHF
  • Modern cuisine • Elegant •
  An elegant address on the first floor. Warm colours, carefully selected furniture
  and elegant details set the tone. Serves seasonal, modern cuisine.

XXX   **Baur** – Hotel Savoy Baur en Ville   ✿ AC
  Poststr. 12 (at Paradeplatz) ✉ *8001 – ☎ 044 215 25 25*   Plan: **C2**
  – www.savoy-zuerich.ch – Closed Saturday-Sunday
  Menu 72 CHF (weekday lunch) – Carte 66/146 CHF
  • French classic • Elegant • Formal •
  This restaurant has a stylish, elegant setting that is perfect for Baur's classic
  French cuisine. Details such as the unusual rock crystal chandeliers together
  with the luxury fittings and smart table settings set the scene.

XXX   **Hummer- & Austernbar** – Hotel St. Gotthard   AC
  Bahnhofstr. 87 ✉ *8021 – ☎ 044 211 76 21*   Plan: **C1**
  – www.hummerbar.ch
  – Closed 13 July-9 August and Sunday lunch
  Menu 55 CHF (lunch) – Carte 69/208 CHF
  • French classic • Elegant • Cosy •
  A real Zürich institution that first opened its doors in 1935. The elegant interior
  and signed postcards from celebrities bear witness to the cult status of this res-
  taurant. Serves largely seafood.

XX   **Sein** (Martin Surbeck)   🍴 AC ⇔
✨   *Schützengasse 5* ✉ *8001 – ☎ 044 221 10 65*   Plan: **C1**
  – www.zuerichsein.ch
  – Closed 24 December-4 January, 19 March-3 April, 16 July-7 August and
  Saturday-Sunday, mid November-December: Saturday lunch, Sunday
  Menu 84 CHF (lunch)/175 CHF – Carte 98/138 CHF
  • French classic • Fashionable •
  After a little shopping on Zürich's famous Bahnhofstrasse, sit down to the crea-
  tive cuisine of Martin Surbeck (who runs the restaurant with partner Patricia
  Lackner) and Ken Nakano. The set menu comes in a separate vegetarian ver-
  sion. And if you fancy something a little lighter, try some of the tasty "Seinigkei-
  ten" served in the Tapas Bar.
  → Störcarpaccio auf Kartoffelstock mit Kaviar und Sauerrahmsauce. Wach-
  tel-Bohnenrisotto mit roh marinierter Entenleber und Pfefferminze. Am
  Knochen gebratene Challans-Entenbrust mit Kartoffelpüree und gelben
  Räben.
  🍴 **Tapas Bar** – See restaurant listing

XX **Lindenhofkeller**

Pfalzgasse 4 ✉ *8001* – ✆ *044 211 70 71*   Plan: **C2**
– *www.lindenhofkeller.ch – Closed 3 weeks end July-August, 1 week Christmas, Saturday-Sunday and Bank Holidays*
Menu 69/115 CHF – Carte 59/138 CHF
• French classic • Elegant • Romantic •
With its homely romantic touch, this elegant cellar restaurant with wine lounge fits harmoniously into the contemplative old town scene. Classic cooking with modern elements.

XX **Widder Restaurant** – Hotel Widder

Rennweg 7 ✉ *8001* – ✆ *044 224 24 12*   Plan: **C2**
– *www.widderhotel.ch – Closed mid July-mid August and Sunday-Monday*
Menu 85 CHF (lunch)/195 CHF – Carte 81/137 CHF
• Modern cuisine • Cosy •
Choose between the smart, elegant atmosphere of the Widder Restaurant or the more relaxed Turmstübli (smokers welcome!) with its upholstered leather benches. Seasonal, modern cuisine.

XX **Tao's**

Augustinergasse 3 ✉ *8001* – ✆ *044 448 11 22*   Plan: **C2**
– *www.tao-group.ch – Closed Sunday*
Menu 51 CHF (weekday lunch) – Carte 63/120 CHF
• Fusion • Exotic • Elegant •
A touch of the exotic in the middle of Zurich! Elegant upstairs, a little more informal on the ground floor. Smokers can use Tao's Lounge Bar that offers a Euro-Asian menu. Grilled meats.

XX **Kaiser's Reblaube**

Glockengasse 7 ✉ *8001* – ✆ *044 221 21 20*   Plan: **C2**
– *www.kaisers-reblaube.ch – Closed 25 July-14 August, January-October: Saturday lunch, Sunday-Monday and November-December: Saturday lunch, Sunday*
Menu 58 CHF (lunch)/120 CHF (weekday lunch) – Carte 62/104 CHF
• Classic cuisine • Rustic • Cosy •
Enjoy modern cooking with a traditional influence in this house that was built in 1260 along a small, narrow alley. Comfortable little restaurant on the first-floor and a wine bar on the ground floor.

XX **Rive Gauche** – Hotel Baur au Lac

Talstr. 1 ✉ *8001* – ✆ *044 220 50 60* – *www.agauche.ch*   Plan: **C3**
Carte 79/144 CHF
• International • Cosy •
One of the places to be seen in the city centre. The great cosmopolitan interior attracts a trendy young and young at heart crowd to eat and drink (grilled meats) but also to see and be seen.

XX **Orsini** – Hotel Savoy Baur en Ville

Poststr. 12 (at Paradeplatz) ✉ *8001* – ✆ *044 215 25 25*   Plan: **C2**
– *www.savoy-zuerich.ch*
Menu 72 CHF (lunch) – Carte 74/146 CHF – *(booking advisable)*
• Italian • Elegant •
This elegant restaurant has been serving classic Italian cuisine for over 30 years. The sumptuous poppy design on the carpet, repeated in the filigree motif in the oil paintings on the walls, adds a special touch.

XX **Parkhuus** – Hotel Park Hyatt

Beethoven Str. 21 ✉ *8002* – ✆ *043 883 10 75*   Plan: **C3**
– *www.zurich.park.hyatt.ch – Closed Saturday lunch, Sunday*
Menu 59 CHF (weekday lunch) – Carte 57/183 CHF
• Modern cuisine • Fashionable •
In keeping with the rest of the hotel, the restaurant is modern and international. It has a large show kitchen producing creative, contemporary cuisine, as well as an impressive glazed wine shop accessed via a spiral staircase.

XX **Le Poisson** – Hotel Glärnischhof AC P

Claridenstr. 30 ⊠ 8022 – ℰ 044 286 22 22 Plan: **C3**
– www.lepoisson.ch
Menu 88/149 CHF – Carte 78/129 CHF – *(Saturday-Sunday dinner only)*
• Fish and seafood • Classic •

As the name implies, the specialities on offer in this restaurant come from the water. Enjoy friendly service at your beautifully laid table.

XX **Rôtisserie** – Hotel Storchen ≤ �ⓗ

Weinplatz 2 (access via Storchengasse 16) ⊠ 8001 Plan: **C2**
– ℰ 044 227 21 13 – www.storchen.ch
Menu 85 CHF (dinner) – Carte 71/99 CHF
• French classic • Cosy •

Take a seat in the tasteful restaurant and marvel first at the wonderful painted ceiling. Then look out of the window (if you aren't already on the terrace) at the wonderful views of the River Limmat and the Great Minster.

X **Heugümper** ⓗ ＆ AC ⇔

Waaggasse 4 ⊠ 8001 – ℰ 044 211 16 60 Plan: **C2**
*– www.restaurantheuguemper.ch – Closed 24-26 December, 11-
17 January, mid July- mid August and Sunday, Mai-September: Saturday-
Sunday*
Menu 115 CHF (dinner) – Carte 55/95 CHF
• Fusion • Fashionable • Bistro •

This venerable townhouse in the heart of Zurich serves international cuisine with a Southeast Asian flair. Small lunch menu. Smart modern bistro on the ground floor and an elegant restaurant upstairs.

X **AuGust** – Hotel Widder ⓗ

ⓐ *Rennweg 7 ⊠ 8001 – ℰ 044 224 28 28* Plan: **C2**
– www.au-gust.ch
Carte 48/97 CHF
• French classic • Brasserie •

AuGust offers fresh and flavoursome cuisine – including some great terrines and delicious sausages – served in a friendly, classic brasserie atmosphere. The local slow-cooked dishes are also very good.

X **AURA** AC ⇔

Bleicherweg 5 ⊠ 8001 – ℰ 044 448 11 44 Plan: **C3**
– www.aura-zurich.ch – Closed Sunday
Menu 60 CHF (weekday dinner) – Carte 54/114 CHF
• International • Trendy •

A stylishly urban restaurant, a top-flight events venue, a lounge or a club? AURA is a little bit of each, but above all the place to be for lovers of modern crossover cuisine with a weakness for grilled food – just watch the chefs at work! Located on Paradeplatz in the old stock exchange building.

X **Kaufleuten** ⓗ ⇔

ⓐ *Pelikanplatz ⊠ 8001 – ℰ 044 225 33 33* Plan: **C2**
– www.kaufleuten.ch – Closed Sunday lunch
Menu 75/85 CHF – Carte 54/98 CHF
• Regional • Brasserie •

This lively brasserie located in the fashionable venue of the same name is much in demand, not least thanks to its good food. Try the duck ravioli with leek salad or the veal cutlet – sliced for you at your table – before moving on to the club or the bar.

X **Kindli** – Hotel Kindli ⓗ

Pfalzgasse 1 ⊠ 8001 – ℰ 043 888 76 78 – www.kindli.ch Plan: **C2**
– Closed Sunday and Bank Holidays
Carte 61/111 CHF – *(booking advisable)*
• French classic • Inn •

The restaurant's charming character comes in part from its wonderful old wood panelling and the bistro-style, communal arrangement of its beautifully laid tables.

X **Sala of Tokyo** 🍴 AC ⟷
Limmatstr. 29 ✉ 8005 – ℰ 044 271 52 90 Plan: **C1**
– www.sala-of-tokyo.ch – Closed 3 weeks July-August, 2 weeks Christmas-New Year
Menu 72/140 CHF – Carte 51/136 CHF
• Japanese • Friendly • Exotic •
This restaurant has been serving authentic Japanese cuisine for over 30 years. In the air-conditioned Sankaiyaki Room meat is grilled at your table in traditional-style. And of course there is a sushi bar.

X **Le Jardin Suisse** – Hotel Sheraton Neues Schloss Zürich 🍴 AC
Stockerstr. 17 ✉ 8002 – ℰ 044 286 94 00 Plan: **C3**
– www.sheraton.com/neuesschloss – Closed Sunday
Carte 52/90 CHF
• Regional • Bistro •
A hint of bistro-style pervades this restaurant with its striking exposed stone wall. It offers traditional Swiss specialities that you can enjoy on the terrace (in summer) that skirts round the building.

X **Tapas Bar** – Restaurant Sein 🍴 AC
😊 *Schützengasse 5 – ℰ 044 221 10 65* Plan: **C1**
– www.zuerichsein.ch – Closed 24 December-4 January, 19 March-3 April, 16 July-7 August and Saturday-Sunday
Carte 46/80 CHF
• Modern cuisine • Tapas bar •
This friendly, modern restaurant boasts a light and airy interior and tapas-style food. Try the ravioli with rosemary butter or the Pilze mit Kakaoerde und Mimolette (a mushroom speciality).

NEAR THE AIRPORT PLAN I

🏨 **Radisson BLU Zurich Airport** 𝕏 Ĺ5 🏊 ♿ AC 🛎
(directly access to the terminals) ✉ 8058 Plan: **B1**
– ℰ 044 800 40 40 – www.radissonblu.com/hotel-zurichairport
323 rm – 🛏250/750 CHF 🛏🛏250/750 CHF – ⊊ 38 CHF – 7 suites
• Business • Conference hotel • Modern •
This is the closest hotel to the airport and it has a 16m-high Wine Tower rising from the imposing atrium lobby. During dinner, marvel as the 'Wine Angels' perform their artistic show at the Angels restaurant (as well as during brunch on Sundays). The Filini restaurant serves Italian specialities.

🏨 **Swissôtel** 𝕏 ≤ Ĺ5 🏊 🔲 ♿ AC 🛎 🚗
Schulstr. 44 (at Marktplatz) – ℰ 044 317 31 11 Plan: **A2**
– www.swissotel.com/hotels/zurich/
336 rm – 🛏160/420 CHF 🛏🛏160/420 CHF – ⊊ 35 CHF – 11 suites
• Business • Chain hotel • Contemporary •
This high-rise hotel is located at the Marktplatz. It boasts an indoor swimming pool on the 32nd floor with views over the whole city and a 19-room convention centre. The Le Muh restaurant is divided into two parts: one casual, the other more elegant.

🏨 **Dorint Airport Zürich** 𝕏 ♿ AC 🛎 ⟷ 🚗
Riethofstr. 40 – ℰ 044 808 10 00 Plan: **B1**
– www.dorint.com/zuerich
235 rm – 🛏150/350 CHF 🛏🛏180/380 CHF – ⊊ 30 CHF
• Business • Functional • Modern •
Selling points at this hotel include the location close to the airport, the functional, modern rooms, the well-equipped conference facilities and an airport shuttle service. Mediterranean and regional cuisine is served in the restaurant. The building is interesting in itself - it takes the form of a Swiss cross. Try the Park, Sleep & Fly option.

Holiday Inn Messe

Plan: **B2**

Wallisellenstr. 48 – ℰ 044 316 11 00
– www.holidayinn.com/zurichmesse
164 rm – †169/361 CHF ††169/361 CHF – ⌑ 28 CHF
• Business • Modern • Functional •

This hotel stands out chiefly for its convenient location opposite the conference centre. The spacious rooms are functionally equipped. The 'Bits & Bites' brasserie serves Swiss and international cuisine.

Hofwiesen

Plan: **A2**

Hofwiesenstr. 265 ⌗ 8057
– ℰ 043 433 80 88 – www.hofwiesen.ch
– Closed Saturday lunch, Sunday
Carte 48/95 CHF
• Austrian • Fashionable •

Hofwiesen promises a little bit of Austria in Zurich. Find dishes like boiled beef in broth, Wiener schnitzel and apricot dumplings on the menu. The food is fresh, uncomplicated and influenced by the Mediterranean, while the decor is warm, modern and minimalist in style.

ENVIRONS OF ZURICH

PLAN I

The Dolder Grand

Plan: **B3**

Kurhausstr. 65 ⌗ 8032 – ℰ 044 456 60 00
– www.thedoldergrand.com
161 rm – †540/740 CHF ††700/1150 CHF – ⌑ 46 CHF – 12 suites
• Grand Luxury • Modern • Historic •

The embodiment of exclusivity. Emanating from the 'Curhaus' of 1899 and committed to this tradition just as much as to the requirements of today. The crème de la crème is the 400 m² Maestro suite high above Zurich. There are 4000 m² of various spa facilities in purist style. Panoramic view from the terrace of the Garden Restaurant. Brunch is served on Sundays.
✿✿ **The Restaurant • Garden Restaurant** – See restaurant listing

Sheraton Zürich

Plan: **A2**

Pfingstweidstr.100 ⌗ 8005 – ℰ 044 285 40 00
– www.sheratonzurichhotel.com
193 rm – †300/400 CHF ††300/400 CHF – ⌑ 35 CHF – 4 suites
• Business • Design • Functional •

Popular with business guests, the rooms at the Sheraton are functional, stylish and urban in design, and all have free use of the Nespresso machine as a little extra. The view from the Club Lounge on the 10th floor is fabulous. 'Route twenty-six' offers typical fare from all 26 Swiss cantons while the 'NUOVO' bistro serves breakfast, panini and pasta in the evenings.

Renaissance Tower Hotel

Plan: **A2**

Turbinenstr. 20 ⌗ 8005
– ℰ 044 630 33 30
– www.renaissancezurichtower.com
252 rm – †345/615 CHF ††345/615 CHF – ⌑ 39 CHF – 48 suites
• Luxury • Business • Modern •

The reception area with its smart minimalist design in light and dark contrasting tones sets the "urban lifestyle" tone which continues throughout the hotel in the rooms, the restaurant and the lobby bar. The Executive Club Lounge and 24hr health club and fitness suite on the top floor offer magnificent views.

SWITZERLAND - ZURICH

B2 Boutique Hotel+Spa

Brandschenkenstr. 152 ✉ *8002 –* ☎ *044 567 67 67* Plan: **A3**
– www.b2boutiquehotels.com
60 rm ☷ – ♦320/550 CHF ♦♦370/590 CHF – 8 suites
• Historic • Design •

Housed in a listed brewery building constructed in 1866, this strikingly chic hotel will appeal predominantly to younger guests and architecture enthusiasts. The Bibliothek bar (over 30 000 books) serves Spanischbrödlis (hazelnut and carrot pastries) dubbed 'SWaPPa's' or Swiss tapas. The thermal bath and spa are particularly impressive (additional charge).

Alden Luxury Suite Hotel

Splügenstr. 2 ✉ *8002 –* ☎ *044 289 99 99* Plan: **A3**
– www.alden.ch
22 suites – ♦450/800 CHF ♦♦450/800 CHF – ☷ 39 CHF
• Luxury • Design •

A great little hotel housed in a magnificent listed building dating back to 1895 with individual, exquisitely designed guestrooms. Non-alcoholic drinks from the mini-bar are included in the price. Two loft suites with a roof terrace.
Alden – See restaurant listing

Kameha Grand Zürich

Dufaux-Str. 1 – ☎ *044 525 50 00* Plan: **B3**
– www.kamehagrandzuerich.com
224 rm – ♦320/380 CHF ♦♦320/380 CHF – ☷ 39 CHF – 21 suites
• Business • Luxury • Design •

A lifestyle hotel set in the middle of the Glattpark. The Kameha Grand is anything but run of the mill with its striking façade, imposing lobby complete with smart bar, and classy, tasteful interior. The service is strikingly straightforward and attentive.
❀ **Yu Nijyo • L'Unico** – See restaurant listing

Zürichberg

Orellistr. 21 ✉ *8044 –* ☎ *044 268 35 35* Plan: **B2**
– www.zuerichberg.ch
66 rm ☷ – ♦240/590 CHF ♦♦300/590 CHF
• Traditional • Design •

On the outside the classical assembly rooms (1900) contrast with the timber-clad elliptical annexe. On the inside find chic clean-lined design, art and comfort. Enjoy the peace and the view of the city, lake and region from the restaurant terrace. Brunch is served on Sundays.
R21 – See restaurant listing

Steigenberger Bellerive au Lac

Utoquai 47 ✉ *8008 –* ☎ *044 254 40 00* Plan: **B3**
– www.steigenberger.com/zuerich
50 rm – ♦279/529 CHF ♦♦279/529 CHF – ☷ 35 CHF – 1 suite
• Business • Elegant • Modern •

This hotel has been extensively renovated and upgraded over recent years. It now offers not only a fine, lakefront location but also comfortable, elegant Art Deco guestrooms with the latest technology and tasteful bathrooms, particularly the Grand Suite with its wonderful roof terrace. The restaurant serves Swiss cuisine with international influences.

Ascot

Tessinerplatz 9 ✉ *8002 –* ☎ *044 208 14 14* Plan: **A3**
– www.ascot.ch
74 rm ☷ – ♦195/485 CHF ♦♦247/577 CHF
• Traditional • Classic •

The rooms in this hotel in the business district offer modern style and technology. They are all equipped with tea/coffee machines and some have balconies. The restaurant, very "British" with its leather upholstery, mahogany and chequered carpet, serves steaks and seafood. Its speciality is classic roast beef carved from the trolley.

Engimatt
★ ※ 🏋 🚗
Engimattstr. 14 ✉ 8002 – 𝒞 044 284 16 16 – www.engimatt.ch
Plan: **A3**
71 rm ⌂ – 🛏250/400 CHF 🛏🛏290/460 CHF
• Business • Personalised •
Despite its location close to the city centre this hotel is a green oasis in the district of Enge. A dedicated, family-run hotel with individual guestrooms in cosy colours and each with its own balcony. The restaurant is located in an airy conservatory overlooking the garden.
Orangerie – See restaurant listing

25Hours Zürich West
★ ⋒ 🕭 AC 🏋 🚗
Pfingstweidstr. 102 ✉ 8005 – 𝒞 044 577 25 25
Plan: **A2**
– www.25hours-hotels.com/zuerich
126 rm – 🛏190/280 CHF 🛏🛏190/280 CHF – ⌂ 25 CHF
• Business • Design •
This modern business hotel in the city's fast-growing development area is designer Alfredo Häberli's homage to the city of Zürich. The rooms, which come in Platinum, Gold and Silver categories, are brightly coloured, curvaceous and very urban. NENI offers a minimalist feel and Israeli/Oriental cuisine.

Krone Unterstrass
★ 🕭 AC 🏋 🅿
Schaffhauserstr. 1 ✉ 8006 – 𝒞 044 360 56 56
Plan: **A2**
– www.hotel-krone.ch
74 rm – 🛏154/290 CHF 🛏🛏216/450 CHF – ⌂ 19 CHF
• Business • Contemporary •
Hotel above the city centre. Technically well-equipped rooms, the newer ones in the town house have a small kitchen and face the courtyard. Simple daytime restaurant or more refined restaurant with fireplace and bar. Good parking facilities in the nearby public car park.

Plattenhof
★ 🕭 🏋
Plattenstr. 26 ✉ 8032 – 𝒞 044 251 19 10
Plan: **B3**
– www.plattenhof.ch
37 rm ⌂ – 🛏135/355 CHF 🛏🛏185/385 CHF
• Business • Design • Minimalist •
This hotel is in a residential quarter on the edge of the city centre. Find distinctly personal service and functional rooms in a modern, plain, designer style. Sento has a bistro atmosphere and serves Italian cuisine.

Helvetia
★ 🚗
Stauffacherquai 1 ✉ 8004 – 𝒞 044 297 99 99
Plan: **A3**
– www.hotel-helvetia.ch
16 rm – 🛏165/375 CHF 🛏🛏215/475 CHF – ⌂ 17 CHF
• Townhouse • Cosy • Contemporary •
Your host at the Helvetia is relaxed and friendly, just like his hotel where you will quickly feel at home. The rooms are charming with their mix of Art Nouveau and modern touches, as is the restaurant with its stylish upmarket decor and Swiss/French brasserie-style cuisine.
Helvetia – See restaurant listing

XXxX The Restaurant – Hotel The Dolder Grand
🥂 ≤ 🍴 🕭 AC 🚗
❀❀ *Kurhausstr. 65 ✉ 8032 – 𝒞 044 456 60 00*
Plan: **B3**
– www.thedoldergrand.com – Closed 23 February-5 March, 26 July-
13 August and Saturday lunch, Sunday-Monday
Menu 98/298 CHF – Carte 159/202 CHF – *(booking advisable)*
• Creative • Fashionable • Elegant •
In the venerable old part of the Dolder Grand, The Restaurant has much that is pleasing to the eye. Inside, the lovely contrast between the old coffered ceiling and the modern elegant style; outside, the view from the wonderful terrace; and on the plate, Heiko Nieder's excellent cuisine. More than just visually attractive, his food is also an exciting combination of textures, temperatures and aromas. The impressive wine cabinet holds a first-class selection, some of which are available by the glass.
→ Hummer mit Erdbeeren, Rande, Estragon und Senf. Reh mit Gartenkräutern, Kürbiskernen und Angostura. Mispeln mit Topfen, Ampfer und Wacholder.

XxX · ✿

Rigiblick - Spice

❀ ⇦ ♨ ⇐ 🛏 & 🚗

Germaniastr. 99 ✉ 8044 – ℰ 043 255 15 70 — Plan: **B2**
– www.restaurantrigiblick.ch – Closed 20 December-4 January and Sunday-Monday

7 rm 🖵 – 🚹350/550 CHF 🚹🚹350/550 CHF
Menu 54 CHF (lunch)/180 CHF – *(booking advisable)*
• Creative • Minimalist • Formal •

Creative without being pretentious, delicate and a real joy to behold… That just about describes the evening menu (up to nine courses) produced by young Berlin chef Dennis Puchert here. If you are eating on a budget, come for lunch. And don't miss the terrace with the wonderful view over the city. Even if most of the diners come for the excellent food, the exclusive, modern apartments also make a great place to spend the night.

➔ Bison, Oona Caviar, Topinambur, Majoran, Buttermilch. Milchlamm, Spargel, Morcheln, Ei, Senf. Stadtmilch, Rhabarber, Haselnuss, Hibiskus, Himbeercryo.

🄑 **Bistro Quadrino** – See restaurant listing

XxX

Sonnenberg

❀ ⇐ 🛏 & 🏧 ⇧ 🅿

Hitzigweg 15 ✉ 8032 – ℰ 044 266 97 97 — Plan: **B3**
– www.sonnenberg-zh.ch – Closed 1-14 January
Carte 54/132 CHF – *(booking advisable)*
• French classic • Formal •

A bright, elegant restaurant with attentive table service and an impressive view over Zürich and the lake. The house specialities are veal and beef dishes.

XxX

Alden – Alden Luxury Suite Hotel

🛏 & 🏧 🅿

Splügenstr. 2 ✉ 8002 – ℰ 044 289 99 99 — Plan: **A3**
– www.alden.ch – Closed Sunday
Menu 70/99 CHF – Carte 66/99 CHF
• Mediterranean • Elegant •

Clear, straight lines set the tone here and one of the dining rooms has a lovely stuccoed ceiling, which marries perfectly with the modern look. The Mediterranean cuisine on offer includes fillet of sea bass with wild garlic gnocchi, while at lunchtime you can enjoy the beef ribs from the trolley.

XX · ✿

mesa

🛏 & 🏧

Weinbergstr. 75 ✉ 8006 – ℰ 043 321 75 75 — Plan: **A2**
– www.mesa-restaurant.ch – Closed 24 December-6 January, 17 July-10 August and Saturday lunch, Sunday-Monday
Menu 65 CHF (lunch)/168 CHF – *(booking advisable)*
• Mediterranean • Minimalist •

The interior at this restaurant is pleasantly light and bright and the service is relaxed and friendly, attentive and professional. As for the cuisine, you can expect top quality ingredients combined with consummate skill.

➔ Erbsenflan, Zitronenluft und Velouté. Artischocke, Peperoni, Blüten, Datterini Tomate. Passionsfrucht, Gurke, Gin, Ricotta, Haselnuss, Minze.

XX · ✿

Yu Nijyo – Hotel Kameha Grand Zürich

🛏 🏧 🚗

Dufaux-Str. 1 – ℰ 044 525 50 00 — Plan: **B3**
– www.kamehagrandzuerich.com – Closed 3 weeks July-August and Sunday-Monday
Menu 159/179 CHF – Carte 82/136 CHF – *(dinner only) (booking advisable)*
• Modern cuisine • Exotic • Fashionable •

Just like the unusual interior, the cuisine at Yu Nijyo has a style all of its own. Namely, modern with a strong Far Eastern influence and featuring a mix of local and Japanese ingredients that are beautifully matched and attractively presented.

➔ Kalbsherzmilken mit Yamwurzel, Yuzu und Horenso. Rind mit Zwiebel "Texturen", Ume-Pflaume und Topinambur. Weisse Schokolade mit Sauerampfer, Granny Smith und Rhabarber.

XX **Garden Restaurant** – Hotel The Dolder Grand
Kurhausstr. 65 ⊠ 8032 – ☏ 044 456 60 00
– www.thedoldergrand.com   Plan: **B3**
Menu 60 CHF (weekday lunch)/80 CHF – Carte 85/236 CHF
• International • Fashionable •
The international and Mediterranean style cuisine and fantastic panoramic terrace are strong arguments for trying this restaurant. It also has a modern design and exclusive service. Brunch served on Sundays.

XX **R21** – Hotel Zürichberg
Orellistr. 21 ⊠ 8044 – ☏ 044 268 35 65
– www.zuerichberg.ch   Plan: **B2**
Carte 58/93 CHF
• Modern cuisine • Fashionable •
An interesting restaurant in an exposed position dominated by strong design features. Diners have a front row view as the chefs set about their work in the exemplary show kitchen. Brunch on Sundays.

XX **Rias**
🌳 *Gerbegasse 6 – ☏ 044 814 26 52 – www.rias.ch – Closed*   Plan: **B1**
24 December-11 January, 18 July-2 August, Saturday-Sunday and Bank Holidays
Menu 65 CHF – Carte 55/109 CHF
• Regional • Fashionable •
Tucked away in one of Kloten's side streets, Rias promises the chance to sample flavoursome food in an appealing contemporary setting. Chef Hansruedi Nef's offerings include dishes such as braised calves' cheeks, slow-cooked beef stew Italian-style and pears in mulled wine with champagne sabayon. You will also find the friendly waiting staff on hand with good wine suggestions (by the glass).

XX **Da Angela**
🌳 *Hohlstr. 449 ⊠ 8048 – ☏ 044 492 29 31*   Plan: **A3**
– www.daangela.ch – Closed end July-early August and Sunday
Carte 62/106 CHF – *(booking essential at lunch)*
• Italian • Traditional •
A very traditional Italian restaurant with a lovely terrace under shady chestnut trees. Home-made pasta is among the dishes prepared from fresh produce.

XX **L'Unico** – Hotel Kameha Grand Zürich
Dufaux-Str. 1 – ☏ 044 525 50 00   Plan: **B3**
– www.kamehagrandzuerich.com – Closed Sunday dinner
Menu 29/55 CHF – Carte 48/85 CHF
• Italian • Trendy •
L'Unico boasts a number of attractive decorative details including prettily tiled walls and tables, round booths and above you on the ceiling, what is probably the largest pasta plate in the world! As you might expect, fresh pasta such as the brasato ravioli is the focus of the traditional Italian cuisine on offer here.

XX **Caduff's Wine Loft**
Kanzleistr. 126 ⊠ 8004 – ☏ 044 240 22 55   Plan: **A3**
– www.wineloft.ch – Closed 24 December-5 January, Saturday lunch and Sunday
Menu 30 CHF (lunch)/120 CHF – Carte 40/108 CHF – *(booking advisable)*
• French classic • Trendy •
This fashionable venue has a modern loft atmosphere. As well as the delicious fresh cooking made from quality products, there is an impressive wine selection, with over 2,000 labels on offer.

SWITZERLAND - ZURICH

XX **Blaue Ente**   🏠 ♿ 🄰🄺 ⇦

Seefeldstr. 223 ✉ *8008*   Plan: **B3**
– ☎ 044 388 68 40 – www.blaue-ente.ch
– Closed Saturday lunch, Sunday
Carte 51/105 CHF *– (booking advisable)*
• Regional • Trendy • Friendly •

Outside a historic building and inside a fashionable, lively restaurant (complete with old generator!) with a very friendly, attentive front-of-house team. Guests may either order a tasty meal – try the coq au vin, for example – from the brasserie kitchen or, in the evenings, something a little more upmarket – veal filet tartare with black truffles, say – from the gourmet menu. Attractive tables in the courtyard.

XX **Orangerie** – Hotel Engimatt   🏠 ♿ 🚗

Engimattstr. 14 ✉ *8002 – ☎ 044 284 16 16*   Plan: **A3**
– www.engimatt.ch
Menu 68 CHF – Carte 39/96 CHF
• Traditional cuisine • Friendly •

In winter and summer alike eating at the Orangerie is like sitting out under a beautiful open sky. The restaurant consists of an elegant, light and airy conservatory, as well as a beautifully appointed terrace. Traditional cuisine.

XX **Le Chef by Meta**   🄰🄺

Kanonengasse 29 ✉ *8004 – ☎ 044 240 41 00*   Plan: **A3**
– www.restaurant-lechef.ch
– Closed during Christmas, during Easter, 3 weeks July-August and Sunday-Monday
Menu 81 CHF – Carte 48/111 CHF
• International • Cosy •

Le Chef manages to be modern yet warm and welcoming thanks to its combination of clean, straight lines, warm wood and purple tones. Meta Hiltebrand offers a range of delicious dishes including roast tomato soup and beef fillet stroganoff.

X   **Sankt Meinrad**   🏠
🕸

Stauffacherstr. 163 ✉ *8004 – ☎ 043 534 82 77*   Plan: **A3**
– www.equi-table.ch – Closed 1 week early January, mid July-mid August and Sunday-Monday
Menu 100 CHF (Vegetarian)/180 CHF
– Carte 88/119 CHF – (dinner only) (booking advisable)
• Modern cuisine • Fashionable •

Just as Sankt Meinrad's parent company deals only in fair trade and organic products, so its kitchen team under Fabian Fuchs uses nothing but the best ingredients in its good modern cuisine. The whole experience is rounded off by the friendly service and informal atmosphere.
➔ Kalbsmilken, Linsen, Wirz, Dörraprikosen. Sanddorn, Haselnuss, Kaffee, Passionsfrucht. Avocado, Rhabarber, Frischkäse, Couscous.

X   **Helvetia** – Hotel Helvetia

Stauffacherquai 1 (1st floor) ✉ *8004 – ☎ 044 297 99 99*   Plan: **A3**
– www.hotel-helvetia.ch
Carte 50/99 CHF
• Traditional cuisine • Cosy •

A floor above the popular and lively bar, Helvetia shares the same wooden floors and panelling and warm, welcoming atmosphere. The friendly and straightforward front-of-house style fits in perfectly here as you sample a delicious crayfish cocktail or fillet of pata negra pork freshly prepared in the kitchen by Françoise Wicki.

✗ 🕄
Maison Manesse
🏠
Hopfenstr. 2 ✉ 8045 – ☎ 044 462 01 01
– www.maisonmanesse.ch – Closed 24 December-10 January, 17 July-
7 August and Sunday-Monday
Menu 148/180 CHF – *(dinner only) (booking advisable)*
• Creative • Rustic •
The latest hot place to eat on the Zurich culinary scene, Maison Manesse is as informal as it is unusual. The predominantly white interior is comfortable and rustic, while the cuisine - based on top quality produce - is creative and aromatic. The lunchtime menu features salads, pasta and steaks.
→ Morchel, Erbse, Minze. Saibling, Ananas, Dashi. Spanferkel, Jackfrucht, Tamarinde.

✗
Nachtjäger
🏠
Badenerstr. 310 ✉ 8004 – ☎ 043 931 77 90
– www.nachtjaeger.ch – Closed 24 December-2 January, 26 July-
13 August, Sunday-Monday and Bank Holidays
Carte 54/72 CHF – *(dinner only)*
• Regional • Cosy •
This charming little restaurant a little outside the city centre serves "comfort food" – fresh, light cuisine that is highly prized by its guests. The flavoursome fare chalked up on the blackboard includes veal and wheat beer pie and shin of beef with chickpeas and paprika.

✗
Bistro Quadrino – Restaurant Rigiblick
🏠 ♿ 🚗
🐕
Germaniastr. 99 ✉ 8044 – ☎ 043 255 15 70
– www.restaurantrigiblick.ch – Closed 20 December-4 January and
Monday
Menu 62 CHF – Carte 52/83 CHF
• Regional • Bistro • Fashionable •
The Rigiblick, it would appear, has more to offer than exquisite gourmet cuisine and classy apartments. The informal Bistro Quadrino also has its fans who come here for the braised calves' cheeks with potato mash, for example, or a simple flammekueche. In summer the best tables are outside with a view over the city.

✗
Café Boy
🏠
Kochstr. 2 ✉ 8004 – ☎ 044 240 40 24
– www.cafeboy.ch – Closed 2 weeks end December and Saturday-Sunday
Menu 60 CHF (dinner) – Carte 51/90 CHF
• Traditional cuisine • Bistro •
Once the haunt of left-wing political activists, restaurateur Stefan Iseli's Café Boy now serves up the fresh, traditional cuisine of his partner Jann M. Hoffmann in a lively, minimalist bistro setting. Wine is his passion, as you will see when you are given the extensive wine list. Simpler menu at lunchtimes.

✗
Riviera
🏠 ♧
Dufourstr. 161 ✉ 8008 – ☎ 044 422 04 26
– www.enoteca-riviera.ch – Closed 1-10 January, 24 July-14 August and
Saturday lunch, Sunday
Menu 78/130 CHF – Carte 60/112 CHF
• Italian • Rustic •
Luca Messina, no newcomer to the Zurich restaurant scene, has opened up his new restaurant here. The setting is authentically rustic and the cuisine is Italian. It includes homemade pasta and osso buco, as well as an ambitious seasonal tasting menu.

✗
Hopfenau
🏠
Hopfenstr. 19 ✉ 8045 – ☎ 044 211 70 60
– www.hopfenau.ch – Closed 24 December-3 January
Carte 49/101 CHF
• Traditional cuisine • Simple •
A really friendly local eatery serving some excellent food, all of which is freshly cooked and delicious to boot. Try the delicious sounding braised shin of beef or Toblerone mousse.

UNITED KINGDOM
UNITED KINGDOM

→ **AREA:**
244 157 km² (94 269 sq mi).

→ **POPULATION:**
64 596 800 inhabitants.
Density = 265 per km².

→ **CAPITAL:** London.

→ **CURRENCY:**
Pound Sterling (£).

→ **GOVERNMENT:**
Constitutional parliamentary
monarchy (since 1707). Member
of European Union since 1973.

→ **LANGUAGE:** English.

→ **PUBLIC HOLIDAYS:**
New Year's Day (1 Jan); Good Friday
(late Mar/Apr); Easter Monday
(late Mar/Apr); Early May Bank
Holiday (first Mon in May); Spring
Bank Holiday (last Mon in May);
Summer Bank Holiday (last Mon
in Aug); Christmas Day (25 Dec);
Boxing Day (26 Dec).

→ **LOCAL TIME:**
GMT in winter and GMT
+1 hour in summer.

→ **CLIMATE:**
Temperate maritime with cool
winters and mild summers
(London: January 3°C; July
17°C), rainfall evenly distributed
throughout the year.

→ **EMERGENCY:**
Police, Medical Assistance, Fire
Brigade ✆ **999** – also used for
Mountain, Cave, Coastguard and
Sea Rescue. (Dialling **112** within
any EU country will redirect your
call and contact the emergency
services.)

Glasgow

Edinburgh

Birmingham

LONDON

→ **ELECTRICITY:**
230 volts AC, 50Hz; 3 flat pin
sockets.

→ **FORMALITIES:**
Travellers from the European
Union (EU), Switzerland, Iceland,
the main countries of North
and South America and some
Commonwealth countries need
a national identity card or passport
(except for Irish nationals; America:
passport required) to visit the
United Kingdom for less than
three months (tourism or business
purpose).
For visitors from other countries
a visa may be required, in addition
to a passport, especially for those
wishing to stay for longer than
three months. We advise you to
check with your embassy before
travelling.

LONDON

LONDON

Population: 8 600 000

Marc Pinter/Fotolia.com

The term 'world city' could have been invented for London. Time zones radiate from Greenwich, global finances zap round the Square Mile and its international restaurants are the equal of anywhere on earth. A stunning diversity of population is testament to the city's famed tolerance; different lifestyles and languages are as much a part of the London scene as cockneys and black cabs. London grew over time in a pretty haphazard way, swallowing up surrounding villages, but retaining an enviable acreage of green 'lungs': a comforting 30 per cent of London's area is made up of open space.

The drama of the city is reflected in its history. From Roman settlement to banking centre to capital of a 19C empire, the city's pulse has never missed a beat; it's no surprise that a dazzling array of theatres, restaurants, museums, markets and art galleries populate its streets. London's piecemeal character has endowed it with distinctly different areas, often breathing down each other's necks. North of Piccadilly lie the playgrounds of Soho and Mayfair, while south is the gentleman's clubland of St James's. On the other side of town are Clerkenwell and Southwark, artisan areas that have been scrubbed down and freshened up. The cool sophistication of Kensington and Knightsbridge is to the west, while a more touristy aesthetic is found in the heaving piazza zone of Covent Garden.

LONDON IN...

→ **ONE DAY**
British Museum, Tower of London, St Paul's Cathedral, Tate Modern.

→ **TWO / THREE DAYS**
National Gallery, London Eye, Natural History Museum, a walk along the Southbank.

→ **THREE DAYS**
Science Museum, Victoria and Albert Museum, National Portrait Gallery.

PRACTICAL INFORMATION

ARRIVAL-DEPARTURE

✈ Heathrow Airport (20mi west). Heathrow Express to Paddington takes 15 min; or take the Piccadilly Line.

✈ Gatwick Airport (28mi south). Gatwick Express to Victoria Station takes 30 min.

✈ Stansted Airport (34mi northeast).

✈ Luton Airport (35mi north).

✈ London City Airport (10mi east).

GETTING AROUND

If you're in London for any period it's worth investing in an Oyster Card, much beloved by locals: these are smartcards with electronically stored pre-pay credit, and they offer good savings on fares. The Underground, known colloquially as the Tube, has 270 stations across the capital and beyond; get yourself a tube map – it's invaluable and also a design classic. Buses can often be the quickest way to travel short distances, especially during the day; or else pick up a 'Boris Bike' from one of the various docking points around the city.

CALENDAR HIGHLIGHTS

February
London Fashion Week.

March
The Boat Race.

April
London Marathon.

May
Chelsea Flower Show.

June
Wimbledon, Trooping the Colour.

August
Notting Hill Carnival.

October
London Film Festival.

November
Lord Mayor's Show.

December
Ice Rinks open across London.

EATING OUT

London is one of the food capitals of the world, where you can eat everything from Turkish to Thai and Polish to Peruvian. Those wishing to sample classic British dishes also have more choice these days as more and more chefs are rediscovering home-grown ingredients, regional classics and traditional recipes. Eating in the capital can be pricey, so check out good value pre- and post-theatre menus, or try lunch at one of the many eateries that drop their prices, but not their standards, in the middle of the day. "Would I were in an alehouse in London! I would give all my fame for a pot of ale and safety", says Shakespeare's Henry V. Samuel Johnson agreed, waxing lyrical upon the happiness produced by a good tavern or inn. Pubs are often open these days from 11am to 11pm (and beyond), so this particular love now knows no bounds, and any tourist is welcome to come along and enjoy the romance. It's not just the cooking that has improved in pubs but wine too; woe betide any establishment in this city that can't distinguish its Gamay from its Grenache.

HOTELS - ALPHABETICAL LIST

Schweizerhof ⚐ ⒶⒸ 🛎 🚗

Bahnhofplatz 7 ✉ *8021* – ℰ *044 218 88 88*　　　Plan: **C1**
– www.hotelschweizerhof.com
107 rm ⌸ – � 365/475 CHF ♦♦580/790 CHF – 11 suites
• Luxury • Classic •
Established in the 19C, this city hotel with its imposing façade stands at the entrance to the pedestrian zone and is just a few steps from the railway station. It offers excellent service with lots of extras and some particularly comfortable junior suites. Snacks in the Café Gourmet.
La Soupière – See restaurant listing

 ### Sheraton Neues Schloss Zürich ⚐ ⅙ ⒶⒸ 🛎

Stockerstr. 17 ✉ *8002* – ℰ *044 286 94 00*　　　Plan: **C3**
– www.sheraton.com/neuesschloss
60 rm – ♦199/599 CHF ♦♦199/599 CHF – ⌸ 39 CHF – 1 suite
• Business • Contemporary •
Just a stone's throw from Lake Zurich, this hotel features straight lines and bright, warm natural tones. The walls of the property are adorned with paintings by Swiss artist Thomas Irniger.
Le Jardin Suisse – See restaurant listing

 ### Glärnischhof ⚐ ⒶⒸ 🛎 🅿

Claridenstr. 30 ✉ *8022* – ℰ *044 286 22 22*　　　Plan: **C3**
– www.hotelglaernischhof.ch
62 rm ⌸ – ♦240/380 CHF ♦♦295/450 CHF
• Business • Classic •
This well-run business hotel in the banking quarter offers attentive service and contemporary, functional rooms. Extras include free Wi-Fi, coffee machine and an iPod dock in some rooms.
Le Poisson – See restaurant listing

St. Gotthard ⚐ ⒶⒸ 🛎

Bahnhofstr. 87 ✉ *8021* – ℰ *044 227 77 00*　　　Plan: **C1**
– www.hotelstgotthard.ch
135 rm – ♦256/318 CHF ♦♦282/406 CHF – ⌸ 34 CHF – 3 suites
• Traditional • Modern •
Providing traditional hospitality since 1889, the St Gotthard's guestrooms offer modern elegance in a classical setting. A great location just a stone's throw from the main station. The Manzoni Bar serves excellent coffee.
Hummer- & Austernbar – See restaurant listing

Kindli ⚐

Pfalzgasse 1 ✉ *8001* – ℰ *043 888 76 78* – *www.kindli.ch*　　Plan: **C2**
20 rm ⌸ – ♦220/340 CHF ♦♦300/420 CHF
• Traditional • Cosy • Personalised •
For over 500 years pilgrims visited this site, now guests looking for some individuality have taken their place. Although the three single rooms in the eaves don't have en-suites, they do enjoy a lovely view over Zürich. If you want to stay a little longer, try one of the excellent little apartments.
Kindli – See restaurant listing

 ### Townhouse ⚐

Schützengasse 7 ✉ *8001* – ℰ *044 200 95 95*　　　Plan: **C1**
– www.townhouse.ch
25 rm – ♦160/415 CHF ♦♦190/435 CHF – ⌸ 25 CHF
• Townhouse • Classic • Cosy •
The Townhouse is an exclusive hotel in an almost perfect location – just a few steps from the famed Bahnhofstrasse. The furniture and wallpaper will delight enthusiasts of the English style. Breakfast is served in your room or in the bar on the ground floor.

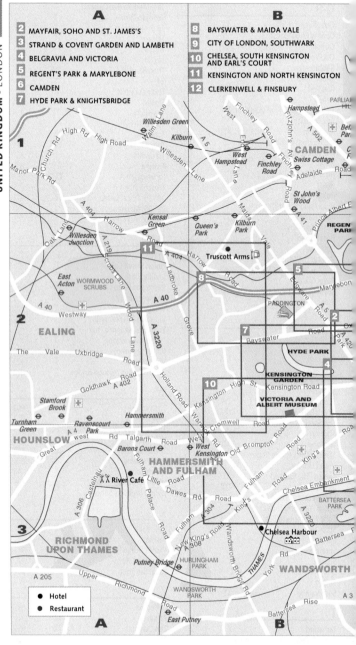

A

2 MAYFAIR, SOHO AND ST. JAMES'S
3 STRAND & COVENT GARDEN AND LAMBETH
4 BELGRAVIA AND VICTORIA
5 REGENT'S PARK & MARYLEBONE
6 CAMDEN
7 HYDE PARK & KNIGHTSBRIDGE

B

8 BAYSWATER & MAIDA VALE
9 CITY OF LONDON, SOUTHWARK
10 CHELSEA, SOUTH KENSINGTON AND EARL'S COURT
11 KENSINGTON AND NORTH KENSINGTON
12 CLERKENWELL & FINSBURY

● Hotel
● Restaurant

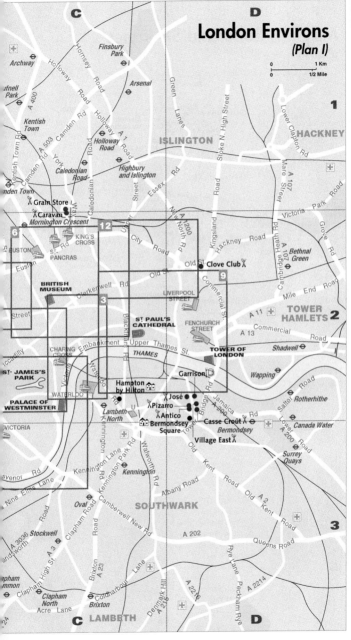

London Environs
(Plan I)

0 — 1 Km
0 — 1/2 Mile

1

C   **D**

Archway

Finsbury Park

utnell Park

Holloway Road

Arsenal

A 400

Kentish Town

Camden Rd

Holloway Road

A 1

Green Lanes

Stoke N. High Street

HACKNEY

Lower Clapton Rd

ISLINGTON

Holloway Road

Caledonian Road

Highbury and Islington

Essex Road

New North Rd

Kingsland Road

Hackney Road

Victoria Park Road

A 107 Mare Street

A 107 Camborne

Gilpe Rd

Bethnal Green

Kentish Town Rd

Camden Rd A 503

York Way

Caledonian Road

A 200

Mile End Road

nden Town

Grain Store

Caravan

Mornington Crescent

12

KING'S CROSS

City Road

Old St

Clove Club

9

TOWER HAMLETS

2

6

EUSTON

Euston

ST PANCRAS

BRITISH MUSEUM

Clerkenwell Rd

3

LIVERPOOL STREET

Commercial St

A 11

Commercial Road

A 13

Mile End Road

Shadwell

Street

CHARING CROSS

Blackfriars Rd

ST PAUL'S CATHEDRAL

Upper Thames St.

THAMES

FENCHURCH STREET

TOWER OF LONDON

Wapping

Saltier Road

Rotherhithe

ST JAMES'S PARK

Piccadilly

WATERLOO

Victoria Embankment

Waterloo Rd

Garrison

Tower Bridge Rd

Jamaica Rd

Casse Croût

Canada Water

A 200

PALACE OF WESTMINSTER

Hampton by Hilton

José

Pizarro

Antico

Lambeth North

Kennington

Bermondsey Square

Bermondsey

Village East

Surrey Quays

VICTORIA

Kennington Lane

Kennington Park Rd

Walworth Rd

Old Kent Road

svenor Rd

Nine Elms Lane

Kennington Lane

Kennington

Albany Road

Old Kent Road

A 2

Old Kent Road

3

Oval

Camberwell New Rd

Camberwell Road

SOUTHWARK

A 202

Queens Road

A 3036 Stockwell

Clapham Road

A 3

Brixton Road

Rye Lane

Peckham Rye

A 2214

apham mmon

Clapham North

Brixton A 23

Coldharbour Lane

Denmark Hill

A 215

A 216

A 24

Clapham High St

Acre Lane

Brixton

LAMBETH

C

D

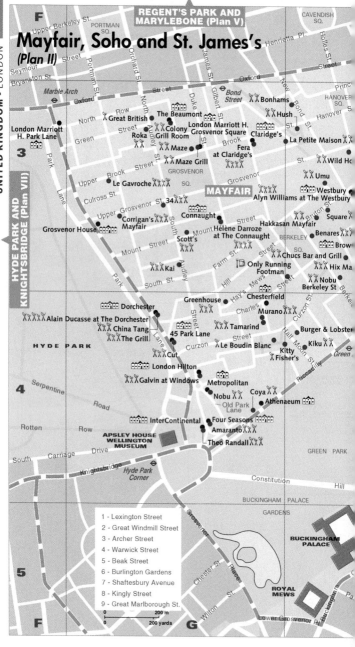

Mayfair, Soho and St. James's
(Plan II)

REGENT'S PARK AND MARYLEBONE (Plan V)

CAVENDISH SQ.

HANOVER SQ.

PORTMAN SQ.

Upper Berkeley St.

Seymour Street

Bryanston St.

Marble Arch

Oxford Street

Oxford Street

Henrietta Pl.

Hollis St.

Princ

Bond Street

✗✗ Bonhams

✗✗ Hush

North Row

Great British ✗✗

Green Street

The Beaumont

Colony Grill Room

London Marriott H. Grosvenor Square

Claridge's

La Petite Maison ✗✗

London Marriott H. Park Lane

Roka ✗✗

✗✗ Maze

Brook

Fera at Claridge's ✗✗✗✗

✗✗ Wild Ho

Upper Brook Street

✗✗ Maze Grill

GROSVENOR SQ.

Grosvenor Street

MAYFAIR

✗✗ Umu

Le Gavroche ✗✗✗

Culross St.

34 ✗✗✗

✗✗✗ Westbury

Alyn Williams at The Westbury

Upper Grosvenor St.

Connaught

Corrigan's Mayfair ✗✗✗

Grosvenor Street

Hakkasan Mayfair

Square ✗✗

Grosvenor House

Mount Street

Hélène Darroze at The Connaught ✗✗✗✗

BERKELEY SQ.

Benares ✗✗✗

Brow

Mount Street

Scott's ✗✗✗

✗✗ Chucs Bar and Grill

HYDE PARK AND KNIGHTSBRIDGE (Plan VIII)

✗✗✗ Kai

Farm Street

Only Running Footman

✗✗ Hix Ma

South St.

✗✗ Nobu Berkeley St

Chesterfield

✗✗✗ Greenhouse

Charles

Murano ✗✗✗

Dorchester

Hay's Mews

Street

Curzon

✗✗✗✗ Alain Ducasse at The Dorchester

✗✗✗ China Tang

45 Park Lane

Tamarind

Burger & Lobster

✗✗✗ The Grill

Curzon Street

Le Boudin Blanc ✗

Kiku ✗✗

HYDE PARK

✗✗✗ Cut

Kitty Fisher's ✗

Half Moon St.

Green

London Hilton

✗✗✗ Galvin at Windows

Metropolitan

Coya ✗✗

Serpentine

Road

Nobu ✗✗

Old Park Lane

Athenaeum

Rotten Row

InterContinental

Four Seasons

Amaranto ✗✗✗

APSLEY HOUSE WELLINGTON MUSEUM

Theo Randall ✗✗✗

GREEN PARK

South Carriage Drive

Knightsbridge

Hyde Park Corner

Constitution Hill

BUCKINGHAM PALACE GARDENS

1 - Lexington Street
2 - Great Windmill Street
3 - Archer Street
4 - Warwick Street
5 - Beak Street
6 - Burlington Gardens
7 - Shaftesbury Avenue
8 - Kingly Street
9 - Great Marlborough St.

BUCKINGHAM PALACE

ROYAL MEWS

Chester St.

Wilton

Lower Grosvenor Pl.

0   200 m
0   200 yards

G

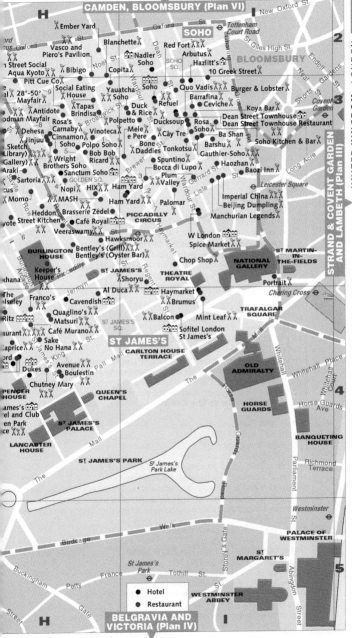

Mayfair

Dorchester

Park Ln. ✉ *W1K 1QA – Ⓜ Hyde Park Corner – ✆ (020) 76298888 – www.dorchestercollection.com* Plan: **G4**

250 rm – †£ 355/895 ††£ 415/955 – ☕ £ 35 – 50 suites

• Grand Luxury • Classic • Stylish •

One of the capital's iconic properties offering every possible facility and exemplary levels of service. The striking marbled and pillared promenade provides an elegant backdrop for afternoon tea. Bedrooms are eminently comfortable; some overlook Hyde Park. The Grill is for all things British; Alain Ducasse waves Le Tricolore; China Tang celebrates the cuisine of the Orient.

✿✿✿ **Alain Ducasse at The Dorchester • The Grill • China Tang** – See restaurant listing

Claridge's

Brook St ✉ *W1K 4HR – Ⓜ Bond Street – ✆ (020) 76298860 – www.claridges.co.uk* Plan: **G3**

197 rm – †£ 480/1140 ††£ 480/1140 – ☕ £ 34 – 62 suites

• Grand Luxury • Historic • Classic •

Claridge's has a long, illustrious history dating back to 1812 and this iconic and very British hotel has been a favourite of the royal family over generations. Its most striking decorative feature is its art deco. The hotel also moves with the times: its restaurant was re-launched in 2014 as Fera.

✿ **Fera at Claridge's** – See restaurant listing

Connaught

Carlos Pl. ✉ *W1K 2AL – Ⓜ Bond Street – ✆ (020) 74997070 – www.the-connaught.co.uk* Plan: **G3**

121 rm ☕ – †£ 510/840 ††£ 600/960 – 26 suites

• Grand Luxury • Townhouse • Classic •

One of London's most famous hotels; restored and renovated but still retaining an elegant British feel. All the luxurious bedrooms come with large marble bathrooms and butler service. There's a choice of two stylish bars and Espelette is an all-day venue for classic French and British dishes.

✿✿ **Hélène Darroze at The Connaught** – See restaurant listing

Four Seasons

Hamilton Pl, Park Ln ✉ *W1J 7DR – Ⓜ Hyde Park Corner – ✆ (020) 7499 0888 – www.fourseasons.com/london* Plan: **G4**

193 rm – †£ 385/960 ††£ 385/960 – ☕ £ 30 – 33 suites

• Grand Luxury • Business • Modern •

Reopened in 2011 after a huge refurbishment project and has raised the bar for luxury hotels. Striking lobby sets the scene; sumptuous bedrooms have a rich, contemporary look and boast every conceivable comfort. Great views from the stunning rooftop spa.

Amaranto – See restaurant listing

InterContinental London Park Lane

1 Hamilton Pl, Park Ln ✉ *W1J 7QY – Ⓜ Hyde Park Corner – ✆ (020) 74093131 – www.london.intercontinental.com* Plan: **G4**

447 rm – †£ 275/790 ††£ 275/790 – ☕ £ 28 – 48 suites

• Business • Luxury • Modern •

International hotel whose position facing the park is an impressive feature. Everything leads off from the large, open-plan lobby. English-style bedrooms with hi-tech equipment; luxurious suites. Casual, family-friendly Cookbook Café.

Theo Randall – See restaurant listing

London Hilton
🎍 ⬸ ⅓ 🖥 & 🎬 🛎 🚗
Plan: **G4**

22 Park Ln. ✉ *W1K 1BE* – Ⓜ *Hyde Park Corner*
– ℰ *(020) 74938000 – www.hilton.co.uk/londonparklane*
453 rm – ♦£ 322/869 ♦♦£ 322/869 – ☲ £ 27 – 56 suites
• Business • Luxury • Classic •
The bedrooms at this 28 storey hotel, which celebrated 50 years in 2013, now come with a sharper and more contemporary edge. For Polynesian food and a Mai Tai, head to the iconic brand that is Trader Vic's; for casual, all-day dining, try Podium. Extensive banqueting and conference facilities.
❀ **Galvin at Windows** – See restaurant listing

Grosvenor House
🎍 ⅓ & 🎬 🛎 🚗
Plan: **G3**

Park Ln ✉ *W1K 7TN* – Ⓜ *Marble Arch* – ℰ *(020)*
7499 6363 – www.londongrosvenorhouse.co.uk
494 rm – ♦£ 199/599 ♦♦£ 199/599 – ☲ £ 29 – 73 suites
• Business • Luxury • Classic •
A large, landmark property occupying a commanding position by Hyde Park. Uniform, comfortable but well proportioned bedrooms in classic Marriott styling. Busy banqueting department boasts the largest ballroom in Europe. JW Steakhouse is the place for beer, bourbon and beef.

The Beaumont
🎍 ⅓ 🖥 & 🎬 🛎 🚗
Plan: **G3**

Brown Hart Gdns ✉ *W1K 6TF* – Ⓜ *Bond Street*
– ℰ *(020) 7499 1001 – www.thebeaumont.com*
73 rm ☲ – ♦£ 395/480 ♦♦£ 395/480 – 10 suites
• Luxury • Art Deco • Personalised •
From a 1926 former garage, restaurateurs Chris Corbin and Jeremy King fashioned their first hotel; art deco inspired, it's stunning, stylish and exudes understated luxury. The attention to detail is exemplary, from the undeniably masculine bedrooms to the lively, cool cocktail bar and busy brasserie.
Colony Grill Room – See restaurant listing

45 Park Lane
🎍 ⬸ ⅓ 🔟 & 🎬 🚗
Plan: **G4**

45 Park Ln ✉ *W1K 1PN* – Ⓜ *Hyde Park Corner*
– ℰ *(020) 7493 4545 – www.45parklane.com*
46 rm – ♦£ 495/834 ♦♦£ 495/834 – ☲ £ 19 – 10 suites
• Luxury • Townhouse • Stylish •
It was the original site of the Playboy Club and has been a car showroom but now 45 Park Lane has been reborn as The Dorchester's sister hotel. The bedrooms, all with views over Hyde Park, are wonderfully sensual and the marble bathrooms are beautiful.
Cut – See restaurant listing

Westbury
🎍 ⅓ & 🎬 🛎
Plan: **H3**

Bond St ✉ *W1S 2YF* – Ⓜ *Bond Street* – ℰ *(020)*
76297755 – www.westburymayfair.com
246 rm – ♦£ 600 ♦♦£ 600 – 13 suites
• Business • Luxury • Modern •
Now as stylish as when it opened in the 1950s. Smart, comfortable bedrooms with terrific art deco inspired suites. Elegant, iconic Polo bar and bright, fresh sushi bar. All the designer brands outside the front door.
❀ **Alyn Williams at The Westbury** – See restaurant listing

Brown's
🎍 ⅓ & 🎬 🛎
Plan: **H3**

33 Albemarle St ✉ *W1S 4BP* – Ⓜ *Green Park* – ℰ *(020)*
7493 6020 – www.roccofortehotels.com
117 rm – ♦£ 415/905 ♦♦£ 445/945 – ☲ £ 32 – 12 suites
• Luxury • Traditional • Stylish •
Opened in 1837 by James Brown, Lord Byron's butler. This urbane and very British hotel with an illustrious past offers a swish bar with Terence Donovan prints, bedrooms in neutral hues and a classic English sitting room for afternoon tea.
Hix Mayfair – See restaurant listing

London Marriott H. Grosvenor Square

84-86 Duke St ✉ W1K 6JP – Ⓜ Bond Street – ✆ (020) 74931232 – www.marriottgrosvenorsquare.com Plan: **G3**

237 rm – †£ 249/599 ††£ 249/599 – ☕ £ 18 – 11 suites

• Business • Functional • Modern •

A well-appointed international hotel that benefits from an excellent location in the heart of Mayfair. Bedrooms are specifically equipped for business travellers. Ask for a Balcony room: they have access to a private roof garden.

Maze Grill Mayfair – See restaurant listing

London Marriott H. Park Lane

140 Park Ln ✉ W1K 7AA – Ⓜ Marble Arch – ✆ (020) 74937000 – www.londonmarriottparklane.co.uk Plan: **F3**

152 rm – †£ 549/699 ††£ 549/699 – ☕ £ 13 – 14 suites

• Luxury • Business • Design •

International hotel located close to Hyde Park and Oxford Street and the only one on Park Lane with a pool. Fresh, contemporary look to the bedrooms after a major refurb. Lanes offers Indian, Lebanese, Vietnamese and British dishes.

Metropolitan

Old Park Ln ✉ W1K 1LB – Ⓜ Hyde Park Corner – ✆ (020) 74471000 – www.comohotels.com/metropolitanlondon Plan: **G4**

144 rm – †£ 350/580 ††£ 350/580 – ☕ £ 28 – 3 suites

• Business • Luxury • Modern •

It's not quite as hip as it once was but it still has an appealing, crisp and uncluttered design-led look. Decent sized bedrooms have plenty of hi-tech touches; an all-day menu is served in the Met Bar and London's original Nobu is upstairs.

Nobu – See restaurant listing

Athenaeum

116 Piccadilly ✉ W1J 7BJ – Ⓜ Hyde Park Corner – ✆ (020) 7499 3464 – www.athenaeumhotel.com Plan: **G4**

164 rm – †£ 295/500 ††£ 295/500 – ☕ £ 23 – 24 suites

• Townhouse • Traditional • Contemporary •

1920s building opposite the park; its smart bedrooms come in cool pastel shades and have floor to ceiling windows. Bright restaurant and a bar offering over 270 different whiskies. The hotel also organises events for kids.

Chesterfield

35 Charles St ✉ W1J 5EB – Ⓜ Green Park – ✆ (020) 74912622 – www.chesterfieldmayfair.com Plan: **G4**

107 rm ☕ – †£ 195/390 ††£ 220/510 – 4 suites

• Townhouse • Traditional • Classic •

An assuredly English feel to this Georgian house. Discreet lobby leads to a clubby bar and wood panelled library. Individually decorated bedrooms, with some antique pieces. Intimate and pretty restaurant.

Alain Ducasse at The Dorchester – Dorchester Hotel

Park Ln ✉ W1K 1QA – Ⓜ Hyde Park Corner – ✆ (020) 76298866 – www.alainducasse-dorchester.com – Closed 9-30 August, 26-30 December, 1-5 January, 25-26 March, Saturday lunch, Sunday and Monday Plan: **G4**

Menu £ 60/95 – *(booking essential)*

• French • Elegant • Luxury •

Elegance, luxury and attention to detail are the hallmarks of Alain Ducasse's London outpost, where the atmosphere is warm and relaxed. The kitchen uses the best seasonal produce, whether British or French, to create visually striking, refined, modern dishes. The 'Table Lumière' with its shimmering curtain affords an opulent, semi-private dining experience.

➜ Sauté of lobster, chicken quenelles and pasta. Simmered halibut with winkles, cockles and razor clams marinière. 'Baba like in Monte Carlo'.

XXXX **Sketch (The Lecture Room & Library)**   🕸 AK 🄸🄾
🕸🕸 *9 Conduit St (1st floor)* ⊠ *W1S 2XG* – Ⓜ *Oxford Circus*   Plan: **H3**
   – 𝒞 *(020) 76594500*
   – *www.sketch.london*
   – *Closed last 2 weeks August, Saturday lunch, Sunday and Monday*
Menu £ 40/110 – Carte £ 101/129 – *(booking essential)*
• **French** • **Luxury** • **Elegant** •
Mourad Mazouz and Pierre Gagnaire's 18C funhouse is awash with colour, energy and vim and the luxurious 'Lecture Room & Library' provides the ideal setting for the sophisticated French cooking. Relax and enjoy artfully presented, elaborate dishes that provide many varieties of flavours and textures.
→ Foie gras terrine with lime, green bean salad, langoustine consommé and rocket Chantilly. Wild turbot with black pepper. Dragon fruit syrup with lemon and olive oil jelly, lemon curd, pink praline and kirsch.

XXXX **Hélène Darroze at The Connaught** – Connaught Hotel
🕸🕸 *Carlos Pl.* ⊠ *W1K 2AL* – Ⓜ *Bond Street*   🕸 AK ⇔
   – 𝒞 *(020) 71078880*   Plan: **G3**
   – *www.the-connaught.co.uk*
   – *Closed 3 weeks August, 1 week January, Saturday lunch, Sunday and Monday*
Menu £ 30/92 – *(booking essential)*
• **Modern cuisine** • **Luxury** • **Elegant** •
From a Solitaire board of 13 marbles, each bearing the name of an ingredient, you choose 5, 7 or 9; this highlights the quality of produce used. The cooking is lighter these days yet still with the occasional unexpected flavour. The warm service ensures the wood-panelled room never feels too formal.
→ Oyster 'fine de claire' with Oscietra caviar and white coco beans. Scallop, tandoori spices, carrot, citrus and coriander. Savarin Armagnac, raspberry and pepper.

XXXX **Le Gavroche** (Michel Roux Jnr)   🕸 AK ⇔
🕸🕸 *43 Upper Brook St* ⊠ *W1K 7QR* – Ⓜ *Marble Arch*   Plan: **G3**
   – 𝒞 *(020) 74080881*
   – *www.le-gavroche.co.uk*
   – *Closed Christmas-January, Saturday lunch, Sunday and bank holidays*
Menu £ 55/126 – Carte £ 63/164 – *(booking essential)*
• **French** • **Formal** • **Luxury** •
Classical, rich and indulgent French cuisine is the draw at Michel Roux's renowned London institution. The large, smart basement room has a clubby, masculine feel; service is formal and structured but also has charm.
→ Mousseline de homard au champagne et caviar. Râble de lapin et galette au parmesan. Soufflé aux fruits de la passion et glace Ivoire.

XXXX **Square** (Philip Howard)   🕸 AK ⇔ 🄸🄾
🕸🕸 *6-10 Bruton St.* ⊠ *W1J 6PU* – Ⓜ *Green Park* – 𝒞 *(020)*   Plan: **H3**
74957100 – *www.squarerestaurant.com* – *Closed 24-26 December and Sunday lunch*
Menu £ 38/90 – Carte £ 75/120
• **French** • **Formal** • **Classic** •
A restaurant that demands respect, and not just because it's approaching its quarter century. The cooking is rooted in classic French cuisine but displays more than a healthy understanding of contemporary mores. The room is smart without being stuffy and the service professional yet warm.
→ White asparagus with Dorset crab, Grelot onions and beach herbs. Saddle of West Country lamb with purple garlic, thyme gnocchetti and Italian artichokes. Milk chocolate délice with salted caramel, peanuts and banana.

UNITED KINGDOM - LONDON

XxXX
☼

Fera at Claridge's – Claridge's Hotel   🕸 ё 🅰🅒 ⇔ 🅘♡

Brook St ⊠ W1K 4HR – 🌀 *Bond Street –* ℰ *(020)*   Plan: **G3**
7107 8888 – www.feraatclaridges.co.uk
Menu £ 39/105 – Carte £ 51/74 – *(booking advisable)*
• **British creative** • **Elegant** • **Luxury** •
Earth-father, forager supreme and gastronomic alchemist Simon Rogan
brings his wonderfully natural, unforced style of cooking to the capital. The
deftly balanced and cleverly textured dishes deliver multi-dimensional
layers of flavours and the grand room has been transformed into a thing
of beauty.
→ Grilled and smoked salad with Isle of Mull truffle custard and sunflo-
wer seeds. Cornish lamb, sheep's milk, white asparagus, ramson flowers
and alliums. Compressed strawberries with sweet cicely, buttermilk and
sorrel.

XxXX
☼

Alyn Williams at The Westbury – Westbury Hotel   🕸 ё

37 Conduit St ⊠ W1S 2YF – 🌀 *Bond Street –* ℰ *(020)*   🅰🅒 ⇔ 🅘♡
71836426 – www.alynwilliams.com   Plan: **H3**
*– Closed first 2 weeks January, last 2 weeks August, Sunday
and Monday*
Menu £ 30/60
• **Modern cuisine** • **Design** • **Elegant** •
Confident, cheery service ensures the atmosphere never strays into terminal
seriousness; rosewood panelling and a striking wine display add warmth. The
cooking is creative and even playful but however elaborately constructed the
dish, the combinations of flavours and textures always work.
→ Roast Scottish scallops with cauliflower and winter truffle. Wiltshire
pigeon with carrot and fennel pollen. Mascarpone with caramelised apple,
ginger and hibiscus.

XxX
☼☼

Greenhouse   🕸 🅰🅒 ⇔

27a Hay's Mews ⊠ W1J 5NY   Plan: **G4**
– 🌀 *Hyde Park Corner –* ℰ *(020) 74993331*
– www.greenhouserestaurant.co.uk
– Closed Saturday lunch, Sunday and bank holidays
Menu £ 40/110 – Carte £ 98/120
• **Creative** • **Fashionable** • **Neighbourhood** •
Chef Arnaud Bignon's cooking is confident, balanced and innovative and uses
the best from Europe's larder; his dishes exude an exhilarating freshness. The
breadth and depth of the wine list is astounding. This is a discreet, sleek and
contemporary restaurant with well-judged service.
→ Cornish crab, mint jelly, cauliflower, Granny Smith apple and curry. Presa
Ibérico, aubergine, Sobrasada, onion and smoked pimento. Guanaja chocolate, praline, lemon and finger lime.

XxX
☼☼

Hibiscus (Claude Bosi)   🅰🅒 ⇔

29 Maddox St ⊠ W1S 2PA – 🌀 *Oxford Circus*   Plan: **H3**
– ℰ (020) 76292999 – www.hibiscusrestaurant.co.uk
*– Closed 3 days Christmas, Monday except December, Sunday and bank
holidays*
Menu £ 50/90
• **Creative** • **Elegant** • **Formal** •
Choose 3, 6 or 8 courses and be prepared for a surprise as the kitchen will choose the dishes. Claude Bosi's cooking is as innovative as ever; the combinations
of flavours and textures are well-judged and dishes are underpinned by fine
ingredients. The last revamp left the room brighter and lighter.
→ Mylor prawn, smoked butter, lemon and Beluski caviar. Cornish sea
bass à la Grenobloise. Chocolate millefeuille, Indonesian basil and star
anise.

XxX
ⁿⁿ

Umu
&& AC

14-16 Bruton Pl. ✉ *W1J 6LX –* Ⓜ *Bond Street*
Plan: **H3**
– ℰ (020) 74998881
– www.umurestaurant.com
– Closed Christmas, New Year, Saturday lunch, Sunday
and bank holidays
Menu £ 25/125 – Carte £ 41/151
• Japanese • Fashionable • Design •
Stylish, discreet interior using natural materials, with central sushi bar. Extensive choice of Japanese dishes; choose one of the seasonal kaiseki menus for the full experience. Over 160 different labels of sake.
→ Line-caught squid, tosasu and ginger. Wild lobster, homemade shichimi pepper and tofu miso bisque. Japanese seasonal tiramisu, green tea, sake and blood orange.

XxX
ⁿ

Murano (Angela Hartnett)
ら AC

20 Queen St ✉ *W1J 5PP –* Ⓜ *Green Park*
Plan: **G4**
– ℰ (020) 74951127 – www.muranolondon.com
– Closed Christmas and Sunday
Menu £ 33/65
• Italian • Fashionable • Elegant •
Angela Hartnett's Italian influenced cooking exhibits an appealing lightness of touch, with assured combinations of flavours, borne out of confidence in the ingredients. This is a stylish, elegant room run by a well-organised, professional and friendly team who put their customers at ease.
→ Sweetbreads, farfalle, broad beans and apple compote. Hake with roast cauliflower, kale, pata negra and garlic. Pistachio panna cotta, chocolate, pistachio and mandarin.

XxX
ⁿ

Galvin at Windows – London Hilton Hotel
≤ ら AC

22 Park Ln (28th floor) ✉ *W1K 1BE*
Plan: **G4**
– Ⓜ *Hyde Park Corner*
– ℰ (020) 72084021 – www.galvinatwindows.com
– Closed Saturday lunch and Sunday dinner
Menu £ 30 (weekday lunch)/70
• Modern cuisine • Formal • Romantic •
The cleverly laid out room makes the most of the spectacular views across London from the 28th floor. Relaxed service takes the edge off the somewhat corporate atmosphere. The bold cooking uses superb ingredients and the classically based food comes with a pleasing degree of flair and innovation.
→ Scallop ceviche, caviar, orange, pomelo, pickled kohlrabi and sweet soy. Fillet of sea bass with potato crust, chicken oyster and jus gras. Guanaja chocolate mousse with blood orange curd and passion fruit sorbet.

XxX
ⁿ

Benares (Atul Kochhar)
&& AC ⇔ ⑩

12a Berkeley Square House, Berkeley Sq. ✉ *W1J 6BS*
Plan: **H3**
– Ⓜ *Green Park – ℰ (020) 76298886*
– www.benaresrestaurant.com
– Closed 24-26 December, 1-2 January and Sunday October-March
Menu £ 30/82 – Carte £ 45/71
• Indian • Formal • Intimate •
No Indian restaurant in London enjoys a more commanding location or expansive interior. Atul Kochhar's influences are many and varied; his spicing is deft and he makes excellent use of British ingredients like Scottish scallops and New Forest venison. The Chef's Table has a window into the kitchen.
→ Coriander and sesame spiced scallops with ginger and grape dressing. Rump of lamb with baby spinach and chickpea stew. Rose and raspberry bhapa doi, pistachio burfi.

853

XxX · ✿

Tamarind

AC IⓋ

20 Queen St. ⊠ W1J 5PR – Ⓜ *Green Park – ℰ (020)* Plan: **G4**
76293561 – www.tamarindrestaurant.com – Closed 25-26 December,
1 January and Saturday lunch
Menu £ 25/72 – Carte £ 35/67
· Indian · Formal · Exotic ·

Makes the best use of its basement location through smoked mirrors, gilded columns and a somewhat exclusive feel. The appealing northern Indian food is mostly traditionally based; kebabs and curries are the specialities, the tandoor is used to good effect and don't miss the carefully judged vegetable dishes.
→ Chickpeas, wheat crisps, blueberries and tamarind chutney. Slow-cooked lamb shank with turmeric and yoghurt. Heritage carrot cake and fudge with vanilla ice cream.

XxX · ✿

Kai

ẞ AC ⇔ IⓋ

65 South Audley St ⊠ W1K 2QU – Ⓜ *Hyde Park Corner* Plan: **G3**
– ℰ (020) 74938988 – www.kaimayfair.co.uk – Closed 25-26 December
and 1 January
Carte £ 39/110 – *(booking essential)*
· Chinese · Intimate · Formal ·

There are a few classics on the menu but Chef Alex Chow's strengths are his modern creations and re-workings of Chinese recipes. His dishes have real depth, use superb produce and are wonderfully balanced. The interior is unashamedly glitzy and the service team anticipate their customers' needs well.
→ Ibérico pork in a Cos lettuce wrap with plum and lime dressing, cashew, and shallots. Kagoshima Wagyu cooked on a salt block with soy, garlic and a coriander & chilli sauce. Durian and vanilla soufflé with salted caramel sauce.

XxX

The Grill – Dorchester Hotel

ẞ & AC

Park Ln ⊠ W1K 1QA – Ⓜ *Hyde Park Corner – ℰ (020)* Plan: **G4**
7317 6531 – www.dorchestercollection.com
Menu £ 39 (weekday lunch) – Carte £ 54/89 – *(booking advisable)*
· French · Elegant · Design ·

The re-launched Grill is relaxed yet formal, with an open kitchen and a striking, hand-blown Murano glass chandelier as its centrepiece. Grill favourites sit alongside modern day classics on the menu; sharing dishes are a good choice, as are the speciality soufflés. Service is smooth and highly professional.

XxX

Cut – 45 Park Lane Hotel

& AC

45 Park Ln ⊠ W1K 1PN – Ⓜ *Hyde Park Corner* Plan: **G4**
– ℰ (020) 7493 4545 – www.45parklane.com
Menu £ 45 (weekday lunch) – Carte £ 48/177 – *(booking essential)*
· Meats · Design · Formal ·

The first European venture from Wolfgang Puck, the US-based Austrian celebrity chef, is this very slick, stylish and sexy room where glamorous people come to eat meat. The not-inexpensive steaks are cooked over hardwood and charcoal and finished off in a broiler.

XxX

34

AC ⇔

34 Grosvenor Sq (entrance on South Audley St) Plan: **G3**
⊠ *W1K 2HD –* Ⓜ *Marble Arch – ℰ (020) 3350 3434*
– www.34-restaurant.co.uk – Closed 25-26 December, dinner 24 December
and lunch 1 January
Carte £ 33/61
· Meats · Brasserie · Fashionable ·

A wonderful mix of art deco styling and Edwardian warmth makes it feel like a glamorous brasserie. A parrilla grill is used for fish, game and beef –choose from Scottish dry-aged, US prime, organic Argentinian and Australian Wagyu.

XxX **Bentley's (Grill)** 🔲 ⇔

11-15 Swallow St. ⊠ W1B 4DG – Ⓜ *Piccadilly Circus* Plan: **H3**
– ℰ *(020) 77344756 – www.bentleys.org – Closed 25 December, 1 January,*
Saturday lunch and Sunday
Menu £ 25 (weekday lunch) – Carte £ 33/74
• Fish and seafood • Elegant • Fashionable •
Enter into the striking bar and take the panelled staircase to the richly decorated restaurant. Carefully sourced seafood or meat dishes are enhanced by clean, crisp cooking. Unruffled service.

XxX **Theo Randall** – Intercontinental Hotel 🔲 ⇔ 🎩 🍸

1 Hamilton Pl, Park Ln ⊠ W1J 7QY Plan: **G4**
– Ⓜ *Hyde Park Corner –* ℰ *(020) 73188747 – www.theorandall.com*
– Closed Christmas, Easter, Saturday lunch, Sunday dinner and bank
holidays
Menu £ 27/33 – Carte £ 46/72
• Italian • Fashionable • Design •
Expect simple, flavoursome and seasonal Italian dishes, using much produce imported from Italy. The pleasingly rustic nature of the food is somewhat at odds with the formal service and the corporate feel of the dining room.

XxX **Scott's** 🔲 ⇔ 🍸

20 Mount St ⊠ W1K 2HE – Ⓜ *Bond Street –* ℰ *(020)* Plan: **G3**
74957309 – www.scotts-restaurant.com – Closed 25-26 December
Carte £ 39/67
• Fish and seafood • Fashionable • Formal •
Stylish yet traditional and one of London's most fashionable addresses, so getting a table can be tricky. Oak panelling is juxtaposed with vibrant artwork from young British artists. Enticing choice of top quality fish and shellfish.

XxX **Corrigan's Mayfair** �& 🔲 ⇔

28 Upper Grosvenor St. ⊠ W1K 7EH – Ⓜ *Marble Arch* Plan: **G3**
– ℰ *(020) 74999943 – www.corrigansmayfair.com*
– Closed 25-30 December, Saturday lunch and bank holidays
Menu £ 25 (weekday lunch)/75 – Carte £ 35/73
• British modern • Elegant •
Richard Corrigan's flagship celebrates British and Irish cooking, with game a speciality. The room is comfortable, clubby and quite glamorous and feels as though it has been around for years.

XxX **Sartoria** �& 🔲 ⇔

20 Savile Row ⊠ W1S 3PR – Ⓜ *Oxford Circus –* ℰ *(020)* Plan: **H3**
75347000 – www.sartoria-restaurant.co.uk – Closed
25 December, Saturday lunch, Sunday and bank holidays
Menu £ 25 – Carte £ 30/62
• Italian • Formal • Elegant •
In the street renowned for English tailoring, a coolly sophisticated and stylish restaurant to suit those looking for classic Italian cooking with some modern touches thrown in. It also comes with confident service.

XxX **Hix Mayfair** – Brown's Hotel �& 🔲 🍸

33 Albemarle St ⊠ W1S 4BP – Ⓜ *Green Park –* ℰ *(020)* Plan: **H3**
75184004 – www.hixmayfair.com
Menu £ 33 – Carte £ 34/69
• British traditional • Formal • Intimate •
This wood-panelled dining room is lightened with the work of current British artists. Mark Hix's well-sourced menu of British classics will appeal to the hunter-gatherer in every man.

XxX **China Tang** – Dorchester Hotel   🕭 ⓐ ⇔

Park Ln ✉ *W1K 1QA* – ⓂHyde Park Corner – 𝓒 *(020)*   Plan: **G4**
76299988 – *www.chinatanglondon.co.uk* – *Closed 24-25 December*
Menu £ 28 (lunch) – Carte £ 28/79
• **Chinese** • **Fashionable** • **Elegant** •

Sir David Tang's atmospheric, art deco-inspired Chinese restaurant, downstairs at The Dorchester, is always abuzz with activity. Be sure to see the terrific bar, before sharing the traditional Cantonese specialities.

XxX **Amaranto** – Four Seasons Hotel   🍽 🕭 ⓐ ⇔ 🚗

Hamilton Pl, Park Ln ✉ *W1J 7DR*   Plan: **G4**
– ⓂHyde Park Corner – 𝓒 *(020) 7499 0888*
– *www.fourseasons.com/london/dining*
Menu £ 20 (lunch) – Carte £ 29/55
• **Italian** • **Fashionable** • **Trendy** •

It's all about flexibility as the Italian influenced menu is served in the stylish bar or the comfortable lounge, on the great terrace or in the restaurant decorated in the vivid colours of the amaranth plant.

XX **Araki** (Mitsuhiro Araki)   ⓐ ⇔
❀❀ *12 New Burlington St* ✉ *W1S 3BF* – ⓂOxford Circus   Plan: **H3**
– 𝓒 *(020) 7287 2481* – *www.the-araki.com* – *Closed 1 January and Monday*
Menu £ 300 – *(dinner only) (booking essential) (set menu only)*
• **Japanese** • **Intimate** • **Minimalist** •

Mitsuhiro Araki is one of Japan's great Sushi Masters who closed his Tokyo restaurant to relocate to London because he wanted a fresh challenge. From one of 9 seats at his beautiful cypress counter, watch him deftly prepare Edomae sushi using European seafood. It's very expensive but the different cuts of tuna are stunning and the rice, grown by his father-in-law back in Japan, is also excellent.

→ Sea bream with wasabi and ponzu. 3 kinds of bluefin tuna sushi. Squid with caviar.

XX **Wild Honey**   ⓐ
❀ *12 St George St.* ✉ *W1S 2FB* – ⓂOxford Circus   Plan: **H3**
– 𝓒 *(020) 7758 9160* – *www.wildhoneyrestaurant.co.uk*
– *Closed 25-26 December, 1 January and Sunday*
Menu £ 30 (lunch and early dinner) – Carte £ 40/64
• **Modern cuisine** • **Design** • **Intimate** •

Skilled kitchen uses seasonal ingredients at their peak to create dishes full of flavour and free from ostentation. Attractive and comfortable oak-panelled room. Personable and unobtrusive service adds to the relaxed feel.

→ Hand dived Scottish scallops, roast and dumpling, fermented ramsons. Slow-cooked shin of Limousin veal, spinach and pommes Anna. English custard tart, salted butter and golden sultanas.

XX **Pollen Street Social** (Jason Atherton)   🕃 ⓐ ⇔ 🝙
❀ *8-10 Pollen St* ✉ *W1S 1NQ* – ⓂOxford Circus   Plan: **H3**
– 𝓒 *(020) 7290 7600* – *www.pollenstreetsocial.com* – *Closed Sunday and bank holidays*
Menu £ 35 (lunch) – Carte £ 56/66 – *(booking essential)*
• **Creative** • **Fashionable** • **Elegant** •

The restaurant where it all started for Jason Atherton when he went solo. Top quality British produce lies at the heart of the menu and the innovative dishes are prepared with great care and no little skill. The room has plenty of buzz, helped along by the 'dessert bar' and views of the kitchen pass.

→ Crab salad with apple, coriander, black garlic, lemon purée and brown crab on toast. Loin of lamb with braised neck, roast artichoke and Merguez sausage. Lincolnshire apple cake, ice wine vinegar ice cream and sweet pickled Opal apples.

XX ⌘
Bonhams   ⛯ ⟐ 🄰🄲
Plan: **H3**
101 New Bond St (lower ground floor) (For breakfast
before 9am and dinner entrance via Haunch of Venison Yard off Brook St)
✉ *W1S 1SR* – Ⓜ *Bond Street* – ℰ *(020) 7468 5868* – *www.bonhams.com*
– *Closed 25-26 December, 1 January, Saturday, Sunday and bank holidays*
Menu £ 45 *(dinner)* – Carte £ 30/52 – *(lunch only and set menu Thursday*
dinner) (booking advisable)
• **Modern cuisine** • **Minimalist** • **Intimate** •
Established in 1793, Bonhams is now one of the world's largest fine art and
antique auctioneers. Its restaurant is bright, modern and professionally run.
Dishes are elegant and delicate and there is real clarity to the flavours. The
wine list has also been very thoughtfully compiled.
→ Flamed mackerel with pickled black radish, baby gem, avocado and
sesame. Duck breast and confit leg with beetroot purée, caramelised
endive, blood orange and five spice. Vanilla panna cotta, ginger-poached
rhubarb and rhubarb sorbet.

XX ⌘
Gymkhana   🄰🄲 ⟐ 🕼 🗓
Plan: **H3**
42 Albemarle St ✉ *W1S 4JH* – Ⓜ *Green Park* – ℰ *(020)*
3011 5900 – *www.gymkhanalondon.com* – *Closed first 2 weeks January,*
25-28 December and Sunday
Menu £ 25 *(lunch and early dinner)/75* – Carte £ 23/57 – *(booking*
essential)
• **Indian** • **Intimate** • **Fashionable** •
If you enjoyed Trishna then you'll love Karam Sethi's Gymkhana – that's if you
can get a table. Inspired by Colonial India's gymkhana clubs, the interior is full of
wonderful detail and plenty of wry touches; ask to sit downstairs. The North
Indian dishes have a wonderful richness and depth of flavour.
→ Kid goat methi keema, salli and pao. Wild muntjac biryani with pomegranate and mint raita. Rose kulfi falooda.

XX ⌘
Hakkasan Mayfair   ⛯ ⟐ 🄰🄲 ⟐ 🗓
Plan: **H3**
17 Bruton St ✉ *W1J 6QB* – Ⓜ *Green Park* – ℰ *(020)*
79071888 – *www.hakkasan.com* – *Closed 25 December*
Menu £ 35/128 – Carte £ 36/75 – *(booking essential)*
• **Chinese** • **Minimalist** • **Trendy** •
Less a copy, more a sister to the original; a sister who's just as fun but lives in a
nicer part of town. This one has a funky, more casual ground floor to go with the
downstairs dining room. You can expect the same extensive choice of top quality, modern Cantonese cuisine; dim sum is a highlight.
→ Crispy duck salad with pomelo, pine nut and shallot. Stir-fry black pepper rib-eye beef with Merlot. Jivara bomb.

XX
Colony Grill Room – The Beaumont Hotel   ⛯ 🄰🄲
Brown Hart Gdns. ✉ *W1K 6TF* – Ⓜ *Bond Street*
Plan: **G3**
– ℰ *(020) 7499 9499* – *www.colonygrillroom.com*
Carte £ 22/66 – *(booking essential)*
• **British traditional** • **Brasserie** • **Fashionable** •
Based on 1920s London and New York grill restaurants, The Beaumont's Colony
Grill comes with leather booths, striking age-of-speed art deco murals and cle-
ver lighting. By making the room and style of service so defiantly old fashioned,
Chris Corbin and Jeremy King have created somewhere effortlessly chic.

XX
Hawksmoor   ⛯ ⛯ 🄰🄲 🕼
Plan: **H3**
5a Air St ✉ *W1B 4EA* – Ⓜ *Piccadilly Circus* – ℰ *(020)*
7406 3980 – *www.thehawksmoor.com* – *Closed 24-26 December*
Menu £ 27 *(lunch and early dinner)* – Carte £ 28/80 – *(booking advi-*
sable)
• **Meats** • **Fashionable** • **Retro** •
The best of the Hawksmoors is large, boisterous and has an appealing art deco
feel. Expect top quality, 35-day aged Longhorn beef but also great seafood,
much of which is charcoal grilled. The delightful staff are well organised.

XX

Momo 🈴 AC

25 Heddon St. ⊠ *W1B 4BH –* Ⓜ *Oxford Circus* Plan: **H3**
– ℰ *(020) 7434 4040 – www.momoresto.com – Closed 25 December and
1 January*
Menu £ 16 (weekdays)/58 – Carte £ 25/82
• **Moroccan** • **Exotic** • **Intimate** •
An authentic Moroccan atmosphere comes courtesy of the antiques, kilim rugs,
Berber artwork, bright fabrics and lanterns – you'll feel you're eating near the
souk. Go for the classic dishes: zaalouk, briouats, pigeon pastilla, and tagines
with mountains of fluffy couscous.

XX

Heddon Street Kitchen 🈴 ሌ AC ⇦

3-9 Heddon St ⊠ *W1B 4BN –* Ⓜ *Oxford Circus* Plan: **H3**
– ℰ *(020) 7592 1212 – www.gordonramsay.com/heddon-street – Closed
25 December*
Menu £ 26 – Carte £ 27/58
• **Modern cuisine** • **Brasserie** • **Trendy** •
Gordon Ramsay's follow up to Bread Street is spread over two floors and is all
about all-day dining: breakfast covers all tastes, there's weekend brunch, and an
à la carte offering an appealing range of European dishes executed with palpable care.

XX

Roka 🈴 AC

30 North Audley St ⊠ *W1K 6ZF –* Ⓜ *Bond Street* Plan: **G3**
– ℰ *(020) 7305 5644 – www.rokarestaurant.com*
Carte £ 21/132
• **Japanese** • **Elegant** • **Fashionable** •
London's third Roka ventures into the rarefied surroundings of Mayfair and the
restaurant's seductive looks are a good fit. All the favourites from their modern
Japanese repertoire are here, with the robata grill taking centre stage.

XX

Sketch (The Gallery) AC

9 Conduit St ⊠ *W1S 2XG –* Ⓜ *Oxford Circus –* ℰ *(020)* Plan: **H3**
76594500 – www.sketch.london – Closed 25 December
Carte £ 43/80 – *(dinner only) (booking essential)*
• **Modern cuisine** • **Trendy** • **Intimate** •
The striking 'Gallery' has a new look from India Mahdavi and artwork from David
Shrigley. At dinner the room transmogrifies from art gallery to fashionable res-
taurant, with a menu that mixes the classic, the modern and the esoteric.

XX

Maze 🎏 ሌ AC ⇦ 🕸

10-13 Grosvenor Sq ⊠ *W1K 6JP –* Ⓜ *Bond Street* Plan: **G3**
– ℰ *(020) 71070000 – www.gordonramsay.com/maze*
Menu £ 33 (lunch and early dinner) – Carte £ 35/46
• **Modern cuisine** • **Fashionable** • **Design** •
This Gordon Ramsay restaurant still offers a glamorous night out, thanks to its
great cocktails, effervescent atmosphere and small plates of Asian influenced
food. Three or four dishes per person is about the going rate.

XX

Nobu Berkeley St AC 🕸

15 Berkeley St. ⊠ *W1J 8DY –* Ⓜ *Green Park –* ℰ *(020)* Plan: **H3**
*72909222 – www.noburestaurants.com – Closed 25 December, 1 January
and Sunday lunch except December*
Menu £ 29 – Carte £ 32/121 – *(booking essential)*
• **Japanese** • **Fashionable** • **Trendy** •
This branch of the glamorous chain is more of a party animal than its elder sibling at The Metropolitan. Start with cocktails then head upstairs for Japanese
food with South American influences; try dishes from the wood-fired oven.

XX **Veeraswamy** 🔲 ⟷ 🐗 🍽

Victory House, 99 Regent St (Entrance on Swallow St.) Plan: **H3**
✉ *W1B 4RS –* Ⓜ *Piccadilly Circus –* ℰ *(020) 77341401*
– www.veeraswamy.com
Menu £ 28 (weekday lunch) – Carte £ 35/65
• **Indian** • **Design** • **Fashionable** •
May have opened back in 1926 but this Indian restaurant feels fresh and is
awash with vibrant colours and always full of bustle. Skilled kitchen cleverly
mixes the traditional with more contemporary creations.

XX **Coya** 🔲 ⟷

118 Piccadilly ✉ *W1J 7NW –* Ⓜ *Hyde Park Corner* Plan: **G4**
– ℰ *(020) 7042 7118 – www.coyarestaurant.com – Closed 24-26 December
and 1 January*
Menu £ 30 (lunch) – Carte £ 34/57 – *(booking advisable)*
• **Peruvian** • **Individual** • **Exotic** •
From the people behind Zuma and Roka comes this lively, loud and enthusias-
tically run basement restaurant that celebrates all things Peruvian. Try their cevi-
che and their skewers, as well as their Pisco Sours in the fun bar.

XX **La Petite Maison** 🍴 🔲

54 Brooks Mews ✉ *W1K 4EG –* Ⓜ *Bond Street* Plan: **H3**
– ℰ *(020) 74954774 – www.lpmlondon.co.uk – Closed Christmas-New
Year*
Carte £ 29/69 – *(booking essential)*
• **French** • **Bistro** • **Neighbourhood** •
A little piece of southern France and Ligurian Italy in Mayfair. The slickly run sis-
ter to the Nice original has a buzzy, glamorous feel, with prices to match. Just
reading the menus of Mediterranean dishes will improve your tan.

XX **Keeper's House** 🍴 ⚐ 🔲 ⟷

Royal Academy of Arts, Burlington House, Piccadilly Plan: **H3**
✉ *W1J 0BD –* Ⓜ *Green Park –* ℰ *(020) 7300 5881*
– www.keepershouse.org.uk – Closed 25-26 December and Sunday
Menu £ 30 – Carte £ 29/57 – *(dinner only)*
• **British modern** • **Individual** • **Intimate** •
Built in 1860 and fully restored, this house is part of the Royal Academy. Two
intimate dining rooms are lined with green baize and hung with architectural
casts. The emphasis is on seasonality, freshness and contrasts in textures.

XX **Maze Grill Mayfair** – London Marriott Hotel Grosvenor Square

10-13 Grosvenor Sq ✉ *W1K 6JP –* Ⓜ *Bond Street* 🏛 ⚐ 🔲
– ℰ *(020) 74952211* Plan: **G3**
– www.gordonramsay.com/mazegrill
Menu £ 27 (lunch) – Carte £ 29/88
• **Meats** • **Retro** • **Fashionable** •
Next door to Maze and specialising in steaks cooked on the Josper grill. Expect a
good range of aged meat, including Aberdeen Angus (28 days), Dedham Vale
(31), USDA Prime (36) and Wagyu 9th Grade (49), served on wooden boards.

XX **Goodman Mayfair** 🔲

26 Maddox St ✉ *W1S 1QH –* Ⓜ *Oxford Circus* Plan: **H3**
– ℰ *(020) 7499 3776 – www.goodmanrestaurants.com – Closed Sunday
and bank holidays*
Carte £ 26/97 – *(booking essential)*
• **Meats** • **Brasserie** • **Classic** •
A worthy attempt at recreating a New York steakhouse; all leather and wood
and macho swagger. Beef is dry or wet aged in-house and comes with a choice
of four sauces; rib-eye the speciality.

XX **Hush** 🛱 🕭 AC ⟷

8 Lancashire Ct., Brook St. ✉ *W1S 1EY –* Ⓜ *Bond Street*   Plan: **H3**
*– ℰ (020) 76591500 – www.hush.co.uk – Closed 25 December and
1 January*
Carte £ 21/28 *– (booking essential)*

• **Modern cuisine** • **Fashionable** • **Brasserie** •

Appealing and all-purpose European brasserie-style menu served in a busy
room with smart destination bar upstairs and plenty of private dining. Tucked
away in a charming courtyard, with a pleasant summer terrace.

XX **Nobu** – Metropolitan Hotel ≤ 🕭 AC ⟷ 🕅

19 Old Park Ln ✉ *W1Y 1LB –* Ⓜ *Hyde Park Corner*   Plan: **G4**
– ℰ (020) 74474747 – www.noburestaurants.com
Menu £ 30 *–* Carte £ 24/73 *– (booking essential)*

• **Japanese** • **Fashionable** • **Minimalist** •

Nobu restaurants are now all over the world but this was Europe's first and
opened in 1997. It retains a certain exclusivity and is buzzy and fun. The menu
is an innovative blend of Japanese cuisine with South American influences.

XX **Kiku** 🕭 AC

17 Half Moon St. ✉ *W1J 7BE –* Ⓜ *Green Park*   Plan: **H4**
– ℰ (020) 74994208 – www.kikurestaurant.co.uk
*– Closed 25-27 December, 1 January, Sunday and lunch on
bank holidays*
Menu £ 20 (weekday lunch) *–* Carte £ 28/78

• **Japanese** • **Neighbourhood** • **Simple** •

For over 35 years this earnestly run, authentically styled, family owned restaurant has been providing every style of Japanese cuisine to its homesick Japanese customers, from shabu shabu to sukiyaki, yakitori to teriyaki.

XX **Chucs Bar and Grill** 🛱 AC

30b Dover St. ✉ *W1S 4NB –* Ⓜ *Green Park – ℰ (020)*   Plan: **H3**
3763 2013 – www.chucsrestaurant.com
– Closed Sunday dinner
Carte £ 38/59 *– (booking essential)*

• **Italian** • **Elegant** • **Cosy** •

Like the shop to which it's attached, Chucs caters for those who summer on the
Riviera and are not afraid of showing it. It's decked out like a yacht and the concise but not inexpensive menu offers classic Mediterranean dishes.

X **Bentley's (Oyster Bar)** 🛱 AC ⟷

11-15 Swallow St ✉ *W1B 4DG –* Ⓜ *Piccadilly Circus*   Plan: **H3**
*– ℰ (020) 77344756 – www.bentleys.org – Closed 25 December and
1 January*
Carte £ 33/70

• **Fish and seafood** • **Bistro** • **Fashionable** •

Sit at the counter to watch white-jacketed staff open oysters by the bucket load.
Interesting seafood menus feature tasty fish pies; lots of daily specials on blackboard.

X **Le Boudin Blanc** 🛱 AC ⟷ 🕭

5 Trebeck St ✉ *W1J 7LT –* Ⓜ *Green Park – ℰ (020)*   Plan: **G4**
*74993292 – www.boudinblanc.co.uk – Closed 24-26 December and
1 January*
Menu £ 15 *–* Carte £ 28/58

• **French** • **Rustic** • **Neighbourhood** •

Appealing, lively French bistro in Shepherd Market, spread over two floors.
Satisfying French classics and country cooking is the draw, along with authentic
Gallic service. Good value lunch menu.

X

Little Social   ♿ AK ⇔ ⑰

5 Pollen St ⊠ W1S 1NE – Ⓜ *Oxford Circus –* ℰ *(020)*   Plan: **H3**
7870 3730 – www.littlesocial.co.uk – Closed Sunday and bank holidays
Menu £ 21/25 – Carte £ 34/58 – *(booking essential)*
• French • Bistro • Fashionable •
Jason Atherton's lively French bistro, opposite his Pollen Street Social restaurant, has a clubby feel and an appealing, deliberately worn look. Service is breezy and capable and the food is mostly classic with the odd modern twist.

X

Kitty Fisher's

10 Shepherd Mkt ⊠ W1J 7QF – Ⓜ *Green Park*   Plan: **H4**
– ℰ (020) 3302 1661 – www.kittyfishers.com – Closed Christmas, Saturday lunch, Sunday and Monday
Carte £ 32/57 – *(booking essential)*
• Modern cuisine • Bistro • Cosy •
Warm, intimate and unpretentious restaurant – the star of the show is the wood grill which gives the dishes added depth. Named after an 18C courtesan, presumably in honour of the profession for which Shepherd Market was once known.

X

Peyote   ♿ AK ⇔

13 Cork St ⊠ W1S 3NS – Ⓜ *Green Park – ℰ (020)*   Plan: **H3**
7409 1300 – www.peyoterestaurant.com – Closed Saturday lunch and Sunday
Menu £ 24/80 – Carte £ 28/63 – *(booking essential)*
• Mexican • Trendy • Design •
From the people behind Zuma and Roka comes a 'refined interpretation of Mexican cuisine' at this fun, glamorous spot. There's an exhilarating freshness to the well-judged dishes; don't miss the great guacamole or the cactus salad.

X

28°-50° Mayfair   🕸 ♿ AK

17-19 Maddox St ⊠ W1S 2QH – Ⓜ *Oxford Circus*   Plan: **H3**
– ℰ (020) 7495 1505 – www.2850.co.uk – Closed 25 December, 1 January and Sunday
Menu £ 20 (lunch) – Carte £ 26/39
• Modern cuisine • Wine bar • Classic •
The group's third wine-bar-restaurant is possibly their best and, as this is Mayfair, almost certainly their most profitable. Modern, unfussy dishes provide great accompaniment to the thoughtfully put-together wine list.

X

Mayfair Chippy   AK ⇔

14 North Audley St ⊠ W1K 6WE – Ⓜ *Marble Arch*   Plan: **G3**
– ℰ (020) 7741 2233 – www.eatbrit.com – Closed 25 December, 1 January and Sunday dinner
Carte £ 20/42
• British traditional • Bistro • Traditional •
When it was called 'The Great British', fish and chips was the top-selling dish so the owners decided to change the restaurant name and specialise in fish dishes, along with a few other British classics. Takeaway is available.

X

Burger & Lobster   AK

29 Clarges St ⊠ W1J 7EF – Ⓜ *Green Park. – ℰ (020)*   Plan: **H4**
7409 1699 – www.burgerandlobster.com – Closed Sunday dinner and bank holidays
Menu £ 20
• Meats • Simple • Rustic •
Choose a burger, a lobster or a lobster roll, with chips, salad and sauces, and mousse for dessert – an ingeniously simple idea. The lobsters are Canadian and the burgers 10oz. It's a well organised bunfight in an old pub.

Only Running Footman   ♿ ⇔

5 Charles St ✉ *W1J 5DF –* Ⓜ *Green Park. –* ☎ *(020)*   Plan: **H3**
74992988 – www.therunningfootmanmayfair.com
Menu £ 45 – Carte £ 25/45
• British traditional • Pub • Neighbourhood •
The busy ground floor bar with its appealing menu of pub classics doesn't take
bookings. By contrast, upstairs is formal and its menu more European and ambitious but the simpler dishes are still the best.

Soho

 Soho   ♤ ⅃ᴓ ♿ Ⅲ ⅍

4 Richmond Mews ✉ *W1D 3DH*   Plan: **I3**
– Ⓜ *Tottenham Court Road –* ☎ *(020) 7559 3000 – www.sohohotel.com*
91 rm – ♦£ 300/610 ♦♦£ 300/610 – ⛌ £ 14 – 5 suites
• Luxury • Stylish • Contemporary •
Stylish and fashionable hotel that mirrors the vibrancy of the neighbourhood.
Boasts two screening rooms, a comfortable drawing room and up-to-the-
minute bedrooms; some vivid, others more muted but all with hi-tech extras.
Refuel – See restaurant listing

Ham Yard   ♤ ⅃ᴓ ❀ ♿ Ⅲ ⅍ ⇋

1 Ham Yard, ✉ *W1D 7DT –* Ⓜ *Piccadilly Circus*   Plan: **I3**
– ☎ *(020) 3642 2000 – www.firmdalehotels.com*
91 rm – ♦£ 318/515 ♦♦£ 318/515 – ⛌ £ 14 – 2 suites
• Family • Business • Stylish •
Opened in 2014, this stylish hotel from the Firmdale group is set around a courtyard – a haven of tranquillity in the West End. Each of the rooms is different but
all are supremely comfortable. There's also a great roof terrace, a theatre, a fully
stocked library and bar... and even a bowling alley.
Ham Yard – See restaurant listing

Café Royal   ♤ ⅃ᴓ ❀ ⋒ ⊡ ♿ Ⅲ ⅍

68 Regent St ✉ *W1B 4DY –* Ⓜ *Piccadilly Circus*   Plan: **H3**
– ☎ *(020) 7406 3333 – www.hotelcaferoyal.com*
160 rm – ♦£ 320/600 ♦♦£ 320/600 – ⛌ £ 32 – 25 suites
• Grand Luxury • Palace • Historic •
One of the most famous names of the London social scene for the last 150 years
is now a luxury hotel. The bedrooms are beautiful, elegant and discreet and the
wining and dining options many and varied – they include the gloriously
rococo Oscar Wilde bar, once home to the iconic Grill Room.

W London   ♤ ⅃ᴓ ❀ ♿ Ⅲ ⅍

10 Wardour St ✉ *W1D 6QF –* Ⓜ *Leicester Square*   Plan: **I3**
– ☎ *(020) 77581000 – www.wlondon.co.uk*
192 rm – ♦£ 339 ♦♦£ 339 – ⛌ £ 18 – 15 suites
• Luxury • Design • Stylish •
An achingly trendy hotel bang in the heart of Leicester Square. A DJ plays in the
lobby lounge at weekends; there's an over-subscribed bar with low slung
tables and slick, uber cool bedrooms in categories called 'Fantastic' or 'Spectacular'.
Spice Market – See restaurant listing

 Sanctum Soho   ♤ Ⅲ ⅍

20 Warwick St. ✉ *W1B 5NF –* Ⓜ *Piccadilly Circus*   Plan: **H3**
– ☎ *(020) 7292 6100 – www.sanctumsoho.com*
30 rm – ♦£ 190/550 ♦♦£ 190/550 – ⛌ £ 14
• Townhouse • Modern • Design •
Plenty of glitz and bling at this funky, self-styled rock 'n' roll hotel, with some
innovative touches such as TVs behind mirrors. Rooftop lounge and hot tub.
Relaxed and comfortable dining with plenty of classic dishes.

Dean Street Townhouse

69-71 Dean St. ⊠ W1D 3SE – **Ⓜ** *Piccadilly Circus*
– ℰ (020) 74341775 – www.deanstreettownhouse.com
39 rm – **♦**£ 225/250 **♦♦**£ 400/500

• Townhouse • Classic • Stylish •

In the heart of Soho and where bedrooms range from tiny to bigger; the latter have roll-top baths in the room. All are well designed and come with a good range of extras. Cosy ground floor lounge.
Dean Street Townhouse Restaurant – See restaurant listing

Nadler Soho

10 Carlisle St ⊠ W1D 3BR – **Ⓜ** *Tottenham Court Road*
– ℰ (020) 3697 3697 – www.thenadler.com
78 rm – **♦**£ 185/215 **♦♦**£ 220/275 – ⊡ £ 14 – 1 suite

• Business • Townhouse • Contemporary •

On a quiet lane, but in the heart of Soho, is a townhouse with a concept: no bar nor restaurant, just comfortable, very well-equipped bedrooms, most of which have a small kitchenette. The smart receptionists double as concierge.

Hazlitt's

6 Frith St ⊠ W1D 3JA – **Ⓜ** *Tottenham Court Road*
– ℰ (020) 74341771 – www.hazlittshotel.com
30 rm – **♦**£ 222 **♦♦**£ 288/834 – ⊡ £ 12

• Townhouse • Traditional • Historic •

Dating from 1718, the former house of essayist and critic William Hazlitt still welcomes many a writer today in its role as a charming townhouse hotel. It has plenty of character and is warmly run. No restaurant so breakfast in bed really is the only option – and who is going to object to that?

Quo Vadis

26-29 Dean St ⊠ W1D 3LL – **Ⓜ** *Tottenham Court Road*
– ℰ (020) 74379585 – www.quovadissoho.co.uk – Closed 25-26 December, 1 January and bank holidays
Menu £ 19 – Carte £ 31/49

• British traditional • Fashionable • Brasserie •

Owned by the Hart brothers, this Soho institution dates from the 1920s and is as stylish and handsome as ever. The menu reads like a selection of all your favourite British dishes – game is always a highlight. They also do a good breakfast and a great value theatre menu.

Gauthier - Soho

21 Romilly St ⊠ W1D 5AF – **Ⓜ** *Leicester Square*
– ℰ (020) 74943111 – www.gauthiersoho.co.uk – Closed Monday lunch, Sunday and bank holidays except Good Friday
Menu £ 18/60

• French • Intimate • Neighbourhood •

Tucked away from the mischief of Soho is this charming Georgian townhouse, with dining spread over three floors. Alex Gauthier offers assorted menus of his classically based cooking, with vegetarians particularly well looked after.

Red Fort

77 Dean St. ⊠ W1D 3SH – **Ⓜ** *Tottenham Court Road*
– ℰ (020) 74372525 – www.redfort.co.uk – Closed lunch Saturday-Sunday
Menu £ 15 – Carte £ 32/65 – *(bookings advisable at dinner)*

• Indian • Fashionable • Formal •

A feature in Soho since 1983 but the last makeover gave it a stylish, contemporary look. Balanced Indian cooking uses much UK produce such as Herdwick lamb; look out for more unusual choices like rabbit.

XxX **Imperial China** 　　　　　　　　　　AC ⇔

White Bear Yard, 25a Lisle St ⊠ *WC2H 7BA* 　　　Plan: I3
– ⊕ *Leicester Square* – ℰ *(020) 7734 3388*
– *www.imperialchina-london.com* – *Closed 25 December*
Menu £ 20/36 – Carte £ 16/96 – *(booking advisable)*
• Chinese • Elegant •
Sharp service and comfortable surroundings are not the only things that set this
restaurant apart: the Cantonese cooking exudes freshness and vitality, whether
that's the steamed dumplings or the XO minced pork with fine beans.

XX **Yauatcha Soho** 　　　　　　　　　　　　　AC
✿ *15 Broadwick St* ⊠ *W1F 0DL* 　　　　　　Plan: I3
– ⊕ *Tottenham Court Road* – ℰ *(020) 74948888* – *www.yauatcha.com*
– *Closed 25 December*
Menu £ 29/55 – Carte £ 16/61
• Chinese • Design • Trendy •
Refined, delicate and delicious dim sum; ideal for sharing in a group. It's over 10
years old yet the surroundings are still as slick and stylish as ever: choose the
lighter, brighter ground floor or the darker, more atmospheric basement.
→ Spicy soft shell crab. Sweet and sour pork. Raspberry délice.

XX **Brasserie Zédel** 　　　　　　　　　　　AC
☺ *20 Sherwood St* ⊠ *W1F 7ED* – ⊕ *Piccadilly Circus* 　Plan: H3
– ℰ *(020) 7734 4888* – *www.brasseriezedel.com* – *Closed 24-25 December
and 1 January*
Menu £ 13/20 – Carte £ 19/41 – *(booking advisable)*
• French • Brasserie •
A grand French brasserie, which is all about inclusivity and accessibility, in a
bustling subterranean space restored to its original art deco glory. Expect a
roll-call of classic French dishes and some very competitive prices.

XX **Bob Bob Ricard** 　　　　　　　　　　　AC
1 Upper James St ⊠ *W1F 9DF* – ⊕ *Oxford Circus* 　Plan: H3
– ℰ *(020) 31451000* – *www.bobbobricard.com*
Carte £ 31/94
• Modern cuisine • Retro • Elegant •
Everyone needs a little glamour now and again and this place provides it. The
room may be quite small but it sees itself as a grand salon – ask for a booth. The
menu is all-encompassing – oysters and caviar to pies and burgers.

XX **Ham Yard** – Ham Yard Hotel 　　　　🛋 & AC
1 Ham Yard, ⊠ *W1D 7DT* – ⊕ *Piccadilly Circus* 　Plan: I3
– ℰ *(020) 3642 2000* – *www.firmdalehotels.com*
Carte £ 24/35
• Modern cuisine • Brasserie • Design •
An exuberantly decorated restaurant; start with a cocktail – the bitters and
syrups are homemade with herbs from the hotel's roof garden. The menu
moves with the seasons and the kitchen has the confidence to keep dishes simple.

XX **Dean Street Townhouse Restaurant** 　🛋 AC 📶 📺
69-71 Dean St. ⊠ *W1D 3SE* – ⊕ *Piccadilly Circus* 　Plan: I3
– ℰ *(020) 74341775* – *www.deanstreettownhouse.com*
Menu £ 17/28 – Carte £ 28/83 – *(booking essential)*
• British modern • Brasserie • Elegant •
Georgian house now home to a fashionable bar and restaurant that is busy
from breakfast onwards. Appealingly classic British food includes some retro
dishes and satisfying puddings.

XX **Aqua Kyoto**　　　　　　　　　　　　　　&. 🅰🅲 ⇧ 🈂
240 Regent St. (5th floor) (entrance on Argyll St.)　Plan: **H3**
🖂 *W1F 7EB –* Ⓜ *Oxford Circus*
– ℰ (020) 7478 0540 – www.aquakyoto.co.uk
– Closed 25 December and 1 January
Menu £ 17 (lunch)/50 – Carte £ 27/64
• Japanese • Trendy • Exotic •
The louder and more boisterous of the two large restaurants on the 5th floor of
Aqua London. It's ideally suited to a night out with a group of friends as many of
the contemporary Japanese dishes are designed for sharing.

XX **Vasco and Piero's Pavilion**　　　　　　　　🅰🅲 ⇧
15 Poland St 🖂 *W1F 8QE –* Ⓜ *Oxford Circus – ℰ (020)*　Plan: **H2**
7437 8774 – www.vascosfood.com
– Closed Saturday lunch, Sunday and bank holidays
Menu £ 17 (lunch and early dinner) – Carte £ 25/46 – *(booking essential
at lunch)*
• Italian • Friendly •
Regulars and tourists have been flocking to this institution for over 40 years; its
longevity is down to a twice daily changing menu of Umbrian-influenced dishes
rather than the matter-of-fact service or simple decoration.

XX **Plum Valley**　　　　　　　　　　　　　　　⇧
20 Gerrard St. 🖂 *W1D 6JQ –* Ⓜ *Leicester Square*　Plan: **I3**
– ℰ (020) 74944366 – Closed 23-24 December
Menu £ 38 – Carte £ 19/37
• Chinese • Design •
Its striking black façade makes this modern Chinese restaurant easy to spot in
Chinatown. Mostly Cantonese cooking, with occasional forays into Vietnam and
Thailand; dim sum is the strength.

XX **Refuel** – Soho Hotel　　　　　　　　　　　&. 🅰🅲
4 Richmond Mews 🖂 *W1D 3DH*　　　　　　　　Plan: **I3**
– Ⓜ *Tottenham Court Road – ℰ (020) 75593007 – www.sohohotel.com*
Menu £ 20 – Carte £ 30/53
• British modern • Fashionable • Brasserie •
At the heart of the cool Soho hotel is their aptly named bar and restaurant. With
a menu to suit all moods and wallets, from Dover sole to burgers, and a cocktail
list to lift all spirits, it's a fun and bustling spot.

XX **Spice Market** – W London Hotel　　　　　🅰🅲 ⇧ 🕥
10 Wardour St 🖂 *W1D 6QF –* Ⓜ *Leicester Square*　Plan: **I3**
– ℰ (020) 77581000 – www.wlondon.co.uk
Carte £ 32/50
• Asian • Fashionable • Exotic •
Spread over two floors and as strikingly decorated and fun as Jean-Georges
Vongerichten's original in Manhattan's Meatpacking district. Influences are
from across Asia; dishes are meant for sharing and curries are a highlight.

XX **HIX**　　　　　　　　　　　　　　　　　🅰🅲 ⇧ 🈂 🕥
66-70 Brewer St. 🖂 *WIF 9UP –* Ⓜ *Piccadilly Circus*　Plan: **H3**
– ℰ (020) 72923518 – www.hixsoho.co.uk
– Closed 25-26 December
Menu £ 20 (weekday lunch)/28 – Carte £ 27/65
• British traditional • Fashionable • Trendy •
The exterior may hint at exclusivity but inside this big restaurant the atmo-
sphere is fun, noisy and sociable. The room comes decorated with the works of
eminent British artists. Expect classic British dishes and ingredients.

UNITED KINGDOM - LONDON

XX

MASH

77 Brewer St ⊠ W1F 9ZN – **Ⓜ** *Piccadilly Circus*   Plan: **H3**
– ℰ *(020) 7734 2608 – www.mashsteak.co.uk – Closed 23-25 December
and Sunday lunch*
Menu £ 25 – Carte £ 50/75

• **Meats** • **Brasserie** • **Fashionable** •

A team from Copenhagen raised the old Titanic and restored the art deco to
create this striking 'Modern American Steak House', offering Danish, Nebraskan
and Uruguayan beef. A great bar and slick service add to the grown up feel.

X
❁

Social Eating House

58 Poland St ⊠ W1F 7NR – **Ⓜ** *Oxford Circus* – ℰ *(020)*   Plan: **H3**
*79933251 – www.socialeatinghouse.com – Closed Christmas, Sunday and
bank holidays*
Menu £ 23 (lunch) – Carte £ 39/56 – *(booking advisable)*

• **Modern cuisine** • **Fashionable** • **Brasserie** •

There's a something of a Brooklyn vibe to this Jason Atherton restaurant, with
its bare brick and raw plastered walls. It's great fun, very busy and gloriously
unstuffy; the menu is an eminently good read, with the best dishes being the
simplest ones.

→ Smoked Lincolnshire eel, salt and vinegar Jersey Royals, macadamia
nuts and land seaweed. Rump of Kentish salt marsh lamb, confit shoulder,
miso caramel, smoked aubergine and asparagus. Jelly and ice cream.

X
❁

Arbutus

63-64 Frith St. ⊠ W1D 3JW – **Ⓜ** *Tottenham Court Road*   Plan: **I3**
– ℰ *(020) 77344545 – www.arbutusrestaurant.co.uk – Closed 25-
26 December and 1 January*
Menu £ 23 (weekday lunch)/25 – Carte £ 34/54 – *(booking advisable)*

• **Modern cuisine** • **Bistro** • **Neighbourhood** •

A relaxed setting, enthusiastic service, a terrific wine list that doesn't break the
bank, and wonderfully flavoursome cooking – what's not to like? The technically
confident kitchen has an innate understanding of the 'less is more' principle
along with an appreciation of what-goes-with-what.

→ Warm crisp pig's head with potato purée, black radish and pistachio.
Saddle of rabbit with peas, wild mushrooms and slow-cooked shoulder
'cottage pie'. Warm chocolate soup with almond milk sorbet.

X
❁

Barrafina

54 Frith St. ⊠ W1D 3SL – **Ⓜ** *Tottenham Court Road*   Plan: **I3**
– ℰ *(020) 7813 8016 – www.barrafina.co.uk – Closed 25 December and
1 January*
Carte £ 11/29 – *(bookings not accepted)*

• **Spanish** • **Tapas bar** • **Fashionable** •

For proof that great food is about great sourcing, come to this terrific, warmly
run tapas bar from the Hart brothers – but be prepared to queue for gaps at the
counter. Wonderful, fresh ingredients and expert cooking allow natural flavours
to shine – the seafood is particularly stunning.

→ Ham croquetas. Gambas, ajetes y setas tortilla. Santiago tart.

X
☺

Dehesa

25 Ganton St ⊠ W1F 9BP – **Ⓜ** *Oxford Circus* – ℰ *(020)*   Plan: **H3**
74944170 – www.dehesa.co.uk – Closed Christmas
Carte £ 19/29

• **Mediterranean** • **Tapas bar** • **Fashionable** •

Repeats the success of its sister restaurant, Salt Yard, by offering flavoursome
and appealingly priced Spanish and Italian tapas. Busy, friendly atmosphere in
appealing corner location. Terrific drinks list too.

X

Nopi   ⅌ ⓐⅭ ⓥ

21-22 Warwick St. ⊠ W1B 5NE – ⓜ *Piccadilly Circus*   Plan: **H3**
*– ℰ (020) 74949584 – www.nopi-restaurant.com – Closed 25-
26 December, 1 January and Sunday dinner*
Carte £ 30/44
• Mediterranean • Design • Fashionable •
The bright, clean look of Yotam Ottolenghi's charmingly run all-day restaurant
matches the fresh, invigorating food. The sharing plates take in the Mediterra-
nean, the Middle East and Asia and the veggie dishes stand out.

X

Ember Yard   ⒶⒸ ⇦

60 Berwick St ⊠ W1F 8DX – ⓜ *Oxford Circus – ℰ (020)*   Plan: **H2**
*7439 8057 – www.emberyard.co.uk – Closed 25-26 December and
1 January*
Carte approx. £ 20 – *(booking advisable)*
• Mediterranean • Tapas bar • Fashionable •
Those familiar with the Salt Yard Group will recognise the Spanish and Italian
themed menus – but their 4th fun outlet comes with a focus on cooking over
charcoal or wood. There's even a seductive smokiness to some of the cocktails.

X
ⓐ

Polpetto   ⒶⒸ

11 Berwick St ⊠ W1F 0PL – ⓜ *Tottenham Court Road*   Plan: **I3**
– ℰ (020) 7439 8627 – www.polpetto.co.uk – Closed Sunday
Carte £ 15/23 – *(bookings not accepted at dinner)*
• Italian • Simple • Rustic •
Re-opened by Russell Norman in bigger premises. The style of food is the per-
fect match for this relaxed environment: the small, seasonally inspired Italian
dishes are uncomplicated, appealingly priced and deliver great flavours.

X
ⓐ

Polpo Soho   ⒶⒸ ⇦

41 Beak St. ⊠ W1F 9SB – ⓜ *Oxford Circus – ℰ (020)*   Plan: **H3**
*7734 4479 – www.polpo.co.uk – Closed dinner 24 December, 25-26 and
31 December, 1 January and Sunday dinner*
Carte £ 12/26 – *(bookings not accepted at dinner)*
• Italian • Tapas bar • Rustic •
A fun and lively Venetian bacaro, with a stripped-down, faux-industrial look. The
small plates, from arancini and prosciutto to fritto misto and Cotechino sausage,
are so well priced that waiting for a table is worth it.

X
ⓐ

Copita   ⒶⒸ

27 D'Arblay St ⊠ W1F 8EP – ⓜ *Oxford Circus*   Plan: **H3**
*– ℰ (020) 7287 7797 – www.copita.co.uk – Closed Sunday and bank
holidays*
Carte £ 17/28 – *(bookings not accepted)*
• Mediterranean • Tapas bar • Rustic •
Perch on one of the high stools or stay standing and get stuck into the daily
menu of small, colourful and tasty dishes. Staff add to the atmosphere and ever-
ything on the Spanish wine list comes by the glass or copita.

X
ⓐ

Palomar   ⅌ ⒶⒸ

34 Rupert St ⊠ W1D 6DN – ⓜ *Piccadilly Circus*   Plan: **I3**
*– ℰ (020) 7439 8777 – www.thepalomar.co.uk – Closed 25-26 December
and Sunday dinner*
Carte £ 23/36 – *(booking advisable)*
• World cuisine • Trendy • Cosy •
A hip slice of modern-day Jerusalem in the heart of theatreland, with a zinc kit-
chen counter running back to an intimate, wood-panelled dining room. Like the
atmosphere, the contemporary Middle Eastern cooking is fresh and vibrant.

X
Mele e Pere
46 Brewer St ⊠ W1F 9TF – Ⓜ *Piccadilly Circus* – ℰ *(020)*   Plan: **I3**
7096 2096 – www.meleepere.co.uk – Closed 25-26 December and
1 January
Menu £ 20 (dinner) – Carte £ 26/39
• Italian • Friendly • Neighbourhood •
Head downstairs – the 'apples and pears'? – to a vaulted room in the style of a
homely Italian kitchen, with an appealing Vermouth bar. The owner-chef has
worked in some decent London kitchens but hails from Verona so expect
gutsy Italian dishes.

X
Blanchette
9 D'Arblay St ⊠ W1F 8DR – Ⓜ *Oxford Circus* – ℰ *(020)*   Plan: **H2**
7439 8100 – www.blanchettesoho.co.uk
Carte £ 14/22 – *(booking essential)*
• French • Simple • Fashionable •
Run by three frères, Blanchette takes French bistro food and gives it the 'small
plates' treatment. It's named after their mother – the ox cheek bourguignon is
her recipe. Tiles and exposed brick add to the rustic look.

X
Bocca di Lupo
12 Archer St ⊠ W1D 7BB – Ⓜ *Piccadilly Circus* – ℰ *(020)*   Plan: **I3**
7734 2223 – www.boccadilupo.com – Closed Christmas, 1 January and
31 August
Carte £ 21/46 – *(booking essential)*
• Italian • Tapas bar •
Atmosphere, food and service are all best when sitting at the marble counter,
watching the chefs at work. Specialities from across Italy come in large or small
sizes and are full of flavour and vitality. Try also their gelato shop opposite.

X
Wright Brothers Soho
13 Kingly St. ⊠ W1B 5PW – Ⓜ *Oxford Circus* – ℰ *(020)*   Plan: **H3**
7434 3611 – www.thewrightbrothers.co.uk – Closed bank holidays
Menu £ 22 (weekdays) – Carte £ 30/80
• Fish and seafood • Neighbourhood • Mediterranean •
A seafood restaurant with a utilitarian look; avoid downstairs which is meant to
resemble a lobster pot. Oysters are a speciality; fish is from Cornwall; and the
'surfboards' are ideal for anyone wanting a quick one course lunch.

X
10 Greek Street
10 Greek St ⊠ W1D 4DH – Ⓜ *Tottenham Court Road*   Plan: **I2/3**
– ℰ (020) 7734 4677 – www.10greekstreet.com – Closed Christmas, Easter
and Sunday
Carte £ 27/62
• Modern cuisine • Bistro • Neighbourhood •
With just 28 seats and a dozen at the counter, the challenge is getting a table at
this modishly sparse-looking bistro (no bookings taken at dinner). The chef-
owner's blackboard menu comes with Anglo, Med and Middle Eastern elements.

X
Haozhan
8 Gerrard St ⊠ W1D 5PJ – Ⓜ *Leicester Square* – ℰ *(020)*   Plan: **I3**
7434 3838 – www.haozhan.co.uk – Closed 24-25 December
Menu £ 15/48 – Carte £ 20/78
• Chinese • Design •
Interesting fusion-style dishes, with mostly Cantonese but other Asian influences too. Specialities like jasmine ribs or wasabi prawns reveal a freshness that
marks this place out from the plethora of Chinatown mediocrity.

X **Cinnamon Soho**   🛱 ⛄ ♿

5 Kingly St ⊠ *W1B 5PF –* Ⓜ *Oxford Circus –* ☏ *(020)*   Plan: **H3**
7437 1664 – www.cinnamonsoho.com – Closed 1 January
Menu £ 10/16 – Carte £ 17/31
• **Indian** • **Friendly** • **Fashionable** •
Younger and more fun than its sister the Cinnamon Club. Has a great selection
of classic and more modern Indian dishes like Rogan Josh Shepherd's pie. High
Chai in the afternoon and a pre-theatre menu that's a steal.

X **Duck & Rice**   ⛄

90 Berwick St ⊠ *WIF 0QB –* Ⓜ *Tottenham Court Road*   Plan: **I3**
– ☏ *(020) 3327 7888 – www.theduckandrice.com*
Carte £ 35/45
• **Chinese** • **Intimate** • **Romantic** •
Alan Yau is one of our most innovative restaurateurs and once again he's created something different – a modern pub with a Chinese kitchen. Beer is the
thing on the ground floor; upstairs is for Chinese favourites and comforting classics.

X **Tapas Brindisa**   ⑩

46 Broadwick St. ⊠ *W1F 7AF –* Ⓜ *Oxford Circus*   Plan: **H3**
– ☏ *(020) 7534 1690 – www.brindisatapaskitchens.com – Closed dinner*
24-27 December
Menu £ 13 (weekday lunch) – Carte £ 15/40 – *(bookings not accepted at*
dinner)
• **Spanish** • **Tapas bar** • **Neighbourhood** •
One of the first in Soho to have a no-bookings policy. This sister to the Borough
Market original also brought with it – in true tapas style – small plates using terrific produce and that great atmosphere you get when places are packed out.

X **Burger & Lobster**   ⛄

36 Dean St ⊠ *W1D 4PS –* Ⓜ *Leicester Square –* ☏ *(020)*   Plan: **I3**
7432 4800 – www.burgerandlobster.com – Closed 25 December and
4 January
Menu £ 20
• **Meats** • **Fashionable** •
A sizeable place, yet as busy as the first branch in Mayfair. Choose a lobster roll
in a brioche bun, a 1½lb Maine or Canadian lobster, or a 280g burger of Irish or
Nebraskan beef. Bookings only taken for parties of 6 or more.

X **Vinoteca**   😷 ♿ ⛄

53-55 Beak St ⊠ *W1F 9SH –* Ⓜ *Oxford Circus –* ☏ *(020)*   Plan: **H3**
3544 7411 – www.vinoteca.co.uk
– Closed 24-26 December and 1 January
Carte £ 26/43 – *(booking essential)*
• **Modern cuisine** • **Wine bar** • **Bistro** •
The terrific wine list mixes the classic with the esoteric and emerging markets
are also covered. The food isn't forgotten – cured meats and cheeses are a high-
light and dishes like venison and bacon pie also hit the spot.

X **Antidote**   😷 🛱

12A Newburgh St ⊠ *W1F 7RR –* Ⓜ *Oxford Circus*   Plan: **H3**
– ☏ *(020) 7287 8488 – www.antidotewinebar.com – Closed Sunday*
Menu £ 19/40 – Carte £ 34/55 – *(booking advisable)*
• **Modern cuisine** • **Individual** • **Wine bar** •
On the ground floor is a wine bar serving cheese, charcuterie and 'small plates'.
The keenly run upstairs restaurant offers fresh, vibrant and contemporary cui-
sine, with the kitchen under the guidance of Mikael Jonsson of Hedone.

UNITED KINGDOM - LONDON

X **Jinjuu**   AC

15 Kingly St ☒ W1B 5PS – ◉ Oxford Circus – ℰ (020)   Plan: H3
8181 8887 – www.jinjuu.com – Closed 25 December
Menu £ 17/42 – Carte £ 18/69
• Asian • Design • Fashionable •
American-born celebrity chef Judy Joo's first London restaurant is a celebration
of her Korean heritage. The vibrant dishes, whether Bibimbap bowls or Ssam
platters, burst with flavour and are as enjoyable as the fun surroundings.

X **Spuntino**   AC

61 Rupert St. ☒ W1D 7PW – ◉ Piccadilly Circus   Plan: I3
*– www.spuntino.co.uk – Closed dinner 24 December, 25-26, 31 December
and 1 January*
Carte £ 15/22 – *(bookings not accepted)*
• North-American • Rustic • Individual •
Influenced by Downtown New York, with its no-booking policy and industrial
look. Sit at the counter and order classics like mac 'n' cheese or mini burgers.
The staff, who look like they could also fix your car, really add to the fun.

X **Bibigo**   AC ⇔

58-59 Great Marlborough St ☒ W1F 7JY   Plan: H3
– ◉ Oxford Circus – ℰ (020) 7042 5225 – www.bibigouk.com
Menu £ 13 (lunch) – Carte £ 20/29
• Korean • Friendly • Fashionable •
The enthusiastically run Bibigo represents Korea's largest food company's first
foray into the UK market. Watch the kitchen send out dishes such as kimchi,
Bossam (simmered pork belly) and hot stone galbi (chargrilled short ribs).

X **Ceviche**   AC

17 Frith St ☒ W1D 4RG – ◉ Tottenham Court Road   Plan: I3
– ℰ (020) 72922040 – www.cevicheuk.com
Menu £ 18 (weekday lunch) – Carte £ 14/24 – *(booking essential)*
• Peruvian • Friendly • Fashionable •
Based on a Lima Pisco bar, Ceviche is as loud as it is fun. First try the deliriously
addictive drinks based on the Peruvian spirit Pisco, and then share some thinly
sliced sea bass or octopus, along with anticuchos skewers.

X **Cây Tre**   AC ⓥ

42-43 Dean St ☒ W1D 4PZ – ◉ Tottenham Court Road   Plan: I3
– ℰ (020) 7317 9118 – www.caytresoho.co.uk
Menu £ 22/29 – Carte £ 17/28 – *(booking advisable)*
• Vietnamese • Minimalist •
Bright, sleek and bustling surroundings where Vietnamese standouts include
Cha La Lot (spicy ground pork wrapped in betel leaves), slow-cooked Mekong
catfish with a well-judged sweet and spicy sauce, and 6 versions of Pho (noodle
soup).

X **Rosa's Carnaby**   AC

23a Ganton Street ☒ W1F 9BW – ◉ Oxford Circus   Plan: H3
– ℰ (020) 7287 9617 – www.rosasthaicafe.com – Closed 25 December
Menu £ 20 (lunch and early dinner) – Carte £ 17/30 – *(booking essential)*
• Thai • Simple • Cosy •
A bright, bustling café celebrating traditional Thai flavours, with the occasional
modern twist. Perch on low stools and rub elbows with your neighbours while
the unfailingly polite staff cope capably with the rush of customers.

X **Rosa's Soho**   X

48 Dean St ☒ W1D 5BF – ◉ Leicester Square – ℰ (020)   Plan: I3
7494 1638 – www.rosasthaicafe.com – Closed 25 December
Menu £ 20 – Carte £ 17/30 – *(booking advisable)*
• Thai • Simple • Friendly •
The worn-in, pared down look of this authentic Thai café adds to its intimate
feel. Signature dishes include warm minced chicken salad and a sweet pumpkin
red curry. Tom Yam soup comes with a lovely balance of sweet, sour and spice.

X **Bone Daddies** ⬛

30-31 Peter St ✉ *W1F OAR –* Ⓜ *Piccadilly Circus* Plan: I3
– ℰ (020) 7287 8581 – www.bonedaddies.com – Closed 25 December
Carte £ 17/26 *– (bookings not accepted)*
• **Asian** • **Fashionable** • **Neighbourhood** •
Maybe ramen is the new rock 'n' roll. The charismatic Aussie chef-owner feels
that combinations are endless when it comes to these comforting bowls. Be
ready to queue then share a table. It's a fun place, run by a hospitable bunch.

X **Soho Kitchen & Bar** ⬛

19-21 Old Compton St. ✉ *W1D 5JJ* Plan: I3
– ℰ Leicester Square – ℰ (020) 7734 5656 – www.sohodiner.com
Carte £ 17/32
• **North-American** • **Simple** • **Trendy** •
Most punters who pack out this appealing retro-style diner are here for the
comforting American classics like mac & cheese, a hot dog or a burger. The
buzz is great, the cocktails are on tap and it's open till the wee small hours.

X **Barshu** ⬛ ⇔

28 Frith St. ✉ *W1D 5LF –* Ⓜ *Leicester Square – ℰ (020)* Plan: I3
72878822 – www.barshurestaurant.co.uk – Closed 24-25 December
Carte £ 21/52 *– (booking advisable)*
• **Chinese** • **Exotic** •
The fiery and authentic flavours of China's Sichuan province are the draw here;
help is at hand as the menu has pictures. It's decorated with carved wood and
lanterns; downstairs is better for groups.

X **Ba Shan** ⬛ ⇔

24 Romilly St. ✉ *W1D 5AH –* Ⓜ *Leicester Square* Plan: I3
– ℰ (020) 72873266 – Closed 24-25 December
Carte £ 15/37 *– (booking advisable)*
• **Chinese** • **Cosy** •
Whilst there are some Sichuan dishes, this bigger-than-it-looks Chinese restau-
rant excels in specialities from Hunan. That means plenty of heat but also pick-
ling, curing and smoking; dishes arrive when ready so sharing is best.

X **Baozi Inn** ⬛

25-26 Newport Court ✉ *WC2H 7JS –* Ⓜ *Leicester Square* Plan: I3
– ℰ (020) 72876877 – Closed 24-25 December
Carte £ 12/18 *– (bookings not accepted)*
• **Chinese** • **Rustic** • **Simple** •
Buzzy, busy little place that's great for a quick bite, especially if you like pork
buns, steaming bowls of noodles, a hit of Sichuan fire and plenty of beer or
tea. You'll leave feeling surprisingly energised and rejuvenated.

X **Manchurian Legends** ⬛

16 Lisle St ✉ *WC2H 7BE –* Ⓜ *Leicester Square – ℰ (020)* Plan: I3
72876606 – www.manchurianlegends.com – Closed Christmas
Menu £ 16/25 *–* Carte £ 20/38
• **Chinese** • **Simple** • **Friendly** •
Try specialities from a less familiar region of China: Dongbei, the 'north east'. As
winters there are long, stews and BBQ dishes are popular, as are pickled ingredients and chilli heat. Further warmth comes from the sweet natured staff.

X **Koya Bar**

50 Frith St ✉ *W1D 4SQ –* Ⓜ *Tottenham Court Road* Plan: I3
– ℰ (020) 74334463 – www.koyabar.co.uk – Closed Christmas
Carte £ 16/28 *– (bookings not accepted)*
• **Japanese** • **Simple** • **Friendly** •
A simple, sweet place serving authentic Udon noodles and small plates; they
open early for breakfast. Counter seating means everyone has a view of the
chefs; bookings aren't taken and there is often a queue, but the short wait is
worth it.

X **Beijing Dumpling** · AC ·
23 Lisle St. ✉ *WC2H 7BA –* Ⓜ *Leicester Square*   Plan: I3
– 𝒞 *(020) 7287 6888 – Closed 24-25 December*
Carte £ 10/40
• Chinese • Neighbourhood • Simple •
This relaxed little place serves freshly prepared dumplings of both Beijing and Shanghai styles. Although the range is not as comprehensive as the name suggests, they do stand out, especially varieties of the famed Siu Lung Bao.

X **Tonkotsu** · AC · ·
63 Dean St ✉ *W1D 4QG –* Ⓜ *Tottenham Court Road*   Plan: I3
– 𝒞 *(020) 7437 0071 – www.tonkotsu.co.uk*
Carte approx. £ 22 – *(bookings not accepted)*
• Japanese • Rustic • Cosy •
Some things are worth queuing for. Good ramen is all about the base stock: 18 hours goes into its preparation here to ensure the bowls of soup and wheat-based noodles reach a depth of flavour that seems to nourish one's very soul.

X **Ducksoup** · AC ·
41 Dean St ✉ *W1D 4PY –* Ⓜ *Leicester Square –* 𝒞 *(020)*   Plan: I3
7287 4599 – www.ducksoupsoho.co.uk – Closed Christmas, Easter, Sunday dinner and bank holidays
Carte £ 19/35
• Modern cuisine • Trendy • Neighbourhood •
It's compact, with bar seating; decoratively it's knowingly underwhelming; and the menu is handwritten each day – yes, every 'on-trend' box is ticked here. Dishes are all about the produce and are confidently unadorned.

X **Pitt Cue Co.** · AC ·
1 Newburgh St ✉ *W1F 7RB –* Ⓜ *Oxford Circus*   Plan: H3
– 𝒞 *(020) 7287 5578 – www.pittcue.co.uk – Closed 25-26 December,1 January, 4 April and 3 October*
Carte £ 18/30 – *(bookings not accepted)*
• Meats • Simple •
The owners started out selling their American barbecue dishes from a van before finding this tiny spot. The ribs are smoked in-house for 6 hours before roasting; the pulled pork is excellent. It's messy, filling and fun; be ready to queue.

ST JAMES'S

 Ritz ⚑ ⓕ₆ AC ⓢₐ
150 Piccadilly ✉ *W1J 9BR –* Ⓜ *Green Park –* 𝒞 *(020)*   Plan: H4
74938181 – www.theritzlondon.com
134 rm – ♦£ 450/1300 ♦♦£ 450/1300 – ⚏ £ 39 – 45 suites
• Grand Luxury • Classic • Stylish •
World famous hotel, opened in 1906 as a fine example of Louis XVI architecture and decoration. Elegant Palm Court famed for its afternoon tea. Many of the lavishly appointed and luxurious rooms and suites overlook the park.
Ritz Restaurant – See restaurant listing

Haymarket ⚑ ⓕ₆ ▢ ⓖ AC ⓢₐ ⌂
1 Suffolk Pl. ✉ *SW1Y 4HX –* Ⓜ *Piccadilly Circus*   Plan: I4
– 𝒞 *(020) 74704000 – www.haymarkethotel.com*
50 rm – ♦£ 336/595 ♦♦£ 336/595 – ⚏ £ 20 – 3 suites
• Luxury • Stylish •
Smart and spacious hotel in John Nash Regency building, with a stylish blend of modern and antique furnishings. Large, comfortable bedrooms in soothing colours. Impressive basement pool is often used for private parties.
Brumus – See restaurant listing

Sofitel London St James

6 Waterloo Pl. ✉ SW1Y 4AN – Ⓜ Piccadilly Circus – ✆ (020) 77472200 – www.sofitelstjames.com Plan: **I4**

183 rm – †£ 240/400 ††£ 240/400 – ☕ £ 25 – 18 suites

• Luxury • Elegant •

Great location for this international hotel in a Grade II former bank. The triple-glazed bedrooms are immaculately kept; the spa is one of the best around. The bar is inspired by Coco Chanel; the lounge by an English rose garden.

Balcon – See restaurant listing

Dukes

35 St James's Pl. ✉ SW1A 1NY – Ⓜ Green Park – ✆ (020) 74914840 – www.dukeshotel.com Plan: **H4**

90 rm – †£ 285/365 ††£ 365/650 – ☕ £ 24 – 6 suites

• Traditional • Luxury • Classic •

The wonderfully located Dukes has been steadily updating its image over the last few years, despite being over a century old. Bedrooms are now fresh and uncluttered and the atmosphere less starchy. The basement restaurant offers a modern menu, with dishes that are original in look and elaborate in construction.

Stafford

16-18 St James's Pl. ✉ SW1A 1NJ – Ⓜ Green Park – ✆ (020) 7493 0111 – www.thestaffordlondon.com Plan: **H4**

104 rm – †£ 280/750 ††£ 280/750 – ☕ £ 25 – 15 suites

• Townhouse • Luxury • Stylish •

Styles itself as a 'country house in the city'; its bedrooms are divided between the main house, converted 18C stables and a more modern mews. Legendary American bar a highlight; traditional British food served in the restaurant.

St James's Hotel and Club

7-8 Park Pl. ✉ SW1A 1LS – Ⓜ Green Park – ✆ (020) 73161600 – www.stjameshotelandclub.com – Closed 24-29 December Plan: **H4**

60 rm – †£ 295/520 ††£ 295/520 – ☕ £ 24 – 10 suites

• Business • Modern •

1890s house, formerly a private club in a wonderfully central yet quiet location. Modern, boutique-style interior with over 300 European works of art from the '20s to the '50s. Fine finish to the compact but well-equipped bedrooms.

✿ **Seven Park Place** – See restaurant listing

Cavendish

81 Jermyn St ✉ SW1Y 6JF – Ⓜ Piccadilly Circus – ✆ (020) 7930 2111 – www.thecavendishlondon.com Plan: **H4**

230 rm ☕ – †£ 290/480 ††£ 290/480 – 2 suites

• Business • Luxury • Classic •

There's been a hotel on this site since the 18C; this one was built in the '60s but is smart and contemporary inside. Great location, bistro-style dining with British menu and good views across London from the top five floors.

Ritz Restaurant – Ritz Hotel

150 Piccadilly ✉ W1J 9BR – Ⓜ Green Park – ✆ (020) 74938181 – www.theritzlondon.com Plan: **H4**

Menu £ 49 (weekday lunch) – Carte £ 69/116

• British traditional • Elegant • Formal •

Grand and lavish restaurant, with Louis XVI decoration, trompe l'oeil and ornate gilding. Delightful terrace over Green Park. Structured, formal service. Classic, traditional dishes are the highlight of the menu. Jacket and tie required.

UNITED KINGDOM - LONDON

XxX   **Seven Park Place** – St James's Hotel and Club   🆑 ⇔
❀   *7-8 Park Pl* ✉ *SW1A 1LS –* Ⓜ *Green Park –* ✆ *(020)*   Plan: **H4**
   73161615 – www.stjameshotelandclub.com – Closed 24-29 December,
   Sunday and Monday
   Menu £ 30 (weekday lunch)/61 – *(booking essential)*
   • **Modern cuisine** • **Cosy** • **Fashionable** •
   William Drabble's cooking is all about the quality of the produce, much of which
   comes from the Lake District, and his confident cooking allows natural flavours
   to shine. This diminutive restaurant is concealed within the hotel and divided
   into two; ask for the warmer, gilded back room.
   → Poached native lobster tail, cauliflower purée and Périgord truffle sauce.
   Assiette of Lune Valley lamb with turnips and thyme. Mango and passion
   fruit cream, elderflower jelly and raspberries.

XxX   **The Wolseley**   🆑 ⇔ 🛇
   160 Piccadilly ✉ *W1J 9EB –* Ⓜ *Green Park –* ✆ *(020)*   Plan: **H4**
   74996996 – www.thewolseley.com – Closed dinner 24 December
   Carte £ 23/78 – *(booking essential)*
   • **Modern cuisine** • **Fashionable** •
   This feels like a grand and glamorous European coffee house, with its pillars
   and high vaulted ceiling. Appealing menus offer everything from caviar to a
   hot dog. It's open from early until late and boasts a large celebrity following.

XxX   **Chutney Mary**   🆑 ⇔ 🛇
   73 St James's St ✉ *SW1A 1PH –* Ⓜ *Green Park*   Plan: **H4**
   – ✆ *(020) 7629 6688 – www.chutneymary.com – Closed Sunday lunch*
   Menu £ 30 (lunch) – Carte £ 29/61
   • **Indian** • **Elegant** • **Friendly** •
   After 25 years in Chelsea, one of London's pioneering Indian restaurants is now
   establishing itself in a more central position. Spicing is understated; classics are
   done well; and some regional dishes have been subtly updated.

XX   **Balcon** – Sofitel London St James Hotel   🆑
   8 Pall Mall. ✉ *SW1Y 4AN –* Ⓜ *Piccadilly Circus*   Plan: **I4**
   – ✆ *(020) 73897820 – www.thebalconlondon.com*
   Menu £ 20 (lunch) – Carte £ 25/45
   • **French** • **Brasserie** •
   A former banking hall with vast chandeliers and a grand brasserie look. It's open
   from breakfast onwards and the menu features French classics like snails and
   cassoulet; try the charcuterie from Wales and France.

XX   **Matsuri**   🆑 ⇔
   15 Bury St. ✉ *SW1Y 6AL –* Ⓜ *Green Park –* ✆ *(020)*   Plan: **H4**
   78391101 – www.matsuri-restaurant.com – Closed 25 December and
   1 January
   Carte £ 33/144
   • **Japanese** • **Friendly** •
   Sweet natured service at this long-standing, traditional Japanese stalwart. Teppan-yaki is their speciality, with Scottish beef the highlight; sushi counter also
   available. Good value lunch menus and bento boxes.

XX   **Le Caprice**   🍴 🆑 🐾 🛇
   Arlington House, Arlington St. ✉ *SW1A 1RJ*   Plan: **H4**
   – Ⓜ *Green Park –* ✆ *(020) 76292239 – www.le-caprice.co.uk – Closed 24-*
   26 December
   Menu £ 25 (early dinner) – Carte £ 32/61
   • **Modern cuisine** • **Fashionable** •
   For over 30 years Le Caprice's effortlessly sophisticated atmosphere and sur-
   roundings have attracted a confident and urbane clientele. Perennials on their
   catch-all menu include their famous burger and rich salmon fishcake.

XX **Sake No Hana**   AC

23 St James's St ✉ *SW1A 1HA* – Ⓜ *Green Park*   Plan: **H4**
– ✆ *(020) 7925 8988 – www.sakenohana.com*
– *Closed 25 December and Sunday*
Menu £ 29/65 – Carte £ 21/99
• Japanese • Minimalist • Fashionable •
A modern Japanese restaurant within a Grade II listed '60s edifice – and proof
that you can occasionally find good food at the end of an escalator. As with the
great cocktails, the menu is best enjoyed when shared with a group.

XX **Boulestin**   �транспорт ✿ 🐾

5 St James's St ✉ *SW1A 1EF* – Ⓜ *Green Park* – ✆ *(020)*   Plan: **H4**
7930 2030 – www.boulestin.com
– *Closed Sunday and bank holidays*
Menu £ 20 (weekday dinner) – Carte £ 32/56
• French • Elegant • Neighbourhood •
Nearly a century after Xavier Marcel Boulestin opened his eponymous restau-
rant showcasing 'Simple French Cooking for English homes', his spirit has been
resurrected at this elegant brasserie, with its lovely courtyard terrace.

XX **Cafe Murano**   AC ✿ 🐾

33. St. James's St ✉ *SW1A 1HD* – Ⓜ *Green Park*   Plan: **H4**
– ✆ *(0203) 371 5559 – www.cafemurano.co.uk*
– *Closed Sunday dinner*
Menu £ 18 (weekdays)/30 – Carte £ 25/58 – *(booking essential)*
• Italian • Fashionable •
Angela Hartnett and her chef have created an appealing and flexible menu of
delicious North Italian delicacies – the lunch menu is very good value. It's cer-
tainly no ordinary café and its popularity means pre-booking is essential.

XX **Franco's**   AC 🐾

61 Jermyn St ✉ *SW1Y 6LX* – Ⓜ *Green Park* – ✆ *(020)*   Plan: **H4**
74992211 – www.francoslondon.com – Closed Sunday and bank holidays
Menu £ 24 (lunch and early dinner) – Carte £ 38/60 – *(booking essential)*
• Italian • Formal • Romantic •
Open from breakfast until late, with café at the front leading into smart, clubby
restaurant. Menu covers all parts of Italy and includes popular grill section and
plenty of classics.

XX **Avenue**   🏇 ₺ AC ✿ 🐾

7-9 St James's St. ✉ *SW1A 1EE* – Ⓜ *Green Park*   Plan: **H4**
– ✆ *(020) 7321 2111 – www.avenue-restaurant.co.uk – Closed Saturday
lunch, Sunday dinner and bank holidays*
Menu £ 20 (lunch and early dinner) – Carte dinner £ 27/49
• Modern cuisine • Elegant •
Avenue has gone all American, with a new look from Russell Sage and a contemporary menu inspired by what's cooking in Manhattan. Wine is also made
more of a feature; and, of course, the cocktails at the long, lively bar are great.

XX **Mint Leaf**   AC 🐾

Suffolk Pl ✉ *SW1Y 4HX* – Ⓜ *Piccadilly Circus* – ✆ *(020)*   Plan: **I4**
*79309020 – www.mintleaflondon.com – Closed 25-26 December,
1 January and lunch Saturday-Sunday*
Menu £ 30/58 – Carte £ 25/35
• Indian • Design • Fashionable •
Cavernous and moodily lit basement restaurant incorporating trendy bar with
lounge music and extensive cocktail list. Contemporary Indian cooking with curries the highlight.

XX **Al Duca**
4-5 Duke of York St ⊠ SW1Y 6LA – ⓜ Piccadilly Circus Plan: **H4**
– ℰ (020) 7839 3090 – www.alduca-restaurant.co.uk – Closed Easter, 25-26 December, 1 January, Sunday and bank holidays
Menu £ 25/34
• Italian • Friendly •
Cooking which focuses on flavour continues to draw in the regulars at this warm and spirited Italian restaurant. Prices are keen when one considers the central location and service is brisk and confident.

XX **Quaglino's**
16 Bury St ⊠ SW1Y 6AJ – ⓜ Green Park – ℰ (020) Plan: **H4**
79306767 – www.quaglinos-restaurant.co.uk – Closed 25 December, Easter Monday and Sunday
Menu £ 21/30 – Carte £ 23/63
• Modern cuisine • Design •
An updated look, a new bar and live music have added sultriness and energy to this vast, glamorous and colourful restaurant. The kitchen specialises in contemporary brasserie-style food.

XX **Brumus** – Haymarket Hotel
1 Suffolk Pl ⊠ SW1Y 4HX – ⓜ Piccadilly Circus Plan: **I4**
– ℰ (020) 74704000 – www.haymarkethotel.com
Menu £ 20 – Carte £ 22/53
• Modern cuisine • Fashionable • Romantic •
Pre-theatre dining is an altogether less frenzied activity when you can actually see the theatre from your table. This is a modern, elegant space with switched-on staff. Stick to the good value set menu or the 'dish of the day'.

X **Portrait**
National Portrait Gallery (3rd floor), St Martin's Pl. Plan: **I3**
⊠ WC2H 0HE – ⓜ Charing Cross – ℰ (020) 73122490
– www.npg.org.uk/portraitrestaurant – Closed 24-26 December
Menu £ 20 – Carte £ 34/53 – *(lunch only and dinner Thursday-Saturday) (booking essential)*
• Modern cuisine • Design •
On the top floor of National Portrait Gallery with rooftop local landmark views: a charming spot for lunch. Modern British/European dishes; weekend brunch.

X **Chop Shop**
66 Haymarket ⊠ SW1Y 4RF – ⓜ Piccadilly Circus Plan: **I3**
– ℰ (020) 7842 8501 – www.chopshopuk.com
Menu £ 22 (weekday lunch)/35 – Carte £ 17/44
• Meats • Trendy • Friendly •
Spread over two floors and with an ersatz industrial look, this lively spot could be in Manhattan's Meatpacking district. Start with a cocktail, then order 'jars', 'crocks' or 'planks' of mousses, meatballs and cheeses; then it's the main event – great steaks and chops.

X **Shoryu**
9 Regent St. ⊠ SW1Y 4LR – ⓜ Piccadilly Circus Plan: **I4**
– www.shoryuramen.com – Closed 25 December and 1 January
Menu £ 10 (weekday lunch) – Carte £ 16/37 – *(bookings not accepted)*
• Japanese • Simple •
Owned by Japan Centre opposite and specialising in Hakata tonkotsu ramen. The base is a milky broth made from pork bones to which is added hosomen noodles, egg, and assorted toppings. Its restorative powers are worth queuing for. There are a two larger branches in Soho.

STRAND AND COVENT GARDEN

Savoy

Strand ⊠ *WC2R 0EU –* Ⓜ *Charing Cross –* ℰ *(020)*   Plan: **J3**
78364343 – www.fairmont.com/savoy
268 rm – ♦£ 350/550 ♦♦£ 370/570 – ⌣ £ 30 – 45 suites
• Grand Luxury • Stylish •

A legendary hotel renewed after a 3 year renovation; its luxurious bedrooms and stunning suites come in Edwardian or art deco styles. Have tea in the Thames Foyer, the hotel's heart, or drinks in the famous American Bar or the moodier Beaufort Bar. Along with the Savoy Grill is Kaspar's, an informal seafood bar and grill which replaced the River restaurant.

One Aldwych

1 Aldwych ⊠ *WC2B 4BZ –* Ⓜ *Temple –* ℰ *(020)*   Plan: **J3**
73001000 – www.onealdwych.com
105 rm – ♦£ 265/450 ♦♦£ 265/450 – ⌣ £ 19 – 12 suites
• Grand Luxury • Modern • Stylish •

Former 19C bank, now a stylish hotel with lots of artwork; the lobby changes its look seasonally and doubles as a bar. Stylish, contemporary bedrooms with the latest mod cons; the deluxe rooms and suites are particularly desirable. Impressive leisure facilities. Light, accessible menu at Indigo.

ME London

336-337 Strand ⊠ *WC2R 1HA –* Ⓜ *Temple –* ℰ *(020)*   Plan: **J3**
7395 3400 – www.melondonuk.com
157 rm – ♦£ 300/600 ♦♦£ 330/720 – ⌣ £ 25 – 16 suites
• Chain hotel • Business • Functional •

On the site of the Gaiety theatre and Marconi House, now a striking hotel designed by Fosters + Partners. Eye-catching pyramid shaped reception; bedrooms that are crisply decorated, cleverly lit and very comfortable. Steaks in the glitzy STK; Cucina Asellina offers a contemporary setting for Italian food; Radio has a simple menu and comes with a stunning rooftop bar.

Waldorf Hilton

Aldwych ⊠ *WC2B 4DD –* Ⓜ *Temple –* ℰ *(020)*   Plan: **J3**
7836 2400 – www.hilton.co.uk/waldorf
298 rm – ♦£ 259/329 ♦♦£ 309/369 – ⌣ £ 23 – 12 suites
• Historic • Elegant •

Impressive curved and columned façade: an Edwardian landmark in a great location. Stylish, contemporary bedrooms in calming colours have superb bathrooms and all mod cons. Tea dances in the Grade II listed Palm Court Ballroom. Stylish 'Homage' is popular for afternoon tea and relaxed brasserie style dining.

St Martins Lane

45 St Martin's Ln ⊠ *WC2N 3HX –* Ⓜ *Charing Cross*   Plan: **I3**
– ℰ *(020) 7300 5500 – www.stmartinslane.com*
206 rm – ♦£ 222/479 ♦♦£ 222/479 – ⌣ £ 26 – 2 suites
• Luxury • Design •

The unmistakable hand of Philippe Starck is evident at this most contemporary of hotels. Unique and stylish, from the starkly modern lobby to the state-of-the-art bedrooms, which come in a blizzard of white.

Delaunay

55 Aldwych ⊠ *WC2B 4BB –* Ⓜ *Temple –* ℰ *(020)*   Plan: **J3**
74998558 – www.thedelaunay.com – Closed 25 December and dinner 24 December
Carte £ 17/67 – *(booking essential)*
• Modern cuisine • Elegant • Fashionable •

The Delaunay was inspired by the grand cafés of Europe but, despite sharing the same buzz and celebrity clientele as its sibling The Wolseley, is not just a mere replica. The all-day menu is more mittel-European, with great schnitzels and wieners.

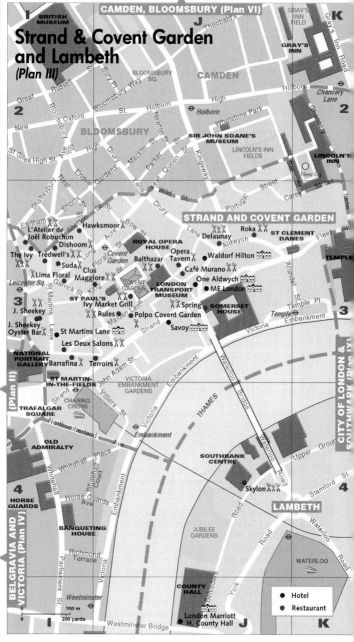

UNITED KINGDOM - LONDON

CAMDEN, BLOOMSBURY (Plan VI)

Strand & Covent Garden
and Lambeth
(Plan III)

BRITISH MUSEUM

GRAY'S INN FIELD

GRAY'S INN

CAMDEN

Chancery Lane

BLOOMSBURY SQ.

Holborn

Whetstone Park

BLOOMSBURY

SIR JOHN SOANE'S MUSEUM

LINCOLN'S INN FIELDS

LINCOLN'S INN

STRAND AND COVENT GARDEN

Hawksmoor
L'Atelier de Joël Robuchon
Dishoom
The Ivy   Tredwell's
Suda   Clos
Lima Floral   Maggiore
ROYAL OPERA HOUSE
Covent Garden
Balthazar   Opera Tavern
Delaunay   Roka   ST CLEMENT DANES
Aldwych
Waldorf Hilton
Café Murano
One Aldwych
ME London

TEMPLE

ST PAUL'S
Ivy Market Grill
J. Sheekey
J. Sheekey Oyster Bar
Rules
St Martins Lane
Les Deux Salons
LONDON TRANSPORT MUSEUM
COVENT GARDEN
Polpo Covent Garden
Savoy
Spring
SOMERSET HOUSE
Temple Pl.
Temple

NATIONAL PORTRAIT GALLERY
Barrafina   Terroirs
ST MARTIN-IN-THE-FIELDS
CHARING CROSS
VICTORIA EMBANKMENT GARDENS

TRAFALGAR SQUARE

OLD ADMIRALTY

HORSE GUARDS

THAMES

SOUTHBANK CENTRE

Skylon

LAMBETH

BANQUETING HOUSE

JUBILEE GARDENS

WATERLOO

COUNTY HALL

London Marriott H. County Hall

Westminster Bridge

● Hotel
● Restaurant

200 m
200 yards

XXX **The Ivy**   AC ⇔ 🍷

1-5 West St ⊠ *WC2H 9NQ –* Ⓜ *Leicester Square*   Plan: I3
– ℰ *(020) 78364751 – www.the-ivy.co.uk – Closed 25 December*
Menu £ 27 – Carte £ 29/75
• **British traditional** • **Fashionable** •
This landmark restaurant has had a facelift and while the glamorous clientele
remain, it now has an oval bar as its focal point. The menu offers international
dishes alongside the old favourites and personable staff anticipate your every
need.

XX **L'Atelier de Joël Robuchon**   AC 🍷
🐦
13-15 West St. ⊠ *WC2H 9NE –* Ⓜ *Leicester Square*   Plan: I3
– ℰ *(020) 70108600 – www.joelrobuchon.co.uk – Closed 25-*
26 December,1 January and August bank holiday Monday
Menu £ 38 (lunch and early dinner)/129 – Carte £ 43/107
• **French** • **Fashionable** • **Trendy** •
Creative, skilled and occasionally playful cooking; dishes may look delicate but
pack a punch. Ground floor 'Atelier' comes with counter seating and chefs on
view. More structured 'La Cuisine' upstairs and a cool bar above that.
→ Salmon tartare with Sologne Imperial caviar. Free range stuffed quail
with pomme purée and herb salad. Manjari chocolate mousse, dark chocolate sorbet and Oreo cookie crumb.

XX **J. Sheekey**   🍴 AC

28-34 St Martin's Ct. ⊠ *WC2 4AL –* Ⓜ *Leicester Square*   Plan: I3
– ℰ *(020) 72402565 – www.j-sheekey.co.uk – Closed 25-26 December*
Carte £ 33/74 – (booking essential)
• **Fish and seafood** • **Fashionable** • **Individual** •
Festooned with photographs of actors and linked to the theatrical world since
opening in 1890. Wood panels and alcove tables add famed intimacy. Accom-
plished seafood cooking.

XX **Spring**   & AC ⇔

New Wing, Somerset House, Strand (Entrance on   Plan: J3
Lancaster Pl) ⊠ *WC2R 1LA –* Ⓜ *Temple –* ℰ *(020) 3011 0115*
– www.springrestaurant.co.uk – Closed Sunday dinner
Menu £ 26 (lunch) – Carte £ 33/62 – (booking advisable)
• **Italian** • **Fashionable** • **Elegant** •
Spring occupies the 'new wing' of Somerset House that for many years was
inhabited by the Inland Revenue. It's a bright, feminine space under the aegis
of chef Skye Gyngell. Her cooking is Italian influenced and ingredient-led.

XX **Rules**   AC ⇔

35 Maiden Ln ⊠ *WC2E 7LB –* Ⓜ *Leicester Square*   Plan: J3
– ℰ *(020) 78365314 – www.rules.co.uk – Closed 25-26 December*
Carte £ 34/65 – (booking essential)
• **British traditional** • **Formal** •
London's oldest restaurant boasts a fine collection of antique cartoons, draw-
ings and paintings. Tradition continues in the menu, specialising in game from
its own estate.

XX **Clos Maggiore**   🍸 AC ⇔ 🍷

33 King St ⊠ *WC2E 8JD –* Ⓜ *Leicester Square –* ℰ *(020)*   Plan: J3
7379 9696 – www.closmaggiore.com – Closed 24-25 December
Menu £ 20 (weekdays)/35 – Carte £ 32/58
• **French** • **Formal** •
One of London's most romantic restaurants – but be sure to ask for the enchanting conservatory with its retractable roof. The sophisticated French cooking is
joined by a wine list of great depth. Good value and very popular pre/post
theatre menus.

XX **Roka** ⒶⒸ

71 Aldwych ✉ *WC2B 4HN* – Ⓜ *Temple* – ✆ *(020)*   Plan: **J3**
7294 7636 – www.rokarestaurant.com
– Closed 25 December
Menu £ 27 (lunch) – Carte approx. £ 55
• **Japanese** • **Fashionable** • **Design** •
This is the fourth and largest Roka in the group. It shares the same stylish look, efficient service and modern Japanese food, although there are some dishes unique to this branch. Consider the Tasting menu for a good all-around experience.

XX **Les Deux Salons** ⓯ ⒶⒸ ⇔ 🕮

40-42 William IV St ✉ *WC2N 4DD* – Ⓜ *Charing Cross*   Plan: **I3**
– ✆ *(020) 7420 2050 – www.lesdeuxsalons.co.uk – Closed 25-26 December and 1 January*
Menu £ 13/30 – Carte £ 23/57
• **French** • **Bistro** • **Design** •
Sir Terence Conran took over this handily-placed site in 2015 and injected a tidy sum into its redesign. On the ground floor is a café, a bistro serving all the French classics, a bar, épicerie, and a more formal restaurant upstairs.

XX **Cafe Murano** ⒶⒸ 🕮

34-36 Tavistock St ✉ *WC2E 7PB* – Ⓜ *Charing Cross*   Plan: **J3**
– ✆ *(020) 7240 3654 – www.cafemurano.co.uk*
– Closed Sunday dinner
Menu £ 21 – Carte £ 23/38
• **Italian** • **Neighbourhood** • **Fashionable** •
The second Café Murano is in the heart of Covent Garden, in a space much larger than the St James's original; head for the smart marble-topped counter at the back. Appealing menu of Northern Italian dishes cooked with care and respect.

XX **Ivy Market Grill** 🕮 ⓯ ⒶⒸ ⇔ 🕮

1 Henrietta St ✉ *WC2E 8PS* – Ⓜ *Leicester Square*   Plan: **J3**
– ✆ *(020) 3301 0200 – www.theivymarketgrill.com*
Menu £ 21 (early dinner) – Carte £ 25/47
• **British traditional** • **Design** • **Brasserie** •
Mere mortals can now experience a little of that Ivy glamour by eating here at the first of their diffusion line. Breakfast, a menu of largely British classics and afternoon tea keep it busy all day. There's another branch in Chelsea.

XX **Balthazar** ⒶⒸ ⇔

4-6 Russell St. ✉ *WC2B 5HZ* – Ⓜ *Covent Garden*   Plan: **J3**
– ✆ *(020) 3301 1155 – www.balthazarlondon.com – Closed 25 December*
Carte £ 26/65 – *(booking essential)*
• **French** • **Brasserie** • **Classic** •
Those who know the original Balthazar in Manhattan's SoHo district will find the London version of this classic brasserie uncannily familiar in looks, vibe and food. The Franglais menu keeps it simple and the cocktails are great.

X **Barrafina** ⒶⒸ ⇔

10 Adelaide St ✉ *WC2N 4HZ* – Ⓜ *Charing Cross*   Plan: **I3**
– ✆ *(020) 7440 1450 – www.barrafina.co.uk – Closed Christmas and New Year*
Carte £ 11/29 – *(bookings not accepted)*
• **Spanish** • **Tapas bar** • **Trendy** •
The second Barrafina is not just brighter than the Soho original – it's bigger too, so you can wait inside with a drink for counter seats to become available. Try more unusual tapas like ortiguillas, frit Mallorquin or the succulent meats.

X

J. Sheekey Oyster Bar

33-34 St Martin's Ct. ✉ *WC2 4AL –* Ⓜ *Leicester Square*   Plan: I3
– ℰ (020) 72402565 – www.j-sheekey.co.uk – Closed 25-26 December
Carte £ 22/39
• Fish and seafood • Intimate •
An addendum to J. Sheekey restaurant. Sit at the bar to watch the chefs prepare
the same quality seafood as next door but at slightly lower prices; fish pie and
fruits de mer are the popular choices. Open all day.

X

Hawksmoor

11 Langley St ✉ *WC2H 9JG –* Ⓜ *Covent Garden*   Plan: I3
– ℰ (020) 7420 9390 – www.thehawksmoor.com – Closed 24-26 December
Menu £ 24 (weekdays)/27 – Carte £ 24/73
• Meats • Rustic • Brasserie •
Steaks from Longhorn cattle lovingly reared in North Yorkshire and dry-aged for
at least 35 days are the stars of the show. Atmospheric, bustling basement res-
taurant in former brewery cellars.

X

Tredwell's

4 Upper St Martin's Ln ✉ *WC2H 9EF*   Plan: I3
– Ⓜ *Leicester Square – ℰ (020) 3764 0840 – www.tredwells.com – Closed
25-26 December*
Menu £ 20 (lunch and early dinner) – Carte £ 25/44
• British modern • Brasserie • Fashionable •
A modern brasserie with a hint of art deco courtesy of Marcus Wareing. Cooking
is best described as modern English; dishes show a degree of refinement, and a
commendable amount of thought has gone into addressing allergen issues.

X

Lima Floral

14 Garrick St ✉ *WC2E 9BJ –* Ⓜ *Leicester Square*   Plan: I3
*– ℰ (020) 7240 5778 – www.limafloral.com – Closed bank holiday
Mondays*
Menu £ 18 (weekday lunch) – Carte £ 35/47
• Peruvian • Fashionable • Friendly •
This second Lima branch has a light and airy feel by day and a cosy, candlelit
vibe in the evening; regional Peruvian dishes are served alongside the more
popular causa and ceviche. Basement Pisco Bar for Peruvian tapas and Pisco
sours.

X
☺

Terroirs

5 William IV St ✉ *WC2N 4DW –* Ⓜ *Charing Cross*   Plan: J3
*– ℰ (020) 70360660 – www.terroirswinebar.com – Closed 25-26 December,
1 January, Sunday and bank holidays*
Menu £ 10 – Carte £ 25/34
• Mediterranean • Bistro •
Eat in the ground floor bistro/wine bar or from a slightly different menu two
floors below at 'Downstairs at Terroirs'. Flavoursome French cooking, with
extra Italian and Spanish influences. Thoughtfully compiled wine list.

X
☺

Opera Tavern

23 Catherine St. ✉ *WC2B 5JS –* Ⓜ *Covent Garden*   Plan: J3
*– ℰ (020) 7836 3680 – www.operatavern.co.uk – Closed 25 December and
1 January*
Carte £ 13/24
• Mediterranean • Tapas bar • Wine bar •
Shares the same appealing concept of small plates of Spanish and Italian delica-
cies as its sisters, Salt Yard and Dehesa. All done in a smartly converted old boo-
zer which dates from 1879; ground floor bar and upstairs dining room.

Polpo Covent Garden

6 Maiden Ln. ✉ *WC2E 7NA* – Ⓜ *Leicester Square* Plan: **J3**
– ✆ (020) 7836 8448 – www.polpo.co.uk – Closed 25-26 December
Carte £ 12/26 – *(bookings not accepted at dinner)*
• Italian • Simple • Trendy •
First Soho, now Covent Garden gets a fun Venetian bacaro. The small plates are surprisingly filling, with delights such as pizzette of white anchovy vying with fennel and almond salad, fritto misto competing with spaghettini and meatballs.

Dishoom

12 Upper St Martin's Ln ✉ *WC2H 9FB* Plan: **I3**
– Ⓜ Leicester Square – ✆ (020) 7420 9320 – www.dishoom.com – Closed 24 December dinner, 25-26 December and 1-2 January
Menu £ 22/40 – Carte £ 13/33 – *(booking advisable)*
• Indian • Individual • Trendy •
A facsimile of a Bombay café, of the sort opened by Persian immigrants in the early 20C. Try baked roti rolls with chai, vada pav – Bombay's version of the chip butty; a curry or grilled meats. There's another branch in Shoreditch.

Suda

23 Slingsby Pl, St Martin's Courtyard ✉ *WC2E 9AB* Plan: **I3**
– Ⓜ Covent Garden – ✆ (020) 72408010 – www.suda-thai.com – Closed 25 December and 1 January
Menu £ 11/25 – Carte £ 19/34
• Thai • Friendly •
This shiny Thai restaurant in a new development may look like a branded chain but the quality of its food far exceeds one's expectations. Come in a group, sit upstairs, order cocktails and share plenty of dishes.

Lambeth

London Marriott H. County Hall

Westminster Bridge Rd ✉ *SE1 7PB* – Ⓜ *Westminster*
– ✆ (020) 79285200 – www.marriott.co.uk/lonch Plan: **J5**
200 rm – †£ 420/540 ††£ 600/900 – ☕ £ 22 – 5 suites
• Luxury • Business • Classic •
Occupying the historic County Hall building. Many of the spacious and comfortable bedrooms enjoy river and Parliament outlooks. Impressive leisure facilities. World famous views too from Gillray's, which specialises in steaks.

Skylon

1 Southbank Centre, Belvedere Rd ✉ *SE1 8XX* Plan: **J4**
– Ⓜ Waterloo – ✆ (020) 76547800 – www.skylon-restaurant.co.uk – Closed 25 December
Menu £ 18/48 – Carte £ 26/54
• Modern cuisine • Design • Trendy •
Ask for a window table here at the Royal Festival Hall. Informal grill-style operation on one side, a more formal and expensive restaurant on the other, with a busy cocktail bar in the middle.

BELGRAVIA – VICTORIA PLAN IV

Belgravia

Berkeley

Wilton Pl ✉ *SW1X 7RL* – Ⓜ *Knightsbridge – ✆ (020) 72356000 – www.the-berkeley.co.uk* Plan: **G4**
210 rm – †£ 270/720 ††£ 330/840 – ☕ £ 32 – 28 suites
• Grand Luxury • Business • Stylish •
Discreet and very comfortable hotel with impressive rooftop pool and opulently decorated, immaculately kept bedrooms. Relax in the gilded, panelled Caramel Room or have a drink in the ice cool Blue Bar. Choice of two restaurants.
✿✿ **Marcus** • **Koffmann's** – See restaurant listing

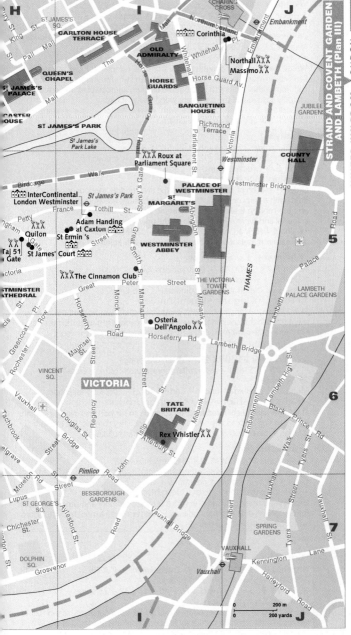

CHARING CROSS

Embankment

Corinthia

Northall ✕✕✕
Massimo ✕✕

Northumberland Pl.

Whitehall

Horse Guard Av.

JUBILEE GARDENS

BANQUETING HOUSE

HORSE GUARDS

OLD ADMIRALTY

CARLTON HOUSE TERRACE

ST JAMES'S SQ.

QUEEN'S CHAPEL

ST JAMES'S PALACE

CASTER HOUSE

ST JAMES'S PARK

St James's Park Lake

Richmond Terrace

COUNTY HALL

Roux at ✕✕✕
Parliament Square

Westminster

Westminster Bridge

PALACE OF WESTMINSTER

ST MARGARET'S

Birdcage Walk

InterContinental
London Westminster

St James's Park

Adam Handing
at Caxton

St Ermin's

St James' Court

Quilon ✕✕✕

Taj 51
Gate

WESTMINSTER ABBEY

WESTMINSTER CATHEDRAL

THE VICTORIA TOWER GARDENS

The Cinnamon Club ✕✕✕

LAMBETH PALACE GARDENS

THAMES

Osteria
Dell'Angolo ✕✕

Horseferry Rd

Lambeth Bridge

VINCENT SQ.

VICTORIA

TATE BRITAIN

Rex Whistler ✕✕

Pimlico

BESSBOROUGH GARDENS

ST GEORGE'S SQ.

DOLPHIN SQ.

Vauxhall Bridge

Lambeth High St.

Black Prince Rd

Embankment

Lambeth Walk

Vauxhall Street

Tyers St.

SPRING GARDENS

VAUXHALL

Vauxhall

Kennington

Harleyford Road

0   200 m
0   200 yards

885

UNITED KINGDOM - LONDON

XxX
❀
Ametsa – Halkin Hotel
5 Halkin St ✉ SW1X 7DJ – Ⓜ *Hyde Park Corner*   Plan: **G5**
– ℰ (020) 73331234 – www.comohotels.com/thehalkin – *Closed 24-26 December, 1 January, lunch 31 December, Sunday and lunch Monday*
Menu £ 28/52 – Carte £ 55/78
• **Creative** • **Elegant** • **Fashionable** •
Whilst the father and daughter team from the celebrated Arzak restaurant in San Sebastián are behind it, Ametsa has its own style. Most ingredients are sourced from within the British Isles but the flavours, combinations and colours are typically Basque and the dishes are wonderfully vibrant.
➜ Scallops at home. Sea bass with celery illusion. Clove custard with toasted milk and pineapple ice cream.

XxX
❀
Amaya
Halkin Arcade, 19 Motcomb St ✉ SW1X 8JT   Plan: **F5**
– Ⓜ *Knightsbridge* – ℰ (020) 78231166 – www.amaya.biz
Menu £ 23 (weekday lunch) – Carte £ 39/84
• **Indian** • **Design** • **Minimalist** •
Order a selection of small dishes from the tawa griddle, tandoor or sigri grill and finish with a curry or biryani. Dishes like lamb chops are aromatic and satisfying and the cooking is skilled and consistent. This busy Indian restaurant is bright, colourful and lively; ask for a table by the open kitchen.
➜ Chargrilled Madagascan prawn. Slow-roasted leg of baby lamb, cumin and garam masala. Spiced black fig brûlée with kokum sherbet.

XxX
Koffmann's – Berkeley Hotel
Wilton Pl ✉ SW1X 7RL – Ⓜ *Knightsbridge* – ℰ (020)   Plan: **G4**
72351010 – www.the-berkeley.co.uk
Menu £ 28 (lunch and early dinner) – Carte £ 43/71
• **French** • **Elegant** • **Fashionable** •
Pierre Koffmann, one of London's most fêted chefs, was enticed out of retirement to open this comfortable, well run and spacious restaurant. Expect classic signature dishes and plenty of gutsy flavours true to his Gascon roots.

XxX
Zafferano
15 Lowndes St ✉ SW1X 9EY – Ⓜ *Knightsbridge*   Plan: **F5**
– ℰ (020) 72355800 – www.zafferanorestaurant.co.uk – *Closed 25 December*
Menu £ 25 (weekday lunch) – Carte £ 40/73 – *(booking essential)*
• **Italian** • **Fashionable** • **Neighbourhood** •
The immaculately coiffured regulars continue to support this ever-expanding, long-standing and capably run Italian restaurant. They come for the reassuringly familiar, if rather steeply priced dishes from all parts of Italy.

🍴
Pantechnicon
10 Motcomb St ✉ SW1X 8LA – Ⓜ *Knightsbridge.*   Plan: **G5**
– ℰ (020) 77306074 – www.thepantechnicon.com – *Closed 25 December*
Carte £ 29/38 – *(booking advisable)*
• **British modern** • **Pub** • **Neighbourhood** •
Urbane, enthusiastically run pub with a busy ground floor and altogether more formal upstairs dining room. Traditional dishes are given a modern twist; oysters and Scottish steaks are perennials.

VICTORIA

Corinthia
Whitehall Pl. ✉ SW1A 2BD – Ⓜ *Embankment* – ℰ (020)   Plan: **J4**
7930 8181 – www.corinthia.com/london
294 rm – ♦£ 342/1140 ♦♦£ 342/1140 – ☲ £ 32 – 23 suites
• **Grand Luxury** • **Stylish** •
The restored Victorian splendour of this grand, luxurious hotel cannot fail to impress. Tasteful and immaculately finished bedrooms are some of the largest in town; suites come with butlers. The stunning spa is over four floors.
Northall • Massimo – See restaurant listing

Goring

15 Beeston Pl ✉ SW1W 0JW – Ⓜ Victoria – ✆ (020) 7396 9000 – www.thegoring.com Plan: **H5**

69 rm – †£ 490/710 ††£ 600/715 – ☕ £ 32 – 8 suites

• Luxury • Townhouse • Elegant •

Under the stewardship of the founder's great grandson, this landmark hotel has been restored and renovated while maintaining its traditional atmosphere and pervading sense of Britishness. Expect first class service and immaculate, very comfortable bedrooms, many of which overlook the garden.

✿ **Dining Room at The Goring** – See restaurant listing

InterContinental London Westminster

22-28 Broadway ✉ SW1H 9JS – Ⓜ St James's Park – ✆ (020) 3301 8080 – www.conradhotels.com/london Plan: **I5**

256 rm – †£ 199/699 ††£ 199/699 – ☕ £ 35 – 12 suites

• Luxury • Business • Contemporary •

Its proximity to the seat of power is a recurring theme at this hotel which opened in 2013. Apart from its façade, little remains of the original 19C building. A cool, crisp reception area sets the tone; bedrooms are stylish and contemporary. The Smokehouse specialises in ribs, pulled pork and steaks.

St James' Court

45 Buckingham Gate ✉ SW1E 6BS – Ⓜ St James's Park – ✆ (020) 7834 6655 – www.tajhotels.com/stjamescourt Plan: **H5**

318 rm – †£ 198/594 ††£ 198/594 – ☕ £ 21 – 20 suites

• Luxury • Classic •

Built in 1897 as serviced accommodation for visiting aristocrats. Behind the impressive Edwardian façade lies an equally elegant interior. Quietest bedrooms overlook a courtyard. Relaxed, bright Bistro 51 comes with an international menu; Bank offers brasserie classics in a conservatory.

✿ **Quilon** – See restaurant listing

Taj 51 Buckingham Gate

51 Buckingham Gate ✉ SW1E 6AF – Ⓜ St James's Park – ✆ (020) 77697766 – www.taj51buckinghamgate.co.uk Plan: **H5**

85 suites – †£ 300/6300 ††£ 300/6300 – ☕ £ 40

• Luxury • Townhouse • Contemporary •

In the courtyard of the Crowne Plaza but offering greater levels of comfort and service. Contemporary in style, suites range from one to nine bedrooms. Butler service available. Restaurants located in adjacent hotel.

St Ermin's

2 Caxton St. ✉ SW1H 0QW – Ⓜ St James's Park – ✆ (020) 7222 7888 – www.sterminshotel.co.uk Plan: **I5**

331 rm – †£ 209/499 ††£ 209/499 – 41 suites

• Luxury • Stylish •

Built as an apartment block in 1897 but has spent most of its life as a hotel and is a favoured spot for many a politician. A comprehensive refurbishment restored many of its original features, including the stunning rococo lobby. The restaurant specialises in meat cooked on the Josper grill.

Adam Handling at Caxton – See restaurant listing

41

41 Buckingham Palace Rd. ✉ SW1W 0PS – Ⓜ Victoria – ✆ (020) 73000041 – www.41hotel.com Plan: **H5**

30 rm ☕ – †£ 340/479 ††£ 360/539 – 6 suites

• Luxury • Classic •

Smart, discreet addendum to The Rubens hotel next door. Attractively decorated and quiet lounge where breakfast is served; comfortable bedrooms boast fireplaces and plenty of extras. Light lunches and dinners for residents only.

UNITED KINGDOM - LONDON

The Rubens at The Palace

39 Buckingham Palace Rd ✉ *SW1W 0PS* – 🚇 *Victoria*
– 𝒞 (020) 78346600 – www.rubenshotel.com
161 rm – 🛏£ 149/259 🛏🛏£ 159/269 – ⌂ £ 20 – 1 suite
• Traditional • Luxury • Classic •

Plan: **H5**

Discreet, comfortable hotel in great location for tourists. Constant reinvestment ensures bright and contemporary bedrooms. 'Old Masters' for a buffet-style carvery; fine dining in cosy 'Library'; South African themed 'bbar'.

Eccleston Square

37 Eccleston Sq ✉ *SW1V 1PB* – 🚇 *Victoria* – 𝒞 *(020)*
3489 1001 – www.ecclestonsquarehotel.com
39 rm – 🛏£ 210/350 🛏🛏£ 210/350 – ⌂ £ 15
• Townhouse • Stylish • Contemporary •

Plan: **H6**

Attractive townhouse in a smart square, with a crisp, contemporary interior. Bedrooms are decorated to a high standard and come full of assorted electronic gadgetry. Varied international menu in Bistrot; afternoon tea a feature.

Artist Residence

52 Cambridge St ✉ *SW1V 4QQ* – 🚇 *Victoria* – 𝒞 *(020)*
79318946 – www.artistresidencelondon.co.uk
10 rm – 🛏£ 160/375 🛏🛏£ 160/375 – ⌂ £ 10
• Townhouse • Stylish •

Plan: **H6**

A converted pub made into a comfortable, quirky townhouse hotel, with stylish bedrooms featuring mini Smeg fridges, retro telephones, reclaimed furniture and pop art. Cool bar and sitting room beneath the busy 64° restaurant.

Lord Milner

111 Ebury St ✉ *SW1W 9QU* – 🚇 *Victoria* – 𝒞 *(020)*
78819880 – www.lordmilner.com
11 rm – 🛏£ 125 🛏🛏£ 160/255 – ⌂ £ 8.50
• Townhouse • Classic •

Plan: **G6**

A four storey terraced house, with individually decorated bedrooms, three with four-poster beds and all with smart marble bathrooms. Garden Suite is the best room; it has its own patio. Breakfast served in your bedroom.

Dining Room at The Goring – Goring Hotel

15 Beeston Pl ✉ *SW1W 0JW* – 🚇 *Victoria* – 𝒞 *(020)*
73969000 – www.thegoring.com – Closed Saturday lunch
Menu £ 43/53
• British traditional • Elegant • Classic •

Plan: **H5**

A paean to all things British and the very model of discretion and decorum – the perfect spot for those who 'like things done properly' but without the stuffiness. The menu is an appealing mix of British classics and lighter, more modern dishes, all prepared with great skill and understanding.
→ Cured sea trout with English asparagus and smoked mayonnaise. Fillet of Suffolk pork with suckling pig belly, pickled turnip, beetroot and eel fritter. Eton mess, crème fraîche and lime.

Quilon – St James' Court Hotel

41 Buckingham Gate ✉ *SW1E 6AF* – 🚇 *St James's Park*
– 𝒞 (020) 78211899 – www.quilon.co.uk – Closed 25 December
Menu £ 27/59 – Carte £ 33/59
• Indian • Design • Elegant •

Plan: **H5**

A meal here will remind you how fresh, vibrant, colourful and healthy Indian food can be. Chef Sriram Aylur and his team focus on India's southwest coast, so the emphasis is on seafood and a lighter style of cooking. The room is stylish and comfortable and the service team, bright and enthusiastic.
→ Coconut cream chicken with chilli and cumin. Spiced, baked black cod. Chai latte crème brûlée.

XxX **Roux at Parliament Square**   🕭 🅰🅒 ⇌

Royal Institution of Chartered Surveyors, Parliament Sq.   Plan: I5
✉ *SW1P 3AD –* Ⓜ *Westminster –* 𝒞 *(020) 73343737*
– www.rouxatparliamentsquare.co.uk – Closed Saturday, Sunday and
bank holidays
Menu £ 35 (weekday lunch)/79 – Carte £ 47/64 – *(bookings advisable at*
lunch)
• **Modern cuisine • Elegant •**
Light floods through the Georgian windows of this comfortable restaurant within the offices of the Royal Institution of Chartered Surveyors. Carefully crafted,
contemporary cuisine, with some interesting flavour combinations.

XxX **Northall** – Corinthia Hotel   🕭 🅰🅒 🗄

Whitehall Pl. ✉ *WC2N 5AE –* Ⓜ *Embankment –* 𝒞 *(020)*   Plan: J4
7321 3100 – www.thenorthall.co.uk
Menu £ 24/75 – Carte £ 26/73
• **British traditional • Bistro •**
The Corinthia Hotel's British restaurant champions our indigenous produce, and
its menu is an appealing document. It occupies two rooms: head for the more
modern one with its bar and booths, which is less formal than the other section.

XxX **The Cinnamon Club**   🅰🅒 ⇌ 🗄 🛈

30-32 Great Smith St ✉ *SW1P 3BU –* Ⓜ *St James's Park*   Plan: I5
– 𝒞 *(020) 7222 2555 – www.cinnamonclub.com – Closed Sunday and*
bank holidays
Menu £ 22 (lunch and early dinner) – Carte £ 30/66
• **Indian • Elegant •**
Tourists and locals, politicians and business types – this smart Indian restau-
rant housed in the listed former Westminster Library attracts all types. The fairly
elaborate dishes arrive fully garnished and the spicing is quite subtle.

XxX **Santini**   🕭 🅰🅒 🗄

29 Ebury St ✉ *SW1W 0NZ –* Ⓜ *Victoria –* 𝒞 *(020)*   Plan: G5
7730 4094 – www.santinirestaurant.com – Closed 23-26 December,
1 January and Easter
Menu £ 25 (dinner) – Carte £ 30/67
• **Italian • Fashionable •**
Santini has looked after its many immaculately coiffured regulars for 30 years.
The not inexpensive menu of classic Italian dishes is broadly Venetian in style;
the daily specials, pasta dishes and desserts are the standout courses.

XxX **Grand Imperial**   🕭 🅰🅒 ⇌

Grosvenor Hotel, 101 Buckingham Palace Rd   Plan: H5
✉ *SW1W 0SJ –* Ⓜ *Victoria –* 𝒞 *(020) 7821 8898*
– www.grandimperiallondon.com – Closed 25-26 December
Menu £ 18 (weekday lunch) – Carte £ 21/110
• **Chinese • Elegant •**
Grand it most certainly is, as this elegant restaurant is in the Grosvenor Hotel's
former ballroom. It specialises in Cantonese cuisine, particularly the version
found in Hong Kong; steaming and frying are used to great effect.

XX **Massimo** – Corinthia Hotel   🕭 🅰🅒 ⇌

10 Northumberland Ave. ✉ *WC2N 5AE*   Plan: J4
– Ⓜ *Embankment –* 𝒞 *(020) 73213156 – www.corinthia.com/london*
– Closed Sunday
Menu £ 30 – Carte £ 28/57
• **Italian • Elegant • Fashionable •**
Opulent, visually impressive room with an oyster bar on one side. On offer are
traditional dishes true to the regions of Italy; fish and seafood dishes stand out.
Impressive private dining room comes with its own chef.

XX **Tinello**

87 Pimlico Rd ⊠ *SW1W 8PH –* Ⓜ *Sloane Square*   Plan: **G6**
– ℰ (020) 77303663 – www.tinello.co.uk – Closed Sunday and bank holidays
Carte £ 17/50 *– (booking essential at dinner)*
• Italian • Design • Friendly •
The brothers Sali have created a warm, friendly, romantic and very popular Italian restaurant. Their native Tuscany informs the cooking, so expect dishes like ribollita, liver crostini, and pappardelle with wild boar ragout.

XX **Adam Handling at Caxton** – St. Ermin's Hotel   ᴀᴄ

2 Caxton St. ⊠ *SW1H 0QW –* Ⓜ *St James's Park*   Plan: **I5**
– ℰ (020) 7222 7888 – www.caxtongrill.co.uk
Menu £ 25 (weekday lunch)/49 – Carte £ 31/59 *– (closed lunch Saturday-Sunday)*
• Modern cuisine • Brasserie •
The eponymous chef – a past finalist on 'MasterChef' – creates skilful, intricate and quite delicate dishes, looking to Asia for many of his influences. Small plates, steaks and a tasting menu are also on offer; lunch is a simpler affair.

XX **Osteria Dell' Angolo**   ᴀᴄ ⇔

47 Marsham St ⊠ *SW1P 3DR –* Ⓜ *St James's Park*   Plan: **I6**
– ℰ (020) 32681077 – www.osteriadellangolo.co.uk – Closed 1-4 January, Easter, 24-28 December, Saturday lunch, Sunday and bank holidays
Menu £ 18 (weekday lunch) – Carte £ 23/43 *– (booking essential)*
• Italian • Neighbourhood • Brasserie •
At lunch, this Italian opposite the Home Office is full of bustle and men in suits; at dinner it's a little more relaxed. Staff are personable and the menu is reassuringly familiar; homemade pasta and seafood dishes are good.

XX **Rex Whistler**   ⅋⅋ ⅋ ᴀᴄ

Tate Britain, Millbank ⊠ *SW1P 4RG Victoria –* Ⓜ *Pimlico*   Plan: **I6**
– ℰ (020) 78878825 – www.tate.org.uk – Closed 24-26 December
Menu £ 27 *– (lunch only)*
• British traditional • Classic • Traditional •
The £ 45million renovation of Tate Britain included a freshening up of its restaurant and restoration of Whistler's mural, 'The Expedition in Pursuit of Rare Meats', which envelops the room. The monthly menu is stoutly British and the remarkably priced wine list has an unrivalled 'half bottle' selection.

XX **Il Convivio**   ᴀᴄ ⇔

143 Ebury St ⊠ *SW1W 9QN –* Ⓜ *Sloane Square*   Plan: **G6**
– ℰ (020) 77304099 – www.ilconvivio.co.uk – Closed Christmas-New Year, Easter, Sunday and bank holidays
Menu £ 18/23 – Carte £ 30/47
• Italian • Neighbourhood •
Handsome Georgian townhouse with a retractable roof and Dante's poetry embossed on the walls. All of the pasta is made on the top floor; the squid ink spaghetti is a staple. Dishes are artfully presented and flavoursome.

XX **Boisdale of Belgravia**   ⌂ ᴀᴄ ⇔

15 Eccleston St ⊠ *SW1W 9LX –* Ⓜ *Victoria – ℰ (020)*   Plan: **G6**
7730 6922 – www.boisdale.co.uk – Closed 25 December, Saturday lunch, Sunday and bank holidays
Menu £ 18 (lunch and early dinner) – Carte £ 27/59
• British traditional • Individual • Musical •
A proudly Scottish restaurant with acres of tartan and a charmingly higgledy-piggledy layout. Stand-outs are the smoked salmon and the 28-day aged Aberdeenshire cuts of beef. Live nightly jazz.

XX **The Ebury Restaurant & Wine Bar** [AC]

139 Ebury St. ⊠ SW1W 9QU – Ⓜ Victoria – ℰ (020)   Plan: **G6**
7730 5447 – www.eburyrestaurant.co.uk – Closed Christmas-New Year
Menu £ 23/29 – Carte £ 28/41
• French • Neighbourhood •
Going strong for over 50 years and as likeable as ever. Some imaginative touches but generally quite classic cooking. Dairy and gluten free menus offered, along with a keenly-priced wine list.

X **A. Wong**   🛜 [AC]

⊛ *70 Wilton Rd ⊠ SW1V 1DE – Ⓜ Victoria – ℰ (020)*   Plan: **H6**
*7828 8931 – www.awong.co.uk – Closed 23 December-4 January, Sunday
and Monday lunch*
Menu £ 14 (lunch) – Carte £ 16/38 – *(booking essential)*
• Chinese • Friendly • Neighbourhood •
Andrew Wong transformed his mother's restaurant into a modern and lively Chinese restaurant. He's taken classics from across China and introduced the odd twist here and there, whilst keeping the original combinations intact.

X **Kouzu** [AC]

21 Grosvenor Gdns ⊠ SW1 0BD – Ⓜ Victoria – ℰ (020)   Plan: **G5**
*7730 7043 – www.kouzu.co.uk – Closed 24-25 December, 1 January,
Saturday lunch and Sunday*
Menu £ 40/65 – Carte £ 33/114
• Japanese • Design •
Occupying two floors of an attractive 19C Grade II building is this modern Japanese restaurant. Those who know Zuma or Nobu will not only recognise the style of the food but will also find the stylish surroundings familiar.

X **Olivocarne** [AC]

61 Elizabeth St ⊠ SW1W 9PP – Ⓜ Sloane Square   Plan: **G6**
– ℰ (020) 7730 7997 – www.olivorestaurants.com
Menu £ 18 (lunch) – Carte £ 31/47
• Italian • Individual • Neighbourhood •
Just when you thought Mauro Sanno had this part of town sewn up he opens another restaurant. This one focuses on meat dishes, along with a selection of satisfying Sardinian specialities and is smarter and larger than his others.

X **Olivo** [AC]

21 Eccleston St ⊠ SW1W 9LX – Ⓜ Victoria – ℰ (020)   Plan: **G6**
*77302505 – www.olivorestaurants.com – Closed lunch Saturday-Sunday
and bank holidays*
Menu £ 25 (weekday lunch) – Carte £ 33/47 – *(booking essential)*
• Italian • Neighbourhood • Bistro •
Carefully prepared, authentic Sardinian specialities are the highlight at this popular Italian restaurant. Simply decorated in blues and yellows, with an atmosphere of bonhomie.

X **Olivomare**   🛜 [AC]

10 Lower Belgrave St ⊠ SW1W 0LJ – Ⓜ Victoria   Plan: **G5**
– ℰ (020) 77309022 – www.olivorestaurants.com – Closed bank holidays
Carte £ 33/45
• Fish and seafood • Design • Neighbourhood •
Expect understated and stylish piscatorial decoration and seafood with a Sardinian base. Fortnightly changing menu, with high quality produce, much of which is available in the deli next door.

🏠 **Thomas Cubitt**

44 Elizabeth St ⊠ SW1W 9PA – Ⓜ Sloane Square.   Plan: **G6**
– ℰ (020) 77306060 – www.thethomascubitt.co.uk
Carte £ 29/44 – *(booking essential)*
• Modern cuisine • Pub •
A pub of two halves: choose the busy ground floor bar with its accessible menu or upstairs for more ambitious, quite elaborate cooking with courteous service and a less frenetic environment.

The Orange

37 Pimlico Rd ⌗ *SW1W 8NE* – Ⓜ *Sloane Square.* ⌂ Plan: **G6**
– 𝄢 *(020) 78819844* – *www.theorange.co.uk*
Carte £ 28/40
• **Mediterranean** • **Friendly** • **Neighbourhood** •

The old Orange Brewery is as charming a pub as its stucco-fronted façade suggests. Try the fun bar or book a table in the more sedate upstairs room. The menu has a Mediterranean bias; spelt or wheat-based pizzas are a speciality. Bedrooms are stylish and comfortable.

REGENT'S PARK & MARYLEBONE   **PLAN V**

The Landmark London

222 Marylebone Rd ⌗ *NW1 6JQ* – Ⓜ *Edgware Road* Plan: **F1**
– 𝄢 *(020) 76318000* – *www.landmarklondon.co.uk*
300 rm – †£ 252/780 ††£ 252/780 – ⌷ £ 29 – 9 suites
• **Business** • **Classic** •

Imposing Victorian Gothic building with a vast glass-enclosed atrium which is overlooked by many of the well-equipped bedrooms. Dining options include the Winter Garden and a wood-panelled room with a global menu.
Winter Garden – See restaurant listing

The London Edition

10 Berners Street ⌗ *W1T 3NP*
– Ⓜ *Tottenham Court Road* – 𝄢 *(020) 7781 0000* Plan: **H2**
– *www.editionhotels.com*
173 rm – †£ 345/450 ††£ 345/450 – ⌷ £ 26 – 9 suites
• **Business** • **Luxury** • **Design** •

Berners, a classic Edwardian hotel, strikingly reborn through a partnership between Ian Schrager and Marriott – the former's influence most apparent in the stylish lobby and bar. Slick, understated rooms; the best ones have balconies.
Berners Tavern – See restaurant listing

Langham

1c Portland Pl., Regent St. ⌗ *W1B 1JA*
– Ⓜ *Oxford Circus* – 𝄢 *(020) 76361000* – *www.langhamhotels.com* Plan: **H2**
380 rm – †£ 360/960 ††£ 360/960 – ⌷ £ 30 – 24 suites
• **Luxury** • **Palace** • **Stylish** •

Was one of Europe's first purpose-built grand hotels when it opened in 1865. Now back to its best, with its famous Palm Court for afternoon tea, a stylish Artesian bar and bedrooms that are not without personality and elegance.
Roux at The Landau – See restaurant listing

Hyatt Regency London-The Churchill

30 Portman Sq ⌗ *W1H 7BH* – Ⓜ *Marble Arch* – 𝄢 *(020)*
7486 5800 – *www.london.churchill.hyatt.com* Plan: **G2**
434 rm – †£ 220/660 ††£ 220/660 – ⌷ £ 32 – 47 suites
• **Luxury** • **Business** • **Modern** •

Smart well-located property whose best bedrooms overlook the attractive square opposite. Elegant marbled lobby with plenty of staff. Well-appointed and refurbished bedrooms have the international traveller in mind. A British menu and afternoon tea served in The Montagu.

Chiltern Firehouse

1 Chiltern St ⌗ *W1U 7PA* – Ⓜ *Baker Street* – 𝄢 *(020)*
7073 7676 – *www.chilternfirehouse.com* Plan: **G2**
26 rm – †£ 495/1020 ††£ 495/1020 – ⌷ £ 20 – 6 suites
• **Townhouse** • **Luxury** • **Stylish** •

From Chateau Marmont in LA to The Mercer in New York, André Balazs' hotels are effortlessly cool. For his London entrance, he has sympathetically restored and extended a gothic Victorian fire station. The style comes with an easy elegance; it's an oasis of calm and hardly feels like a hotel at all.
Chiltern Firehouse – See restaurant listing

Charlotte Street

15 Charlotte St ✉ *W1T 1RJ* – Ⓜ *Goodge Street*
– ℰ *(020) 78062000 – www.charlottestreethotel.co.uk*
Plan: **I2**
52 rm – †£ 276/342 ††£ 276/342 – ☑ £ 20 – 4 suites
• **Luxury** • **Townhouse** • **Stylish** •
Stylish interior designed with a charming, understated English feel. Impeccably kept and individually decorated bedrooms. Popular in-house screening room. Colourful restaurant whose terrace spills onto Charlotte Street; grilled meats a highlight.

Sanderson

50 Berners St ✉ *W1T 3NG* – Ⓜ *Oxford Circus* – ℰ *(020)*
73001400 – www.morganshotelgroup.com
Plan: **H2**
150 rm – †£ 234/538 ††£ 234/538 – ☑ £ 18
• **Luxury** • **Business** • **Minimalist** •
Originally designed by Philippe Starck and his influence is still evident. The Purple Bar is dark and moody; the Long Bar is bright and stylish. Bedrooms are crisply decorated and come complete with all mod cons.

Montcalm

34-40 Great Cumberland Pl. ✉ *W1H 7TW*
– Ⓜ *Marble Arch*
– ℰ *(020) 7402 4288 – www.montcalm.co.uk*
Plan: **F2**
126 rm – †£ 380 ††£ 380/750 – ☑ £ 20 – 17 suites
• **Business** • **Family** • **Stylish** •
Named after an 18C French general, the Montcalm forms part of a crescent of townhouses with a Georgian façade. A top-to-toe refurbishment has created smart, contemporary bedrooms in lively colours. Seasonal British dishes served in Crescent restaurant.
sixtyone – See restaurant listing

Durrants

26-32 George St ✉ *W1H 5BJ* – Ⓜ *Bond Street*
– ℰ *(020) 7935 8131 – www.durrantshotel.co.uk*
Plan: **G2**
92 rm – †£ 235 ††£ 300/420 – ☑ £ 20 – 4 suites
• **Traditional** • **Business** • **Classic** •
Traditional, privately owned hotel with friendly, long-standing staff. Bedrooms are now brighter in style but still retain a certain English character. Clubby dining room for mix of British classics and lighter, European dishes.

Dorset Square

39-40 Dorset Sq ✉ *NW1 6QN* – Ⓜ *Marylebone*
– ℰ *(020) 77237874 – www.dorsetsquarehotel.co.uk*
Plan: **F1**
38 rm – †£ 200/240 ††£ 250/460 – ☑ £ 13
• **Townhouse** • **Business** • **Contemporary** •
Having reacquired this Regency townhouse, Firmdale refurbished it fully before reopening it in 2012. It has a contemporary yet intimate feel and visiting MCC members will appreciate the cricketing theme, which even extends to the cocktails in their sweet little basement brasserie.

Marble Arch by Montcalm

31 Great Cumberland Pl. ✉ *W1H 7TA* – Ⓜ *Marble Arch*
– ℰ *(020) 7258 0777 – www.themarblearch.co.uk*
Plan: **F2**
42 rm – †£ 175/201 ††£ 201/300 – ☑ £ 20
• **Townhouse** • **Business** • **Stylish** •
Bedrooms at this 5-storey Georgian townhouse come with the same high standards of stylish, contemporary design as its parent hotel opposite, the Montcalm, but are just a little more compact.

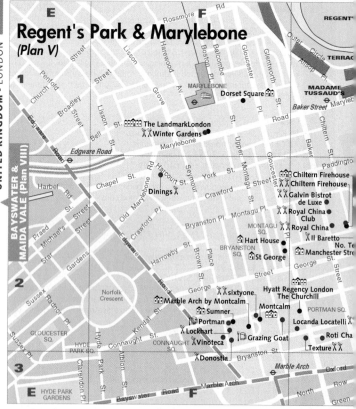

Regent's Park & Marylebone
(Plan V)

🏨 **Mandeville**　　　　　　　　　　　　　　　　✿ 🕭 AK 🐟

Mandeville Pl ⊠ W1U 2BE – ⓂBond Street　　　　Plan: **G2**
– ℰ (020) 7935 5599
– www.mandeville.co.uk
142 rm – †£ 216/600 ††£ 240/600 – ⌑ £ 16 – 2 suites
• Business • Family • Design •
Usefully located hotel with a marbled reception leading into a very colourful
and comfortable bar. Stylish rooms have flat screen TVs and make good use of
the space available. Steaks are the highlight of the classic menu.

🏨 **No. Ten Manchester Street**　　　　　　　　　✿ 🕭 AK

10 Manchester St ⊠ W1U 4DG – ⓂBaker Street　　Plan: **G2**
– ℰ (020) 73175900
– www.tenmanchesterstreethotel.com
44 rm – †£ 225/375 ††£ 225/375 – ⌑ £ 15 – 9 suites
• Townhouse • Business • Modern •
Converted Edwardian house in an appealing, central location. Discreet entrance
leads into little lounge and Italian-themed bistro; semi-enclosed cigar bar also a
feature. Neat, well-kept bedrooms.

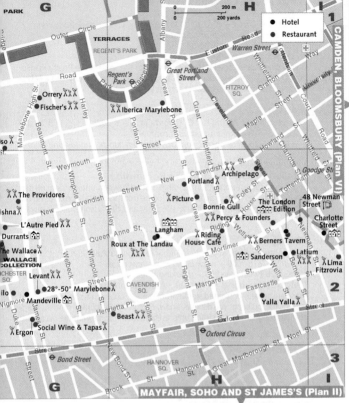

MAYFAIR, SOHO AND ST JAMES'S (Plan II)

🏠 **Sumner**   ♿ 🆎

54 Upper Berkeley St ⊠ W1H 7QR – Ⓜ Marble Arch   Plan: **F2**
– ℰ (020) 77232244 – www.thesumner.com
19 rm 🖙 – ♦£ 160/300 ♦♦£ 160/300
• Townhouse • Business • Personalised •
Two Georgian terrace houses in central location. Comfy, stylish sitting room;
basement breakfast room. Largest bedrooms, 101 and 201, benefit from
having full-length windows.

XXX **Locanda Locatelli**   🍴 ♿ 🆎 ⇔
🌸   8 Seymour St ⊠ W1H 7JZ – Ⓜ Marble Arch – ℰ (020)   Plan: **G2**
79359088 – www.locandalocatelli.com – Closed 25-26 December and 1 January
Carte £ 34/60
• Italian • Fashionable • Elegant •
Giorgio Locatelli's Italian restaurant may be into its second decade but still looks
as dapper as ever. The service is smooth and the room was designed with conviviality in mind. The hugely appealing menu covers all regions; unfussy presentation and superb ingredients allow natural flavours to shine.
➜ Calf's foot salad with red onion and peppers. Roast rabbit with polenta
and radicchio. Sicilian cannoli with orange sauce and pistachio ice cream.

XxX **Roux at The Landau** – Langham Hotel   AC ⇔

1c Portland Pl., Regent St. ✉ *W1B 1JA*   Plan: **H2**
– Ⓜ *Oxford Circus –* ℰ *(020) 76361000 – www.rouxatthelandau.com*
– Closed Saturday lunch and Sunday
Menu £ 35/65 – Carte £ 36/88
• **French** • **Formal** • **Elegant** •
Grand, oval-shaped hotel restaurant run under the aegis of the Roux organisation. Classical, French-influenced cooking is the order of the day, but a lighter style of cuisine using the occasional twist is also emerging.

XxX **Latium**   AC

21 Berners St. ✉ *W1T 3LP –* Ⓜ *Oxford Circus –* ℰ *(020)*   Plan: **H2**
7323 9123 – www.latiumrestaurant.com
– Closed 25-26 December, 1 January, Saturday lunch, Sunday and bank holidays
Menu £ 23 (weekdays)/36
• **Italian** • **Neighbourhood** • **Romantic** •
Bright and contemporary surroundings but with warm and welcoming service. Owner-chef from Lazio but dishes come from across Italy, often using British produce. Ravioli is the house speciality and the fassone beef is always good.

XxX **Orrery**   🌳 AC ⇔

55 Marylebone High St ✉ *W1U 5RB –* Ⓜ *Regent's Park*   Plan: **G1**
– ℰ *(020) 7616 8000 – www.orrery-restaurant.co.uk*
Menu £ 28 (weekdays)/55 – *(booking essential)*
• **Modern cuisine** • **Formal** • **Neighbourhood** •
These are actually converted stables from the 19C but, such is the elegance and style of the building, you'd never know. Featured is elaborate, modern European cooking; dishes are strong on presentation and come with the occasional twist.

XX **Texture** (Agnar Sverrisson)   🥂 AC ⇔
❀

34 Portman St ✉ *W1H 7BY –* Ⓜ *Marble Arch –* ℰ *(020)*   Plan: **G2**
72240028 – www.texture-restaurant.co.uk
– Closed first 2 weeks August, 1 week Easter, Christmas-New Year, Sunday and Monday
Menu £ 30/79 – Carte £ 54/82
• **Creative** • **Design** • **Fashionable** •
Technically skilled but light and invigorating cooking from Icelandic chef-owner, who uses ingredients from home. Bright restaurant with high ceiling and popular adjoining champagne bar. Pleasant service from keen staff, ready with a smile.
→ Scottish scallops, coconut, ginger, lime leaf and lemongrass. Lightly salted Icelandic cod, bisque, prawns, barley and grapefruit. Skyr with vanilla, rye bread crumbs and Muscatel grapes.

XX **L'Autre Pied**   AC 🍸
❀

5-7 Blandford St. ✉ *W1U 3DB –* Ⓜ *Bond Street*   Plan: **G2**
– ℰ *(020) 74869696 – www.lautrepied.co.uk – Closed 4 days Christmas, 1 January and Sunday dinner*
Menu £ 24/75 – Carte £ 52/63
• **Modern cuisine** • **Design** •
Dishes are visual and easy to eat and provide pleasing contrasts in textures; venison dishes are a particular speciality. This sibling of Pied à Terre has a more relaxed, neighbourhood atmosphere; ask for a table by the window to better enjoy the local 'village' feel.
→ Scallop ceviche with cucumber, balsamic and crème fraîche. Blackface lamb, red pepper ketchup and violet artichoke. Chocolate crémeux with honeycomb and pistachio.

XX **Berners Tavern** – The London Edition Hotel   ⅏ AC ⇔

10 Berners St ✉ *WIT 3NP* – Ⓜ *Tottenham Court Road*   Plan: **H2**
– ℰ (020) 7908 7979 – www.bernerstavern.com
Carte £ 33/117
• **British modern** • **Brasserie** • **Elegant** •
What was once a hotel ballroom is now a very glamorous restaurant, with every inch of wall filled with gilt-framed pictures. Jason Atherton has put together an appealing, accessible menu and the cooking is satisfying and assured.

XX **Royal China Club**   AC ⅏

40-42 Baker St ✉ *W1U 7AJ* – Ⓜ *Baker Street* – ℰ *(020)*   Plan: **G2**
7486 3898 – www.royalchinagroup.co.uk – Closed 25-27 December
Carte £ 25/70
• **Chinese** • **Elegant** • **Romantic** •
'The Club' is the glittering bauble in the Royal China chain but along with the luxurious feel of the room comes an appealing sense of calm. Their lunchtime dim sum is very good; at dinner try their more unusual Cantonese dishes.

XX **Galvin Bistrot de Luxe**   🌿 ⅏ AC ⇔ ⅏

66 Baker St. ✉ *W1U 7DJ* – Ⓜ *Baker Street* – ℰ *(020)*   Plan: **G2**
7935 4007 – www.galvinrestaurants.com – Closed dinner
24 December, 25-26 December and 1 January
Menu £ 22/24 – Carte £ 32/54
• **French** • **Bistro** • **Formal** •
Firmly established modern Gallic bistro with ceiling fans, globe lights and wood-panelled walls. Satisfying and precisely cooked classic French dishes from the Galvin brothers. The elegant basement cocktail bar adds to the comfy feel.

XX **Chiltern Firehouse** – Chiltern Firehouse Hotel   🌿 AC ⇔

1 Chiltern St ✉ *WIU 7PA* – Ⓜ *Baker Street* – ℰ *(020)*   Plan: **G2**
7073 7676 – www.chilternfirehouse.com
Carte £ 36/61
• **World cuisine** • **Individual** • **Design** •
How appropriate – the hottest ticket in town is a converted fire station. The room positively bursts with energy but what makes this celebrity hangout unusual is that the food is rather good. Nuno Mendes' menu is full of vibrant North and South American dishes that are big on flavour.

XX **Beast**   ⅏ AC

3 Chapel Pl ✉ *W1G 0BG* – Ⓜ *Bond Street* – ℰ *(020)*   Plan: **H2**
7495 1816 – www.beastrestaurant.co.uk – Closed Sunday, lunch Monday-Wednesday and bank holidays
Menu £ 85 – *(booking essential) (set menu only)*
• **Meats** • **Elegant** • **Fashionable** •
An underground banquet hall with three exceedingly long tables set for communal dining. The main event is a perfectly cooked hunk of rib eye steak and a large platter of succulent warm king crab. Bring a big appetite and a fat wallet.

XX **sixtyone** – Montcalm Hotel   ⅏ AC ⇔

61 Upper Berkeley St ✉ *W1H 7TW* – Ⓜ *Marble Arch*   Plan: **F2**
– ℰ (020) 7958 3222 – www.montcalm.co.uk – Closed Sunday dinner
Menu £ 18/61 – Carte £ 32/47
• **British modern** • **Elegant** • **Design** •
A joint venture between chef Arnaud Stevens and Searcy's, in a space leased from the Montcalm hotel. The room is stylish and slick; the modern cooking is elaborate and quite playful, although the best dishes are often the simplest.

XX **Percy & Founders**   🌿 ⅏ AC ⇔

1 Pearson Sq, (off Mortimer St) ✉ *W1T 3BF*   Plan: **H2**
– Ⓜ Goodge Street – ℰ (020) 3761 0200 – www.percyandfounders.co.uk
Carte £ 28/51
• **Modern cuisine** • **Brasserie** • **Fashionable** •
Where Middlesex hospital once stood is now a residential development that includes this all-day operation. It's a mix between a smart pub and a modern brasserie and the kitchen brings quite a refined touch to the seasonal menu.

UNITED KINGDOM - LONDON

XX **Archipelago** [AC]

53 Cleveland St ✉ W1T 4JJ – Ⓜ Goodge Street   Plan: **H2**
– ℰ (020) 7383 3346 – www.archipelago-restaurant.co.uk – Closed 24-28 December, Saturday lunch, Sunday and bank holidays
Carte £ 29/44
• Creative • Exotic •
New premises for this true one-off, but the same eccentric decoration that makes you feel you're in a bazaar. The exotic menu reads like an inventory at an omnivore's safari park; it could include crocodile, zebra and wildebeest.

XX **Winter Garden** – The Landmark London Hotel   [AC] 🚗

222 Marylebone Rd ✉ NW1 6JQ – Ⓜ Edgware Road   Plan: **F1**
– ℰ (020) 76318000 – www.landmarklondon.co.uk
Menu £ 30/40 – Carte £ 36/50
• Mediterranean • Friendly •
Dining options north of Marylebone Road can be limited, so the Winter Garden, in the vast atrium of the Landmark Hotel, is a useful spot for a business lunch. The kitchen has a lightness of touch and the confidence not to overcrowd a plate.

XX **Fischer's** [AC]

50 Marylebone High St ✉ W1U 5HN – Ⓜ Baker Street   Plan: **G1**
– ℰ (020) 7466 5501 – www.fischers.co.uk – Closed 24-25 December and 1 January
Carte £ 15/43
• Austrian • Individual • Fashionable •
An Austrian café and konditorei that summons the spirit of old Vienna, from the owners of The Wolseley et al. Open all day; breakfast is a highlight – the viennoiserie are great. Schnitzels are also good – upgrade to a Holstein.

XX **The Providores** [AC]

109 Marylebone High St. ✉ W1U 4RX – Ⓜ Bond Street   Plan: **G2**
– ℰ (020) 7935 6175 – www.theprovidores.co.uk – Closed 25-26 December
Carte £ 35/47
• Creative • Trendy • Romantic •
Packed ground floor for tapas; upstairs for innovative fusion cooking, with spices and ingredients from around the world, including Australasia. Starter-sized dishes at dinner allow for greater choice.

XX **Iberica Marylebone** [AC] ⇗

195 Great Portland St ✉ W1W 5PS   Plan: **H1**
– Ⓜ Great Portland Street – ℰ (020) 76368650 – www.ibericalondon.co.uk – Closed 24-26 December, Sunday dinner and bank holidays
Menu £ 18/36 – Carte £ 14/46
• Spanish • Family • Neighbourhood •
Some prefer the intimacy of upstairs, others the bustle of the ground floor with its bar and deli. Along with an impressive array of Iberico hams are colourful dishes to share, such as glossy black rice with cuttlefish and prawns.

XX **Levant** [AC]

Jason Ct., 76 Wigmore St. ✉ W1U 2SJ – Ⓜ Bond Street   Plan: **G2**
– ℰ (020) 7224 1111 – www.levant.co.uk – Closed 25-26 December
Menu £ 14/35 – Carte £ 18/41
• Lebanese • Exotic • Individual •
Come in a group to best enjoy the Lebanese and Middle Eastern specialities; it's worth ordering one of the 'Feast' menus. Belly dancing, a low slung bar, lanterns and joss sticks add to the exotic feel of this basement restaurant.

XX **Royal China** [AC] 🏵

24-26 Baker St ✉ W1U 7AB – Ⓜ Baker Street – ℰ (020)   Plan: **G2**
74874688 – www.royalchinagroup.co.uk
Menu £ 30/38 – Carte £ 18/74
• Chinese • Exotic • Family •
Barbequed meats, assorted soups and stir-fries attract plenty of large groups to this smart and always bustling Cantonese restaurant. Over 40 different types of dim sum served during the day.

UNITED KINGDOM - LONDON

✕ **Trishna** (Karam Sethi)   AC ⟳ ⓥ
✿ *15-17 Blandford St. ⊠ W1U 3DG –* ❶ *Baker Street*   Plan: **G2**
– ℰ (020) 79355624 – www.trishnalondon.com – Closed 25-28 December and 1-3 January
Menu £ 24/60 – Carte £ 29/51
• **Indian** • **Neighbourhood** • **Simple** •
Double-fronted, modern Indian restaurant dressed in an elegant, understated style. The coast of southwest India provides the influences and the food is balanced, satisfying and executed with care - the Tasting menus provide a good all-round experience.
→ Aloo tokri chaat. Dorset brown crab with butter, pepper and wild garlic. Mango bappa doi with mango and star anise chutney.

✕ **Portland**   ✿ AC ⟳
✿ *113 Great Portland St ⊠ W1W 6QQ*   Plan: **H2**
– ❶ *Great Portland Street – ℰ (020) 7436 3261*
– www.portlandrestaurant.co.uk – Closed Sunday
Carte £ 29/39 – *(booking essential)*
• **Modern cuisine** • **Intimate** • **Simple** •
A no-frills, pared down restaurant that exudes honesty. One look at the menu and you know you'll eat well: it twists and turns on a daily basis and the combinations just sound right together. Dishes are crisp and unfussy but with depth and real understanding – quite something for such a young team.
→ Sea trout, peas, beans and lemon verbena. Pigeon with parsley root and enoki. Brown butter ice cream, fresh almonds and grilled pear.

✕ **Lima Fitzrovia**   AC ⓥ
✿ *31 Rathbone Pl ⊠ W1T 1JH –* ❶ *Goodge Street*   Plan: **I2**
– ℰ (020) 3002 2640 – www.limalondon.com – Closed 24-27 December-3 January, Sunday dinner and bank holidays
Menu £ 20 (lunch and early dinner)/55 – Carte £ 38/52
• **Peruvian** • **Neighbourhood** • **Exotic** •
Lima Fitzrovia is one of those restaurants that just makes you feel good about life – and that's even without the Pisco Sours. The Peruvian food at this informal, fun place is the ideal antidote to times of austerity: it's full of punchy, invigorating flavours and fantastically vivid colours.
→ Sea bream ceviche with tiger's milk, sweet potato, red onion and cancha corn. Beef with wild black quinoa, Cuzco corn and aji panca juice. Dulce de Leche ice cream.

✕ **Social Wine & Tapas**   AC
39 James St ⊠ W1U 1DL – ❶ *Bond Street – ℰ (020)*   Plan: **G2**
7993 3257 – www.socialwineandtapas.com – Closed 25 December
Carte £ 20/38 – *(bookings not accepted)*
• **Mediterranean** • **Neighbourhood** • **Trendy** •
The latest in the Jason Atherton stable, and the name says it all. Urban styling, with wines on display; sit in the moodily lit basement. A mix of Spanish and Mediterranean dishes, with some Atherton classics too; desserts are a highlight.

✕ **Picture**   AC
⊛ *110 Great Portland St. ⊠ W1W 6PQ –* ❶ *Oxford Circus*   Plan: **H2**
– ℰ (020) 76377892 – www.picturerestaurant.co.uk – Closed Sunday and bank holidays
Menu £ 35 – Carte £ 23/32
• **British modern** • **Simple** • **Retro** •
An ex Arbutus and Wild Honey triumvirate have created this cool, great-value restaurant. The look may be a little stark but the delightful staff add warmth. The small plates are vibrant and colourful, and the flavours are assured.

899

The Wallace

Hertford House, Manchester Sq ⊠ *W1U 3BN*   Plan: **G2**
– ⓜ *Bond Street* – ℰ *(020) 75639505*
– *www.peytonandbyrne.co.uk/the-wallace-restaurant/index.html – Closed 24-26 December*
Menu £ 25 (lunch) – Carte £ 30/47 – *(lunch only and dinner Friday-Saturday)*
• French • Friendly •

Large glass-roofed courtyard on the ground floor of Hertford House, home to the splendid Wallace Collection. French-influenced menu, with fruits de mer section; terrines are the house speciality.

Roti Chai   AC

3 Portman Mews South ⊠ *W1H 6HS* – ⓜ *Marble Arch*   Plan: **G2**
– ℰ *(020) 74080101* – *www.rotichai.com* – *Closed 25 December*
Carte £ 15/31
• Indian • Trendy • Simple •

Representing the new wave of modern, casual Indian restaurants, in appropriately vivid colours. The ground floor is for quick and easy pan-Indian street food; downstairs is swankier and offers a contemporary update of Indian home cooking.

Il Baretto   AC

43 Blandford St. ⊠ *W1U 7HF* – ⓜ *Baker Street*   Plan: **G2**
– ℰ *(020) 74867340* – *www.ilbaretto.co.uk*
Menu £ 26 – Carte £ 35/83
• Italian • Neighbourhood • Simple •

The robata grill is the star of the show at this lively Italian restaurant. The extensive and variably priced menu offers something for everyone, from pizzas to succulent lamb chops. The basement setting adds to the 'local' feel.

28°-50° Marylebone   ✿ AC ♨

15-17 Marylebone Ln. ⊠ *W1U 2NE* – ⓜ *Bond Street*   Plan: **G2**
– ℰ *(020) 74867922* – *www.2850.co.uk* – *Closed 25-26 and 31 December, 1 January and Sunday*
Menu £ 20 (lunch and early dinner) – Carte £ 26/39
• Modern cuisine • Wine bar • Neighbourhood •

This second wine bar from the owners of Texture restaurant offers a great choice of wines by the glass and a terrific "Collectors' List". Most plump for the grilled meats from the coal burning oven. Service is as bright as the room.

Riding House Café   AC ⇔

43-51 Great Titchfield St ⊠ *W1W 7PQ* – ⓜ *Oxford Circus*   Plan: **H2**
– ℰ *(020) 79270840* – *www.ridinghousecafe.co.uk* – *Closed 25-26 December*
Menu £ 28 – Carte £ 25/41
• Modern cuisine • Rustic • Fashionable •

It's less a café, more a large, quirkily designed, all-day New York style brasserie and cocktail bar. The 'small plates' have more zing than the main courses. The 'unbookable' side of the restaurant is the more fun part.

Opso   ⌂ & ⇔

10 Paddington St ⊠ *W1U 5QL* – ⓜ *Baker Street*   Plan: **G1**
– ℰ *(020) 7487 5088* – *www.opso.co.uk* – *Closed Sunday dinner*
Menu £ 27/50 – Carte £ 21/46
• Greek • Neighbourhood • Individual •

A modern Greek restaurant which has proved a good fit for the neighbourhood – and not just because it's around the corner from the Hellenic Centre. It serves small sharing plates that mix the modern with the traditional.

Donostia

10 Seymour Pl ⊠ *W1H 7ND* – ⓜ *Marble Arch* – ℰ *(020)*   Plan: **F2**
3620 1845 – *www.donostia.co.uk* – *Closed Christmas, Easter and Monday lunch*
Carte £ 19/43
• Basque • Tapas bar • Fashionable •

The two young owners were inspired by the food of San Sebastiàn to open this pintxos and tapas bar. Sit at the counter for Basque classics like cod with pil-pil sauce, chorizo from the native pig Kintoa and slow-cooked pig's cheeks.

X **Ergon**   🅰🄲
16 Picton Pl ⊠ WIU 1BP – Ⓜ *Bond Street –* ℰ *(020)*   Plan: **G2**
7486 9210 – www.ergonproducts.com
Carte £ 25/38
• **Greek** • **Friendly** • **Simple** •
The London branch of this successful group in Greece is a bright eatery with a
downstairs deli stocked with Hellenic produce. The menu is a blend of classic
and modern Greek dishes designed for sharing; the wine list is all Greek too.

X **Vinoteca**   🕸 🄲
15 Seymour Pl. ⊠ W1H 5BD – Ⓜ *Marble Arch –* ℰ *(020)*   Plan: **F2**
*7724 7288 – www.vinoteca.co.uk – Closed Christmas, bank holidays and
Sunday dinner*
Menu £ 13 – Carte £ 21/36 – *(booking advisable)*
• **Modern cuisine** • **Wine bar** • **Neighbourhood** •
Follows the formula of the original: great fun, great wines, gutsy and wholesome food, enthusiastic staff and almost certainly a wait for a table. Influences
from sunnier parts of Europe, along with some British dishes.

X **Bonnie Gull**
21a Foley St ⊠ W1W 6DS – Ⓜ *Goodge Street*   Plan: **H2**
– ℰ (020) 7436 0921 – www.bonniegull.com
Carte £ 23/56 – *(booking essential)*
• **Fish and seafood** • **Simple** • **Traditional** •
Sweet Bonnie Gull calls itself a 'seafood shack' – a reference perhaps to its
modest beginnings as a pop-up. Start with an order from the raw bar then go
for a classic like Cullen skink, a whole Devon cock crab or fish and chips.

X **Lockhart**   🍴 🄲
22-24 Seymour Pl ⊠ W1H 7NL – Ⓜ *Marble Arch*   Plan: **F2**
– ℰ (020) 3011 5400 – www.lockhartlondon.com – Closed Sunday dinner
Carte £ 23/43
• **World cuisine** • **Individual** • **Friendly** •
Owned by two Texan couples, this fun spot specialises in the fiery flavours of
Texas, Louisiana and New Mexico. Start with a mezcal-based cocktail then tuck
into a wonderfully smoky meat dish like the lip-smackingly good BBQ chicken.

X **Yalla Yalla**   🄲
12 Winsley St. ⊠ W1W 8HQ – Ⓜ *Oxford Circus*   Plan: **H2**
*– ℰ (020) 7637 4748 – www.yalla-yalla.co.uk – Closed 25-26 December,
1 January and Sunday*
Carte £ 19/29
• **Lebanese** • **Rustic** • **Simple** •
It's fun, loud and you can't book, but the name means "Hurry up!" so you won't
wait long. This is Beirut street food, meant for sharing. Try homemade soujoc
(spicy sausages), sawda djej (chicken livers) and a succulent lamb dish.

X **Dinings**
22 Harcourt St. ⊠ W1H 4HH – Ⓜ *Edgware Road*   Plan: **F2**
– ℰ (020) 77230666 – www.dinings.co.uk – Closed Christmas and Sunday
Carte £ 36/74 – *(booking essential)*
• **Japanese** • **Cosy** • **Simple** •
It's hard not to be charmed by this sweet little Japanese place, with its ground
floor counter and basement tables. Its strengths lie with the more creative, con-
temporary dishes; sharing is recommended but prices can be steep.

X **Zoilo**   🄲 ⇆
9 Duke St. ⊠ W1U 3EG – Ⓜ *Bond Street –* ℰ *(020)*   Plan: **G2**
7486 9699 – www.zoilo.co.uk
Menu £ 10 (weekdays) – Carte £ 14/42
• **Argentinian** • **Friendly** • **Wine bar** •
It's all about sharing so plonk yourself at the counter and discover Argentina's
regional specialities. Typical dishes include braised pig head croquettes, grilled
scallops with pork belly, and refreshing watermelon salad with ricotta.

901

48 Newman Street

48 Newman St ✉ *W1T 1QQ –* Ⓜ *Goodge Street.*   Plan: **H2**
– ℰ (020) 3667 1445 – www.newmanstreettavern.co.uk – Closed 25-26 December and Easter Monday
Menu £ 20 – Carte £ 17/35
• British traditional • Neighbourhood • Rustic •
The experienced team behind this Edwardian pub have created a warm, welcoming spot. The kitchen celebrates the best of British and the menu is instantly appealing. Eat in the busy bar or in the more sedate first floor dining room.

Grazing Goat   ⇐ 🏠

6 New Quebec St ✉ *W1H 7RQ –* Ⓜ *Marble Arch.*   Plan: **F2**
– ℰ (020) 7724 7243 – www.thegrazinggoat.co.uk
8 rm – †£ 210 ††£ 250 – ⌑ £ 7
Carte £ 30/37 – *(booking essential at dinner)*
• British traditional • Pub • Fashionable •
A smart city facsimile of a country pub; it's first-come-first-served in the bar but you can book in the upstairs dining room. Proper pub classics such as pies and Castle of Mey steaks are on offer. Bedrooms with Nordic style bathrooms.

Portman

51 Upper Berkeley St ✉ *W1H 7QW –* Ⓜ *Marble Arch.*   Plan: **F2**
– ℰ (020) 7723 8996 – www.theportmanmarylebone.com
Menu £ 35/40 – Carte £ 26/41
• Modern cuisine • Pub • Friendly •
The condemned on their way to Tyburn Tree gallows would take their last drink here. Now it's an urbane pub with a formal upstairs dining room. The ground floor is more fun for enjoying the down-to-earth menu.

CAMDEN   PLAN VI

BLOOMSBURY

Covent Garden   🛝 ⅃ゟ ẢC 🔊

10 Monmouth St ✉ *WC2H 9HB –* Ⓜ *Covent Garden*   Plan: **I3**
– ℰ (020) 7806 1000 – www.firmdalehotels.com
58 rm – †£ 235/460 ††£ 235/460 – ⌑ £ 20 – 1 suite
• Luxury • Townhouse • Stylish •
Popular with those of a theatrical bent. Boldly designed, stylish bedrooms, with technology discreetly concealed. Boasts a very comfortable first floor oak-panelled drawing room with its own honesty bar.
Brasserie Max – See restaurant listing

Radisson Blu Edwardian Mercer Street   🛝 ⅃ゟ ẢC 🔊

20 Mercer St ✉ *WC2H 9HD –* Ⓜ *Covent Garden*   Plan: **I3**
– ℰ (020) 7836 4300 – www.radissonblu-edwardian.com
137 rm – †£ 180/450 ††£ 195/675 – ⌑ £ 23
• Business • Modern • Contemporary •
Smart, modern group-owned hotel in an excellent central location. The best rooms are at the apex of the V-shaped building. Informal 1st floor restaurant offers British classics. Popular for afternoon tea.

Bloomsbury   🛝 ⅃ゟ & ẢC 🔊

16-22 Gt Russell St ✉ *WC1B 3LR*   Plan: **I2**
– Ⓜ *Tottenham Court Road – ℰ (020) 7347 1000*
– www.doylecollection.com/bloomsbury
153 rm – †£ 185/450 ††£ 185/450 – ⌑ £ 19
• Business • Luxury • Historic •
Neo-Georgian building by Edward Lutyens, built for the YWCA in 1929. Now boasts a smart, comfortable interior, from the lobby to the contemporary bedrooms. Restaurant with largely British menu and clubby bar.

DoubleTree by Hilton London - West End

92 Southampton Row ✉ *WC1B 4BH* – ⓜ *Holborn* – ☏ *(020)*
7242 2828 – *www.doubletree3.hilton.com*

Plan: **J2**

216 rm ⌑ – †£ 130/230 ††£ 150/270 – 8 suites

• Business • Chain hotel • Contemporary •

A modern, corporate hotel behind a traditional façade. The spacious ground floor includes an open-plan bar which flows into a restaurant offering a simple British menu. Rooms vary in size but all have a clean, branded feel.

Pied à Terre

34 Charlotte St ✉ *W1T 2NH* – ⓜ *Goodge Street*

Plan: **I2**

– ☏ *(020) 76361178* – *www.pied-a-terre.co.uk* – *Closed last week December-5 January, Saturday lunch, Sunday and bank holidays*
Menu £ 36/65 – *(booking essential)*

• Creative • Elegant • Intimate •

For well over two decades David Moore's restaurant has stood apart in Charlotte Street, confident in its abilities and in the loyalty of its regulars. Subtle decorative changes keep it looking fresh and vibrant, while delivering elegant food with punchy flavours.

➔ Roast breast, crispy leg and Kiev of quail, Douglas Fir purée and hazelnut vinaigrette. Monkfish with sea purslane, salsify and Morteau sausage broth. Caramel parfait with vanilla ice cream, toasted oats, whiskey crème anglaise and popcorn.

Hakkasan Hanway Place

8 Hanway Pl. ✉ *W1T 1HD* – ⓜ *Tottenham Court Road*

Plan: **I2**

– ☏ *(020) 79277000* – *www.hakkasan.com* – *Closed 24-25 December*
Menu £ 35/128 – Carte £ 36/106

• Chinese • Trendy • Fashionable •

There are now Hakkasans all over the world but this was the original. It has the sensual looks, air of exclusivity and glamorous atmosphere synonymous with the 'brand'. The exquisite Cantonese dishes are prepared with care and consistency by the large kitchen team; lunch dim sum is a highlight.

➔ Crispy duck salad with pomelo, pine nuts and shallots. Spicy prawn with lily bulb and almond. Coconut semifreddo.

Kitchen Table at Bubbledogs (James Knappett)

70 Charlotte St ✉ *W1T 4QG* – ⓜ *Goodge Street*

Plan: **H1/2**

– ☏ *(020) 76377770* – *www.kitchentablelondon.co.uk* – *Closed 1-14 January, 17 August-2 September, 23-27 December, Sunday and Monday*
Menu £ 88 – *(dinner only) (booking essential) (set menu only)*

• Modern cuisine • Individual • Fashionable •

Fight through the crowds enjoying a curious mix of hot dogs and champagne and head for the curtain – behind it is a counter for 19 diners. Chef-owner James prepares a no-choice menu of around 12 dishes. The produce is exemplary; the cooking has a clever creative edge; and the dishes have real depth.

➔ Crispy chicken skin with rosemary mascarpone and bacon jam. Aged Dexter beef with yoghurt, wild garlic and caper sauce. Sorrel granité, custard cream and pear.

Mon Plaisir

19-21 Monmouth St. ✉ *WC2H 9DD* – ⓜ *Covent Garden*

Plan: **I3**

– ☏ *(020) 78367243* – *www.monplaisir.co.uk* – *Closed Christmas-New Year, Sunday and bank holidays*
Menu £ 14 *(early dinner)* – Carte £ 28/43

• French • Family •

This proud French institution opened in the 1940s. Enjoy satisfyingly authentic classics in any of the four contrasting rooms, full of Gallic charm; apparently the bar was salvaged from a Lyonnais brothel.

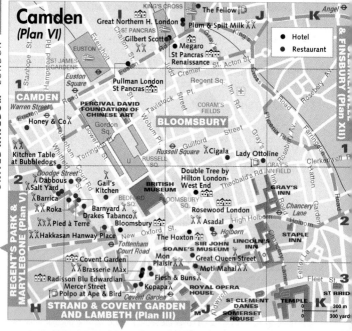

Camden
(Plan VI)

CAMDEN

XX   **Roka**

37 Charlotte St ⊠ W1T 1RR – Ⓜ *Goodge Street*   Plan: I2
– 𝒞 *(020) 75806464 – www.rokarestaurant.com – Closed 25 December*
Carte £ 16/109

• **Japanese • Fashionable • Design •**

Bright, atmospheric interior of teak and oak; bustling and trendy feel. Contemporary touches added to Japanese dishes; try specialities from the on-view Robata grill. Capable and chatty service.

XX   **Brasserie Max** – Covent Garden Hotel

10 Monmouth St ⊠ WC2H 9HB – Ⓜ *Covent Garden*   Plan: I3
– 𝒞 *(020) 78061007 – www.firmdalehotels.com*
Menu £ 24 (lunch and early dinner) – Carte £ 29/72 – *(booking essential)*

• **British modern • Fashionable • Brasserie •**

A boldly decorated and busy brasserie with an appealing and accessible menu of modern dishes with some Mediterranean influences. Very popular afternoon teas; cocktails at the large zinc bar and a weekend film club.

X   **Dabbous** (Ollie Dabbous)
ॐ

39 Whitfield St ⊠ W1T 2SF – Ⓜ *Goodge Street*   Plan: I2
– 𝒞 *(020) 7323 1544 – www.dabbous.co.uk – Closed 10 days Christmas-New Year, Easter and Sunday*
Menu £ 35/69 – *(booking essential) (set menu only)*

• **Modern cuisine • Design • Neighbourhood •**

One of the hottest tickets in town – the kitchen adopts the 'less is more' approach; the food comes with elegantly restrained finesse and a bewitching purity. Most have the 7-course menu with its stimulating and sublime combinations of ingredients. The ersatz industrial room has a simple elegance.

→ Alliums in chilled pine broth. Braised halibut with lemon verbena. Barley sponge soaked in red tea with vanilla cream.

X **Kopapa** ⛱ & 🅰🅲
32-34 Monmouth St ✉ *WC2H 9HA –* Ⓜ *Covent Garden*   Plan: I3
– 𝒞 (020) 7240 6076 – www.kopapa.co.uk – Closed 25-26 December
Carte £ 29/49 – *(booking advisable)*
• Asian • Bistro • Individual •
Kopapa, a Maori word for a gathering, is Peter Gordon's just-drop-in-anytime place. It's busy but fun, with breakfast morphing into all-day dining. Go for the 'fusion'-inspired dishes - they'll give your taste buds the best workout.

X **Gail's Kitchen** ⛱ & 🅰🅲
🐼 *11-13 Bayley St* ✉ *WC1B 3HD –* Ⓜ *Goode Street*   Plan: I2
– 𝒞 (020) 73239694 – www.gailskitchen.co.uk – Closed 25 December
Menu £ 14/19 – Carte approx. £ 18
• Mediterranean • Bistro • Friendly •
From the bakery people comes this engagingly run eatery that occupies a rather small space within the Myhotel. The enticing Mediterranean dishes are prepared with care and designed for sharing; the snacks are great too.

X **Drakes Tabanco** 🅰🅲
3 Windmill St ✉ *W1T 2HY –* Ⓜ *Goode Street – 𝒞 (020)*   Plan: I2
7637 9388 – www.drakestabanco.com – Closed Sunday and bank holidays
Menu £ 15/50 – Carte £ 14/30
• Spanish • Simple • Rustic •
Taking advantage of our newfound fondness for fino is this simple tabanco, from the people behind nearby Barrica and Copita. The small, Andalusian-inspired tapas menu uses imported produce from Spain alongside British ingredients.

X **Salt Yard** 🕸 🅰🅲
🐼 *54 Goodge St.* ✉ *W1T 4NA –* Ⓜ *Goodge Street*   Plan: H2
– 𝒞 (020) 76370657 – www.saltyard.co.uk – Closed 25 and dinner 24 and 31 December, 1 January
Carte £ 17/28
• Mediterranean • Tapas bar • Intimate •
Ground floor bar and buzzy basement restaurant specialising in good value plates of tasty Italian and Spanish dishes, ideal for sharing; charcuterie a speciality. Super wine list.

X **Honey & Co** 🅰🅲 🕅
🐼 *25a Warren St* ✉ *W1T 5LZ –* Ⓜ *Warren Street – 𝒞 (020)*   Plan: H1
73886175 – www.honeyandco.co.uk – Closed 25-26 December and Sunday
Menu £ 16 (weekdays)/27 – Carte £ 24/31 – *(booking essential)*
• World cuisine • Simple • Neighbourhood •
The husband and wife team at this sweet little café were both Ottolenghi head chefs so expect cooking full of freshness and colour. Influences stretch beyond Israel to the wider Middle East. Open from 8am; packed at night.

X **Barrica** ⛱ 🅰🅲
🐼 *62 Goodge St* ✉ *W1T 4NE –* Ⓜ *Goodge Street*   Plan: H2
– 𝒞 (020) 7436 9448 – www.barrica.co.uk – Closed 25-26 December,
1 January, Sunday and bank holidays
Menu £ 20/25 – Carte £ 19/48 – *(booking essential)*
• Spanish • Tapas bar • Friendly •
All the staff at this lively little tapas bar are Spanish, so perhaps it's national pride that makes them run it with a passion lacking in many of their competitors. When it comes to the food authenticity is high on the agenda.

X **Cigala** 🕸 ⛱ 🅰🅲 ⇄
54 Lamb's Conduit St. ✉ *WC1N 3LW*   Plan: J1
– Ⓜ *Russell Square – 𝒞 (020) 74051717 – www.cigala.co.uk – Closed 25-26 December, 1 January, Easter Sunday and Easter Monday*
Menu £ 18 (weekday lunch) – Carte £ 23/51 – *(booking essential)*
• Spanish • Neighbourhood • Friendly •
Longstanding Spanish restaurant, with a lively and convivial atmosphere, friendly and helpful service and an appealing and extensive menu of classics. The dried hams are a must and it's well worth waiting the 30 minutes for a paella.

Polpo at Ape & Bird

142 Shaftesbury Ave ✉ WC2H 8HJ – Ⓜ Leicester Square Plan: I3
– ✆ (020) 7836 3119 – www.polpo.co.uk
Carte £ 12/25 – *(bookings not accepted)*
• Italian • Rustic • Simple •
Even experienced restaurateurs have to sometimes have a rethink. When Russell Norman found his Ape & Bird pub wasn't working, he simply turned it into another Polpo. Expect the same style of small plates, just in a bigger place with a couple of bars.

Barnyard

18 Charlotte St ✉ W1T 2LZ – Ⓜ Goodge Street Plan: I2
– ✆ (020) 7580 3842 – www.barnyard-london.com – Closed 25-26 December
Carte £ 17/33 – *(bookings not accepted)*
• British traditional • Rustic • Design •
Dude food prepared with integrity draws the crowds to this fun little place co-owned by Ollie Dabbous. The food arrives all at once on enamel plates, and dishes are full of rustic, artery-hardening goodness yet are prepared with precision and care. Just be ready to queue, as it seats fewer than 50.

Flesh & Buns

41 Earlham St ✉ WC2H 9LX – Ⓜ Leicester Square Plan: I3
– ✆ (020) 7632 9500 – www.fleshandbuns.com – Closed 24-25 December
Menu £ 19 (lunch and early dinner)/40 – Carte £ 18/46 – *(booking advisable)*
• Asian • Trendy • Fashionable •
A loud, fun basement next to the Donmar. There's plenty of Japanese dishes but star billing goes to the hirata bun – the soft Taiwanese-style steamed pillows of delight that sandwich your choice of meat or fish filling.

Lady Ottoline

11a Northington St ✉ WC1N 2JF – Ⓜ Chancery Lane. Plan: J1
– ✆ (020) 78310008 – www.theladyottoline.com – Closed 25 December-2 January and bank holiday Mondays
Carte £ 22/43
• British traditional • Cosy • Neighbourhood •
A charming traditional feel and a palpable sense of history have always defined this classic Victorian pub. Stout British dishes are served in the ground floor bar and the more sedate upstairs dining room.

Holborn

Rosewood London

252 High Holborn ✉ WC1V 7EN Holborn – Ⓜ Holborn Plan: J2
– ✆ (020) 77818888 – www.rosewoodhotels.com/london
306 rm – †£ 345 ††£ 365 – ☕ £ 25 – 44 suites
• Historic • Luxury • Elegant •
A beautiful Edwardian building that was once the HQ of Pearl Assurance. The styling is very British and the bedrooms are uncluttered and smart. Cartoonist Gerald Scarfe's work adorns the walls of his eponymous bar. A classic brasserie with a menu of British favourites occupies the former banking hall.

The Hoxton

199 - 206 High Holborn ✉ WC1V 7BD – Ⓜ Holborn Plan: J2
– ✆ (020) 7661 3000 – www.thehoxton.com
174 rm ☕ – †£ 69/299 ††£ 69/299
• Townhouse • Contemporary • Design •
When the room categories are Shoebox, Snug, Cosy and Roomy, you know you're in a hip hotel. A great location and competitive rates plus a retro-style diner, a buzzy lobby and a 'Chicken Shop' in the basement.

XX **Moti Mahal**   🕭 AC ⑩

45 Great Queen St. ✉ *WC2B 5AA –* Ⓜ *Holborn*   Plan: J3
– 𝒞 (020) 72409329 – www.motimahal-uk.com – Closed 25-28 December,
Saturday lunch, Saturday lunch and bank holidays
Menu £ 16 (weekday lunch) – Carte £ 39/54
• **Indian** • **Design** • **Fashionable** •
The menu follows the path of the 16C Grand Trunk Road, stretching from Bengal through northern India to the mountains of the northwest frontier. The tandoor features heavily but there are also plenty of unfamiliar dishes to try.

X **Great Queen Street**

⊛ *32 Great Queen St* ✉ *WC2B 5AA –* Ⓜ *Holborn*   Plan: J2
– 𝒞 (020) 72420622 – www.greatqueenstreetrestaurant.co.uk – Closed
Christmas-New Year, Sunday dinner and bank holidays
Menu £ 18 (weekday lunch) – Carte £ 21/41 – *(booking essential)*
• **British modern** • **Rustic** • **Neighbourhood** •
The menu is a model of British understatement and is dictated by the seasons; the cooking, confident and satisfying with laudable prices and generous portions. Lively atmosphere and enthusiastic service.

X **Asadal**   AC ⇆

227 High Holborn ✉ *WC1V 7DA –* Ⓜ *Holborn – 𝒞 (020)*   Plan: J2
7430 9006 – www.asadal.co.uk – Closed 25-26 December, 1 January
and Sunday lunch
Carte £ 20/30
• **Korean** • **Friendly** •
Sharing is the key in this busy basement, where you'll be oblivious to its unprepossessing location. Hotpots, dumplings and barbeques are the highlights from the easy-to-follow menu. Staff cope well with the evening rush.

🏨 **St Pancras Renaissance**   🛎 ᵭ ⑩ 🕭 ᵭ AC 🕭 ⇆

Euston Rd ✉ *NW1 2AR –* Ⓜ *King's Cross St Pancras*   Plan: J0
– 𝒞 (020) 7841 3540 – www.stpancrasrenaissance.co.uk
245 rm – 🛏£ 390/450 🛏🛏£ 390/450 – ⊵ £ 19 – 10 suites
• **Business** • **Historic** • **Stylish** •
This restored Gothic jewel was built in 1873 as the Midland Grand hotel and reopened in 2011 under the Marriott brand. A former taxi rank is now a spacious lobby and all-day dining is in the old booking office. Luxury suites in Chambers wing; Barlow wing bedrooms are a little more functional.
Gilbert Scott – See restaurant listing

🏨 **Great Northern H. London**   🛎 ᵭ AC

Pancras Rd ✉ *N1C 4TB –* Ⓜ *King's Cross St Pancras*   Plan: J0
– 𝒞 (020) 3388 0800 – www.gnhlondon.com
91 rm ⊵ – 🛏£ 189/489 🛏🛏£ 208/508 – 1 suite
• **Townhouse** • **Traditional** • **Stylish** •
Built as a railway hotel in 1854; reborn as a stylish townhouse. Connected to King's Cross' western concourse and just metres from Eurostar check-in. Bespoke furniture in each of the modern bedrooms, and a pantry on each floor.
Plum + Spilt Milk – See restaurant listing

🏨 **Pullman London St Pancras**   🛎 ᵭ ᵰ ᵭ AC 🕭

100-110 Euston Rd ✉ *NW1 2AJ*   Plan: I0
– Ⓜ *Kings Cross St Pancras – 𝒞 (020) 76669000 – www.pullmanhotels.com*
312 rm – 🛏£ 200/450 🛏🛏£ 200/450 – ⊵ £ 20 – 2 suites
• **Business** • **Conference hotel** • **Modern** •
Designed primarily for the business traveller, Pullman is a stylish and modern brand from the Accor group. The open-plan reception and chic lounge lead into a relaxed eatery offering the brasserie classics. State-of-the-art conference facilities include a theatre. Ideally located for Eurostar.

Megaro
23-27 Euston Rd ((entrance on Belgrove St)) ✉ *WC1H 8AB*   Plan: **J0**
– **Ⓜ** *King's Cross St Pancras*
– *℘ (020) 7843 2222* – *www.hotelmegaro.co.uk*
49 rm – **†**£ 165/260 – **††**£ 165/260 – 🖵 £ 13
• **Townhouse** • **Contemporary** • **Personalised** •
Contemporary hotel fashioned out of a converted bank. The rooms are unfussy and the bathrooms smart. Daily 'absinthe hour' in the basement bar; simple seasonal modern European menu. Pastries for breakfast from their on-site bakery.

Gilbert Scott – St Pancras Renaissance Hotel
Euston Rd ✉ *NW1 2AR* – **Ⓜ** *King's Cross St Pancras*   Plan: **J0**
– *℘ (020) 7278 3888* – *www.thegilbertscott.co.uk*
Menu £ 21 (lunch and early dinner) – Carte £ 28/61
• **British traditional** • **Brasserie** • **Elegant** •
Run under the aegis of Marcus Wareing and named after the architect of this Gothic masterpiece, the restaurant has the look of a Grand Salon but the buzz of a brasserie. It celebrates the UK's many regional and historic specialities.

Plum + Spilt Milk – Great Northern Hotel London
Pancras Rd ✉ *N1C 4TB* – **Ⓜ** *King's Cross St Pancras*   Plan: **J0**
– *℘ (020) 3388 0818* – *www.plumandspiltmilk.com*
Menu £ 25 – Carte £ 21/45
• **British modern** • **Brasserie** • **Friendly** •
Bright brasserie in the Grade II listed Great Northern hotel; ideal for those who've just arrived, or are about to leave, by train. Classic British dishes like potted shrimps and 'pie of the day'. Start with a drink in the GNH bar.

Grain Store
Granary Sq, 1-3 Stable St ✉ *N1C 4AB*   Plan: **C2**
– **Ⓜ** *King's Cross St Pancras* – *℘ (020) 73244466* – *www.grainstore.com*
– *Closed 24-25 December, 1 January and Sunday dinner*
Carte £ 21/33
• **Modern cuisine** • **Individual** • **Fashionable** •
Big, buzzy 'canteen' from Bruno Loubet and the Zetter hotel people. Eclectic, clever dishes – influenced by Bruno's experiences around the world – are packed with interesting flavours and textures; vegetables often take the lead role.

Caravan
The Granary Building, 1 Granary Sq. ✉ *N1C 4AA*   Plan: **C2**
– **Ⓜ** *King's Cross St Pancras* – *℘ (020) 71017661*
– *www.caravankingscross.co.uk* – *Closed Sunday dinner*
Menu £ 30/50 – Carte £ 27/39 – *(booking essential)*
• **World cuisine** • **Simple** • **Fashionable** •
This second Caravan pitched up near King's Cross in an old granary warehouse. The industrial-chic look is matched by a great atmosphere – crowds flock here for breakfast, brunch, great coffee, pizza and globally influenced dishes.

Fellow
24 York Way ✉ *N1 9AA* – **Ⓜ** *King's Cross St Pancras.*   Plan: **J0**
– *℘ (020) 78334395* – *www.thefellow.co.uk*
– *Closed 25-27 December*
Carte £ 26/75
• **Modern cuisine** • **Rustic** • **Traditional** •
Anonymous façade but moody and atmospheric inside, with a cool cocktail bar. The lean menu of European dishes uses well-sourced ingredients. Fish from Cornish day boats is a highlight; cheeses are British and puds worth a flutter.

Mandarin Oriental Hyde Park

Plan: F4

66 Knightsbridge ⊠ *SW1X 7LA –* Ⓜ *Knightsbridge*
– ℰ (020) 72352000
– www.mandarinoriental.com/london
194 rm – ♦£ 414/798 ♦♦£ 414/798 – ☲ £ 26 – 25 suites
• Grand Luxury • Classic •

The Rosebery, a salon for afternoon tea, is the newest addition to this celebrated hotel which dates from 1889. The luxurious spa now includes a pool; the service is as strong as ever; and the bedrooms, many of which have views of Hyde Park, are spacious and comfortable.

❀❀ **Dinner by Heston Blumenthal • Bar Boulud** – See restaurant listing

Bulgari

Plan: F4

171 Knightsbridge ⊠ *SW7 1DW*
– Ⓜ *Knightsbridge – ℰ (020) 7151 1010*
– www.bulgarihotels.com/london
85 rm – ♦£ 510/790 ♦♦£ 510/890 – ☲ £ 34 – 23 suites
• Luxury • Stylish • Design •

Impeccably tailored hotel making stunning use of materials like silver, mahogany, silk and marble. Luxurious bedrooms with sensual curves, sumptuous bathrooms and a great spa – and there is substance behind the style. Down a sweeping staircase to the Alain Ducasse restaurant.
Rivea – See restaurant listing

Dinner by Heston Blumenthal – Mandarin Oriental Hyde Park Hotel

Plan: F4

66 Knightsbridge ⊠ *SW1X 7LA –* Ⓜ *Knightsbridge*
– ℰ (020) 7201 3833 – www.dinnerbyheston.com
Menu £ 38 (weekday lunch) – Carte £ 63/111
• British modern • Design • Fashionable •

Don't come expecting 'molecular gastronomy' – this is all about respect for, and a wonderful renewal of, British food, with just a little playfulness thrown in. Each one of the meticulously crafted and deceptively simple looking dishes comes with a date relating to its historical provenance.
→ Mandarin, chicken liver parfait and grilled bread, (c.1500). Chicken with lettuce, grilled onion emulsion, spiced celeriac sauce and oyster leaves, (c.1670). Tipsy cake with spit-roast pineapple, (c.1810).

Bar Boulud

Plan: F4

66 Knightsbridge ⊠ *SW1X 7LA –* Ⓜ *Knightsbridge*
– ℰ (020) 72352000 – www.mandarinoriental.com/london
Menu £ 19 (weekday lunch) – Carte £ 26/57
• French • Brasserie • Fashionable •

Daniel Boulud's London outpost is fashionable, fun and frantic. His hometown is Lyon but he built his considerable reputation in New York, so charcuterie, sausages and burgers are the highlights.

Rivea – Bulgari Hotel

Plan: F4

171 Knightsbridge ⊠ *SW7 1DW –* Ⓜ *Knightsbridge*
– ℰ (020) 7151 1025 – www.rivealondon.com
Menu £ 35 (lunch) – Carte £ 21/42
• Mediterranean • Design • Fashionable •

Elegant basement restaurant where blues and whites make reference to warmer climes – and also to its sister in St Tropez. Precise, unfussy cooking focuses on the French and Italian Riviera, with an interesting range of vibrant small plates.

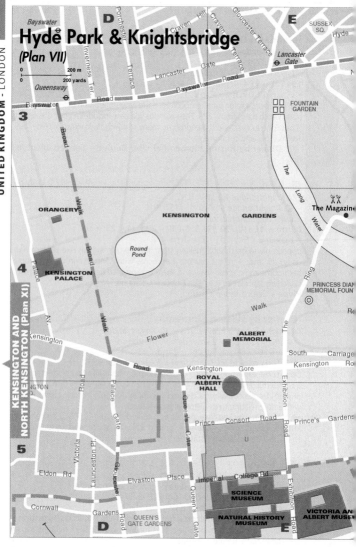

Hyde Park & Knightsbridge
(Plan VII)

KENSINGTON AND NORTH KENSINGTON (Plan XI)

XX **The Magazine** 🛱 🛒 ♿ 🅰🅲

Serpentine Sackler Gallery, West Carriage Dr, Kensington Plan: **E4**
Gardens ⊠ W2 2AR – ⓂLancaster Gate – ℘ (020) 7298 7552
– www.magazine-restaurant.co.uk – Closed Monday and dinner in winter
Menu £ 22 (lunch) – Carte £ 27/51 – (lunch only and dinner Friday-Saturday)
• Modern cuisine • Design • Individual •
Designed by Zaha Hadid, the Serpentine Sackler Gallery comprises a restored
1805 gunpowder store and a modern tensile extension. The Magazine is a bright
open space which serves modern European cuisine.

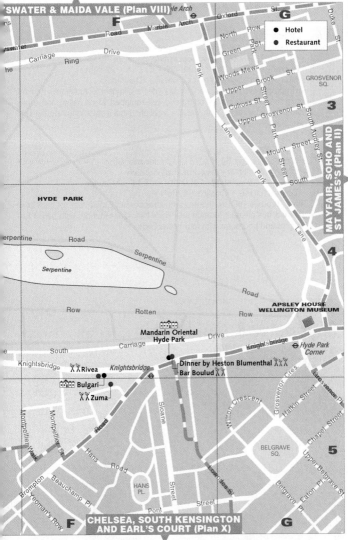

SWATER & MAIDA VALE (Plan VIII) *le Arch*

F **G**

● Hotel
● Restaurant

HYDE PARK

Serpentine

APSLEY HOUSE
WELLINGTON MUSEUM

Mandarin Oriental
Hyde Park

✗✗ **Rivea**

Bulgari
✗✗ **Zuma**

Dinner by Heston Blumenthal ✗✗✗
Bar Boulud ✗✗

Hyde Park
Corner

GROSVENOR
SQ.

3

4

BELGRAVE
SQ.

HANS
PL.

5

F **G**

CHELSEA, SOUTH KENSINGTON
AND EARL'S COURT (Plan X)

MAYFAIR, SOHO AND
ST JAMES'S (Plan II)

✗✗ **Zuma**   AC

5 Raphael St ⊠ SW7 1DL – Ⓜ Knightsbridge – ℰ (020)   Plan: **F5**
75841010 – www.zumarestaurant.com
– Closed 25 December
Carte £ 33/79 – *(booking essential)*
• Japanese • Fashionable •

Now a global brand but this was the original. The glamorous clientele come for the striking surroundings, bustling atmosphere and easy-to-share food. Go for the more modern dishes and those cooked on the robata grill.

Lancaster London

※ ≤ ⅙ ಓ ㎉ ⅍ 🄿

Lancaster Terr ⊠ *W2 2TY –* Ⓜ *Lancaster Gate*
– ℰ *(020) 75516000 – www.lancasterlondon.com*

Plan: **E3**

416 rm – †£ 129/429 ††£ 129/429 – ☲ £ 16 – 22 suites
• Business • Conference hotel • Classic •

An imposing 1960s hotel overlooking Hyde Park, known for its extensive conference suites. Bedrooms are bright and well-equipped. Island has an accessible, Med-influenced menu, with steaks a highlight; Nipa is their longstanding Thai restaurant.

Royal Park

㎉ 🄿

3 Westbourne Terr ⊠ *W2 3UL –* Ⓜ *Lancaster Gate*
– ℰ *(020) 74796600 – www.theroyalpark.com*

Plan: **E3**

48 rm – †£ 191/299 ††£ 191/299 – ☲ £ 14 – 11 suites
• Townhouse • Cosy • Stylish •

Three attractive 19C townhouses, with an appealing English feel, set back from the road, in a pleasant location near Hyde Park. Quiet lounges with period furnishings and bedrooms with four-poster beds.

Hotel Indigo London Paddington

16 London St ✉ W2 1HL – Ⓜ Paddington Plan: **E2**
– ✆ (020) 7706 4444
– www.hotelindigo.com
64 rm – †£ 109/279 ††£ 129/379 – ☕ £ 20
• Business • Modern •

Behind the period façade is a modern, corporate townhouse themed around the Golden ratio, a mathematical formula. Bright rooms have feature walls depicting scenes of the local area. All-day menu of steaks, pasta and brasserie classics.

Angelus

4 Bathurst St ✉ W2 2SD – Ⓜ Lancaster Gate Plan: **E3**
– ✆ (020) 74020083 – www.angelusrestaurant.co.uk
– Closed 24 December-2 January
Menu £ 22 (lunch) – Carte £ 42/59
• French • Brasserie • Neighbourhood •

Hospitable owner has created an attractive French brasserie within a 19C former pub, with a warm and inclusive feel. Satisfying and honest French cooking uses seasonal British ingredients.

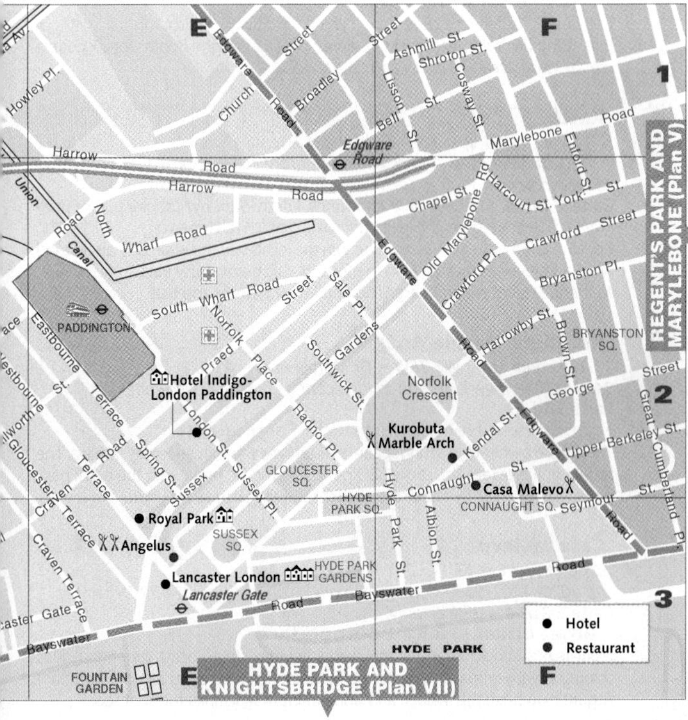

XX **Marianne** AC
104a Chepstow Rd ⊠ *W2 5QS –* ⓜ *Westbourne Park* Plan: **C2**
– ℰ (020) 3675 7750 – www.mariannerestaurant.com – Closed Christmas-New Year, 26-28 August and Monday
Menu £ 65/85 – *(dinner only and lunch Friday-Sunday) (booking essential) (set menu only)*
• French • Cosy • Individual •
The eponymous Marianne was a finalist on MasterChef. Her restaurant is a sweet little place with just 6 tables. A concise daily menu lets her own cooking style come through – it's classically based but keeps things quite light.

XX **Toa Kitchen** AC
100 Queensway ⊠ *W2 3RR –* ⓜ *Bayswater – ℰ (020)* Plan: **D3**
77929767 – www.toakitchen.com – Closed 25 December
Carte £ 14/58
• Chinese • Friendly • Traditional •
There's an overwhelming number of Chinese restaurants on Queensway so search out Toa Kitchen and head for the Chef's Specials for good, authentic Cantonese dishes. Service from owner Mr Fung and his team is also a cut above average.

X **Hereford Road** AC
ⓐ *3 Hereford Rd* ⊠ *W2 4AB –* ⓜ *Bayswater – ℰ (020)* Plan: **C2**
77271144 – www.herefordroad.org – Closed 24 December-3 January and 27-29 August
Menu £ 14 (weekday lunch) – Carte £ 23/32 – *(booking essential)*
• British traditional • Neighbourhood •
Converted butcher's shop specialising in tasty British dishes without frills, using first-rate, seasonal ingredients; offal a highlight. Booths for six people are the prized seats. Friendly and relaxed feel.

X **Kateh** AC
ⓐ *5 Warwick Pl* ⊠ *W9 2PX –* ⓜ *Warwick Avenue* Plan: **D1**
– ℰ (020) 7289 3393 – www.katehrestaurant.co.uk – Closed 25-26 December
Carte £ 19/36 – *(dinner only and lunch Friday-Sunday) (booking essential)*
• Mediterranean • Neighbourhood • Intimate •
Booking is imperative if you want to join the locals who have already discovered what a little jewel they have in the form of this buzzy, busy Persian restaurant. Authentic stews, expert chargrilling and lovely pastries and teas.

X **Kurobuta Marble Arch** AC
17-20 Kendal St ⊠ *W2 2AW –* ⓜ *Marble Arch – ℰ (020)* Plan: **F2**
3475 4158 – www.kurobuta-london.com – Closed 25 December
Carte £ 17/32
• Japanese • Neighbourhood • Fashionable •
The Aussie owner-chef's fun Japanese restaurant was influenced by izakaya. The robata grill provides the sticky BBQ pork belly for the pork buns; the black pepper soft shell crabs fly out of the kitchen; and the yuzu tart is good.

X **Casa Malevo** AC
23 Connaught St ⊠ *W2 2AY –* ⓜ *Marble Arch* Plan: **F2**
– ℰ (020) 74021988 – www.casamalevo.com – Closed 24-29 December
Carte £ 21/44 – *(dinner only)*
• Argentinian • Neighbourhood •
Meat lovers should head for this warm, country style 'cocina Argentina'. Kick things off with empanadas or homemade chorizo then order a cut of premium Argentinian beef; the Malbec and bone marrow sauce hits the spot too.

Truscott Arms

Plan: B2

55 Shirland Rd ✉ W9 2JD – Ⓜ Warwick Avenue.
– ✆ (020) 7266 9198 – www.thetruscottarms.com
Menu £ 18/36 – Carte £ 24/33
• Modern cuisine • Neighbourhood •
A Victorian pub resuscitated and restored by a husband and wife team. Pub classics on the ground floor; local artwork in upstairs dining room where the ambitious kitchen uses modern techniques to produce quite elaborate dishes.

CITY OF LONDON – SOUTHWARK PLAN IX

City of London

Andaz Liverpool Street

Plan: M2

40 Liverpool St. ✉ EC2M 7QN – Ⓜ Liverpool Street
– ✆ (020) 79611234 – www.andaz.com
267 rm – †£ 173/683 ††£ 189/699 – ☕ £ 18 – 3 suites
• Business • Design • Contemporary •
A contemporary and stylish interior hides behind the classic Victorian façade. Bright and spacious bedrooms boast state-of-the-art facilities. Various dining options include a brasserie specialising in grilled meats, a compact Japanese restaurant and a traditional pub.
1901 – See restaurant listing

Threadneedles

Plan: M3

5 Threadneedle St. ✉ EC2R 8AY – Ⓜ Bank – ✆ (020) 7657 8080 – www.hotelthreadneedles.co.uk
74 rm ☕ – †£ 199/499 ††£ 199/499
• Business • Townhouse • Modern •
A converted bank, dating from 1856, with a smart, boutique feel and a stunning stained-glass cupola in the lounge. Bedrooms are very stylish and individual, featuring Egyptian cotton sheets, iPod docks and thoughtful extras. Spacious bar and restaurant; a striking backdrop to the classical menu.

Apex Temple Court

Plan: K3

1-2 Serjeant's Inn, Fleet St ✉ EC4Y 1LL – Ⓜ Blackfriars
– ✆ (020) 3004 4141 – www.apexhotels.co.uk
184 rm – †£ 120/500 ††£ 120/500 – ☕ £ 21
• Business • Chain hotel • Contemporary •
Smart, corporate hotel fashioned out of former law firm offices and tucked away in a courtyard. Chambers is a well-kept brasserie with a Mediterranean menu. Four grades of bedroom, but all are bright, light and a good size.

Montcalm London City at The Brewery

Plan: M2

52 Chiswell St ✉ EC1Y 4SA – Ⓜ Barbican – ✆ (020) 7614 0100 – www.themontcalmlondoncity.co.uk
235 rm – †£ 168/350 ††£ 168/350 – ☕ £ 25 – 7 suites
• Business • Stylish • Historic •
The majority of the contemporary rooms are in the original part of the Whitbread Brewery, built in 1714; ask for a quieter one overlooking the courtyard, or one of the 25 found in the 4 restored Georgian townhouses across the road.
Chiswell Street Dining Rooms – See restaurant listing

Hotel Indigo London - Tower Hill

Plan: N3

142 Minories ✉ EC3N 1LS – Ⓜ Aldgate – ✆ (020) 7265 1014 – www.hotelindigo.com/lontowerhill
46 rm – †£ 155/395 ††£ 155/395 – ☕ £ 9
• Business • Modern • Design •
Quieter than its city location would suggest, this business hotel comes with funky modern bedrooms equipped with iPod docks and coffee machines. Tower Bridge and Tower Hill suites have skyline views. Popular menu in Square Mile brasserie.

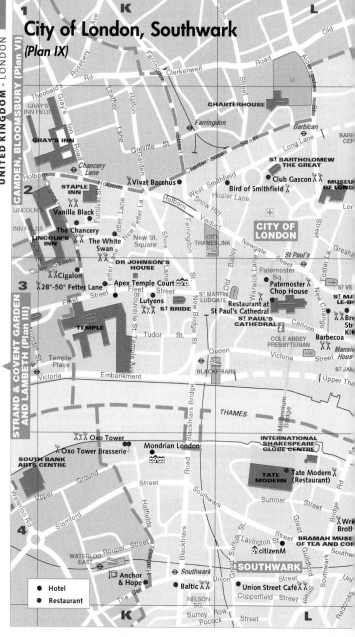

City of London, Southwark
(Plan IX)

CHARTERHOUSE

GRAY'S INN FIELD

GRAY'S INN

Farringdon

Barbican

BARB CEN

ST BARTHOLOMEW THE GREAT

Club Gascon

MUSEUM OF LOND

Lor

STAPLE INN

LINCOLN'S INN FIELDS

Vivat Bacchus

Bird of Smithfield

Hosier Lane

Vanilla Black

The Chancery

LINCOLN'S INN

The White Swan

CITY OF LONDON

CITY THAMESLINK

St Paul's

Gresha

Cigalon

DR JOHNSON'S HOUSE

Apex Temple Court

Paternoster Sq.

ST VE

28°-50° Fetter Lane

Lutyens

ST BRIDE

Restaurant at St Paul's Cathedral

Paternoster Chop House

ST MA LE-B

St Br Str Kit

TEMPLE

ST MARTIN LUDGATE

ST PAUL'S CATHEDRAL

Barbecoa

COLE ABBEY PRESBYTERIAN

Mansi Hous

Temple Place

BLACKFRIARS

Victoria

ST JAM

Upper Th

THAMES

Millennium Bridge

INTERNATIONAL SHAKESPEARE GLOBE CENTRE

Oxo Tower

Oxo Tower Brasserie

Mondrian London

SOUTH BANK ARTS CENTRE

TATE MODERN

Tate Modern (Restaurant)

Wr Broth

WATERLOO EAST

BRAMAH MUSE OF TEA AND COF

citizenM

SOUTHWARK

Anchor & Hope

Southwark

Baltic

Union Street Café

NELSON SQ.

Copperfield Street

Surrey Row

Pocock

●	Hotel
●	Restaurant

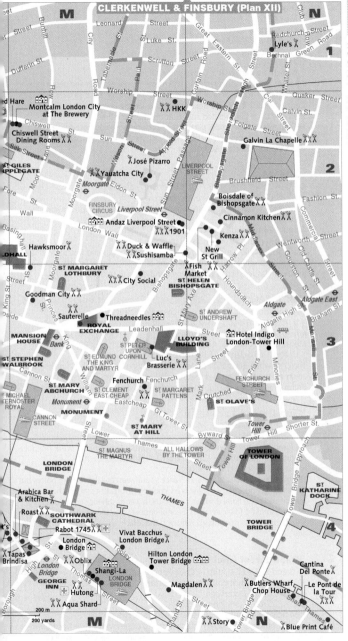

Leonard   Street

Luke   St.

Scrutton   Street

Worship   Street

×× HKK

Galvin La Chapelle ×××

Montcalm London City
at The Brewery

Chiswell Street
Dining Rooms ××

×× José Pizarro

×× Yauatcha City

Moorgate

Boisdale of
Bishopsgate ××

Cinnamon Kitchen ×××

Kenza ××

Andaz Liverpool Street

×××1901

New
St Grill

Hawksmoor ×

×× Duck & Waffle
×× Sushisamba

St Margaret
Lothbury

××× City Social

Goodman City ××

Fish
Market
××

St Helen
Bishopsgate

St Andrew
Undershaft

Aldgate

Aldgate East

Sauterelle ● Threadneedles

Royal
Exchange

Mansion
House

Bank

Hotel Indigo
London-Tower Hill

Leadenhall

St Peter
Upon
Cornhill

Lloyd's
Building

St Stephen
Walbrook

St Edmund
The King
and Martyr

Luc's
Brasserie ××

Fenchurch

St Clement
East Cheap

Fenchurch

St Margaret
Pattens

St Olave's

St Mary
Abchurch

Monument ⊖

Eastcheap

Monument

Cannon
Street

St Mary
at Hill

Tower
Hill   Hill   Shorter St.

London
Bridge

St Magnus
The Martyr

All Hallows
By The Tower

Tower of
London

St Katharine
Dock

Arabica Bar
& Kitchen ×

THAMES

Roast ××

Southwark
Cathedral

Tower
Bridge

Rabot 1745 ×××

Vivat Bacchus
London Bridge ×

London
Bridge

Hilton London
Tower Bridge

×× Oblix

× Tapas
Brindisa

London
Bridge

Shangi-La

Cantina
Del Ponte ×

George
Inn

Magdalen ××

× Butlers Wharf
Chop House

Le Pont de
la Tour
×××

×× Hutong

×× Aqua Shard

200 m
200 yards

×× Story ●

× Blue Print Café

917

UNITED KINGDOM - LONDON

XxX **City Social**   🕸 ≼ 🕭 🄰🄲 ⇔
盟   *Tower 42 (24th floor), 25 Old Broad St ✉ EC2N 1HQ*   Plan: **M3**
   – 🚇 *Liverpool Street*
   – 𝒞 *(020) 78777703 – www.citysociallondon.com*
   – *Closed Sunday and bank holidays*
   Carte £ 34/70
   • Modern cuisine • Elegant • Design •
   Jason Atherton took over in 2014 and made the place bigger and better looking
   with a darker, moodier feel. The City views are as impressive as ever, especially
   from tables 10 & 15. The flexible menu is largely European and the cooking
   manages to be both refined and robust at the same time.
   → Yellow fin tuna tataki, cucumber salad, radish and avocado. Saddle and
   sausage of Lincolnshire rabbit with mustard mash and garlic. Pistachio
   soufflé with chocolate sorbet.

XxX **Lutyens**   🕸 🄰🄲 ⇔
   85 Fleet St. ✉ EC4Y 1AE – 🚇 Blackfriars – 𝒞 (020)   Plan: **K3**
   7583 8385 – www.lutyens-restaurant.com
   – *Closed 1 week Christmas-New Year, Saturday, Sunday and bank
   holidays*
   Menu £ 24 (weekday lunch)/30 – Carte £ 28/62
   • Modern cuisine • Fashionable •
   The unmistakable hand of Sir Terence Conran: timeless and understated good
   looks mixed with functionality, and an appealing Anglo-French menu with
   plenty of classics such as fruits de mer and game in season.

XxX **1901** – Andaz Liverpool Street Hotel   🕭 🄰🄲
   Liverpool St. ✉ EC2M 7QN – 🚇 Liverpool Street   Plan: **M2**
   – 𝒞 *(020) 76187000 – www.andaz.com – Closed Christmas, Saturday
   lunch, Sunday and bank holidays*
   Menu £ 26 – Carte £ 34/53
   • British modern • Elegant • Luxury •
   The crisp white decoration and judicious lighting highlight the immense Doric
   columns, the cornicing and the beautiful cupola above. The menu champions
   British produce and the cooking is modern and quite ambitious in its reach.

XX **Club Gascon** (Pascal Aussignac)   🕸 🄰🄲
盟 *57 West Smithfield ✉ EC1A 9DS – 🚇 Barbican*   Plan: **L2**
   – 𝒞 *(020) 76006144 – www.clubgascon.com*
   – *Closed Christmas-New Year, Saturday lunch, Sunday and bank holidays*
   Menu £ 29 (lunch)/65 – Carte £ 36/63 – *(booking essential)*
   • French • Intimate • Elegant •
   The gastronomy of Gascony and France's southwest are the starting points but
   the assured and intensely flavoured cooking also pushes at the boundaries.
   Marble and huge floral displays create suitably atmospheric surroundings.
   → Pine-smoked foie gras with Génépi liqueur, croissant and hay ice cream.
   Squab pigeon with rhubarb, chicory and black garlic. Chocolate 'million-
   aire'.

XX **Bread Street Kitchen**   🄰🄲
   10 Bread St ✉ EC4M 9AJ – 🚇 St Paul's – 𝒞 (020)   Plan: **L3**
   3030 4050 – www.breadstreetkitchen.com
   – *Closed 25-26 December*
   Carte £ 27/65 – *(booking advisable)*
   • Modern cuisine • Trendy • Brasserie •
   Gordon Ramsay's take on NY loft-style dining comes with a large bar, thumping
   music, an open kitchen and enough zinc ducting to kit out a small industrial
   estate. For the food, think modern bistro dishes with an element of refinement.

XX **New St Grill** 🏨 ☕ 🕭 AC

16a New St ✉ *EC2M 4TR –* Ⓜ *Liverpool Street*   Plan: **N2**
– ℰ (020) 3503 0785 – www.newstreetgrill.com – Closed 23 December-
7 January except dinner 31 December and Sunday dinner
Menu £ 27 (lunch and early dinner) – Carte £ 32/66
• Meats • Friendly • Intimate •
D&D converted an 18C warehouse to satisfy our increasing appetite for red
meat. They use Black Angus beef: grass-fed British, aged for 28 days, or corn-
fed American, aged for 40 days. Start with a drink in the Old Bengal Bar.

XX **Sauterelle** 🕭 ✿ 🕼

The Royal Exchange ✉ *EC3V 3LR –* Ⓜ *Bank – ℰ (020)*   Plan: **M3**
76182483 – www.royalexchange-grandcafe.co.uk – Closed Easter,
Saturday, Sunday and bank holidays
Menu £ 29 – Carte £ 37/55
• French • Design •
Impressive location on the mezzanine floor of The Royal Exchange; ask for a
table overlooking the Grand Café which was the original trading floor. A largely
French-inspired contemporary menu makes good use of luxury ingredients.

XX **Sushisamba** ⪕ ☕ AC

Heron Tower (38th and 39th Floor), 110 Bishopsgate   Plan: **M2**
✉ *EC2N 4AY –* Ⓜ *Liverpool Street – ℰ (020) 3640 7330*
– www.sushisamba.com
Carte £ 30/66 – *(booking essential)*
• Japanese • Trendy • Fashionable •
Stunning views, a great destination bar and a menu that blends Japanese, Peru-
vian and Brazilian influences – it may not come cheap but this US import is all
about giving its young, fashionable fan base a fun night out.

XX **The Chancery** AC ✿

9 Cursitor St ✉ *EC4A 1LL –* Ⓜ *Chancery Lane – ℰ (020)*   Plan: **K2**
78314000 – www.thechancery.co.uk – Closed 23 December-4 January,
Saturday lunch, Sunday and bank holidays
Menu £ 40/47
• Modern cuisine • Formal • Neighbourhood •
An elegant restaurant that's so close to the law courts you'll assume your fellow
diners are barristers, jurors or the recently acquitted. The menu is appealingly
concise; dishes come with a classical backbone and bold flavours.

XX **Fenchurch** ⪕ 🕭 AC ✿

Level 37, 20 Fenchurch St ✉ *EC3M 3BY*   Plan: **M3**
– Ⓜ *Monument – ℰ (0333) 772 0020 – www.skygarden.london – Closed*
Sunday dinner
Carte £ 41/63 – *(booking advisable)*
• Modern cuisine • Design •
Arrive at the 'Walkie Talkie' early so you can first wander round the Sky Garden
and take in the views. The smartly dressed restaurant is housed in a glass box
within the atrium. Dishes are largely British; flavour combinations are comple-
mentary and ingredients top drawer.

XX **Vanilla Black** AC 🕼

17-18 Tooks Ct. ✉ *EC4A 1LB –* Ⓜ *Chancery Lane*   Plan: **K2**
– ℰ (020) 72422622 – www.vanillablack.co.uk – Closed 2 weeks Christmas
and bank holidays
Menu £ 25/42
• Creative • Intimate • Individual •
Proving that vegetarian food can be flavoursome, creative and satisfying, with a
menu that is varied, imaginative and, at times, ambitious. This is a well-run,
friendly restaurant with understated décor, run by a husband and wife.

UNITED KINGDOM - LONDON

UNITED KINGDOM - LONDON

XX **Yauatcha City** 🛱 & 🄰🄲 ⟷

Broadgate Circle ⊠ *EC2M 2QS –* Ⓜ *Liverpool Street* Plan: **M2**
*– ℰ (020) 38179880 – www.yauatcha.com – Closed 25 December and
Sunday*
Menu £ 40 – Carte £ 24/56
• Chinese • Fashionable •
A more corporate version of the stylish Soho original, with a couple of bars and
a terrace at both ends. All the dim sum greatest hits are on the menu but the
chefs have some work to match the high standard found in Broadwick Street.

XX **Cinnamon Kitchen** 🛱 & 🄰🄲 ⟷ 🕾

9 Devonshire Sq ⊠ *EC2M 4YL –* Ⓜ *Liverpool Street* Plan: **N2**
*– ℰ (020) 76265000 – www.cinnamon-kitchen.com – Closed Saturday
lunch, Sunday and bank holidays*
Menu £ 19 (lunch and early dinner) – Carte £ 26/50
• Indian • Trendy • Minimalist •
Sister to The Cinnamon Club. Contemporary Indian cooking, with punchy fla-
vours and arresting presentation. Sprightly service in large, modern surroun-
dings. Watch the action from the Tandoor Bar.

XX **Kenza** 🄰🄲 ⟷

10 Devonshire Sq. ⊠ *EC2M 4YP –* Ⓜ *Liverpool Street* Plan: **N2**
*– ℰ (020) 79295533 – www.kenza-restaurant.com – Closed 24-
25 December, Saturday lunch and bank holidays*
Menu £ 30/50 – Carte £ 29/71
• Lebanese • Exotic • Design •
Exotic basement restaurant, with lamps, carvings, pumping music and nightly
belly dancing. Lebanese and Moroccan cooking are the menu influences and
the food is authentic and accurate.

XX **Cigalon** 🄰🄲 ⟷

115 Chancery Ln ⊠ *WC2A 1PP –* Ⓜ *Chancery Lane* Plan: **K3**
*– ℰ (020) 7242 8373 – www.cigalon.co.uk – Closed Christmas and New
Year, Saturday, Sunday and bank holidays*
Menu £ 22 (weekdays)/33 – Carte £ 25/43
• French • Intimate • Formal •
Pays homage to the food and wine of Provence, in an appropriately bright
space that was a once an auction house. All the classics are here, from bouilla-
baisse to pieds et paquets. Busy bar in the cellar.

XX **Boisdale of Bishopsgate** 🄰🄲

Swedeland Crt, 202 Bishopsgate ⊠ *EC2M 4NR* Plan: **N2**
– Ⓜ *Liverpool Street – ℰ (020) 72831763 – www.boisdale.co.uk – Closed
Saturday lunch, Sunday and bank holidays*
Carte £ 29/59
• British traditional • Intimate • Cosy •
It's champagne and oysters on the ground floor and Scottish hospitality and live
jazz in the clubby, unapologetically masculine vaulted restaurant below. Enjoy
smoked salmon, roast haggis and dry-aged, grass-fed Aberdeenshire beef.

XX **The White Swan** 🄰🄲

108 Fetter Ln (1st floor) ⊠ *EC4A 1ES* Plan: **K2**
– Ⓜ *Chancery Lane – ℰ (020) 72429696 – www.thewhiteswanlondon.com
– Closed 25-26 December, Saturday, Sunday and bank holidays*
Menu £ 29 (lunch and early dinner) – Carte £ 27/48
• Modern cuisine • Elegant • Intimate •
The classically educated kitchen uses British ingredients but also flavours from
the Med. To reach this clubby, part-panelled first floor room – a haven of sere-
nity – one must fight through the hordes of drinkers on the ground floor.

XX **Manicomio** `AC`

6 Gutter Ln ⊠ EC2V 8AS – Ⓜ St Paul's   Plan: **L3**
– ℰ (020) 77265010 – www.manicomio.co.uk
– Closed 1 week Christmas, Saturday, Sunday and bank holidays
Carte £ 28/51
• Italian • Brasserie • Fashionable •

They serve breakfast, cater for private parties, operate a café, provide takeaway, serve drinks and run a restaurant – all within this Norman Foster designed building. The regional Italian fare makes good use of quality ingredients.

XX **Luc's Brasserie**

17-22 Leadenhall Mkt ⊠ EC3V 1LR – Ⓜ Bank   Plan: **M3**
– ℰ (020) 76210666 – www.lucsbrasserie.com
– Closed Christmas, New Year, Saturday, Sunday and bank holidays
Menu £ 18 (lunch) – Carte £ 26/71 – (lunch only and dinner Tuesday-Thursday) (booking essential)
• French • Brasserie • Elegant •

A classic French brasserie looking down on the Victorian splendour of Leadenhall Market and run with impressive efficiency. The menu has all the French favourites you'll ever need, along with steaks in all sizes and chops aplenty.

XX **Barbecoa** `AC`

20 New Change Passage ⊠ EC4M 9AG – Ⓜ St Paul's   Plan: **L3**
– ℰ (020) 3005 8555 – www.barbecoa.com
– Closed 1 January, 31 August and 24-26 December
Menu £ 55/85 – Carte £ 32/64 – (booking essential)
• Meats • Design • Brasserie •

Set up by Jamie Oliver, to show us what barbecuing is all about. The prime meats, butchered in-house, are just great; go for the pulled pork shoulder with cornbread on the side. By dessert you may be willing to share.

XX **Goodman City** ♿ `AC` ⇪

11 Old Jewry ⊠ EC2R 8DU – Ⓜ Bank – ℰ (020)   Plan: **M3**
7600 8220 – www.goodmanrestaurants.com
– Closed Saturday, Sunday and bank holidays
Menu £ 22 (lunch) – Carte £ 43/66
• Meats • Design • Bistro •

Machismo reigns at this archetypal steakhouse with corn-fed, wet-aged USDA steaks and grass-fed, dry-aged Irish and Scottish steaks. All are perfectly cooked on the Josper grill, although starters and sides aren't quite as good.

XX **Chiswell Street Dining Rooms** – Montcalm London City

56 Chiswell St ⊠ EC1Y 4SA – Ⓜ Barbican   ♿ `AC` 🐾
– ℰ (020) 7614 0177 – www.chiswellstreetdining.com   Plan: **M2**
– Closed 25-26 December, 1 January, Saturday and Sunday
Menu £ 27 – Carte £ 29/55
• British modern • Individual • Brasserie •

The Martin brothers used their Botanist restaurant as the model for this corner of the old Whitbread Brewery. The cocktail bar comes alive at night. Makes good use of British produce, especially fish from nearby Billingsgate.

XX **Duck & Waffle**　　　　　　　　≼ 🖢 🄰🄲 ⇔

Heron Tower (40th floor), 110 Bishopsgate　　　Plan: **M2**
✉ *EC2N 4AY –* Ⓜ *Liverpool Street – 𝒞 (020) 3640 7310*
– www.duckandwaffle.com
Carte £ 26/68 *– (booking essential)*
• **Modern cuisine** • **Trendy** • **Romantic** •
The UK's highest restaurant, on the 40th floor of Heron Tower, is a cheaper and
less excitable alternative to Sushisamba one floor down. The menu is varied and
offal is done well – try the crispy pig's ears. It's open 24 hours a day.

X **Bird of Smithfield**　　　　　　　　🄰🄲 ⇔

26 Smithfield St ✉ *EC1A 9LB –* Ⓜ *Farringdon – 𝒞 (020)*　Plan: **L2**
*7559 5100 – www.birdofsmithfield.com – Closed Christmas, New Year,
Sunday and bank holidays*
Carte £ 28/46 *– (booking essential)*
• **British traditional** • **Design** • **Intimate** •
Feels like a private members' club but without the smugness. Five floors of fun
include a cocktail bar, lounge, rooftop terrace and small, friendly restaurant. The
appealing British menu makes good use of the country's larder.

X **Hawksmoor**　　　　　　　　🕸 🄰🄲 ⇔

10-12 Basinghall St ✉ *EC2V 5BQ –* Ⓜ *Bank – 𝒞 (020)*　Plan: **M3**
*7397 8120 – www.thehawksmoor.com – Closed 24 December-2 January,
Saturday, Sunday and bank holidays*
Menu £ 27 (lunch and early dinner) – Carte £ 23/83 *– (booking essential)*
• **Meats** • **Traditional** • **Brasserie** •
Fast and furious, busy and boisterous, this handsome room is the backdrop for
another testosterone filled celebration of the serious business of beef eating.
Nicely aged and rested Longhorn steaks take centre-stage.

X **José Pizarro**　　　　　　　　🍴 🖢 🄰🄲

36 Broadgate Circle ✉ *EC2M 1QS –* Ⓜ *Liverpool Street*　Plan: **M2**
– 𝒞 (020) 72565333 – www.josepizarro.com – Closed Sunday
Carte £ 24/31
• **Spanish** • **Tapas bar** •
The eponymous chef's third operation is a good fit here: it's well run, flexible
and fairly priced – and that includes the wine list. The Spanish menu is nicely
balanced, with the fish and seafood dishes being the standouts.

X **Fish Market**　　　　　　　　🍴 🖢 🄰🄲

16b New St ✉ *EC2M 4TR –* Ⓜ *Liverpool Street*　Plan: **N2**
*– 𝒞 (020) 3503 0790 – www.fishmarket-restaurant.co.uk – Closed 25-
26 December, 1 January, Sunday and bank holidays*
Menu £ 20 – Carte £ 26/68 *– (booking advisable)*
• **Fish and seafood** • **Friendly** • **Individual** •
How to get to the seaside from Liverpool Street? Simply step into this bright fish
restaurant, in an old warehouse of the East India Company, and you'll almost
hear the seagulls. The menu is lengthy and the cooking style classic.

X **Vivat Bacchus**　　　　　　　　🕸 🄰🄲 ⇔

47 Farringdon St ✉ *EC4A 4LL –* Ⓜ *Farringdon*　Plan: **K2**
*– 𝒞 (020) 73532648 – www.vivatbacchus.co.uk – Closed Christmas and
New Year, Saturday, Sunday and bank holidays*
Carte £ 21/92
• **Meats** • **Wine bar** • **Friendly** •
Wine is the star at this bustling City spot: from 4 cellars come 500 labels and
15,000 bottles. The menu complements the wine: steaks, charcuterie, sharing
platters and South African specialities feature along with great cheese.

✗ **Paternoster Chop House** 🏠 AC

Warwick Ct., Paternoster Sq. ✉ *EC4M 7DX* — Plan: **L3**
— Ⓜ *St Paul's* – ✆ *(020) 70299400 – www.paternosterchophouse.co.uk*
– *Closed Christmas and dinner Saturday and Sunday*
Menu £ 20 (lunch and early dinner) – Carte £ 22/54
• **British traditional** • **Brasserie** • **Trendy** •
Appropriately British menu in a restaurant lying in the shadow of St Paul's Cathedral. Large, open room with full-length windows; busy bar attached. Kitchen uses thoughtfully sourced produce.

✗ **28°-50° Fetter Lane** 🍸 AC ⇔

140 Fetter Ln ✉ *EC4A 1BT* – Ⓜ *Temple* – ✆ *(020)* — Plan: **K3**
72428877 – www.2850.co.uk – Closed Saturday, Sunday and bank holidays
Menu £ 20 (weekday lunch) – Carte £ 27/33
• **Modern cuisine** • **Wine bar** • **Simple** •
From the owners of Texture comes this cellar wine bar and informal restaurant. The terrific wine list is thoughtfully compiled and the grills, cheeses, charcuterie and European dishes are designed to allow the wines to shine.

✗ **Restaurant at St Paul's Cathedral** ⇔

St Paul's Churchyard ✉ *EC4M 8AD* – Ⓜ *St Paul's* — Plan: **L3**
– ✆ *(020) 72481574 – www.restaurantatstpauls.co.uk – Closed 25 December and Good Friday*
Menu £ 15/45 – Carte £ 23/36 – *(lunch only) (booking advisable)*
• **British modern** • **Bistro** • **Simple** •
Tucked away in a corner of the crypt of Sir Christopher Wren's 17C masterpiece, offering respite to tired tourists and weary worshippers. The monthly menu is reassuringly concise, seasonal and a celebration of all things British.

🍴 **Jugged Hare** AC ⇔ 📷

42 Chiswell St ✉ *EC1Y 4SA* – Ⓜ *Barbican.* – ✆ *(020)* — Plan: **M2**
7614 0134 – www.thejuggedhare.com – Closed 25-26 December
Menu £ 22 (early dinner) – Carte £ 29/59 – *(booking advisable)*
• **British traditional** • **Pub** • **Trendy** •
Vegetarians may feel ill at ease – and not just because of the taxidermy. The atmospheric dining room, with its open kitchen down one side, specialises in stout British dishes, with meats from the rotisserie a highlight.

BERMONDSEY

 Shangri-La 🏊 ≤ Ⅰ₅ 📺 ᕫ AC ♨ 🚗

The Shard, 31 St Thomas St ✉ *SE1 9QU* — Plan: **M4**
– Ⓜ *London Bridge* – ✆ *(020) 7234 8000 – www.shangri-la.com/london*
202 rm – 🛏£ 350/575 🛏🛏£ 350/575 – ☲ £ 32 – 17 suites
• **Luxury** • **Chain hotel** • **Elegant** •
When your hotel occupies floors 34-52 of The Shard, you know it's going to have the wow factor. The pool is London's highest and north-facing bedrooms have the best views. An East-meets-West theme includes the restaurant's menu and afternoon tea when you have a choice of traditional English or Asian.

Hilton London Tower Bridge 🏊 Ⅰ₅ ᕫ AC ♨

5 More London, Tooley St ✉ *SE1 2BY* — Plan: **M4**
– Ⓜ *London Bridge* – ✆ *(020) 30024300 – www.towerbridge.hilton.com*
245 rm – 🛏£ 129/529 🛏🛏£ 129/629 – ☲ £ 20
• **Business** • **Modern** •
Usefully located new-style Hilton hotel with boldly decorated open-plan lobby. Contemporary bedrooms boast well-designed features; 4 floors of executive rooms. The Larder has an international menu.

Bermondsey Square
Bermondsey Sq, Tower Bridge Rd ⊠ SE1 3UN   Plan: **D2**
– Ⓜ London Bridge – ℰ (020) 7378 2450
– www.bermondseysquarehotel.co.uk
80 rm – †£ 99/300 ††£ 99/300 – ⌺ £ 14
• Business • Modern • Design •
Cleverly designed hotel in a regenerated square, with subtle '60s influences and a relaxed, hip feel. Well-equipped bedrooms, including stylish loft suites. British food and grilled meats in the open-plan GB Grill & Bar.

London Bridge
8-18 London Bridge St ⊠ SE1 9SG – Ⓜ London Bridge   Plan: **M4**
– ℰ (020) 78552200 – www.londonbridgehotel.com
138 rm – †£ 430 ††£ 430 – 3 suites
• Business • Historic • Contemporary •
Independently owned hotel with an ornate façade dating from 1915, in one of the oldest parts of London. Modern interior with contemporary bedrooms. Londinium for brasserie dining; Quarter for cocktails.

Le Pont de la Tour
36d Shad Thames, Butlers Wharf ⊠ SE1 2YE   Plan: **N4**
– Ⓜ London Bridge – ℰ (020) 74038403 – www.lepontdelatour.co.uk
– Closed 1 January
Menu £ 15/25 – Carte £ 33/64
• French • Elegant •
Providing, since 1991, seasonal French cooking, an urbane atmosphere and a wonderful riverside location, with views of Tower Bridge. Simpler dishes served in the livelier cocktail bar and grill.

Story (Tom Sellers)
201 Tooley St. ⊠ SE1 2JX – Ⓜ London Bridge – ℰ (020)   Plan: **N5**
7183 2117 – www.restaurantstory.co.uk – Closed 2 weeks Christmas-New Year, Easter, Sunday, Monday and bank holidays
Menu £ 39 (weekday lunch)/95 – (booking essential) (set menu only)
• Modern cuisine • Design • Neighbourhood •
Amazing what you can create out of an old public toilet on a traffic island. In what looks like a Nordic eco-lodge, Tom Sellers offers 6 or 10 courses of earthy yet delicate, playful yet easy to eat dishes; go for 10, as 6 is too few. With just 13 tables, getting a booking is another story.
→ Onion, apple and gin. Herdwick lamb, sheep's yoghurt and ramson. Almond and dill.

Magdalen
152 Tooley St. ⊠ SE1 2TU – Ⓜ London Bridge   Plan: **M4**
– ℰ (020) 74031342 – www.magdalenrestaurant.co.uk – Closed Sunday, Saturday lunch and bank holidays
Menu £ 17 (lunch) – Carte £ 30/42
• British modern • Neighbourhood •
The clever sourcing and confident British cooking will leave you satisfied. Add genial service, an affordable lunch menu and a food-friendly wine list and you have the favourite restaurant of many.

Hutong
Level 33, The Shard, 31 St Thomas St ⊠ SE1 9RY   Plan: **M4**
– Ⓜ London Bridge – ℰ (020) 3011 1257 – www.hutong.co.uk – Closed 25-26 December and 1 January
Menu £ 28 (weekday lunch) – Carte £ 30/62 – (booking essential)
• Chinese • Intimate • Exotic •
You no longer need to fly to Hong Kong to get a view with your Peking duck. On the 33rd floor of The Shard – ask to sit in 'Beijing' – you'll find a menu focusing on the more northerly Chinese regions; specialities include de-boned lamb ribs, soft shell crab and roast duck. Prices are equally vertiginous.

XX **Oblix**

Level 32, The Shard, 31 St Thomas St. ✉ *SE1 9RY*   Plan: **M4**
– Ⓜ *London Bridge* – ✆ *(020) 72686700 – www.oblixrestaurant.com*
Menu £ 29 (weekday lunch)/58 – Carte £ 31/105
• Meats • Trendy • Design •
From the Zuma/Roka people comes this New York grill restaurant, where meat
and fish from the rotisserie, grill and Josper oven are the stars of the show.
Views are far-reaching and there's live music in the adjacent lounge bar.

XX **Aqua Shard**

Level 31, The Shard, 31 St Thomas St ✉ *SE1 9RY*   Plan: **M4**
– Ⓜ *London Bridge* – ✆ *(020) 3011 1256 – www.aquashard.co.uk – Closed
25 December and 1 January*
Menu £ 31 (weekday lunch)/48 – Carte £ 36/65
• Modern cuisine • Fashionable • Design •
The Shard's most accessible restaurant covers all bases by serving breakfast,
brunch, lunch, afternoon tea and dinner. If you don't mind queuing, you can
even come just for a drink. The contemporary cooking makes good use of British ingredients and comes with a degree of finesse in flavour and looks.

X **Blueprint Café**

Design Museum, Shad Thames, Butlers Wharf   Plan: **N5**
✉ *SE1 2YD* – Ⓜ *London Bridge* – ✆ *(020) 73787031*
– www.blueprintcafe.co.uk – Closed 1 January and Sunday dinner
Menu £ 23/25 – Carte £ 30/42
• Modern cuisine • Brasserie •
Large retractable windows make the most of the river views from this bright
restaurant above the Design Museum. The first change of head chef in 16
years was seamless: the cooking remains light, seasonally pertinent and easy
to eat.

X **Village East**

171-173 Bermondsey St ✉ *SE1 3UW*   Plan: **D2**
– Ⓜ *London Bridge* – ✆ *(020) 7357 6082 – www.villageeast.co.uk – Closed
24-26 December*
Carte £ 20/43
• Modern cuisine • Trendy • Neighbourhood •
Counter dining is the focus in the main room; those celebrating can tuck them-
selves away in a separate bar. Cooking mixes contemporary dishes with Medi-
terranean-inspired plates; the confit turkey leg is the house speciality.

X **Cantina Del Ponte**

36c Shad Thames, Butlers Wharf ✉ *SE1 2YE*   Plan: **N4**
– Ⓜ *London Bridge* – ✆ *(020) 74035403 – www.cantina.co.uk – Closed
25 December*
Menu £ 13/23 – Carte £ 20/50
• Italian • Rustic •
This Italian stalwart offers an appealing mix of classic dishes and reliable favouri-
tes from a sensibly priced menu, in pleasant faux-rustic surroundings. Its plea-
sant terrace takes advantage of its riverside setting.

X **Butlers Wharf Chop House**

36e Shad Thames, Butlers Wharf ✉ *SE1 2YE*   Plan: **N4**
– Ⓜ *London Bridge* – ✆ *(020) 7403 3403*
– www.chophouse-restaurant.co.uk – Closed 1 January
Carte £ 29/64
• British traditional • Brasserie • Simple •
Grab a table on the terrace in summer and dine in the shadow of Tower Bridge.
Rustic feel to the interior; noisy and fun. The menu focuses on traditional Eng-
lish ingredients and dishes; grilled meats a speciality.

UNITED KINGDOM - LONDON

X **Vivat Bacchus London Bridge** 🕸

4 Hays Ln ✉ *SE1 2HB –* Ⓜ *London Bridge*   Plan: **M4**
– 𝒞 (020) 72340891 – www.vivatbacchus.co.uk
– Closed Christmas-New Year, Saturday lunch, Sunday and bank holidays
Carte £ 24/47
• Meats • Wine bar • Friendly •
Wines from the South African owners' homeland feature strongly and are well-suited to the meat dishes – the strength here. Choose one of the sharing boards themed around various countries, like Italian hams or South African BBQ.

X **Pizarro** 🆎 ⇄

171-173 Bermondsey St ✉ *SE1 3UW –* Ⓜ *Borough*   Plan: **D2**
– 𝒞 (020) 73789455 – www.josepizarro.com
– Closed 24-28 December
Menu £ 35 – Carte £ 26/55
• Mediterranean • Neighbourhood •
José Pizarro has a refreshingly simple way of naming his establishments: after José, his tapas bar, comes Pizarro, a larger restaurant a few doors down. Go for the small plates, like prawns with piquillo peppers and jamón.

X **Antico** 🆎 🐝

214 Bermondsey St ✉ *SE1 3TQ –* Ⓜ *London Bridge*   Plan: **D2**
– 𝒞 (020) 7407 4682 – www.antico-london.co.uk
– Closed 25 December, 1 January and Monday
Menu £ 15 (lunch and early dinner) – Carte £ 23/38
• Italian • Neighbourhood •
Once an antiques warehouse – hence the name – Antico is fun, bright and breezy, with honest and straightforward Italian food; the homemade pasta is good. Check out the seasonal ragu, risotto and sorbet on the blackboard.

X **Casse Croûte**

109 Bermondsey St ✉ *SE1 3XB –* Ⓜ *London Bridge*   Plan: **D2**
– 𝒞 (020) 7407 2140 – www.cassecroute.co.uk
– Closed Sunday dinner
Carte £ 28/35 – *(booking essential)*
• French • Bistro • Friendly •
Squeeze into this tiny bistro and you'll find yourself transported to rural France. A blackboard menu offers three choices for each course but new dishes are added as others run out. The cooking is rustic, authentic and heartening.

X **José** 🅶 🆎
☺

104 Bermondsey St ✉ *SE1 3UB –* Ⓜ *London Bridge*   Plan: **D2**
– 𝒞 (020) 7403 4902 – www.josepizarro.com – Closed 24-26 December and Sunday dinner
Carte approx. £ 25
• Spanish • Minimalist • Tapas bar •
Standing up while eating tapas feels so right, especially at this small, fun bar that packs 'em in like boquerones. Five dishes each should suffice; go for the daily fish dishes from the blackboard. There's a great list of sherries too.

🛏 **Garrison** 🆎 ⇄

99-101 Bermondsey St ✉ *SE1 3XB –* Ⓜ *London Bridge.*   Plan: **D2**
– 𝒞 (020) 70899355 – www.thegarrison.co.uk – Closed 25-26 December
Carte £ 24/34 – *(booking essential at dinner)*
• Mediterranean • Pub •
Known for its charming vintage look, booths and sweet-natured service, The Garrison boasts a warm, relaxed vibe. Open from breakfast until dinner, when a Mediterranean-led menu pulls in the crowd.

Southwark

Mondrian London

20 Upper Ground ✉ SE1 9PD – Ⓜ Southwark – ✆ (020) 3747 1000 – www.mondrianlondon.com
Plan: K4

359 rm – †£ 195 ††£ 220/600 – ☕ £ 16 – 5 suites

• Business • Design • Stylish •

The former Sea Containers house now has slick, stylish look evoking the golden age of the transatlantic liner. Rooms come with a bright splash of colour; Suites have balconies and Superiors, a river view. Globally influenced small plates in smart restaurant, with meat and fish from the grill & clay oven.

citizenM

20 Lavington St ✉ SE1 0NZ – Ⓜ Southwark – ✆ (020) 3519 1680 – www.citizenm.com
Plan: L4

192 rm – †£ 120/249 ††£ 120/249 – ☕ £ 13

• Business • Design • Functional •

A new type of budget hotel with an eye for the aesthetic. Relaxing, open-plan lobby with sofas, books, tables, desks and a bar for snacks and drinks. Upstairs, the bedrooms may be pod-like but are well-lit and cleverly designed.

Hampton by Hilton

157 Waterloo Rd ✉ SE1 8XA – Ⓜ Waterloo – ✆ (020) 7401 8080 – www.hamptoninn3.hilton.com/en/hotels/united-kingdom/hampton-by-
Plan: C2

297 rm ☕ – †£ 109/299 ††£ 109/299

• Chain hotel • Functional •

A useful budget hotel from Hilton, near the Old Vic and Waterloo. Crisply decorated rooms and plenty of lounge space on the ground floor. Assado is a big, bright restaurant from Cyrus Todiwala fusing Indian and Portuguese cuisine.

Oxo Tower

Oxo Tower Wharf (8th floor), Barge House St ✉ SE1 9PH – Ⓜ Southwark – ✆ (020) 78033888 – www.harveynichols.com – Closed 25 December
Plan: K4

Menu £ 34 (lunch) – Carte £ 42/71

• Modern cuisine • Minimalist •

Top of a converted iconic factory, providing stunning views of the Thames and beyond. Stylish, minimalist interior with huge windows. Expect quite ambitious, mostly European, cuisine.

Oxo Tower Brasserie – See restaurant listing

Roast

The Floral Hall, Borough Mkt ✉ SE1 1TL – Ⓜ London Bridge – ✆ (020) 30066111 – www.roast-restaurant.com – Closed 25-26 December and 1 January
Plan: M4

Carte £ 31/56 – *(booking essential)*

• British modern • Fashionable •

Known for its British food and for promoting UK producers – not surprising considering the restaurant's in the heart of Borough Market. The 'dish of the day' is often a highlight; service is affable and there's live music at night.

Baltic

74 Blackfriars Rd ✉ SE1 8HA – Ⓜ Southwark – ✆ (020) 79281111 – www.balticrestaurant.co.uk – Closed 24-26 December and Monday lunch
Plan: K4

Menu £ 18 (lunch and early dinner) – Carte £ 22/38 – *(bookings advisable at dinner)*

• World cuisine • Brasserie •

In this converted 18C coach builder's works you'll find a big, bright restaurant specialising in Eastern European food – from Poland, Russia, Bulgaria, even Siberia. Dumplings and meat dishes stand out, as do the great vodkas.

UNITED KINGDOM - LONDON

XX **Union Street Café** ₠ 🅐🅚 ⇄

47 - 51 Great Suffolk Street ✉ *SE1 0BS* Plan: **L4**
– Ⓜ *London Bridge* – ℰ *(020) 7592 7977* – *www.gordonramsay.com*
Menu £ 19/29 – Carte £ 26/44
• Italian • Trendy • Design •

Occupying a former warehouse, this Gordon Ramsay restaurant has been busy since day one and comes with a New York feel, a faux industrial look and a basement bar. The Italian menu keeps things simple and stays true to the classics.

XX **Rabot 1745** 🍽 ₠ 🅐🅚 ⇄

2-4 Bedal St, Borough Mkt ✉ *SE1 9AL* Plan: **M4**
– Ⓜ *London Bridge* – ℰ *(020) 73788226* – *www.rabot1745.com* – *Closed 25-26 December, Sunday and Monday*
Carte £ 22/39
• Modern cuisine • Design • Fashionable •

Want something different? How about cocoa cuisine? Rabot 1745 is from the owners of Hotel Chocolat and is named after their estate in St Lucia. They take the naturally bitter, spicy flavours of the bean and use them subtly in classically based dishes. The chocolate mousse dessert is pretty good too!

X **Oxo Tower Brasserie** ≤ 🍽 🅐🅚

Oxo Tower Wharf (8th floor), Barge House St Plan: **K4**
✉ *SE1 9PH* – Ⓜ *Southwark* – ℰ *(020) 78033888*
– *www.harveynichols.com* – *Closed 25 December*
Menu £ 30 (lunch and early dinner) – Carte £ 31/55
• Modern cuisine • Design •

Less formal but more fun than the next-door restaurant. Open-plan kitchen produces modern, colourful and easy-to-eat dishes with influences from the Med. Great views too from the bar.

X **Elliot's**
🐝

12 Stoney St., Borough Market ✉ *SE1 9AD* Plan: **L4**
– Ⓜ *London Bridge* – ℰ *(020) 74037436* – *www.elliotscafe.com* – *Closed Sunday and bank holidays*
Carte £ 19/31 – *(booking advisable)*
• Modern cuisine • Rustic • Friendly •

Open from breakfast onwards, this busy and unpretentious café sources most of its ingredients from Borough Market, in which it stands. The appealing menu is concise and the cooking is earthy, pleasingly uncomplicated and very satisfying.

X **Tate Modern (Restaurant)** ≤ ⇄

Tate Modern (6th floor), Bankside ✉ *SE1 9TG* Plan: **L4**
– Ⓜ *Southwark* – ℰ *(020) 7887 8888* – *www.tate.org.uk* – *Closed 24-26 December*
Menu £ 25 – Carte £ 29/42 – *(lunch only and dinner Friday-Saturday)*
• British modern • Design •

Ask for a front window table facing St Paul's at this big, bright restaurant on Level 6. The menu is seasonal and the influences largely British; the kitchen has a light touch and each dish comes with a suggested wine pairing.

X **Tapas Brindisa** 🍽

18-20 Southwark St, Borough Market ✉ *SE1 1TJ* Plan: **M4**
– Ⓜ *London Bridge* – ℰ *(020) 73578880*
– *www.brindisatapaskitchens.com*
Carte £ 20/32 – *(bookings not accepted)*
• Spanish • Tapas bar •

A blueprint for many of the tapas bars that subsequently sprung up over London. It has an infectious energy and the well-priced, robust dishes include Galician-style hake and black rice with squid; do try the hand-carved Ibérico hams.

Wright Brothers

11 Stoney St., Borough Market ✉ SE1 9AD Plan: **L4**
– Ⓜ London Bridge
– ✆ (020) 74039554 – www.thewrightbrothers.co.uk – Closed bank holidays
Carte £ 29/71 – *(booking advisable)*
• Fish and seafood • Cosy •
Originally an oyster wholesaler; now offers a wide range of oysters along with porter, as well as fruits de mer, daily specials and assorted pies. It fills quickly and an air of contentment reigns.

Arabica Bar & Kitchen

3 Rochester Walk, Borough Mkt ✉ SE1 9AF Plan: **M4**
– Ⓜ London Bridge – ✆ (020) 3011 5151
– www.arabicabarandkitchen.com – Closed 25-27 December, 1 January and Sunday October-March
Carte £ 15/32 – *(bookings advisable at dinner)*
• World cuisine • Rustic • Simple •
The owner-chef once sold mezze in Borough Market so it's no surprise he opened his Levantine-inspired restaurant under a railway arch here. This fun, cavernous place serves sharing plates from Egypt, Syria, Iraq, Jordan and Lebanon.

Anchor & Hope

36 The Cut ✉ SE1 8LP – Ⓜ Southwark. Plan: **K4**
– ✆ (020) 79289898 – www.anchorandhopepub.co.uk
– Closed Christmas-New Year, Sunday dinner, Monday lunch and bank holidays
Menu £ 15 (weekday lunch) – Carte £ 22/41 – *(bookings not accepted)*
• British modern • Pub •
As popular as ever thanks to its congenial feel and lived-in looks but mostly because of the appealingly seasonal menu and the gutsy, bold cooking that delivers on flavour. No reservations so be prepared to wait at the bar.

CHELSEA – SOUTH KENSINGTON – EARL'S COURT PLAN X

Chelsea

Jumeirah Carlton Tower

Cadogan Pl ✉ SW1X 9PY – Ⓜ Knightsbridge – ✆ (020) 72351234 – jumeirah.com/jct Plan: **F5**
216 rm – †£ 350/835 ††£ 350/835 – ☕ £ 32 – 50 suites
• Grand Luxury • Business • Modern •
Imposing international hotel overlooking a leafy square and just yards from all the swanky boutiques. Well-equipped rooftop health club has great views. Generously proportioned bedrooms boast every conceivable facility.
Rib Room – See restaurant listing

Chelsea Harbour

Chelsea Harbour ✉ SW10 0XG – Ⓜ Imperial Wharf Plan 1: **B3**
– ✆ (020) 78233000 – www.thechelseaharbourhotel.co.uk
157 rm – †£ 220/300 ††£ 220/300 – ☕ £ 24
• Luxury • Modern • Contemporary •
Formerly called Wyndham Grand. Modern hotel within an exclusive marina and retail development. Many of the large, well-appointed rooms have balconies for views across the Thames. Bright restaurant offers a wide-ranging menu.

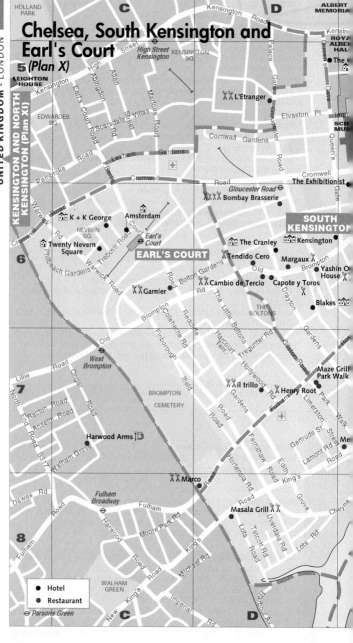

Chelsea, South Kensington and Earl's Court

5 (Plan X)

HOLLAND PARK

ALBERT MEMORIA

LEIGHTON HOUSE

EDWARDES SQ.

High Street Kensington

KENSINGTON SQ.

Kensington Road

The

L'Etranger

Elvaston Pl.

Cornwall Gardens

IMP
SCIE
MUS

Gardens

Cromwell

Road

Cromwell

The Exhibitionist

Gloucester Road

Bombay Brasserie

K + K George

Amsterdam

Earl's Court

NEVERN SQ.

Twenty Nevern Square

EARL'S COURT

The Cranley

Kensington

SOUTH KENSINGTON

Tendido Cero

Margaux

Yashin O
House

Old

Capote y Toros

Blakes

Garnier

Cambio de Tercio

Bolton Gardens

THE BOLTONS

Maze Grill
Park Walk

West Brompton

Old

il trillo

Henry Root

BROMPTON CEMETERY

Harwood Arms

Me

Marco

Fulham Broadway

Fulham

Masala Grill

King's

WALHAM GREEN

● Hotel
● Restaurant
⊖ Parsons Green

UNITED KINGDOM - LONDON

KENSINGTON AND NORTH KENSINGTON (Plan XI)

930

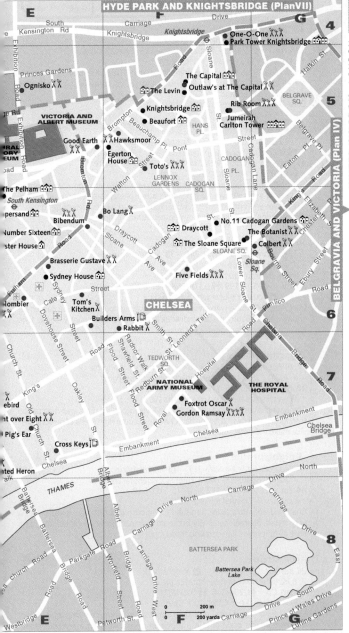

E

South
Kensington Rd

Carriage   Drive

Knightsbridge   Knightsbridge

F

One-O-One
Park Tower Knightsbridge

G

4

Exhibition
Road

Princes Gardens

Ognisko

VICTORIA AND
ALBERT MUSEUM

RAL
ORY
UM
ad

The Pelham

South Kensington

persand

Number Sixteen

ster House

Halkin St

Sloane   Road

The Capital

The Levin   Outlaw's at The Capital

BELGRAVE
SQ.

Knightsbridge

Brompton   Beauchamp

Beaufort

Good Earth

HANS
PL.

Hawksmoor

Egerton
House

Walton   Street

Toto's

Pont   Street

LENNOX
GARDENS

Rib Room

Jumeirah
Carlton Tower

St.   Cadogan   Lane

CADOGAN

CADOGAN
SQ.

BELGRAVE
SQ.

Belgrave Pl.

Eaton   Pl.

King's   Road

Elizabeth   St.

Bo Lang

Draycott

Sloane

Cadogan

Draycott   St.

No.11 Cadogan Gardens

The Botanist

Bibendum

Brasserie Gustave

Sydney House

lombier

Fulham   Road

Sydney   Street

Cale   Street

Tom's
Kitchen

Builders Arms

Rabbit

Draycott   The Sloane Square

Ave   SLOANE SQ.

Ave   Five Fields

Lower Sloane St.

Colbert

Sloane
Sq.

Bourne Street   Ebury   Street

Chester   Street

5

6

CHELSEA

Church St.

King's

ebird

t over Eight

Pig's Ear

Cross Keys

ated Heron

alk

Oakley   Street

Dovehouse Street

Flood   Street

Radnor Walk

Shawfield St.

Redburn St.

Flood St.

Smith   St.

St. Leonard's   Terr.

TEDWORTH
SQ.

NATIONAL
ARMY
MUSEUM

Royal   Hospital   Road

Foxtrot Oscar

Gordon Ramsay

THE ROYAL
HOSPITAL

Chelsea   Embankment

Chelsea
Bridge

Embankment

Chelsea   Bridge

North

7

Church Road   Old   Church   St.

Albert   Bridge   Road

THAMES

Parkgate   Road

Battersea   Bridge   Road

Worfield   Street

Albert   Bridge

Carriage   Drive   North

Carriage   Drive   West

BATTERSEA PARK

Battersea Park
Lake

Carriage   Drive

Prince of Wales Drive

Lurline Gardens

8

Westbridge   Road

Petworth St.

E

0   200 m
0   200 yards

F

Carriage

G

Park Tower Knightsbridge

101 Knightsbridge ⊠ *SW1X 7RN* – Ⓜ *Knightsbridge* — Plan: **F4**
– ℰ *(020) 72358050*
– *www.theparktowerknightsbridge.com*
258 rm – †£ 279/759 ††£ 279/759 – ⊑ £ 29 – 22 suites
• Luxury • Business • Modern •
Built in the 1970s in a unique cylindrical shape. The well-equipped bedrooms
are all identical in size. Top floor executive rooms come with commanding
views of Hyde Park and The City.
One-O-One – See restaurant listing

The Capital

22-24 Basil St. ⊠ *SW3 1AT* – Ⓜ *Knightsbridge* – ℰ *(020)* — Plan: **F5**
75895171 – *www.capitalhotel.co.uk*
49 rm – †£ 250/355 ††£ 295/550 – ⊑ £ 17 – 1 suite
• Luxury • Traditional • Classic •
This fine, thoroughly British hotel has been under the same private ownership
for over 40 years. Known for its discreet atmosphere, conscientious and attentive service and immaculately kept bedrooms courtesy of different designers.
❀ **Outlaw's at The Capital** – See restaurant listing

Draycott

26 Cadogan Gdns ⊠ *SW3 2RP* – Ⓜ *Sloane Square* — Plan: **F6**
– ℰ *(020) 77306466*
– *www.draycotthotel.com*
35 rm – †£ 192/199 ††£ 378/558 – ⊑ £ 22
• Townhouse • Luxury • Stylish •
Charming 19C house with elegant sitting room overlooking tranquil garden for
afternoon tea. Bedrooms are individually decorated in a country house style
and are named after writers or actors.

Egerton House

17-19 Egerton Terr ⊠ *SW3 2BX* – Ⓜ *South Kensington* — Plan: **F5**
– ℰ *(020) 75892412* – *www.egertonhousehotel.com*
28 rm – †£ 295/425 ††£ 295/425 – ⊑ £ 29
• Townhouse • Luxury • Classic •
Compact but comfortable townhouse in a very good location, well-maintained
throughout and owned by the Red Carnation group. High levels of personal service make the hotel stand out.

Knightsbridge

10 Beaufort Gdns ⊠ *SW3 1PT* – Ⓜ *Knightsbridge* — Plan: **F5**
– ℰ *(020) 75846300* – *www.knightsbridgehotel.com*
44 rm – †£ 234/250 ††£ 264/475 – ⊑ £ 18
• Luxury • Townhouse • Stylish •
Charming and attractively furnished townhouse in a Victorian terrace, with a
very stylish, discreet feel. Every bedroom is immaculately appointed and has a
style all of its own; fine detailing throughout.

The Levin

28 Basil St. ⊠ *SW3 1AS* – Ⓜ *Knightsbridge* – ℰ *(020)* — Plan: **F5**
75896286 – *www.thelevinhotel.co.uk*
12 rm ⊑ – †£ 204/316 ††£ 204/316
• Townhouse • Classic • Stylish •
Little sister to The Capital next door. Impressive façade, contemporary interior
and comfortable bedrooms in a subtle art deco style, with marvellous champagne mini bars. Simple dishes served all day down in basement restaurant Le
Metro.

No.11 Cadogan Gardens 🌣 🕭 🖛 🐾 AC
11 Cadogan Gdns ✉ *SW3 2RJ* – ⓜ *Sloane Square*   Plan: F6
– ℰ (020) 7730 7000 – www.no11cadogangardens.com
56 rm – †£ 270/450 ††£ 270/450 – ☲ £ 22 – 19 suites
• Townhouse • Stylish • Personalised •
Townhouse hotel fashioned out of four red-brick houses and exuberantly dressed in bold colours and furnishings. Theatrically decorated bedrooms vary in size from cosy to spacious. Intimate basement Italian restaurant with accomplished and ambitious cooking.

Beaufort AC
33 Beaufort Gdns ✉ *SW3 1PP* – ⓜ *Knightsbridge*   Plan: F5
– ℰ (020) 75845252 – www.thebeaufort.co.uk
29 rm – †£ 168/228 ††£ 228/312 – ☲ £ 16
• Traditional • Classic • Personalised •
A vast collection of English floral watercolours adorn this 19C townhouse, set in a useful location. Modern and co-ordinated rooms. Tariff includes all drinks and afternoon tea.

Sydney House AC
9-11 Sydney St. ✉ *SW3 6PU* – ⓜ *South Kensington*   Plan: E6
– ℰ (020) 73767711 – www.sydneyhousechelsea.co.uk – Closed 25-29 December
21 rm – †£ 125/355 ††£ 125/355 – ☲ £ 12
• Townhouse • Modern • Cosy •
Stylish and compact Georgian townhouse made brighter through plenty of mirrors and light wood. Thoughtfully designed bedrooms; Room 43 has its own terrace. Part of the Abode group.

The Sloane Square 🌣 ⅙ AC 🛋
7-12 Sloane Sq. ✉ *SW1W 8EG* – ⓜ *Sloane Square*   Plan: F6
– ℰ (020) 7896 9988 – www.sloanesquarehotel.co.uk
102 rm – †£ 150/250 ††£ 170/295 – ☲ £ 15
• Business • Modern •
Well-placed, red-brick hotel boasting bright, contemporary décor. Stylish, co-ordinated bedrooms, with laptops; library of DVDs and games available. Rooms at the back are slightly quieter.

Gordon Ramsay (Clare Smyth) 🕸 AC 🍷
68-69 Royal Hospital Rd. ✉ *SW3 4HP*   Plan: F7
– ⓜ Sloane Square – ℰ (020) 73524441 – www.gordonramsay.com
– Closed 21-28 December, Saturday and Sunday
Menu £ 65/110 – *(booking essential)*
• French • Formal •
Attention to detail ensures that Gordon Ramsay's flagship restaurant still provides the consummate dining experience. Composed, reassuring and discreet service adds to the calmness of the room; Clare Smyth's cooking is poised, elegant and a little more daring.
➔ Cornish crab with radish, kombu and sesame & oyster emulsion. Roast pigeon with fennel, foie gras, lavender, honey and orange. Poached Yorkshire rhubarb with Tahitian vanilla parfait, lemon balm and olive oil.

Bibendum 🕸 AC 🍷
Michelin House, 81 Fulham Rd. ✉ *SW3 6RD*   Plan: E6
– ⓜ South Kensington – ℰ (020) 75815817 – www.bibendum.co.uk
– Closed dinner 24 December, 25-26 December and 1 January
Menu £ 34 (weekdays) – Carte £ 27/63
• French • Design • Fashionable •
Located on the 1st floor of a London landmark – Michelin's former HQ, dating from 1911. French food comes with a British accent and there's fresh seafood served in the oyster bar below. It's maintained a loyal following for over 20 years.

UNITED KINGDOM - LONDON

XXX Rib Room – Jumeirah Carlton Tower Hotel

Cadogan Pl ⊠ *SW1X 9PY –* Ⓜ *Knightsbridge*
– ℰ (020) 7858 7250 – www.theribroom.co.uk
Plan: **F5**
Menu £ 28 (weekday lunch) – Carte £ 50/120
• Meats • Elegant • Intimate •
Rib of Aberdeen Angus, steaks and other classic British dishes attract a prosperous, international crowd; few of whom appear to have a beef with the prices at this swish veteran.

XXX Five Fields

8-9 Blacklands Terr ⊠ *SW3 2SP –* Ⓜ *Sloane Square*
– ℰ (020) 7838 1082 – www.fivefieldsrestaurant.com
Plan: **F6**
– Closed Christmas-mid January, first 2 weeks August, Sunday and Monday
Menu £ 45/80 – *(dinner only)*
• Modern cuisine • Formal • Intimate •
Expect some rather daring combinations on the plate, along with bold flavours; desserts have a unique identity all of their own. This formally run restaurant may be comparatively small but it comes with a warm, intimate feel.

XXX One-O-One – Park Tower Knightsbridge Hotel

101 Knightsbridge ⊠ *SW1X 7RN –* Ⓜ *Knightsbridge*
– ℰ (020) 72907101 – www.oneoonerestaurant.com
Plan: **F4**
Menu £ 23 (lunch and early dinner) – Carte £ 47/107
• Fish and seafood • Formal •
Smart ground floor restaurant; it might be lacking a little in atmosphere but the seafood is good. Much of the excellent produce is from Brittany and Norway; don't miss the King crab legs which are the stars of the show.

XXX Toto's

Walton House, Lennox Garden Mews (off Walton St)
⊠ *SW3 2JH –* Ⓜ *South Kensington – ℰ (020) 75892062*
Plan: **F5**
– www.totosrestaurant.com
Carte £ 43/91 – *(booking essential at dinner)*
• Italian • Elegant • Neighbourhood •
A Chelsea institution returned in 2014, when new owners reopened this discreet Italian restaurant for grown-ups. The kitchen has made the food more contemporary without doing anything to alarm those with more traditional tastes.

XX Outlaw's at The Capital – The Capital Hotel
ॐ
22-24 Basil St. ⊠ *SW3 1AT –* Ⓜ *Knightsbridge*
– ℰ (020) 75911202 – www.capitalhotel.co.uk

Plan: **F5**
– Closed Sunday
Menu £ 27/55 – *(booking essential)*
• Fish and seafood • Formal • Cosy •
Chef Nathan Outlaw brings his award-winning formula up from Cornwall: great seafood where the quality of the fish shines through and the flavours harmonise perfectly. The well-structured wine list features the ever popular Levin Sauvignon Blanc from the owner's own estate in the Loire.
→ Lobster risotto, orange, basil and spring onion. Hake with crab, asparagus and crab dressing. Raspberry and treacle tart with clotted cream.

XX **Medlar**
438 King's Rd ⊠ *SW10 0LJ* – Ⓜ *South Kensington*   Plan: **E7**
– ℰ (020) 73491900 – www.medlarrestaurant.co.uk
– Closed 24-26 December and 1 January
Menu £ 28 (weekday lunch)/46
• Modern cuisine • Neighbourhood • Romantic •
A charming, comfortable and very popular restaurant with a real sense of neighbourhood, from two alumni of Chez Bruce. The service is engaging and unobtrusive; the cooking is quite elaborate and comes with a classical base.

XX **Masala Grill**   AC ⇔
535 King's Rd ⊠ *SW10 0SZ* – Ⓜ *Fulham Broadway*   Plan: **D8**
– ℰ (020) 7351 7788 – www.masalagrill.co.uk
Carte £ 28/39 – *(dinner only and Sunday lunch)*
• Indian • Exotic •
When the owners moved Chutney Mary to St James's after 25 years they wisely installed another Indian restaurant in her place. It's still awash with colour and vitality but is less expensive and more varied in its influences.

XX **Le Colombier**   ⇔
145 Dovehouse St. ⊠ *SW3 6LB* – Ⓜ *South Kensington*   Plan: **E6**
– ℰ (020) 73511155 – www.le-colombier-restaurant.co.uk
Menu £ 20 (lunch) – Carte £ 34/66
• French • Neighbourhood •
Proudly Gallic corner restaurant in an affluent residential area. Attractive enclosed terrace. Bright and cheerful surroundings and service; traditional French cooking.

XX **Eight over Eight**   AC ⇔
392 King's Rd ⊠ *SW3 5UZ* – Ⓜ *South Kensington*   Plan: **E7**
– ℰ (020) 73499934 – www.rickerrestaurants.com – Closed 25 December
and 1 January
Menu £ 35/50 – Carte £ 15/45
• Asian • Fashionable •
Reopened after a fire, with a slightly plusher feel; still as popular as ever with the fashionable crowds. Influences stretch across South East Asia and dishes are designed for sharing.

XX **Painted Heron**
112 Cheyne Walk ⊠ *SW10 0DJ*   Plan: **E7/8**
– ⓂFulham Broadway
– ℰ (020) 73515232 – www.thepaintedheron.com
– Closed 1 January and lunch bank holidays
Menu £ 15 (lunch) – Carte £ 25/35
• Indian • Formal • Neighbourhood •
Smart, well-supported and quite formally run Indian restaurant. Nooks and crannies create an intimate atmosphere; and there's a heated cigar terrace. Fish and game dishes are the highlights of the contemporary cooking.

XX **Bluebird**
350 King's Rd. ⊠ *SW3 5UU* – ⓂSouth Kensington   Plan: **E7**
– ℰ (020) 75591000
– www.bluebird-restaurant.co.uk
Menu £ 20 (lunch and early dinner) – Carte £ 27/69
• British modern • Design •
Not just for a night out with friends – with a foodstore, cellar, bakery, café and courtyard there's enough here for a day out too. Big menu to match the big room: everything from British classics to steaks, salads and shellfish.

935

XX **Hawksmoor** 　　　　　　　　　　　　　　　　　　AC

3 Yeoman's Row ⊠ *SW3 2AL –* Ⓜ *South Kensington* 　　Plan: **F5**
*– ℰ (020) 7590 9290 – www.thehawksmoor.com – Closed 24-26 December
and 1 January*
Menu £ 27 (weekday lunch) – Carte £ 28/163
• Meats • Brasserie •
The Hawksmoor people turned to rarefied Knightsbridge for their 5th London
branch. Steak is still the star of the show but here there's also plenty of fish
and seafood. Art deco elegance and friendly service compensate for the basement site.

XX **Maze Grill Park Walk** 　　　　　　　　　　　　　AC

11 Park Walk ⊠ *SW10 0AJ –* Ⓜ *South Kensington* 　　Plan: **D7**
– ℰ (020) 7255 9299 – www.gordonramsay.com/mazegrill/park-walk
Carte £ 24/60
• Meats • Fashionable • Neighbourhood •
The site of Aubergine, where it all started for Gordon Ramsay, now specialises in
steaks. Dry-aged in-house, the meats are cooked on a fierce bit of kit called a
Montague grill. There's another Maze Grill close by in Royal Hospital Road.

XX **Brasserie Gustave** 　　　　　　　　　　　　AC ✿

4 Sydney St ⊠ *SW3 6PP –* Ⓜ *South Kensington* 　　Plan: **E6**
– ℰ (020) 7352 1712 – www.brasserie-gustave.com
Menu £ 39 – Carte £ 29/68
• French • Brasserie •
All the traditional French favourites are here, from snails to boeuf Bourguignon
and rum baba, all prepared in a way to make Escoffier proud. Studded leather
seating and art deco style posters complete the classic brasserie look.

XX **il trillo** 　　　　　　　　　　　　　　　　　🍽 AC

4 Hollywood Rd ⊠ *SW10 9HY –* Ⓜ *Earl's Court* 　　Plan: **D7**
– ℰ (020) 3602 1759 – www.iltrillo.net
– Closed 25-26 December
Menu £ 29 – Carte £ 29/57 – *(dinner only and lunch Saturday-Sunday)*
• Italian • Friendly • Neighbourhood •
The Bertuccelli family have been making wine and running a restaurant in the
Tuscan Hills for over 30 years. Two of the brothers now run this smart local
which showcases the produce and wine from their region. Delightful courtyard.

XX **Colbert** 　　　　　　　　　　　　　　　　　　AC

50-52 Sloane Sq ⊠ *SW1W 8AX –* Ⓜ *Sloane Square* 　　Plan: **G6**
*– ℰ (020) 7730 2804 – www.colbertchelsea.com – Closed 25 December
and dinner 24 December*
Carte £ 19/65 – *(booking advisable)*
• French • Brasserie • Neighbourhood •
With its posters, chessboard tiles and red leather seats, Colbert bears more than
a passing resemblance to a Parisian pavement café. It's an all-day, every day
operation with French classics from croque monsieur to steak Diane.

XX **Good Earth** 　　　　　　　　　　　　　　AC 🕅

233 Brompton Rd. ⊠ *SW3 2EP –* Ⓜ *Knightsbridge* 　　Plan: **E5**
*– ℰ (020) 75843658 – www.goodearthgroup.co.uk – Closed 23-
31 December*
Carte £ 27/51
• Chinese • Elegant •
The menu might appear predictable but this long-standing Chinese has always
proved a reliable choice in this area. Although there's no particular geographical
bias, the cooking is carefully executed and dishes are authentic.

XX **Marco** 🔤

Stamford Bridge, Fulham Rd. ✉ *SW6 1HS* Plan: **D8**
– Ⓜ *Fulham Broadway* – ℰ *(020) 79152929 – www.marcogrill.com*
– *Closed Sunday-Monday*
Carte £ 24/44 – *(dinner only) (booking advisable)*
• French • Brasserie •

Marco Pierre White's brasserie at Chelsea Football Club offers an appealing range of classics, from British favourites to satisfying French and Italian fare; puddings are a highlight. Comfortable and well-run room.

XX **The Botanist** 🔤 😋

7 Sloane Sq ✉ *SW1W 8EE* – Ⓜ *Sloane Square* Plan: **F6**
– ℰ *(020) 77300077 – www.thebotanistlondon.com – Closed 25-26 December*
Menu £ 21 (dinner) – Carte £ 29/54
• Modern cuisine • Trendy • Neighbourhood •

Push through the busy bar to get to this stylish, comfortable restaurant. An extensive menu; the simplest dishes are usually the best ones. Open all day and useful for a bite before curtain-up at The Royal Court or Cadogan Hall.

X **Bo Lang** 🔤

100 Draycott Ave ✉ *SW3 3AD* – Ⓜ *South Kensington* Plan: **F6**
– ℰ *(020) 7823 7887 – www.bolangrestaurant.com*
Menu £ 22 (weekday lunch) – Carte £ 25/48
• Chinese • Trendy •

It's all about dim sum at this diminutive Hakkasan wannabe. The kitchen has a deft touch but stick to the more traditional combinations; come with friends for the cocktails and to mitigate the effects of some ambitious pricing.

X **Rabbit**

172 King's Rd ✉ *SW3 4UP* – Ⓜ *Sloane Square* Plan: **F6**
– ℰ *(020) 3750 0172 – www.rabbit-restaurant.com – Closed 22 December-2 January*
Menu £ 28/42 – Carte £ 22/32
• British modern • Rustic •

The Gladwin brothers have followed the success of The Shed with another similarly rustic and warmly run restaurant. Share satisfying, robustly flavoured plates; game is a real highlight, particularly the rabbit dishes.

X **Henry Root** 🐟 🍽 🔤

9 Park Walk ✉ *SW10 0AJ* – Ⓜ *South Kensington* Plan: **D7**
– ℰ *(020) 7352 7040 – www.thehenryroot.com*
– *Closed 25-28 December*
Carte £ 22/41 – *(booking advisable)*
• French • Neighbourhood • Intimate •

William Donaldson satirised many of the good and the great of his day through the letters of his alter ego, Henry Root. His name lives on in this cheery local spot, with its appealing menu that includes small plates and charcuterie.

X **Tom's Kitchen**

27 Cale St. ✉ *SW3 3QP* – Ⓜ *South Kensington* Plan: **E6**
– ℰ *(020) 73490202 – www.tomskitchen.co.uk*
– *Closed 25-26 December*
Carte £ 26/48
• Modern cuisine • Neighbourhood •

A converted pub, whose white tiles and mirrors help to give it an industrial feel. Appealing and wholesome dishes come in man-sized portions. The eponymous Tom is Tom Aikens.

Cross Keys

1 Lawrence St ✉ SW3 5NB – Ⓜ Sloane Square. Plan: **E7**
– ✆ (020) 73510686 – www.thecrosskeyschelsea.co.uk – Closed 25 and dinner 24 December
Menu £ 20 (weekday lunch) – Carte £ 28/50
• Modern cuisine • Pub • Neighbourhood •
Chelsea's oldest pub, dating from 1708, reopened in 2015 having been saved from property developers. The place has genuine character and warmth. The style of cooking is largely contemporary, although there are also dishes for traditionalists.

Builders Arms

13 Britten St ✉ SW3 3TY – Ⓜ South Kensington. Plan: **E6**
– ✆ (020) 73499040 – www.geronimo-inns.co.uk
Carte £ 18/41 – *(bookings not accepted)*
• British traditional • Pub • Trendy •
Smart looking and busy pub for the Chelsea set; drinkers are welcomed as much as diners. Cooking reveals the effort put into sourcing decent ingredients; rib of beef for two is a favourite. Thoughtfully compiled wine list.

Pig's Ear

35 Old Church St ✉ SW3 5BS – Ⓜ South Kensington. Plan: **E7**
– ✆ (020) 73522908 – www.thepigsear.info – Closed 25 December
Carte £ 27/43
• British traditional • Pub • Rustic •
Honest pub, with rough-and-ready ground floor bar for lunch; more intimate, wood-panelled upstairs dining room for dinner. Robust, confident and satisfying cooking with a classical bent.

South Kensington

Blakes

33 Rowland Gdns ✉ SW7 3PF – Ⓜ Gloucester Road Plan: **D6**
– ✆ (020) 73706701 – www.blakeshotels.com
45 rm – †£ 285/598 ††£ 285/598 – ☕ £ 16 – 8 suites
• Luxury • Design • Contemporary •
Behind the Victorian façade is one of London's first 'boutique' hotels. Dramatic, bold and eclectic décor, with oriental influences and antiques from around the world. Ambitious, Asian-influenced cooking in the intimate restaurant.

The Pelham

15 Cromwell Pl ✉ SW7 2LA – Ⓜ South Kensington Plan: **E6**
– ✆ (020) 7589 8288 – www.pelhamhotel.co.uk
51 rm – †£ 180/335 ††£ 260/480 – ☕ £ 18 – 1 suite
• Luxury • Stylish • Personalised •
Great location if you're in town for museum visiting. It's a mix of English country house and city townhouse, with a panelled sitting room and library with honesty bar. Sweet and intimate basement restaurant with Mediterranean menu.

Kensington

109-113 Queen's Gate ✉ SW7 5LR Plan: **D6**
– Ⓜ South Kensington – ✆ (020) 7589 6300 – www.doylecollection.com
150 rm ☕ – †£ 200/400 ††£ 200/400 – 24 suites
• Business • Contemporary • Stylish •
Grand façade to this well-placed, corporate hotel fashioned from several townhouses. Appealing superior rooms and studios; quite compact singles. Pleasant drawing room with fireplace; brasserie-style dining and popular afternoon tea.

Number Sixteen

16 Sumner Pl. ✉ *SW7 3EG –* Ⓜ *South Kensington*
– ℰ (020) 7589 5232 – www.firmdalehotels.co.uk
Plan: **E6**
41 rm – 🛏£ 175/250 🛏🛏£ 285/400 – ☕ £ 18
• Townhouse • Luxury • Stylish •
Elegant and delightfully furnished 19C townhouses in smart neighbourhood. Discreet entrance, comfortable sitting room, charming breakfast terrace and pretty little garden at the back. Bedrooms in an English country house style.

Ampersand

10 Harrington Rd ✉ *SW7 3ER –* Ⓜ *South Kensington.*
– ℰ (020) 7589 5895 – www.ampersandhotel.com
Plan: **E6**
111 rm – 🛏£ 170 🛏🛏£ 216/288 – ☕ £ 15 – 5 suites
• Luxury • Contemporary • Stylish •
A bright, elegant converted Victorian hotel in London's cultural centre – the nearby museums inspire the bedroom decoration. Rooms aren't the largest but they're smart and well-lit. Basement restaurant has a Mediterranean menu.

The Exhibitionist

8-10 Queensberry Pl ✉ *SW7 2EA –* Ⓜ *South Kensington*
– ℰ (020) 7915 0000 – www.theexhibitionisthotel.com
Plan: **E6**
37 rm ☕ – 🛏£ 240/460 🛏🛏£ 240/460 – 2 suites
• Townhouse • Stylish • Contemporary •
A funky, design-led boutique hotel fashioned out of several 18C townhouses. The modern artwork changes every few months and the bedrooms are individually furnished – several have their own roof terrace.

The Gore

190 Queen's Gate ✉ *SW7 5EX –* Ⓜ *Gloucester Road*
– ℰ (020) 7584 6601 – www.gorehotel.com
Plan: **D5**
50 rm – 🛏£ 180/650 🛏🛏£ 180/650 – ☕ £ 15
• Townhouse • Traditional • Classic •
Idiosyncratic, hip Victorian house close to the Royal Albert Hall, whose charming lobby is covered with pictures and prints. Individually styled bedrooms have plenty of character and fun bathrooms. Bright and casual bistro.

The Cranley

10 Bina Gdns ✉ *SW5 0LA –* Ⓜ *Gloucester Road*
– ℰ (020) 7373 0123 – www.cranleyhotel.com
Plan: **D6**
39 rm – 🛏£ 135/215 🛏🛏£ 155/235 – ☕ £ 18 – 2 suites
• Townhouse • Stylish • Homely •
Delightful Regency townhouse combines charm and period details with modern comforts and technology. Individually styled bedrooms; some with four-posters. Breakfast served in bedrooms.

Aster House

3 Sumner Pl. ✉ *SW7 3EE –* Ⓜ *South Kensington*
– ℰ (020) 75815888 – www.asterhouse.com
Plan: **E6**
13 rm ☕ – 🛏£ 90/180 🛏🛏£ 120/350
• Townhouse • Luxury • Cosy •
An end of terrace Victorian house in a charming neighbourhood and great location for visiting museums. Pretty little rear garden; breakfast served in first floor conservatory. Ground floor bedrooms available.

Bombay Brasserie

Courtfield Rd. ✉ *SW7 4QH –* Ⓜ *Gloucester Road*
– ℰ (020) 73704040 – www.bombayb.co.uk – Closed 25 December
Plan: **D6**
Menu £ 24 (weekday lunch) – Carte £ 30/48 – *(bookings advisable at dinner)*
• Indian • Exotic • Formal •
Plush new look for this well-run, well-known and comfortable Indian restaurant; very smart bar and conservatory with a show kitchen. More creative dishes now sit alongside the more traditional.

XX **L'Etranger**
36 Gloucester Rd. ⊠ SW7 4QT – Ⓜ Gloucester Road
– ℰ (020) 75841118 – www.etranger.co.uk
Menu £ 25/34 – Carte £ 27/88 – (booking essential)
• Creative • Neighbourhood • Romantic •
Plan: **D5**
Eclectic menu mixes French dishes with techniques and flavours from Japanese cooking. Impressive wine and sake lists. Moody and atmospheric room; ask for a corner table.

XX **Cambio de Tercio**
163 Old Brompton Rd. ⊠ SW5 0LJ
– Ⓜ Gloucester Road – ℰ (020) 72448970 – www.cambiodetercio.co.uk
– Closed 2 weeks December and 2 weeks August
Carte £ 32/68
• Spanish • Cosy • Family •
Plan: **D6**
A long-standing, ever-improving Spanish restaurant. Start with small dishes like the excellent El Bulli inspired omelette, then have the popular Pluma Iberica. There are super sherries and a wine list to prove there is life beyond Rioja.

XX **Yashin Ocean House**
117-119 Old Brompton Rd ⊠ SW7 3RN
– Ⓜ Gloucester Road – ℰ (020) 7373 3990 – www.yashinocean.com
– Closed 24-25 and 31 December and 1 January
Menu £ 20/70 – Carte £ 21/72
• Japanese • Individual • Elegant •
Plan: **D6**
The USP of this chic Japanese restaurant is 'head to tail' eating although, as there's nothing for carnivores, 'fin to scale' would be more precise. Stick with specialities like the whole dry-aged sea bream for the full umami hit.

XX **Ognisko**
55 Prince's Gate, Exhibition Rd ⊠ SW7 2PN
– Ⓜ South Kensington – ℰ (020) 7589 0101
– www.ogniskorestaurant.co.uk – Closed 24-26 December and 1 January
Menu £ 20 (lunch and early dinner) – Carte £ 24/36
• Polish • Bistro • Traditional •
Plan: **E5**
Ognisko Polskie Club was founded in 1940 in this magnificent townhouse – its restaurant is now open to the public. The gloriously traditional Polish menu celebrates cooking that is without pretence and truly from the heart.

X **Tendido Cero**
174 Old Brompton Rd. ⊠ SW5 0LJ
– Ⓜ Gloucester Road – ℰ (020) 73703685 – www.cambiodetercio.co.uk
– Closed 2 weeks Christmas-New Year
Menu £ 35/40 – Carte £ 20/61
• Spanish • Tapas bar • Neighbourhood •
Plan: **D6**
It's all about the vibe here at Abel Lusa's tapas bar, just across the road from his Cambio de Tercio restaurant. Colourful surroundings, well-drilled service and a menu of favourites all contribute to the fun and lively atmosphere.

X **Capote y Toros**
157 Old Brompton Road ⊠ SW5 0LJ
– Ⓜ Gloucester Road – ℰ (020) 73730567 – www.cambiodetercio.co.uk
– Closed 2 weeks Christmas, Sunday and Monday
Carte £ 18/45 – (dinner only)
• Spanish • Tapas bar • Cosy •
Plan: **D6**
Expect to queue at this compact and vividly coloured spot which celebrates sherry, tapas, ham... and bullfighting. Sherry is the star; those as yet unmoved by this most underappreciated of wines will be dazzled by the variety.

Margaux
152 Old Brompton Rd ⊠ *SW5 0BE –* Ⓜ *Gloucester Road* Plan: **D6**
– ℰ (020) 7373 5753 – www.barmargaux.co.uk – Closed 1 week Christmas
Menu £ 15 (weekday lunch)/55 – Carte £ 30/52
• Mediterranean • Trendy • Bistro •
Spain and Italy are the primary influences at this modern bistro. There are classics aplenty alongside more unusual dishes. The wine list provides a good choice of varietals and the ersatz industrial look is downtown Manhattan.

EARL'S COURT

K + K George
1-15 Templeton Pl ⊠ *SW5 9NB –* Ⓜ *Earl's Court* Plan: **C6**
– ℰ (020) 75988700 – www.kkhotels.com
154 rm ⌕ – †£ 150/330 ††£ 150/375
• Business • Modern • Functional •
In contrast to its period façade, this hotel's interior is stylish, colourful and contemporary. The hotel is on a quiet street, yet close to the Tube and has a large rear garden where you can enjoy breakfast in summer. Comfortable bar/lounge and a spacious restaurant serving a wide-ranging menu.

Twenty Nevern Square
20 Nevern Sq. ⊠ *SW5 9PD –* Ⓜ *Earl's Court – ℰ (020)* Plan: **C6**
75659555 – www.twentynevernsquare.co.uk
20 rm ⌕ – †£ 80/250 ††£ 100/300
• Townhouse • Luxury • Personalised •
Privately owned townhouse overlooking an attractive Victorian garden square. It's decorated with original pieces of hand-carved Indonesian furniture; breakfast in a bright conservatory. Some bedrooms have their own terrace.

Amsterdam
7-9 Trebovir Rd. ⊠ *SW5 9LS –* Ⓜ *Earl's Court – ℰ (020)* Plan: **C6**
7370 2814 – www.amsterdam-hotel.com
19 rm ⌕ – †£ 80/160 ††£ 100/220
• Townhouse • Functional • Minimalist •
Basement breakfast room and a small secluded garden. The brightly decorated bedrooms are light and airy. Some have smart wood floors; some boast their own balcony.

Garnier
314 Earl's Court Rd ⊠ *SW5 9QB –* Ⓜ *Earl's Court* Plan: **C6**
– ℰ (020) 7370 4536 – www.garnier-restaurant-london.co.uk
Menu £ 18/22 – Carte £ 34/56
• French • Neighbourhood • Brasserie •
A wall of mirrors, rows of simply dressed tables and imperturbable service lend an authentic feel to this Gallic brasserie. The extensive menu of comforting French classics is such a good read, you'll find it hard to choose.

KENSINGTON – NORTH KENSINGTON – NOTTING HILL **PLAN XI**

KENSINGTON

Royal Garden
2-24 Kensington High St ⊠ *W8 4PT* Plan: **D4**
– Ⓜ *High Street Kensington – ℰ (020) 79378000*
– www.royalgardenhotel.co.uk
394 rm – †£ 300/500 ††£ 350/500 – ⌕ £ 25 – 17 suites
• Business • Luxury • Functional •
A tall, modern hotel with many of its rooms enjoying enviable views over the adjacent Kensington Gardens. All the modern amenities and services, with well-drilled staff. Bright, spacious Park Terrace offers an international menu as well as afternoon tea for which you're accompanied by a pianist.
Min Jiang – See restaurant listing

UNITED KINGDOM - LONDON

UNITED KINGDOM - LONDON

The Milestone ✿ ⅃♿ 🐾 AC

1-2 Kensington Ct ⊠ W8 5DL — Plan: **D4**
– **Ⓜ** *High Street Kensington* – ℰ *(020) 79171000*
– *www.milestonehotel.com*
62 rm ⊡ – **†**£ 348/480 **†††**£ 400/1000 – 6 suites
• Luxury • Townhouse • Personalised •

Elegant and enthusiastically run hotel with decorative Victorian façade and a very British feel. Charming oak-panelled sitting room is popular for afternoon tea; snug bar in former stables. Meticulously decorated bedrooms offer period detail. Ambitious cooking in discreet Cheneston's restaurant.

Baglioni ✿ ⅃♿ AC 🏋

60 Hyde Park Gate ⊠ SW7 5BB — Plan: **D4**
– **Ⓜ** *High Street Kensington* – ℰ *(020) 73685700*
– *www.baglionihotels.com*
67 rm – **†**£ 300/500 **†††**£ 300/500 – ⊡ £ 30 – 15 suites
• Luxury • Stylish •

Opposite Kensington Palace and no escaping the fact that this is an Italian owned hotel. The interior is bold and ornate and comes with a certain swagger. Stylish bedrooms have a masculine feel and boast impressive facilities.
Brunello – See restaurant listing

XxX Launceston Place 🍴 AC ⟷

❀ *1a Launceston Pl ⊠ W8 5RL* – **Ⓜ** *Gloucester Road* — Plan: **D5**
– ℰ *(020) 7937 6912* – *www.launcestonplace-restaurant.co.uk*
– *Closed 19-30 December 1 January, Tuesday lunch and Monday*
Menu £ 34/55 – *(bookings advisable at dinner)*
• Modern cuisine • Neighbourhood •

Under the aegis of the D&D group, this long-standing and smoothly run neighbourhood restaurant continues to engender loyalty and goodwill from its many customers. The cooking is polished and at times original; it also produces rewardingly robust flavours.
➔ Veal sweetbread, allium, Morteau sausage and crispy potatoes. Monkfish with caramelised cauliflower, English crayfish and Indian spices. Gold Rush apple with butterscotch, crispy pastry and praline sorbet.

XxX Min Jiang – Royal Garden Hotel ⋜ AC ⟷

2-24 Kensington High St (10th Floor) ⊠ W8 4PT — Plan: **D4**
– **Ⓜ** *High Street Kensington* – ℰ *(020) 73611988*
– *www.minjiang.co.uk*
Menu £ 40/80 – Carte £ 24/92
• Chinese • Elegant • Design •

The cooking at this stylish 10th floor Chinese restaurant covers all provinces, but Cantonese and Sichuanese dominate. Wood-fired Beijing duck is a speciality. The room's good looks compete with the great views of Kensington Gardens.

XX Kitchen W8 AC

❀ *11-13 Abingdon Rd ⊠ W8 6AH* — Plan: **C5**
– **Ⓜ** *High Street Kensington*
– ℰ *(020) 79370120* – *www.kitchenw8.com*
– *Closed 25-26 December and bank holidays*
Menu £ 23 (lunch and early dinner)/60 – Carte £ 35/53
• Modern cuisine • Neighbourhood •

A joint venture between restaurateur Rebecca Mascarenhas and Philip Howard of The Square. Not as informal as the name suggests but still refreshingly free of pomp. The cooking has depth and personality and prices are quite restrained considering the quality of the produce and the kitchen's skill.
➔ Smoked eel with Cornish mackerel, golden beetroot and sweet mustard. 55-day aged Middle White pork with smoked celeriac, charred pear and bacon dauphine. Vanilla parfait with mango, white chocolate and lime.

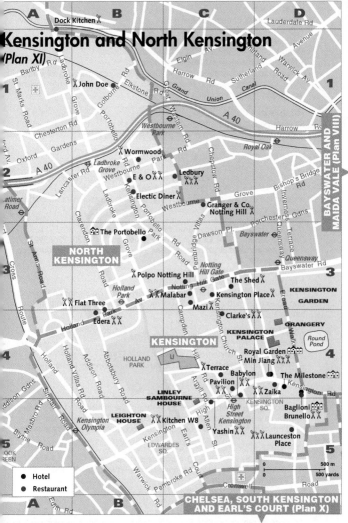

Kensington and North Kensington

(Plan XI)

Dock Kitchen

John Doe

Wormwood

E & O

Ledbury

Electic Diner

Granger & Co. Notting Hill

The Portobello

NORTH KENSINGTON

Polpo Notting Hill

The Shed

Flat Three

Malabar

Kensington Place

Mazi

Edera

Clarke's

KENSINGTON GARDEN

ORANGERY

Round Pond

KENSINGTON PALACE

Royal Garden

Min Jiang

KENSINGTON

HOLLAND PARK

Terrace

Babylon

Pavilion

Zaika

The Milestone

LINLEY SAMBOURNE HOUSE

LEIGHTON HOUSE

Kitchen W8

Kensington Olympia

Baglioni

Brunello

High Street Kensington

Yashin

Launceston Place

EDWARDES SQ.

KENSINGTON SQ.

● Hotel
● Restaurant

0   500 m
0   500 yards

CHELSEA, SOUTH KENSINGTON AND EARL'S COURT (Plan X)

XX   **Pavilion**   AC

96 Kensington High St ⊠ W8 4SG   Plan: **C4**
– Ⓜ High Street Kensington – ℰ (020) 7221 2000
– www.kensingtonpavilion.com
– Closed Christmas-New Year
Menu £ 25 (lunch) – Carte £ 27/59
• Modern cuisine • Fashionable • Design •
Attractive and stylish room with a smart central bar and a separate marble
counter in front of the open kitchen. An appealing contemporary menu comes
with a certain originality and the produce is exemplary – especially the steaks.

943

XX **Clarke's** 🔥 AC ⇔

124 Kensington Church St ✉ *W8 4BH* Plan: **C4**
– **Ⓜ** *Notting Hill Gate* – ℰ *(020) 72219225 – www.sallyclarke.com*
– *Closed 2 weeks August, Christmas-New Year, Sunday and bank holidays*
Menu £ 25/39 – Carte £ 38/51 – *(booking advisable)*
• **Modern cuisine** • **Neighbourhood** •
Forever popular restaurant that has enjoyed a loyal local following for over 30
years. Sally Clarke uses the freshest seasonal ingredients and her cooking
has a famed lightness of touch.

XX **Brunello** – Baglioni Hotel AC

60 Hyde Park Gate ✉ *SW7 5BB* Plan: **D4**
– **Ⓜ** *High Street Kensington* – ℰ *(020) 73685900*
– *www.baglionihotels.com*
Menu £ 23 (lunch) – Carte £ 41/71
• **Italian** • **Design** •
Brunello now seems to have sensibly settled on a kitchen that is less about sho-
winess and more about delivering recognisable Italian classics. This works
because there's frankly more than enough drama in the exuberant decoration.

XX **Babylon** ≤ AC ⇔

The Roof Gardens, 99 Kensington High St (entrance on Plan: **C4**
Derry St) ✉ *W8 5SA* – **Ⓜ** *High Street Kensington* – ℰ *(020) 73683993*
– *www.roofgardens.virgin.com – Closed 24-30 December, 1-2 January and*
Sunday dinner
Menu £ 24/50 – Carte £ 35/56
• **Modern cuisine** • **Fashionable** •
Found on the 7th floor and affording great views of the city skyline and an ama-
zing 1.5 acres of rooftop garden. Stylish modern décor in keeping with the con-
temporary, British cooking.

XX **Zaika** AC 🍽

1 Kensington High St. ✉ *W8 5NP* Plan: **D4**
– **Ⓜ** *High Street Kensington* – ℰ *(020) 77956533*
– *www.zaikaofkensington.com – Closed 25-26 December, 1 January*
and Monday lunch
Menu £ 22 (lunch) – Carte £ 31/65
• **Indian** • **Exotic** •
The cooking focuses on the North of India and the influences of Mughal and
Nawabi, so expect rich and fragrantly spiced dishes. The softly-lit room makes
good use of its former life as a bank, with its wood-panelling and ornate ceiling.

XX **Yashin** AC

1A Argyll Rd. ✉ *W8 7DB* – **Ⓜ** *High Street Kensington* Plan: **C5**
– ℰ *(020) 79381536 – www.yashinsushi.com – Closed 24-25 and*
31 December, 1 January
Carte £ 39/81 – *(booking essential)*
• **Japanese** • **Design** • **Fashionable** •
Ask for a counter seat to watch the chefs prepare the sushi; choose 8, 11 or 15
pieces, to be served together. The quality of fish is clear; tiny garnishes and the
odd bit of searing add originality.

XX **Malabar** AC

27 Uxbridge St. ✉ *W8 7TQ* – **Ⓜ** *Notting Hill Gate* Plan: **C3**
– ℰ *(020) 77278800 – www.malabar-restaurant.co.uk – Closed 1 week*
Christmas
Menu £ 19 (lunch and early dinner) – Carte £ 17/39 – *(buffet lunch Sun-*
day)
• **Indian** • **Neighbourhood** •
Opened in 1983 in a residential Notting Hill street, but keeps up its appearance,
remaining fresh and good-looking. Balanced menu of carefully prepared and
sensibly priced Indian dishes.

X **Terrace**

33c Holland St ✉ *W8 4LX* – Ⓜ *High Street Kensington*   Plan: **C4**
– ✆ (020) 7937 9252 – www.theterraceonhollandstreet.co.uk
Menu £ 18 (weekday lunch) – Carte £ 28/54
• **Modern cuisine** • **Neighbourhood** • **Friendly** •
A sweet little neighbourhood restaurant, tucked away in a corner spot on a quiet residential street. The short menu changes daily and concentrates on seasonal, British-inspired dishes with classic combinations and bold flavours.

X **Kensington Place**

201-209 Kensington Church St. ✉ *W8 7LX*   Plan: **C3**
– Ⓜ Notting Hill Gate – ✆ (020) 77273184
– www.kensingtonplace-restaurant.co.uk – Closed Sunday dinner, Monday lunch and bank holidays
Menu £ 25 (lunch and early dinner) – Carte £ 27/49
• **Modern cuisine** • **Neighbourhood** • **Brasserie** •
An iconic restaurant which opened in 1987 as a big, boisterous, brasserie; these days a little less noisy but it remains well run. The menu offers a wide choice of modern European favourites, with the emphasis on very fresh fish.

X **The Shed**

122 Palace Gardens Terr. ✉ *W8 4RT*   Plan: **C3**
– Ⓜ Notting Hill Gate – ✆ (020) 7229 4024
– www.theshed-restaurant.com – Closed Monday lunch and Sunday
Menu £ 25 (dinner) – Carte £ 21/27
• **British modern** • **Rustic** •
It's more than just a shed but does have a higgledy-piggledy charm and a healthy dose of the outdoors. One brother cooks, one manages and the third runs the farm which supplies the produce for the earthy, satisfying dishes.

X **Mazi**

12-14 Hillgate St ✉ *W8 7SR* – Ⓜ *Notting Hill Gate*   Plan: **C3**
– ✆ (020) 72293794 – www.mazi.co.uk – Closed 24-26 December and 1-2 January
Menu £ 13 (weekday lunch) – Carte £ 28/52
• **Greek** • **Friendly** • **Neighbourhood** •
It's all about sharing at this simple, bright Greek restaurant where traditional recipes are given a modern twist to create vibrant, colourful and fresh tasting dishes. The garden terrace at the back is a charming spot in summer.

NORTH KENSINGTON

🏠 **The Portobello**

22 Stanley Gdns. ✉ *W11 2NG* – Ⓜ *Notting Hill Gate*   Plan: **B3**
– ✆ (020) 77272777 – www.portobellohotel.com – Closed 24-27 December
21 rm ⌂ – ✝£ 125/175 ✝✝£ 175/385
• **Townhouse** • **Luxury** • **Personalised** •
An attractive Victorian townhouse in an elegant terrace. Original and theatrical décor. Circular beds, half-testers, Victorian baths: no two bedrooms are the same.

XXX **Ledbury** (Brett Graham)   🕸 🛋 🅰🅒
❀❀

127 Ledbury Rd. ✉ *W11 2AQ* – Ⓜ *Notting Hill Gate*   Plan: **C2**
– ✆ (020) 7792 9090 – www.theledbury.com – Closed 25-26 December, August bank holiday and lunch Monday-Tuesday
Menu £ 50/85
• **Modern cuisine** • **Neighbourhood** • **Wine bar** •
Brett Graham's husbandry skills and close relationship with his suppliers ensure the quality of the produce shines through and flavour combinations linger long in the memory. This smart yet unshowy restaurant comes with smooth and engaging service. Only a tasting menu is served at dinner on weekends.
➙ Warm pheasant's egg with celeriac, dried ham, Arbois and truffle. Herdwick lamb with ewe's milk, Padrón and salt-baked Kabu turnip. Tartlet of strawberries with English flowers and vanilla cream.

XX **Flat Three** 🔼 🛇

120-122 Holland Park Ave ✉ *W11 4UA*   Plan: **B3/4**
– Ⓜ *Holland Park* – ✆ *(020) 7792 8987 – www.flatthree.london – Closed 2 weeks Christmas, 1 week August, Sunday and Monday*
Menu £ 65 – Carte £ 30/52 – *(dinner only and lunch Friday-Saturday)*
• **Creative** • **Design** • **Minimalist** •
Basement restaurant blending the cuisines of Scandinavia, Korea and Japan. Not everything works but there's certainly ambition. They make their own soy and miso and serve more foraged ingredients than you'll find in Ray Mears' pocket.

XX **E&O** 🔼 ⇔

14 Blenheim Cres. ✉ *W11 1NN* – Ⓜ *Ladbroke Grove*   Plan: **B2**
– ✆ *(020) 72295454 – www.rickerrestaurants.com – Closed 25 December*
Carte £ 22/45
• **Asian** • **Trendy** •
Mean, moody and cool and that's just the customers. Sophisticated, chic and noisy, thanks to contented groups of diners. Menus scour the Far East, with dishes designed for sharing.

XX **Edera** 🔼 ⇔

148 Holland Park Ave. ✉ *W11 4UE* – Ⓜ *Holland Park*   Plan: **B4**
– ✆ *(020) 72216090 – www.edera.co.uk*
Carte £ 33/52
• **Italian** • **Neighbourhood** •
Warm and comfortable neighbourhood restaurant with plenty of local regulars and efficient, well-marshalled service. Robust cooking has a subtle Sardinian accent and comes in generous portions.

X **Dock Kitchen** 🏠 & ⇔

Portobello Dock, 342-344 Ladbroke Grove ✉ *W10 5BU*   Plan: **A1**
– Ⓜ *Ladbroke Grove*
– ✆ *(020) 8962 1610 – www.dockkitchen.co.uk*
– *Closed Christmas, Sunday dinner and bank holidays*
Menu £ 18 (weekday lunch)/50 – Carte £ 30/44
• **Mediterranean** • **Design** • **Trendy** •
What started as a 'pop-up' became a permanent feature in this open-plan former Victorian goods yard. The chef's peregrinations inform his cooking, which relies on simple, natural flavours.

X **Granger & Co Notting Hill** & 🔼

175 Westbourne Grove ✉ *W11 2SB* – Ⓜ *Bayswater*   Plan: **C2**
– ✆ *(020) 7229 9111 – www.grangerandco.com – Closed August bank holiday weekend and 25-26 December*
Carte £ 19/44 – *(bookings not accepted)*
• **Modern cuisine** • **Friendly** • **Simple** •
When Bill Granger moved from sunny Sydney to cool Notting Hill he opened a local restaurant too. He's brought with him that delightful 'matey' service that only Aussies do, his breakfast time ricotta hotcakes and a fresh, zesty menu.

X **Polpo Notting Hill** & 🔼

126-128 Notting Hill Gate ✉ *W11 3QG*   Plan: **C3**
– Ⓜ *Notting Hill Gate* – ✆ *(020) 7229 3283 – www.polpo.co.uk – Closed 25-26 December and 1 January*
Carte £ 13/27
• **Italian** • **Trendy** • **Wine bar** •
The fourth Polpo is Russell Norman's most commercially minded one but is shares the same appealing lack of pretence – and the no booking policy. It's about the whole package, from the shared plates to the appealing vibe.

X **Wormwood**

16 All Saints Rd ✉ *W11 1HH –* Ⓜ *Westbourne Park*   Plan: **B2**
– ℰ (020) 7854 1808 – www.wormwoodrestaurant.com – Closed 28 August-3 September 24-28 December, 1-2 January, Monday lunch and Sunday
Menu £ 35 (lunch) – Carte £ 27/51
• **Mediterranean** • **Neighbourhood** • **Friendly** •
The look is New England with a Moorish edge and it's named after the primary herb in absinthe; throw in North African dominated Mediterranean food with a creative edge and you have a restaurant doing something a little different.

X **Electric Diner**   ⅊ 🆎

191 Portobello Rd ✉ *W11 2ED –* Ⓜ *Ladbroke Grove*   Plan: **B2**
– ℰ (020) 7908 9696 – www.electricdiner.com
– Closed 30-31 August and 25 December
Carte £ 19/35
• **Meats** • **Rustic** • **Neighbourhood** •
Next to the iconic Electric Cinema is this loud, brash and fun all-day operation with an all-encompassing menu; the flavours are as big as the portions. The long counter and red leather booths add to the authentic diner feel.

X **John Doe**   🆎

46 Golborne Rd ✉ *W10 5PR –* Ⓜ *Westbourne Park*   Plan: **B1**
– ℰ (020) 8969 3280 – www.johndoerestaurants.com
– Closed 25-26 December, 30-31 August, Sunday and Monday
Carte £ 24/41
• **Meats** • **Bistro** • **Simple** •
The name is nothing to do with anonymity and everything to do with venison and game – wild British ingredients cooked in the big Bertha oven, using sustainable charcoal and wood from renewable forests, so that dishes burst with flavour.

CLERKENWELL - FINSBURY

CLERKENWELL

🏨 **Malmaison**   ✿ ⅊ 🆎 ♨

18-21 Charterhouse Sq ✉ *EC1M 6AH –* Ⓜ *Barbican*   Plan: **L2**
– ℰ (020) 7012 3700 – www.malmaison.com
97 rm – ♥£ 150/350 ♥♥£ 150/360 – ⌷ £ 15
• **Townhouse** • **Modern** • **Personalised** •
Striking early 20C red-brick building overlooking pleasant square. Stylish, comfy public areas. Bedrooms in vivid, bold colours, with plenty of extra touches. Modern brasserie with international menu; grilled meats a highlight.

🏠 **The Rookery**   🆎

12 Peters Ln, Cowcross St ✉ *EC1M 6DS –* Ⓜ *Farringdon*   Plan: **L2**
– ℰ (020) 73360931 – www.rookeryhotel.com
33 rm – ♥£ 228 ♥♥£ 294/672 – ⌷ £ 12
• **Townhouse** • **Luxury** • **Personalised** •
A row of charmingly restored 18C houses which remain true to their roots courtesy of wood panelling, flagstone flooring, open fires and antique furnishings. Highly individual bedrooms have feature beds and Victorian bathrooms.

X **St John**   🆎 ⇦
❀

26 St John St ✉ *EC1M 4AY –* Ⓜ *Farringdon – ℰ (020)*   Plan: **L2**
7251 0848 – www.stjohnrestaurant.com – Closed Christmas-New Year, Saturday lunch, Sunday dinner and bank holidays
Carte £ 26/54 – *(booking essential)*
• **British traditional** • **Minimalist** • **Brasserie** •
A glorious celebration of British fare and a champion of 'nose to tail eating'. Utilitarian surroundings and a refreshing lack of ceremony ensure the food is the focus; it's appealingly simple, full of flavour and very satisfying.
➜ Roast bone marrow and parsley salad. Braised ox cheek, red wine and celeriac. Eccles cake and Lancashire cheese.

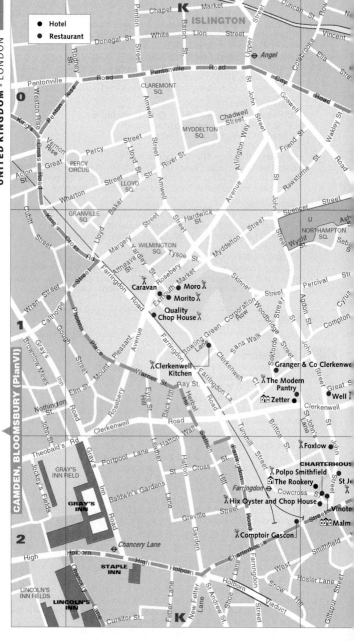

Hotel
Restaurant

ISLINGTON

Chapel

Market

Duncan St.

Vincent

Penton

White

Baron St.

Lion Street

Jeddo

Colebrooke

Ella

Stre

Donegal St.

Rodney St.

Angel

City

Pentonville Road

Road

Goswell

Wakley St.

Pentonville

Weston Rise

King's

Penton Rise

Road

CLAREMONT SQ.

Amwell

Chadwell Street

John Street

Friend St.

Road

Acton St.

Vernon Rise

Great

King's Cross Road

Percy

Street

Lloyd St.

River St.

MYDDELTON SQ.

Arlington Way

St

Rawstorne St.

PERCY CIRCUS

Street

Amwell

Spencer

Street

Wharton

Baker

Street

LLOYD SQ.

John

U

NORTHAMPTON SQ.

Ash

GRANVILLE SQ.

Lloyd

Hardwick St.

Street

Myddelton

Wyclif

Sebs

Cubitt Street

King's Cross Rd

Margery

WILMINGTON SQ.

Tysoe St.

Street

Percival

Str

Wren Street

Calthorpe

Phoenix

Tarrington Road

Yardley St.

Attneave St.

Rosebery

Exmouth Market

Skinner

Street

Street

Agdon St.

Cyrus

Compton

Caravan ● **Moro** ✕

● **Morito**

Corporation Row

Woodbridge Street

Gough Street

Grays Inn

Place

Mount Pleasant

Avenue

Farringdon

Quality Chop House ✕

Bowling Green Lane

Clerkenwell

sans walk

Spencer Street

Granger & Co Clerkenwe

Nothindon St.

Rosebery Avenue

Elm St.

Warner St.

Eyre St. Hill

Back Hill

Ray St.

Herbal Hill

Farringdon La.

Clerkenwell Kitchen ✕

✕ **The Modern Pantry**

🏠 **Zetter** ●

Well ✕

John's St

Clerkenwell

Theobald's Rd

Clerkenwell Road

Hatton Wall

Saffron

Britton St.

Turnmill St.

St. John's Lane

GRAY'S INN FIELD

Jockey's Fields

Portpool Lane

Leather Lane

Hatton

Cross St.

Farringdon

✕ **Foxlow**

CHARTERHOUS

John

GRAY'S INN

Baldwin's Gardens

Hill

✕ **Polpo Smithfield**

🏠 **The Rookery**

St J

✕

GRAY'S INN FIELDS

Greville Street

Garden

Farringdon

Cowcross

✕ **Hix Oyster and Chop House**

Vinote

🏠 **Malm**

Chancery Lane

High

Holborn

High

Holborn

✕ **Comptoir Gascon**

Chart erhouse

Farringdon Rd

Smithfield

STAPLE INN

Snow Hill

Hosier Lane

LINCOLN'S INN FIELDS

LINCOLN'S INN

Cursitor St.

Fetter Lane

New Fetter Lane

St Andrew's Street

Holborn Viaduct

Glitspur Street

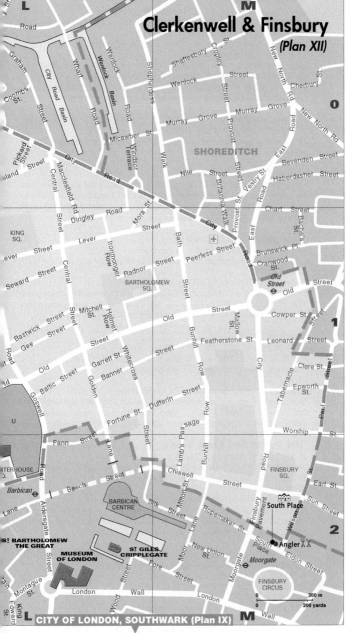

Clerkenwell & Finsbury
(Plan XII)

M

L

O

Road

Graham

Coombs St.

Street

Pickard Street

eland Street

Central

KING SQ.

Lever Street

Seward Street

Bastwick Street

Gee Street

Old Street

Baltic Street

Goswell

Road

U

TERHOUSE Q.

Barbican ⊖

Lane

Aldersgate

Street

ST BARTHOLOMEW THE GREAT

MUSEUM OF LONDON

Montague

King Edward St.

City Road Basin

Wharf

Wenlock Basin

Wenlock

Road

Macclesfield Rd

Central Street

Dingley Road

Lever Street

Ironmonger Row

Radnor Street

BARTHOLOMEW SQ.

Mitchell St.

Helmet Row

Garrett St.

Whitecross

Banner Street

Golden Lane

Fann Street

Fortune St.

Beech Street

BARBICAN CENTRE

Silk Street

ST GILES CRIPPLEGATE

Fore

London Wall

Shepherdess

Micawber St.

Windsor Terrace

Walk

Mora St.

Bath Street

Old Street

Bunhill Row

Dufferin Street

Lamb's Passage

Chiswell Street

Milton St.

Bunhill Row

Silk Street

Moor Lane

New Union St.

Moorgate

Moorgate

London Wall

Shaftesbury St.

Wenlock

Murray Grove

Nile Street

Britannia Walk

City Road

Peerless Street

Old Street

Mallow St.

Featherstone St.

City Road

Ropemaker St.

South Place

Cropley St.

Street

Murray Grove

Provost Street

East Road

East Road

Vestry St.

New North Rd

New North Road

Cherbury St.

Bevenden Street

Haberdasher Street

Chart Street

Bache's St.

SHOREDITCH

Brunswick Pl.

Cranwood St.

Old Street ⊖ Old Street

Cowper St.

Leonard Street

Clere St.

Tabernacle

Epworth St.

Worship St.

FINSBURY SQ.

Finsbury Pavement

Earl St.

Sun Street

South Place

Angler ✕✕

Eldon Street

Wilson St.

Paul Street

Street

1

2

FINSBURY CIRCUS

0 ___ 200 m
0 ___ 200 yards

X
🐸
Comptoir Gascon   AC

61-63 Charterhouse St. ✉ EC1M 6HJ – Ⓜ Farringdon   Plan: **K2**
– ℰ (020) 7608 0851 – www.comptoirgascon.com – Closed Christmas-New Year, Sunday, Monday and bank holidays
Menu £ 16 (weekday lunch) – Carte £ 23/44 – *(booking essential)*
• **French • Bistro • Rustic •**
Buzzy restaurant; sister to Club Gascon. Rustic and satisfying specialities from the SW of France include wine, bread, cheese and plenty of duck, with cassoulet and duck rillettes perennial favourites and the duck burger popular at lunch. Great value set 3 course menu. Produce on display to take home.

X
🐸
Polpo Smithfield   🍴 AC

3 Cowcross St ✉ EC1M 6DR – Ⓜ Farringdon. – ℰ (020)   Plan: **L2**
7250 0034 – www.polpo.co.uk – Closed Christmas, New Year and Sunday dinner
Carte £ 12/26
• **Italian • Friendly • Wine bar •**
For his third Venetian-style bacaro, Russell Norman converted an old meat market storage facility; it has an elegantly battered feel. Head first for the Negroni bar downstairs; then over-order tasty, uncomplicated and very satisfying dishes to share. Bookings only taken up to 5.30pm.

X
Granger & Co Clerkenwell   ♿ AC

50 Sekforde St ✉ EC1R 0HA – Ⓜ Farringdon – ℰ (020)   Plan: **K1**
7251 9032 – www.grangerandco.com – Closed Sunday dinner
Carte £ 28/30
• **Modern cuisine • Family • Elegant •**
Aussie food writer and restaurateur Bill Granger's 2nd London branch is a stylish affair. His food is inspired by his travels, with the best dishes being those enlivened with the flavours of SE Asia; his breakfasts are also renowned.

X
Foxlow   ♿

69-73 St John St ✉ EC1M 4AN – Ⓜ Farringdon   Plan: **L2**
– ℰ (020) 7014 8070 – www.foxlow.co.uk – Closed 24 December-1 January, Sunday dinner and bank holidays
Carte £ 19/38
• **Meats • Neighbourhood • Individual •**
From the clever Hawksmoor people comes this fun and funky place where the staff ensure everyone's having a good time. There are steaks available but plenty of other choices with influences from Italy, Asia and the Middle East.

X
Hix Oyster and Chop House   🍴

36-37 Greenhill Rents ✉ EC1M 6BN – Ⓜ Farringdon   Plan: **L2**
– ℰ (020) 70171930 – www.hixoysterandchophouse.co.uk – Closed 25-29 December, Saturday lunch and bank holidays
Carte £ 30/55
• **British traditional • Bistro • Traditional •**
Appropriately utilitarian surroundings put the focus on seasonal and often underused British ingredients. Cooking is satisfying and unfussy, with plenty of oysters and aged beef served on the bone.

X
Vinoteca

7 St John St. ✉ EC1M 4AA – Ⓜ Farringdon – ℰ (020)   Plan: **L2**
72538786 – www.vinoteca.co.uk – Closed 25 December, 1 January, Sunday and bank holidays
Carte £ 20/33
• **Modern cuisine • Bistro • Cosy •**
This cosy and enthusiastically run 'bar and wine shop' is always busy and full of life. The thrilling wine list is constantly evolving and the classic European dishes, cured meats and cheeses are ideal accompaniments.

FINSBURY

 South Place   ⬕ ⬕ ⬕ ⬕ ⬕ ⬕

3 South Pl ✉ EC2M 2AF – Ⓜ Moorgate   Plan: **M2**
– ℰ (020) 35030000 – www.southplacehotel.com
80 rm – ♦£ 200/450 ♦♦£ 350/450 – ⬓ £ 25 – 1 suite
• Business • Stylish • Design •
Restaurant group D&D's first venture into the hotel business is a stylish affair;
unsurprising as its interior was designed by Conran & Partners. Bedrooms are a
treat for those with an eye for aesthetics and no detail has been forgotten. The
ground floor hosts 3 South Place, a bustling bar and grill.
❀ **Angler** – See restaurant listing

 Zetter   ⬕ ⬕ ⬕ ⬕ ⬕

St John's Sq, 86-88 Clerkenwell Rd. ✉ EC1M 5RJ
– Ⓜ Farringdon   Plan: **K1**
– ℰ (020) 7324 4444 – www.thezetter.com
59 rm – ♦£ 186/270 ♦♦£ 186/270 – ⬓ £ 14
• Townhouse • Modern • Retro •
A trendy and discreet converted 19C warehouse with well-equipped bedrooms
that come with pleasant touches, such as Penguin paperbacks. The more idio-
syncratic Zetter Townhouse across the square is used as an overflow.

 Angler – South Place Hotel   ⬕ ⬕ ⬕ ⬕

3 South Pl ✉ EC2M 2AF – Ⓜ Moorgate   Plan: **M2**
– ℰ (020) 32151260 – www.anglerrestaurant.com
– Closed 26-30 December, Saturday lunch and Sunday
Menu £ 35 (weekdays) – Carte £ 37/73 – (booking advisable)
• Fish and seafood • Elegant • Friendly •
The rooftop restaurant of D&D's South Place hotel is a bright, light and very
comfortable space; its adjoining bar and terrace the perfect spot for a pre-pran-
dial cocktail. The menu champions the best of British seafood and the freshness
of the ingredients really shines through.
➔ Yellowfin tuna tartare, lime, chilli and avocado. Steamed wild sea bass,
crab-crushed Pink Fir potatoes and sauce vierge. Chocolate fondant and
pistachio ice cream.

Quality Chop House   ⬕ ⬕ ⬕ ⬕

92-94 Farringdon Rd ✉ EC1R 3EA – Ⓜ Farringdon   Plan: **K1**
– ℰ (020) 7278 1452 – www.thequalitychophouse.com – Closed Sunday
dinner and bank holidays
Menu £ 39 (weekday dinner) – Carte £ 22/62 – (booking advisable)
• British traditional • Classic • Bistro •
Back in the hands of owners who respect its history, this 'progressive working
class caterer' is once again championing gutsy British grub. It also has a terrific,
concise wine list with plenty of gems. The Grade II listed room, with its trade-
mark booths, has been an eating house since 1869.

Moro   ⬕ ⬕ ⬕ ⬕

34-36 Exmouth Mkt ✉ EC1R 4QE – Ⓜ Farringdon   Plan: **K1**
– ℰ (020) 78338336 – www.moro.co.uk
– Closed dinner 24 December-2 January, Sunday dinner and bank holidays
Carte £ 32/42 – (booking essential)
• Mediterranean • Friendly • Simple •
It's the stuff of dreams – pack up your worldly goods, drive through Spain, Por-
tugal, Morocco and the Sahara, and then back in London, open a restaurant and
share your love of Moorish cuisine. The wood-fired oven and chargrill fill the air
with wonderful aromas and food is vibrant and colourful.

Morito

32 Exmouth Mkt ✉ *EC1R 4QE –* Ⓜ *Farringdon* Plan: **K1**
– ℰ (020) 72787007
– www.morito.co.uk
– Closed 24 December-2 January, Sunday dinner
and bank holidays
Carte £ 14/26 *– (bookings not accepted at dinner)*
• Spanish • Intimate • Tapas bar •
From the owners of next door Moro comes this authentic and appealingly down to earth little tapas bar. Seven or eight dishes between two should suffice but over-ordering is easy and won't break the bank.

The Modern Pantry

47-48 St John's Sq. ✉ *EC1V 4JJ –* Ⓜ *Farringdon* Plan: **K1**
– ℰ (020) 75539210
– www.themodernpantry.co.uk
– Closed August bank holiday and 25-26 December
Menu £ 23 (weekday lunch)/45 – Carte £ 26/39
– (booking advisable)
• World cuisine • Design • Bistro •
Fusion cooking that uses complementary flavours to create vibrant, zesty dishes. The simple, crisp ground floor of this Georgian building has the buzz; upstairs is more intimate. Clued-up service.

Caravan

11-13 Exmouth Market ✉ *EC1R 4QD –* Ⓜ *Farringdon* Plan: **K1**
– ℰ (020) 78338115
– www.caravanonexmouth.co.uk
Carte £ 19/45 *– (booking advisable)*
• World cuisine • Trendy •
A discernible Antipodean vibe pervades this casual eatery, from the laid-back charm of the service to the kitchen's confident combining of unusual flavours. Cooking is influenced by owner's travels – hence the name.

Clerkenwell Kitchen

27-31 Clerkenwell Cl ✉ *EC1R 0AT –* Ⓜ *Farringdon* Plan: **K1**
– ℰ (020) 71019959
– www.theclerkenwellkitchen.co.uk
– Closed Christmas-New Year, Saturday, Sunday
and bank holidays
Carte £ 15/26 *– (lunch only) (booking advisable)*
• Modern cuisine • Friendly •
The owner of this simple, friendly, tucked away eatery worked with Hugh Fearnley-Whittingstall and is committed to sustainability. Daily changing, well-sourced produce; fresh, flavoursome cooking.

Well

180 St John St ✉ *EC1V 4JY –* Ⓜ *Farringdon.* Plan: **L1**
– ℰ (020) 72519363
– www.downthewell.com
– Closed 25-26 December
Carte £ 23/41
• British modern • Pub • Neighbourhood •
This well-supported local pub from the Martin Brothers comes with the sort of food that is reassuringly familiar yet done well, and service that instils confidence. Eat on the ground floor, rather than in the less welcoming basement.

CHISWICK

XX ✪ **Hedone** (Mikael Jonsson)   🅰🅲 ⇧

301-303 Chiswick High Rd ✉ W4 4HH – Ⓜ Chiswick Park – ☎ (020)
8747 0377 – www.hedonerestaurant.com – Closed two weeks summer,
two weeks Christmas-New Year, Sunday and Monday
Menu £ 45/125 – (dinner only and Saturday lunch) (set menu only)
• Modern cuisine • Design • Friendly •

Mikael Jonsson, former lawyer turned chef, is not one for complacency so his
restaurant continues to evolve. The content of his set menus is governed entirely by what ingredients are in their prime – and it is this passion for produce
which underpins the superlative and very flavoursome cooking.
→ Pertuis asparagus with pistachio, avocado, wild garlic and primrose.
Roast breast and leg of squab pigeon, with offal sauce, smoked Jersey
pearls, parsley and almond. Fresh raspberries with cinnamon and aromatic
vinegar.

XX ✪ **La Trompette**   🕃 🏠 🅰🅲 ⇧

5-7 Devonshire Rd ✉ W4 2EU – Ⓜ Turnham Green – ☎ (020) 87471836
– www.latrompette.co.uk – Closed 24-26 December and 1 January
Menu £ 30 (lunch and early dinner)/48 – (booking essential)
• British modern • Neighbourhood • Fashionable •

Chez Bruce's sister is a delightful neighbourhood restaurant that's now a little
roomier. The service is charming and the food terrific. Dishes at lunch are quite
simple but great value; the cooking at dinner is a tad more elaborate.
→ Roast Isle of Orkney scallops with barley, buttermilk, miso and grilled
cabbage. Shoulder of suckling pig, sprouting broccoli, white polenta and
grapes. Rhubarb crumble soufflé with rhubarb ripple ice cream.

FULHAM

🏠 ✪ **Harwood Arms**   🕃 🅰🅲

Walham Grove ✉ SW6 1QP – Ⓜ Fulham Broadway.   Plan X: **C7**
– ☎ (020) 73861847 – www.harwoodarms.com – Closed 24-27 December,
1 January and Monday lunch except Bank Holidays
Menu £ 20 (weekday lunch)/40
• British modern • Pub • Neighbourhood •

Its reputation may have spread like wildfire but this remains a proper, down-to-
earth pub that just happens to serve really good food. The cooking is very seasonal, proudly British, full of flavour and doesn't seem out of place in this environment. Service is suitably relaxed and friendly.
→ Berkshire game faggots with Jerusalem artichokes, pickled walnut and
Muscat grapes. Roast and braised Herdwick lamb with artichoke, creamed
spinach and black garlic. Warm heritage carrot cake with orange, lovage
and stem ginger.

HAMMERSMITH

XX ✪ **River Café** (Ruth Rogers)   🕃 🏠 ⇧

Thames Wharf, Rainville Rd ✉ W6 9HA   Plan I: **A3**
– Ⓜ Barons Court – ☎ (020) 73864200 – www.rivercafe.co.uk – Closed
Christmas-New Year, Sunday dinner and bank holidays
Carte £ 61/80 – (booking essential)
• Italian • Fashionable • Design •

It's all about the natural Italian flavours of the superlative ingredients. The on-
view kitchen with its wood-fired oven dominates the stylish riverside room;
the contagiously effervescent atmosphere is helped along by very charming
service.
→ Wood-roasted langoustines, chilli and oregano. Roast turbot tranche
with an anchovy and rosemary sauce and broad beans. Chocolate Nemesis.

XX
❀ **The Glasshouse** &ﾟ AC

14 Station Par. ⊠ *TW9 3PZ –* ⓜ *Kew Gardens –* ℰ *(020) 89406777
– www.glasshouserestaurant.co.uk – Closed 24-26 December and
1 January*
Menu £ 30 (weekday lunch)/48
• Modern cuisine • Fashionable • Neighbourhood •
The Glasshouse is the very model of a modern neighbourhood restaurant and
sits in the heart of lovely, villagey Kew. Food is confident yet unshowy – much
like the locals – and comes with distinct Mediterranean flavours along with the
occasional Asian hint. Service comes with the eagerness of youth.
→ Assiette of rabbit with pancetta, rainbow chard, carrot purée and
Madeira jus. Loin of lamb with braised shoulder, boulangère potatoes,
peas and wild garlic. Dark chocolate mousse with hazelnut nougatine, bergamot and caramel ice cream.

SHOREDITCH

XX
❀ **HKK** ⅋ AC ⇔ |۞

88 Worship St ⊠ *EC2A 2BE –* ⓜ *Liverpool Street*   Plan IX : **M2**
– ℰ *(020) 3535 1888 – www.hkklondon.com – Closed 25 December and
Sunday*
Menu £ 35/98 – Carte lunch £ 24/65
• Chinese • Elegant • Design •
Cantonese has always been considered the finest of the Chinese cuisines and
here at HKK it is given an extra degree of refinement. Expect classic flavour com-
binations yet delivered in a modern way. The room is elegant and graceful; the
service smooth and assured.
→ Cherry wood roasted Peking duck. King soy seared Wagyu beef with jas-
mine tea. Jasmine panna cotta with rhubarb sorbet.

X
❀ **Clove Club** (Isaac McHale) AC |۞

380 Old St ⊠ *EC1V 9LT –* ⓜ *Old Street –* ℰ *(020)*   Plan 1 : **D2**
77296496 – www.thecloveclub.com
*– Closed 2 weeks Christmas-New Year, August bank holiday, Monday
lunch and Sunday*
Menu £ 35/65 – *(bookings advisable at dinner) (set menu only)*
• Modern cuisine • Trendy • Individual •
An unrelentingly sparse room at Shoreditch Town Hall is the chosen site for
three friends who made their names in pop-ups. The set menu showcases
expertly sourced produce in dishes that are full of originality, verve and flair
– but where flavours are expertly judged and complementary.
→ Raw Orkney scallop, hazelnut, clementine, brown butter and Périgord
truffle. Slow-cooked North Ronaldsay lamb with seaweed sauce and purple
sprouting broccoli. Amalfi lemonade with Sarawak pepper ice cream.

X
❀ **Lyle's** (James Lowe) AC

Tea Building, 56 Shoreditch High St ⊠ *E1 6JJ*   Plan IX : **N1**
– ⓜ *Shoreditch High Street –* ℰ *(020) 30115911 – www.lyleslondon.com
– Closed Sunday and bank holidays*
Menu £ 39 (dinner) – Carte lunch £ 23/31 – *(set menu only at dinner)*
• British modern • Simple • Individual •
The young chef-owner is an acolyte of Fergus Henderson and delivers similarly
unadulterated flavours from seasonal British produce, albeit from a set menu at
dinner. This pared-down approach extends to a room that's high on functiona-
lity, but considerable warmth comes from the keen young service team.
→ Pumpkin, whey butter and hazelnut. Monkfish and seaweed. Pear, ginger loaf and caramel.

SPITALFIELDS

XXX Galvin La Chapelle

35 Spital Sq ⊠ *E1 6DY –* Ⓜ *Liverpool Street* Plan IX : **N2**
– 𝒞 (020) 7299 0400 – www.galvinrestaurants.com – Closed dinner 24-26 December and 1 January
Menu £ 29 (lunch and early dinner) – Carte £ 45/73
• French • Individual • Elegant •

The Victorian splendour of St Botolph's Hall, with its vaulted ceiling, arched windows and marble pillars, lends itself perfectly to its role as a glamorous restaurant. The food is bourgeois French with a sophisticated edge and is bound to satisfy.

→ Lasagne of Dorset crab with beurre Nantais. Tagine of Bresse pigeon, couscous, confit lemon and harissa sauce. Tarte Tatin with crème Normande.

WANDSWORTH

XX Chez Bruce (Bruce Poole)

2 Bellevue Rd ⊠ *SW17 7EG –* Ⓜ *Tooting Bec – 𝒞 (020) 86720114*
– www.chezbruce.co.uk – Closed 24-26 December and 1 January
Menu £ 30/48 – *(booking essential)*
• French • Brasserie • Neighbourhood •

Flavoursome, uncomplicated French cooking with hints of the Mediterranean prepared with innate skill; well-organised, personable service and an easygoing atmosphere - some of the reasons why Chez Bruce remains a favourite of so many.

→ Cod brandade with smoked haddock, crisp egg, wild garlic and sea kale. Anjou pigeon with stuffed onion, pearl barley, sauce poivrade and foie gras. Apple and Calvados trifle with spiced raisin fritter.

HEATHROW AIRPORT

☖☖☖☖ Sofitel

Terminal 5, Heathrow Airport ⊠ *TW6 2GD –* Ⓜ *Heathrow Terminal 5*
– 𝒞 (020) 87577777 – www.sofitelheathrow.com
605 rm – ♦£ 150/289 ♦♦£ 150/289 – ☲ £ 20 – 27 suites
• Luxury • Business • Modern •

Smart and well-run contemporary hotel, designed around a series of atriums, with direct access to T5. Crisply decorated, comfortable bedrooms with luxurious bathrooms. Choice of restaurant: international or classic French cuisine.

☖☖☖☖ Hilton London Heathrow Airport Terminal 5

Poyle Rd, Colnbrook (West: 2.5 mi by A
3113) ⊠ *SL3 OFF – 𝒞 (01753) 686860 – www.hilton.com/heathrowt5*
350 rm – ♦£ 119/259 ♦♦£ 119/259 – ☲ £ 21 – 3 suites
• Chain hotel • Business • Functional •

A feeling of light and space pervades this modern, corporate hotel. Soundproofed rooms are fitted to a good standard; the spa offers wide-ranging treatments. Open-plan Gallery for British comfort food.
Mr Todiwala's Kitchen – See restaurant listing

☖☖☖☖ Hilton London Heathrow Airport

Terminal 4 ⊠ *TW6 3AF –* Ⓜ *Heathrow Terminal 4 – 𝒞 (020)*
87597755 – www.hilton.com/heathrow
398 rm – ♦£ 92/255 ♦♦£ 96/260 – ☲ £ 21 – 5 suites
• Business • Contemporary •

Group hotel with a striking modern exterior and linked to Terminal 4 by a covered walkway. Good-sized bedrooms, with contemporary styled suites. Casual dining in Aromi which occupies part of the vast atrium.
Zen Oriental – See restaurant listing

London Heathrow Marriott

Bath Rd, Hayes ✉ UB3 5AN – Ⓜ Heathrow Terminal 1,2,3 – ✆ (020) 89901100 – www.londonheathrowmarriott.co.uk

393 rm – †£ 125/209 ††£ 125/209 – ☕ £ 18 – 2 suites

• Chain hotel • Business • Contemporary •

Built at the end of 20C, this modern, comfortable hotel is centred around a large atrium, with comprehensive business facilities: there is an exclusive Executive floor. Italian cuisine in bright and convivial Tuscany. Grill favourites in Allie's.

Mr Todiwala's Kitchen – Hilton London Heathrow Airport Terminal 5

Poyle Rd, Colnbrook (West: 2.5 mi by A 3113) ✉ SL3 OFF – ✆ (01753) 766482 – www.hilton.com/heathrowterminal5 – Closed 19 December-2 January and Sunday

Menu £ 45 – Carte £ 28/39 – *(dinner only and lunch Thursday-Saturday)*

• Indian • Individual • Design •

Secreted within the Hilton is Cyrus Todiwala's appealingly stylish, fresh-looking restaurant. The choice ranges from street food to tandoor dishes, Goan classics to Parsee specialities; order the 'Kitchen menu' for the full experience.

Zen Oriental – Hilton London Heathrow Airport Hotel

Terminal 4 ✉ TW6 3AF – Ⓜ Heathrow Terminal 4 – ✆ (020) 87597755 – www.hilton.com/heathrow – Closed 25-26 December

Carte £ 34/63 – *(booking essential at dinner)*

• Asian • Fashionable •

With its capable service and appealing menu of authentically executed classics, Zen Oriental has long been a favourite at the Hilton. Popular for business lunches; busy at dinner with hotel guests.

BIRMINGHAM

BIRMINGHAM

Population: 1 101 360

J. Lorieau/Loop Images/Photononstop

It's hard to visualise Birmingham as an insignificant market town, but England's second city was just such a place throughout much of its history. Then came the boom times of the Industrial Revolution; the town fattening up on the back of the local iron and coal trades. In many people's minds that legacy lives on, the city seen as a rather dour place with shoddy Victorian housing, but 21C Brum has swept away much of its factory grime and polished up its civic face. Its first 'makeover' was nearly a century ago, when the mayor, Joseph Chamberlain, enlarged the city's boundaries to make it the second largest in the country.

Today it's feeling the benefits of a second modernist surge – a multi-million pound regeneration, typified by shopping arcades and appealing squares; it now boasts more canal miles than Venice and more trees than inhabitants. It's pretty much in the centre of England, surrounded by Stratford-on-Avon in the south and Bridgnorth and Ironbridge in the west, with Wolverhampton and Coventry in its hinterland. Former resident JRR Tolkien would be lost nowadays, with the undulating contours of the flyovers, the self-important muscle of the sporting, conference and exhibition centres – the NIA, the ICC and the NEC – and the trendy makeover of the Bullring and the Gas Street Basin. Perhaps he would feel more at home in the elegant Jewellery Quarter further north.

BIRMINGHAM IN...

→ ONE DAY
The Rag, The Bullring, Birmingham Museum.

→ TWO DAYS
Brindleyplace, a trip on the water-bus to The Mailbox, a cycle ride along the canals.

→ THREE DAYS
Take the Shakespeare Express to Stratford, Aston Hall.

PRACTICAL INFORMATION

ARRIVAL-DEPARTURE

✈ Birmingham International Airport is 8 miles east of the city. There's a free AirRail connection to Birmingham International Station every 2min. From there, frequent trains to New St Station take 20min.

GETTING AROUND

There is no central bus station –instead, buses depart from various points all over the city; maps are available from tourist offices, libraries and Network West Midlands. For a single ticket, be sure to have the correct fare ready to pay the driver, as they don't give change. Birmingham New Street Railway Station, located within the Grand Central shopping centre, provides train links all over the country,

while Birmingham Snow Hill and Moor Street run mainly local services. The Midland Metro light railway links Snow Hill Station with Wolverhampton.

CALENDAR HIGHLIGHTS

March
St Patrick's Day Parade, Crufts Dog Show.

April
St George's Day Celebration.

May-June
Birmingham Pride.

August
Birmingham International Carnival (Biannual).

October
Comedy Festival.

November
The Motor Show.

EATING OUT

To the southwest of the city is Cadbury World, the UK's only purpose-built visitor centre devoted entirely to chocolate. It's located in the evocative sounding Bourneville area and staff are on hand to tell visitors the history of chocolate and how it's made, but, let's face it, most people go along to get a face full of the stuff in fresh liquid form straight from the vat. More conventionally, many people who come to Birmingham make for the now legendary area of Sparkbrook, Balsall Heath and Moseley, to the

south of the centre. In itself that may not sound too funky, but over the last 30 years it's become the area known as the Balti Triangle. The balti was 'officially' discovered in Birmingham in 1976, a full-on dish of aromatic spices, fresh herbs and rich curries, and The Triangle now boasts over 50 establishments dedicated to the dish. For those after something a little more subtle, the city offers a growing number of lively and fashionable restaurants, offering assured and contemporary cuisine.

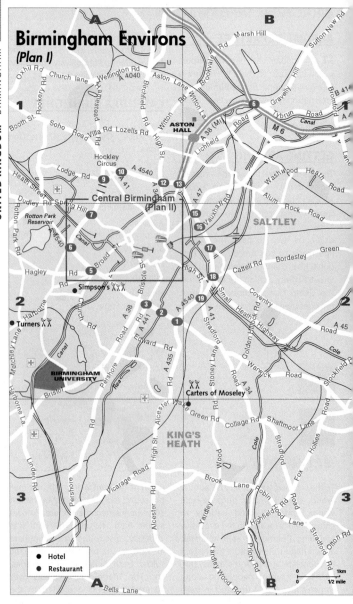

Birmingham Environs
(Plan I)

United Kingdom - Birmingham

Oxhil Rd
Church lane
Rookery Rd
Booth St.
Wellington Rd
A 4040
Aston Lane
Marsh Hill
Sutton New Rd
B 41
Bromford
Gravelly Hill
Tybrun
Road
Brookvale
Witton La.
Witton Rd
High St.
Birchfield
Soho Road
Villa Rd
Lozells Rd
ASTON HALL
A 38 (M)
Lichfield
Road
M 6
Canal
Washwood Heath Road
Hockley Circus
A 4540
A 41
Heath Street
Lodge Rd
10
9
12 **13**
A 47
Alum Rock Road
SALTLEY
Dudley Rd
Spring Hill
Central Birmingham
(Plan II)
Rotton Park Rd
Rotton Park Reservoir
7
15
16
Vauxhall Rd
A 4540
Canal
6
Broad
17
Bordesley Green
Hagley
Rd
5
Broad St
High St.
18
Cattell Rd
Simpson's
Harborne
Church Rd
A 38
A 441
3
2
1
19
A 4540
A 41
Small Heath Highway
Coventry
A 45
Road
Turners
Matchley Lane
Canal
Edward Rd
Stratford Lane
Golden Hillock Road
Warwick Road
Cole
Stockfield
BIRMINGHAM UNIVERSITY
Pershore
Bristol
Rea
A 435
Alcester
A 34
Carters of Moseley
Rd
Stoney
Road
Shaftmoor Lane
Hollies Road
Green Rd
Collage Rd
Stratford
Fox
KING'S HEATH
Cole
Linden Rd
Pershore
Vicarage Road
High St.
Alcester Rd
Wood
Brook
Lane
Robin
Road
Yardley
Highfield Rd
Hood Lane
Stratford
Otton Rd
Priory Rd
Yardley Wood Rd

| ● | Hotel |
| ● | Restaurant |

Bells Lane

0 ___ 1km
0 ___ 1/2 mile

Hyatt Regency
2 Bridge St ⊠ B1 2JZ – ℰ (0121) 6431234   Plan: **D2**
– www.birmingham.regency.hyatt.com
325 rm – †£ 117/219 ††£ 117/219 – ☑ £ 18 – 4 suites
• Business • Luxury • Contemporary •
An eye-catching, mirror-fronted, tower block hotel in a prime city centre location, with a covered link to the International Convention Centre. Spacious bedrooms have floor to ceiling windows and an excellent level of facilities. Aria restaurant, in the atrium, offers modern European menus.

Hotel Du Vin
25 Church St ⊠ B3 2NR – ℰ (0844) 7364 250   Plan: **E2**
– www.hotelduvin.com
66 rm ☑ – †£ 120/185 ††£ 130/195
• Business • Luxury • Design •
Characterful former eye hospital with a relaxed, boutique style. Richly hued bedrooms are named after wine companies and estates; one suite boasts an 8 foot bed, 2 roll-top baths and a gym. Kick-back in the small cellar pub or comfy champagne bar. The classical bistro has a lively buzz and a French menu.

Hotel La Tour
Albert St ⊠ B5 5JE – ℰ (0121) 718 8000   Plan: **F2**
– www.hotel-latour.co.uk – Closed 23-30 December
174 rm – †£ 85/249 ††£ 89/359 – ☑ £ 16
• Business • Modern • Design •
Striking modern building with a stylish lobby featuring state-of-the-art self-check-in terminals. With their media hubs and TV recording facilities, bedrooms are ideal for business travellers; the smart bathrooms are shower-only. There are extensive events facilities, and a chic café, bar and brasserie.

Malmaison
Mailbox, 1 Wharfside St ⊠ B1 1RD – ℰ (0121) 2465000   Plan: **E2**
– www.malmaison.com
192 rm ☑ – †£ 80/200 ††£ 80/250 – 1 suite
• Business • Luxury • Modern •
A smart new-build with dark, moody décor, set next to designer clothes and homeware shops, on the site of the old Royal Mail sorting office. Bedrooms are spacious and stylish; the Penny Black suite has a mini-cinema and a steam room. The bustling black brasserie serves an accessible British menu.

Hotel Indigo
The Cube ⊠ B1 1PR – ℰ (0121) 6432010   Plan: **E3**
– www.hotelindigobirmingham.com
52 rm – †£ 89/200 ††£ 89/200 – ☑ £ 14
• Business • Design • Stylish •
Stylish, modern hotel on the top two floors of the eye-catching 'Cube'. Appealingly styled guest areas and bedrooms are decorated in one of four bright colours. The smart steakhouse serves classic dishes and comes with a champagne bar, terrace and great views from every table.

Hilton Garden Inn Birmingham
1 Brunswick Sq, Brindley Place ⊠ B1 2HW – ℰ (0121)   Plan: **D2**
6431003 – www.birminghambrindleyplace.hgi.com
238 rm ☑ – †£ 59/195 ††£ 69/205
• Business • Chain hotel • Stylish •
Stylish, modern business hotel in the heart of the lively Brindley Place development. Brightly coloured reception and small, contemporary bar. Well-kept, well-equipped bedrooms; facilities include Apple iMac computers. Popular City Café opens onto a terrace.

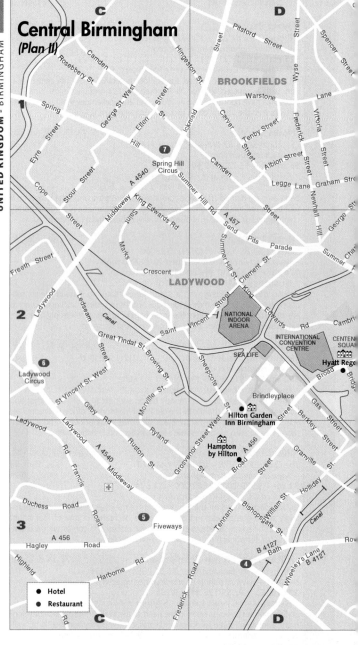

Central Birmingham
(Plan II)

BROOKFIELDS

LADYWOOD

7 Spring Hill Circus

NATIONAL INDOOR ARENA

INTERNATIONAL CONVENTION CENTRE

SEA LIFE

CENTENARY SQUARE

Hyatt Rege

Brindleyplace

Hilton Garden Inn Birmingham

Hampton by Hilton

6 Ladywood Circus

5 Fiveways

4

● Hotel
● Restaurant

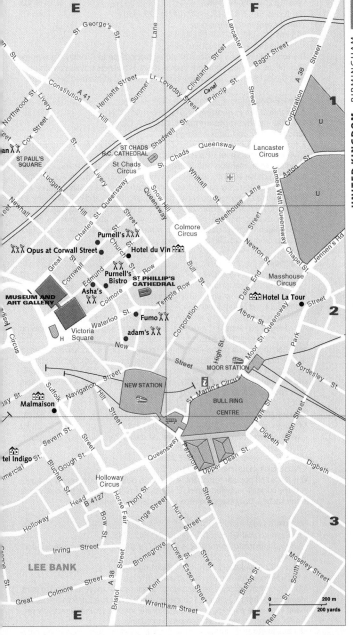

E

F

St George's St.

Lane

Northwood St.

Livery St.

Constitution

A 41

Hill

Henrietta Street

Summer

Lancaster

Cleveland Street

Lr. Loveday Street

Bagot Street

Corporation

A 38

Street

Princip St.

Canal

Street

St. Paul's St.

Cox Street

Northwood St.

Street

an X X

ST PAUL'S
SQUARE

Ludgate

Newhall

Livery St.

Hill

Shadwell St.

ST CHADS
R.C. CATHEDRAL

St Chads
Circus

Snow Hill

Queensway

Queensway

St. Chads

Whittall St.

St.

Queensway

Lancaster
Circus

James Watt Queensway

Aston St.

Jennen's Rd

U

1

U

Charles St.

Great

Charles St. Queensway

Church

Purnell's X X X

Street

Colmore
Circus

Steelhouse Lane

Newton St.

Chapel St.

Masshouse
Circus

2

Jennen's Rd

Newhall

Cornwall

X X X Opus at Corwall Street

Hotel du Vin

Edmund

Purnell's
Bistro

Colmore

Asha's

X X

St

Row

ST PHILLIP'S
CATHEDRAL

Bull St.

Temple Row

Dale End

Hotel La Tour

Street

MUSEUM AND
ART GALLERY

Waterloo

St.

Fumo X X

Temple Row

Corporation

Albert St.

Moor St. Queensway

Park

Bordesley St.

Circus

H

Victoria
Square

New

adam's X X

Street

High St.

St.

MOOR STATION

Navigation

Hill Street

Street

NEW STATION

St. Martin's Circus

i

BULL RING
CENTRE

Park St.

Allison Street

Digbeth

Digbeth

ay St.

Suffolk

Severn St.

Malmaison

Queensway

Pershore

Upper Dean St.

tel Indigo

St.

Blucher St.

Gough St.

Head

B 4127

Holloway
Circus

Holloway

Bow St.

Horse Fair

Thorp St.

Inge Street

Hurst

Street

Street

Street

3

Bishop St.

South

Moseley Street

LEE BANK

Irving

Street

A 38 Street

Bromsgrove Street

Lower Essex Street

Great

Colmore

Street

Bristol

Kent

Street

Wrentham Street

Rea St.

0   200 m
0   200 yards

E

F

Hampton by Hilton　　　　　ᴸᴮ ㅎ AC P

200 Broad St ⊠ B15 1SU – ℰ *(0121) 329 7450*　　Plan: **D3**
– www.hamptonbyhilton.com
285 rm ☲ – ♦£ 49/149 ♦♦£ 49/149
• Chain hotel • Functional •
The top 17 floors of a modern 20 storey block, close to Brindley Place in the heart of the city. Bedrooms are geared towards business travellers, with good work desks, free wi-fi, comfortable beds and smart, part-marbled bathrooms.

Simpsons (Andreas Antona and Luke Tipping)　　⇦ 倫 🏠 ㅎ AC

ಇ
20 Highfield Rd, Edgbaston ⊠ B15 3DU – ℰ *(0121)*　　⇎ 🕪 P
4543434 – www.simpsonsrestaurant.co.uk – Closed　　Plan: **A2**
Sunday dinner and bank holidays
3 rm ☲ – ♦£ 125/175 ♦♦£ 125/175　　Menu £ 45 (lunch) – Carte £ 48/65
• Modern cuisine • Fashionable • Formal •
Smart Georgian mansion with a pleasant garden-facing terrace and a summer house; which has recently undergone a stylish refurbishment. Service is formal and efficient. Classically based menus showcase excellent quality produce and display subtle contemporary twists; flavours are distinct and combinations are carefully judged. The spacious bedrooms have French country styling.
→ Crab risotto, smoked haddock, Granny Smith apples and sea herbs. Squab pigeon with cabbage, onions, morels, wild rice and sauce Albufera. Rhubarb crumble soufflé and rhubarb sorbet.

Purnell's (Glynn Purnell)　　　　　ㅎ AC ⇎

ಇ
55 Cornwall St ⊠ B3 2DH – ℰ *(0121) 2129799*　　Plan: **E2**
– www.purnellsrestaurant.com – Closed 2 weeks August, 1 week Easter,
1 week Christmas, Saturday lunch, Sunday and Monday
Menu £ 32 (weekday lunch)/85
• Modern cuisine • Design • Fashionable •
A well-regarded restaurant with a passionate owner and a keen local following – you're encouraged to relax and enjoy your time here. Start with a drink in the large bar, then move to the sleek dining room. Cooking is modern and refined; choose from the 'Now' or 'Reminisce' menu. Service is smooth and friendly.
→ Salad of Cornish crab with sumac honeycomb "Ice"berg lettuce. Vanilla and cardamom confit pork belly with crisp pickled apple and Savoy salt. Mint chocolate chip with aerated chocolate.

Opus at Cornwall Street　　　　　ㅎ AC ⇎

54 Cornwall St ⊠ B3 2DE – ℰ *(0121) 200 2323*　　Plan: **E2**
– www.opusrestaurant.co.uk – Closed 24 December-3 January, Saturday
lunch, Sunday dinner and bank holidays
Menu £ 14 (weekdays) – Carte £ 26/44
• Modern cuisine • Design • Formal •
Very large and popular restaurant with floor to ceiling windows; enjoy an aperitif in the cocktail bar before dining in the stylish main room or at the chef's table in the kitchen. Daily changing menu of modern brasserie dishes.

adam's (Adam Stokes)　　　　　ㅎ AC

ಇ
21a Bennetts Hill ⊠ B2 5QP – ℰ *(0121) 643 3745*　　Plan: **E2**
– www.adamsrestaurant.co.uk – Closed Christmas-New Year, Sunday and
Monday
Menu £ 32 (weekday lunch)/80 *– (booking advisable)*
• Modern cuisine • Individual • Elegant •
A bright, contemporary restaurant, which is planning to move as we go to print. Menus range from a 3-choice, 3 course set lunch menu to a 5 or 9 course tasting menu with wine pairings. Cooking is intricate, innovative and attractively presented, relying on top quality seasonal ingredients.
→ Cauliflower with smoked eel and mint. Venison, pearl barley and charred onions. Rhubarb with cardamom and blood orange.

XX
&

Turners (Richard Turner)   &. AC

69 High St, Harborne ⊠ B17 9NS – ℰ (0121) 4264440   Plan: **A2**
– www.turnersrestaurantbirmingham.co.uk – Closed Sunday and Monday
Menu £ 35/55 – *(dinner only and lunch Friday-Saturday) (booking essential)*
• **Modern cuisine** • **Neighbourhood** • **Intimate** •
Busy neighbourhood restaurant in a suburban parade, smartly decorated with etched mirrors and velvet chairs; there are just 8 neatly set tables. Visually impressive, confidently crafted, flavoursome dishes use top quality seasonal ingredients. Cooking is classically based but has a modern touch.
➔ Ceviche of scallop with salt baked beetroot, apple, yoghurt and horseradish. Tasting of new season lamb, wild garlic, morels and lamb jus. Rhubarb crumble soufflé and custard ice cream.

XX
&

Carters of Moseley (Brad Carter)   &. AC 🔟

2c St Mary's Row, Wake Green Rd ⊠ B13 9EZ   Plan: **B3**
– ℰ (0121) 449 8885 – www.cartersofmoseley.co.uk – Closed 1-7 January, 10-23 August, Monday and Tuesday
Menu £ 28/50 – *(booking advisable) (set menu only)*
• **British modern** • **Neighbourhood** • **Friendly** •
Lovely little neighbourhood restaurant with black ash tables and a glass-fronted cabinet running down one wall. Each dish is made up of three key components – which can include some unusual ingredients; combinations are well-balanced and flavours are intense. The young team are friendly and engaging.
➔ Devilled crab with Jersey Royals and samphire. Cornish lamb with sea vegetables and seaweed sauce. Wye Valley rhubarb and custard.

XX

Lasan   AC 🔟

3-4 Dakota Buildings, James St, St Pauls Sq ⊠ B3 1SD   Plan: **E1**
– ℰ (0121) 2123664 – www.lasan.co.uk – Closed 25 December
Carte £ 27/57
• **Indian** • **Design** • **Fashionable** •
An industrial-style restaurant in an old Jewellery Quarter art gallery. Original cooking takes authentic Indian flavours and delivers them in creative modern combinations; there are some particularly interesting vegetarian choices.

XX

Purnell's Bistro   AC

Ground Floor, Newater House, 11 Newhall St ⊠ B3 3NY   Plan: **E2**
– ℰ (0121) 200 1588 – www.purnellsbistro-gingers.com – Closed 25-30 December and Sunday dinner
Menu £ 20 (weekdays) – Carte £ 26/35
• **Modern cuisine** • **Brasserie** • **Wine bar** •
Just around the corner from Glynn Purnell's eponymous restaurant is his bistro – a simply styled, low-ceilinged eatery fronted by a lively cocktail bar. Cooking is clever and modern and dishes arrive in original combinations.

XX

Asha's   &. AC ⟷ 🔟

12-22 Newhall St ⊠ B3 3LX – ℰ (0121) 2002767   Plan: **E2**
– www.ashasuk.co.uk – Closed 26 December, 1 January and lunch Saturday-Sunday
Carte £ 27/68
• **Indian** • **Exotic** • **Fashionable** •
A stylish, passionately run Indian restaurant with exotic décor; owned by renowned artiste/gourmet Asha Bhosle. Extensive menus cover most parts of the Subcontinent, with everything cooked to order. Tandoori kebabs are a speciality.

XX

Fumo   &. AC

1 Waterloo St ⊠ B2 5PG – ℰ (0121) 643 8979   Plan: **E2**
– www.sancarlofumo.co.uk
Carte £ 18/35 – *(bookings not accepted)*
• **Italian** • **Tapas bar** • **Friendly** •
Set in a smart area; an elegant Italian restaurant with a 1930s edge and a lovely bar. Tables are closely set and waiters bustle around delivering good value 'cicchetti' – tasty Venetian small plates that are designed for sharing.

EDINBURGH
EDINBURGH

Population: 495 360

Doug Pearson/Agency Jon Arnold Images/Age Fotostock

The beautiful Scottish capital is laid out on seven, formerly volcanic, hills – a contrast to the modern city, which is elegant, cool and sophisticated. It's essentially two cities in one: the medieval Old Town, huddled around and beneath the crags and battlements of the castle, and the smart Georgian terraces of the New Town, overseen by the 18C architect Robert Adam. You could also say there's now a third element to the equation: the revamped port of Leith, just two miles away.

This is a city that's been attracting tourists since the 19C; and since 1999 it's been the home of the Scottish Parliament, adding a new dimension to its worldwide reputation. It accepts its plaudits with the same ease that it accepts an extra half million visitors at the height of summer, and its status as a UNESCO World Heritage site confirms it as a city that knows how to be both ancient and modern. In the middle is the castle, to the south is the old town and to the north is the new town. There's a natural boundary to the north at the Firth of Forth, while to the south lie the rolling Pentland Hills. Unless you've had a few too many drams, it's just about impossible to get lost here, as prominent landmarks like the Castle, Arthur's Seat and Calton Hill access all areas. Bisecting the town is Princes Street, one side of which invites you to shop, the other, to sit and relax in your own space.

EDINBURGH IN...

→ **ONE DAY**
Calton Hill, Royal Mile, Edinburgh Castle, New Town café, Old Town pub.

→ **TWO DAYS**
Water of Leith, Scottish National Gallery of Modern Art, Leith.

→ **THREE DAYS**
Arthur's Seat, National Museum of Scotland, Holyrood Park, Pentland Hills.

PRACTICAL INFORMATION

ARRIVAL-DEPARTURE

✈ Edinburgh International Airport is 8 miles west of the city centre. There is an Airlink Bus Service to Waverley Bridge every 10min. You can also catch the tram; it takes 35min to reach York Place in the city centre.

GETTING AROUND

There's no underground or tram system, so it might be wise to invest in a DAYticket for the buses; you'll have the freedom of Edinburgh for 24 hours. There are plenty of guided options for looking around: choose from an open-top bus, a walking or cycling tour, or even a ghost tour of the old town. All bus tours leave from Waverley Bridge and the hop-on, hop-off nature of the ticket will last 24 hours.

CALENDAR HIGHLIGHTS

March-April
International Science Festival.

July
Jazz and Blues Festival.

August
Edinburgh Festival Fringe (shows, exhibitions, comedy), International Book Festival.

August-September
International Festival (dance, music, theatre), Edinburgh Art Festival.

December
Markets and funfairs, Four-day Hogmanay celebration (torchlight procession, carnival and street party).

EATING OUT

Edinburgh enjoys a varied and interesting restaurant culture so, whatever the occasion, you should find somewhere that fits the bill. The city is said to have more restaurants per head than anywhere in the UK and they vary from lavish establishments in grand hotels to cosy little bistros; you can dine with ghosts in a basement eatery or admire the city from a rooftop table. Scotland's great larder provides much of the produce, and cooking styles range from the innovative and contemporary to the simple and traditional. There are also some good pubs to explore in the old town, and drinking dens also abound in Cowgate and Grassmarket. Further away, in West End, you'll find enticing late-night bars, while the stylish variety, serving cocktails, are more in order in the George Street area of the new town. If you'd rather drink something a little more special then try the 19C Cadenhead's on the Royal Mile – it's the place to go for whiskies and it sells a mindboggling range of rare distillations. The peaty flavoured Laphroaig is a highly recommended dram.

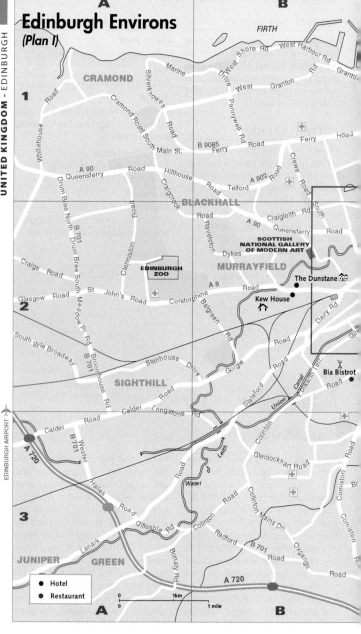

Edinburgh Environs
(Plan I)

A   **B**

FIRTH

West Harbour Rd

West Shore Rd

Granton

CRAMOND

Marine

Silverknowes

West Granton Rd

Drive

West Pennywell Rd

Crewe Rd South

Ferry Road

1

Whitehouse Road

Cramond Road South

Main St.

B 9085 Ferry Road

A 902 Road

Telford

Ferry Road

A 90 Queensferry Road

Hillhouse Road

Craigcrook

Drum Brae North

Craigcrook Road

Ravelston Dykes

BLACKHALL

Craigleith Rd

A 90 Queensferry Road

Road

B 701

Clermiston

Craigs Road

Drum Brae South

St John's Road

EDINBURGH ZOO

SCOTTISH NATIONAL GALLERY OF MODERN ART

MURRAYFIELD

The Dunstane 🏨

2

Glasgow Road

Drum Meadow Pl. Rd

Broomhouse Rd

Corstorphine Road

A 8

Balgreen Rd

Kew House 🏨

Dairy Rd

South gyle Broadway

B 701

Stenhouse Drive

Gorgie Road

Road

Union Canal

SIGHTHILL

Road

Slateford Road

Colinton Road

Bia Bistrot 🍴

3

Calder Road

Longstone Rd

Wester B 701

Calder

Water of Leith

Colinton Road

Gleniockhart Road

Comiston Road

EDINBURGH AIRPORT ✈

A 720

Hailes Road

Gillespie Rd

Bonaly Rd

Colinton Mains Dri.

Redford

B 701

Oxgangs Road

Lanark Road

JUNIPER GREEN

A 720

Road

● Hotel

● Restaurant

0 ___ 1km
0 ___ 1 mile

A   **B**

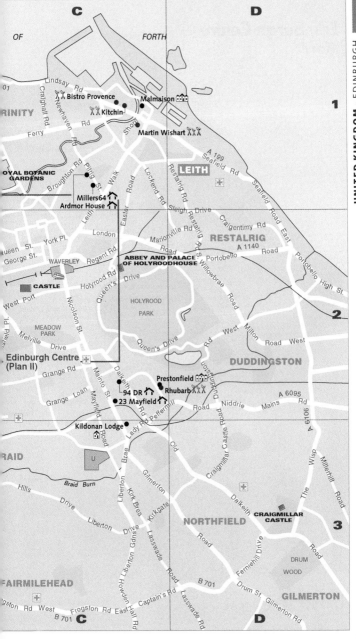

OF FORTH

Lindsay Rd
01
Craighall Rd
Newhaven
Ferry Rd
TRINITY
Rd

X̂X̂ Bistro Provence
X̂X̂ Kitchin
Malmaison ⌂

Martin Wishart X̂X̂X̂

A 199 Seafield Rd

LEITH ✚

Seafield Road East

ROYAL BOTANIC GARDENS

Broughton Rd
Pirig Rd
Leith Walk
Easter Road
Lockend Rd
Restalrig Rd
Sleigh Drive
Craigentimy Rd

Portobello High St.

Millers64 ⌂
Ardmor House ⌂

London Rd
Marionville Rd
Restalrig Road

RESTALRIG
A 1140 Road

Queen St.
York Pl.
George St.

WAVERLEY
Regent Rd

ABBEY AND PALACE OF HOLYROODHOUSE ⌂

Portobello

Willowbrae

West Port
CASTLE
Holyrood Rd
Nicolson St.
Queen's Drive

HOLYROOD PARK

West Milton Road West

Pleasance Pl.
MEADOW PARK
Melville Drive
Queen's Drive

DUDDINGSTON

Duddingston Rd

Edinburgh Centre (Plan II) ✚
Grange Rd
Grange Loan
Mainto St.
Mayfield Road
Dalkeith Rd

94 DR ⌂
23 Mayfield ⌂

Prestonfield ⌂
Rhubarb X̂X̂X̂

Niddrie Mains Rd
A 6095

Kildonan Lodge ⌂
Brae Lady Rd
Peffermill Road
Old

Craigmillar Castle Road

BRAID
U
Braid Burn
Hills
Drive
Liberton

Gilmerton
Kirk Brae
Kirkgate
Liberton Drive
Lasswade

NORTHFIELD
Road
Dalkeith
CRAIGMILLAR CASTLE ✚

The Wisp
Millerhill Road
A 6019

FAIRMILEHEAD
✚
gston Rd West
Frogston Rd East
Howden Hall Rd
Captain's Rd
Hallhead
B 701
Lasswade Rd
B 701
Drum St.
Gilmerton Rd

DRUM WOOD

Fernihill Drive

GILMERTON

C   D

969

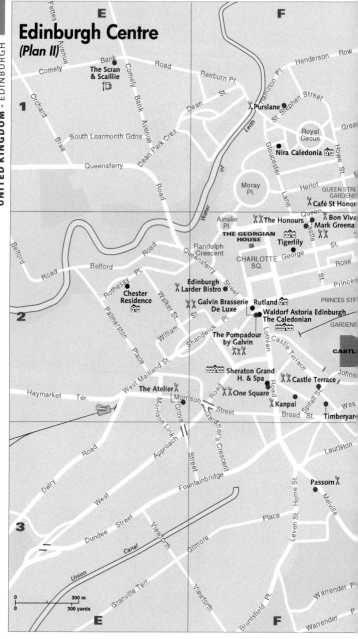

Edinburgh Centre
(Plan II)

The Scran & Scaillie

Purslane

Nira Caledonia

Café St Honor

The Honours

Bon Viva

Mark Greena

Tigerlily

THE GEORGIAN HOUSE

CHARLOTTE SQ.

Edinburgh Larder Bistro

Chester Residence

Galvin Brasserie De Luxe

Rutland

Waldorf Astoria Edinburgh

The Caledonian

The Pompadour by Galvin

Sheraton Grand H. & Spa

Castle Terrace

The Atelier

One Square

Kanpai

Timberyar

Passorn

0   300 m
0   300 yards

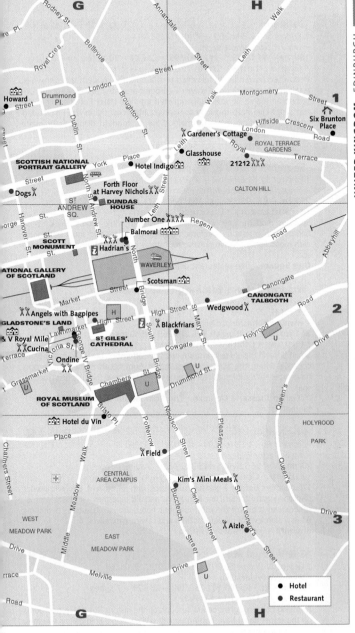

1

Howard

Rodney St.

Royal Cres.

Bellevue

Drummond Pl.

London Street

Annandale Street

Leith Walk

Montgomery Street

Hillside Crescent

London Road

Six Brunton Place

ROYAL TERRACE GARDENS

Gardener's Cottage

Glasshouse

21212

SCOTTISH NATIONAL PORTRAIT GALLERY

Hotel Indigo

Dogs

Forth Floor at Harvey Nichols

DUNDAS HOUSE

York Place

Leith Street

Royal Terrace

CALTON HILL

ST ANDREW SQ.

Number One

Balmoral

SCOTT MONUMENT

Hadrian's

NATIONAL GALLERY OF SCOTLAND

WAVERLEY

Regent Road

Abbeyhill

Market Street

North Bridge

Scotsman

Wedgwood

CANONGATE TALBOOTH

Canongate

2

Angels with Bagpipes

GLADSTONE'S LAND

& V Royal Mile

Cucina

Ondine

ROYAL MUSEUM OF SCOTLAND

Lawnmarket

High Street

St GILES' CATHEDRAL

Victoria St.

George IV Bridge

High Street

South Bridge

Blackfriars

St Mary's St.

Cowgate

Holyrood

HOLYROOD PARK

Queen's Drive

Hotel du Vin

Chambers Street

Bristo Pl.

Potterrow

Nicolson Street

Drummond St.

Pleasance

Field

CENTRAL AREA CAMPUS

Kim's Mini Meals

Clerk Street

Buccleuch Street

St. Leonard's Street

Queen's Drive

3

WEST MEADOW PARK

EAST MEADOW PARK

Middle Meadow Walk

Melville Drive

Aizle

Chalmers Street

● Hotel
● Restaurant

G   **H**

UNITED KINGDOM - EDINBURGH

Balmoral ⭐ 🕍 🌐 🛎 🖥 ☕ 🏧 🧖 🛥

1 Princes St ⊠ EH2 2EQ – ✆ (0131) 5562414   Plan: **G2**
– www.roccofortehotels.com
188 rm – ♦£ 190/595 ♦♦£ 190/595 – � £ 21 – 20 suites
• Grand Luxury • Chain hotel • Classic •
Renowned Edwardian hotel which provides for the modern traveller whilst retaining its old-fashioned charm. Bedrooms are classical with a subtle contemporary edge; JK Rowling completed the final Harry Potter book in the top suite! Live harp music accompanies afternoon tea in the Palm Court and 'Scotch' offers over 460 malts. Dine on modern dishes or brasserie classics.
❀ **Number One** – See restaurant listing

Sheraton Grand H. & Spa ⭐ 🕍 🌐 🛎 🖥 ☕ 🏧 🧖 🅿

1 Festival Sq ⊠ EH3 9SR – ✆ (0131) 2299131   Plan: **F2**
– www.sheratonedinburgh.co.uk
269 rm – ♦£ 195/595 ♦♦£ 195/595 – ⊻ £ 15 – 12 suites
• Grand Luxury • Business • Modern •
Spacious modern hotel with castle views from some rooms. Sleek, stylish bedrooms boast strong comforts, the latest mod cons and smart bathrooms with mood lighting. An impressive four-storey glass cube houses the stunning spa.
One Square – See restaurant listing

Waldorf Astoria Edinburgh The Caledonian ⭐ 🕍

Princes St ⊠ EH1 2AB   🌐 🛎 🖥 ☕ 🏧 🧖 🅿
– ✆ (0131) 222 8888   Plan: **F2**
– www.waldorfastoriaedinburgh.com
241 rm ⊻ – ♦£ 195/749 ♦♦£ 215/769 – 6 suites
• Historic • Luxury • Design •
Smart hotel in the old railway terminus: have afternoon tea in the forecourt or cocktails where the trains once pulled in. Sumptuous modern bedrooms have excellent facilities; ask for a castle view. They have the UK's first Guerlain spa.
 Galvin Brasserie De Luxe • **The Pompadour by Galvin** – See restaurant listing

Prestonfield ⭐ 🐾 ≼ 🍴 🖥 🏧 🧖 🅿

Priestfield Rd ⊠ EH16 5UT – ✆ (0131) 2257800   Plan: **C2**
– www.prestonfield.com
23 rm ⊻ – ♦£ 325/425 ♦♦£ 325/425 – 5 suites
• Luxury • Country house • Stylish •
17C country house in a pleasant rural spot, with an opulent, dimly lit interior displaying warm colours, fine furnishings and old tapestries – it's hugely atmospheric and is one of the most romantic hotels around. Luxurious bedrooms boast a high level of modern facilities and service is excellent.
Rhubarb – See restaurant listing

G & V Royal Mile ⭐ ≼ 🕍 ☕ 🏧 🧖

1 George IV Bridge ⊠ EH1 1AD – ✆ (0131) 2206666   Plan: **G2**
– www.gandvhotel.com
136 rm – ♦£ 150/390 ♦♦£ 150/390 – ⊻ £ 21 – 7 suites
• Luxury • Design • Stylish •
A striking hotel in a great central location on the historic Royal Mile. Bedrooms on the upper floors have impressive city skyline views. Bold colour schemes, modern furnishings and clever design features can be seen throughout.
Cucina – See restaurant listing

UNITED KINGDOM - EDINBURGH

Howard
⚐ ♨ **P**
34 Great King St ✉ *EH3 6QH –* ℰ *(0131) 5573500*
Plan: **G1**
– www.thehoward.com
18 rm ⬚ – 🛏£ 120/450 🛏🛏£ 140/450 – 3 suites
• Townhouse • Luxury • Classic •
A series of three Georgian townhouses with many characterful original features still in situ; situated in the heart of the New Town. Bedrooms vary in size and have classic furnishings and a contemporary edge; every room is assigned a butler. Formal dining from modern menus in the elegant restaurant.

Hotel du Vin
⚐ �& 🆎 ♨
11 Bristo Pl ✉ *EH1 1EZ –* ℰ *(0131) 2474900*
Plan: **G3**
– www.hotelduvin.com/edinburgh
47 rm ⬚ – 🛏£ 105/305 🛏🛏£ 115/330
• Luxury • Design • Contemporary •
Boutique hotel located close to the Royal Mile, featuring unique modern murals and wine-themed bedrooms furnished with dark wood. Guest areas include a whisky snug and a mezzanine bar complete with glass-fronted cellars and a wine tasting room. The traditional bistro offers classic French cooking.

Scotsman
⚐ ♬ ☕ 🜚 🔲 ♨
20 North Bridge ✉ *EH3 1TR –* ℰ *(0131) 5565565*
Plan: **G2**
– www.thescotsmanhotel.co.uk
69 rm ⬚ – 🛏£ 115/380 🛏🛏£ 130/395 – 2 suites
• Business • Historic • Classic •
Characterful Victorian hotel within the old Scotsman newspaper offices. Period guest areas feature lovely wood panelling and stained glass, while traditional bedrooms are accessed via an impressive marble staircase. The stunning brasserie boasts a beautiful ceiling and a minstrels' gallery.

Tigerlily
⚐ ᴖ 🆎
125 George St ✉ *EH2 4JN –* ℰ *(0131) 2255005*
Plan: **F2**
– www.tigerlilyedinburgh.co.uk – Closed 25 December
33 rm ⬚ – 🛏£ 100/260 🛏🛏£ 100/260
• Townhouse • Design • Stylish •
Classical Georgian townhouse concealing a funky, boutique interior. Large, individually designed bedrooms are luxurious, boasting seductive lighting, quality furnishings and superb wet rooms. The busy open-plan bar and dining room have similarly stylish modern décor and offer a worldwide menu.

Glasshouse
🛌 ᴖ 🆎 ♨
2 Greenside Pl ✉ *EH1 3AA –* ℰ *(0131) 5258200*
Plan: **H1**
– www.theglasshousehotel.co.uk
77 rm – 🛏£ 120/455 🛏🛏£ 120/455 – ⬚ £ 19
• Business • Luxury • Modern •
A striking combination of a 150 year old church and sleek glass, topped by an impressive two acre roof garden. Stylish bedrooms feature floor to ceiling windows and lots of wood and leather; the suites open onto a sweeping balcony. Contemporary Scottish fare served in smart Observatory restaurant.

Chester Residence
9 Rothesay Pl ✉ *EH3 7SL –* ℰ *(0131) 226 2075*
Plan: **E2**
– www.chester-residence.com – Closed 23-26 December
23 suites – 🛏£ 135/550 🛏🛏£ 145/365 – ⬚ £ 12
• Townhouse • Stylish • Contemporary •
A series of smart Georgian townhouses in a quiet street. The luxurious, individually furnished suites come with kitchens and state-of-the-art facilities include video entry and integrated sound systems; the Mews apartments are the best.

Nira Caledonia
6 and 10 Gloucester Pl ✉ *EH3 6EF* – ℰ *(0131) 2252720*   Plan: **F1**
– www.niracaledonia.com
28 rm ⌙ – †£ 100/205 ††£ 140/325
• Townhouse • Luxury • Stylish •
Two luxurious townhouses with romantic interiors and stunningly restored staircases. Bedrooms boast top class furnishings and are decorated in gold, black and silver colour schemes; some have jacuzzis in the rooms. The sleek, modern dining room – in the main house – offers meats cooked on the Josper grill.

Rutland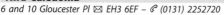
1-3 Rutland St ✉ *EH1 2AE* – ℰ *(0131) 2293402*   Plan: **F2**
– www.therutlandhotel.com – Closed 25 December
11 rm ⌙ – †£ 110/190 ††£ 120/220
• Townhouse • Design • Modern •
Boutique hotel occupying a commanding position at the top of Princes Street. Stylish modern bedrooms have bold décor, bluetooth media hubs and slate-floored shower rooms. The restaurant is a contemporary take on a steakhouse and the smart cocktail bar shares its cellar with the Edinburgh Gin Distillery.

Hotel Indigo
51-59 York Pl ✉ *EH1 3JD* – ℰ *(0131) 556 5577*   Plan: **G1**
– www.hiedinburgh.co.uk
60 rm ⌙ – †£ 119/349 ††£ 119/349
• Townhouse • Business • Contemporary •
Hotel Indigo comprises five interconnecting Georgian townhouses (one was previously a famous tea and coffee merchant's) and has a stylish, contemporary feel. Bedrooms have bold feature walls and good amenities; those to the front are the largest. The simple bistro serves an accessible all-day menu.

The Dunstane
4 West Coates ✉ *EH12 5JQ* – ℰ *(0131) 3376169*   Plan: **B2**
– www.thedunstane.co.uk
38 rm ⌙ – †£ 79/139 ††£ 89/249
• Townhouse • Contemporary • Personalised •
An impressive house which used to be a training centre for the Royal Bank of Scotland. Guest areas retain original Victorian features and the smart modern bedrooms have designer touches; some are located across a busy road. Small restaurant with a stylish cocktail bar; the menu champions local produce.

Kildonan Lodge
27 Craigmillar Pk. ✉ *EH16 5PE* – ℰ *(0131) 6672793*   Plan: **C3**
– www.kildonanlodgehotel.co.uk – Closed 25-26 December
12 rm ⌙ – †£ 75/159 ††£ 79/220
• Townhouse • Traditional • Classic •
Large detached Victorian house on the main road into the city. Cosy drawing room with an open fire and an honesty bar. Comfy, traditionally furnished bedrooms: some have four-posters or jacuzzis; those in the basement are more contemporary. Appealing, classical dishes with Italian influences.

Six Brunton Place
6 Brunton Place ✉ *EH7 5EG* – ℰ *(0131) 6220042*   Plan: **H1**
– www.sixbruntonplace.com
4 rm ⌙ – †£ 89/179 ††£ 109/199
• Townhouse • Luxury • Contemporary •
This late Georgian townhouse – run by a charming owner – was once home to Frederick Ritchie, who designed the One O'Clock Gun and Time Ball. Inside you'll find flagged floors, columns, marble fireplaces and a cantilevered stone staircase; these contrast with contemporary furnishings and vibrant modern art.

94 DR   **P**

94 Dalkeith Rd ✉ *EH16 5AF* – ℰ *(0131) 6629265*
– www.94dr.com – Closed 4-18 January and 25-26 December

6 rm ⌂ – **†**£ 80/125 **††**£ 85/220

Plan: **C2**

• Townhouse • Stylish • Personalised •

Charming owners welcome you to this very stylish and individual hotel in a Victorian terraced house. Retro lounge with honesty bar; breakfast conservatory with decked terrace. Well-equipped bedrooms named after Islay whisky distilleries.

23 Mayfield   **P**

23 Mayfield Gdns ✉ *EH9 2BX* – ℰ *(0131) 667 5806*
– www.23mayfield.co.uk

8 rm ⌂ – **†**£ 75/130 **††**£ 80/190

Plan: **C2**

• Traditional • Classic •

Lovingly restored Victorian house with a very welcoming, helpful owner and an outdoor hot-tub. Spacious lounge has an honesty bar and a collection of old and rare books. Sumptuous bedrooms come with coordinated soft furnishings, some mahogany features and luxurious bathrooms. Extravagant breakfast choices.

Millers64

64 Pilrig St ✉ *EH6 5AS* – ℰ *(0131) 454 3666*
– www.millers64.co.uk

3 rm ⌂ – **†**£ 85/95 **††**£ 95/150

Plan: **C1**

• Townhouse • Stylish •

A modernised Victorian terraced house in an up and coming part of the city. Smart, spacious bedrooms boast good quality linens; those on the first floor are the best. Complimentary drinks in the lounge. Communal breakfasts.

Kew House   **P**

1 Kew Terr, Murrayfield ✉ *EH12 5JE* – ℰ *(0131)*
3130700 – www.kewhouse.com – Closed 4-31 January and 25-26 December

7 rm ⌂ – **†**£ 82/99 **††**£ 99/185

Plan: **B2**

• Townhouse • Personalised •

A warm, welcoming stone house with a neat lounge and a wood-furnished breakfast room; very personally run by its charming owners. Modern, immaculately kept bedrooms come with chocolates, a decanter of sherry and fresh flowers.

Ardmor House

74 Pilrig St ✉ *EH6 5AS* – ℰ *(0131) 554 4944*
– www.ardmorhouse.com

5 rm ⌂ – **†**£ 65/95 **††**£ 95/170

Plan: **C1**

• Townhouse • Personalised •

Comfy, laid-back guesthouse on a residential street; the owner has good local knowledge. Variously sized bedrooms boast bright décor, original plaster ceilings and granite fireplaces. Homemade cakes and preserves feature at breakfast.

XXXX   Number One – Balmoral Hotel   🕸 ♿ **AK** 🔽

ॐ *1 Princes St* ✉ *EH2 2EQ* – ℰ *(0131) 5576727*
– www.restaurantnumberone.com – Closed 2 weeks mid-January

Menu £ 70 – *(dinner only)*

Plan: **G2**

• Modern cuisine • Formal • Intimate •

A stylish, long-standing restaurant with a chic cocktail bar, set in the basement of a grand hotel. Richly upholstered banquettes and red lacquered walls give it a plush, luxurious feel. Cooking is modern and intricate and prime Scottish ingredients are key. Service is professional and has personality.

→ Balvenie-smoked salmon with lemon butter, quail's egg and caviar. Fillet of Orkney beef with baba ganoush and braised oxtail. Valrhona chocolate tart, praline and white chocolate.

XxX
⊗

21212 (Paul Kitching)   ⇦ 🕭 Ⓐ 🄲 ⇔ 🕼
3 Royal Terr ⊠ EH7 5AB – ☏ (0131) 523 1030   Plan: **H1**
– www.21212restaurant.co.uk – Closed 10 days January, 10 days summer,
Sunday and Monday
4 rm ⊑ – ♦£ 115/325 ♦♦£ 115/325
Menu £ 32/69 – (booking essential)
• Creative • Elegant • Design •
Stunningly refurbished Georgian townhouse designed by William Playfair. The
glass-fronted kitchen is the focal point of the stylish, high-ceilinged dining
room. Cooking is skilful, innovative and features quirky combinations; '21212'
reflects the number of dishes per course at lunch – at dinner it's '31313'. Some
of the luxurious bedrooms overlook the Firth of Forth.
→ Lamb curry, chilli, coriander, currants and courgettes. Oriental sea bass,
chestnuts, soy and beansprouts. Peach, apricot, coconut, anglaise and nut-
meg.

XxX
Rhubarb – Prestonfield Hotel   ⊛ 🕭 🕭 Ⓐ 🄿
Priestfield Rd ⊠ EH16 5UT – ☏ (0131) 2251333   Plan: **C2**
– www.prestonfield.com
Menu £ 20/35 – Carte £ 38/72
• Modern cuisine • Elegant • Formal •
Two sumptuous, richly decorated dining rooms set within a romantic 17C
country house; so named as this was the first place in Scotland where rhubarb
was grown. The concise menu lists modern dishes with some innovative touches and is accompanied by an interesting wine list, with a great selection by
the glass.

XxX
The Pompadour by Galvin – Waldorf Astoria Edinburgh The Caledonian
Princes St ⊠ EH1 2AB – ☏ (0131) 222 8975   🕭 Ⓐ 🕼 🄿
– www.galvinrestaurants.com   Plan: **F2**
– Closed first two weeks January, 26 December, dinner 25 December,
Sunday and Monday
Carte £ 43/67 – (dinner only)
• French • Formal • Intimate •
A grand, first floor hotel restaurant which opened in the 1920s and is modelled
on a French salon. Classic Gallic dishes showcase Scottish produce, using tech-
niques introduced by Escoffier, and are executed with a lightness of touch.

XX
Castle Terrace   🕭 Ⓐ 🕼
33-35 Castle Terr ⊠ EH1 2EL – ☏ (0131) 2291222   Plan: **F2**
– www.castleterracerestaurant.com – Closed Christmas, New Year, Sunday
and Monday
Menu £ 29 (lunch) – Carte £ 50/74
• Modern cuisine • Intimate • Elegant •
Set in the shadow of the castle, an understated restaurant with a gilded ceiling.
Ambitious cooking uses seasonal local produce and follows a 'nature to plate'
philosophy. The accompanying wine list offers a great selection.

XX
Mark Greenaway   ⇔ 🕼
69 North Castle St ⊠ EH2 3LJ – ☏ (0131) 226 1155   Plan: **F2**
– www.markgreenaway.com – Closed 25-26 December, 1-2 January,
Sunday and Monday
Menu £ 22 (lunch and early dinner) – Carte £ 39/54 – (booking advisable)
• Modern cuisine • Formal • Individual •
Smart restaurant located in an old Georgian bank – they store their wine in the
old vault. The well-travelled chef employs interesting texture and flavour combinations. Dishes are modern, ambitious and attractively presented.

XX **The Honours**   🅰🅲 ⬡

58A North Castle St ⊠ *EH2 3LU* – ☎ *(0131) 220 2513*   Plan: **F2**
– www.thehonours.co.uk – Closed 25-26 December, 1-3 January,
Sunday and Monday
Menu £ 19 (lunch and early dinner) – Carte £ 36/64
• Classic cuisine • Brasserie • Fashionable •
Bustling brasserie with a smart, stylish interior and a pleasingly informal atmo-
sphere. Classical brasserie menus have French leanings but always offer some
Scottish dishes too; meats cooked on the Josper grill are popular.

XX **Cucina** – G & V Royal Mile Hotel   🍴 🅰🅲 ⬡

1 George IV Bridge ⊠ *EH1 1AD* – ☎ *(0131) 2206666*   Plan: **G2**
– www.gandvhotel.com
Menu £ 19 – Carte £ 23/50
• Italian • Design • Fashionable •
A buzzy mezzanine restaurant in a chic hotel, featuring red and blue glass-topped tables and striking kaleidoscope-effect blocks on the walls. Italian dishes
follow the seasons – some are classically based and others are more modern.

XX **Galvin Brasserie De Luxe** – Waldorf Astoria Edinburgh The Caledonian

Princes St ⊠ *EH1 2AB* – ☎ *(0131) 222 8988*   🅰🅲 🅿
– www.galvinrestaurants.com   Plan: **F2**
Menu £ 20 – Carte £ 26/42
• French • Brasserie • Formal •
Accurately described by its name: a simply styled restaurant which looks like a
brasserie of old but with the addition of a smart shellfish counter and formal
service. There's an appealing daily menu of French classics and a concise,
good value set selection; dishes are refined, flavoursome and a good size.

XX **One Square** – Sheraton Grand Hotel & Spa   🍴 🅰🅲 ⬡ 🅿

1 Festival Sq ⊠ *EH3 9SR* – ☎ *(0131) 2216422*   Plan: **F2**
– www.onesquareedinburgh.co.uk
Menu £ 16 (lunch) – Carte £ 30/53
• Traditional cuisine • Classic • Brasserie •
So named because it covers one side of the square, this smart hotel restaurant
offers casual dining from an all-encompassing menu, accompanied by views
towards Edinburgh Castle. Its stylish bar also stocks over 50 varieties of gin.

XX **Ondine**   🅰🅲 ⬡

2 George IV Bridge (1st floor) ⊠ *EH1 1AD* – ☎ *(0131)*   Plan: **G2**
2261888 – www.ondinerestaurant.co.uk – Closed 1 week early January
and 24-26 December
Menu £ 20 (lunch and early dinner) – Carte £ 33/74
• Fish and seafood • Brasserie • Elegant •
Smart, lively restaurant dominated by an impressive horseshoe bar and a crustacean counter. Classic menus showcase prime Scottish seafood in tasty,
straightforward dishes which let the ingredients shine. Service is well-structured.

XX **Forth Floor at Harvey Nichols**   ⬡ 🍴 🅰🅲 ⬡

30-34 St Andrew Sq ⊠ *EH2 2AD* – ☎ *(0131) 5248350*   Plan: **G1**
– www.harveynichols.com – Closed 25 December, 1 January and dinner
Sunday-Monday
Menu £ 33 (lunch and early dinner) – Carte £ 35/49
• Modern cuisine • Fashionable • Trendy •
A buzzy fourth floor eatery and terrace offering wonderful rooftop views. Dine
on accomplished modern dishes in the restaurant or on old favourites in the all-
day bistro. Arrive early and start with a drink in the smart cocktail bar.

XX **Angels with Bagpipes**

343 High St, Royal Mile ⊠ *EH1 1PW* – *(0131)*   Plan: **G2**
220 1111 – *www.angelswithbagpipes.co.uk* – *Closed 4-19 January and 24-26 December*
Menu £ 15 (lunch) – Carte £ 29/49
• Modern cuisine • Bistro • Design •
Small, stylish restaurant named after the wooden sculpture in St Giles Cathedral, opposite. Dishes are more elaborate than the menu implies; modern interpretations of Scottish classics could include 'haggis, neeps and tattiesgine'.

X **Timberyard**

10 Lady Lawson St ⊠ *EH3 9DS* – *(0131) 221 1222*   Plan: **F2**
– *www.timberyard.co* – *Closed Christmas, 1 week April, 1 week October, Sunday and Monday*
Menu £ 27 (lunch) – Carte £ 44/51 – *(booking essential at dinner)*
• Modern cuisine • Rustic • Simple •
Trendy warehouse restaurant; its spacious, rustic interior incorporating wooden floors and wood-burning stoves. Scandic-influenced menu offers 'bites', 'small' and 'large' sizes, with some home-smoked dishes and an emphasis on distinct, punchy flavours. Cocktails are made with vegetable purées and foraged herbs.

X **Aizle**

107-109 St Leonard's St ⊠ *EH8 9QY* – *(0131)*   Plan: **H3**
662 9349 – *www.aizle.co.uk* – *Closed 4-19 July, 25-31 December, Monday and Tuesday*
Menu £ 45 – *(dinner only) (set menu only)*
• Modern cuisine • Simple • Neighbourhood •
Modest little suburban restaurant whose name means 'ember' or 'spark'. Well-balanced, skilfully prepared dishes are, in effect, a surprise, as the set menu is presented as a long list of ingredients – the month's 'harvest'.

X **Passorn**

23-23a Brougham Pl ⊠ *EH3 9JU* – *(0131) 229 1537*   Plan: **F3**
– *www.passornthai.com* – *Closed 25-26 December, 1-2 January, Sunday and Monday lunch*
Menu £ 16 (weekday lunch) – Carte £ 23/36 – *(booking essential)*
• Thai • Friendly • Neighbourhood •
The staff are super-friendly at this extremely popular neighbourhood restaurant, whose name means 'Angel'. Authentic menus feature Thai classics and old family recipes; the seafood dishes are a highlight and presentation is first class. Spices and other ingredients are flown in from Thailand.

X **Dogs**

110 Hanover St (1st Floor) ⊠ *EH2 1DR* – *(0131)*   Plan: **G1**
220 1208 – *www.thedogsonline.co.uk* – *Closed 25 December and 1 January*
Carte £ 14/21
• Traditional cuisine • Bistro • Rustic •
Cosy, slightly bohemian-style eatery on the first floor of a classic Georgian mid-terrace, with two high-ceilinged, shabby chic dining rooms and an appealing bar. Robust, good value comfort food is crafted from local, seasonal produce; dishes such as cock-a-leekie soup and devilled ox livers feature.

X **The Atelier**

159 Morrison St ⊠ *EH3 8AG* – *(0131) 6291344*   Plan: **E2**
– *www.theatelierrestaurant.co.uk* – *Closed 2-3 weeks January and 25-26 December*
Menu £ 20 (lunch) – Carte £ 24/46
• Mediterranean • Bistro • Neighbourhood •
Attractive little restaurant with bright orange chairs and a stone feature wall. The chef is Polish but his dishes have French and Italian influences; fresh ingredients are prepared with care and cooking has a subtle modern slant.

✗ ### Edinburgh Larder Bistro   AC 🍴

1a Alva St ✉ *EH2 4PH –* ☏ *(0131) 225 4599*   Plan: **F2**
– www.edinburghlarder.co.uk
– Closed 3-8 January, Sunday and Monday
Menu £ 15 (weekday lunch) – Carte £ 24/36
• **Regional** • **Bistro** • **Simple** •
Sustainability and provenance are key here: the chef is a forager and fisherman, the tables are crafted from scaffold boards, old lobster creels act as lampshades, and the daily menu features carefully prepared seasonal dishes.

✗ ### Blackfriars

57-61 Blackfriars St ✉ *EH1 1NB –* ☏ *(0131) 558 8684*   Plan: **H2**
– www.blackfriarsedinburgh.co.uk – Closed 25-26 December, 1 January,
Monday and Tuesday except August
Menu £ 19 (lunch) – Carte dinner £ 25/40
• **Regional** • **Neighbourhood** • **Intimate** •
Hidden behind the castle is this intimate, nature-themed, neighbourhood restaurant, which is well run by its experienced owners. Produce is seasonal and dishes take their influences from around the world; the local game is a must-try.

✗ ### Purslane

33a St Stephen St ✉ *EH3 5AH –* ☏ *(0131) 226 3500*   Plan: **F1**
– www.purslanerestaurant.co.uk – Closed 25-26 December, 1 January and
Monday
Menu £ 18/30 – *(booking essential)*
• **Modern cuisine** • **Neighbourhood** • **Rustic** •
Set in a residential area, in the basement of a terraced Georgian house; an intimate restaurant of just 7 tables, with wallpaper featuring a pine tree motif. The chef carefully prepares modern dishes using well-practiced techniques.

✗ ### Gardener's Cottage

1 Royal Terrace Gardens ✉ *EH7 5DX –* ☏ *(0131)*   Plan: **H1**
558 1221 – www.thegardenerscottage.co – Closed Tuesday and
Wednesday
Menu £ 35 (dinner) – Carte lunch £ 16/24 – *(bookings advisable at dinner)*
• **Traditional cuisine** • **Individual** • **Simple** •
This quirky little eatery was once home to a royal gardener. Two cosy, simply furnished rooms have long communal tables. Lunch is light and dinner offers a 7 course, no-choice set menu; much of the produce is from the kitchen garden.

✗ ### Field

41 West Nicholson St ✉ *EH8 9DB –* ☏ *(0131) 667 7010*   Plan: **G3**
– www.fieldrestaurant.co.uk – Closed Monday
Menu £ 15 (lunch and early dinner) – Carte £ 22/28
• **Modern cuisine** • **Simple** • **Rustic** •
A rustic restaurant run by two young owners, comprising just 8 tables – which are overlooked by a huge canvas of a prized cow. The appealing menu changes slightly each day, offering original modern cooking with a playful element.

✗ ### Bon Vivant   🍸

55 Thistle St ✉ *EH2 1DY –* ☏ *(0131) 225 3275*   Plan: **F1**
– www.bonvivantedinburgh.co.uk – Closed 25-26 December and 1 January
Carte £ 17/30
• **Traditional cuisine** • **Wine bar** • **Individual** •
A relaxed wine bar in the city backstreets, with a dimly lit interior, tightly packed tables and a cheery, welcoming team. The appealing, twice daily menu has an eclectic mix of influences; start with some of the bite-sized nibbles.

X **Kanpai**

8-10 Grindlay St ✉ *EH3 9AS –* ☏ *(0131) 228 1602*   Plan: **F2**
– www.kanpaisushi.co.uk – Closed Monday
Carte £ 15/38
• Japanese • Simple • Design •
Uncluttered, modern Japanese restaurant with a smart sushi bar and cheerful service. Colourful, elaborate dishes have clean, well-defined flavours; the menu is designed to help novices feel confident and experts feel at home.

X **Kim's Mini Meals**   ⅠⓋ ⇥

5 Buccleuch St ✉ *EH8 9JN –* ☏ *(0131) 6297951*   Plan: **H3**
– www.kimsminimeals.com
Carte approx. £ 17 – *(booking essential at dinner)*
• Korean • Simple • Friendly •
A delightfully quirky little eatery filled with bric-a-brac and offering good value, authentic Korean home cooking. Classic dishes like bulgogi, dolsot and jjigae come with your choice of meat or vegetables as the main ingredient.

X **Bia Bistrot**   ☷

19 Colinton Rd ✉ *EH10 5DP –* ☏ *(0131) 4528453*   Plan: **B2**
– www.biabistrot.co.uk – Closed first week January, 1 week July, Sunday and Monday
Menu £ 10 (lunch and early dinner)/26 – Carte £ 19/33
• Classic cuisine • Neighbourhood • Bistro •
A simple, good value neighbourhood bistro with a buzzy vibe. Unfussy, flavoursome dishes range in their influences due to the friendly owners' Irish-Scottish and French-Spanish heritages; they are husband and wife and cook together.

X **Café St Honoré**

34 North West Thistle Street Ln. ✉ *EH2 1EA –* ☏ *(0131)*   Plan: **F1**
2262211 – www.cafesthonore.com – Closed 24-26 December and 1-2 January
Menu £ 16/19 – Carte £ 30/41 – *(booking essential)*
• French classic • Bistro • Neighbourhood •
Long-standing French bistro, tucked away down a side street. The interior is cosy, with wooden marquetry, mirrors on the walls and tightly packed tables. Traditional Gallic menus use Scottish produce and they even smoke their own salmon.

X **Wedgwood**   🅰🄲 ⅠⓋ

267 Canongate ✉ *EH8 8BQ –* ☏ *(0131) 5588737*   Plan: **H2**
– www.wedgwoodtherestaurant.co.uk – Closed 2-22 January and 25-26 December
Menu £ 17 (lunch) – Carte £ 30/49
• Modern cuisine • Friendly •
Atmospheric bistro hidden away at the bottom of the Royal Mile. Well-presented dishes showcase produce foraged from the surrounding countryside and feature some original, modern combinations. It's personally run by a friendly team.

🍴 **The Scran & Scallie**   ६ 🅰🄲

1 Comely Bank Rd, Stockbridge ✉ *EH4 1DT –* ☏ *(0131)*   Plan: **E1**
332 6281 – www.scranandscallie.com – Closed 25 December
Menu £ 15 (weekday lunch) – Carte £ 20/43 – *(booking advisable)*
• British traditional • Neighbourhood • Family •
A more casual venture from Tom Kitchin and Dominic Jack, with a wood furnished bar and a dining room which blends rustic and contemporary décor. Extensive menus follow a 'Nature to Plate' philosophy and focus on the classical and the local.

Malmaison   🕃 ⬚ ⬚ ⬚ 🅿

1 Tower Pl ⊠ EH6 7BZ – 𝒞 (0844) 693 0652
Plan: **C1**
– www.malmaison.com
100 rm – †£ 89/300 ††£ 89/300 – ⬚ £ 14
• Business • Luxury • Stylish •

Impressive former seamen's mission located on the quayside; the first of the Malmaison hotels. The décor is a mix of bold stripes and contrasting black and white themes. Comfy, well-equipped bedrooms; one with a four-poster and a tartan roll-top bath. Intimate bar and a popular French brasserie and terrace.

Martin Wishart   ⬚ 🄰🄲 🛇
✿
54 The Shore ⊠ EH6 6RA – 𝒞 (0131) 5533557
Plan: **C1**
– www.martin-wishart.co.uk – Closed 31 December-19 January, 25-26 December, Sunday and Monday
Menu £ 29 (weekday lunch)/75 – *(booking essential)*
• Modern cuisine • Formal • Elegant •

Elegant modern restaurant with immaculately set tables and attentive, professional service. Three 6 course menus – Tasting, Seafood and Vegetarian – and a concise à la carte. Fine ingredients are used in well-judged, flavourful combinations. Dishes display a classical base and elaborate, original touches.

➙ Scallops with Jerusalem artichoke, sweet potato, hazelnut and truffle velouté. Roe deer with braised lettuce, carrot, date and BBQ winter onion. Valrhona dark chocolate and passion fruit délice, banana and yuzu sorbet, cocoa tuille.

Kitchin (Tom Kitchin)   ⬚ 🄰🄲 ⬚ 🛇
✿
78 Commercial Quay ⊠ EH6 6LX – 𝒞 (0131) 5551755
Plan: **C1**
– www.thekitchin.com – Closed Christmas, New Year, Sunday and Monday
Menu £ 30/75 – Carte £ 53/87 – *(booking essential)*
• Classic cuisine • Design • Fashionable •

Set in a smart, converted whisky warehouse. 'From nature to plate' is the eponymous chef-owner's motto and the use of natural features like bark wall coverings, alongside the more traditional Harris tweed, reflect his passion for using the freshest and best quality Scottish ingredients. Refined, generously proportioned classic French dishes are packed with vivid flavours.

➙ Local shellfish and sea vegetables with shellfish consommé. Boudin of Inverurie ox tongue, braised shin, bone marrow potato and Vallum Farm carrots. Yoghurt panna cotta with apple sorbet and local sea buckthorn.

Bistro Provence   ⬚
88 Commercial St ⊠ EH6 6LX – 𝒞 (0131) 344 4295
Plan: **C1**
– www.bistroprovence.co.uk – Closed 4-14 January and Monday
Menu £ 10/36
• French classic • Bistro • Friendly •

This converted warehouse brings a taste of France to the cobbled quayside of Leith. It's very personally run by a gregarious owner and a welcoming team, and offers an appealing range of unfussy dishes with Provençal leanings.

GLASGOW
GLASGOW

Population: 598 830

Steve Vidler/Prisma/Age Fotostock

The Clyde played a pivotal role in the original growth of Glasgow: in the 18C as a source of trade with the Americas, and in the 19C as a centre of the world's major shipbuilding industries. During this period many of the imposing buildings on show today were constructed; a testament to the city's wealth. This all changed post-World War II, however, as Glasgow's industry fell into tatters and it gained a troubled, poverty-stricken reputation. But Glasgow is also one of the greatest urban success stories: the 1990 City of Culture award turned its image upside down and since then it has grown immensely as an arts, business and retail centre, and tourists have discovered for themselves its grand Victorian façade and eye-catching riverside milieu.

Cocooned within the curving arm of the M8 motorway, the centre is arranged in a neat grid system – and is home to Glasgow's main cultural venues. The 'Merchant City', just to the east, was the original medieval centre but is now a thriving arts quarter, while the West End – a bohemian district filled with cafés, bars and restaurants – has practically reinvented itself as a town in its own right; it's also where you'll find the Kelvingrove Art Gallery and Museum. Cross the Clyde, to the south, and amongst the sprawling suburbs you come across gems like The Burrell Collection and Charles Rennie Mackintosh's House for an Art Lover.

GLASGOW IN...

→ **ONE DAY**
Kelvingrove Art Gallery, Sauchiehall Street, Glasgow School of Art, West End.

→ **TWO DAYS**
Glasgow Green, Provand's Lordship, Necropolis, Science Centre, trip on the Clyde.

→ **THREE DAYS**
Train journey to the Clyde Valley, Pollok Country Park.

PRACTICAL INFORMATION

ARRIVAL-DEPARTURE

 Glasgow International Airport is 8 miles west of the city. The Glasgow Shuttle runs every 10min and takes 25min.

GETTING AROUND

Glasgow has a circular underground system covering the centre and west of the city – to go right round it only takes 24 minutes. You can buy single or return fares as well as all day and 7 day tickets. A good idea on the buses is to buy a FirstDay ticket from your driver; this will let you hop on or off buses right through until midnight. Black cabs are easy to hail all over the city.

CALENDAR HIGHLIGHTS

January
Celtic Connections.

March
Comedy Festival.

June
West End Festival, International Jazz Festival.

July
Merchant City Festival.

August
World Pipe Band Championships.

November
Whisky Live.

EATING OUT

The dreaded legend of the deep-fried Mars bar did no favours for the reputation of the Scottish diet. Don't mention it in Glasgow, though, because in the last decade the place has undergone a gourmet revolution, and these days you can enjoy good food in restaurants from all areas of the world. There are now many establishments specialising in modern Scottish cooking and fish menus have come of age. If you go to the trendy West End or Merchant City quarters you'll find bistros and brasseries that wouldn't be out of place in France or Italy. Glasgow makes the most of the glorious natural larder on its doorstep: spring lamb from the Borders, Perthshire venison, fresh fish and shellfish from the Western Highlands and Aberdeen Angus beef. It's also always had a lot of respect for its liquid refreshment: if you fancy a beer, you can't go far wrong with a pint of Deuchar's, the award-winning 'Bitter & Twisted' or a Dark Island 'imported' from the Orkneys; the locals have taken to real ale from the Scottish regions in a big way.

983

Hotel du Vin at One Devonshire Gardens

1 Devonshire Gdns ✉ G12 OUX – ✆ (0844) 7364256 – www.hotelduvin.com Plan: **A1**

49 rm – †£ 109/300 ††£ 109/300 – ☕£ 18 – 4 suites

• Townhouse • Luxury • Stylish •

Collection of adjoining townhouses boasting original 19C stained glass, wood panelling and a labyrinth of corridors. Furnished in dark, opulent shades but with a modern, country house air. Luxurious bedrooms; one with a small gym and sauna.

Bistro – See restaurant listing

Blythswood Square

11 Blythswood Sq ✉ G2 4AD – ✆ (0141) 2488888 – www.blythswoodsquare.com Plan: **D2**

100 rm ☕ – †£ 120/400 ††£ 120/400 – 1 suite

• Historic • Luxury • Design •

Stunning property on a delightful Georgian square; once the Scottish RAC HQ. Modern décor contrasts with original fittings. Dark, moody bedrooms have marble bathrooms; the Penthouse Suite features a bed adapted from a snooker table.

Blythswood Square – See restaurant listing

Radisson Blu

301 Argyle St. ✉ G2 8DL – ✆ (0141) 2043333 – www.radissonblu.co.uk/hotel-glasgow Plan: **D2**

247 rm ☕ – †£ 99/305 ††£ 99/325 – 1 suite

• Business • Chain hotel • Modern •

Stylish commercial hotel with an impressive glass atrium. Bedrooms come in three styles – Modern, City, and Gallery – and all are spacious and contemporary with a Scandinavian edge. The restaurant has a central buffet breakfast area and an all-encompassing menu; Peter Blake's artwork decorates the walls.

Malmaison

278 West George St ✉ G2 4LL – ✆ (0141) 5721000 – www.malmaison.com Plan: **C2**

72 rm ☕ – †£ 99/185 ††£ 109/195 – 8 suites

• Business • Historic • Stylish •

Impressive-looking former church with moody, masculine décor. Stylish, boldly coloured bedrooms offer good facilities; some are duplex suites. The Big Yin Suite – named after Billy Connolly – has a roll-top bath in the room.

The Honours – See restaurant listing

Grand Central

99 Gordon St ✉ G1 3SF – ✆ (0141) 2403700 – www.grandcentralhotel.co.uk Plan: **D2**

240 rm ☕ – †£ 99/369 ††£ 99/369 – 3 suites

• Historic • Business • Modern •

Renowned hotel built into the main station; the first TV signal broadcast from London was to this hotel. Smart bedrooms are aimed at the corporate market. Original plasterwork features in the ballroom and marble floors in the champagne bar. The contemporary restaurant boasts Murano chandeliers.

Hotel Indigo

75 Waterloo St ✉ G2 7DA – ✆ (0141) 2267700 – www.hotelindigoglasgow.com Plan: **C2**

94 rm – †£ 100/250 ††£ 120/300 – ☕£ 17

• Business • Chain hotel • Design •

Stylish, corporate hotel in a grand 19C building which started life as the city's first power station. Bright colour schemes and bold murals of city sights feature in the well-equipped bedrooms; each floor has a different colour theme. The huge, vibrantly decorated restaurant offers a classic brasserie menu.

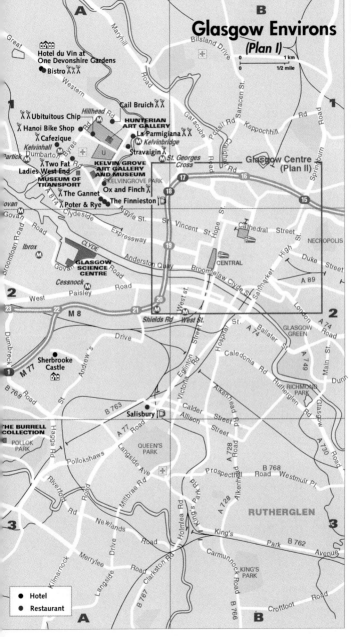

Glasgow Environs
(Plan I)

Bilsland Drive

Maryhill

Great

Western

Road

Hotel du Vin at
One Devonshire Gardens

Bistro ✕✕✕

0   1 km
0   1/2 mile

Hillhead

Cail Bruich ✕✕

Ubuituitous Chip ✕

HUNTERIAN
ART GALLERY

Hanoi Bike Shop ✕

La Parmigiana ✕✕

Cafezique ✕

Kelvinbridge

Kelvinhall

Stravaigin ✕

Dumbarton

Partick

St. Georges
Cross

Glasgow Centre
(Plan II)

KELVIN GROVE
KELVINGROVE PARK

Gairscube Rd

Saracen St.

Keppochhill

Caldarvil Rd

Springburn

Two Fat
Ladies West End

KELVIN GROVE
ART GALLERY
AND MUSEUM

MUSEUM OF
TRANSPORT

The Gannet ✕

Ox and Finch ✕

Poter & Rye ✕

The Finnieston

16

17

18

15

NECROPOLIS

Govan

Govan

Clydeside

Argyle St.

Expressway

St. Vincent St.

Hope St.

Cathedral
Street

Duke
Street

CLYDE

19

Anderston Quay

Broomielaw Clyde St.

CENTRAL

High

Saltmarket

A 89

Ibrox

M

GLASGOW
SCIENCE
CENTRE

Govan Road

Cessnock

M

West

Paisley

23

22

M 8

21

20

West St.

West St.

Shields Rd

Hospital St.

London

A 74
Road

Dumbreck

M 77

Sherbrooke
Castle

St Andrew's

Drive

Edinton Street

Victoria Road

A 74

GLASGOW
GREEN

Ballater St.

Caledonia Rd

RICHMOND
PARK

Main St.

Glasgow Road

Dunn

B 768

Road

B 763

Salisbury

Calder Street

Aitkenhead Rd

Allison Street

Rutherglen Rd

THE BURRELL
COLLECTION

POLLOK
PARK

Haggs Rd

Pollokshaws

Riverford Road

Langside Ave

QUEEN'S
PARK

Millbrae Rd

King's Park Rd

Prospecthill Road

A 728

A 728

Road

B 768

Westmuir Pl.

A 730 Road

RUTHERGLEN

Newlands

Kilmarnock Road

Merrylee

Langside

Road

Drive

Road

B 767

Clarkston Rd

Holmlea Rd

King's Park Rd

King's
Park

Carmunnock Road

KING'S
PARK

B 762
Avenue

Crottfoot

Road

B 766

- ● Hotel
- ● Restaurant

A

B

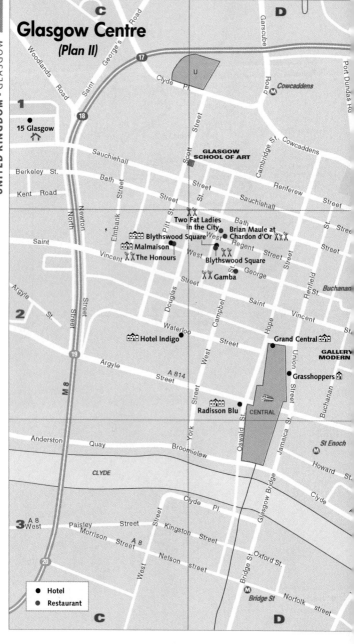

Glasgow Centre
(Plan II)

15 Glasgow

GLASGOW SCHOOL OF ART

Cowcaddens

Two Fat Ladies
in the City

Brian Maule at
Chardon d'Or

Blythswood Square

Malmaison

The Honours

Blythswood Square

Gamba

Hotel Indigo

Grand Central

GALLERY MODERN

Grasshoppers

Radisson Blu

CENTRAL

St Enoch

Bridge St

● Hotel
● Restaurant

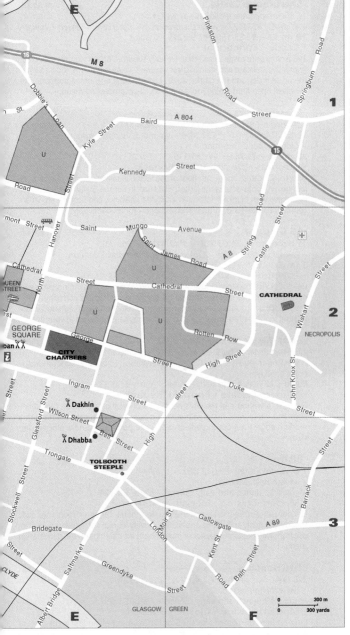

E

F

M 8

Dobbie's Loan

16

St.

Baird

A 804

Kyle Street

Street

1

15

U

Kennedy

Street

Road

Street

mont Street

Saint

Mungo

Avenue

A 8

Stirling

Castle

Street

Hanover

Saint

James

Road

Wishart Street

Cathedral

North

Street

Street

Cathedral

Street

CATHEDRAL

QUEEN STREET

U

U

Cathedral

Street

2

st

U

U

Rotten

Row

NECROPOLIS

GEORGE SQUARE

George

High

Street

John Knox St.

Ingram

Street

Street

Duke

ban

CITY CHAMBERS

CITY CHAMBERS

Street

Wilson Street

Dakhin

Glassford Street

Bell

High

street

Street

Barrack

Street

Dhabba

Trongate

Street

TOLBOOTH STEEPLE

Stockwell Street

Bridgate

Gallowgate

A 89

3

London

St.

Kent St.

Bain Street

Saltmarket

Greendyke

Road

Albert Bridge

CLYDE

Street

Street

GLASGOW GREEN

0   300 m
0   300 yards

E

F

Sherbrooke Castle

11 Sherbrooke Ave, Pollokshields ✉ *G41 4PG*   Plan: **A2**
– ℰ (0141) 4274227 – www.sherbrookecastlehotel.com – Closed 1 January
18 rm ⌣ – **†**£ 85/150 **††**£ 95/245 – 1 suite
• Castle • Functional •

19C pink granite castle, in an attractive leafy suburb. Original features include an impressive staircase and stained glass windows. Large bedrooms add a touch of the present day and the garden suites provide additional home comforts. The panelled, open-fired dining room offers an all-encompassing menu.

Grasshoppers

Caledonian Chambers (6th Floor), 87 Union St   Plan: **D2**
✉ *G1 3TA – ℰ (0141) 222 2666 – www.grasshoppersglasgow.com*
– Closed 3 days Christmas
29 rm ⌣ – **†**£ 75/95 **††**£ 85/115
• Business • Design • Functional •

Unusually located, on the 6th floor of the Victorian railway station building; the lounge overlooks what is the largest glass roof in Europe. Stylish, well-designed bedrooms with bespoke Scandinavian-style furnishings and Scottish art. Smart, compact shower rooms. Three course suppers for residents only.

15 Glasgow

15 Woodside Pl. ✉ *G3 7QL – ℰ (0141) 3321263*   Plan: **C1**
– www.15glasgow.com – Closed 25 December and 3 January
5 rm ⌣ – **†**£ 99/135 **††**£ 99/145
• Townhouse • Luxury • Stylish •

Delightful Victorian townhouse on a quiet square, run by a charming, professional owner. Original features include mosaic floors and ornate cornicing. Extremely spacious, luxurious bedrooms have top quality furnishings and underfloor heating in the bathrooms. Cooked breakfast trays are delivered to your door.

XxX   Brian Maule at Chardon d'Or

176 West Regent St. ✉ *G2 4RL – ℰ (0141) 2483801*   Plan: **D2**
– www.brianmaule.com – Closed 25 December, 1 January, Sunday and bank holidays
Menu £ 22 (lunch and early dinner) – Carte £ 36/53
• Modern cuisine • Formal • Elegant •

Georgian townhouse in the city's heart, with original pillars, ornate carved ceilings and white walls hung with vibrant modern art. Classical cooking with a modern edge; luxurious ingredients and large portions. Friendly, efficient service.

XxX   Bistro – Hotel du Vin at One Devonshire Gardens

1 Devonshire Gdns ✉ *G12 0UX – ℰ (0844) 7364256*   Plan: **A1**
– www.hotelduvin.com
Menu £ 22 (lunch and early dinner) – Carte £ 31/74
• Modern cuisine • Elegant • Intimate •

Elegant oak-panelled restaurant in a luxurious hotel. The three rooms are dark, moody and richly appointed, and there's a lovely lounge and whisky snug. Choose from well-prepared classics or more ambitious offerings on the degustation menu.

XX   The Honours – Malmaison Hotel

278 West George St ✉ *G2 4LL – ℰ (0141) 5721001*   Plan: **C2**
– www.thehonours.co.uk
Menu £ 19 (lunch and early dinner) – Carte £ 33/57
• Modern cuisine • Classic • Brasserie •

Intimate brasserie named after the Scottish Crown Jewels and set in the crypt of an old Greek Orthodox Church. Sit on leather banquettes under a vaulted ceiling and beside gilded columns. Classic brasserie dishes have a modern edge.

XX **Cail Bruich**   ☒ ⑰

725 Great Western Rd. ✉ *G12 8QX –* ✆ *(0141) 3346265*   Plan: **A1**
– www.cailbruich.co.uk – Closed 25-26 December, 1-2 January and lunch
Monday and Tuesday
Menu £ 21 (lunch and early dinner)/25 – Carte £ 32/53 – *(booking advisable)*
• **Modern cuisine** • **Intimate** • **Neighbourhood** •
High ceilinged restaurant with red leather banquettes and low hanging copper
lamps. Menus range from a market selection to tasting options; cooking is
modern and creative, with BBQ dishes a specialty. Its name means 'to eat well'.

XX **Gamba**   ⑬

225a West George St. ✉ *G2 2ND –* ✆ *(0141) 5720899*   Plan: **D2**
– www.gamba.co.uk – Closed 25 December and first 2 weeks January
Menu £ 19 (lunch and early dinner) – Carte £ 26/53
• **Fish and seafood** • **Brasserie** •
Tucked away in a basement but well-known by the locals. Appealing seafood
menu of unfussy, classical dishes with the odd Asian influence; lemon sole is a
speciality. Cosy bar-lounge and contemporary dining room hung with fish
prints.

XX **La Parmigiana**   ☒ ⑬

447 Great Western Rd, Kelvinbridge ✉ *G12 8HH*   Plan: **A1**
– ✆ *(0141) 3340686 – www.laparmigiana.co.uk – Closed 25-*
26 December, 1 January and Sunday dinner
Menu £ 17 (lunch) – Carte £ 29/50 – *(booking essential)*
• **Italian** • **Neighbourhood** • **Classic** •
Unashamedly classic in terms of its décor and its dishes, this well-regarded, professionally run Italian restaurant celebrated its 35th birthday in 2013. Red walls,
white linen and efficient service. Refined cooking delivers bold flavours.

XX **Ubiquitous Chip**   ⌘ ⅚ ☒ ⑬

12 Ashton Ln ✉ *G12 8SJ –* ✆ *(0141) 334 5007*   Plan: **A1**
– www.ubiquitouschip.co.uk – Closed 25 December and 1 January
Menu £ 20 (lunch and early dinner) – Carte £ 29/64 – *(bookings advisable at dinner)*
• **Modern cuisine** • **Bistro** • **Individual** •
An iconic establishment on a cobbled street. The restaurant – with its ponds,
fountains and greenery – offers modern classics which showcase local ingredients, while the mezzanine-level brasserie serves tasty Scottish favourites.

XX **Blythswood Square** – Blythswood Square Hotel   ⅚ ☒ ⑬

11 Blythswood Sq ✉ *G2 4AD –* ✆ *(0141) 2488888*   Plan: **D2**
– www.blythswoodsquare.com
Menu £ 22 (lunch and early dinner) – Carte £ 28/58
• **Modern cuisine** • **Fashionable** • **Brasserie** •
Stylish hotel restaurant in the ballroom of the old RAC building; chic in black
and white, with a zinc-topped bar and Harris Tweed banquettes. Classic menu
with meats from the Josper grill. Desserts showcase the kitchen's ambitious
side.

XX **Two Fat Ladies in the City**   ⅚ ⑬

118a Blythswood St ✉ *G2 4EG –* ✆ *(0141) 8470088*   Plan: **D2**
– www.twofatladiesrestaurant.com
Menu £ 16 (lunch and early dinner) – Carte £ 30/56
• **Traditional cuisine** • **Classic** • **Brasserie** •
Intimate restaurant which resembles an old-fashioned brasserie, courtesy of its
wooden floor, banquettes and mirrors. Classically based dishes are straightforward in style, with a modern edge, and fresh Scottish seafood is a feature.

XX **Urban**   🅰🄲 ⇔ 🕾

23-25 St Vincent Pl. ✉ G1 2DT – ℰ (0141) 2485636   Plan: **E2**
– www.urbanbrasserie.co.uk – Closed 25 December and 1 January
Menu £ 16 (lunch and early dinner) – Carte £ 22/63
• British traditional • Brasserie • Classic •
Formerly the Bank of England's HQ. The grand dining room has booths, vibrant
artwork and an impressive illuminated glass and wrought iron ceiling. Classic
British dishes feature, along with live music every Friday and Saturday evening.

X **The Gannet**   &. 🄲 🕾
🍃
1155 Argyle St ✉ G3 8TB – ℰ (0141) 2042081   Plan: **A1**
*– www.thegannetglasgow.com – Closed first week January, 20-28 July, 25-
26 December, Sunday dinner and Monday*
Menu £ 25 (lunch and early dinner) – Carte £ 23/36
• British modern • Rustic • Neighbourhood •
You may well feel like a gannet after a visit to this appealingly rustic restaurant,
where the tasty menus are constantly evolving. Classic dishes are presented in a
modern style and are brought to the table by a charming team. Exposed stone,
untreated wood and corrugated iron feature throughout.

X **Ox and Finch**   🄲 ⇔ 🕾
🍃
920 Sauchiehall St ✉ G3 7TF – ℰ (0141) 339 8627   Plan: **A1**
– www.oxandfinch.com – Closed 25 December
Carte £ 15/25
• British modern • Design • Retro •
A bright, breezy team run this likeable rustic restaurant, with its tile-backed
open kitchen and wines displayed in a huge metal cage. The Scottish and European small plates will tempt one and all: cooking centres around old favourites
but with added modern twists, and the flavours really shine through.

X **Porter & Rye**   &. 🄲
1131 Argyle St ✉ G3 8ND – ℰ (0141) 572 1212   Plan: **A1**
– www.porterandrye.com – Closed 25 December and 1 January
Carte £ 22/85 – *(booking advisable)*
• Meats • Trendy • Bistro •
Small, well-run loft style operation where wooden floors and exposed bricks
blend with steel balustrades and glass screens. Menus offer creative modern
small plates and a good range of aged Scottish steaks, from onglet to porterhouse.

X **Stravaigin**   🕾 &. 🄲
🍃
28 Gibson St, ✉ G12 8NX – ℰ (0141) 3342665   Plan: **A1**
– www.stravaigin.co.uk – Closed 25 December and 1 January
Carte £ 23/37 – *(booking essential at dinner)*
• International • Simple • Individual •
Well-run eatery with a relaxed shabby-chic style, a bustling café bar and plenty
of nooks and crannies. Interesting menus uphold the motto 'think global, eat
local', with dishes ranging from carefully prepared Scottish favourites to tasty
Asian-inspired fare. Monthly 'theme' nights range from haggis to tapas.

X **Two Fat Ladies West End**   🕾
88 Dumbarton Rd ✉ G11 6NX – ℰ (0141) 339 1944   Plan: **A1**
*– www.twofatladiesrestaurant.com – Closed 25-26 December and 1-
2 January*
Menu £ 18 (lunch and early dinner) – Carte £ 27/48
• Fish and seafood • Neighbourhood • Bistro •
Quirky neighbourhood restaurant – the first in the Fat Ladies group – with red
velour banquettes, bold blue and gold décor, and a semi open plan kitchen in
the window. Cooking is simple and to the point, focusing on classical fish
dishes.

Dhabba
🕇   ⅙ Ⓐℂ ⑂

44 Candleriggs ✉ *G1 1LE* – ☎ *(0141) 5531249*   Plan: **E3**
– www.thedhabba.com – Closed 25 December and 1 January
Menu £ 10 (weekday lunch) – Carte £ 20/38
• Indian • Exotic •
Stylish, modern restaurant in the heart of the Merchant City; its walls decorated with huge photos of Indian street scenes. Menus focus on northern India, with interesting breads and lots of tandoor dishes – the speciality is 'dum pukht'.

Hanoi Bike Shop
🕇   ⅙ Ⓐℂ

8 Ruthven Ln (off Byres Road) ✉ *G12 9BG* – ☎ *(0141)*   Plan: **A1**
334 7165 – www.thehanoibikeshop.co.uk – Closed 25 December and 1 January
Carte £ 20/27
• Vietnamese • Simple • Individual •
Relaxed Vietnamese café; head to the lighter upstairs room with its fine array of lanterns. Simple menu of classic Vietnamese dishes including street food like rice paper summer rolls. Charming, knowledgeable staff offer recommendations.

Dakhin
🕇   ⅙ ⑂

89 Candleriggs ✉ *G1 1NP* – ☎ *(0141) 5532585*   Plan: **E2**
– www.dakhin.com – Closed 25 December and 1 January
Menu £ 10 (weekday lunch) – Carte £ 18/35
• South-indian • Simple • Friendly •
It's all about the cooking at this modest, brightly decorated restaurant: authentic, southern Indian dishes might include seafood from Kerala, lamb curry from Tamil Nadu, and their speciality, dosas – available with a variety of fillings.

Cafezique
🕇   ⅙ Ⓐℂ

66 Hyndland St ✉ *G11 5PT* – ☎ *(0141) 339 7180*   Plan: **A1**
– www.delizique.co.uk – Closed 25-26 December and 1 January
Carte £ 21/28
• Modern cuisine • Bistro • Friendly •
Behind the old Hargan's Dairy sign is a buzzy shabby-chic eatery with stone walls, original wood floors and striking monotone screen prints. All-day breakfasts and Mediterranean light bites are followed by vibrant dishes in two sizes.

The Finnieston
🕇   🍴 &

1125 Argyle St ✉ *G3 8ND* – ☎ *(0141) 2222884*   Plan: **A1**
– www.thefinniestonbar.com – Closed 25-26 December and 1 January
Carte £ 19/51
• Fish and seafood • Friendly • Cosy •
Small, cosy pub specialising in Scottish seafood and gin cocktails; with an intriguing ceiling, a welcoming fire and lots of booths. Dishes are light, tasty and neatly presented, relying on just a few ingredients so that flavours are clear.

Salisbury
🕇   Ⓐℂ

72 Nithsdale Rd ✉ *G41 2AN* – ☎ *(0141) 423 0084*   Plan: **A2**
– www.salisburybar.com – Closed 25 December and 1 January
Carte £ 19/43
• British modern • Neighbourhood • Rustic •
A bijou pub on the south side of the city. Its interior is modern and cosy; the staff are friendly; and the monthly menu has an eclectic mix of Scottish and international flavours. Local seafood is given an original modern twist.

The MICHELIN Guide
A collection to savour!

Belgïe • Belgique & Luxembourg
Deutschland
España & Portugal
France
Great Britain & Ireland
Italia
Nederland • Netherlands
Suisse • Schweiz • Svizzera
Main Cities of Europe

Also:

Chicago
Hong Kong · Macau
Kyoto · Osaka
London
New York City
Nordic Guide
Paris
Rio de Janeiro & São Paulo
San Francisco
Tokyo

Europe in maps and numbers

Eurozone : €

 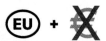

 EU states

Schengen Countries

Area of free movement between member states

  + Schengen

  + Sche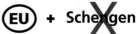**gen**

  + Schengen

1001

Driving in Europe

The information panels which follow give the principal motoring regulations in force when this guide was prepared for press; an explanation of the symbols is given below, together with some additional notes.

Speed restrictions in kilometres per hour applying to:

 motorways

 dual carriageways

 single carriageways

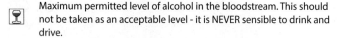 urban areas

Maximum permitted level of alcohol in the bloodstream. This should not be taken as an acceptable level - it is NEVER sensible to drink and drive.

Whether tolls are payable on motorways and/or other parts of the road network.

Whether seatbelts are compulsory for the driver and all passengers in both front and back seats.

Whether headlights must be on at all times.

		🛣️	🛣️	🛣️	🛣️	🍷	🛣️	🦺	�
AUSTRIA	Ⓐ	130		100	50	0,5	●	●	●
BELGIUM	Ⓑ	120	120	90	50	0,5		●	●
CZECH REPUBLIC	ⒸⓏ	130		90	50	0,0	●	●	●
DENMARK	ⒹⓀ	130		80	50	0,5		●	●
FINLAND	ⒻⒾⓃ	120		80	50	0,5		●	●
FRANCE	Ⓕ	130	110	90	50	0,5	●	●	
GERMANY	Ⓓ			100	50	0,5		●	●
GREECE	ⒼⓇ	130		90	50	0,5		●	
HUNGARY	Ⓗ	130	110	90	50	0,0	●	●	●
IRELAND	ⒾⓇⓁ	120	100	80	50	0,5		●	
ITALY	Ⓘ	130	110	90	50	0,5		●	●
LUXEMBOURG	Ⓛ	130		90	50	0,5		●	●
NETHERLANDS	ⓃⓁ	120	100	80	50	0,5		●	
NORWAY	Ⓝ	100		80	50	0,2		●	●
POLAND	ⓅⓁ	140	120	90	50	0,2		●	●
PORTUGAL	Ⓟ	120		90	50	0,5		●	●
SPAIN	Ⓔ	120	120	90	50	0,5		●	●
SWEDEN	Ⓢ	110		70	50	0,2		●	●
SWITZERLAND	ⒸⒽ	120	100	80	50	0,5	●	●	
UNITED KINGDOM (Scotland)	ⒼⒷ	112	112	96	48	0,8 0,5		●	

● Compulsory

Distances

123 : distances by road in kilometers

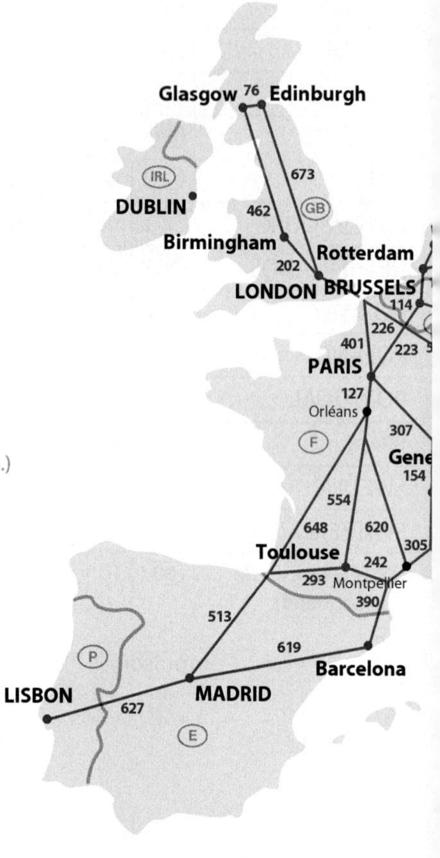

Glasgow 76 Edinburgh

(IRL)

673

DUBLIN 462 (GB)

Birmingham

202 Rotterdam

LONDON BRUSSELS

114

226

401 223

PARIS

127

Orléans

307

(F) Gene

154

554

648 620

305

Toulouse 242

293 Montpellier

390

513

619

Barcelona

LISBON 627 MADRID

(P)

(E)

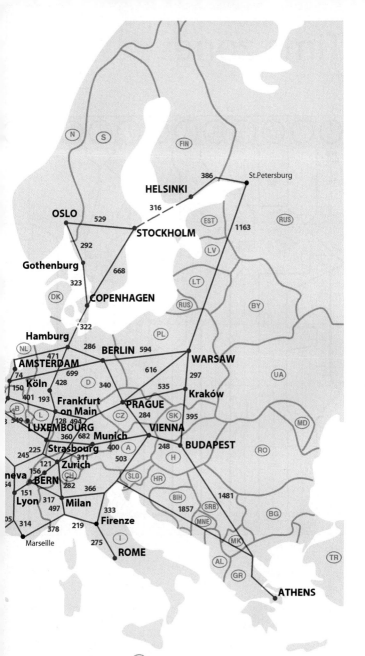

Time zones

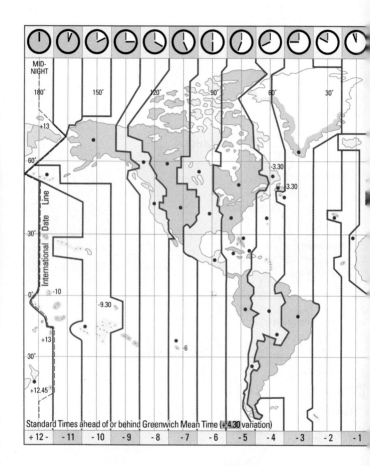

Standard Times ahead of or behind Greenwich Mean Time (± 4.30 variation)

| + 12 - | - 11 | - 10 | - 9 | - 8 | - 7 | - 6 | - 5 | - 4 | - 3 | - 2 | - 1 |

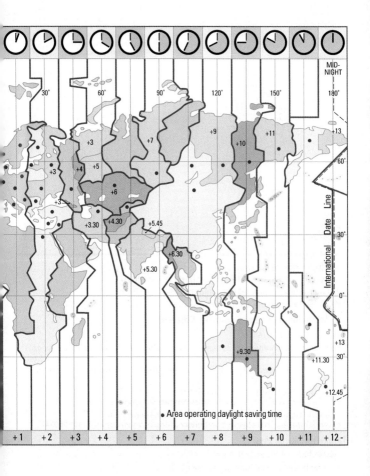

- Area operating daylight saving time

Michelin Travel Partner
Société par actions simplifiées au capital de 11 288 880 EUR
27 Cours de l'Île Seguin - 92100 Boulogne Billancourt (France)
R.C.S. Nanterre 433 677 721

© **Michelin et Cie, Propriétaires-Éditeurs**

Dépôt légal : 02-2016

No part of this publication may be reproduced in any form without the prior permission of the publisher.

"Based on Ordnance Survey Ireland by permission of the Government Permit No 8908 © Government of Ireland"

City plans of Bern, Basle, Geneva and Zürich:
with the permission of Federal directorate for cadastral surveys

"Based on Ordnance Survey of Great Britain with the permission
of the Controller of Her Majesty's Stationery Office, © Crown Copyright 100000247"

Printed in Italy: 02-2016

Typesetting: JOUVE, Saran (France)

Printing-binding: LEGO Print, Lavis (Italie)

Printed on paper from sustainably managed forests